Taxation of Business Entities

McGraw Hill's

Taxation of Business Entities

Brian C. Spilker
Brigham Young University
Editor

Benjamin C. Ayers
The University of Georgia

Troy K. Lewis
Brigham Young University

Connie D. Weaver
Texas A&M University

John A. Barrick
Brigham Young University

John R. Robinson
Texas A&M University

Ron G. Worsham
Brigham Young University

McGRAW HILL'S TAXATION OF BUSINESS ENTITIES, 2023 EDITION, FOURTEENTH EDITION

Published by McGraw Hill LLC, 1325 Avenue of the Americas, New York, NY 10019.

This book is printed on acid-free paper.

1 2 3 4 5 6 7 8 9 LWI 26 25 24 23 22

ISBN 978-1-265-62200-8 (bound edition)
MHID 1-265-62200-0 (bound edition)
ISBN 978-1-265-62693-8 (loose-leaf edition)
MHID 1-265-62693-6 (loose-leaf edition)
ISSN 1946-7737

Executive Portfolio Manager: *Kathleen Klehr*
Product Developers: *Sarah Wood, Katie Ward*
Marketing Manager: *Clare McLemore*
Content Project Managers: *Jill Eccher, Brian Nacik*
Buyer: *Susan K. Culbertson*
Designer: *Beth Blech*
Content Licensing Specialist: *Melissa Homer*
Cover Image: *Joseph De Sciose/Pixtal/age fotostock*
Compositor: *Aptara®, Inc.*

mheducation.com/highered

Dedications

We dedicate this book to:

My family and to Professor Dave Stewart for his great example and friendship.

Brian Spilker

My wife Marilyn, daughters Margaret Lindley and Georgia, son Benjamin, and parents Bill and Linda.

Ben Ayers

My wife Jill and my children Annika, Corinne, Lina, Mitch, and Connor.

John Barrick

My wife Mindy; sons Tyler, Braden, and Connor; and parents Kent and Wendy.

Troy Lewis

JES, Tommy, and Laura.

John Robinson

My family: Dan, Travis, Alix, Alan, Anna, and Avery.

Connie Weaver

My wife Anne, sons Matthew and Daniel, and daughters Whitney and Hayley.

Ron Worsham

About the Authors

Courtesy of Brian Spilker

Brian C. Spilker (PhD, University of Texas at Austin, 1993) is the Robert Call/Deloitte Professor in the School of Accountancy at Brigham Young University. He teaches taxation at Brigham Young University. He received both BS (Summa Cum Laude) and MAcc (tax emphasis) degrees from Brigham Young University before working as a tax consultant for Arthur Young & Co. (now Ernst & Young). After his professional work experience, Brian earned his PhD at the University of Texas at Austin. He received the Price Waterhouse Fellowship in Tax Award and the American Taxation Association and Arthur Andersen Teaching Innovation Award for his work in the classroom. Brian has also been awarded for his use of technology in the classroom at Brigham Young University. Brian researches issues relating to tax information search and professional tax judgment. His research has been published in journals such as *The Accounting Review, Organizational Behavior and Human Decision Processes, Journal of the American Taxation Association, Behavioral Research in Accounting, Issues in Accounting Education, Accounting Horizons, Journal of Accounting Education, Journal of Corporate Taxation, Journal of Accountancy,* and *The Tax Adviser.*

Courtesy of Ben Ayers

Ben Ayers (PhD, University of Texas at Austin, 1996) holds the Earl Davis Chair in Taxation and is the dean of the Terry College of Business at the University of Georgia. He received a PhD from the University of Texas at Austin and an MTA and BS from the University of Alabama. Prior to entering the PhD program at the University of Texas, Ben was a tax manager at KPMG in Tampa, Florida, and a contract manager with Complete Health, Inc., in Birmingham, Alabama. He is the recipient of 11 teaching awards at the school, college, and university levels, including the Richard B. Russell Undergraduate Teaching Award, the highest teaching honor for University of Georgia junior faculty members. His research interests include the effects of taxation on firm structure, mergers and acquisitions, and capital markets and the effects of accounting information on security returns. He has published articles in journals such as *The Accounting Review, Journal of Finance, Journal of Accounting and Economics, Contemporary Accounting Research, Review of Accounting Studies, Journal of Law and Economics, Journal of the American Taxation Association,* and *National Tax Journal.* Ben was the 1997 recipient of the American Accounting Association's Competitive Manuscript Award, the 2003 and 2008 recipient of the American Taxation Association's Outstanding Manuscript Award, and the 2016 recipient of the American Taxation Association's Ray M. Sommerfeld Outstanding Tax Educator Award.

Courtesy of John Barrick

John Barrick (PhD, University of Nebraska at Lincoln, 1998) is currently an associate professor in the Marriott School at Brigham Young University. He served as an accountant at the U.S. Congress Joint Committee on Taxation during the 110th and 111th Congresses. He teaches taxation in the graduate and undergraduate programs at Brigham Young University. He received both BS and MAcc (tax emphasis) degrees from Brigham Young University before working as a tax consultant for Price Waterhouse (now PricewaterhouseCoopers). After his professional work experience, John earned his PhD at the University of Nebraska at Lincoln. He was the 1998 recipient of the American Accounting Association, Accounting, Behavior, and Organization Section's Outstanding Dissertation Award. John researches issues relating to tax corporate political activity. His research has been published in journals such as *Organizational Behavior and Human Decision Processes, Contemporary Accounting Research,* and *Journal of the American Taxation Association.*

Courtesy of Troy K Lewis

Troy K. Lewis (CPA, CGMA, MAcc, Brigham Young University, 1995) is an associate teaching professor in the School of Accountancy at Brigham Young University—Marriott School of Business. He teaches graduate and undergraduate courses in introductory taxation, property transactions, pass-through entity taxation, advanced individual taxation, and accounting for income taxes. He is the past chair of the Tax Executive Committee of the American Institute of CPAs (AICPA) in Washington, D.C., as well as the president of the Utah Association of CPAs (UACPA). He has testified six times before the U.S. Senate Finance Committee and the House Committee on Small Business. Prior to joining the faculty at BYU, he was a tax manager at Arthur Andersen and KPMG in Salt Lake City, Utah. In addition, he was employed for over a decade as the CERMO and Tax Director of Heritage Bank in St. George, Utah. He is the recipient of the AICPA Tax Section Distinguished Service Award, the BYU Marriott Ethics Teaching Award, and the UACPA Distinguished Service Award. Troy researches and publishes in professional tax journals in the areas of individual and pass-through taxation, qualified business income deduction, and property transactions as well as professional tax practice standards. His work has been published in journals such as *Practical Tax Strategies, Journal of Accountancy, Issues in Accounting Education,* and *The Tax Adviser.*

Courtesy of John Robinson

John Robinson (PhD, University of Michigan, 1981) is the Patricia '77 and Grant E. Sims '77 Eminent Scholar Chair in Business. Prior to joining the faculty at Texas A&M, John was the C. Aubrey Smith Professor of Accounting at the University of Texas at Austin, Texas, and he taught at the University of Kansas, where he was the Arthur Young Faculty Scholar. In 2009–2010 John served as the Academic Fellow in the Division of Corporation Finance at the Securities and Exchange Commission. He has been the recipient of the Henry A. Bubb Award for outstanding teaching, the Texas Blazer's Faculty Excellence Award, and the MPA Council Outstanding Professor Award. John also received the 2012 Outstanding Service Award from the American Taxation Association (ATA) and in 2017 was named the Ernst & Young and ATA Ray Sommerfeld Outstanding Educator. John served as the 2015–2016 president of the ATA. John conducts research in a broad variety of topics involving financial accounting, mergers and acquisitions, and the influence of taxes on financial structures and performance. His scholarly articles have appeared in *The Accounting Review, The Journal of Accounting and Economics, Journal of Finance, National Tax Journal, Journal of Law and Economics, Journal of the American Taxation Association, The Journal of the American Bar Association,* and *The Journal of Taxation.* John's research was honored with the 2003 and 2008 ATA Outstanding Manuscript Awards. In addition, John was the editor of *The Journal of the American Taxation Association* from 2002–2005. Professor Robinson received his JD (*Cum Laude*) from the University of Michigan in 1979, and he teaches courses on individual and corporate taxation and advanced accounting.

Courtesy of Connie Weaver

Connie Weaver (PhD, Arizona State University, 1997) is the KPMG Professor of Accounting at Texas A&M University. She received a PhD from Arizona State University, an MPA from the University of Texas at Arlington, and a BS (chemical engineering) from the University of Texas at Austin. Prior to entering the PhD program, Connie was a tax manager at Ernst & Young in Dallas, Texas, where she became licensed to practice as a CPA. She teaches taxation in the Professional Program in Accounting and the Executive MBA program at Texas A&M University. She has also taught undergraduate and graduate students at the University of Wisconsin–Madison and the University of Texas at Austin. She is the recipient of several teaching awards, including the American Taxation Association/Deloitte Teaching Innovations award, the David and Denise Baggett Teaching award, and the college and university level Association of Former Students Distinguished Achievement award in teaching. Connie's current research interests include the effects of tax and financial incentives on corporate decisions and reporting. She has published articles in journals such as *The Accounting Review, Contemporary Accounting Research, Journal of the American Taxation Association, National Tax Journal, Accounting Horizons, Journal of Corporate Finance,* and *Tax Notes*. Connie is an editor of *The Accounting Review* and has served as the senior editor of *The Journal of the American Taxation Association* and on the editorial board of *Contemporary Accounting Research.*

Ron Worsham (PhD, University of Florida, 1994) is an associate professor in the School of Accountancy at Brigham Young University. He teaches taxation in the graduate program at Brigham Young University. He has also taught as a visiting professor at the University of Chicago. He received both BS and MAcc (tax emphasis) degrees from Brigham Young University before working as a tax consultant for Arthur Young & Co. (now Ernst & Young) in Dallas, Texas. While in Texas, he became licensed to practice as a CPA. After his professional work experience, Ron earned his PhD at the University of Florida. He has been honored for outstanding innovation in the classroom at Brigham Young University. Ron has published academic research in the areas of taxpayer compliance and professional tax judgment. He has also published legal research in a variety of areas. His work has been published in journals such as *Journal of the American Taxation Association, The Journal of International Taxation, The Tax Executive, Tax Notes, The Journal of Accountancy,* and *Practical Tax Strategies*.

Courtesy of Ron Worsham

In Memoriam

On May 20, 2019, we lost one of our beloved authors, Edmund (Ed) Outslay, aged 67. During his tenure at Michigan State University from 1980 to 2019, Ed was known as a passionate academic, impactful mentor, and devoted community volunteer.

Over the course of his long and distinguished career, Ed gathered a remarkable list of accomplishments. He coauthored three tax textbooks, testified before the U.S. Senate Finance Committee, and presented to the Treasury, the IRS, and the Office of Tax Analysis. He won numerous awards from the Eli Broad College of Business at MSU, including the Distinguished Faculty Award, the Presidential Award for Outstanding Community Service, the Withrow Teacher-Scholar Award, and the Curricular Service-Learning and Civic Engagement Award, in addition to numerous departmental teaching and research awards.

Ed enjoyed volunteering his time and was involved in many community programs, such as Lansing's Meals on Wheels program and MSU's Volunteer Income Tax Assistance (VITA) program. He was also an assistant baseball coach at East Lansing High School.

Ed was an avid reader and enjoyed visiting baseball parks and the zoo; he enjoyed coaching baseball and celebrating Halloween.

He earned his bachelor's degree from Furman University in Greenville, South Carolina, and his MBA and PhD from the University of Michigan.

Ed's guidance, energy, and contributions will be deeply missed.

Courtesy Ed Outslay

TEACHING THE CODE IN CONTEXT

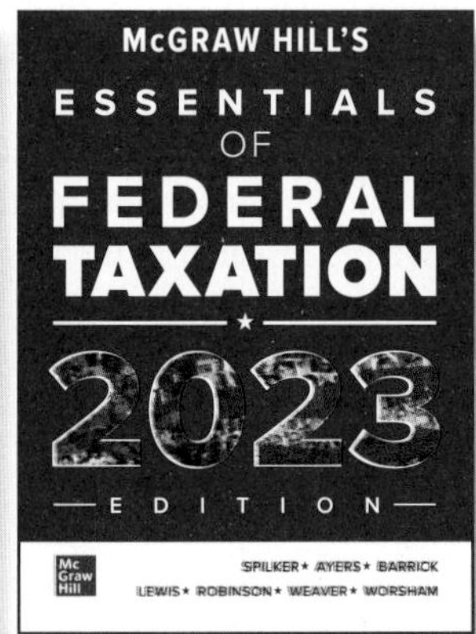

The bold, innovative approach used by McGraw Hill's Taxation *series has become the most popular choice of course materials among instructors and students—a remarkable achievement in just over 10 years since first publishing. It's apparent why the clear, organized, and engaging delivery of content, paired with the most current and robust tax code updates, has been adopted by more than 650 schools across the country.*

McGraw Hill's Taxation is designed to provide a unique, innovative, and engaging learning experience for students studying taxation. The breadth of the topical coverage, **the storyline approach to presenting the material,** the emphasis on the tax and nontax consequences of multiple parties involved in transactions, and the integration of financial and tax accounting topics make this book ideal for the modern tax curriculum.

"Do you want the best tax text? This is the one to use. It has a storyline in each chapter that can relate to real life issues."

Leslie A. Mostow
– University of Maryland—College Park

"This text provides broad coverage of important topics and does so in a manner that is easy for students to understand. The material is very accessible for students."

Kyle Post
–Tarleton State University

Since the first manuscript was written in 2005, 450 professors have contributed 500 book reviews, in addition to 30 focus groups and symposia. Throughout this preface, their comments on the book's organization, pedagogy, and unique features are a testament to the **market-driven nature of *Taxation*'s development.**

"I think this is the best book available for introductory and intermediate courses in taxation."

Shane Stinson
– University of Alabama

A MODERN APPROACH FOR TODAY'S STUDENT

McGraw Hill's Taxation series was built around the following five core precepts:

1. **Storyline Approach:** Each chapter begins with a storyline that introduces a set of characters or a business entity facing specific tax-related situations. Each chapter's examples are related to the storyline, providing students with opportunities to **learn the code in context.**

2. **Integrated Examples:** In addition to providing examples in context, we provide **"What if"** scenarios within many examples to **illustrate how variations in the facts might or might not change the answers.**

3. **Conversational Writing Style:** The authors took special care to write *McGraw Hill's Taxation* in a way that fosters a friendly dialogue between the content and each individual student. The tone of the presentation is intentionally conversational—creating the impression of ***speaking with* the student,** as opposed to *lecturing to* the student.

4. **Superior Organization of Related Topics:** *McGraw Hill's Taxation* provides two alternative topic sequences. In the *McGraw Hill's Taxation of Individuals and Business Entities* volume, the individual topics generally follow the tax form sequence, with an individual overview chapter and then chapters on income, deductions, investment-related issues, and the tax liability computation. The topics then transition into business-related topics that apply to individuals. This volume then provides a group of specialty chapters dealing with topics of particular interest to individuals (including students), including separate chapters on home ownership, compensation, and retirement savings and deferred compensation. Alternatively, in the *Essentials of Federal Taxation* volume, the topics follow a more traditional sequence, with topics streamlined (no specialty chapters) and presented in more of a life-cycle approach.

5. **Real-World Focus:** Students learn best when they see how concepts are applied in the real world. For that reason, real-world examples and articles are included in **Taxes in the Real World** boxes throughout the book. These vignettes demonstrate current issues in taxation and show the relevance of tax issues in all areas of business.

A STORYLINE APPROACH THAT RESONATES WITH STUDENTS

mentatdgt/Shutterstock

Storyline Summary

Elise Brandon (she/her/hers)

Employment status: Tax associate for a large public accounting firm.

Assigned to prepare the federal income tax provision and income-tax-related balance sheet accounts and footnote disclosures for Premiere Computer Corporation, a nonaudit client.

Premiere Computer Corporation
Medium-sized publicly traded company.
Manufactures and sells computers and computer-related equipment. Calendar-year taxpayer.

Tax rate: 21 percent.

Elise felt a great sense of accomplishment when she completed her review of the federal income tax return for Premiere Computer Corporation (PCC). She was glad the return was filed on time and did not need to be extended. With the tax return filed, Elise was assigned to help the PCC tax department compute the federal **income tax provision** (financial income tax expense) for the company's soon-to-be-published income statement and to determine the correct amounts in the company's

Elise was aware that, as a result of the stringent independence requirements imposed by the Sarbanes-Oxley Act, her colleagues in the tax group were getting a lot of engagements to help prepare the income tax provision for nonaudit clients. In fact, her firm considered accounting for income taxes to be a "core competency" for all tax staff and prepared a training course for everyone. Having recently attended the firm's training on the subject, Elise was eager to apply her new knowledge to an actual client

Each chapter begins with a storyline that introduces a set of characters facing specific tax-related situations. This revolutionary approach to teaching tax emphasizes real people facing real tax dilemmas. Students learn to apply practical tax information to specific business and personal situations. As their situations evolve, the characters are brought further to life.

Examples

Examples are the cornerstone of any textbook covering taxation. For this reason, *McGraw Hill's Taxation* authors took special care to create clear and helpful examples that relate to the storyline of the chapter. Students learn to refer to the facts presented in the storyline and apply them to other scenarios—in this way, they build a greater base of knowledge through application. Many examples also include "What if" scenarios that add more complexity to the example or explore related tax concepts.

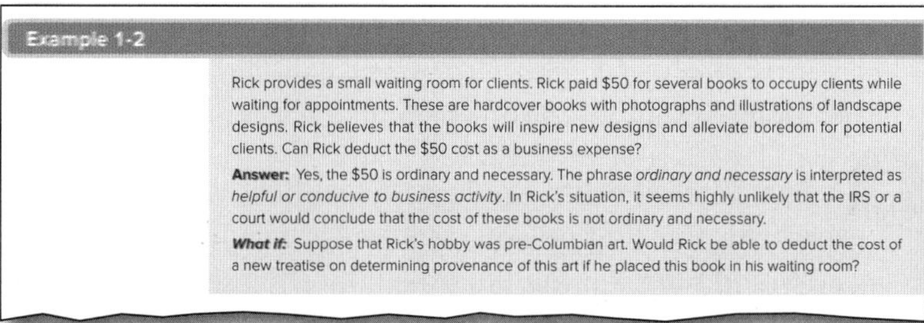

Example 1-2

Rick provides a small waiting room for clients. Rick paid $50 for several books to occupy clients while waiting for appointments. These are hardcover books with photographs and illustrations of landscape designs. Rick believes that the books will inspire new designs and alleviate boredom for potential clients. Can Rick deduct the $50 cost as a business expense?

Answer: Yes, the $50 is ordinary and necessary. The phrase *ordinary and necessary* is interpreted as *helpful or conducive to business activity*. In Rick's situation, it seems highly unlikely that the IRS or a court would conclude that the cost of these books is not ordinary and necessary.

What if: Suppose that Rick's hobby was pre-Columbian art. Would Rick be able to deduct the cost of a new treatise on determining provenance of this art if he placed this book in his waiting room?

THE PEDAGOGY YOUR STUDENTS NEED TO PUT THE CODE IN CONTEXT

Taxes in the Real World

Taxes in the Real World are short boxes used throughout the book to demonstrate the real-world use of tax concepts. Current articles on tax issues, the real-world application of chapter-specific tax rules, and short vignettes on popular news about tax are some of the issues covered in Taxes in the Real World boxes.

TAXES IN THE REAL WORLD Is a *Hard Fork* a taxable event?

A hard fork refers to a radical change to the protocols of a blockchain network. In simple terms, a hard fork splits a single cryptocurrency into two. On August 1, 2017, Bitcoin experienced a hard fork, and a second cryptocurrency, called Bitcoin Cash, was created. Every holder of a unit of Bitcoin received the same number of Bitcoin Cash units.

In 2021, the IRS concluded that the Bitcoin hard fork is a taxable event if the taxpayer had control over the resulting second cryptocurrency. Hence, a taxpayer who held 1 Bitcoin unit with a private key was subject to tax in 2017 on the value of the Bitcoin Cash unit received in the hard fork.

In contrast, another taxpayer owned Bitcoin through an account at CEX, a cryptocurrency

sole control over the private key to 100 units of Bitcoin. The taxpayer owned one unit of the 100 total Bitcoin units held by CEX. Because CEX was uncertain of Bitcoin Cash's security and viability, it chose not to support Bitcoin Cash at the time of the hard fork. As a result, the taxpayer was unable to access any Bitcoin Cash through the account with CEX. The taxpayer was only subject to tax in 2018 on the value of the Bitcoin Cash unit after CEX initiated support for Bitcoin Cash in 2018, allowing the taxpayer to buy, sell, send, receive, transfer, or exchange the 1 unit in their account. The IRS noted that the character of the gain depended on whether the virtual currency is a capital asset in the hands of the taxpayer.

The Key Facts

The Key Facts provide quick synopses of the critical pieces of information presented throughout each chapter.

Inventories

When producing, buying, or selling goods is an income-producing activity, taxpayers are required to keep inventories of goods, including raw materials and work in process, to determine the cost of goods sold. In addition, taxpayers who are required to keep inventory records also must use the accrual method of accounting for purchases and sales.[43] This requirement applies regardless of whether the taxpayer uses the cash or the accrual method as the overall method of accounting. Hence, the cost of inventory must include the purchase price of raw materials (minus any discounts), direct costs (manufacturing), shipping costs, and any indirect costs allocated to the inventory under the **uniform cost**

THE KEY FACTS

Inventories

- C corporations and partnerships with C corporation partners must use the accrual method to account for inventories unless they qualify as a small business under the gross

Exhibits

Today's students are visual learners, and *McGraw Hill's Taxation* understands this student need by making use of clear and engaging charts, diagrams, and tabular demonstrations of key material.

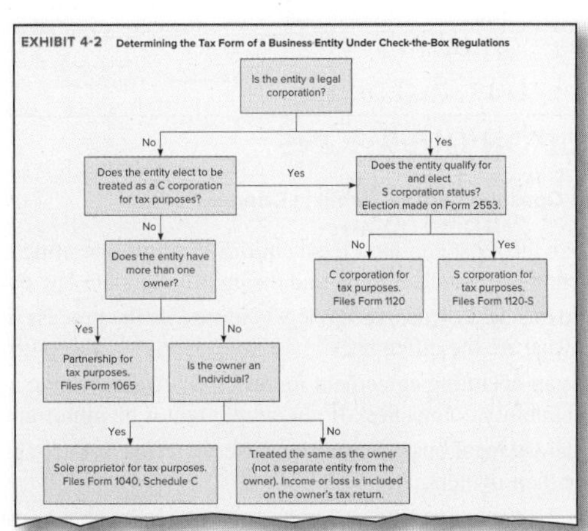

Top: Imageroller/Alamy Stock Photo; Bottom left: Jill Braaten/McGraw Hill

"This is the best text I have found for both my students and myself. Easier to read than other textbooks I have looked at, good examples, and, as mentioned before, I appreciate the instructor resources."

Esther Ehrlich, CPA
– The University of Texas at El Paso

PRACTICE MAKES PERFECT WITH A WIDE VARIETY OF ASSIGNMENT MATERIAL

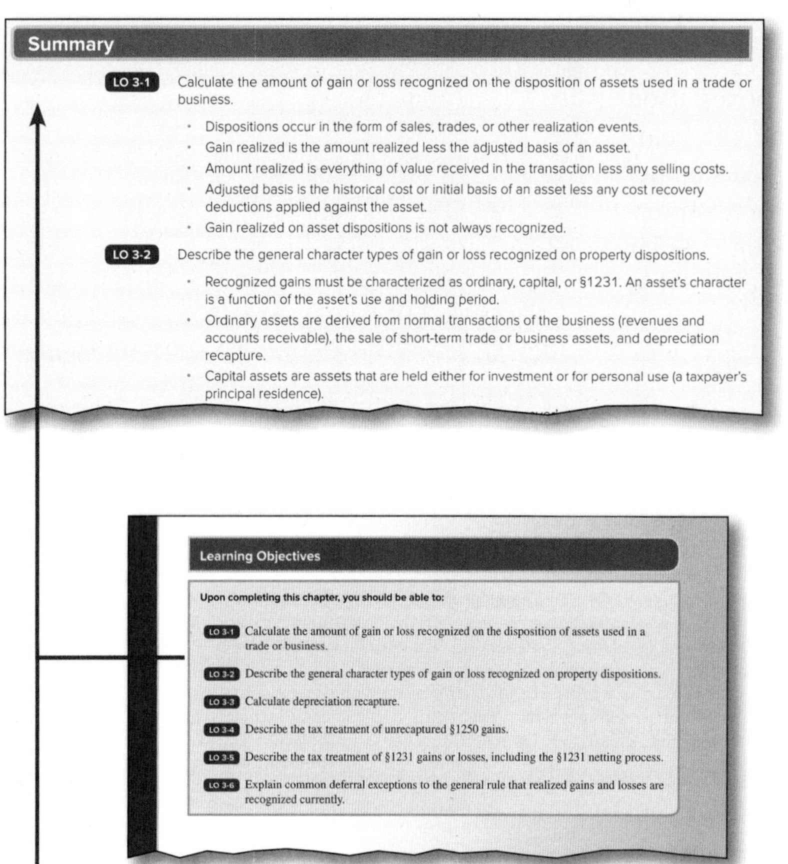

Summary

LO 3-1 Calculate the amount of gain or loss recognized on the disposition of assets used in a trade or business.

- Dispositions occur in the form of sales, trades, or other realization events.
- Gain realized is the amount realized less the adjusted basis of an asset.
- Amount realized is everything of value received in the transaction less any selling costs.
- Adjusted basis is the historical cost or initial basis of an asset less any cost recovery deductions applied against the asset.
- Gain realized on asset dispositions is not always recognized.

LO 3-2 Describe the general character types of gain or loss recognized on property dispositions.

- Recognized gains must be characterized as ordinary, capital, or §1231. An asset's character is a function of the asset's use and holding period.
- Ordinary assets are derived from normal transactions of the business (revenues and accounts receivable), the sale of short-term trade or business assets, and depreciation recapture.
- Capital assets are assets that are held either for investment or for personal use (a taxpayer's principal residence).

Learning Objectives

Upon completing this chapter, you should be able to:

LO 3-1 Calculate the amount of gain or loss recognized on the disposition of assets used in a trade or business.

LO 3-2 Describe the general character types of gain or loss recognized on property dispositions.

LO 3-3 Calculate depreciation recapture.

LO 3-4 Describe the tax treatment of unrecaptured §1250 gains.

LO 3-5 Describe the tax treatment of §1231 gains or losses, including the §1231 netting process.

LO 3-6 Explain common deferral exceptions to the general rule that realized gains and losses are recognized currently.

Summary

A unique feature of *McGraw Hill's Taxation* is the end-of-chapter summary organized around learning objectives. Each objective has a brief, bullet-point summary that covers the major topics and concepts for that chapter, including references to critical exhibits and examples. All end-of-chapter material is tied to learning objectives.

DISCUSSION QUESTIONS

Discussion Questions are available in Connect®. 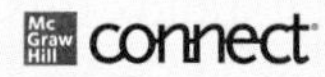

LO 4-1 1. What are the most common legal entities used for operating a business? How are these entities treated similarly and differently for state law purposes?

LO 4-1 2. How do business owners create legal entities? Is the process the same for all entities? If not, what are the differences?

LO 4-1 3. What is an operating agreement for an LLC? Are operating agreements required for limited liability companies? If not, why might it be important to have one?

LO 4-1 4. Explain how legal business entities differ in terms of the liability protection they provide their owners.

LO 4-1 5. Why is it a nontax advantage for corporations to be able to trade their stock on the stock market?

Discussion Questions

Discussion questions, available in Connect, are provided for each of the major concepts in each chapter, providing students with an opportunity to review key parts of the chapter and answer evocative questions about what they have learned.

Problems

Problems are designed to test the comprehension of more complex topics. Each problem at the end of the chapter is tied to one of that chapter's learning objectives, with multiple problems for critical topics.

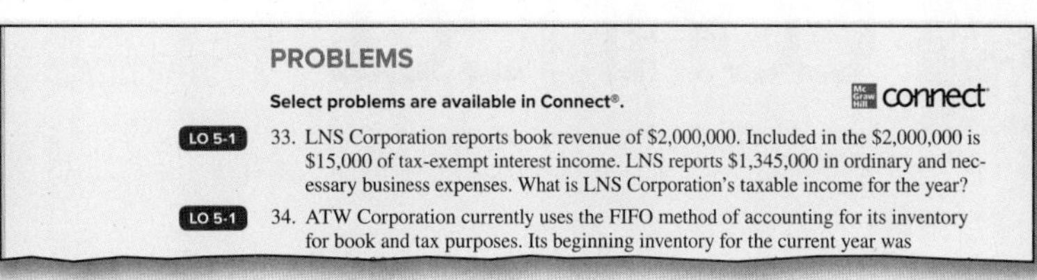

PROBLEMS

Select problems are available in Connect®. connect

LO 5-1 33. LNS Corporation reports book revenue of $2,000,000. Included in the $2,000,000 is $15,000 of tax-exempt interest income. LNS reports $1,345,000 in ordinary and necessary business expenses. What is LNS Corporation's taxable income for the year?

LO 5-1 34. ATW Corporation currently uses the FIFO method of accounting for its inventory for book and tax purposes. Its beginning inventory for the current year was

Tax Form Problems

Tax form problems are a set of requirements included in the end-of-chapter material of the 2023 edition. These problems require students to complete a tax form (or part of a tax form), providing students with valuable experience and practice with filling out these forms. These requirements—and their relevant forms—are also included in Connect, with select problems available in both static and algorithmic format. Each tax form problem includes an icon to differentiate it from regular problems.

Research Problems

Research problems are special problems throughout the end-of-chapter assignment material. These require students to do both basic and more complex research on topics outside of the scope of the book. Each research problem includes an icon to differentiate it from regular problems.

60. Mustafa, Mickayla, and Taylor are starting a new business (MMT). To get the business started, Mustafa is contributing $200,000 for a 40 percent ownership interest, Mickayla is contributing a building with a value of $200,000 and a tax basis of $150,000 for a 40 percent ownership interest, and Taylor is contributing legal services for a 20 percent ownership interest. What amount of gain or income is each owner required to recognize under each of the following alternative situations? [*Hint:* Look at §§351 and 721.] LO 4-3 research

a) MMT is formed as a C corporation.

Planning Problems

Planning problems are another unique set of problems included in the end-of-chapter assignment material. These require students to test their tax planning skills after covering the chapter topics. Each planning problem includes an icon to differentiate it from regular problems.

14. Daria is considering investing in one of two partnerships that will build, own, and operate a hotel. One is located in Canada and one is located in Arizona. Assuming both investments will generate the same before-tax rate of return, which entity should Daria invest in when considering the after-tax consequences of the investment? Assume Daria's marginal tax rate is 37 percent, she will be a passive investor in the business, and she will report the flow-through income from either entity on her tax return. Explain (ignore any foreign tax credit issues). LO 4-3 planning

15. Is business income allocated from a flow-through business entity to its owner's self-employment income? Explain. LO 4-3

Comprehensive and Tax Return Problems

Comprehensive and tax return problems address multiple concepts in a single problem. Comprehensive problems are ideal for cumulative topics; for this reason, they are located at the end of all chapters. **Tax return problems are also available in *Connect* and *Instructor Resource Center.* These problems range from simple to complex and cover individual taxation, corporate taxation, partnership taxation, and S corporation taxation.**

Instructors: Student Success Starts with You

Tools to enhance your unique voice

Want to build your own course? No problem. Prefer to use an OLC-aligned, prebuilt course? Easy. Want to make changes throughout the semester? Sure. And you'll save time with Connect's auto-grading too.

65%
Less Time Grading

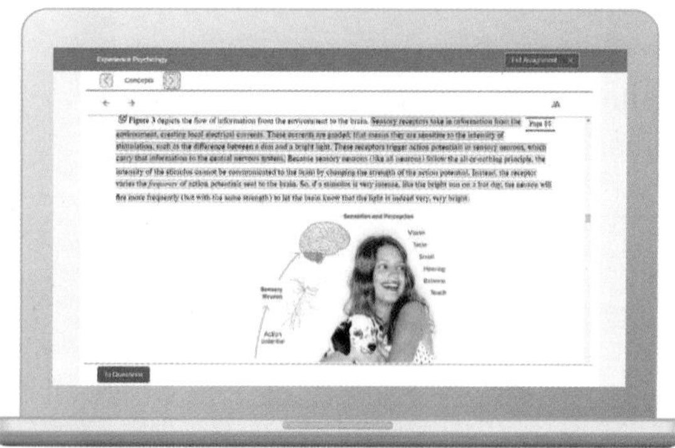

Laptop: McGraw Hill; Woman/dog: George Doyle/Getty Images

Study made personal

Incorporate adaptive study resources like SmartBook® 2.0 into your course and help your students be better prepared in less time. Learn more about the powerful personalized learning experience available in SmartBook 2.0 at **www.mheducation.com/highered/connect/smartbook**

Affordable solutions, added value

Make technology work for you with LMS integration for single sign-on access, mobile access to the digital textbook, and reports to quickly show you how each of your students is doing. And with our Inclusive Access program you can provide all these tools at a discount to your students. Ask your McGraw Hill representative for more information.

Padlock: Jobalou/Getty Images

Solutions for your challenges

A product isn't a solution. Real solutions are affordable, reliable, and come with training and ongoing support when you need it and how you want it. Visit **www.supportateverystep.com** for videos and resources both you and your students can use throughout the semester.

Checkmark: Jobalou/Getty Images

Students: Get Learning that Fits You

Effective tools for efficient studying

Connect is designed to help you be more productive with simple, flexible, intuitive tools that maximize your study time and meet your individual learning needs. Get learning that works for you with Connect.

Study anytime, anywhere

Download the free ReadAnywhere app and access your online eBook, SmartBook 2.0, or Adaptive Learning Assignments when it's convenient, even if you're offline. And since the app automatically syncs with your Connect account, all of your work is available every time you open it. Find out more at **www.mheducation.com/readanywhere**

"I really liked this app—it made it easy to study when you don't have your text-book in front of you."

- Jordan Cunningham,
Eastern Washington University

Calendar: owattaphotos/Getty Images

Everything you need in one place

Your Connect course has everything you need—whether reading on your digital eBook or completing assignments for class, Connect makes it easy to get your work done.

Learning for everyone

McGraw Hill works directly with Accessibility Services Departments and faculty to meet the learning needs of all students. Please contact your Accessibility Services Office and ask them to email accessibility@mheducation.com, or visit **www.mheducation.com/about/accessibility** for more information.

Top: Jenner Images/Getty Images, Left: Hero Images/Getty Images, Right: Hero Images/Getty Images

DIGITAL LEARNING ASSETS TO IMPROVE STUDENT OUTCOMES

> "The quality of the online materials in Connect and Learnsmart are market-leading and unmatched in the tax arena."
>
> Jason W. Stanfield
> – Ball State University

Connect helps students learn more efficiently by providing feedback and practice material when they need it, where they need it. Connect grades homework automatically and gives immediate feedback on any questions students may have missed. The extensive assignable, gradable end-of-chapter content includes problems, comprehensive problems (available as auto-graded tax forms), and discussion questions. Also, select questions have been redesigned to test students' knowledge more fully. They now include tables for students to work through rather than requiring that all calculations be done offline.

Auto-Graded Tax Forms

The auto-graded **Tax Forms,** also called the Comprehensive Problems—Static (Tax Form) in Connect, provide a much-improved student experience when solving the tax form–based problems. The tax form simulation allows students to apply tax concepts by completing the actual tax forms online with automatic feedback and grading for both students and instructors.

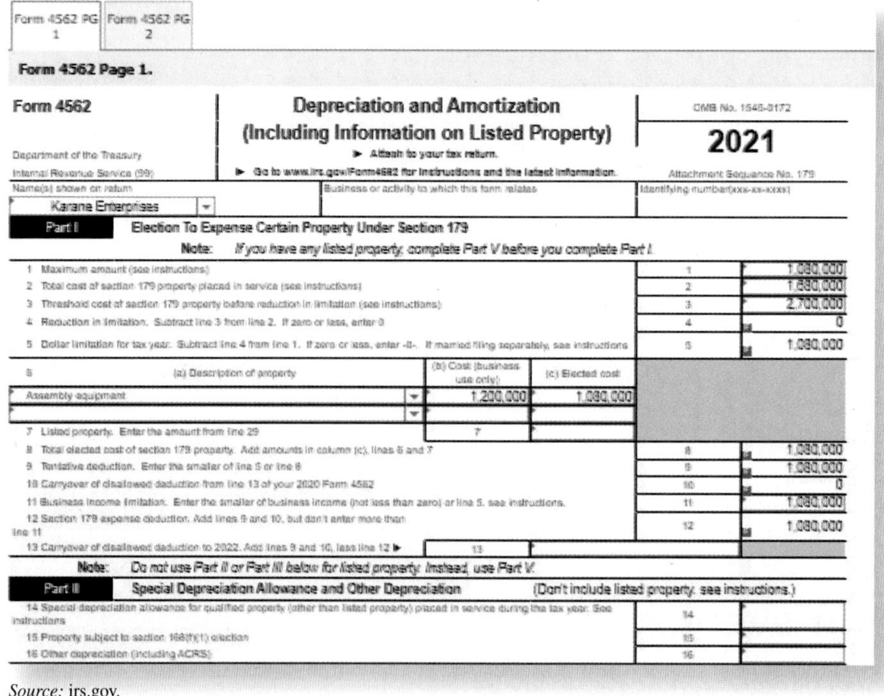

Form 4562 PG 1 | Form 4562 PG 2

Form 4562 Page 1.

Form 4562 — **Depreciation and Amortization (Including Information on Listed Property)** — OMB No. 1545-0172 — **2021**

Department of the Treasury
Internal Revenue Service (99)

► Attach to your tax return.
► Go to www.irs.gov/Form4562 for instructions and the latest information.

Attachment Sequence No. 179

Name(s) shown on return	Business or activity to which this form relates	Identifying number(xxx-xx-xxxx)
Karane Enterprises		

Part I — Election To Expense Certain Property Under Section 179

Note: *If you have any listed property, complete Part V before you complete Part I.*

1 Maximum amount (see instructions)			1	1,080,000
2 Total cost of section 179 property placed in service (see instructions)			2	1,680,000
3 Threshold cost of section 179 property before reduction in limitation (see instructions)			3	2,700,000
4 Reduction in limitation. Subtract line 3 from line 2. If zero or less, enter 0			4	0
5 Dollar limitation for tax year. Subtract line 4 from line 1. If zero or less, enter -0-. If married filing separately, see instructions			5	1,080,000
6 (a) Description of property	(b) Cost (business use only)	(c) Elected cost		
Assembly equipment	1,200,000	1,080,000		
7 Listed property. Enter the amount from line 29	7			
8 Total elected cost of section 179 property. Add amounts in column (c), lines 6 and 7			8	1,080,000
9 Tentative deduction. Enter the smaller of line 5 or line 8			9	1,080,000
10 Carryover of disallowed deduction from line 13 of your 2020 Form 4562			10	0
11 Business income limitation. Enter the smaller of business income (not less than zero) or line 5. see instructions.			11	1,080,000
12 Section 179 expense deduction. Add lines 9 and 10, but don't enter more than line 11			12	1,080,000
13 Carryover of disallowed deduction to 2022. Add lines 9 and 10, less line 12 ►	13			

Note: *Do not use Part II or Part III below for listed property. Instead, use Part V.*

Part II — Special Depreciation Allowance and Other Depreciation (Don't include listed property. see instructions.)

14 Special depreciation allowance for qualified property (other than listed property) placed in service during the tax year. See instructions	14	
15 Property subject to section 168(f)(1) election	15	
16 Other depreciation (including ACRS)	16	

Source: irs.gov.

Guided Examples

The **Guided Examples,** or "hint" videos, in Connect provide a narrated, animated, step-by-step walk-through of select problems similar to those assigned. These short presentations can be turned on or off by instructors and provide reinforcement when students need it most.

Tableau Dashboard Activities

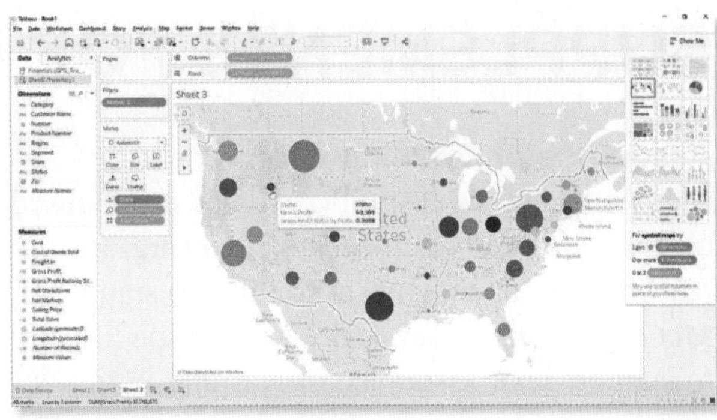

Tableau Dashboard Activities allow students to explore live Tableau dashboards directly integrated into Connect through interactive filters and menus as well as auto-graded questions focused on both calculations and analysis. Students can check their understanding and apply what they are learning within the framework of analytics and critical thinking.

TaxACT®

TaxAct Professional

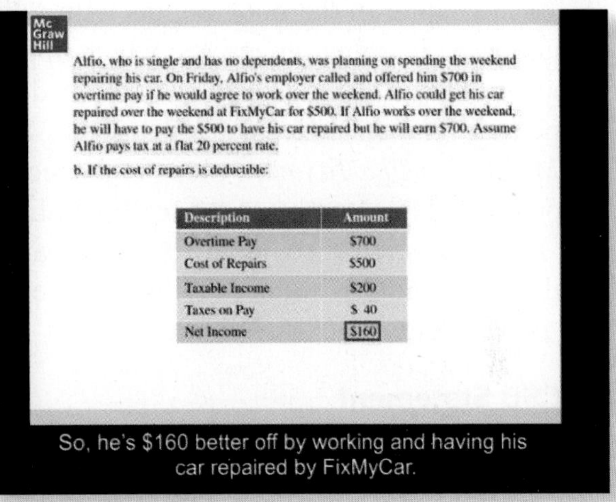

McGraw Hill's Taxation features an integrated software package from TaxAct, one of the leading preparation software companies in the market today. TaxAct features in-depth form instructions that supplement *Individuals* and *Business Entities,* making it easier than ever to integrate software into the classroom. Students are provided with the latest tax forms via the Check for Updates from the Online tab in the program so that at the start of the semester, each student will be prepared to work with the most up-to-date information available. With over 120 tax forms, schedules, and worksheets, TaxAct is sure to have the course materials you will need throughout the semester.

Please note, TaxAct is only compatible with PCs and not Macs. However, we offer easy-to-complete licensing agreement templates that are accessible within Connect and the Instructor Resources Center to enable school computer labs to download the software onto campus hardware for free.

Roger CPA

UWorld | ROGER CPA Review

McGraw Hill has partnered with Roger CPA Review (Powered by UWorld), a global leader in CPA Exam preparation, to provide students a smooth transition from the accounting classroom to successful completion of the CPA Exam. While many aspiring accountants wait until they have completed their academic studies to begin preparing for the CPA Exam, research shows that those who become familiar with exam content earlier in the process have a stronger chance of successfully passing the CPA Exam. Accordingly, students using these McGraw Hill materials will have access to Roger CPA Review multiple choice questions supported by explanations written by CPAs focused on exam preparation. McGraw Hill and Roger CPA Review are dedicated to supporting every accounting student along their journey, ultimately helping them achieve career success in the accounting profession. For more information about the full Roger CPA Review program, exam requirements, and exam content, visit www.rogercpareview.com.

McGraw Hill Customer Experience Group Contact Information

At McGraw Hill, we understand that getting the most from new technology can be challenging. That's why our services don't stop after you purchase our products. You can contact our Product Specialists 24 hours a day to get product training online. Or you can search the knowledge bank of Frequently Asked Questions on our support website. For Customer Support, call **800-331-5094,** or visit www.mhhe.com/support. One of our Technical Support Analysts will be able to assist you in a timely fashion.

SUPPLEMENTS FOR INSTRUCTORS

Assurance of Learning Ready

Many educational institutions today are focused on the notion of *assurance of learning,* an important element of many accreditation standards. *McGraw Hill's Taxation* is designed specifically to support your assurance of learning initiatives with a simple, yet powerful, solution.

Each chapter in the book begins with a list of numbered learning objectives, which appear throughout the chapter as well as in the end-of-chapter assignments. Every test bank question for *McGraw Hill's Taxation* maps to a specific chapter learning objective in the textbook. Each test bank question also identifies topic area, level of difficulty, Bloom's Taxonomy level, and AICPA and AACSB skill area.

AACSB Statement

McGraw Hill Education is a proud corporate member of AACSB International. Understanding the importance and value of AACSB accreditation, *McGraw Hill's Taxation* recognizes the curriculum guidelines detailed in the AACSB standards for business accreditation by connecting selected questions in the text and the test bank to the general knowledge and skill guidelines in the revised AACSB standards.

The statements contained in *McGraw Hill's Taxation* are provided only as a guide for the users of this textbook. The AACSB leaves content coverage and assessment within the purview of individual schools, the mission of the school, and the faculty. While *McGraw Hill's Taxation* and the teaching package make no claim of any specific AACSB qualification or evaluation, we have, within the text and test bank, labeled selected questions according to the eight general knowledge and skill areas.

Tegrity: Lectures 24/7

Tegrity in Connect is a tool that makes class time available 24/7 by automatically capturing every lecture. With a simple one-click start-and-stop process, you capture all computer screens and corresponding audio in a format that is easy to search, frame by frame. Students can replay any part of any class with easy-to-use, browser-based viewing on a PC, Mac, iPod, or other mobile device.

Educators know that the more students can see, hear, and experience class resources, the better they learn. In fact, studies prove it. Tegrity's unique search feature helps students efficiently find what they need, when they need it, across an entire semester of class recordings. Help turn your students' study time into learning moments immediately supported by your lecture. With Tegrity, you also increase intent listening and class participation by easing students' concerns about note-taking. Using Tegrity in Connect will make it more likely you will see students' faces, not the tops of their heads.

Test Builder in Connect

Available within Connect, Test Builder is a cloud-based tool that enables instructors to format tests that can be printed or administered within an LMS. Test Builder offers a modern, streamlined interface for easy content configuration that matches course needs, without requiring a download.

Test Builder allows you to:

- access all test bank content from a particular title.
- easily pinpoint the most relevant content through robust filtering options.
- manipulate the order of questions or scramble questions and/or answers.
- pin questions to a specific location within a test.
- determine your preferred treatment of algorithmic questions.
- choose the layout and spacing.
- add instructions and configure default settings.

Test Builder provides a secure interface for better protection of content and allows for just-in-time updates to flow directly into assessments.

Four Volumes to Fit Four Course Approaches

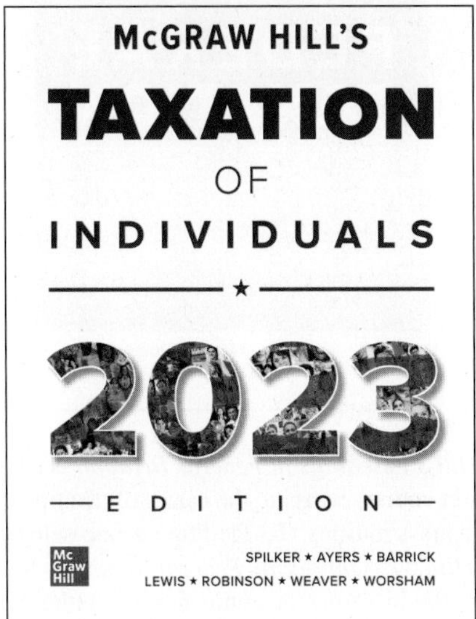

McGraw Hill's Taxation of Individuals is organized to emphasize topics that are most important to undergraduates taking their first tax course. The first three chapters provide an introduction to taxation and then carefully guide students through tax research and tax planning. Part II discusses the fundamental elements of individual income tax, starting with the tax formula in Chapter 4 and then proceeding to more discussion on income, deductions, investments, and computing tax liabilities in Chapters 5–8. Part III then discusses tax issues associated with business-related activities. Specifically, this part addresses business income and deductions, accounting methods, and tax consequences associated with purchasing assets and property dispositions (sales, trades, or other dispositions). Part IV is unique among tax textbooks; this section combines related tax issues for compensation, retirement savings, and home ownership.

Part I: Introduction to Taxation

1. An Introduction to Tax
2. Tax Compliance, the IRS, and Tax Authorities
3. Tax Planning Strategies and Related Limitations

Part II: Basic Individual Taxation

4. Individual Income Tax Overview, Dependents, and Filing Status
5. Gross Income and Exclusions
6. Individual Deductions
7. Investments
8. Individual Income Tax Computation and Tax Credits

Part III: Business-Related Transactions

9. Business Income, Deductions, and Accounting Methods
10. Property Acquisition and Cost Recovery
11. Property Dispositions

Part IV: Specialized Topics

12. Compensation
13. Retirement Savings and Deferred Compensation
14. Tax Consequences of Home Ownership

McGraw Hill's Taxation of Business Entities begins with the process for determining gross income and deductions for businesses, and the tax consequences associated with purchasing assets and property dispositions (sales, trades, or other dispositions). Part II provides a comprehensive overview of entities and the formation, reorganization, and liquidation of corporations. Unique to this series is a complete chapter on accounting for income taxes, which provides a primer on the basics of calculating the income tax provision. Included in the narrative is a discussion of temporary and permanent differences and their impact on a company's book "effective tax rate." Part III provides a detailed discussion of partnerships and S corporations. The last part of the book covers state and local taxation, multinational taxation, and transfer taxes and wealth planning.

Part I: Business-Related Transactions

1. Business Income, Deductions, and Accounting Methods
2. Property Acquisition and Cost Recovery
3. Property Dispositions

Part II: Entity Overview and Taxation of C Corporations

4. Business Entities Overview
5. Corporate Operations
6. Accounting for Income Taxes
7. Corporate Taxation: Nonliquidating Distributions
8. Corporate Formation, Reorganization, and Liquidation

Part III: Taxation of Flow-Through Entities

9. Forming and Operating Partnerships
10. Dispositions of Partnership Interests and Partnership Distributions
11. S Corporations

Part IV: Multijurisdictional Taxation and Transfer Taxes

12. State and Local Taxes
13. The U.S. Taxation of Multinational Transactions
14. Transfer Taxes and Wealth Planning

McGraw Hill's Taxation of Individuals and Business Entities covers all chapters included in the two split volumes in one convenient volume. See Table of Contents.

Part I: Introduction to Taxation
1. An Introduction to Tax
2. Tax Compliance, the IRS, and Tax Authorities
3. Tax Planning Strategies and Related Limitations

Part II: Basic Individual Taxation
4. Individual Income Tax Overview, Dependents, and Filing Status
5. Gross Income and Exclusions
6. Individual Deductions
7. Investments
8. Individual Income Tax Computation and Tax Credits

Part III: Business-Related Transactions
9. Business Income, Deductions, and Accounting Methods
10. Property Acquisition and Cost Recovery
11. Property Dispositions

Part IV: Specialized Topics
12. Compensation
13. Retirement Savings and Deferred Compensation
14. Tax Consequences of Home Ownership

Part V: Entity Overview and Taxation of C Corporations
15. Business Entities Overview
16. Corporate Operations
17. Accounting for Income Taxes
18. Corporate Taxation: Nonliquidating Distributions
19. Corporate Formation, Reorganization, and Liquidation

Part VI: Taxation of Flow-Through Entities
20. Forming and Operating Partnerships
21. Dispositions of Partnership Interests and Partnership Distributions
22. S Corporations

Part VII: Multijurisdictional Taxation and Transfer Taxes
23. State and Local Taxes
24. The U.S. Taxation of Multinational Transactions
25. Transfer Taxes and Wealth Planning

McGraw Hill's Essentials of Federal Taxation is designed for a one-semester course, covering the basics of taxation of individuals and business entities. To facilitate a one-semester course, *McGraw Hill's Essentials of Federal Taxation* folds the key topics from the investments, compensation, retirement savings, and home ownership chapters in *Taxation of Individuals* into three individual taxation chapters that discuss gross income and exclusions, for AGI deductions, and from AGI deductions, respectively. The essentials volume also includes a two-chapter C corporation sequence that uses a life-cycle approach covering corporate formations and then corporate operations in the first chapter and nonliquidating and liquidating corporate distributions in the second chapter. This volume is perfect for those teaching a one-semester course and for those who struggle to get through the 25-chapter comprehensive volume.

Part I: Introduction to Taxation
1. An Introduction to Tax
2. Tax Compliance, the IRS, and Tax Authorities
3. Tax Planning Strategies and Related Limitations

Part II: Individual Taxation
4. Individual Income Tax Overview, Dependents, and Filing Status
5. Gross Income and Exclusions
6. Individual For AGI Deductions
7. Individual From AGI Deductions
8. Individual Income Tax Computation and Tax Credits

Part III: Business-Related Transactions
9. Business Income, Deductions, and Accounting Methods
10. Property Acquisition and Cost Recovery
11. Property Dispositions

Part IV: Entity Overview and Taxation of C Corporations
12. Business Entities Overview
13. Corporate Formations and Operations
14. Corporate Nonliquidating and Liquidating Distributions

Part V: Taxation of Flow-Through Entities
15. Forming and Operating Partnerships
16. Dispositions of Partnership Interests and Partnership Distributions
17. S Corporations

A HEARTFELT THANKS TO THE MANY COLLEAGUES WHO SHAPED THIS BOOK

The version of the book you are reading would not be the same book without the valuable suggestions, keen insights, and constructive criticisms of the reviewers below. Each professor listed here contributed in substantive ways to the organization of chapters, coverage of topics, and use of pedagogy. We are grateful to them for taking the time to read chapters or attend reviewer conferences, focus groups, and symposia in support of the development for the book:

Previous Edition Reviewers

Donna Abelli, *Mount Ida College*
Joseph Assalone, *Rowan College at Gloucester County*
Dr. Valeriya Avdeev, *William Paterson University*
Victoria Badura, *Metropolitan Community College*
Robyn Barrett, *St. Louis Community College*
Kevin Baugess, *ICDC College*
Christopher Becker, *Coastal Carolina University*
Jeanne Bedell, *Keiser University*
Marcia Behrens, *Nichols College*
Michael Belleman, *St. Clair County Community College*
David Berman, *Community College of Philadelphia*
Tim Biggart, *Berry College*
Cynthia Bird, *Tidewater Community College*
Lisa Blum, *University of Louisville*
Rick Blumenfeld, *Sierra College*
Cindy Bortman Boggess, *Babson College*
William A. Bottiglieri, *Iona College*
Cathalene Bowler, *University of Northern Iowa*
Justin Breidenbach, *Ohio Wesleyan University*
Suzon Bridges, *Houston Community College*
Stephen Bukowy, *UNC Pembroke*
Esther Bunn, *Stephen F. Austin State University*
Megan Burke, *Texas Woman's University*
Holly Caldwell, *Bridgewater College*
James Campbell, *Thomas College*
Alisa Carini, *University of California San Diego Extension*
Ronald Carter, *Patrick Henry Community College*
Cynthia Caruso, *Endicott College*
Al Case, *Southern Oregon University*
Paul Caselton, *University of Illinois–Springfield*
Machiavelli (Max) Chao, *University of California–Irvine*
Amy Chataginer, *Mississippi Gulf Coast Community College*
Christine Cheng, *Louisiana State University*
Lisa Church, *Rhode Island College*
Marilyn Ciolino, *Delgado Community College*
Wayne Clark, *Southwest Baptist University*
Ann Cohen, *University at Buffalo, SUNY*
Sharon Cox, *University of Illinois–Urbana-Champaign*
Terry Crain, *University of Oklahoma–Norman*
Roger Crane, *Indiana University East*
Cheryl Crespi, *Central Connecticut State University*
Brad Cripe, *Northern Illinois University*
Curtis J. Crocker, *Southern Crescent Technical College*
Richard Cummings, *University of Wisconsin–Whitewater*
Joshua Cutler, *University of Houston*
William Dams, *Lenoir Community College*
Nichole Dauenhauer, *Lakeland Community College*
Susan Snow Davis, *Green River College*
Ginger DeLatte, *Texas A&M—Corpus Christi*
Jim Desimpelare, *University of Michigan–Ann Arbor*
Julie Dilling, *Moraine Park Technical College*
Steve Dombrock, *Carroll University*
Dr. Vicky C. Dominguez, *College of Southern Nevada*
Keith Donnelly, *SUNY Brockport*
Michael P. Donohoe, *University of Illinois–Urbana-Champaign*
John Dorocak, *California State University–San Bernardino*
Katharine Drake, *University of Arizona*
Amy Dunbar, *University of Connecticut–Storrs*
Bob Duquette, *Lehigh University*
John Eagan, *Morehouse College*
Reed Easton, *Seton Hall University*
Esther Ehrlich, CPA, *The University of Texas at El Paso*
Elizabeth Ekmekjian, *William Paterson University*
Ann Esarco, *Columbia College Columbia*
Frank Faber, *St. Joseph's College*
Michael Fagan, *Raritan Valley Community College*
Frank Farina, *Catawba College*
Andrew Finley, *Claremont McKenna*
Tim Fogarty, *Case Western Reserve University*
Wilhelmina Ford, *Middle Georgia State University*
Michele Frank, *Miami University*
George Frankel, *San Francisco State University*
Lawrence Friedken, *Penn State University*
Stephen Gara, *Drake University*
Lauren Garrett, *Shippensburg University*
Robert Gary, *University of New Mexico*
Sheri Geddes, *Hope College*
Greg Geisler, *Indiana University*
Alex Gialanella, *Fordham University*
Earl Godfrey, *Gardner Webb University*
Thomas Godwin, *Purdue University*
David Golub, *Northeastern University*
Marina Grau, *Houston Community College*
Brian Greenstein, *University of Delaware*
Patrick Griffin, *Lewis University*
Lillian Grose, *University of Holy Cross*
Thomas Guarino, *Plymouth State University*
Rosie Hagen, *Virginia Western Community College*
Joni Hammond, *Georgia Southwestern State University*
Marcye Hampton, *University of Central Florida*
Connie Hardgrove, *College of Central Florida*
Cass Hausserman, *Portland State University*
Rebecca Helms, *Ivy Tech Community College*
Melanie Hicks, *Liberty University*
Mary Ann Hofmann, *Appalachian State University*
Robert Joseph Holdren, *Muskingum University*
Bambi Hora, *University of Central Oklahoma*
David Horn, *Metropolitan State University*
Carol Hughes, *Asheville Buncombe Technical Community College*
Helen Hurwitz, *Saint Louis University*
Rik Ichiho, *Dixie State University*

Kerry Inger, *Auburn University*
Paul Johnson, *Mississippi Gulf Coast CC–JD Campus*
Athena Jones, *University of Maryland Global Campus*
Andrew Junikiewicz, *Temple University*
Susan Jurney, *University of Arkansas–Fayetteville*
Beth R. Kane, *Northwestern University and Johnson Wales University*
Sandra Kemper, *Regis University*
Jon Kerr, *Baruch College–CUNY*
Lara Kessler, *Grand Valley State University*
Janice Klimek, *University of Central Missouri*
Pamela Knight, *Columbus Technical College*
Satoshi Kojima, *East Los Angeles College*
Dawn Konicek, *Idaho State University*
Jack Lachman, *Brooklyn College*
Brandon Lanciloti, *Freed-Hardeman University*
Stacie Laplante, *University of Wisconsin–Madison*
Suzanne Laudadio, *Durham Tech*
Stephanie Lewis, *Ohio State University–Columbus*
Teresa Lightner, *University of North Texas*
Robert Lin, *California State University–East Bay*
Chris Loiselle, *Cornerstone University*
Bruce Lubich, *Penn State–Harrisburg*
Elizabeth Lyon, *California State University–Sacramento*
Narelle Mackenzie, *San Diego State University, National University*
Michael Malmfeldt, *Shenandoah University*
Kate Mantzke, *Northern Illinois University*
Robert Martin, *Kennesaw State University*
Anthony Masino, *East Tennessee State University*
Paul Mason, *Baylor University*
Lisa McKinney, *University of Alabama at Birmingham*
Allison McLeod, *University of North Texas*
Lois McWhorter, *Somerset Community College*
Janet Meade, *University of Houston*
Michele Meckfessel, *University of Missouri–St. Louis*
Frank Messina, *University of Alabama at Birmingham*
R. Miedaner, *Lee University*
Ken Milani, *University of Notre Dame*
Syed M Moiz, *University of Wisconsin, Platteville*
Karen Morris, *Northeast Iowa Community College*
Stephanie Morris, *Mercer University*
Michelle Moshier, *University at Albany*
Leslie Mostow, *University of Maryland–College Park*
James Motter, *Indiana University–Purdue University Indianapolis*
Jackie Myers, *Sinclair Community College*
Michael Nee, *Cape Cod Community College*
Liz Ott, *Casper College*
Sandra Owen, *Indiana University–Bloomington*
Edwin Pagan, *Passaic County Community College*
Jeff Paterson, *Florida State University*
Ronald Pearson, *Bay College*
Martina Peng, *Franklin University*
Michael Wayne Penn Jr., *University of Illinois–Urbana-Champaign*
Dr. Theresa Phipps, *Slippery Rock University*
James Pierson, *Franklin University*
Sonja Pippin, *University of Nevada–Reno*
Jonathan David Pittard, *University of California–Riverside*
Anthony Pochesci, *Rutgers University*
Kyle Post, *Tarleton State University*
Christopher Proschko, *Texas State University*
Joshua Racca, *University of Alabama*
Nirmalee Raddatz, *University of Memphis*
Francisco Rangel, *Riverside City College*
Pauline Ash Ray, *Thomas University*
Luke Richardson, *University of South Florida*
Rodney Ridenour, *Montana State University Northern*
John Robertson, *Arkansas State University*
Jennifer Robinson, *Trident Technical College*
Nicholas Robinson, *Eastern Illinois University*
Susan Robinson, *Georgia Southwestern State University*
Morgan Rockett, *Moberly Area Community College*
Miles Romney, *Michigan State University*
Abbie Sadler, *University of Richmond*
Ananth Seetharaman, *Saint Louis University*
Alisa Shapiro, *Raritan Valley Community College*
Deanna Sharpe, *University of Missouri*
Wayne Shaw, *Southern Methodist University*
Sonia Singh, *University of Florida*
Georgi Smatrakalev, *Florida Atlantic University*
Lucia Smeal, *Georgia State University*
Pamela Smith, *University of Texas at San Antonio*
Adam Spoolstra, *Johnson County Community College*
Joe Standridge, *Sonoma State*
Jason Stanfield, *Ball State University*
George Starbuck, *McMurry University*
James Stekelberg, *University of Arizona*
Teresa Stephenson, *University of Alaska Anchorage*
Shane Stinson, *University of Alabama*
Terrie Stolte, *Columbus State Community College*
Pamela J. Strickland, *Campbell University*
Gloria Jean Stuart, *Georgia Southern University*
Kenton Swift, *University of Montana*
MaryBeth Tobin, *Bridgewater State University*
Erin Towery, *University of Georgia*
Ronald Unger, *Temple University*
Glenn Walberg, *University of Vermont*
Karen Wallace, *Ramapo College*
Stephanie Walton, *Louisiana State University*
Natasha Ware, *Southeastern University*
Luke Watson, *University of Florida*
Sarah Webber, *University of Dayton*
Cassandra Weitzenkamp, *Peru State College*
Marvin Williams, *University of Houston–Downtown*
Chris Woehrle, *American College*
Jennifer Wright, *Drexel University*
Massood Yahya-Zadeh, *George Mason University*
James Yang, *Montclair State University*
Scott Yetmar, *Cleveland State University*
Xiaoli (Charlie) Yuan, *Elizabeth City State University*
Zhen Zhang, *Towson University*
Mingjun Zhou, *DePaul University*

Acknowledgments

We would like to thank the many talented people who made valuable contributions to the creation of this fourteenth edition. William A. Padley of Madison Area Technical College, Deanna Sharpe of the University of Missouri–Columbia, and Troy Lewis of Brigham Young University checked the page proofs and solutions manual for accuracy; we greatly appreciate the hours they spent checking tax forms and double-checking our calculations throughout the book. Troy Lewis, Deanna Sharpe, and Teressa Farough accuracy checked the test bank. Thank you to Troy Lewis, Matt Lowenkron, and Jason Stanfield for your contributions to the Smartbook revision for this edition. Special thanks to Troy Lewis for his sharp eye and valuable feedback throughout the revision process. Finally, Deanna Sharpe, Troy Lewis, Nancy Osborne of University of Massachusetts Dartmouth, and Vivian Paige of Christopher Newport University greatly contributed to the accuracy of McGraw Hill's Connect for the 2023 edition.

We are especially grateful to J. T. Eagan for his contributions to the Tableau Dashboard Activities and Guided Examples, as well as Temple University instructors Wayne Williams, David Jones, and Ronald Unger for their assistance developing the Data Analytics Problems.

We also appreciate the expert attention given to this project by the staff at McGraw Hill Education, especially Tim Vertovec, Managing Director; Kathleen Klehr, Executive Portfolio Manager; Sarah Wood and Katie Ward, Freelance Product Developers; Brian Nacik and Jill Eccher, Content Project Managers; Beth Blech, Designer; Natalie King, Marketing Director; Claire McLemore, Marketing Manager; and Sue Culbertson, Senior Buyer.

Changes in *Taxation of Business Entities,* 2023 Edition

For the 2023 edition of McGraw Hill's *Taxation of Business Entities,* many changes were made in response to feedback from reviewers and focus group participants:

- All tax forms have been **updated for the latest available tax form as of 2022.** In addition, **chapter content** throughout the text has been **updated to reflect tax law changes through February 8, 2022.**

Other notable changes in the 2023 edition include:

Chapter 1

- Updated tax forms from 2020 to 2021.
- Updated examples and problems for changes in inflation limit on gross receipts test.
- Added new Taxes in the Real World on whether cost of goods sold is subject to the test for economic performance.
- Clarified exception for prohibition of expense deduction by cannabis businesses.
- Explained and illustrated new small business accounting regulations.
- Integrated gross receipts test into accounting limitations.
- Added explanations of new regulations limiting entertainment and travel deductions including revised examples.
- Described and illustrated accounting for nonincidental material.
- Updated mileage deductions for travel in 2022.
- Added new Taxes in the Real World on Cryptocurrency and Income from a Hard Fork.

Chapter 2

- Updated Exhibit 2-2 for Weyerhaueser's 2020 assets.
- Updated tax rates to 2022 rates.
- Revised section on §179 amounts to reflect the inflation adjustments for 2022.
- Updated examples for 2022 §179 amounts.
- Updated discussion and Exhibit 2-10 relating to automobile depreciation limits.
- Updated §179 amount for SUVs for 2022 inflation amount changes.
- Updated tax forms to 2021.
- Updated and revised end-of-chapter problems for §179 amounts and bonus depreciation rules.
- Revised discussion of research and experimentation expenditures to reflect disallowance of the immediate expensing option in 2022.
- Added new Taxes in the Real World: The Case of How Sports Owners Pay Lower Tax Rates Than the Stadium Beer Server.

Chapter 3

- Updated tax rates for 2022.
- Updated tax forms from 2020 to 2021 forms.
- Added new Taxes in the Real World: Buyer Beware.

Chapter 4

- Added discussion and new example illustrating double taxation of C corporations and single taxation of flow-through entities (including basis in ownership interest in entity).
- Added discussion on the qualified business income (QBI) deduction, including two new examples.
- Enhanced QBI-related problems to include limitations.
- Added discussion and new example on self-employment tax.
- Added discussion relating to tax-exempt organizations.
- Added new discussion question dealing with tax-exempt organizations.
- Added new exhibit comparing tax characteristics by tax entity type.
- Added discussion and new example on owner compensation when owners provide services.
- Added new Taxes in the Real World dealing with unreasonable compensation paid to S corporation shareholder/employees.
- Updated Social Security wage base limitation for 2022, including related calculations.
- Updated inflation-adjusted numbers for excess business loss threshold and gross receipts test to reflect 2022 numbers.
- Added and/or revised several discussion questions and problems, including adding a new comprehensive problem.
- Updated tax forms to 2021 in problem solutions.

Chapter 5

- Revised section dealing with book–tax difference on an investment held for trading.
- Added summary of temporary book–tax differences for installment sales and like-kind exchanges.

- Added example on the book-tax differences associated with organizational expenditures.
- Revised net operating loss discussion.
- Added new Taxes in the Real World about whether large corporations are paying enough taxes.
- Added note to Exhibit 5-6 to mention that NOL deductions may be limited when there is an ownership change.
- Revised charitable deduction limitation discussion and example to reflect differences in charitable contribution limit between 2021 and 2022.
- Updated the gross receipts test for the cash method to reflect the inflation-adjusted threshold for 2022.
- Updated dates in examples and problems from 2021 to 2021.
- Updated tax forms to 2022.

Chapter 6

- Added new discussion of ASC 740 objectives.
- Added new Examples 6-1 and 6-2 to illustrate the importance of ASC 740 and its objectives.
- Revised net operating loss discussion in the valuation allowance section to describe tax law changes relating to net operating losses under the CARES Act.
- Updated text discussion for tax law changes introduced by the Consolidated Appropriations Act (CAA), 2021, signed on December 27, 2020. This includes updating the deductibility of the cost of meals purchased at a restaurant and updating the income percentage limitation for qualified charitable contributions.
- Updated examples and problems to reflect the tax law changes introduced by the CAA.
- Revised and streamlined the Tax Provision Process to five steps.
- Added new Exhibit 6-6 for the current tax expense formula.
- Revised discussion of the calculation of the current income tax expense.
- Revised discussion of the determination of the deferred tax assets and liabilities.
- Added new Exhibit 6-7 to illustrate taxable and deductible temporary differences.
- Added new Exhibit 6-8 to provide PCC's tax basis balance sheet.
- Added new discussion of tax basis liabilities and the balance sheet method of determining the deferred tax assets and liabilities.
- Revised Examples 6-7 through 6-13 to illustrate the balance sheet approach.
- Added formula for the total tax expense.
- Revised the discussion of the required journal entries to book the current and deferred income tax expense or benefit.
- Expanded the discussion of the journal entries related to the valuation allowance.
- Added discussion of journal entries related to uncertain tax positions.
- Updated dates in examples and problems from 2021 to 2022.
- Updated the Subsequent Events discussion for uncertain tax benefits.
- Updated Exhibit 6-9 for Microsoft uncertain tax benefit footnote disclosure.
- Added new Taxes in the Real World: Material Weaknesses in Tax Reporting.

Chapter 7

- Modified examples and discussion to clarify distinction between calculating accumulated and current earnings and profits.
- Added new Taxes in the Real World describing the importance of record keeping in calculating the tax basis of shares of corporate stock.
- Clarified examples of stock attribution from entities to owners or beneficiaries.
- Added new Taxes in the Real World illustrating the substance-over-form doctrine.
- Clarified homework problems on calculation of current earnings and profits.

Chapter 8

- Clarified discussion and example of receipt of stock for services in §351.
- Modified version of ethics question on accommodation transfers.
- Revised explanation of corporate basis calculation when shareholders receive boot in a §351 transaction.
- Clarified that merger negotiations must simultaneously consider both the form and the price of a corporate acquisition.
- Added new Taxes in the Real World on reverse Special Purpose Acquisition Company (SPAC) mergers.
- Added new alternatives to corporate liquidation problems.

Chapter 9

- Updated discussion on excess business loss limitation to reflect inflation adjustments of threshold amounts.
- Updated discussion on the availability of the cash method to partnerships with corporate partners to

reflect inflation adjustments to the average annual gross receipts test.
- Updated discussion on the applicability of the limitation on business interest expense to partners and partnerships to reflect inflation adjustments to the average annual gross receipts test.
- Added new discussion of forms K-2 and K-3 filed by partnerships.
- Added a new discussion of how passive activity losses carried forward are used when a partner sells their interest in a partnership.
- Updated tax forms to 2021.
- Revised end-of-chapter problems to reflect inflation adjustments.

Chapter 10

- Updated Form 1065 late filing penalty amounts.
- Added a new Taxes in the Real World item describing how owners of sports franchises utilize special basis adjustments available to partners to deduct a substantial amount of their purchase price.
- Added a new discussion of partnership terminations and their implications.

Chapter 11

- Updated excess business loss limitation for 2022.
- Added a new Taxes in the Real World on S corporation elections and venture capital.
- Updated Social Security tax wage base for 2022.
- Updated tax forms to 2021.

Chapter 12

- Updated economic sales tax nexus for updates related to *South Dakota v. Wayfair, Inc.*
- Updated nexus discussion to reflect sales tax nexus and income tax nexus being different.

Chapter 13

- Updated the discussion on the OECD base erosion and profit-shifting project to reflect the recent adoption by OECD countries of a worldwide minimum tax rate.
- Updated the discussion on the level of foreign investment in the U.S and the level of U.S. investment in foreign countries.
- Updated tax forms to 2021.

Chapter 14

- Revised text and Exhibit 14-2 for changes in the applicable exclusion amount.
- Revised for inflation adjustment for annual gift tax exclusion.
- Explained and illustrated calculation of applicable credit in event that the applicable exclusion amount is reduced in the future.
- Explained and illustrated calculation of deceased spousal unused exclusion (DSUE) for changes in the applicable exclusion amount at the death of the surviving spouse.
- Added new homework problem on use of the DSUE portability election.
- Modified homework problem on calculation of estate tax in a contemplation of death transfer.
- Clarified and illustrated shortcut method to calculate transfer taxes.
- Updated 2020 tax forms with 2021 forms.

As We Go to Press

The 2023 Edition includes tax law enacted as part of the Consolidated Appropriations Act, 2021 (CAA), signed into law on December 27, 2020, and the American Rescue Plan Act of 2021 (ARP), signed into law on March 11, 2021. The 2023 Edition is current through February 8, 2022. You can visit the *Connect Library* for updates that occur after this date.

Table of Contents

6 Accounting for Income Taxes

7 Corporate Taxation: Nonliquidating Distributions

8 Corporate Formation, Reorganization, and Liquidation

9 Forming and Operating Partnerships

10 Dispositions of Partnership Interests and Partnership Distributions

11 S Corporations

12 State and Local Taxes

13 The U.S. Taxation of Multinational Transactions

14 Transfer Taxes and Wealth Planning

chapter

1

Business Income, Deductions, and Accounting Methods

Learning Objectives

Upon completing this chapter, you should be able to:

LO 1-1 Identify common business deductions.

LO 1-2 Determine the limits on deducting business expenses.

LO 1-3 Describe accounting periods available to businesses.

LO 1-4 Apply cash and accrual methods to determine business income and expense deductions.

Tony Anderson/DigitalVision/Getty Images

Storyline Summary

Taxpayer:	Rick Grime (he/him/his)
Location:	San Antonio, Texas
Family description:	Unmarried
Employment status:	Rick quit his landscaping job in Dallas and moved to San Antonio to start a business as a self-employed landscaper.

Rick Grime graduated from Texas A&M University with a degree in agronomy, and for the past few years has been employed by a landscape architect in Dallas. Nearly every day Rick shared ideas with his employer about improving the business. Rick finally decided to take his ideas and start his own landscaping business in his hometown of San Antonio, Texas. In mid-April, Rick left his job and moved to San Antonio. Once in town, Rick discovered a lot of things are necessary to start a business. First, Rick registered his new business name (Green Acres Landscaping, LLC) and established a bank account for the business. Next, Rick rented a used sport utility vehicle (SUV) and a shop for the place of business. Rick didn't know much about accounting for business activities, so a CPA, Jane Bronson, was hired to advise Rick. Jane and Rick decided that Green Acres would operate as a sole proprietorship, but Jane suggested that as the business grew, Rick might want to consider organizing it as a different type of legal entity. Operating as a corporation, for instance, would allow Rick to invite new investors or business partners to help fund future expansion. Rick formally started his business on May 1. Initially, Rick spent a lot of time attracting new customers, and figured he would hire employees as needs warranted.

(to be continued . . .)

This chapter describes the process for determining income for *businesses*. Keep in mind that the concepts in this chapter generally apply to all types of tax entities, including sole proprietorships (such as Green Acres), partnerships, entities taxed as partnerships (such as LLCs), S corporations, and C corporations.[1] Because Rick is a sole proprietor, our examples emphasize business income and deductions from his personal perspective. Proprietors report business income on Schedule C of their individual income tax returns.

Schedule C income is subject to both individual income and self-employment taxes. Entities, other than sole proprietorships, report income on tax forms separate from the owners' tax returns. For example, partnerships report taxable income on Form 1065, S corporations report taxable income on Form 1120-S, and C corporations report taxable income on Form 1120. Of all these entity types, generally only C corporations pay taxes on their income.

BUSINESS GROSS INCOME

In most respects, the rules for determining business gross income are the same as for determining gross income for individuals. Gross income includes "all income from whatever source derived."[2] Generally speaking, income from a business includes gross profit from inventory sales (i.e., sales minus cost of goods sold), income from services provided to customers, and income from renting property to customers. Just like individuals, a business is allowed to exclude certain types of realized income from gross income, such as municipal bond interest. Unlike wage earners, businesses can be subject to complex rules and limitations discussed later in this chapter. However, most *small* businesses are exempt from these rules as determined under a gross receipts test.

Gross Receipts Test for Determining Small Businesses

A business that qualifies as a *small* business under a **gross receipts test** is exempt from certain complex accounting provisions (discussed later in the chapter) for each year in which it meets the test. A business meets the gross receipts test for 2022 if its average annual gross receipts for the three prior taxable years does not exceed $27 million.[3] For example, if a corporation reported gross receipts of $26 million, $25 million, and $29 million in 2019, 2020, and 2021, respectively, it would meet the gross receipts test for 2022 ($26.7 million in average gross receipts over the prior three years). However, if it reported $32 million of gross receipts in 2021, rather than $29 million, it would fail the gross receipts test for 2022 ($27.7 million in average gross receipts over the prior three years) and would not qualify as a small business for 2022. For purposes of the test, gross receipts includes total sales (net of returns and allowances but not cost of goods sold), amounts received for services, and income from investments (including tax-exempt interest).[4] When the business has not been in existence for three prior tax years, the test is conducted for the years that it was in existence. Also, in the case of a taxable year of less than 12 months (a *short* year), the amount of gross receipts must be annualized by multiplying the gross receipts for the short period by 12 and dividing the result by the number of months in the short period.

[1]S corporations are treated as flow-through entities (S corporation income is taxed to its owners), while C corporations are taxed as separate taxable entities. The choice of the organizational form for a business is a complex decision that is beyond the scope of this chapter.

[2]§61(a).

[3]§448(c). The gross receipts threshold amount is indexed for inflation. The gross receipts threshold was $25 million for 2018 and $26 million for 2019 through 2021.

[4]Temp. Reg. §1.448-1T(f)(2)(iv)(A). Gross receipts from the sale of a capital asset is reduced by the adjusted basis in the asset.

The gross receipts test is an annual test. It is possible a business might qualify under the the gross receipts test in year 1 but experience a surge in gross receipts and not qualify in year 2. Hence, businesses that experience volatile gross receipts may find that they qualify in one year but not the next if gross receipts vary substantially around the $27 million cutoff.

Example 1-1

What if: Suppose that Green Acres is a C corporation and a calendar-year taxpayer. Suppose further that Green Acres reported gross receipts of $20 million in 2019, $25 million in 2020, and $30 million in 2021. In 2022, is Green Acres a small business under the gross receipts test?

Answer: Yes. The average of gross receipts for the previous three-tax-year period is $25 million ($75 million divided by 3). Because average gross receipts doesn't exceed $27 million, Green Acres qualifies as a small business under the gross receipts test in 2022.

What if: Suppose that Green Acres began business operations on January 1, 2020, and reported $22 million in gross receipts for that year. In 2021, Green Acres reported $30 million in gross receipts. Is Green Acres a small business in 2022 under the gross receipts test?

Answer: Yes. The average of gross receipts for the two-tax-year period in which Green Acres conducted business is $26 million ($52 million divided by 2). Because average gross receipts doesn't exceed $27 million, Green Acres qualifies as a small business in 2022.

What if: Suppose that Green Acres began business operations on July 1, 2021, and reported $15 million in gross receipts for the six months of 2021, a short year. Does Green Acres qualify as a small business in 2022 under the gross receipts test?

Answer: No. For purposes of the gross receipts test, the gross receipts for the six-month 2021 tax year is annualized by multiplying $15 million by 12 and dividing the result by 6 (the number of months in the short period 2021). Thus, gross receipts for Green Acres in 2021 is $30 million ($180 million divided by 6). Because average gross receipts is more than $27 million, Green Acres is not considered to be a small business in 2022.

TAXES IN THE REAL WORLD Is a *Hard Fork* a taxable event?

A hard fork refers to a radical change to the protocols of a blockchain network. In simple terms, a hard fork splits a single cryptocurrency into two. On August 1, 2017, Bitcoin experienced a hard fork, and a second cryptocurrency, called Bitcoin Cash, was created. Every holder of a unit of Bitcoin received the same number of Bitcoin Cash units.

In 2021, the IRS concluded that the Bitcoin hard fork is a taxable event if the taxpayer had control over the resulting second cryptocurrency. Hence, a taxpayer who held 1 Bitcoin unit with a private key was subject to tax in 2017 on the value of the Bitcoin Cash unit received in the hard fork.

In contrast, another taxpayer owned Bitcoin through an account at CEX, a cryptocurrency exchange. Rather than the taxpayer, CEX had sole control over the private key to 100 units of Bitcoin. The taxpayer owned one unit of the 100 total Bitcoin units held by CEX. Because CEX was uncertain of Bitcoin Cash's security and viability, it chose not to support Bitcoin Cash at the time of the hard fork. As a result, the taxpayer was unable to access any Bitcoin Cash through the account with CEX. The taxpayer was only subject to tax in 2018 on the value of the Bitcoin Cash unit after CEX initiated support for Bitcoin Cash in 2018, allowing the taxpayer to buy, sell, send, receive, transfer, or exchange the 1 unit in their account. The IRS noted that the character of the gain depended on whether the virtual currency is a capital asset in the hands of the taxpayer.

Source: Chief Counsel Advice CCA 202114020.

BUSINESS DEDUCTIONS

LO 1-1

Because Congress intended for taxable income to reflect the *net* increase in wealth from a business, it is only fair that a business is allowed to deduct expenses incurred to generate business income. Typically, Congress provides *specific* statutory rules authorizing

THE KEY FACTS

Business Expenses

- Business expenses must be incurred in pursuit of profits, not personal goals.
- A deduction must be ordinary and necessary (appropriate and helpful).
- Only reasonable amounts are allowed as deductions.

deductions. However, as you can see from the following excerpt from §162, the provision authorizing business deductions is relatively broad and ambiguous:

> There shall be allowed as a deduction all the ordinary and necessary expenses paid or incurred during the taxable year in carrying on any trade or business. . . .[5]

Taxpayers can deduct expenses for "trade or business" activities, but the law does not define the phrase "trade or business."[6] However, it is implicit that the primary objective of a "business" activity is to make a profit. Thus, the law requires that a business expense be made in the pursuit of profit rather than the pursuit of other, presumably personal, motives.

Ordinary and Necessary

Business expenditures must be both **ordinary and necessary** to be deductible. An *ordinary* expense is an expense that is normal or appropriate for the business under the circumstances.[7] To be considered ordinary, an expense need not be typical or repetitive in nature. For example, a business could deduct the legal fees it expends to defend itself in an antitrust suit. Although an antitrust suit would be atypical and unusual for most businesses, defending the suit would probably be deemed ordinary because it would be expected under the circumstances. A *necessary* expense is an expense that is helpful or conducive to the business activity, but the expenditure need not be essential or indispensable. For example, a deduction for metric tools would qualify as ordinary and necessary even if there was only a small chance that a repair would require these tools. The "ordinary and necessary" requirements are applied on a case-by-case basis, and while the deduction depends on individual circumstances, the IRS is often reluctant to second-guess business decisions. Exhibit 1-1 presents examples of expenditures that are ordinary and necessary for typical businesses.

EXHIBIT 1-1 Examples of Typical Ordinary and Necessary Business Expenses

• Advertising	• Office expenses
• Car and truck expenses	• Rent
• Depreciation	• Repairs
• Employee compensation and benefits	• Supplies
• Insurance	• Travel
• Interest	• Utilities
• Legal fees	• Wages

Example 1-2

Rick provides a small waiting room for clients. Rick paid $50 for several books to occupy clients while waiting for appointments. These are hardcover books with photographs and illustrations of landscape designs. Rick believes that the books will inspire new designs and alleviate boredom for potential clients. Can Rick deduct the $50 cost as a business expense?

Answer: Yes, the $50 is ordinary and necessary. The phrase *ordinary and necessary* is interpreted as *helpful or conducive to business activity*. In Rick's situation, it seems highly unlikely that the IRS or a court would conclude that the cost of these books is not ordinary and necessary.

What if: Suppose that Rick's hobby was pre-Columbian art. Would Rick be able to deduct the cost of a new treatise on determining provenance of this art if he placed this book in his waiting room?

[5]§162(a). It is important to note that the cost of goods sold is not a deduction. Instead, it automatically reduces gross income from sales and requires no statutory authority. See *Doyle v. Mitchell Brothers Co.,* 247 U.S. 179 (1918), *aff'g* 235 Fed. 686 (6th Cir. 1916).

[6]§212 contains a sister provision to §162 allowing deductions for ordinary and necessary expenses incurred for the production of income ("investment expenses") and for the management and maintenance of property (including expenses incurred in renting property in situations when the rental activity is not considered to be a trade or business). A business activity, sometimes referred to as a trade or business, requires a relatively high level of involvement or effort from the taxpayer. Unlike business activities, investments are profit-motivated activities that don't require a high degree of taxpayer involvement or effort.

[7]*Welch v. Helvering,* 290 U.S. 111 (1933).

Answer: No. It seems unlikely that Rick's prospective clients would share Rick's interest in pre-Columbian art, much less how to determine provenance. Hence, it seems highly likely that the IRS or a court would conclude that Rick purchased the treatise for personal rather than business reasons and that the cost of this book is not ordinary and necessary.

ETHICS

Sheri is an attorney who operates as a sole practitioner. Despite a busy schedule, in the past Sheri found time for family. This year Sheri took on two new important clients and hired a personal assistant to help manage Sheri's schedule and make timely court filings. Occasionally, Sheri asked the assistant to assist with personal tasks such as buying groceries. Do you think that Sheri should treat the assistant's entire salary as a business expense? Would your answer be any different if personal assistants were to commonly perform these tasks for other busy professionals, such as corporate executives and accountants? How would the cost of a personal assistant differ from the cost of having groceries delivered?

Reasonable in Amount

Ordinary and necessary business expenses are deductible only *to the extent* they are **reasonable in amount.** The courts have interpreted this requirement to mean that an expenditure is not reasonable when it is extravagant or exorbitant.[8] If the expenditure is extravagant in amount, the courts presume the excess amount is spent for personal rather than business reasons and is not deductible.

Determining whether an expenditure is reasonable is not an exact science, and, not surprisingly, taxpayers and the IRS may have different opinions. Generally, the courts and the IRS test for extravagance by comparing the amount of the expense to a market price or an **arm's-length amount.** An amount is reasonable if it is within the range of amounts typically charged in the market by unrelated persons. When an amount exceeds this range, the underlying issue becomes *why* a profit-motivated taxpayer would make an excessive payment. Hence, reasonableness is most likely to be an issue when a payment is made to an individual related to the taxpayer or when the taxpayer enjoys some incidental benefit from the expenditure.

Example 1-3

During the busy part of the year, Rick could not keep up with all the work. Therefore, he hired four part-time employees and paid them the market rate of $20 an hour to mow and trim lawns. When things finally slowed down in late fall, Rick released his four part-time employees. Rick paid a total of $21,000 in compensation to the four employees.

Rick still needed some extra help now and then, so he hired his brother, Tom, on a part-time basis. Tom performed the same duties as the prior part-time employees. However, Rick paid Tom $35 per hour because Tom is a college student and Rick wanted to provide some additional support for Tom's education. At year-end, Tom had worked a total of 100 hours and received $3,500 from Rick. What amount can Rick deduct for the compensation he paid to his employees?

Answer: $23,000. Rick can deduct the entire $21,000 paid to the four part-time employees. However, he can only deduct $20 an hour for Tom's compensation because the extra $15 per hour Rick paid Tom is unreasonable in amount.[9] The remaining $15 per hour is considered a personal (nondeductible) gift from Rick to Tom. Hence, Rick can deduct a total of $23,000 for compensation expense this year [$21,000 + ($20 × 100)].

(continued on page 1-6)

[8]§162(a); *Comm'r v. Lincoln Elec. Co.*, 176 F.2d 815 (6th Cir. 1949).

[9]In practice, this distinction is rarely cut and dried. Rick may be able to argue for various reasons that Tom's work is worth more than $20 an hour, but perhaps not as much as $35 per hour. We use this example to illustrate the issue of reasonable expenses and not to discuss the merits of what actually is reasonable compensation to Tom.

What if: Suppose that Tom was able to mow twice as many lawns as other employees in the same amount of time and also provide the same quality of work. What is the deductible amount of the $3,500 under these circumstances?

Answer: $3,500. Rick can now deduct an additional $1,500 because Tom's quality of work justifies twice the salary paid to other employees.

LO 1-2

LIMITATIONS ON BUSINESS DEDUCTIONS

THE KEY FACTS

Limitations on Business Deductions

- No business deductions are allowable for expenditures that are against public policy (bribes) or are political contributions.
- Expenditures that benefit a period longer than 12 months generally must be capitalized.
- No deductions are allowable for expenditures associated with the production of tax-exempt income.
- Personal expenditures are not deductible.

For a variety of reasons, Congress specifically prohibits or limits a business's ability to deduct certain expenditures that appear to otherwise meet the general business expense deductibility requirements.

Expenditures against Public Policy

Businesses occasionally incur fines and penalties and may even pay illegal bribes and kickbacks. However, these payments are not deductible for tax purposes.[10] Congress disallows these expenditures under the rationale that allowing them would subsidize illegal activities and frustrate public policy. Interestingly enough, businesses conducting an illegal activity (i.e., selling stolen goods or conducting illegal gambling) are allowed to offset gross income with the cost of the illegal goods (the cost of goods sold) and deduct other ordinary and necessary business expenses incurred in conducting the illegal business activity. However, they are not allowed to deduct fines, penalties, bribes, or illegal kickbacks.[11] Of course, the IRS is probably more concerned that many illegal businesses fail to report *any* income than that illegal businesses overstate deductions.[12]

Example 1-4

In July, the city fined Rick $200 for violating the city's watering ban when he watered a newly installed landscape. Later, Rick donated $250 to the mayor's campaign for reelection. Can Rick deduct these expenditures?

Answer: No. Rick cannot deduct either the fine or the political contribution as a business expense because the tax laws specifically prohibit deductions for these expenditures.

Political Contributions and Lobbying Costs

Perhaps to avoid the perception that the federal government subsidizes taxpayer efforts to influence politics, the tax laws prohibit deductions for political contributions and most lobbying expenses.[13]

[10]§162(c); Reg. §1.162-21. This prohibition applies to fines and penalties imposed by a government or governmental unit unless the taxpayer establishes that the payment is either restitution, remediation, or required to come into compliance with the law. Fines and penalties imposed by other organizations, such as a fine levied by NASCAR or the NFL, would be fully deductible if the payment otherwise qualified as an ordinary and necessary business expense.

[11]*Comm'r v. Sullivan,* 356 U.S. 27 (1958). In addition, no deduction is allowed for any settlement, payout, or attorney fees related to sexual harassment or abuse if the payments are subject to a nondisclosure agreement.

[12]§280E explicitly prohibits dealers in illegal drugs from deducting any business expenses associated with this "business" activity. This prohibition remains on marijuana producers despite the legalization of marijuana under some state laws. However, drug dealers and marijuana producers are still able to deduct cost of goods sold because cost of goods sold is technically a reduction in gross income (return of capital) and not a business expense. See Reg. §1.61-3(a).

[13]§162(e).

Capital Expenditures

Whether a business uses the cash or the accrual method of accounting, it must capitalize expenditures for *tangible* assets such as buildings, machinery and equipment, furniture and fixtures, and similar property that have useful lives of more than one year (12 months).[14] For tax purposes, businesses recover the cost of capitalized tangible assets (other than land) either by immediate expensing (when allowed by law) or through depreciation.

Businesses also capitalize the cost to create or acquire *intangible* assets such as patents, purchased goodwill, start-up costs, and organizational expenditures.[15] They recover the costs of capitalized intangible assets either through amortization (when the tax laws allow them to do so) or upon disposition of the assets.[16] Prepaid expenses are also subject to capitalization, but there is a special exception that we discuss under accounting methods later in this chapter.

Expenses Associated with the Production of Tax-Exempt Income

Expenses that generate *tax-exempt* income are not allowed to offset taxable income. For example, this restriction disallows interest expense deductions for businesses that borrow money and invest the loan proceeds in municipal (tax-exempt) bonds. It also disallows deductions for life insurance premiums businesses pay on policies that cover the lives of officers or other key employees and compensate the business for the disruption and lost income related to a key employee's death. Because the death benefit from the life insurance policy is not taxable, a business is not allowed to deduct the insurance premium expense associated with this nontaxable income.

Example 1-5

Rick employs Joan, an arborist who specializes in trimming trees and treating local tree ailments. Joan generates a great deal of revenue for Rick's business, but Joan is over 60 and suffers from MS. In November, Rick purchased a "key employee" term life insurance policy on Joan's life. Rick paid $720 in premiums for a policy that pays Rick (Green Acres) a $20,000 death benefit if Joan passes away during the next 12 months. Can Rick deduct the life insurance premium?

Answer: No. Rick cannot deduct the $720 premium on the life insurance policy because the life insurance proceeds from the policy are tax-exempt.

What if: Suppose Rick purchased the life insurance policy on Joan's life and allowed Joan to name the beneficiary. Again, Rick paid a $720 premium for a policy that pays the beneficiary a $20,000 death benefit if Joan dies in the next 12 months. What amount of life insurance policy premium can Rick deduct?

Answer: $720. In this scenario, Rick can deduct the entire premium of $720 as a *compensation* expense because the benefit of the policy inures to Joan (she names the beneficiary), and not to Rick's business.

Personal Expenditures

Taxpayers are not allowed to deduct **personal expenses** unless the expenses are "expressly" authorized by a provision in the law.[17] While the tax laws do not expressly define what constitutes a *personal* expense, the statute identifies "personal, living, or family expenses" as nondeductible examples. Hence, at a minimum, the costs of food, clothing, and shelter are assumed to be personal and nondeductible. Of course, there are the inevitable exceptions when otherwise personal items are specially adapted to business use. For example, taxpayers may deduct the cost of uniforms or special clothing they purchase for use in their business if the clothing is not appropriate to wear as ordinary clothing outside the place of business. However, when the clothing is adaptable as ordinary clothing, the cost of the clothing is a nondeductible personal expenditure.

[14]Reg. §1.263(a)-2(d)(4). The act of recording the asset is sometimes referred to as *capitalizing* the expenditure.

[15]Reg. §1.263(a)-4(b). The extent to which expenditures for intangible assets must be capitalized is explored in *Indopco v. Comm'r,* 503 U.S. 79 (1992).

[16]See §§195, 197, and 248 for provisions that allow taxpayers to amortize the cost of certain intangible assets such as start-up costs and purchased goodwill.

[17]§262(a).

Example 1-6

Rick spent $500 to purchase special coveralls that identify his landscaping service and provide a professional appearance. How much of the cost for the clothing can Rick deduct as a business expense?

Answer: $500. While the cost of clothing is inherently personal, Rick can deduct the $500 cost of the coveralls because, due to the design and labeling on the coveralls, they are not suitable for ordinary use.

Many business owners, particularly small business owners such as sole proprietors, may be tempted to use business funds to pay for items that are entirely personal in nature. For example, a sole proprietor could use the business checking account to pay for family groceries. These expenditures, even though funded by the business, are not deductible.

Educational expenses constitute another exception. Expenditures made by a taxpayer for business education, including tuition and books, may be motivated by business aspirations. However, educational expenditures are not deductible as business expenses unless the taxpayer is self-employed and the education *maintains or improves skills* required by the individual in an *existing* trade or business. Education expenses necessary to meet minimum requirements for an occupation are not deductible. For example, tuition payments for courses to satisfy the education requirement to sit for the CPA exam are not deductible. These courses would qualify the taxpayer for a *new* trade or business rather than improving his skills in an existing trade or business.

THE KEY FACTS

Mixed-Motive Expenditures

- Special limits are imposed on expenditures that have both personal and business benefits.
- Entertainment expenses are generally not deductible.
- For 2022, the cost of business meals provided by restaurants is 100 percent deductible. Other business meals are typically 50 percent deductible.
- Contemporaneous written records of business purpose are required.

Mixed-Motive Expenditures

Business owners in general, and owners of small or closely held businesses in particular, often make expenditures that are motivated by *both* business and personal concerns. These **mixed-motive expenditures** are of particular concern to lawmakers and the IRS because of the tax incentive to disguise nondeductible personal expenses as deductible business expenses. Thus, deductions for business expenditures accompanied by personal benefits are closely monitored and restricted. The rules for determining the amount of *deductible* mixed-motive expenditures depend on the type of expenditure. The most common restrictions determine the deductible portion of mixed-motive expenditures for meals, travel and transportation, and the use of property for both business and personal purposes.

Like personal expenses, entertainment expenditures are generally not deductible as business expenses. Entertainment is defined in the regulations as any activity that is of a type generally considered to constitute entertainment, amusement, or recreation. Activities at night clubs, theaters, country clubs, and sporting events are all considered entertainment.[18] Two notable exceptions to the ban on deducting entertainment expenses include expenditures primarily for the benefit of the taxpayer's employees and entertainment expenses designed and treated as compensation. For example, an employer could deduct as compensation an all-expense paid holiday provided to an outstanding employee.

Some business expenditures are deductible despite being related to personal, living, or family needs of an individual; for example, the cost of a hotel room maintained by an employer for lodging of his employees while in business travel status. Another example is the cost for using an automobile in the active conduct of trade or business even though the auto might also be used for routine personal purposes such as commuting to and from work.

Because everyone needs to eat, meals also contain a significant personal element. In addition, meals are also often associated with entertainment activities. However, the cost or a portion of the cost of a meal can sometimes qualify as a business expense. To qualify as a business expense, the cost of food and beverages must meet several requirements. First, as with all business expenses, a meal must be ordinary and necessary under the circumstances and the amount must be reasonable (not extravagant). Second, the taxpayer or an employee must be present when the meal is furnished, and the meal must be provided to a current or potential client or business contact. Finally, if the meal is provided during or at an entertainment activity, the meal must be purchased separately from the entertainment or the cost stated separately on invoices or receipts.[19]

[18]Reg. §§1.274-2(b) and 1.274-11.

[19]§274(k), (n); Notices 2018-76 and 2021-25; Prop. Reg. §1.274-11(b)(ii).

Business deductions for food and beverages are generally limited to 50 percent of the cost. However, for 2022 (and 2021) the cost of food and beverages for business meals is 100 percent deductible as long as the expense is for food or beverages provided by a *restaurant* (presumably including take-out and delivery).[20] Also fully deductible are the costs of food and beverages when the amounts paid are treated as employee compensation.[21] For example, when a business rewards a high-performing salesperson with an all-inclusive vacation, the cost of the vacation including food and beverages is fully deductible. Likewise, the cost of food and beverages provided during employee recreational activities is fully deductible when the activity is not limited to highly compensated individuals. For example, the cost of meals and beverages would be fully deductible for a buffet and open bar at a holiday party for employees.

Example 1-7

Rick invited two prospective clients to a professional basketball game. Rick purchased tickets to attend the game in a suite where food and beverages would be provided by a wine and cheese specialty store that does not qualify as a restaurant. Rick paid $850 for the tickets and $540 for the food and beverages. Assuming that these amounts were not extravagant, what amount can Rick deduct as a business expense?

Answer: Rick can deduct $270 [$540 × 50%] as a business expense because the cost of the food was stated separately from the cost of the tickets. The cost of the tickets to the game is a nondeductible entertainment expense. If the food and beverages were provided by a restaurant, then Rick could deduct their full cost ($540).

What if: Suppose that Rick purchased the tickets for $1,500 and that the cost of the tickets included food and beverages. What amount of the expenditures can Rick deduct as a business expense?

Answer: Zero. The cost of meals must be stated separately from the cost of the entertainment.

What if: Suppose that Rick invited all of his employees to a company picnic where he paid $1,250 for food and beverages. What amount of the expenditures can Rick deduct as a business expense?

Answer: $1,250. The cost of food and beverages is fully deductible for employee recreational events that are not limited to highly compensated employees.

What if: Suppose Rick took a prospective client to his favorite restaurant and paid $200 for a meal. What amount could Rick deduct as a business expense?

Answer: $200 if the meal was not extravagant. For 2022, the entire cost of a business meal is deductible when provided by a restaurant.

Travel and Transportation Under certain conditions, sole proprietors and self-employed taxpayers may deduct the cost of travel and transportation for business purposes. *Transportation* expenses relate to the direct cost of transporting the taxpayer to and from remote business sites. In contrast, the cost of commuting between the taxpayer's home and regular place of business is personal and, therefore, not deductible. If the taxpayer uses a vehicle for business, the taxpayer can deduct the costs of operating the vehicle plus depreciation on the vehicle's tax basis. Alternatively, in lieu of deducting these costs, the taxpayer may simply deduct a standard amount for each business mile driven. The standard mileage rate represents the per-mile cost of operating an automobile (including depreciation or lease payments).[22] For 2022, the standard mileage rate is 58.5 cents per mile. To be deductible, the transportation must be for business reasons. If the transportation is primarily for personal purposes, the cost is not deductible.

[20]Section 210 of the Taxpayer Certainty and Disaster Tax Relief Act of 2020 amends Code Sec. 274(n)(2) to allow for 100 percent deduction of expenses for food and beverages paid to or incurred at a restaurant after December 31, 2020, and prior to January 1, 2023. Notice 2021-15 defines restaurant to mean a business that sells food or beverages to retail customers for immediate consumption regardless of whether the food or beverages are consumed on the business's premises.

[21]§274(e)(20) and Reg. §1.274-12(c). Importantly, the cost of food and beverages is only 50 percent deductible for breakroom snacks because this benefit does not qualify as compensation or recreational activities.

[22]This mileage rate is updated periodically (sometimes more than once a year) to reflect changes in the cost of operating a vehicle. Once a taxpayer uses the actual cost method including depreciation for determining automobile deductions, the taxpayer is not allowed to switch to the standard mileage rate method. If the taxpayer uses the mileage method, they can switch to the cost method in a subsequent year but must compute depreciation using the straight-line method.

Example 1-8

Rick decided to lease an SUV to drive between his shop and various work sites. Rick carefully documents the business use of the SUV (8,100 miles this year) and his operating expenses ($5,335 this year, including $3,935 for gas, oil, and repairs and $1,400 for lease payments). At no time does Rick use the SUV for personal purposes. What amount of these expenses may Rick deduct as business expenses?

Answer: $5,335. Because Rick uses the SUV in his business activities, he can deduct (1) the $5,335 cost of operating and leasing the SUV or (2) $4,739 for the 8,100 business miles driven this year (58.5 cents per mile × 8,100 miles). Assuming Rick chooses to deduct operating expenses and lease payments in lieu of using the mileage rate, he can deduct $5,335. However, by choosing to deduct the actual operating expense, Rick will forgo the option of using the mileage rate in the future.

In contrast to transportation expenses, *travel* expenses are only deductible if the taxpayer is *away from home* overnight while traveling. This distinction is important because, besides the cost of transportation, the deduction for **travel expenses** includes the cost of meals (limited to 50 percent unless provided by a restaurant), lodging, and incidental expenses. A taxpayer is considered to be away from home overnight if the travel is away from the primary place of business and of sufficient duration to require sleep or rest (typically this will be overnight).

When a taxpayer travels solely for business purposes, *all* of the costs of travel are deductible (but only 50 percent of meals unless provided by a restaurant). When the travel has both business and personal aspects, the deductibility of the transportation costs depends upon whether business is the *primary* purpose for the trip. If the primary purpose of a trip is business, the transportation costs are fully deductible, but meals (50 percent unless provided by a restaurant), lodging, and incidental expenditures are limited to those incurred during the business portion of the travel.[23] If the taxpayer's primary purpose for the trip is personal, the taxpayer may not deduct *any* transportation costs to arrive at the location but may deduct meals (limited to 50 percent unless provided by a restaurant), lodging, transportation, and incidental expenditures for the *business* portion of the trip. The primary purpose of a trip depends upon facts and circumstances and is often the subject of dispute.

The rule for business travel is modified somewhat if a trip abroad includes both business and personal activities. Like the rule for domestic travel, if foreign travel is primarily for personal purposes, then only those expenses directly associated with business activities are deductible. However, unlike the rule for domestic travel, when foreign travel is primarily for business purposes, a portion of the round-trip transportation costs is not deductible. The nondeductible portion is typically computed based on a ratio of the proportion of personal days to total days (travel days count as business days).[24]

Example 1-9

Rick paid a $300 registration fee for a three-day course in landscape design. The course was held in upstate New York (Rick paid $625 for airfare to attend) and he spent four days away from home. He spent the last day sightseeing. During the trip, Rick paid $150 a night for three nights' lodging, $50 a day for meals at restaurants, and $70 a day for a rental car. What amount of these travel-related expenditures may Rick deduct as business expenses?

[23]Note that travel days are considered business days. Also, special limitations apply to a number of travel expenses that are potentially abusive, such as luxury water travel, foreign conventions, conventions on cruise ships, and travel expenses associated with taking a companion.

[24]Foreign transportation expense is deductible without prorating under special circumstances detailed in §274(c). For example, the cost of getting abroad is fully deductible if the travel is for one week or less or if the personal activity constitutes less than one-fourth of the travel time.

Answer: $1,435 for business travel and $300 for business education. The primary purpose for the trip appears to be business because Rick spent three days on business activities versus one day on personal activities. He can deduct travel costs, computed as follows:

Deductible Travel Costs

Description	Amount	Explanation
Airfare	$ 625	Primary purpose is business
Lodging	450	3 business days × $150 a day
Meals	150	3 business days × $50 a day
Rental car	210	3 business days × $70 a day
Total business travel expenses	**$1,435**	

What if: Assume Rick stayed in New York for 10 days, spending 3 days at the seminar and 7 days sightseeing. What amount could he deduct?

Answer: In this scenario Rick can deduct $810 for the lodging, meals, and rental car and $300 for business education. Rick would not be able to deduct the $625 cost of airfare because the trip is primarily personal, as evidenced by the seven days of personal activities compared to only three days of business activities.

Deductible Travel Costs

Description	Amount	Explanation
Airfare	$ 0	Primary purpose is personal
Lodging	450	3 business days × $150 a day
Meals	150	3 business days × $50 a day
Rental car	210	3 business days × $70 a day
Total business travel expenses	**$810**	

What if: Assume the original facts in the example except Rick traveled to London (rather than upstate New York) for 10 days, spending 6 days at the seminar and 4 days sightseeing. What amount could he deduct?

Answer: In this scenario, Rick can deduct $1,995 for travel (computed below) and $300 for business education.

Deductible Travel Costs

Description	Amount	Explanation
Airfare to London	$ 375	6 business days/10 total days × $625
Lodging in London	900	6 business days × $150 a day
Meals	300	6 business days × $50 a day
Rental car	420	6 business days × $70 a day
Total business travel expenses	**$1,995**	

Rick is allowed to deduct $375 of the $625 airfare (60 percent) because he spent 6 of the 10 days on the trip conducting business activities.

Property Use Several types of property may be used for both business and personal purposes. For example, business owners often use automobiles, computers, or cell phones for both business and personal purposes.[25] However, because expenses relating to these assets are deductible only to the extent the assets are used for business purposes, taxpayers must allocate the expenses between the business and personal use portions. For example, if a full year's expense for a business asset is $1,000, but the asset is only used for business purposes 90 percent of the time, then only $900 of expense can be deducted ($1,000 × 90%).

[25]These types of assets are referred to as "listed property." However, cell phones and computers are specifically exempted from the definition of listed property under §280F(d)(4)(A).

Example 1-10

Rick occasionally uses his personal auto (a BMW) to drive to interviews with prospective clients and to drive back and forth between his shop and various work sites. This year Rick carefully recorded that the BMW was driven 500 miles for business activities and 10,000 miles in total. What expenses associated with the BMW may Rick deduct if Rick incurred $6,120 in operating costs for his BMW?

Answer: $306. Rick can deduct the business portion (of his total operating costs based upon the percentage of business miles driven to total miles driven [500 business miles/10,000 total miles]). Hence, Rick will deduct 5 percent of $6,120, or $306, as business travel. Alternatively, Rick could use the business mileage rate of 58.5 cents a mile to determine his business travel expense.

Record Keeping and Other Requirements Because distinguishing business purposes from personal purposes is a difficult and subjective task, the tax laws include provisions designed to help the courts and the IRS determine the business element of mixed-motive transactions. Under these provisions, taxpayers must maintain specific, written, contemporaneous records (of time, amount, and business purpose) for mixed-motive expenses. For example, the cost of business meals is deductible (limited to 50% unless provided by a restaurant), but only if the taxpayer can properly document the five requirements described above.[26]

THE KEY FACTS

Business Interest Limitation

- The deduction of business interest expense is limited to business interest income plus 30 percent of the business's adjusted taxable income.
- The business interest limitation does not apply to businesses qualifying as small businesses under the $27 million gross receipts test.
- Adjusted taxable income is taxable income allocable to the business computed without interest income and before depreciation and interest expense deductions.
- Disallowed business interest expense can be carried forward indefinitely.

Limitation on Business Interest Deductions

The deduction of interest paid or accrued on indebtedness allocable to a trade or business is subject to limitation. The purpose of this limitation is to limit the extent to which a business utilizes debt to avoid income taxes. Specifically, business interest is broadly defined as an amount that is paid, received, or accrued as compensation for the use or forbearance of money under the terms of an instrument or contractual arrangement. The amount of the deduction is, in general, limited to the sum of (1) *business interest income* and (2) 30 percent of the *adjusted taxable income* of the taxpayer for the taxable year. As a matter of equity, Congress allows business interest deductions to offset business interest income. The latter is defined as the amount of interest income includable in gross income that is properly allocable to a trade or business. The limitation does not apply to a business that qualifies as a small business under the $27 million gross receipts test discussed in the gross income section of the chapter.

Calculating the Interest Limitation Adjusted taxable income represents the taxable income allocable to the business activity. This income is defined as taxable income of the taxpayer computed without regard to (1) any item of income, gain, deduction, or loss that is not properly allocable to a trade or business; (2) any business interest expense or business interest income; (3) the amount of any net operating loss deduction; (4) deductions allowable for depreciation, amortization, or depletion; and (5) any deduction for qualified business income under §199A.[27]

When computing the limit, business interest expense does not include investment interest expense, and business interest income does not include investment income. For example, business interest expense would include interest paid on a loan used to purchase business equipment, but it would not include interest paid on a loan to purchase stock or bonds for investment purposes. The amount of any business interest expense not allowed as a deduction for any taxable year is carried forward indefinitely. If the average gross receipts of the business in any given year falls below a three-year average of $27 million indexed for inflation, then the interest (including any carryforwards) becomes fully deductible (i.e., it is no longer subject to the business interest limitation).

[26]§274 requires substantiation of all elements of travel, including sufficient corroborating evidence. Although there are a few exceptions to this rule, approximations and estimates are generally not sufficient. Also, taxpayers must maintain records to deduct the business portion of mixed-use assets such as cars used for both business and personal purposes. Note that when the taxpayer is unable to substantiate other deductions, the court may estimate the deductible amount under the *Cohan* rule [*George Cohan v. Comm'r,* 39 F.2d 540 (2d Cir. 1930)].

[27]Adjusted taxable income of the taxpayer cannot be less than zero. Under §163(j), the interest expense disallowance is determined at the filer level, but special rules apply to pass-through entities. For years before 2022, adjusted taxable income was also reduced for depreciation, amortization, and depletion.

Example 1-11

What if: Suppose that at the beginning of the year Rick borrowed $300,000 to provide liquidity for starting up Green Acres. Suppose further that at year-end Rick had reported $9,000 in interest expense on the business loan. In addition, Green Acres reported $70,000 of revenue from services and incurred $47,000 of other deductible expenses (excluding interest expense and $5,000 of depreciation). What amount of interest can Rick deduct as a business expense for Green Acres?

Answer: $9,000. Green Acres is not subject to the business interest expense limitation because Rick's gross receipts do not exceed the $27 million average gross receipts test.

What if: Suppose the interest expense limitation applies to Green Acres. What amount of business interest expense could Rick deduct for Green Acres?

Answer: $6,900. Green Acres generated $23,000 of adjusted taxable income. Adjusted taxable income is the amount of revenue less expense before interest expense and after adding back depreciation ($70,000 – ($47,000)). The 2022 business interest limitation is 30 percent of the $23,000 of adjusted taxable income, or $6,900. The $2,100 of disallowed interest expense from 2022 would be carried over to 2023.

Losses on Dispositions of Business Property

Businesses are generally allowed to deduct losses incurred when selling or disposing of business assets. The calculation of losses from business property dispositions can be complex, but the main idea is that businesses realize and recognize a loss when the asset's tax basis exceeds the sale proceeds. To prevent businesses and related persons from working together to defer taxes, the tax laws generally limit the deduction of business losses when property is sold to a related person. For this purpose, related persons generally include family members, partnerships, and controlled corporations. Related persons are discussed in more detail in the next section of this chapter, and the calculation of the loss limitation is discussed in the Property Dispositions chapter.

Example 1-12

What if: Assume that in late October, Rick purchased a used trailer to transport equipment to work sites. Rick bought the trailer for what he thought was a bargain price of $1,000. However, shortly after Rick acquired it, the axle snapped and was not repairable. Rick was forced to sell the trailer to a parts shop for $325. What amount can Rick deduct as a loss from the trailer sale?

Answer: $675 is deductible as a business loss because the trailer was a business asset. The loss is calculated as the amount realized of $325 minus adjusted basis of $1,000. (Note that Rick is not allowed to deduct depreciation on the trailer because he disposed of it in the same year he acquired it.)

What if: Suppose that Rick sold the trailer to a parts shop owned by his father. What amount can Rick deduct as a loss from the trailer sale?

Answer: Zero. However, Rick's father may be able to utilize Rick's loss if the trailer is later sold by the father.

Business Casualty Losses

Businesses can also incur deductible losses when their assets are stolen, damaged, or completely destroyed by a force outside the control of the business. These events are called casualties.[28] Businesses deduct casualty losses in the year the casualty occurs or, in the case of theft, the year the theft is discovered. The amount of the loss deduction depends on whether the asset is completely destroyed or only partially destroyed. When its asset is *completely* destroyed (or stolen), the business calculates the loss by substituting the insurance proceeds, if any, for the amount realized. That is, the loss is the amount of insurance proceeds minus the adjusted tax basis of the asset. If the asset is damaged but not completely destroyed, the amount of the loss is the amount of the insurance proceeds

[28]Casualties are unexpected events driven by forces outside the control of the taxpayer that damage or destroy a taxpayer's property. §165 lists "fire, storm, and shipwreck" as examples of casualties.

minus the *lesser* of (1) the asset's adjusted tax basis or (2) the decline in the value of the asset due to the casualty. For individuals, business casualty losses and casualty losses associated with rentals and royalties are deducted for AGI.

Example 1-13

What if: Suppose Rick acquires business equipment this year for $5,000, but a fire damages the equipment shortly after it is acquired and before it can be placed in service. After the fire the equipment was worth $3,500 and insurance reimbursed Rick for $1,000. What would be the amount of his business casualty loss?

Answer: $500. The loss is the insurance proceeds ($1,000) reduced by the lesser of the decline in value, $1,500 (computed as $5,000 − $3,500), or the adjusted tax basis, $5,000. The calculation follows:

Insurance proceeds	$ 1,000
Minus decline in value	−1,500
Casualty loss deduction	**$ (500)**

What if: Suppose that the fire completely destroyed the equipment. What would be the amount of Rick's business casualty loss?

Answer: $4,000. The loss is the insurance proceeds ($1,000) reduced by the adjusted tax basis, $5,000.

LO 1-3

ACCOUNTING PERIODS

After identifying a business's taxable income and deductible business expenses, it is necessary to identify the period in which income and deductions are to be measured. Businesses must report their income and deductions over a fixed **accounting period** or **tax year.** A full tax year consists of 12 full months. A tax year can consist of a period less than 12 months (a short tax year) in certain circumstances. For instance, a business may report income for such a short year in its first year of existence (for example, it reports income on a calendar year-end and starts business after January 1) or in its final year of existence (for example, a calendar-year business ends its business before December 31). Short tax years in a business's initial or final year are treated the same as full years. A business also may have a short year when it changes its tax year, and this can occur when the business is acquired by new owners. In these situations, special rules may apply for computing taxable income and the tax liability of the business.[29]

There are three types of tax years, each with different year-ends:

1. A calendar year ends on December 31.
2. A **fiscal year** ends on the last day of a month other than December.
3. A 52/53-week year. This is a fiscal year that ends on the same day of the week that is the last such day in the month or on the same day of the week nearest the end of the month. For example, a business could adopt a 52/53-week fiscal year that (1) ends on the last Saturday in July each year or (2) ends on the Saturday closest to the end of July (although this Saturday might be in August rather than July).[30]

THE KEY FACTS

Accounting Periods

- Individuals and proprietorships generally account for income using a calendar year-end.
- Corporations are allowed to choose a fiscal year.
- Partnerships and other flow-through entities generally use a tax year consistent with their owners' tax years.

Not all types of tax years are available to all types of businesses. The rules for determining the tax years available to the business depend on whether the business is a sole proprietorship, a **flow-through entity,** or a C corporation. These rules are summarized as follows:

- *Sole proprietorships:* Because individual proprietors must report their business income on their individual returns, proprietorships use a calendar-year-end to report their business income on their tax returns.[31]

[29]§443. Discussion of tax consequences associated with these short years is beyond the scope of this text.

[30]Businesses with inventories, such as retailers, can benefit from 52/53-week year-ends. These year-ends can facilitate inventory counts (e.g., the store is closed, such as over a weekend) and financial reporting.

[31]Virtually all individual taxpayers use a calendar-year tax year.

- *Flow-through entities:* Partnerships and S corporations are flow-through entities (partners and S corporation owners report the entity's income directly on their own tax returns), and these entities generally must adopt tax years consistent with the owners' tax years.[32] Because owners are allocated income from flow-through entities on the last day of the entity's taxable year, the tax laws impose the tax year consistency requirement to minimize income tax deferral opportunities for the owners.
- *C corporations:* C corporations are generally allowed to select a calendar, fiscal, or 52/53-week year-end.

A business adopts a calendar year-end or fiscal year-end by filing its initial tax return. In contrast, a business adopts a 52/53-week year-end by filing a special election with the IRS. Once a business establishes its tax year, it generally must receive permission from the IRS to change.

Example 1-14

Rick is a calendar-year taxpayer. What tax year must Rick use to report income from Green Acres?

Answer: Calendar year. This is true even though Rick began his business in May of this year. He will calculate income and expense for his landscaping business over the calendar year and include business income and deductions from May through December of this year on Schedule C of his individual tax return.

What if: Suppose that Rick formed Green Acres as a C corporation for tax purposes at the time he began his business. What tax year could Green Acres adopt?

Answer: If Green Acres were operated as a C corporation, it could elect a calendar year-end, a fiscal year-end, or a 52/53-week year-end. If it were an S corporation, it likely would use a calendar year-end. If Rick opted to have Green Acres adopt a calendar year-end, the first tax return for Green Acres would only cover the eight months from May through December (a short year).

ACCOUNTING METHODS

LO 1-4

Once a business adopts a tax year, it must determine which items of income and deduction to recognize during a particular year. Generally speaking, the taxpayer's **accounting methods** determine the tax year in which a business recognizes a particular item of income or deduction. Because accounting methods affect the *timing* of when a taxpayer reports income and deductions, these methods are especially important for taxpayers considering a timing strategy to defer taxable income or accelerate deductions.[33]

Financial and Tax Accounting Methods

Many businesses are required to generate financial statements for nontax business reasons. For example, publicly traded corporations must file financial statements with the Securities and Exchange Commission (SEC) based on generally accepted accounting principles (GAAP). Also, privately owned businesses borrowing money from banks are often required to generate financial statements under GAAP so that the lender can evaluate the business's creditworthiness. In reporting financial statement income, businesses have incentives to select accounting methods permissible under GAAP that *accelerate income* and *defer deductions.*

In contrast, for tax planning purposes, businesses have incentives to choose accounting methods that defer income and accelerate deductions. This natural tension between financial reporting incentives and tax reporting incentives may be the reason the tax laws generally require businesses to use the same accounting methods for tax purposes that they use for

[32]See §706 for the specific restrictions on year-ends for partnerships and §1378 for restrictions on S corporations. If they can show a business purpose (a difficult task), both partnerships and S corporations can adopt year-ends other than those used by their owners.

[33]Accounting methods determine *when* income or a deduction is recognized but do not determine *whether* an item of income is taxable or an expense is deductible.

financial accounting purposes, a *consistency* requirement. In other words, in many circumstances, if businesses want to defer taxable income, they must also defer book income.[34]

Sometimes the tax laws require businesses to use specific accounting methods for tax purposes regardless of what accounting method is used for financial reporting purposes. With certain restrictions, businesses first select their *overall* accounting method and then choose accounting methods for *specific* items or transactions.

Overall Accounting Method

Businesses must choose an overall method of accounting to track and report their business activities for tax purposes. The overriding requirement for all tax accounting methods is that the method must "clearly reflect income" and be applied consistently.[35] The two overall methods of accounting are the cash method and the accrual method. Although businesses are generally free to choose either the cash or accrual method, C corporations and partnerships with C corporation partners are generally required to use the accrual method if they do not qualify as a small business under the gross receipts test discussed previously.[36] Businesses that qualify under the gross receipts test do not need to request the consent of the IRS to elect the cash method. Businesses also may choose to keep some accounts on the cash method and others on the accrual method. This method is sometimes called a hybrid or mixed accounting method, but technically the method is still classified as a form of cash method.

Cash Method A business using the cash method of accounting recognizes revenue when property or services are actually or constructively received. This is generally true no matter when the business sells the goods or performs the service that generates the revenue. Keep in mind that a cash-method business receiving payments in *noncash* form (as property or services) must recognize the noncash payments as gross income when the goods or services are received.

Likewise, a business adopting the cash method generally recognizes deductions when the expense is paid. Thus, the timing of the liability giving rise to the expense is usually irrelevant. For example, a cash-method business would deduct office supply expense when payment is made rather than when the supplies are ordered or received. Also, in certain circumstances, a business expending cash on ordinary and necessary business expenses may not be allowed to *currently* deduct the expense at the time of the payment. For example, cash-method taxpayers (and accrual-method taxpayers) are not allowed to deduct expenditures that create future benefits. Hence, a business using either the cash or accrual method must generally capitalize prepaid interest and other prepayments that create tangible or intangible assets.

However, it can be difficult and time-consuming for small businesses to capitalize the multitude of prepaid expenditures that create benefits for a relatively brief period of time. For this reason, regulations provide a **12-month rule** that simplifies the process of determining whether to capitalize or immediately expense payments that create benefits for a relatively brief period of time, such as insurance, security, rent, and warranty service contracts. When a business prepays business expenses, it may *immediately* deduct the prepayment if (1) the contract period does not last more than a year *and* (2) the contract period does not extend beyond the end of the taxable year following the tax year in which the taxpayer makes the payment.[37] If the prepaid expense does not meet both these

[34]§446(a). Businesses that use different accounting methods for book and tax income must typically file a Schedule M-1 or Schedule M-3 that reconciles the results from the two accounting methods.

[35]§446(b).

[36]Businesses that are defined as tax shelters cannot qualify for the cash method under §448(a). A business on the cash basis that fails the gross receipts test must change to the accrual method of accounting. However, if the same business qualifies under the gross receipts test in a subsequent year, the business may elect to use the cash basis again.

[37]§263(a).

criteria, the business must capitalize the prepaid amount and amortize it over the length of the contract whether the business uses the cash or accrual method of accounting.[38]

Example 1-15

On July 1 of this year, Rick paid $1,200 for a 12-month insurance policy that covers his business property from accidents and casualties from July 1 of this year through June 30 of next year. How much of the $1,200 expenditure may Rick deduct this year if he uses the cash method of accounting for his business activities?

Answer: $1,200. Because the insurance coverage does not exceed 12 months and does not extend beyond the end of next year, Rick is allowed to deduct the entire premium payment under the 12-month rule.

What if: Suppose the insurance policy was for 12 months, but the policy ran from February 1 of next year through January 31 of the following year. How much of the expenditure may Rick deduct this year if he uses the cash method of accounting for his business activities?

Answer: $0. Even though the contract period is 12 months or less, Rick is required to capitalize the cost of the prepayment for the insurance policy because the contract period extends beyond the end of next year. Hence, he will amortize the cost beginning next year.

What if: Suppose Rick had paid $1,200 for an *18-month* policy beginning July 1 of this year and ending December 31 of next year. How much may he deduct this year if he uses the cash method of accounting for his business activities?

Answer: $400. In this scenario, because the policy exceeds 12 months, Rick is allowed to deduct the portion of the premium pertaining to this year. Hence, this year, he would deduct $400 [(6 months/18 months) × $1,200]. He would deduct the remaining $800 in the next year.

(continued from page 1-1 . . .)

Rick's CPA, Jane, informed him that he needs to select an overall method of accounting for Green Acres to compute its taxable income. Jane advised Rick to use the cash method. However, Rick wanted to prepare GAAP financial statements and use the accrual method of accounting. Rick believed that if Green Acres was going to become a big business, it needed to act like a big business. Finally, after much discussion, Rick and Jane reached a compromise. For the first year, they decided they would track Green Acres's business activities using both the cash *and* the accrual methods. In addition, they would also keep GAAP-based books for financial purposes. When filing time comes, Rick must choose which method to use in reporting taxable income. Jane told Rick that he could wait until he filed his tax return to select the overall accounting method for tax purposes. ■

Accrual Method Businesses using the accrual method to determine taxable income follow rules similar to GAAP with two basic differences. First, the requirements for recognizing taxable income tend to be structured to recognize income earlier than the recognition rules for financial accounting. Second, the requirements for accruing tax deductions tend to be structured to recognize less accrued expenses than the recognition rules for financial reporting purposes. These differences reflect the underlying objectives of financial accounting income and taxable income. The objective of financial accounting is to provide useful information to stakeholders such as creditors, prospective investors, and shareholders. Because financial accounting methods are designed to guard against businesses overstating their profitability to these users, financial accounting tends to bias against *overstating* income. In contrast, the government's main objective for writing tax laws is to collect revenues. Thus, tax accounting rules for accrual-method businesses tend to bias against *understating* income.

[38] Reg §1.263(a)-4(f). This 12-month rule applies to both cash-method and accrual-method taxpayers. However, for accrual-method taxpayers to deduct prepaid expenses, they must meet both the 12-month rule requirements and the economic performance requirements discussed in the Accrual Deductions section.

Accrual Income

Businesses using the accrual method of accounting generally recognize income when they meet the *all-events test.* This test is sometimes referred to as the fixed and determinable test.

All-Events Test for Income The all-events test requires that businesses recognize income when (1) all events have occurred that determine or fix their right to receive the income and (2) the amount of the income can be determined with reasonable accuracy.[39] Assuming the amount of income can be determined with reasonable accuracy, businesses meet the all-events requirement on the *earliest* of the following three dates:

1. When they complete the task required to earn the income. Businesses earn income for services as they provide the services, and they generally earn income from selling property when the title of the property passes to the buyer.
2. When the payment for the task is due from the customer.
3. When the business receives payment for the task.

Alternatively, the all-events test is deemed to be satisfied when an income item is recognized on an applicable financial statement (AFS), even if it has yet to satisfy any of the above three criteria.[40]

Example 1-16

In early fall, Rick contracted with a dozen homeowners to landscape their yards. Rick agreed to do the work for an aggregate of $11,000. Rick and his crew started in the fall and completed the jobs in December of this year. However, he didn't mail the bills until after the holidays and didn't receive any payments until the following January. When must Rick recognize the income from this work?

Answer: Under the accrual method, Rick would recognize the entire $11,000 as income this year because his right to the income is fixed at year-end, when Rick and his crew complete the work. Under the cash method, however, Rick would not recognize the $11,000 as income until next year, when he receives it.

THE KEY FACTS

Revenue Recognition under the Accrual Method

- Income is recognized when earned (all-events) or received (if earlier).
- Under the all-events test, income is earned when the business has the right to receive payment or when recognized in the applicable financial statement, if earlier.
- Taxpayers can generally elect to defer recognition of prepaid (unearned) income if the income is also deferred for financial accounting purposes.
- However, the deferral of income is an accounting method election and deferred income must be recognized in the year after deferral (e.g., the tax deferral only lasts for one year).

Taxation of Advance Payments of Income (Unearned Income)

In some cases, taxpayers receive income payments before they actually earn the income.[41] Taxpayers using the cash method include these payments in gross income in the year the payment is received. When an accrual-method taxpayer must include unearned income in gross income depends, in part, on the type of income. For example, all taxpayers must recognize interest and rental income immediately upon receipt (i.e., the income is taxable when received even if is not yet earned).

For other types of income, accrual-method businesses can elect to defer recognition of unearned income for one year. Specifically, businesses using the accrual method may elect to defer recognizing advance payments for goods or services until the next tax year.[42] This one-year deferral method does not apply if the income is actually earned by the end of the year of receipt or if the unearned income is recognized for financial reporting purposes. In addition, this is an accounting method election that once elected can only be revoked with the permission of the Commissioner.

[39]Reg. §1.451-1(a).

[40]§451(b). Applicable financial statements are described in §451(b)(3).

[41]Unlike advance payments, businesses are not required to recognize security deposits as income because there is an obligation to return the deposit [*Comm'r v. Indianapolis Power & Light Co.,* 493 U.S. 203 (1990)].

[42]§451(c).

Example 1-17

In late November 2022, Rick received a $7,200 payment in advance from a client for monthly landscaping services from December 1, 2022, through November 30, 2024 ($300 a month for 24 months). When must Rick recognize the income from the advance payment for services?

Answer: Under the accrual method, if Rick elects the deferral method to account for advance payments, he would initially recognize the $300 income he earned in December 2022. In 2023, he would recognize the remaining $6,900 (rather than only the $3,600 related to 2022) because he is not allowed to defer the prepayments for more than a year. If Rick does not elect the deferral method, he would recognize the entire prepayment of $7,200 as income upon receipt in 2022. Under the cash method, Rick would recognize the entire prepayment, $7,200, as income upon receipt in 2022.

What if: Suppose that rather than receiving payment in advance for services, Rick's client paid $7,200 in 2022 for landscape supplies that Rick purchased in 2022 and provided in 2023. When must Rick recognize the income from the advance payment for goods?

Answer: Using the accrual method, if Rick elects the deferral method to account for advance payments, he would not recognize any income in 2022 because none of the income had been earned in 2022. Rick would then recognize the entire $7,200 (less the cost of goods sold) in 2023. If Rick did not elect the deferral method, he would recognize the entire $7,200 (less the cost of the goods) in 2022. Under the cash method, Rick would recognize the entire $7,200 (less the cost of goods sold) in 2022.

Inventories

When producing, buying, or selling goods is an income-producing activity, taxpayers are required to keep inventories of goods, including raw materials and work in process, to determine the cost of goods sold. In addition, taxpayers who are required to keep inventory records also must use the accrual method of accounting for purchases and sales.[43] This requirement applies regardless of whether the taxpayer uses the cash or the accrual method as the overall method of accounting. Hence, the cost of inventory must include the purchase price of raw materials (minus any discounts), direct costs (manufacturing), shipping costs, and any indirect costs allocated to the inventory under the **uniform cost capitalization (UNICAP) rules** (discussed next).[44]

However, under §471(c), small businesses qualifying under the gross receipts test discussed previously can opt to account for goods as nonincidental materials or use the accounting method that conforms to the taxpayer's financial accounting treatment of inventory. Generally, nonincidental materials are tracked on the taxpayer's books and records, either through records of consumption or by periodic physical inventory. Amounts paid to acquire or produce nonincidental materials are generally deductible in the tax year in which the materials are used in the taxpayer's operations or are consumed in the taxpayer's operations. The IRS interprets "used or consumed" to mean that nonincidental materials are deductible when taxpayers sell the inventory.

For example, suppose a company stores machine repair parts for which it keeps records of purchases and consumption. The company can choose to treat the parts either under the method conforming to its financial accounting or as nonincidental materials. If the parts are treated as nonincidental materials and the parts are used in the business, the company can deduct the costs of parts in the tax year the part is removed from storage. If, however, the parts are a component of a finished good, then the cost of the part can only be deducted at the time the taxpayer incurs the cost or delivers the finished goods, whichever is later.[45]

THE KEY FACTS

Inventories

- C corporations and partnerships with C corporation partners must use the accrual method to account for inventories unless they qualify as a small business under the gross receipts test. Small businesses can account for inventories either as nonincidental materials or use the inventory method used for financial reporting.
- The UNICAP rules require capitalization of most indirect costs of production, but businesses that qualify as a small business under the gross receipts test are exempt from UNICAP.
- The LIFO method is allowed if it is also used for financial reporting purposes (a conformity rule).

[43]Reg. §1.446-1(c)(2).

[44]Inventory valuation allowances are generally not allowed, but taxpayers can adopt the lower of cost or market method of inventory valuation. In addition, under certain conditions specific goods not salable at normal prices can be valued at bona fide selling prices less direct cost of disposition.

[45]Reg. §1.162-3(a)(1); Prop. Reg. §1.471-1(b)(4). Note that nonincidental materials can only be accounted for using the first-in, first-out (FIFO); specific identification; or average cost methods. The last-in, first-out (LIFO) method and the lower of cost or market method may not be used.

The ability to account for goods as nonincidental materials was intended to simplify accounting for small businesses by exempting them from having to allocate indirect costs to inventory. However, small businesses are still required to record beginning and ending inventories even when the business chooses to treat goods as nonincidental materials or use the inventory method on the taxpayer's books. In addition, small business accounting for inventories is subject to the overriding requirement that all accounting methods must ultimately clearly reflect income.

Example 1-18

What if: Suppose that Green Acres (Rick) commences to manufacture an organic lawn supplement. Green Acres would purchase compost from local farms and blend the compost with minerals. Green Acres would then package the mix and sell the packages to local retailers. Under these circumstances, would Green Acres be required to keep inventories of raw materials, work in process, and goods for sale?

Answer: Yes. Green Acres must keep inventories because producing and selling goods is an income-producing activity. However, because it is a small business under the gross receipts test, Green Acres need not use the accrual method of accounting for its purchases and sales. Green Acres either can elect to treat the raw materials, work-in-process, and finished products as nonincidental materials or can use the accounting method that conforms to the method Green Acres uses for financial reporting. In either case, Green Acres must keep records of its beginning and ending inventories.

What if: Suppose that Green Acres purchased and paid for compost in 2022 and elected to account for the purchase as nonincidental materials. However, the compost was used in producing lawn supplements sold in 2023. Can Green Acres deduct the cost of the compost in 2022?

Answer: No, the cost of the compost used is deducted in 2023. While Green Acres incurred the cost in 2022, the deduction is allowed in the year the goods were delivered because it is the later date.

Uniform Capitalization The tax laws require large businesses that account for inventories to capitalize certain direct and indirect costs associated with inventories (called the UNICAP rules for uniform capitalization). However, businesses that qualify as a small business under the gross receipts test need not apply UNICAP rules.[46] Congress enacted UNICAP primarily for two reasons. First, the rules accelerate tax revenues for the government by deferring deductions for the capitalized costs until the business sells the associated inventory. Thus, there is generally a one-year lag between when businesses initially capitalize the costs and when they deduct them. Second, Congress designed the "uniform" rules to reduce variation in the costs businesses include in inventory, and Congress intended these provisions to apply to large manufacturers and resellers.

Under these uniform cost capitalization rules, large businesses are generally required to capitalize more costs to inventory for tax purposes than they capitalize under financial accounting rules. Under GAAP, businesses generally include in inventory only those costs incurred within their production facility. In contrast, the UNICAP rules require businesses to allocate to inventory the costs they incur inside the production facility and the costs they incur outside the facility to support production (or inventory acquisition) activities. For example, under the UNICAP provisions, a business must capitalize at least a portion of the compensation paid to employees in its purchasing department, general and administrative department, and even its information technology department, to the extent these groups provide support for the production process. In contrast, businesses immediately expense these items as period costs for financial accounting purposes. The regulations provide guidance on the costs that must be allocated to inventory. Selling, advertising, and research are specifically identified as costs that do not have to be allocated to inventory under the UNICAP provisions.[47]

[46]§263A(i).

[47]Reg. §1.263A–1(e)(3)(iii).

Example 1-19

What if: Green Acres sells trees, but Rick anticipates that the business will sell flowers, shrubs, and other plants in future years. Ken is Rick's employee in charge of purchasing inventory. Ken's compensation this year is $30,000, and Rick estimates that Ken spends about 5 percent of his time acquiring inventory and the remaining time working on landscaping projects. Assuming Green Acres is required to apply the UNICAP rules, how would Ken's compensation be allocated?

Answer: If the UNICAP rules applied to Green Acres (Rick), $1,500 ($30,000 × 5%) of Ken's compensation would be allocated to the cost of the inventory Green Acres acquired this year. In contrast, Ken's entire salary would be expensed as a period cost for financial accounting purposes.

What if: Suppose that Green Acres began operations on September 1, 2021, and reported $5 million in gross receipts from services and sales of trees, flowers, shrubs, and other plants for the four months in the 2021 short year. Is Green Acres required to apply the UNICAP rules in 2022?

Answer: No, because average annual gross receipts in the period prior to 2022 is less than $27 million. For purposes of the gross receipts test, the gross receipts for the four-month 2021 tax year is annualized by multiplying $5 million by 12 and dividing the result by 4 (the number of months in the short period 2021). Thus, gross receipts for Green Acres in 2021 is $15 million ($60 million divided by 4).

Inventory Cost-Flow Methods Once a business determines the cost of its inventory, it must use an inventory cost-flow method to determine its cost of goods sold. Three primary cost-flow methods are (1) the **first-in, first-out (FIFO) method;** (2) the **last-in, first-out (LIFO) method;** and (3) the **specific identification method,** although the LIFO method cannot be used to account for inventories of nonincidental materials. Businesses might be inclined to use FIFO or LIFO methods when they sell similar, relatively low-cost, high-volume products such as cans of soup or barrels of oil. These methods simplify inventory accounting because the business need not track the individual cost of each item it sells. In contrast, businesses that sell distinct, relatively high-cost, low-volume products might be more likely to adopt the specific identification method. For example, jewelry and used-car businesses would likely use the specific identification method to account for their cost of sales. In general terms, when costs are increasing, a business using the FIFO method will report a higher gross margin than if it used the LIFO method. The opposite is true if costs are decreasing.

Example 1-20

In late August, Green Acres (Rick) purchased 10 oak saplings (immature trees) for a total purchase price of $3,000. In September, 12 more were purchased for a total price of $3,900, and in late October, 15 more were purchased for $5,000. The total cost of each lot of trees was determined as follows:

Purchase Date	Trees	Direct Cost	Other Costs	Total Cost
August 20	10	$ 3,000	$ 350	$ 3,350
September 15	12	3,900	300	4,200
October 22	15	5,000	400	5,400
Totals	37	$11,900	$1,050	$12,950

Before the end of the year, Green Acres sold 20 of the oak saplings (5 from the August lot, 5 from the September lot, and 10 from the October lot) for cash. To illustrate the effects of inventory accounting, assume that Green Acres is considering keeping inventory records for financial reporting purposes under various methods. What is Green Acres's gross profit from sales of oak saplings if the sales revenue totaled $14,000 (all collected by year-end), and what is its ending oak sapling inventory under the FIFO, LIFO, and specific identification cost-flow methods?

(continued on page 1-22)

Answer: Under the accrual method, Rick's (Green Acres) gross profit from sapling sales and its ending inventory balance for the remaining oak saplings under the FIFO, LIFO, and specific identification cost-flow methods are as follows:

Description	FIFO	LIFO	Specific ID
Sales	$14,000	$14,000	$14,000
Cost of goods sold	−6,850	−7,150	−7,025
Gross profit	$ 7,150	$ 6,850	$ 6,975
Ending inventory:			
August 20 trees	$ 0	$ 3,350	$ 1,675
September 15 trees	700	2,450	2,450
October 22 trees	5,400	0	1,800
Total ending inventory	**$ 6,100**	**$ 5,800**	**$ 5,925**

If the gross receipts test is satisfied, Rick could record the trees as nonincidental materials. However, Rick would still need to count the trees and adopt a flow assumption. For example, Rick could adopt the average cost method and calculate the average cost of trees by summing the cost of trees in inventory at the beginning of the year with the cost of purchased trees and dividing by the total trees (beginning inventory plus purchases). In this example, the cost of purchasing 37 trees was $12,950 (average of $350 per tree), so the cost of selling 20 trees would be $7,000 (20 times $350).

When costs are subject to inflation over time, a business would get the best of both worlds if it adopted the FIFO method for financial reporting purposes and the LIFO method for tax purposes. Not surprisingly, the tax laws require that a business can use LIFO for tax purposes only if it also uses LIFO for financial reporting purposes.[48] While this "conformity" requirement may not matter to entities not required to generate financial reports, it can be very restrictive to publicly traded corporations.

Accrual Deductions

Generally, when accrual-method businesses incur an expense, they account for it by crediting a liability account or by crediting cash if the expense is paid. Sometimes the amount of the expense must be estimated. For example, a business might have to estimate the expenses associated with future warranty claims to match with current sales. Typically, estimated expenses result in a reserve account, which can be described as a contingent liability.

To claim a tax deduction for an accrued expense, the expense must meet two tests: (1) an **all-events test** *and* (2) an **economic performance test.**[49] The all-events test for recognizing deductions is similar to the all-events test for recognizing income. That is, the events that establish the liability giving rise to the deduction must have occurred and the amount of the liability must be determinable with reasonable accuracy. However, the additional economic performance requirement makes the deduction recognition rules more stringent than the income recognition rules. As a result, businesses are generally prohibited from deducting estimated expenses or reserves. In other words, economic performance must have occurred for a business to claim a deduction.[50]

[48]§472(c).

[49]§461(h).

[50]§461.

TAXES IN THE REAL WORLD Economic Performance and Cost of Goods Sold

During 2008 and 2009, a limited liability company called Bluescape paid around $180 million to acquire hundreds of thousands of acres of mineral and lease interests in four states. Bluescape planned to explore for natural gas on these leases and produce the gas for sale. Bluescape claimed on its tax return for those years about $160 million in cost of goods sold for natural gas exploration and mining. However, during those years, Bluescape did not actually drill for gas and did not report any gross receipts or sales attributable to the sale of natural gas.

Upon audit, the IRS disallowed the cost of goods sold arguing that Bluescape did not satisfy the all-events test and the economic performance requirement in §461(h)(1). Bluescape responded by arguing that the economic performance requirement does not apply to amounts included in cost of goods sold. They claimed, instead, that the cost of goods sold is an offset against gross receipts used to compute gross income. Hence, cost of goods sold is governed by §451 and not subject to economic performance.

Bluescape petitioned the Tax Court, which then posed a question to both parties: Can a taxpayer recognize cost of goods sold before it has any gross receipts from the sale of goods? In his opinion, Judge Pugh noted that under Reg §1.61-3(a), gross income is calculated by subtracting the cost of goods sold from gross receipts. Bluescape argued, however, that "matching" of cost of goods sold and gross receipts is not required under the regulations and that cost of goods sold should be recognized in the year the taxpayer assumes the obligations to drill the wells.

In finding for the IRS, the judge noted the gap in the taxpayer's logic that cost of goods sold serves as an offset against gross receipts but that cost of goods sold need not "match" gross receipts. The court held that taxpayers can only offset cost of goods sold against gross receipts from sales of goods. Unfortunately, the court did not answer the dispute over whether the economic performance requirement applies to the cost of goods sold.

Source: BRC Operating Co. LLC v. Comm'r, TC Memo 2021-59.

Example 1-21

On November 1 of this year, Rick agreed to a one-year $6,000 contract with Ace Advertising to produce a radio ad campaign. Ace agreed that Rick would owe nothing under the contract unless the sales for Green Acres increase a minimum of 25 percent over the next six months. What amount, if any, may Rick deduct this year for this contract under the accrual and cash methods?

Answer: Under the accrual method, Rick is not allowed to recognize *any* deduction this year for the liability. Even though Ace will have completed two months of advertising for Green Acres by the end of the year, the guarantee means that the liability is not fixed until and unless the sales increase by 25 percent. Under the cash method, Rick would not deduct any of the cost of the campaign this year because he has not paid anything to Ace.

THE KEY FACTS

Accrual of Business-Expense Deductions

- Both all-events and economic performance tests are required for deducting accrued business expenses.
- The all-events test requires the events that establish the liability giving rise to the expense must have occurred and the amount of the liability must be determinable with reasonable accuracy.
- Economic performance generally requires that the underlying activity generating the liability has occurred in order for the associated expense to be deductible.

Economic Performance Even when businesses meet the all-events test, they still must clear the economic performance hurdle to recognize the tax deduction. Congress added the economic performance requirement because in some situations, taxpayers claimed current deductions under the all events test, but delayed the event triggering payment of the associated cash expenditures for years. Thus, the delayed payment reduced the real (present value) cost of the deduction. This requirement specifies that businesses cannot deduct an expense until the underlying activity generating the associated liability has occurred. Thus, an accrual-method business is not allowed to deduct a prepaid business expense even if it qualifies to do so under the 12-month rule (discussed above) unless it also has met the economic performance test with respect to the liability associated with the expense.

The specific requirements for the economic performance test differ based on whether the liability has arisen from:

- Receiving goods or services *from* another person.
- Use of property (renting or leasing property *from* another person).
- Providing goods or services *to* another person.
- Certain activities creating **payment liabilities.**

Receiving goods or services from another person. When a business receives goods or services from another person, the business deducts the expense associated with the liability when the other person provides the goods or services (assuming the all-events test is met for the liability). However, there is an exception when a business actually pays the liability before the other person provides the goods or services. In this circumstance, the business can elect to treat the actual payment as economic performance as long as it reasonably expects the other person to provide the goods or the services within 3½ months after the payment.[51]

Example 1-22

On December 22, 2022, Rick signed a contract with PickUp LLC to clean and sweep Rick's shop during 2023. Rick agreed to pay PickUp $300 per month for the service, a total of $3,600. Rick paid $1,000 of the cost as a down payment and agreed to pay the remaining $2,600 in 2023. What amount associated with this service is Rick allowed to deduct in 2022 and 2023 under the accrual method and, alternatively, under the cash method?

Answer: Under the accrual method, Rick is not entitled to a deduction in 2022. Rick will deduct his full $3,600 service costs in 2023. Even though Rick paid for part of the services in 2022, economic performance only occurs as the services are provided to the taxpayer. Under the cash method, Rick would deduct $1,000 (his down payment) in 2022 and the remainder in 2023 when he pays the remainder on the contract.

What if: Suppose that Rick only contracted with PickUp to provide cleaning services for the first three months of 2023 and paid $900 on December 22, 2022. What amount associated with this service is Rick allowed to deduct in 2022 and 2023?

Answer: Under the accrual method, Rick is allowed to deduct $900 in 2022 because Rick actually paid this amount in 2022 and he reasonably expected YNF to complete the services within 3½ months after he made the payment. Under the cash method, Rick also deducts the $900 payment in 2022.

Renting or leasing property from another person. When a business enters into an agreement to use property (rent or lease property) from another person, economic performance occurs over the term of the lease. Thus, the business is allowed to deduct the rental expense over the term of the lease.

Example 1-23

On May 1, 2022, Rick paid $7,200 in advance to rent his shop for 12 months ($600 per month). What amount may Rick deduct for rent in 2022 if he accounts for his business activities using the accrual method?

Answer: $4,800 ($600 × 8 months' use). Even though the rent is a prepaid business expense under the 12-month rule (the contract period is for 12 months and the contract period does not extend beyond 2023), he can only deduct the rent expense over the term of the lease because that is when economic performance occurs.

[51]Reg. §1.461-4(d)(6).

What if: Assuming the original facts, what amount of the $7,200 rental payment may Rick deduct in 2022 if he is using the cash method of accounting for his business?

Answer: $7,200. In this case, Rick may deduct the expense under the 12-month rule. Rick is not required to meet the economic performance requirement to deduct the expense because the economic performance requirements apply to accrual-method taxpayers, but not cash-method taxpayers.

Example 1-24

On November 1, 2022, Rick paid $2,400 to rent a trailer for 24 months. What amount of this payment may Rick deduct and when may he deduct it?

Answer: Under the accrual method, even though Rick paid the entire rental fee in advance, economic performance occurs over the 24-month rental period. Thus, Rick deducts $200 for the trailer rental in 2022, $1,200 in 2023, and $1,000 in 2024. Because the rental period exceeds 12 months, the amount and timing of the deductions are the same under the cash method.

Providing goods or services to another person. Businesses liable for providing goods or services to other persons meet the economic performance test as they provide the goods or services that satisfy the liability.

Example 1-25

In the summer, Rick landscaped a city park. As part of this contract, Rick agreed to remove a fountain from the park if requested by the city parks committee. In December 2022, the committee decided to have Rick remove the fountain. Rick began the removal in December, and he accrued $850 of expenses associated with this work on December 31. Rick completed the removal work in the spring of 2023 and paid accrued expenses of $1,500 on March 31. What amounts will Rick deduct for the removal project and when may he deduct them?

Answer: Under the accrual method, Rick is allowed to deduct his accrued expenses as he provides the services. Consequently, in 2022 Rick can deduct $850 for the cost of the services provided in 2022 and the additional $650 in 2023. In 2023, Rick can deduct the remaining $685 cost of the services. Under the cash method, Rick can only deduct the $1,500 of expenses when paid in 2023.

Payment liabilities. Economic performance occurs for certain liabilities only when the business actually pays the liability. Thus, accrual-method businesses incurring payment liabilities are essentially on the cash method for deducting the associated expenses. Exhibit 1-2 describes different categories of these payment liabilities.

EXHIBIT 1-2 Categories of Payment Liabilities

Economic performance occurs when the taxpayer pays liabilities associated with:

- Workers' compensation, tort, breach of contract, or violation of law.
- Rebates and refunds.
- Awards, prizes, and jackpots.
- Insurance, warranties, and service contracts provided *to* the business. (*Note:* This relates to insurance, warranties, and product service contracts that cover the taxpayer and *not* a warranty that the taxpayer provides to others.)
- Taxes.[52]
- Other liabilities not provided for elsewhere.

[52]While taxes are generally not deducted until they are paid, §461(c) allows businesses to elect to accrue the deduction for real property taxes ratably over the tax period instead of deducting them when they actually pay them.

Exhibit 1-3 describes the requirements for economic performance for the different types of liabilities.

EXHIBIT 1-3 Economic Performance

Taxpayer incurs liability from	Economic performance occurs
Receiving goods and services *from* another person.	When the goods or services are provided to the taxpayer or with payment if the taxpayer reasonably expects actual performance within 3½ months.
Renting or leasing property *from* another person.	Ratably over the time period during which the taxpayer is entitled to use the property or money.
Providing goods and services *to* another person.	When the taxpayer incurs costs to satisfy the liability or provide the goods and services.
Activities creating "payment" liabilities.	When the business actually makes payment.
Interest expense.	As accrued. This technically does not fall within the economic performance rules, but it is a similar concept.

Recurring item exception. One of the most common exceptions to economic performance is the **recurring item** exception. This exception is designed to reduce the administrative cost of applying economic performance to expenses that occur on a regular basis. Under this exception, accrual-method taxpayers can deduct certain accrued expenses even if economic performance has not occurred by year-end.[53] A recurring item is a liability that is expected to recur in future years and either the liability is not material in amount or deducting the expense in the current year more properly matches with revenue. Payment liabilities, such as insurance, rebates, and refunds, are deemed to meet the matching requirement.[54] In addition, the all-events test must be satisfied at year-end and actual economic performance of the item must occur within a reasonable time after year-end (but prior to the filing of the tax return, which could be up to 8½ months after year-end with an extension). As a final note, the recurring item exception does not apply to workers' compensation or tort liabilities.

Example 1-26

If clients are not completely satisfied with his landscaping work, Rick offers a $200 refund with no questions asked. Near the end of 2022, Rick had four clients request refunds, so Rick incurred the liability for the refunds this year. However, Rick was busy during the holiday season, so he didn't pay the refunds until January 2023. Ignoring the recurring item exception, when can Rick deduct the customer refunds under the cash and accrual methods?

Answer: Because refunds are payment liabilities, under the accrual method economic performance does not occur until Rick actually pays the refunds. Consequently, Rick deducts the $800 of refunds in 2023 even though the liability for the refunds met the all-events test in 2022. Under the cash method, Rick would not deduct the refunds until he paid them in 2023.

What if: Suppose that Rick received $800 of refund requests at year-end. Under what conditions could Rick deduct the refunds in 2022 if he elects to use accrual accounting and the recurring item exception?

Answer: Typically, to claim accrual method deductions under the recurring item exception, either the accrued expense must not be material in amount or a 2022 deduction must better match 2022 revenue than 2023 revenue. Rick doesn't need to worry about the matching requirement because under the regulations, refunds are deemed to meet the matching requirement for purposes of the recurring item exception. Also, actual economic performance (payment) must occur within a reasonable time after year-end (but not longer than 8½ months or the filing of the tax return). Note once Rick elects to use the recurring item exception for refunds, he must follow this method for refunds in future periods.

[53]§461(h)(3).

[54]Reg. §1.461-5(b)(5)(ii).

Bad Debt Expense When accrual method businesses sell a product or a service on credit, they debit accounts receivable and credit sales revenue for both financial and tax purposes. However, when a business is unable to collect the full amount of their accounts receivable, they incur bad debt expense (a customer owes them a debt that the customer will not or can not pay). For financial reporting purposes, the business estimates the amount of the bad debt at year end and creates a reserve account, the allowance for doubtful accounts. However, for tax purposes, businesses are only allowed to deduct bad debt expense when the debt actually becomes worthless within the taxable year.[55] Consequently, for tax purposes, when businesses determine which specific debts are uncollectible, they are entitled to a deduction. This method of determining bad debt expense for tax purposes is called the **direct write-off method.** In contrast, the method used for financial reporting purposes is called the **allowance method.** As an aside, businesses using the cash method of accounting are *not* allowed to deduct bad debt expenses because they do not include receivables in taxable income.

Example 1-27

At year-end, Rick estimates that about $900 of the receivables for his services will be uncollectible, but he has identified only one client, Jared, who will definitely not pay his bill. Jared, who has skipped town, owes Rick $280 for landscaping this fall. What amount of bad debt expense may Rick deduct for the year under the accrual method?

Answer: For financial reporting purposes, Rick recognizes a $900 bad debt expense. However, for tax purposes, under the direct write-off method, Rick can deduct only $280—the amount associated with specifically writing off Jared's receivable. Under the cash method, Rick would not be able to claim any deduction because he did not receive a payment from Jared and thus did not recognize income on the amount Jared owed him.

Limitations on Accruals To prevent businesses and related persons from working together to defer taxes, the tax laws prevent an accrual-method business from accruing (and deducting) an expense for a liability owed to a related person using the cash method until the related person recognizes the income associated with the payment.[56] For this purpose, related persons include:

- Family members, including parents, siblings, and spouses.
- Shareholders and C corporations when the shareholder owns more than 50 percent of the corporation's stock.[57]
- Owners of partnerships and S corporations no matter the ownership percentage.[58]

This issue frequently arises in situations in which a business using the accrual method employs the owner or a relative of an owner. The business is not allowed to deduct compensation expense owed to the related person until the year in which the related person includes the compensation in income. However, this related-person limit extends beyond compensation to any accrued expense the business owes to a related cash-method taxpayer.

For compensation paid to unrelated persons, an accrual method business generally deducts compensation expense as employees perform services. However, a business is not allowed to deduct compensation accrued at year-end unless it actually pays the compensation (including bonuses, vacation pay, and other forms of compensation) within 2½ months of year-end.

Example 1-28

In December, Rick asked his retired father, Lee, to help him finish a landscaping job. By the end of 2022, Rick owed Lee $2,000 of (reasonable) compensation for his efforts, which he paid in January 2023. What amount of this compensation may Rick deduct and when may he deduct it?

(continued on page 1-28)

[55]§166(a).

[56]§267(a).

[57]Certain constructive ownership rules apply in determining ownership percentages for this purpose. See §267(c).

[58]See §267(b) for related-person definitions.

Answer: If Rick uses the accrual method and Lee the cash method, Rick will not be able to deduct the $2,000 compensation expense until 2023. Rick is Lee's son, so Rick and Lee are "related" persons for tax purposes. Consequently, Rick can deduct the compensation only when Lee includes the payment in his taxable income in 2023. If Rick uses the cash method, he will deduct the expense when he pays it in January 2023.

What if: Suppose that Rick owed the $2,000 in compensation to Megan, an unrelated employee, instead of Lee. Can Rick deduct the compensation in 2022 even though he did not pay the compensation until January 2023?

Answer: Yes, Rick can deduct compensation in the year accrued (2022) if the compensation is paid within the *first* 2½ months following the end of Rick's taxable year. If Rick waits to pay the compensation until after March 15, 2023, he would deduct the compensation in the year he pays it.

Comparison of Accrual and Cash Methods

From a business perspective, the two primary advantages of adopting the cash method over the accrual method are that (1) the cash method provides the business with more flexibility to time income and deductions by accelerating or deferring payments (timing tax planning strategy) and (2) bookkeeping for the cash method is easier. For example, a cash-method taxpayer could defer revenue by waiting to bill clients for goods or services until after year-end, thereby increasing the likelihood that customers would send payment after year-end. There are some concerns with this tax strategy. For example, delaying the bills might increase the likelihood that the customers will not pay their bills at all.

The primary advantage of the accrual method over the cash method is that it better matches revenues and expenses. For that reason, external financial statement users who want to evaluate a business's financial performance prefer the accrual method. Consistent with this idea, the cash method is not allowed for financial reporting under GAAP.

Although the cash method is by far the predominate accounting method among sole proprietors, it is less common in other types of businesses. As we noted previously, tax laws generally prohibit large C corporations and large partnerships with corporate partners from using the cash method of accounting.[59] Exhibit 1-4 details the basic differences in accounting for income and deductions under the accrual and cash methods of accounting.

Example 1-29

At year-end, Rick determined that Green Acres had collected a total of $78,000 of service revenue and $12,575 in other expenses (not described elsewhere in examples but listed in Exhibit 1-5). Rick is debating whether to adopt the cash or accrual method. To help him resolve his dilemma, Jane calculates Green Acres's taxable income under the cash and accrual methods assuming that Rick elects to account for the cost of goods as nonincidental materials (summarized in Exhibit 1-5). What are the differences between the two calculations?

Answer: Jane provided the following summary of the differences between taxable income under the cash method and taxable income under the accrual method:

Description	(1) Accrual	(2) Cash	(1) − (2) Difference	Example
Revenue:				
Credit sales	11,000	0	+11,000	1-16
Prepaid revenue	300	7,200	−6,900	1-17
Expenses:				
Prepaid services	0	−1,000	+1,000	1-22
Prepaid rent expense	−4,800	−7,200	+2,400	1-23
Bad debts	−280	0	−280	1-27
Total difference (accrual income > cash income)			**+7,220**	

After comparing the revenue and expenses recognized under the two accounting methods, Jane explains that the selection of the accrual method for Green Acres means that Rick will be taxed on an additional $7,220 of income this year.

[59]Recall businesses are able to adopt the cash method when they qualify as a small business under the gross receipts test.

EXHIBIT 1-4 Comparison of Cash and Accrual Methods

Income or Expense Item	Cash Method	Accrual Method
Income recognition.	Actually or constructively received.	Taxable once the all-events test is satisfied or the income is recognized in the financial statements.
Unearned rent and interest income.	Taxable on receipt.	Taxable on receipt.
Advance payment for goods and services.	Taxable on receipt.	Taxed when received, or taxpayers can elect to be taxed in the year following receipt if not earned by end of year of receipt.
General deduction recognition.	Deduct when paid; economic performance does not apply.	Deduct once all-events test and economic performance test are both satisfied.
Expenditures for tangible assets with a useful life of more than one year.	Capitalize and apply cost recovery.	Same as the cash method.
Expenditures for intangible assets other than prepaid business expenses.	Capitalize and amortize if provision in code allows it.	Same as the cash method.
Prepaid business expenses.	Immediately deductible. However, amortize if contract period exceeds 12 months or extends beyond the end of the next taxable year.	Same as cash method for payment liabilities; otherwise, apply all-events and economic performance tests to ascertain when to capitalize and amortize.
Prepaid interest expense.	Not deductible until interest accrues.	Same as the cash method.
Bad debt expense.	Not deductible because sales on account not included in income.	Deduct under direct write-off method.

The business income for Green Acres under the accrual and cash methods is summarized in Exhibit 1-5. After reflecting on these numbers and realizing that he would recognize $7,220 more taxable income (and self-employment income subject to self-employment tax) this year under the accrual method, Rick determined that it made sense to instead adopt the cash method of accounting for Green Acres. Rick would make this election when he includes Green Acres's business income calculated using the cash method on Schedule C of his individual tax return. Exhibit 1-6 presents Rick's Schedule C for Green Acres using the cash method of accounting.

Adopting an Accounting Method

We've seen that businesses use overall accounting methods (cash, accrual, or hybrid) and many specific accounting methods (inventory cost-flow assumption, methods of accounting for prepaid income for goods and services, and methods for accounting for prepaid expenses, among other methods) to account for their business activities. For tax purposes, it's important to understand how and when a business technically adopts an accounting method because once it does so, it must get the IRS's permission to change the method.

Businesses generally elect their accounting methods by using them on their tax returns. However, when the business technically adopts a method depends on whether it is a **permissible accounting method** or an **impermissible accounting method.** So far, our discussion has emphasized accounting methods permissible under the tax laws. A business adopts a permissible accounting method by using and reporting the tax results of the method for at least one year. However, businesses may unwittingly (or intentionally) use impermissible accounting methods. For example, a business using the allowance method for determining bad debt expense for tax purposes is using an impermissible accounting method because the tax laws prescribe the use of the direct write-off method for determining bad debt expense. A business adopts an impermissible method by using and reporting the results of the method for two consecutive years.

EXHIBIT 1-5 Green Acres's Net Business Income

Description	Cash	Accrual	Example
Income			
Service revenue:			
Landscaping revenue	$78,000	$ 78,000	1-29
December landscape service	0	11,000	1-16
Prepaid landscape services	7,200	300	1-17
Sales of inventory:			
Tree sales	14,000	14,000	1-20
Total receipts and sales	**$99,200**	**$103,300**	
Cost of Goods Sold (non-incidental materials)	−7,000	−7,000	1-20
Gross Profit	**$92,200**	**$ 96,300**	
Car and truck expense:			
SUV operating expense	5,335	5,335	1-8
BMW operating expense	306	306	1-10
Insurance	1,200	1,200	1-15
Rent:			
Shop	7,200	4,800	1-23
Trailer	200	200	1-24
Travel and business meals:			
Travel to NY seminar	1,435	1,435	1-9
Business dinner with clients	270	270	1-7
Wages and subcontractor fees:			
Part-time employees	23,000	23,000	1-3
Full-time employee (Ken)	30,000	30,000	1-19
Fountain removal (part-time employee)	850	850	1-25
Fence installation (prepaid subcontractor)	1,000	0	1-22
Other expenses:			
Books for waiting room	50	50	1-2
Education—seminar	300	300	1-9
Uniforms	500	500	1-6
Bad debts	0	280	1-27
Other expenses (not in examples):			
Advertising	1,160	1,160	
Depreciation	4,000	4,000	
Interest	300	300	
Legal and professional services	1,040	1,040	
Office expense	1,500	1,500	
Repairs and maintenance	1,975	1,975	
Taxes and licenses	400	400	
Utilities	2,200	2,200	
Total deductions	**$91,221**	**$ 88,101**	
Net Business Income	**$ 7,979**	**$ 15,199**	

Changing Accounting Methods

Once a business has adopted an accounting method, it must generally receive permission to change the method, regardless of whether it is a permissible or an impermissible method. There are three important exceptions to this general rule that apply to small businesses that qualify under the gross receipts test. Small businesses are allowed to switch to use the cash method, treat inventories as nonincidental materials, and ignore the UNICAP rules when the gross receipts test is satisfied.[60]

[60]§§448(d)(7), 471(c)(4), 263A(i)(3), respectively. These changes in accounting method are treated as initiated by the taxpayer and no longer need the consent of the Secretary.

EXHIBIT 1-6 Green Acres Schedule C

SCHEDULE C (Form 1040)
Department of the Treasury Internal Revenue Service (99)

Profit or Loss From Business
(Sole Proprietorship)

▶ Go to *www.irs.gov/ScheduleC* for instructions and the latest information.
▶ Attach to Form 1040, 1040-SR, 1040-NR, or 1041; partnerships must generally file Form 1065.

OMB No. 1545-0074
2021
Attachment Sequence No. 09

Name of proprietor: **RICK GRIME**
Social security number (SSN): **000-00-0000**

A Principal business or profession, including product or service (see instructions): **LANDSCAPING**
B Enter code from instructions ▶ 5 7 1 6 3 0

C Business name. If no separate business name, leave blank.: **GREEN ACRES LANDSCAPING**
D Employer ID number (EIN) (see instr.): 0 0 0 0 0 0 0 0 0

E Business address (including suite or room no.) ▶ **BUCKSNORT STREET**
City, town or post office, state, and ZIP code: **SAN ANTONIO TX 78208**

F Accounting method: (1) ☑ Cash (2) ☐ Accrual (3) ☐ Other (specify) ▶

G Did you "materially participate" in the operation of this business during 2021? If "No," see instructions for limit on losses . ☑ Yes ☐ No

H If you started or acquired this business during 2021, check here . . . ▶ ☑

I Did you make any payments in 2021 that would require you to file Form(s) 1099? See instructions . . . ☐ Yes ☑ No

J If "Yes," did you or will you file required Form(s) 1099? . . . ☐ Yes ☐ No

Part I Income

Line	Description		Amount
1	Gross receipts or sales. See instructions for line 1 and check the box if this income was reported to you on Form W-2 and the "Statutory employee" box on that form was checked . . . ▶ ☐	1	99,200
2	Returns and allowances	2	
3	Subtract line 2 from line 1	3	99,200
4	Cost of goods sold (from line 42)	4	7,000
5	**Gross profit.** Subtract line 4 from line 3	5	92,200
6	Other income, including federal and state gasoline or fuel tax credit or refund (see instructions)	6	
7	**Gross income.** Add lines 5 and 6 . . . ▶	7	92,200

Part II Expenses. Enter expenses for business use of your home **only** on line 30.

Line	Description		Amount	Line	Description		Amount
8	Advertising	8	1,160	18	Office expense (see instructions)	18	1,500
9	Car and truck expenses (see instructions)	9	5,641	19	Pension and profit-sharing plans	19	
10	Commissions and fees	10		20	Rent or lease (see instructions):		
11	Contract labor (see instructions)	11	1,000	a	Vehicles, machinery, and equipment	20a	7,400
12	Depletion	12		b	Other business property	20b	
13	Depreciation and section 179 expense deduction (not included in Part III) (see instructions)	13	4,000	21	Repairs and maintenance	21	1,975
				22	Supplies (not included in Part III)	22	
				23	Taxes and licenses	23	400
				24	Travel and meals:		
14	Employee benefit programs (other than on line 19)	14		a	Travel	24a	1,435
15	Insurance (other than health)	15	1,200	b	Deductible meals (see instructions)	24b	270
16	Interest (see instructions):			25	Utilities	25	2,200
a	Mortgage (paid to banks, etc.)	16a	300	26	Wages (less employment credits)	26	53,850
b	Other	16b		27a	Other expenses (from line 48)	27a	850
17	Legal and professional services	17	1,040	b	**Reserved for future use**	27b	

Line	Description		Amount
28	**Total expenses** before expenses for business use of home. Add lines 8 through 27a . . . ▶	28	84.221
29	Tentative profit or (loss). Subtract line 28 from line 7	29	7,979
30	Expenses for business use of your home. Do not report these expenses elsewhere. Attach Form 8829 unless using the simplified method. See instructions. **Simplified method filers only:** Enter the total square footage of (a) your home: ______ and (b) the part of your home used for business: ______ . Use the Simplified Method Worksheet in the instructions to figure the amount to enter on line 30	30	0
31	**Net profit or (loss).** Subtract line 30 from line 29. • If a profit, enter on both **Schedule 1 (Form 1040), line 3,** and on **Schedule SE, line 2.** (If you checked the box on line 1, see instructions). Estates and trusts, enter on **Form 1041, line 3.** • If a loss, you **must** go to line 32.	31	7,979

32 If you have a loss, check the box that describes your investment in this activity. See instructions.
• If you checked 32a, enter the loss on both **Schedule 1 (Form 1040), line 3,** and on **Schedule SE, line 2.** (If you checked the box on line 1, see the line 31 instructions.) Estates and trusts, enter on **Form 1041, line 3.**
• If you checked 32b, you **must** attach **Form 6198.** Your loss may be limited.

32a ☑ All investment is at risk.
32b ☐ Some investment is not at risk.

For Paperwork Reduction Act Notice, see the separate instructions. Cat. No. 11334P **Schedule C (Form 1040) 2021**

Source: irs.gov.

For accounting method changes unrelated to qualifying as a small business under the gross receipts test, a taxpayer must request permission to change accounting methods by filing Form 3115 with the IRS. The IRS automatically approves certain types of accounting method changes (such as described above), but for others the business must provide a good business purpose for the change and pay a fee. The IRS also requires permission when a business must change from using an impermissible method; this requirement helps the IRS to certify that the business properly makes the transition to a permissible method. In essence, the IRS requires the business to report its own noncompliance. Why would a business do so? Besides complying with the tax laws, a business might report its own noncompliance to receive leniency from the IRS. Without getting into the details, the IRS is likely to assess fewer penalties and less interest expense for noncompliance when the business reports the noncompliance before the IRS discovers it on its own.

Tax Consequences of Changing Accounting Methods When a business changes from one accounting method to another, the business determines its taxable income for the year of change using the new method. Furthermore, the business must make an adjustment to taxable income that effectively represents the cumulative difference, as of the beginning of the tax year, between the amount of income (or deductions) recognized under the old accounting method and the amount that would have been recognized for all prior years if the new method had been applied. This adjustment is called a **§481 adjustment.** The §481 adjustment prevents the duplication or omission of items of income or deduction due to a change in accounting method. If the §481 adjustment increases taxable income, the taxpayer generally recognizes the total adjustment spread evenly over four years beginning with the year of the change (25 percent of the full adjustment each year).[61] If the adjustment decreases taxable income, the taxpayer typically recognizes it entirely in the year of change.

Example 1-30

What if: Suppose that at the end of 2022, Green Acres has $24,000 of accounts receivable. Assuming Green Acres uses the cash method of accounting in 2022, it would not include the $24,000 of receivables in income in determining its 2022 taxable income. Suppose further that Rick decides to switch Green Acres to the accrual method of accounting in 2023 by filing a Form 3115 and receiving permission from the IRS. What is Rick's §481 adjustment for his change in accounting method from the cash to the accrual method, and when will he include the full adjustment in his taxable income?

Answer: Rick's positive §481 full adjustment is $24,000, which will be added to his taxable income over four years in equal increments. Hence, Rick will have a $6,000 annual increase to income beginning in 2023 and ending in 2026. Because Rick is using the accrual method in 2023, he would *not* include payments he receives for the $24,000 in receivables from sales made in 2022. Instead, Rick would be required to make a §481 adjustment to ensure that he does not *omit* these items from taxable income.

What if: Suppose that at the end of 2022, Green Acres has $4,000 of accounts payable instead of $24,000 of accounts receivable. What is the full §481 adjustment and when will he include the adjustment in his taxable income?

Answer: In this instance, Green Acres would have a negative (income-decreasing) §481 adjustment of $4,000 because the $4,000 of expenses would have accrued in 2022 but would not have been deducted in 2022. Hence, Green Acres would be entitled to deduct the full $4,000 as a negative §481 adjustment amount in 2023 (income-decreasing adjustments are made in the year of change rather than spread over four years).

[61]Rev. Proc. 2015-13. There are multiple exceptions to the general rule. For example, taxpayers with positive §481 adjustments less than $25,000 can elect to recognize the entire amount in the year of change. Rev. Proc. 2002-19.

CONCLUSION

This chapter discusses issues relating to business income and deductions. We learned that the income rules for businesses are very similar to those for individuals and that businesses may deduct only ordinary and necessary business expenses and other business expenses specifically authorized by law. We also described several business expense limitations and discussed the accounting periods and methods businesses may use in reporting taxable income to the IRS. The issues described in this chapter are widely applicable to all types of business entities, including sole proprietorships, partnerships, S corporations, and C corporations.

Summary

Identify common business deductions. LO 1-1

- Ordinary and necessary business expenses are allowed as deductions to calculate net income from activities entered into with a profit motive.
- Only reasonable amounts are allowed as business expense deductions. Extravagant or excessive amounts are likely to be characterized by personal motives and are disallowed.

Determine the limits on deducting business expenses. LO 1-2

- To pass the gross receipts test for 2022, a business cannot have average annual gross receipts in excess of $27 million for the three prior years. This limit is indexed for inflation.
- The law specifically prohibits deducting expenses that are against public policy (such as fines or bribes) and expenses that produce tax-exempt income.
- Entertainment is not a deductible business expense, but the cost of business meals is 50 percent deductible (100 percent if purchased from a restaurant) under specific circumstances.
- Expenses benefiting more than 12 months must be capitalized, and special limits and recordkeeping requirements are applied to business expenses that may have personal benefits, such as meals and travel.
- Except for businesses qualifying under the gross receipts test, business interest can only be deducted to the extent of business interest income plus 30 percent of the business's adjusted taxable income. Adjusted taxable income is taxable income before depreciation and interest deductions allocable to the business activity. Disallowed business interest expense can be carried forward indefinitely.
- Losses on the sale of business assets are typically deductible. However, losses on sales to related persons, such as family members, cannot be deducted in the year of sale.
- Special calculations are necessary for deductions such as the deduction for casualty losses. The deduction when an asset is damaged (not destroyed) is limited to the lesser of the reduction in value or the adjusted tax basis of the asset.

Describe accounting periods available to businesses. LO 1-3

- Accounting periods and methods are chosen at the time of filing the first tax return.
- There are three types of tax years—calendar year, fiscal year, and 52/53-week year—and each tax year is distinguished by year-end.

Apply cash and accrual methods to determine business income and expense deductions. LO 1-4

- Under the cash method, taxpayers recognize revenue when they actually or constructively receive property or services and they recognize deductions when they actually pay the expense. C corporations and partnerships with C corporation partners, but not tax shelters, can elect to use the cash method if the business passes the gross receipts test.
- Under the accrual method, the all-events test requires that income be recognized when all the events have occurred that are necessary to fix the right to receive payments and the amount of the payments can be determined with reasonable accuracy, but no later than the income is recognized in the financial statements.
- Businesses where sales are an income-producing factor must elect an inventory method and account for sales and purchases under the accrual method.

- Taxpayers who meet the gross receipts test, however, can account for sales either under the method used for financial reporting or as nonincidental materials.
- Under the accrual method, accrued expenses can be deducted only when the all-events test and the economic performance test both have been met. The application of the economic performance test depends, in part, on the type of business expense.
- Changes in accounting method or accounting period typically require the consent of the IRS and a §481 adjustment to taxable income. A negative adjustment is included in income for the year of change, whereas a positive adjustment is spread over four years.

KEY TERMS

§481 adjustment (1-32)
12-month rule (1-16)
accounting methods (1-15)
accounting period (1-14)
all-events test (1-22)
allowance method (1-27)
arm's-length amount (1-5)
direct write-off method (1-27)
economic performance test (1-22)
first-in, first-out (FIFO) method (1-21)
fiscal year (1-14)
flow-through entity (1-14)
gross receipts test (1-2)
impermissible accounting method (1-29)
last-in, first-out (LIFO) method (1-21)
mixed-motive expenditures (1-8)
ordinary and necessary (1-4)
payment liabilities (1-24)
permissible accounting method (1-29)
personal expenses (1-7)
reasonable in amount (1-5)
recurring item (1-26)
specific identification method (1-21)
tax year (1-14)
travel expenses (1-10)
uniform cost capitalization (UNICAP) rules (1-19)

DISCUSSION QUESTIONS

Discussion Questions are available in Connect®.

LO 1-1 1. What is an "ordinary and necessary" business expenditure?

LO 1-1 2. Explain how cost of goods is treated when a business sells inventory.

LO 1-1 3. Whether a business expense is "reasonable in amount" is often a difficult question. Explain why determining reasonableness is difficult, and describe a circumstance where reasonableness is likely to be questioned by the IRS.

LO 1-1 4. Jake is a professional dog trainer who purchases and trains dogs for use by law enforcement agencies. Last year Jake purchased 500 bags of dog food from a large pet food company at an average cost of $30 per bag. This year, however, Jake purchased 500 bags of dog food from a local pet food company at an average cost of $45 per bag. Under what circumstances would the IRS likely challenge the cost of Jake's dog food as unreasonable?

LO 1-2 5. What kinds of deductions are prohibited as a matter of public policy? Why might Congress deem it important to disallow deductions for expenditures that are against public policy?

LO 1-2 6. Provide an example of an expense associated with the production of tax-exempt income, and explain what might happen if Congress repealed the prohibition against deducting expenses incurred to produce tax-exempt income.

LO 1-2 research 7. Peggy is a rodeo clown, and this year she expended $1,000 on special "funny" clothes and outfits. Peggy would like to deduct the cost of these clothes as work-related because she refuses to wear the clothes unless she is working. Under what circumstances can Peggy deduct the cost of her clown clothes?

LO 1-2 8. Jimmy is a sole proprietor of a small dry-cleaning business. This month Jimmy paid for his groceries by writing checks from the checking account dedicated to the dry-cleaning business. Why do you suppose Jimmy is using his business checking account rather than his personal checking account to pay for personal expenditures?

LO 1-2 9. Troy operates an editorial service that often entertains prospective authors to encourage them to use Troy's service. This year Troy paid $3,000 for the cost of meals and

$6,200 for the cost of entertaining authors. Describe the conditions under which Troy can deduct a portion of the cost of the meals as a business expense.

10. Susmita purchased a car this year and uses it for both business and personal purposes. Susmita drove the car 11,000 miles on business trips and 9,000 miles for personal transportation. Describe how Susmita will determine the amount of deductible expenses associated with the auto. LO 1-2
11. What expenses are deductible when a taxpayer combines both business and personal activities on a trip? How do the rules for international travel differ from the rules for domestic travel? LO 1-1 LO 1-2
12. Clyde lives and operates a sole proprietorship in Dallas, Texas. This year Clyde found it necessary to travel to Fort Worth (about 25 miles away) for legitimate business reasons. Is Clyde's trip likely to qualify as "away from home"? Why would this designation matter? LO 1-2
13. Describe the record-keeping requirements for deducting business expenses, including mixed-motive expenditures. LO 1-2
14. Describe the computation of the limit placed on the business interest deduction. Is the disallowed business interest ever deductible? LO 1-2
15. Describe the gross receipts test and identify how this test relates to the business interest deduction. LO 1-2
16. Explain the difference between calculating a loss deduction for a business asset that was partially damaged in an accident and calculating a loss deduction for a business asset that was stolen or completely destroyed in an accident. LO 1-2
17. How does a casualty loss on a business asset differ when the asset is stolen as opposed to destroyed in a fire? LO 1-2
18. What is the difference between a full tax year and a short tax year? Describe circumstances in which a business may have a short tax year. LO 1-3
19. Explain why a taxpayer might choose one tax year-end over another if given a choice. LO 1-3
20. Compare and contrast the different year-ends available to sole proprietorships, flow-through entities, and C corporations. LO 1-3
21. Why does the law generally require partnerships to adopt a tax year consistent with the year used by the partners? LO 1-3
22. How does an entity choose its tax year? Is it the same process no matter the type of tax year-end the taxpayer adopts? LO 1-3
23. Explain when an expenditure should be "capitalized" based upon accounting principles. From time to time, it is suggested that all business expenditures should be deducted when incurred for tax purposes. Do you agree with this proposition, and if so, why? LO 1-4
24. Describe the 12-month rule for determining whether and to what extent businesses should capitalize or immediately deduct prepaid expenses such as insurance or security contracts. Explain the apparent rationale for this rule. LO 1-4
25. Explain why Congress sometimes mandates that businesses use particular accounting methods while other times Congress is content to require businesses to use the same accounting methods for tax purposes that they use for financial accounting purposes. LO 1-4
26. Why is it not surprising that specific rules differ between tax accounting and financial accounting? LO 1-4
27. The cash method of accounting is generally preferred by taxpayers. Describe two types of businesses that are not allowed to use the cash method. LO 1-4
28. Fred is considering using the accrual method for his next business venture. Explain to Fred the conditions for recognizing income for tax purposes under the accrual method. LO 1-4
29. Describe the all-events test for determining income, and describe how to determine the date on which the all-events test has been met. LO 1-4

LO 1-4 30. Compare and contrast the tax treatment for rental income received in advance with advance payments for goods and services.

LO 1-4 research 31. Jack operates a large home repair business as a sole proprietorship. Besides providing services, Jack also sells home repair supplies to homeowners. However, these sales constitute a relatively small portion of Jack's income. Describe the conditions under which Jack would need to account for sales and purchases of plumbing supplies using the accrual method. (*Hint:* Read §471(c) and Reg. §1.471-1.)

LO 1-4 32. Describe why Congress enacted the UNICAP rules, and describe an exception to these rules.

LO 1-4 33. Compare and contrast financial accounting rules with the tax rules under UNICAP (§263A). Explain whether the UNICAP rules tend to accelerate or defer income relative to the financial accounting rules.

LO 1-4 34. Compare and contrast the tests for accruing income and those for accruing deductions for tax purposes.

LO 1-4 35. Compare and contrast when taxpayers are allowed to deduct the cost of warranties provided by others to the taxpayer (i.e., purchased by the taxpayer) and when taxpayers are allowed to deduct the costs associated with warranties they provide (sell) to others.

LO 1-4 36. Describe when economic performance occurs for the following expenses:

a) Workers' compensation

b) Rebates and refunds

c) Insurance, warranties, and service contracts provided *to* the business

d) Taxes

LO 1-4 37. On December 31 of the current year, a taxpayer prepays an advertising company to provide advertising services for the next 10 months. Using the 12-month rule and the economic performance rules, contrast when the taxpayer would be able to deduct the expenditure if the taxpayer uses the cash method of accounting versus if the taxpayer uses the accrual method of accounting.

LO 1-4 38. Compare and contrast how bad debt expense is determined for financial accounting purposes and how the deduction for bad debts is determined for accrual-method taxpayers. How do cash-method taxpayers determine their bad debt expense for accounts receivable?

LO 1-4 39. Describe the related-person limitation on accrued deductions. What tax savings strategy is this limitation designed to thwart?

LO 1-4 40. What are the relative advantages of the cash and accrual methods of accounting?

LO 1-4 41. Describe how a business adopts a permissible accounting method. Explain whether a taxpayer can adopt an impermissible accounting method.

LO 1-4 42. Describe why the IRS might be skeptical of permitting requests for changes in accounting method without a good business purpose.

LO 1-4 43. Describe two specific accounting methods that are treated as initiated by the taxpayer without any need for consent of the IRS when the business qualifies under the gross receipts test.

LO 1-4 44. What is a §481 adjustment, and what is the purpose of this adjustment?

PROBLEMS

Select problems are available in Connect®. 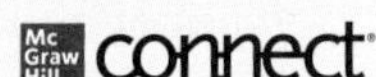

LO 1-1 45. Manny hired his brother's firm to provide accounting services to his business. During the current year, Manny paid his brother's firm $82,000 for services even though other firms were willing to provide the same services for $40,000. How much of this expenditure, if any, is deductible as an ordinary and necessary business expenditure?

46. Michelle operates several food trucks. Indicate the amount (if any) that she can deduct as an ordinary and necessary business deduction in each of the following situations, and explain your solution. LO 1-1 LO 1-2

a) Michelle moves her food truck between various locations on a daily rotation. Last week, Michelle was stopped for speeding. She paid a fine of $125 for speeding, including $80 for legal advice in connection with the ticket.

b) Michelle paid $750 to reserve a parking place for her food truck for the fall football season outside the local football stadium. Michelle also paid $95 for tickets to a game for her children.

c) Michelle provided a candidate with free advertising painted on her truck during the candidate's campaign for city council. Michelle paid $500 to have the ad prepared and an additional $200 to have the ad removed from the truck after the candidate lost the election.

d) Michelle realized a $1,200 loss when she sold one of her food trucks to her father, a related party.

47. Indicate the amount (if any) that Josh can deduct as an ordinary and necessary business deduction in each of the following situations, and explain your solution. LO 1-1 LO 1-2

a) Josh borrowed $50,000 from First State Bank using his business assets as collateral. He used the money to buy City of Blanksville bonds. Over the course of a year, Josh paid interest of $4,200 on the borrowed funds, but he received $3,500 of interest on the bonds.

b) Josh purchased a piece of land for $45,000 in order to get a location to expand his business. He also paid $3,200 to construct a new driveway for access to the property.

c) This year Josh paid $15,000 to employ the mayor's son in the business. Josh would typically pay an employee with these responsibilities about $10,000, but the mayor assured Josh that after his son was hired, some city business would be coming his way.

d) Josh paid his brother, a mechanic, $3,000 to install a robotic machine for Josh's business. The amount he paid to his brother is comparable to what he would have paid to an unrelated person to do the same work. Once the installation was completed by his brother, Josh began calibrating the machine for operation. However, by the end of the year, he had not started using the machine in his business.

48. Armelio operates a business that acts as a sales representative for firms that produce and sell precious metals to electronics manufacturers. Armelio contacts manufacturers and convinces them to sign contracts for the delivery of metals. Armelio's company earns a commission on the sales. This year, Armelio contacted a jeweler to engrave small lapel buttons for each client. Armelio paid $20 each for the lapel buttons, and the jeweler charged Armelio an additional $7 for engraving. The electronics manufacturers, however, prohibit their employees from accepting gifts related to sales contracts. Can Armelio deduct the cost of the lapel buttons as business gifts? LO 1-2 research

49. Melissa recently paid $400 for round-trip airfare to San Francisco to attend a business conference for three days. Melissa also paid the following expenses: $250 fee to register for the conference, $300 per night for three nights' lodging, $200 for meals in restaurants, and $150 for cab fare. LO 1-2

a) What amount of these costs can Melissa deduct as business expenses?

b) Suppose that while Melissa was on the coast, she also spent two days sightseeing the national parks in the area. To do the sightseeing, she paid $1,000 for transportation, $800 for lodging, and $450 for meals during this part of her trip, which she considers personal in nature. What amount of these costs can Melissa deduct as business expenses?

c) Suppose that Melissa made the trip to San Francisco primarily to visit the national parks and only attended the business conference as an incidental benefit of being present on the coast at that time. What amount of the airfare can Melissa deduct as a business expense?

d) Suppose that Melissa's permanent residence and business were located in San Francisco. She attended the conference in San Francisco and paid $250 for the registration fee. She drove 100 miles over the course of three days and paid $90 for parking at the conference hotel. In addition, she spent $150 for breakfast and dinner over the three days of the conference. She bought breakfast on the way to the conference hotel, and she bought dinner on her way home each night from the conference. What amount of these costs can Melissa deduct as business expenses?

LO 1-2

50. Sasha is a self-employed taxpayer. They recently spent $1,000 for airfare to travel to Italy. What amount of the airfare is deductible in each of the following alternative scenarios?

a) Sasha's trip was entirely for personal purposes.

b) On the trip, Sasha spent eight days on personal activities and two days on business activities.

c) On the trip, Sasha spent seven days on business activities and three days on personal activities.

d) Sasha's trip was entirely for business purposes.

LO 1-2

51. Ryan is self-employed. This year Ryan used his personal auto for several long business trips. Ryan paid $1,500 for gasoline on these trips. His depreciation on the car if he was using it fully for business purposes would be $3,000. During the year, he drove his car a total of 12,000 miles (a combination of business and personal travel).

a) Ryan can provide written documentation of the business purpose for trips totaling 3,000 miles. What business expense amount can Ryan deduct (if any) for these trips?

b) Ryan estimates that he drove approximately 1,300 miles on business trips, but he can only provide written documentation of the business purpose for trips totaling 820 miles. What business expense amount can Ryan deduct (if any) for these trips?

LO 1-1 LO 1-2

52. Haru is a self-employed cash-method, calendar-year taxpayer who made the following cash payments related to his business this year. Calculate the after-tax cost of each payment assuming Haru has a 37 percent marginal tax rate.

a) $500 fine for speeding while traveling to a client meeting.

b) $800 of interest on a short-term loan incurred in September and repaid in November. Half of the loan proceeds was used immediately to pay salaries and the other half was invested in municipal bonds until November.

c) $600 for office supplies in May of this year. Haru used half of the supplies this year, and he will use the remaining half by February of next year.

d) $450 for several pairs of work boots. Haru expects to use the boots about 80 percent of the time in his business and the remainder of the time for hiking. Consider the boots to be a form of clothing.

LO 1-2

53. Heather is an attorney who paid $15,000 to join a country club in order to meet potential clients. This year she also paid $4,300 in greens fees when golfing with clients and paid an additional $1,700 for meals with clients in the clubhouse. Under what circumstances, if any, can Heather deduct all or part of the $21,000 paid to the country club this year?

54. Sarah is a cash-method, calendar-year taxpayer, and she is considering making the following cash payments related to her business. Calculate the after-tax cost of each payment assuming she is subject to a 37 percent marginal tax rate. LO 1-1 LO 1-2
 a) $2,000 payment for next year's property taxes on her place of business.
 b) $800 to reimburse the cost of meals at restaurants incurred by employees while traveling for the business.
 c) $1,200 for football tickets to entertain out-of-town clients during contract negotiations.
 d) $500 contribution to the mayor's reelection campaign.

55. Red Inc. is a C corporation and a calendar-year taxpayer. Red reports sales of $24 million in 2019, $28.3 million in 2020, and $32 million in 2021. LO 1-2
 a) Is Red subject to the business interest limitation in 2022?
 b) Suppose that besides sales, Red also reports sales returns of $3.1 million in each year 2019–2021. Is Red subject to the business interest limitation in 2022?
 c) Suppose that Red began business on January 1, 2020, and reported gross receipts of $25.3 million in 2020 and $28.9 million in 2021. Is Red subject to the business interest limitation in 2022?
 d) Suppose that Red began business operations on October 1, 2021, and reported $6.2 million in gross receipts for the three-month 2021 short year. Is Red subject to the business interest limitation in 2022?

56. Renee operates a proprietorship selling collectibles over the Web. This year, Renee's business reported revenue of $95.5 million and deducted $88.6 million in expenses and loss carryovers. Her business deductions included cost of goods sold of $48.5 million, sales commissions paid of $16.9 million, $10.5 million of interest paid on a mortgage, $10.7 million of depreciation, and $2 million deduction for a net operating loss carryover. LO 1-2
 a) What is Renee's adjusted taxable income for purposes of calculating the limitation on business interest expense?
 b) What is the maximum amount of business interest expense that Renee can deduct this year, and how is the disallowed interest expense (if any) treated?
 c) Suppose that Renee's revenue includes $5 million of business interest income. What is the maximum amount of business interest expense that could be deducted this year under the business interest limitation?

57. This year, Amy purchased $2,000 of equipment for use in her business. However, the machine was damaged in a traffic accident while Amy was transporting the equipment to her business. Note that because Amy did not place the equipment into service during the year, she does not claim any depreciation or cost recovery expense for the equipment. LO 1-2
 a) After the accident, Amy had the choice of repairing the equipment for $1,800 or selling the equipment to a junk shop for $300. Amy sold the equipment. What amount can Amy deduct for the loss of the equipment?
 b) Suppose that after the accident, Amy repaired the equipment for $800. What amount can Amy deduct for the loss of the equipment?
 c) Suppose that after the accident, Amy could not replace the equipment so she had the equipment repaired for $2,300. What amount can Amy deduct for the loss of the equipment?

58. In July of this year, Stephen started a proprietorship called ECR (which stands for electric car repair). ECR uses the cash method of accounting, and Stephen has produced the following financial information for this year: LO 1-3

- ECR collected $81,000 in cash for repairs completed during the year and an additional $3,200 in cash for repairs that will commence after year-end.

- Customers owe ECR $14,300 for repairs completed this year, and while Stephen isn't sure which bills will eventually be paid, he expects to collect all but about $1,900 of these revenues next year.

ECR has made the following expenditures:

Interest expense	$ 1,250
Shop rent ($1,500 per month)	27,000
Utilities	1,075
Contract labor	8,250
Compensation	21,100
Liability insurance premiums ($350 per month)	4,200
Term life insurance premiums ($150 per month)	1,800

The interest paid relates to interest accrued on a $54,000 loan made to Stephen in July of this year. Stephen used half of the loan to pay for 18 months of shop rent, and the remainder he used to upgrade his personal wardrobe. In July, Stephen purchased 12 months of liability insurance to protect against liability should anyone be injured in the shop. ECR has only one employee (the remaining workers are contract labor), and this employee thoroughly understands how to repair an electric propulsion system. On November 1 of this year, Stephen purchased a 12-month term life policy that insures the life of this "key" employee. Stephen paid Gecko Insurance Company $1,800; in return, Gecko promises to pay Stephen a $40,000 death benefit if this employee dies any time during the next 12 months.

Complete a draft of the front page of Stephen's Schedule C.

LO 1-4 planning

59. Nicole is a calendar-year taxpayer who accounts for her business using the cash method. On average, Nicole sends out bills for about $12,000 of her services on the first of each month. The bills are due by the end of the month, and typically 70 percent of the bills are paid on time and 98 percent are paid within 60 days.
    a) Suppose that Nicole is expecting a 2 percent reduction in her marginal tax rate next year. Ignoring the time value of money, estimate the tax savings for Nicole if she postpones mailing the December bills until January 1 of next year.
    b) Describe how the time value of money affects your calculations.
    c) Would this tax savings strategy create any additional business risks? Explain.

LO 1-4

60. Jeremy is a calendar-year taxpayer who sometimes leases his business equipment to local organizations. He recorded the following receipts this year. Indicate the extent to which these payments are taxable income to Jeremy this year if Jeremy is (1) a cash-method taxpayer and (2) an accrual-method taxpayer.
    a) $1,000 deposit from the Ladies' Club, which wants to lease a trailer. The club will receive the entire deposit back when the trailer is returned undamaged.
    b) $800 from the Ladies' Club for leasing the trailer from December of this year through March of next year ($200 per month).
    c) $300 lease payment received from the Men's Club this year for renting Jeremy's trailer last year. Jeremy billed the club last year, but recently he determined that the Men's Club would never pay him, so he was surprised when he received the check.

LO 1-4

61. Brown Thumb Landscaping is a calendar-year, accrual-method taxpayer. In September, Brown Thumb negotiated a $14,000 contract for services it would provide to the city in November of the current year. The contract specifies that Brown Thumb will receive $4,000 in October as a down payment for these services, and it will receive the remaining $10,000 in January of next year.
    a) How much income from this $14,000 contract will Brown Thumb recognize in the current year? Explain.
    b) How much income from this $14,000 contract will Brown Thumb recognize in the current year if it uses the cash method of accounting?

c) Suppose that the total amount to be paid under the contract with the city is estimated at $14,000 but may be adjusted to $12,000 next year during the review of the city budget. What amount from the contract, if any, should Brown Thumb recognize as income this year? Explain.

d) Suppose that in addition to the basic contract, Brown Thumb will be paid an additional $3,000 if its city landscape design wins the annual design competition next year. Should Brown Thumb accrue $3,000 revenue this year? Why or why not?

62. In January of year 0, Justin paid $4,800 for an insurance policy that covers his business property for accidents and casualties. Justin is a calendar-year taxpayer who uses the cash method of accounting. What amount of the insurance premium may Justin deduct in year 0 in each of the following alternative scenarios? LO 1-4

a) The policy covers the business property from April 1 of year 0 through March 31 of year 1.

b) The policy begins on February 1 of year 1 and extends through January 31 of year 2.

c) Justin pays $6,000 for a 24-month policy that covers the business from April 1, year 0, through March 31, year 2.

d) Instead of paying an insurance premium, Justin pays $4,800 to rent his business property from April 1 of year 0 through March 31 of year 1.

63. Binu teaches golf lessons at a country club under a business called Binu's Pure Swings (BPS). Binu operates this business as a sole proprietorship on the accrual basis of accounting. Use the following accounting information for BPS to complete the firm's Schedule C: LO 1-4

This year BPS billed clients for $86,700 and collected $61,000 in cash for golf lessons completed during the year. In addition, BPS collected an additional $14,500 in cash for lessons that will commence after year-end. Binu hopes to collect about half of the outstanding billings next year, but the rest will likely be written off.

Besides providing private golf lessons, BPS also contracted with the country club to staff the driving range. This year, BPS billed the country club $27,200 for the service. The club paid $17,000 of the amount but disputed the remainder. By year-end, the dispute had not been resolved, and while Binu believes BPS is entitled to the money, the remaining $10,200 has not been paid.

BPS has accrued the following expenses (explained below):

Advertising (in the clubhouse)	$13,150
Pro golf teachers' membership fees	860
Supplies (golf tees, balls, etc.)	4,720
Club rental	6,800
Malpractice insurance	2,400
Accounting fees	8,820

The expenditures were all paid for this calendar year, with several exceptions. First, Binu initiated his golfer's malpractice insurance on June 1 of this year. The $2,400 insurance bill covers the last six months of this calendar year and the first six months of next year. At year-end, Binu had only paid $600 but has assured the insurance agent the remaining $1,800 will be paid early next year. Second, the amount paid for club rental ($100 per week) represents rental charges for the last 6 weeks of the previous year, the 52 weeks in this calendar year, and the first 10 weeks of next year. Binu has also mentioned that BPS only pays for supplies that are used at the club. Although BPS could buy the supplies for half the cost elsewhere, Binu likes to "throw some business" to the golf pro shop because it is operated by his brother.

Complete a draft of Parts I and II on the front page of a Schedule C for BPS.

LO 1-4 64. Stephanie began her consulting business this year, and on April 1 Stephanie received a $9,000 payment for full payment on a three-year service contract (under the contract, Stephanie is obligated to provide advisory services for the next three years). Stephanie has elected to use the accrual method of accounting for her business.

a) What is the minimum amount of income Stephanie should recognize for tax purposes this year if she recognizes $2,250 of income for financial accounting purposes?

b) What is the minimum amount of income Stephanie will recognize next year for tax purposes?

LO 1-4 65. This year, Amber purchased a business that processes and packages landscape mulch. Approximately 20 percent of management time, space, and expenses are spent on this manufacturing process.

		Costs	Tax Inventory
Material:	Mulch and packaging	$ 500,000	?
	Administrative supplies	25,000	?
Salaries:	Factory labor	1,200,000	?
	Sales & advertising	350,000	?
	Administration	520,000	?
Property taxes:	Factory	460,000	?
	Offices	270,000	?
Depreciation:	Factory	800,000	?
	Offices	150,000	?

a) At the end of the year, Amber's accountant indicated that the business had processed 10 million bags of mulch, but only 1 million bags remained in the ending inventory. What is Amber's tax basis in her ending inventory if the UNICAP rules are used to allocate indirect costs to inventory? (Assume direct costs are allocated to inventory according to the level of ending inventory. In contrast, indirect costs are first allocated by time spent and then according to level of ending inventory.)

b) Under what conditions could Amber's business avoid having to apply UNICAP rules to allocate indirect costs to inventory for tax purposes?

LO 1-4 66. Suppose that David has elected to account for inventories and has adopted the last-in, first-out (LIFO) inventory-flow method for his business inventory of widgets (purchase prices below).

Widget	Purchase Date	Direct Cost	Other Costs	Total Cost
#1	August 15	$2,100	$100	$2,200
#2	October 30	2,200	150	2,350
#3	November 10	2,300	100	2,400

In late December, David sold one widget, and next year David expects to purchase three more widgets at the following estimated prices:

Widget	Purchase Date	Estimated Cost
#4	Early spring	$2,600
#5	Summer	2,260
#6	Fall	2,400

a) What cost of goods sold and ending inventory would David record if he elects to use the LIFO method this year?

b) If David sells two more widgets next year, what will be his cost of goods sold and ending inventory next year under the LIFO method?

c) How would you answer (a) and (b) if David had initially selected the first-in, first-out (FIFO) method instead of LIFO?

d) Suppose that David initially adopted the LIFO method but wants to apply for a change to FIFO next year. What would be his §481 adjustment for this change, and in what year(s) would he make the adjustment?

67. On November 1 of this year, Jaxon borrowed $50,000 from Bucksnort Savings and Loan for use in his business. In December, Jaxon paid interest of $4,500 relating to the 12-month period from November of this year through October of next year. LO 1-4

a) How much interest, if any, can Jaxon deduct this year if his business uses the cash method of accounting for tax purposes?

b) How much interest, if any, can Jaxon deduct this year if his business uses the accrual method of accounting for tax purposes?

68. Matt hired Apex Services to repair his business equipment. On November 1 of this year, Matt paid $2,000 for the repairs that he expects to begin in early March of next year. LO 1-4

a) What amount of the cost of the repairs can Matt deduct this year if he uses the cash method of accounting for his business?

b) What amount of the cost of the repairs can Matt deduct this year if he uses the accrual method of accounting for his business?

c) What amount of the cost of the repairs can Matt deduct this year if he uses the accrual method, and he expects the repairs to be done by early February?

d) What amount of the cost of the repairs can Matt deduct this year if he uses the cash method of accounting, and he expects the repairs to be done by early February?

69. Circuit Corporation (CC) is a calendar-year, accrual-method taxpayer. CC manufactures and sells electronic circuitry. On November 15 of this year, CC enters into a contract with Equip Corp (EC) that provides CC with exclusive use of EC's specialized manufacturing equipment for the five-year period beginning on January 1 of next year. Pursuant to the contract, CC pays EC $100,000 on December 30 of this year. How much of this expenditure is CC allowed to deduct this year and next year? LO 1-4

70. This year Elizabeth agreed to a three-year service contract with an engineering consulting firm to improve efficiency in her factory. The contract requires Elizabeth to pay the consulting firm $1,500 for each instance that Elizabeth requests its assistance. The contract also provides that Elizabeth only pays the consultants if their advice increases efficiency as measured 12 months from the date of service. This year Elizabeth requested advice on three occasions, and she has not yet made any payments to the consultants. LO 1-4

a) How much should Elizabeth deduct this year under this service contract if she uses the accrual method of accounting?

b) How much should Elizabeth deduct this year under this service contract if she uses the cash method of accounting?

71. Travis is a professional landscaper. He provides his clients with a one-year (12-month) warranty for retaining walls he installs. In June of this year, Travis installed a wall for an important client, Sheila. In early November, Sheila informed Travis that the retaining wall had failed. To repair the wall, Travis paid $700 cash for additional stone that he delivered to Sheila's location on November 20 of this year. Travis also offered to pay a mason $800 to repair the wall. Due to some bad weather and the mason's work backlog, the mason agreed to begin the work by the end of January of the next year. Even though Travis expected the mason to finish LO 1-4

the project by the end of February, Travis informed the mason that he would only pay the mason the $800 when he completed the job.

a) Assuming Travis is an accrual-method taxpayer, how much can he deduct this year from these activities?

b) Assuming Travis is a cash-method taxpayer, how much can he deduct this year from these activities?

LO 1-4 research

72. Adam elects the accrual method of accounting for his business. What amount of deductions does Adam recognize this year for the following transactions?

a) Adam guarantees that he will refund the cost of any goods sold to a client if the goods fail within a year of delivery. In December of this year, Adam agreed to refund $2,400 to clients, and he expects to make payment in January of next year.

b) On December 1 of this year, Adam paid $480 for a one-year contract with CleanUP Services to clean his store. The agreement calls for services to be provided on a weekly basis.

c) Adam was billed $240 for annual personal property taxes on his delivery van. Because this was the first time Adam was billed for these taxes, he did not make payment until January of next year. However, he considers the amounts immaterial.

LO 1-4

73. Rebecca is a calendar-year taxpayer who operates a business. She made the following business-related expenditures in December of this year. Indicate the amount of these payments that she may deduct this year under both the cash method of accounting and the accrual method of accounting.

a) $2,000 for an accountant to evaluate the accounting system of Rebecca's business. The accountant spent three weeks in January of next year working on the evaluation.

b) $2,500 for new office furniture. The furniture was delivered on January 15 of next year.

c) $3,000 for property taxes payable on her factory.

d) $1,500 for interest on a short-term bank loan relating to the period from November 1 of this year through March 31 of next year.

LO 1-4

74. BCS Corporation is a calendar-year, accrual-method taxpayer. BCS was formed and started its business activities on January 1 of this year. It reported the following information for the year. Indicate BCS's deductible amount for this year in each of the following alternative scenarios.

a) BCS provides two-year warranties on products it sells to customers. For its current-year sales, BCS estimated and accrued $200,000 in warranty expense for financial accounting purposes. During this year, BCS actually spent $30,000 repairing its product under the warranty.

b) BCS accrued an expense of $50,000 for amounts it anticipated it would be required to pay under the workers' compensation act. During the year, BCS actually paid $10,000 for workers' compensation–related liabilities.

c) In June of this year, a display of BCS's product located in its showroom fell and injured a customer. The customer sued BCS for $500,000. The case is scheduled to go to trial next year. BCS anticipates that it will lose the case and this year accrued a $500,000 expense on its financial statements.

d) Assume the same facts as in (c) except that BCS was required to pay $500,000 to a court-appointed escrow fund this year. If BCS loses the case next year, the money from the escrow fund will be transferred to the customer suing BCS.

e) On December 1 of this year, BCS acquired equipment from Equip Company. As part of the purchase, BCS signed a separate contract that provided that Equip would warranty the equipment for two years (starting on December 1 of this year). The extra cost of the warranty was $12,000, which BCS finally paid to Equip in January of next year.

75. This year William provided $4,200 of services to a large client on credit. Unfortunately, this client has recently encountered financial difficulties and has been unable to pay William for the services. Moreover, William does not expect to collect for his services. William has "written off" the account and would like to claim a deduction for tax purposes. LO 1-4
   a) What amount of deduction for bad debt expense can William claim this year if he uses the accrual method?
   b) What amount of deduction for bad debt expense can William claim this year if he uses the cash method?

76. Dustin has a contract to provide services to Dado Enterprises. In November of this year, Dustin billed Dado $10,000 for the services he rendered during the year. Dado is an accrual-method proprietorship that is owned and operated by Dustin's father. LO 1-4
   a) What amount of revenue must Dustin recognize this year if Dustin uses the cash method and Dado remits payment and Dustin receives payment for the services in December of this year? What amount can Dado deduct this year?
   b) What amount of revenue must Dustin recognize this year if Dustin uses the accrual method and Dado remits payment for the services in December of this year? What amount can Dado deduct this year?
   c) What amount of revenue must Dustin recognize this year if Dustin uses the cash method and Dado remits payment for the services in January of this year? What amount can Dado deduct this year?
   d) What amount of revenue must Dustin recognize this year if Dustin uses the accrual method and Dado remits payment for the services in January of next year? What amount can Dado deduct this year?

77. Nancy operates a business that uses the accrual method of accounting. In December, Nancy asked her brother, Hank, to provide her business with consulting advice. Hank billed Nancy for $5,000 of consulting services in year 0 (a reasonable amount), but Nancy was only able to pay $3,000 of the bill by the end of this year. However, Nancy paid the remainder of the bill in the following year. LO 1-4
   a) How much of the $5,000 consulting services will Hank include in his income this year if he uses the cash method of accounting? What amount can Nancy deduct this year for the consulting services?
   b) How much of the $5,000 consulting services will Hank include in his income this year if he uses the accrual method of accounting? What amount can Nancy deduct this year for the consulting services?

78. Erin is considering switching her business from the cash method to the accrual method at the beginning of next year. Determine the amount and timing of her §481 adjustment assuming the IRS grants Erin's request in the following alternative scenarios. LO 1-4
   a) At the end of this year, Erin's business has $15,000 of accounts receivable and $18,000 of accounts payable that have not been recorded for tax purposes.
   b) At the end of this year, Erin's business reports $25,000 of accounts receivable and $9,000 of accounts payable that have not been recorded for tax purposes.

COMPREHENSIVE PROBLEMS

Select problems are available in Connect®.

79. Joe operates a business that locates and purchases specialized assets for clients, among other activities. Joe uses the accrual method of accounting, but he doesn't keep any significant inventories of the specialized assets that he sells. Joe reported

the following financial information for his business activities during this year. Determine the effect of each of the following transactions on the taxable business income.

a) Joe has signed a contract to sell gadgets to the city. The contract provides that sales of gadgets are dependent upon a test sample of gadgets operating successfully. In December of this year, Joe delivers $12,000 worth of gadgets to the city that will be tested in March of next year. Joe purchased the gadgets especially for this contract and paid $8,500.

b) Joe paid $180 in July of this year to entertain a visiting out-of-town client. The client didn't discuss business with Joe during this visit, but Joe wants to maintain good relations to encourage additional business next year.

c) On November 1 of this year, Joe paid $600 for premiums providing for $40,000 of "key man" insurance on the life of Joe's accountant over the next 12 months.

d) At the end of this year, Joe's business reports $9,000 of accounts receivable. Based upon past experience, Joe believes that at least $2,000 of his new receivables will be uncollectible.

e) In December of this year, Joe rented equipment to complete a large job. Joe paid $3,000 in December because the rental agency required a minimum rental of three months ($1,000 per month). Joe completed the job before year-end, but he returned the equipment at the end of the lease.

f) Joe hired a new sales representative as an employee and sent them to Dallas for a week to contact prospective out-of-state clients. Joe ended up reimbursing his employee $300 for airfare, $350 for lodging, and $250 for meals at restaurants (the sales representative provided adequate documentation to substantiate the business purpose for the meals). Joe requires the employee to account for all expenditures to be reimbursed.

g) Joe uses his BMW (a personal auto) to travel to and from his residence to his factory. However, he switches to a business vehicle if he needs to travel after he reaches the factory. In September of this year, the business vehicle broke down and he was forced to use the BMW both to travel to and from the factory and to visit work sites. He drove 120 miles visiting work sites and 46 miles driving back and forth between the factory and his home. Joe uses the standard mileage rate to determine his auto-related business expenses.

h) Joe paid a visit to his parents in Dallas over the Christmas holidays this year. While he was in the city, Joe spent $50 to attend a half-day business symposium. Joe paid $200 for airfare, $50 for meals provided during the symposium, and $20 on cab fare to the symposium.

80. Jack, a geologist, had been debating for years whether or not to venture out on his own and operate his own business. He had developed a lot of solid relationships with clients, and he believed that many of them would follow him if he were to leave his current employer. As part of a New Year's resolution, Jack decided he would finally do it. Jack put his business plan together, and on January 1 of this year, Jack opened his doors for business as a C corporation called Geo-Jack (GJ). Jack is the sole shareholder. Jack reported the following financial information for the year (assume GJ reports on a calendar year, uses the accrual method of accounting, and elects to account for inventory).

a) In January, GJ rented a small business office about 12 miles from Jack's home. GJ paid $10,000, which represented a damage deposit of $4,000 and rent for two years ($3,000 annually).

b) GJ earned and collected $290,000 performing geological-related services and selling its specialized digging tool [see part (i)].

c) GJ received $50 interest from municipal bonds and $2,100 interest from other investments.

d) GJ purchased some new equipment in February for $42,500. It claimed depreciation on these assets during the year in the amount of $6,540.

e) GJ paid $7,000 to buy luxury season tickets for Jack's parents for State U football games.

f) GJ paid Jack's father $10,000 for services that would have cost no more than $6,000 if Jack had hired any other local business to perform the services. While Jack's dad was competent, he does not command such a premium from his other clients.

g) In an attempt to get his name and new business recognized, GJ paid $7,000 for a one-page ad in the *Geologic Survey*. It also paid $15,000 in radio ads to be run through the end of December.

h) GJ leased additional office space in a building downtown. GJ paid rent of $27,000 for the year.

i) In November, Jack's office was broken into, and equipment valued at $5,000 was stolen. The tax basis of the equipment was $5,500. Jack received $2,000 of insurance proceeds from the theft.

j) GJ incurred a $4,000 fine from the state government for digging in an unauthorized digging zone.

k) GJ contributed $3,000 to lobbyists for their help in persuading the state government to authorize certain unauthorized digging zones.

l) On July 1, GJ paid $1,800 for an 18-month insurance policy for its business equipment. The policy covers the period July 1 of this year through December 31 of next year.

m) GJ borrowed $20,000 to help with the company's initial funding needs. GJ used $2,000 of funds to invest in municipal bonds. At the end of the year, GJ paid the $1,200 of interest expense that accrued on the loan during the year.

n) Jack lives 12 miles from the office. He carefully tracked his mileage and drove his truck 6,280 miles between the office and his home. He also drove an additional 7,200 miles traveling between the office and client sites. Jack did not use the truck for any other purposes. He did not keep track of the specific expenses associated with the truck. However, while traveling to a client site, Jack received a $150 speeding ticket. GJ reimbursed Jack for business mileage and for the speeding ticket.

o) GJ purchased two season tickets (20 games) to attend State U baseball games for a total of $1,100. Jack took existing and prospective clients to the games to maintain contact and find further work. This was very successful for Jack as GJ gained many new projects through substantial discussions with the clients following the games.

p) GJ paid $3,500 for meals at restaurants when sales employees met with prospective clients.

q) GJ had a client who needed Jack to perform work in Florida. Because Jack had never been to Florida before, he booked an extra day and night for sightseeing. Jack spent $400 for airfare and booked a hotel for three nights ($120/night). (Jack stayed two days for business purposes and one day for personal purposes.) He also rented a car for $45 per day. The client provided Jack's meals while Jack was doing business, but GJ paid all expenses.

r) GJ paid a total of $10,000 of wages to employees during the year, and cost of goods sold was $15,000.

Required:

a) What is GJ's net business income for tax purposes for the year?

b) As a C corporation, does GJ have a required tax year? If so, what would it be?

c) If GJ were a sole proprietorship, would it have a required tax year-end? If so, what would it be?
d) If GJ were an S corporation, would it have a required tax year-end? If so, what would it be?

81. Rex loves to work with his hands and is very good at making small figurines. Three years ago, Rex opened Bronze Age Miniatures (BAM) for business as a sole proprietorship. BAM produces miniature characters ranging from sci-fi characters (his favorite) to historical characters like George Washington (the most popular). Business has been going very well for him, and he has provided the following information relating to his business. Calculate the business taxable income for BAM assuming that BAM elects to account for its inventory of miniatures.
   a) Rex received approval from the IRS to switch from the cash method of accounting to the accrual method of accounting effective January 1 of this year. At the end of last year, BAM reported accounts receivable that had not been included in income under the accrual method of $14,000 and accounts payable that had not been deducted under the accrual method of $5,000.
   b) In March, BAM sold 5,000 miniature historical figures to History R Us Inc. (HRU), a retailer of historical artifacts and figurines, for $75,000.
   c) HRU was so impressed with the figurines that it purchased in March that it wanted to contract with BAM to continue to produce the figurines for it for the next three years. HRU paid BAM $216,000 ($12 per figurine) on October 30 of this year to produce 500 figurines per month for 36 months beginning on November 1 of this year. BAM delivered 500 figurines on November 30 and again on December 30. Rex elects to use the deferral method to account for the transaction.
   d) Though the sci-fi figurines were not quite as popular, BAM sold 400 figurines at a sci-fi convention in April. Rex accepted cash only and received $11,000 for these sales.
   e) In January, BAM determined that it would not be able to collect on $2,000 of its beginning-of-the-year receivables, so it wrote off $2,000 of specific receivables. BAM sold 100,000 other figurines on credit for $120,000. BAM estimates that it will be unable to collect 5 percent of the sales revenue from these sales, but it has not been able to specifically identify any accounts to write off.
   f) Assume that BAM correctly determined that its cost of goods sold using an appropriate inventory method is $54,000 this year.
   g) The sci-fi convention in April was held in Chicago, Illinois. Rex attended the convention because he felt it was a good opportunity to gain new customers and to get new ideas for figurines. He paid $350 round-trip airfare, $100 for entrance to the convention, $210 for lodging, $65 for cab fare, and $110 for meals at restaurants during the trip. He was busy with business activities the entire trip.
   h) On August 1, BAM purchased a 12-month insurance policy that covers its business property for accidents and casualties through July 31 of next year. The policy cost BAM $3,600.
   i) BAM reported depreciation expense of $8,200 for this year.
   j) Rex had previously operated his business out of his garage, but in January he decided to rent a larger space. He entered into a lease agreement on February 1 and paid $14,400 ($1,200 per month) to possess the space for the next 12 months (February of this year through January of next year).
   k) Before he opened his doors for business, Rex spent $30,000 investigating and otherwise getting ready to do business. He expensed $5,000 immediately and is amortizing the remainder using the straight-line method over 180 months.
   l) In December, BAM agreed to a 12-month, $8,000 contract with Advertise-With-Us (AWU) to produce a radio ad campaign. BAM paid $3,000 up front

(in December of this year), and AWU agreed that BAM would owe the remaining $5,000 only if BAM's sales increased by 15 percent over the 9-month period after the contract was signed.

m) In November of this year, BAM paid $2,500 in business property taxes (based on asset values) covering the period December 1 of this year through November 30 of next year. In November of last year, BAM paid $1,500 for business property taxes (based on asset values) covering the period December 1 of last year through November 30 of this year.

82. Bryan followed in his father's footsteps and entered into the carpet business. He owns and operates I Do Carpet (IDC). Bryan prefers to install carpet only, but in order to earn additional revenue, he also cleans carpets and sells carpet-cleaning supplies. Compute his taxable income for the current year considering the following items:

a) IDC contracted with a homebuilder in December of last year to install carpet in 10 new homes being built. The contract price of $80,000 includes $50,000 for materials (carpet). The remaining $30,000 is for IDC's service of installing the carpet. The contract also stated that all money was to be paid up front. The homebuilder paid IDC in full on December 28 of last year. The contract required IDC to complete the work by January 31 of this year. Bryan purchased the necessary carpet on January 2 and began working on the first home January 4. He completed the last home on January 27 of this year.

b) IDC entered into several other contracts this year and completed the work before year-end. The work cost $130,000 in materials, and IDC elects to immediately deduct supplies. Bryan billed out $240,000 but only collected $220,000 by year-end. Of the $20,000 still owed to him, Bryan wrote off $3,000 he didn't expect to collect as a bad debt from a customer experiencing extreme financial difficulties.

c) IDC entered into a three-year contract to clean the carpets of an office building. The contract specified that IDC would clean the carpets monthly from July 1 of this year through June 30 three years hence. IDC received payment in full of $8,640 ($240 a month for 36 months) on June 30 of this year.

d) IDC sold 100 bottles of carpet stain remover this year for $5 per bottle (it collected $500). Rex sold 40 bottles on June 1 and 60 bottles on November 2. IDC had the following carpet-cleaning supplies on hand for this year, and IDC has elected to use the LIFO method of accounting for inventory under a perpetual inventory system:

Purchase Date	Bottles	Total Cost
November last year	40	$120
February this year	35	112
July this year	25	85
August this year	40	140
Totals	140	$457

e) On August 1 of this year, IDC needed more room for storage and paid $900 to rent a garage for 12 months.

f) On November 30 of this year, Bryan decided it was time to get his logo on the sides of his work van. IDC hired We Paint Anything Inc. (WPA) to do the job. It paid $500 down and agreed to pay the remaining $1,500 upon completion of the job. WPA indicated it wouldn't be able to begin the job until January 15 of next year, but the job would only take one week to complete. Due to circumstances beyond its control, WPA wasn't able to complete the job until April 1 of next year, at which time IDC paid the remaining $1,500.

g) In December, Bryan's son, Aiden, helped him finish some carpeting jobs. IDC owed Aiden $600 (reasonable) compensation for his work. However, Aiden did not receive the payment until January of next year.

h) IDC also paid $1,000 for interest on a short-term bank loan relating to the period from November 1 of this year through March 31 of next year.

83. Hank started a new business, Hank's Donut World (HW for short), in June of last year. He has requested your advice on the following specific tax matters associated with HW's first year of operations. Hank has estimated HW's income for the first year as follows:

Revenue:		
Donut sales	$252,000	
Catering revenues	71,550	$ 323,550
Expenditures:		
Donut supplies	$124,240	
Catering expense	27,910	
Salaries to shop employees	52,500	
Rent expense	40,050	
Accident insurance premiums	8,400	
Other business expenditures	6,850	−259,950
Net income		$ 63,600

HW operates as a sole proprietorship, and Hank reports on a calendar year. Hank uses the cash method of accounting and plans to do the same with HW (HW has no inventory of donuts because unsold donuts are not salable). HW does not purchase donut supplies on credit, nor does it generally make sales on credit. Hank has provided the following details for specific first-year transactions:

- A small minority of HW clients complained about the catering service. To mitigate these complaints, Hank's policy is to refund dissatisfied clients 50 percent of the catering fee. By the end of the first year, only two HW clients had complained but had not yet been paid refunds. The expected refunds amount to $1,700, and Hank reduced the reported catering fees for the first year to reflect the expected refund.
- In the first year, HW received a $6,750 payment from a client for catering a monthly breakfast for 30 consecutive months beginning in December. Because the payment didn't relate to last year, Hank excluded the entire amount when he calculated catering revenues.
- In July, HW paid $1,500 to ADMAN Co. for an advertising campaign to distribute fliers advertising HW's catering service. Unfortunately, this campaign violated a city code restricting advertising by fliers, and the city fined HW $250 for the violation. HW paid the fine, and Hank included the fine and the cost of the campaign in "other business" expenditures.
- In July, HW also paid $8,400 for a 24-month insurance policy that covers HW for accidents and casualties beginning on August 1 of the first year. Hank deducted the entire $8,400 as accident insurance premiums.
- In May of the first year, Hank signed a contract to lease the HW donut shop for 10 months. In conjunction with the contract, Hank paid $2,000 as a damage deposit and $8,050 for rent ($805 per month). Hank explained that the damage deposit was refundable at the end of the lease. At this time, Hank also paid $30,000 to lease kitchen equipment for 24 months ($1,250 per month). Both leases began on June 1 of the first year. In his estimate, Hank deducted these amounts ($40,050 in total) as rent expense.
- Hank signed a contract hiring WEGO Catering to help cater breakfasts. At year-end, WEGO asked Hank to hold the last catering payment for the year, $9,250, until after January 1 (apparently because WEGO didn't want to report the income on its tax return). The last check was delivered to WEGO in January after the end of the first year. However, because the payment related to the first year of operations, Hank included the $9,250 in last year's catering expense.

- Hank believes that the key to the success of HW has been hiring Jimbo Jones to supervise the donut production and manage the shop. Because Jimbo is such an important employee, HW purchased a "key-employee" term life insurance policy on his life. HW paid a $5,100 premium for this policy, and it will pay HW a $40,000 death benefit if Jimbo passes away any time during the next 12 months. The term of the policy began on September 1 of last year, and this payment was included in "other business" expenditures.
- In the first year, HW catered a large breakfast event to celebrate the city's anniversary. The city agreed to pay $7,100 for the event, but Hank forgot to notify the city of the outstanding bill until January of this year. When he mailed the bill in January, Hank decided to discount the charge to $5,500. On the bill, Hank thanked the mayor and the city council for their patronage and asked them to "send a little more business our way." This bill is not reflected in Hank's estimate of HW's income for the first year of operations.

Required:

a) Hank files his personal tax return on a calendar year, but he has not yet filed last year's personal tax return, nor has he filed a tax return reporting HW's results for the first year of operations. Explain when Hank should file the tax return for HW, and calculate the amount of taxable income generated by HW last year.

b) Determine the taxable income that HW will generate if Hank chooses to account for the business under the accrual method.

c) Describe how your solution might change if Hank incorporated HW before he commenced business last year.

84. R.E.M., a calendar-year corporation and Athens, Georgia, band, recently sold tickets ($20,000,000) for concerts scheduled in the United States for next year and the following two years. For financial statement purposes, R.E.M. will recognize the income from the ticket sales when it performs the concerts, and R.E.M is obligated to return the ticket payments should a concert be cancelled. For tax purposes, R.E.M. uses the accrual method and would prefer to defer the income from the ticket sales until after the concerts are performed. This is the first time that it has sold tickets one or two years in advance. Michael Stipe has asked for your advice. Write a memo to Michael explaining your findings.

UWorld Roger CPA Review

Sample CPA Exam questions from Roger CPA Review are available in Connect as support for the topics in this text. These Multiple Choice Questions and Task-Based Simulations include expert-written explanations and solutions and provide a starting point for students to become familiar with the content and functionality of the actual CPA Exam.

chapter **2**

Property Acquisition and Cost Recovery

Learning Objectives

Upon completing this chapter, you should be able to:

- **LO 2-1** Describe the cost recovery methods for recovering the cost of personal property, real property, intangible assets, and natural resources.
- **LO 2-2** Determine the applicable cost recovery (depreciation) life, method, and convention for tangible personal and real property and the deduction allowable under basic MACRS.
- **LO 2-3** Calculate the deduction allowable under the additional special cost recovery rules (§179, bonus, and listed property).
- **LO 2-4** Calculate the deduction for amortization.
- **LO 2-5** Explain cost recovery of natural resources and the allowable depletion methods.

Adam Sternin/Cavan Images/Image Source

Storyline Summary

Taxpayer:	Teton Mountaineering Technology, LLC (Teton)—a calendar-year, single-member LLC (treated as a sole proprietorship for tax purposes)
Location:	Cody, Wyoming
President/ Founder:	Steve Dallimore (he/him/his)
Current situation:	Teton has acquired property for its manufacturing operations and wants to understand the tax consequences of property acquisitions.

Several years ago while climbing the Black Ice Couloir (pronounced "cool-wahr") in Grand Teton National Park, Steve Dallimore and his buddy got into a desperate situation. The climbers planned to move fast and light and be home before an approaching storm reached the Tetons. But just shy of the summit, climbing conditions forced them to turn back. Huddled in a wet sleeping bag in a dark snow cave waiting for the tempest to pass, Steve had an epiphany—he conceived of a design for a better ice-climbing tool. Since that moment, Steve has been working toward making his dream—designing and selling his own line of climbing equipment—a reality. Steve spent the next few years planning his business while continuing his current sales career. In December 2020, Steve decided to exercise his stock options, leave his sales position, and start Teton Mountaineering Technology (Teton). At the beginning of 2021, Steve identified a location for his business in Cody, Wyoming, and purchased a building and some equipment to begin his business. He soon discovered that he needed help dealing with the tax issues related to his business assets.

(to be continued . . .)

Steve obviously has many issues to address and decisions to make. In this chapter, we focus on the tax issues relating to the assets Steve acquires for use in his new business. In particular, we explain how Teton determines its cost recovery (depreciation, amortization, and depletion) deductions for the assets in the year the business begins and in subsequent years.[1] These deductions can generate significant tax savings for companies in capital-intensive industries.

This chapter explores the tax consequences of acquiring new or used property, depreciation methods businesses may use to recover the cost of their assets, and other special cost recovery incentives. The Tax Cuts and Jobs Act of 2017 (TCJA) made many changes to the way taxpayers determine their depreciation deductions. Although these changes dramatically accelerate the depreciation deductions for many assets, they do not apply to all assets. Therefore, it is important to understand the basic depreciation rules as we discuss in more detail later in the chapter. To begin, we discuss the amount that is subject to cost recovery. We then discuss the basic depreciation rules using the assets Steve acquires for his business in 2021. We follow basic depreciation rules by discussing the special incentives using Steve's 2022 asset acquisitions.[2] We also address the tax consequences of using intangible assets and natural resources in business activities.

COST RECOVERY AND TAX BASIS FOR COST RECOVERY

LO 2-1

Most businesses make a significant investment in property, plant, and equipment that is expected to provide benefits over a number of years. Both for financial accounting and generally for tax accounting purposes, businesses must capitalize the cost of assets with a useful life of more than one year (on the balance sheet) rather than expense the cost immediately. Businesses are allowed to use various methods to allocate the cost of these assets over time because the assets are subject to wear, tear, and obsolescence.

The method of **cost recovery** depends on the nature of the underlying asset. **Depreciation** is the method of deducting the cost of *tangible* personal and real property (other than land) over time. **Amortization** is the method of deducting the cost of **intangible assets** over time. Finally, **depletion** is the method of deducting the cost of natural resources over time. Exhibit 2-1 summarizes these concepts.

EXHIBIT 2-1 Assets and Cost Recovery

Asset Type	Cost Recovery Method
Personal property comprises tangible assets such as automobiles, equipment, and machinery.	Depreciation
Real property comprises buildings and land (although land is nondepreciable).	Depreciation
Intangible assets are nonphysical assets such as goodwill and patents.	Amortization
Natural resources are commodities that are considered valuable in their natural form such as oil, coal, timber, and gold.	Depletion

Generally, a significant portion of a firm's assets consists of property, plant, equipment, intangibles, or even natural resources. In most cases, this holds true for small businesses like Teton and also for large publicly traded companies. For example, Exhibit 2-2 describes the assets held by Weyerhaeuser, a publicly traded timber company. As indicated in Exhibit 2-2, Weyerhaeuser has over $2 billion in property and equipment (net of depreciation) and $11.8 billion in timber (net of depletion), together comprising over 80 percent of its assets.

[1]Cost recovery is the common term used to describe the process by which businesses allocate the cost of their fixed assets over the time period in which the assets are used.

[2]The rules for basic depreciation that we discuss for the 2021 assets are the same as for assets acquired in 2022.

EXHIBIT 2-2 Weyerhaeuser Assets

Assets (in millions) per 2020 10-K Statement	2020	2019
Total current assets	$ 1,609	$ 1,611
Property and equipment, net (Note 7)	2,013	1,969
Construction in progress	73	130
Timber and timberlands at cost, less depletion charged to disposal	11,827	11,929
Minerals and mineral rights, less depletion	268	281
Deferred tax assets (Note 20)	120	72
Other assets	401	414
Total assets	$16,311	$16,406

Attention to detail is important because the **tax basis** of an asset must be reduced by the cost recovery deductions allowed or *allowable.* If a business fails to deduct (by mistake or error) the allowable amount of depreciation for the year, the business still must reduce the asset's tax basis by the depreciation the taxpayer could have deducted under the method the business is using to depreciate the asset. This means that the business will never receive a tax benefit for the amount of depreciation it failed to deduct.[3]

THE KEY FACTS

Initial Basis

- An asset's initial basis includes all costs needed to purchase the asset, prepare it for use, and begin using it.
- Initial basis is usually the same for book and tax purposes.
- Special basis rules apply when personal-use assets are converted to business use and when assets are acquired through tax-deferred transactions, gifts, or inheritances.

Basis for Cost Recovery

Businesses may begin recouping the cost of purchased business assets once they begin using the asset in their business (i.e., they place it in service).[4] Once the business establishes its cost in an asset, the business recovers the cost of the asset through cost recovery deductions such as depreciation, amortization, or depletion. The amount of an asset's cost that has yet to be recovered through cost recovery deductions is called the asset's **adjusted basis** or tax basis.[5] An asset's adjusted basis can be computed by subtracting the accumulated depreciation (or amortization or depletion) from the asset's initial or historical basis.[6]

For most assets, the initial basis is the cost plus all the expenses to purchase, prepare for use, and begin using the asset. These expenses include sales tax, shipping costs, and installation costs. The financial accounting and tax rules for computing an asset's basis are very similar. Thus, a purchased asset's initial basis is generally the same for both tax

[3]If a business discovers that it failed to claim allowable depreciation in a previous year, it can deduct the depreciation it failed to claim in prior years in the current year by filing an automatic consent to a change in accounting method using Form 3115 (Rev. Procs. 2002-9, 2004-11, and 2015-14).

[4]Basis is defined under §1012. The mere purchase of an asset does not trigger cost recovery deductions. A business must begin using the asset for business purposes (place it in service) in order to depreciate the asset. However, because businesses generally acquire and place assets in service at the same time, we refer to these terms interchangeably throughout the chapter.

[5]Throughout the chapter, we use several different terms to refer to an asset's tax basis. The differences in these terms are somewhat subtle but can often be important. For example, an asset's initial basis refers to the tax basis of an asset at the time the taxpayer initially acquires the asset. If a taxpayer purchases the asset, the initial basis is the same as its cost. However, if a taxpayer acquires the asset through means other than purchase (e.g., gift, inheritance, tax-deferred transaction, or conversion from personal use), the initial basis will typically differ from the asset's cost. We discuss some of these differences in the Property Dispositions chapter. The broad term *tax basis* refers to an asset's carrying value for tax purposes at a given point in time. When an asset's initial basis is recovered through depreciation, amortization, or depletion, the asset's tax basis is often referred to as the adjusted tax basis, or sometimes simply the adjusted basis. It is not common to use the term adjusted tax basis for assets that are not subject to cost recovery. For example, the tax basis for a common stock investment would typically be referred to simply as its tax basis rather than its adjusted tax basis. Finally, the depreciable basis of an asset refers to the amount of the initial basis that can be depreciated over time using the regular depreciation rules. In many cases, the depreciable basis and the initial basis are the same—for example, in the case of real property (i.e., buildings). However, the depreciable basis may differ from the initial basis when taxpayers take advantage of special incentives (such as §179 expensing or bonus depreciation, discussed later in the chapter) that accelerate an asset's cost recovery in the year it is placed in service.

[6]§1011.

and book purposes.[7] So how do taxpayers know whether they should immediately deduct the cost of an asset or capitalize and depreciate it? Taxpayers generally capitalize assets with useful lives over one year, but there are exceptions to this rule. The Treasury has issued regulations that are quite lengthy (over 200 pages) and complex to guide taxpayers in answering this question.[8] The regulations provide a *de minimis* safe harbor that allows taxpayers to immediately deduct low-cost personal property items used in their business. The definition of "low-cost" depends on whether the taxpayer has an applicable financial statement, which generally means a certified, audited financial statement. If taxpayers have an applicable financial statement, they may use the *de minimis* safe harbor to immediately deduct amounts paid for tangible property up to $5,000 per invoice or item.[9] If taxpayers don't have an applicable financial statement, they may use the safe harbor to deduct amounts up to $2,500 per invoice or item. Taxpayers generally use the invoice amount to determine whether they meet the safe harbor; however, if the total invoice amount exceeds the $5,000/$2,500 threshold and the invoice provides detailed cost information about each item, taxpayers may immediately deduct individual items that are less than the threshold amount. Taxpayers must capitalize the cost of personal property that does not fall under the *de minimis* safe harbor provision.[10]

When a business acquires multiple assets for one purchase price, the tax laws require the business to determine a cost basis for each separate asset. For example, for Teton's building purchase, Teton must treat the building and land as separate assets. In these types of acquisitions, businesses determine the initial basis of each asset by allocating a portion of the purchase price to each asset based on that asset's value relative to the total value of all the assets the business acquired in the same purchase. The asset values are generally determined by an appraisal.[11]

Example 2-1

Steve determined that he needed machinery and office furniture for a manufacturing facility and a design studio (located in Cody, Wyoming). During 2021, Steve purchased the following assets and incurred the following costs to prepare the assets for business use. His cost basis in each asset is determined as follows:

Asset	Date Acquired	(1) Purchase Price	(2) Business Preparation Costs	(1) + (2) Cost Basis
Office furniture	2/3/21	$ 20,000		$ 20,000
Warehouse	5/1/21	270,000*	$5,000 (minor modifications)	275,000
Land (10 acres)	5/1/21	75,000*		75,000
Machinery	7/22/21	600,000	$10,000 (delivery and setup)	610,000
Delivery truck (used)	8/17/21	25,000		25,000

*Note that the warehouse and the land were purchased together for $345,000. Steve and the seller determined that the value (and cost) of the warehouse was $270,000 and the value (and cost) of the land was $75,000.

What if: Assume Steve acquired a printer for $800 on July 9. Would he immediately deduct the cost of the printer or capitalize it?

Answer: Assuming that Steve has a policy to expense items costing $2,500 or less for nontax purposes, he would be able to immediately deduct the cost of the printer under the *de minimis* safe harbor.[12]

[7]However, special basis rules apply when an asset is acquired through a tax-deferred transaction. See discussion in the Property Dispositions chapter.

[8]Reg. §§1.263(a)-1, -2, -3.

[9]Taxpayers must have accounting procedures in place at the beginning of the year treating items costing less than a specified dollar figure as an expense for nontax purposes.

[10]Separate rules apply when taxpayers purchase materials and supplies to be used in their business (Reg. §1.162-3).

[11]Reg. §1.167(a)-5.

[12]Later in this chapter, we discuss alternative ways to immediately deduct the cost of certain assets (§179 expensing and bonus depreciation). The first step, however, is to determine if it must be capitalized or immediately deducted under the Treasury regulations for §263.

When a business incurs additional costs associated with an asset after the asset has been placed in service, are these costs immediately deducted or are they capitalized? In general, the answer depends on whether the expenditure constitutes routine maintenance on the asset or whether it results in a "betterment, restoration, or new or different use for the property."[13] Taxpayers can immediately deduct the costs if they meet the routine maintenance safe harbor rules provided in the Treasury regulations.[14] Routine maintenance is defined as preventative or cyclical maintenance that is an essential part of the ongoing care and upkeep of a building or building system. Building systems include the critical systems of a building such as electrical, HVAC, security, and lighting. Costs related to the replacement of damaged or worn parts with comparable and commercially available replacement parts arising from inspecting, cleaning, and testing of the property are immediately deductible when the taxpayer fully expects to perform the activity more than once during a 10-year period (for buildings and structures related to buildings), or more than once during the property's class life (for property other than buildings).

Example 2-2

What if: Suppose that Steve's business requires an annual safety certification on all its equipment and machinery. As a result of a required inspection of the machinery, Steve finds a defect in the engine blade (not a major component) of one of his machines and must replace the engine blade at a cost of $3,000. Can Steve immediately deduct the cost of the new engine blade?

Answer: Steve's business requires an annual safety certification inspection; thus, Steve meets the requirement of reasonably expecting to perform the activity more than once during the machinery's class life. Assuming that Steve replaces the engine blade with a comparable, commercially available part, he may immediately deduct the $3,000 cost of the new engine blade.

If the routine maintenance safe harbor rules do not apply, then taxpayers must determine whether the costs result in a betterment, restoration, or adaptation for a new or different use for the property.[15] If so, they must capitalize the costs; if not, they may immediately deduct the costs.[16] For example, if the roof of Teton's warehouse was completely replaced because it was leaking, Steve would be required to capitalize the costs to replace the roof as a restoration because a significant portion (100 percent) of a major component was replaced. If Teton needed to replace only 10 percent of the roof, Steve would most likely be able to immediately deduct the costs.[17]

Special rules apply when determining the tax basis of assets converted from personal to business use or assets acquired through a tax-deferred exchange, gift, or inheritance. If an asset is used for personal purposes and is later converted to business (or rental) use, the basis for cost recovery purposes is the *lesser* of (1) the cost basis of the asset or (2) the fair market value of the asset on the date of conversion to business use.[18] This rule prevents taxpayers from converting a nondeductible personal loss into a deductible business loss. For example, if Steve had purchased a truck for $20,000 several

[13]Reg. §1.263(a)-3.

[14]The routine maintenance safe harbor is discussed in Reg. §1.263(a)-3(i). In addition to the routine maintenance safe harbor, the regulations provide an additional safe harbor for small taxpayers. This safe harbor allows taxpayers with average annual gross receipts over the last three years of $10 million or less to immediately deduct amounts paid for maintenance and improvement on buildings with an unadjusted basis of $1 million or less if the amounts expended are less than the lesser of 2 percent of the building's unadjusted basis or $10,000 [Reg. §1.263(a)-3(h)].

[15]Reg. §1.263(a)-3.

[16]The regulations provide detailed guidelines for taxpayers to use to establish when they have expenditures related to these three distinct concepts. Coverage of these concepts is beyond the scope of this chapter. See Reg. §1.263(a)-3 for details.

[17]Steve may have an opportunity to expense the cost of the roof under §179 (discussed later in the chapter) if the property meets the definition of real property for purposes of the expensing provision.

[18]Reg. §§1.167(g)-1, 1.168(i)-4(b). However, this rule creates an interesting situation when selling converted assets. The taxpayer uses the lower of the adjusted basis or the fair market value at the time of the conversion for computing loss but uses the adjusted basis to compute a gain.

years ago for personal use but decided to use it as a delivery truck when its value had declined to $15,000, his basis in the truck for cost recovery purposes would be $15,000. The $5,000 decline in the truck's value from $20,000 to $15,000 would be a nondeductible personal loss to Steve, and the reduction in basis ensures that he will not be allowed to deduct the loss as a business loss.

Assets acquired through a tax-deferred transaction, such as a like-kind exchange (like-kind exchanges are discussed later in the Property Dispositions chapter), generally take the same basis the taxpayer had in the property that the taxpayer transferred in the transaction. Assets acquired by gift have a carryover basis. This means that the taxpayer's basis in property received through a gift is generally the same basis the transferor had in the property.[19] For example, if Steve's parents gave him equipment worth $45,000 to help him start his business and his parents had purchased the equipment 10 years earlier for $25,000, Steve's basis in the equipment would be $25,000 (the same basis his parents had in the equipment). Assets acquired through inheritance generally receive a basis equal to the fair market value on the transferor's date of death.[20] For example, if Steve inherited a building worth $90,000 from his grandfather, who originally paid $35,000 for it, Steve's basis would be $90,000 (its fair market value at date of death) because Steve acquired it through an inheritance.

ETHICS

Catherine Travis is starting a new business. She has several assets that she wants to use in her business that she has been using personally. Because she plans to convert several assets from personal to business use, she will need to find out how much each asset is worth so she can determine her basis for depreciating the assets. Catherine has decided that getting an appraisal would be too costly, so she simply uses her cost basis for the assets. What do you think of Catherine's strategy for determining her business asset bases?

DEPRECIATION

LO 2-2

THE KEY FACTS

Tax Depreciation

To depreciate an asset, a business must determine:

- Original basis
- Depreciation method
- Recovery period
- Depreciation convention

As a preface to this section, the TCJA made many changes to how taxpayers will recover the cost of their assets for the next several years. In this chapter, we discuss the depreciation provisions both before and after the TCJA effective dates for several reasons. First, existing assets continue to follow the rules in place before the tax law change; therefore, for assets placed in service before the effective dates of the TCJA, taxpayers will need to understand the rules in effect at the time the assets were placed in service. Second, the new provisions provide very generous deductions for personal property; however, taxpayers may opt out of these provisions and instead follow the pre-TCJA rules. Taxpayers with losses may opt to forgo the large depreciation deductions provided under the TCJA to reduce their losses, which may be subject to limitations (e.g., NOL limitations and excess business loss limitations). These taxpayers would then use the standard depreciation methods used prior to the TCJA. Third, for assets that do not qualify for the special provisions in the TCJA, taxpayers must fall back to the standard depreciation methods used under prior law. For example, some states do not allow the additional depreciation provided by the TCJA. Taxpayers doing business in these states will need to follow the basic depreciation rules in place prior to TCJA. Finally, the TCJA expanded §179 expensing (effective for assets placed in service after December 31, 2017) and extended bonus depreciation (effective for assets placed in service after September 27, 2017); however, bonus depreciation is temporary and is scheduled to begin phasing out for assets placed in service after December 31, 2022. Therefore, it is important to understand the rules in effect both before and after the effective date of the TCJA.

With that in mind, we proceed by discussing the basic rules for determining depreciation. In this section, we consider how Steve can depreciate the assets he acquired in 2021

[19]§1015. The basis may be increased if the transferor is required to pay gift tax on the transfer [see §1015(d)]. In addition, special dual basis rules apply if the basis in the gifted property at the gift date is greater than its fair market value.

[20]§1014. In certain circumstances, the estate can elect an alternative valuation date six months after death.

assuming he does not want to use any of the special depreciation provisions. We then discuss the special rules (§179, bonus depreciation, and listed property), which were modified and expanded by the TCJA.

Since 1986, businesses have calculated their tax depreciation using the **Modified Accelerated Cost Recovery System (MACRS)**—which is pronounced "makers" by tax accountants.[21] Compared to financial (book) depreciation, MACRS tax depreciation is quite simple. To compute MACRS depreciation for an asset, the business need only know the asset's *depreciable basis,* the date it was placed in service, the applicable *depreciation method,* the asset's **recovery period** (or depreciable "life"), and the applicable depreciation *convention* (used to compute the amount of depreciation deductible in the year of acquisition and the year of disposition). The method, recovery period, and convention vary based on whether the asset is **personal property** or **real property.** Before we turn our attention to the determination of the depreciation deduction for personal property, it is important to emphasize that there may be a difference in when an asset is acquired and when it is placed in service. Being placed in service requires that the property is in a condition or state of readiness and availability for a specifically assigned function. This requirement is often met when an asset is acquired but may not be when additional installation is required or modifications must be made to ready the asset for its intended use.[22]

Personal Property Depreciation

Personal property includes all tangible property, such as computers, automobiles, furniture, machinery, and equipment, other than real property. Note that *personal* property and *personal-use* property are not the same thing. Personal property denotes any property that is not real property (e.g., building and land), while personal-use property is any property used for personal purposes (e.g., a personal residence is personal-use property even though it is real property). Personal property is relatively short-lived and subject to obsolescence, as compared to real property.

Depreciation Method MACRS provides three acceptable methods for depreciating personal property: 200 percent (double) declining balance (DB), 150 percent declining balance, and straight-line.[23] The 200 percent declining balance method is the default method. This method takes twice the straight-line percentage of depreciation in the first year and continues to take twice the straight-line percentage on the asset's declining basis until switching to the straight-line method in the year that the straight-line method over the remaining life provides a greater depreciation expense. Fortunately, as we describe below, the IRS provides depreciation tables to simplify the calculations.

Profitable businesses with relatively high marginal tax rates generally choose to use the 200 percent declining balance method because it generates the largest depreciation deduction in the early years of the asset's life and, thus, the highest current-year, after-tax cash flows. For tax planning purposes, taxpayers that currently have lower marginal tax rates but expect their marginal tax rates to increase in the near future may elect to use the straight-line method because that method generates less depreciation in the early years of the asset's life, relatively, and more depreciation in the later years when their marginal tax rates may increase.

Example 2-3

If Teton wants to accelerate its current MACRS depreciation deductions to the extent possible, what method should it use to depreciate its office furniture, machinery, and delivery truck?

Answer: The 200 percent declining balance method (default). Teton could elect to use either the 150 percent declining balance or the straight-line method if it wants a less-accelerated method for determining its depreciation deductions.

[21]IRS Publication 946 provides a useful summary of MACRS depreciation.

[22]Reg. §1.167(a)-11(e)(1)(1); *Brown v. Comm'r,* TC Memo 2013-275.

[23]MACRS includes two depreciation systems: the general depreciation system (GDS) and the alternative depreciation system (ADS). MACRS provides three methods under GDS (200 percent DB, 150 percent DB, and straight-line) and one method under ADS (straight-line).

Each year, businesses elect the depreciation method for the assets placed in service during *that year*. Specifically, businesses elect one depreciation method for all similar assets they acquire that year.[24] Thus, if a business acquires several different machines during the year, it must use the same method to depreciate all of the machines. However, the methods may differ for machines acquired in different tax years.

Depreciation Recovery Period For financial accounting purposes, an asset's recovery period (depreciable life) is based on its taxpayer-determined estimated useful life. In contrast, for tax purposes, an asset's recovery period is predetermined by the IRS in Rev. Proc. 87-56. This revenue procedure helps taxpayers categorize each of their assets based upon the property's description. Once the business has determined the appropriate categories for its assets, it can use the revenue procedure to identify the recovery period for all assets in a particular category. For example, Teton placed office furniture in service during the year. By examining the excerpt from Rev. Proc. 87-56 provided in Exhibit 2-3, you can see that Category or Asset Class 00.11 includes office furniture and that assets in this category, including Teton's office furniture, have a recovery period of seven years (emphasis in excerpt added through bold text).[25]

EXHIBIT 2-3 Excerpt from Revenue Procedure 87-56

Description of Assets Included	Years		
Specific depreciable assets used in all business activities, except as noted:	Class Life	General Recovery Period	Alternative Recovery Period
00.11 Office Furniture, Fixtures, and Equipment: Includes furniture and fixtures that are not a structural component of a building. Includes such assets as desks, files, safes, and communications equipment. Does not include communications equipment that is included in other classes.	10	7	10
00.12 Information Systems: Includes computers and their peripheral equipment used in administering normal business transactions and the maintenance of business records.	6	5	5
00.241 Light General Purpose Trucks: Includes trucks for use over the road (actual unloaded weight less than 13,000 pounds) . . .	4	5	5
34.0 Manufacture of Fabricated Metal Products Special Tools: Includes assets used in the production of metal cans, tinware . . .	12	7	12

While even this small excerpt from Rev. Proc. 87-56 may seem a bit intimidating, you can classify the vast majority of business assets acquired by knowing a few common recovery periods. Exhibit 2-4 lists the most commonly purchased assets and their recovery periods.

To this point, our discussion has emphasized computing regular MACRS depreciation for new assets. Does the process change when businesses acquire used assets? No, it is exactly the same. For example, Teton purchased a *used* delivery truck. The fact that the truck is used does not change its MACRS recovery period. No matter how long the

[24]Technically, similar assets are assets in the same property class (with the same recovery period).

[25]The "alternative" recovery period in Rev. Proc. 87-56 refers to an asset's life under the alternative depreciation system referred to as ADS (which we discuss later in this chapter). The class life referred to in Rev. Proc. 87-56 refers to the midpoint of the asset depreciation range (ADR) applicable under pre-ACRS and has little or no meaning under MACRS.

previous owner used the truck, Teton will restart the five-year recovery period for light general-purpose trucks to depreciate the delivery truck (see Exhibit 2-4).

Under MACRS, the tax recovery period for machinery and equipment is seven years. Using Rev. Proc. 87-56, Teton has determined the cost recovery periods for the personal property it purchased and placed in service during 2021. Exhibit 2-5 summarizes this information.

EXHIBIT 2-4 Recovery Period for Most Common Business Assets

Asset Description (Summary of Rev. Proc. 87-56)	Recovery Period
Cars, light general-purpose trucks, and computers and peripheral equipment	5 years
Office furniture, fixtures, and equipment	7 years
Qualified improvement property (straight-line method)	15 years

EXHIBIT 2-5 Teton Personal Property Summary (Base Scenario)

Asset	Date Acquired	Quarter Acquired	Cost Basis	Recovery Period	Reference
Office furniture	2/3/21	1st	$ 20,000	7	Example 2-1; Exhibit 2-3
Machinery	7/22/21	3rd	610,000	7	Example 2-1; Exhibit 2-3
Delivery truck	8/17/21	3rd	25,000	5	Example 2-1; Exhibit 2-3
Total personal property			**$655,000**		

Depreciation Conventions Once a business has determined the depreciation methods and recovery periods for the assets it placed in service during the year, it then must determine the applicable depreciation conventions. The depreciation convention specifies the portion of a full-year's depreciation the business can deduct for an asset in the year the asset is first placed in service *and* in the year the asset is sold. For *personal property,* taxpayers must use either the **half-year convention** or the **mid-quarter convention.** But taxpayers are *not* free to choose between the two conventions. The half-year convention applies most of the time; however, under certain conditions, taxpayers are required to use the mid-quarter convention (discussed below). The depreciation convention is determined annually for the assets placed in service in that year. Once the convention is determined for the assets acquired during the year, the convention remains the same for the entire recovery period for those assets. For example, if a taxpayer placed assets in service in year 1 and was required to use the mid-quarter convention for year 1, depreciation calculated in year 2 for these assets would continue using the mid-quarter convention even though the taxpayer may not be required to use the mid-quarter convention for assets placed in service in year 2.

Before MACRS, taxpayers were required to use the half-year convention for all personal property placed in service during the year. However, Congress believed that many businesses took unfair advantage of the half-year convention by purposely acquiring assets at the end of the year that they otherwise would have acquired at the beginning of the next taxable year. Thus, businesses received one-half of a year's depreciation for assets that they used for only a small portion of the year. Even though the half-year convention is the default convention, policy makers introduced the *mid-quarter convention* under MACRS to limit or prevent this type of opportunistic behavior. Nevertheless, as we discuss below, the new tax laws allow taxpayers to accelerate their cost recovery deductions no matter when during the year the assets are placed in service. Consequently, the mid-quarter convention may have limited application to assets placed in service under current law.

Half-year convention. The half-year convention allows one-half of a full-year's depreciation in the year the asset is placed in service (and in the year in which it is disposed), regardless of when it was actually placed in service. For example, when the half-year convention applies to a calendar-year business, an asset placed in service on either February 3 or August 17 is treated as though it was placed in service on July 1, which is the middle of the calendar year. Thus, under this convention, Teton would deduct one-half of a year's depreciation for the machinery, office furniture, and delivery truck even though it acquired the machinery, delivery truck, and office furniture at various times during the year (see Exhibit 2-5). The half-year convention is built into the depreciation tables provided by the IRS, which simplifies the depreciation calculation for the year the asset is placed into service.

THE KEY FACTS

Half-Year Convention

- One-half of a year's depreciation is allowed in the first and the last years of an asset's life.
- The IRS depreciation tables automatically account for the half-year convention in the acquisition year.
- If an asset is disposed of before it is fully depreciated, only one-half of the table's applicable depreciation percentage is allowed in the year of disposition.

Mid-quarter convention. Businesses must use the mid-quarter convention when *more* than 40 percent of their total *tangible personal property* that they place in service during the year is placed in service during the *fourth* quarter. Under the mid-quarter convention, businesses treat assets *as though* they were placed in service during the middle of the *quarter* in which the business actually placed the assets into service. For example, when the mid-quarter convention applies, if a business places an asset in service on December 1 (in the fourth quarter), it must treat the asset as though it was placed in service on November 15, which is the middle of the fourth quarter. Consequently, the business deducts only one-half of a quarter's depreciation in the year the asset is placed in service (depreciation for the second half of November and the entire month of December). In addition, if the mid-quarter convention applies, businesses must use the convention for *all* tangible personal property placed in service during the year—even assets placed in service in quarters other than the fourth quarter. The mid-quarter test is applied after the §179 expense but before bonus depreciation (discussed later in the chapter), meaning that to the extent property is expensed under §179, it is not included in the mid-quarter test. The IRS depreciation tables have built in the mid-quarter convention to simplify the calculations.

For assets placed in service under the TCJA regime (effective for assets acquired after September 27, 2017), the mid-quarter convention will be largely irrelevant as businesses can use either §179 or 100 percent bonus depreciation to recover the cost in full in the year of acquisition. However, for assets placed in service before TCJA and for assets that fail to qualify for §179 and bonus depreciation, the mid-quarter convention continues to apply.

Calculating Depreciation for Personal Property Once a business has identified the applicable method, recovery period, and convention for personal property, tax depreciation is relatively easy to calculate because the Internal Revenue Service provides depreciation percentage tables in Rev. Proc. 87-57. The percentages in the depreciation tables for tangible personal property incorporate the method and convention. Accordingly, there are separate tables for each combination of depreciation method (200 percent declining balance, 150 percent declining balance, and straight-line) and convention (half-year and mid-quarter; each quarter has its own table). To determine the depreciation for an asset for the year, use the following steps:

Step 1: Determine the appropriate convention (half-year or mid-quarter) by determining whether more than 40 percent of qualified property was placed in service in the last quarter of the tax year.

Step 2: Locate the applicable table provided in Rev. Proc. 87-57 (reproduced in Appendix A of this chapter).

Step 3: Select the column that corresponds with the asset's recovery period.

Step 4: Find the row identifying the year of the asset's recovery period.

The tables are constructed so that the intersection of the row and column provides the percentage of the asset's *depreciable basis* that is deductible as depreciation expense for the particular year. As we discuss later, the depreciable basis used for basic depreciation is the initial basis less the amount of §179 expense and bonus depreciation taken on the asset. Thus, depreciation expense for a particular asset is the product of the percentage from the table and the asset's *depreciable basis.*

Applying the Half-Year Convention Consider Table 1 in Appendix A at the end of the chapter that shows the depreciation percentages for MACRS 200 percent declining balance using the half-year convention. If a seven-year asset is placed into service during the current year, the depreciation percentage is 14.29 percent [the intersection of row 1 (year 1) and the seven-year property column].

Notice from Table 1 that the depreciation percentages for five-year property extend for six years and the percentages for seven-year property extend for eight years. Why does it take six years to fully depreciate an asset with a five-year recovery period and eight years for a seven-year asset? Because the business does not deduct a full-year's depreciation in the first year, an entire year of depreciation is effectively split between the first and last years. For example, when the half-year convention applies to a five-year asset, the taxpayer deducts one-half of a year's depreciation in year 1 and one-half of a year's depreciation in year 6.

Example 2-4

Teton is using the 200 percent declining balance method and half-year convention to compute depreciation on its 2021 personal property additions. What is Teton's 2021 depreciation deduction for these assets?

Answer: $95,027, computed as follows:

Asset	Date Placed in Service	(1) Original Basis	(2) Rate	(1) × (2) Depreciation
Office furniture	February 3	$ 20,000	14.29%	$ 2,858
Machinery	July 22	610,000	14.29%	87,169
Used delivery truck	August 17	25,000	20.00%	5,000
Total				**$95,027**

Because the office furniture and machinery have a seven-year recovery period and it is the first year for depreciation, the depreciation rate is 14.29 percent (see Table 1). The depreciation rate for the used delivery truck (five-year property) is 20 percent (see Table 1) and is determined in a similar manner.

Calculating depreciation for assets in years after the year of acquisition is also relatively simple. Again, using Table 1 to compute depreciation for the second year, the taxpayer would multiply the asset's initial basis by the percentage in the *year 2* row; in the following year, the taxpayer would use the percentage in the *year 3* row; and so on.

Example 2-5

What if: Assume that Teton holds the tangible personal property it acquired and placed in service in 2021 until the assets are fully depreciated. Using the IRS-provided tables (see Table 1), how would Teton determine its depreciation expense for 2021 through 2028?

Answer: See the following table:

(continued on page 2-12)

Depreciation over Asset Recovery Period

Recovery Period	Year	7-Year Office Furniture	7-Year Machinery	5-Year Delivery Truck	Yearly Total
1	2021	$ 2,858	$ 87,169	$ 5,000	$ 95,027
2	2022	4,898	149,389	8,000	162,287
3	2023	3,498	106,689	4,800	114,987
4	2024	2,498	76,189	2,880	81,567
5	2025	1,786	54,473	2,880	59,139
6	2026	1,784	54,412	1,440	57,636
7	2027	1,786	54,473	N/A	56,259
8	2028	892	27,206	N/A	28,098
Accumulated Depreciation		$20,000	$610,000	$25,000	$655,000

Half-year convention for year of disposition. Businesses often sell or dispose of assets before they fully depreciate them. Recall that the half-year convention applies in both the year of acquisition and the year of disposition. Note, however, that the tables can't anticipate when a business may dispose of an asset. Accordingly, the tables only provide depreciation percentages for assets assuming the asset won't be disposed of before it is fully depreciated. That is, for each year in the asset's recovery period, the tables provide a percentage for an entire year's depreciation. So, to calculate the depreciation for the year of disposition, the business first calculates depreciation for the *entire year* as if the property had not been disposed of. Then the business applies the half-year convention by multiplying the full-year's depreciation by 50 percent (one-half of a year's depreciation).[26] Note, however, that if a business acquires and disposes of an asset in the same tax year, it is not allowed to claim any depreciation on the asset.

Example 2-6

What if: Assume that Teton sells all of its office furniture in 2022 (the year after it buys it). What is Teton's depreciation for the office furniture in the year of disposition (2022)?

Answer: $2,449, calculated using the MACRS Half-Year Convention table (Table 1) as follows:

Asset	Amount	Explanation
(1) Office furniture	$20,000	Original basis
(2) Depreciation percentage	24.49%	Seven-year property, year 2
(3) Full year of depreciation	$ 4,898	(1) × (2)
(4) Half-year convention percentage	50%	Depreciation limit in year of disposal
Depreciation in year of disposal	**$ 2,449**	(3) × (4)

What if: Assume that Teton sold all of its office furniture in year 1 (the year it bought it and placed it in service). How much depreciation expense can Teton deduct for the office furniture in year 1?

Answer: $0. A business is not allowed to claim any depreciation expense for assets it acquires and disposes of in the same tax year.

[26]Suppose Teton sells the five-year delivery truck in year 6 on January 5. What depreciation percentage should Teton use for purposes of determining year 6 depreciation? Teton should take one-half year's depreciation on the truck. The percentage shown in Table 1 for the year of an asset's recovery period (in this case, year 6) already reflects the half-year convention, so Teton would take $1,440 of depreciation regardless of when during year 6 the truck was sold.

Applying the Mid-Quarter Convention When the mid-quarter convention applies, the process for computing depreciation is the same as it is when the half-year convention applies, except that businesses use a separate table for each quarter. After categorizing the assets by recovery period and grouping them into quarters, businesses consult the Mid-Quarter Convention tables (Tables 2a–2d in Appendix A to this chapter) to determine the depreciation percentage for each asset group.

The depreciation deduction for an asset is the product of the asset's original basis and the percentage from the table.

Example 2-7

What if: For this example, assume the machinery Teton placed in service in Exhibit 2-5 was placed in service on November 1, 2021, rather than July 22. What is Teton's 2021 depreciation for its personal property additions?

Answer: $30,527, computed as follows:

Asset	Purchase Date	Quarter	Original Basis	Rate	Depreciation
Office furniture (7-year)	February 3	1st	$ 20,000	25.00%	$ 5,000
Delivery truck (5-year)	August 17	3rd	25,000	15.00%	3,750
Machinery (7-year)	November 1	4th	610,000	3.57%	21,777
					$30,527

The mid-quarter convention applies because more than 40 percent of the assets were placed in service during the last quarter of the year ($610,000/$655,000 = 93% placed in service in the last quarter). The office furniture percentage of 25 percent is located in Table 2a. See the columns for property placed into service during the first quarter (first two columns); select the seven-year recovery period column (last column), and the year 1 row. The process for determining the percentage for the delivery truck and machinery follows the same method, using Table 2c and Table 2d, respectively.

THE KEY FACTS

Mid-Quarter Convention

- The mid-quarter convention is required when more than 40 percent of personal property is placed in service during the fourth quarter of the tax year.
- Each quarter has its own depreciation table. Once the mid-quarter convention applies, the taxpayer must continue to use it over the assets' entire recovery period.
- If an asset is disposed of before it is fully depreciated, use the formula given to determine the allowable depreciation in the year of disposition.

The process for calculating depreciation for assets in years after acquisition is the same as the process we described for the half-year convention except the taxpayer uses the MACRS Mid-Quarter Convention tables for the appropriate quarter rather than the MACRS Half-Year Convention table (Table 1).

Mid-quarter convention for year of disposition. Calculating depreciation expense in the year of sale or disposition is a bit more involved when the mid-quarter convention applies than when it does not. When the mid-quarter convention applies, the asset is treated as though it is sold in the middle of the quarter of which it was actually sold. The process for calculating mid-quarter convention depreciation for the year of sale is exactly the same as the process for using the half-year convention, except that instead of multiplying the full-year's depreciation by 50 percent, the business multiplies the amount of depreciation it would have been able to claim on the asset if it had not sold the asset (a full-year's depreciation) by the applicable percentage in Exhibit 2-6.

EXHIBIT 2-6 Mid-Quarter Convention Percentage of Full-Year's Depreciation in Year of Disposition

Quarter of Disposition	Percentage	Calculation*
1st	12.5%	1.5/12
2nd	37.5	4.5/12
3rd	62.5	7.5/12
4th	87.5	10.5/12

*The calculation is the number of months the taxpayer is deemed to have held the asset in the year of disposition divided by 12 months in the year.

Example 2-8

What if: Assume that Teton depreciates its personal property under the mid-quarter convention (Example 2-7) and that it sells its office furniture in the third quarter of 2022. The office furniture ($20,000 original basis) was placed into service during the first quarter of 2021 and has a seven-year recovery period. What is Teton's 2022 depreciation deduction for the office furniture?

Answer: $2,679, computed as follows:

Description	Amount	Explanation
(1) Original basis	$20,000	Example 2-7
(2) 2022 depreciation percentage	21.43%	Table 2a, mid-quarter, first quarter table, 7-year property, year 2
(3) Full-year's depreciation	$ 4,286	(1) × (2)
(4) Percentage of full-year's depreciation in year of disposition if mid-quarter convention applies	62.5%	From Exhibit 2-6; asset disposed of in third quarter
Depreciation in year of disposition	**$ 2,679**	(3) × (4)

THE KEY FACTS

Real Property Depreciation

- Real property is depreciated using the straight-line method.
- Real property uses the mid-month convention.
- Residential property has a recovery period of 27.5 years.
- Nonresidential property placed in service on or after May 13, 1993, has a life of 39 years.
- Nonresidential property placed in service after December 31, 1986, but before May 13, 1993, has a recovery period of 31.5 years.

Real Property

For depreciation purposes, real property is classified as land, *residential rental property,* or *nonresidential property.* Land is nondepreciable. Residential rental property consists of dwelling units such as houses, condominiums, and apartment complexes. Residential rental property has a 27.5-year recovery period. Nonresidential property consists of all other buildings (office buildings, manufacturing facilities, shopping malls, and the like). Nonresidential property placed in service on or after May 13, 1993, has a 39-year recovery period, and nonresidential property placed in service after December 31, 1986, but before May 13, 1993, has a 31.5-year recovery period. Exhibit 2-7 summarizes the recovery periods for real property.[27]

EXHIBIT 2-7 Recovery Period for Real Property

Asset Description (Summary from Rev. Proc. 87-57)	Recovery Period
Residential	27.5 years
Nonresidential property placed in service on or after May 13, 1993	39 years
Nonresidential property placed in service after December 31, 1986, but before May 13, 1993	31.5 years

If a building is substantially improved (e.g., expanded) at some point after the initial purchase, the building addition is treated as a new asset with the same recovery period of the original building. For example, if Teton expanded its warehouse 10 years after the building was placed in service, the expansion or building addition would be depreciated as a *new, separate* asset over 39 years because it is nonresidential property.

An important area of tax practice related to real property is cost segregation (see Taxes in the Real World on this later in the chapter). This practice attempts to partition or divide the costs of a building into two or more categories. The first category is the building itself, which has a recovery period as noted in Exhibit 2-7. The second category is building components (tangible personal property associated with the building such as electrical and plumbing fixtures that have a shorter recovery period and accelerated depreciation

[27]§179(f)(2) classifies the following improvements to nonresidential real property as eligible for immediate expensing: roofs; heating, ventilation, and air-conditioning systems; fire protection and alarm systems; and security systems. In addition, §179(f)(1) allows qualified improvements (any improvement to an interior portion of a nonresidential building placed in service after the date the building was placed in service) to be eligible for §179. Qualified improvements do not include expansions, additions of elevators/escalators, or improvements to the internal structural framework of the building; therefore, these items are not eligible to be immediately deducted under §179 [§168(e)(6)(B)].

method). Cost segregation utilizes engineers and construction experts who divide the costs between real and tangible personal property. This can generate significant tax savings due to the difference in the present value of the tax savings from the accelerated depreciation deductions associated with personal property relative to real property.

TAXES IN THE REAL WORLD Cost Segregation

Consider a taxpayer who purchases a strip mall for $1 million, excluding land, in July. Typically, the taxpayer records the purchase as a 39-year asset and depreciates it using a straight-line method according to the MACRS rules for depreciating real property. After five years, the taxpayer would have claimed $114,330 of depreciation deductions on the property. Is it possible for the taxpayer to accelerate the depreciation deductions on the property to take advantage of the timing tax planning strategy? Yes, with the help of a cost segregation study!

Cost segregation is the process of identifying personal property assets that are included in the purchase price of real property such as a strip mall. Cost segregation separates out the personal property from the real property for tax reporting purposes. Personal property includes a building's nonstructural elements, exterior land improvements, and indirect construction costs. Now suppose a cost segregation study on the strip mall identifies 5-year property of $200,000, 15-year property of $250,000, and 39-year property of $550,000. The taxpayer would claim $345,562 of depreciation expense over the 5-year period, even without considering bonus depreciation on the identified personal property. Taking bonus depreciation into consideration, the total depreciation over the five years would be $512,882, an increase of almost $398,552 in deductions over the 5-year period!

Applicable Method All depreciable real property is depreciated for tax purposes using the straight-line method. This is generally consistent with depreciation methods used for financial accounting purposes.

Applicable Convention All real property is depreciated using the mid-month convention. The **mid-month convention** allows the owner of real property to expense one-half of a month's depreciation for the month in which the property was placed in service (and in the month of the year it is sold as well). This is true regardless of whether the asset was placed in service at the beginning or at the end of the month. For example, if Teton placed its warehouse into service on May 1 (or on *any* other day in May), it would deduct *one-half* of a month's depreciation for May and then full depreciation for the months June through December.

Depreciation Tables Just as it does for personal property, the IRS provides depreciation tables for real property. The depreciation tables for 27.5-year, 31.5-year, and 39-year real property are reproduced as Tables 3, 4, and 5, respectively, in Appendix A. The percentage of the asset's basis that is depreciated in a particular year is located at the intersection of the month the asset was placed in service (column) and the year of depreciation (row).

Example 2-9

As indicated in Example 2-1, Teton's cost basis in the warehouse it purchased on May 1, 2021, is $275,000. What is Teton's 2021 and 2022 depreciation on its warehouse?

Answer: $4,414 in 2021 and $7,051 in 2022, calculated as follows:

Warehouse	Method	Recovery Period	Date Placed in Service	(1) Basis	(2) Rate*	(1) × (2) Depreciation
2020	SL	39	5/1/2021	$275,000	1.605%	**$4,414**
2021	SL	39	5/1/2021	275,000	2.564%	**7,051**

(continued on page 2-16)

What if: What would be Teton's 2021 and 2022 depreciation if, instead of a warehouse, the building was an apartment building that it rented to Teton's employees?

Answer: $6,251 in 2021 and $9,999 in 2022, calculated as follows:

Apartment Bldg.	Method	Recovery Period	Date Placed in Service	(1) Basis	(2) Rate†	(1) × (2) Depreciation
2020	SL	27.5	5/1/2021	$275,000	2.273%	**$6,251**
2021	SL	27.5	5/1/2022	275,000	3.636%	**9,999**

*The 1.605 percent for the year is found in the 39-year table (Table 5, in Appendix A) in the fifth column (fifth month) and first row (first year).

†The 2.273 percent for the year is found in the 27.5-year table (Table 3, in Appendix A) in the fifth column (fifth month) and first row (first year).

When using depreciation tables for real property, it is important to stay in the month column corresponding with the month the property was originally placed in service.[28] Thus, to calculate depreciation for real property placed in service in May (the fifth month), businesses will *always* (for each year of depreciation) find the current-year rate factor in the fifth column for that asset. This is true even if the asset is sold in a subsequent year in July (it's easy to make the mistake of using the seventh column to calculate the depreciation for the year of disposition in this situation).

Mid-month convention for year of disposition. Businesses deduct one-half of a month's depreciation in the month they sell or otherwise dispose of real property. For example, if Teton sold its warehouse on March 5 of year 2, it would deduct two and one-half months of depreciation in that year for the warehouse (depreciation for January, February, and one-half of March). Calculating depreciation deduction in the year of sale or disposition for mid-month convention assets is similar to the calculation under the mid-quarter convention. When the mid-month convention applies, the asset is treated as though it is sold in the *middle of the month* in which it was actually sold. The simplest process for calculating mid-month convention depreciation for the year of sale consists of the following four steps:

Step 1: Determine the amount of depreciation deduction for the asset as if the asset was held for the entire year.

Step 2: Subtract one-half of a month from the month in which the asset was sold (if sold in the third month, subtract .5 from 3 to get 2.5). (Subtract half of a month because the business is treated as though the asset was disposed of in the middle of the third month—not the end.)

Step 3: Divide the amount determined in Step 2 by 12 months (2.5/12). This is the fraction of the full-year's depreciation the business is eligible to deduct.

Step 4: Multiply the Step 3 outcome by the full depreciation determined in Step 1.

These steps are summarized in the following formula:

Mid-month depreciation for year of disposition

$$= \text{Full-year's depreciation} \times \frac{(\text{Month in which asset was disposed of} - .5)}{12}$$

[28]Failure to do so will result in the wrong depreciation expense and is technically a change in accounting method (which requires filing of Form 3115 with the IRS).

(continued from page 2-1 . . .)

During 2021, Teton had huge success, generating a large profit. To continue to grow the business and increase Teton's production capacity, Steve acquired more assets in 2022. He has heard about ways to "write off" the costs of business assets and wants to learn more.

(to be continued . . .)

Example 2-10

What if: Assume that Teton sells its warehouse on March 5, 2022 (the year after Teton buys it). What is Teton's depreciation for the warehouse in the year of disposition?

Answer: $1,469, computed using the four-step procedure outlined above as follows.

Step 1: Determine full-year's depreciation: $275,000 × 2.564%* = $7,051

Step 2: 3 (month sold) – .5 = 2.5

Step 3: 2.5/12

Step 4: $7,051 × 2.5/12 = **$1,469** (see formula above)

*The 2.564 percent (full-year percentage) in Step 1 is obtained from the MACRS Mid-Month table for 39-year property (Table 5) placed in service during the fifth month (year 2 row).

SPECIAL RULES RELATING TO COST RECOVERY

LO 2-3

In addition to the basic MACRS rules, several additional provisions affect the depreciation of personal property. Congress often uses these special rules for economic stimulus or to curb perceived taxpayer abuses. For many businesses, the calculation of MACRS depreciation for personal property will become a thing of the past due to the recent expansion of these special rules. It is worth noting, however, that Congress did not make all of the provisions permanent. For example, bonus depreciation is effective for property placed in service before January 1, 2023, with a subsequent four-year phase-out. We discuss these special rules below.

Immediate Expensing (§179) Policy makers created §179 as an incentive to help small businesses purchasing qualified property. This incentive is commonly referred to as the **§179 expense** or *immediate expensing* election.[29] This provision will have limited application because bonus depreciation (discussed below) allows taxpayers to immediately deduct assets' initial bases. As discussed earlier in the chapter, businesses must generally depreciate an asset's initial basis over the asset's recovery period. However, under §179, businesses may elect to immediately expense up to $1,080,000 (up from $1,050,000 in 2021) of qualified property placed in service during 2022.[30,31] Businesses can also use immediate expensing for off-the-shelf computer software and qualified real property.[32] Qualified property does not include property with prior use by the taxpayer reacquiring the property. Businesses may also elect to deduct less than the maximum. When businesses elect to deduct a certain amount of §179 expense, they immediately expense all or a portion of an asset's basis or several assets' bases. To reflect this immediate depreciation, they must reduce the basis of the asset or assets (to which they applied the §179 amount) *before* they compute MACRS depreciation (from the tables).

Exhibit 2-8 shows the assets Teton acquires in 2022.

EXHIBIT 2-8 Teton's 2022 Asset Acquisitions

Asset	Cost	Date Placed in Service
Computers & information systems	$ 920,000	March 3
Delivery truck	80,000	May 26
Machinery	1,200,000	August 15
Total	$2,200,000	

[29]Intangibles and tangible personal property that are used less than 50 percent for business and most real property are not eligible for immediate expensing.

[30]The maximum allowable expense under §179 is indexed for inflation beginning with years after 2018.

[31]These maximum amounts are per tax return. Thus, if an individual has multiple businesses with asset acquisitions, the taxpayer may only deduct up to these maximum amounts for the combined businesses.

[32]Qualified real property means improvements to nonresidential real property placed in service after the date the building was placed in service, including roofs; heating, ventilation, and air-conditioning; fire protection and alarm systems; and security systems.

Example 2-11

What if: Assume Teton is eligible for and elects to immediately deduct $800,000 of §179 expense against the basis of the machinery acquired in 2022 (see Exhibit 2-8). (Note that Teton could have elected to deduct up to $1,080,000.) What is the amount of Teton's current-year depreciation deduction, including regular MACRS depreciation and the §179 expense on its machinery (assuming the half-year convention applies and that Teton elects out of bonus depreciation)?

Answer: $857,160, computed as follows:

Description	Amount	Explanation
(1) Machinery	$1,200,000	Exhibit 2-8
(2) §179 expense	800,000	
(3) Remaining basis in machinery	$ 400,000	(1) − (2)
(4) MACRS depreciation rate for 7-year machinery	14.29%	Rate from Table 1
(5) MACRS depreciation expense on machinery	$ 57,160	(3) × (4)
Total depreciation on machinery	**$ 857,160**	(2) + (5)

What if: Assume that Teton was eligible for and elected to claim the maximum amount of §179 expense. What would be its total current-year depreciation deduction, including MACRS depreciation and §179 expense (assuming the half-year convention applies and that Teton elects out of bonus depreciation)?

Answer: $1,097,148, computed as follows:

Description	Amount	Explanation
(1) Machinery	$ 1,200,000	Exhibit 2-8
(2) §179 expense	1,080,000	Maximum expense in 2022
(3) Remaining basis in machinery	$ 120,000	(1) − (2)
(4) MACRS depreciation rate for 7-year machinery	14.29%	Rate from Table 1
(5) MACRS depreciation expense on machinery	$ 17,148	(3) × (4)
Total depreciation on machinery	**$1,097,148**	(2) + (5)

Limits on immediate expensing. The maximum amount of §179 expense a business may elect to claim for the year is subject to a phase-out limitation. Under the phase-out limitation, businesses must reduce the $1,080,000 maximum available expense dollar-for-dollar for the amount of *qualified property* placed in service during 2022 over a $2,700,000 threshold (up from $2,620,000 in 2021).[33] Thus, if a business places $3,780,000 ($2,700,000 threshold plus $1,080,000) or more of tangible personal property into service during 2022, its maximum available §179 expense for the year is $0. The phased-out portion of the maximum expense disappears and does *not* carry over to a subsequent year.

Businesses may elect to claim the §179 expense for the year up to the maximum amount available (after computing the phase-out—see the previous example). When a business elects to claim a certain amount of §179 expense, it must reduce the basis of the asset(s) to which the expense is applied. It then computes regular depreciation on the remaining basis after reducing the basis of the asset(s) for the §179 expense.

[33]The threshold under §179 is indexed for inflation beginning with years after 2018.

Example 2-12

What if: Let's assume that during 2022, Teton placed into service $2,400,000 of machinery (up from the $1,200,000 amount in Exhibit 2-8), $920,000 of computers, and an $80,000 delivery truck, for a total of $3,400,000 tangible *personal* property placed in service for the year. What is Teton's maximum §179 expense after applying the phase-out limitation?

Answer: $380,000, computed as follows:

Description	Amount	Explanation
(1) Property placed in service in 2022	$3,400,000	
(2) Threshold for §179 phase-out	2,700,000	2022 amount [§179(b)(2)]
(3) Phase-out of maximum §179 expense	700,000	(1) – (2)
(4) Maximum §179 expense before phase-out	1,080,000	§179(b)(1)
Maximum §179 expense after phase-out*	**$ 380,000**	(4) – (3)

*Note that this is the maximum expense after phase-out but *before* the taxable income limitation we discuss next.

What if: Assume further that on November 13, Teton acquired and placed in service a storage building costing $400,000. Taking the building into account, what is Teton's maximum §179 amount after the phase-out?

Answer: $380,000, the same answer as above. The phase-out is based on the amount of qualified property placed in service during the year. Because the warehouse is *real property* (not qualified), its acquisition has no effect on Teton's maximum §179 expense.

A business's *deductible* §179 expense is limited to the taxpayer's business income after deducting all expenses (including regular and bonus depreciation) except the §179 expense. Consequently, the §179 expense cannot create or extend a business's net operating loss. Taxpayers' business income includes income from all businesses. For example, a sole proprietor's business income for purposes of §179 would include the income not only from all Schedules C but also from regular wages. If a business claims more §179 expense than it is allowed to deduct due to the taxable income limitation, it carries the excess forward (indefinitely) and deducts it in a subsequent year, subject to the taxable income limitation (but not the phase-out limitation) in the subsequent year.[34]

Example 2-13

What if: Let's assume the facts in Example 2-12, where Teton's maximum §179 expense after applying the phase-out limitation is $380,000. Also assume that Teton elects to claim the entire $380,000 expense and it chooses to apply it against the machinery. Further assume that Teton elects out of bonus depreciation and reports $400,000 of taxable income before deducting any §179 expense and depreciation. What amount of total depreciation (including §179 expense) is Teton able to deduct on the machinery for the year?

Answer: $400,000, computed as follows:

Description	Amount	Explanation
(1) Machinery	$2,400,000	Example 2-12
(2) Elected §179 expense	380,000	
(3) Remaining basis	$2,020,000	(1) – (2)
(4) MACRS depreciation rate for 7-year machinery, year 1	14.29%	See Table 1
(5) MACRS depreciation expense on machinery	$ 288,658	(3) × (4)
(6) Deductible §179 expense	111,342	Taxable income limitation ($400,000 – $288,658)
(7) Total depreciation expense on machinery for the year	**$ 400,000**	(5) + (6)
(8) Excess §179 expense	$ 268,658	(2) – (6)

(continued on page 2-20)

THE KEY FACTS

§179 Expenses

- $1,080,000 of tangible personal property can be immediately expensed in 2022.
- Businesses are eligible for the full amount of this expense when tangible personal property placed in service is less than $2,700,000. Beginning at $2,700,000, the §179 expense is phased out, dollar-for-dollar. When assets placed in service reach $3,780,000, no §179 expense can be taken.
- §179 expenses are also limited to a business's taxable income before the §179 expense. §179 expenses cannot create losses.

[34]Businesses typically elect to expense only the currently deductible amount because the taxable income limitation may also limit their §179 expense in future years just as it does for the current year. Electing the amount deductible after the taxable income limitation also maximizes the current-year depreciation deduction.

What is the amount of Teton's excess §179 expense (elected expense in excess of the deductible amount due to the taxable income limitation), and what does Teton do with it for tax purposes?

Answer: $268,658. See the above table for the computation (line 8). Teton carries this $268,658 excess §179 expense forward to future years and may deduct it subject to the taxable income limitation. Note that the depreciable basis of the machinery remaining after the §179 expense is $2,020,000 because the depreciable basis is reduced by the full $380,000 of §179 expense elected even though the deductible §179 expense was limited to $111,342 in the current year.

Choosing the assets to immediately expense. Businesses qualifying for immediate expensing are allowed to choose the asset or assets (from tangible personal property placed in service during the year) they immediately expense under §179. If a business's objective is to maximize its current depreciation deduction, it should immediately expense the asset with the lowest first-year cost recovery percentage including bonus depreciation (discussed in the next section).[35,36]

Example 2-14

What if: Let's assume that on June 1, Teton placed into service five-year property costing $1,400,000 and seven-year property costing $1,400,000 and had no other fixed asset additions during the year. Further assume that Teton is not subject to the taxable income limitation for the §179 expense. What is Teton's depreciation deduction (including §179 expense) if it elects to apply the full §179 expense against the five-year property (Scenario A)? What is its depreciation deduction if it applies the full §179 expense against its seven-year property (Scenario B)? Assume Teton elects out of bonus depreciation.

Answer: $1,344,060 if it applies the full §179 expense to the five-year property (Scenario A) and $1,405,728 if it applies it to the seven-year property (Scenario B). See the computations below:

Description	(Scenario A) §179 Expense on 5-Year Property	(Scenario B) §179 Expense on 7-Year Property	Explanation
(1) Original basis	$1,400,000	$1,400,000	
(2) Elected §179 expense	1,080,000	1,080,000	Maximum expense
(3) Remaining basis	320,000	320,000	(1) − (2)
(4) MACRS depreciation rate	20%	14.29%	See Table 1
(5) MACRS depreciation expense	$ 64,000	$ 45,728	(3) × (4)
(6) Deductible §179 expense	1,080,000	1,080,000	Maximum §179 expense allowed this year.
(7) MACRS depreciation on other property	200,060	280,000	This is the depreciation on the $1,400,000 7-year property in the 5-year column ($1,400,000 × 14.29% = $200,060) and on the $1,400,000 5-year property in the 7-year column ($1,400,000 × 20% = $280,000).
Total depreciation expense	**$1,344,060**	**$1,405,728**	(5) + (6) + (7)

Note that Teton deducts $61,668 more in depreciation expense if it applies the §179 expense to the seven-year property.

[35]Reg. §1.168(d)-1(b)(4)(i).

[36]Looking at Tables 2a and 2c in Appendix A, if a business has to choose between immediately expensing seven-year property placed in service in the first quarter or five-year property placed in service in the third quarter, which asset should it elect to expense under §179 if it wants to maximize its current-year depreciation expense? The answer is the five-year asset because its first-year depreciation percentage is 15 percent, while the seven-year asset's first-year depreciation percentage is 25 percent. Finally, note that businesses reduce the basis of the assets for the §179 expense before computing whether the mid-quarter convention applies.

Bonus Depreciation Since 2001, businesses have had the ability to immediately deduct a percentage of the acquisition cost of qualifying assets under rules known as **bonus depreciation.**[37] The percentage allowable for each tax year during this period has changed many times, ranging from 30 percent to 100 percent. Just prior to the TCJA, the bonus percentage was 50 percent. However, the TCJA increased the percentage to 100 percent for qualified property acquired after September 27, 2017. This provision (and the enhancement of §179) simplifies the depreciation calculation for many businesses because they can deduct the full amount of certain assets placed in service during the year.[38] There are several nuances of this provision that businesses need to consider. We discuss them in this section.

Bonus depreciation is mandatory for all taxpayers that qualify. However, taxpayers may elect out of bonus depreciation (on a property class basis) by attaching a statement to their tax return indicating they are electing not to claim bonus depreciation.[39] That is, taxpayers can elect out of bonus depreciation for all of their five-year class property but still claim bonus depreciation for all of their seven-year property acquisitions. The election to opt out of bonus depreciation is made annually. Businesses in a loss position may want to elect out of bonus depreciation to reduce these losses because their ability to deduct the losses in the future may be limited by other provisions of the tax code. In addition, businesses may want to elect out of bonus depreciation and use §179 instead because §179 allows taxpayers to pick and choose carefully which assets to expense, whereas bonus depreciation is all-or-nothing based on property class. For taxpayers claiming the deduction, bonus depreciation is calculated after the §179 expense but before regular MACRS depreciation.[40] Bonus depreciation is a temporary provision, and the percentage phases out as shown in Exhibit 2-9.[41]

Qualified property. Taxpayers must first determine whether the assets acquired during the year are eligible for bonus depreciation. To qualify, property must be new or used property (as long as the property has not previously been used by the taxpayer within the past five years)[42] and must generally have a regular depreciation life of 20 years or less.

EXHIBIT 2-9 Bonus Depreciation Percentages

Placed in Service	Bonus Depreciation Percentage
September 28, 2017–December 31, 2022	100 percent
2023	80 percent
2024	60 percent
2025	40 percent
2026	20 percent
2027 and after	None

[37]§168(k)(1).

[38]Many states do not allow bonus depreciation, so businesses will be required to calculate their depreciation using basic MACRS for those state tax returns.

[39]§168(k)(7). Property classes are broader categories of the asset classes discussed in Rev. Proc. 87-56. There are eight property classes of assets: 3-year, 5-year, 7-year, 10-year, 15-year, 20-year, residential rental property, and nonresidential real property.

[40]Reg. §1.168(k)-1(a)(2)(iii), (d)(3) Example (2).

[41]§168(k)(6).

[42]§168(k)(2)(E)(ii). Taxpayers may not use bonus depreciation for assets received as a gift or inheritance, for like-kind property (unless the taxpayer pays money in addition to the exchanged property), for property received in tax-deferred exchanges (reorganizations), or for property acquired from a related entity.

Example 2-15

What if: Assume that Teton claims bonus depreciation for the eligible personal property acquired in Exhibit 2-8.

Asset	Date Acquired	Cost Basis	Recovery Period
Computers & information systems	3/3/2022	$ 920,000	5
Delivery truck	5/26/2022	80,000	5
Machinery	8/15/2022	1,200,000	7
Total		$2,200,000	

Assuming Teton elects no §179 expense, what is Teton's bonus depreciation?

Answer: $2,200,000, computed as follows:

Description	Amount	Explanation
(1) Qualified property	$ 2,200,000	
(2) Bonus depreciation rate	100%	§168(k)(1)(A), (6)(A)(i)
Bonus depreciation	**$2,200,000**	(1) × (2)

What if: Assume that the delivery truck does not qualify for bonus depreciation and that Teton elects the maximum §179 expense. What is Teton's bonus depreciation?

Answer: $1,150,000, computed as follows:

Description	Amount	Explanation
(1) §179 qualified property	$ 2,200,000	
(2) §179 expense	1,080,000	Maximum expense
(3) Remaining basis	$ 1,120,000	(1) – (2)
(4) Remaining amount eligible for bonus depreciation	1,120,000	Remaining amount relates to the computers and the machinery. Because the truck is not eligible for bonus depreciation, we apply $80,000 of §179 expense first to the truck to maximize the current-year depreciation deduction. We next apply the remaining $1,000,000 of §179 expense ($1,080,000 – $80,000) to the machinery (7-year), which reduces its basis to $200,000 ($1,200,000 – $1,000,000).
(5) Bonus depreciation rate	100%	§168(k)(1)(A), (6)(A)(i)
Bonus depreciation	**$1,120,000**	(4) × (5)

What if: Assuming Teton elects the maximum §179 and bonus depreciation, what is Teton's total depreciation on its personal property?

Answer: $2,200,000. Teton is able to fully depreciate its tangible personal property placed in service in 2022 due to a combination of §179 ($1,080,000) and bonus depreciation ($1,120,000). Teton does not need to calculate regular MACRS depreciation on any of its tangible personal property. Alternatively, Teton could elect to take §179 on the delivery truck only and use bonus depreciation on the remaining assets. This option would produce $80,000 of §179 expense and $2,120,000 of bonus depreciation, for a total of $2,200,000.

THE KEY FACTS

Listed Property

- When an asset is used for both personal and business use, calculate the business-use percentage.
- If the business-use percentage is above 50 percent, the allowable depreciation is limited to the business-use percentage.
- If a listed property's business-use percentage ever falls to or below 50 percent, depreciation for all previous years is retroactively restated using the MACRS straight-line method.

Listed Property Most business-owned assets are used for business rather than personal purposes. For example, Weyerhaeuser employees probably have little or no personal interest in using Weyerhaeuser's timber-harvesting equipment during their free time. In contrast, business owners and employees may find some business assets, such as company automobiles or laptop computers, conducive to personal use.

Business assets that tend to be used for both business and personal purposes are referred to as **listed property.** For example, automobiles, other means of transportation (planes, boats, and recreation vehicles), and even digital cameras are considered to be listed property. The tax law limits the allowable depreciation on listed property to the portion of the asset used for business purposes.

How do taxpayers compute depreciation for listed property? First, they must determine the percentage of business versus personal use of the asset for the year. If the business-use percentage for the year exceeds 50 percent, the deductible depreciation is limited to the full annual depreciation multiplied by the business-use percentage for the year. Listed property used in trade or business more than 50 percent of the time is eligible for the §179 expensing election and bonus depreciation (limited to the business-use percentage).

Example 2-16

What if: Assume that, in addition to the assets Teton purchased in 2022 presented in Exhibit 2-8, it also purchased a new digital camera for $4,000 that its employees use for business on weekdays. On weekends, Steve uses the camera for his photography hobby. Because the camera is listed property, Teton must assess the business-use percentage to properly calculate its deductible depreciation for the camera. Assuming that Teton determines the business-use percentage to be 75 percent, what is Teton's depreciation deduction on the camera for the year (ignoring bonus depreciation and §179 expensing)?

Answer: $600, computed as follows:

Description	Amount	Explanation
(1) Initial basis of camera	$4,000	
(2) MACRS depreciation rate	20%	5-year property, year 1, half-year convention
(3) Full MACRS depreciation expense	$ 800	(1) × (2)
(4) Business-use percentage	75%	
Depreciation deduction for year	**$ 600**	(3) × (4)

When the business-use percentage of an asset is 50 percent or less, the business must compute depreciation for the asset using the MACRS *straight-line* method over the MACRS ADS (alternative depreciation system) recovery period.[43] For five-year assets such as automobiles, the assets on which the personal-use limitation is most common, the MACRS ADS recovery period is also 5 years. However, for seven-year assets, the ADS recovery period is generally 10 years.[44]

If a business initially uses an asset more than 50 percent of the time for business (and appropriately adopts the 200 percent declining balance method, §179, or bonus depreciation) but subsequently its business use drops to 50 percent or below, the depreciation expense for all prior years must be recomputed as if the business had been using the straight-line depreciation over the ADS recovery period the entire time. The business must then recapture any excess accelerated depreciation (including §179 and bonus depreciation) it deducted over the straight-line depreciation that it should have deducted by adjusting the current-year depreciation. In practical terms, taxpayers can use the following five steps to determine their current depreciation expense for the asset:

Step 1: Compute depreciation for the year it drops to 50 percent or below using the straight-line method (this method also applies to all subsequent years).

Step 2: Compute the amount of depreciation the taxpayer would have deducted if the taxpayer had used the straight-line method over the ADS recovery period for

[43]This is the alternative recovery period listed in Rev. Proc. 87-56. See §168(g)(3)(C); Reg. §1.280F-3T(d)(1).

[44]However, there are exceptions to this general rule. For example, the ADS recovery period for certain machinery for food and beverages is 12 years and the ADS recovery period for machinery for tobacco products is 15 years. Thus, it is important to check Rev. Proc. 87-56 to verify the ADS recovery period in these situations.

all prior years (recall that depreciation is limited to the business-use percentage in those years).

Step 3: Compute the amount of depreciation (including §179 and bonus depreciation) the taxpayer actually deducted on the asset for all prior years.

Step 4: Subtract the amount from Step 2 from the amount in Step 3. The difference is the prior-year accelerated depreciation in excess of straight-line depreciation.

Step 5: Subtract the excess accelerated depreciation determined in Step 4 from the current-year, straight-line depreciation in Step 1. This is the taxpayer's allowable depreciation expense on the asset for the year. If the prior-year excess depreciation from Step 4 exceeds the current-year, straight-line depreciation in Step 1, the taxpayer is not allowed to deduct any depreciation on the asset for the year and must recognize additional ordinary income for the amount of the excess.

This five-step process is designed to place the taxpayer in the same position it would have been in had it used straight-line depreciation during all years of the asset's life.

Example 2-17

What if: Assume that, consistent with Example 2-16, in 2022 Teton used the camera 75 percent of the time for business purposes and deducted $600 depreciation expense on the camera. However, in year 2, Teton's business-use percentage falls to 40 percent. What is Teton's depreciation deduction for the camera in year 2?

Answer: $20, computed using the five-step process described above as follows:

Description	Amount	Explanation*
(1) Straight-line depreciation in current year	$320	$4,000/5 years × 40 percent business-use percentage (Step 1)
(2) Prior-year, straight-line depreciation	300	$4,000/5 × 50 percent (half-year convention) × 75 percent business-use percentage (Step 2)
(3) Prior-year accelerated depreciation	600	Example 2-16 (prior example)
(4) Excess accelerated depreciation	300	(3) − (2) (Step 4)
Allowable current-year depreciation	**$ 20**	(1) − (4) (Step 5)

*Note that the MACRS ADS recovery period (five years) for digital cameras (qualified technological equipment) is the same as the standard MACRS recovery period (five years).

What if: Now assume that, in 2022, Teton took bonus depreciation and deducted $3,000 depreciation expense ($4,000 × 100% × 75%) on the camera. However, in year 2, Teton's business-use percentage falls to 40 percent. What is Teton's depreciation deduction for the camera in year 2?

Answer: $0 depreciation deduction and $2,380 of ordinary income because excess accelerated depreciation exceeds current-year straight-line depreciation, computed as follows:

Description	Amount	Explanation
(1) Straight-line depreciation in current year	$ 320	$4,000/5 years × 40 percent business use (Step 1)
(2) Prior-year, straight-line depreciation	300	$4,000/5 × 50 percent (half-year convention) × 75 percent business-use percentage from year 1 (Step 2)
(3) Prior-year accelerated depreciation	3,000	Bonus depreciation
(4) Excess accelerated depreciation	2,700	(3) − (2) (Step 4)
Income required to be recognized	**$(2,380)**	(1) − (4) (Step 5)

Luxury Automobiles As we discussed in the Business Income, Deductions, and Accounting Methods chapter, §162 limits business deductions to those considered to be "ordinary, necessary, and reasonable" to prevent subsidizing (i.e., giving a tax deduction for) unwarranted business expenses. Although these terms are subject to interpretation, most taxpayers agree that for purposes of simply transporting passengers for business-related purposes, the cost of acquiring and using a Ford Focus is more likely to be ordinary, necessary, and reasonable than the cost of acquiring and using a Ferrari California—although perhaps not as exhilarating. Because either vehicle should be able to transport an employee or business owner from the office to a business meeting, the Ford Focus should be just as effective at accomplishing the business purpose as the Ferrari.

THE KEY FACTS

Luxury Vehicles

- Depreciation on automobiles weighing less than 6,000 pounds is subject to luxury auto provisions.
- Luxury automobiles have a maximum depreciation limit for each year.
- Listed property rules are also applicable to luxury automobiles.

If this is true, why should the government help taxpayers pay for expensive cars with tax savings from large depreciation deductions associated with automobiles? Congress decided it shouldn't. Therefore, with certain exceptions we discuss below, the tax laws generally limit the annual depreciation deduction for automobiles. Each year, the IRS provides a maximum depreciation schedule for automobiles placed in service during that particular year.[45] In 2022, taxpayers are allowed to expense $8,000 of bonus depreciation above the otherwise allowable maximum depreciation (maximum depreciation of $18,200).[46] Exhibit 2-10 summarizes these schedules for automobiles placed in service for each year from 2022 back to 2019.

EXHIBIT 2-10 Automobile Depreciation Limits

Recovery Year	Year Placed in Service			
	2022*	2021	2020	2019
1	10,200**	10,200**	10,100**	10,100**
2	16,400	16,400	16,100	16,100
3	9,800	9,800	9,700	9,700
4 and after	5,860	5,860	5,760	5,760

*As of press date, the IRS had not released the 2022 limitations for automobiles, so throughout the chapter we use the same limitations as in 2021 for 2022.

**$8,000 additional depreciation is allowed when bonus depreciation is claimed [§168(k)(2)(F)].

Ignoring bonus depreciation for a moment, taxpayers placing automobiles into service during the year determine depreciation for the automobiles by first computing regular MACRS depreciation (using the appropriate convention). They then compare it to the maximum depreciation amount for the first year of the recovery period based on the IRS-provided tables. Taxpayers are allowed to deduct the lesser of the two. Each subsequent year, taxpayers should compare the regular MACRS amount with the limitation amount and deduct the lesser of the basic MACRS depreciation or the limitation. In 2022, if the half-year convention applies, the table limits the depreciation on automobiles placed in service during the year costing more than $51,000.[47] Automobiles to which the depreciation

[45]These limitations are indexed for inflation and change annually. Section 280F(a)(1)(A) provides the 2018 limitations for automobiles.

[46]§168(k)(2)(F)(i).

[47]Using the 2021 limitation amounts for 2022, the full first-year depreciation on an automobile costing $51,000 is $10,200 ($50,500 × 20 percent). This is the amount of the first-year limit for automobiles placed in service in 2021.

limits apply are commonly referred to as **luxury automobiles.**[48] Comparing the lifetime depreciation for two cars—say, a 2023 Honda Civic and a 2023 Porsche 911—we can see that the annual depreciation deduction is lower and the recovery period much shorter for the Civic than for the Porsche. As the next example illustrates, the Porsche will take 16 years to fully depreciate!

Example 2-18

What is the maximum annual depreciation deduction available for 2022 (year 1) on a 2023 Honda Civic costing $19,150 and a 2023 Porsche 911 costing $112,000 (ignoring bonus depreciation)?

Answer: $3,830 for the Honda and $10,200 for the Porsche. See the following depreciation schedules for each automobile.

Luxury Auto Depreciation*

Year/Make	2023 Honda Civic	2023 Porsche 911
Model	DX 2dr Coupe	Carrera 4S
Price	$19,150	$112,000
Depreciation		
Year 1	**$ 3,830**	**$ 10,200**
Year 2	6,128	16,400
Year 3	3,677	9,800
Year 4	2,206	5,860
Year 5	2,206	5,860
Year 6	1,103	5,860
Years 7–15		5,860
Year 16		5,280

The depreciation schedule for the Honda Civic follows the standard depreciation amounts calculated under MACRS because these annual amounts are lower than the limitations. The Honda is fully depreciated in year 6. The MACRS depreciation amounts for the Porsche, however, exceed the limitations, so the schedule shows the limited amount of depreciation each year. The limitations extend the recovery period for the Porsche to 16 years—however, it is unlikely the business will actually hold the Porsche for that long.

*Note that we use the 2021 limitations for the 2022 amounts in this example.

The luxury automobile limitations don't apply to vehicles weighing more than 6,000 pounds (for example, large SUVs) and those that charge for transportation, such as taxi cabs, limousines, and hearses. It also excludes delivery trucks and vans. Thus, taxpayers owning these vehicles are allowed to claim §179, bonus, and regular MACRS depreciation expense for these vehicles.[49]

Just like taxpayers using other types of listed property, taxpayers using automobiles exceeding the automobile limitation for business and personal purposes may deduct depreciation on the asset only to the extent of business use. Business use is determined by miles driven for business purposes relative to total miles driven for the year.[50] Consequently,

[48]Correspondingly, the depreciation limits on automobiles are commonly referred to as the *luxury auto depreciation limits.*

[49]§280F(d)(5)(A).

[50]As an alternative to deducting depreciation expense and other costs of operating an automobile, taxpayers using automobiles for both personal and business purposes may deduct a standard mileage rate for each mile of business use. In 2022 the business mileage rate is 58.5 cents per mile. Once a taxpayer uses the standard mileage rate, they may not switch back to actual costs.

if a taxpayer places a luxury automobile into service in 2022 and uses the automobile 90 percent of the time for business purposes during the year (9,000 miles for business and 1,000 miles of personal use), the owner's depreciation (ignoring bonus depreciation) on the auto for the year is limited to $9,180 (year 1 full depreciation of $10,200 × 90 percent business use—see Exhibit 2-10).[51] Further, if the business use falls to 50 percent or less in any subsequent year, just as with other listed property, the taxpayer must use the straight-line method of depreciation and reduce depreciation expense by the amount of excess accelerated depreciation (see Example 2-17). However, because straight-line depreciation is also limited by the luxury auto depreciation limits, it may turn out that the taxpayer doesn't have any excess accelerated depreciation.

Automobiles and §179. Are taxpayers allowed to deduct §179 expensing on luxury automobiles? The answer is yes, but . . . the luxury car limitation in 2022 is $10,200, and this limit applies regardless of whether the taxpayer claims regular MACRS depreciation or §179 expensing on the car. So, for cars that cost more than $51,000, the taxpayer doesn't benefit by electing §179 because the regular MACRS depreciation deduction would be greater than $10,200 and would be limited to $10,200. For cars that cost less than $51,000, taxpayers could benefit by electing to take $10,200 of §179 expense on the car to boost the depreciation deduction in the first year. For instance, in Example 2-18, the regular MACRS depreciation amount for the Honda Civic in the first year was $3,830. By electing §179, a taxpayer could increase the first-year depreciation deduction to $10,200.

Recall that large SUVs (those weighing more than 6,000 pounds) are not subject to the luxury car limitations. Therefore, a taxpayer will calculate its regular MACRS depreciation each year without the limitations for passenger cars. For these vehicles, taxpayers may take a §179 expense amount of $27,000 in 2022 (up from $26,200 in 2021) in the acquisition year in addition to their MACRS depreciation (calculated after the §179 expense).[52]

Automobiles and bonus depreciation. But wait! Why don't taxpayers simply use bonus depreciation to fully recover the cost of their automobiles in the year they buy the vehicle? For passenger cars (automobiles weighing 6,000 pounds or less), the luxury automobile limitations still apply. With bonus depreciation, taxpayers are allowed to increase the limitation in the first year by $8,000, making the first-year limit $18,200 in 2022.

Example 2-19

What if: Suppose Teton purchases a $60,000 car, which is used 100 percent of the time for business purposes. Teton would like to claim bonus depreciation. What is Teton's depreciation deduction for the car in 2022?

Answer: $18,200, calculated as follows:

Description	Amount	Explanation
(1) Automobile	$ 60,000	
(2) Bonus percentage	100%	§168(k)(1), (6)(A)(i)
(3) Bonus depreciation	$60,000	(1) × (2)
(4) Luxury automobile limitation	18,200	Luxury automobile limitation {$10,200 [§280F(a)(1)] + $8,000 [§168(k)(2)(F)]}
Year 1 depreciation	**$18,200**	Lesser of (3) or (4)

[51]Even if the business-use percentage multiplied by the MACRS depreciation is greater than the $10,200 maximum, the depreciation amount is limited to the maximum depreciation amount times the business-use percentage.

[52]This amount is indexed for inflation for years after 2018 [§179(b)(6)].

However, in years 2–6 (recovery period for passenger cars), taxpayers must again compare the regular MACRS amount in each year to the automobile limitation in Exhibit 2-10 for the year. If the taxpayer claims bonus depreciation, then, technically, all of the allowable depreciation was taken in year 1 (100 percent bonus depreciation) even though the taxpayer was limited by the automobile limitations. This means that there is no regular depreciation remaining for years 2–6. So, absent a special rule, taxpayers would not be allowed to claim *any* depreciation for those years. The remaining cost to be recovered would occur beginning in year 7 using the limitation for year 4 and after ($5,860 per Exhibit 2-10). Fortunately, the IRS provides a way (safe harbor) for taxpayers to continue to take depreciation in years 2–6 when they claim bonus depreciation.[53] This method applies to automobiles that have an initial basis greater than $18,200 (the first-year depreciation limitation for luxury automobiles) when taxpayers have not elected out of 100 percent bonus depreciation.

Under the IRS method, taxpayers first subtract the annual first-year limitation ($18,200) from the initial basis to determine the asset's adjusted depreciable basis. The taxpayer then multiplies the asset's adjusted depreciable basis by the applicable percentage in the MACRS table for each year (years 2–6) and then compares that to the annual depreciation limitation for each year (see Exhibit 2-10). The depreciation deduction for years 2–6 is the lesser of these two numbers. Starting in year 7, the taxpayer may deduct up to the year 4 and after automobile limitation until the auto is fully depreciated. This method is illustrated in the following example:

Example 2-20

What if: Assume the same facts as in Example 2-19. What is Teton's annual depreciation deduction on the car after the first year?

Answer: Determined as follows:

Taxable Year	Depreciation Limitations	Annual Depreciation	Deductible Depreciation under the Safe Harbor
2022	$18,200	$18,200 ($10,200 limitation + $8,000 additional bonus depreciation)	$18,200
2023	16,400	$13,376 [adjusted depreciable basis of $41,800 ($60,000 less $18,200 depreciation taken in the first year) × 32% depreciation rate from Appendix Table 1]	13,376
2024	9,800	$8,026 ($41,800 × 19.2%)	8,026
2025	5,860	$4,815 ($41,800 × 11.52%)	4,815
2026	5,860	$4,815 ($41,800 × 11.52%)	4,815
2027	5,860	$2,408 ($41,800 × 5.76%)	2,408
2028	5,860	N/A	$5,860 (lesser of limitation or remaining basis of $8,360)
2029	5,860	N/A	$2,500 (lesser of limitation of $5,860 or remaining basis of $2,500)

Can taxpayers avoid this calculation? Yes! There are at least two ways to avoid having to calculate depreciation on cars in this way. First, taxpayers can elect out of bonus depreciation. By electing out of bonus, taxpayers would calculate the depreciation on automobiles as the lesser of the regular MACRS depreciation or the limitation amount from Exhibit 2-10 for each year. The downside of electing out of bonus depreciation for automobiles is that the election must be done on a property class basis. Automobiles are in the five-year property class, but so are computers and office machinery (calculators and

[53]Rev. Proc. 2019-13.

copiers). So, if taxpayers elect out of bonus for automobiles, they also elect out for other assets included in the five-year property class. The second way to avoid this calculation is to purchase SUVs that weigh more than 6,000 pounds instead of passenger cars. These large SUVs are not subject to the listed property automobile limitations. Taxpayers can deduct the full cost of these vehicles in the first year under the bonus depreciation rules.

Depreciation for the Alternative Minimum Tax Individuals are subject to tax under the alternative minimum tax (AMT) system.[54] In determining their alternative minimum taxable income, individuals may be required to recalculate their depreciation expense. For AMT purposes, the allowable recovery period and conventions are the same for all depreciable assets as they are for regular tax purposes.[55] However, for AMT purposes, businesses are not allowed to use the 200 percent declining balance method to depreciate tangible personal property. Rather, they must choose from the 150 percent declining balance method or the straight-line method to depreciate the property for AMT purposes. The difference between regular tax depreciation and AMT depreciation is an adjustment that is either added to or subtracted from regular taxable income in computing the alternative minimum tax base.[56] In contrast, the §179 expense and bonus depreciation are equally deductible for both regular tax and AMT purposes. If a taxpayer claims bonus depreciation, there is no adjustment for AMT. Depreciation of real property is the same for both regular tax and AMT purposes.

Depreciation Summary Teton's depreciation for 2022 on all its assets is summarized in Exhibit 2-11, and Exhibit 2-12 presents Teton's depreciation as it would be reported on its tax return on Form 4562 (assuming Teton does not elect §179 and elects out of bonus depreciation for assets acquired in 2021). We use the 2021 forms for Teton's depreciation because the 2022 forms are not yet available.

EXHIBIT 2-11 Teton's 2022 Depreciation Expense

	Date Acquired	Original Basis	§179 Expense	Remaining Basis	Bonus Depreciation	Remaining Basis	Depreciation Expense	Reference
2021 Assets								
Machinery	7/22/2021	$ 610,000	–	$610,000	–	$610,000	$ 149,389	Example 2-5
Office furniture	2/3/2021	20,000	–	20,000	–	20,000	4,898	Example 2-5
Delivery truck	8/17/2021	25,000	–	25,000	–	25,000	8,000	Example 2-5
Warehouse	5/1/2021	275,000	–	275,000	–	275,000	7,051	Example 2-9
Land	5/1/2021	75,000	–	75,000	–	75,000	–	N/A
2022 Assets								
Computers & info systems	3/3/2022	920,000	–	920,000	920,000	–	–	Example 2-15 *What if* scenario
Delivery truck	5/26/2022	80,000	80,000	–	–	–	–	Example 2-15 *What if* scenario
Machinery	8/15/2022	1,200,000	1,000,000	200,000	200,000	–	–	Example 2-15 *What if* scenario
§179 Expense							1,080,000	Example 2-15 *What if* scenario
Bonus depreciation							1,120,000	Example 2-15 *What if* scenario
Total 2022 Depreciation Expense							**$2,369,338**	

[54]Corporations are not subject to the alternative minimum tax.

[55]This is true for assets placed in service after 1998.

[56]If the taxpayer elected either the 150 percent declining balance or the straight-line method for regular tax depreciation of tangible personal property, then there is no AMT adjustment with respect to that property.

EXHIBIT 2-12 Teton's Form 4562 Parts I–IV for Depreciation (Assumes $1,500,000 of taxable income before the §179 expense)

Form **4562**
Department of the Treasury
Internal Revenue Service (99)

Depreciation and Amortization
(Including Information on Listed Property)
▶ Attach to your tax return.
▶ Go to *www.irs.gov/Form4562* for instructions and the latest information.

OMB No. 1545-0172
2021
Attachment Sequence No. 179

Name(s) shown on return	Business or activity to which this form relates	Identifying number
Steve Dallimore	Teton Mountaineering Technologies LLC	

Part I Election To Expense Certain Property Under Section 179
Note: If you have any listed property, complete Part V before you complete Part I.

		Line	Amount
1	Maximum amount (see instructions)	1	1,080,000
2	Total cost of section 179 property placed in service (see instructions)	2	2,200,000
3	Threshold cost of section 179 property before reduction in limitation (see instructions)	3	2,700,000
4	Reduction in limitation. Subtract line 3 from line 2. If zero or less, enter -0-	4	-0-
5	Dollar limitation for tax year. Subtract line 4 from line 1. If zero or less, enter -0-. If married filing separately, see instructions	5	1,080,000

6 (a) Description of property	(b) Cost (business use only)	(c) Elected cost
Machinery	1,200,000	1,000,000
Delivery Truck	80,000	80,000
7 Listed property. Enter the amount from line 29	7	

		Line	Amount
8	Total elected cost of section 179 property. Add amounts in column (c), lines 6 and 7	8	1,080,000
9	Tentative deduction. Enter the **smaller** of line 5 or line 8	9	1,080,000
10	Carryover of disallowed deduction from line 13 of your 2020 Form 4562	10	
11	Business income limitation. Enter the smaller of business income (not less than zero) or line 5. See instructions	11	1,080,000
12	Section 179 expense deduction. Add lines 9 and 10, but don't enter more than line 11	12	1,080,000
13	Carryover of disallowed deduction to 2022. Add lines 9 and 10, less line 12 ▶	13	

Note: Don't use Part II or Part III below for listed property. Instead, use Part V.

Part II Special Depreciation Allowance and Other Depreciation (Don't include listed property. See instructions.)

		Line	Amount
14	Special depreciation allowance for qualified property (other than listed property) placed in service during the tax year. See instructions	14	1,120,000
15	Property subject to section 168(f)(1) election	15	
16	Other depreciation (including ACRS)	16	

Part III MACRS Depreciation (Don't include listed property. See instructions.)

Section A

		Line	Amount
17	MACRS deductions for assets placed in service in tax years beginning before 2021	17	169,338
18	If you are electing to group any assets placed in service during the tax year into one or more general asset accounts, check here ▶ ☐		

Section B—Assets Placed in Service During 2021 Tax Year Using the General Depreciation System

(a) Classification of property	(b) Month and year placed in service	(c) Basis for depreciation (business/investment use only—see instructions)	(d) Recovery period	(e) Convention	(f) Method	(g) Depreciation deduction
19a 3-year property						
b 5-year property						
c 7-year property						
d 10-year property						
e 15-year property						
f 20-year property						
g 25-year property			25 yrs.		S/L	
h Residential rental property			27.5 yrs.	MM	S/L	
			27.5 yrs.	MM	S/L	
i Nonresidential real property			39 yrs.	MM	S/L	
				MM	S/L	

Section C—Assets Placed in Service During 2021 Tax Year Using the Alternative Depreciation System

(a) Classification of property	(b) Month and year placed in service	(c) Basis for depreciation	(d) Recovery period	(e) Convention	(f) Method	(g) Depreciation deduction
20a Class life					S/L	
b 12-year			12 yrs.		S/L	
c 30-year			30 yrs.	MM	S/L	
d 40-year			40 yrs.	MM	S/L	

Part IV Summary (See instructions.)

		Line	Amount
21	Listed property. Enter amount from line 28	21	
22	**Total.** Add amounts from line 12, lines 14 through 17, lines 19 and 20 in column (g), and line 21. Enter here and on the appropriate lines of your return. Partnerships and S corporations—see instructions	22	2,369,388
23	For assets shown above and placed in service during the current year, enter the portion of the basis attributable to section 263A costs	23	

For Paperwork Reduction Act Notice, see separate instructions. Cat. No. 12906N Form **4562** (2021)

Source: irs.gov.

AMORTIZATION

LO 2-4

Businesses recover the cost of intangible assets through amortization rather than depreciation. Intangible assets in the form of capitalized expenditures, such as capitalized **research and experimentation (R&E) costs** or **covenants not to compete,** do not have physical characteristics. Nonetheless, they may have determinable lives. While research and experimentation costs may have an indeterminate life, a covenant not to compete, for example, would have a life equal to the stated term of the contractual agreement. When the life of intangible assets cannot be determined, taxpayers recover the cost of the assets when they dispose of them—unless they are assigned a specific tax recovery period.

For tax purposes, an intangible asset can be placed into one of the following four general categories:

1. §197 purchased intangibles.
2. Organizational expenditures and start-up costs.
3. Research and experimentation costs.
4. Patents and copyrights.

Businesses amortize all intangible assets in these categories using the straight-line method for both financial accounting and tax purposes.

Section 197 Intangibles

When a business purchases the *assets* of another business for a single purchase price, the business must determine the initial basis of each of the assets it acquired in the transaction. To determine basis, the business must allocate a portion of the purchase price to each of the individual assets acquired in the transaction. Generally, under this approach, each asset acquired (cash, machinery, and real property, for example) takes an initial basis equal to its fair market value. However, some of the assets acquired in the transaction may not appear on the seller's balance sheet. In fact, a substantial portion of a business's value may exist in the form of intangible assets such as customer lists, patents, trademarks, trade names, goodwill, going-concern value, covenants not to compete, and so forth. Nearly all these assets are amortized according to §197 of the Internal Revenue Code—hence, they are often referred to as **§197 intangibles.**

THE KEY FACTS

§197 Intangible Assets

- Purchased intangibles are amortized over a period of 180 months, regardless of their explicitly stated lives.
- The full-month convention applies to amortizable assets.

According to §197, these assets have a recovery period of 180 months (15 years), *regardless of their useful life.*[57] For example, when a business buys an existing business, the owner selling the business often signs a covenant not to compete for a specified period such as 5 years.[58] Even though a five-year covenant not to compete clearly has a fixed and determinable life, it must be amortized over 180 months (15 years). The **full-month convention** applies to the amortization of purchased intangibles. This convention allows taxpayers to deduct an entire month's amortization for the month of purchase and all subsequent months in the year. The full-month convention also applies in the month of sale or disposition.[59]

[57]Section 197 was Congress's response to taxpayers manipulating the valuation and recovery periods assigned to these purchased intangibles.

[58]A covenant not to compete is a contract between the seller of a business and its buyer that the seller will not operate a similar business that would compete with the previous business for a specified period of time.

[59]Reg. §1.197-2(g)(l)(i) illustrates the special rules that apply when a taxpayer sells a §197 intangible or the intangible becomes worthless and the taxpayer's basis in the asset exceeds the sale proceeds (if any). A business may recognize a loss on the sale or disposition only when the business does not hold any other §197 assets that the business acquired in the *same initial transaction*. Otherwise, the taxpayer may not deduct the loss on the sale or disposition until the business sells or disposes of *all* of the other §197 intangibles that it purchased in the same initial transaction. The same loss disallowance rule applies if a §197 intangible expires before it is fully amortized.

Example 2-21

What if: Assume that on January 30, 2022, Teton acquires a competitor's assets for $350,000.[60] Of the $350,000 purchase price, $125,000 is allocated to tangible assets and $225,000 is allocated to §197 intangible assets (patent, $25,000; customer list with a three-year life, $50,000; and goodwill, $150,000).[61] For each of the first three years, Teton would deduct one-fifteenth of the basis of each asset as amortization expense. What is Teton's accumulated amortization and remaining basis in each of these §197 intangibles after three years?

Answer: See the table below:

Description	Patent	Customer List	Goodwill
Initial basis	$25,000	$50,000	$150,000
Accumulated amortization (3/15 of original basis)	(5,000)	(10,000)	(30,000)
Remaining basis	$20,000	$40,000	$120,000

When a taxpayer sells a §197 intangible for more than its basis, the taxpayer recognizes gain. We describe how to characterize this type of gain in the next chapter.

TAXES IN THE REAL WORLD The Case of How Sports Owners Pay Lower Tax Rates Than the Stadium Beer Server

ProPublica, an investigative journalism nonprofit, obtained proprietary IRS data on thousands of America's wealthiest individuals. Among other things, these data revealed the tax rates of some of the sports team owners and compared them to the tax rates of players and even stadium employees. Their analysis showed that the owners often paid the lowest tax rate! As an example, Steve Ballmer, owner of the Los Angeles Clippers, had a federal income tax rate of 12 percent on $656 million in 2019. That same year, LeBron James (LA Lakers) paid a federal income tax rate of 35.9 percent on $124 million, and Adelaide Avila (Staples Center employee) had a federal income tax rate of 14.1 percent on $44,810. So, how does this happen? The answer relates to how the price of a sports franchise is treated under the U.S. tax code. A sports team's most valuable assets are generally its TV and player contracts. These assets can represent upward of 90 percent of the team's value. When the franchise is acquired, the purchase price is allocated to the team's assets, which are then subject to depreciation or, more importantly in this instance, amortization rules. Under §197, the intangible assets acquired with a business purchase are amortized and deducted over a 15-year period. These amortization deductions can turn profits into what looks like a huge tax loss. As the owner of the franchise, Ballmer and others can use these losses to offset other income. LeBron James's and Adelaide Avila's incomes are typically subject to ordinary income tax rates with no benefit from amortization.

Source: Based on Robert Faturechi, Justin Elliott, and Ellis Simani, "The Billionaire Playbook: How Sports Owners Use Their Teams to Avoid Millions in Taxes," *ProPublica* (July 8, 2021), www.propublica.org/article/the-billionaire-playbook-how-sports-owners-use-their-teams-to-avoid-millions-in-taxes.

Organizational Expenditures and Start-Up Costs

Organizational expenditures include expenditures to form and organize a business in the form of a corporation or an entity taxed as a partnership.[62] Organizational expenditures typically include costs of organizational meetings, state fees, accounting service costs incident to organization, and legal service expenditures such as document drafting,

[60]If a business acquires a corporation's stock (rather than assets), there is no goodwill assigned for tax purposes, and the purchase price simply becomes the basis of the stock purchased.

[61]A customer list is the value assigned to current customers (i.e., the lists that will allow the new owner to capture future benefits from the current customers).

[62]§248 for corporations and §709 for partnerships. Sole proprietorships cannot deduct organizational expenditures.

taking minutes of organizational meetings, and creating terms of the original stock certificates. These costs are generally incurred prior to the starting of business (or shortly thereafter) but relate to creating the business entity. The costs of selling or marketing stock do *not* qualify as organizational expenditures and cannot be amortized.[63]

Example 2-22

What if: Suppose Teton was organized as a corporation rather than a sole proprietorship (sole proprietorships cannot deduct organizational expenditures). Steve paid $35,000 of legal costs to Scott, Tang, and Malan to draft the corporate charter and articles of incorporation; $10,000 to Harvey and Stratford for accounting fees related to the organization; and $7,000 for organizational meetings, $5,000 for stock issuance costs, and $1,000 for state fees related to the incorporation. What amounts of these expenditures qualify as organizational expenditures?

Answer: $53,000, computed as follows (with the exception of the stock issuance costs, each of Teton's expenses qualifies as an amortizable organizational expenditure):

Description	Qualifying Organizational Expenditures
Legal drafting of corporate charter and articles of incorporation	$ 35,000
Accounting fees related to organization	10,000
Organizational meetings	7,000
Stock issuance costs	0
State incorporation fees	1,000
Total	**$53,000**

THE KEY FACTS

Organizational Expenditures and Start-Up Costs

- Taxpayers may immediately expense up to $5,000 of organizational expenditures and $5,000 of start-up costs.
- The immediate expense rule has a dollar-for-dollar phase-out that begins at $50,000 for organizational expenditures and for start-up costs. Thus, when organizational expenditures or start-up costs exceed $55,000, there is no immediate expensing.

Businesses may *immediately expense* up to $5,000 of organizational expenditures.[64] However, corporations and partnerships incurring more than $50,000 in organizational expenditures must phase out (reduce) the $5,000 immediate expense amount dollar-for-dollar for expenditures exceeding $50,000. Thus, businesses incurring at least $55,000 of organizational expenditures are not allowed to immediately expense any of the expenditures.

Example 2-23

What if: Suppose Teton is a corporation and it wants to maximize its first-year organizational expenditure deduction. As described in Example 2-22, Teton incurred $53,000 of organizational expenditures in year 1. How much of the organizational expenditures can Teton immediately deduct in year 1?

Answer: $2,000, computed as follows:

Description	Amount	Explanation
(1) Maximum immediate expense	$ 5,000	§248(a)(1)
(2) Total organizational expenditures	53,000	Example 2-22
(3) Phase-out threshold	50,000	§248(a)(1)(B)
(4) Immediate expense phase-out	$ 3,000	(2) – (3)
(5) Allowable immediate expense	**$ 2,000**	(1) – (4), but not below zero
Remaining organizational expenditures	$51,000*	(2) – (5)

*As we discuss below, Teton amortizes the remaining organizational expenditures over 180 months beginning in the month it starts business.

(continued on page 2-34)

[63]These costs are called syndication costs and are capitalized and deducted on the final tax return.

[64]§248(a)(1) for corporations or §709 for partnerships.

What if: Assuming that Teton is a corporation and that it incurred $41,000 of organizational expenditures in year 1, how much of the organizational expenditures could Teton immediately expense in year 1?

Answer: $5,000, computed as follows:

Description	Amount	Explanation
(1) Maximum immediate expense	$ 5,000	§248(a)(1)
(2) Total organizational expenditures	41,000	
(3) Phase-out threshold	50,000	§248(a)(1)(B)
(4) Immediate expense phase-out	$ 0	(2) – (3), limit to zero
(5) Allowable immediate expense	**$ 5,000**	(1) – (4)
Remaining organizational expenditures	$36,000*	(2) – (5)

*As we discuss below, Teton amortizes the remaining organizational expenditures over 180 months beginning in the month it starts business.

What if: Assuming that Teton is a corporation and it incurred $60,000 of organizational expenditures in year 1, how much of the organizational expenditures could Teton immediately expense in year 1?

Answer: $0, computed as follows:

Description	Amount	Explanation
(1) Maximum immediate expense	$ 5,000	§248(a)(1)
(2) Total organizational expenditures	60,000	
(3) Phase-out threshold	50,000	§248(a)(1)(B)
(4) Immediate expense phase-out	$10,000	(2) – (3)
(5) Allowable immediate expense	**$ 0**	(1) – (4), limited to zero
Remaining organizational expenditures	$60,000*	(2) – (5)

*As we discuss below, Teton amortizes the remaining organizational expenditures over 180 months beginning in the month it starts business.

Businesses amortize organizational expenditures that they do not immediately expense using the straight-line method over a recovery period of 15 years (180 months beginning in the month it starts business).

Example 2-24

What if: Assume Teton is a corporation and it amortizes the $51,000 of organizational expenditures remaining after it immediately expenses $2,000 of the costs (see the first *what if* scenario in Example 2-23). If Teton began business on February 1 of year 1, how much total cost recovery expense for the organizational expenditures is Teton able to deduct in year 1? How much cost recovery expense will Teton be able to deduct in year 2?

Answer: $5,117 in year 1 and $3,400 in year 2, computed as follows:

Description	Amount	Explanation
(1) Total organizational expenditures	$53,000	Example 2-22
(2) Amount immediately expensed	2,000	Example 2-23
(3) Expenditures subject to straight-line amortization	$51,000	(1) – (2)
(4) Recovery period in months	180	15 years; §248(a)(2)
(5) Monthly straight-line amortization	283.33	(3)/(4)
(6) Teton business months during year 1	× 11	February through December
(7) Year 1 straight-line amortization	$ 3,117	(5) × (6) (using full-month convention)
Total year 1 cost recovery expense for organizational expenditures	**$ 5,117**	(2) + (7)
Total year 2 cost recovery expense	**$ 3,400**	(3)/15 years

Start-up costs are costs businesses incur to, not surprisingly, start up a business.[65] Start-up costs apply to sole proprietorships, entities taxed as partnerships, and corporations.[66] These costs include costs associated with investigating the possibilities of and actually creating or acquiring a trade or business. For example, costs Teton incurs in deciding whether to locate the business in Cody, Wyoming, or Bozeman, Montana, are start-up costs. Start-up costs also include costs that would normally be deductible as ordinary business expenses except that they don't qualify as business expenses because they are incurred before the trade or business activity actually begins. For example, costs Teton incurs to train its employees before the business begins are start-up costs.

The rules for immediately expensing and amortizing start-up costs are the same as those for immediately expensing and amortizing organizational expenditures. Consequently, businesses incurring at least $55,000 of start-up costs are not allowed to immediately expense any of the costs. The limitations are computed separately for organizational expenditures and for start-up costs. Thus, a business could immediately expense $5,000 of organizational expenditures and $5,000 of start-up costs in its first year of business in addition to the 15-year amortization amount.

Example 2-25

What if: Assume that in January of year 1 (before it began business on February 1), Teton spent $4,500 investigating the climbing hardware market, creating company logos, and determining the locations for both the office and manufacturing facility. The $4,500 of expenditures qualify as start-up costs. How much of the $4,500 of start-up costs is Teton allowed to immediately expense?

Answer: All $4,500. Teton is allowed to immediately expense the entire $4,500 because its total start-up costs do not exceed $50,000.

Exhibit 2-13 illustrates the timing of organizational expenditures, start-up costs, and normal trade or business expenses.

EXHIBIT 2-13 Summary of Timing for Organizational Expenditures, Start-Up Costs, and Normal Trade or Business Expenses

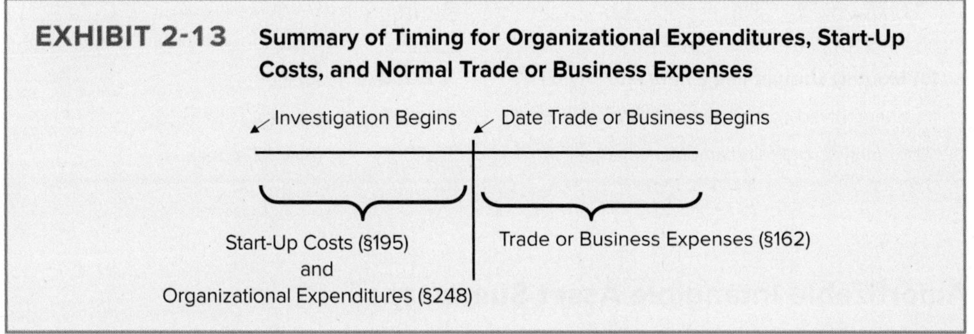

Research and Experimentation Expenditures

To stay competitive, businesses often invest in activities they believe will generate innovative products or significantly improve their current products or processes. These research and experimentation costs include expenditures for research laboratories, including salaries, materials, and other related expenses. In tax years beginning after December 31, 2021, these costs are capitalized and amortized ratably over 5 years beginning with the midpoint of the year in which the costs were incurred. Research and experimentation expenditures attributable to research conducted outside the United States are capitalized and amortized ratably over a period of 15 years for tax years beginning after December 31, 2021.[67] However, when

[65] §195.

[66] Recall that rules for amortizing organizational expenditures apply only to corporations and partnerships.

[67] See §174. For tax years beginning before January 1, 2022, businesses could immediately expense research and experimentation costs or elect to capitalize the costs and amortize them. The research and experimentation credit is also available to some businesses.

a business receives a patent relating to the expenditures, it must stop amortizing the costs. When the business obtains a patent, it adds any remaining basis in the costs to the basis of the patent and it amortizes the basis of the patent over the patent's life (see discussion below).

Patents and Copyrights

The manner in which a business amortizes a patent or copyright depends on whether the business directly purchases the patent or copyright or whether it creates it. Businesses directly purchasing patents or copyrights (not in an asset acquisition to which §197 applies) amortize the cost over the remaining life of the patents or copyrights.[68] Businesses that create patents or copyrights amortize the cost or basis of the self-created intangible assets over their legal lives. The costs included in the basis of a self-created patent or copyright include legal costs, fees, and, as we discussed above, unamortized research and experimentation expenditures associated with the creation of the patent or copyright. However, because the patent approval process is slow, the unamortized research and experimentation costs included in the patent's basis are likely to be relatively small because, with a five-year recovery period, the research and experimentation costs would likely be mostly or even fully amortized by the time the patent is approved.

Example 2-26

In September of year 1, Teton purchased a patent with a remaining life of 10 years from Chouinard Equipment for $60,000. What amount of amortization expense is Teton allowed to deduct for the patent in year 1? In year 2?

Answer: $2,000 in year 1 and $6,000 in year 2, computed as follows:

Description	Amount	Explanation
(1) Cost of patent	$60,000	
(2) Remaining life of patent in months	120	10 years
(3) Monthly amortization	$ 500	(1)/(2)
(4) Months in year 1 Teton held patent	× 4	September through December
(5) Monthly straight-line amortization (year 1)	**$ 2,000**	(3) × (4)
(6) Unamortized cost of patent at end of year 1	$58,000	(1) – (5)
(7) Monthly straight-line amortization (year 2)	$ 6,000	(3) × 12 months

Amortizable Intangible Asset Summary

Exhibit 2-14 summarizes the different types of amortizable intangible assets, identifies the recovery period of these assets, and describes the applicable amortization method for each asset. Exhibit 2-14 also identifies the applicable convention for each type of amortizable intangible asset and identifies the financial accounting treatment for recovering the cost of the intangible assets under GAAP.

Exhibit 2-15 presents Teton's amortization expense as it would be reported on its tax return on Form 4562 (the exhibit assumes that Teton is a corporation so it can amortize organizational expenditures). We use the 2021 form because the 2022 form is not yet available. The amortization is reported on line 43 because it is Teton's second year in business. The amortization amount of $9,400 is from organizational expenditures of $3,400 (Example 2-24) and a patent, $6,000 (Example 2-26). The amortization would be reported on line 42 (with more detail) had this been Teton's first year in business.

[68]§167(f).

EXHIBIT 2-14 Summary of Amortizable Assets

Asset Description	Recovery Period	Applicable Method	Applicable Convention	Financial Accounting Treatment
§197 purchased intangibles, including goodwill, trademarks, patents, and covenants not to compete[69]	180 months	Straight-line	Full-month, beginning with month of purchase	ASC 350 tests for annual impairment
Organizational expenditures and start-up costs that are required to be capitalized	180 months	Straight-line	Full-month, in month business begins	AICPA SOP 98-5
Research and experimentation costs	Ratably over 5 years	Straight-line	Midpoint of the tax year in which the costs are paid or incurred	Expensed
Self-created patents and copyrights	Actual life	Straight-line	Full-month, in month intangible is obtained	Expensed
Purchased patents and copyrights	Remaining life	Straight-line	Full-month, in month intangible is obtained	Expensed

EXHIBIT 2-15 Teton Form 4562 Part VI for Amortization of Organizational Expenditures and Patent

Part VI Amortization

(a) Description of costs	(b) Date amortization begins	(c) Amortizable amount	(d) Code section	(e) Amortization period or percentage	(f) Amortization for this year
42 Amortization of costs that begins during your 2021 tax year (see instructions):					
43 Amortization of costs that began before your 2021 tax year . . .				43	9,400
44 Total. Add amounts in column (f). See the instructions for where to report . . .				44	9,400

Form **4562** (2021)

Source: irs.gov.

(continued from page 2-16 . . .)
Teton was developing some additional employee parking on a lot adjacent to the warehouse when the excavation crew discovered a small gold deposit. Steve called his friend Ken, who had some experience in mining precious metals, to see what Ken thought of the find. Ken was impressed and offered Steve $1,500,000 for the rights to the gold. Steve accepted the offer on Teton's behalf. ■

DEPLETION

LO 2-5

Depletion is the method taxpayers use to recover their capital investment in natural resources. Depletion is a particularly significant deduction for businesses in the mining, oil and gas, and forestry industries. These businesses generally incur depletion expense as they use the natural resource. Specifically, businesses compute annual depletion expense under both the cost and percentage depletion methods and deduct the larger of the two.[70]

[69]A patent or copyright that is part of a basket purchase (several assets together) is treated as a §197 intangible. A patent or copyright that is purchased separately is simply amortized over its remaining life [§167(f)].

[70]Depletion of timber and major integrated oil companies must be calculated using only the cost depletion method (i.e., no percentage depletion is available).

Under **cost depletion,** taxpayers must estimate or determine the number of recoverable units or reserves (tons of coal, barrels of oil, or board feet of timber, for example) that remain at the beginning of the year and allocate a pro rata share of the property's adjusted basis to each unit. To determine the cost depletion amount, taxpayers then multiply the per-unit basis amount by the number of units sold during the year.[71]

Example 2-27

THE KEY FACTS

Depletion

- Cost depletion involves estimating resource reserves and allocating a pro rata share of basis based on the number of units extracted.
- Percentage depletion is determined by a statutory percentage of gross income that is permitted to be expensed each year. Different resources have different statutory percentages (e.g., gold, tin, coal).
- Taxpayers may expense the larger of cost or percentage depletion.

Ken's cost basis in the gold is the $1,500,000 he paid for it. Based on a mining engineer's estimate that the gold deposit probably holds 1,000 ounces of gold, Ken can determine his cost depletion. What is Ken's cost depletion for year 1 and year 2, assuming he extracts and sells 300 and 700 ounces of gold in year 1 and year 2, respectively?

Answer: $450,000 in year 1 and $1,050,000 in year 2, computed as follows:

Description	Amount	Explanation
(1) Cost basis in gold	$ 1,500,000	
(2) Estimated ounces of gold	1,000	
(3) Per-ounce cost depletion rate	1,500	(1)/(2)
(4) Year 1 ounces sold	300	
(5) Year 1 cost depletion	**$ 450,000**	(3) × (4)
(6) Basis remaining after year 1 depletion	1,050,000	(1) – (5)
(7) Year 2 ounces sold	700	
(8) Year 2 cost depletion	**$1,050,000**	(7) × (3)
Basis remaining after year 2 depletion	$ 0	(6) – (8)

Ken is not eligible for cost depletion after year 2 because as of the end of year 2, his cost basis has been reduced to $0.

Because the cost depletion method requires businesses to estimate the number of units of the resource they will actually extract, it is possible that their estimate will prove to be inaccurate. If they underestimate the number of units, they will fully deplete the cost basis of the resource before they have fully extracted the resource. Once they have recovered the entire cost basis of the resource, businesses are not allowed to use cost depletion to determine depletion expense. They may, however, continue to use percentage depletion (see discussion below). If a business overestimates the number of units to be extracted, it will still have basis remaining after the resource has been fully extracted. In these situations, the business deducts the unrecovered basis once it has sold all the remaining units.

The amount of **percentage depletion** for a natural resource business activity is determined by multiplying the *gross income* from the resource extraction activity by a fixed percentage based on the type of natural resource, as indicated in Exhibit 2-16.[72]

EXHIBIT 2-16 Applicable Percentage Depletion Rates

Statutory Percentage	Natural Resources (partial list)
5 percent [§613(b)(6)]	Gravel, pumice, and stone
14 percent [§613(b)(3)]	Asphalt rock, clay, and other metals
15 percent [§613(b)(2)]	Gold, copper, oil shale, and silver
15 percent [§613A(c)(1)]	Domestic oil and gas
22 percent [§613(b)(1)]	Platinum, sulfur, uranium, and titanium

[71]§612.
[72]§613.

In many cases, percentage depletion may generate *larger* depletion deductions than cost depletion. Recall that taxpayers are allowed to deduct the greater of cost or percentage depletion. Businesses reduce their initial basis in the resource when they deduct percentage depletion. However, once the initial basis is exhausted, they are allowed to continue to deduct percentage (but not cost) depletion. This provides a potentially significant governmental subsidy to extraction businesses that have completely recovered their costs in a natural resource.[73]

Note that businesses deduct percentage depletion when they *sell* the natural resource, and they deduct cost depletion in the year they *produce* or *extract* the natural resource. Also, percentage depletion cannot exceed 50 percent (100 percent in the case of oil and gas properties) of the taxable income from the natural resource business activity before considering the depletion expense, while cost depletion has no such limitation.

Example 2-28

In Example 2-27, Ken determined his cost depletion expense for the gold. However, because he is allowed to deduct the greater of cost or percentage depletion each year, he set out to determine his percentage depletion for year 2. Assuming that Ken has gross (taxable) income from the gold mining activity before depletion expense of $2,000,000 ($500,000), $6,000,000 ($4,500,000), and $6,000,000 ($5,000,000) in year 1, year 2, and year 3, respectively, what is his percentage depletion expense for each of these three years?

Answer: $250,000, $900,000, and $900,000 for years 1, 2, and 3, respectively, computed as follows:

Description	Year 1	Year 2	Year 3	Explanation
(1) Taxable income from activity (before depletion expense)	$ 500,000	$4,500,000	$5,000,000	
(2) Gross income	$2,000,000	$6,000,000	$6,000,000	
(3) Percentage	× 15%	× 15%	× 15%	Exhibit 2-16
(4) Percentage depletion expense before limit	$ 300,000	$ 900,000	$ 900,000	(2) × (3)
(5) 50 percent of taxable income limitation	$ 250,000	$2,250,000	$2,500,000	(1) × 50%
Allowable percentage depletion	**$ 250,000**	**$ 900,000**	**$ 900,000**	Lesser of (4) or (5)

Finally, as we discussed above, a business's depletion deduction is the greater of either the annual cost or percentage depletion.

Example 2-29

Based on his computations of cost depletion and percentage depletion, Ken was able to determine his deductible depletion expense. Using the cost and percentage depletion computations from Examples 2-27 and 2-28, what is Ken's deductible depletion expense for years 1, 2, and 3?

Answer: $450,000 for year 1, $1,050,000 for year 2, and $900,000 for year 3, computed as follows:

Tax Depletion Expense	Year 1	Year 2	Year 3	Explanation
(1) Cost depletion	$ 450,000	$ 1,050,000	$ 0	Example 2-27
(2) Percentage depletion	$ 250,000	$ 900,000	$ 900,000	Example 2-28
Allowable expense	**$450,000**	**$1,050,000**	**$900,000**	Greater of (1) or (2)

[73]Percentage depletion in excess of basis is an AMT preference item.

CONCLUSION

This chapter describes and discusses how businesses recover the costs of their tangible and intangible assets. Cost recovery is important because it represents a significant tax deduction for many businesses. Businesses must routinely make choices that affect the amount and timing of these deductions. Further understanding cost recovery basics helps businesses determine how to compute and characterize the gain and loss they recognize when they sell or otherwise dispose of business assets. We address the interaction between cost recovery deductions and gain and loss on property dispositions in the next chapter.

Appendix A MACRS Tables

TABLE 1 **MACRS Half-Year Convention**

	Depreciation Rate for Recovery Period					
Year	3-Year	5-Year	7-Year	10-Year	15-Year	20-Year
1	33.33%	20.00%	14.29%	10.00%	5.00%	3.750%
2	44.45	32.00	24.49	18.00	9.50	7.219
3	14.81	19.20	17.49	14.40	8.55	6.677
4	7.41	11.52	12.49	11.52	7.70	6.177
5		11.52	8.93	9.22	6.93	5.713
6		5.76	8.92	7.37	6.23	5.285
7			8.93	6.55	5.90	4.888
8			4.46	6.55	5.90	4.522
9				6.56	5.91	4.462
10				6.55	5.90	4.461
11				3.28	5.91	4.462
12					5.90	4.461
13					5.91	4.462
14					5.90	4.461
15					5.91	4.462
16					2.95	4.461
17						4.462
18						4.461
19						4.462
20						4.461
21						2.231

TABLE 2a **MACRS Mid-Quarter Convention:** *For property placed in service during the first quarter*

	Depreciation Rate for Recovery Period	
Year	5-Year	7-Year
1	35.00%	25.00%
2	26.00	21.43
3	15.60	15.31
4	11.01	10.93
5	11.01	8.75
6	1.38	8.74
7		8.75
8		1.09

TABLE 2b **MACRS Mid-Quarter Convention:** *For property placed in service during the second quarter*

Depreciation Rate for Recovery Period		
Year	**5-Year**	**7-Year**
1	25.00%	17.85%
2	30.00	23.47
3	18.00	16.76
4	11.37	11.97
5	11.37	8.87
6	4.26	8.87
7		8.87
8		3.34

TABLE 2c **MACRS Mid-Quarter Convention:** *For property placed in service during the third quarter*

Depreciation Rate for Recovery Period		
Year	**5-Year**	**7-Year**
1	15.00%	10.71%
2	34.00	25.51
3	20.40	18.22
4	12.24	13.02
5	11.30	9.30
6	7.06	8.85
7		8.86
8		5.53

TABLE 2d **MACRS Mid-Quarter Convention:** *For property placed in service during the fourth quarter*

Depreciation Rate for Recovery Period		
Year	**5-Year**	**7-Year**
1	5.00%	3.57%
2	38.00	27.55
3	22.80	19.68
4	13.68	14.06
5	10.94	10.04
6	9.58	8.73
7		8.73
8		7.64

TABLE 3 Residential Rental Property Mid-Month Convention Straight-Line—27.5 Years

	Month Property Placed in Service											
Year	**1**	**2**	**3**	**4**	**5**	**6**	**7**	**8**	**9**	**10**	**11**	**12**
1	3.485%	3.182%	2.879%	2.576%	2.273%	1.970%	1.667%	1.364%	1.061%	0.758%	0.455%	0.152%
2–9	3.636	3.636	3.636	3.636	3.636	3.636	3.636	3.636	3.636	3.636	3.636	3.636
10	3.637	3.637	3.637	3.637	3.637	3.637	3.636	3.636	3.636	3.636	3.636	3.636
11	3.636	3.636	3.636	3.636	3.636	3.636	3.637	3.637	3.637	3.637	3.637	3.637
12	3.637	3.637	3.637	3.637	3.637	3.637	3.636	3.636	3.636	3.636	3.636	3.636
13	3.636	3.636	3.636	3.636	3.636	3.636	3.637	3.637	3.637	3.637	3.637	3.637
14	3.637	3.637	3.637	3.637	3.637	3.637	3.636	3.636	3.636	3.636	3.636	3.636
15	3.636	3.636	3.636	3.636	3.636	3.636	3.637	3.637	3.637	3.637	3.637	3.637
16	3.637	3.637	3.637	3.637	3.637	3.637	3.636	3.636	3.636	3.636	3.636	3.636
17	3.636	3.636	3.636	3.636	3.636	3.636	3.637	3.637	3.637	3.637	3.637	3.637
18	3.637	3.637	3.637	3.637	3.637	3.637	3.636	3.636	3.636	3.636	3.636	3.636
19	3.636	3.636	3.636	3.636	3.636	3.636	3.637	3.637	3.637	3.637	3.637	3.637
20	3.637	3.637	3.637	3.637	3.637	3.637	3.636	3.636	3.636	3.636	3.636	3.636
21	3.636	3.636	3.636	3.636	3.636	3.636	3.637	3.637	3.637	3.637	3.637	3.637
22	3.637	3.637	3.637	3.637	3.637	3.637	3.636	3.636	3.636	3.636	3.636	3.636
23	3.636	3.636	3.636	3.636	3.636	3.636	3.637	3.637	3.637	3.637	3.637	3.637
24	3.637	3.637	3.637	3.637	3.637	3.637	3.636	3.636	3.636	3.636	3.636	3.636
25	3.636	3.636	3.636	3.636	3.636	3.636	3.637	3.637	3.637	3.637	3.637	3.637
26	3.637	3.637	3.637	3.637	3.637	3.637	3.636	3.636	3.636	3.636	3.636	3.636
27	3.636	3.636	3.636	3.636	3.636	3.636	3.637	3.637	3.637	3.637	3.637	3.637
28	1.97	2.273	2.576	2.879	3.182	3.485	3.636	3.636	3.636	3.636	3.636	3.636
29							0.152	0.455	0.758	1.061	1.364	1.667

TABLE 4 Nonresidential Real Property Mid-Month Convention Straight-Line—31.5 Years (for assets placed in service before May 13, 1993)

	Month Property Placed in Service											
Year	1	2	3	4	5	6	7	8	9	10	11	12
1	3.042%	2.778%	2.513%	2.249%	1.984%	1.720%	1.455%	1.190%	0.926%	0.661%	0.397%	0.132%
2–7	3.175	3.175	3.175	3.175	3.175	3.175	3.175	3.175	3.175	3.175	3.175	3.175
8	3.175	3.174	3.175	3.174	3.175	3.174	3.175	3.175	3.175	3.175	3.175	3.175
9	3.174	3.175	3.174	3.175	3.174	3.175	3.174	3.175	3.174	3.175	3.174	3.175
10	3.175	3.174	3.175	3.174	3.175	3.174	3.175	3.174	3.175	3.174	3.175	3.174
11	3.174	3.175	3.174	3.175	3.174	3.175	3.174	3.175	3.174	3.175	3.174	3.175
12	3.175	3.174	3.175	3.174	3.175	3.174	3.175	3.174	3.175	3.174	3.175	3.174
13	3.174	3.175	3.174	3.175	3.174	3.175	3.174	3.175	3.174	3.175	3.174	3.175
14	3.175	3.174	3.175	3.174	3.175	3.174	3.175	3.174	3.175	3.174	3.175	3.174
15	3.174	3.175	3.174	3.175	3.174	3.175	3.174	3.175	3.174	3.175	3.174	3.175
16	3.175	3.174	3.175	3.174	3.175	3.174	3.175	3.174	3.175	3.174	3.175	3.174
17	3.174	3.175	3.174	3.175	3.174	3.175	3.174	3.175	3.174	3.175	3.174	3.175
18	3.175	3.174	3.175	3.174	3.175	3.174	3.175	3.174	3.175	3.174	3.175	3.174
19	3.174	3.175	3.174	3.175	3.174	3.175	3.174	3.175	3.174	3.175	3.174	3.175
20	3.175	3.174	3.175	3.174	3.175	3.174	3.175	3.174	3.175	3.174	3.175	3.174
21	3.174	3.175	3.174	3.175	3.174	3.175	3.174	3.175	3.174	3.175	3.174	3.175
22	3.175	3.174	3.175	3.174	3.175	3.174	3.175	3.174	3.175	3.174	3.175	3.174
23	3.174	3.175	3.174	3.175	3.174	3.175	3.174	3.115	3.174	3.175	3.174	3.175
24	3.175	3.174	3.175	3.174	3.175	3.174	3.175	3.174	3.175	3.174	3.175	3:174
25	3.174	3.175	3.174	3.175	3.174	3.175	3.174	3.175	3.174	3.175	3.174	3.175
26	3.175	3.174	3.175	3.174	3.175	3.174	3.175	3.174	3.175	3.174	3.175	3.174
27	3.174	3.175	3.174	3.175	3.174	3.175	3.174	3.175	3.174	3.175	3.174	3.175
28	3.175	3.174	3.175	3.174	3.175	3.174	3.175	3.174	3.175	3.174	3.175	3.174
29	3.174	3.175	3.174	3.175	3.174	3.175	3.174	3.175	3.174	3.175	3.174	3.175
30	3.175	3.174	3.175	3.174	3.175	3.174	3.175	3.174	3.175	3.174	3.175	3.174
31	3.174	3.175	3.174	3.175	3.174	3.175	3.174	3.175	3.174	3.175	3.174	3.175
32	1.720	1.984	2.249	2.513	2.778	3.042	3.175	3.174	3.175	3.174	3.175	3.174
33							0.132	0.397	0.661	0.926	1.190	1.455

TABLE 5 Nonresidential Real Property Mid-Month Convention Straight-Line—39 Years (for assets placed in service on or after May 13, 1993)

	Month Property Placed in Service											
Year	1	2	3	4	5	6	7	8	9	10	11	12
1	2.461%	2.247%	2.033%	1.819%	1.605%	1.391%	1.177%	0.963%	0.749%	0.535%	0.321%	0.107%
2–39	2.564	2.564	2.564	2.564	2.564	2.564	2.564	2.564	2.564	2.564	2.564	2.564
40	0.107	0.321	0.535	0.749	0.963	1.177	1.391	1.605	1.819	2.033	2.247	2.461

Summary

LO 2-1 Describe the cost recovery methods for recovering the cost of personal property, real property, intangible assets, and natural resources.

- Tangible personal and real property (depreciation), intangibles (amortization), and natural resources (depletion) are all subject to cost recovery.
- An asset's initial basis is the amount that is subject to cost recovery. Generally, an asset's initial basis is its purchase price, plus the cost of any other expenses incurred to get the asset in working condition.
- The taxpayer's basis of assets acquired in a tax-deferred exchange is the same basis the taxpayer transferred to acquire the property received.
- Expenditures on an asset are either expensed currently or capitalized as a new asset. Expenditures for routine or general maintenance of the asset are expensed currently. Expenditures that better, restore, or adapt an asset to a new use are capitalized.
- When acquiring a business and purchasing a bundle of property, the basis of each asset is determined as the fair market value of the asset.

LO 2-2 Determine the applicable cost recovery (depreciation) life, method, and convention for tangible personal and real property and the deduction allowable under basic MACRS.

- Tax depreciation is calculated under the Modified Accelerated Cost Recovery System (MACRS).
- MACRS for tangible personal property is based upon the recovery period (Rev. Proc. 87-56), method (200 percent declining balance, 150 percent declining balance, and straight-line), and convention (half-year or mid-quarter).
- Real property is divided into two groups for tax purposes: residential rental and nonresidential. The recovery period is 27.5 years for residential property and 31.5 years or 39 years for nonresidential property, depending on when the property was placed in service. The depreciation method is straight-line and the convention is mid-month.

LO 2-3 Calculate the deduction allowable under the additional special cost recovery rules (§179, bonus, and listed property).

- §179 allows taxpayers to expense qualified property. The deduction is limited by the amount of property placed in service and taxable income.
- Bonus depreciation allows taxpayers to immediately deduct 100 percent of qualified property in the year of acquisition.
- Listed property includes automobiles, other means of transportation, and assets that tend to be used for both business and personal purposes. Depreciation is limited to the expense multiplied by business-use percentage. Special rules apply if business use is less than or equal to 50 percent.
- Additional limitations apply to luxury automobiles.

LO 2-4 Calculate the deduction for amortization.

- Intangible assets (such as patents, goodwill, and trademarks) have their costs recovered through amortization.
- Intangible assets are amortized (straight-line method) using the full-month convention except research and experimentation costs, which use a mid-year convention.
- Intangibles are divided into four types (§197 purchased intangibles, start-up costs and organizational expenditures, research and experimentation, and self-created intangibles).

LO 2-5 Explain cost recovery of natural resources and the allowable depletion methods.

- Depletion allows a taxpayer to recover their capital investment in natural resources.
- Two methods of depletion are available, and the taxpayer must calculate both and take the one that results in the larger depletion deduction each year.
- Cost depletion allows taxpayers to estimate the number of units and then allocate a pro rata share of the basis to each unit extracted during the year.
- Percentage depletion allows the taxpayer to take a statutory determined percentage of gross income as an expense. Deductions are not limited to basis.

KEY TERMS

§179 expense (2-17)
§197 intangibles (2-31)
adjusted basis (2-3)
amortization (2-2)
bonus depreciation (2-21)
cost depletion (2-38)
cost recovery (2-2)
covenants not to compete (2-31)
depletion (2-2)
depreciation (2-2)
full-month convention (2-31)
half-year convention (2-9)
intangible assets (2-2)
listed property (2-23)
luxury automobiles (2-26)
mid-month convention (2-15)
mid-quarter convention (2-9)
Modified Accelerated Cost Recovery System (MACRS) (2-7)
organizational expenditures (2-32)
percentage depletion (2-38)
personal property (2-7)
real property (2-7)
recovery period (2-7)
research and experimentation (R&E) costs (2-31)
start-up costs (2-35)
tax basis (2-3)

DISCUSSION QUESTIONS

Discussion Questions are available in Connect®.

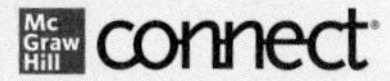

1. Explain why certain long-lived assets are capitalized and recovered over time rather than immediately expensed. LO 2-1
2. Explain the differences and similarities between personal property, real property, intangible property, and natural resources. Also, provide an example of each type of asset. LO 2-1
3. Explain the similarities and dissimilarities between depreciation, amortization, and depletion. Describe the cost recovery method used for each of the four asset types (personal property, real property, intangible property, and natural resources). LO 2-1
4. Is an asset's initial or cost basis simply its purchase price? Explain. LO 2-1
5. Compare and contrast the basis of property acquired via purchase, conversion from personal use to business or rental use, tax-deferred exchange, gift, and inheritance. LO 2-1
6. Explain why the expenses incurred to get an asset in place and operable should be included in the asset's basis. LO 2-1
7. Graber Corporation runs a long-haul trucking business. Graber incurs the following expenses: replacement tires, oil changes, and a transmission overhaul. Which of these expenditures may be deducted currently and which must be capitalized? Explain. LO 2-1
8. MACRS depreciation requires the use of a recovery period, method, and convention to depreciate tangible personal property assets. Briefly explain why each is important to the calculation. LO 2-2
9. Can a taxpayer with very little current-year income choose to not claim any depreciation deduction for the current year and thus save depreciation deductions for the future when the taxpayer expects to be more profitable? LO 2-2
10. What depreciation methods are available for tangible personal property? Explain the characteristics of a business likely to adopt each method. LO 2-2 planning
11. If a business places several different assets in service during the year, must it use the same depreciation method for all assets? If not, what restrictions apply to the business's choices of depreciation methods? LO 2-2
12. Describe how you would determine the MACRS recovery period for an asset if you did not already know it. LO 2-2

research LO 2-2 13. Compare and contrast the recovery periods used by MACRS and those used under generally accepted accounting principles (GAAP).

LO 2-2 14. What are the two depreciation conventions that apply to tangible personal property under MACRS? Explain why Congress provides two methods.

LO 2-2 15. A business buys two identical tangible personal property assets for the same price. It buys one at the beginning of the year and one at the end of the year. Under what conditions would the taxpayer's depreciation on each asset be exactly the same? Under what conditions would it be different?

LO 2-2 16. AAA Inc. acquired a machine in year 1. In May of year 3, it sold the asset. Can AAA find its year 3 depreciation percentage for the machine on the MACRS table? If not, what adjustment must AAA make to its full-year depreciation percentage to determine its year 3 depreciation?

LO 2-2 17. There are two recovery period classifications for real property. What reasons might Congress have to allow residential real estate a shorter recovery period than nonresidential real property?

LO 2-2 18. Discuss why Congress has instructed taxpayers to depreciate real property using the mid-month convention as opposed to the half-year convention used for tangible personal property.

research LO 2-2 19. If a taxpayer has owned a building for 10 years and decides that it should make significant improvements to the building, what is the recovery period for the improvements?

LO 2-2 20. Compare and contrast computing the depreciation deduction for tangible personal property versus computing the depreciation deduction for real property under both the regular tax and alternative tax systems.

LO 2-3 21. Discuss how the property limitation restricts large businesses from taking the §179 expense.

LO 2-3 22. Explain the two limitations placed on the §179 deduction. How are they similar? How are they different?

LO 2-3 23. Compare and contrast the types of businesses that would and would not benefit from the §179 expense.

LO 2-3 24. What strategies will help a business maximize its current depreciation deductions (including §179)? Why might a taxpayer choose *not* to maximize its current depreciation deductions?

LO 2-3 25. Why might a business claim a reduced §179 expense amount in the current year rather than claiming the maximum amount available?

LO 2-3 26. Describe assets that are listed property. Why do you think Congress requires them to be "listed"?

LO 2-3 27. Are taxpayers allowed to claim depreciation on assets they use for both business and personal purposes? What are the tax consequences if the business use drops from above 50 percent in one year to below 50 percent in the next?

LO 2-3 28. Discuss why Congress limits the amount of depreciation deduction businesses may claim on certain automobiles.

LO 2-3 29. Compare and contrast how a Land Rover SUV and a Mercedes-Benz sedan are treated under the luxury auto rules. Also include a discussion of the similarities and differences in available §179 expense.

LO 2-4 30. What is a §197 intangible? How do taxpayers recover the costs of these intangibles? How do taxpayers recover the cost of a §197 intangible that expires (such as a covenant not to compete)?

31. Compare and contrast the tax and financial accounting treatment of goodwill. Are taxpayers allowed to deduct amounts associated with self-created goodwill? LO 2-4

32. Compare and contrast the similarities and differences between organizational expenditures and start-up costs for tax purposes. LO 2-4

33. Discuss the method used to determine the amount of organizational expenditures or start-up costs that may be immediately expensed in the year a taxpayer begins business. LO 2-4

34. Explain the amortization convention applicable to intangible assets. LO 2-4

35. Compare and contrast the recovery periods of §197 intangibles, organizational expenditures, start-up costs, and research and experimentation expenses. LO 2-4

36. Compare and contrast the cost and percentage depletion methods for recovering the costs of natural resources. What are the similarities and differences between the two methods? LO 2-5

37. Explain why percentage depletion has been referred to as a government subsidy. LO 2-5

PROBLEMS

Select problems are available in Connect®.

McGraw Hill connect

38. Jose purchased a delivery van for his business through an online auction. His winning bid for the van was $24,500. In addition, Jose incurred the following expenses before using the van: shipping costs of $650; paint to match the other fleet vehicles at a cost of $1,000; registration costs of $3,200, which included $3,000 of sales tax and an annual registration fee of $200; wash and detailing for $50; and an engine tune-up for $250. What is Jose's cost basis for the delivery van? LO 2-1

39. Emily purchased a building to store inventory for her business. The purchase price was $760,000. Emily also paid legal fees of $300 to acquire the building. In March, Emily incurred $2,000 to repair minor leaks in the roof (from storm damage earlier in the month) and $5,000 to make the interior suitable for her finished goods. What is Emily's cost basis in the new building? LO 2-1 research

40. In January, Prahbu purchased for $90,000 a new machine for use in an existing production line of his manufacturing business. Assume that the machine is a unit of property and is not a material or supply. Prahbu pays $2,500 to install the machine, and after the machine is installed, he pays $1,300 to perform a critical test on the machine to ensure that it will operate in accordance with quality standards. On November 1, the critical test is complete, and Prahbu places the machine in service on the production line. On December 3, Prahbu pays another $3,300 to perform periodic quality control testing after the machine is placed in service. How much will Prahbu be required to capitalize as the cost of the machine? LO 2-1 research

41. Dennis contributed business assets to a new business in exchange for stock in the company. The exchange did not qualify as a tax-deferred exchange. The fair market value of these assets was $287,000 on the contribution date. Dennis's original basis in the assets he contributed was $143,000, and the accumulated depreciation on the assets was $78,000. LO 2-1
    a) What is the business's basis in the assets it received from Dennis?
    b) What would be the business's basis if the transaction qualified as a tax-deferred exchange?

42. Brittany started a law practice as a sole proprietor. She owned a computer, printer, desk, and file cabinet she purchased during law school (several years ago) that she is planning to use in her business. What is the depreciable basis LO 2-1

that Brittany should use in her business for each asset, given the following information?

Asset	Purchase Price	FMV at Time Converted to Business Use
Computer	$5,500	$3,800
Printer	3,300	3,150
Desk	4,200	4,000
File cabinet	3,200	3,225

LO 2-1 43. Meg O'Brien received a gift of some small-scale jewelry manufacturing equipment that her father had used for personal purposes for many years. Her father originally purchased the equipment for $1,500. Because the equipment is out of production and no longer available, the property is currently worth $4,000. Meg has decided to begin a new jewelry manufacturing trade or business. What is her depreciable basis for depreciating the equipment?

LO 2-1 44. Gary inherited a Maine summer cabin on 10 acres from his grandmother. His grandparents originally purchased the property for $500 in 1950 and built the cabin at a cost of $10,000 in 1965. His grandfather died in 1980, and when his grandmother recently passed away, the property was appraised at $500,000 for the land and $700,000 for the cabin. Because Gary doesn't currently live in New England, he decided that it would be best to put the property to use as a rental. What is Gary's basis in the land and in the cabin?

LO 2-1 45. Wanting to finalize a sale before year-end, on December 29, WR Outfitters sold to Bob a warehouse and the land for $125,000. The appraised fair market value of the warehouse was $75,000, and the appraised value of the land was $100,000.

a) What is Bob's basis in the warehouse and in the land?

b) What would be Bob's basis in the warehouse and in the land if the appraised value of the warehouse was $50,000 and the appraised value of the land was $125,000?

c) Which appraisal would Bob likely prefer?

LO 2-2 46. At the beginning of the year, Poplock began a calendar-year, dog-boarding business called Griff's Palace. Poplock bought and placed in service the following assets during the year:

Asset	Date Acquired	Cost Basis
Computer equipment	3/23	$ 5,000
Dog-grooming furniture	5/12	7,000
Pickup truck	9/17	10,000
Commercial building	10/11	270,000
Land (one acre)	10/11	80,000

Assuming Poplock does not elect §179 expensing and elects not to use bonus depreciation, answer the following questions:

a) What is Poplock's year 1 depreciation deduction for each asset?

b) What is Poplock's year 2 depreciation deduction for each asset?

LO 2-2 47. DLW Corporation acquired and placed in service the following assets during the year:

Asset	Date Acquired	Cost Basis
Computer equipment	2/17	$ 10,000
Furniture	5/12	17,000
Commercial building	11/1	270,000

Assuming DLW does not elect §179 expensing and elects not to use bonus depreciation, answer the following questions:

a) What is DLW's year 1 cost recovery for each asset?

b) What is DLW's year 3 cost recovery for each asset if DLW sells these assets on 1/23 of year 3?

48. At the beginning of the year, Anna began a calendar-year business and placed in service the following assets during the year: LO 2-2

Asset	Date Acquired	Cost Basis
Computers	1/30	$ 28,000
Office desks	2/15	32,000
Machinery	7/25	75,000
Office building	8/13	400,000

Assuming Anna does not elect §179 expensing and elects not to use bonus depreciation, answer the following questions:

a) What is Anna's year 1 cost recovery for each asset?

b) What is Anna's year 2 cost recovery for each asset?

49. Parley needs a new truck to help him expand Parley's Plumbing Palace. Business has been booming, and Parley would like to accelerate his tax deductions as much as possible (ignore §179 expense and bonus depreciation for this problem). On April 1, Parley purchased a new delivery van for $25,000. It is now September 26 and Parley, already in need of another vehicle, has found a deal on buying a truck for $22,000 (all fees included). The dealer tells him if he doesn't buy the truck (Option 1), it will be gone tomorrow. There is an auction (Option 2) scheduled for October 5 where Parley believes he can get a similar truck for $21,500, but there is also a $500 auction fee. Parley makes no other asset acquisitions during the year. LO 2-2 planning

a) Which option allows Parley to generate more depreciation deductions this year (the vehicles are not considered to be luxury autos)?

b) Assume the original facts, except that the delivery van was placed in service one day earlier on March 31 rather than April 1. Which option generates more depreciation deduction?

50. Way Corporation disposed of the following tangible personal property assets in the current year. Assume that the delivery truck is not a luxury auto. Calculate Way Corporation's 2022 depreciation deduction (ignore §179 expense and bonus depreciation for this problem). LO 2-2

Asset	Date Acquired	Date Sold	Convention	Original Basis
Furniture (7-year)	5/12/18	7/15/22	HY	$ 55,000
Machinery (7-year)	3/23/19	3/15/22	MQ	72,000
Delivery truck* (5-year)	9/17/20	3/13/22	HY	20,000
Machinery (7-year)	10/11/21	8/11/22	MQ	270,000
Computer (5-year)	10/11/22	12/15/22	HY	80,000

*Used 100 percent for business.

51. On November 10 of year 1, Javier purchased a building, including the land it was on, to assemble his new equipment. The total cost of the purchase was $1,200,000; $300,000 was allocated to the basis of the land, and the remaining $900,000 was allocated to the basis of the building. LO 2-2

a) Using MACRS, what is Javier's depreciation deduction on the building for years 1 through 3?

b) What would be the year 3 depreciation deduction if the building was sold on August 1 of year 3?

c) Answer the question in part (a), except assume the building was purchased and placed in service on March 3 instead of November 10.

d) Answer the question in part (a), except assume that the building is residential property.

e) What would be the depreciation for 2022, 2023, and 2024 if the property were nonresidential property purchased and placed in service November 10, 2005 (assume the same original basis)?

LO 2-2

52. Carl purchased an apartment complex for $1.1 million on March 17 of year 1. Of the purchase price, $300,000 was attributable to the land the complex sits on. He also installed new furniture into half of the units at a cost of $60,000.

a) What is Carl's allowable depreciation deduction for his real property for years 1 and 2?

b) What is Carl's allowable depreciation deduction for year 3 if the real property is sold on January 2 of year 3?

LO 2-2 LO 2-3

53. Evergreen Corporation (calendar-year-end) acquired the following assets during the current year:

Asset	Date Placed in Service	Original Basis
Machinery	October 25	$ 70,000
Computer equipment	February 3	10,000
Used delivery truck*	August 17	23,000
Furniture	April 22	150,000

*The delivery truck is not a luxury automobile.

a) What is the allowable depreciation on Evergreen's property in the current year, assuming Evergreen does not elect §179 expense and elects out of bonus depreciation?

b) What is the allowable depreciation on Evergreen's property in the current year if Evergreen does not elect out of bonus depreciation?

LO 2-2 LO 2-3

54. Convers Corporation (calendar-year-end) acquired the following assets during the current tax year:

Asset	Date Placed in Service	Original Basis
Machinery	October 25	$ 70,000
Computer equipment	February 3	10,000
Delivery truck*	March 17	23,000
Furniture	April 22	150,000
Total		$253,000

*The delivery truck is not a luxury automobile.

In addition to these assets, Convers installed qualified real property (MACRS, 15 year, 150% DB) on May 12 at a cost of $300,000.

a) What is the allowable MACRS depreciation on Convers's property in the current year assuming Convers does not elect §179 expense and elects out of bonus depreciation?

b) What is the allowable MACRS depreciation on Convers's property in the current year assuming Convers does not elect out of bonus depreciation (but does not take §179 expense)?

55. Harris Corp. is a technology start-up in its second year of operations. The company didn't purchase any assets this year but purchased the following assets in the prior year: LO 2-2 LO 2-3

Asset	Placed in Service	Basis
Office equipment	August 14	$10,000
Manufacturing equipment	April 15	68,000
Computer system	June 1	16,000
Total		$94,000

Harris did not know depreciation was tax deductible until it hired an accountant this year and didn't claim any depreciation deduction in its first year of operation.

a) What is the maximum amount of depreciation deduction Harris Corp. can deduct in its second year of operation?

b) What is the basis of the office equipment at the end of the second year?

56. AMP Corporation (calendar-year-end) has 2022 taxable income of $1,900,000 for purposes of computing the §179 expense. During 2022, AMP acquired the following assets: LO 2-2 LO 2-3

Asset	Placed in Service	Basis
Machinery	September 12	$1,550,000
Computer equipment	February 10	365,000
Office building	April 2	480,000
Total		$2,395,000

a) What is the maximum amount of §179 expense AMP may deduct for 2022?

b) What is the maximum total depreciation, including §179 expense, that AMP may deduct in 2022 on the assets it placed in service in 2022, assuming no bonus depreciation?

57. Assume that TDW Corporation (calendar-year-end) has 2022 taxable income of $650,000 for purposes of computing the §179 expense. The company acquired the following assets during 2022: LO 2-2 LO 2-3

Asset	Placed in Service	Basis
Machinery	September 12	$2,270,000
Computer equipment	February 10	263,000
Furniture	April 2	880,000
Total		$3,413,000

a) What is the maximum amount of §179 expense TDW may deduct for 2022?

b) What is the maximum total depreciation, including §179 expense, that TDW may deduct in 2022 on the assets it placed in service in 2022, assuming no bonus depreciation?

58. Assume that Timberline Corporation has 2022 taxable income of $240,000 for purposes of computing the §179 expense. It acquired the following assets in 2022: LO 2-2 LO 2-3

Asset	Purchase Date	Basis
Furniture (7-year)	December 1	$ 450,000
Computer equipment (5-year)	February 28	90,000
Copier (5-year)	July 15	30,000
Machinery (7-year)	May 22	480,000
Total		$1,050,000

a) What is the maximum amount of §179 expense Timberline may deduct for 2022? What is Timberline's §179 carryforward to 2023, if any?

b) What would Timberline's maximum depreciation deduction be for 2022 assuming no bonus depreciation?

c) What would Timberline's maximum depreciation deduction be for 2022 if the machinery cost $3,500,000 instead of $480,000 and assuming no bonus depreciation?

LO 2-2 LO 2-3 planning

59. Dain's Diamond Bit Drilling purchased the following assets this year. Assume its taxable income for the year was $53,000 for purposes of computing the §179 expense (assume no bonus depreciation).

Asset	Purchase Date	Original Basis
Drill bits (5-year)	January 25	$ 90,000
Drill bits (5-year)	July 25	95,000
Commercial building	April 22	220,000

a) What is the maximum amount of §179 expense Dain's may deduct for the year?

b) What is Dain's maximum depreciation deduction for the year (including §179 expense)?

c) If the January drill bits' original basis was $2,875,000, what is the maximum amount of §179 expense Dain's may deduct for the year?

d) If the January drill bits' original basis was $3,875,000, what is the maximum amount of §179 expense Dain's may deduct for the year?

LO 2-2 LO 2-3 research

60. Assume that ACW Corporation has 2022 taxable income of $1,500,000 for purposes of computing the §179 expense. The company acquired the following assets during 2022 (assume no bonus depreciation):

Asset	Placed in Service	Basis
Machinery	September 12	$ 470,000
Computer equipment	February 10	70,000
Delivery truck	August 21	93,000
Qualified real property (MACRS, 15 year, 150% DB)	April 2	1,380,000
Total		$2,013,000

a) What is the maximum amount of §179 expense ACW may deduct for 2022?

b) What is the maximum *total* depreciation that ACW may deduct in 2022 on the assets it placed in service in 2022?

LO 2-2 LO 2-3

61. Chaz Corporation has taxable income in 2022 of $312,000 for purposes of computing the §179 expense and acquired the following assets during the year:

Asset	Placed in Service	Basis
Office furniture	September 12	$ 780,000
Computer equipment	February 10	930,000
Delivery truck	August 21	68,000
Qualified real property (MACRS, 15 year, 150% DB)	September 30	1,500,000
Total		$3,278,000

What is the maximum *total* depreciation deduction that Chaz may deduct in 2022?

LO 2-2 LO 2-3 planning research

62. Woolard Supplies (a sole proprietorship) has taxable income in 2022 of $240,000 before any depreciation deductions (§179, bonus, or MACRS) and placed some office furniture into service during the year. The furniture does not qualify for bonus depreciation.

Asset	Placed in Service	Basis
Office furniture (used)	March 20	$1,200,000

a) If Woolard elects $50,000 of §179, what is Woolard's total depreciation deduction for the year?

b) If Woolard elects the maximum amount of §179 for the year, what is the amount of deductible §179 expense for the year? What is the *total* depreciation that Woolard may deduct in 2022? What is Woolard's §179 carryforward amount to next year, if any?

c) Woolard is concerned about future limitations on its §179 expense. How much §179 expense should Woolard expense this year if it wants to maximize its depreciation this year and avoid any carryover to future years?

63. Assume that Sivart Corporation has 2022 taxable income of $1,750,000 for purposes of computing the §179 expense and acquired several assets during the year. Assume the delivery truck does not qualify for bonus depreciation. LO 2-2 LO 2-3 planning

Asset	Placed in Service	Basis
Machinery	June 12	$1,440,000
Computer equipment	February 10	70,000
Delivery truck—used	August 21	93,000
Furniture	April 2	310,000
Total		$1,913,000

a) What is the maximum amount of §179 expense Sivart may deduct for 2022?

b) What is the maximum *total* depreciation (§179, bonus, MACRS) that Sivart may deduct in 2022 on the assets it placed in service in 2022?

64. Acorn Construction (calendar-year-end C corporation) has had rapid expansion during the last half of the current year due to the housing market's recovery. The company has record income and would like to maximize its cost recovery deduction for the current year. Acorn provided you with the following information: LO 2-2 LO 2-3 planning

Asset	Placed in Service	Basis
New equipment and tools	August 20	$3,800,000
Used light-duty trucks	October 17	2,000,000
Used machinery	November 6	525,000
Total		$6,325,000

The used assets had been contributed to the business by its owner in a tax-deferred transaction.

a) What is Acorn's maximum cost recovery deduction in the current year?

b) What planning strategies would you advise Acorn to consider?

65. Phil owns a ranch business and uses four-wheelers to do much of his work. Occasionally, though, he and his boys will go for a ride together as a family activity. During year 1, Phil put 765 miles on the four-wheeler that he bought on January 15 for $6,500. Of the miles driven, only 175 miles were for personal use. Assume four-wheelers qualify to be depreciated according to the five-year MACRS schedule and the four-wheeler was the only asset Phil purchased this year. LO 2-3

a) Calculate the allowable depreciation for year 1 (ignore the §179 expense and bonus depreciation).

b) Calculate the allowable depreciation for year 2 if total miles were 930 and personal-use miles were 400 (ignore the §179 expense and bonus depreciation).

LO 2-3

66. Assume that Ernesto purchased a digital camera on July 10 of year 1 for $3,000. In year 1, 80 percent of his camera usage was for his business and 20 percent was for personal photography activities. This was the only asset he placed in service during year 1. Ignoring any potential §179 expense and bonus depreciation, answer the questions for each of the following alternative scenarios:
   a) What is Ernesto's depreciation deduction for the camera in year 1?
   b) What would be Ernesto's depreciation deduction for the camera in year 2 if his year 2 usage was 75 percent business and 25 percent for personal use?
   c) What would be Ernesto's depreciation deduction for the camera in year 2 if his year 2 usage was 45 percent business and 55 percent for personal use?

LO 2-3

67. Lina purchased a new car for use in her business during 2022. The auto was the only business asset she purchased during the year, and her business was extremely profitable. Calculate her maximum depreciation deductions (including §179 expense unless stated otherwise) for the automobile in 2022 and 2023 (Lina doesn't want to take bonus depreciation for 2022 or 2023) in the following alternative scenarios (assuming half-year convention for all):
   a) The vehicle cost $35,000, and business use is 100 percent (ignore §179 expense).
   b) The vehicle cost $80,000, and business use is 100 percent.
   c) The vehicle cost $80,000, and she used it 80 percent for business.
   d) The vehicle cost $80,000, and she used it 80 percent for business. She sold it on March 1 of year 2.
   e) The vehicle cost $80,000, and she used it 20 percent for business.
   f) The vehicle cost $80,000 and is an SUV that weighs 6,500 pounds. Business use was 100 percent.

LO 2-2 LO 2-3 planning

68. Tamika Meer purchased a new car for use in her business during 2022 for $75,000. The auto was the only business asset she purchased during the year, and her business was very profitable. Calculate Tamika's maximum depreciation deductions for the automobile in 2022 and 2023 under the following scenarios:
   a) Tamika does not want to take §179 expense and she elects out of bonus depreciation.
   b) Tamika wants to maximize her 2022 depreciation using bonus depreciation.

LO 2-2 LO 2-3

69. Burbank Corporation (calendar-year-end) acquired the following property this year:

Asset	Placed in Service	Basis
Used copier	November 12	$ 7,800
New computer equipment	June 6	14,000
Furniture	July 15	32,000
New delivery truck	October 28	19,000
Luxury auto	January 31	70,000
Total		$142,800

Burbank acquired the copier in a tax-deferred transaction when the shareholder contributed the copier to the business in exchange for stock.
   a) Assuming no bonus or §179 expense, what is Burbank's maximum cost recovery deduction for this year?
   b) Assuming Burbank would like to maximize its cost recovery deductions by claiming bonus and §179 expense, which assets should Burbank immediately expense?
   c) What is Burbank's maximum cost recovery deduction this year assuming it elects §179 expense and claims bonus depreciation?

70. Paul Vote purchased the following assets this year (ignore §179 expensing and bonus depreciation when answering the questions below): LO 2-3 research

Asset	Purchase Date	Basis
Machinery	May 12	$ 23,500
Computers	August 13	20,000
Warehouse	December 13	180,000

a) What is Paul's allowable MACRS depreciation for the property?
b) What is Paul's allowable alternative minimum tax (AMT) depreciation for the property? You will need to find the AMT depreciation tables to compute the depreciation.

71. After several profitable years running her business, Ingrid decided to acquire the assets of a small competing business. On May 1 of year 1, Ingrid acquired the competing business for $300,000. Ingrid allocated $50,000 of the purchase price to goodwill. Ingrid's business reports its taxable income on a calendar-year basis. LO 2-4 research
a) How much amortization expense on the goodwill can Ingrid deduct in year 1, year 2, and year 3?
b) In lieu of the original facts, assume that Ingrid purchased only a phone list with a useful life of five years for $10,000. How much amortization expense on the phone list can Ingrid deduct in year 1, year 2, and year 3?

72. Juliette formed a new business to sell sporting goods this year. The business opened its doors to customers on June 1. Determine the amount of start-up costs Juliette can immediately expense (not including the portion of the expenditures that are amortized over 180 months) this year in the following alternative scenarios: LO 2-4
a) She incurred start-up costs of $2,000.
b) She incurred start-up costs of $45,000.
c) She incurred start-up costs of $53,500.
d) She incurred start-up costs of $63,000.
e) How would you answer parts (a) through (d) if she formed a partnership or a corporation and she incurred the same amount of organizational expenditures rather than start-up costs (how much of the organizational expenditures would be immediately deductible)?

73. Nicole organized a new corporation. The corporation began business on April 1 of year 1. She made the following expenditures associated with getting the corporation started: LO 2-4

Expense	Date	Amount
Attorney fees for articles of incorporation	February 10	$32,000
March 1–March 30 wages	March 30	4,500
March 1–March 30 rent	March 30	2,000
Stock issuance costs	April 1	20,000
April 1–May 30 wages	May 30	12,000

a) What is the total amount of the start-up costs and organizational expenditures for Nicole's corporation?
b) What amount of the start-up costs and organizational expenditures may the corporation immediately expense in year 1 (excluding the portion of the expenditures that are amortized over 180 months)?
c) What amount can the corporation deduct as amortization expense for the organizational expenditures and for the start-up costs for year 1 [not including the amount determined in part (b)]?
d) What would be the total allowable organizational expenditures if Nicole started a sole proprietorship instead of a corporation?

LO 2-4

74. Bethany incurred $20,000 in research and experimental costs for developing a specialized product during July 2022. Bethany went through a lot of trouble and spent $10,000 in legal fees to receive a patent for the product in August 2024. Bethany expects the patent to have a remaining useful life of 10 years.
    a) What amount of research and experimental expenses for 2022, 2023, and 2024 may Bethany deduct?
    b) How much *patent* amortization expense would Bethany deduct in 2024?
    c) If Bethany chose to capitalize but *not* amortize the research and experimental expenses she incurred in 2022, how much patent amortization expense would Bethany deduct in2024?

LO 2-5

75. Last Chance Mine (LCM) purchased a coal deposit for $750,000. It estimated it would extract 12,000 tons of coal from the deposit. LCM mined the coal and sold it, reporting gross receipts of $1 million, $3 million, and $2 million for years 1 through 3, respectively. During years 1–3, LCM reported net income (loss) from the coal deposit activity in the amount of ($20,000), $500,000, and $450,000, respectively. In years 1–3, LCM extracted 13,000 tons of coal as follows:

(1) Tons of Coal	(2) Basis	(2)/(1) Depletion Rate	Tons Extracted per Year Year 1	Year 2	Year 3
12,000	$750,000	$62.50	2,000	7,200	3,800

    a) What is LCM's cost depletion for years 1, 2, and 3?
    b) What is LCM's percentage depletion for each year (the applicable percentage for coal is 10 percent)?
    c) Using the cost and percentage depletion computations from parts (a) and (b), what is LCM's actual depletion expense for each year?

COMPREHENSIVE PROBLEMS

Select problems are available with Connect®.

tax forms

76. Karane Enterprises, a calendar-year manufacturer based in College Station, Texas, began business in 2021. In the process of setting up the business, Karane has acquired various types of assets. Below is a list of assets acquired during 2021:

Asset	Cost	Date Placed in Service
Office furniture	$ 150,000	02/03/2021
Machinery	1,560,000	07/22/2021
Used delivery truck*	40,000	08/17/2021

*Not considered a luxury automobile.

During 2021, Karane was very successful (and had no §179 limitations) and decided to acquire more assets in 2022 to increase its production capacity. These are the assets acquired during 2022:

Asset	Cost	Date Placed in Service
Computers & info. system	$ 400,000	03/31/2022
Luxury auto*	80,000	05/26/2022
Assembly equipment	1,200,000	08/15/2022
Storage building	700,000	11/13/2022

*Used 100% for business purposes.

Karane generated taxable income in 2022 of $1,732,500 for purposes of computing the §179 expense limitation.

a) Compute the maximum 2021 depreciation deductions, including §179 expense (ignoring bonus depreciation).
b) Compute the maximum 2022 depreciation deductions, including §179 expense (ignoring bonus depreciation).
c) Compute the maximum 2022 depreciation deductions, including §179 expense, but now assume that Karane would like to take bonus depreciation.
d) Now assume that during 2022, Karane decides to buy a competitor's assets for a purchase price of $1,350,000. Compute the maximum 2022 cost recovery, including §179 expense and bonus depreciation. Karane purchased the following assets for the lump-sum purchase price:

Asset	Cost	Date Placed in Service
Inventory	$220,000	09/15/2022
Office furniture	230,000	09/15/2022
Machinery	250,000	09/15/2022
Patent	198,000	09/15/2022
Goodwill	2,000	09/15/2022
Building	430,000	09/15/2022
Land	20,000	09/15/2022

e) Complete Part I of Form 4562 for part (b) (use the most current form available).

77. While completing undergraduate school work in information systems, Dallin Bourne and Michael Banks decided to start a technology support company called eSys Answers. During year 1, they bought the following assets and incurred the following start-up fees:

Year 1 Assets	Purchase Date	Basis
Computers (5-year)	October 30, Y1	$15,000
Office equipment (7-year)	October 30, Y1	10,000
Furniture (7-year)	October 30, Y1	3,000
Start-up costs	October 30, Y1	17,000

In April of year 2, they decided to purchase a customer list from a company providing virtually the same services, started by fellow information systems students preparing to graduate. The customer list cost $10,000, and the sale was completed on April 30. During their summer break, Dallin and Michael passed on internship opportunities in an attempt to really grow their business into something they could do full time after graduation. In the summer, they purchased a small van (for transportation, not considered a luxury auto) and a pinball machine (to help attract new employees). They bought the van on June 15, Y2, for $15,000 and spent $3,000 getting it ready to put into service. The pinball machine cost $4,000 and was placed in service on July 1, Y2.

Year 2 Assets	Purchase Date	Basis
Van	June 15, Y2	$18,000
Pinball machine (7-year)	July 1, Y2	4,000
Customer list	April 30, Y2	10,000

Assume that eSys Answers does not claim any §179 expense or bonus depreciation.

a) What are the maximum cost recovery deductions for eSys Answers for Y1 and Y2?
b) Complete eSys Answers's Form 4562 for Y1 (use the most current form available).
c) What is eSys Answers's basis in each of its assets at the end of Y2?

78. Diamond Mountain was originally thought to be one of the few places in North America to contain diamonds, so Diamond Mountain Inc. (DM) purchased the land for $1,000,000. Later, DM discovered that the only diamonds on the mountain had been planted there and the land was worthless for mining. DM engineers discovered a new survey technology and discovered a silver deposit estimated at 5,000 pounds on Diamond Mountain. DM immediately bought new drilling equipment and began mining the silver.

    In years 1–3 following the opening of the mine, DM had net (gross) income of $200,000 ($700,000), $400,000 ($1,100,000), and $600,000 ($1,450,000), respectively. Mining amounts for each year were as follows: 750 pounds (year 1), 1,450 pounds (year 2), and 1,800 pounds (year 3). At the end of year 2, engineers used the new technology (which had been improving over time) and estimated there was still an estimated 6,000 pounds of silver deposits.

    DM also began a research and experimentation project with the hopes of gaining a patent for its new survey technology. Diamond Mountain Inc. chose to capitalize research and experimentation expenditures and to amortize the costs over 60 months or until it obtained a patent on its technology. In March of year 1, DM spent $95,000 on research and experimentation. DM spent another $75,000 in February of year 2 for research and experimentation. DM realizes benefits from the research and experimentation expenditures when the costs are incurred. In September of year 2, DM paid $20,000 of legal fees and was granted the patent in October of year 2 (the entire process of obtaining a patent was unusually fast). The patent's life is 20 years.

    Answer the following questions regarding DM's activities (assume that DM tries to maximize its deductions if given a choice).

    a) What is DM's depletion expense for years 1–3?
    b) What is DM's research and experimentation amortization for years 1 and 2?
    c) What is DM's basis in its patent, and what is its amortization for the patent in year 2?

UWorld Roger CPA Review

Sample CPA Exam questions from Roger CPA Review are available in Connect as support for the topics in this text. These Multiple Choice Questions and Task-Based Simulations include expert-written explanations and solutions and provide a starting point for students to become familiar with the content and functionality of the actual CPA Exam.

chapter

3 Property Dispositions

Learning Objectives

Upon completing this chapter, you should be able to:

LO 3-1 Calculate the amount of gain or loss recognized on the disposition of assets used in a trade or business.

LO 3-2 Describe the general character types of gain or loss recognized on property dispositions.

LO 3-3 Calculate depreciation recapture.

LO 3-4 Describe the tax treatment of unrecaptured §1250 gains.

LO 3-5 Describe the tax treatment of §1231 gains or losses, including the §1231 netting process.

LO 3-6 Explain common deferral exceptions to the general rule that realized gains and losses are recognized currently.

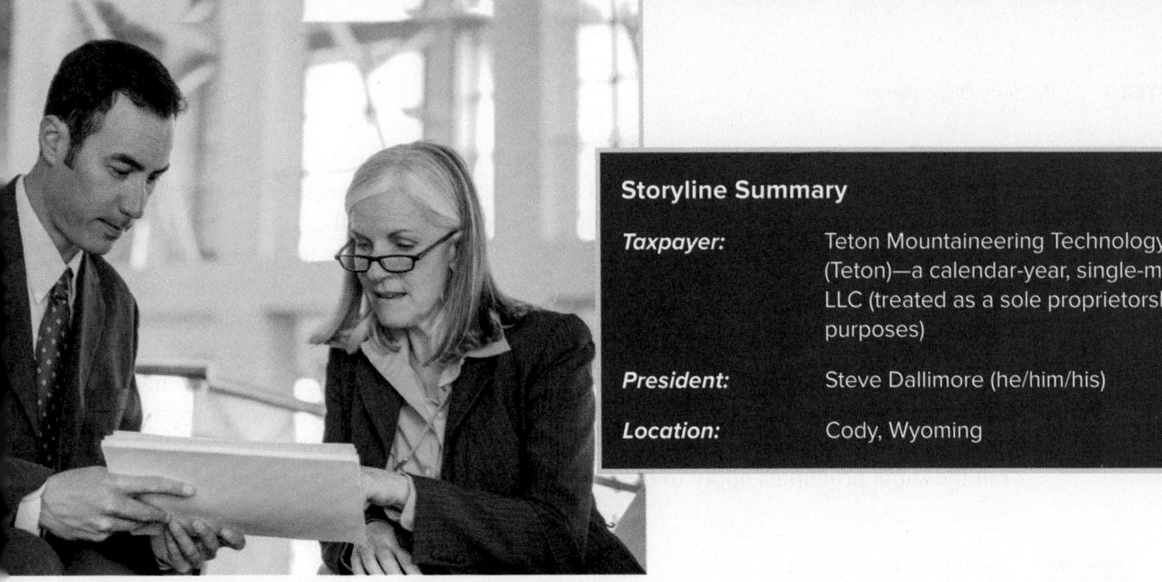
Mike Kemp/Blend Images

Storyline Summary

Taxpayer:	Teton Mountaineering Technology, LLC (Teton)—a calendar-year, single-member LLC (treated as a sole proprietorship for tax purposes)
President:	Steve Dallimore (he/him/his)
Location:	Cody, Wyoming

By most measures, Teton Mountaineering Technology, LLC (Teton), has become a success, with sponsored climbers summiting the world's highest peaks, satisfied customers creating brand loyalty, and profitability improving steadily. However, after several years of operation, some of Teton's machinery is wearing out and must be replaced. Further, because Teton has outgrown its manufacturing capacity, Steve is considering whether to expand the company's current facility or sell it and build a new one in a different location. Steve would like to know how any asset dispositions will affect his tax bill.

Steve has found a willing buyer for some of Teton's land, and he has options for trading the land. For tax purposes, does it matter whether he sells or trades the land? Steve also has questions about how to best manage Teton's acquisitions and dispositions of real property. It all seems a bit overwhelming. . . . He picks up the phone and dials his tax accountant's number. ■

You can imagine why Steve might be eager to reach out to his accountant. Tax accounting widely impacts business decisions: What are the tax consequences of selling, trading, or even abandoning business assets? Are the tax consequences the same whether taxpayers sell machinery, inventory, or investment assets? Does it matter for tax purposes whether Teton is structured as a sole proprietorship or a corporation when it sells its warehouse? If Steve sells his personal sailboat, car, or furniture, what are the tax consequences?

In the previous chapter, we explained the tax consequences associated with purchasing assets and recovering the cost of the assets through depreciation, amortization, or depletion. This chapter explores fundamental tax issues associated with property dispositions (sales, trades, or other dispositions). We focus on the disposition of tangible assets, but the same principles apply to the sale of intangible assets and natural resources.

LO 3-1

DISPOSITIONS

Taxpayers can dispose of assets in many ways. For example, a taxpayer could sell an asset, donate it to charity, trade it for a similar asset, take it to the landfill, or have it destroyed in a natural disaster. No matter how it is accomplished, every asset disposition triggers a realization event for tax purposes. To calculate the amount of gain or loss taxpayers realize when they sell assets, they must determine the amount realized on the sale and the *adjusted basis* of each asset they are selling.

Amount Realized

Simply put, the **amount realized** by a taxpayer from the sale or other disposition of an asset is everything of *value* received from the buyer *less* any selling costs.[1] Although taxpayers typically receive cash when they sell property, they may also accept marketable securities, notes receivable, cryptocurrency, similar assets, or any combination of these items as payment. Additionally, taxpayers selling assets such as real property subject to loans or mortgages may receive some debt relief. In this case, they would increase their amount realized by the amount of debt relief (the buyer's assumption of the seller's liability increases the seller's amount realized). The amount realized computation is captured in the following formula:

Amount realized = Cash received + Fair market value of other property
+ Buyer's assumption of liabilities − Seller's expenses

Example 3-1

Teton wants to upgrade its old manufacturing machinery that is wearing out. On November 1 of the current year, Teton sells the machinery for $230,000 cash and marketable securities valued at $70,500. Teton paid a broker $500 to find a buyer. What is Teton's amount realized on the sale of the machinery?

Answer: $300,000, computed as follows:

Description	Amount	Explanation
(1) Cash received	$ 230,000	
(2) Marketable securities received	70,500	
(3) Broker commission paid	(500)	
Amount realized	**$300,000**	(1) + (2) + (3)

[1] *Chapin v. Comm'r*, 50-1 USTC ¶ 9171 (8th Cir. 1950).

Determination of Adjusted Basis

In the previous chapter, we discussed the basis for cost recovery and focused on purchased assets in which the initial basis is the asset's cost. However, taxpayers may acquire assets without purchasing them. For example, a taxpayer may acquire an asset as a gift or as an inheritance. In either case, the taxpayer does not purchase the asset, so the taxpayer's initial basis in the asset must be computed as something other than purchase price. Although there are many situations when an asset's initial basis is not the asset's cost, we focus on three cases: gifts, inherited assets, and property converted from personal use to business use.

Gifts A gift is defined as a transfer of property proceeding from a detached and disinterested generosity or out of affection, respect, admiration, charity, or like impulses.[2] The initial basis of gift property to a recipient (donee) depends on whether the value of the asset exceeds the donor's basis on the date of the gift. If the fair market value of the asset on the date of the gift is greater than the donor's basis, then the asset's initial basis to the recipient of the gift will be the same as the donor's basis.[3] That is, the donor's basis carries over to the donee.

If the donor's basis is greater than the fair market value of the asset at the date of the gift, then special dual basis rules apply. A dual basis means that the gift property has one basis to the donee if the donee sells the property at a price above the donor's basis and a different basis if the donee sells the property at a price below the fair market value at the date of the gift. Interestingly, the donee will not know the basis for calculating gain or loss until the donee sells the property. Thus, the basis of gifted property that has declined in value depends on the sales price of the asset subsequent to the gift. The donee uses the carryover basis if the asset is sold for a gain (sales price > donor's basis), whereas the donee uses the fair market value at the date of the gift if the asset is sold for a loss (sales price < FMV at date of gift). If the asset sells at a price between the donor's basis and the fair market value at the date of the gift, then the donee's basis at the time of the sale is set equal to the selling price and the donee does not recognize gain or loss on the sale. The dual basis rule prevents the transfer of unrealized losses from one taxpayer to another by gift.

When the dual basis rules apply, the donee's holding period of the asset depends on whether the gift property subsequently sells for a gain or loss. If the donor's basis is used to determine the gain, the holding period includes that of the donor. If the fair market value at the date of the gift is used to figure the loss, the holding period starts on the date of the gift. If the asset subsequently sells at a price between the donor's basis and the fair market value at the date of the gift, the holding period is irrelevant because there is no recognized gain or loss.

Inherited Property For inherited property, the general rule is that the heir's basis in property passing from a decedent to the heir is the fair market value on the date of the decedent's death.[4] The holding period of inherited property is deemed to be long term regardless of how long the heir owns the property.[5]

Property Converted from Personal Use to Business Use The basis for determining the gain or loss on the sale of converted property depends on whether the property appreciated or declined in value during the time the property was used personally. For appreciated property (i.e., the fair market value at the date of the conversion is greater than the taxpayer's basis in the property), the taxpayer will use their basis to calculate depreciation and gain or loss at disposition.

[2] *Comm'r v. Duberstein,* 363 U.S. 278 (1960), *rev'g* 265 F.2d 28 (6th Cir. 1959), *rev'g* TC Memo 1958-4.

[3] §1015(a). The basis to the donee may be increased if the donor is required to pay gift tax on the gift.

[4] §1014(a)(1). An alternate valuation date may be used to determine the basis to the heirs if elected by the estate.

[5] §1223(9).

For property with a basis greater than value, taxpayers may try to convert nondeductible personal losses to business losses by converting the property into business property and then selling it. In order to prevent this from occurring, the dual basis rules apply. If the fair market value at the date of conversion is below the taxpayer's basis, the taxpayer will use the fair market value at the date of conversion as the basis for calculating loss and will use the basis at date of conversion to calculate gain. The fair market value at the date of conversion is also the basis used to calculate depreciation on property that has declined in value prior to the conversion regardless of whether the taxpayer subsequently sells the property for a gain or a loss. After conversion, the taxpayer adjusts the basis (whether gain or loss) for depreciation deductions from the date of conversion to the date of disposition. If the property later sells for an amount that falls between the adjusted basis for gain and the adjusted basis for loss, the basis for the sale is treated as the sales price so that the taxpayer does not recognize gain or loss on the sale.[6]

Example 3-2

Assume that Steve received 100 shares of FZL stock from his grandfather on January 8. On the date of the gift, the stock was worth $15,000. Steve's grandfather originally purchased the stock 10 years earlier for $10,000. What is Steve's initial basis in the stock?

Answer: Because the stock had appreciated in value while Steve's grandfather owned it, Steve's initial basis is a carryover basis of $10,000.

What if: Assume that on the date of the gift, the fair market value of the stock was $8,000. What is Steve's initial basis in the stock?

Answer: Steve's initial basis depends on the price for which he later sells the stock. If Steve sells the stock six months later at a price greater than $10,000, his basis is the $10,000 carryover basis. He will recognize a long-term capital gain because his holding period is 10½ years (i.e., it includes the time his grandfather owned the stock). If he sells the stock six months later at a price less than $8,000, his basis is $8,000, the fair market value at the date of the gift. He will recognize a short-term capital loss because his holding period is only six months (i.e., it begins on the date of the gift). If he sells the stock for a price that is between $10,000 and $8,000, his basis is the sales price and he recognizes no gain or loss (his holding period does not matter).

What if: Assume that Steve inherited the stock from his grandfather on January 8. What is Steve's initial basis if the fair market value is (a) $15,000 and (b) $8,000 at the time of his grandfather's death?

Answer: Steve's initial basis is the fair market value at the date of his grandfather's death regardless of whether the value is greater or less than his grandfather's original cost. If the fair market value is $15,000, Steve's initial basis is $15,000. If the fair market value is $8,000, Steve's initial basis is $8,000. Steve's holding period is long-term regardless of how long he actually holds the stock because it is inherited property.

What if: Assume Steve owns some mountaineering equipment that he uses personally and purchased two years ago for $4,000. On March 20, he converts the equipment into business-use property when the fair market value of the equipment is $5,000. What is Steve's initial basis in the equipment for business purposes?

Answer: Because the equipment appreciated in value before Steve converted it to business use, his basis is his original cost of $4,000. Steve will use the $4,000 as his initial basis for calculating cost recovery and determining his adjusted basis when he sells or otherwise disposes of the equipment.

What if: Assume that the equipment that Steve converts from personal to business use has a fair market value of $3,000 at the date of conversion. What is Steve's initial basis in the equipment for business purposes?

Answer: The equipment declined in value before Steve converted it to business use. In order to prevent Steve from converting his $1,000 personal loss into a business loss, his initial basis for business purposes will depend on whether he subsequently sells the equipment at a gain or loss. His initial basis for loss (and cost recovery) is the $3,000 fair market value at the conversion date. His initial basis for gain is his $4,000 original cost.

[6]Reg. §§1.165-9(b)(2), 1.167(g)-1.

What if: Assume that the equipment that Steve converts from personal to business use has a fair market value of $3,000 at the date of conversion. Two years later, after taking $500 of depreciation deductions, he sells the equipment for $3,300. What is Steve's adjusted basis in the equipment for purposes of determining the gain or loss on the disposition?

Answer: Steve's initial basis for loss was the $3,000 fair market value at the conversion date, and his initial basis for gain was the $4,000 original cost. At the time of the sale, the adjusted basis for loss is $2,500, and the adjusted basis for gain is $3,500. Because the sales price falls between the adjusted basis for gain and the adjusted basis for loss, the adjusted basis is assumed to be equal to the sales price of $3,300, resulting in no gain or loss.

The **adjusted basis** for determining the gain or loss on the sale of an asset is the initial basis (however determined) reduced by depreciation or other types of cost recovery deductions allowed (or allowable) on the property. The adjusted basis of an asset can be determined using the following formula:

Adjusted basis = Initial basis − Cost recovery allowed (or allowable)

Example 3-3

To determine its realized gain or loss on the sale, Teton must calculate the adjusted basis of the machinery it sold in Example 3-1 for $300,000. Teton originally purchased the machinery for $610,000 three years ago. For tax purposes, Teton depreciated the machinery using MACRS (seven-year recovery period, 200 percent declining-balance method, and half-year convention).

The machinery's adjusted basis at the time of the sale is $228,658, computed as follows:

Description	Basis	Explanation
(1) Initial basis	$ 610,000	Example 2-1
(2) Year 1	(87,169)	Example 2-5
(3) Year 2	(149,389)	Example 2-5
(4) Year 3	(106,689)	Example 2-5
(5) Year 4	(38,095)	$76,189 (Example 2-5) × 50% (half-year convention)
(6) Accumulated depreciation	(381,342)	(2) + (3) + (4) + (5)
Adjusted basis	**$228,658**	(1) + (6)

Because businesses generally use more highly accelerated depreciation methods for tax purposes than they do for book purposes, the adjusted tax basis of a particular asset is likely to be lower than the adjusted book basis.

Realized Gain or Loss on Disposition

The amount of gain or loss taxpayers realize on a sale or other disposition of assets is simply the amount they realize minus their adjusted basis in the disposed assets.[7] The formula for computing **realized gain or loss** is as follows:

Gain or (loss) realized = Amount realized − Adjusted basis

Example 3-4

In Example 3-1 we learned that Teton sold machinery for a total amount realized of $300,000, and in Example 3-3 we learned that its basis in the machinery was $228,658. What is Teton's realized gain or loss on the sale of the machinery?

(continued on page 3-6)

[7]§1001(a).

Answer: $71,342, computed as follows:

Description	Amount	Explanation
(1) Amount realized	$300,000	Example 3-1
(2) Adjusted basis	(228,658)	Example 3-3
Gain realized	**$ 71,342**	(1) + (2)

Exhibit 3-1 details the important formulas necessary to determine realized tax gains and losses.

EXHIBIT 3-1 Summary of Formulas for Computing Gain or Loss Realized on an Asset Disposition

Gain (loss) realized = Amount realized − Adjusted basis; where

- Amount realized = Cash received + Fair market value of other property + Buyer's assumption of seller's liabilities − Seller's expenses
- Adjusted basis = Initial basis − Cost recovery deductions

So far, our examples have used one of Teton's asset sales to demonstrate how to compute gain or loss realized when property is sold. However, as we describe in Exhibit 3-2, Teton disposed of several assets during the year. We refer to this exhibit throughout the chapter as a reference point for discussing the tax issues associated with property dispositions.

EXHIBIT 3-2 Teton's Asset Dispositions:* Realized Gain (Loss) for Tax Purposes

Assets	(1) Amount Realized	(2) Initial Basis	(3) Accumulated Depreciation	(4) [(2) − (3)] Adjusted Basis	(5) [(1) − (4)] Gain (Loss) Realized
Machinery	$300,000	$610,000	$381,342	$228,658	$ 71,342
Office furniture	23,000	20,000	14,000	6,000	17,000
Delivery truck	2,000	25,000	17,500	7,500	(5,500)
Warehouse	350,000	275,000	15,000	260,000	90,000
Land	175,000	75,000	0	75,000	100,000
Total gain realized					$272,842

*These are the assets initially purchased by Teton in Example 2-1. In this chapter, we assume that Teton has been in business for four years. For simplicity, we assume Teton did not previously elect any §179 immediate expensing and opted out of bonus depreciation.

Recognized Gain or Loss on Disposition

THE KEY FACTS

- Realized gain or loss:
  - Amount realized less adjusted basis.
- Recognized gain or loss:
  - A realized gain or loss reported on the taxpayer's current-year return.

As a general rule, taxpayers realizing gains and losses during a year must recognize the gains or losses. **Recognized gains or losses** are gains (losses) that increase (decrease) taxpayers' gross income.[8] Thus, taxpayers must report recognized gains and losses on their tax returns. Although taxpayers must immediately recognize the vast majority of realized gains and losses, in certain circumstances they may be allowed to defer recognizing gains to subsequent periods, or they may be allowed to permanently exclude the gains from taxable income. However, taxpayers may also be required to defer losses to later periods and, in more extreme cases, they may have their realized losses permanently disallowed. We address certain tax-deferred provisions later in the chapter.

[8]Recall under the return of capital principle we discussed in the Gross Income and Exclusions chapter, when a taxpayer sells an asset, the taxpayer's adjusted basis is a return of capital and not a deductible expense.

CHARACTER OF GAIN OR LOSS

LO 3-2

In order to determine how a recognized gain or loss affects a taxpayer's income tax liability, the taxpayer must determine the *character* or type of gain or loss recognized. Ultimately, every gain or loss is characterized as either ordinary or capital (long-term or short-term gains or losses). As described below, businesses may recognize §1231 gains or losses on property dispositions that require some intermediary steps, but even these gains or losses are eventually characterized as ordinary or capital (long-term).

The character of a gain or loss is important because gains and losses of different characters are treated differently for tax purposes. For example, ordinary income (loss) is generally taxed at ordinary rates (fully deductible against ordinary income). However, capital gains may be taxed at preferential (lower) rates, while deductions for capital losses are subject to certain restrictions. The character of the gains or losses taxpayers recognize when they sell assets depends on the character of the assets they are selling. The character of an asset depends on how the taxpayer used the asset and how long the taxpayer owned the asset (i.e., the holding period) before selling it.

In general terms, property can be used in a trade or business, treated as inventory or accounts receivable of a business, held for investment, or used for personal purposes. The holding period may be short term (one year or less) or long term (more than a year). Exhibit 3-3 provides a table showing the character of assets (ordinary, capital, or §1231) depending on how taxpayers used the assets and the length of time they held the property before selling it.

THE KEY FACTS

Character of Assets

- Ordinary assets
  - Assets created or used in a taxpayer's trade or business.
  - Business assets held for one year or less.
- Capital assets
  - Assets held for investment purposes.
  - Assets held for personal-use purposes.
- §1231 assets
  - Depreciable assets and land used in a trade or business held for *more* than one year.

EXHIBIT 3-3 Character of Assets Depending on Property Use and Holding Period

	Property Use		
Holding Period	**Trade or Business**	**Investment or Personal-Use Assets***	**Inventory and Accounts Receivable**
Short term (one year or less)	Ordinary	Short-term capital	Ordinary
Long term (more than one year)	§1231†	Long-term capital	Ordinary

*Gains on the sale of personal-use assets are taxable, but losses on the sale of personal-use assets are not deductible.
†As we describe later in the chapter, gain or loss is eventually characterized as ordinary or capital (long-term).

TAXES IN THE REAL WORLD Buyer Beware!

In February 2021, Elon Musk, Tesla's CEO, announced that Tesla would accept Bitcoin as payment in exchange for its products. But buyer beware! If buyers choose to pay with Bitcoin, they may face a higher tax bill. The IRS treats Bitcoin as property and not currency. What that means is that when taxpayers use Bitcoin to pay for products or services, the IRS treats it as a sale of an asset. Because Bitcoin's price has increased from about $11,000 in September 2020 to $58,000 in February 2021, most uses of Bitcoin will require taxpayers to report a gain on their tax return. For example, if a taxpayer acquired a Tesla Model S in February 2021 for $58,000 in Bitcoin purchased three months earlier for $18,000, they would have a gain of $40,000. The tax on the gain at a rate of 37 percent (short-term capital gains rate) would be $14,800, increasing the price of the car by 25.5 percent!

Source: Based on Spencer Jakab, "Tesla Versus the Taxman," *The Wall Street Journal* (March 26, 2021), www.wsj.com/articles/tesla-versus-the-taxman-11616767630.

Ordinary Assets

Ordinary assets are generally assets created or used in a taxpayer's trade or business. For example, inventory is an **ordinary asset** because it is held for sale to customers in the ordinary course of business. Accounts receivable are ordinary assets because receivables are generated from the sale of inventory or business services. Other assets used in a trade or business such as machinery and equipment are also considered to be ordinary assets if they have been used in a business for *one year or less.* For example, if Teton purchased a forklift for the warehouse but sold it six months later, the gain or loss would be ordinary. When taxpayers sell ordinary assets at a gain, they recognize an ordinary gain that is taxed at ordinary rates. When taxpayers sell ordinary assets at a loss, they deduct the loss against other ordinary income.

Capital Assets

A **capital asset** is generally something held for investment (e.g., stocks and bonds) for the **production of income** (i.e., a for-profit activity that doesn't rise to the level of a trade or business) or for personal use (e.g., your car, house, or personal computer).[9] Whether an asset qualifies as a capital asset depends on the purpose for which the taxpayer uses the asset. Thus, the same asset may be considered a capital asset to one taxpayer and an ordinary asset to another taxpayer. For example, a piece of land held as an investment because it is expected to appreciate in value over time is a capital asset to that taxpayer. However, the same piece of land held as inventory by a real estate developer would be an ordinary asset. Finally, the same piece of land would be a §1231 asset if the taxpayer held it for more than one year and used it in a trade or business (e.g., as a parking lot).

Individual taxpayers generally prefer capital gains to ordinary income because certain capital gains are taxed at lower rates and capital gains may offset capital losses that cannot be deducted against ordinary income. Individuals also prefer ordinary losses to capital losses because ordinary losses are deductible without limit, while individuals may deduct only $3,000 of net capital losses against ordinary income each year. Corporate taxpayers may prefer capital gains to ordinary income because capital gains may offset capital losses that they would not be allowed to offset otherwise. C corporations are not allowed to deduct net capital losses, but they are allowed to carry net capital losses back three years and forward five years to offset net gains from capital assets in those years. Exhibit 3-4 reviews the treatment of capital gains and losses for individuals and corporations.

Section 1231 Assets

Section 1231 assets are depreciable assets and land used in a trade or business (including rental property) held by taxpayers for *more* than one year.[10] At a general level, when a taxpayer sells a §1231 asset, the taxpayer recognizes a §1231 gain or loss. As discussed above, however, ultimately §1231 gains or losses are characterized as ordinary or capital on a taxpayer's return. When taxpayers sell multiple §1231 assets during the year, they combine or "net" their §1231 gains and §1231 losses together. If the netting results in a net §1231 gain, the net gain is treated as a long-term capital gain. If the netting results in a net §1231 loss, the net loss is treated as an ordinary loss. Because net §1231 gains are treated as capital gains and §1231 losses are treated as ordinary losses, §1231 assets are tax-favored relative to other types of assets.

As we discuss below, §1231 gains on individual depreciable assets may be recharacterized as ordinary income under the depreciation recapture rules. However, because land is not depreciable, when taxpayers sell or otherwise dispose of land that qualifies as §1231 property, the gain or loss from the sale is always characterized as a §1231 gain or loss. Thus, we refer to land as a pure §1231 asset.

[9]§1221 defines what is not a capital asset. Broadly speaking, a *capital asset* is any property *other than* property used in a trade or business (e.g., inventory, manufacturing equipment) or accounts (or notes) receivable acquired in a business from the sale of services or property.

[10]As noted above, property used in a trade or business and held for one year or less is ordinary income property.

EXHIBIT 3-4 Review of Capital Gains and Losses

Taxpayer Type	Preferential Rates	Loss Limitations
Individuals	• Net capital gains on assets held more than one year are taxed at 15% (0% to the extent taxable income including the gain is below the maximum 0% breakpoint and 20% to the extent taxable income including capital gains is above the maximum 15% breakpoint). When determining which capital gains tax rate applies, capital gains that fall within the range of taxable income specified in the tax rate schedules are included in taxable income last.) • Unrecaptured §1250 gains on real property held more than one year remaining after the netting process are taxed at a maximum rate of 25%. • Net gains on collectibles held for more than a year and qualified small business stock (§1202) are taxed at a maximum rate of 28%. • Net gains from capital assets held one year or less are taxed at ordinary rates.	• Individuals may annually deduct up to $3,000 of net capital losses against ordinary income. • Losses can be carried forward indefinitely but not carried back.
C Corporations	• No preferential rates; taxed at ordinary rates.	• No offset against ordinary income. • Net capital losses can generally be carried back three years and forward five years to offset net gains from capital assets in those years.

Example 3-5

In order to acquire another parcel of land to expand its manufacturing capabilities, Teton sold five acres of land that it had been using in its trade or business for $175,000. Teton purchased the land several years ago for $75,000. What are the amount and character of Teton's gain recognized on the land?

Answer: $100,000 §1231 gain, calculated as follows:

Description	Amount	Explanation
(1) Amount realized	$ 175,000	
(2) Original basis and current adjusted basis	75,000	
Gain (loss) realized and recognized	**$100,000**	(1) – (2) §1231 gain

What if: Assume that Teton sold the land for $50,000. What would be the character of the $25,000 loss it would recognize?

Answer: §1231 loss.

What if: Assume that the land was the only asset Teton sold during the year. How would the §1231 gain or §1231 loss on the sale ultimately be characterized on its tax return?

Answer: If Teton recognized a §1231 gain on the sale, it would be characterized as a long-term capital gain on its return. If Teton recognized a §1231 loss on the sale, it would be characterized as an ordinary loss.

LO 3-3

DEPRECIATION RECAPTURE

Although Congress intended for businesses to receive favorable treatment on economic gains from the economic *appreciation* of §1231 assets, it did not intend for this favorable treatment to apply to gains that were created artificially through depreciation deductions that offset ordinary income. For example, if a taxpayer purchases an asset for $100 and sells it three years later for the same amount, we would generally agree that there is no economic gain on the disposition of the asset. However, if the taxpayer claimed depreciation deductions of $70 during the three years of ownership, the taxpayer would recognize a $70 gain on the disposition simply because the depreciation deductions reduced the asset's adjusted basis. Depreciation is an ordinary deduction that offsets income that would otherwise be taxed at ordinary rates.

Absent tax rules to the contrary, the gain recognized by the taxpayer upon the sale of the asset would be treated as long-term capital gain and would be taxed at a preferential rate (for individuals). Thus, depreciation deductions save taxes at the ordinary rate, but the gains created by depreciation generate income taxed at a preferential rate. This potential asymmetrical treatment led Congress to implement the concept of **depreciation recapture.** Depreciation recapture potentially applies to gains (but not losses) on the sale of depreciable or amortizable business property. When depreciation recapture applies, it changes the character of the gain on the sale of a §1231 asset (all or a portion of the gain) from §1231 gain into ordinary income. Note, however, that depreciation recapture does not affect losses recognized on the disposition of §1231 assets.

The method for computing the amount of depreciation recapture depends on the type of §1231 asset the taxpayer is selling (personal property or real property). As presented in Exhibit 3-5, §1231 assets can be categorized as pure §1231 assets (land), §1245 assets (personal property), or §1250 assets (real property). Whether personal or real property is sold, it is important to understand that depreciation recapture changes only the *character* but not the *amount* of gain recognized.

EXHIBIT 3-5 §1231 Asset Types

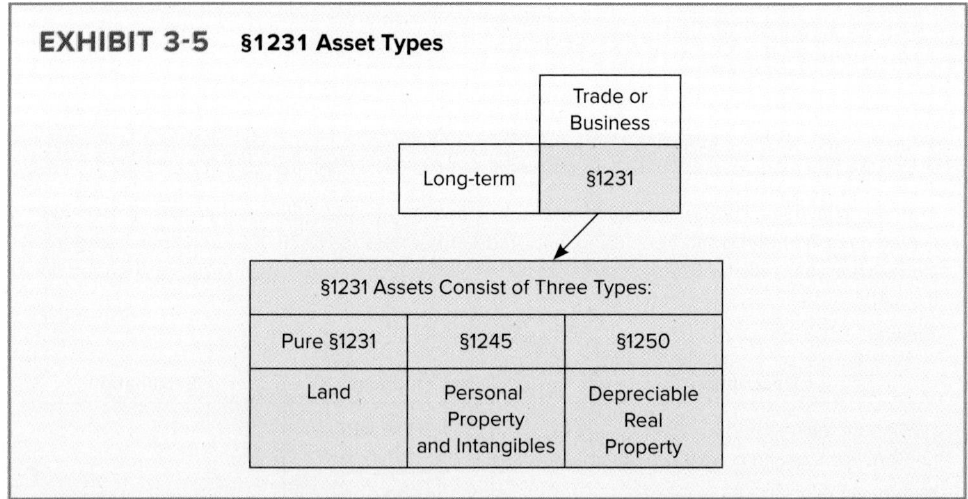

Section 1245 Property

Tangible personal property (e.g., machinery, equipment, and automobiles) and amortizable intangible property (e.g., patents, copyrights, and purchased goodwill) are a subset of §1231 property known as **§1245 property.**[11] The gain from the sale of §1245 property is characterized as ordinary income to the extent the gain was created by depreciation or amortization deductions. The amount of *ordinary income* (§1245 depreciation recapture) taxpayers

[11]An exception in the law is that §1245 property also includes nonresidential real property placed in service between 1981 and 1986 (ACRS) for which the taxpayer elected accelerated depreciation.

recognize when they sell §1245 property is the lesser of (1) recognized gain on the sale *or* (2) total accumulated depreciation (or amortization) on the asset.[12] The remainder of any recognized gain is characterized as §1231 gain.[13] The sum of the ordinary income (due to depreciation recapture) and the §1231 gain on the sale equals the *total* gain recognized because depreciation recapture changes only the character of the gain, not the amount.

When taxpayers sell or dispose of §1245 property, they encounter one of the following three scenarios involving gain or loss:

Scenario 1: They recognize a gain created solely through depreciation deductions.

Scenario 2: They recognize a gain created through both depreciation deductions and actual asset appreciation.

Scenario 3: They recognize a loss.

The following discussion considers each of these scenarios.

THE KEY FACTS

§1245 Assets

- Personal property and amortizable intangible assets are §1245 assets.
- The lesser of (1) gain recognized or (2) accumulated depreciation is recaptured (characterized) as ordinary income under §1245.
- Any remaining gain is §1231 gain.
- There is no depreciation recapture on assets sold at a loss.

Scenario 1: Gain Created Solely through Cost Recovery Deductions Most §1231 assets that experience wear and tear or obsolescence generally do not appreciate in value. Thus, when a taxpayer sells these types of assets at a gain, the gain is usually created because the taxpayer's depreciation deductions associated with the asset reduced the asset's adjusted basis faster than the real decline in the asset's economic value. That is, the entire gain is artificially generated through depreciation, and absent these deductions, the taxpayer would recognize a loss on the sale of the asset. Therefore, the entire gain on the disposition is recaptured (or recharacterized) as ordinary income under §1245 (recall that without depreciation recapture, the gain would be §1231 gain, which can generate long-term capital gain and could create a double benefit for the taxpayer: ordinary depreciation deductions and preferentially taxed capital gain upon disposition).

Example 3-6

As indicated in Exhibit 3-2, Teton sold machinery for $300,000. What are the amount and character of the gain Teton recognizes on the sale?

Answer: $71,342 of ordinary income under the §1245 depreciation recapture rules and $0 of §1231 gain, computed as follows:

Machinery Sale: Scenario 1
(Original scenario sales price = $300,000)

Description	Amount	Explanation
(1) Amount realized	$300,000	Exhibit 3-2
(2) Original basis	610,000	Exhibit 3-2
(3) Accumulated depreciation	381,342	Exhibit 3-2
(4) Adjusted basis	$228,658	(2) – (3)
(5) Gain (loss) recognized	71,342	(1) – (4)
(6) Ordinary income (§1245 depreciation recapture)	**$ 71,342**	Lesser of (3) or (5)
§1231 gain	**0**	(5) – (6)

Note that in this situation, because Teton's entire gain is created through depreciation deductions reducing the basis, the entire gain is treated as ordinary income under §1245.

(continued on page 3-12)

[12]Section 1245 recapture is commonly referred to as "full" depreciation recapture because it may cause a taxpayer to recapture the entire accumulated depreciation amount as ordinary income. Section 1245 recapture applies notwithstanding any other provision of the Internal Revenue Code (i.e., depreciation recapture takes precedence over all other tax rules, such as installment sales).

[13]As a practical matter, taxpayers are unlikely to recognize any §1231 gain on the disposition of personal property because the real economic value of most tangible personal property does not increase over time as the property is used.

What if: What would be the amount and character of Teton's gain without the depreciation recapture rules?

Answer: $71,342 of §1231 gain. Note that the recapture rules change the character of the gain but not the amount of the gain.

Both §179 expensing and bonus depreciation allow taxpayers to accelerate the depreciation taken on assets in the year of acquisition. Under current law, many taxpayers will fully deduct the cost of acquired assets. These provisions, however, require that taxpayers reduce the basis of the assets by the amount of accumulated depreciation. When taxpayers deduct the full cost of an asset under these rules, the asset's basis is reduced to zero. As a result, taxpayers will have larger gains than under prior law, and the gains will typically be ordinary in character.

Scenario 2: Gain Due to Both Cost Recovery Deductions and Asset Appreciation Assets subject to cost recovery deductions may actually *appreciate* in value over time. When these assets are sold, the recognized gain must be divided into ordinary gain from depreciation recapture and §1231 gain. The portion of the gain created through cost recovery deductions is recaptured as ordinary income. The remaining gain (i.e., the gain due to economic appreciation) is §1231 gain.

Example 3-7

What if: Let's assume the same facts as in Example 3-6 and Exhibit 3-2, except that Teton sells the machinery for $620,000. What are the amount and character of the gain Teton would recognize on this sale?

Answer: $381,342 of ordinary income under the §1245 depreciation recapture rules and $10,000 of §1231 gain due to the asset's economic appreciation, computed as follows:

Machinery Sale: Scenario 2
(Assumed sales price = $620,000)

Description	Amount	Explanation
(1) Amount realized	$ 620,000	
(2) Original basis	610,000	Exhibit 3-2
(3) Accumulated depreciation	381,342	Exhibit 3-2
(4) Adjusted basis	$ 228,658	(2) − (3)
(5) Gain (loss) recognized	391,342	(1) − (4)
(6) Ordinary income (§1245 depreciation recapture)	**$381,342**	Lesser of (3) or (5)
§1231 gain	**$ 10,000**	(5) − (6)

Note that taxpayers can quickly determine their §1231 gain (if any) when they sell §1245 property by subtracting the asset's *initial* basis from the amount realized. For example, in Example 3-7, the §1231 gain is $10,000 ($620,000 amount realized less the $610,000 original basis).

Scenario 3: Asset Sold at a Loss Many §1231 assets, such as computer equipment or automobiles, tend to decline in value faster than the corresponding depreciation deductions reduce the asset's adjusted basis. When taxpayers sell or dispose of these assets before the assets are fully depreciated, they recognize a loss on the disposition. Because the depreciation recapture rules don't apply to losses, taxpayers selling §1245 property at a loss recognize a §1231 loss.

Example 3-8

What if: Let's assume the same facts as in Example 3-6 and Exhibit 3-2, except that Teton sells the machinery for $180,000. What are the amount and character of the gain or loss Teton would recognize on this sale?

Answer: A $48,658 §1231 loss, computed as follows:

Machinery Sale: Scenario 3 (Assumed sales price = $180,000)		
Description	**Amount**	**Explanation**
(1) Amount realized	$180,000	
(2) Initial basis	610,000	Exhibit 3-2
(3) Accumulated depreciation	381,342	Exhibit 3-2
(4) Adjusted basis	$228,658	(2) – (3)
(5) Gain (loss) recognized	(48,658)	(1) – (4)
(6) Ordinary income (§1245 depreciation recapture)	$ 0	Lesser of (3) or (5) (limited to $0)
§1231 (loss)	**$(48,658)**	(5) – (6)

Exhibit 3-6 graphically illustrates the §1245 depreciation recapture computations for the machinery sold in Scenarios 1, 2, and 3, presented in Examples 3-6, 3-7, and 3-8, respectively.[14]

EXHIBIT 3-6 Machinery §1245 Depreciation Recapture Scenarios 1, 2, and 3

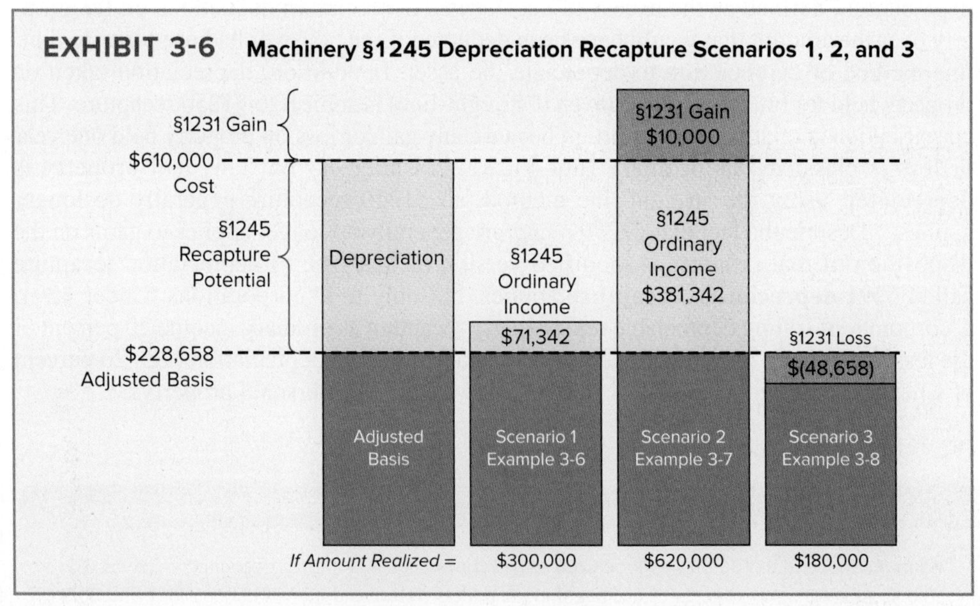

Example 3-9

In Example 3-6 (Scenario 1), we characterized the gain Teton recognized when it sold its machinery. For completeness, let's characterize the gain or loss Teton recognized on the other two §1245 assets it sold during the year (see Exhibit 3-2). Teton sold its office furniture for $23,000 and its delivery truck for $2,000. What are the amount and character of gain or loss Teton recognizes on the sale of the office furniture and the delivery truck?

(continued on page 3-14)

[14]The authors thank PwC for allowing us to use this exhibit.

Answer: Office furniture: $14,000 ordinary income and $3,000 §1231 gain. Delivery truck: $5,500 §1231 loss. The computations supporting the answers are as follows:

Description	Office Furniture	Delivery Truck	Explanation
(1) Amount realized	$ 23,000	$ 2,000	Exhibit 3-2
(2) Initial basis	20,000	25,000	Exhibit 3-2
(3) Accumulated depreciation	14,000	17,500	Exhibit 3-2
(4) Adjusted basis	$ 6,000	$ 7,500	(2) – (3)
(5) Gain (loss) recognized	17,000	(5,500)	(1) – (4)
(6) Ordinary income (§1245 depreciation recapture)	**$14,000**	**$ 0**	Lesser of (3) or (5), limited to $0
§1231 gain (loss)	**$ 3,000**	**$(5,500)**	(5) – (6)

Section 1250 Depreciation Recapture for Real Property

Depreciable real property, such as an office building or a warehouse, sold at a gain is *not* subject to §1245 depreciation recapture. Rather, it is potentially subject to a different type of recapture called §1250 depreciation recapture. Thus, depreciable real property is frequently referred to as **§1250 property.** Under §1250, when depreciable real property is sold at a gain, the amount of gain recaptured as ordinary income is limited to *additional* depreciation, defined as the excess of *accelerated* depreciation deductions on the property over the amount that would have been deducted if the taxpayer had used the straight-line method of depreciation to depreciate the asset. In addition, depreciation taken on property held for one year or less (even if straight-line) is subject to §1250 recapture. This classification is relatively unimportant because any gain or loss on property held one year or less is classified as ordinary (not §1231).[15] Under current law, real property is depreciated using the straight-line method, so §1250 recapture generally no longer applies.[16] Despite the fact that *§1250 recapture* generally no longer applies to gains on the disposition of real property, a modified version of this type of depreciation recapture called **§291 depreciation recapture** applies, but only to C corporations. Under §291, C corporations selling depreciable real property recapture as ordinary income 20 percent of the lesser of (1) the recognized gain or (2) the accumulated depreciation (i.e., 20 percent of what §1245 recapture would be if the asset was tangible personal property).

Example 3-10

What if: Suppose that Teton was organized as a C corporation and that, as described in Exhibit 3-2, it sold its existing warehouse. Let's assume the same facts: Teton sold the warehouse for $350,000, it initially purchased the warehouse for $275,000, and it has deducted $15,000 of straight-line depreciation deductions as of the date of the sale. What is Teton's recognized gain on the sale and what is the character of its gain on the sale?

[15]Section 1250 recapture is commonly referred to as *partial depreciation recapture*.

[16]Accelerated depreciation was allowed for real property placed in service before 1987. Such property had a maximum recovery period of 19 years, which means that as of 2005 all of this property is now fully depreciated under both the accelerated and straight-line depreciation methods. One instance where §1250 recapture might apply is for qualified leasehold improvements placed in service before 2018 and depreciated over 15 years.

Answer: $90,000 gain recognized; $3,000 ordinary income and $87,000 §1231 gain, computed as follows:

Description	Amount	Explanation
(1) Amount realized	$350,000	Exhibit 3-2
(2) Initial basis	275,000	Exhibit 3-2
(3) Accumulated depreciation	15,000	Exhibit 3-2
(4) Adjusted basis	$260,000	(2) − (3)
(5) Gain (loss) recognized	**$ 90,000**	(1) − (4)
(6) Lesser of accumulated depreciation or recognized gain	15,000	Lesser of (3) or (5)
(7) §291 recapture (ordinary income)	**$ 3,000**	20% × (6)
§1231 gain	**$ 87,000**	(5) − (7)

OTHER PROVISIONS AFFECTING THE RATE AT WHICH GAINS ARE TAXED

LO 3-4

Other provisions, other than depreciation recapture, may affect the rate at which gains are taxed. The first potentially applies when individuals sell §1250 property at a gain, and the second potentially applies when taxpayers sell property to related persons at a gain.

Unrecaptured §1250 Gain for Individuals

Except for assets held one year or less and select instances for qualified leasehold property, neither C corporations nor individuals recognize §1250 recapture on the sale of §1250 property when it is sold at a gain. Instead, C corporations recognize §291 recapture as ordinary income on the sale of these assets. Individuals, however, do not recognize ordinary income from the sale of §1250 property when it is held long term. Rather, individual taxpayers treat a gain resulting from the disposition of §1250 property as a §1231 gain and combine it with other §1231 gains and losses to determine whether a net §1231 gain or a net §1231 loss results for the year.

After the §1231 netting process (described below), if the gain on the sale of the §1250 property is ultimately determined to be a long-term capital gain, the taxpayer must determine the rate at which the gain will be taxed. Tax policy makers have determined that the portion of the gain caused by depreciation deductions reducing the basis, called **unrecaptured §1250 gain,** should be taxed at a maximum rate of 25 percent (taxed at the ordinary rate if the ordinary rate is lower than 25 percent) and not the 0/15/20 percent rate generally applicable to other types of long-term capital gains. Consequently, when an individual sells §1250 property at a gain, the amount of the gain taxed at a maximum rate of 25 percent is the *lesser* of (1) the recognized gain or (2) the accumulated depreciation on the asset.[17] Thus, the amount of unrecaptured §1250 gain is the same as the depreciation recapture would be if it were §1245 property. The remainder of the gain is taxed at a maximum rate of 0/15/20 percent.[18]

THE KEY FACTS

Unrecaptured §1250 Gains

- Depreciable real property sold at a gain is §1250 property but is no longer subject to §1250 recapture unless it is held 12 months or less and bought and sold in different years.
- The lesser of the (1) recognized gain or (2) accumulated depreciation on the assets is called *unrecaptured* §1250 gain.
- Unrecaptured §1250 gain is §1231 gain that, if ultimately characterized as a long-term capital gain, is taxed at a maximum rate of 25 percent.

Example 3-11

Teton bought its warehouse for $275,000, depreciated it $15,000, and sold it for $350,000. What are the amount and character of the gain Teton (and thus Steve) reports on the sale? (Recall that income of sole proprietorships is taxed directly to the owner of the business.)

(continued on page 3-16)

[17]The amount taxed at a maximum rate of 25 percent cannot exceed the amount of the taxpayer's net §1231 gain.

[18]These rates (25 or 0/15/20 percent) apply to net §1231 gains after a netting process for capital gains, which we discuss in a different chapter.

Answer: $90,000 of §1231 gain, which includes $15,000 of unrecaptured §1250 gain, computed as follows:

Description	Amount	Explanation
(1) Amount realized	$350,000	Exhibit 3-2
(2) Original basis	275,000	Exhibit 3-2
(3) Accumulated depreciation	15,000	Exhibit 3-2
(4) Adjusted basis	$260,000	(2) − (3)
(5) Gain (loss) recognized	90,000	(1) − (4)
(6) Unrecaptured §1250 gain	$ 15,000	Lesser of (3) or (5)
(7) Remaining §1231 gain	$ 75,000	(5) − (6)
Total §1231 gain	**$ 90,000**	(6) + (7)

What if: Suppose Steve's marginal ordinary tax rate is 32 percent. What amount of tax will he pay on the gain (assuming no other asset dispositions)?

Answer: $15,000, computed as follows:

Description	(1) Gain	(2) Rate	(1) × (2) Tax	Explanation
Long-term capital gain (unrecaptured §1250 gain portion)	$15,000	25%	$ 3,750	This is the gain due to depreciation deductions.
Long-term capital gain (15% portion)	75,000	15%	11,250	Taxed at 15% because Steve's taxable income including the capital gain is below the maximum 15%/20% breakpoint.
Totals	$90,000		**$15,000**	

Because Steve did not sell any other §1231 assets during the year, the entire §1231 gain is treated as a long-term capital gain that is split into a portion taxed at 25 percent and a portion taxed at 15 percent.

THE KEY FACTS

§1239 Related-Person Transactions

- All gain recognized from selling property that is a depreciable asset to a related buyer is ordinary income (regardless of the character of the asset to the seller).
- Related persons are defined in §1239 and include:
  - An individual and the individual's controlled corporation or partnership.
  - A taxpayer and any trust in which the taxpayer (or spouse) is a beneficiary.

Characterizing Gains on the Sale of Depreciable Property to Related Persons

Under §1239, when a taxpayer sells property to a *related person* and the property is depreciable property to the *buyer,* the entire gain on the sale is characterized as ordinary income to the *seller*.[19] Without this provision, related taxpayers could create tax savings by currently generating capital or §1231 gains through selling appreciated assets to related persons who would receive future ordinary deductions through depreciation expense on the basis of the property (stepped up to fair market value through the sale) acquired in the transaction.

The §1239 provision is different from depreciation recapture in the sense that the seller is required to recognize ordinary income for depreciation deductions the buyer will receive *in the future,* while depreciation recapture requires taxpayers to recognize ordinary income for depreciation deductions they have received *in the past.* In both cases, however, the tax laws are designed to provide symmetry between the character of deductions an asset generates and the character of income the asset generates when it is sold.

[19]§1239. §707(b)(2) contains a similar provision for partnerships.

For purposes of §1239, a related person includes an individual and their controlled (more than 50 percent owned) corporation or partnership or a taxpayer and any trust in which the taxpayer (or spouse) is a beneficiary.[20]

Example 3-12

What if: Suppose that Teton is organized as a C corporation and Steve is the sole shareholder. Steve sells equipment that he was using for personal purposes to Teton for $90,000 (he originally purchased the equipment for $80,000). The equipment was a capital asset to Steve because he had been using it for personal purposes (he did not depreciate it). What are the amount and character of the gain Steve would recognize on the sale?

Answer: $10,000 of ordinary income (amount realized $90,000 – $80,000 adjusted basis). Even though Steve is selling what is a capital asset to him, because it is a depreciable asset to Teton and because Steve and Teton are considered to be related persons, Steve is required to characterize the entire amount of gain as ordinary under §1239. Without the §1239 provision, Steve would have recognized a capital gain.

Exhibit 3-7 provides a flowchart for determining the character of gains and losses on the taxable sale of assets used in a trade or business.

CALCULATING NET §1231 GAINS OR LOSSES

LO 3-5

Once taxpayers determine the amount and character of gain or loss they recognize on *each* §1231 asset they sell during the year, they still have work to do to determine whether the gains or losses will be treated as ordinary or capital. After recharacterizing §1231 gain as ordinary income under the §1245 and §291 (if applicable) depreciation recapture rules and the §1239 recharacterization rules, the remaining §1231 gains and losses are netted together.[21] Recall that a portion of the §1231 gains may include unrecaptured §1250 gains that are taxed at a maximum of 25 percent. When netting the §1231 losses against §1231 gains, the losses first offset regular §1231 gains before offsetting unrecaptured §1250 gains. If the gains exceed the losses, the net gain becomes a long-term capital gain (a portion of which may be taxed at the maximum rate of 25 percent). If the losses exceed the gains, the net loss is treated as an ordinary loss.

A taxpayer could obtain significant tax benefits by discovering a way to have all §1231 gains treated as long-term capital gains and all §1231 losses treated as ordinary losses. The *annual* netting process makes this task impossible for a *particular* year. However, a taxpayer who owns multiple §1231 assets could sell the §1231 loss assets at the end of year 1 and the §1231 gain assets at the beginning of year 2. The taxpayer could benefit from this strategy in three ways: (1) accelerating losses into year 1, (2) deferring gains until year 2, and (3) favorably characterizing the gains and losses due to the §1231 netting process. The **§1231 look-back rule** limits the benefits from implementing this strategy.

THE KEY FACTS

Netting and Look-Back Rule

- §1231 gains and losses from individual asset dispositions are annually netted together.
- Net §1231 gains may be recharacterized as ordinary income under the §1231 look-back rule.

Section 1231 Look-Back Rule

The §1231 look-back rule is a *nondepreciation* recapture rule that applies in situations like the one we just described to turn what would otherwise be §1231 gain into ordinary income. That is, the rule affects the character but not the amount of gains on which a

[20]Additional related persons for purposes of §1239 include two corporations that are members of the same controlled group, a corporation and a partnership if the same person owns more than 50 percent of both entities, two S corporations controlled by the same person, and an S corporation and a C corporation controlled by the same person.

[21]If any of the §1231 gains and losses result from casualty or theft, these gains and losses are netted together first. If a net loss results, the net loss from §1231 casualty and theft events is treated as ordinary loss. Net gains from casualty and theft are treated as other §1231 gains and continue through the normal §1231 netting process.

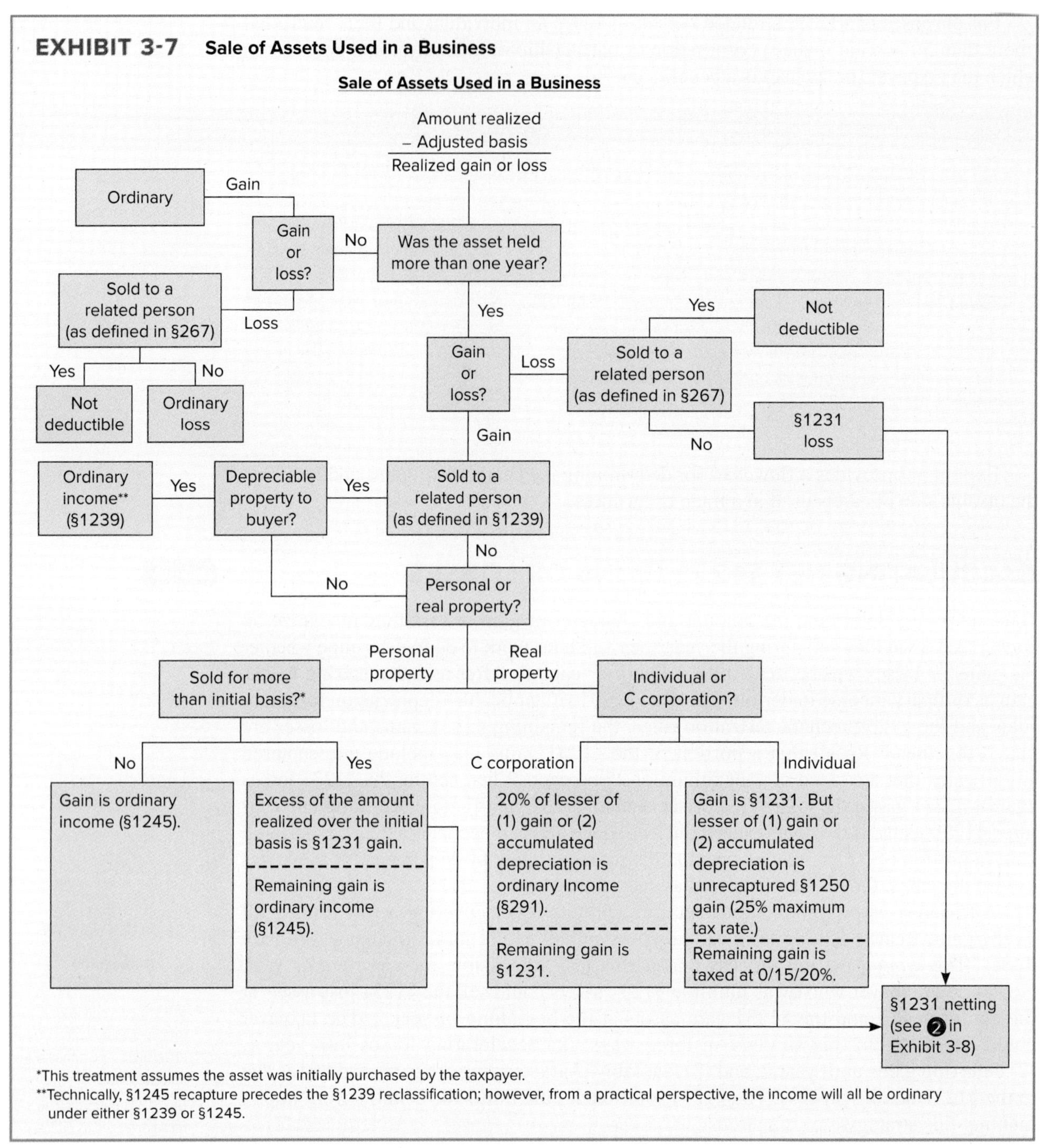

EXHIBIT 3-7 **Sale of Assets Used in a Business**

*This treatment assumes the asset was initially purchased by the taxpayer.

**Technically, §1245 recapture precedes the §1239 reclassification; however, from a practical perspective, the income will all be ordinary under either §1239 or §1245.

taxpayer is taxed. In general terms, the §1231 look-back rule is designed to require taxpayers who recognize net §1231 gains in the current year to recapture (recharacterize) current-year gains as ordinary to the extent the taxpayer deducted ordinary net §1231 losses in prior years. Without the look-back rule, taxpayers could carefully time the year in which the §1231 assets were sold to maximize the tax benefits.

In specific terms, the §1231 look-back rule indicates that when a taxpayer recognizes a net §1231 gain for a year, the taxpayer must "look back" to the *five-year* period preceding the current tax year to determine whether, during that period, the taxpayer recognized any **nonrecaptured net §1231 losses,** which are losses that were deducted as ordinary losses that have not caused subsequent §1231 gains to be recharacterized as ordinary income. The taxpayer starts the process by looking back to the year five years prior to the beginning of the current year. If the taxpayer has recognized a net §1231 loss in that period and has not previously recaptured the loss (by causing a subsequent §1231 gain to be recharacterized as ordinary) in a subsequent year (but prior to the current year), the taxpayer must recharacterize the *current-year* net §1231 gain as ordinary income to the extent of that prior-year nonrecaptured net §1231 loss. If the current-year net §1231 gain includes unrecaptured §1250 gains, the look-back rule requires the unrecaptured §1250 gains to be recharacterized as ordinary before other §1231 gains. The prior-year loss is then considered "recaptured," to the extent it caused the current-year gain to be treated as ordinary income.

If the current-year net §1231 gain exceeds the nonrecaptured net §1231 loss from the year five years prior, the taxpayer repeats the process for the year four years prior, and then three years prior, and so on. A prior year's nonrecaptured net losses are not netted against the current year's gains (they don't offset the current-year gains); rather, they cause the taxpayer to recharacterize a net §1231 gain or a portion of that gain (that would otherwise be characterized as a long-term capital gain) as ordinary income in the current year.

Example 3-13

What if: Suppose that Teton began business in year 1 and that it recognized a $7,000 net §1231 loss in year 1. Assume that the current year is year 6 and that Teton reports a ***net*** §1231 gain of $25,000 for the year. Teton did not recognize any §1231 gains or losses in years 2–5. For year 6, what would be the ultimate character of the $25,000 net §1231 gain?

Answer: $7,000 ordinary income and $18,000 long-term capital gain. Because it recognized a net §1231 loss in year 1, it must recharacterize $7,000 of its net §1231 gain in year 6 as ordinary income. The remaining $18,000 §1231 gain is taxed as long-term capital gain.

What if: Assume the same facts as above, except that Teton also recognized a $2,000 net §1231 loss in year 5. For year 6, what would be the ultimate character of the $25,000 net §1231 gain?

Answer: $9,000 ordinary income and $16,000 long-term capital gain. Note that the overall gain is still $25,000, but to the extent of the $7,000 loss in year 1 and the $2,000 loss in year 5, the §1231 gain is recharacterized as ordinary income under the §1231 look-back rule.

ETHICS

Emma Bean operates a real estate development company and wants to sell some of her business equipment and a piece of land that is used as a parking lot for her business. She expects to realize a $10,000 loss on the equipment and a $15,000 gain on the land. Emma has talked to her accountant and has learned about the look-back rule for §1231 property. To avoid any negative effects, she has decided to game the system and sell the land this year and then sell the equipment early next year. What do you think about her strategy to avoid the look-back rule?

As we've mentioned before, ultimately, all of a taxpayer's §1231 gains and losses must be characterized as ordinary or capital for purposes of determining the taxpayer's tax liability. Exhibit 3-8 summarizes the process of characterizing §1231 gains and losses as ordinary or capital.

The following provides details on Steps 1–3 from Exhibit 3-8:

Step 1: Apply the *depreciation* recapture rules (and the §1239 rule) to §1231 assets sold at a gain (any recaptured amounts become ordinary).

Step 2: Net the remaining §1231 gains with the §1231 losses. The §1231 losses offset regular §1231 gains before the unrecaptured §1250 gains. If the netting process yields a §1231 loss, the net §1231 loss becomes an ordinary loss.

Step 3: If the netting process produces a net §1231 gain, the taxpayer applies the §1231 look-back rule to determine if any of the remaining §1231 gain should be recharacterized as ordinary gain. Under the look-back rule, the unrecaptured §1250 gains will be recharacterized before the regular §1231 gains. Any gain remaining after applying the look-back rule is treated as long-term capital gain (including unrecaptured §1250 gain). This gain is included in the capital gains netting process.

EXHIBIT 3-8 §1231 Netting Process

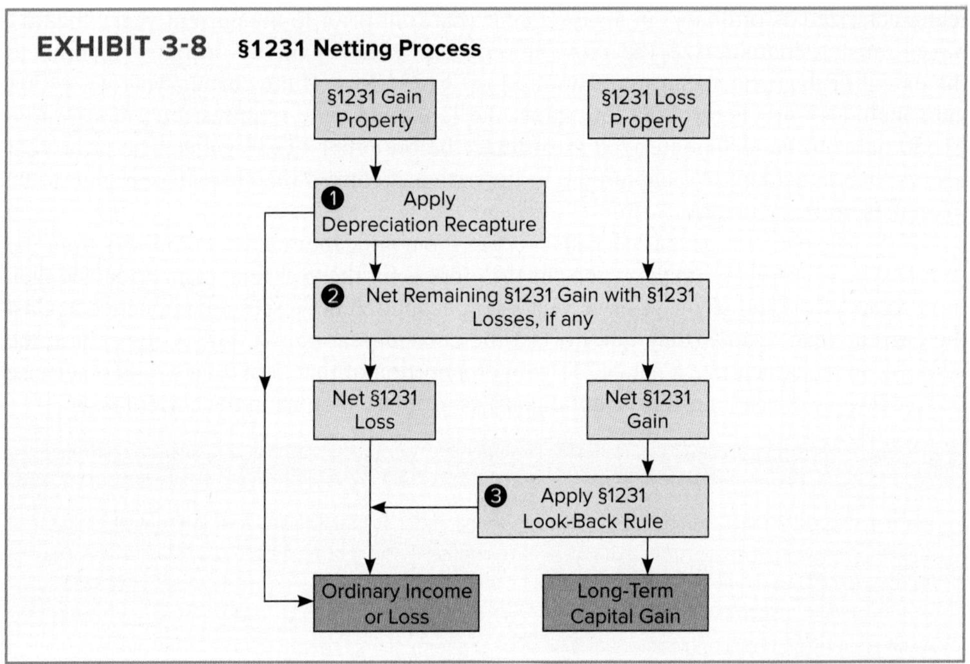

GAIN OR LOSS SUMMARY

As indicated in Exhibit 3-2, Teton sold several assets during the year. Exhibit 3-9 summarizes the character of the gain or loss Teton (and thus Steve) recognized on each asset sale.

So, how would this information be reported on Steve's tax return? Exhibit 3-10 provides Steve's Form 4797, which summarizes Teton's property transactions and divides the gains and losses between the ordinary gain of $95,342 and the §1231 gain of $177,500. Because the net §1231 gain is treated as a long-term capital gain, it flows to Steve's Schedule D (the form for reporting capital gains and losses). Steve's Schedule D is presented in Exhibit 3-11.

EXHIBIT 3-9 Summary of Teton Gains and Losses on Property Dispositions

Asset	(1) §1245 Ordinary Gain	(2) Total Ordinary Gain	(3) §1231 Gain (Loss)	(2) + (3) Total Gain
Machinery	$71,342	$71,342	$ 0	$ 71,342
Office furniture	14,000	14,000	3,000	17,000
Delivery truck	0	0	(5,500)	(5,500)
Warehouse	0	0	90,000*	90,000
Land	0	0	100,000	100,000
§1231 look-back	0	10,000	(10,000)†	0
Totals	$85,342	$95,342	$177,500*	$272,842

*Because the warehouse is §1231 property, the $90,000 gain is included in the §1231 gain (loss) column. Further, $15,000 of the $90,000 gain is considered unrecaptured §1250 gain (see Example 3-11).

†This exhibit assumes that Teton had $10,000 of net §1231 losses in the prior five years. Following the application of the look-back rule, $172,500 of the §1231 gains will be treated as long-term capital gains taxed at 0/15/20 percent and $5,000 of the §1231 gains will be treated as long-term capital gains taxed at a maximum rate of 25 percent.

EXHIBIT 3-10 Teton's (on Steve's return) Form 4797

Form **4797**

Department of the Treasury
Internal Revenue Service

Sales of Business Property

(Also Involuntary Conversions and Recapture Amounts Under Sections 179 and 280F(b)(2))

► **Attach to your tax return.**

► **Go to *www.irs.gov/Form4797* for instructions and the latest information.**

OMB No. 1545-0184

2021

Attachment Sequence No. **27**

Name(s) shown on return: **Steve Dallimore (Teton Mountaineering Technology, LLC)**

Identifying number

1a	Enter the gross proceeds from sales or exchanges reported to you for 2021 on Form(s) 1099-B or 1099-S (or substitute statement) that you are including on line 2, 10, or 20. See instructions	1a	
b	Enter the total amount of gain that you are including on lines 2, 10, and 24 due to the partial dispositions of MACRS assets	1b	
c	Enter the total amount of loss that you are including on lines 2 and 10 due to the partial dispositions of MACRS assets	1c	

Part I **Sales or Exchanges of Property Used in a Trade or Business and Involuntary Conversions From Other Than Casualty or Theft—Most Property Held More Than 1 Year** (see instructions)

2 (a) Description of property	(b) Date acquired (mo., day, yr.)	(c) Date sold (mo., day, yr.)	(d) Gross sales price	(e) Depreciation allowed or allowable since acquisition	(f) Cost or other basis, plus improvements and expense of sale	(g) Gain or (loss) Subtract (f) from the sum of (d) and (e)
Delivery truck	**Yr 0**	**Yr 4**	**2,000**	**17,500**	**25,000**	**(5,500)**
Land	**Yr 0**	**Yr 4**	**175,000**	**0**	**75,000**	**100,000**

3	Gain, if any, from Form 4684, line 39	3	
4	Section 1231 gain from installment sales from Form 6252, line 26 or 37	4	
5	Section 1231 gain or (loss) from like-kind exchanges from Form 8824	5	
6	Gain, if any, from line 32, from other than casualty or theft	6	**93,000**
7	Combine lines 2 through 6. Enter the gain or (loss) here and on the appropriate line as follows	7	**187,500**

Partnerships and S corporations. Report the gain or (loss) following the instructions for Form 1065, Schedule K, line 10, or Form 1120-S, Schedule K, line 9. Skip lines 8, 9, 11, and 12 below.

Individuals, partners, S corporation shareholders, and all others. If line 7 is zero or a loss, enter the amount from line 7 on line 11 below and skip lines 8 and 9. If line 7 is a gain and you didn't have any prior year section 1231 losses, or they were recaptured in an earlier year, enter the gain from line 7 as a long-term capital gain on the Schedule D filed with your return and skip lines 8, 9, 11, and 12 below.

8	Nonrecaptured net section 1231 losses from prior years. See instructions	8	**10,000**
9	Subtract line 8 from line 7. If zero or less, enter -0-. If line 9 is zero, enter the gain from line 7 on line 12 below. If line 9 is more than zero, enter the amount from line 8 on line 12 below and enter the gain from line 9 as a long-term capital gain on the Schedule D filed with your return. See instructions	9	**177,500**

Part II **Ordinary Gains and Losses** (see instructions)

10 Ordinary gains and losses not included on lines 11 through 16 (include property held 1 year or less):

11	Loss, if any, from line 7	11	( )
12	Gain, if any, from line 7 or amount from line 8, if applicable	12	**10,000**
13	Gain, if any, from line 31	13	**85,342**
14	Net gain or (loss) from Form 4684, lines 31 and 38a	14	
15	Ordinary gain from installment sales from Form 6252, line 25 or 36	15	
16	Ordinary gain or (loss) from like-kind exchanges from Form 8824	16	
17	Combine lines 10 through 16	17	**95,342**
18	For all except individual returns, enter the amount from line 17 on the appropriate line of your return and skip lines a and b below. For individual returns, complete lines a and b below.		
a	If the loss on line 11 includes a loss from Form 4684, line 35, column (b)(ii), enter that part of the loss here. Enter the loss from income-producing property on Schedule A (Form 1040), line 16. (Do not include any loss on property used as an employee.) Identify as from "Form 4797, line 18a." See instructions	18a	
b	Redetermine the gain or (loss) on line 17 excluding the loss, if any, on line 18a. Enter here and on Schedule 1 (Form 1040), Part I, line 4	18b	**95,342**

For Paperwork Reduction Act Notice, see separate instructions. Cat. No. 13086I Form **4797** (2021)

EXHIBIT 3-10 Teton's (on Steve's return) Form 4797 (*continued*)

Form 4797 (2021) Page **2**

Part III **Gain From Disposition of Property Under Sections 1245, 1250, 1252, 1254, and 1255** (see instructions)

19 (a) Description of section 1245, 1250, 1252, 1254, or 1255 property:	(b) Date acquired (mo., day, yr.)	(c) Date sold (mo., day, yr.)
A Machinery	Yr 0	Yr 4
B Office furniture	Yr 0	Yr 4
C Warehouse	Yr 0	Yr 4
D		

These columns relate to the properties on lines 19A through 19D. ▶		Property A	Property B	Property C	Property D
20 Gross sales price (**Note:** *See line 1a before completing.*)	20	300,000	23,000	350,000	
21 Cost or other basis plus expense of sale	21	610,000	20,000	275,000	
22 Depreciation (or depletion) allowed or allowable	22	381,342	14,000	15,000	
23 Adjusted basis. Subtract line 22 from line 21	23	228,658	6,000	260,000	
24 Total gain. Subtract line 23 from line 20	24	71,342	17,000	90,000	
25 **If section 1245 property:**					
a Depreciation allowed or allowable from line 22	25a	381,342	14,000		
b Enter the **smaller** of line 24 or 25a	25b	71,342	14,000		
26 **If section 1250 property:** If straight line depreciation was used, enter -0- on line 26g, except for a corporation subject to section 291.					
a Additional depreciation after 1975. See instructions	26a				
b Applicable percentage multiplied by the **smaller** of line 24 or line 26a. See instructions	26b				
c Subtract line 26a from line 24. If residential rental property **or** line 24 isn't more than line 26a, skip lines 26d and 26e	26c				
d Additional depreciation after 1969 and before 1976	26d				
e Enter the **smaller** of line 26c or 26d	26e				
f Section 291 amount (corporations only)	26f				
g Add lines 26b, 26e, and 26f	26g			0	
27 **If section 1252 property:** Skip this section if you didn't dispose of farmland or if this form is being completed for a partnership.					
a Soil, water, and land clearing expenses	27a				
b Line 27a multiplied by applicable percentage. See instructions	27b				
c Enter the **smaller** of line 24 or 27b	27c				
28 **If section 1254 property:**					
a Intangible drilling and development costs, expenditures for development of mines and other natural deposits, mining exploration costs, and depletion. See instructions	28a				
b Enter the **smaller** of line 24 or 28a	28b				
29 **If section 1255 property:**					
a Applicable percentage of payments excluded from income under section 126. See instructions	29a				
b Enter the **smaller** of line 24 or 29a. See instructions	29b				

Summary of Part III Gains. Complete property columns A through D through line 29b before going to line 30.

30 Total gains for all properties. Add property columns A through D, line 24	30	178,342
31 Add property columns A through D, lines 25b, 26g, 27c, 28b, and 29b. Enter here and on line 13	31	85,342
32 Subtract line 31 from line 30. Enter the portion from casualty or theft on Form 4684, line 33. Enter the portion from other than casualty or theft on Form 4797, line 6	32	93,000

Part IV **Recapture Amounts Under Sections 179 and 280F(b)(2) When Business Use Drops to 50% or Less** (see instructions)

		(a) Section 179	(b) Section 280F(b)(2)
33 Section 179 expense deduction or depreciation allowable in prior years	33		
34 Recomputed depreciation. See instructions	34		
35 Recapture amount. Subtract line 34 from line 33. See the instructions for where to report	35		

Form **4797** (2021)

Source: irs.gov.

EXHIBIT 3-11 **Steve's Schedule D (Assumes Steve had no other capital gains and losses other than those incurred by Teton)**

SCHEDULE D (Form 1040)

Department of the Treasury Internal Revenue Service (99)

Capital Gains and Losses

▶ Attach to Form 1040, 1040-SR, or 1040-NR.
▶ Go to *www.irs.gov/ScheduleD* for instructions and the latest information.
▶ Use Form 8949 to list your transactions for lines 1b, 2, 3, 8b, 9, and 10.

OMB No. 1545-0074

2021

Attachment Sequence No. **12**

Name(s) shown on return: **Steve Dallimore** | **Your social security number**

Did you dispose of any investment(s) in a qualified opportunity fund during the tax year? ☐ **Yes** ☐ **No**
If "Yes," attach Form 8949 and see its instructions for additional requirements for reporting your gain or loss.

Part I **Short-Term Capital Gains and Losses—Generally Assets Held One Year or Less** (see instructions)

See instructions for how to figure the amounts to enter on the lines below. This form may be easier to complete if you round off cents to whole dollars.	**(d)** Proceeds (sales price)	**(e)** Cost (or other basis)	**(g)** Adjustments to gain or loss from Form(s) 8949, Part I, line 2, column (g)	**(h) Gain or (loss)** Subtract column (e) from column (d) and combine the result with column (g)
1a Totals for all short-term transactions reported on Form 1099-B for which basis was reported to the IRS and for which you have no adjustments (see instructions). However, if you choose to report all these transactions on Form 8949, leave this line blank and go to line 1b .				
1b Totals for all transactions reported on Form(s) 8949 with **Box A** checked				
2 Totals for all transactions reported on Form(s) 8949 with **Box B** checked				
3 Totals for all transactions reported on Form(s) 8949 with **Box C** checked				

4 Short-term gain from Form 6252 and short-term gain or (loss) from Forms 4684, 6781, and 8824 . .	**4**	
5 Net short-term gain or (loss) from partnerships, S corporations, estates, and trusts from Schedule(s) K-1	**5**	
6 Short-term capital loss carryover. Enter the amount, if any, from line 8 of your **Capital Loss Carryover Worksheet** in the instructions	**6**	( )
7 **Net short-term capital gain or (loss).** Combine lines 1a through 6 in column (h). If you have any long-term capital gains or losses, go to Part II below. Otherwise, go to Part III on the back	**7**	

Part II **Long-Term Capital Gains and Losses—Generally Assets Held More Than One Year** (see instructions)

See instructions for how to figure the amounts to enter on the lines below. This form may be easier to complete if you round off cents to whole dollars.	**(d)** Proceeds (sales price)	**(e)** Cost (or other basis)	**(g)** Adjustments to gain or loss from Form(s) 8949, Part II, line 2, column (g)	**(h) Gain or (loss)** Subtract column (e) from column (d) and combine the result with column (g)
8a Totals for all long-term transactions reported on Form 1099-B for which basis was reported to the IRS and for which you have no adjustments (see instructions). However, if you choose to report all these transactions on Form 8949, leave this line blank and go to line 8b .				
8b Totals for all transactions reported on Form(s) 8949 with **Box D** checked				
9 Totals for all transactions reported on Form(s) 8949 with **Box E** checked				
10 Totals for all transactions reported on Form(s) 8949 with **Box F** checked.				

11 Gain from Form 4797, Part I; long-term gain from Forms 2439 and 6252; and long-term gain or (loss) from Forms 4684, 6781, and 8824	**11**	177,500
12 Net long-term gain or (loss) from partnerships, S corporations, estates, and trusts from Schedule(s) K-1	**12**	
13 Capital gain distributions. See the instructions	**13**	
14 Long-term capital loss carryover. Enter the amount, if any, from line 13 of your **Capital Loss Carryover Worksheet** in the instructions	**14**	( )
15 **Net long-term capital gain or (loss).** Combine lines 8a through 14 in column (h). Then, go to Part III on the back	**15**	177,500

For Paperwork Reduction Act Notice, see your tax return instructions. Cat. No. 11338H **Schedule D (Form 1040) 2021**

Source: irs.gov.

LO 3-6

TAX-DEFERRED TRANSACTIONS

Taxpayers realizing gains and losses when they sell or exchange property must immediately recognize the gain for tax purposes unless a specific provision in the tax code says otherwise. Under certain tax provisions, taxpayers defer or delay recognizing a gain or loss until a subsequent period. We first explore tax provisions that allow taxpayers to defer recognizing realized gains. Congress allows taxpayers to defer recognizing gains in certain types of exchanges because the exchange itself does not provide the taxpayers with the wherewithal (cash) to pay taxes on the realized gain if the taxpayers were required to immediately recognize the gain. Also, taxpayers are in the same economic position before and after the exchange (e.g., owning similar property). In particular, we discuss common **tax-deferred transactions** such as like-kind exchanges, involuntary conversions, installment sales, and other business-related transactions such as business formations and reorganizations.

Like-Kind Exchanges

Taxpayers involved in a business may have valid reasons to trade business assets to others for similar business assets. For example, a taxpayer may want to trade land used in its business for a different parcel of land in a better location. As we discussed earlier in this chapter, taxpayers exchanging property *realize* gains (or losses) on exchanges just as taxpayers do by selling property for cash. However, taxpayers exchanging property for property are in a different situation than taxpayers selling the same property for cash. Taxpayers exchanging one piece of business property for another haven't changed their relative economic position because both before and after the exchange they hold similar assets for use in their business. Further, exchanges of property do not generate the wherewithal (cash) for the taxpayers to pay taxes on the gain they realize and recognize on the exchanges. While taxpayers selling property for cash must immediately recognize gain on the sale, taxpayers exchanging property for assets other than cash must defer recognizing gain (or loss) realized on the exchange if they meet certain requirements. This type of deferred gain (or loss) transaction is commonly referred to as a **like-kind exchange** or §1031 exchange.[22]

Like-kind exchange treatment can provide taxpayers with significant tax advantages by allowing them to defer gain (and current taxes payable) that would otherwise be recognized immediately.[23] For an exchange to qualify as a like-kind exchange for tax purposes, the transaction must meet the following three criteria:

1. Real property is exchanged "solely for like-kind" property.
2. Both the real property given up and the real property received in the exchange by the taxpayer are and will be either "used in a trade or business" or "held for investment" by the taxpayer.
3. The exchange must meet certain time restrictions.[24]

Below, we discuss each of these requirements in detail.

Definition of Like-Kind Property Real property is eligible for like-kind treatment while personal property is not.[25] Real property is considered to be like-kind with any other type of real property as long as the real property is used in a trade or business or held for

[22]Like-kind exchanges are defined in §1031 of the Internal Revenue Code.

[23]Financial accounting rules require businesses to recognize (for financial accounting purposes) any gain they realize in a like-kind exchange transaction.

[24]Prior to 2018, personal property could be exchanged under the like-kind exchange rules.

[25]Regulations under §1031 issued in December 2020 provide clarification and guidance as to what constitutes real property. Property that is considered inherently permanent (e.g., in-ground swimming pools, parking facilities, fences, silos) is listed in Reg. §1.1031(a)-3(a)(2).

investment. For example, from Teton's perspective, its warehouse on 10 acres is considered to be like-kind with a nearby condominium, a 20-acre parcel of raw land across town, or even a Manhattan skyscraper. Real property held for sale in the course of ordinary business is not eligible for like-kind treatment, so taxpayers whose business is to buy and sell real property cannot do so using the like-kind exchange rules.[26] In addition, real property located in the United States and real property located outside the United States are not like-kind.

THE KEY FACTS

Like-Kind Property

- Real property
  - All real property used in a trade or business or held for investment is considered "like-kind" with other real property used in a trade or business or held for investment.
- Ineligible property
  - Personal property.
  - Domestic property exchanged for property used in a foreign country and all property used in a foreign country.
  - Real property held for sale.

Property Use Even when property meets the definition of like-kind property, taxpayers can exchange the property in a qualifying like-kind exchange only if they used the transferred property in a trade or business or for investment *and* they will use the property received in the exchange in a trade or business or for investment. For example, Teton could exchange its warehouse on 10 acres for a 200-acre parcel of land it intends to hold as an investment in a qualifying like-kind exchange because Teton was using the warehouse in its business and it will hold the land as an investment. However, if Steve exchanged his cabin in Maine for a personal residence in Wyoming, the exchange would not qualify because Steve used the Maine residence for personal purposes, and he would be using the Wyoming property for personal rather than business or investment purposes. In fact, even if Steve were renting out his Maine cabin (meaning it qualifies as investment property) when he exchanged it for his principal residence in Wyoming, the exchange would not qualify for like-kind exchange treatment because *both* properties must meet the use test for Steve (the personal residence does not qualify as business or investment property).

Timing Requirements for a Like-Kind Exchange The like-kind rules require an exchange of real property for real property; however, a simultaneous exchange may not be practical or possible. For example, taxpayers may not always be able to immediately (or even eventually) find another party who is willing to exchange properties with them. In these situations, taxpayers often use **third-party intermediaries** to facilitate like-kind exchanges.

When a third party is involved, the taxpayer transfers the like-kind property to the intermediary, who then sells the property and uses the proceeds to acquire the new property for the taxpayer.[27] Because the third party must sell the taxpayer's old property and locate and purchase suitable replacement property, this process is subject to delay. Does a delay in the completion of the exchange disqualify an otherwise allowable like-kind exchange? Not necessarily. The tax laws do not require a simultaneous exchange of assets, but they do impose some timing requirements to ensure that a transaction is completed within a reasonable time in order to qualify as a **deferred like-kind exchange** (not simultaneous)—often referred to as a "*Starker* exchange."[28]

THE KEY FACTS

Timing Requirements

- Like-kind property exchanges may involve intermediaries.
- Taxpayers must identify replacement like-kind property within 45 days of giving up their real property.
- Like-kind property must be received within 180 days of when the taxpayer transfers real property in a like-kind exchange.

The two timing rules applicable to like-kind exchanges are that (1) the taxpayer must *identify* the like-kind replacement property within 45 days after transferring the property given up in the exchange and (2) the taxpayer must receive the replacement like-kind property within 180 days (or the due date of the tax return including extensions) after the taxpayer initially transfers property in the exchange.[29,30] The time limits force the

[26]§1031(a)(2).

[27]Exchanges involving third-party intermediaries are very common with real estate exchanges. For real estate, taxpayers must use a "qualified exchange intermediary," such as a title company, and cannot use a personal attorney (because attorneys are considered to be the taxpayer's agent).

[28]The term "*Starker* exchange" refers to a landmark court case that first allowed deferred exchanges [*Starker v. United States,* 79-2 USTC ¶ 9541 (9th Cir. 1979)]. The rules for deferred exchanges are found in §1031(a)(3). The tax laws also allow for reverse like-kind exchanges, where replacement property is acquired before the taxpayer transfers the like-kind property.

[29]The taxpayer must identify at least one like-kind asset; however, because failure to obtain the asset disqualifies the transaction from having deferred like-kind exchange status, the taxpayer may identify up to three alternatives to hedge against the inability to obtain the first identified asset. Generally, a taxpayer must obtain only one to facilitate the exchange [see Reg. §1.1031(k)-1(c)(4)].

[30]The identification period begins on the date the taxpayer transfers the property and ends at midnight on the 45th day after the transfer. Similarly, the exchange period begins on the date of the transfer and ends at midnight on the earlier of the 180th day after the transfer or the due date (including extensions) for the taxpayer's tax return. Reg. §1.1031(k)-1(b)(2).

taxpayer to close the transaction within a specified time period in order to be able to report the tax consequences of the transaction. Exhibit 3-12 provides a diagram of a like-kind exchange involving a third-party intermediary.

EXHIBIT 3-12 Diagram of Deferred or *Starker* Exchange

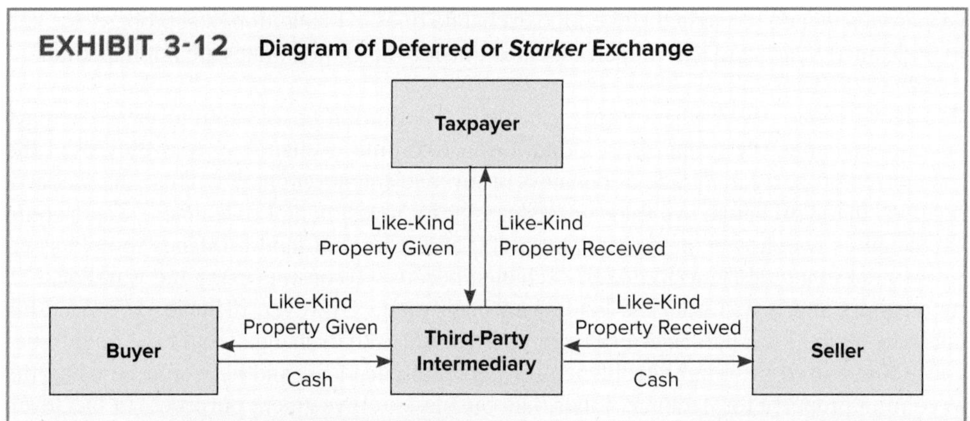

When a taxpayer fails to meet the timing requirements, the exchange fails to qualify for like-kind treatment and is fully taxable.

Example 3-14

What if: Suppose that on August 4 of year 1 Steve transferred a parcel of real property that he was holding as an investment to a third-party intermediary with the intention of exchanging the property for another suitable investment property. By what date does Steve need to identify the replacement property?

Answer: September 18 of year 1, which is 45 days after Steve transferred the property to the intermediary.

Assuming Steve identifies the replacement property within the 45-day time period, by what date does he need to receive the replacement property in order to qualify for like-kind exchange treatment?

Answer: January 31 of year 2, which is 180 days from August 4, the date he transferred the property to the intermediary.

Tax Consequences When Like-Kind Property Is Exchanged Solely for Like-Kind Property As we've discussed, when taxpayers exchanging property meet the like-kind exchange requirements, they do not recognize gain or loss on the exchange. They also establish or receive a **substituted basis** in the like-kind property they receive. That is, they exchange the basis they have in the property they are giving up and transfer it to the basis of the property they are receiving.[31]

Example 3-15

Teton trades land worth $29,500 (tax basis of $18,000) for land in a different location that is also worth $29,500. How much gain does Teton recognize on this exchange?

Answer: $0. Teton's exchange qualifies as a like-kind exchange, and the $11,500 realized gain ($29,500 amount realized − $18,000 tax basis) is deferred.

What is Teton's tax basis in the new land?

Answer: $18,000, the basis it had in the old land it exchanged.

[31]If the real property received is depreciable, the taxpayer continues to depreciate the new property as if it were the old property.

Tax Consequences of Transfers Involving Like-Kind and Non-Like-Kind Property (Boot) A practical problem with like-kind exchanges is that the value of the like-kind property the taxpayer transfers may differ from the value of the like-kind property the taxpayer receives in the exchange. In these situations, the party transferring the lesser-valued asset must also transfer additional property to the other party to equate the values. When this additional property or **boot** (non-like-kind property) is transferred, the party giving the boot recognizes gain or loss on the transfer of the boot portion of the exchange. If the boot transferred is cash, there is no gain or loss for the transferor. However, the like-kind property exchanged will still qualify for gain deferral.

When a taxpayer receives boot, it appears as though the transaction fails the first like-kind exchange requirement that like-kind property be exchanged solely for like-kind property. Nevertheless, if a taxpayer receives boot in addition to like-kind property, the transaction can still qualify for like-kind exchange treatment, but the taxpayer is required to recognize realized gain *to the extent of the boot received*.[32] As a practical matter, this means the taxpayer's recognized gain is the *lesser of* (1) gain realized or (2) boot received.

The reason a taxpayer must recognize gain is that the taxpayer is essentially selling a portion of the like-kind property for the boot in a taxable exchange. The receipt of boot triggers taxable gain (but not taxable loss) in an otherwise qualifying like-kind exchange. If the taxpayer transfers loss property (adjusted basis is greater than fair market value) in a qualifying like-kind exchange, the taxpayer defers recognition of the loss until the taxpayer sells or disposes of the loss property in a taxable transaction—so it may be important for tax planning purposes to avoid the like-kind exchange rules if the taxpayer wishes to currently recognize the loss.[33] When a taxpayer recognizes gain in a like-kind exchange, the character of the gain depends on the character of the asset transferred by the taxpayer (the depreciation recapture rules apply when characterizing gains).

THE KEY FACTS

Like-Kind Exchanges Involving Boot

- Non-like-kind property is known as *boot*.
- When boot is given as part of a like-kind transaction:
  - The asset received is recorded in two parts: (1) property received in exchange for like-kind property and (2) property received in a sale (bought by the boot).
- When boot is received:
  - Boot received usually creates recognized gain.
  - Gain recognized is lesser of gain realized or boot received.

Example 3-16

What if: Suppose that Teton trades land with a value of $29,500 and a tax basis of $18,000 for land in a different location valued at $27,500. To equate the value of the property exchanged, the other party also pays Teton $2,000. What gain or loss does Teton realize on the exchange and what gain or loss does Teton recognize on the exchange?

Answer: $11,500 realized gain and $2,000 recognized gain, calculated as follows:

Description	Amount	Explanation
(1) Amount realized from land	$ 27,500	Fair market value of new land
(2) Amount realized from boot (cash)	2,000	
(3) Total amount realized	29,500	(1) + (2)
(4) Adjusted basis	18,000	
(5) Gain realized	**$11,500**	(3) − (4)
Gain recognized	**$ 2,000**	Lesser of (2) or (5)

What is the character of Teton's $2,000 gain?

Answer: §1231 gain. Teton includes the gain in its §1231 netting process.

What if: Suppose the same facts as above, except that Teton's tax basis in the land was $29,000. What amount of gain would Teton recognize on the exchange?

Answer: $500. Teton recognizes the lesser of (1) $500 gain realized ($29,500 − $29,000) or (2) $2,000 boot received.

[32] §1031(b).

[33] §1031(a) states that no gain or loss is recognized in a qualifying like-kind exchange.

When taxpayers receive like-kind property and boot in a like-kind exchange, their basis in the like-kind property can be computed in two ways, as shown in Exhibit 3-13.

EXHIBIT 3-13 Like-Kind Basis Calculation

Simplified Method	Method under §1031(d)
Fair market value of like-kind property received	Adjusted basis of like-kind property surrendered
– Deferred gain, or	+ Adjusted basis of boot given
+ Deferred loss	+ Gain recognized
= Basis of like-kind property received	– Fair market value of boot received
	– Loss recognized
	= Basis of like-kind property received

The basis of boot received in the exchange is the boot's fair market value. The formula for computing basis ensures that the taxpayer's deferred gain or loss on the exchange (i.e., the gain or loss realized that is not recognized) is captured in the difference between the value and the basis of the new property received. Consequently, taxpayers defer realized gains or losses on qualifying like-kind exchanges; they do not exclude them. Taxpayers will ultimately recognize the entire gain or loss when they dispose of the new asset in a fully taxable transaction.[34]

Example 3-17

What if: Assume the facts in Example 3-16, where Teton exchanged land with a value of $29,500 and tax basis of $18,000 for land valued at $27,500 and $2,000 cash. Teton recognized $2,000 of gain on the exchange. What is Teton's basis in the new land it received from the dealer?

Answer: $18,000, computed using the simplified method, as follows:

Description	Amount	Explanation
(1) Amount realized from land	$ 27,500	Fair market value of new land
(2) Amount realized from boot (cash)	2,000	
(3) Total amount realized	$ 29,500	(1) + (2)
(4) Tax basis of land	18,000	
(5) Gain realized	$ 11,500	(3) – (4)
(6) Gain recognized	$ 2,000	Lesser of (2) or (5)
(7) Deferred gain	9,500	(5) – (6)
Basis in new land	**$18,000**	(1) – (7)

Anything a taxpayer receives in an exchange other than like-kind property is considered boot. This includes cash, other property, or even the amount of a taxpayer's liability transferred to (assumed by) the other party in the exchange. Let's return to the previous example. If, instead of paying Teton $2,000 in cash, the buyer had assumed Teton's $2,000 liability secured by Teton's old land, the tax consequences would have been identical. The buyer relieved Teton of $2,000 of debt, and the debt relief would be treated the same as if the buyer had paid Teton cash and Teton had paid off its $2,000 liability. Generally, when a taxpayer both transfers and receives boot in an otherwise qualifying like-kind exchange, the taxpayer must recognize any realized gain to the extent of the boot received. That is, the taxpayer is not allowed to offset boot received with boot paid.[35]

[34]Additionally, the deferred gain is subject to depreciation recapture when the asset is eventually disposed of in a taxable disposition.

[35]However, Reg. §1.1031(j)-1 provides an exception where multiple like-kind exchanges are made in a single exchange.

EXHIBIT 3-14 Form 8824, Part III (From exchange in Example 3-15)

Form 8824 (2021) Page 2

Name(s) shown on tax return. Do not enter name and social security number if shown on other side. | Your social security number

Steve Dallimore (Teton Mountaineering Technologies, LLC)

Part III **Realized Gain or (Loss), Recognized Gain, and Basis of Like-Kind Property Received**

Caution: If you transferred **and** received **(a)** more than one group of like-kind properties, or **(b)** cash or other (not like-kind) property, see ***Reporting of multi-asset exchanges*** in the instructions.

Note: Complete lines 12 through 14 **only** if you gave up property that was not like-kind. Otherwise, go to line 15.

12	Fair market value (FMV) of other property given up. See instructions	12			
13	Adjusted basis of other property given up	13			
14	Gain or (loss) recognized on other property given up. Subtract line 13 from line 12. Report the gain or (loss) in the same manner as if the exchange had been a sale			14	
	Caution: If the property given up was used previously or partly as a home, see ***Property used as home*** in the instructions.				
15	Cash received, FMV of other property received, plus net liabilities assumed by other party, reduced (but not below zero) by any exchange expenses you incurred. See instructions			15	0
16	FMV of like-kind property you received			16	29,500
17	Add lines 15 and 16			17	29,500
18	Adjusted basis of like-kind property you gave up, net amounts paid to other party, plus any exchange expenses **not** used on line 15. See instructions			18	18,000
19	**Realized gain or (loss).** Subtract line 18 from line 17			19	11,500
20	Enter the smaller of line 15 or line 19, but not less than zero			20	0
21	Ordinary income under recapture rules. Enter here and on Form 4797, line 16. See instructions			21	0
22	Subtract line 21 from line 20. If zero or less, enter -0-. If more than zero, enter here and on Schedule D or Form 4797, unless the installment method applies. See instructions			22	0
23	**Recognized gain.** Add lines 21 and 22			23	0
24	Deferred gain or (loss). Subtract line 23 from line 19. If a related party exchange, see instructions			24	11,500
25	**Basis of like-kind property received.** Subtract line 15 from the sum of lines 18 and 23. See instructions			25	18,000

Source: irs.gov.

However, when the taxpayer receives boot in the form of liability relief, the taxpayer is allowed to net any boot paid against the (liability) boot received when determining gain recognized.[36]

Reporting Like-Kind Exchanges Like-kind exchange transactions are reported on Form 8824. Exhibit 3-14 presents the computations from Form 8824 reflecting the like-kind exchange of the land in Example 3-15.

THE KEY FACTS

Exchanged Basis

- The basis of like-kind property received is the fair market value of the new asset minus deferred gain or plus deferred loss on the exchange (unless boot is given).
  - When no gain is recognized on the exchange, the basis of the new property is the same as the taxpayer's basis in the old like-kind property.
- The basis of boot received is the fair market value of the boot.

Involuntary Conversions

Usually, when taxpayers sell, exchange, or abandon property, they intend to do so. However, sometimes taxpayers may involuntarily dispose of property due to circumstances beyond their control. The tax law refers to these types of property dispositions as **involuntary conversions.**[37] Involuntary conversions occur when property is partially or wholly destroyed by a natural disaster or accident, stolen, condemned, or seized via eminent domain by a governmental agency. Tragic examples of this include the results of Hurricanes Harvey, Irma, and Maria in 2017 and the wildfires in California in 2020. Even in situations when taxpayers experience a loss of property due to theft, disaster, or other circumstances, they might realize a gain for tax purposes if they receive replacement property or insurance proceeds in excess of their basis in the property that was stolen or destroyed.

Taxpayers may experience a tremendous financial hardship if they are required to recognize the realized gain in these circumstances. For example, let's consider a business

[36]Further details of this important exception are beyond the scope of our discussion. See the examples provided in Reg. §1.1031(d)-2 for further guidance.

[37]§1033.

THE KEY FACTS

Involuntary Conversions

- Gain is deferred when appreciated property is involuntarily converted in an accident or natural disaster.
- Basis of property directly converted is carried over from the old property to the new property.
- In an indirect conversion, gain recognized is the lesser of:
  - Gain realized or
  - Amount of reimbursement the taxpayer does not reinvest in qualified property.
- Qualified replacement property must be of a similar or related use to the original property.

that acquired a building for $100,000. The building appreciates in value, and when it is worth $150,000, it is destroyed by fire. The building is fully insured at its replacement cost, so the business receives a check from the insurance company for $150,000. The problem for the business is that it realizes a $50,000 gain on this involuntary conversion ($150,000 insurance proceeds minus $100,000 basis in property without considering depreciation). Assuming the business's income is taxed at a 32 percent marginal rate, it must pay $16,000 of tax on the insurance money it receives. That leaves it with only $134,000 to replace property worth $150,000. This hardly seems equitable. Congress provides special tax laws to allow taxpayers to defer the gains on such *involuntary* conversions.

Taxpayers may defer realized gains on both direct and indirect involuntary conversions. **Direct conversions** occur when taxpayers receive a direct property replacement for the involuntarily converted property. For example, a municipality that is widening its streets may seize land from a taxpayer through its eminent domain and compensate the taxpayer with another parcel of similar value. In this case, the taxpayer would not recognize gain on the exchange of property and would take a basis in the new parcel of land equal to the taxpayer's basis in the land that was claimed by the municipality. Just as with like-kind exchanges, an exchanged basis (basis of old property exchanged for basis of new property) ensures that the gain built into the new property (i.e., fair market value minus adjusted basis) includes the same gain that was built into the old property.

Indirect conversions occur when taxpayers receive money for the involuntarily converted property through insurance reimbursement or some other type of settlement. Taxpayers meeting the involuntary conversion requirements may *elect* to either recognize or defer realized gain on the conversions. Indirect conversions are more common than direct conversions. Taxpayers can defer realized gains on indirect conversions *if* they acquire **qualified replacement property** within a prescribed time limit, which is generally two years (three years in the case of condemnation) after the close of the tax year in which they receive the proceeds.[38,39]

In contrast to the like-kind exchange rules, both personal and real property can qualify for the tax treatment under the involuntary conversion rules. Qualified replacement property is defined somewhat narrowly; to qualify, it must be similar *and* related in service or use.[40] For example, a bowling alley is not qualified replacement property for a pool hall, even though both are real properties used for entertainment purposes. This definition is stricter than the like-kind exchange rules that would allow the bowling alley to be exchanged for any other real property, including a pool hall. In addition, the involuntary conversion rules allow a taxpayer's personal residence (personal-use property) to qualify for gain deferral; however, qualified replacement property of a personal residence is restricted to another residence. Taxpayers recognize realized gain to the extent that they do not reinvest the reimbursement proceeds in qualified property. However, just as in like-kind exchanges, taxpayers do not recognize more gain than they realize on involuntary conversions. That is, a taxpayer's recognized gain on an involuntary conversion can be determined by the following formula: Recognized gain on an involuntary conversion is equal to the *lesser of* (1) the gain realized on the conversion or (2) the amount of reimbursement the taxpayer does *not reinvest* in qualified property.

The character of any gain recognized in an involuntary conversion depends on the nature of the asset that was converted—including depreciation recapture, if applicable. The basis of the replacement property in an involuntary conversion is calculated using the

[38]Condemnation occurs when a local, state, or federal government seizes private property and compensates the owner but does not require the owner's approval. Governments accomplish a condemnation through the power of eminent domain, which essentially means the government takes private property for public use.

[39]§1033(a)(2)(B). The time period varies depending on the type of property converted. Additionally, the IRS may consent to an extension of the time period for replacement.

[40]The similar and related-use test has been developed through a variety of administrative pronouncements and judicial law.

simplified method described for like-kind exchange property (see Exhibit 3-13, Simplified Method). That is, the basis of the replacement property is the fair market value of the new property minus the deferred gain on the conversion.

Example 3-18

What if: Assume that one of Teton's employees was in a traffic accident while driving a delivery van. The employee escaped without serious injury, but the van was totally destroyed. Before the accident, Teton's delivery van had a fair market value of $15,000 and an adjusted basis of $11,000 (the cost basis was $15,000 and accumulated depreciation on the van was $4,000). Teton received $15,000 of insurance proceeds to cover the loss. Teton was considering two alternatives for replacing the van: Alternative 1 was to purchase a new delivery van for $20,000 and Alternative 2 was to purchase a used delivery van for $14,000. What gain or loss does Teton recognize under Alternative 1 and Alternative 2?

Answer: $0 gain recognized under Alternative 1 and $1,000 gain recognized under Alternative 2 (see computations below). Teton qualifies for a deferral because the new property (delivery van) has a similar and related use to the old property (delivery van). But it must recognize gain under Alternative 2 because it did not reinvest all of the insurance proceeds in a replacement van.

What is Teton's basis in the replacement property it acquired under Alternative 1 and Alternative 2?

Answer: $16,000 in Alternative 1 and $11,000 in Alternative 2, computed as follows:

Description	Alternative 1 Amount	Alternative 2 Amount	Explanation
(1) Amount realized	$15,000	$15,000	
(2) Adjusted basis	11,000	11,000	
(3) Gain realized	4,000	4,000	(1) – (2)
(4) Insurance proceeds	15,000	15,000	
(5) Proceeds reinvested	15,000	14,000	
(6) Amount not reinvested	0	1,000	(4) – (5)
(7) Gain recognized	**0**	**1,000**	Lesser of (3) or (6)*
(8) Deferred gain	4,000	3,000	(3) – (7)
(9) Value of replacement property	20,000	14,000	
Basis of replacement property	**16,000**	**11,000**	(9) – (8)

*The character of the $1,000 recognized gain is ordinary income under §1245 (lesser of gain recognized or accumulated depreciation).

Involuntary conversions share several characteristics with like-kind exchanges, such as the concept of qualified property, time period restrictions, the method of computing gain recognized (lesser of realized gain or cash received in addition to qualifying property), and basis calculation (gain or loss from old property remains built into new property). However, there are two important differences between like-kind exchanges and involuntary conversions. First, involuntary conversion rules allow taxpayers to defer gains on both personal and real property (business, investment, or personal-use property), whereas the like-kind exchange rules limit the deferral treatment to only real property (business or investment use). Second, taxpayers experiencing a loss from involuntary conversion may immediately deduct the loss as a casualty loss, either as a business loss or as a personal loss, if incurred in a federally declared disaster area, depending on the nature of the loss.

Installment Sales

In general, when taxpayers sell property for cash and collect the entire sale proceeds in one lump-sum payment, they immediately recognize gain or loss for tax purposes. However, taxpayers selling property don't always collect the sale proceeds in one lump sum from the buyer. For example, the buyer may make a down payment in the year of sale and

THE KEY FACTS

Installment Sales

- Sale of property where the seller receives at least one payment in a taxable year subsequent to the year of disposition of the property.
- Must recognize a portion of gain on each installment payment received.
- Gains from installment sales are calculated as follows:
  - Gross profit percentage = Gross profit/Contract price
  - Gain recognized = Gross profit percentage × Principal payment received in the year
- Inventory, marketable securities, and depreciation recapture cannot be accounted for under installment sale rules.
- Installment sale rules do not apply to losses.

then agree to pay the remainder of the sale proceeds over a period of time. This type of arrangement is termed an **installment sale.** For tax purposes, an installment sale is any sale of property where the seller receives at least one payment in a taxable year subsequent to the year of disposition of the property.[41]

Taxpayers selling property via an installment sale realize gains to the extent the selling price (the amount realized) exceeds their adjusted basis in the property sold. The installment sale rules stay true to the wherewithal-to-pay concept and allow taxpayers selling property in this manner to use the installment method of recognizing *gain* on the sale over time.[42] The installment method does not apply to property sold at a loss. Under the installment method, taxpayers determine the amount of realized gain on the transaction, and they recognize the gain pro rata as they receive the installment payments. So, by the time they have received all the installment payments, they will have recognized all the initial realized gain.[43] For financial accounting purposes, businesses selling property on an installment basis generally immediately recognize the realized gain on their financial statements.[44]

To calculate the amount of gain the taxpayer (seller) must recognize on each installment payment received, the seller must compute the gross profit percentage on the transaction. The gross profit percentage is calculated as follows:

$$\text{Gross profit percentage} = \frac{\text{Gross profit}}{\text{Contract price}}$$

Gross profit is calculated as the sales price minus the adjusted basis of the property being sold. The contract price is the sales price less the seller's liabilities that are assumed by the buyer. The gross profit percentage indicates the percentage of the contract price that will ultimately be recognized as gain. To calculate the portion of a particular payment that is currently recognized as gain, the seller multiplies the amount of the payments received during the year (including the year of sale) by the gross profit percentage (note that once established, the gross profit percentage does not change). As in fully taxable transactions, the character of gain recognized by taxpayers using the installment method is determined by the character of the asset sold.

The formula for determining the basis of an installment note receivable is:

$$(1 - \text{Gross profit percentage}) \times \text{Remaining principal payments on note}$$

Because the gross profit percentage reflects the percentage of the installment payments that will be recognized as gain, (1 – Gross profit percentage) is the percentage that is not recognized as gain because it reflects a return of capital (basis).

Example 3-19

What if: Suppose Teton decides to sell five acres of land adjacent to the warehouse for $100,000. The basis for the land is $37,500. Teton agrees to sell the property for four equal payments of $25,000—one now (in year 1) and the other three on January 1 of the next three years—plus interest. What amount of gain does Teton realize on the sale and what amount of gain does it recognize in year 1?

[41]§453(b)(1).

[42]For tax purposes, a taxpayer selling qualifying property on an installment basis at a gain is required to use the installment method of reporting the recognized gain from the transaction. However, taxpayers are allowed to elect out of using the installment method [§453(d)].

[43]Because the seller in an installment sale is essentially lending money to the buyer, the buyer makes the required installment payments to the seller and the buyer pays interest to the seller for the money the buyer is borrowing. Any interest income received by the seller is immediately taxable as ordinary income. Special rules apply regarding interest for installment sales of more than $150,000 (see §453A).

[44]One exception is that the installment sale method, similar to the tax installment method, is used for financial accounting purposes when there is doubt that the business will collect the receivable.

Answer: The realized gain on the transaction is $62,500 ($100,000 amount realized less $37,500 adjusted basis), and the year 1 recognized gain is $15,625, computed as follows:

Description	Amount	Explanation
(1) Sales price	$100,000	
(2) Adjusted basis	37,500	
(3) Gross profit	**$ 62,500**	(1) − (2)
(4) Contract price	$100,000	(1) − assumed liabilities (-0-)
(5) Gross profit percentage	62.5%	(3)/(4)
(6) Payment received in year 1	$ 25,000	
Gain recognized in year 1	**$ 15,625**	(5) × (6)

Because Teton used the land in its trade or business and it held the land for more than a year, the character of the gain is §1231 gain.

Gains Ineligible for Installment Reporting

Not all gains are eligible for installment sale reporting. Taxpayers selling marketable securities or inventory on an installment basis may not use the installment method to report gain on the sales. Similarly, any depreciation recapture (including §1245, §1250, and §291 depreciation recapture) is not eligible for installment reporting and must be recognized in the year of sale.[45] However, the §1231 gain remaining after the depreciation recapture can be recognized using the installment method. To ensure that any depreciation recapture is not taxed twice (once immediately and then a second time as payments are received), taxable recapture-related gains that are taxable in the year of sale are *added to* the adjusted basis of the property sold to determine the gross profit percentage. The increase in basis reduces the gain realized, which also reduces the gross profit percentage and the amount of future gain that will ultimately be recognized as the taxpayer receives the installment payments. Installment sales are reported on Form 6252.

Example 3-20

What if: Assume that Teton agrees to sell some of its machinery for $90,000 for two equal payments of $45,000 plus interest. Teton's original basis was $80,000 and accumulated depreciation on the machinery was $30,000. Teton will receive one payment in year 1 (the current year) and the other payment in year 2. What are the amount and character of the gain Teton recognizes on the sale in year 1?

Answer: $30,000 ordinary income and $5,000 of §1231 gain, computed as follows:

Description	Amount	Explanation
(1) Sales price	$ 90,000	
(2) Initial basis	80,000	
(3) Accumulated depreciation	(30,000)	
(4) Adjusted basis	$ 50,000	(2) + (3)
(5) Realized gain (loss)	$ 40,000	(1) − (4)
(6) Ordinary income from depreciation recapture (not eligible for installment reporting)	**$30,000**	Ordinary income; lesser of (3) or (5)
(7) Gain eligible for installment reporting	$ 10,000	(5) − (6)
(8) Contract price	$ 90,000	(1) − assumed liabilities (-0-)
(9) Gross profit percentage	11.11%	(7)/(8)
(10) Payment received in year 1	$ 45,000	
Installment (§1231) gain recognized in year 1	**$ 5,000**	(10) × (9)

What are the amount and character of the gain Teton recognized upon receipt of the payment in year 2?

Answer: $5,000 of §1231 gain ($45,000 payment received × 11.11% gross profit percentage).

[45]§453(i). Unrecaptured §1250 gain is eligible for deferral but is recognized first upon gain recognition when cash payments are received [Reg. §1.453-12(a)].

Other Tax-Deferred Provisions

Several tax law provisions allow businesses to change the form or organization of their business while deferring the realized gains for tax purposes. For example, a sole proprietor can form the business as a corporation or contribute assets to an existing corporation and defer the gain realized on the exchange of assets for an ownership interest in the business entity.[46] Without the tax-deferred provision, the tax cost of forming a corporation may be large enough to deter taxpayers from doing so. Tax-deferral rules also apply to taxpayers forming partnerships or contributing assets to partnerships.[47] In still other corporate transactions, such as mergers or reorganizations, corporations can often do so in tax-deferred transactions.[48] While these transactions generally result in deferred gain or loss for the involved parties, the specific details of these topics can easily fill entire chapters. Further coverage is beyond the scope of this chapter (see later chapters for coverage of §351 and §721 tax-deferred transactions).

THE KEY FACTS

Related-Person Losses

- Related persons are defined in §267 and include certain family members, related corporations, and other entities.
- Losses on sales to related persons are not deductible by the seller.
- The related-person buyer may subsequently deduct the previously disallowed loss *to the extent of the gain* on the sale to an unrelated third party.

Related-Person Loss Disallowance Rules

Taxpayers selling business or investment property at a loss to unrelated persons are generally able to deduct the loss.[49] This makes sense in most situations because taxpayers are selling the property for less than their remaining investment (adjusted basis) in the property, and after the sale, the taxpayer's investment in the property is completely terminated. In contrast, when a taxpayer sells property at a loss to a related person, they effectively retain some element of control over the property through the related person. Consistent with this idea, §267(a) disallows recognition of losses on sales to related persons. Under §267, related persons include individuals with family relationships, including siblings, spouses, ancestors, and lineal descendants. Related persons also include an individual and a corporation if the individual owns more than 50 percent of the value of the stock of the corporation.[50]

Example 3-21

What if: Suppose Teton is formed as a C corporation and Steve is its sole shareholder. Teton is looking to make some long-term investments to fund its anticipated purchase of a new manufacturing facility. Steve currently owns 1,000 shares of stock in his previous company, Northeastern Corp., which he intends to sell in the near future. Steve initially paid $40 a share for the stock, but the stock is currently valued at $30 a share. While Steve believes the stock has good long-term potential, he needs cash now to purchase a personal residence in Cody, Wyoming. Steve believes selling the shares to Teton makes good sense because he can deduct the loss and save taxes now, and Teton can benefit from the expected long-term appreciation of the stock. If Steve sells 1,000 shares of Northeastern Corp. stock to Teton for $30 per share, what amount of loss will he realize and what amount of loss will he recognize for tax purposes?

Answer: $10,000 loss realized and $0 loss recognized, determined as follows:

Description	Amount	Explanation
(1) Amount realized on sale	$30,000	(1,000 × $30)
(2) Adjusted basis in stock	40,000	(1,000 × $40)
(3) Loss realized on sale	**(10,000)**	(1) – (2)
Loss recognized on sale	**$ 0**	Losses on sales to related persons are disallowed.

Because Steve owns more than 50 percent of Teton (he owns 100 percent), Steve and Teton are considered to be related persons. Consequently, Steve is not allowed to recognize any loss on the sale.

[46]§351.

[47]§721.

[48]Section 368(a) contains the numerous variations and requirements of these tax-deferred reorganizations.

[49]Capital losses are subject to certain limitations for individuals and corporate taxpayers (§1211).

[50]§267(a). The related-person rules include both direct ownership as well as indirect ownership (ownership attributed to the taxpayer from related persons). See §267(c) for a description of the indirect ownership rules.

Although taxpayers are not allowed to immediately deduct losses when they sell property to the related person, the related-person buyer may be able to subsequently deduct the disallowed loss by selling the property to an *unrelated* third party at a gain. The rules follow:

- If the related-person buyer sells the property at a gain (the related-person buyer sells it for more than their purchase price) greater than the disallowed loss, the entire loss that was disallowed for the related-person seller is deductible by the buyer.
- If the related-person buyer subsequently sells the property and the related-person seller's disallowed loss exceeds the related-person buyer's gain on the subsequent sale, the related-person buyer may only deduct or offset the previously disallowed loss *to the extent of the gain* on the sale to the unrelated third party—the remaining disallowed loss expires unused.
- If the related-person buyer sells the property for less than their purchase price from the related-person seller, the disallowed loss expires unused.
- The holding period for the related-person buyer begins on the date of the sale between the related persons.[51]

Example 3-22

What if: Let's return to Example 3-21, where Steve sold 1,000 shares of Northeastern Corp. stock to Teton for $30,000. As we discovered in that example, Steve realized a $10,000 loss on the sale, but he was not allowed to deduct it because Steve and Teton are related persons. Let's assume that a few years after Teton purchased the stock from Steve, Teton sells the Northeastern Corp. stock to an unrelated third party. What gain or loss does *Teton* recognize when it sells the stock in each of three scenarios, assuming it sells the stock for $37,000 in Scenario 1, $55,000 in Scenario 2, and $25,000 in Scenario 3?

Answer: $0 gain or loss in Scenario 1, $15,000 gain in Scenario 2, and $5,000 loss in Scenario 3, computed as follows:

Description	Scenario 1	Scenario 2	Scenario 3	Explanation
(1) Amount realized	$37,000	$ 55,000	$25,000	
(2) Adjusted basis	30,000	30,000	30,000	Example 3-21 (Teton's purchase price)
(3) Realized gain (loss)	$ 7,000	$ 25,000	$ (5,000)	(1) − (2)
(4) Benefit of Steve's ($10,000) disallowed loss	(7,000)	(10,000)	0	Loss benefit limited to realized gain.
Recognized gain (loss)	**$ 0**	**$15,000**	**$ (5,000)**	(3) + (4)

In Scenario 1, $3,000 of Steve's $10,000 remaining disallowed loss expires unused. In Scenario 3, Steve's entire $10,000 disallowed loss expires unused.

CONCLUSION

This chapter describes and discusses the tax consequences associated with sales and other types of property dispositions. We've learned how to determine the amount of gain or loss taxpayers recognize when they sell or otherwise dispose of property, and we've learned how to determine the character of these gains and losses. Tax accountants who understand the rules and concepts of property dispositions are able to comply with the tax law and advise clients of potential tax planning opportunities and avoid pitfalls associated with various tax-deferred provisions.

[51]Reg. §1.267(d)-1(c)(3).

Summary

LO 3-1 Calculate the amount of gain or loss recognized on the disposition of assets used in a trade or business.

- Dispositions occur in the form of sales, trades, or other realization events.
- Gain realized is the amount realized less the adjusted basis of an asset.
- Amount realized is everything of value received in the transaction less any selling costs.
- Adjusted basis is the historical cost or initial basis of an asset less any cost recovery deductions applied against the asset.
- Gain realized on asset dispositions is not always recognized.

LO 3-2 Describe the general character types of gain or loss recognized on property dispositions.

- Recognized gains must be characterized as ordinary, capital, or §1231. An asset's character is a function of the asset's use and holding period.
- Ordinary assets are derived from normal transactions of the business (revenues and accounts receivable), the sale of short-term trade or business assets, and depreciation recapture.
- Capital assets are assets that are held either for investment or for personal use (a taxpayer's principal residence).
- Section 1231 assets consist of property used in a taxpayer's trade or business that has been held for more than one year.
- Net §1231 gains are treated as long-term capital gains, and net §1231 losses are treated as ordinary losses.

LO 3-3 Calculate depreciation recapture.

- Section 1231 assets, other than land, are subject to cost recovery deductions (depreciation), which generate ordinary deductions.
- Gains that are created through depreciation deductions are subject to depreciation recapture. Any remaining gain is §1231 gain.
- Depreciation recapture does not change the amount of the gain but simply converts or recharacterizes the gain from §1231 to ordinary.
- Different recapture rules apply to tangible personal property (§1245) and real property (§291 for C corporations only and §1250).

LO 3-4 Describe the tax treatment of unrecaptured §1250 gains.

- When individuals sell §1250 property at a gain, the portion of the gain generated by depreciation deductions is called unrecaptured §1250 gain.
- This gain is a §1231 gain that, when treated as a capital gain after the §1231 netting process, flows into the capital gain/loss process (see the Investments chapter) and is taxed at a maximum rate of 25 percent.
- If a taxpayer sells an asset at a gain to a related person and the asset is a depreciable asset to the related person, the seller must characterize the entire gain as ordinary income.

LO 3-5 Describe the tax treatment of §1231 gains or losses, including the §1231 netting process.

- After applying the depreciation recapture rules, taxpayers calculate the net §1231 gain or loss.
- If a net §1231 loss results, the loss will become ordinary and offset ordinary income.
- If a net §1231 gain results, the §1231 look-back rule must be applied.
- After applying the look-back rule, any remaining net §1231 gain is a long-term capital gain.

LO 3-6 Explain common deferral exceptions to the general rule that realized gains and losses are recognized currently.

- Like-kind exchanges involve trading or exchanging real property used in a business or held for investment for similar real property. The gain is deferred unless boot or non-like-kind property is received.

- Involuntary conversions are the losses on property through circumstances beyond taxpayers' control. Reasons include natural disasters, accidents, theft, or condemnation.
- Installment sales occur when any portion of the amount realized is received in a year subsequent to the disposition. A portion of the gain is initially deferred but then recognized over time as payments are received.
- §267 related-person losses are disallowed, but the related-person buyer may be able to deduct the disallowed loss if they subsequently sell the property at a gain.

KEY TERMS

§291 depreciation recapture (3-14)
§1231 assets (3-8)
§1231 look-back rule (3-17)
§1245 property (3-10)
§1250 property (3-14)
adjusted basis (3-5)
amount realized (3-2)
boot (3-27)
capital asset (3-8)
deferred like-kind exchange (3-25)
depreciation recapture (3-10)
direct conversions (3-30)
indirect conversions (3-30)
installment sale (3-32)
involuntary conversions (3-29)
like-kind exchange (3-24)
nonrecaptured net §1231 losses (3-18)
ordinary asset (3-7)
production of income (3-8)
qualified replacement property (3-30)
realized gain or loss (3-5)
recognized gains or losses (3-6)
substituted basis (3-26)
tax-deferred transactions (3-24)
third-party intermediaries (3-25)
unrecaptured §1250 gain (3-15)

DISCUSSION QUESTIONS

Discussion Questions are available in Connect®.

Mc Graw Hill connect

1. Compare and contrast different ways in which a taxpayer triggers a realization event by disposing of an asset. LO 3-1
2. Potomac Corporation wants to sell a warehouse that it has used in its business for 10 years. Potomac is asking $450,000 for the property. The warehouse is subject to a mortgage of $125,000. If Potomac accepts Wyden Inc.'s offer to give Potomac $325,000 in cash and assume full responsibility for the mortgage on the property, what amount does Potomac realize on the sale? LO 3-1
3. Montana Max sells a 2,500-acre ranch for $1,000,000 in cash, a note receivable of $1,000,000, and debt relief of $2,400,000. He also pays selling commissions of $60,000. In addition, Max agrees to build a new barn on the property (cost $250,000) and spend $100,000 upgrading the fence on the property before the sale. What is Max's amount realized on the sale? LO 3-1
4. Hawkeye sold farming equipment for $55,000. It bought the equipment four years ago for $75,000, and it has since claimed a total of $42,000 in depreciation deductions against the asset. Explain how to calculate Hawkeye's adjusted basis in the farming equipment. LO 3-1
5. When a taxpayer sells an asset, what is the difference between realized and recognized gain or loss on the sale? LO 3-1
6. What does it mean to characterize a gain or loss? Why is characterizing a gain or loss important? LO 3-2
7. Explain the difference between ordinary, capital, and §1231 assets. LO 3-2
8. Discuss the reasons why individuals generally prefer capital gains over ordinary gains. Explain why corporate taxpayers might prefer capital gains over ordinary gains. LO 3-2
9. Dakota Conrad owns a parcel of land he would like to sell. Describe the circumstances in which the sale of the land would generate §1231 gain or loss, ordinary gain or loss, or capital gain or loss. Also, describe the circumstances under which Dakota would not be allowed to deduct a loss on the sale. LO 3-2

LO 3-2 10. Lincoln Brown has used a piece of land in their business for the past five years. The land qualifies as §1231 property. It is unclear whether Lincoln will have to recognize a gain or loss when they eventually sell the asset. Lincoln asks their accountant how the gain or loss would be characterized if they decide to sell. The accountant says that selling §1231 assets gives sellers "the best of both worlds." Explain what the accountant means by this statement.

LO 3-3 11. Explain Congress's rationale for depreciation recapture.

LO 3-3 12. Compare and contrast §1245 recapture and §1250 recapture.

LO 3-3 13. Why is depreciation recapture not required when assets are sold at a loss?

LO 3-3 14. What are the similarities and differences between the tax benefit rule and depreciation recapture?

LO 3-3 LO 3-4 15. Are both corporations and individuals subject to depreciation recapture when they sell depreciable real property at a gain? Explain.

LO 3-4 16. How is unrecaptured §1250 gain for individuals similar to depreciation recapture? How is it different?

LO 3-4 17. Explain why gains from depreciable property sold to a related taxpayer are treated as ordinary income under §1239.

LO 3-5 18. Bingaman Resources sold two depreciable §1231 assets during the year. One asset resulted in a large gain (the asset was sold for more than it was purchased) and the other resulted in a small loss. Describe the §1231 netting process for Bingaman.

LO 3-5 19. Jeraldine believes that when the §1231 look-back rule applies, the taxpayer deducts a §1231 loss in a previous year against §1231 gains in the current year. Explain whether Jeraldine's description is correct.

LO 3-5 20. Explain the purpose behind the §1231 look-back rule.

LO 3-5 21. Does a taxpayer apply the §1231 look-back rule in a year when the taxpayer recognizes a net §1231 loss? Explain.

LO 3-4 LO 3-5 22. Describe the circumstances in which an individual taxpayer with a net §1231 gain will have different portions of the gain taxed at different rates.

LO 3-6 23. Rocky and Bullwinkle Partnership sold a parcel of land during the current year and realized a gain of $250,000. Rocky and Bullwinkle did not recognize gain related to the sale of the land on its tax return. Is this possible? Explain how a taxpayer could realize a gain but not recognize it.

LO 3-6 24. Why does the tax code allow taxpayers to defer gains on like-kind exchanges? How do the tax laws ensure that the gains (or losses) are deferred and not permanently excluded from a taxpayer's income?

LO 3-6 25. Describe the like-kind property requirements for real property for purposes of qualifying for a like-kind exchange. Explain whether land held for investment by a corporation will qualify as like-kind property with land held by an individual for personal use.

LO 3-6 26. Salazar Inc., a Colorado company, is relocating to a nearby town. It would like to trade its real property for some real property in the new location. While Salazar has found several prospective buyers for its real property and has also located several properties that are acceptable in the new location, it cannot find anyone willing to trade Salazar Inc. for its property in a like-kind exchange. Explain how a third-party intermediary could facilitate Salazar's like-kind exchange.

LO 3-6 27. Minuteman wants to enter into a like-kind exchange by exchanging its old New England manufacturing facility for a ranch in Wyoming. Minuteman is using a third-party intermediary to facilitate the exchange. The purchaser of the manufacturing facility wants to complete the transaction immediately, but, for various reasons, the ranch transaction will not be completed for three to four months. Will this delay cause a problem for Minuteman's desire to accomplish this through a like-kind exchange? Explain.

28. Olympia Corporation, of Kittery, Maine, wants to exchange its manufacturing facility for Bangor Company's warehouse. Both parties agree that Olympia's building is worth $100,000 and that Bangor's building is worth $95,000. Olympia would like the transaction to qualify as a like-kind exchange. What could the parties do to equalize the value exchanged but still allow the exchange to qualify as a like-kind exchange? How would the necessary change affect the tax consequences of the transaction? LO 3-6
29. Compare and contrast the similarities and differences between like-kind exchanges and involuntary conversions for tax purposes. LO 3-6
30. What is an installment sale? How do the tax laws ensure that taxpayers recognize all the gain they realize on an installment sale? How is depreciation recapture treated in an installment sale? Explain the gross profit ratio and how it relates to gains recognized under installment method sales. LO 3-6
31. Mr. Kyle owns stock in a local publicly traded company. Although the stock price has declined since he purchased it two years ago, he likes the long-term prospects for the company. If Kyle sells the stock to his sister because he needs some cash for a down payment on a new home, is the loss deductible? If Kyle is right and the stock price increases in the future, how is his sister's gain computed if she sells the stock? LO 3-6

PROBLEMS

Select problems are available in Connect®.

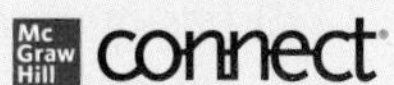

32. Rafael sold an asset to Jamal. What is Rafael's amount realized on the sale in each of the following alternative scenarios? LO 3-1
    a) Rafael received $80,000 cash and a vehicle worth $10,000. Rafael also paid $5,000 in selling expenses.
    b) Rafael received $80,000 cash and was relieved of a $30,000 mortgage on the asset he sold to Jamal. Rafael also paid a commission of $5,000 on the transaction.
    c) Rafael received $20,000 cash, a parcel of land worth $50,000, and marketable securities of $10,000. Rafael also paid a commission of $8,000 on the transaction.
33. Alan Meer inherits a hotel from his grandmother, Mary, on February 11 of the current year. Mary bought the hotel for $730,000 three years ago. Mary deducted $27,000 of cost recovery on the hotel before her death. The fair market value of the hotel in February is $725,000. (Assume that the alternative valuation date is not used.) LO 3-1
    a) What is Alan's adjusted basis in the hotel?
    b) If the fair market value of the hotel at the time of Mary's death was $500,000, what is Alan's basis?
34. Shasta Corporation sold a piece of land to Bill for $45,000. Shasta bought the land two years ago for $30,600. What gain or loss does Shasta realize on the transaction? LO 3-1
35. Lassen Corporation sold a machine to a machine dealer for $25,000. Lassen bought the machine for $55,000 and has claimed $15,000 of depreciation expense on the machine. What gain or loss does Lassen realize on the transaction? LO 3-1
36. Hannah Tywin owns 100 shares of MM Inc. stock. She sells the stock on December 11 for $25 per share. She received the stock as a gift from her Aunt Pam on March 20 of this year when the fair market value of the stock was $18 per share. Aunt Pam originally purchased the stock seven years ago at a price of $12 per share. What are the amount and character of Hannah's recognized gain on the stock? LO 3-1 LO 3-2

LO 3-1 LO 3-2

37. On September 30 of last year, Rex received some investment land from Holly as a gift. Holly's basis was $50,000 and the land was valued at $40,000 at the time of the gift. Holly acquired the land five years ago. What are the amount and character of Rex's recognized gain (loss) if he sells the land on May 12 this year at the following prices?
    a) $32,000
    b) $70,000
    c) $45,000

LO 3-1 LO 3-2

38. Franco converted a building from personal to business use in May 2019 when the fair market value was $55,000. He purchased the building in July 2016 for $80,000. On December 15 of this year, Franco sells the building for $40,000. On the date of sale, the accumulated depreciation on the building is $5,565. What is Franco's recognized gain or loss on the sale?

LO 3-2

39. Identify each of Avery Corporation's following assets as an ordinary, capital, or §1231 asset.
    a) Two years ago, Avery used its excess cash to purchase a piece of land as an investment.
    b) Two years ago, Avery purchased land and a warehouse. It uses these assets in its business.
    c) Manufacturing machinery Avery purchased earlier this year.
    d) Inventory Avery purchased 13 months ago that is ready to be shipped to a customer.
    e) Office equipment Avery has used in its business for the past three years.
    f) 1,000 shares of stock in Plaid Corporation that Avery purchased two years ago because it was a good investment.
    g) Account receivable from a customer with terms 2/10, net 30.
    h) Machinery Avery held for three years and then sold at a loss of $10,000.

LO 3-3 LO 3-4

40. In year 0, Canon purchased a machine to use in its business for $56,000. In year 3, Canon sold the machine for $42,000. Between the date of the purchase and the date of the sale, Canon depreciated the machine by $32,000.
    a) What are the amount and character of the gain or loss Canon will recognize on the sale, assuming that it is a partnership?
    b) What are the amount and character of the gain or loss Canon will recognize on the sale, assuming that it is a corporation?
    c) What are the amount and character of the gain or loss Canon will recognize on the sale, assuming that it is a corporation and the sale proceeds were increased to $60,000?
    d) What are the amount and character of the gain or loss Canon will recognize on the sale, assuming that it is a corporation and the sale proceeds were decreased to $20,000?

LO 3-3 LO 3-4

41. In year 0, Longworth Partnership purchased a machine for $40,000 to use in its business. In year 3, Longworth sold the machine for $35,000. Between the date of the purchase and the date of the sale, Longworth depreciated the machine by $22,000.
    a) What are the amount and character of the gain or loss Longworth will recognize on the sale?
    b) What are the amount and character of the gain or loss Longworth will recognize on the sale if the sale proceeds are increased to $45,000?
    c) What are the amount and character of the gain or loss Longworth will recognize on the sale if the sale proceeds are decreased to $15,000?

42. On August 1 of year 0, Dirksen purchased a machine for $20,000 to use in its business. On December 4 of year 0, Dirksen sold the machine for $18,000. LO 3-3 LO 3-4
    a) What are the amount and character of the gain or loss Dirksen will recognize on the sale?
    b) Dirksen depreciated the machinery using MACRS (seven-year recovery period). What are the amount and character of the gain or loss Dirksen will recognize on the sale if the machine is sold on January 15 of year 1 instead?
43. Rayburn Corporation has a building that it bought during year 0 for $850,000. It sold the building in year 5. During the time it held the building, Rayburn depreciated it by $100,000. What are the amount and character of the gain or loss Rayburn will recognize on the sale in each of the following alternative situations? LO 3-3 LO 3-4
    a) Rayburn receives $840,000.
    b) Rayburn receives $900,000.
    c) Rayburn receives $700,000.
44. Moran owns a building he bought during year 0 for $150,000. He sold the building in year 6. During the time he held the building, he depreciated it by $32,000. What are the amount and character of the gain or loss Moran will recognize on the sale in each of the following alternative situations? LO 3-3 LO 3-4
    a) Moran received $145,000.
    b) Moran received $170,000.
    c) Moran received $110,000.
45. Hart, an individual, bought an asset for $500,000 and has claimed $100,000 of depreciation deductions against the asset. Hart has a marginal tax rate of 32 percent. Answer the questions presented in the following alternative scenarios (assume Hart had no property transactions other than those described in the problem): LO 3-3 LO 3-4 LO 3-5 planning
    a) What are the amount and character of Hart's recognized gain or loss if the asset is tangible personal property sold for $450,000? What effect does the sale have on Hart's tax liability for the year?
    b) What are the amount and character of Hart's recognized gain or loss if the asset is tangible personal property sold for $550,000? What effect does the sale have on Hart's tax liability for the year?
    c) What are the amount and character of Hart's recognized gain or loss if the asset is tangible personal property sold for $350,000? What effect does the sale have on Hart's tax liability for the year?
    d) What are the amount and character of Hart's recognized gain or loss if the asset is a nonresidential building sold for $450,000? What effect does the sale have on Hart's tax liability for the year?
    e) Now assume that Hart is a C corporation. What are the amount and character of its recognized gain or loss if the asset is a nonresidential building sold for $450,000? What effect does the sale have on Hart's tax liability for the year (assume a 21 percent tax rate)?
    f) Assuming that the asset is real property, which entity type should be used to minimize the taxes paid on real estate gains?
46. Luke sold a building and the land on which the building sits to his wholly owned corporation, Studemont Corp., at fair market value. The fair market value of the building was determined to be $325,000; Luke built the building several years ago at a cost of $200,000. Luke had claimed $45,000 of depreciation on the building. The fair market value of the land was determined to be $210,000 at the time of the sale; Luke purchased the land many years ago for $130,000. LO 3-4
    a) What are the amount and character of Luke's recognized gain or loss on the building?
    b) What are the amount and character of Luke's recognized gain or loss on the land?

LO 3-5

47. Buckley, an individual, began business two years ago and has never sold a §1231 asset. Buckley has owned each of the assets since he began the business. In the current year, Buckley sold the following business assets:

Asset	Accumulated Original Cost	Depreciation	Gain/Loss
Computers	$ 6,000	$ 2,000	$(3,000)
Machinery	10,000	4,000	(2,000)
Furniture	20,000	12,000	7,000
Building	100,000	10,000	(1,000)

Assuming Buckley's marginal ordinary income tax rate is 32 percent, answer the questions for the following alternative scenarios:

a) What is the character of Buckley's gains or losses for the current year? What effect do the gains and losses have on Buckley's tax liability?

b) Assume that the amount realized increased so that the building was sold at a $6,000 gain instead. What is the character of Buckley's gains or losses for the current year? What effect do the gains and losses have on Buckley's tax liability?

c) Assume that the amount realized increased so that the building was sold at a $15,000 gain instead. What is the character of Buckley's gains or losses for the current year? What effect do the gains and losses have on Buckley's tax liability?

LO 3-3 LO 3-4 LO 3-5

48. Lily Tucker (single) owns and operates a bike shop as a sole proprietorship. In 2022, she sells the following long-term assets used in her business:

Asset	Sales Price	Cost	Accumulated Depreciation
Building	$230,000	$200,000	$52,000
Equipment	80,000	148,000	23,000

Lily's taxable income before these transactions is $190,500. What are Lily's taxable income and tax liability for the year?

LO 3-3 LO 3-4 LO 3-5

49. Shimmer Inc. is a calendar-year-end, accrual-method corporation. This year, it sells the following long-term assets:

Asset	Sales Price	Cost	Accumulated Depreciation
Building	$650,000	$642,000	$37,000
Sparkle Corporation stock	130,000	175,000	n/a

Shimmer does not sell any other assets during the year, and its taxable income before these transactions is $800,000. What are Shimmer's taxable income and tax liability for the year?

LO 3-5
planning

50. Aruna, a sole proprietor, wants to sell two assets that she no longer needs for her business. Both assets qualify as §1231 assets. The first is machinery and will generate a $10,000 §1231 loss on the sale. The second is land that will generate a $7,000 §1231 gain on the sale. Aruna's ordinary marginal tax rate is 32 percent.

a) Assuming she sells both assets in December of year 1 (the current year), what effect will the sales have on Aruna's tax liability?

b) Assuming that Aruna sells the land in December of year 1 and the machinery in January of year 2, what effect will the sales have on Aruna's tax liability for each year?

c) Explain why selling the assets in separate years will result in greater tax savings for Aruna.

51. Bourne Guitars, a corporation, reported a $157,000 net §1231 gain for year 6. LO 3-5
    a) Assuming Bourne reported $50,000 of nonrecaptured net §1231 losses during years 1–5, what amount of Bourne's net §1231 gain for year 6, if any, is treated as ordinary income?
    b) Assuming Bourne's nonrecaptured net §1231 losses from years 1–5 were $200,000, what amount of Bourne's net §1231 gain for year 6, if any, is treated as ordinary income?

52. Tonya Jefferson (single), a sole proprietor, runs a successful lobbying business in Washington, D.C. She doesn't sell many business assets, but she is planning on retiring and selling her historic townhouse, from which she runs her business, to buy a place somewhere sunny and warm. Tonya's townhouse is worth $1,000,000 and the land is worth another $1,000,000. The original basis in the townhouse was $600,000, and she has claimed $250,000 of depreciation deductions against the asset over the years. The original basis in the land was $500,000. Tonya has located a buyer that would like to finalize the transaction in December of the current year. Tonya's marginal ordinary income tax rate is 35 percent, and her capital gains tax rate is 20 percent. LO 3-5 planning
    a) What amount of gain or loss does Tonya recognize on the sale? What is the character of the gain or loss? What effect does the gain or loss have on her tax liability?
    b) In addition to the original facts, assume that Tonya reports the following nonrecaptured net §1231 loss:

Year	Net §1231 Gains/(Losses)
Year 1	$(200,000)
Year 2	0
Year 3	0
Year 4	0
Year 5	0
Year 6 (current year)	?

    What amount of gain or loss does Tonya recognize on the sale? What is the character of the gain or loss? What effect does the gain or loss have on her year 6 (the current year) tax liability?
    c) As Tonya's tax adviser, you suggest that Tonya sell the townhouse in year 7 in order to reduce her taxes. What amount of gain or loss does Tonya recognize on the sale in year 7?

53. Morgan's Water World (MWW), an LLC, opened several years ago. MWW has reported the following net §1231 gains and losses since it began business. Net §1231 gains shown are before the look-back rule. LO 3-5

Year	Net §1231 Gains/(Losses)
Year 1	$ (11,000)
Year 2	5,000
Year 3	(21,000)
Year 4	(4,000)
Year 5	17,000
Year 6	(43,000)
Year 7 (current year)	113,000

What amount, if any, of the current year (year 7) $113,000 net §1231 gain is treated as ordinary income?

LO 3-5

54. Hans runs a sole proprietorship. Hans has reported the following net §1231 gains and losses since he began business. Net §1231 gains shown are before the look-back rule.

Year	Net §1231 Gains/(Losses)
Year 1	$(65,000)
Year 2	15,000
Year 3	0
Year 4	0
Year 5	10,000
Year 6	0
Year 7 (current year)	50,000

a) What amount, if any, of the year 7 (current year) $50,000 net §1231 gain is treated as ordinary income?

b) Assume that the $50,000 net §1231 gain occurs in year 6 instead of year 7. What amount of the gain would be treated as ordinary income in year 6?

LO 3-6

55. Independence Corporation needs to replace some of the assets used in its trade or business and is contemplating the following exchanges:

Exchange	Asset Given Up by Independence	Asset Received by Independence
A	Office building in Chicago, IL	Piece of land in Toronto, Canada
B	Large warehouse on 2 acres	Small warehouse on 22 acres
C	Office building in Green Bay, WI, used in the business	Apartment complex in Newport Beach, CA, that will be held as an investment

Determine whether each exchange qualifies as a like-kind exchange. Also, explain the rationale for why each qualifies or does not qualify as a like-kind exchange.

LO 3-6

56. Kase, an individual, purchased some property in Potomac, Maryland, for $150,000 approximately 10 years ago. Kase is approached by a real estate agent representing a client who would like to exchange a parcel of land in North Carolina for Kase's Maryland property. Kase agrees to the exchange. What is Kase's realized gain or loss, recognized gain or loss, and basis in the North Carolina property in each of the following alternative scenarios?

a) The transaction qualifies as a like-kind exchange, and the fair market value of each property is $675,000.

b) The transaction qualifies as a like-kind exchange, and the fair market value of each property is $100,000.

LO 3-6
research

57. Longhaul Real Estate exchanged a parcel of land it held for sale in Bryan, Texas, for a warehouse in College Station, Texas. Will the exchange qualify for like-kind treatment?

LO 3-6
research
planning

58. Twinbrook Corporation needed to upgrade to a larger manufacturing facility. Twinbrook first acquired a new manufacturing facility for $2,100,000 cash and then transferred the facility it was using (building and land) to White Flint Corporation for $2,000,000 three months later. Does the exchange qualify for like-kind exchange treatment? (*Hint:* Examine Revenue Procedures 2000-37 and 2004-51.) If not, can you propose a change in the transaction that will allow it to qualify?

LO 3-6
research

59. Woodley Park Corporation currently owns two parcels of land (parcel 1 and parcel 2). It owns a warehouse facility on parcel 1. Woodley needs to acquire a new and larger manufacturing facility. Woodley was approached by Blazing Fast Construction (which specializes in prefabricated warehouses) about acquiring Woodley's existing warehouse on parcel 1. Woodley indicated that it would prefer to exchange its

existing facility for a new and larger facility in a qualifying like-kind exchange. Blazing Fast indicated that it could construct a new manufacturing facility on parcel 2 to Woodley's specification within four months. Woodley and Blazing Fast agreed to the following arrangement. First, Blazing Fast would construct the new warehouse on parcel 2 and then relinquish the property to Woodley within four months. Woodley would then transfer the warehouse facility and land parcel 1 to Blazing Fast. All of the property exchanged in the deal was identified immediately and the construction was completed within 180 days. Does the exchange of the new building for the old building and parcel 1 qualify as a like-kind exchange? [*Hint*: See *DeCleene v. Comm'r*, 115 TC 457 (2000).]

60. Metro Corp. traded building A for building B. Metro originally purchased building A for $50,000, and building A's adjusted basis was $25,000 at the time of the exchange. What is Metro's realized gain or loss, recognized gain or loss, and adjusted basis in building B in each of the following alternative scenarios? LO 3-6
    a) The fair market value of building A and of building B is $40,000 at the time of the exchange. The exchange does not qualify as a like-kind exchange.
    b) The fair market value of building A and of building B is $40,000. The exchange qualifies as a like-kind exchange.
    c) The fair market value of building A is $35,000, and building B is valued at $40,000. Metro exchanges building A and $5,000 cash for building B. Building A and building B are like-kind property.
    d) The fair market value of building A is $45,000, and Metro trades building A for building B valued at $40,000 and $5,000 cash. Building A and building B are like-kind property.
61. Prater Inc. enters into an exchange in which it gives up its warehouse on 10 acres of land and receives a tract of land. A summary of the exchange is as follows: LO 3-6

Transferred	FMV	Original Basis	Accumulated Depreciation
Warehouse	$300,000	$225,000	$45,000
Land	50,000	50,000	
Mortgage on warehouse	30,000		
Cash	20,000	20,000	
Assets received	**FMV**		
Land	$340,000		

What are Prater's realized and recognized gain on the exchange and its basis in the assets it received in the exchange?

62. Baker Corporation owned a building located in Kansas. Baker used the building for its business operations. Last year, a tornado hit the property and completely destroyed it. This year, Baker received an insurance settlement. Baker had originally purchased the building for $350,000 and had claimed a total of $100,000 of depreciation deductions against the property. What are Baker's realized and recognized gain or (loss) on this transaction and what is its basis in the new building in the following alternative scenarios? LO 3-6
    a) Baker received $450,000 in insurance proceeds and spent $450,000 rebuilding the building during the current year.
    b) Baker received $450,000 in insurance proceeds and spent $500,000 rebuilding the building during the current year.
    c) Baker received $450,000 in insurance proceeds and spent $400,000 rebuilding the building during the current year.
    d) Baker received $450,000 in insurance proceeds and spent $450,000 rebuilding the building during the next three years.

LO 3-6

63. Russell Corporation sold a parcel of land valued at $400,000. Its basis in the land was $275,000. For the land, Russell received $50,000 in cash in year 0 and a note providing that Russell will receive $175,000 in year 1 and $175,000 in year 2 from the buyer.
    a) What is Russell's realized gain on the transaction?
    b) What is Russell's recognized gain in year 0, year 1, and year 2?

LO 3-6

64. In year 0, Javens Inc. sold machinery with a fair market value of $400,000 to Chris. The machinery's original basis was $317,000, and Javens's accumulated depreciation on the machinery was $50,000, so its adjusted basis to Javens was $267,000. Chris paid Javens $40,000 immediately (in year 0) and provided a note to Javens indicating that Chris would pay Javens $60,000 a year for six years beginning in year 1. What are the amount and character of the gain that Javens will recognize in year 0? What amount and character of the gain will Javens recognize in years 1 through 6?

LO 3-6
research

65. Ken sold a rental property for $500,000. He received $100,000 in the current year and $100,000 each year for the next four years. Of the sales price, $400,000 was allocated to the building, and the remaining $100,000 was allocated to the land. Ken purchased the property several years ago for $300,000. When he initially purchased the property, he allocated $225,000 of the purchase price to the building and $75,000 to the land. Ken has claimed $25,000 of depreciation deductions over the years against the building. Ken had no other sales of §1231 or capital assets in the current year. For the year of the sale, determine Ken's recognized gain or loss and the character of Ken's gain, and calculate Ken's tax due because of the sale (assuming his marginal ordinary tax rate is 32 percent). (*Hint:* See the examples in Reg. §1.453-12.)

LO 3-6
planning

66. Hill Corporation is in the leasing business and faces a marginal tax rate of 21 percent. It has leased a building to Whitewater Corporation for several years. Hill bought the building for $150,000 and claimed $20,000 of depreciation deductions against the asset. The lease term is about to expire and Whitewater would like to acquire the building. Hill has been offered two options:

Option	Details
Like-kind exchange	Whitewater would provide Hill with a like-kind building. The like-kind building has a fair market value of $135,000.
Installment sale	Whitewater would provide Hill with two payments of $69,000. It would use the proceeds to purchase another building that it could also lease.

    Ignoring time value of money, which option provides the greater after-tax value for Hill, assuming it is indifferent between the proposals based on nontax factors?

LO 3-6

67. Deirdre sold 100 shares of stock to her brother, James, for $2,400. Deirdre purchased the stock several years ago for $3,000.
    a) What gain or loss does Deirdre recognize on the sale?
    b) What amount of gain or loss does James recognize if he sells the stock for $3,200?
    c) What amount of gain or loss does James recognize if he sells the stock for $2,600?
    d) What amount of gain or loss does James recognize if he sells the stock for $2,000?

COMPREHENSIVE PROBLEMS

Select problems are available in Connect®. 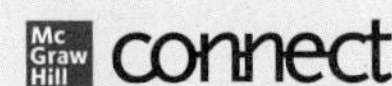

68. Two years ago, Bethesda Corporation bought a delivery truck for $30,000 (not subject to the luxury auto depreciation limits). Bethesda used MACRS 200 percent declining balance and the half-year convention to recover the cost of the truck, but it did not elect §179 expensing and opted out of bonus depreciation. Answer the questions for the following alternative scenarios.
   a) Assuming Bethesda used the truck until it sold it in March of year 3, what depreciation expense can it claim on the truck for years 1 through 3?
   b) Assume that Bethesda claimed $18,500 of depreciation expense on the truck before it sold it in year 3. What are the amount and character of the gain or loss if Bethesda sold the truck in year 3 for $17,000 and incurred $2,000 of selling expenses on the sale?
   c) Assume that Bethesda claimed $18,500 of depreciation expense on the truck before it sold it in year 3. What are the amount and character of the gain or loss if Bethesda sold the truck in year 3 for $35,000 and incurred $3,000 of selling expenses on the sale?
69. Hauswirth Corporation sold (or exchanged) a warehouse in year 0. Hauswirth bought the warehouse several years ago for $65,000, and it has claimed $23,000 of depreciation expense against the building.
   a) Assuming that Hauswirth receives $50,000 in cash for the warehouse, compute the amount and character of Hauswirth's recognized gain or loss on the sale.
   b) Assuming that Hauswirth exchanges the warehouse in a like-kind exchange for some land with a fair market value of $50,000, compute Hauswirth's realized gain or loss, recognized gain or loss, deferred gain or loss, and basis in the new land.
   c) Assuming that Hauswirth receives $20,000 in cash in year 0 and a $50,000 note receivable that is payable in year 1, compute the amount and character of Hauswirth's gain or loss in year 0 and in year 1.
70. Fontenot Corporation sold some machinery to its majority owner Gray (an individual who owns 60 percent of Fontenot). Fontenot purchased the machinery for $100,000 and has claimed a total of $40,000 of depreciation expense deductions against the property. Gray will provide Fontenot with $10,000 cash today and provide a $100,000 note that will pay Fontenot $50,000 one year from now and $50,000 two years from now. 
   a) What gain or loss does Fontenot realize on the sale?
   b) What are the amount and character of the gain or loss that Fontenot must recognize in the year of sale (if any) and each of the two subsequent years? (*Hint:* Use the Internal Revenue Code and start with §453; please give appropriate citations.)
71. Moab Inc. manufactures and distributes high-tech biking gadgets. It has decided to streamline some of its operations so that it will be able to be more productive and efficient. Because of this decision, it has entered into several transactions during the year. **tax forms**

   Part (1): Determine the gain/loss realized and recognized in the current year for each of these events. Also determine whether the gain/loss recognized will be §1231, capital, or ordinary.
   a) Moab Inc. sold a machine that it used to make computerized gadgets for $27,300 cash. It originally bought the machine for $19,200 three years ago and has taken $8,000 in depreciation.
   b) Moab Inc. held stock in ABC Corp., which had a value of $12,000 at the beginning of the year. That same stock had a value of $15,230 at the end of the year.
   c) Moab Inc. sold some of its inventory for $7,000 cash. This inventory had a basis of $5,000.

d) Moab Inc. disposed of an office building with a fair market value of $75,000 for another office building with a fair market value of $55,000 and $20,000 in cash. It originally bought the office building seven years ago for $62,000 and has taken $15,000 in depreciation.

e) Moab Inc. sold some land held for investment for $28,000. It originally bought the land for $32,000 two years ago.

f) Moab Inc. sold another machine for a note payable in four annual installments of $12,000. The first payment was received in the current year. It originally bought the machine two years ago for $32,000 and has claimed $9,000 in depreciation expense against the machine.

g) Moab Inc. sold stock it held for eight years for $2,750. It originally purchased the stock for $2,100.

h) Moab Inc. sold another machine for $7,300. It originally purchased this machine six months ago for $9,000 and has claimed $830 in depreciation expense against the asset.

Part (2): From the recognized gains/losses determined in part (1), determine the net §1231 gain/loss, the net ordinary gain/loss, and the net capital gain/loss Moab will recognize on its tax return. Moab Inc. also has $2,000 of nonrecaptured net §1231 losses from previous years.

Part (3): Complete Moab Inc.'s Form 4797 for the year. Use the most current form available.

research

72. Vertovec Inc., a large local consulting firm in Utah, hired several new consultants from out of state last year to help service its expanding list of clients. To aid in relocating the consultants, Vertovec Inc. purchased the consultants' homes in their prior location if the consultants were unable to sell their homes within 30 days of listing them for sale. Vertovec Inc. bought the homes from the consultants for 5 percent less than the list price and then continued to list the homes for sale. Each home Vertovec Inc. purchased was sold at a loss. By the end of last year, Vertovec had suffered a loss totaling $250,000 from the homes. How should Vertovec treat the loss for tax purposes? Write a memo to Vertovec Inc. explaining your findings and any planning suggestions that you may have if Vertovec Inc. continues to offer this type of relocation benefit to newly hired consultants.

tax forms

73. WAR (We Are Rich) has been in business since 1989. WAR is an accrual-method sole proprietorship that deals in the manufacturing and wholesaling of various types of golf equipment. Hack & Hack CPAs has filed accurate tax returns for WAR's owner since WAR opened its doors. The managing partner of Hack & Hack (Jack) has gotten along very well with the owner of WAR—Mr. Someday Woods (single). However, in early 2022, Jack Hack and Someday Woods played a round of golf, and Jack, for the first time ever, beat Mr. Woods. Mr. Woods was so upset that he fired Hack & Hack and has hired you to compute his 2022 taxable income. Mr. Woods was able to provide you with the following information from prior tax returns. The taxable income numbers reflect the results from all of Mr. Woods's activities *except for the items separately stated.* You will need to consider how to handle the separately stated items for tax purposes. Also, note that the 2017–2021 numbers do not reflect capital loss carryovers.

Description	2017	2018	2019	2020	2021
Ordinary taxable income	$ 4,000	$ 2,000	$94,000	$170,000	$250,000
Other items not included in ordinary taxable income					
Net gain (loss) on disposition of §1231 assets	3,000	10,000		(6,000)	
Net long-term capital gain (loss) on disposition of capital assets	(15,000)	1,000	(7,000)		(7,000)

In 2022, Mr. Woods had taxable income in the amount of $480,000 *before* considering the following events and transactions that transpired in 2022:

a) On January 1, 2022, WAR purchased a plot of land for $100,000 with the intention of creating a driving range where patrons could test their new golf equipment. WAR never got around to building the driving range; instead, WAR sold the land on October 1, 2022, for $40,000.

b) On August 17, 2022, WAR sold its golf testing machine, "Iron Byron," and replaced it with a new machine, "Iron Tiger." "Iron Byron" was purchased and installed for a total cost of $22,000 on February 5, 2018. At the time of sale, "Iron Byron" had an adjusted tax basis of $4,000. WAR sold "Iron Byron" for $25,000.

c) In the months October through December 2022, WAR sold various assets to come up with the funds necessary to invest in WAR's latest and greatest invention—the three-dimple golf ball. Data on these assets are provided below:

Asset	Placed in Service (or Purchased)	Sold	Initial Basis	Accumulated Depreciation	Selling Price
Someday's black leather sofa (used in office)	4/4/21	10/16/22	$ 3,000	$ 540	$ 2,900
Someday's office chair	3/1/20	11/8/22	8,000	3,000	4,000
Marketable securities	2/1/19	12/1/22	12,000	0	20,000
Land held for investment	7/1/21	11/29/22	45,000	0	48,000
Other investment property	11/30/20	10/15/22	10,000	0	8,000

d) Finally, on May 7, 2022, WAR decided to sell the building where it tested its plutonium shaft and lignite head drivers. WAR purchased the building on January 5, 2010, for $190,000 ($170,000 for the building, $20,000 for the land). At the time of the sale, the accumulated depreciation on the building was $50,000. WAR sold the building (with the land) for $300,000. The fair market value of the land at the time of sale was $45,000.

Part (1): Compute Mr. Woods's taxable income *after* taking into account the transactions described above.

Part (2): Compute Mr. Woods's tax liability for the year. (Ignore any net investment income tax for the year and assume the 20 percent qualified business income deduction is included in taxable income before these transactions.)

Part (3): Complete Mr. Woods's Form 8949, Schedule D, and Form 4797 (use the most current version of these schedules) to be attached to his Form 1040. Assume that asset bases are not reported to the IRS.

74. Fizbo Corporation is in the business of breeding and racing horses. Fizbo has taxable income of $5,000,000 other than from these transactions. It has nonrecaptured §1231 losses of $10,000 from 2018 and $13,000 from 2016.

Consider the following transactions that occur during 2022:

a) A building with an adjusted basis of $300,000 is totally destroyed by fire. Fizbo receives insurance proceeds of $400,000 but does not plan to replace the building. The building was built 12 years ago at a cost of $420,000 and was used to provide lodging for employees.

b) Fizbo sells four acres of undeveloped farmland (used for grazing) for $50,000. Fizbo purchased the land 15 years ago for $15,000.

c) Fizbo sells a racehorse for $250,000. The racehorse was purchased four years ago for $200,000. Total depreciation taken on the racehorse was $160,000.

d) Fizbo exchanges equipment that was purchased three years ago for $300,000 for $100,000 of IBM common stock. The adjusted basis of the equipment is $220,000. If straight-line depreciation had been used, the adjusted basis would be $252,000.

e) On November 1, Fizbo sold XCON stock for $50,000. Fizbo had purchased the stock on December 12, 2021, for $112,000.

Part (1): After *all* netting is complete, what is Fizbo's total amount of income from these transactions to be treated as ordinary income or loss? What is its capital gain or loss?

Part (2): What is Fizbo's taxable income for the year after including the effects of these transactions?

UWorld Roger CPA Review

Sample CPA Exam questions from Roger CPA Review are available in Connect as support for the topics in this text. These Multiple Choice Questions and Task-Based Simulations include expert-written explanations and solutions and provide a starting point for students to become familiar with the content and functionality of the actual CPA Exam.

chapter

4 Business Entities Overview

Learning Objectives

Upon completing this chapter, you should be able to:

LO 4-1 Discuss the legal and other nontax characteristics of different types of legal business entities.

LO 4-2 Describe the different types of business entities for tax purposes.

LO 4-3 Identify fundamental differences in tax characteristics across business entity types.

Gyorgy Barna/Shutterstock

Storyline Summary

Taxpayer:	Nicole Johnson (she/her/hers)
Location:	Salt Lake City, Utah
Employment status:	State government employee with entrepreneurial ambitions

Nicole Johnson is currently employed by the Utah Chamber of Commerce in Salt Lake City, Utah. While she enjoys the relatively short workweeks, she eventually would like to work for herself. In her current position, she deals with a lot of successful entrepreneurs who have become role models for her. Nicole has also developed an extensive list of contacts that should prove valuable when she starts her own business. It has taken a while, but Nicole believes she has finally developed a viable new business idea. Her idea is to design and manufacture bed sheets that have various colored patterns and are made of unique fabric blends. The sheets look great and are extremely comfortable whether the bedroom is warm or cool. She has had several friends try out her prototype sheets, and they have consistently given the sheets rave reviews. With this encouragement, Nicole started giving serious thought to making "Color Comfort Sheets" a moneymaking enterprise.

Nicole has enough business background to realize that she is embarking on a risky path, but one, she hopes, with significant potential rewards. After creating some initial income projections, Nicole realized that it will take a few years for the business to become profitable.

While Nicole's original plan was to start the business by herself, she is considering seeking out another equity owner so that she can add financial resources and business experience to the venture. Nicole feels like she has a grasp on her business plan, but she still needs to determine how to organize the business for tax purposes. After doing some research, Nicole learned that she should consider many factors in order to determine the "best" entity type for her business. Each type of entity has advantages and disadvantages from both tax and nontax perspectives, and the best entity for a business depends on the goals, outlook, and strategy for that particular business and its owners. She understands that she has more work to do to make an informed decision.

(to be continued . . .)

This chapter explores various types of legal business entities and then discusses business entities available for tax purposes. We outline some of the pros and cons of each business entity type from both nontax and tax perspectives, as we help Nicole determine how she will organize her business to best accomplish her goals. Subsequent chapters provide additional detail concerning the tax characteristics of each business entity type.

LO 4-1

BUSINESS ENTITY LEGAL CLASSIFICATION AND NONTAX CHARACTERISTICS

When forming new business ventures, entrepreneurs can choose to house their operations under one of several basic business entity types. These business entities differ in terms of their legal and tax considerations. In fact, as we discuss in more depth below, the legal classification of a business may be different from its tax classification. These business entities differ in terms of the formalities that entrepreneurs must follow to create them, the legal rights and responsibilities conferred on the entities and their owners, and the tax rules that determine how the business entities and owners will be taxed on income generated by the entities. CPAs are frequently asked to help clients choose the best entity choice for their businesses.

Legal Classification

Generally, a business entity legally may be classified as a **corporation,** a **limited liability company (LLC),** a **general partnership (GP),** a **limited partnership (LP),** or a **sole proprietorship** (not formed as an LLC).[1] Under state law, corporations are recognized as legal entities separate from their owners (i.e., shareholders). Business owners legally form corporations by filing **articles of incorporation** with the state in which they organize the business. State laws also recognize limited liability companies (LLCs) as legal entities separate from their owners (i.e., members). Business owners create limited liability companies by filing either, depending on the state, a **certificate of organization** or **articles of organization** with the state in which they are organizing the business.

Partnerships are formed under state partnership statutes, and the degree of formality required depends on the type of partnership being formed. General partnerships may be formed by written agreement among the partners, called a **partnership agreement,** or they may be formed informally without a written agreement when two or more owners join together in an activity to generate profits. Although general partners are not required to file partnership agreements with the state, general partnerships are still considered to be legal entities separate from their owners under state laws. Unlike general partnerships, limited partnerships are usually organized by written agreement and typically must file a **certificate of limited partnership** to be recognized by the state.[2]

Finally, for state law purposes, sole proprietorships are *not* treated as legal entities separate from their individual owners, unless they are formed as a single-member LLC. As a result, sole proprietors are not required to formally organize their businesses with the state, and they hold title to business assets in their own names rather than in the name of their businesses.

Nontax Characteristics

Rather than identify and discuss all possible nontax entity characteristics, we compare and contrast several prominent nontax characteristics across the different legal entity types.

[1]Variations of these entities include limited liability partnerships (LLPs), limited liability limited partnerships (LLLPs), professional limited liability companies (PLLCs), and professional corporations (PCs).

[2]Similar to limited partnerships, LLPs, LLLPs, PLLCs, and PCs must register with the state to receive formal recognition.

Responsibility for Liabilities Whether the business entity or the owner(s) is ultimately responsible for paying the liabilities of the business depends on the type of entity. Under state law, the corporation itself, not its shareholders, is responsible for payment of its liabilities.[3] Similarly, LLCs and not their members are responsible for the liabilities of the business.[4] For entities formed as partnerships, all general partners are ultimately responsible for the liabilities of the partnership. In contrast, limited partners are not responsible for the partnership's liabilities.[5] However, limited partners are not allowed to actively participate in the activities of the business.

Finally, if a business is conducted as a sole proprietorship, the individual owner is responsible for the liabilities of the business. However, individual business owners may organize their businesses as single-member LLCs. In exchange for observing the formalities of organizing as an LLC, they receive the liability protection available to LLC members.[6]

Rights, Responsibilities, and Legal Arrangements among Owners State corporation laws specify the rights and responsibilities of corporations and their shareholders. For example, to retain limited liability protection for shareholders, corporations must create, regularly update, and comply with a set of bylaws (i.e., internal rules governing how the corporation is run). They must have a board of directors. They must have regular board meetings and regular (at least annual) shareholder meetings, and they must keep minutes of these meetings. They must also issue shares of stock to owners (i.e., shareholders) and maintain a stock ledger reflecting stock ownership. They must comply with annual filing requirements specified by the state of incorporation, pay required filing fees, and pay required corporate taxes, if any. Consequently, shareholders have no flexibility to alter their legal treatment with respect to one another (rights are determined solely by stock ownership, not by agreements), with respect to the corporation, or with respect to outsiders. In contrast, while state laws provide default provisions specifying rights and responsibilities of LLCs and their members, members have the flexibility to alter their arrangement by spelling out, through an operating agreement, the management practices of the entity and the rights and responsibilities of the members consistent with their wishes. Thus, LLCs allow more flexible business arrangements than do corporations.

Like LLC statutes, state partnership laws provide default provisions specifying the partners' legal rights and responsibilities for dealing with each other absent an agreement to the contrary. Because partners have the flexibility to depart from the default provisions, they frequently craft partnership agreements that are consistent with their preferences.

Although in many instances having the flexibility to customize business arrangements is desirable, sometimes inflexible governance rules mandated by state statute are needed to limit the participation of owners in management when their participation becomes impractical. For example, when businesses decide to "go public" with an **initial public offering (IPO)** on one of the public securities exchanges, they usually solicit a

THE KEY FACTS

Legal Classification and Nontax Characteristics of Business Entities

- State law generally classifies business entities as either corporations, limited liability companies, general partnerships, limited partnerships, or sole proprietorships.
- Corporations and limited liability companies shield all their owners against the entity's liabilities.
- Corporations are less flexible than other business entities but are generally better suited to going public.

[3]Payroll tax liabilities are an important exception to this general rule. Shareholders of closely held corporations may be held responsible for these liabilities.

[4]When closely held corporations and LLCs borrow from banks or other lenders, shareholders or members are commonly asked to personally guarantee the debt. To the extent they do this, they become personally liable to repay the loan in the event the corporation or LLC is unable to repay it.

[5]Limited liability limited partnerships (LLLPs) are limited partnerships in which general and limited partners are protected from the liabilities of the entity. Also, professional service businesses such as accounting firms and law firms are generally not allowed to operate as corporations, LLCs, or limited partnerships. These businesses are frequently organized as limited liability partnerships (LLPs), professional limited liability companies (PLLCs), or professional corporations (PCs). Owners of a PLLC or a PC are protected from liabilities of the entity other than liabilities stemming from their own negligence. LLPs do not provide protection against liabilities stemming from a partner's own negligence or from the LLP's contractual liabilities.

[6]Shareholders of corporations and LLC members are responsible for liabilities stemming from their own negligence.

vast pool of potential investors to become corporate shareholders.[7] State corporation laws prohibit shareholders from directly amending corporate governance rules and from directly participating in management—they have only the right to vote for corporate directors or officers. In comparison, LLC members generally have the right to amend the LLC operating agreement, provide input, and manage LLCs. Obviously, managing a publicly traded business would be next to impossible if thousands of owners had the legal right to change operating rules and directly participate in managing the enterprise.

Exhibit 4-1 summarizes several nontax characteristics of different types of legal business entities.

EXHIBIT 4-1 Business Types: Legal Entities and Nontax Characteristics

Nontax Characteristics	Corporation	LLC	General Partnership	Limited Partnership	Sole Proprietorship
Must formally organize with state	Yes	Yes	No	Yes	No*
Responsibility for liabilities of business	Entity	Entity	General partner(s)	General partner(s)	Owner†
Legal arrangement among owners	Not flexible	Flexible	Flexible	Flexible	Not applicable
Suitable for initial public offering	Yes	No	No	No‡	No

*A sole proprietor must organize with the state if forming a single-member LLC.

†The owner is not responsible for the liabilities of the business if the sole proprietorship is organized as an LLC. However, the owner is responsible for liabilities stemming from personal negligence and for any liabilities the owner personally guarantees.

‡While it is uncommon, certain limited partnerships are eligible for IPOs.

As summarized in Exhibit 4-1, corporations and LLCs have the advantage in liability protection, LLCs and partnerships have an advantage over other entities in terms of legal flexibility, and corporations have the advantage when owners want to take a business public.

(continued from page 4-1 . . .)

As an initial step in the process of selecting the type of legal entity to house Color Comfort Sheets (CCS), Nicole began to research other nontax issues that might be relevant to her decision. Early in her research she realized that the other nontax benefits unique to traditional corporations were relevant primarily to large, publicly traded corporations. Although Nicole was very optimistic about CCS's prospects, she knew it would likely be a long time, if ever, before CCS would go public. However, she remained interested in limiting her own and other potential investors' liability in the new venture, so she began to dig a little deeper. As she perused the State of Utah website, she learned that corporations and LLCs are the only legal business entities that can completely shield investors from liabilities. Although Nicole doesn't anticipate any trouble from her future creditors, she decides to limit her choice of legal entity to either a corporation or LLC.

At this point in her information-gathering process, Nicole is leaning toward the LLC option because she is not sure she wants to deal with board meetings and all the other formalities of operating a corporation; however, she decides to assemble a five-year forecast of CCS's expected operating results and to learn a little more about the way corporations and LLCs are taxed before making a final decision.

(to be continued . . .)

[7]The vast majority of IPOs involve corporate shares; however, limited partnership interests are occasionally sold in IPOs. Like shareholders, limited partners are typically not allowed to participate in management. Limited partnerships are used for public offerings in lieu of corporations when they qualify for favorable partnership tax treatment available to some publicly traded partnerships.

BUSINESS ENTITY TAX CLASSIFICATION

LO 4-2

A business's legal form may be different from its tax form. We discussed the legal form of business entities in the previous section. We now discuss the tax form of business entities. In general terms, for tax purposes, business entities can be classified as either separate taxpaying entities or **flow-through entities.** Separate taxpaying entities pay tax on their own income. In contrast, flow-through entities generally don't pay taxes because income from these entities flows through to their business owners, who are responsible for paying tax on the income.

How do we determine whether a particular business entity is treated as a separate taxpaying entity or as a flow-through entity for tax purposes? According to Treasury Regulations, commonly referred to as the "check-the-box" regulations, entities that are legal corporations under state law are treated as **C corporations** for tax purposes by default. These corporations and their shareholders are subject to tax provisions in Subchapter C (and not Subchapter S) of the Internal Revenue Code.[8] C corporations report their taxable income to the IRS on Form 1120, "U.S. Corporation Income Tax Return." However, shareholders of *legal* corporations may qualify to make a special tax election known as an "S" election, thus permitting the corporation to be taxed as a flow-through entity called an **S corporation.**[9] S corporations and their shareholders are subject to tax provisions in Subchapter S of the Internal Revenue Code. S corporations report the results of their operations to the IRS on Form 1120-S, "U.S. Income Tax Return for an S Corporation."

Also under the check-the-box regulations, unincorporated entities are, by default, treated as flow-through entities.[10] However, owners of an unincorporated entity can still elect to have their business taxed as a C corporation instead of as the default flow-through entity.[11] In fact, the owner(s) of an unincorporated entity could elect to have the business taxed as a C corporation and then make a second election to have the "C corporation" taxed as an S corporation (provided that it meets the S corporation eligibility requirements).[12] Before making such elections, however, the business owner(s) would need to be convinced that the move makes sense from a tax perspective.[13] Tax entity elections do not change nontax entity choice considerations because tax elections do not affect the legal classification of the entity.

Finally, entities that are not taxed as C or S corporations are treated for tax purposes as either partnerships, sole proprietorships, or **disregarded entities** (considered to be the same entity as the owner).[14] Entities with more than one owner are taxed as partnerships.[15] Partnerships report their operating results to the IRS on Form 1065, "U.S. Return of Partnership Income." Entities with only one *individual* owner such as sole proprietorships and **single-member LLCs** are taxed as sole proprietorships.[16] Income from businesses taxed as sole proprietorships is reported on Schedule C, "Profit or Loss from Business," of Form 1040, "U.S. Individual Income Tax Return." Similarly, unincorporated entities with only one *corporate* owner, typically a single-member LLC, are disregarded for tax purposes. Thus, income and losses from this single, corporate-member LLC are reported as if they had originated from a division of the corporation and are reported directly on the single-member corporation's tax return. Exhibit 4-2 provides a flowchart for determining the tax form of a business entity under the check-the-box regulations. Taxpayers check the box by filing Form 8832, "Entity Classification Election."

THE KEY FACTS

Tax Classification of Legal Entities

- Incorporated entities (i.e., legal corporations) are C corporations for tax purposes unless they make a valid S election.
- Unincorporated entities are taxed as partnerships if they have more than one owner.
- Unincorporated entities are taxed as sole proprietorships if held by a single individual or as disregarded entities if held by a single entity.
- Unincorporated entities may elect to be treated as C corporations, or they may elect to be taxed as S corporations, if eligible.

[8]Reg. §301.7701-3(a).

[9]§1362(a). Because §1361 limits the number and type of shareholders of corporations qualifying to make an S election, some corporations are ineligible to become S corporations.

[10]Reg. §301.7701-3(b). However, §7704 mandates that unincorporated publicly traded entities be taxed as corporations unless their income predominately consists of certain types of passive income.

[11]Reg. §301.7701-3(a).

[12]In general, a noncorporate entity that is eligible to elect to be treated as a corporation can elect to be treated as a corporation for tax purposes and as an S corporation in one step by filing a timely S corporation election.

[13]As presented in Exhibit 4-3, compared to corporations, unincorporated entities taxed as partnerships have more favorable ownership requirements and more favorable tax treatment on nonliquidating and liquidating distributions of noncash property.

[14]Reg. §301.7701-3(a).

[15]Reg. §301.7701-3(b)(i).

[16]Reg. §301.7701-3(b)(ii).

EXHIBIT 4-2 Determining the Tax Form of a Business Entity Under Check-the-Box Regulations

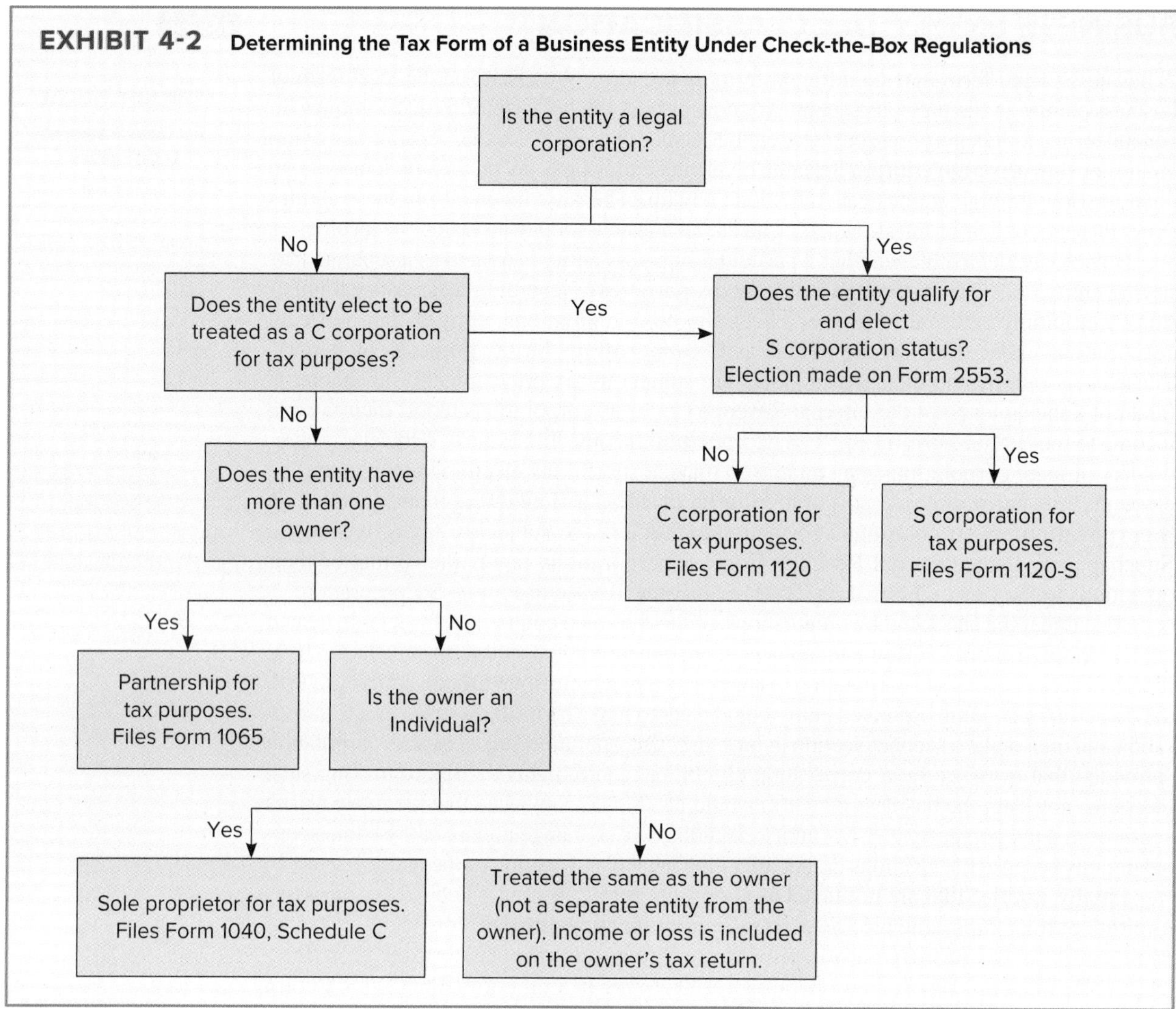

To summarize, although there are other types of legal entities, there are really only four categories of business entities recognized by the U.S. tax system, as follows:

1. C corporation (separate taxpaying entity; income reported on Form 1120).
2. S corporation (flow-through entity; income reported on Form 1120-S).
3. Partnership (flow-through entity; income reported on Form 1065).
4. Sole proprietorship (flow-through entity; income reported on Form 1040, Schedule C).

Example 4-1

What if: Assume Nicole legally forms CCS as a corporation (with only common stock) by filing articles of incorporation with the state. What are her options for classifying CCS for tax purposes if she is the only shareholder of CCS?

Answer: Nicole may treat CCS as either a C corporation or an S corporation. The default classification is a C corporation for tax purposes. However, given the facts provided, CCS is eligible to make an election to be taxed as an S corporation.[17]

[17]§1361(b).

What if: Assume Nicole legally forms CCS as an LLC (with only one class of ownership rights) by filing articles of organization with the state. What are her options for classifying CCS for tax purposes if she is the only member of CCS?

Answer: The default classification for CCS is a sole proprietorship because CCS is unincorporated with one individual member. However, Nicole may elect to have CCS taxed as a C corporation or as an S corporation. CCS can be taxed as a C corporation because unincorporated entities may elect to be taxed as corporations. Further, eligible entities taxed as corporations can elect to be taxed as S corporations. Later in the chapter, we discuss reasons why LLC owners may prefer to be taxed as S corporations.

What if: Assume Nicole legally forms CCS as an LLC and allows other individuals or business entities to become members in return for contributing their cash, property, or services to CCS. What is the default tax classification of CCS under these assumptions?

Answer: Partnership. The default tax classification for unincorporated entities with more than one owner is a partnership.

It might seem at this point that owners of business entities classified as flow-through entities would be treated the same for tax purposes; however, that is true only in a general sense. We see in this and other chapters that there are subtle and not-so-subtle differences in ways the owners of ventures classified as S corporations, partnerships, and sole proprietorships are taxed.[18]

BUSINESS ENTITY TAX CHARACTERISTICS

LO 4-3

In choosing from the available options for the tax form of business entities, owners and their advisers must carefully consider whether tax rules that apply to a particular tax classification would be either more or less favorable than tax rules under alternative tax classifications. The specific tax rules they must compare and contrast are unique to their situations; however, certain key differences in the tax rules tend to be relevant in many scenarios. We turn our attention to the taxation of business entity income, owner compensation, and the tax treatment of entity losses because these are a few of the most important tax characteristics to consider when selecting the tax form of the entity. Later in the chapter we preview other tax factors that differ between entities, and we identify the chapter where each factor is discussed in more detail.

Taxation of Business Entity Income

The taxation of a business entity's income depends on whether the entity is a flow-through entity or a C corporation. The income of a flow-through entity is taxed once to the owner when the income "flows through" or is allocated (on paper) to entity owners at the end of the year, whether or not the income is distributed to them. The income is included on the owners' tax returns as if they had earned the income themselves. The income also increases the owners' basis in their ownership interest in the entity to ensure that the income is not taxed a second time if an owner sells their partnership interest or if the owner receives a distribution from the entity. A distribution from a flow-through entity reduces the owner's basis in their ownership interest and is therefore treated as a nontaxable return of capital rather than a taxable distribution of income. C corporation income, however, is taxed twice. The income is first taxed to the corporation at the corporate tax rate. A C corporation's income is taxed a second time (taxed to the shareholders) when the shareholders sell their stock or the corporation distributes the income as a dividend.[19]

[18]The Business Income, Deductions, and Accounting Methods chapter explains how sole proprietors are taxed, and the Forming and Operating Partnerships and Dispositions of Partnership Interests and Partnership Distributions chapters describe how partners are taxed. Finally, the S Corporations chapter explains how S corporation shareholders are taxed.

[19]Distributions to C corporation shareholders are taxed as dividends to the extent they come from the "earnings and profits" (similar to economic income) of corporations.

Example 4-2

What if: Suppose Nicole formed CCS by contributing $100,000 in cash in exchange for CCS stock. In the first year of operations, CCS reported $10,000 of business income. On the last day of the year, CCS distributed $6,000 to Nicole. How much taxable income will Nicole recognize for the year on these transactions, and what is her stock basis in CCS at year-end assuming she operated CCS as a C corporation compared to operating it as an S corporation (flow-through entity)?

Answer: If CCS is organized as a C corporation, Nicole will recognize $6,000 of dividend income on the distribution and her basis in her CCS stock at year-end will be $100,000 (the amount of her original contribution). If CCS is organized as an S corporation, Nicole will be personally taxed on the $10,000 of business income allocated to her, but she will not be taxed on the $6,000 distribution because the distribution will be treated as a return of capital. Nicole's basis in her S corporation stock at the end of the year will be $104,000 ($100,000 original basis for contribution + $10,000 income allocation − $6,000 distribution). See the following for computations:

Description	C Corporation	S Corporation (flow-through)	Explanation
(1) Original basis in CCS ownership interest (stock)	$ 100,000	$ 100,000	Basis is equal to the cost (cash contributed)
(2) Business income	10,000	10,000	
(3) Income taxed at entity level	10,000	0	C corporation income taxed at corporate level
(4) Flow-through income taxed to Nicole	0	10,000	Nicole is a 100% owner and thus is taxed on 100% of the S corporation income.
(5) Nicole's stock basis at end of year before distribution	100,000	110,000	(1) + (4)
(6) Distribution	6,000	6,000	
(7) Taxable portion of distribution	**6,000**	**0**	Distribution from C corporation is a taxable dividend to Nicole. Distribution from S corporation is not taxable because distribution does not exceed basis [i.e., (6) is not greater than (5)].
(8) Nontaxable portion of distribution	0	6,000	(6) − (7)
Nicole's basis in CCS stock at year-end after distribution	**$100,000**	**$104,000**	(5) − (8)

In this example, all $10,000 of business income is taxed at the entity level for the C corporation and $6,000 of the $10,000 is also taxed to Nicole when she receives the dividend distribution. In the C corporation form, the $4,000 that was not taxed twice this year will eventually be taxed to Nicole as a dividend when it is distributed to her or as a capital gain when she sells her stock [the corporation stock has appreciated in value by $4,000 during the year ($104,000 FMV end of year − $100,000 FMV beginning of year)]. If CCS is organized as an S corporation, the $10,000 business income earned by CCS is taxed only once. That is, the income is taxed to Nicole, not CCS, when it is allocated to Nicole. The distribution to Nicole is not taxed because it represents a return of her capital (investment).

The Taxation of Flow-Through Entity Business Income The tax that flow-through entity owners pay on the entity's business income depends in large part on the owner's marginal income tax rate. The top marginal individual tax rate is currently 37 percent. Nevertheless, flow-through entity owners' tax burden on the flow-through income also depends on whether the income is eligible for the deduction for qualified business income, whether it is subject to the net investment income tax, whether it is subject to self-employment tax, and/or whether it is subject to the additional Medicare tax. Below, we discuss the deduction for qualified business income, the net investment income tax, the self-employment tax, the additional Medicare tax, and the overall tax rate on flow-through entity income (assuming the owners are individuals).

Deduction for qualified business income. The deduction for **qualified business income (QBI)** is deductible by individuals but not by business entities.[20] However, the amount of the deduction is based on the amount of QBI allocated to individuals from flow-through entities (i.e., S corporations, partnerships, and sole proprietorships). The QBI deduction is a from AGI deduction (i.e., it does not impact AGI) and is deductible by taxpayers even if they claim the standard deduction instead of itemizing deductions. Qualified business income is generally the net business income from a qualified trade or business conducted in the United States. Subject to a taxable income limit and to a wage-based limitation (the wage-based limitation is discussed after the next example), taxpayers can deduct 20 percent of the amount of QBI allocated to them from the business entity reduced by other deductions attributable to the QBI such as the taxpayer's self-employment tax deduction, self-employed health insurance deduction, and self-employed retirement plan contribution deductions [i.e., the QBI deduction before the wage-based limitation is {(QBI − self-employment tax deduction − self-employed health insurance deduction − self-employment retirement plan contributions) × 20 percent}]. Note that, as discussed below, guaranteed payments are not included in the calculation of the QBI deduction. Thus, the deduction for the self-employment tax on the guaranteed payment does not reduce QBI.[21]

The taxable income limit for the QBI deduction is 20 percent of the taxpayer's taxable income before the QBI deduction that is taxed at ordinary rates (net capital gains and qualified dividends are not included in the QBI tax base because they are taxed at a preferential tax rate). The taxable income limit represents the maximum deduction the taxpayer can claim after applying the specified service requirement and the wage-based limitation (both discussed below) to the QBI deduction.

To qualify as QBI, the business income must be from a business *other than* a **specified service trade or business.** In general, a specified service trade or business includes certain service businesses such as services in the fields of health, law, accounting, actuarial science, performing arts, consulting, athletics, financial services, brokerage services, or any trade or business where the principal asset of such trade or business is the reputation or skill of one or more of its employees or that involves the performance of services that consist of investing and investment management trading or dealing in securities, partnership interests, or commodities.[22] Qualified business income does not include income earned as an employee, guaranteed payments received by a partner (see owner compensation discussion below), or investment-type income such as capital gains, dividends, and investment interest income. In 2022, if the taxpayer's taxable income before the QBI deduction is less than $170,050 ($340,100 if married filing jointly), the specified service requirement does not apply. That is, the taxpayer is allowed to claim the QBI deduction even if the business income is from a specified service trade or business, but employee income, guaranteed payments, and investment income are not eligible for the QBI no matter the taxpayer's income level. However, for taxpayers with taxable income above $170,050 ($340,100 if married filing jointly), the specified service trade or business requirement phases in pro rata (i.e., the deduction phases out) over a $50,000 range ($100,000 if married filing jointly). Thus, the specified service requirement is completely phased in (i.e., the

[20]§199A.

[21]Reg. §1.199A-3(b)(1)(vi). The self-employment tax deduction is allocated between the guaranteed payment (not QBI) and the business income allocation (QBI) based on the relative amounts of these income items included in the taxpayer's gross income.

[22]§199A(d)(2). See Reg. §1.199A-5 for discussion of what constitutes a specified trade or business in each of the fields referenced in §199A(d)(2).

deduction is fully phased out if the business income is from a specified service trade or business) for taxpayers with taxable income before the QBI deduction of at least $220,050 ($440,100 if married filing jointly).[23]

Example 4-3

What if: Assume that CCS allocates $50,000 of business income to Nicole and the business income is from a specified service trade or business. Also, assume that Nicole's deduction for self-employment taxes paid on the business income allocation included in QBI is $3,532, Nicole is married and files a joint return with her spouse, and the taxable income on their joint tax return is $600,000 before the QBI deduction (all of the income is taxed at ordinary rates). What is Nicole's QBI deduction before considering the wage-based limitation?

Answer: $0 QBI deduction. Because the income is from a specified service trade or business and the taxable income on Nicole's joint tax return of $600,000 is greater than $440,100, the specified service trade or business requirement is fully phased in. Consequently, the QBI deduction is fully phased out.

What if: Assume that CCS allocates $50,000 of business income to Nicole and that the business income is from a specified service trade or business. Also, assume that Nicole's deduction for self-employment taxes paid on the business allocation included in QBI is $3,532, Nicole is married and files a joint tax return with her spouse, and the taxable income on their joint tax return is $300,000 before the QBI deduction (all of the taxable income is taxed at ordinary rates). What is Nicole's QBI deduction before considering the wage-based limitation but after considering the taxable income limitation?

Answer: $9,294 QBI deduction, computed as follows:

Description	Amount	Explanation
(1) Qualified business income	$ 50,000	Not from a specified service
(2) Self-employment tax deduction	3,532	Based on self-employment taxes paid on self-employment income included in QBI
(3) Base for QBI deduction	$ 46,468	(1) – (2)
(4) QBI deduction rate	20%	
(5) QBI deduction before specified service requirement	9,294	(3) × (4)
(6) Deduction phase-out due to specified service requirement	0	Taxable income before QBI deduction is less than $340,100
(7) QBI deduction before the taxable income limitation	$ 9,294	(5) – (6)
(8) Taxable income limitation	$300,000	Taxable income (before QBI deduction) taxed at ordinary rates
QBI deduction	**$ 9,294**	Lesser of (7) or (8)

What if: Assume that CCS allocates $50,000 of business income to Nicole and that the business income is from a specified service trade or business. Also, assume that Nicole's deduction for self-employment taxes paid on the business allocation included in QBI is $3,532, Nicole is married and files a joint return with her spouse, and the taxable income on their joint tax return is $400,000 before the QBI deduction. All of the taxable income is taxed at ordinary rates except for $15,000 of qualified dividends. What is Nicole's QBI deduction before considering the wage-based limitation but after considering the taxable income limitation?

[23]The phase-out thresholds for both the specified service trade or business requirement and the wage-based limitation are indexed for inflation.

Answer: $3,727 QBI deduction, computed as follows:

Description	Amount	Explanation
(1) Qualified business income	$ 50,000	Not from a specified service
(2) Self-employment tax deduction	3,532	Based on self-employment taxes paid on self-employment income included in QBI
(3) Base for QBI deduction	$ 46,468	(1) – (2)
(4) QBI deduction rate	20%	
(5) QBI deduction before specified service requirement	$ 9,294	(3) × (4)
(6) Taxable income before QBI deduction	400,000	
(7) Taxable income threshold for specified service T or B requirement phase-in	340,100	
(8) Taxable income over threshold	$ 59,900	(6) – (7)
(9) Percentage through specified service T or B requirement phase-in (deduction phase-out) range for MFJ tax return	59.9%	(8)/100,000
(10) Deduction phase-out due to specified service requirement	5,567	(5) × (9)
(11) QBI deduction before the taxable income limit	$ 3,727	(5) – (10)
(12) Taxable income limitation	$385,000	Taxable income (before QBI deduction) taxed at ordinary rates ($400,000 – $15,000)
QBI deduction	**$ 3,727**	Lesser of (11) or (12)

Under the wage-based limitation, the QBI deduction cannot exceed the greater of (1) 50 percent of the wages paid with respect to the qualified trade or business or (2) the sum of 25 percent of the wages with respect to the qualified trade or business plus 2.5 percent of the unadjusted basis of all qualified property used in the qualified trade or business immediately after the acquisition.[24] For purposes of the wage-based limitation, each partner or S corporation shareholder is treated as having paid wages for the year equal to their allocable share from the partnership or S corporation. The wage-based limitation only applies to taxpayers with taxable income in 2022 in excess of $170,050 ($340,100 if married filing jointly). The wage-based limitation phases in pro rata (i.e., the amount that would be deductible without the limit phases out) over a $50,000 range ($100,000 if married filing jointly). Thus, the wage-based limitation is completely phased in for taxpayers with taxable income before the QBI deduction of at least $220,050 ($440,100 if married filing jointly).

Example 4-4

What if: Assume that CCS allocates $50,000 of business income to Nicole, the business income is *not* from a specified service trade or business, and CCS allocated $15,000 of wages to Nicole for purposes of determining the wage-based limitation (assume there is no qualified property). Also, assume that Nicole's deduction for self-employment taxes paid on the business allocation included in

(continued on page 4-12)

[24]Qualified property is generally tangible, depreciable property used in a qualified trade or business during the year.

QBI is $3,532, Nicole is married and files a joint return with her spouse, and the taxable income on their joint tax return is $600,000 before the QBI deduction (all taxable income is taxed at ordinary rates). What is Nicole's QBI deduction?

Answer: $7,500 QBI deduction, computed as follows:

Description	Amount	Explanation
(1) Qualified business income	$ 50,000	Not from a specified service
(2) Self-employment tax deduction	− 3,532	Based on self-employment taxes paid on self-employment income included in QBI
(3) Base for QBI deduction	$ 46,468	(1) − (2)
(4) QBI deduction rate	20%	
(5) QBI deduction before wage limit	$ 9,294	(3) × (4)
(6) 50% of wages paid allocated to Nicole	7,500	$15,000 wages allocated to Nicole × 50%
(7) QBI deduction before taxable income limit	7,500	Lesser of (5) or (6)
(8) Taxable income limit	$600,000	
QBI deduction	**$ 7,500**	Lesser of (7) or (8)

Because Nicole's taxable income before the QBI deduction of $600,000 exceeds $440,100, the wage-based limitation is fully phased in (the limit applies in full), so Nicole's QBI deduction is limited to $7,500, which is 50% of the wages she is allocated from CCS.

What if: Assume the original facts except that the business income allocated to Nicole was from a specified service trade or business. What would be Nicole's QBI deduction?

Answer: $0 QBI deduction. The income is from a specified service trade or business and Nicole's taxable income on her joint tax return before the QBI deduction is greater than $440,100. Consequently, the specified service requirement is fully phased in and the deduction is fully phased out before considering the wage-based limitation.

What if: Assume the original facts (business income is not from a specified service trade or business) except Nicole's taxable income on her joint tax return is $300,000 before the QBI deduction and all the income is taxed at ordinary rates.

Answer: $9,294 QBI deduction. Because Nicole's joint taxable income before the QBI deduction is below $340,100, the wage-based limitation does not apply and Nicole would be able to claim a $9,294 QBI deduction.

What if: Assume the same facts as the prior what-if scenario except that $292,000 of the $300,000 of taxable income is qualified dividends and long-term capital gains taxed at the preferential 15% tax rate. That is, only $8,000 of the $300,000 is taxed at ordinary rates. What would be Nicole's QBI deduction?.

Answer: $8,000 QBI deduction. Without imposing the taxable income limitation, the QBI deduction would be $9,294. However, the taxable income limitation is $8,000 because that was the amount of taxable income before the QBI deduction taxed at ordinary rates. Consequently, the taxable income limitation restricts the QBI deduction to $8,000 in this scenario.

What if: Assume the original facts (business income is not from a specified service trade or business) except that Nicole's taxable income is $410,000 before the QBI deduction (all income taxed at ordinary rates). What would be Nicole's QBI deduction?

Answer: $8,040 QBI deduction, computed as follows:

Description	Amount	Explanation
(1) Qualified business income	$ 50,000	Not from a specified service
(2) Self-employment tax deduction	3,532	Based on self-employment taxes paid on self-employment income included in QBI
(3) Base for QBI deduction	$ 46,468	(1) – (2)
(4) QBI deduction rate	20%	
(5) QBI deduction before wage-based limit	$ 9,294	(3) × (4)
(6) Full wage-based limitation	7,500	
(7) Deduction disallowed if wage-based limit applies in full	$ 1,794	(5) – (6) (limited to $0)
(8) Taxable income before QBI deduction	410,000	
(9) Taxable income threshold for phase-in of wage-based limitation (phase-out of deduction)	340,100	
(10) Taxable income over threshold	$ 69,900	(8) – (9)
(11) Percentage through wage-based limitation phase-in (deduction phase-out)	69.9%	(10)/$100,000
(12) Deduction disallowed after partial phase-in of wage-based limitation	1,254	(7) × (11)
(13) QBI deduction before taxable income limit	$ 8,040	(5) – (12)
(14) Taxable income limit	$410,000	
QBI deduction	**$ 8,040**	Lesser of (13) or (14)

When the business income is from a specified service trade or business, both the specified service trade or business limitation and the wage-based limitation are phased in based on taxable income before the QBI. The QBI deduction computation can become complex when both limits are partially phased in. Describing the process of partial phase-in of both limitations simultaneously is beyond the scope of this text.

Net investment income tax. When an owner of a business entity taxed as a partnership or a shareholder of an S corporation does not work for the entity (that is, the owner is a passive owner or investor in the entity), the business income allocated to the taxpayer is considered to be "passive" income.[25] Because passive income is considered to be investment income for purposes of the net investment income tax, passive owners of flow-through entities may be required to pay net investment income tax on income allocated to them from the business (minus related investment expenses). Note that traditional types of investment income such as dividends, capital gains and interest income are also included in the net investment income tax base. The net investment income tax rate is 3.8 percent of the lesser of (1) net investment income (gross investment income minus investment expenses) or (2) AGI in excess of a threshold amount. The threshold amount is $250,000 for married taxpayers filing jointly and surviving spouses, $125,000 for married taxpayers filing separately, and $200,000 for all other taxpayers.[26]

[25]§469. We discuss specific tests for determining when an owner is a passive investor in the Forming and Operating Partnerships chapter.

[26]§1411. The thresholds are not indexed for inflation.

Self-employment tax. Business owners who receive and/or are allocated self-employment income from their businesses are subject to self-employment tax on the income. Whether a flow-through entity's business income allocated to an owner is considered to be self-employment income to the owner depends on the type of entity and the owner's involvement in the entity's business activities. An S corporation's business income allocated to a shareholder is not self-employment income to the shareholder. In contrast, a sole proprietorship's income is self-employment income to the sole proprietor. For owners of entities taxed as partnerships, the determination of whether business income allocations are subject to self-employment tax isn't as clear as it is for S corporations and sole proprietorships. For entities taxed as partnerships, whether business income is self-employment income to an owner depends on the owner's involvement in the entity's business activities.[27]

The tax base for the self-employment tax is **net earnings from self-employment.** Net earnings from self-employment is 92.35 percent of the taxpayer's self-employment income (from all sources).[28] For example, if a taxpayer reported net income of $100,000 as a sole proprietor on Schedule C, was allocated $50,000 of business income from a partnership in which the taxpayer was actively involved in the business (assume no guaranteed payment—we discuss guaranteed payments later in the chapter), and was allocated $10,000 of business income from an S corporation in which the taxpayer was actively involved in the business, the taxpayer's self-employment income would be $150,000 [$100,000 sole proprietor income + $50,000 business income from partnership (business income from S corporation is not self-employment income)]. The taxpayer's tax base for the self-employment tax would be $138,525 ($150,000 × .9235). For 2022, the first $147,000 of net earnings from self-employment is taxed at 15.3 percent, and net earnings from self-employment above $147,000 is taxed at 2.9 percent.[29] The $147,000 is called the **social security wage base limitation** (adjusted annually based on the national average wage index). The $147,000 limitation is reduced by the amount of employee compensation received during the year (i.e., wages or salary) when computing the self-employment tax. Taxpayers can deduct 50 percent of the self-employment tax paid as a for AGI deduction (i.e., deducted when computing AGI). Consequently, a taxpayer who paid $20,000 of self-employment tax would deduct $10,000 of the tax for AGI ($20,000 × .50). Finally, it is important to note that the self-employment tax is computed separately for each spouse even if a married couple files a joint return (i.e., the self-employment tax is an individual computation rather than a joint computation).

Example 4-5

What if: Assume that Nicole chooses to form CCS as an S corporation. In 2022, assume that Nicole is allocated $30,000 of business income from CCS and $20,000 of business income from a partnership in which Nicole is actively involved in the business. What are Nicole's self-employment tax liability and self-employment tax deduction for the year?

[27]We discuss more details of determining whether business income allocated to partners is self-employment income in the Forming and Operating Partnerships chapter.

[28]§1402. Taxing 92.35 percent of self-employment income for self-employment tax and additional Medicare tax purposes provides the taxpayer with a built-in 7.65 percent deduction for the employer's portion of the 15.3 percent self-employment tax.

[29]The 15.3 percent rate consists of a 12.4 percent Social Security portion (6.2 percent of the 12.4 percent is the employer portion of the self-employment tax and the other 6.2 percent is the employee portion) and a 2.9 percent Medicare portion (1.45 percent of the 2.9 percent is the employer portion and the other 1.45 percent is the employee portion). There is no limit on the 2.9 percent Medicare portion of the self-employment tax.

Answer: $2,826 self-employment tax liability and $1,413 self-employment tax deduction, computed as follows:

Description	Amount	Explanation
(1) Self-employment income	$20,000	$20,000 allocation from partnership is self-employment income, but $30,000 allocation from the S corporation is not.
(2) Net earnings from self-employment (SE tax base)	18,470	(1) × 92.35%
(3) Self-employment tax rate	15.3%	Rate is 15.3% on first $147,000 of net earnings from self-employment and 2.9% on the amount over $147,000.
(4) Self-employment tax liability	**$ 2,826**	**(2) × (3)**
Self-employment tax deduction	**$ 1,413**	(4) × 50 percent

What if: Assume the original facts except that the income allocation from the partnership is $200,000. What would be Nicole's self-employment tax liability and self-employment tax deduction?

Answer: $23,584 self-employment tax liability and $11,792 self-employment tax deduction, computed as follows:

Description	Amount	Explanation
(1) Self-employment income	$200,000	$200,000 allocation from partnership is self-employment income, but $30,000 allocation from S corporation is not.
(2) Net earnings from self-employment (SE tax base)	184,700	(1) × 92.35 percent
(3) Self-employment tax rate up to $147,000	15.3%	Rate on first $147,000 of net earnings from self-employment
(4) Self-employment tax rate on net earnings from self-employment above $147,000	2.9%	Rate on net earnings from self-employment above $147,000
(5) Self-employment tax liability	**$ 23,584**	(3) × $147,000 + (4) × [(2) − $147,000] (i.e., $22,491 + $1,093)
Self-employment tax deduction	**$ 11,792**	(5) × 50 percent

What if: Assume the same facts as in the previous what-if except that Nicole also received $170,000 in salary compensation from an employer (not CCS). What would be Nicole's self-employment tax liability and self-employment tax deduction?

Answer: $5,356 self-employment tax liability ($184,700 × 2.9%) and $2,678 self-employment tax deduction ($5,356 × 50%). Because Nicole's salary exceeds the $147,000 social security wage base limitation for 2022, the remaining wage base limit is reduced to zero for purposes of determining her self-employment tax, and the entire amount of earnings from self-employment is taxed at 2.9%.

Additional Medicare tax. In addition to the self-employment tax, business owners who receive or are allocated self-employment income from their businesses potentially must pay additional Medicare tax on the income. The tax rate for the additional Medicare tax is .9 percent and the tax base is the sum of the taxpayer's (and spouse's, if married filing jointly) net earnings from self-employment (from all sources) and compensation earned as an employee minus a threshold amount. The threshold amount is $250,000 for married taxpayers filing jointly and surviving spouses, $125,000 for married taxpayers filing separately, and $200,000 for all other taxpayers. Thus, for example, a single taxpayer who was allocated $240,000 of self-employment income (assuming no other self-employment income and no employee compensation) would have $221,640 of net earnings from self-employment ($240,000 × .9235) and would owe $195 of additional Medicare tax [($221,640 – $200,000) × .009].[30]

The additional Medicare tax is computed jointly for married couples filing a joint return. Thus, net earnings from self-employment from both spouses (and compensation earned as employees, if any) is combined to determine the excess of net earnings from self-employment over the $250,000 threshold amount for married taxpayers filing a joint tax return. Taxpayers are not allowed to deduct any of the additional Medicare tax they pay.

Example 4-6

What if: Assume that Nicole chooses to form CCS as an S corporation. She makes the following assumptions:

- CCS's taxable income is $500,000, and all of the income is business income.
- Nicole's marginal ordinary tax rate is 37 percent (this assumes she has other sources of income).
- Nicole is eligible for the full deduction for qualified business income on the flow-through income from CCS (i.e., no limitations apply).
- The income is not passive income and is therefore not subject to the net investment income tax.
- Because CCS is an S corporation, the flow-through business income from CCS is not self-employment income to Nicole.

What is the overall tax rate on CCS's business income?

Answer: 29.6 percent, computed as follows:

Description	Amount	Explanation
(1) Business income allocated to Nicole	$500,000	
(2) Deduction for qualified business income	(100,000)	(1) × 20 percent
(3) Net taxable income to Nicole from CCS	$400,000	(1) + (2)
(4) Owner's marginal income tax rate	37%	
(5) Owner-level income tax	$148,000	(3) × (4)
Overall tax rate on business income allocation	**29.6%**	(5)/(1)

What if: Assume the original facts except that the income from CCS is not eligible for the deduction for qualified business income. What is the overall tax rate on CCS's business income?

Answer: 37 percent. The entire $500,000 business income is taxed to Nicole at her marginal ordinary tax rate of 37 percent.

What if: Assume the original facts except the income from CCS is not eligible for the deduction for qualified business income and Nicole is a passive investor in CCS and must pay the 3.8 percent net investment income tax on the income. What is the overall tax rate on the income of CCS?

Answer: 40.8 percent. The full $500,000 of business income is taxed to Nicole at her marginal ordinary tax rate of 37 percent plus the net investment income tax rate of 3.8 percent.

[30]The threshold amounts are not indexed for inflation.

Example 4-7

What if: Assume that Nicole forms CCS as an LLC with another investor (as equal owners) so that CCS is taxed as a partnership. Nicole makes the following assumptions:

- CCS earns business income of $1,000,000, and Nicole's share of the business income is $500,000 (i.e., Nicole is allocated 50 percent of the CCS business income).
- Nicole's marginal ordinary tax rate is 37 percent.
- Nicole is entitled to the deduction for qualified business income on the flow-through income from CCS (minus her self-employment tax deduction) without limitation.
- Because Nicole works full time for the entity, the business income allocated to her is self-employment income.
- The CCS business income is Nicole's only source of self-employment income.
- Nicole's spouse received $300,000 of salary for the year.
- Nicole's entire net earnings from self-employment from the income allocation is subject to the .9 percent additional Medicare tax (i.e., Nicole's spouse's salary is over the $250,000 threshold amount, so the entire amount of Nicole's net earnings from self-employment is subject to the additional Medicare tax).

What is the overall tax rate on the CCS business income allocated to Nicole?

Answer: 35.82 percent, computed as follows:

Description	Amount	Explanation
(1) Business income allocated to Nicole	$500,000	$1,000,000 × .5
(2) Net earnings from self-employment	461,750	(1) × .9235
(3) Deduction for 50 percent of self-employment tax (for AGI deduction)	(15,809)	(7) × .5
(4) Deduction for qualified business income (from AGI deduction)	(96,838)	[(1) + (3)] × 20%
(5) Income net of Nicole's deductions	$387,353	(1) + (3) + (4)
(6) Owner-level income tax	143,321	(5) × 37%
(7) Self-employment tax	31,619	$147,000 × .153 + [(2) − $147,000] × .029
(8) Additional Medicare tax	4,156	(2) × .009 [Nicole's spouse's employee compensation income exceeds $250,000 threshold amount before considering (2)]
(9) Total tax paid on CCS business income allocations	$179,096	(6) + (7) + (8)
Overall tax rate on business income allocation	**35.82%**	(9)/(1)

What if: Assume the original facts except that the business income allocation is not qualified business income (QBI). That is, assume Nicole does not claim the QBI deduction. What is the overall tax rate on the CCS business income allocated to Nicole?

Answer: 42.99 percent. The only difference between the original and new facts in this what-if example is that Nicole would pay an additional $35,830 in income tax ($96,838 QBI deduction × 37 percent tax rate). Consequently, the overall taxes due on the business income allocation would be $214,926 ($179,096 + $35,830), and the overall tax rate would be 42.99 percent ($214,926/$500,000).

What if: Assume the original facts except Nicole's marginal self-employment tax rate is 2.9 percent because she has other sources of self-employment income that put her net earnings from self-employment over the $147,000 cutoff for the 15.3 percent rate.

What is the overall tax rate on the CCS business income allocated to Nicole?

(continued on page 4-18)

Answer: 32.71 percent, computed as follows:

Description	Amount	Explanation
(1) Business income allocated to Nicole	$500,000	$1,000,000 × .5
(2) Net earnings from self-employment	461,750	(1) × .9235
(3) Deduction for 50 percent of self-employment tax (for AGI deduction)	(6,695)	(7) × .5
(4) Deduction for qualified business income (from AGI deduction)	(98,661)	[(1) + (3)] × 20 percent
(5) Income net of Nicole's deductions	$394,644	(1) + (3) + (4)
(6) Owner-level income tax	146,018	(5) × 37%
(7) Self-employment tax	13,391	(2) × .029
(8) Additional Medicare tax	4,156	(2) × .009
(9) Total tax paid on CCS business income allocations	$163,565	(6) + (7) + (8)
Overall tax rate on business income allocation	**32.71%**	(9)/(1)

What if: Assume the original facts except the income from CCS is not eligible for the QBI deduction and Nicole is a passive investor in CCS. Consequently, she must pay the net investment income tax on the entire income allocation, but she is not required to pay the self-employment tax or the additional Medicare tax on the income allocation. What is the overall tax rate on the CCS business income allocated to Nicole?

Answer: 40.8 percent. The entire $500,000 business income allocation is taxed to Nicole at her marginal ordinary tax rate of 37 percent plus the net investment income tax rate of 3.8 percent.

In summary, while income from a flow-through entity is taxed only once, the overall tax rate on the entity's business income depends on whether the income (and thus the owner) qualifies for the QBI deduction and whether the income is subject to the net investment tax or is considered to be self-employment income.

Overall Tax Rate of C Corporation Income C corporations are taxed on their taxable income at a flat 21 percent rate. The tax rate on the second level of tax on a C corporation's income depends on whether the shareholder is an individual (or S corporation because S corporation income flows through to shareholders who are individuals), a C corporation, an **institutional shareholder,** a tax-exempt entity, or a foreign entity. Determining the overall tax rate on a tax entity's income is an important factor when making the tax entity choice for a business.

Individual shareholders. The tax rate on dividends to individual taxpayers depends on the individual's taxable income. High-income taxpayers are taxed on dividends at a 20 percent rate, low-income taxpayers are taxed at a 0 percent rate, and others are taxed on dividends at a 15 percent rate.[31] Also, as discussed above, taxpayers with (modified) AGI in excess of a threshold amount pay an additional 3.8 percent net investment income tax on dividends.

[31]To the extent the dividend income increases a taxpayer's taxable income beyond specific "breakpoints," the dividend is taxed at a higher rate. For 2022, the breakpoint between the 0 and 15 percent rates is $83,350 for married taxpayers filing jointly, $55,800 for head of household filers, and $41,675 for all other taxpayers. The breakpoint between the 15 percent and 20 percent rates is $517,200 for married taxpayers filing jointly, $258,600 for married taxpayers filing separately, $459,750 for single taxpayers, and $488,500 for head of household filers.

Example 4-8

What if: Assume that Nicole operates CCS as a C corporation and she makes the following assumptions:

- CCS earns taxable income of $500,000.
- CSS will distribute all of its after-tax earnings annually as a dividend.
- Nicole's marginal ordinary tax rate is 37 percent and her dividend tax rate is 23.8 percent (20% income tax on the dividend plus an additional 3.8% of net investment tax on the dividend).

What is the overall tax rate on CCS's taxable income?

Answer: 39.8 percent, computed as follows:

Description	Amount	Explanation
(1) Taxable income	$500,000	
(2) Corporate tax rate	21%	Flat corporate tax rate
(3) Corporate-level tax	$105,000	(1) × (2) [first level of tax]
(4) Income remaining after taxes and amount distributed as a dividend	$395,000	(1) − (3)
(5) Dividend tax rate	23.8%	20% dividend rate + 3.8% net investment income tax rate
(6) Shareholder-level tax on dividend	$ 94,010	(4) × (5) [second level of tax]
(7) Total tax paid on corporate taxable income	$199,010	(3) + (6)
Overall tax rate on corporate taxable income	**39.8%**	(7)/(1)

Note that the overall rate is not 44.8 percent (21 percent corporate rate + 23.8 percent shareholder rate) because the amount of corporate-level tax (i.e., $105,000) is income that is not taxed twice (it is paid to the government, not to the shareholders).

What if: Assume that Nicole operates CCS as a C corporation and she makes the following assumptions:

- CCS earns taxable income of $500,000.
- CCS distributes 25 percent of its after-tax earnings as a dividend and retains the rest to grow the business.
- Nicole's marginal ordinary tax rate is 37 percent and her dividend tax rate is 23.8 percent (including both income and net investment income tax.

What is the overall tax rate on CCS's taxable income?

Answer: 25.7 percent, computed as follows:

Description	Amount	Explanation
(1) Taxable income	$500,000	
(2) Corporate tax rate	21%	Flat corporate tax rate
(3) Corporate-level tax	$105,000	(1) × (2) [first level of tax]
(4) Income remaining after taxes	$395,000	(1) − (3)
(5) Dividend	$ 98,750	(4) × 25% distributed
(6) Tax rate on dividend	23.8%	20% dividend rate + 3.8% net investment income tax rate
(7) Shareholder-level tax on dividend	$ 23,503	(5) × (6) [second level of tax]
(8) Total tax paid on corporate taxable income	$128,503	(3) + (7)
Overall tax rate on corporate taxable income	**25.7%**	(8)/(1)

The overall tax rate is lower in this situation because CCS retains most of its after-tax income and thus protects that portion of its income from immediate double taxation. If CCS retained all of its after-tax earnings, the current overall tax rate on its income would have been 21 percent (the corporate tax rate). Also, note that while the overall tax rate is lower when CCS distributes less of its income, Nicole also receives less cash from the business.

Shareholders that are C corporations. Shareholders that are C corporations are taxed on dividends at 21 percent, the same rate as they are taxed on other income. In addition, dividends received by a corporation are potentially subject to another (third) level of tax when the corporation receiving the dividend distributes its earnings as dividends to its shareholders. This potential for more than two levels of tax on the same before-tax earnings prompted Congress to allow corporations to claim the **dividends-received deduction (DRD).** In the next chapter, we discuss the DRD in detail, but the underlying concept is that a corporation *receiving* a dividend is allowed to deduct a certain percentage of the dividend from its taxable income to offset the potential for additional layers of taxation on the dividend when it distributes the dividend to its shareholders. The dividends-received deduction percentage is 50, 65, or 100 percent of the dividend received, depending on the level of the recipient corporation's ownership in the dividend-paying corporation's stock. The DRD is 50 percent if the shareholder corporation owns less than 20 percent of the distributing corporation; 65 percent if it owns at least 20 percent but less than 80 percent of the distributing corporation; and 100 percent if the shareholder corporation owns at least 80 percent of the distributing corporation. Thus, a corporation's net tax rate on a dividend received is 10.5 percent if it claims a 50 percent DRD [.21 tax rate × (1 − .5 DRD)], 7.35 percent if it claims a 65 percent DRD [.21 tax rate × (1 − .65 DRD)], and 0 percent if it claims a 100 percent DRD [.21 × (1 − 1.0 DRD)].

Example 4-9

What if: Assume that Nicole invites a C corporation to invest in CCS in exchange for a 10 percent share in the company. Nicole makes the following assumptions as part of her calculations:

- CCS is a C corporation.
- CCS earns taxable income of $500,000.
- CCS will pay out all of its after-tax earnings annually as a dividend.

Given these assumptions, what would be the overall tax rate on a C corporate investor's share of CCS's income given that the shareholder corporation would be eligible for the 50 percent dividends-received deduction?

Answer: 29.3 percent, computed as follows:

Description	Amount	Explanation
(1) Taxable income	$500,000	
(2) Corporate tax rate	21%	Flat corporate tax rate
(3) Entity-level tax	$105,000	(1) × (2) [first level of tax]
(4) After-tax income	$395,000	(1) − (3)
(5) Corporate investor's dividend	$ 39,500	(4) × 10%
(6) Dividend income net of DRD	$ 19,750	(5) × (1 − 50% DRD)
(7) Corporate investor's share of entity-level tax	$ 10,500	(3) × 10% investor's share
(8) Corporate investor's tax on dividend net of DRD	$ 4,148	(6) × 21% corporate tax rate
(9) Total tax paid on corporate taxable income	$ 14,648	(7) + (8)
Overall tax rate on corporate taxable income	**29.3%**	(9)/[(1) × 10% investor's share]

Note: The income of the corporate shareholder will be taxed again when the corporate shareholder distributes it to its own shareholders.

Institutional shareholders. Pension and retirement funds are some of the largest institutional shareholders of corporations. However, these entities do not pay shareholder-level tax on the dividends they receive. Ultimately, retirees pay the second tax on this income when they receive retirement distributions from these funds. While retirees pay the second tax at ordinary rates, not reduced dividend rates, they are able to defer the tax until they receive distributions.

Tax-exempt organizations. Tax-exempt organizations such as charitable organizations, churches, universities, and political organizations are exempt from tax on their investment income, including dividend income from investments in corporate stock. In general, tax-exempt organizations are required to annually file Form 990, "Return of Organization Exempt from Income Tax."[32] While tax-exempt organizations don't pay tax on their investment income, they may be required to pay tax on unrelated business income (UBI) they generate. The tax is called the unrelated business income tax (UBIT). **Unrelated business income** is income from a trade or business, regularly carried on, that is not substantially related to the charitable, educational, or other purpose that is the basis of the organization's exemption. The tax rate is equal to the C corporation tax rate (21 percent). The UBIT is imposed so that tax-exempt organizations don't have an unfair tax advantage compared to taxable businesses when the taxable and tax-exempt entities are both involved in business activities. If an organization has $1,000 or more of gross income for the year from unrelated business activities, the organization must file Form 990-T, "Exempt Organization Business Income Tax Return" (generally due the 15th day of the 5th month after the end of its tax year). Further, tax-exempt organizations must pay estimated tax if they expect their tax for the year to be $500 or more.[33]

Foreign shareholders. Foreign investors may be eligible for reduced rates on dividend income depending on the tax treaty, if any, their country of residence has signed with the United States.

Double tax on C corporation income. As we discuss and illustrate above, C corporation income is subject to **double taxation.** The first tax is paid by the corporation when it earns the income, and the second tax is paid by the shareholders when the earnings are distributed to shareholders as dividends. Can C corporations avoid the second level of tax entirely by not paying dividends? The answer is generally no. Even when corporations retain after-tax income, their shareholders pay the second level of tax at capital gains rates on the undistributed income when they sell their stock because the undistributed income indirectly increases the value of their stock and thus increases shareholders' gains when they sell the stock. Assuming the shareholder is an individual and the shareholder owns stock in a corporation for more than a year, the gain is taxed at the same rates as the tax rates on qualified dividends discussed above (0, 15, or 20 percent plus 3.8 percent net investment income tax for higher-income taxpayers). Because this second level of tax is deferred until taxpayers sell their stock, the longer they hold the stock, the less the tax cost is on a present value basis. In the extreme, taxpayers can avoid the second level of income tax completely on their stock appreciation by holding the stock until death. At death, gain built into the stock is eliminated because the stock takes basis equal to the value of the stock on the date of death.[34]

[32]See www.irs.gov/charities-non-profits/annual-exempt-organization-return-who-must-file for exceptions as to which tax-exempt entities are required to file Form 990.

[33]A detailed discussion of tax-exempt organizations is beyond the scope of this text. See www.irs.gov/charities-non-profits/exempt-organization-types and related links for more details.

[34]§1014. High net worth taxpayers may be required to pay estate tax on the value of the stock at death.

Shareholders other than individuals face different tax consequences when they sell their shares. When shareholders that are C corporations eventually sell the stock, they are taxed on capital gains at the corporate rate of 21 percent. Consequently, income from stock appreciation may expose income to *more* than two levels of taxation because capital gains from selling stock do not qualify for the dividends-received deduction. Also, institutional shareholders don't pay tax when they sell their stock and recognize capital gains. However, retirees generally pay tax on the gains at ordinary rates when they receive distributions from their retirement accounts. Also, tax-exempt shareholders do not pay tax on capital gains from selling stock, and foreign investors are generally not subject to U.S. tax on their capital gains from selling corporate stock.

Finally, the tax law provides incentives for C corporations to distribute income rather than to retain it for the purpose of avoiding the second level of tax. First, **personal holding companies** (closely held corporations generating primarily investment income) are subject to a 20 percent **personal holding company tax** on their undistributed income.[35] Second, corporations that retain earnings for the purpose of avoiding the second level of tax are subject to a 20 percent **accumulated earnings tax** on the retained earnings.[36] Corporations are not considered to be retaining earnings for tax avoidance purposes and are not subject to the accumulated earnings tax to the extent they (1) reinvest the earnings in assets necessary for their business or (2) retain liquid assets for reasonable planned needs of the business.

Under the tax rate system prior to 2018, flow-through entities were generally considered to be superior to corporations for tax purposes because they generated income that was taxed only once, while corporations produced income that was taxed twice, with the first level of tax imposed at a rate comparable to the individual tax rate. However, for years after 2017, the corporate tax rate is significantly lower than the maximum individual tax rate. Further, as described above, tax law effective beginning in 2018 provides a deduction for qualified business income (QBI) for individuals who are owners of flow-through entities. This tax legislation makes the optimal choice of entity based on overall tax rates of the entity's business income less clear than it was under prior law. It is important to note, however, that the corporate tax rate reduction is a permanent change, while the QBI deduction is scheduled to expire in 2026.[37] The overall tax rate on a flow-through entity's business income depends on whether the flow-through entity's business income is eligible for the QBI deduction and whether the income is subject to the net investment income tax or the self-employment tax and the additional Medicare tax. For C corporations, the overall tax rate depends in large part on the extent to which the corporation distributes its after-tax earnings as a dividend to its shareholders. As we saw in Example 4-6, the overall tax rate on CCS's taxable income as a flow-through entity (S corporation) ranged from 29.6 percent to 40.8 percent, depending on whether the QBI deduction and the net investment income tax applied. In Example 4-8, the overall tax rate on CCS's taxable income as a C corporation ranged from 21 percent, when CCS retained all of its after-tax income, to 39.8 percent, when it distributed all of its after-tax income.

Owner Compensation Entity owners who work for the entity are compensated in different ways, depending on the entity type. Owners of S corporations and C corporations receive compensation as employees. Owners of entities taxed as partnerships receive compensation in the form of guaranteed payments. Sole proprietors don't receive separate compensation payments because a sole proprietorship is the same taxable entity as the individual sole proprietor (this is true even when the proprietorship is organized as a single-member LLC).

S corporations and C corporations deduct the wages paid to employees (including shareholders who are employees) to calculate the entity's business income. They also pay

[35]§541.

[36]§§531–533.

[37]While the corporate tax rate has no scheduled expiration date, future legislation could change the rate.

(and deduct) the employer's portion of the FICA tax (Social Security tax plus Medicare tax) on the employee's behalf. In 2022, the employer's portion of the tax is 7.65 percent of the employee's first $147,000 of employee compensation plus 1.45 percent of employee compensation above $147,000. The shareholder-employee is taxed on the wages received at ordinary rates and is required to pay the employee's portion of the FICA tax, which is generally the same as the employer's portion. When considering both the employer's and the employee's portions of the FICA tax, the overall FICA tax rate is 15.3 percent of the first $147,000 of wages and 2.9 percent of the rest. This is the same rate as the self-employment tax rate. Also, similar to self-employment income, employee compensation is subject to the additional Medicare tax when the taxpayer's AGI is over the threshold amount (discussed previously).

Entities taxed as partnerships deduct guaranteed payments made to owners working for the entity. However, the entity is not required to pay FICA tax on the owner-worker's behalf because guaranteed payments are self-employment income to the recipient, and self-employment taxes are the sole responsibility of the owner-worker.[38] The owner-workers are taxed on the amount of the guaranteed payment at ordinary rates and are required to pay self-employment tax and potentially additional Medicare tax on the income, depending on their income level (see prior discussion on computing the self-employment tax and additional Medicare tax). A sole proprietorship does not pay deductible compensation to the sole proprietor. In general, all of the income of a sole proprietorship is self-employment income and, consequently, is subject to self-employment tax and additional Medicare tax.

Owner compensation from certain entity types provides potential tax planning opportunities. For S corporations, business income allocations to owners are not subject to FICA or self-employment tax. However, salary and wages paid to owner-employees are subject to FICA tax. (Recall that the combined employer/employee FICA rate is the same as the self-employment tax rate.) Consequently, as we discuss in the S Corporations chapter, S corporations have a tax incentive to pay lower salary/wages to shareholder-employees who are subject to FICA tax so there is more business income to allocate to shareholder-employees who are not subject to FICA tax (lower deductible wages mean higher business income allocations). Further, S corporations have an incentive to reduce wages to shareholder-employees in order to increase business income because employee compensation is not eligible for the deduction for qualified business income, but business income allocations to shareholders are eligible. In the extreme, S corporations may prefer to pay zero wages to shareholder-employees in order to maximize business income allocations to them. However, to the extent an S corporation pays an S corporation shareholder an unreasonably low salary for services provided, the IRS may reclassify some of the shareholder's business income allocation as salary.[39]

In contrast to S corporations, entities taxed as partnerships don't have an incentive to decrease guaranteed payments in order to increase business income allocations in an attempt to save self-employment taxes to owners. This is because both guaranteed payments and business income allocations are self-employment income to the owner-worker. However, similar to S corporations, entities taxed as partnerships have an incentive to reduce guaranteed payments to owner-workers in order to increase business income allocations to them because guaranteed payments are not eligible for the qualified business income deduction, but allocations of business income are eligible. Finally, relative to both S corporations and entities taxed as partnerships, sole proprietorships may be the most advantageous for purposes of maximizing the qualified business income deduction in certain situations. This is because the sole proprietorship's qualified business income is not reduced by a deduction for compensation paid to the owner/sole proprietor (but it is reduced by the sole proprietor's deduction for self-employment taxes paid).

[38] Taxpayers pay self-employment tax on self-employment income and FICA taxes on employee compensation.

[39] See www.forbes.com/sites/anthonynitti/2014/02/04/tax-geek-tuesday-reasonable-compensation-in-the-s-corporation-arena/#2f467d5f4790 for a more detailed discussion of this potential tax planning strategy.

Example 4-10

What if: Assume that Nicole and a second investor are equal (50%) owners in CCS. Both Nicole and the other investor provide similar services to CCS, and both receive the same amount of annual compensation. For the year, CCS's business income before the compensation deduction is $200,000 (Nicole's share is $100,000). What are the total FICA/self-employment tax and income taxes payable by Nicole and CCS as they relate to Nicole's services, assuming CCS is either an S corporation (S Corp 1) that pays $10,000 of compensation for Nicole's services, an S corporation (S Corp 2) that pays $6,000 for Nicole's services, or a partnership (Partnership) that pays $10,000 for Nicole's services? Further assume that Nicole's marginal ordinary income tax rate is 35% and that her marginal self-employment tax rate is 2.9% (she has self-employment income from other sources that exceed the $147,000 Social Security wage base limit).

Note: The numbers in computations below provide entity-related information as it pertains to Nicole only. The results for the second investor would be exactly the same as the results for Nicole, but results for the second investor are not included here for simplicity. The overall tax numbers for the entity (for both owners combined) can be calculated simply by doubling the number in each cell in the example results.

Answer: Total FICA/self-employment tax and income taxes payable by Nicole are $36,262 for S Corp 1, $35,757 for S Corp 2, and $37,209 for Partnership.

Description	S Corp 1	S Corp 2	Partnership	Explanation
(1) Business income before compensation deduction (Nicole's portion only)	$100,000	$100,000	$100,000	Nicole's share of entity income before compensation deduction ($200,000 × 50%) for Nicole's share
(2) Compensation deduction for services provided by Nicole only	10,000	6,000	10,000	Treated as salary to Nicole in S corporation scenarios and as a guaranteed payment in the partnership scenario
(3) FICA tax rate for employer on employee's salary	7.65%	7.65%	N/A	FICA rate on employer's portion of FICA liability based on salary. No employer FICA liability on guaranteed payments.
(4) FICA paid and deducted by employer	765	459	N/A	(2) × (3)
(5) Business income (Nicole's portion)	$ 89,235	$ 93,541	$ 90,000	(1) − (2) − (4)
(6) Nicole's FICA tax on salary	765	459	N/A	(2) × (3). Employee's portion is same as employer's portion (7.65%).
(7) Self-employment tax	0	0	2,678	[(2) + (5)] × .9235 × .029. Business income and compensation are self-employment income for partner but not for S corporation shareholder.
(8) Self-employment tax deduction	0	0	1,339	(7) × 50%
(9) Combined entity and owner FICA (or self-employment) tax	$ 1,530	$ 918	$ 2,678	(4) + (6) + (7)
(10) Income taxed at ordinary tax rates	$ 99,235	$ 99,541	$ 98,661	(2) + (5) − (8)
(11) Income taxes	$ 34,732	$ 34,839	$ 34,531	(10) × 35%
Total FICA/self-employment tax and income taxes	**$ 36,262**	**$ 35,757**	**$ 37,209**	(9) + (11)

S Corp 2 has a lower tax burden than S Corp 1 ($35,757 vs. $36,262, respectively). S Corp 2's tax burden is lower than S Corp 1's tax burden solely due to S Corp 2 paying less compensation (salary) to Nicole than does S Corp 1. Also, both S Corp 1 and S Corp 2 have a lower tax burden compared to Partnership ($36,262 and $35,757 vs. $37,209, respectively). The primary reason for this is that all of the partnership income is subject to self-employment tax at 2.9%, and for the S corporations, only the salary is subject to FICA tax (combined employer and employee rate is 15.3%). The difference would be much larger if CCS were Nicole's only source of self-employment income because the self-employment tax rate on the partnership income would be 15.3% rather than 2.9%.

What if: What is Nicole's QBI deduction based on the income from each of the three entities assuming that the business income is QBI and that the QBI wage-based limitations do not apply?

Answer: For the S corporation entities, the QBI deduction is the business income [line (5)] × 20%. The QBI deduction based on S Corp 1's income is $17,847, and the QBI deduction based on S Corp 2's income is $18,708. However, in the case of the partnership, the business income must be reduced by the deduction for self-employment taxes paid to arrive at QBI. Nicole's QBI deduction under the partnership entity form is $17,732 {[(5) – (8)] × 20%}.

In this example, the S corporation tax form provides more tax benefits than the partnership tax form. This example illustrates a reason why taxpayers who form an LLC may elect to have the entity taxed as an S corporation rather than as a partnership. The LLC legal form of entity can protect owners from liability while the S corporation tax form can reduce taxes. However, the tax entity form decision should be made based on the facts specific to the situation rather than a general rule of thumb.

TAXES IN THE REAL WORLD Reasonable Compensation Must Be, Well, Reasonable

As we've discussed in this chapter, an S corporation shareholder who also works as an employee for the business must pay FICA tax on the salary received. Further, the S corporation must also pay payroll taxes on the salary. In contrast, neither the shareholder nor the business pays payroll tax on business income allocated to S corporation shareholders. Thus, shareholders and the S corporation have incentives to keep salaries low so that less income is subject to payroll taxes. The IRS insists that shareholders providing services be paid a reasonable salary for their services, and the IRS is likely to challenge the amount of the salary when it identifies a salary that may be unreasonably low. The IRS and taxpayers have had many court battles over whether salary paid to the shareholders is unreasonably low based on the extent and nature of the services the shareholder provides to the S corporation. In *David E. Watson, P.C. v. United States,* Mr. Watson, an employee/shareholder in an S corporation, received only $24,000 in annual salary from the S corporation but received distributions of almost $200,000 per year (in 2002 and 2003 when the Social Security wage base limitation was $84,900 and $87,000, respectively). At trial, an expert witness for the IRS testified that the value of the taxpayer's services to the business was about $91,000 per year. The court concluded that any reasonable person in Mr. Watson's position would expect to earn significantly more than what he was being paid in salary and that his $24,000 salary wasn't enough to support Mr. Watson's lifestyle. The court ruled for the IRS, resulting in a portion of the distributions being recast as taxable salary. Further, Mr. Watson (and the S corporation) was required to pay employment taxes, penalties, and interest.

In *J.D. & Associates v. United States,* Mr. Dahl, the sole shareholder of an S corporation, J.D. & Associates, was paid a salary between $19,000 and $30,000 each year but received annual distributions in the $50,000 range. It turns out that the salary paid to Mr. Dahl, a CPA, was lower than the salary paid to other employees who were providing only administrative services to the business. Needless to say, the taxpayer lost that case too and ended up paying payroll taxes on distributions that were recast as salary.

In these types of cases, the S corporation bears the burden of proving that the compensation paid to the shareholder is reasonable. Obviously, the burden is much easier to manage when the salaries are actually reasonable.

Sources: David E. Watson, P.C. v. United States, 109 AFTR2d 2012-1059 (8th Cir. 2012); and *J.D. & Associates v. United States,* No. 3:04-cv-59, 2006 U.S. Dist. LEXIS 117266 (D.N.D. June 5, 2006).

For C corporations, tax planning opportunities have potentially shifted with the steep reduction in the corporate tax rate relative to individual rates, effective beginning in 2018. Prior to the rate reduction, corporations could avoid the heavy cost of double taxation of their income by paying deductible salaries to shareholder-employees. This income would be taxed once to the employee at ordinary rates that were similar to the corporate rate. The IRS could evaluate compensation to an employee-shareholder to determine if the compensation was unreasonably high for the work the employee-shareholder was doing and, to the extent it was, reclassify the excess compensation as nondeductible dividends. Currently, however, with the corporate tax rate significantly lower than the maximum individual rate, corporations have an incentive to pay lower salaries to shareholder-employees in order to have more of their income taxed at the lower corporate rate. By reducing deductible salaries, more of the corporate income is subject to tax at the lower 21 percent tax rate. If the income is paid in the form of salaries, it is subject to the individual rate (the top rate is 37 percent) and subject to both the employer's and the employee's portions of the FICA tax. This type of strategy is more likely to be useful for closely held corporations where all of the owners work for the corporation. It remains to be seen how the IRS will respond to such strategies.

While the overall tax rate of an entity's income and the tax treatment of owner compensation are important entity choice factors, it is also important to consider the tax treatment of the entity's losses and other tax characteristics when choosing a tax entity for a new business.

ETHICS

Meghna is the sole shareholder and CEO of BQT. BQT is a very profitable S corporation. Until recently, Meghna's salary was in line with the salaries of comparable CEOs. However, Meghna recently learned that she could reduce her tax burden if she were to reduce her salary. In particular, by lowering her salary, Meghna would receive less employee compensation that is subject to FICA tax and is not eligible for the qualified business income deduction, and she would be allocated more business income that is not subject to FICA tax and qualifies for the qualified business income deduction. After considering the potential benefits, Meghna decided to cut her salary in half. Do you think Meghna's decision is ethical? Why or why not?

Deductibility of Entity Losses When a C corporation's tax deductions exceed its income for the year, the excess is called a **net operating loss (NOL).** While NOLs provide no tax benefit to C corporations for the year they incur them, corporations may use NOLs to offset corporate taxable income and reduce corporate taxes in other years. The specific tax treatment for an NOL depends on when the NOL was generated. For NOLs generated in tax years beginning before 2018, the carry forward period is 20 years and the carry back period is two years. These carryovers can offset up to 100 percent of taxable income before the NOL deduction in carryover years. For NOLs generated in tax years beginning after 2017 and before 2021, the carryforward period is indefinite and the carryback period is five years. The NOL carryovers can offset up to 100 percent of taxable income before the NOL deduction in tax years beginning before 2021. However, in tax years beginning after 2020, the NOL carryovers from 2018–2020 tax years can offset up to only 80 percent of taxable income remaining after deducting NOL carryovers from NOLs incurred in tax years beginning before 2018. Finally, for NOLs generated in tax years beginning after 2020, the NOLs may be carried forward indefinitely but may not be carried back. In carryover years, the NOL can offset up to only 80 percent of taxable income remaining after deducting NOL carryovers from NOLs incurred in tax years beginning before 2018.[40] NOL carryovers are deducted on a FIFO basis (oldest first, to the extent deductible). In any event, losses from C corporations are *not* available to offset shareholders' personal income.

[40]We discuss the net operating loss deduction in more detail in the Corporate Operations chapter.

In contrast to losses generated by C corporations, losses generated by sole proprietorships and other flow-through entities are generally available to offset owners' personal income, subject to certain restrictions. For example, the owner of an entity taxed as a partnership or an S corporation shareholder may deduct losses from the entity only to the extent of the owner's basis in their ownership interest in the flow-through entity. In addition, deductibility of losses from flow-through entities may be further limited by the at-risk limitation and/or the passive activity loss limitation. The at-risk limitation is similar to the basis limitation but is slightly more restrictive (i.e., the amount at risk is generally the same as the owner's basis in their ownership interest). Consequently, if the taxpayer clears the basis limitation, they typically clear the at-risk limitation for deduction. The passive activity loss limitation typically applies to individual investors who are passive investors in the flow-through entities. For passive investors, the business activities of the entity are called passive activities. In these circumstances, taxpayers can deduct losses from passive activities only to the extent they have income from other passive activities (or when they sell their interest in the activity). Due to the complex nature of these limitations, we defer a detailed discussion of these limitations until the Forming and Operating Partnerships chapter.

Individual taxpayers are also not allowed to deduct an "excess business loss" for the year. An **excess business loss** is the excess of aggregate business deductions for the year over the sum of aggregate business gross income or gain of the taxpayer plus a threshold amount. The threshold amount for 2022 is $540,000 for married taxpayers filing jointly and $270,000 for other taxpayers. The amounts are adjusted annually for inflation. Excess business losses include business losses from sole proprietorships, entities taxed as partnerships, and S corporations. In the case of an S corporation or an entity taxed as a partnership, the limit applies at the owner level. Excess business losses are carried forward and used in subsequent years. The excess business loss limitation applies to losses that are otherwise deductible after applying the basis, at-risk, and passive loss rules. See the Forming and Operating Partnerships chapter for more details.

The ability to deduct flow-through losses against other sources of income can be a significant issue for owners of new businesses because new businesses tend to report losses early on as the businesses get established. If owners form a new business as a C corporation, the corporate-level losses provide no current tax benefit to the shareholders. The fact that C corporation losses are trapped at the corporate level can impose a higher tax cost for shareholders initially doing business as a C corporation relative to a flow-through entity such as an S corporation or an entity taxed as a partnership.

THE KEY FACTS

Taxation of Entity Income

- Flow-through entity income is taxed at the owner's tax rate. Individuals are taxed at a top marginal income rate of 37 percent on business income allocated to them from a flow-through entity.
- Flow-through entity owners who receive qualified business income from a flow-through entity are allowed to claim a qualified business income deduction equal to 20 percent of the qualified business income allocated to them (reduced by certain deductions and subject to certain limitations).
- Business income allocations to passive owners of flow-through entities may be subject to the 3.8 percent net investment income tax.
- Business income allocated to S corporation shareholders is not subject to self-employment tax.
- Owners of entities taxed as a partnership may be subject to self-employment tax on business income allocations, depending on the owner's involvement in the business activities.
- Sole proprietors are subject to self-employment tax on the sole proprietorship's income.
- C corporation taxable income is subject to a flat 21 percent tax rate.
- The maximum tax rate on dividends for Individuals who are C corporation shareholders is generally 20 percent. Further, certain taxpayers may be charged a 3.8 percent net investment income tax on dividends and capital gains.
- C corporation shareholders that are themselves C corporations are generally eligible to receive a 50 percent or greater dividends-received deduction (DRD).

(continued)

TAXES IN THE REAL WORLD Will Entity Selection Be Affected by the Tax Law Changes Effective in 2018?

In its Statistics of Income Tax Report (see below), the Internal Revenue Service reported the following information relating to tax entity selection by business owners as of 2015 (the most recent year reported). Sole proprietorships were the most common, followed by S corporations, entities taxed as partnerships, and then C corporations. Nevertheless, C corporations by far generated the most business entity receipts and net income. Under tax legislation effective in 2018, the C corporation tax rate has been reduced from 35 percent to 21 percent and owners of flow-through entities are allowed a new deduction for qualified business income generated by the entity. Going forward, how do you expect the percentage of each entity type to change, if at all, under the new tax system? Is it likely we will see a shift toward C corporations as the entity of choice?

The Blackstone Group Inc., the largest alternative investment firm in the world, converted from a publicly traded partnership to a corporation (C corporation for tax purposes), effective July 1, 2019. By converting, Blackstone expects to provide value to its shareholders. Stephen Schwarzman, Blackstone chairperson, CEO, and co-founder, said, "We are converting our firm from a publicly traded partnership to a

(continued)

- C corporation shareholders who are individuals generally pay capital gains taxes when shares are sold at a gain.
- S corporation and C corporation shareholders receive employee compensation for work they do for the entity.
- Owner-workers for entities taxed as a partnership receive compensation in the form of guaranteed payments. Guaranteed payments are self-employment income.

corporation. This change will make it vastly easier to buy and own Blackstone stock. It eliminates the burdensome K-1 tax forms. Blackstone will also become eligible for several market indicies. And these benefits come at what we expect to be a modest tax cost."* Mr. Schwarzman's comments suggest that while Blackstone had important nontax reasons to convert to a corporation, the recent reduction in the corporate tax rate from 35 percent to 21 percent significantly reduced the tax cost of converting to the point that the conversion made sense from an economical perspective. Would Blackstone have converted if the rate hadn't dropped? Probably not, but who knows for sure?

	Number of Entities	**Business Receipts**	**Net Income (including deficits)**
Totals for all entities	35,060,997	$33,812,762,216	$3,145,991,627
Entity Type	**Percentage**	**Percentage**	**Percentage**
C corporations	4.60	59.58	36.71
S corporations	12.80	21.73	17.79
General partnerships	1.66	1.08	2.89
Limited partnerships	1.16	2.92	7.76
LLCs (taxed as partnerships)	7.17	9.28	7.87
Sole proprietorships (nonfarm)	71.95	4.27	10.55
Other	.66	1.14	16.43

*Blackstone.com, April 18, 2019,http://site-174789.bcvpOrtal.com/.
Source: www.irs.gov/statistics/soi-tax-stats-integrated-business-data,Table 3: Selected financial data on businesses, 2015.

Example 4-11

What if: Assume that Nicole organizes CCS as a C corporation and that, in spite of her best efforts as CEO of the company, CCS reports a tax loss of $50,000 in its first year of operation (2022). Also assume that Nicole's marginal tax rate is 37 percent and the taxable income on her joint tax return is $500,000 (all ordinary income) before considering the CCS tax loss. How much tax will CCS pay for 2022, and how much tax will Nicole (and her spouse) pay on the $500,000 of other taxable income on their joint return if CCS is organized as a C corporation?

Answer: CCS will pay $0 in taxes because it reports a loss for tax purposes. However, CCS can carry the loss over to future years and can use the loss to offset up to 80 percent of its taxable income in a given year (before the NOL deduction itself). Because Nicole may not use the CCS loss to offset any of the ordinary income on her joint return, Nicole (and her spouse) must pay $185,000 in taxes. See the computations in the table below.

What if: Suppose CCS is organized as an S corporation and Nicole's stock basis in CCS before the 2022 loss is $100,000. How much tax will CCS pay for 2022, and how much tax will Nicole (and her spouse) pay on the $500,000 of ordinary income on the joint tax return?

Answer: CCS will pay $0 taxes (S corporations are not tax-paying entities) and Nicole (and spouse) will pay $166,500 in taxes. See the computations in the table below.

Description	C Corporation	S Corporation (flow-through)	Explanation
(1) Taxable income (loss)	$ (50,000)	$ (50,000)	
(2) CCS corporate-level tax	**$ 0**	**$ 0**	No taxable income
(3) Nicole's other income	$ 500,000	$ 500,000	
(4) CCS loss available to offset Nicole's other income	$ 0	$ (50,000)	$0 if C corporation; (1) if S corporation (flow-through entity)
(5) Nicole's other income reduced by entity loss	$ 500,000	$ 450,000	(3) + (4)
(6) Nicole's marginal ordinary tax rate	37%	37%	
Nicole's tax on other income	**$185,000**	**$166,500**	(5) × (6)

What if: Suppose CCS is organized as an S corporation and Nicole's stock basis before the $50,000 loss in 2022 is $100,000. Further, assume that Nicole does not participate in CCS's business activities; that is, assume she is a passive investor in the business entity. How much tax will Nicole (and her spouse) pay on the $500,000 of other ordinary income?

Answer: $185,000. Because Nicole is a passive investor, she is not allowed to deduct the loss allocated to her this year. She must carry it over and use it in future years (this assumes neither Nicole nor her spouse has income from other investments in which they are passive investors).

As the example above illustrates, owners' ability to immediately use start-up losses from flow-through entities to offset income from other sources is a tax advantage of flow-through entities over C corporations.

Exhibit 4-3 summarizes general rules for different tax characteristics by tax entity type.

EXHIBIT 4-3 General Rules for Tax Characteristics by Tax Entity Type*

Tax Characteristic	C Corporation	S Corporation	Partnership	Sole Proprietorship
Tax Form (or schedule) filed	Form 1120	Form 1120-S	Form 1065	Schedule C (Form 1040)
Taxation of entity income	Entity pays tax on its income and shareholders pay tax on dividends or when they sell their stock (i.e., double taxation).	Flows through to owners and is taxed once to owners as if owners had earned income (no double taxation). Income allocation increases each owner's stock basis and loss allocation decreases stock basis.	Flows through to owners and is taxed once to owners as if owners had earned income (no double taxation). Income allocation increases each owner's basis in ownership interest and loss allocation decreases basis in ownership interest.	Taxed once on the owner's tax return.** Owner does not have separate ownership basis in sole proprietorship even if the entity is formed as an LLC.
Are owners (who are individuals) potentially eligible for QBI deduction based on entity's income?	N/A	Yes, potentially eligible for QBI deduction based on business income allocation to owner.	Yes, potentially eligible for QBI deduction based on business income allocation to owner.	Yes
Compensation paid to owners for services	Treated as salary to owner/employee. Deductible by entity in computing entity's taxable income.	Treated as salary to owner/employee. Deductible by entity in computing entity's business income.	Guaranteed payment to partner providing service. Deductible by entity in computing entity's business income.	No compensation paid to owner.
Are owners subject to self-employment tax on compensation received for services provided to entity?	No***	No***	Yes	N/A
Is business income allocation to or earned by owners subject to self-employment tax?	N/A	No.	Yes, for general partners. No for limited partners. Yes, for LLC members who provide significant services for entity.	Yes.

(continued)

Tax Characteristic	C Corporation	S Corporation	Partnership	Sole Proprietorship
Are owners potentially subject to the additional Medicare tax on compensation received from the entity and on the entity's business income allocated to or earned by owner?	Yes, for compensation. N/A for business income.	Yes, for compensation. No, for business income allocation.	Yes, for compensation (guaranteed payment). Yes, for business income allocation that is subject to self-employment tax.	N/A for compensation. Yes, for business income.
Are distributions taxable to owners?	Yes, distributions are taxable as dividends.	No, to the extent of shareholder's basis in stock. Amount in excess of stock basis is capital gain.	No, to the extent of owner's basis in ownership interest. Amount above basis in ownership interest is capital gain.	N/A
Are owners potentially subject to net investment income tax on entity's income?	Yes, for dividends received and capital gain on sale of stock.	Yes, for capital gain on sale of stock, traditional investment income that flows through to shareholder, and business income allocated to shareholder to the extent the shareholder is a passive investor in the entity.	Yes, for capital gain on sale of ownership interest, traditional investment income that flows through to partner, and business income allocated to partner to the extent the shareholder is a passive investor in the entity.	N/A
Entity losses	Net losses (NOLs) stay at the entity level carry over to offset income in other years.	Deductible at the owner level to extent losses clear basis, at-risk, and passive loss hurdles. Amount of deductible loss for a year is restricted to annual excess loss limitation (based on filing status). Loss over limit carries over to next year. Limit applies to individual taxpayers.	Deductible at the owner level to extent losses clear basis, at-risk, and passive loss hurdles. Deduction for losses are subject to the excess loss deduction limitation as described in the S Corp. column.	Net loss can potentially offset individual's income from other sources. Net loss can carry over to other years under individual NOL provisions. Deduction for losses are subject to the at-risk, passive loss, and excess loss deduction limitations.
Is contribution of appreciated property to entity taxable (includes entity formation)?****	No to shareholder and no to corporation if shareholder(s) has control of corporation after property contribution.	No to shareholder and no to corporation if shareholder(s) has control of corporation after property contribution.	No to partner (member) and no to partnership. Control not required.	N/A
Are liquidations taxable?****	Generally, entity gain to extent FMV of property distributed exceeds property's basis. Shareholder recognizes capital gain (loss) to extent value of property received exceeds (is less than) stock basis in entity. Liquidations of 80%+ owned subsidiary into parent are not taxable.	Yes, entity gain that flows through to shareholders to extent FMV of property distributed exceeds property's basis. Shareholder recognizes capital gain (loss) to extent value of property received exceeds (is less than) stock basis.	No to entity or to owners.	N/A
Other	See Exhibit 4-4.	See Exhibit 4-4.	See Exhibit 4-4.	See Exhibit 4-4.

*This table provides the general rules. There are exceptions to most of the general rules. Exceptions are covered elsewhere in text.

**Entity and owner are same. Income flows from Schedule C to front page of Form 1040.

***Salary is not subject to self-employment tax, but it is subject to FICA tax. The employee pays half the FICA tax, and the entity pays the other half.

****This topic is not covered in detail in this chapter but is included here for completeness. See Exhibit 4-4 for text chapters that cover these topics in more detail.

OTHER TAX CHARACTERISTICS

There are many tax factors that differ across entities and can influence the entity selection decision. Exhibit 4-4 provides an overview of these tax characteristics. The exhibit describes the general rules for each tax characteristic as it relates to C corporations, S corporations, entities taxed as partnerships, and sole proprietorships, and it ranks the entities on each characteristic (1 is most tax favorable). Finally, it identifies the chapters where detail on these tax characteristics can be found.

Converting to Other Business Entity Types

With the significant reduction in corporate tax rates from tax legislation effective beginning in 2018, owners of existing flow-through entities may reevaluate their entity status and determine whether they prefer to have their entity taxed as a C corporation rather than as a flow-through entity (see the Taxes in the Real World box in this chapter discussing The Blackstone Group's conversion from a partnership to a C corporation). Fortunately for flow-through entity owners wanting to change entity type, it is easy and inexpensive to convert flow-through entities, including sole proprietorships, into C corporations. Owners of S corporations can revoke their election to be taxed as an S corporation and be taxed as a C corporation (see the S Corporations chapter for details on this process). As we discussed in the Business Entity Tax Classification section of this chapter, owners of entities taxed as partnerships and sole proprietors doing business as an LLC can retain the same legal entity type but make a check-the-box election to be taxed as a C corporation. Alternatively, owners of entities taxed as a partnership and sole proprietors can contribute the assets of the business entity to a newly formed corporation in a tax-deferred transaction without any special tax elections.[41] However, because this alternative involves creating a new legal entity, nontax factors (e.g., the cost of creating a new entity, changing the asset title to a new entity, etc.) may make this option less desirable than the check-the-box election to be taxed as a C corporation.

Conversely, because tax laws currently allow a deduction for qualified business income and slightly lower individual tax rates, C corporation shareholders may prefer to have their business taxed as a flow-through entity rather than as a C corporation. Shareholders of existing corporations really have only two options for converting into flow-through entities. First, shareholders of C corporations could make an election to treat the corporation as an S corporation (flow-through entity), if they are eligible to do so. This option is not available for many corporations due to the tax rule restrictions prohibiting certain corporations from operating as S corporations.[42] The only other option is for the shareholders to liquidate the corporation and form the business as an entity taxed as a partnership or sole proprietorship for tax purposes. This may not be a viable option, however, because the taxes imposed on liquidating corporations with appreciated assets can be punitive, even with the low current corporate tax rate. As described in Exhibit 4-4, liquidating corporations are taxed on the appreciation in the assets they distribute to their shareholders in liquidation. Further, shareholders of liquidating corporations are also taxed on the difference between the fair market value of the assets they receive from the liquidating corporation and the tax basis in their stock. Effectively, the total double-tax cost of liquidating a corporation can swamp expected tax savings from operating as a flow-through entity. The tax cost of liquidating an entity is a factor to consider when making the tax entity choice for a business.

[41]§351; Rev. Rul. 84-111.

[42]See the S Corporations chapter for details on making the S corporation election.

EXHIBIT 4-4 Comparison of Tax Characteristics across Entities

Tax Characteristic	C Corporation	Entity Taxed as Partnership	S Corporation	Sole Proprietorship	Summary
Owner limits	At least one shareholder.	At least two owners.	Not more than 100 shareholders; no corporations, partnerships, nonresident aliens, or certain trusts.	Not applicable.	Limitations are least strict for C corporations and most strict for S corporations. S corporations are the only entity with significant owner limitations. More detail for this factor is discussed in the S Corporations chapter.
Rank[1]	1	2	3	N/A	
Owner contributions of appreciated property to entity	Tax deferred to shareholder if certain requirements are met.	Tax deferred to owner.	Tax deferred to shareholder if certain requirements are met.	Not applicable.	This factor favors entities taxed as partnerships because partners are not required to meet special requirements in order to avoid recognizing gain on the contribution of appreciated property to the partnership, but shareholders of both C and S corporations are required to meet certain requirements to avoid recognizing gain on such contributions to the corporation. More detail for this factor is provided in the Corporate Formation, Reorganization, and Liquidation, the Forming and Operating Partnerships, and the S Corporations chapters.
Rank	2	1	2	N/A	
Accounting periods	Generally, any tax year that ends on the last day of any month.[2]	Generally, must use tax year that matches tax year of owners (special rules when not all owners have same tax year-end).	Calendar year.	Generally a calendar year.	C corporations generally have the most flexibility to select their year-end. But because C corporations are not flow-through entities, this is not a real advantage or disadvantage from a tax perspective. Partnerships generally are not free to choose their year-end, but they can have a year-end that is a different year-end from some of the owners. Because this allows some partners to defer reporting income, this factor favors partnerships over S corporations. S corporations generally have the same calendar year-end as their shareholders. More detail for this factor is provided in the Business Income, Deductions, and Accounting Methods, the Forming and Operating Partnerships, and the S Corporations chapters.
Rank	2	1	2	2	
Overall accounting method	Must use accrual method unless average annual gross receipts are $27 million or less.[3,4]	Generally, allowed to use cash or accrual method.	Generally, allowed to use cash or accrual method.	Cash or accrual method.	Entities taxed as partnerships, S corporations, and sole proprietorships generally have more flexibility to choose their overall accounting method than do C corporations with average annual gross receipts over $27 million. The cash method makes it easier for these entities to plan the timing of income and expenses than does the accrual method. More detail for this factor is provided in the Business Income, Deductions, and Accounting Methods, the Corporate Operations, the Forming and Operating Partnerships, and the S Corporations chapters.
Rank	4	1	1	1	
Allocation of income or loss items to owners	Not applicable	Allocations based on partnership agreement (can differ from ownership percentages).	Allocations based on stock ownership percentages.	Not applicable	This factor applies to partnerships and S corporations only. Partnerships have more flexibility than S corporations to determine how to allocate income and loss items to entity owners. More detail for this factor is provided in the Forming and Operating Partnerships and the S Corporations chapters.
Rank	N/A	1	2	N/A	

Tax Characteristic	C Corporation	Entity Taxed as Partnership	S Corporation	Sole Proprietorship	Summary
Share of flow-through entity debt included in basis of owner's equity interest	Not applicable	Increase basis in ownership interest by owner's share of entity's debt.	No increase in stock basis for debt of entity (special rules if shareholder lends money to S corporation).	Not applicable	Partners are allowed to increase the basis in their ownership interest by their share of the partnership's debt; S corporation shareholders generally are not. This factor favors partnerships over S corporations. More detail for this factor is provided in the the Forming and Operating Partnerships and the S Corporations chapters.
Rank	N/A	1	2	N/A	
Nonliquidating distributions of noncash property	Gains recognized on distributions of appreciated property and losses disallowed on distributions of depreciated property.	Generally no gain or loss recognized on noncash property distributions.	Same as C corporation.	Not applicable	This factor favors partnerships for distributions of appreciated and depreciated property. More detail for this factor is provided in the Corporate Taxation: Nonliquidating Distributions, the Dispositions of Partnership Interests and Partnership Distributions, and the S Corporations chapters.
Rank	2	1	1	N/A	
Liquidating distributions	Gain and loss generally recognized (certain losses disallowed). Liquidations of 80+ owned subsidiary into parent are tax deferred.	Generally no gain or loss recognized.	Gain and loss recognized (certain losses disallowed).	Not applicable	This factor tends to favor partnerships if the liquidating entities have gain assets, and it tends to favor corporations if the entities have loss assets. More detail for this factor is provided in the Corporate Formation, Reorganization, and Liquidation, the Dispositions of Partnership Interests and Partnership Distributions, and the S Corporations chapters.
Rank	1	1	1	N/A	

[1]"Rank" orders the entities based on the particular characteristic (1 is most favorable).

[2]C corporations that qualify as personal service corporations (PSCs) are generally required to use a calendar year. In general, a personal service corporation is a corporation whose shareholders perform professional services such as law, engineering, and accounting. See §448(d)(2) for more detail.

[3]The $27 million limit applies for tax years beginning in 2022, and the limit is indexed for inflation. The entity meets the gross receipts test for a taxable year if its annual gross receipts for the three-taxable-year period ending with the taxable year that precedes such taxable year does not exceed $27 million.

[4]C corporations that are qualified personal service corporations are required to use the cash method.

Example 4-12

What if: Assume we are years down the road and that Nicole is the sole shareholder of CCS (a C corporation). CCS's assets have a fair market value of $10 million and adjusted tax basis of $6 million ($4 million built-in gain). Further assume that the corporate tax rate is 21 percent, Nicole's stock basis in CCS is $2 million, and her marginal tax rate on long-term capital gains is 23.8 percent (20 percent capital gains rate + 3.8 percent net investment income tax). How much tax would CCS and Nicole be required to pay if CCS were to liquidate in order to form an LLC?

Answer: $2,544,080. This would be a steep tax price to pay for changing from a C corporation to an LLC.

Description	Amount	Explanation
(1) FMV of CCS assets	$10,000,000	
(2) Adjusted basis of CCS assets	6,000,000	
(3) CCS taxable income on liquidation	$ 4,000,000	(1) − (2)
(4) Corporate tax rate	21%	
(5) Entity-level tax	$ 840,000	(3) × (4)
(6) After-tax assets distributed to Nicole	9,160,000	(1) − (5)
(7) Nicole's stock basis	2,000,000	
(8) Nicole's long-term capital gain on distribution	$ 7,160,000	(6) − (7)
(9) Nicole's marginal tax rate on gain	23.8%	
(10) Shareholder-level tax	$ 1,704,080	(8) × (9)
Total entity- and shareholder-level tax on liquidation	**$ 2,544,080**	(5) + (10)

(continued from page 4-4 . . .)
Nicole quickly determined she would legally form CCS as an LLC in Utah. This would provide her with limited liability and allow her complete flexibility for determining the tax entity type of CCS. If at some point she wanted to convert CCS into a corporation in Utah, she was advised that she could make the conversion simply by filing some paperwork.

Nicole's five-year forecast of CCS's expected operating results showed that CCS would generate losses for the first three years and then become very profitable thereafter. With these projections in hand, Nicole first considered forming CCS as a partnership for tax purposes (she was planning on bringing in another investor) or electing to become an S corporation. Nicole determined that income allocated to her from CCS would be eligible for the deduction for qualified business income whether she operated CCS as a partnership or an S corporation. She then compared the specific tax rules applicable to partnerships and S corporations before deciding her preference between the two tax entity types. She identified some differences that could sway her decision one way or the other. Supporting a decision to select a partnership, Nicole learned she would likely be able to deduct the projected losses in the early years from CCS more quickly with a partnership compared with an S corporation because she could include a share of the partnership's debt in her tax basis in her ownership interest (whereas she would not be able to include a share of the S corporation's debt in the tax basis of her ownership interest). Nicole also hoped to attract corporate investors, and she discovered that a partnership can have corporate partners but that S corporations are not permitted to have corporate shareholders. Supporting a decision to select an S corporation, Nicole learned that S corporations appear to have a compelling advantage over partnerships in reducing the self-employment tax of owners active in managing their businesses. Nicole decided that she preferred a partnership over an S corporation because she would be willing to potentially incur additional self-employment taxes with a partnership in exchange for the ability to deduct her losses sooner and for the freedom to solicit corporate investors.

Nicole then turned her attention to whether she preferred to operate CCS as a C corporation or a partnership for tax purposes. Favoring the partnership tax entity choice was the fact that Nicole would be able to immediately deduct initial losses of the business against her personal taxable income. Favoring the C corporation choice was the overall tax rate on the CCS income when it becomes profitable. She reasoned that the corporate tax rate is significantly lower than her marginal individual tax rate and she planned to grow CCS by having CCS retain rather than distribute its income and subject it to a second level of tax. Consequently, Nicole determined that the overall tax rate to CCS income would be significantly lower if she operated CCS as a C corporation. Further, as a C corporation she would be able to solicit corporate owners and eventually take CCS public if the opportunity were to present itself (to do this she would have to convert to a legal corporation). After much thought and analysis, Nicole chose to make the election necessary to have CCS taxed as a C corporation. With this big decision out of the way, Nicole could focus on applying for a small business loan from her local bank and on having her attorney take the necessary steps to formally organize CCS as a limited liability company. ■

CONCLUSION

Any time a new business is formed, and periodically thereafter as circumstances change (such as relevant tax law), business owners must carefully evaluate what type of business entity will maximize the after-tax profits from their business ventures. Many of the key factors to consider in the entity selection decision-making process are outlined in this chapter. When making the entity selection decision, owners must carefully balance the tax and nontax characteristics unique to the entities available to them. This chapter explains how various legal entities are treated for tax purposes and how certain tax characteristics differ between entity types. Moreover, it also identifies some of the more important nontax issues that come to bear on the choice of entity decision. With this understanding, taxpayers and their advisers will be better prepared to face this frequently encountered business decision. In the Forming and Operating Partnerships chapter, we return to Nicole and Color Comfort Sheets LLC to examine the tax rules that apply to Nicole and other members in CCS as they form the entity for tax purposes and begin business operations.

Summary

Discuss the legal and other nontax characteristics of different types of legal business entities. LO 4-1

- Business entities that differ in terms of their legal characteristics include corporations, limited liability companies, general partnerships, limited partnerships, and sole proprietorships.
- Corporations are formally organized by filing articles of incorporation with the state. They are legally separate entities and protect their shareholders from the liabilities of the corporation. State corporation laws dictate interactions between corporations and shareholders.

As a result, shareholders have limited flexibility to customize their business arrangements with the corporation and other shareholders. State corporate governance rules do, however, facilitate initial public offerings.

- Limited liability companies are formally organized by filing articles of organization with the state. Like corporations, they are separate legal entities that shield their members from liabilities. In contrast to corporations, state LLC statutes give members a great deal of latitude in customizing their business arrangements with the LLC and other members.
- General partnerships may be organized informally without state approval, but limited partnerships must file a certificate of limited partnership with the state to organize. Although they are considered to be legally separate entities, they provide either limited or no liability protection for partners. While limited partners in limited partnerships have liability protection, general partners are fully exposed to the liabilities of the partnership. General and limited partnerships are given a great deal of latitude in customizing their partnership agreements.
- Sole proprietorships are businesses legally indistinguishable from their sole individual owners. As such, they are very flexible but provide no liability protection. Sole proprietors can obtain liability protection by converting to a single-member LLC.

LO 4-2 Describe the different types of business entities for tax purposes.

- The four categories of business entities recognized by our tax system include C corporations, S corporations, partnerships, and sole proprietorships.
- Legal corporations that don't make the S election are treated as C corporations and therefore pay taxes. All other entities recognized for tax purposes are flow-through entities.
- Legal corporations that qualify for and make the S election are treated as S corporations.
- Unincorporated entities with more than one owner are treated as partnerships unless they elect to be taxed as a corporation. If the entity elects to be taxed as a corporation, it can further elect to be taxed as an S corporation if it meets the S corporation requirements.
- Unincorporated entities with one owner are treated as sole proprietorships, where the sole owner is an individual, or as disregarded entities otherwise. If a sole proprietor converts to a single-member LLC, the LLC can elect to be taxed as a corporation. It can further elect to be taxed as an S corporation.

LO 4-3 Identify fundamental differences in tax characteristics across business entity types.

- Flow-through entity income is taxed once at the owner level. For individual owners, the top rate is 37 percent. Flow-through income may also be subject to the net investment income tax for passive investors or the self-employment tax for those involved in the business activities of a partnership or sole proprietorship.
- Flow-through business owners are eligible to deduct 20 percent of their qualified business income (minus the self-employed health insurance deduction, the self-employment tax deduction, and the deduction for contributions to self-employed retirement plans) as a from AGI deduction that is not an itemized deduction. The deduction is subject to certain limitations determined at the individual level.
- Qualified business income is generally nonservice business income generated in the United States. The deduction is subject to a wage-based limitation and a taxable income limitation.
- Flow-through entity business income allocated to passive owners is subject to the 3.8 percent net investment income tax for taxpayers with AGI over a threshold dependent on filing status.
- Self-employment income is subject to self-employment tax and additional Medicare tax.
- S corporation business income allocated to shareholders is not self-employment income.
- Sole proprietorship income is self-employment income to the sole proprietor.
- Whether business income of entities taxed as a partnership is self-employment income to an owner depends on the owner's involvement in the entity's business activities.
- Corporate taxable income is taxed at the corporate level and again at the shareholder level. The corporate tax rate is a flat 21 percent. The second level of tax is paid at the shareholder level when the corporation distributes after-tax earnings as a dividend or when the shareholder sells the stock. The tax rate for the second level of tax depends on the type of shareholder.

- Dividends and long-term capital gains are taxed at a top rate of 23.8 percent (20 percent dividend plus 3.8 percent net investment income tax). Corporate shareholders are taxed on dividends and capital gains at the corporate tax rate. However, corporations are entitled to deduct 50, 65, or 100 percent of dividends received based on the extent of their ownership in the distributing corporation.
- Corporations can defer the second level of tax by not distributing their after-tax income. However, corporations that retain earnings for tax avoidance rather than business purposes may be subject to the accumulated earnings tax or the personal holding company tax. These taxes reduce the incentive for corporations to retain earnings in order to avoid the second level of tax. Corporations are allowed to retain earnings to invest in their business.
- Business entity owners who work for the entity are compensated in different ways, depending on the type of entity.
- S corporation and C corporation shareholders who work for the entity receive employee compensation.
- Owners who work for entities taxed as partnerships receive guaranteed payments that are self-employment income to the owner-worker.
- Sole proprietors don't receive compensation from the business because the sole proprietorship and the sole proprietor are the same entity for tax purposes.
- Operating losses from S corporations and entities taxed as partnerships flow through to the owners. Owners may deduct these losses only to the extent of the basis in their ownership interest. The losses must also clear "at-risk" limitations and passive activity loss limitations in order for the owners to deduct the loss.
- The at-risk limitation is similar to the basis limitation. The passive activity loss limitations typically apply to individual investors who do little, if any, work relating to the business activities of the flow-through entity (referred to as *passive* activities to the individual investors). In these circumstances, taxpayers can deduct such losses only to the extent they have income from other passive activities.
- Flow-through entity individual owners are not allowed to deduct an excess business loss for the year ($540,000 for married couples filing jointly; $270,000 for other taxpayers). This provision potentially limits losses that would otherwise be deductible after applying the at-risk and passive activity loss limitations.
- Shareholders can mitigate the double tax by increasing the time they hold shares before selling.
- C corporation losses are referred to as net operating losses (NOLs).
- The specific tax rules for a corporation's ability to deduct net operating losses depends on the year in which the NOL is incurred. Different rules apply for NOLs originating in tax years beginning before 2018, beginning after 2017 and before 2021, and beginning after 2020.
- C corporations may have one or many shareholders. S corporations may have one shareholder and as many as 100 unrelated shareholders; but corporations, nonresident aliens, partnerships, and certain trusts may not be S corporation shareholders. Partnerships must have at least two partners but are not restricted to a maximum number of partners. Sole proprietorships may have only one owner.
- Gains and income from contributing appreciated property to business entities are more easily deferred with partnerships compared to C and S corporations.
- S corporations, partnerships, and sole proprietorships are generally required to use tax year-ends conforming to the tax year-ends of their owners. C corporations may use any tax year-end.
- C corporations generally must use the accrual method unless they are a smaller corporation (average gross receipts of $27 million or less in the prior three years). S corporations may use either the cash or accrual method of accounting. Partnerships generally may use either the cash or accrual method. Sole proprietorships may use either the cash or accrual method.
- Income and losses may be specially allocated to partners based on the partnership agreement. This gives partnerships a great deal of flexibility in determining how the risks and rewards of the enterprise are shared among partners. In contrast, income and losses must be allocated pro rata to S corporation shareholders consistent with their ownership percentages.

- Partners, but not S corporation shareholders, may add their share of entity debt to the basis in their ownership interest.
- Generally, distributions of appreciated property trigger gain at both the corporate and shareholder levels when made to shareholders of C corporations, trigger gain at the corporate level when made to S corporation shareholders, and don't trigger any gain at all when made to partners.
- On liquidation, C and S corporations will generally recognize gains and losses on distributed assets. In contrast, partnerships and their partners generally do not recognize gains or losses on liquidating distributions.
- Converting a flow-through entity into a C corporation for tax purposes is generally fairly easy and inexpensive to do. S corporation shareholders can revoke the S corporation election; partnerships (and sole proprietorships formed as LLCs) can check the box to be taxed as a corporation; and partnerships and sole proprietors can contribute assets to a corporate entity in tax-deferred transactions.
- C corporations wanting to convert to a flow-through entity have two options. They may elect to become an S corporation if eligible, or they may liquidate the corporation and organize as a new entity. Taxes from liquidating C corporations can be significant when C corporations have appreciated assets.

KEY TERMS

accumulated earnings tax (4-22)
articles of incorporation (4-2)
articles of organization (4-2)
C corporations (4-5)
certificate of limited partnership (4-2)
certificate of organization (4-2)
corporation (4-2)
disregarded entities (4-5)
dividends-received deduction (DRD) (4-20)
double taxation (4-21)
excess business loss (4-27)
flow-through entities (4-5)
general partnership (GP) (4-2)
initial public offering (IPO) (4-3)
institutional shareholder (4-18)
limited liability company (LLC) (4-2)
limited partnership (LP) (4-2)
net earnings from self-employment (4-14)
net operating loss (NOL) (4-26)
partnership agreement (4-2)
personal holding companies (4-22)
personal holding company tax (4-22)
qualified business income (QBI) (4-9)
S corporation (4-5)
single-member LLCs (4-5)
social security wage base limitation (4-14)
sole proprietorship (4-2)
specified service trade or business (4-9)
unrelated business income (4-21)

DISCUSSION QUESTIONS

Discussion Questions are available in Connect®.

LO 4-1 1. What are the most common legal entities used for operating a business? How are these entities treated similarly and differently for state law purposes?

LO 4-1 2. How do business owners create legal entities? Is the process the same for all entities? If not, what are the differences?

LO 4-1 3. What is an operating agreement for an LLC? Are operating agreements required for limited liability companies? If not, why might it be important to have one?

LO 4-1 4. Explain how legal business entities differ in terms of the liability protection they provide their owners.

LO 4-1 5. Why is it a nontax advantage for corporations to be able to trade their stock on the stock market?

LO 4-1 6. How do legal corporations protect shareholders from liability? If you formed a small corporation, would you be able to avoid repaying a bank loan from your community bank if the corporation went bankrupt? Explain.

LO 4-1 LO 4-2 7. Other than corporations, are there other legal business entities that offer liability protection? Are any of them taxed as flow-through entities? Explain.

8. In general, how are unincorporated business entities classified for tax purposes? LO 4-2
9. Can unincorporated legal business entities ever be treated as corporations for tax purposes? Can legal corporations ever be treated as flow-through entities for tax purposes? Explain. LO 4-2
10. What are the differences, if any, between the legal and tax classifications of business entities? LO 4-2
11. What types of business entities does the U.S. tax system recognize? LO 4-2
12. For flow-through business entities with individual owners, how many times is flow-through entity income taxed, who pays the tax, and what is the tax rate? LO 4-3
13. What is the qualified business income deduction, and how does it affect the tax rate on flow-through business entity income? LO 4-3
14. Daria is considering investing in one of two partnerships that will build, own, and operate a hotel. One is located in Canada and one is located in Arizona. Assuming both investments will generate the same before-tax rate of return, which entity should Daria invest in when considering the after-tax consequences of the investment? Assume Daria's marginal tax rate is 37 percent, she will be a passive investor in the business, and she will report the flow-through income from either entity on her tax return. Explain (ignore any foreign tax credit issues). LO 4-3 planning
15. Is business income allocated from a flow-through business entity to its owner's self-employment income? Explain. LO 4-3
16. Did tax lax law changes effective in 2018 increase or decrease the amount of the double tax on C corporation income? Explain. LO 4-3
17. Who pays the first level of tax on a C corporation's income? What is the tax rate applicable to the first level of tax? LO 4-3
18. Who pays the second level of tax on a C corporation's income? What is the tax rate applicable to the second level of tax, and when is it levied? LO 4-3
19. Is it possible for shareholders to defer or avoid the second level of tax on corporate income altogether? Briefly explain. LO 4-3
20. How does a corporation's decision to pay dividends affect its overall tax rate? LO 4-3
21. Is it possible for the overall tax rate on corporate taxable income to be lower than the tax rate on flow-through entity taxable income? If so, under what conditions would you expect the overall corporate tax rate to be lower? LO 4-3
22. Assume Congress increases individual tax rates on ordinary income while leaving all other tax rates unchanged. How would this change affect the overall tax rate on corporate taxable income? How would this change affect overall tax rates for owners of flow-through business entities? LO 4-3
23. Assume Congress increases the dividend tax rate to the ordinary tax rate while leaving all other tax rates unchanged. How would this change affect the overall tax rate on corporate taxable income? LO 4-3
24. Evaluate the following statement: "When dividends and long-term capital gains are taxed at the same rate, the overall tax rate on corporate income is the same whether the corporation distributes its after-tax earnings as a dividend or whether it reinvests the after-tax earnings to increase the value of the corporation." LO 4-3
25. If XYZ Corporation is a shareholder of BCD Corporation, how many times will BCD's before-tax income potentially be taxed? Has Congress provided any tax relief for this result? Explain. LO 4-3
26. How many times is income from a C corporation taxed if a retirement fund is the owner of the corporation's stock? Explain. LO 4-3
27. Do tax-exempt organizations pay tax on dividends received from C corporations? Do tax-exempt organizations pay tax on business income earned? Explain. LO 4-3

LO 4-3 28. For tax purposes, how is the compensation paid to an S corporation shareholder similar to compensation paid to an owner of an entity taxed as a partnership? How is it different?

LO 4-3 29. Why might it be a good tax planning strategy for an S corporation with one shareholder to pay a salary to the shareholder on the low end of what the services are potentially worth?

LO 4-3 30. When a C corporation reports a loss for the year, can shareholders use the loss to offset their personal income? Why or why not?

LO 4-3 31. Is a current-year net operating loss of a C corporation available to offset income from the corporation in other years? Explain.

LO 4-3 32. Would a corporation with a small amount of current-year taxable income (before the net operating loss deduction) and a large net operating loss carryover have a tax liability for the current year? Explain.

LO 4-3 33. In its first year of existence, SMS, an S corporation, reported a business loss of $10,000. Sewon, SMS's sole shareholder, reports $50,000 of taxable income from sources other than SMS. What must you know to determine whether she can deduct the $10,000 loss against her other income? Explain.

LO 4-3 34. ELS, an S corporation, reported a business loss of $1,000,000. Ethan, ELS's sole shareholder, is involved in ELS's daily business activities, and he reports $1,200,000 of taxable income from sources other than ELS. What must you know in order to determine how much, if any, of the $1,000,000 loss Ethan may deduct in the current year? Explain.

LO 4-3 35. Why are S corporations less favorable than C corporations and entities taxed as partnerships in terms of owner-related limitations?

LO 4-3 36. Are C corporations or flow-through entities (S corporations and entities taxed as partnerships) more flexible in terms of selecting a tax year-end? Why are the tax rules in this area different for C corporations and flow-through business entities?

LO 4-3 37. Which tax entity types are generally allowed to use the cash method of accounting?

LO 4-3 38. According to the tax rules, how are profits and losses allocated to owners of entities taxed as partnerships (partners or LLC members)? How are they allocated to S corporation shareholders? Which entity permits greater flexibility in allocating profits and losses?

LO 4-3 39. Compare and contrast the FICA tax burden of S corporation shareholder-employees and LLC members (assume the LLC is taxed as a partnership) receiving compensation for working for the entity (guaranteed payments) and business income allocations to S corporation shareholders and LLC members assuming the owners are actively involved in the entity's business activities. How does your analysis change if the owners are not actively involved in the entity's business activities?

LO 4-3 40. Explain how liabilities of an LLC (taxed as a partnership) or an S corporation affect the amount of tax losses from the entity that limited liability company members and S corporation shareholders may deduct. Do the tax rules favor LLCs or S corporations?

LO 4-3 41. Compare the entity-level tax consequences for C corporations, S corporations, and business entities taxed as partnerships for both nonliquidating and liquidating distributions of noncash property. Do the tax rules tend to favor one entity type more than the others? Explain.

LO 4-3 42. If business entities taxed as partnerships and S corporations are both flow-through entities for tax purposes, why might an owner prefer one form over the other for tax purposes? List separately the tax factors supporting the decision to operate a business entity as an entity taxed either as a partnership or as an S corporation.

LO 4-3 43. What are the tax advantages and disadvantages of converting a C corporation into an LLC taxed as a partnership?

PROBLEMS

Select problems are available in Connect®. connect

44. Visit your state's official website and review the information there related to forming and operating business entities in your state. Write a short report explaining the steps for organizing a business in your state and summarizing any tax-related information you found. LO 4-1 research

45. Kiyara (single) is a 50 percent shareholder of Guardian Corporation (an S corporation). Kiyara does not do any work for Guardian Corp. Guardian Corp. reported $300,000 of business income for the year (2022). Before considering her business income allocation from Guardian Corp. and the self-employment tax deduction (if any), Kiyara's adjusted gross income was $250,000 (all employee salary). Kivara has $40,000 in itemized deductions. Answer the following questions for Kiyara. LO 4-3
    a) What is Kiyara's self-employment tax liability?
    b) Assuming the income allocated to Kiyara is qualified business income, what is Kiyara's deduction for qualified business income? Assume Kiyara's share of wages paid by Guardian Corp. is $50,000 and her share in the unadjusted basis of qualified property used by Guardian was $200,000.
    c) What is Kiyara's net investment income tax liability (assume no investment expenses)?
    d) What is Kiyara's additional Medicare tax liability (include all earned income in computing the tax)?

46. Mason (single) is a 50 percent shareholder in Angels Corp. (an S Corporation). Mason receives a $180,000 salary working full time for Angels Corp. Angels Corp. reported $400,000 of taxable business income for the year (2022). Before considering his business income allocation from Angels and the self-employment tax deduction (if any), Mason's adjusted gross income is $180,000 (all salary from Angels Corp.). Mason claims $50,000 in itemized deductions. Answer the following questions for Mason. LO 4-3
    a) What is Mason's self-employment tax liability?
    b) Assuming the business income allocated to Mason is income from a specified service trade or business, what is Mason's deduction for qualified business income? Ignore the wage-based limitation when computing the deduction.
    c) Assume the same facts as question (b), except that Angels Corp. reported $150,000 of taxable business income for the year. What is Mason's deduction for qualified business income? Ignore the wage-based limitation when computing the deduction.
    d) Assuming the original facts, what is Mason's net investment income tax liability (assume no investment expenses)?
    e) Assuming the original facts, what is Mason's additional Medicare tax liability?

47. Sofia (single) is a 50 percent owner in Beehive LLC (taxed as a partnership). Sofia does not do any work for Beehive. Beehive LLC reported $600,000 of taxable business income for the year (2022). Before considering her 50 percent business income allocation from Beehive and the self-employment tax deduction (if any), Sofia's adjusted gross income is $150,000 (all employee salary). Sofia has $35,000 in itemized deductions. Answer the following questions for Sofia. LO 4-3
    a) What is Sofia's self-employment tax liability?
    b) Assuming the income allocated to Sofia is not from a specified service trade or business, what is Sofia's deduction for qualified business income? Assume Sofia's share of wages paid by Beehive LLC is $130,000 and her share in the unadjusted basis of qualified property used by Beehive was $300,000.

c) What is Sofia's net investment income tax liability (assume no investment expenses)?

d) What is Sofia's additional Medicare tax liability?

LO 4-3

48. Omar (single) is a 50 percent owner in Cougar LLC (taxed as a partnership). Omar works half time for Cougar and receives guaranteed payment of $50,000. Cougar LLC reported $450,000 of business income for the year (2022). Before considering his 50 percent business income allocation from Cougar and the self-employment tax deduction (if any), Omar's adjusted gross income is $210,000 (includes $50,000 guaranteed payment from Cougar and $160,000 salary from a different employer). Omar reports itemized deductions of $40,000. Answer the following questions for Omar.

a) What is Omar's self-employment tax liability?

b) What would be Omar's self-employment tax liability if he didn't receive any salary.

c) Assume the original facts and that the business income allocated to Omar is not from a specified service. What is Omar's deduction for qualified business income? Assume that 81.82 percent of the self-employment tax is from self-employment income included in QBI [i.e., $225,000 business income allocation/$275,000 (business income allocation plus guaranteed payment)]. That is, the $50,000 guaranteed payment is not qualified business income. Ignore the wage-based limitation.

d) What is Omar's net investment income tax liability (assume no investment expenses)?

e) What is Omar's additional Medicare tax liability?

LO 4-3

49. Jacob is a member of WCC (an LLC taxed as a partnership). Jacob was allocated $100,000 of business income from WCC for the year. Jacob's marginal income tax rate is 37 percent. The business allocation is subject to 2.9 percent of self-employment tax and .9 percent additional Medicare tax.

a) What is the amount of tax Jacob will owe on the income allocation if the income is not qualified business income?

b) What is the amount of tax Jacob will owe on the income allocation if the income is qualified business income (QBI) and Jacob qualifies for the full QBI deduction?

LO 4-3

50. Amanda would like to organize BAL as either an LLC (taxed as a sole proprietorship) or a C corporation. In either form, the entity is expected to generate an 8 percent annual before-tax return on a $500,000 investment. Amanda's marginal income tax rate is 37 percent, and her tax rate on qualified dividends and net capital gains is 20%. Assume that BAL will distribute half of its after-tax earnings every year as a dividend if it is formed as a C corporation. Assume the income is not eligible for the QBI deduction. Further, when computing your answers, include the self-employment tax (use a 2.9% marginal rate for self-employment income because Amanda has salary over $147,000 from her employer) but not the additional Medicare tax or the net investment income tax.

a) How much cash after taxes would Amanda receive from her investment in the first year if BAL is organized as an LLC? What if BAL is organized as a C corporation?

b) What is the overall tax rate on BAL's income in the first year if BAL is organized as an LLC or as a C corporation?

c) At a high level, explain the primary factors contributing to differences between entities in cash flow and overall tax rate on business income.

51. Sandra would like to organize LAB (a legal corporation) as either an S corporation or a C corporation for tax purposes. In either form, the entity is expected to generate an 8 percent annual before-tax return on a $500,000 investment. Sandra's marginal income tax rate is 37 percent and her tax rate on qualified dividends and net capital gains is 20 percent. LAB's income is not qualified business income (QBI), so Sandra is not allowed to claim the QBI deduction. Assume that LAB will distribute all of its earnings after entity-level taxes every year. Ignore the additional Medicare tax and the net investment income tax when computing your answers. LO 4-3

 a) How much cash after taxes would Sandra receive from her investment in the first year if LAB is organized as either an S corporation or a C corporation?
 b) What is the overall tax rate on LAB's income in the first year if LAB is organized as an S corporation or as a C corporation?
 c) At a high level, explain the differences between entity types in after-tax cash flow and overall tax rate on business income.

52. Tremaine would like to organize UTA as either an S Corporation or a C corporation. In either form, the entity will generate a 9 percent annual before-tax return on a $1,000,000 investment. Tremaine's marginal income tax rate is 37 percent, and his tax rate on dividends and capital gains is 23.8 percent (including the net investment income tax). If Tremaine organizes UTA as an S corporation, he will be allowed to claim the deduction for qualified business income. Also, because Tremaine will participate in UTA's business activities, the income from UTA will not be subject to the net investment income tax. Assume that UTA will pay out 25 percent of its after-tax earnings every year as a dividend if it is formed as a C corporation. LO 4-3 research

 a) How much cash after taxes would Tremaine receive from his investment in the first year if UTA is organized either as an S corporation or as a C corporation?
 b) What is the overall tax rate on UTA's income in the first year if UTA is organized as an S corporation or as a C corporation?
 c) What is the overall tax rate on UTA's income in the first year if it is organized as an S corporation, but UTA's income is not qualified business income?
 d) What is the overall tax rate on UTA's income if it is organized as an S corporation, UTA's income is not qualified business income, and Tremaine is a passive investor in UTA?

53. Marathon Inc. (a C corporation) reported $1,000,000 of taxable income in the current year. During the year, it distributed $100,000 as dividends to its shareholders as follows: LO 4-3

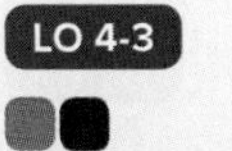
tax forms

 - $5,000 to Guy, a 5 percent individual shareholder.
 - $15,000 to Little Rock Corp., a 15 percent shareholder (C corporation).
 - $80,000 to other shareholders.

 a) How much of the dividend payment did Marathon deduct in determining its taxable income?
 b) Assuming Guy's marginal ordinary tax rate is 37 percent, how much tax will he pay on the $5,000 dividend he received from Marathon Inc. (including the net investment income tax)?
 c) What amount of tax will Little Rock Corp. pay on the $15,000 dividend it received from Marathon Inc. (50 percent dividends-received deduction)?
 d) Complete Form 1120 Schedule C for Little Rock Corp. to reflect its dividends-received deduction (use the most recent Form 1120 Schedule C available).
 e) On what line on page 1 of Little Rock Corp.'s Form 1120 is the dividend from Marathon Inc. reported, and on what line of Little Rock Corp.'s Form 1120 is its dividends-received deduction reported?

LO 4-3 research

54. After several years of profitable operations, Javell, the sole shareholder of JBD Inc., a C corporation, sold 22 percent of her JBD stock to ZNO Inc., a C corporation in a similar industry. During the current year, JBD reports $1,000,000 of after-tax income. JBD distributes all of its after-tax earnings to its two shareholders in proportion to their shareholdings. How much tax will ZNO pay on the dividend it receives from JBD? What is ZNO's tax rate on the dividend income (after considering the DRD)? [*Hint:* See §243.]

LO 4-3

55. Mackenzie is considering conducting her business, Mac561, as either a single-member LLC or an S corporation. Assume her marginal ordinary income tax rate is 37 percent, her marginal FICA rate on employee compensation is 1.45 percent, her marginal self-employment tax rate is 2.9 percent (her other self-employment income and/or salary exceeds the $147,000 wage base limit for the 12.4 percent Social Security tax portion of the self-employment tax), and any employee compensation or self-employment income she receives is subject to the .9 percent additional Medicare tax. Also, assume Mac561 generated $200,000 of business income before considering the deduction for compensation Mac561 pays to Mackenzie and Mackenzie can claim the full qualified business income deduction on Mac561's business income allocated to her. Determine Mackenzie's after-tax cash flow from the entity's business income and any compensation she receives from the business under the following assumptions:

a) Mackenzie conducted Mac561 as a single-member LLC.

b) Mackenzie conducted Mac561 as an S corporation and she received a salary of $100,000. All business income allocated to her is also distributed to her.

c) Mackenzie conducted Mac561 as an S corporation and she received a salary of $20,000. All business income allocated to her is also distributed to her.

d) Which entity/compensation combination generated the most after-tax cash flow for Mackenzie? What are the primary contributing factors favoring this combination?

LO 4-3

56. SCC corporation (a calendar-year C corporation) has a net operating loss (NOL) carryover to 2022 in the amount of $30,000. How much tax will SCC pay for 2022 if it reports taxable income from operations of $20,000 before considering loss carryovers under the following assumptions?

a) The NOL originated in 2017.

b) The NOL originated in 2018.

LO 4-3

57. Willow Corp. (a calendar-year C corporation) reported taxable income before the net operating loss deduction (NOL) in the amount of $100,000 in 2022. Willow had an NOL carryover of $90,000 to 2022. How much tax will Willow Corp. pay in 2022, what is its NOL carryover to 2023, and when will the NOL expire under the following assumptions?

a) $50,000 of the NOL carryover was generated in 2016 and $40,000 of the NOL carryover was generated in 2017.

b) $40,000 of the NOL was generated in 2016 and $50,000 was generated in 2021.

LO 4-3

58. Damarcus is a 50 percent owner of Rockit (a business entity). In the current year, Rockit reported a $100,000 business loss. Answer the following questions associated with each of the following alternative scenarios.

a) Rockit is organized as a C corporation and Damarcus works full time as an employee for Rockit. Damarcus has a $20,000 basis in his Rockit stock. How much of Rockit's loss is Damarcus allowed to deduct against his other income?

b) Rockit is organized as an LLC taxed as a partnership. Fifty percent of Rockit's loss is allocated to Damarcus. Damarcus works full time for Rockit (he is not considered to be a passive investor in Rockit). Damarcus has a $20,000 basis and at-risk amount in his ownership interest in Rockit. Damarcus does not report income or loss from any other business activity investments. How much of the $50,000 loss allocated to him by Rockit is Damarcus allowed to deduct this year?

c) Rockit is organized as an LLC taxed as a partnership. Fifty percent of Rockit's loss is allocated to Damarcus. Damarcus does not work for Rockit at all (he is a passive investor in Rockit). Damarcus has a $20,000 basis and at-risk amount in his ownership interest in Rockit. Damarcus does not report income or loss from any other business activity investments. How much of the $50,000 loss allocated to him by Rockit is Damarcus allowed to deduct this year?

d) Rockit is organized as an LLC taxed as a partnership. Fifty percent of Rockit's loss is allocated to Damarcus. Damarcus works full time for Rockit (he is not considered to be a passive investor in Rockit). Damarcus has a $70,000 basis and at-risk amount in his ownership interest in Rockit. Damarcus does not report income or loss from any other business activity investments. How much of the $50,000 loss allocated to him by Rockit is Damarcus allowed to deduct this year?

e) Rockit is organized as an LLC taxed as a partnership. Fifty percent of Rockit's loss is allocated to Damarcus. Damarcus does not work for Rockit at all (he is a passive investor in Rockit). Damarcus has a $20,000 basis and at-risk amount in his ownership interest in Rockit. Damarcus reports $10,000 of income from another business activity in which he is a passive investor. How much of the $50,000 loss allocated to him by Rockit is Damarcus allowed to deduct this year?

59. Danni is a single 30 percent owner of Kolt (a business entity). In the current year, Kolt reported a $1,000,000 business loss. Answer the following questions associated with each of the following alternative scenarios: LO 4-3

a) Kolt is organized as a C corporation and Danni works 20 hours a week as an employee for Kolt. Danni has a $200,000 basis in her Kolt stock. How much of Kolt's loss is Danni allowed to deduct this year against her other income?

b) Kolt is organized as an LLC taxed as a partnership. Thirty percent of Kolt's loss is allocated to Danni. Danni works 20 hours a week on Kolt business activities (she is not considered to be a passive investor in Kolt). Danni has a $400,000 basis in her Kolt ownership interest, and she also has a $400,000 at-risk amount in her investment in Kolt. Danni does not report income or loss from any other business activity investments. How much of the $300,000 loss allocated to her from Kolt is Danni allowed to deduct this year?

c) Kolt is organized as an LLC taxed as a partnership. Thirty percent of Kolt's loss is allocated to Danni. Danni is not involved in Kolt business activities. Consequently, she is considered to be a passive investor in Kolt. Danni has a $400,000 basis and at-risk amount in her ownership interest in Kolt. Danni does not report income or loss from any other business activity investments. How much of the $300,000 loss allocated to her from Kolt is Danni allowed to deduct this year?

60. Mustafa, Mickayla, and Taylor are starting a new business (MMT). To get the business started, Mustafa is contributing $200,000 for a 40 percent ownership interest, Mickayla is contributing a building with a value of $200,000 and a tax basis of $150,000 for a 40 percent ownership interest, and Taylor is contributing legal services for a 20 percent ownership interest. What amount of gain or income is each owner required to recognize under each of the following alternative situations? [*Hint:* Look at §§351 and 721.] LO 4-3

a) MMT is formed as a C corporation.

b) MMT is formed as an S corporation.

c) MMT is formed as an LLC (taxed as a partnership).

61. Dave and his friend Stewart each owns 50 percent of KBS. During the year, Dave received $75,000 compensation for services he performed for KBS during the year. He performed a significant amount of work for the entity, and he was heavily LO 4-3

involved in management decisions for the entity (he was not a passive investor in KBS). After deducting Dave's compensation, KBS reported taxable income of $30,000. How much FICA and/or self-employment tax is Dave required to pay on his compensation and his share of the KBS income if KBS is formed as a C corporation, an S corporation, or a limited liability company (taxed as a partnership) (ignore the .9 percent additional Medicare tax)? How much FICA tax would the entity be required to pay on the compensation paid to Dave?

LO 4-3
research

62. Rondo and his business associate, Larry, are considering forming a business entity called R&L, but they are unsure about whether to form it as a C corporation, an S corporation, or an LLC taxed as a partnership for tax purposes. Rondo and Larry would each invest $50,000 in the business. Thus, each owner would take an initial basis in his ownership interest of $50,000 no matter which entity type is formed. Shortly after the formation of the entity, the business borrowed $30,000 from the bank. If applicable, this debt will be shared equally between the two owners.
    a) After taking the loan into account, what is Rondo's tax basis in his R&L stock if R&L is formed as a C corporation?
    b) After taking the loan into account, what is Rondo's tax basis in his R&L stock if R&L is formed as an S corporation?
    c) After taking the loan into account, what is Rondo's tax basis in his R&L ownership interest if R&L is formed as an LLC and taxed as a partnership?

LO 4-3

63. Haruki and Bob have owned and operated SOA as a C corporation for a number of years. When they formed the entity, Haruki and Bob each contributed $100,000 to SOA. Each has a current basis of $100,000 in his SOA ownership interest. Information on SOA's assets at the end of year 5 is as follows (SOA does not have any liabilities):

Assets	FMV	Adjusted Basis	Built-in Gain
Cash	$200,000	$200,000	$ 0
Inventory	80,000	40,000	40,000
Land and building	220,000	170,000	50,000
Total	$500,000		

At the end of year 5, SOA liquidated and distributed half of the land and building, half of the inventory, and half of the cash remaining after paying taxes (if any) to each owner. Assume that, excluding the effects of the liquidating distribution, SOA's taxable income for year 5 is $0.
    a) What are the amount and character of gain or loss SOA will recognize on the liquidating distribution?
    b) What are the amount and character of gain or loss Haruki will recognize when he receives the liquidating distribution of cash and property? Recall that his stock basis is $100,000 and he is treated as having sold his stock for the liquidation proceeds.

COMPREHENSIVE PROBLEMS

Select problems are available with Connect®.

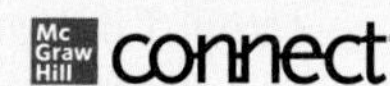

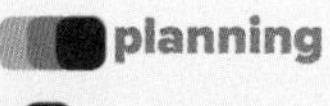

64. Daisy Taylor has developed a viable new business idea. Her idea is to design and manufacture cookware that remains cool to the touch when in use. She has had several family members and friends try out her prototype cookware, and they have consistently given the cookware rave reviews. With this encouragement, Daisy started giving serious thought to starting up a business called "Cool Touch Cookware" (CTC).

Daisy understands that it will take a few years for the business to become profitable. She would like to grow her business and perhaps at some point "go public" or sell the business to a large retailer.

Daisy, who is single, decided to quit her full-time job so that she could focus all of her efforts on the new business. Daisy had some savings to support her for a while, but she did not have any other source of income. She was able to recruit Kesha and Aryan to join her as initial equity investors in CTC. Kesha has an MBA and a law degree. She was employed as a business consultant when she decided to leave that job to work with Daisy and Aryan. Aryan owns a *very* profitable used car business. Because buying and selling used cars takes all his time, he is interested in becoming only a passive investor in CTC. He wanted to get in on the ground floor because he really likes the product and believes CTC will be wildly successful. While CTC originally has three investors, Daisy and Kesha have plans to grow the business and seek more owners and capital in the future.

The three owners agreed that Daisy would contribute land and cash for a 30 percent interest in CTC, Kesha would contribute services (legal and business advisory) for the first two years for a 30 percent interest, and Aryan would contribute cash for a 40 percent interest. The plan called for Daisy and Kesha to be actively involved in managing the business, while Aryan would not be. The three equity owners' contributions are summarized as follows:

Daisy Contributed	FMV	Adjusted Basis	Ownership Interest
Land (held as investment)	$120,000	$70,000	30%
Cash	30,000		
Kesha Contributed			
Services	$150,000		30
Aryan Contributed			
Cash	$200,000		40

Working together, Daisy and Kesha made the following five-year income and loss projections for CTC. They anticipate the business will be profitable and that it will continue to grow after the first five years.

Cool Touch Cookware
5-Year Income and Loss Projections

Year	Income (Loss)
1	$(200,000)
2	(80,000)
3	(20,000)
4	60,000
5	180,000

With plans for Daisy and Kesha to spend a considerable amount of their time working for and managing CTC, the owners would like to develop a compensation plan that works for all parties. Down the road, they plan to have two business locations (in different cities). Daisy would take responsibility for the activities of one location and Kesha would take responsibility for the other. Finally, they would like to arrange for some performance-based financial incentives for each location.

To get the business activities started, Daisy and Kesha determined CTC would need to borrow $800,000 to purchase a building to house its manufacturing facilities and its administrative offices (at least for now). Also, in need of additional cash, Daisy and Kesha arranged to have CTC borrow $300,000 from a local bank and borrow $200,000 cash from Aryan. CTC would pay Aryan a market rate of interest on the loan, but there was no fixed date for principal repayment.

Required:

Identify significant tax and nontax issues or concerns that may differ across entity types and discuss how they are relevant to the choice of entity decision for CTC.

65. Cool Touch Cookware (CTC) has been in business for about 10 years now. Daisy and Kesha are each 50 percent owners of the business. They initially established the business with cash contributions. CTC manufactures unique cookware that remains cool to the touch when in use. CTC has been fairly profitable over the years. Daisy and Kesha have both been actively involved in managing the business. They have developed very good personal relationships with many customers (both wholesale and retail) that, Daisy and Kesha believe, keep the customers coming back.

On September 30 of the current year, CTC had all of its assets appraised. Below is CTC's balance sheet, as of September 30, with the corresponding appraisals of the fair market value of all of its assets. Note that CTC has several depreciated assets. CTC uses the hybrid method of accounting. It accounts for its gross margin–related items under the accrual method, and it accounts for everything else using the cash method of accounting.

Assets	Adjusted Tax Basis	FMV
Cash	$150,000	$150,000
Accounts receivable	20,000	15,000
Inventory*	90,000	300,000
Equipment	120,000	100,000
Investment in XYZ stock	40,000	120,000
Land (used in the business)	80,000	70,000
Building	200,000	180,000
Total assets	$700,000	$935,000†
Liabilities		
Accounts payable	$ 40,000	
Bank loan	60,000	
Mortgage on building	100,000	
Equity	500,000	
Total liabilities and equity	$700,000	

*CTC uses the LIFO method for determining the adjusted basis of its inventory. Its basis in the inventory under the FIFO method would have been $110,000.

†In addition, Daisy and Kesha had the entire business appraised at $1,135,000, which is $200,000 more than the value of the identifiable assets.

From January 1 of the current year through September 30, CTC reported the following income:

Ordinary business income	$530,000
Dividends from XYZ stock	12,000
Long-term capital losses	15,000
Interest income	3,000

Daisy and Kesha are considering changing the business form of CTC.

Required:

a) Assume CTC is organized as a C corporation. Identify significant tax and nontax issues associated with converting CTC from a C corporation to an S corporation. [*Hint:* See §§1374 and 1363(d).]

b) Assume CTC is organized as a C corporation. Identify significant tax and nontax issues associated with converting CTC from a C corporation to an LLC. Assume CTC converts to an LLC (taxed as a partnership) by distributing its assets to its shareholders, who then contribute the assets to a new LLC. [*Hint:* See §§331, 336, and 721(a).]

c) Assume that CTC is a C corporation with a net operating loss carryforward as of the beginning of the year in the amount of $500,000 and that the NOL originated in 2019. Identify significant tax and nontax issues associated with converting CTC from a C corporation to an LLC (taxed as a partnership). Assume CTC converts to an LLC by distributing its assets to its shareholders, who then contribute the assets to a new LLC. [*Hint:* See §§172(a), 331, 336, and 721(a).]

66. Amy is evaluating the cash flow consequences of organizing her business entity SHO as an LLC (taxed as a sole proprietorship), an S corporation, or a C corporation. She used the following assumptions to make her calculations:

a) For all entity types, the business reports $22,000 of business income before deducting compensation paid to Amy and payroll taxes SHO pays on Amy's behalf.

b) All entities use the cash method of accounting.

c) If Amy organizes SHO as an S corporation or a C corporation, SHO will pay Amy a $5,000 annual salary (assume the salary is reasonable for purposes of this problem). For both the S and C corporations, Amy will pay 7.65 percent FICA tax on her salary and SHO will also pay 7.65 percent FICA tax on Amy's salary (the FICA tax paid by the entity is deductible by the entity).

d) Amy's marginal ordinary income tax rate is 35 percent, and her income tax rate on qualified dividends and net capital gains is 15 percent.

e) Amy's marginal self-employment tax rate is 15.3 percent.

f) Amy pays a .9 percent additional Medicare tax on salary and net earnings from self-employment (i.e., her salary and net earnings from self-employment are over the threshold for the tax).

g) Amy pays a 3.8 percent net investment income tax on dividends and net capital gains (i.e., AGI on joint tax return is over threshold by more than any net investment income she receives).

h) Assume that for purposes of the qualified business income deduction, the business income is not from a specified service and neither the wage-based limitation nor the taxable income limitation applies to limit the deduction.

i) If SHO is formed as an S corporation or a C corporation, SHO will distribute all of its earnings after paying entity level taxes and after deducting salary and related FICA taxes paid to Amy.

Required:

a) Fill in the cells in the table below to identify cash flows associated with the income from the business if the business is formed as an LLC (sole proprietorship), S corporation, or C corporation for tax purposes. Enter cash outflows as negative numbers.

Cash flow	LLC (Sole prop)	S Corporation	C Corporation
Business income	$22,000	$22,000	$22,000
FICA taxes paid by Amy			
FICA taxes paid by SHO			
Self-employment tax paid by Amy			
Federal income tax paid by SHO			
Additional Medicare tax paid by Amy			
Net investment income tax paid by Amy			
Federal income tax paid by Amy*			
Cash remaining after taxes			

*Remember to consider account flow-through income, qualified dividends, the self-employment tax deduction, and the qualified business income deduction in calculation.

b) At a high level, describe the factors causing differences in the after-tax cash flows from each entity, given that the before-tax cash flows are the same (don't use dollar amounts in the explanation).

UWorld Roger CPA Review

Sample CPA Exam questions from Roger CPA Review are available in Connect as support for the topics in this text. These Multiple Choice Questions and Task-Based Simulations include expert-written explanations and solutions and provide a starting point for students to become familiar with the content and functionality of the actual CPA Exam.

chapter

5 Corporate Operations

Learning Objectives

Upon completing this chapter, you should be able to:

LO 5-1 Describe the corporate income tax formula and discuss tax considerations relating to corporations' accounting periods and accounting methods.

LO 5-2 Identify common permanent and temporary book–tax differences and compute a corporation's taxable income and associated income tax liability.

LO 5-3 Describe a corporation's tax return reporting and estimated tax payment obligations.

mentatdgt/Shutterstock

Storyline Summary

Premiere Computer Corporation (PCC)

Medium-sized publicly traded company

Manufactures and sells computers and computer-related equipment

Calendar-year taxpayer

Elise Brandon (she/her/hers)

Newly hired tax associate for a large public accounting firm

Currently assigned to review the federal income tax return for PCC

Today was Elise's first day on the job as a tax associate for a large public accounting firm. Shortly after she arrived, Aminah, a tax manager, introduced herself and took Elise around the office to meet some of the people with whom Elise would be working. After the introductions, Aminah told Elise she would like her to review the federal tax return for Premiere Computer Corporation (PCC).

PCC is a medium-sized publicly traded C corporation that manufactures computers and computer-related equipment. PCC has been a client of the firm for several years. Overall, PCC has been a fairly profitable company, but last year the company experienced a bit of a setback, incurring its first tax loss in many years.

Elise was excited about her opportunity. She was confident her accounting education had adequately prepared her to successfully complete the assignment. When Aminah spoke with Elise about the assignment, Aminah advised Elise to first review PCC's tax return and tax return workpapers from last year to get an idea about how to review the current-year tax return. Next, she should start with the audited numbers on the income statement and examine the book-to-tax adjustments that caused taxable income to differ from PCC's book net income before income taxes. Aminah counseled Elise to identify those book and tax differences as being "temporary" or "permanent" because Elise was eventually going to compute the company's accounting "income tax provision" from this information. Aminah encouraged Elise to keep her posted on her progress and ask questions when necessary to keep the project on budget. ■

In this chapter we explore the process of computing and reporting taxable income for C corporations. As we discussed in the Business Entities Overview chapter, C corporations are taxpaying entities separate from their shareholders. Each year, C corporations are required to compute their taxable income and pay tax on the income. In contrast to individuals, C corporations often compute taxable income by starting with their book (financial accounting) income and making adjustments for book–tax differences.

LO 5-1 CORPORATE TAXABLE INCOME FORMULA

The formulas for computing corporate taxable income and individual taxable income are similar in some respects and different in others. Exhibit 5-1 compares the corporate income tax formula with the individual tax formula.

EXHIBIT 5-1 Corporate and Individual Tax Formulas

	Corporate Tax Formula	Individual Tax Formula
	Gross income	Gross income
Minus	Deductions	For AGI deductions
Equals		Adjusted gross income
Minus		From AGI deductions: (1) Greater of: (a) Standard deduction or (b) Itemized deductions (2) Charitable contribution deduction for taxpayers who do not itemize deductions* (3) Deduction for qualified business income
Equals	Taxable income	Taxable income
Times	Tax rates	Tax rates
Equals	Regular income tax liability	Regular income tax liability
Add	Other taxes	Other taxes
Equals	Total tax	Total tax
Minus	Credits	Credits
Minus	Prepayments	Prepayments
Equals	Taxes due (or refund)	Taxes due (or refund)

*The charitable contribution for nonitemizers applies for 2021 but, as of press time, the deduction had not been extended to 2022.

THE KEY FACTS

Corporate Taxable Income Formula and Accounting Periods and Methods

- The corporate tax formula is similar to the individual tax formula, but corporations don't claim the deduction for qualified business income and they don't itemize deductions or deduct the standard deduction.
- In 2022, corporations with annual average gross receipts of $27 million or less over the three prior tax years (or a shorter period for new corporations) may use the cash method.

Corporations compute gross income in the same way as other types of business entities and individual taxpayers. Similar to other businesses, corporations are permitted to deduct ordinary and necessary business expenditures (see discussion in the Business Income, Deductions, and Accounting Methods chapter). However, in contrast to individuals, corporations cannot claim the deduction for qualified business income and corporations do not itemize deductions or deduct a standard deduction. Consequently, the formula for computing a corporation's taxable income is relatively straightforward.

Accounting Periods and Methods

In the Business Income, Deductions, and Accounting Methods chapter, we discussed accounting periods and methods for all types of business entities. We learned that corporations measure their taxable income over a tax year and that their tax year must be the same as their financial accounting year. A C corporation generally elects its tax year when it files its first income tax return. A C corporation is able to adopt a calendar or any fiscal year-end that matches its financial accounting year-end.

A corporation's choice of accounting methods determines when income and deductions are recognized. As we discuss in the Business Income, Deductions, and Accounting Methods chapter, accounting methods include overall methods of accounting (accrual method, cash method, or hybrid method) and accounting methods for individual items such as inventory (for example, LIFO or FIFO) or depreciation (accelerated or straight-line). For tax purposes, corporations have some flexibility in choosing methods of accounting for individual items or transactions. However, corporations generally are required to use the accrual method of accounting.[1] For tax purposes, corporations with annual average gross receipts of $27 million or less for the three years prior to the current tax year (2022) can elect to use the cash method of accounting.[2] Corporations that have not been in existence for at least three years compute their annual average gross receipts over the prior periods they have been in existence to determine if they are permitted to use the cash method of accounting.

COMPUTING CORPORATE TAXABLE INCOME

LO 5-2

To compute taxable income, most corporations begin with **book (financial reporting) income** after income tax expense and then make adjustments for **book–tax differences** to reconcile to the tax numbers.[3]

Book–Tax Differences

Many items of income and expense are accounted for differently for book and tax purposes. The following discussion describes common book–tax differences applicable to corporations. Each book–tax difference can be classified as "unfavorable" or "favorable" depending on its effect on taxable income relative to book income. A book–tax difference that requires an add-back to book income to compute taxable income is an **unfavorable book–tax difference** because it increases taxable income (and, therefore, taxes payable) relative to book income. A book–tax difference that requires corporations to subtract the difference from book income in computing taxable income is a **favorable book–tax difference** because it decreases taxable income (and, therefore, taxes payable) relative to book income.

In addition to the favorable or unfavorable distinction, book–tax differences can be categorized as permanent or temporary. **Permanent book–tax differences** arise from items that are income or deductions during the year for either book or tax purposes but not both. Permanent differences *do not reverse* over time, so over the long term, the *total* amount of income or deductions for the items differs for book and tax purposes. In contrast, **temporary book–tax differences** reverse over time such that, over the long term, corporations recognize the same amount of income or deductions for the items on their income statements as they recognize on their tax returns. Temporary book–tax differences arise because the income or deduction items are included in financial accounting income in one year and in taxable income in a different year. Temporary book–tax differences that are *initially* favorable (unfavorable) become unfavorable (favorable) in future years when they reverse.

[1]See the Business Income, Deductions, and Accounting Methods chapter for a detailed discussion of determining the timing of taxable income and tax deductions under the accrual method.

[2]§448. Other special types of corporations such as qualified family farming corporations and qualified personal service corporations may use the cash method of accounting. A C corporation that fails the $27 million gross receipts test is precluded from using the cash method for the year in which the test is not satisfied but can resume using the cash method in future years in which the test is satisfied. The $27 million annual average gross receipts test threshold is indexed for inflation.

[3]This chapter generally assumes that generally accepted accounting principles (GAAP) are used to determine book income numbers.

THE KEY FACTS

Computing Corporate Regular Taxable Income

- Corporations reconcile from book income to taxable income.
  - Favorable (unfavorable) book–tax differences decrease (increase) taxable income relative to book income.
  - Permanent book–tax differences arise in one year and never reverse.
  - Temporary book–tax differences arise in one year and reverse in subsequent years.

Distinguishing between permanent and temporary book–tax differences is important for several reasons. First, as we discuss later in the chapter, large corporations are *required to disclose* their permanent and temporary book–tax differences on a schedule attached to their tax returns. Second, the distinction is useful for those responsible for tracking book–tax differences for purposes of computing the corporation's income tax expense on its income statement. For temporary book–tax differences, it is important to understand how the items were accounted for in previous years to appropriately account for current-year reversals. In contrast, for permanent book–tax differences, corporations need only consider current-year amounts to determine book–tax differences. Finally, as we discuss in more detail in the Accounting for Income Taxes chapter, permanent differences impact a company's effective tax rate whereas temporary differences generally do not. Below we describe common book–tax differences.

Common Permanent Book–Tax Differences As we describe in the Business Income, Deductions, and Accounting Methods chapter, businesses, including corporations, exclude certain income items from gross income, and they are not allowed to deduct certain expenditures for tax purposes. Because these income items are included in book income, and the expenditures are deductible for financial reporting purposes, they generate permanent book–tax differences. Exhibit 5-2 identifies several permanent book–tax differences associated with items we discuss in the Business Income, Deductions, and Accounting Methods chapter; explains their tax treatment; and identifies whether the items create favorable or unfavorable book–tax differences.

EXHIBIT 5-2 Common Permanent Book–Tax Differences Associated with Items Discussed in the Business Income, Deductions, and Accounting Methods Chapter

Description	Explanation	Difference
Interest income from municipal bonds	Income included in book income but excluded from taxable income	Favorable
Death benefit from life insurance on key employees	Income included in book income but excluded from taxable income	Favorable
Interest expense on loans to acquire investments generating tax-exempt income	Deductible for book purposes, but expenses incurred to generate tax-exempt income are not deductible for tax purposes	Unfavorable
Life insurance premiums for which corporation is beneficiary	Deductible for book purposes, but expenses incurred to generate tax-exempt income (life insurance death benefit) are not deductible for tax purposes	Unfavorable
Meals expense	Fully deductible for book purposes but generally only 50 percent deductible for tax purposes. However, for 2022 (and 2021), the cost of meals purchased from restaurants (including take-out and delivery) is fully deductible for tax purposes.[4]	Unfavorable
Fines and penalties and political contributions	Deductible for book purposes but not for tax purposes	Unfavorable
Entertainment expense	Deductible for book purposes but not deductible for tax purposes	Unfavorable
Federal income tax expense	Deductible for book purposes but not deductible for tax purposes	Unfavorable

[4]IRS Notice 2021-25 provides guidance on what is and is not considered to be a restaurant.

Example 5-1

Elise reviewed PCC's prior-year tax return and its current-year trial balance. She discovered that PCC earned $12,000 of interest income from City of San Diego municipal bonds, expensed $34,000 for premiums on key employee life insurance policies, and expensed $28,000 for business-related meals purchased from restaurants. What amount of permanent book–tax differences does PCC report from these transactions? Are the differences favorable or unfavorable?

Answer: See Elise's summary of these items below:

Item	Adjustment (Favorable) Unfavorable	Notes
Interest income from City of San Diego municipal bonds	$(12,000)	Income excluded from gross income.
Premiums paid for key employee life insurance policies	34,000	Premiums paid to insure lives of key company executives are not deductible for tax purposes.
Meals expense	0	No book–tax difference because meals were purchased from restaurants.

Federal income tax expense. Corporations deduct federal income tax expense (called a "provision for income taxes") in determining their book income [determined under FASB ASC (Accounting Standards Codification) Topic 740]. However, they are not allowed to deduct federal income tax expense for tax purposes.[5] Federal income tax expense is an unfavorable, permanent difference when the corporation is reconciling after-tax book income with taxable income.

Example 5-2

What if: Assume that PCC's audited financial reporting income statement indicates that its federal income tax provision (expense) is $2,000,000.[6] What is PCC's book–tax difference for the year associated with this expense? Is the difference favorable or unfavorable? Is it permanent or temporary?

Answer: $2,000,000 unfavorable, permanent book–tax difference because PCC is not allowed to deduct federal income tax expense for tax purposes.

Common Temporary Book–Tax Differences Corporations experience temporary book–tax differences because the accounting methods they apply to determine certain items of income and expense for financial reporting purposes differ from those they use for tax purposes. Unlike permanent book–tax differences, temporary book–tax differences balance out over time, so corporations eventually recognize the same amount of income or deduction for the particular item. Exhibit 5-3 identifies common temporary book–tax differences associated with items we discuss in other chapters. Exhibit 5-4 summarizes PCC's temporary book–tax differences described in Exhibit 5-3.

[5]§275(a)(1).

[6]Note that this example is presented in what-if form because this is not the income tax expense PCC will report in its financial statements. We compute PCC's actual income tax expense in the Accounting for Income Taxes chapter.

EXHIBIT 5-3 Common Temporary Book–Tax Differences Associated with Items Discussed in Other Chapters

Description	Explanation	Initial Difference*
Depreciation expense (Property Acquisition and Cost Recovery chapter)	Difference between depreciation expense for tax purposes and depreciation expense for book purposes.	Favorable
Gain or loss on disposition of depreciable assets (Property Dispositions chapter)	Difference between gain or loss for tax and book purposes when a corporation sells or disposes of depreciable property. Difference generally arises because depreciation expense, and thus the adjusted basis of the asset, is different for tax and book purposes. This difference is essentially the reversal of the book–tax difference for the depreciation expense on the asset sold or disposed of.	Unfavorable
Bad debt expense (Business Income, Deductions, and Accounting Methods chapter)	Direct write-off method for tax purposes; allowance method for book purposes.	Unfavorable
Unearned rent revenue (Business Income, Deductions, and Accounting Methods chapter)	Taxable on receipt but recognized when earned for book purposes.	Unfavorable
Deferred compensation (Business Income, Deductions, and Accounting Methods chapter)	Deductible when accrued for book purposes but deductible when paid for tax purposes if accrued but not paid within 2.5 months after year-end. Also, accrued compensation to shareholders owning more than 50 percent of the corporation is not deductible until paid.	Unfavorable
Organizational expenditures and start-up costs (Property Acquisition and Cost Recovery chapter)	Immediately deducted for book purposes but capitalized and amortized for tax purposes (limited immediate expensing allowed for tax).	Unfavorable
Warranty expense and other estimated expenses (Business Income, Deductions, and Accounting Methods chapter)	Estimated expenses deducted for book purposes, but actual expenses deducted for tax purposes.	Unfavorable
UNICAP (§263A) (Business Income, Deductions, and Accounting Methods chapter)	Certain expenditures deducted for book purposes but capitalized to inventory for tax purposes. Difference reverses when inventory is sold. There is an exception for taxpayers with an annual average of $27 million or less in gross receipts over the three prior years.	Unfavorable
Interest expense [§163(j)] (Business Income, Deductions, and Accounting Methods chapter)	The deduction for interest expense is disallowed to the extent it exceeds the sum of business interest income and 30 percent of adjusted taxable income (ATI). There is an exception for taxpayers with an annual average of $27 million or less in gross receipts over the three prior years. Unused amounts can be carried forward indefinitely. ATI is defined as taxable income computed without regard to any business interest expense or business interest income. It also excludes depreciation and amortization.	Unfavorable
Installment sales (§453) (Property Dispositions chapter)	When qualifying property is sold and the selling taxpayer receives payment in a taxable year subsequent to the year of disposition, under the installment method, the taxpayer recognizes realized gain (but not loss) pro rata over time as the payments are collected. Gain from property dispositions are generally recognized for book purposes in the year of disposition.	Favorable
Like-kind exchange (§1031) (Property Dispositions chapter)	Realized gain (or loss) is deferred for tax purposes when a taxpayer exchanges property for other qualifying real property in an exchange that meets certain timing requirements. Gain or loss is generally recognized immediately for book purposes.	Favorable

*Note that each of the initial book–tax differences will reverse over time [the initially favorable (unfavorable) book–tax differences will reverse to become unfavorable (favorable) book–tax differences in the future].

EXHIBIT 5-4 PCC's Temporary Book–Tax Differences Associated with Items Discussed in Other Chapters

Item	(1) Books (Dr) Cr	(2) Tax (Dr) Cr	(2) − (1) Difference (Favorable) Unfavorable
Depreciation expense	$(2,400,000)	$(3,100,000)	$(700,000)
Gain on fixed-asset disposition	54,000	70,000	16,000
Bad debt expense	(165,000)	(95,000)	70,000
Warranty expense	(580,000)	(410,000)	170,000
Deferred compensation	(300,000)	(450,000)	(150,000)

Example 5-3

What if: Assume that PCC started business on July 1, 2021. PCC incurred $100,000 of organizational expenditures that it expensed immediately for books and capitalized to amortize over 180 months for tax purposes. What was PCC's book–tax difference associated with organizational expenditures in 2021? What is the book–tax difference associated with organizational expenditures for 2022? Are these book–tax differences favorable or unfavorable? Are they permanent or temporary?

Answer: For 2021, the book–tax difference is $96,667 unfavorable ($100,000 book expense and $3,333 amortization tax deduction) temporary difference. For books the entire $100,000 was expensed in 2021, but for tax only $3,333 was amortized ($100,000 × 6/180 months). After 2021, the remaining basis in the organizational expenditures was $0 for books and $96,667 for tax. For 2022, the book–tax difference is $6,667 favorable ($0 book expense and $6,667 amortization tax deduction) temporary difference. Because the entire amount of organizational expenditures was expensed on the books in 2021, there are no organizational expenditures remaining to expense for book purposes. However, for tax purposes, PCC can deduct $6,667 of amortization for tax purposes ($100,000 × 12/180 months). PCC will continue amortizing the organizational expenditures for 162 more months (13.5 years). All of the tax amortization will result in a favorable, temporary book–tax difference after 2021.

TAXES IN THE REAL WORLD Are Large Corporations Paying Enough in Taxes?

In a report dated April 2021, the Institute of Taxation and Economic Policy (ITEP) indicated that, based on an analysis of financial statements and notes to the financial statements, 55 corporations paid $0 taxes in 2020 despite reporting significant pre-tax profit for book purposes. Corporations on the list included Archer Daniels Midland, FedEx, Nike, Dish Network, and Salesforce. The report indicates that "tax breaks" such as deducting the bargain element of nonqualified stock options or accelerated depreciation on business asset purchases (e.g., 100% bonus depreciation) or the Research and Experimentation Credit (for research and development) are the reason(s) some corporations are not paying taxes, even though they are reporting profits on their financial statements. Some may perceive this as an injustice and determine that the system is flawed because large, profitable corporations aren't paying their fair share of taxes. In an article published by the Tax Foundation, the author points out that there may be legitimate reasons why a corporation may pay $0 taxes despite reporting profits for book purposes. The article points out that, first and foremost, the accounting rules (GAAP) that determine book income are different from tax laws that determine taxable income. Book and taxable income serve different purposes. For example, tax laws allow accelerated depreciation deductions or tax credits for research to companies that invest in capital or perform research and development because Congress wants to encourage companies to invest in business and research and development. The article also points out that the IRS is closely watching large corporations. The IRS audit rate for large corporations is

(continued on page 5-8)

near 50 percent, while the overall audit rate for other corporations is 0.7 percent. Further, the Joint Committee on Taxation reviews C corporation refunds in excess of $5 million. Finally, large companies pay taxes in foreign countries that add to their overall tax bill without increasing their U.S. tax bill. The article concludes that it is a mistake to determine that something is amiss when a corporation has a $0 tax bill because Congress makes the tax laws that corporations are following and Congress could change the tax rules to conform more closely to book rules, if it wished to do so. In the end, different people have different opinions about whether large corporations are paying enough taxes. What's your opinion?

Sources: Matthew Gardner and Steve Wamhoff, "55 Corporations Paid $0 Federal Taxes on 2020 Profits," ITEP, April 2, 2021, https://itep.org/55-profitable-corporations-zero-corporate-tax/; and Erica York, "Explaining the GAAP between Book and Taxable Income," Tax Foundation, June 3, 2021, https://taxfoundation.org/corporations-zero-corporate-tax/.

Dividends and stock ownership related. Corporations receiving dividends from other corporations may account for the dividends in different ways for book and tax purposes. For tax purposes, corporations receiving dividends include the dividends in gross income.[7] For financial reporting purposes, accounting for the dividend depends on the receiving corporation's level of stock ownership in the distributing corporation. The *general* rules for such investments are summarized as follows:

- If the receiving (shareholder) corporation owns less than 20 percent of the stock of the distributing corporation, the receiving corporation includes the dividend in both book and taxable income (i.e., no book–tax difference on the dividend). In addition, if the corporate shareholder is holding the stock investment for trading (i.e., purchased the stock with the intent to sell it within a short period, usually less than a year), the shareholder corporation includes the unrealized gain or loss for the year on that stock in book income but not taxable income. The unrealized gain or loss for the year results in a temporary book–tax difference that will completely reverse when the shareholder corporation sells the stock.
- If the receiving corporation owns at least 20 percent but not more than 50 percent of the distributing corporation's stock, the receiving corporation usually includes a pro rata portion of the distributing corporation's earnings in its book income under the "equity method of accounting" (ASC Topic 323) and does not include the dividend in its income, resulting in a temporary favorable or unfavorable book–tax difference for the difference between the pro rata share of equity income reported on the books and the dividend amount reported on the tax return.
- If the receiving corporation owns more than 50 percent of the distributing corporation's stock, the receiving corporation and the distributing corporation usually consolidate their financial reporting books (ASC Topic 810) and the intercompany dividend is eliminated (book–tax difference beyond the scope of this text).[8]

Example 5-4

What if: Assume that PCC owns 30 percent of the stock of BCS, a U.S. corporation, and applies the equity method of accounting for book purposes. During 2022, BCS distributed a $40,000 dividend to PCC. Also, BCS reported $100,000 of net income for 2022 on its financial statements. Based on this information, what is PCC's 2022 book–tax difference relating to the dividend and its investment in BCS (ignore the dividends-received deduction)? Is the difference favorable or unfavorable?

[7] As we discuss later in the chapter, corporations are generally entitled to deduct a certain percentage of the dividends received based on the level of the receiving corporation's ownership in the distributing corporation.

[8] Note that at least 80 percent ownership is required to file a consolidated tax return.

Answer: $10,000 unfavorable book–tax difference, computed as follows:

Description	Amount	Explanation
(1) Dividend received in 2022 (included in 2022 taxable income but not in book income)	$ 40,000	
(2) BCS 2022 net income on financial statements	$ 100,000	
(3) PCC's ownership in BCS stock	30%	
(4) PCC's book income from BCS investment	$ 30,000	(2) × (3)
Unfavorable book–tax difference associated with dividend	**$ 10,000**	(1) − (4)

What if: Assume the same facts as above, except that PCC owns 10 percent of BCS rather than 30 percent. What would be PCC's 2022 book–tax difference relating to the $40,000 dividend and its investment in BCS (ignore the dividends-received deduction)? Assume that PCC's basis (and value) in its BCS stock on January 1 is $1,000,000 and its value in its BCS stock on December 31 is $1,050,000.

Answer: $0 book–tax difference on the dividend because PCC includes the $40,000 dividend in income for both book and tax purposes. $50,000 favorable book–tax difference for the unrealized gain in PCC's BCS stock that is recognized for book purposes but not for tax purposes.

Goodwill acquired in an acquisition. When a corporation acquires the stock of another corporation in a cash (taxable) transaction, the tax basis of each asset of the target corporation remains unchanged. Self-created intangibles such as a patent retain a tax basis of zero or close to zero and do not get written up to fair value as they do for book purposes. The accounting rules (ASC Topic 805) require the target corporation's identifiable assets to be reported at fair value, with any residual amount allocated to book goodwill. This book goodwill will not have a corresponding tax basis. Such book goodwill generally is subject to impairment testing (private companies can elect to amortize the book goodwill over 10 years, however). A book–tax difference does not arise until the goodwill is written off as impaired, at which time the book expense creates a (permanent) unfavorable difference.

In less-frequent acquisitions, the acquiring corporation may acquire the assets of another business directly in a taxable transaction. When this occurs, the assets acquired are assigned a tax basis equal to their fair market value. Any excess of the consideration paid over the net fair value of the tangible and intangible assets acquired is allocated to tax goodwill, which is amortizable over 15 years (180 months).[9] In this case, the goodwill has both a tax and a book basis, which may be the same or different because of differences in the purchase price computation. As the corporation amortizes the goodwill for tax purposes, the resulting book–tax difference is treated as a favorable temporary difference (if book and tax goodwill are different, the accounting becomes more complex and is beyond the scope of this book). If the corporation writes the goodwill off as impaired in a future period, the excess of book goodwill impaired over the remaining goodwill tax basis is treated as an unfavorable temporary book–tax difference (assuming the original tax and book goodwill were equal).

Example 5-5

What if: Suppose that on July 1, 2022, PCC acquired the assets of another business in a taxable acquisition. As part of the transaction, PCC recognized $180,000 of goodwill for both financial accounting and tax purposes. During 2022, PCC amortized $6,000 of the goodwill for tax purposes ($180,000/180 months × 6 months during the year) and did not impair any of the goodwill for financial accounting purposes. What was PCC's book–tax difference associated with this goodwill in 2022? Is it a favorable or unfavorable difference? Is the difference permanent or temporary?

(continued on page 5-10)

[9]§197. Self-created goodwill is not amortizable for tax purposes.

Answer: $6,000 favorable, temporary book–tax difference. The amount of capitalized goodwill is the same for book and tax purposes, and PCC deducted $6,000 of the goodwill for tax purposes and none for book purposes.

What if: Assume that at the end of 2023, PCC recorded a $30,000 goodwill impairment expense on its income statement. What is PCC's book–tax difference associated with its goodwill during 2023? Is the difference favorable or unfavorable? Is the difference permanent or temporary?

Answer: $18,000 unfavorable, temporary book–tax difference, computed as follows:

Description	Amount	Explanation
(1) Goodwill initially recorded on 7/1/22 acquisition	$180,000	
(2) Goodwill impairment recorded in 2023	$ 30,000	This write-down is expensed for book purposes.
(3) Months over which goodwill is amortized for tax purposes.	180	15 years × 12 months = 180 months
(4) Tax goodwill amortization expense for 2023	$ 12,000	[(1)/(3)] × 12 months
Unfavorable book–tax temporary difference associated with goodwill in 2023	**$ 18,000**	(2) − (4)

Corporate-Specific Deductions and Associated Book–Tax Differences

Certain deductions and corresponding limitations apply specifically to corporations. In this section, we introduce these deductions and identify book–tax differences associated with the deductions.

Stock Options Corporations often compensate executives and other employees with stock options. Stock options allow recipients to acquire stock in the corporation issuing the options at a predetermined price over a specified period of time. To acquire the stock, employees exercise the options and pay the **exercise price.** The exercise price is usually at or above the stock price on the day the options are issued to the employee. For example, when a corporation's stock is trading for $10 per share, a corporation might issue (or grant) 100 stock options to an employee that allow the employee to purchase up to 100 shares of the corporation's stock for $10 a share. In most cases, after receiving the options, employees must wait a certain amount of time (called the **requisite service period)** before they are able to exercise them (they must wait until the options **vest** before they can exercise them). If employees stop working for the corporation before the options vest, they forfeit the options.

Stock options are valuable to employees when the stock price appreciates above the exercise price because, when the options vest, employees can purchase the stock at a below-market price. Stock options are a popular form of compensation because they provide incentives for employees receiving the options to work to increase the value of the corporation's stock and thereby benefit themselves and other stockholders.

For tax purposes, the tax treatment to the corporation (and the employee) depends on whether the options are **incentive stock options (ISOs)** (less common, more administrative requirements for the corporation to qualify) or **nonqualified stock options (NQOs)** (more common, options that don't qualify as ISOs).[10] Corporations issuing ISOs

[10]Employees do not recognize any compensation income when they exercise incentive stock options. However, for nonqualified options, they recognize compensation (ordinary) income for the difference between the value of the stock and the exercise price on the date of exercise. This chapter emphasizes the tax treatment of the options from the corporation's perspective. Requirements for options to qualify as incentive stock options are more restrictive than the requirements for nonqualified stock options. The formal requirements for incentive stock options are beyond the scope of this text.

generally do not deduct compensation expense associated with the options for tax purposes. In contrast, for NQOs, corporations deduct for tax purposes the difference between the fair market value of the stock and the exercise price of the option (called the **bargain element**) as compensation expense in the year in which employees exercise the stock options.

For book purposes (ASC Topic 718), corporations are required to recognize *book expense* for stock options they grant. Corporations are required to estimate the fair value of the options at the time they issue them (i.e., on the **grant date**). They then deduct (or expense) the value of the options for book purposes as employee compensation over the employee's requisite service period (i.e., over the **vesting period**). For ISOs, the book compensation expense is an unfavorable permanent difference (book deduction but no tax deduction).

Example 5-6

What if: Assume that on January 1, 2022, PCC issued 10,000 incentive stock options (ISOs) with an estimated fair value of $6 per option. The options vest at the end of four years. For 2022, PCC records a $15,000 compensation expense related to the ISOs (10,000 options × $6/4 years). What is PCC's 2022 book–tax difference associated with the incentive stock options? Would the difference be favorable or unfavorable? Would the difference be permanent or temporary?

Answer: $15,000 unfavorable, permanent difference. PCC does not deduct compensation expense related to the ISOs for tax purposes.

Nonqualified options (NQOs) can generate both temporary and permanent book–tax differences. Corporations recognize unfavorable book–tax difference each year equal to the value of the options that vest during the year but are not exercised (book deduction but no tax deduction). The unfavorable book–tax differences completely reverse (corporations recognize a favorable temporary book–tax difference equal to the previous unfavorable book–tax differences) in the year the employee exercises the stock options.

When an employee exercises an NQO, the tax deduction, which is the difference between the fair market value of the stock purchased and the exercise price on the exercise date, likely will differ from the compensation expense recorded on the income statement over the requisite service period (i.e., the estimated value of the options for book purposes). The corporation recognizes a favorable permanent book–tax difference in the amount by which the tax deduction exceeds the total book expense for the options, and the corporation recognizes an unfavorable permanent book–tax difference in the amount by which the total book expenses for the options exceed the tax deduction.

Example 5-7

On January 1, 2022, PCC granted 20,000 NQOs with an estimated $10 fair value per option ($200,000 total fair value). Each option entitled the recipient to purchase one share of PCC stock for $10 a share (the per share price of PCC stock on January 1, 2022, when the options were granted). The options vested at the end of the day on December 31, 2023. No options were exercised in 2022 or 2023. For 2022 and 2023, PCC deducts compensation expense of $100,000 for book purposes. What is PCC's book–tax difference associated with the nonqualified options in 2022? in 2023? Is the difference favorable or unfavorable? Is it permanent or temporary?

Answer: $100,000 unfavorable, temporary book–tax difference in both 2022 and 2023. PCC reports $100,000 of compensation expense for book purposes in 2022 and 2023 and $0 for tax purposes (no options were exercised in 2022 or 2023).

(continued on page 5-12)

What if: Assume the same facts as above and that on March 1, 2024, employees exercised all 20,000 options at a time when the PCC stock was trading at $25 per share. What is PCC's book–tax difference associated with the stock options in 2024? Is it a permanent difference or a temporary difference? Is it favorable or unfavorable?

Answer: $200,000 favorable, temporary book–tax difference in 2024 and a $100,000 favorable permanent book–tax difference. PCC claims a $300,000 tax deduction in 2024, equal to the number of shares purchased (20,000) times the bargain element of $15 per option exercised ($25 – $10). PCC does not deduct any additional compensation expense for book purposes in 2024 because the vesting period ended in 2023. $200,000 of the tax deduction is a reversal of the total 2022–2023 unfavorable, temporary book–tax difference. The excess $100,000 tax deduction is a favorable permanent difference.

Exhibit 5-5 summarizes the book and tax treatments of stock options.

EXHIBIT 5-5 Book and Tax Treatment of Stock Options

Description	Book Deduction	Tax Deduction	Book–Tax Difference
Incentive stock option	Initial estimated fair value of stock options/ requisite service period	No deduction	Unfavorable, permanent
Nonqualified stock option (in years before exercise)	Initial estimated fair value of stock options/ requisite service period	No deduction until exercise	Unfavorable, temporary
Nonqualified stock option (in year of exercise)	Initial estimated fair value of stock options/ requisite service period	Bargain element*	Favorable, temporary (reversing unfavorable, temporary difference in prior years)
			Favorable, permanent difference if the bargain element exceeds the initial estimated value of stock options; unfavorable permanent difference otherwise

*The bargain element is the difference between the fair market value of the stock and the exercise price on the date the employee exercises the stock options.

TAXES IN THE REAL WORLD Facebook's NQO Tax Benefits

When Facebook filed its registration statement for its initial public offering (IPO) in February 2012, it was revealed that CEO Mark Zuckerberg had been granted nonqualifying stock options (NQOs) to purchase 120 million additional shares of the company for 6 cents per share. The company also informed potential investors that Mr. Zuckerberg intended to exercise these options when the company became a publicly traded company. Mr. Zuckerberg subsequently exercised his option to purchase 60 million additional Facebook shares prior to the IPO at a time when the value of the shares was $2,276,677,500. This transaction (fair value of the Facebook stock on the exercise date less the exercise price) simultaneously created a tax deduction for Facebook and compensation income to Mr. Zuckerberg of approximately $2.3 billion! The company's tax benefit of $800 million also created an $800 million tax bill for Mr. Zuckerberg. In total, employees of Facebook exercised 135.5 million NQOs in 2012, resulting in a tax benefit to the company of more than $1 billion, of which $451 million was recovered as a refund for taxes paid in 2010–2011. The cash proceeds received by the company from the employees' exercise of the NQOs was only $17 million.

In 2018, 2019, and 2020, Facebook employees exercised stock options and provided the company with excess tax benefits of approximately $659 million, $174 million, and $531 million, respectively. Since going public, Facebook has reported more than $50 billion of U.S. net income, yet the company reports a federal net operating loss carryover as of December 31, 2020, of $10.62 billion! Most of this difference results from the book–tax differences in stock option compensation reported on the income statements and the tax returns over this period.

Source: All of the information is publicly available on Facebook's Form 10-K and Proxy Statement for 2012, 2018, 2019, and 2020.

Net Capital Losses For corporations, all net capital gains (long- and short-term) are included in taxable income and taxed at the 21 percent corporate tax rate. Nevertheless, corporations generally prefer capital gains to ordinary income capital gains because corporations can deduct capital losses only to the extent of capital gains.[11] That is, corporations cannot deduct a net capital loss for the year (excess of capital losses over capital gains for the year). In contrast, individual taxpayers may deduct up to $3,000 ($1,500 if married filing separately) of net capital losses in computing taxable income.[12]

When corporations recognize net capital losses for a year, they are permitted to carry the capital losses back three years, called a **net capital loss carryback,** and forward five years, called a **net capital loss carryover,** to offset net capital gains in the three years before the current tax year and then to offset net capital gains in the five years after the current tax year.[13] The net capital loss carrybacks and carryovers must be applied in a particular order. If a corporation reports a net capital loss in year 4, it must first carry back the loss to year 1, then year 2, and then year 3. If the net capital loss remains after the carryback period, the corporation carries the loss forward to year 5 first, then year 6, then year 7, then year 8, and finally year 9. If the net capital loss carryover has not been fully absorbed by the end of the fifth year after it was incurred (i.e., year 9), the carryover expires unused.

Although corporations may carry back net capital losses, they may not carry back a net capital loss if doing so creates or increases a net operating loss of the corporation (excess of deductions over income) in the year to which it is carried back (see discussion of net operating losses in the next section).[14]

For financial reporting purposes, corporations deduct net capital losses in the year they are incurred. Thus, corporations recognizing net capital losses report unfavorable book–tax differences in the year they incur the losses and favorable book–tax differences in the year they use net capital loss carrybacks or carryovers to offset net capital gains.

Example 5-8

During 2022, PCC sold Intel stock at a $12,000 gain and also reported a $40,000 capital loss on the disposition of land held for investment. PCC has not recognized a net capital gain or loss since 2018. PCC has a net operating loss carryover from 2021 in the amount of $24,000. What is PCC's net capital loss for the year?

Answer: $28,000 loss [$12,000 + ($40,000)]. Because PCC did not recognize any net capital gains in 2019, 2020, or 2021, it may not carry back the loss (note that PCC could not carry back the loss to 2021 in any event because it recognized a net operating loss in that year as evidenced by its net operating loss carryover from 2021).

(continued on page 5-14)

[11]§1211(a).

[12]§1211(b). Individuals are also allowed to carry net capital losses forward indefinitely.

[13]§1212(a).

[14]§1212(a)(1)(A)(ii). To allow a corporation to carry back a net capital loss to absorb capital gains in a net operating loss year would increase the NOL carryover amount of the net capital loss used to offset the capital gain. This freed-up NOL would have a 20-year or indefinite carryover (depending on the year incurred) rather than the 5-year carryover of the net capital loss.

What amount of book–tax difference does this loss generate? Is the difference favorable or unfavorable? Is it temporary or permanent?

Answer: $28,000 unfavorable, temporary book–tax difference.

What if: Assume that in 2022, PCC reported a net capital loss of $28,000 and that it reported a $7,000 net capital gain in 2019, no net capital gain or loss in 2020, and a $4,000 net capital gain in 2021. What is the amount of its net capital loss carryover to 2023? PCC reported a net operating loss in 2021 but did not report a net operating loss in either 2019 or 2020.

Answer: $21,000. PCC first carries back the $28,000 loss to 2019, offsetting the $7,000 net capital gain in that year. PCC then carries the remaining $21,000 loss [($28,000) + $7,000] back to 2021. However, because PCC reported a net operating loss in 2021, it is not allowed to offset the $4,000 net capital gain with the net capital loss carryback. Consequently, the $21,000 unused net capital loss carryover is carried forward to 2023.

What if: Suppose PCC did not recognize any net capital gains in prior years but that next year (2023) it recognizes a net capital gain of $5,000 (before considering any capital loss carryovers). What will be its book–tax difference associated with capital gains and losses next year? Is it favorable or unfavorable? Is it temporary or permanent?

Answer: Next year, PCC would report a $5,000 favorable, temporary book–tax difference because it would be allowed to deduct $5,000 of its $28,000 net capital loss carryover for tax purposes. This is a reversal of $5,000 of the $28,000 unfavorable, temporary book–tax difference from the prior year. PCC would carry over the remaining $23,000 loss for up to four more years.

Net Operating Losses Compare the tax burdens of A Corporation and B Corporation. A Corporation reports $1,000,000 of taxable income and pays $210,000 of tax in year 1 and again in year 2. In contrast, B Corporation reports a $2,000,000 loss in year 1 and $4,000,000 of taxable income in year 2. Absent any special tax provisions, B Corporation would pay no tax in year 1 but $840,000 of tax in year 2. Over the same two-year period, both A Corporation and B Corporation reported $2,000,000 of (net) taxable income, yet B Corporation paid twice the tax A Corporation paid ($840,000 vs. $420,000).

The inequity for B Corporation in this situation is that, because it is required to report taxable income on an annual basis, it receives no tax benefit for its $2,000,000 loss (deductions in excess of gross income) in year 1. To ease the tax burden on corporations that aren't consistently profitable (for tax purposes), the tax laws allow those that report deductions in excess of gross income in a particular year to carry over the excess deductions to reduce taxable income and taxes payable in years when gross income exceeds deductions. This excess of deductions over gross income is referred to as a **net operating loss (NOL).** NOLs may be carried forward to deduct against positive taxable income in future years, and certain NOLs may be carried back to deduct against positive taxable income in prior years. When a NOL is carried forward to a future year, it is referred to as a **net operating loss carryover,** and when it is carried back to a prior year, it is called a **net operating loss carryback.**

When computing a corporation's net operating loss for the current year, a corporation may not deduct a NOL generated in a different year. Further, a corporation may deduct a net capital loss carryover against a net capital gain arising in the current year in calculating its current-year NOL, but, as described previously, it may not deduct a net capital loss carryback against a net capital gain in calculating its current-year NOL.

The specific rules for deducting NOL carryovers and carrybacks depend on the year in which the NOL was created.[15] When a corporation has multiple NOL carryovers, it uses the oldest first (i.e., FIFO order). The NOL deduction rules are summarized in Exhibit 5-6.

[15]In certain situations, corporations that experience a "change in ownership" may have NOL deductions limited under §382. Details relating to the §382 limitations are beyond the scope of this text.

EXHIBIT 5-6 Net Operating Loss Carryback and Carryover Summary*

Tax Year NOL Originated	Carrybacks	Carryovers
Beginning before 2018	Back two years.** Can offset 100% of taxable income before the NOL deduction in carryback years.	Forward 20 years. Can offset 100% of taxable income before the NOL deduction.
Beginning after 2017 and before 2021	Back five years.** Can offset up to 100% of taxable income before the NOL deduction in carryback years.	Carried forward indefinitely. Can offset up to 100% of taxable income before the NOL deduction in tax years beginning before 2021. In tax years beginning after 2020, can offset up to 80 percent of taxable income after deducting NOL carryovers from NOLs originating in tax years beginning before 2018.
Beginning after 2020	Not allowed.	Carried forward indefinitely. Can offset up to 80 percent of taxable income remaining after deducting NOL carryovers from NOLs originating in tax years beginning before 2018.

*In certain situations, when a corporation with a NOL experiences an "ownership change," the NOL deduction may be limited beyond the restrictions described in this exhibit (see §382). A discussion of these rules are beyond the scope of this text.

**A corporation can elect to forgo the NOL carryback and simply carry the NOL forward to future years. Also, if a corporation carries back a NOL, it must carry it back to the earliest year first (i.e., two years prior or five years prior, depending on the year the NOL originated).

Example 5-9

What if: In 2022, PCC reported taxable income of $250,000 before the NOL deduction. Assume that PCC has a NOL carryover from 2021 in the amount of $300,000 (this assumes PCC elected to forgo the carryback). What is PCC's 2022 taxable income and its NOL carryover to 2023?

Answer: $50,000 taxable income ($250,000 – $200,000), with a $100,000 NOL carryover to 2023 ($300,000 – $200,000). The NOL can be carried forward indefinitely. PCC can deduct the 2021 NOL carryover against 80 percent of 2022 taxable income before the NOL deduction ($250,000 × 80% = $200,000 limitation on the NOL carryover).

What if: Assume the $300,000 NOL originated in 2017 (the $300,000 is what remained after the two-year carryback) and PCC broke even each year from 2018 through 2021. What are PCC's 2022 taxable income and NOL carryover to 2023?

Answer: $0 taxable income ($250,000 – $250,000), with a $50,000 NOL carryover to 2023 ($300,000 – $250,000). PCC can deduct 100 percent of the pre-2018 NOL against taxable income in carryover years (2023 would be the sixth year of the 20-year carryover period).

What if: Assume that in 2022, PCC reported taxable income of $250,000 before the NOL deduction. Also assume that PCC has a NOL carryover from 2016 in the amount of $210,000 and a NOL carryover from 2019 in the amount of $200,000. What are PCC's 2022 taxable income and its NOL carryover to 2023?

Answer: $8,000 taxable income, with a $168,000 NOL carryover from 2019 to 2023. For 2022, PCC can deduct the full $210,000 NOL carryover from 2016. This leaves $40,000 of taxable income before the deduction for the 2019 NOL ($250,000 – $210,000). PCC can then deduct $32,000 of the 2019 NOL ($40,000 × 80%). Thus, taxable income is $8,000 ($250,000 – $210,000 – $32,000). PCC can carry over indefinitely the remaining $168,000 NOL from 2019 ($200,000 – $32,000), subject to the 80 percent limitation.

What if: Assume that in 2022 PCC reported $120,000 of deductions and $90,000 of gross income (including $6,000 of net capital gain). Also assume PCC has a $15,000 NOL carryover from 2021 and an $8,000 net capital loss carryover from 2021. What are PCC's net operating loss and capital loss carryovers to 2023, and when do they expire?

Answer: $15,000 net operating loss carryover from 2021 that can be carried forward indefinitely, a $36,000 net operating loss carryover from 2022 that can be carried forward indefinitely, and a $2,000 net capital loss carryover from 2021 that expires at the end of 2026 if unused. PCC's 2021 NOL is unused in 2022 because PCC reports a NOL in 2022 and is not allowed to deduct its NOL carryover in determining its 2022 NOL. In 2022, PCC is able to offset the $6,000 net capital gain included in gross income with $6,000 of the $8,000 net capital loss carryover from 2022. This reduces PCC's gross income to $84,000 ($90,000 – $6,000) and increases its deductions in excess of gross income (its current-year NOL) to $36,000 ($120,000 – $84,000). Finally, PCC's 2022 capital loss carryover is reduced by the $6,000 absorbed portion to $2,000 ($8,000 – $6,000 used in 2022).

For financial reporting purposes, corporations report losses in the year they incur them. Consequently, corporations report unfavorable temporary book–tax differences in the year they generate NOLs. Because corporations do not deduct NOL carryovers in determining book income, they report favorable *temporary* book–tax differences in the year they deduct the NOL carryovers for tax purposes. A corporation reports its NOL carryovers on Schedule K (line 12 on 2021 form) of Form 1120.

Example 5-10

What if: Assume that PCC incurred a $24,000 net operating loss in 2021 that it carried over to reduce 2022 taxable income from $100,000 (before the NOL deduction) to $76,000 (after the NOL deduction). What is PCC's current-year book–tax difference associated with its NOL carryover? Is the difference favorable or unfavorable? Is it permanent or temporary?

Answer: $24,000 favorable, temporary book–tax difference. The net operating loss carryover from the prior year is deductible for tax purposes but not for book purposes. The NOL carryover from 2021 is fully deductible because it did not reduce 2022 taxable income by more than 80 percent (it reduced it by 24 percent).

Charitable Contributions Similar to individuals, corporations are allowed to deduct charitable contributions to qualified charitable organizations.[16] However, the income-based deduction limitations and the timing rules are a little different for corporations than they are for individual taxpayers. In general, corporations are allowed to deduct the amount of money they contribute, the fair market value of **capital gain property** they donate (i.e., property that would generate long-term capital gain if sold), and the adjusted basis of **ordinary income property** they donate (i.e., all other property). This chapter emphasizes the tax consequences of cash donations by corporations to qualified charities.

Generally, corporations are allowed to deduct charitable contributions at the time they make payment to charitable organizations (subject to an overall taxable income limitation we discuss below). However, corporations using the accrual method of accounting can deduct contributions in the year *before* they actually pay the contribution when (1) their board of directors approves the payment and (2) they actually pay the contributions within three and one-half months of their tax year (two and one-half months for corporations with a June 30 year-end).[17]

Example 5-11

On December 1, 2022, the PCC board of directors approved a $110,000 cash contribution to the American Red Cross (ARC). For financial reporting purposes, PCC accrued and expensed the donation in 2022 for book purposes. PCC transferred the cash to the ARC on March 1, 2023. Does PCC report a book–tax difference associated with the charitable contribution (assume the taxable income limitation does not apply)?

Answer: No book–tax difference. For tax purposes, as an accrual-method taxpayer, PCC may deduct the $110,000 contribution in 2022 because it paid the donation to the ARC within three and one-half months after year-end.

What if: Assume the same facts as above, except that PCC transferred the cash to the ARC on April 30, 2023. Does PCC report a book–tax difference associated with the charitable contribution (assume the taxable income limitation does not apply)?

Answer: Yes, PCC reports a $110,000 unfavorable, temporary book–tax difference in 2022. A calendar-year-end corporation such as PCC must pay the charitable contribution by the 15th day of the fourth month after its year-end (April 15). This book–tax difference will reverse and become a $110,000 favorable, temporary book–tax difference in 2023 when PCC makes the payment to the ARC and deducts the contribution.

[16]§170(a). The IRS Tax Exempt Organization Search (https://apps.irs.gov/app/eos/) allows you to search an organization to determine if it is a qualified charity eligible to receive tax-deductible charitable contributions.

[17]§170(a)(2).

A corporation's deduction for qualified charitable contributions is limited to a percentage of a corporation's **charitable contribution limit modified taxable income.** For 2022, the percentage is 10 percent. For 2021 (and 2020), the percentage was 25 percent for qualified contributions and 10 percent for nonqualified contributions. For this purpose, qualified charitable contributions are cash contributions made to public charities and private operating foundations (except contributions to donor advised funds or supporting organizations) by a corporation that *elects* to apply the 25 percent limit. A corporation's charitable contribution limit modified taxable income is its taxable income *before* deducting the following:

1. *Any* charitable contributions.
2. The dividends-received deduction (DRD) (discussed below).
3. Net capital loss *carrybacks.*

Net capital loss and NOL *carryovers are deductible* in determining a corporation's charitable contribution limit modified taxable income. Net capital loss *carrybacks* are *not deductible* for charitable contribution limitation purposes because they are unknown when corporations must determine the limitation (they arise in a future year).

Due to the income percentage limitation, a corporation's charitable contribution deduction for the year is the *lower* of (1) the amount of charitable contributions to qualifying charities (including charitable contribution carryovers—discussed below) or (2) the applicable percentage of the corporation's charitable contribution limit modified taxable income.

THE KEY FACTS

Charitable Contributions

- Charitable contribution deductions
  - Deductible when they accrue if approved by board of directors and paid within 3.5 months of year-end (2.5 months for corporations with a June 30 year-end).
- Deductions limited to 10 percent of charitable contribution deduction modified taxable income in 2022. In 2021, deductions limited to 25 percent for qualified contributions from electing corporations and 10 percent otherwise.
- Contributions in excess of the charitable contribution limit are carried forward up to five years.

Example 5-12

What if: Assume that PCC's 2022 taxable income *before* considering the charitable contribution limitation was $100,000. Further, assume the taxable income computation includes an $18,000 charitable contribution deduction, a $10,000 DRD, a $24,000 NOL carryover deduction from 2020, a $4,000 net capital loss carryover deduction (offsets $4,000 of capital gain), and a $25,000 depreciation deduction. Under these circumstances, what would be PCC's 2022 deductible charitable contribution after applying the income percentage limitation?

Answer: $12,800 deductible charitable contribution, computed as follows:

Description	Amount	Explanation
(1) Taxable income before charitable contribution limitation	$100,000	
(2) Charitable contribution deduction before limitation	18,000	Not deductible in computing limitation
(3) Dividends-received deduction	10,000	Not deductible in computing limitation
(4) Charitable contribution limit modified taxable income*	$128,000	Sum of (1) through (3)
(5) Tax deduction limitation percentage	10%	10% limit for 2022
(6) Charitable contribution deduction limitation	$ 12,800	(4) × (5)
(7) Charitable contribution deduction for year	**$ 12,800**	Lesser of (2) or (6)
Charitable contribution carryover (expires if unused by the end of 2027)	$ 5,200	(2) − (7)

*Note that the NOL and net capital loss carryovers are not added back to compute line (4) because they are deductible in determining the charitable contribution limit modified taxable income.

What if: Assume this was a qualified contribution in 2021. What would be PCC's charitable contribution deduction for 2021?

Answer: $18,000. Because this is 2021 and it is a qualified contribution (taxpayer is eligible and elects to use the 25% modified charitable contribution limitation, the deduction is the lesser of (1) $32,000 ($128,000 × 25% charitable deduction limit percentage) or (2) $18,000, the amount of the actual contribution.

Corporations making current-year charitable contributions in excess of the income limitation may carry forward the excess for up to five years after the year in which the carryover arises. Carryovers are absorbed on a first-in, first-out (FIFO) basis and are applied after the current-year contribution deduction. Corporations can deduct the carryover in future years to the extent the income limitation does not restrict deductions for charitable contributions corporations actually make in those years. Unused carryovers expire after five years.

Example 5-13

What if: Assume the same facts as in the previous example, where PCC reported a $12,800 charitable contribution deduction and a $5,200 charitable contribution carryover. What would be PCC's book–tax difference associated with the charitable contribution? Would it be favorable or unfavorable? Would it be permanent or temporary?

Answer: $5,200 unfavorable, temporary book–tax difference. The amount of the carryover was not deductible for tax in the current year, but it was expensed for books. When PCC deducts the charitable contribution carryover, it will report a $5,200 favorable, temporary book–tax difference.

Corporations report *unfavorable, temporary* book–tax differences to the extent the modified taxable income limitation restricts the amount of their charitable contribution tax deduction. That is, they recognize unfavorable, temporary book–tax differences in the amount of the charitable contribution carryover they generate for the year. Conversely, corporations report *favorable, temporary* book–tax differences when they deduct charitable contribution carryovers because they deduct the carryovers for tax purposes but not book purposes.

Example 5-14

In 2022, PCC donated a total of $700,000 of cash to the American Red Cross. Elise knew she had to apply the 10 percent taxable income limitation to verify the amount PCC deducted for tax purposes. For 2022, PCC's taxable income before any charitable contribution, NOL carryovers from prior years, and dividends-received deduction was $6,287,000 (see Exhibit 5-8 later in the text for the computation). What is PCC's charitable contribution deduction for the year, assuming the donation is a qualified charitable contribution? What is its charitable contribution carryover to next year, if any?

Answer: $626,300 charitable contribution deduction and $73,700 charitable contribution carry-over, computed as follows:

Description	Amount	Explanation
(1) Taxable income before *any* charitable contribution, NOL carryover from previous year, and DRD	$6,287,000	Exhibit 5-8
(2) NOL *carryover* from previous year (from Example 5-10)	(24,000)	Deductible in determining taxable income limit
(3) Charitable contribution limit modified taxable income	$6,263,000	(1) + (2)
(4) Total charitable contributions for year	$ 700,000	
(5) Tax deduction limitation percentage	10%	Percentage limitation for qualified contributions
(6) Charitable contribution deduction limitation	$ 626,300	(3) × (5)
(7) Charitable contribution deduction for year	**$ 626,300**	Lesser of (4) or (6)
Charitable contribution carryover (expires if unused by the end of 2027)	**$ 73,700**	(4) − (7)

What is PCC's book–tax difference associated with its charitable contribution? Is the difference favorable or unfavorable? Is it permanent or temporary?

Answer: $73,700 unfavorable, temporary book–tax difference.

Dividends-Received Deduction When corporations receive dividends from other corporations, the dividends are included in taxable income and taxed at the 21 percent corporate tax rate. However, corporations are allowed to claim a dividends-received deduction (DRD) that reduces the actual tax they pay on the dividends.[18] The DRD is designed to mitigate the extent to which corporate earnings are subject to three (or perhaps even more) levels of taxation. Corporate taxable income is subject to triple taxation when a corporation pays tax on its income and then distributes its after-tax income to shareholders that are corporations. Corporate shareholders are taxed on the dividends, creating the second tax. When corporate shareholders distribute their after-tax earnings as dividends to their shareholders, the income is taxed for a third time. The dividends-received deduction reduces the amount of the second-level tax and thus mitigates the impact of triple taxation (or more) of earnings that corporations distribute as dividends.

Corporations generally compute their dividends-received deduction by multiplying the dividend amount by 50 percent, 65 percent, or 100 percent, depending on the receiving corporation's level of ownership in the distributing corporation's stock. Exhibit 5-7 summarizes the stock ownership thresholds and the corresponding dividends-received deduction percentage. Only dividends received from domestic corporations are eligible for this DRD. Certain dividends from 10-percent-or-more-owned foreign corporations are eligible for a 100 percent DRD, which is discussed in the chapter The U.S. Taxation of Multinational Transactions.

THE KEY FACTS

Dividends-Received Deduction

- Dividends-received deduction
  - Generally lesser of deduction percentage (50 percent, 65 percent, or 100 percent) based on ownership × DRD modified taxable income.
  - Limitation doesn't apply if full DRD creates or increases a corporation's NOL.
  - Generates favorable, permanent book–tax difference.

EXHIBIT 5-7 Stock Ownership and Dividends-Received Deduction Percentage

Receiving Corporation's Stock Ownership in Distributing Corporation's Stock	Dividends-Received Deduction Percentage
Less than 20 percent	50%
At least 20 percent but less than 80 percent	65
80 percent or more[19]	100

Example 5-15

During 2022, PCC received a $30,000 dividend from Apple Inc. PCC owns less than 1 percent of the Apple Inc. stock. What is PCC's DRD associated with the dividend?

Answer: $15,000 ($30,000 × 50%).

What if: PCC's marginal tax rate on the dividend *before* considering the effect of the dividends-received deduction is 21 percent. What is PCC's marginal tax rate on the Apple Inc. dividend income *after* considering the dividends-received deduction?

Answer: 10.5 percent marginal tax rate on dividend income, computed as follows:

Description	Amount	Explanation
(1) Dividend from Apple	$ 30,000	
(2) The percentage DRD	50%	Less than 20 percent ownership in Apple
(3) Dividends-received deduction	**$15,000**	(1) × (2)
(4) Dividend subject to taxation after DRD	$ 15,000	(1) − (3)
(5) Marginal ordinary tax rate	21%	
(6) Taxes payable on dividend *after* DRD	$ 3,150	(4) × (5)
Marginal tax rate on dividend *after* DRD	**10.5%**	(6)/(1)

[18]§243. Also, §246(c) describes certain dividends that are ineligible for the dividends-received deduction.

[19]To qualify for the 100 percent dividends-received deduction, the receiving and distributing corporations must be in the same affiliated group, as described in §1504. The 80 percent ownership requirement is the minimum ownership level required for inclusion in the same affiliated group.

Deduction limitation. The dividends-received deduction is limited to the product of the applicable dividends-received deduction percentage (see Exhibit 5-7) and **DRD modified taxable income.**[20] DRD modified taxable income is the dividend-receiving corporation's taxable income *before* deducting the following:

- DRD.
- NOL deduction.
- Net capital loss carrybacks (but after deducting net capital loss carryovers).[21]

Example 5-16

What if: Suppose that during 2022, PCC received a $30,000 dividend from Apple Inc. and that PCC owns less than 1 percent of the Apple Inc. stock. Further assume that PCC's taxable income before the dividends-received deduction was $50,000 in Scenario A and $25,000 in Scenario B. To arrive at the taxable income under both scenarios (before the DRD), PCC deducted a $3,000 NOL carryover and a $4,000 net capital loss carryover. What is PCC's dividends-received deduction associated with the dividend in Scenario A and in Scenario B?

Answer: $15,000 in Scenario A and $14,000 in Scenario B, computed as follows:

Description	Scenario A	Scenario B	Explanation
(1) Taxable income before the dividends-received deduction (includes dividend income)	$ 50,000	$ 25,000	
(2) NOL carryover	3,000	3,000	
(3) DRD modified taxable income	$ 53,000	$ 28,000	(1) + (2)
(4) Dividend income	$ 30,000	$ 30,000	
(5) Dividends-received deduction percentage based on ownership	50%	50%	§243(a)
(6) Dividends-received deduction before limitation	$ 15,000	$ 15,000	(4) × (5)
(7) Dividends-received deduction limitation	$ 26,500	$ 14,000	(3) × (5)
DRD deductible	**$15,000**	**$14,000**	Lesser of (6) or (7)

Note that the net capital loss carryover is deductible in determining the DRD modified taxable income, so it is not added back to taxable income to arrive at DRD modified taxable income.

The modified taxable income limitation *does not apply* if, after deducting the *full* dividends-received deduction (dividend × DRD percentage), a corporation reports a current-year net operating loss. That is, if, after deducting the full dividends-received deduction, the corporation has a net operating loss, the corporation is allowed to deduct the *full* dividends-received deduction no matter the amount of the modified taxable income limitation.[22] As the following example illustrates, this rule can cause some unusual results.

Example 5-17

What if: Let's assume that PCC reports gross income of $80,000, *including* $40,000 of dividend income from TOU Corp. PCC owns 25 percent of TOU Corp. stock, so its applicable DRD percentage is 65 percent (see Exhibit 5-7). Finally, let's consider two alternative scenarios. In Scenario A, PCC reports $54,000 of business expenses deductible in determining its DRD modified taxable income. In Scenario B, PCC reports $55,000 of business expenses deductible in determining its DRD modified taxable income. For each scenario, what is PCC's DRD modified taxable income? For each scenario, what is PCC's dividends-received deduction?

[20]When corporations receive dividends from multiple corporations with different deduction percentages, according to §246(b)(3), the limitations first apply to the 65 percent dividends-received deduction and then the 50 percent dividends-received deduction.

[21]§246(b)(1).

[22]§246(b)(2).

Scenario A Answer: $26,000 DRD modified taxable income; $16,900 dividends-received deduction (see computation below).

Scenario B Answer: $25,000 DRD modified taxable income; $26,000 dividends-received deduction, computed as follows:

Description	Scenario A	Scenario B	Explanation
(1) Gross income other than dividends	$ 40,000	$ 40,000	
(2) Dividend income	40,000	40,000	
(3) Gross income	$ 80,000	$ 80,000	(1) + (2)
(4) Business expenses deductible in determining the DRD modified taxable income	54,000	55,000	
(5) DRD modified taxable income (note this is taxable income before the DRD)	**$26,000**	**$25,000**	(3) – (4)
(6) Full dividends-received deduction	$ 26,000	$ 26,000	(2) × 65%
(7) DRD modified taxable income limitation	16,900	16,250	(5) × 65%
(8) Taxable income (loss) after deducting full DRD	0	(1,000)	(5) – (6)
DRD deductible	**$16,900**	**$26,000**	Lesser of (6) or (7) unless (8) is negative, then (6)

Compare the results in Scenario A and Scenario B in the previous example. In Scenario B, PCC's DRD is $9,100 larger than it is in Scenario A ($26,000 – $16,900), despite the fact that the only difference in the two scenarios is that PCC reports $54,000 of business expenses in Scenario A and $55,000 of business expenses in Scenario B. Interestingly, in this example, PCC is able to increase its DRD by $9,100 for a $40,000 dividend simply by incurring $1,000 more in expenses (or potentially even $1 more).

Because the dividends-received deduction is strictly a tax deduction and not a book deduction, *any* dividends-received deduction creates a *favorable, permanent* book–tax difference.

Example 5-18

From her review of PCC's dividend income computations, Elise determined that the only dividend PCC received during the year was a $30,000 dividend from Apple Inc., a U.S. corporation. Because PCC owns a very small percentage of Apple Inc. stock (less than 1 percent), Elise determined that PCC was entitled to a 50 percent dividends-received deduction. PCC's modified taxable income before any NOL and DRD is $4,721,250. What is PCC's book–tax difference associated with its dividends-received deduction? Is the difference favorable or unfavorable? Is it permanent or temporary?

Answer: $15,000 favorable, permanent book–tax difference, computed as follows:

Description	Amount	Explanation
(1) Taxable income before NOL and DRD (DRD modified taxable income)	$4,721,250	Exhibit 5-8 ($4,697,250 + 24,000 NOL)
(2) Dividend income	$ 30,000	Exhibit 5-8
(3) Applicable DRD percentage	50%	Owns less than 20 percent of Apple Inc.
(4) Full dividends-received deduction	$ 15,000	(2) × (3)
(5) Dividends-received deduction taxable income limitation	$2,360,625	(1) × (3)
(6) Book deductible dividends-received deduction	0	No book DRD
(7) Tax-deductible dividends-received deduction	$ 15,000	Lesser of (4) or (5)
(Favorable) permanent book–tax difference	**$ (15,000)**	(6) – (7)

Taxable Income Summary

Exhibit 5-8 presents Elise's template for reconciling PCC's book and taxable income. Note that the template does not follow the typical financial accounting

EXHIBIT 5-8 PCC Book–Tax Reconciliation Template

Description	Book Income (Dr) Cr	Book–Tax Adjustments (Dr)[†]		Taxable Income (Dr) Cr
Revenue from sales	$60,000,000			$60,000,000
Cost of goods sold	(38,000,000)			(38,000,000)
Gross profit	$22,000,000			$22,000,000
Other income:				
Dividend income	30,000			30,000
Interest income	120,000	(12,000)[Ex. 1]		108,000
Capital gains (losses)	(28,000)		28,000[Ex. 8]	0
Gain on fixed asset dispositions	54,000		16,000[Exh. 4]	70,000
Gross income	$22,176,000			$22,208,000
Expenses:				
Compensation	(9,868,000)			(9,868,000)
Deferred compensation	(300,000)	(150,000)[Exh. 4]		(450,000)
Stock option compensation	(100,000)		100,000[Ex. 7]	0
Bad debt expense	(165,000)		70,000[Exh. 4]	(95,000)
Charitable contributions	Moved below			
Depreciation	(2,400,000)	(700,000)[Exh. 4]		(3,100,000)
Advertising	(1,920,000)			(1,920,000)
Warranty expenses	(580,000)		170,000[Exh. 4]	(410,000)
Meals	(14,000)			(14,000)
Life insurance premiums	(34,000)		34,000[Ex. 1]	0
Other expenses	(64,000)			(64,000)
Federal income tax expense	(2,000,000)*		2,000,000[Ex. 2]	0
Total expenses *before* charitable contribution, NOL, and DRD	(17,445,000)			(15,921,000)
Income *before* charitable contribution, NOL, and DRD	4,731,000			$ 6,287,000
NOL carryover from prior year		(24,000)[Ex. 10]		(24,000)
Taxable income for charitable contribution limitation purposes				6,263,000
Charitable contributions	(700,000)		73,700[Ex. 14]	(626,300)
Taxable income before DRD				5,636,700
Dividends-received deduction (DRD)		(15,000)[Ex. 18]		(15,000)
Book/taxable income	**$ 4,031,000**	**$(901,000)**	**$2,491,700**	**$5,621,700**

*This number is used only for illustrative purposes. In the Accounting for Income Taxes chapter, we compute the correct federal income tax expense (also referred to as the federal income tax provision).

[†]Note that the superscript by each book–tax difference identifies the example (Ex.) or exhibit (Exh.) where the adjustment is calculated. Also note that the debit numbers are favorable book–tax adjustments while credit numbers are unfavorable book–tax adjustments.

format because it organizes the information to facilitate the taxable income computation. In particular, it puts the deductions in the sequence in which they are deducted for tax purposes.

Corporate Income Tax Liability

Corporations compute their pre-credit federal income tax liability by applying a 21 percent rate to taxable income.

Example 5-19

Elise determined that PCC's taxable income is $5,621,700. What is its income tax liability?

Answer: $1,180,557, computed as $5,621,700 × 21%.

COMPLIANCE

LO 5-3

Corporations report their taxable income on Form 1120. Exhibit 5-9 presents the front page of PCC's current-year Form 1120 through the tax liability.

Form 1120 includes a schedule for corporations to report their book–tax differences and reconcile their book and taxable income. Corporations with total assets of less than $10,000,000 report their book–tax differences on Schedule M-1. Corporations with total assets of $10,000,000 or more are required to report their book–tax differences on Schedule M-3.[23] Because corporations report book–tax differences as adjustments to book income to compute taxable income on either Schedule M-1 or M-3, these book-to-tax adjustments are often referred to as **Schedule M adjustments, M adjustments,** and even "Ms" (plural version of M).

Because PCC's total assets are $9,500,000 (see Exhibit 5-9, line D), it may complete a Schedule M-1 rather than a Schedule M-3. Exhibit 5-10 presents PCC's completed Schedule M-1 based on the information provided in Exhibit 5-8. Schedule M-1 is a relatively short schedule, and it does not require corporations to provide much detail about the nature of their book–tax differences.

The schedule begins on line 1 with book income after taxes. The left-hand column includes all unfavorable book–tax differences (add-backs to book income to arrive at taxable income). In general, the top part of the left column is for income items and the bottom part is for expense items. The right-hand column consists of all favorable book–tax differences. The top part of the right column is for income items and the bottom part includes expense items.

Finally, note that Schedule M-1 (and Schedule M-3) reconciles to taxable income *before* the net operating loss deduction and the dividends-received deduction.[24] Consequently, to fully reconcile book and taxable income, corporations must deduct net operating loss carryovers and dividends-received deductions from line 10 on Schedule M-1 (or the amount on line 30d on Schedule M-3).

[23]Corporations with at least $10 million but less than $50 million in total assets at tax year-end are permitted to file Schedule M-1 in place of Schedule M-3, Parts II and III. Schedule M-3, Part I, lines 1–12 continue to be required for these taxpayers. Corporations with $10 million to $50 million in total assets may voluntarily file Schedule M-3 Parts II and III rather than Schedule M-1.

[24]Schedule M-1 (and Schedule M-3) reconciles to line 28 on Form 1120. Line 28 is taxable income before the net operating loss and special deductions (the dividends-received deduction).

EXHIBIT 5-9 PCC Form 1120 page 1, through tax refund

Form **1120** Department of the Treasury Internal Revenue Service

U.S. Corporation Income Tax Return

For calendar year 2021 or tax year beginning ________, 2021, ending ________, 20 ____

▶ Go to *www.irs.gov/Form1120* for instructions and the latest information.

OMB No. 1545-0123 **2021**

A Check if:	TYPE OR PRINT		
1a Consolidated return (attach Form 851) ☐		Name: **Premier Computer Corporation**	B Employer identification number: **12-3456789**
b Life/nonlife consolidated return ☐		Number, street, and room or suite no. If a P.O. box, see instructions.: **4810 East Crown Drive**	C Date incorporated: **01/01/2001**
2 Personal holding co. (attach Sch. PH) ☐		City or town, state or province, country, and ZIP or foreign postal code: **Denver, CO 80239**	D Total assets (see instructions): $ **9,500,000**
3 Personal service corp. (see instructions) ☐			
4 Schedule M-3 attached ☐	E Check if: (1) ☐ Initial return (2) ☐ Final return (3) ☐ Name change (4) ☐ Address change		

Income	1a	Gross receipts or sales	1a	60,000,000		
	b	Returns and allowances	1b			
	c	Balance. Subtract line 1b from line 1a			1c	60,000,000
	2	Cost of goods sold (attach Form 1125-A)			2	38,000,000
	3	Gross profit. Subtract line 2 from line 1c			3	22,000,000
	4	Dividends and inclusions (Schedule C, line 23)			4	30,000
	5	Interest			5	108,000
	6	Gross rents			6	
	7	Gross royalties			7	
	8	Capital gain net income (attach Schedule D (Form 1120))			8	
	9	Net gain or (loss) from Form 4797, Part II, line 17 (attach Form 4797)			9	70,000
	10	Other income (see instructions—attach statement)			10	
	11	**Total income.** Add lines 3 through 10 ▶			11	22,208,000
Deductions (See instructions for limitations on deductions.)	12	Compensation of officers (see instructions—attach Form 1125-E) ▶			12	1,500,000
	13	Salaries and wages (less employment credits)			13	8,818,000
	14	Repairs and maintenance			14	
	15	Bad debts			15	95,000
	16	Rents			16	
	17	Taxes and licenses			17	
	18	Interest (see instructions)			18	
	19	Charitable contributions			19	626,300
	20	Depreciation from Form 4562 not claimed on Form 1125-A or elsewhere on return (attach Form 4562)			20	3,100,000
	21	Depletion			21	
	22	Advertising			22	1,920,000
	23	Pension, profit-sharing, etc., plans			23	
	24	Employee benefit programs			24	
	25	Reserved for future use			25	
	26	Other deductions (attach statement) Warranties 410,000 + Meals 14,000 + Other expenses 64,000			26	488,000
	27	**Total deductions.** Add lines 12 through 26 ▶			27	16,547,300
	28	Taxable income before net operating loss deduction and special deductions. Subtract line 27 from line 11			28	5,660,700
	29a	Net operating loss deduction (see instructions)	29a	24,000		
	b	Special deductions (Schedule C, line 24)	29b	15,000		
	c	Add lines 29a and 29b			29c	39,000
Tax, Refundable Credits, and Payments	30	**Taxable income.** Subtract line 29c from line 28. See instructions			30	5,621,700
	31	Total tax (Schedule J, Part I, line 11)			31	1,180,557
	32	Reserved for future use			32	
	33	Total payments and credits (Schedule J, Part III, line 23)			33	1,328,000
	34	Estimated tax penalty. See instructions. Check if Form 2220 is attached ▶ ☐			34	
	35	**Amount owed.** If line 33 is smaller than the total of lines 31 and 34, enter amount owed			35	
	36	**Overpayment.** If line 33 is larger than the total of lines 31 and 34, enter amount overpaid			36	147,443
	37	Enter amount from line 36 you want: **Credited to 2022 estimated tax** ▶ **Refunded** ▶			37	147,443

Sign Here

Under penalties of perjury, I declare that I have examined this return, including accompanying schedules and statements, and to the best of my knowledge and belief, it is true, correct, and complete. Declaration of preparer (other than taxpayer) is based on all information of which preparer has any knowledge.

▶ Signature of officer | Date | ▶ Title

May the IRS discuss this return with the preparer shown below? See instructions. ☐ Yes ☐ No

Paid Preparer Use Only

Print/Type preparer's name	Preparer's signature	Date	Check ☐ if self-employed	PTIN
Firm's name ▶			Firm's EIN ▶	
Firm's address ▶			Phone no.	

For Paperwork Reduction Act Notice, see separate instructions. Cat. No. 11450Q Form **1120** (2021)

Source: irs.gov.

EXHIBIT 5-10 Form 1120, Schedule M-1

Schedule M-1 **Reconciliation of Income (Loss) per Books With Income per Return**

Note: The corporation may be required to file Schedule M-3. See instructions.

1	Net income (loss) per books	4,031,000	7	Income recorded on books this year not included on this return (itemize):	
2	Federal income tax per books	2,000,000		Tax-exempt interest $ 12,000	
3	Excess of capital losses over capital gains	28,000			
4	Income subject to tax not recorded on books this year (itemize): gain on disposition of fixed assets	16,000			12,000
5	Expenses recorded on books this year not deducted on this return (itemize):		8	Deductions on this return not charged against book income this year (itemize):	
a	Depreciation $		a	Depreciation $ 700,000	
b	Charitable contributions $ 73,700		b	Charitable contributions $	
c	Travel and entertainment $			deferred compensation 150,000	
	Other 374,000 see statement 1	447,700			850,000
			9	Add lines 7 and 8	862,000
6	Add lines 1 through 5	6,522,700	10	Income (page 1, line 28)—line 6 less line 9	5,660,700

Schedule M-1
Statement 1
Other expenses recorded on books this year not deducted on this return

Compensation expense (stock options)	$100,000
Bad debt expense	70,000
Warranty expense	170,000
Life insurance premiums	34,000
Total other expenses	$374,000

Source: irs.gov.

Example 5-20

In reviewing her work on PCC's tax return, Elise wanted to check to make sure that she could reconcile from the bottom line of Schedule M-1 to PCC's taxable income. She noted that line 10 of PCC's Schedule M-1 was $5,660,700. How should Elise reconcile from this number to PCC's taxable income?

Answer: Start with the amount on line 10 and subtract PCC's NOL carryover and its DRD, as illustrated below:

Description	Amount	Explanation
(1) Schedule M-1 taxable income reconciliation total	$ 5,660,700	Form 1120, Schedule M-1, line 10
(2) Net operating loss deduction	(24,000)	Exhibit 5-8
(3) Dividends-received deduction	(15,000)	Exhibit 5-8
Taxable income	**$5,621,700**	(1) + (2) + (3)

Schedule M-3 requires corporations to report significantly more information than Schedule M-1 does. For example, Schedule M-3 includes more than 60 specific types of book–tax differences, while Schedule M-1 includes only 10 summary lines. Furthermore,

Schedule M-3 requires corporations to identify each book–tax difference as either temporary or permanent. The IRS created Schedule M-3 in hopes of providing a better and more efficient starting point for agents to identify and scrutinize large dollar compliance issues.

Form 1120 also requires corporations to complete Schedule M-2, which provides a reconciliation of the corporation's beginning and ending balance in its unappropriated retained earnings from its financial accounting balance sheet (reported on Schedule L). Corporations with total receipts and total assets of less than $250,000 are not required to complete Schedules L, M-1, and M-2.

ETHICS

Your client traditionally provides free doughnuts and coffee from a local convenience store (not considered to be a restaurant) to its employees every Friday morning to help boost morale. Corporations can generally deduct 50 percent of the cost of food provided to employees. However, food costs at "mentoring events" is 100 percent deductible. Following the tax director's proposal, the Friday events have been recharacterized as "mentoring events" by having someone from management make a few remarks about professional development. What do you think of the corporation's approach to maximizing its deduction for meals on its tax return? Would it matter that the client could easily purchase the coffee and doughnuts from a doughnut shop?

Consolidated Tax Returns An affiliated group of corporations may elect to file a **consolidated tax return**—that is, the group files a tax return as if it were one entity for tax purposes. An **affiliated group** exists when one corporation owns at least 80 percent of (1) the total voting power and (2) the total stock value of another corporation.[25] Filing a consolidated tax return allows the losses of one group member to offset the income of other members. Further, income from certain intercompany transactions is deferred until realized through a transaction outside of the affiliated group. However, losses from certain intercompany transactions are also deferred until realized through a transaction outside of the affiliated group.

Affiliated groups cannot file a consolidated tax return unless they elect to do so. Because the election is binding on subsequent years, it should be made with care. Consolidated tax returns may impose additional administrative and compliance costs on the taxpayers. The consolidated tax return laws are very complex and beyond the scope of this text.[26] Further, the rules for consolidated reporting for financial statement purposes are different from the tax rules.

Corporate Tax Return Due Dates and Estimated Taxes

The tax return due date for most C corporations (those with a tax year-end other than June 30) is three and one-half months after the corporation's year-end. Thus, a calendar-year corporation's unextended tax return due date is April 15. Corporations requesting an

[25]§1504(a).

[26]The tax rules for consolidated tax returns are provided primarily in the regulations under §1502.

extension can extend the due date for filing their tax returns (not for paying the taxes) for six months (October 15 for calendar-year corporations). Corporations with a June 30 year-end have a September 15 due date (the 15th day of the third month following the end of the fiscal year), and the extended due date is seven months after the regular due date (April 15).

Corporations with a federal income tax liability of $500 or more are required to pay their tax liability for the year in quarterly estimated installments.[27] The installments are due on the 15th day of the 4th, 6th, 9th, and 12th months of their tax year.[28] When corporations file their tax returns, they determine whether they must pay estimated tax underpayment penalties. Generally, corporations are subject to underpayment penalties if they did not pay 25 percent, 50 percent, 75 percent, and 100 percent of their required annual payment with their first, second, third, and fourth installment payments, respectively.[29] The required annual payment is the *least* of:

1. 100 percent of the tax liability on the prior year's return, but only if there was a positive tax liability on the return and the prior-year return covered a 12-month period (however, see discussion of the exception that applies to corporations with taxable income above $1 million).
2. 100 percent of the current-year tax liability (corporations usually don't rely on this method to compute the required payment because they won't know what their current-year liability is until they complete their tax returns—after the estimated tax due dates).
3. 100 percent of the estimated current-year tax liability using the annualized income method (discussed below).[30]

From a cash management perspective (considering the time value of money), it generally makes sense for corporations to make the *minimum* required estimated payment installments for each quarter. Thus, as each estimated tax due date approaches, corporations will generally compute the required estimated payment under the prior-year tax method (if available) and under the annualized method and pay the lesser of the two.

The **annualized income method** is perhaps the most popular method of determining estimated tax payments (particularly for corporations that can't use the prior-year tax liability to compute their current-year estimated tax payment obligations) because corporations can use this method as a safe harbor to avoid estimated payment penalties. Under this method, corporations measure their taxable income as of the end of each quarter and then annualize (project) the amount to calculate their estimated taxable income and tax liability for the year. They use the estimated annual tax liability at the end of each quarter to calculate the minimum required estimated payment for that quarter. Corporations use the first-quarter taxable income to project their annual tax liability for the *first- and second-quarter* estimated tax payments. They use taxable income at the end of the second quarter to calculate the third-quarter estimated tax payment requirement, and taxable income at the end of the third quarter to calculate their fourth-quarter payment requirement. Exhibit 5-11 shows the formula for computing estimated taxable income under the annualized income method.

THE KEY FACTS

Tax Compliance

- Corporations report taxable income on Form 1120.
- Corporations with total assets of less than $10M report book–tax differences on Schedule M-1 of Form 1120. Otherwise, they are required to report book–tax differences on Schedule M-3.
- The tax return due date is 3.5 months after year-end (2.5 months for corporations with a June 30 year-end).
  - Extensions extend the due date for filing Form 1120 (not for paying taxes) for six additional months after year-end (seven months for corporations with a June 30 year-end).
- An affiliated group may file a consolidated tax return.
- Corporations pay expected annual tax liability through estimated tax payments.
  - Installments due in the 4th, 6th, 9th, and 12th months of their taxable year.
- Underpayment penalties apply if estimated tax payments are inadequate.

[27]§6655.

[28]§6655(c).

[29]§6665(d).

[30]§6655(e).

EXHIBIT 5-11 Estimated Taxable Income Computation under Annualized Income Method

Installment	(1) Taxable Income (first __ months of year)	(2) Annualization Factor	(1) × (2) Annual Estimated Taxable Income
First quarter	3	12/3 = 4	
Second quarter	3	12/3 = 4	
Third quarter	6	12/6 = 2	
Fourth quarter	9	12/9 = 1.3333	

Example 5-21

PCC determined its taxable income at the close of the first, second, and third quarters as follows:

Quarter-End	Cumulative Taxable Income
First	$1,000,000
Second	3,200,000
Third	4,000,000

What is its annual estimated taxable income for estimated tax payment purposes as of the end of the first, second, third, and fourth quarters, respectively?

Answer: $4,000,000 for the first and second quarters, $6,400,000 for the third quarter, and $6,666,667 for the fourth quarter, computed as follows:

Installment	(1) Taxable Income	(2) Annualization Factor	(1) × (2) Annual Estimated Taxable Income
First quarter	$1,000,000	12/3 = 4	**$4,000,000**
Second quarter	1,000,000	12/3 = 4	**4,000,000**
Third quarter	3,200,000	12/6 = 2	**6,400,000**
Fourth quarter	5,000,000	12/9 = 1.333	**6,666,667**

Once corporations have determined their annual estimated taxable income for each quarter, they can use the formulas in Exhibit 5-12 to compute the required estimated tax installments for each quarter under the annualized income method.

EXHIBIT 5-12 Estimated Taxable Income Computation under Annualized Income Method

Installment	(1) Annual Estimated Taxable Income	(2) Tax on Estimated Taxable Income	(3) Percentage of Tax Required to Be Paid	(4) [(2) × (3)] Required Cumulative Payment	(5) Prior Cumulative Payment	(4) − (5) Required Estimated Tax Payment
First quarter			25%			
Second quarter			50			
Third quarter			75			
Fourth quarter			100			

Example 5-22

Based on the estimated taxable income in the previous example, what are PCC's required estimated tax payments for the year under the annualized income method?

Answer: $210,000 for the first and second quarters, $588,000 for the third quarter, and $392,000 for the fourth quarter, computed as follows:

Installment	(1) Annual Estimated Taxable Income	(2) Tax on Estimated Taxable Income	(3) Percentage of Tax Required to Be Paid	(4) [(2) × (3)] Required Cumulative Payment	(5) Prior Cumulative Payments	(4) – (5) Required Estimated Tax Payment
First quarter	$4,000,000	$ 840,000	25%	$ 210,000	$ 0	**$210,000**
Second quarter	4,000,000	840,000	50	420,000	210,000	**210,000**
Third quarter	6,400,000	1,344,000	75	1,008,000	420,000	**588,000**
Fourth quarter	6,666,667	1,400,000	100	1,400,000	$1,008,000	**392,000**

Can PCC use its prior-year tax liability to determine its current-year estimated tax payments?

Answer: No. PCC reported a net operating loss last year and did not pay taxes, so it may not use its prior-year tax liability to determine its current-year estimated tax payments.

Can PCC use its current-year tax liability to determine its current-year estimated tax payments?

Answer: Yes. As we determined in Example 5-19, PCC's actual tax liability for the year is $1,180,557. So, PCC could have avoided estimated tax penalties by paying in $295,139 each quarter ($1,180,557 × 25%). However, it did not know this amount when it was required to make its estimated tax payments, so it would likely have used the annualized income method of determining its estimated tax payments to protect itself from penalties.

"Large" corporations, defined as corporations with over $1,000,000 of taxable income in *any* of the three years prior to the current year,[31] may use the prior-year tax liability to determine their first-quarter estimated tax payments only. If they use the prior-year tax liability to determine their first-quarter payment, their second-quarter payment must catch up their estimated payments. That is, the second-quarter payment must be large enough for the sum of the first- and second-quarter payments to equal or exceed 50 percent of the corporation's projected current-year tax liability.[32]

Example 5-23

What if: Assume that in 2021 PCC reported taxable income of $2,000,000 and a tax liability of $420,000. Further, PCC determined its required estimated tax payments under the annualized method as described in the previous example. What would be PCC's required minimum estimated tax payments for each quarter for 2022? (Ignore the current-year tax requirement because PCC is unsure what its current-year tax will be.)

(continued on page 5-30)

[31]§6655(g)(2).

[32]§6655(d).

Answer: $105,000 for the first quarter, $315,000 for the second quarter, $588,000 for the third quarter, and $392,000 for the fourth quarter, computed as follows:

Installment	(1) Estimated Tax Payment under Prior-Year Tax Exception	(2) Estimated Tax Payment under Annualized Method	(3) Required Cumulative Payment for Quarter × [sum of the lesser of (1) or (2) through quarter x]	(4) Prior Cumulative Payments	(5) [(3) − (4)] Required Estimated Tax Payment
First quarter	$105,000*	$210,000	$ 105,000	$ 0	**$105,000**
Second quarter	Not applicable*	210,000	420,000	105,000	**315,000**
Third quarter	Not applicable*	588,000	1,008,000	420,000	**588,000**
Fourth quarter	Not applicable*	320,000	1,400,000	1,008,000	**392,000**

*Because PCC is a large corporation, it may determine its first-quarter estimated tax payment using its prior-year liability ($420,000 × 25% = $105,000). However, it must use the annualized method to determine its second-, third-, and fourth-quarter required payments.

With its second installment, PCC must have paid in $420,000. Because it only paid in $105,000 with the first-quarter installment, it must pay $315,000 with its second-quarter payment.

What if: Assume the same facts as above, except that last year PCC paid $200,000 in tax and PCC is not a large corporation. What would be PCC's required minimum estimated tax payments for each quarter (ignore the current-year tax requirement)?

Answer: $50,000 for the first quarter, $50,000 for the second quarter, $50,000 for the third quarter, and $50,000 for the fourth quarter, computed as follows:

Installment	(1) Estimated Tax Payment under Prior Year Tax Exception ($200,000/4)	(2) Estimated Tax Payment under Annualized Method	(3) Required Cumulative Payment for Quarter × [sum of the lesser of (1) or (2) through quarter x]	(4) Prior Cumulative Payments	(5) [(3) − (4)] Required Estimated Tax Payment
First quarter	$50,000	$210,000	$ 50,000	$ 0	**$50,000**
Second quarter	50,000	210,000	100,000	50,000	**50,000**
Third quarter	50,000	588,000	150,000	100,000	**50,000**
Fourth quarter	50,000	320,000	200,000	150,000	**50,000**

PCC can use the prior-year tax to determine its minimum required estimated tax payments.

Corporations that have underpaid their estimated taxes for any quarter must pay an underpayment penalty calculated on Form 2220. The amount of the penalty is based on the underpayment rate (or interest rate), the amount of the underpayment, and the period of the underpayment. The interest rate is generally the federal short-term interest rate plus 3 percent. The period of the underpayment is the due date for the installment through the earlier of (1) the date the payment is made or (2) the due date of the tax return without extensions. The penalties are not deductible.[33]

CONCLUSION

A C corporation is a separate taxpaying entity from its stockholders. Consequently, it must compute and report its own taxable income to the IRS. This chapter described the process of computing a corporation's taxable income and the associated tax liability

[33]§6655(b)(2).

for C corporations. We learned that book income (after taxes) is the starting point for calculating taxable income. Corporations adjust their book income for book–tax differences that arise because they account for many items of income and deduction differently for book purposes than they do for tax purposes. Some of these book–tax differences are temporary (the differences balance out over time), and some are permanent in nature (they don't balance out over the long term). As we discover in the next chapter, the distinction between temporary and permanent book–tax differences is critical for corporations computing their income tax expense or benefit for financial accounting purposes.

Summary

Describe the corporate income tax formula and discuss tax considerations relating to corporations' accounting periods and accounting methods. LO 5-1

- A corporation's taxable income is gross income minus deductions.
- The corporate tax formula is similar to the individual formula except that corporations don't claim the qualified business income deduction and they don't itemize deductions or deduct a standard deduction.
- Corporations may generally elect any tax year for reporting their taxable income, but the year must coincide with their financial accounting year.
- The timing of a corporation's income and deductions depends on the corporation's overall accounting method and its methods for specific transactions.
- Corporations are generally required to use the accrual overall method of accounting. However, smaller corporations may be allowed to use the cash method.

Identify common permanent and temporary book–tax differences and compute a corporation's taxable income and associated income tax liability. LO 5-2

- Corporations typically compute taxable income by starting with book income and adjusting for book–tax differences.
- Book–tax differences are favorable when they reduce taxable income relative to book income and unfavorable when they increase it.
- Book–tax differences are permanent when the amount of an income or deduction item is different for book and tax purposes and the amount will not reverse in the future.
- Book–tax differences are temporary when the amount of an income or deduction item is different for book and tax purposes in the current year but the same for book and tax purposes over the long term. That is, temporary book–tax differences reverse over time.
- Common permanent book–tax differences include interest from municipal bonds (favorable), life insurance premiums on policies covering key employees (unfavorable), one-half of nonrestaurant-provided meals expense, entertainment expense, and federal income tax expense, among others.
- Common temporary book–tax differences include depreciation expense, gain or loss on sale of depreciable assets, bad-debt expense, purchased goodwill amortization, and warranty expense, among others.
- Stock options granted when FASB ASC Topic 718 applies can generate temporary and permanent book–tax differences.
- Corporations may not deduct net capital losses for tax purposes. However, they may carry them back three years and forward five years to offset net capital gains in those other years.
- Net operating losses incurred in tax years beginning before 2018 can be carried forward up to 20 years (and back 2 years) and can offset up to 100 percent of taxable income (before the NOL deduction) in a given year.
- Net operating losses incurred in tax years beginning after 2017 and before 2021 can be carried back five years and forward indefinitely. These NOLs can offset 100 percent of taxable income before the NOL deduction for tax years beginning before 2021. For tax years beginning after 2020, they can offset up to 80 percent of taxable income after deducting NOL carryovers from tax years beginning before 2018.

- Net operating losses incurred in tax years beginning after 2020 can be carried forward indefinitely but may not be carried back. They can offset up to 80 percent of taxable income after deducting NOL carryovers from tax years beginning before 2018.
- When corporations have NOL carryovers from multiple years, they apply the oldest first to offset taxable income in a given year.
- When computing their net operating losses for the year, corporations may not deduct net operating losses from other years or net capital loss carrybacks.
- Subject to limitation, corporations can deduct the amount of money, the fair market value of capital gain property, and the adjusted basis of ordinary income property they donate to charity.
- The charitable contribution deduction limit is 10 percent of taxable income before deducting the charitable contribution, the dividends-received deduction, and net capital loss carrybacks. Amounts in excess of the limitation can be carried forward for up to five years.
- Corporations are allowed a deduction for dividends received to help mitigate potential triple taxation of the income distributed as a dividend. The amount of the deduction depends on the corporation's ownership in the distributing corporation. The deduction is 50 percent if the ownership is less than 20 percent; the deduction is 65 percent if the ownership is at least 20 percent but less than 80 percent; and the deduction is 100 percent if the ownership is 80 percent or more.
- The dividends-received deduction (DRD) is subject to a taxable income limitation. This limitation does not apply if the full DRD extends or creates a net operating loss for the corporation in the current year.
- A corporation's tax rate is 21 percent.

LO 5-3 Describe a corporation's tax return reporting and estimated tax payment obligations.

- Corporations file their tax returns on Form 1120, which is due three and one-half months after the corporation's year-end. Corporations with a June 30 year-end must file within two and one-half months after year-end (through 2026). Corporations can apply for a six-month extension of the due date for filing (seven months for corporations with a June 30 year-end).
- Small corporations report their book–tax differences on Schedule M-1 of Form 1120. Large corporations (assets of $10 million or more) report them on Schedule M-3. Schedule M-3 requires much more detail than Schedule M-1.
- Corporations pay income taxes through estimated tax payments. Each payment should be 25 percent of their required annual payment. The installments are due on the 15th day of the 4th, 6th, 9th, and 12th months of the corporation's taxable year.
- Corporations' required annual payment is the least of (1) 100 percent of their current-year tax liability, (2) 100 percent of their prior-year tax liability (but only if they had a positive tax liability in the prior year), or (3) 100 percent of the estimated current-year tax liability using the annualized income method. Large corporations may rely on (2) only to compute their first-quarter estimated payment requirement.

KEY TERMS

DISCUSSION QUESTIONS

Discussion Questions are available in Connect®.

1. In general terms, identify the similarities and differences between the corporate taxable income formula and the individual taxable income formula. LO 5-1
2. Is a corporation's choice of its tax year independent from its year-end for financial accounting purposes? LO 5-1
3. Can C corporations use the cash method of accounting? Explain. LO 5-1
4. Briefly describe the process of computing a corporation's taxable income assuming the corporation must use GAAP to determine its book income. LO 5-2
5. What role do a corporation's audited financial statements play in determining its taxable income? LO 5-2
6. What is the difference between favorable and unfavorable book–tax differences? LO 5-2
7. What is the difference between permanent and temporary book–tax differences? LO 5-2
8. Why is it important to be able to determine whether a particular book–tax difference is permanent or temporary? LO 5-2
9. Describe the relation between the book–tax differences associated with depreciation expense and the book–tax differences associated with gain or loss on disposition of depreciable assets. LO 5-2
10. A Corporation owns stock in B Corporation, and A Corporation receives a dividend from B Corporation. Ignoring the dividends-received deduction, what book–tax differences will A report for the year relating to its investment in B? Explain. LO 5-2
11. Describe how goodwill with a zero basis for tax purposes but not for book purposes leads to a permanent book–tax difference when the book goodwill is written off as impaired. LO 5-2
12. Describe how purchased goodwill leads to temporary book–tax differences. LO 5-2
13. Describe the book–tax differences that arise from incentive stock options. LO 5-2
14. Describe the book–tax differences that arise from nonqualified stock options. LO 5-2
15. How do corporations account for capital gains and losses for tax purposes? How is this different from the way individuals account for capital gains and losses? LO 5-2
16. What are the common book–tax differences relating to accounting for capital gains and losses? Do these differences create favorable or unfavorable book-to-tax adjustments? LO 5-2
17. What are the carryover and carryback periods for a net operating loss? Does a corporation have the option to choose the years to which it carries back a NOL? Explain. LO 5-2
18. Distinguish the tax treatment of a NOL incurred in 2017, a NOL incurred in 2020, and a NOL incurred in 2022. LO 5-2
19. When a corporation has NOL carryovers arising in different years, can it choose which NOL carryover to deduct first in a given year? Explain. LO 5-2
20. A corporation commissioned an accounting firm to recalculate the way it accounted for leasing transactions. With the new calculations, the corporation was able to file amended tax returns for the past few years that increased the corporation's net operating loss carryover from $3,000,000 to $5,000,000. Was the corporation wise to pay the accountants for their work that led to the increase in the NOL carryover? What factors should be considered in making this determination? LO 5-2
21. Compare and contrast the general rule for determining the amount of the charitable contribution if the corporation contributes capital gain property versus ordinary income property. LO 5-2
22. Which limitations might restrict a corporation's deduction for a cash charitable contribution in 2022? Explain how to determine the amount of the limitation. LO 5-2
23. For tax purposes, what happens to a corporation's charitable contributions that are not deducted in the current year because of the taxable income limitation? LO 5-2

LO 5-2 24. What are common book–tax differences relating to corporate charitable contributions? Are these differences favorable or unfavorable?

LO 5-2 25. Why does Congress provide the dividends-received deduction for corporations receiving dividends?

LO 5-2 26. How does a corporation determine the percentage for its dividends-received deduction? Explain.

LO 5-2 27. What limitations apply to the amount of the allowable dividends-received deduction?

LO 5-2 28. How many tax brackets are there in the corporate tax rate schedule?

LO 5-3 29. How is Schedule M-1 similar to and different from Schedule M-3? How does a corporation determine whether it must complete Schedule M-1 or Schedule M-3 when it completes its tax return?

LO 5-3 30. What is the due date for a calendar-year corporation tax return Form 1120 for 2022? Is it possible to extend the due date? Explain.

LO 5-3 31. How does a corporation determine the minimum amount of estimated tax payments it must make to avoid underpayment penalties? How do these rules differ for large corporations?

LO 5-3 32. Describe the annualized income method for determining a corporation's required estimated tax payments. What advantages does this method have over other methods?

PROBLEMS

Select problems are available in Connect®.

LO 5-1 33. LNS Corporation reports book revenue of $2,000,000. Included in the $2,000,000 is $15,000 of tax-exempt interest income. LNS reports $1,345,000 in ordinary and necessary business expenses. What is LNS Corporation's taxable income for the year?

LO 5-1 34. ATW Corporation currently uses the FIFO method of accounting for its inventory for book and tax purposes. Its beginning inventory for the current year was $8,000,000. Its ending inventory for the current year was $7,000,000. If ATW had been using the LIFO method of accounting for its inventory, its beginning inventory would have been $7,000,000 and its ending inventory would have been $5,500,000.

a) How much more in taxes did ATW Corporation pay for the current year because it used the FIFO method of accounting for inventory rather than the LIFO method?

b) Why would ATW use the FIFO method of accounting if doing so causes it to pay more taxes on a present value basis? (Note that the tax laws don't allow corporations to use the LIFO method of accounting for inventory unless they also use the LIFO method of accounting for inventory for book purposes.)

LO 5-1 35. ELS Corporation reported gross receipts for 2019–2021 for Scenarios A, B, and C as follows:

Year	Scenario A	Scenario B	Scenario C
2019	$26,000,000	$25,000,000	$27,500,000
2020	$27,000,000	$27,000,000	$27,000,000
2021	$27,900,000	$29,500,000	$26,500,000

a) Is ELS allowed to use the cash method of accounting in 2022 under Scenario A?

b) Is ELS allowed to use the cash method of accounting in 2022 under Scenario B?

c) Is ELS allowed to use the cash method of accounting in 2022 under Scenario C?

LO 5-2 36. On its year 1 financial statements, Seatax Corporation, an accrual-method taxpayer, reported federal income tax expense of $570,000. On its year 1 tax return, it reported a tax liability of $650,000. During year 1, Seatax made estimated tax payments of $700,000. What book–tax difference, if any, associated with its federal income tax expense should Seatax have reported when computing its year 1 taxable income? Is the difference favorable or unfavorable? Is it temporary or permanent?

37. Assume Maple Corp. has just completed the third year of its existence (year 3). The table below indicates Maple's ending book inventory for each year and the additional §263A costs it was required to include in its ending inventory. Maple immediately expensed these costs for book purposes. In year 2, Maple sold all of its year 1 ending inventory, and in year 3 it sold all of its year 2 ending inventory. LO 5-2

	Year 1	Year 2	Year 3
Ending book inventory	$2,400,000	$2,700,000	$2,040,000
Additional §263A costs	60,000	70,000	40,000
Ending tax inventory	$2,460,000	$2,770,000	$2,080,000

a) What book–tax difference associated with its inventory did Maple report in year 1? Was the difference favorable or unfavorable? Was it permanent or temporary?
b) What book–tax difference associated with its inventory did Maple report in year 2? Was the difference favorable or unfavorable? Was it permanent or temporary?
c) What book–tax difference associated with its inventory did Maple report in year 3? Was the difference favorable or unfavorable? Was it permanent or temporary?

38. JDog Corporation owns stock in Oscar Inc. valued at $2,000,000 at the beginning of the year and $2,200,000 at year-end. JDog received a $10,000 dividend from Oscar Inc. What temporary book–tax differences associated with its ownership in Oscar stock will JDog report for the year in the following alternative scenarios (income difference only—ignore the dividends-received deduction)? LO 5-2
a) JDog owns 5 percent of the Oscar Inc. stock. Oscar's income for the year was $500,000.
b) JDog owns 40 percent of the Oscar Inc. stock. Oscar's income for the year was $500,000.

39. On July 1 of year 1, Riverside Corp. (RC), a calendar-year taxpayer, acquired the assets of another business in a taxable acquisition. When the purchase price was allocated to the assets purchased, RC determined it had purchased $1,200,000 of goodwill for both book and tax purposes. At the end of year 1, RC determined that the goodwill had not been impaired during the year. In year 2, however, RC concluded that $200,000 of the goodwill had been impaired and wrote down the goodwill by $200,000 for book purposes. LO 5-2
a) What book–tax difference associated with its goodwill should RC report in year 1? Is it favorable or unfavorable? Is it permanent or temporary?
b) What book–tax difference associated with its goodwill should RC report in year 2? Is it favorable or unfavorable? Is it permanent or temporary?

40. Assume that on January 1, year 1, ABC Inc. issued 5,000 stock options with an estimated value of $10 per option. Each option entitles the owner to purchase one share of ABC stock for $25 a share (the per share price of ABC stock on January 1, year 1, when the options were granted). The options vest at the end of the day on December 31, year 2. All 5,000 stock options were exercised in year 3 when the ABC stock was valued at $31 per share. Identify ABC's year 1, 2, and 3 tax deductions and book–tax differences (indicate whether permanent and/or temporary) associated with the stock options under the following alternative scenarios: LO 5-2
a) The stock options are incentive stock options.
b) The stock options are nonqualified stock options.

41. Assume that on January 1, year 1, XYZ Corp. issued 1,000 nonqualified stock options with an estimated value of $4 per option. Each option entitles the owner to purchase one share of XYZ stock for $14 a share (the per share price of XYZ stock on January 1, year 1, when the options were granted). The options vest 25 percent a year (on December 31) for four years (beginning with year 1). All 500 stock options that had vested to that point were exercised in year 3 when the XYZ stock was valued at $20 per share. No other options were exercised in year 3 or year 4. Identify XYZ's LO 5-2

year 1, 2, 3, and 4 tax deductions and book–tax difference (identify as permanent and/or temporary) associated with the stock options.

LO 5-2

42. What book–tax differences in year 1 and year 2 associated with its capital gains and losses would ABD Inc. report in the following alternative scenarios? Identify each book–tax difference as favorable or unfavorable and as permanent or temporary.

a)

	Year 1	Year 2
Capital gains	$20,000	$5,000
Capital losses	8,000	0

b)

	Year 1	Year 2
Capital gains	$ 8,000	$5,000
Capital losses	20,000	0

c)

	Year 1	Year 2
Capital gains	$ 0	$50,000
Capital losses	25,000	30,000

d)

	Year 1	Year 2
Capital gains	$ 0	$40,000
Capital losses	25,000	0

e) Answer for year 6 only.

	Year 1	Years 2–5	Year 6
Capital gains	$ 0	$ 0	$15,000
Capital losses	10,000	0	0

f) Answer for year 7 only.

	Year 1	Years 2–6	Year 7
Capital gains	$ 0	$ 0	$15,000
Capital losses	10,000	0	0

LO 5-2

43. What book–tax differences in year 1 and year 2 associated with its capital gains and losses would DEF Inc. report in the following alternative scenarios? Identify each book–tax difference as favorable or unfavorable and as permanent or temporary.

a) In year 1, DEF recognized a loss of $15,000 on land that it had held for investment. In year 1, it also recognized a $30,000 gain on equipment it had purchased a few years ago. The equipment sold for $50,000 and had an adjusted basis of $20,000. DEF had deducted $40,000 of depreciation on the equipment. In year 2, DEF recognized a capital loss of $2,000.

b) In year 1, DEF recognized a loss of $15,000 on land that it had held for investment. It also recognized a $20,000 gain on equipment it had purchased a few years ago. The equipment sold for $50,000 and had an adjusted basis of $30,000. DEF had deducted $15,000 of tax depreciation on the equipment. There were no capital asset transactions in year 2.

LO 5-2

44. B12 Corp. is currently in the sixth year of its existence (2022). In 2017–2021, it reported the following income and (losses) (before net operating loss carryovers or carrybacks).

2017	$ (70,000)
2018	(30,000)
2019	60,000
2020	140,000
2021	(225,000)
2022	300,000

What is B12's 2022 taxable income after the NOL deduction (assume it does not elect to forgo any carrybacks, if applicable)? What is its 2022 book–tax difference associated with its NOL? Is it favorable or unfavorable? Is it permanent or temporary?

45. In 2022 Hill Corporation reported a net operating loss of $10,000 that it carried forward to 2023. In 2022 Hill also reported a net capital loss of $3,000 that it carried forward to 2023. In 2023, ignoring any carryovers from other years, Hill reported a loss for tax purposes of $50,000. The current-year loss includes a $12,000 net capital gain. What is Hill's 2023 net operating loss? LO 5-2

46. WCC Corp. has a $100,000 net operating loss carryover to 2022 from a previous year. Assume that it reported $75,000 of taxable income in 2022 (before the net operating loss deduction) and $30,000 of taxable income in 2023 (before the net operating loss deduction). LO 5-2
    a) What is WCC's taxable income in 2022 and 2023 (after the net operating loss deduction), assuming the $100,000 NOL carryover originated in 2017?
    b) What is WCC's taxable income in 2022 and 2023 (after the net operating loss deduction), assuming the $100,000 NOL carryover originated in 2020 and WCC elected to forgo the NOL carry back option?
    c) Assuming the same facts as in part (b), what is WCC's book–tax difference associated with the NOL in 2022 and in 2023? Identify the book–tax difference for each year as permanent or temporary.

47. In 2022, SML Corp. reported taxable income of $100,000 before any NOL deductions. SML has a $170,000 NOL carryover that originated in 2017 and a $90,000 NOL carryover that originated in 2020. What is SML's 2022 taxable income after the NOL deduction (assuming it elects to forgo any NOL carryback)? What NOLs can SML carry over to 2023? LO 5-2

48. Cedar Corporation reported a $25,000,000 net operating loss in 2022. It also has a $100,000 NOL carryover from 2017. In 2023, Cedar reported taxable income before any NOL carryovers of $20,000,000. What is Cedar's taxable income in 2023 after the NOL deduction, and what is its NOL carryover, if any, to 2024? LO 5-2

49. Golf Corp. (GC), a calendar-year, accrual-method corporation, held its directors' meeting on December 15 of year 1. During the meeting, the board of directors authorized GC to pay a $75,000 charitable contribution to the World Golf Foundation, a qualifying charity. LO 5-2
    a) If GC actually pays $50,000 of this contribution on January 15 of year 2 and the remaining $25,000 on or before April 15 of year 2, what book–tax difference will it report associated with the contribution in year 1 (assume the income limit does not apply)? Is it favorable or unfavorable? Is it permanent or temporary?
    b) Assuming the same facts as in part (a), what book–tax difference will GC report in year 2 (assume the income limit does not apply)? Is it favorable or unfavorable?
    c) If GC actually pays $50,000 of this contribution on January 15 of year 2 and the remaining $25,000 on May 15 of year 2, what book–tax difference will it report associated with the contribution in year 1 (assume the income limit does not apply)? Is it favorable or unfavorable? Is it permanent or temporary?
    d) Assuming the same facts as in part (c), what book–tax difference will GC report in year 2 (assume the income limit does not apply)? Is it favorable or unfavorable?

50. In 2022, OCC Corp. made a charitable donation of $400,000 to the International Rescue Committee (a qualifying charity). For the year, OCC reported taxable income of $1,500,000 before deducting any charitable contributions, before deducting its $20,000 dividends-received deduction, and before deducting its $40,000 NOL carryover from last year. LO 5-2
    a) What amount of the $400,000 donation is OCC allowed to deduct for tax purposes in 2022, what is the carryover to 2023, and when does the carryover expire?

b) Assume that in 2023, OCC did not make any charitable donations and that it is allowed to deduct its full charitable contribution carryover, if any, from 2022. What book–tax difference associated with the charitable contributions will OCC report in 2023? Is the difference favorable or unfavorable? Is it permanent or temporary?

LO 5-2

51. In 2022, LAA Inc. made a charitable donation of $100,000 to the Trevor Project (a qualifying charity). For the year, LAA reported taxable income of $550,000, which included a $100,000 charitable contribution deduction (before limitation), a $50,000 dividends-received deduction, and a $10,000 net operating loss carryover from 2021. What is LAA Inc.'s charitable contribution deduction for 2022?

LO 5-2
research

52. Coattail Corporation (CC) manufactures and sells women's and children's coats. This year, CC donated 1,000 coats to a qualified public charity. The charity distributed the coats to needy women and children throughout the region. At the time of the contribution, the fair market value of each coat was $80. Determine the amount of CC's charitable contribution (the taxable income limitation does not apply) for the coats, assuming the following:

a) CC's adjusted basis in each coat was $30.

b) CC's adjusted basis in each coat was $10.

LO 5-2
research

53. Maple Corp. owns several pieces of highly valued paintings that are on display in the corporation's headquarters. This year, it donated one of the paintings valued at $100,000 (adjusted basis of $25,000) to a local museum for the museum to display. What is the amount of Maple Corp.'s charitable contribution deduction for the painting (assuming income limitations do not apply)? What would be Maple's deduction if the museum sold the painting one month after it received it from Maple? (Assume Maple Corp. had prior knowledge of the museum's intention to sell the painting after receiving it.)

LO 5-2

54. Riverbend Inc. received a $200,000 dividend from stock it held in Hobble Corporation. Riverbend's taxable income is $2,100,000 before deducting the dividends-received deduction (DRD), a $40,000 NOL carryover, and a $100,000 charitable contribution.

a) What is Riverbend's deductible DRD assuming it owns 10 percent of Hobble Corporation?

b) Assuming the facts in part (a), what is Riverbend's marginal tax rate on the dividend after taking the DRD into account?

c) What is Riverbend's DRD assuming it owns 60 percent of Hobble Corporation?

d) Assuming the facts in part (c), what is Riverbend's marginal tax rate on the dividend?

e) What is Riverbend's DRD assuming it owns 85 percent of Hobble Corporation (and is part of the same affiliated group)?

f) Assuming the facts in part (e), what is Riverbend's marginal tax rate on the dividend?

LO 5-2

55. Wasatch Corp. (WC) received a $200,000 dividend from Tager Corporation (TC). WC owns 15 percent of the TC stock. Compute WC's deductible DRD in each of the following situations:

a) WC's taxable income (loss) without the dividend income or the DRD is $10,000.

b) WC's taxable income (loss) without the dividend income or the DRD is $(10,000).

c) WC's taxable income (loss) without the dividend income or the DRD is $(99,000).

d) WC's taxable income (loss) without the dividend income or the DRD is $(101,000).

e) WC's taxable income (loss) without the dividend income or the DRD is $(500,000).

f) What is WC's book–tax difference associated with its DRD in part (a)? Is the difference favorable or unfavorable? Is it permanent or temporary?

56. Compute SWK Inc.'s tax liability for each of the following scenarios: LO 5-3
   a) SWK's taxable income is $60,000.
   b) SWK's taxable income is $275,000.
   c) SWK's taxable income is $50,000,000.

57. Last year, TBA Corporation, a calendar-year taxpayer, reported a tax liability of $100,000. TBA confidently anticipates a current-year tax liability of $240,000. What minimum estimated tax payments should TBA make for the first, second, third, and fourth quarters, respectively (ignore the annualized income method), assuming the following: LO 5-3
   a) TBA is not considered to be a large corporation for estimated tax purposes.
   b) TBA is considered to be a large corporation for estimated tax purposes.

58. Last year, BTA Corporation, a calendar-year taxpayer, reported a net operating loss of $10,000 and a $0 tax liability. BTA confidently anticipates a current-year tax liability of $240,000. What minimum estimated tax payments should BTA make for the first, second, third, and fourth quarters, respectively (ignore the annualized income method), assuming the following: LO 5-3
   a) BTA is not considered to be a large corporation for estimated tax purposes.
   b) BTA is considered to be a large corporation for estimated tax purposes.

59. For the current year, LNS Corporation reported the following taxable income at the end of its first, second, and third quarters. What are LNS's minimum first-, second-, third-, and fourth-quarter estimated tax payments, using the annualized income method? LO 5-3

Quarter-End	Cumulative Taxable Income
First	$1,000,000
Second	1,600,000
Third	2,400,000

60. Last year, JL Corporation's tax liability was $900,000. For the current year, JL Corporation reported the following taxable income at the end of its first, second, and third quarters (see table below). What are JL's minimum required first-, second-, third-, and fourth-quarter estimated tax payments (ignore the actual current-year tax safe harbor)? LO 5-3 planning

Quarter-End	Cumulative Taxable Income
First	$ 500,000
Second	1,250,000
Third	2,250,000

61. Last year, Cougar Corp. (CC) reported a net operating loss of $25,000. In the current year, CC expected its current-year tax liability to be $260,000, so it made four equal estimated tax payments of $65,000 each. Cougar closed its books at the end of each quarter. The following schedule reports CC's taxable income at the end of each quarter: LO 5-3

Quarter-End	Cumulative Taxable Income
First	$ 300,000
Second	700,000
Third	1,000,000
Fourth	1,500,000

CC's current-year tax liability on $1,500,000 of taxable income is $315,000. Does CC owe underpayment penalties on its estimated tax payments? If so, for which quarters does it owe the penalty?

COMPREHENSIVE PROBLEMS

Select problems are available in Connect®. 

62. Compute MV Corp.'s 2022 taxable income given the following information relating to its year 1 activities. Also, compute MV's Schedule M-1 assuming that MV's federal income tax expense for book purposes is $100,000.
    - Gross profit from inventory sales of $500,000 (no book–tax differences).
    - Dividends MV received from 25 percent–owned corporation of $100,000 (assume this is also MV's pro rata share of the distributing corporation's earnings).
    - Expenses *other than* DRD, charitable contribution (CC), and net operating loss (NOL) are $350,000 (no book–tax differences).
    - NOL carryover from 2021 of $10,000.
    - Cash charitable contribution of $120,000.

63. Compute HC Inc.'s current-year taxable income given the following information relating to its current-year (2022) activities. Also, compute HC's Schedule M-1 assuming that HC's federal income tax expense for book purposes is $30,000.
    - Gross profit from inventory sales of $310,000 (no book–tax differences).
    - Dividends HC received from 28 percent–owned corporation of $120,000 (this is also HC's pro rata share of the corporation's earnings).
    - Expenses *other than* DRD, charitable contribution (CC), and net operating loss (NOL) are $300,000 (no book–tax differences).
    - NOL carryover from prior year of $12,000.
    - Cash charitable contribution of $50,000.

64. Timpanogos Inc. is an accrual-method, calendar-year corporation. For 2022, it reported financial statement income after taxes of $1,342,000. Timpanogos provided the following information relating to its 2022 activities:

Life insurance proceeds as a result of CEO's death	$ 200,000
Revenue from sales (for both book and tax purposes)	2,000,000
Premiums paid on the key-person life insurance policies; the policies have no cash surrender value	21,000
Charitable contributions	180,000
Cost of goods sold for book and tax purposes	300,000
Interest income on tax-exempt bonds	40,000
Interest paid on loan obtained to purchase tax-exempt bonds	45,000
Rental income payments received and earned in 2022	15,000
Rental income payments received in 2021 but earned in 2022	10,000
Rental income payments received in 2022 but not earned by year-end	30,000
Tax depreciation	55,000
Book depreciation	25,000
Net capital loss	42,000
Federal income tax expense for books in 2022	310,000

Required:

a) Reconcile book income to taxable income for Timpanogos Inc. Be sure to start with book income and identify all of the adjustments necessary to arrive at taxable income.
b) Identify each book–tax difference as either permanent or temporary.

c) Complete Schedule M-1 for Timpanogos.
d) Compute Timpanogos Inc.'s tax liability.

65. XYZ is a calendar-year corporation that began business on January 1, 2022. For the year, it reported the following information in its current-year audited income statement. Notes with important tax information are provided below.

Required:

Identify the book-to-tax adjustments for XYZ.

a) Reconcile book income to taxable income and identify each book–tax difference as temporary or permanent.
b) Compute XYZ's income tax liability.
c) Complete XYZ's Schedule M-1.
d) Complete XYZ's Form 1120, page 1 (use the most current form available). Ignore estimated tax penalties when completing this form.
e) Determine the quarters for which XYZ is subject to penalties for the underpayment of estimated taxes (see assumptions and estimated tax information below).

XYZ Corp. Income Statement for Current Year	Book Income	Book to Tax Adjustments (Dr.)	Cr.	Taxable Income
Revenue from sales	$ 40,000,000			
Cost of goods sold	(27,000,000)			
Gross profit	$ 13,000,000			
Other income:				
Income from investment in corporate stock	300,000[1]			
Interest income	20,000[2]			
Capital gains (losses)	(4,000)			
Gain or loss from disposition of fixed assets	3,000[3]			
Miscellaneous income	50,000			
Gross income	$ 13,369,000			
Expenses:				
Compensation	(7,500,000)[4]			
Stock option compensation	(200,000)[5]			
Advertising	(1,350,000)			
Repairs and maintenance	(75,000)			
Rent	(22,000)			
Bad debt expense	(41,000)[6]			
Depreciation	(1,400,000)[7]			
Warranty expenses	(70,000)[8]			
Charitable donations	(500,000)[9]			
Meals (all from restaurants)	(18,000)			
Goodwill impairment	(30,000)[10]			
Organizational expenditures	(44,000)[11]			
Other expenses	(140,000)[12]			
Total expenses	$(11,390,000)			
Income before taxes	$ 1,979,000			
Provision for income taxes	(400,000)[13]			
Net income after taxes	$ 1,579,000			

Notes

1. XYZ owns 30 percent of the outstanding Hobble Corp. (HC) stock. HC reported $1,000,000 of income for the year. XYZ accounted for its investment in HC under the equity method, and it recorded its pro rata share of HC's earnings for the year. HC also distributed a $200,000 dividend to XYZ. For tax purposes, HC reports the actual dividend received as income, not the pro rata share of HC's earnings.
2. Of the $20,000 interest income, $5,000 was from a City of Seattle bond, $7,000 was from a Tacoma City bond, $6,000 was from a fully taxable corporate bond, and the remaining $2,000 was from a money market account.
3. This gain is from equipment that XYZ purchased in February and sold in December (i.e., it does not qualify as §1231 gain).
4. This includes total officer compensation of $2,500,000 (no one officer received more than $1,000,000 compensation).
5. This amount is the portion of incentive stock option compensation that was expensed during the year (recipients are officers).
6. XYZ actually wrote off $27,000 of its accounts receivable as uncollectible.
7. Tax depreciation was $1,900,000.
8. In the current year, XYZ did not make any actual payments on warranties it provided to customers.
9. XYZ made $500,000 of cash contributions to charities during the year.
10. On July 1 of this year, XYZ acquired the assets of another business. In the process, it acquired $300,000 of goodwill. At the end of the year, XYZ wrote off $30,000 of the goodwill as impaired.
11. XYZ expensed all of its organizational expenditures for book purposes. XYZ expensed the maximum amount of organizational expenditures allowed for tax purposes.
12. The other expenses do not contain any items with book–tax differences.
13. This is an estimated tax provision (federal tax expense) for the year. Assume that XYZ is not subject to state income taxes.

Estimated Tax Information

XYZ made four equal estimated tax payments totaling $360,000 ($90,000 per quarter). For purposes of estimated tax liabilities, assume XYZ was in existence in 2021 and that in 2021 it reported a tax liability of $500,000. During 2022, XYZ determined its taxable income at the end of each of the four quarters as follows:

Quarter-End	Cumulative Taxable Income (Loss)
First	$ 400,000
Second	1,100,000
Third	1,400,000

Finally, assume that XYZ is not a large corporation for purposes of estimated tax calculations.

UWorld Roger CPA Review

Sample CPA Exam questions from Roger CPA Review are available in Connect as support for the topics in this text. These Multiple Choice Questions and Task-Based Simulations include expert-written explanations and solutions and provide a starting point for students to become familiar with the content and functionality of the actual CPA Exam.

chapter **6**

Accounting for Income Taxes

Learning Objectives

Upon completing this chapter, you should be able to:

LO 6-1 Describe the objectives of FASB ASC Topic 740, *Income Taxes,* and the income tax provision process.

LO 6-2 Calculate the current and deferred income tax expense or benefit components of a company's income tax provision.

LO 6-3 Determine how to calculate a valuation allowance.

LO 6-4 Explain how a company accounts for its uncertain income tax positions under FASB ASC Topic 740.

LO 6-5 Describe how a company computes and discloses the components of its effective tax rate.

mentatdgt/Shutterstock

Storyline Summary

Elise Brandon (she/her/hers)

Employment status:	Tax associate for a large public accounting firm.

Assigned to prepare the federal income tax provision and income-tax-related balance sheet accounts and footnote disclosures for Premiere Computer Corporation, a nonaudit client.

Premiere Computer Corporation
Medium-sized publicly traded company.
Manufactures and sells computers and computer-related equipment. Calendar-year taxpayer.

Tax rate:	21 percent.

Elise felt a great sense of accomplishment when she completed her review of the federal income tax return for Premiere Computer Corporation (PCC). She was glad the return was filed on time and did not need to be extended. With the tax return filed, Elise was assigned to help the PCC tax department compute the federal **income tax provision** (financial income tax expense) for the company's soon-to-be-published income statement and to determine the correct amounts in the company's income-tax-related balance sheet accounts.[1] She also was given responsibility for helping prepare the income tax note to the financial statements.[2]

Elise was aware that, as a result of the stringent independence requirements imposed by the Sarbanes-Oxley Act, her colleagues in the tax group were getting a lot of engagements to help prepare the income tax provision for nonaudit clients. In fact, her firm considered accounting for income taxes to be a "core competency" for all tax staff and prepared a training course for everyone. Having recently attended the firm's training on the subject, Elise was eager to apply her new knowledge to an actual client situation. She knew that developing her skill set in this complex topic would make her more valuable to her firm and her clients.

(to be continued . . .)

[1]The tax provision is typically completed in the month or two following year-end, whereas the filing date of the tax return is several months later. Due to the chapter sequence, Elise will complete the provision after the tax return from the Corporate Operations chapter. We discuss the timing of the provision and return later in the chapter.

[2]In today's post-Sarbanes-Oxley environment, staff from public accounting firms that are not a company's auditors often are hired to help prepare the company's income tax provision under FASB ASC Topic 740 because many companies do not have staff with the expertise to make this calculation.

Most of the items of income (revenue) and deductions (expenses) that are included in a company's taxable income also are included in the company's net (book) income before taxes. Not all of these items are included in the computations in the same accounting period, however, which creates a "temporary" mismatch of the amounts of these items included in taxable income and pretax book income in a given year. Other items are included in only one of the computations, which creates a "permanent" mismatch of the amount of these items included in taxable income and pretax book income. A company must take these temporary and permanent differences into account in computing its income tax expense or (benefit) on the income statement and its deferred income taxes payable (liabilities) or refundable (assets) on the balance sheet.

FASB Accounting Standards Codification Topic 740, *Income Taxes* (hereafter, ASC 740), governs the computation and disclosure of a company's income tax provision (expense or benefit) and its expected future income tax liabilities or benefits related to "events" that have been recorded on either the financial statement or the tax return. ASC 740 deals with the majority of accounting and reporting guidance related to income taxes. Accounting for income taxes guidance related to accounting for investments under the equity method, stock compensation, business combinations, foreign currency translation, and industry subtopics such as real estate, entertainment, and oil and gas is embedded within the ASC topic that deals with each of these issues. The Emerging Issues Task Force (EITF)[3] and the Securities and Exchange Commission continue to provide guidance on issues related to accounting for income taxes.

A company's failure to accurately compute the income tax provision and related balance sheet accounts can lead to the issuance of a material weakness statement by the auditor and, in some cases, a restatement of the financial statements. Not surprisingly, individuals who understand these complex and sometimes counterintuitive rules are in great demand by public accounting firms and industry.

This chapter discusses the basic rules for how a company computes and discloses its current-year income tax provision and its future income tax consequences, using the facts related to Premiere Computer Corporation in the Corporate Operations chapter. We focus on the portion of the provision that relates to federal income taxes.

LO 6-1

ACCOUNTING FOR INCOME TAXES AND THE INCOME TAX PROVISION PROCESS

In addition to filing its federal, state and local, and non-U.S. income tax returns, Premiere Computer Corporation, along with all other U.S. publicly traded corporations and many privately held corporations, must prepare financial statements in accordance with generally accepted accounting principles (GAAP) issued by the FASB (Financial Accounting Standards Board). Under GAAP, a company includes as part of its income statement a "provision" for the income tax expense or benefit that is associated with the pretax net income or loss reported on the income statement. The income tax provision includes not only current-year taxes payable or refundable, but also future income tax consequences, that result from differences in the timing of when an item is reported on the tax return compared to the financial statement. The company records the amount of future income tax benefits as a **deferred tax asset** and the amount of future income tax obligations as a **deferred tax liability** on its balance sheet. Practitioners use the term "provision" to refer to either all of the income tax expense reported in the financial statements or the specific components of income tax expense such as "the current tax provision" or the "deferred tax provision." It is often a matter of context to determine how the term is being used. In this chapter, we use the term *provision* in both contexts. The income tax provision process refers to the entire income tax process, whereas the current or deferred tax provisions refer to individual components of the process.

[3]The Emerging Issues Task Force is a committee of accounting practitioners who assist the Financial Accounting Standards Board in providing timely guidance on emerging issues and the implementation of existing standards.

TAXES IN THE REAL WORLD Material Weaknesses in Tax Reporting

Taxes remain a primary area for internal control issues due to their size and complexity of the issues. The consequences of errors can be severe. As an example, on October 29, 2019, Mattel Inc. announced the completion of a whistleblower investigation into accounting errors that occurred in 2017. The investigation found that in the third quarter of 2017, Mattel Inc. understated its income tax expense by reducing its deferred tax valuation allowance by $109 million, understating its loss. Rather than disclose the error to the CEO and the board, the company changed its accounting for an intangible asset in the fourth quarter of 2017, which resulted in correcting the third quarter error. As a result of the investigation, Mattel determined there were material weaknesses in its internal control over financial reporting. To remediate the identified issues, Mattel restated its 2016–2018 annual financial statements and replaced several financial employees, including the CFO, controller, and Senior Vice President of Tax. In addition, Mattel's outside auditor replaced its lead audit partner and other key members of the audit team.

Source: Based on Mattel Inc.'s 8-K filing dated October 29, 2019. Available at https://investors.mattel.com/node/31261/html.

Why Is Accounting for Income Taxes So Complex?

The basic principles that underlie ASC 740 are fairly straightforward, but the application of ASC 740 can be very complex. Much of the complexity is due to the fact that the U.S. tax laws are complex and often ambiguous. In addition, companies frequently prepare their financial statements (Form 10-K) much earlier than their corresponding tax returns. For example, a calendar-year corporation generally files its Form 10-K with the SEC in February or early March, but it might not file its federal income tax return (Form 1120) with the Internal Revenue Service (IRS) until October.[4] As a result, management often must exercise a high degree of judgment in estimating the income tax return positions currently and in future years when a tax return position might be challenged by the tax authorities. After the tax return has been filed, it may take a number of years before it is audited by the IRS and the final tax liability is determined.[5] For example, Microsoft Corporation disclosed in its Form 10-K for the year ended June 30, 2021, that the IRS is auditing Microsoft's tax returns for 2004–2017.

Objectives of ASC 740

ASC 740 applies only to *income* taxes levied by the U.S. federal government, U.S. state and local governments, and non-U.S. (foreign) governments. The FASB defines an *income tax* as a tax *based on income*. This definition excludes property taxes, excise taxes, sales taxes, and value-added taxes. Companies report nonincome taxes as expenses in the computation of their net income before taxes.

ASC 740 has two primary objectives. One is to "recognize the amount of taxes payable or refundable in the current year," referred to as the **current tax liability (asset).**[6] A second objective is to "recognize deferred tax liabilities and assets for the future tax consequences of events that have been recognized in an entity's financial statements or tax returns."[7] Both objectives relate to reporting a company's income tax amounts on the balance sheet, not on the income statement. The FASB refers to this method as the "asset

[4]The due date for a federal income tax return filed by a calendar-year corporation is April 15, but corporations can request a six-month extension to October 15 by filing Form 7004 and paying any remaining tax liability.

[5]Although the statute of limitations for a filed income tax return is three years, large corporations often agree to extend the statute for a longer period of time to allow the IRS to audit the return. As a result, a corporation's tax return may not be audited for five or more years from the date it is filed.

[6]ASC 740-10-10-1(a).

[7]Accounting Standards Update No. 2018-05. Income Taxes (Topic 740). March 2018.

and liability approach" to accounting for income taxes.[8] The FASB chose this approach because it is the most consistent with the definitions in FASB Concepts Statement No. 6, *Elements of Financial Statements,* and produces the most useful and understandable information.[9] So, some of the complexity of the income tax provision comes from meeting these two objectives.

To compute the deferred tax liability or asset, a company calculates the future tax effects attributable to temporary book and tax differences and **tax carryovers.**[10] As you learned in the Corporate Operations chapter, temporary differences generally can be thought of as revenue (income) or expenses (deductions) that will appear on both the income statement and the tax return but in different periods. Temporary differences that cause cumulative taxable income to be less than cumulative pretax book income create deferred tax liabilities. Thus, deferred tax liabilities represent future tax obligations resulting from the reversal of favorable originating book–tax differences. In contrast, temporary differences that cause cumulative taxable income to exceed cumulative pretax book income create deferred tax assets, which represent future tax benefits resulting from the reversal of unfavorable originating book–tax differences.

Examples 6-1 and 6-2 illustrate the two objectives of ASC 740.

Example 6-1

What if: Suppose PPC begins business in year 1. PPC uses the accrual method of accounting for book purposes and the cash method for tax purposes and has a 25 percent tax rate. The company has two sources of revenue in year 1: $100 of interest income and $100 from the sale of services on account. In year 2, PPC again earns $100 of interest income but does not sell any additional services. It receives $100 from its customer in payment for the year 1 sale. The company does not have any expenses other than income taxes in years 1 and 2. How would these transactions be reflected in PPC's income statement if PPC reported its income taxes as calculated on its tax return (i.e., no deferred taxes)?

Answer:

	Book (Accrual Method)			**Tax (Cash Method)**	
	Year 1	**Year 2**		**Year 1**	**Year 2**
Revenue	$200	$100	Income	$100	$200
Expenses	0	0	Deductions	0	0
Pretax income	$200	$100	Taxable income	$100	$200
			Tax bill	$ 25	$ 50
Tax expense					
Current tax expense (using tax bill amount)	25	50			
Deferred tax expense	N/A	N/A			
Net income	$175	$ 50			
Effective tax rate (tax expense/ pretax income)	12.5%	50%			

In year 1, PPC has $200 of income for book purposes; however, because PPC did not receive payment for the sale of its services in year 1, it will only report the interest income on its year 1 tax return, resulting in a $25 tax bill ($100 × 25 percent). If PPC reports the $25 tax bill as its financial tax expense, year 1 net income is $175 and its effective tax rate is 12.5 percent ($25/$200). In year 2, PPC reports the $100 of interest income for book purposes and $200 of taxable income because it includes the $100 payment on the sale of services from year 1. At a 25 percent tax rate, PPC's tax bill is $50 ($200 × 25 percent). Consequently, in year 2 PPC reports $50 of net income and an effective tax rate of 50 percent!

[8]FAS 109, ¶63. (This paragraph was not codified in ASC 740.)

[9]FAS 109, ¶63.

[10]ASC 740-10-25-2(b).

As shown in Example 6-1, this reporting causes large swings in net income and the effective tax rate that have little to do with the company's operations, making it difficult for shareholders and other interested parties of the financial statements to interpret the company's performance. To prevent these situations, GAAP requires the use of the accrual method of accounting, which is designed to better align expenses (like taxes) with revenues. So, under accrual accounting, the effects of transactions in specific years should be accounted for in the year of the transaction regardless of the cash flow. ASC 740 provides the guidance for companies to report their income tax expense in accordance with these accrual accounting principles. For PPC's situation, ASC 740 requires PPC to report the tax expense associated with both the interest income and the sale of services in year 1 regardless of when the tax is paid to the taxing authority—that is, it is required to report both the current and deferred income tax expenses.

Example 6-2

What if: How would PPC's income statement be reported using ASC 740 principles?

Answer:

	Book (Accrual Method)			**Tax (Cash Method)**	
	Year 1	**Year 2**		**Year 1**	**Year 2**
Revenue	$200	$100	Revenue	$100	$200
Expenses	0	0	Expenses	0	0
Pretax income	$200	$100	Taxable income	$100	$200
			Tax bill	$ 25	$ 50
Tax expense					
Current tax expense	25	50			
Deferred tax expense*	25	(25)			
Net income	$150	$ 75			
Effective tax rate (tax expense/ pretax income)	25%	25%			

*We will discuss the calculation of the deferred tax expense later in the chapter.

Example 6-2 shows that PPC's net income and effective tax rate now reflect the effects of PPC's operations for each of those years. Notice that the fluctuation in the effective tax rate has disappeared.

The Income Tax Provision Process

The tax provision process refers to the process of determining the current and deferred income tax expense or (benefit) for the income statement and the tax payable or receivable and deferred tax assets and liabilities for the balance sheet. In addition, the process includes preparing the related footnote disclosures for a company's financial reporting. A company typically begins this process by computing the two components of its income tax provision (current and deferred) separately (independently) for each category of income tax (U.S. federal, U.S. state and local, and international) and then combining the components to produce the total income tax expense or (benefit). We can summarize the formula to compute a company's total income tax expense or (benefit) as:

Total income tax expense (benefit) = Current income tax expense (benefit)
+ Deferred income tax expense (benefit)

A company computes its federal income tax provision using a five-step process. These steps are:

1. Identify all permanent and temporary differences and tax carryover amounts and calculate the current income tax provision (ASC 740 Objective 1).
2. Determine the ending balances in the balance sheet deferred tax asset and liability accounts (ASC 740 Objective 2).
3. Calculate the deferred income tax provision and the total income tax provision.
4. Evaluate the need for a valuation allowance for gross deferred tax assets.
5. Evaluate the need for an uncertain tax benefit reserve.

Example 6-3

Before she began the income tax provision process for 2022, Elise knew she needed to get the ending balances in PCC's deferred tax accounts from the prior year. Accordingly, she retrieved PCC's balance sheet for the current and prior years (Exhibit 6-1) and the deferred tax component of the company's income tax note (Exhibit 6-2).

EXHIBIT 6-1 PCC Balance Sheet at 12/31/2022 and 12/31/2021

	12/31/2022	12/31/2021
Assets		
Current Assets		
Cash	$ 6,933,480	$ 10,776,380
Municipal bonds	300,000	300,000
Accounts receivable	20,750,000	17,250,000
Less: Allowance for bad debts	(415,000)	(345,000)
Accounts receivable (net)	20,335,000	16,905,000
Inventory	5,175,000	4,312,500
Total current assets	$ 32,743,480	$ 32,293,880
Noncurrent Assets		
Fixed assets	$ 70,000,000	$ 60,000,000
Less: Accumulated depreciation	(14,400,000)	(12,054,000)
Fixed assets (net)	55,600,000	47,946,000
Investments	1,647,960	1,597,960
Goodwill	180,000	180,000
Total noncurrent assets	$ 57,427,960	$ 49,723,960
Total assets	$ 90,171,440	$ 82,017,840
Liabilities and Shareholders' Equity		
Current Liabilities		
Accounts payable	$ 24,015,600	$ 20,013,000
Reserve for warranties	600,000	430,000
Total current liabilities	$ 24,615,600	$ 20,443,000
Noncurrent Liabilities		
Long-term debt	$ 40,000,000	$ 40,000,000
Deferred compensation	1,050,000	1,200,000
Deferred tax liabilities*	2,187,570	2,187,570
Total noncurrent liabilities	$ 43,237,570	$ 43,387,570
Total liabilities	$ 67,853,170	$ 63,830,570
Shareholders' Equity		
Common stock (par value = $1)	$ 500,000	$ 500,000
Additional paid-in capital	5,100,000	5,000,000
Retained earnings	16,718,270	12,687,270
Total shareholders' equity	$ 22,318,270	$ 18,187,270
Total liabilities and shareholders' equity	$ 90,171,440	$ 82,017,840

*Deferred tax liabilities have not yet been updated for current year.

Looking at Exhibit 6-2, what income tax accounts appear on PCC's balance sheet from the prior year?

Answer: PCC has a net deferred tax liability of $2,187,570, which is the sum of the deferred tax assets and liabilities. A net deferred tax liability results when deferred tax liabilities exceed deferred tax assets. A net deferred tax asset results when deferred tax assets exceed deferred tax liabilities.

Since its inception, has PCC had net favorable or unfavorable temporary differences?

Answer: Because PCC has a net deferred tax liability at the end of 2021, PCC has a future tax obligation related to the reversal of book–tax differences that were favorable when they originated. The future tax obligation indicates that the company has had cumulative pretax net income that has exceeded its cumulative taxable income.

EXHIBIT 6-2 PCC Deferred Tax Accounts at 12/31/2021

Deferred Tax Assets	
Allowance for bad debts	$ 72,450
Reserve for warranties	90,300
Net operating loss carryover	5,040
Deferred compensation	252,000
Net capital loss carryover	—
Contribution carryover	—
Total deferred tax assets	$ 419,790
Valuation allowance for deferred tax assets	—
Deferred tax assets, net of valuation allowance	$ 419,790
Deferred Tax Liabilities	
Depreciation	(2,607,360)
Total deferred tax liabilities	$(2,607,360)
Net deferred tax liabilities	$(2,187,570)

CALCULATING A COMPANY'S INCOME TAX PROVISION

LO 6-2

(continued from page 6-1 . . .)
Elise gathered the financial statement and tax return data she needed to get started, beginning with the workpaper template she reviewed to verify PCC's taxable income. (Exhibit 6-3 reproduces the book–tax reconciliation template from Exhibit 5-8, excluding the estimated book federal income tax expense of $2,000,000.) Elise identified each of the book–tax adjustments as being either permanent (P) or temporary (T). She was ready to begin the process of computing PCC's federal income tax provision using the five-step method she had learned at firm training.

(to be continued . . .)

Step 1: Identify All Permanent and Temporary Differences and Tax Carryover Amounts and Calculate the Current Income Tax Provision (ASC 740 Objective 1)

Permanent Differences As you learned in the Corporate Operations chapter, book–tax differences can be classified into different categories (permanent or temporary). Some differences will appear on either the income statement or the tax return but not on both. ASC 740 does not provide a label for these types of differences; however, in practice they are referred to as **permanent book–tax differences.** Examples of items that affect only the income statement are tax-exempt interest income and nondeductible fines. Items that appear only on the tax return include the dividends-received deduction and the excess tax over book benefit from the exercise of nonqualified stock options.

EXHIBIT 6-3 PCC Book–Tax Reconciliation Template for 2022

Premiere Computer Corporation				
		Book–Tax Adjustments		
Income Statement for Current Year	Book Income	(Dr)	Cr	Taxable Income
Revenue from sales	$ 60,000,000			$ 60,000,000
Cost of goods sold	(38,000,000)			(38,000,000)
Gross profit	$ 22,000,000			$ 22,000,000
Other income:				
Dividend income	30,000			30,000
Interest income (P)	120,000	(12,000)		108,000
Capital gains (losses) (T)	(28,000)		28,000	0
Gain on fixed asset dispositions (T)	54,000		16,000	70,000
Gross income	$ 22,176,000			$ 22,208,000
Expenses:				
Compensation	(9,868,000)			(9,868,000)
Deferred compensation (T)	(300,000)	(150,000)		(450,000)
Stock option compensation (T)	(100,000)		100,000	0
Bad debt expense (T)	(165,000)		70,000	(95,000)
Charitable contributions (T)	(700,000)		73,700	(626,300)
Depreciation (T)	(2,400,000)	(700,000)		(3,100,000)
Advertising	(1,920,000)			(1,920,000)
Warranty expenses (T)	(580,000)		170,000	(410,000)
Meals	(14,000)			(14,000)
Life insurance premiums (P)	(34,000)		34,000	0
Other expenses	(64,000)			(64,000)
Total expenses *before* NOL, DRD	$(16,145,000)			$(16,547,300)
Income *before* NOL, DRD	$ 6,031,000			$ 5,660,700
NOL carryover from prior year (T)	0	(24,000)		(24,000)
Dividends-received deduction (P)	0	(15,000)		(15,000)
Book/taxable income	**$ 6,031,000**	**$(901,000)**	**$491,700**	**$ 5,621,700**

A company does not take permanent differences into account in computing its deferred tax assets and liabilities. Permanent differences enter into the company's computation of taxable income and thus affect the current tax expense or benefit, either increasing or decreasing it. As a result, permanent differences usually affect a company's **effective tax rate**—or its total income tax expense/pretax net income—and appear as part of the company's reconciliation of its effective tax rate with its statutory U.S. tax rate (21 percent). We discuss this and other ASC 740 disclosure requirements in a later section of this chapter.

Exhibit 6-4 provides a list of common permanent differences you will encounter in practice.

EXHIBIT 6-4 Common Permanent Differences

Life insurance proceeds	Disallowed premiums on officers' life insurance
Tax-exempt interest income	Dividends-received deduction
Nondeductible tax penalties and fines	The windfall tax benefit from exercise of nonqualified stock options
Political contributions	Entertainment expenses
Disallowed business-related meals*	Tax credits**

*For 2021 and 2022, meals purchased from restaurants are fully deductible and will not result in a permanent difference.

**Tax credits are permanent differences for ASC 740; however, they are not a book-tax reconciling item. Rather, tax credits reduce tax expense directly.

Example 6-4

Elise went back to the template she used to review PCC's taxable income and identified the book–tax adjustments that were considered permanent in nature. What are PCC's permanent differences, and are they favorable or unfavorable?

Answer: A net unfavorable permanent difference of $7,000, computed as follows:

Permanent Differences	(Favorable) Unfavorable
Tax-exempt interest income	$(12,000)
Life insurance premiums	34,000
Dividends-received deduction	(15,000)
Net unfavorable permanent difference	**$ 7,000**

Example 6-5

Elise used the net unfavorable permanent difference of $7,000 to adjust PCC's pretax income. What is PCC's pretax income adjusted for permanent differences?

Answer: $6,038,000, computed as follows:

PCC pretax income	$ 6,031,000
Net unfavorable permanent difference	$ 7,000
PCC pretax income adjusted for permanent differences	**$ 6,038,000**

Elise remembered that her instructor at ASC 740 training referred to this intermediate computation as a company's **book equivalent of taxable income.** That is, this amount represents the book income that ultimately will be taxable, either currently or in the future.

Temporary Differences and Tax Carryover Amounts In contrast to permanent differences, **temporary book–tax differences** reverse over time such that, over the long term, corporations recognize the same amount of income or deductions for the items on their income statements as they recognize on their tax returns. Temporary book–tax differences arise because the income or deduction items are included in financial accounting income in one year and in taxable income in a different year. Temporary book–tax differences that are *initially* favorable (unfavorable) become unfavorable (favorable) in future years when they reverse. The distinction between permanent and temporary book–tax differences is not all that important in calculating the current tax provision, but it is useful to identify them at this stage because only temporary differences and tax carryovers create deferred tax assets and liabilities and the deferred tax provision.

Exhibit 6-5 lists common temporary differences.[11] Refer to the Corporate Operations chapter for more details on the book and tax treatment of these temporary differences.

EXHIBIT 6-5 Common Temporary Differences

Depreciation	Reserves for bad debts (uncollectible accounts)
Accrued vacation pay	Inventory costs capitalized under §263A
Prepayments of income	Warranty reserves
Installment sale income	Stock option expense
Pension plan deductions	Accrued bonuses and other compensation
Accrued contingency losses	Net operating loss and net capital loss carryovers
Business interest expense	

[11]The standard practice to determine temporary differences is to compare book and tax balance sheet basis differences. Companies that do not keep formal tax balance sheets may "roll forward" cumulative book and tax differences from prior years and must periodically prove out the balances to book and tax bases.

Example 6-6

Elise uses the book–tax reconciliation (see Exhibit 6-3) to identify PCC's temporary differences. What are PCC's temporary differences?

Answer: PCC has several temporary difference in the current year, which Elise summarizes as follows:

Temporary Differences	Amount
Net capital loss carryover	$ 28,000
Gain on fixed asset dispositions	16,000
Deferred compensation	(150,000)
Stock option compensation	100,000
Bad debt expense	70,000
Charitable contribution carryover	73,700
Depreciation	(700,000)
Warranty expense	170,000
NOL carryover from 2021	(24,000)
Total temporary differences	**$(416,300)**

Temporary differences that reduce taxable income are shown in parentheses and represent favorable book–tax differences. For the year, PCC has a net (favorable) temporary difference of $(416,300).

Temporary differences arise in one reporting period and reverse in later periods. Which of PCC's temporary differences are reversals of differences that arose in a prior period?

Answer: The gain on fixed asset dispositions, deferred compensation, and NOL carryover from 2021 are reversals. For example, the NOL carryover originated in a prior year but can be used in the current period to reduce taxable income. The use of the NOL deduction will reverse the deferred tax effects from the prior period. So, it is important to identify these reversals for the calculation of the deferred tax assets and liabilities, which we discuss in Step 2 of the income tax provision process.

Calculate the Current Income Tax Expense or (Benefit) (ASC 740 Objective 1)

In many respects, the computation of the current portion of a company's tax provision appears to be straightforward. **Current income tax expense (benefit)** is generally defined as

> [t]he amount of income taxes paid or payable (or refundable) for a year as determined by applying the provisions of the enacted tax law to the taxable income or excess of deductions over revenues for that year.[12]

In most cases, the major component of a company's current income tax expense or benefit is the income tax liability or refund from its current-year operations. Exhibit 6-6 shows a common formula used to calculate this component of the current income tax expense or benefit.

Although Exhibit 6-6 shows the calculation of the main component of the current income tax expense, there are other items that enter into the computation that do not appear on the company's income tax return (Form 1120), which add to the complexity of the computation. In practice, the tax provision is usually completed several months before the tax

EXHIBIT 6-6 Current Tax Expense Formula

	Pretax book income or loss
+/−	Book–tax permanent differences
+/−	Book–tax temporary differences
=	Taxable income
×	Applicable tax rate
=	Current income tax expense

[12]Statement of Financial Accounting Standards No. 109, Accounting for Income Taxes, February 1992. This definition was not codified in ASC 740.

return is filed and must rely on some estimates of the book–tax differences. These estimates often result in differences between the provision calculations of current tax expense and the tax return amounts, and the differences are corrected in the next year with return to provision adjustments that affect the current tax expense in the year the difference is discovered (usually the subsequent tax year). Other items that produce differences include prior-year income tax refunds from current-year carrybacks of a net capital loss,[13] IRS audit adjustments from prior-year tax returns,[14] and changes in the company's **uncertain tax positions**—a company's reserve for taxes it has not paid but could pay in the future for positions taken on the current- and prior-year income tax returns.[15]

Example 6-7

Elise uses her summary of permanent and temporary differences to verify her earlier computation of PCC's taxable income. Does using her summary of PCC's permanent and temporary differences verify her earlier computation?

Answer: Yes!

	PCC pretax net income	$ 6,031,000
+	Net permanent difference (from Example 6-4)	7,000
−	Net temporary differences (from Example 6-6)	(416,300)
=	**PCC taxable income**	**$5,621,700**

What is PCC's current income tax expense?

Answer: $1,180,557, computed as follows:

PCC taxable income	$ 5,621,700
Applicable tax rate	× 21%
PCC current income tax expense (income tax payable)	**$1,180,557**

Because Elise has completed the tax return (in the Corporate Operations chapter) before our discussion of the income tax provision process, we will not see any differences between the tax return and the provision for book–tax differences, which eliminates the need for any return to provision adjustments.

(continued from page 6-7 . . .)
Having calculated the current portion of PCC's income tax provision, Elise turned her attention to computing the deferred component of PCC's income tax provision. Although not required by ASC 740, firms commonly keep a separate tax basis balance sheet to compute the deferred tax accounts. Fortunately for Elise, PCC had created a formal **tax accounting balance sheet**[16] for computing its deferred tax provision (see Exhibit 6-8). Elise would need to compare the changes in the book–tax basis differences from the beginning of the year to the end of the year for each account she identified as being a temporary difference. ■

[13]Requested on Form 1139, Corporation Application for Tentative Refund, or Form 1120X, Amended U.S. Corporation Income Tax Return.

[14]Agreed to on Form 5701, Notice of Proposed Adjustment.

[15]Calculated in the uncertain tax position workpapers.

[16]Schedule L of Form 1120 requests that the taxpayer report its financial statement balance sheet.

Step 2: Determine the Ending Balances in the Balance Sheet Deferred Tax Asset and Liability Accounts (ASC 740 Objective 2)

Think back to Example 6-1 in which PPC's net income and effective tax rate fluctuated simply because of the tax effects of PPC's temporary difference and Example 6-2, where including the future tax effects of the temporary differences smoothed out the fluctuation. In this section, we determine how to measure the deferred tax assets and liabilities, which is the start to calculating the deferred income tax provision.

THE KEY FACTS

Identifying Taxable and Deductible Temporary Differences

- ASC 740 defines a temporary difference as a difference between the financial reporting and tax basis of an asset or liability that will create a future tax liability or benefit when the difference reverses.
- A taxable temporary difference results from an excess of book carrying value over tax basis for assets and from an excess of tax basis over book carrying value for liabilities.
- The future tax cost associated with a taxable temporary difference is recorded on the balance sheet as a deferred tax liability.
- A deductible temporary difference results from an excess of tax basis over book carrying value for assets and from an excess of book carrying value over tax basis for liabilities.
- The future tax benefit associated with a deductible temporary difference is recorded on the balance sheet as a deferred tax asset.

Identifying Taxable and Deductible Temporary Differences Deferred tax assets and liabilities are a result of temporary differences in which the book and tax treatments of certain items occur in different periods. In the Corporate Operations chapter and in calculating the current tax expense in Step 1 of the income tax provision process, these temporary differences were classified as favorable and unfavorable depending on whether they decreased or increased taxable income relative to book income. Because the standard focuses on the balance sheet, ASC 740 uses different terminology for temporary differences.

ASC 740 formally defines a *temporary difference* as:

> [a] difference between the tax basis of an asset or liability . . . and its reported amount in the financial statements that will result in taxable or deductible amounts in future years when the reported amount of the asset or liability is recovered or settled, respectively.[17]

Note that the standard evaluates temporary differences based on their impact in *future* periods rather than their impact on the current period and thus labels the differences as either taxable or deductible temporary differences based on what effect the temporary difference will have when it reverses. These temporary differences result from differences in the book and tax bases of a company's assets and liabilities and reflect the cumulative amount of temporary differences over the life of the company. Taxable temporary differences (associated with deferred tax liabilities) will increase taxable income in the future when they reverse, whereas deductible temporary differences (associated with deferred tax assets) will reduce taxable income in the future when they reverse.

Taxable Temporary Difference From a balance sheet perspective, a **taxable temporary difference**[18] (TTD) generally arises when the financial reporting (book) basis of an asset exceeds its corresponding tax basis or when the financial reporting (book) basis of a liability is less than its corresponding tax basis. Subsequent recovery of the financial statement balance sheet basis of the asset or payment of the balance sheet liability will cause taxable income to exceed book income, by either creating a tax gain or reducing a tax deduction. The future tax cost associated with a taxable temporary difference is recorded on the balance sheet as a deferred tax liability. The bases differences that produce taxable temporary differences generally arise when (1) revenues or gains are taxable *after* they are recognized in net income (e.g., gross profit from an installment sale) (category 1) and (2) expenses or losses are deductible on the tax return *before* they reduce net income (e.g., excess tax depreciation over financial accounting depreciation) (category 2) (See Exhibit 6-7).[19]

[17]Accounting Standards Update No. 2016-16. Income Taxes (Topic 740). October 2016.

[18]ASC 740-10-25-23.

[19]Consistent with the terminology introduced in the Corporate Operations chapter, a "favorable" book–tax adjustment is one that reduces current-year taxable income compared to current-year net income.

EXHIBIT 6-7 Sources of Taxable and Deductible Temporary Differences

Taxable Temporary Differences	Deductible Temporary Differences
1. Revenues or gains that are taxable after they are recognized in financial income	3. Revenues or gains that are taxable before they are recognized in financial income
2. Expenses or losses that are deductible before they are recognized in financial income	4. Expenses or losses that are deductible after they are recognized in financial income

Deductible Temporary Difference From a balance sheet perspective, a **deductible temporary difference**[20] (DTD) occurs when the financial reporting (book) basis of an asset is less than its corresponding tax basis or the financial reporting (book) basis of a liability exceeds its corresponding tax basis. Subsequent recovery of the financial reporting balance sheet basis of the asset or payment of the balance sheet liability will cause taxable income to be less than book income, by either creating a tax loss or increasing a tax deduction. The future tax benefit associated with a deductible temporary difference is recorded on the balance sheet as a deferred tax asset.

Book and tax basis differences that produce deductible generally arise when (1) revenues or gains are taxable *before* they are recognized in net income (e.g., prepayments of subscriptions) (category 3) and (2) expenses or losses are deductible on the tax return *after* they reduce net income (e.g., reserves for product warranty or uncollectible accounts) (category 4). Deductible temporary differences also can arise from items that cannot be associated with a particular asset or liability for financial accounting purposes but produce revenue (income) or expense (deduction) that has been recognized in the financial statement and will result in taxable or deductible amounts in future years. For example, a net operating loss carryover and a net capital loss carryover create temporary differences in the year they arise without being associated with a specific asset or liability. Temporary differences that do not have balance sheet accounts, such as net operating loss carryovers, net capital loss carryovers, and charitable contribution carryovers, must be tracked to ensure that the appropriate adjustment is made to a company's deferred tax asset accounts when the carryover is used on a future tax return.

In order to determine the taxable and deductible temporary differences, companies must create a tax basis balance sheet. For many of the assets and liabilities listed on the book balance sheet, the tax and book bases will be the same. However, when accounting methods differ between book and tax that result in temporary differences, the tax basis will be different from the book basis. For example, the net carrying value of fixed assets will differ between book and tax due to differences in the way depreciation is calculated: usually straight-line for book and MACRS for tax. Similarly, the book and tax bases of accounts receivable differ because the accounting methods for determining bad debts differs: the allowance method for book and the direct charge off method for tax. Determining the tax basis for liabilities is slightly less straightforward. The regulations provide some guidelines to help determine the tax basis of an obligation.[21] An obligation is a tax liability if and to the extent the obligation:

1. creates or increases basis or results in cash (e.g., bank loan);
2. provides an immediate tax deduction (e.g., accounts payable);[22] or
3. is a nondeductible expense for computing taxable income (e.g., accrued fines expense).

If an obligation meets one of these criteria, it will have a tax basis. Exhibit 6-8 shows PCC's tax basis balance sheet comparing the prior year with current year amounts.

[20]ASC 740-10-25-23.

[21]Reg. §1.752-1(a)(4)

[22]To be immediately deductible, an expense must meet the all events test (fixed and determinable) and the requirements of economic performance. See the Business Income, Deductions, and Accounting Methods chapter for more details.

EXHIBIT 6-8 PCC's Tax Basis Balance Sheet for 12/31/2021 and 12/31/2022

	12/31/2022	12/31/2021
Assets		
Cash	$ 6,933,480	$10,776,380
Municipal bonds	300,000	300,000
Accounts receivable	20,750,000	17,250,000
Less: Allowance for bad debts	–	–
Accounts receivable (net)	20,750,000	17,250,000
Inventory	5,175,000	4,312,500
Fixed assets	70,000,000	60,000,000
Less: Accumulated depreciation	(27,500,000)	(24,470,000)
Fixed assets (net)	42,500,000	35,530,000
Investments	1,647,960	1,597,960
Goodwill	180,000	180,000
Total assets	$77,486,440	$69,946,840
Liabilities		
Accounts payable	$24,015,600	$20,013,000
Reserve for warranties	–	–
Long term debt	40,000,000	40,000,000
Deferred compensation	–	–
Deferred tax liabilities*	N/A	N/A
Total liabilities	$64,015,600	$60,013,000
Shareholders' Equity		
Common stock	$ 500,000	$ 500,000
Additional paid-in capital	5,000,000	5,000,000
Retained earnings*	N/A	N/A
Total liabilities and shareholders' equity	$69,515,600	$65,513,000

*Tax basis balance sheets do not include these accounts

Example 6-8

PCC has provided its book (Exhibit 6-1) and tax (Exhibit 6-8) basis balance sheets. Elise identifies differences in the balances in several accounts. She isolates the accounts with differences as an initial step in determining the taxable and deductible temporary differences and the deferred tax liabilities (DTLs) and deferred tax assets (DTAs). Elise summarizes the differences and produces the following table:

PCC Balance Sheet (select items)	**Book Basis DR/(CR)**		**Tax Basis**	
	12/31/2022	**12/31/2021**	**12/31/2022**	**12/31/2021**
Accounts receivable (net)	$20,335,000	$16,905,000	$20,750,000	$17,250,000
Fixed assets (net)	55,600,000	47,946,000	42,500,000	35,530,000
Reserve for warranties	(600,000)	(430,000)	–	–
Deferred compensation	(1,050,000)	(1,200,000)	–	–
Additional paid-in capital (stock option expense)	(5,100,000)	(5,000,000)	(5,000,000)	(5,000,000)

Why is the tax basis for the reserve for warranties and deferred compensation zero?

Answer: Neither of these book liabilities meets the definition for a tax liability. The warranty reserve and the deferred compensation do not provide an immediate tax deduction because the related expenses do not meet the all events test (not fixed) and therefore do not create tax basis. These items also do not meet the other two criteria because they do not create cash and they will eventually be deductible.

By comparing the book and tax bases of the assets and liabilities, we can determine the taxable and deductible temporary differences. TTDs occur for assets (liabilities) when the book basis is greater (less) than the tax basis. Conversely, DTDs arise for assets (liabilities) when the book basis is less (greater) than the tax basis. For example, using the end of year book and tax bases in the accounts receivable from Example 6-8, the end of year difference is $415,000 ($20,750,000 tax basis less $20,335,000 book basis). Because this difference relates to an asset and the book basis is less than the tax basis, the difference results in a deductible temporary difference.

Example 6-9

What are PCC's taxable and deductible temporary differences at the beginning and end of the year? What is the change in the cumulative temporary differences?

Answer:

	Cumulative Temporary Differences DTD/(TTD)		Change in Cumulative Temporary Differences
	End of Year (Tax – Book)	Beginning of Year (Tax – Book)	(Ending – Beginning)
(1) Accounts receivable (net)	$ 415,000	$ 345,000	$ 70,000
(2) Fixed assets (net)	(13,100,000)	(12,416,000)	(684,000)
(3) Reserve for warranties	600,000	430,000	170,000
(4) Deferred compensation	1,050,000	1,200,000	(150,000)
(5) Additional paid-in capital (stock option expense)	100,000	–	100,000

Elise has set up her workpaper so that positive amounts are deductible temporary differences (DTDs) and negative amounts are taxable temporary differences (TTDs). Because DTDs generate DTAs and TTDs generate DTLs, this formatting convention will help her as she determines how these amounts need to be recorded on the balance sheet.

Some temporary differences are not directly related to an asset or liability on the balance sheet. For example, tax attributes such as NOL carryovers, capital loss carryovers, credit carryovers, and other carryovers are not tied to any specific asset or liability and as a result will not appear on either a book or tax balance sheet. These items produce deductible temporary differences and must be tracked separately in the tax workpapers.

Example 6-10

Elise reviewed her schedules of favorable and unfavorable temporary differences (from Example 6-6) and notices that for the most part, the change in temporary differences for these items matches the temporary differences she identified when calculating the current tax provision. However, Elise notices that the change in the temporary difference for fixed assets is $684,000 and does not match the depreciation book–tax difference she used for the tax provision. Why doesn't the depreciation difference match the cumulative temporary difference change for fixed assets?

Answer: The depreciation temporary difference that Elise used for the current provision of $700,000 only represents part of the cumulative temporary difference related to fixed assets. A missing item is the temporary difference related to the gain on the sale of fixed assets of $16,000. This difference represents the reversal of the difference in depreciation that was taken on the asset while PCC used it. So, this difference is included in the overall fixed asset difference from the book and tax basis balance sheets. Elise reconciles the difference by combining the $(700,000) favorable depreciation difference with the $16,000 unfavorable difference from the sale to obtain a total $684,000 favorable temporary difference for fixed assets, which matches the taxable temporary difference she calculated using the balance sheet approach.

(continued on page 6-16)

Elise also notices that some items are missing from the temporary items she identified in the book–tax reconciliation. Which temporary differences are missing?

Answer: The missing items include the NOL, net capital loss, and charitable contribution carryovers. These items are tax items for which there is no book basis and must be tracked separately in the tax workpapers. Elise adds them to her cumulative temporary differences.

	Cumulative Temporary Differences DTD/(TTD)		**Change in Temporary Differences**
	Ending (Tax − Book)	**Beginning (Tax − Book)**	**(Ending − Beginning)**
(1) NOL carryover	–	$24,000	$(24,000)
(2) Net capital loss carryover	$28,000	–	28,000
(3) Charitable contribution carryover	73,700	–	73,700

Once the TTDs and DTDs are identified, they are used to determine the deferred tax assets and liabilities reported on the book balance sheet. The future tax obligation of a taxable temporary difference is recorded on the balance sheet as a deferred tax liability. Conversely the future tax benefit of a deductible temporary difference is recorded as a deferred tax asset. The company computes its deferred tax assets and liabilities using the **enacted tax rate** that is expected to apply to taxable income in the period(s) in which the deferred tax assets and liabilities are expected to be settled.[23] For example, in Example 6-9, we determined that the end of year DTD related to the accounts receivable balance is $415,000. To calculate the deferred tax asset related to this DTD, we multiply the DTD by the enacted tax rate of 21 percent resulting in a DTA of $87,150 ($415,000 × 21%) at the end of the year.

Example 6-11

Elise's next step is to determine the deferred tax assets and liabilities to be included on the financial balance sheet. Using the temporary differences from Example 6-9 and the enacted tax rate of 21 percent, she determines the beginning and ending DTAs and DTLs.

	DTA/(DTL) @ 21%		
PCC Balance Sheet (select items)	**Ending**	**Beginning**	**Explanation**
Accounts receivable (net) (allowance for bad debts)	$ 87,150	$ 72,450	Example 6-9, line (1) × 21%
Fixed assets (net) (depreciation)	(2,751,000)	(2,607,360)	Example 6-9, line (2) × 21%
Reserve for warranties	126,000	90,300	Example 6-9, line (3) × 21%
Deferred compensation	220,500	252,000	Example 6-9, line (4) × 21%
Additional paid-in capital (stock option expense)	21,000	–	Example 6-9, line (5) × 21%
Other temporary differences			
NOL carryover	–	5,040	Example 6-10, line (1) × 21%
Net capital loss carryover	5,880	–	Example 6-10, line (2) × 21%
Charitable contribution carryover	15,477	–	Example 6-10, line (3) × 21%
Totals	$(2,274,993)	$(2,187,570)	

[23]ASC 740-10-30-2.

Which of the amounts in the table above represent DTAs and which represent DTLs?

Answer: Elise has set up her workpaper such that DTAs are positive amounts and DTLs are negative (i.e., in parentheses). This convention is typical in financial accounting formatting for debits and credits. PCC's DTAs include the accounts receivable (net), reserve for warranties, deferred compensation, additional paid-in capital (representing the stock option expense temporary difference), NOL carryover, net capital loss carryover, and charitable contribution carryover. Fixed assets (depreciation) is the only DTL for PCC.

Summary of PCC's DTAs and DTLs

	Ending	Beginning
DTA	$ 476,007	$ 419,790
DTL	(2,751,000)	(2,607,360)
Totals	(2,274,993)	(2,187,570)

Using a template that tracks the cumulative changes in the book–tax differences related to book and tax balance sheet accounts becomes especially important when a company's enacted tax rate changes. For example, the Tax Cuts and Jobs Act reduced the corporate tax rate to 21 percent for tax years beginning after December 31, 2017. The bill was signed by the president on December 22, 2017. As a result, corporations were required to revalue their U.S. deferred tax assets and liabilities existing on December 22, 2017, to reflect the lower tax rate. This discussion points to the fact that the focus of ASC 740 is to have the balance sheet deferred tax accounts reflect the tax benefit or obligation when the underlying temporary differences reverse in a future period.

THE KEY FACTS

Computing the Deferred Income Tax Expense (Benefit)

- Identify current-year changes in taxable and deductible temporary differences.
- Determine ending balances in each deferred tax asset and liability balance sheet account.
- Identify carryovers (net operating loss, net capital loss, charitable contributions) not on the balance sheet.
- The current-year deferred income tax expense or benefit is the difference between the deferred tax asset and liability balances at the beginning of the year and the end of the year, as well as changes in tax carryovers.

Step 3: Calculate the Deferred Income Tax Provision and the Total Income Tax Provision

Deferred Income Tax Provision The deferred income tax expense or benefit portion of a company's tax provision reflects the change during the year in a company's balance sheet deferred tax liabilities or assets.[24] This information provides investors and other interested parties with a measure of a company's expected future income-tax-related cash inflows or outflows resulting from book-tax differences that are temporary in nature or from tax carryovers. Once the beginning and ending DTAs and DTLs have been determined, calculating the deferred income tax expense or benefit is relatively straightforward. The deferred tax expense or benefit is calculated as the change in the *net* deferred tax asset or liability for the period (EOY net DTL or DTA minus BOY net DTL or DTA). An increase (decrease) in a net DTA produces a deferred tax benefit (expense). Conversely, an increase (decrease) in a net DTL produces a deferred income tax expense (benefit).

Example 6-12

Elise now has the pieces to determine PCC's deferred income tax expense or benefit for 2022. Using the solution from Example 6-11, what is PCC's deferred income tax provision for 2022?

Answer: $87,423 deferred tax expense, computed as follows:

Summary

	Ending	Beginning	Change
DTA	$ 476,007	$ 419,790	$ 56,217
DTL	(2,751,000)	(2,607,360)	(143,640)
Net DTL	$(2,274,993)	$(2,187,570)	**$ (87,423)**

PCC's net deferred tax liability increased during the year, indicating a larger net future tax obligation; thus, the $87,423 increase represents PCC's deferred income tax expense for the year.

[24]ASC 740-10-20 Glossary.

Total Income Tax Provision Recall that ASC 740 has two objectives. The first is to "recognize the amount of tax payable or refundable in the current year,"[25] and the second is to "recognize deferred tax liabilities and assets for the future tax consequences of events that have been recognized in an entity's financial statements or tax returns."[26] The first relates to the current income tax provision and the second to the deferred income tax provision. Although the current income tax expense or benefit and the deferred income tax expense or benefit may be affected by other complexities not yet discussed, once these amounts are determined, the total tax expense is the sum of the two.

Example 6-13

What is PCC's total income tax provision for 2022?

Answer: $1,267,980 total income tax expense, computed as:

Current income tax expense	$ 1,180,557	Example 6-7
Deferred income tax expense	87,423	Example 6-12
Total income tax expense	**$1,267,980**	

There is a straightforward back-of-the-envelope method of verifying the ASC 740 approach to calculating PCC's total tax provision. Under the assumption that all temporary differences will appear on a tax return in a current or future period, the total tax provision should reflect the tax that ultimately will be paid on pretax net income adjusted for permanent differences. Remember from Example 6-5 that this amount is sometimes referred to as a company's *book equivalent of taxable income*. The total income tax provision should equal the company's tax rate times its book equivalent of taxable income. We emphasize that this approach to computing a company's income tax provision is not in accordance with GAAP and will not provide the correct answer when there are changes in a company's income tax rate or other items that affect the current tax expense (e.g., UTPs, carrybacks, return to provision adjustments, and audit adjustments).

Example 6-14

Elise retrieved her computation of PCC's book equivalent of taxable income (from Example 6-5), as follows:

PCC pretax net income	$6,031,000
Net unfavorable permanent difference	7,000
PCC book equivalent of taxable income	$6,038,000

What is PCC's total tax provision using book equivalent of taxable income as a base?

Answer: $1,267,980, computed as follows:

PCC's book equivalent of taxable income	$ 6,038,000
	× 21%
PCC's total tax provision	**$1,267,980**

This computation confirms the computation made under ASC 740 from Example 6-13.

[25]ASC 740-10-10-1(a)

[26]Accounting Standards Update No. 2018-05, Income Taxes (Topic 740), March 2018.

Journal Entries Once the calculations have been completed to determine the current and deferred income tax expense, the journal entries must be made to record the income tax effects on the financial statements. To record a current income tax expense, the journal entry follows this format:

Current income tax expense	*XXX*	
Income taxes payable		*XXX*

If the company instead has a current income tax benefit, the journal entry format would be:

Income taxes receivable	*XXX*	
Current income taxes expense		*XXX*

For the deferred provision, the journal entry records the changes in the deferred tax assets and liabilities as well as the deferred tax expense or benefit. The general format of the journal entry for a company where the change in the deferred tax liabilities is greater than the change in the deferred tax assets is:

Deferred income tax expense	*XXX*	
Deferred tax asset	*XXX*	
Deferred tax liability		*XXX*

The journal entry will change depending on whether the deferred tax assets and liabilities increase or decrease and their relative amounts. The deferred tax expense or benefit is the balancing amount of the entry. For example, if the change in the deferred tax assets is greater than the change in the deferred tax liabilities, the journal entry would appear in the following format:

Deferred tax asset	*XXX*	
Deferred income tax benefit		*XXX*
Deferred tax liability		*XXX*

Example 6-15

What tax accounting journal entry does Elise make to record PCC's current income taxes?

Answer:

Current income tax expense	$1,180,557		Example 6-7
Income taxes payable		$1,180,557	

What tax accounting journal entry does Elise make to record PCC's deferred income taxes?

Answer:

Deferred income tax expense	$87,423		Example 6-12
Deferred income tax asset	$56,217		
Deferred income tax liability		$143,640	

LO 6-3

DETERMINING WHETHER A VALUATION ALLOWANCE IS NEEDED

THE KEY FACTS

Determining Whether a Valuation Allowance Is Needed

- A valuation allowance is required if it is more likely than not that some or all of the deferred tax asset will not be realized in the future.
- To make this determination, a company must determine its sources of future (or past) taxable income.
  - Taxable income in carryback years.
  - Reversing taxable temporary differences in future years.
  - Expected taxable income in future years from other than reversing taxable temporary differences.
  - Expected taxable income in future taxable years from implementing tax planning strategies.
- A company must evaluate positive and negative evidence in deciding whether a valuation allowance is needed.
- A company must monitor whether increases or decreases should be made to the valuation allowance account every quarter.

Step 4: Evaluate the Need for a Valuation Allowance for Gross Deferred Tax Assets

ASC 740 specifically precludes PCC, or any company, from discounting (i.e., recording the present value of) the deferred income tax liability or asset related to a temporary difference based on when the asset is expected to be recovered or the liability settled. The FASB debated whether discounting deferred income tax assets and liabilities would provide more relevant information to investors, but ultimately it decided that the complexity and cost of making the computation outweighed any benefits investors and creditors might receive.[27]

Rather than discounting, ASC 740 requires that a company evaluate each of its gross deferred income tax assets on the balance sheet and assess the likelihood the expected tax benefit will be *realized* in a future period. The income tax benefits reflected in the deferred tax assets can be realized (i.e., converted into cash) only if the company expects to have sufficient taxable income or tax liability in the future or carryback period to absorb the unused tax deductions or credits before they expire.

Determining the Need for a Valuation Allowance

Under ASC 740, if a company determines that it is more likely than not (i.e., a likelihood greater than 50 percent) that some portion or all of the deferred tax assets will not be realized in a future period, it must offset the deferred tax assets with a **valuation allowance** to reflect the amount the company does not expect to realize in the future.[28] Valuation allowances operate as *contra accounts* to the deferred income tax assets on the balance sheet, much like the allowance for bad debts a company must estimate for its accounts receivable. Companies usually disclose the amount of the valuation allowance in the income tax footnote to the financial statements.

Management must assess whether it is more likely than not that a deferred income tax asset will *not* be realized in the future based on all available evidence, both positive and negative. ASC 740 identifies four sources of potential future taxable income, two of which are objective and two of which are subjective and determined by management judgment.[29] The objective sources are (1) future reversals of existing taxable temporary differences and (2) taxable income in prior carryback year(s). The subjective sources are (1) expected future taxable income exclusive of reversing temporary differences and carryovers and (2) tax planning strategies.

Future Reversals of Existing Taxable Temporary Differences Existing taxable temporary differences provide taxable income when they are recovered in a future period. For example, the recovery of the excess of an asset's financial accounting (book) basis over its tax basis, whether through sale or depreciation, will cause taxable income to be higher than pretax net income in the periods in which the excess financial accounting basis is recovered. If the reversing taxable temporary differences provide sufficient future taxable income to absorb the reversing deductible temporary differences, the company does not record a valuation allowance against the deferred tax asset. In the case of NOL carryovers from years beginning after December 31, 2017, only 80 percent of the reversing taxable temporary differences can be used as a source of future taxable income because these NOL carryovers can only offset up to 80 percent of taxable income. Refer to the Corporate Operations chapter for more details related to NOL carryover usage.

[27]FAS 109, ¶¶198–199. (These paragraphs were not codified in ASC 740.)
[28]ASC 740-10-30-5(e).
[29]ASC 740-10-30-18.

Taxable Income in Prior Carryback Year(s) The company does not record a valuation allowance if the tax benefit from the realization of a deferred income tax asset can be carried back to a prior year that has sufficient taxable income (or capital gain net income in the case of a net capital loss carryback) or tax liability (in the case of a credit) to absorb the realized tax benefit.

Expected Future Taxable Income Exclusive of Reversing Temporary Differences and Carryovers ASC 740 allows a company to consider taxable income it expects to earn in future periods in determining whether a valuation allowance is necessary. The company might support its predictions of future taxable income with evidence of existing contracts or a sales backlog that will produce enough taxable income to realize the deferred tax asset when it reverses. In addition, the company could demonstrate that it has a strong earnings history if a deferred tax asset arises from a loss that could be considered out of the ordinary and not from a continuing condition. Firms in cyclical industries, such as automobile manufacturers, builders, and airlines, traditionally have cited a history of past income as evidence of expected future income.

Tax Planning Strategies The most subjective source of future taxable income to support the realization of a deferred income tax asset is the company's ability and willingness to employ tax strategies in those future periods to create the taxable income needed to absorb the deferred tax asset. ASC 740 allows a company to consider actions it might take to create sufficient taxable income to absorb a deferred income tax asset, provided such actions (1) are prudent and feasible, (2) are actions an enterprise would take only to prevent an operating loss or tax credit carryovers from expiring unused, and (3) would result in realization of the deferred tax assets.

The company does not have to implement the strategy to avoid recording a valuation allowance, but management must be willing and able to execute the strategy if the need arises. Tax planning strategies could include (1) selling and leasing back operating assets, (2) changing inventory accounting methods (e.g., from LIFO to FIFO), (3) refraining from making voluntary contributions to the company pension plan, (4) electing to capitalize certain expenditures (e.g., research and development costs) rather than deduct them currently, (5) selling noncore assets, (6) converting tax-exempt investments into taxable investments, and (7) electing the alternative depreciation system (i.e., straight line instead of declining balance).

Negative Evidence That a Valuation Allowance Is Needed ASC 740 requires that a company consider negative evidence as well as positive evidence in determining whether it is more likely than not that a deferred income tax asset will not be realized in the future. Negative evidence includes (1) cumulative (book) losses in recent years; (2) a history of net operating losses, net capital losses, and credits expiring unused; (3) an expectation of losses in the near future; and (4) unsettled circumstances that, if resolved unfavorably, will result in losses from continuing operations in future years (e.g., the loss of a patent on a highly profitable drug).[30] As a general rule, public accounting firms interpret "recent years" with regard to cumulative book losses as a rolling 12 quarters (i.e., 36 months). As with all general rules, there are exceptions depending on the industry.

Valuation Allowance Journal Entries If the company determines that it is more likely than not that its deferred tax assets will not be fully realized, it will need to record the valuation allowance as a contra-asset account to its deferred tax assets as follows:

Deferred tax expense	*XXX*	
Valuation allowance		*XXX*

[30]ASC 740-10-30-21.

When setting up the valuation allowance, the offsetting part of the journal entry is to the deferred income tax expense. It will not affect the current tax provision. Note that this journal entry is similar to the journal entry required to set up an allowance for doubtful accounts (debit: bad debt expense, credit: allowance for doubtful accounts).

Each reporting period, the valuation allowance must be evaluated to determine if it is still needed. If management determines that a deferred tax asset will never be realized (e.g., DTA from a NOL that expires), the DTA will need to be written off. The format for the journal entry would be as follows:

Valuation allowance	*XXX*	
Deferred tax asset		*XXX*

Note that this entry affects only the balance sheet because the income tax expense effect occurred when the valuation allowance was initially set up. There may also be situations when management evaluates new facts and circumstances and determines that the realizability of the deferred tax asset has increased such that the valuation allowance is no longer needed. The valuation allowance would need to be reduced or eliminated using a journal entry of the following form:

Valuation allowance	*XXX*	
Deferred tax benefit		*XXX*

In these situations, the reduction or elimination of the valuation allowance decreases the deferred tax expense and provides a benefit, increasing book income. Because the valuation allowance requires substantial judgment, auditors pay close attention to changes in the account.

TAXES IN THE REAL WORLD Berkshire Hathaway's $29 Billion Gift from Congress

When Berkshire Hathaway released its highly anticipated Form 10-K for 2017, the company announced that its gain in net worth for the year was $65.3 billion, but as CEO Warren Buffett noted, "A large portion of our gain did not come from anything we accomplished at Berkshire. The $65 billion gain is nonetheless real—rest assured of that. But only $36 billion came from Berkshire's operations. The remaining $29 billion was delivered to us in December when Congress rewrote the U.S. Tax Code."[31] What was the source of this $29 billion? Deferred tax accounting! At September 30, 2017, Berkshire Hathaway had a net deferred tax liability on its balance sheet of $85 billion, most of which was tax-effected at 35 percent (the statutory tax rate). When Congress reduced the corporate tax rate to 21 percent, Berkshire Hathaway was required to revalue this liability at 21 percent to the extent the associated taxable temporary differences were associated with U.S. book–tax differences. Using a back-of-the-envelope calculation, the $85 billion deferred tax liability translates to approximately $240 billion of book–tax differences ($85/.35). Valued at 21 percent, this net book–tax difference would translate to a deferred tax liability of $51 billion. Berkshire Hathaway would reduce its net deferred tax liability from $85 billion to $51 billion. The $34 billion reduction in the balance sheet basis would be accompanied by a decrease in deferred tax expense of $34 billion, thus increasing net income after tax and, ultimately, retained earnings (net worth) by $34 billion. The company stated in its Form 10-K that the benefit from revaluing its deferred tax accounts was approximately $30 billion.

[31]Warren Buffett, "Warren Buffett's Letter to the Shareholders of Berkshire Hathaway, Inc.," February 24, 2018. www.berkshirehathaway.com/letters/2017ltr.pdf.

Example 6-16

Elise created a workpaper that listed PCC's ending balances in its deferred tax assets and liabilities at December 31, 2022 (from Example 6-11), as follows:

PCC Deferred Tax Accounts at 12/31/2022

Deferred tax assets	
Allowance for bad debts	$ 87,150
Reserve for warranties	126,000
Net operating loss carryover	0
Deferred compensation	220,500
Stock option compensation	21,000
Net capital loss carryover	5,880
Charitable contribution carryover	15,477
Total deferred tax assets	**$ 476,007**
Deferred tax liabilities	
Depreciation	(2,751,000)
Total deferred tax liabilities	$ (2,751,000)
Net deferred tax liabilities	**$(2,274,993)**

What *positive* evidence should Elise consider in her evaluation as to whether PCC should record a valuation allowance against some or all of the deferred tax assets?

Answer: PCC has an excess of deferred tax liabilities over deferred tax assets of $2,274,993. When the book–tax depreciation difference reverses in the future, this will provide PCC with enough taxable income to absorb the reversing deferred tax assets.

What *negative* evidence should Elise consider in her evaluation as to whether PCC should record a valuation allowance against some or all of the deferred tax assets?

Answer: The deferred tax asset related to the charitable contribution carryover has a short carryover expiration date (five years). Elise may need to schedule out when the depreciation differences will reverse to determine if the reversals alone will provide PCC with enough taxable income to absorb the contribution carryover within the next five years.

More problematic, the net capital loss carryover has both a short carryover expiration date (five years) and requires PCC to recognize net capital gains in future periods to absorb the net capital loss. A reversal of the book–tax depreciation temporary difference will not provide PCC with net capital gain to absorb the net capital loss carryover.

What other sources of *positive* evidence should Elise consider in her evaluation as to whether PCC should record a valuation allowance against the deferred tax asset related to the net capital loss carryover?

Answer: Two additional sources of positive evidence are management's projections of future taxable income from sources other than reversing taxable temporary differences and future taxable income from tax planning strategies. Because PCC is in the business of manufacturing and selling computer-related equipment, any additional taxable income it generates from selling additional equipment will produce ordinary income. The company likely will have to rely on an assertion that management has a "prudent" *tax planning strategy* it would be willing to use to generate net capital gain in the future. An example of such a strategy might be management's willingness to sell a parcel of land held for investment to generate a capital gain sufficient to absorb the net capital loss.

After discussing with management its assessment of the company's sources of future taxable income, Elise concurred with management that the company did not need to record a valuation allowance for 2022.

What if: Assume PCC determined that a valuation allowance is required for the capital loss carryover. What journal entry would be required to reflect the valuation allowance?

Answer: The journal entry PCC would need to make to set up the valuation allowance would be as follows:

Deferred tax expense	$5,880	
Valuation allowance		$5,880

The impact of this journal entry would be to increase PCC's deferred tax expense for the year.

Example 6-17

What if: Assume PCC has had pretax book losses of $5,000,000 and $2,500,000 in 2020 and 2021, respectively. How might this additional fact influence Elise's assessment about the need for a valuation allowance?

Answer: PCC would have a cumulative pretax book loss of $1,469,000 over the past 36 months at December 31, 2022 (combined book losses of $7,500,000 in excess of 2022 pretax book income of $6,031,000 from Exhibit 6-3). ASC 740 states that a cumulative loss "in recent years" is considered objective negative evidence that may be hard to overcome. Elise would have to consider other sources of positive evidence that will outweigh the "significant" negative evidence in this situation. Often, the national office of the public accounting firm will make the determination as to whether a valuation allowance is required when a client experiences a 36-month cumulative loss.

Example 6-18

What if: Assume PCC just lost a big account to its competitor, but the company reported cumulative net income in the current and prior two years. How might this additional fact influence Elise's assessment about the need for a valuation allowance?

Answer: Expectations of future events can outweigh historic results. In this case, Elise would have to seriously consider whether a valuation allowance would be required to the extent that reversing taxable temporary differences would not absorb expected future losses.

LO 6-4

THE KEY FACTS

Accounting for Uncertain Tax Positions

- ASC 740 requires a two-step process for determining whether a tax benefit can be recognized in the financial statements.
  - A company first determines whether it is more likely than not that its tax position on a particular account will be sustained on IRS examination based on its technical merits.
  - A company then computes the amount it expects to be able to recognize.
- The measurement process requires the company to make a cumulative probability assessment of all likely outcomes of the audit and litigation process.
  - The company recognizes the amount that has a greater than 50 percent probability of being sustained on examination and subsequent litigation.
  - The amount not recognized is recorded as a liability on the balance sheet.

ACCOUNTING FOR UNCERTAINTY IN INCOME TAX POSITIONS

Step 5: Evaluate the Need for an Uncertain Tax Benefit Reserve

As you have learned in your study of the U.S. income tax laws, the answer to every tax question is not always certain. Taxpayers and the IRS can differ in their opinions as to whether an expenditure is deductible or must be capitalized, or whether income is taxable or is deferred or exempt from taxation. When irresolvable disputes arise, the taxpayer can petition the courts to resolve the tax treatment of a transaction. Taxpayers and the IRS can appeal decisions of the lower courts to the appellate courts and ultimately to the U.S. Supreme Court.

Taxpayers also take tax positions that can be disputed by state and local taxing authorities and international tax authorities. For example, the taxpayer and a state (international) tax authority may differ on whether the taxpayer has earned income in that jurisdiction and should pay tax on such income. The courts may not resolve this issue for many years after the original transaction takes place. If the courts do not resolve the issue in the taxpayer's favor, the taxpayer will be subject to interest and possible penalties on the tax owed.

For financial accounting purposes, a company must determine whether it can record the current or future tax benefits from an uncertain tax position in its financial statement for the period in which the transaction takes place, knowing that the ultimate resolution of the tax position may not be known until some time in the future.

Statement of Financial Accounting Standards No. 109 as originally written provided no specific guidance on how to deal with uncertain tax positions. As a result, companies generally applied the principles of FAS 5, *Accounting for Contingencies* (codified as ASC Topic 450), to uncertain tax positions. The FASB became concerned that companies were not applying FAS 5 uniformly, leading to diversity in practice and financial statements that were not comparable. After much debate, the FASB issued FASB Interpretation (FIN) No. 48, *Accounting for Uncertainty in Income Taxes—An Interpretation of FASB Statement No. 109,* in July 2006, effective for years beginning after December 15, 2006.

FIN 48 has been codified in ASC 740-10 but continues to be commonly referred to as FIN 48. We use both references (ASC 740-10 (FIN 48)) throughout the chapter to minimize confusion when referring to the topic. The objective of ASC 740-10 (FIN 48) is to provide a uniform approach to recording and disclosing tax benefits resulting from tax positions that are considered to be uncertain.

ASC 740-10 (FIN 48) applies a two-step process to evaluating tax positions. ASC 740-10 refers to the first step as *recognition*.[32] The second step is referred to as *measurement*.[33] Under ASC 740-10, the company records the largest amount of the benefit, as calculated on a cumulative probability basis, which is more likely than not to be realized on the ultimate settlement of the tax position.

Application of ASC Topic 740 to Uncertain Tax Positions

ASC 740 applies to all *tax positions* dealing with income taxes. As a result, it pertains to a tax position taken on a current or previously filed tax return and a tax position that will be taken on a future tax return that is reflected in the financial statements as a deferred tax asset or liability. ASC 740-10 (FIN 48) also applies to tax positions that result in permanent differences (e.g., the dividends-received deduction and credits) and to decisions not to file a tax return in a particular jurisdiction. For example, assume a company deducts an expenditure on its current tax return, which the IRS may challenge on audit in a future period. The deduction produces a net operating loss that will be carried forward and offset against future taxable income. ASC 740-10 (FIN 48) addresses whether the company can *recognize* the deferred tax asset related to the NOL carryover on its balance sheet. Once the recognition hurdle has been overcome, the company must then evaluate whether it is more likely than not that the deferred tax asset will be *realized* in the future period (i.e., whether a valuation allowance should be recorded).

Step 1: Recognition A company first must determine whether it is more likely than not that its tax position on a particular account will be sustained on IRS examination based on its technical merits. If the company believes this threshold has been met, it can record (recognize) the tax benefit of the tax position on its financial statements as a reduction in its current tax expense or an increase in its deferred tax benefit. The company must presume the IRS will examine this tax position with full knowledge of all relevant information. However, in deciding whether the more-likely-than-not threshold has been met, the company can take into account how the tax position might be resolved if litigated. This requires the company to evaluate the sources of authority that address this issue (i.e., the tax law, regulations, legislative history, IRS rulings, and court opinions).

Step 2: Measurement After the company determines that the more-likely-than-not recognition threshold has been met, it must compute the amount of the tax benefit to recognize in its financial statements. ASC 740-10 (FIN 48) states that the tax position is to be measured as:

> the largest amount of tax benefit that is greater than 50 percent likely of being realized upon ultimate settlement with a taxing authority that has full knowledge of all relevant information.[34]

This measurement process requires the company to make a cumulative probability assessment of all likely outcomes of the audit and litigation process. The company then recognizes the amount that has a greater than 50 percent probability of being sustained on examination and subsequent litigation.

[32]ASC 740-10-25-5 through 25-7.

[33]ASC 740-10-30-7.

[34]ASC 740-10-30-7.

Example 6-19

Assume PCC had taken a research credit of $500,000 on its 2022 tax return. There was some discussion about whether all of the company's activities qualified for the credit.

What threshold must be met before PCC can *recognize* any of the tax benefit from the "uncertain" portion of the research credit on its financial statements?

Answer: PCC must determine that it is more likely than not that its tax position on the research credit will be sustained by the IRS on examination based on its technical merits.

Example 6-20

PCC determined that it was more likely than not that the tax position in Example 6-19 would be sustained on audit and litigation. The tax department calculated the probability of receiving a full or partial benefit after resolution of the issue as follows:

Potential Estimated Tax Benefit	Individual Probability of Being Realized (%)	Cumulative Probability of Being Realized (%)
$500,000	60	60
300,000	25	85
200,000	10	95
0	5	100

Based on these probabilities, how much of the uncertain tax benefit of $500,000 can PCC recognize?

Answer: $500,000. PCC can recognize all $500,000 of the research credit tax benefit because this amount is the largest amount that has a greater than 50 percent cumulative probability of being realized on the ultimate settlement of the tax position.

Uncertain Tax Benefit Reserve Journal Entries The amount of the tax benefit that is not recognized ("unrecognized tax benefit") is recorded as a liability on the balance sheet (usually labeled as "Income Taxes Payable"). The corresponding "debit" to record the balance sheet liability is to *current* income tax expense (or a decrease in income tax benefit).

Current income tax expense	*XXX*	
Income taxes payable		*XXX*

If the company expects the uncertain tax position to be resolved in the next 12 months, the balance sheet payable is characterized as current. Otherwise, the payable is characterized as being noncurrent. The increase in tax expense is added to the current portion of the provision under the theory that this is an on-demand liability.

Example 6-21

What if: Assume PCC's tax department had assessed the cumulative probabilities of sustaining the $500,000 research credit tax benefit as follows:

Potential Estimated Tax Benefit	Individual Probability of Being Realized (%)	Cumulative Probability of Being Realized (%)
$500,000	40	40
300,000	30	70
200,000	20	90
0	10	100

Based on these probabilities, how much of the uncertain tax benefit of $500,000 can PCC recognize?

Answer: $300,000. PCC can recognize $300,000 of the research credit tax benefit because this amount is the largest amount that has a greater than 50 percent cumulative probability of being realized on the ultimate settlement of the tax position. This translates into management believing that $300,000 of the uncertain research credit will be sustained on audit.

What would be PCC's journal entry to record the portion of the tax benefit that cannot be recognized?

Answer: PCC would establish a liability for the $200,000 difference between the amount of the benefit received on the current-year tax return ($500,000) and the amount the company ultimately expects to receive ($300,000). PCC would record the following journal entry:

Current income tax expense	$200,000	
Income taxes payable		$200,000

The Income Taxes Payable account is characterized as noncurrent on the balance sheet if PCC does not expect the "uncertain tax position" (UTP) to be resolved within the next 12 months. The uncertain tax benefit is recorded as a current tax expense because this is the additional amount of taxes PCC would pay if it prepared its tax return by deducting only $300,000 of the uncertain research credit instead of $500,000.

Subsequent Events

ASC 740-10 (FIN 48) requires a company to monitor subsequent events (e.g., the issuance of new regulations, rulings, court opinions) that might change the company's assessment that a tax position will be sustained on audit and litigation. As facts and circumstances change, a company must reevaluate the tax benefit amount it expects to realize in the future. For example, the Treasury might issue a regulation or ruling that clarifies its tax position on a particular item. This regulation could change a company's assessment that its tax position meets the more-likely-than-not threshold required for recognition.

In July 2015, the U.S. Tax Court held in favor of Altera, Inc., that the IRS's challenge to its transfer pricing methodology (intercompany cost sharing for the development of intangibles) was invalid. After the decision, the IRS filed an appeal with the U.S. Court of Appeals for the Ninth Circuit. The Ninth Circuit court held 2-1 in favor of the IRS, but one of the judges favoring the IRS died and the case was remanded back to the Ninth Circuit for a new hearing. At that time, Microsoft Corp., which had a similar tax-related uncertain tax position, concluded that no adjustment should be made to the company's uncertain tax benefit balance because there was still uncertainty as to the ultimate outcome of the case. On the other hand, Juniper Networks viewed the *Altera* decision as new information that allowed the company to reduce its uncertain tax benefit related to its cost-sharing arrangements. The different reactions of these two companies to the same court case decision illustrates that the application of this accounting pronouncement is subject to management judgment. On June 7, 2019, a three-judge panel of the Ninth Circuit Court of Appeals reversed the Tax Court decision.[35] The IRS issued a new directive (www.irs.gov/businesses/corporations/withdrawal-of-directive-lbi-04-0118-005) instructing examiners to open new examinations on the issue. On June 22, 2020, the U.S. Supreme Court denied to hear Altera's appeal; thus, the 9th Circuit decision stands (926 F.3d 1061 (2019)). Microsoft Corp.'s 2020 annual report shows continued uncertainty in its uncertain tax positions related to its transfer pricing. Juniper Networks's 2020 annual report (latest available) includes an additional charge of $20.1 million to its uncertain tax benefit reserve in response to the Supreme Court denial to hear the case.

[35]*Altera v. Comm'r,* 926 F.3d 1061 (9th Cir. 2019).

Interest and Penalties

ASC 740-10 (FIN 48) requires a company to accrue interest and any applicable penalties on liabilities it establishes for potential future tax obligations. The interest (net of the tax benefit from deducting it on a future tax return when paid) and penalties (which are not tax deductible) can be treated as part of the company's UTP-related income tax expense and income tax payable or can be recognized as interest or penalties separate from the UTP-related income tax expense. ASC 740-10 (FIN 48) only requires that the company apply its election consistently from period to period. This election creates the potential for diversity in practice. For example, General Motors Corporation treats accrued interest and penalties on its uncertain tax positions as part of its selling, general, and administrative expenses, while Ford Motor Company treats accrued interest and penalties on its uncertain tax positions as part of its income tax provision.

Disclosures of Uncertain Tax Positions

One of the most controversial aspects of ASC 740-10 (FIN 48) is its expansion of the disclosure requirements related to liabilities recorded due to uncertain tax positions (UTPs). ASC 740-10 (FIN 48) requires the company to roll forward all unrecognized tax benefits (UTBs) on a worldwide aggregated basis. Specific line items must disclose (1) the gross amounts of increases and decreases in liabilities related to uncertain tax positions as a result of tax positions taken during a prior period, (2) the gross amounts of increases and decreases in liabilities related to uncertain tax positions as a result of tax positions taken during the current period, (3) the amounts of decreases in liabilities related to uncertain tax positions relating to settlements with taxing authorities, and (4) reductions in liabilities related to uncertain tax positions as a result of a lapse of the applicable statute of limitations (the taxing authority can no longer audit the tax return on which the tax position was taken). The UTP disclosure by Microsoft Corporation is illustrated in Exhibit 6-9.

EXHIBIT 6-9 The UTP Disclosure of Microsoft Corporation

The aggregate changes in the balance of unrecognized tax benefits were as follows:

	(In millions)		
Year Ended June 30,	**2021**	**2020**	**2019**
Balance, beginning of year	**$13,792**	$13,146	$11,961
Decreases related to settlements	**(195)**	(31)	(316)
Increases for tax positions related to the current year	**790**	647	2,106
Increases for tax positions related to prior years	**461**	366	508
Decreases for tax positions related to prior years	**(297)**	(331)	(1,113)
Decreases due to lapsed statutes of limitations	**(1)**	(5)	0
Balance, end of year	**$14,550**	$13,792	$13,146

Source: Microsoft Corporation, "Annual Report 2021," July 31, 2021, Note 12—Income Taxes.

Opponents of ASC 740-10 (FIN 48) worried that the UTB disclosures would provide the IRS with a "roadmap" to a company's uncertain tax positions.[36] The ASC 740-10 (FIN 48) disclosures have not provided the IRS with the hoped-for details because the UTP disclosure does not identify the tax jurisdictions to which the uncertain tax positions relate.

[36]Jesse Drucker, "Lifting the Veil on Tax Risk—New Accounting Rule Lays Bare a Firm's Liability If Transaction Is Later Disallowed by the IRS," *The Wall Street Journal,* May 25, 2007.

Schedule UTP (Uncertain Tax Position) Statement

Since 2010, large corporations have been required to file Schedule UTP, Uncertain Tax Position Statement, with their Form 1120. Schedule UTP was designed to increase transparency and efficiency in identifying audit issues and help the IRS prioritize the selection of issues and taxpayers for audit. Schedule UTP requires corporations to report any federal income tax position for which an unrecognized tax benefit has been recorded in an audited financial statement. A corporation must identify the IRC section or sections relating to the position, indicate whether the position involves a temporary or permanent difference, identify whether the tax position is a major tax position (i.e., 10 percent or more of the total), rank the tax position by size, and provide a "concise" description of the UTP. Corporations with assets of $10 million or more that issue audited financial statements and have one or more reported uncertain tax positions must file Schedule UTP.

ETHICS

Miguel Castillo, senior manager in the tax group in the Boston office of Bean Counters LLP, an international professional services firm, was reviewing the workpapers related to the uncertain tax positions prepared by his biggest client, Pro Vision Inc. Miguel noticed that the client took the position that it did not need to record an uncertain tax benefit for a significant transaction because it had a "should level" opinion from its law firm. (A "should level" tax opinion means that the law firm believes there is a 70 to 90 percent probability that the tax benefit from the transaction will be allowed if litigated.) When Miguel asked to see the tax opinion, he was told by the firm's tax director that the company did not want to disclose the item for fear the IRS also would ask to see the opinion. Miguel has always had a good working relationship with the tax staff at Pro Vision and trusts their integrity.

Should Miguel take the tax director's word when auditing the company's reserve for uncertain tax positions? What would you do if you were in Miguel's position?

FINANCIAL STATEMENT DISCLOSURE AND COMPUTING A CORPORATION'S EFFECTIVE TAX RATE

LO 6-5

Balance Sheet Classification

ASC 740 requires publicly traded and privately held companies to classify all deferred tax assets and liabilities on their balance sheets as noncurrent.

Income Tax Footnote Disclosure

In addition to the above balance sheet disclosure requirements, ASC 740 mandates that a company disclose the components of the net deferred tax assets and liabilities reported on its balance sheet and the total valuation allowance recognized for deferred tax assets.[37] Most companies provide this information in a footnote to the financial statements (often referred to as the *income tax footnote*). Publicly traded companies must disclose the approximate "tax effect" of each type of temporary difference and carryover that gives rise to a *significant* portion of the net deferred tax liabilities and deferred tax assets.[38] Privately held (nonpublic) companies need to disclose only the types of significant temporary differences, without disclosing the tax effects of each type. ASC 740 does not

[37] ASC 740-10-50-2.
[38] ASC 740-10-50-6.

define the term *significant,* although the SEC requires a publicly traded company to disclose separately the components of its total deferred tax assets and liabilities that are 5 percent or more of the total balance.[39] Exhibit 6-10 provides the disclosure of PCC's deferred tax accounts in its income tax footnote.

ASC 740 also requires publicly traded companies to disclose the significant components of their income tax provision (expense or benefit) attributable to continuing operations in

EXHIBIT 6-10 PCC's Income Tax Note to Its Financial Statements

NOTE 5 INCOME TAXES

The Company's income (loss) from continuing operations before the income tax provision by taxing jurisdiction is as follows:

	2022
United States	$6,031,000

The provision (benefit) for income taxes is as follows:

Current tax provision (benefit)	
Federal (U.S.)	$1,180,557
Deferred tax expense (benefit)	
Federal (U.S.)	87,423
Income tax provision	$1,267,980

The significant components of the Company's deferred tax assets and liabilities as of December 31, 2022, are as follows:

	2022
Deferred tax *assets*	
Allowance for bad debts	$ 87,150
Reserve for warranties	126,000
Deferred compensation	220,500
Stock option compensation	21,000
Net capital loss carryover	5,880
Contribution carryover	15,477
Total deferred tax assets	$ 476,007
Valuation allowance	0
Deferred tax assets net of valuation allowance	$ 476,007
Deferred tax *liabilities*	
Depreciation	$(2,751,000)
Total deferred tax liabilities	$(2,751,000)
Net deferred tax liabilities	$(2,274,993)

The net capital loss carryover and the contribution carryover expire after 2027 if unused.

A reconciliation of income taxes computed by applying the statutory U.S. income tax rate to the Company's income before income taxes to the income tax provision is as follows:

	2022
Amount computed at the statutory U.S. tax rate (21%)	$1,266,510
Tax-exempt income	(2,520)
Nondeductible life insurance premiums	7,140
Dividends-received deduction	(3,150)
Income tax provision	$1,267,980

The cash amount paid during 2022 for income taxes, net of refunds, was $1,180,557.

[39] ASC 740-10-50-8; SEC Regulation S-X, §210.4-08(h).

either the financial statements or a note thereto.[40] These components include the (1) current tax expense or benefit, (2) deferred tax expense or benefit, (3) benefits of operating loss carryovers, (4) adjustments of a deferred tax liability or asset for enacted changes in tax laws or rates, and (5) adjustments of the beginning-of-the-year balance of a valuation allowance because of a change in circumstances that causes a change in management's judgment about the realizability of the recognized deferred tax assets.

Computation and Reconciliation of the Income Tax Provision with a Company's *Hypothetical* Tax Provision (Effective Tax Rate Reconciliation) ASC 740 requires a company to reconcile its (a) reported income tax provision attributable to continuing operations with (b) the amount of income tax expense that would result from applying its U.S. statutory tax rate to its pretax net income or loss from continuing operations.[41] Alternately, a company can present the reconciliation in terms of tax rates, comparing its statutory tax rate with its effective tax rate (income tax provision/pretax income from continuing operations).

Differences between a company's income tax provision and its hypothetical tax provision can arise from several sources. Income taxes paid to a state or municipality increase a company's total income tax provision over its hypothetical income tax expense. Income taxes paid to a jurisdiction outside the United States can increase or decrease a company's total income tax provision over its hypothetical income tax expense, depending on whether the jurisdiction taxes the company's income at more or less than the U.S. statutory rate. Permanent differences also affect the computation of a company's income tax provision. Favorable permanent differences (e.g., tax-exempt income) decrease the income tax provision relative to the hypothetical income tax provision. Unfavorable permanent differences (e.g., nondeductible fines and penalties) increase the income tax provision relative to the hypothetical income tax provision.

ASC 740 requires a publicly traded company to disclose the estimated amount and nature of each significant reconciling item, which the SEC defines as an amount equal to or greater than 5 percent of the hypothetical provision. The SEC requires nonpublicly traded companies to disclose the nature of significant reconciling items but not the reconciling amount.

Example 6-22

Elise used her schedule of permanent differences (from Example 6-4) to reconcile PCC's income tax provision ($1,267,980, from Example 6-13) with the company's hypothetical income tax provision. The permanent differences from Example 6-4 are reproduced below:

Permanent Differences	(Favorable) Unfavorable
Tax-exempt interest income	$(12,000)
Life insurance premiums	34,000
Dividends-received deduction	(15,000)

PCC's pretax net income from continuing operations in 2022 is $6,031,000 (from Exhibit 6-10).

What is PCC's *hypothetical* income tax provision for 2022?

Answer: $1,266,510, computed as $6,031,000 × 21 percent.

(continued on page 6-32)

[40] ASC 740-10-50-9.

[41] ASC 740-10-50-12. The income tax provision computed using the statutory tax rate is often referred to as the *hypothetical income tax expense.*

What is PCC's *effective tax rate* for 2022?

Answer: 21.02 percent, computed as $1,267,980/$6,031,000.

PCC's reconciliation of its hypothetical income tax provision with its actual income tax provision in 2022 was presented in Exhibit 6-10. The tax cost or benefit from each permanent difference is computed by multiplying the permanent difference (from above) times 21 percent.

Answer:

	2022
Amount computed at statutory U.S. tax rate (21%)	$1,266,510
Tax-exempt income	(2,520)
Nondeductible life insurance premiums	7,140
Dividends-received deduction	(3,150)
Income tax provision	$1,267,980

The SEC requires its registrants to separately disclose only those components of their effective tax rate reconciliations that equal or exceed 5 percent of the "hypothetical" tax expense. In the above reconciliation, PCC would only be required to separately disclose the items that equal or exceed $63,326 ($1,266,510 × 5%). None of the reconciling items exceed this amount. All of the reconciling items could be netted in the reconciliation.

Provide a reconciliation of PCC's statutory income tax rate (21 percent) with its actual effective tax rate (21.02 percent) in 2022. The percentage effect of each permanent difference is computed by dividing the tax cost or benefit from the item (from above) by PCC's pretax net income ($6,031,000).

Answer:

	2022
Statutory U.S. tax rate	21.00%
Tax-exempt income	(0.042)
Nondeductible life insurance premiums	0.118
Dividends-received deduction	(0.052)
Effective tax rate	21.02%

PCC's income tax note to its financial statements (Exhibit 6-10) provides the disclosure of PCC's reconciliation of its effective tax rate.

Importance of a Corporation's Effective Tax Rate The effective tax rate often serves as a benchmark for companies in the same industry. However, nonrecurring events can sometimes have a significant impact on the effective tax rate. To mitigate the impact of such aberrational events, companies and their investors may use (at least for internal purposes) a different measure of effective tax rate that backs out one-time and nonrecurring events and assumes profitable operations in each jurisdiction in which it operates. This effective tax rate is referred to as the company's **structural tax rate.** The structural effective tax rate often is viewed as more representative of the company's effective tax rate from its normal (recurring) operations. In our example, PCC does not appear to have any nonrecurring reconciling items, which would make its effective tax rate and its structural tax rate the same.

Analysts often compute a company's **cash tax rate,** the cash taxes paid divided by pretax book income, in their evaluation of the company's tax efficiency.[42] As the name implies, the cash tax rate excludes deferred taxes. PCC's cash tax rate in 2022 is 19.57 percent ($1,180,557/$6,031,000). Companies that have significant favorable temporary differences can have a cash tax rate that is much lower than their accounting effective tax rate.

Interim Period Effective Tax Rates

In addition to annual reports (Form 10-K), PCC also must report earnings on a quarterly basis (Form 10-Q). ASC 740-270, *Interim Reporting,* governs the preparation of these quarterly statements. ASC 740-270-30-6 states that "[a]t the end of each interim period the entity should make its best estimate of the effective tax rate expected to be applicable for the full fiscal year"[43] and apply this rate to the income reported in the quarterly statement. A company must reconsider its estimate of the annual rate each quarter. When the estimate changes, the company must adjust the cumulative tax provision for the year-to-date earnings to reflect the new expected annual rate. The adjusting amount becomes the company's income tax provision for the quarter.

FASB PROJECTS RELATED TO ACCOUNTING FOR INCOME TAXES

As part of its Disclosure Framework project, the FASB has proposed expanding the information to be provided in the income tax footnote. In particular, the FASB is considering whether to require companies to report pretax income from continuing operations, the associated income tax provision, and cash taxes paid as either U.S. or non-U.S. The FASB also wants increased disclosure regarding the nature and amounts of the valuation allowance recorded and released during the reporting period. The FASB issued an Accounting Statement Update in December 2019 (ASU No. 2019-12) to simplify certain reporting requirements of ASC 740 relating to loss entities and interim reporting.

CONCLUSION

In this chapter we discussed the basic rules that govern the computation of a company's U.S. income tax provision. As a result of increased SEC and Public Company Accounting Oversight Board (PCAOB) scrutiny, the need for individuals who understand these rules has increased dramatically. The FASB requires a company to take a balance sheet approach to computing its current and future (deferred) tax liabilities or benefits (assets). The income tax provision that appears on a company's income statement becomes the amount necessary to adjust the beginning balances of these accounts to their appropriate ending balances. The FASB and SEC also impose disclosure requirements for how a company reports its tax accounts in the financial statement amounts and notes to the financial statements.

[42]ASC Topic 230, *Statement of Cash Flows,* requires an enterprise to separately disclose income taxes paid as part of the statement itself or in a note to the financial statements (usually the income taxes note or a supplemental cash flow note).

[43]Financial Accounting Foundation, "FASB Exposure Draft: Proposed Accounting Standards Update. Income Taxes (Topic 740)," May 14, 2019. https://asc.fasb.org/imageRoot/07/120320407.pdf.

Summary

LO 6-1 Describe the objectives of FASB ASC Topic 740, *Income Taxes,* and the income tax provision process.

- Objectives of ASC 740:
  - To recognize a current income tax liability or asset for the company's taxes payable or refundable in the current year.
  - To recognize a deferred income tax liability or asset for the income tax effects of the company's temporary differences and carryovers.
- The income tax provision process consists of five steps:
  1. Identify all permanent and temporary differences and tax carryover amounts and calculate the current income tax provision (ASC 740 Objective 1).
  2. Determine the ending balances in the balance sheet deferred tax asset and liability accounts (ASC 740 Objective 2).
  3. Calculate the deferred income tax provision and the total income tax provision.
  4. Evaluate the need for a valuation allowance for gross deferred tax assets.
  5. Evaluate the need for an uncertain tax benefit reserve.

LO 6-2 Calculate the current and deferred income tax expense or benefit components of a company's income tax provision.

- The company first adjusts its pretax net income or loss for permanent and temporary book–tax differences to compute taxable income or loss. The company then applies the appropriate tax rate to taxable income (loss) to compute the tax return current tax expense or benefit.
- The company adjusts its tax return income tax liability or benefit for audit refunds or deficiencies from prior-year tax returns and for income tax benefits from stock option exercises treated as permanent differences.
- A company computes its deferred income tax expense or benefit by applying the applicable tax rate to the change in the cumulative balance sheet temporary differences between the financial accounting basis of an asset or liability and its corresponding tax basis from the beginning of the year to the end of the year.
- The future tax benefits from deductible temporary differences are recorded as deferred tax assets.
- The future tax costs of favorable taxable temporary differences are recorded as deferred tax liabilities.

LO 6-3 Determine how to calculate a valuation allowance.

- If a company determines that it is more likely than not (a greater than 50 percent probability) that some portion or all of the deferred tax assets will not be realized in a future period, it must offset the deferred tax assets with a valuation allowance to reflect the amount the company does not expect to realize in the future.
- The determination as to whether it is more likely than not that a deferred tax asset will not be realized in the future must be based on all available evidence, both positive and negative.
- ASC 740 identifies four sources of prior and future taxable income to consider: (1) future reversals of existing taxable temporary differences, (2) taxable income in prior carryback year(s), (3) expected future taxable income exclusive of reversing temporary differences and carryovers, and (4) expected income from tax planning strategies.

LO 6-4 Explain how a company accounts for its uncertain income tax positions under FASB ASC Topic 740.

- A company must determine whether it can record the tax benefits from an "uncertain" tax position in its financial statement for the period in which the transaction takes place, knowing that the ultimate resolution of the tax position may not be known until some future period.

- ASC 740 applies a two-step process to evaluating uncertain tax positions:
  - Recognition: A company must determine whether it is more likely than not (a greater than 50 percent probability) that a tax position will be sustained upon examination by the IRS or other taxing authority, including resolution of any appeals within the court system, based on the technical merits of the position.
  - Measurement: If the tax position meets the more-likely-than-not threshold (a subjective determination), the company must determine the amount of the benefit to record in the financial statements.
- Under ASC 740, the amount to be recorded is the largest amount of the benefit, as calculated on a cumulative probability basis, that is more likely than not to be realized on the ultimate settlement of the tax position.

Describe how a company computes and discloses the components of its effective tax rate. LO 6-5

- For annual periods beginning after December 15, 2016, ASC 740 requires a business entity to disclose all of its deferred tax liabilities and assets as noncurrent on its balance sheet.
- A company also is required to present the "significant" components of the income tax provision (expense or benefit) attributable to continuing operations.
- ASC 740 requires publicly traded companies to reconcile their reported income tax expense (benefit) from continuing operations with the *hypothetical* tax expense that would have resulted from applying the domestic federal statutory rate to pretax income from continuing operations. Alternatively, the company can compute an *effective tax rate* from its continuing operations and reconcile it with the domestic federal statutory rate (21 percent).
- A company computes its effective tax rate by dividing its income tax provision (benefit) from continuing operations by its pretax net income from continuing operations.
- Items that cause the effective tax rate to differ from the statutory tax rate include permanent differences, audit adjustments, state and local taxes, and international taxes.

KEY TERMS

book equivalent of taxable income (6-9)
cash tax rate (6-33)
current income tax expense (benefit) (6-10)
current tax liability (asset) (6-3)
deductible temporary differences (6-13)
deferred tax asset (6-2)
deferred tax liability (6-2)
effective tax rate (6-8)
enacted tax rate (6-16)
income tax provision (6-1)
permanent book–tax differences (6-7)
structural tax rate (6-32)
tax accounting balance sheet (6-11)
tax carryovers (6-4)
taxable temporary difference (6-12)
temporary book–tax differences (6-9)
uncertain tax positions (6-11)
valuation allowance (6-20)

DISCUSSION QUESTIONS

Discussion Questions are available in Connect®.

Mc Graw Hill connect

1. Identify some of the reasons why accounting for income taxes is complex. LO 6-1
2. True or False: ASC 740 applies to all taxes paid by a corporation. Explain. LO 6-1
3. True or False: ASC 740 is the sole source for the rules that apply to accounting for income taxes. Explain. LO 6-1
4. How does the fact that most corporations file their financial statements several months before they file their income tax returns complicate the income tax provision process? LO 6-1
5. What distinguishes an *income tax* from other taxes? LO 6-1
6. Briefly describe the five-step process by which a company computes its income tax provision. LO 6-1

LO 6-2 7. What are the two components of a company's income tax provision? What does each component represent about a company's income tax provision?

LO 6-2 8. True or False: All differences between book and taxable income, both permanent and temporary, affect a company's effective tax rate. Explain.

LO 6-2 9. When does a temporary difference resulting from an expense (deduction) create a taxable temporary difference? A deductible temporary difference?

LO 6-2 10. When does a temporary difference resulting from income create a taxable temporary difference? A deductible temporary difference?

LO 6-2 11. Briefly describe what is meant by the *asset and liability* or *balance sheet* approach taken by ASC 740 with respect to computing a corporation's deferred tax provision.

LO 6-2 12. Why are cumulatively favorable temporary differences referred to as taxable temporary differences?

LO 6-2 13. Why are cumulatively unfavorable temporary differences referred to as deductible temporary differences?

LO 6-2 14. In addition to the current-year tax return taxes payable or refundable, what other transactions can affect a company's current income tax provision?

LO 6-2 LO 6-4 15. What is an unrecognized tax benefit, and how does it affect a company's current income tax expense?

LO 6-2 16. True or False: When Congress changes the corporate tax rates, only the current-year book–tax temporary differences are measured using the new rates. Explain.

LO 6-2 17. True or False: All temporary differences have a financial accounting basis. Explain.

LO 6-3 18. What is the purpose behind a valuation allowance as it applies to deferred tax assets?

LO 6-3 19. What is the difference between *recognition* and *realization* in the recording of a deferred tax asset on a balance sheet?

LO 6-3 20. Briefly describe the four sources of taxable income a company evaluates in determining if a valuation allowance is necessary.

LO 6-3 21. Which of the four sources of taxable income are considered objective and which are considered subjective? Which of these sources generally receives the most weight in analyzing whether a valuation allowance is necessary?

LO 6-3 22. What are the elements that define a tax planning strategy as it applies to determining if a valuation allowance is necessary? Provide an example where a tax planning strategy may be necessary to avoid recording a valuation allowance.

LO 6-3 23. When does a company remove a valuation allowance from its balance sheet?

LO 6-3 24. What is a company's *book equivalent of taxable income*?

LO 6-4 25. What motivated the FASB to issue ASC 740-10 (FIN 48)?

LO 6-4 26. Briefly describe the two-step process a company must undertake when it evaluates whether it can record the tax benefit from an uncertain tax position under ASC 740-10 (FIN 48).

LO 6-4 27. Distinguish between *recognition* and *measurement* as they relate to the computation of unrecognized tax benefits under ASC 740-10 (FIN 48).

LO 6-4 28. What is a *tax position* as it relates to the application of ASC 740-10 (FIN 48) to uncertain tax positions?

LO 6-4 29. True or False: A company determines its unrecognized tax benefits with respect to a transaction only at the time the transaction takes place; subsequent events are ignored. Explain.

LO 6-4 30. True or False: ASC 740-10 (FIN 48) requires that a company treat potential interest and penalties related to an unrecognized tax benefit as part of its income tax provision. Explain.

LO 6-4 31. Where on the balance sheet does a company report its unrecognized tax benefits?

32. Why did many companies oppose ASC 740-10 (FIN 48) when it was first proposed? LO 6-4
33. How does a company disclose deferred tax assets and liabilities on its balance sheet? LO 6-5
34. Under what conditions can a company net its deferred tax assets with its deferred tax liabilities on the balance sheet? LO 6-5
35. True or False: A publicly traded company must disclose all of the components of its deferred tax assets and liabilities in a footnote to the financial statements. Explain. LO 6-5
36. What is a company's *hypothetical* income tax provision, and what is its importance in a company's disclosure of its income tax provision in the tax footnote? LO 6-5
37. Briefly describe the difference between a company's effective tax rate, cash tax rate, and structural tax rate. LO 6-5

PROBLEMS

Select problems are available in Connect®.

Mc Graw Hill connect

38. Which of the following taxes is *not* accounted for under ASC 740? LO 6-1
    a) Income taxes paid to the U.S. government.
    b) Income taxes paid to the French government.
    c) Income taxes paid to the city of Detroit.
    d) Property taxes paid to the city of Detroit.
    e) All of the above taxes are accounted for under ASC 740.
39. Which of the following organizations can issue rules that govern accounting for income taxes? LO 6-1
    a) FASB.
    b) SEC.
    c) IRS.
    d) Both (a) and (b) above.
    e) All of the above organizations.
40. Find the paragraph(s) in ASC 740 that deals with the following items (access ASC 740 on the FASB website, www.fasb.org, and then click on "Standards"). You will need a username and password from your instructor. LO 6-1 research
    a) The objectives and basic principles that underlie ASC 740.
    b) Examples of book–tax differences that create temporary differences.
    c) The definition of a *tax planning strategy*.
    d) Examples of positive evidence in the valuation allowance process.
    e) Rules relating to financial statement disclosure.
41. Bautista Corporation reported pretax book income of $1,000,000. Included in the computation were favorable temporary differences of $200,000, unfavorable temporary differences of $50,000, and favorable permanent differences of $100,000. Compute the company's current income tax expense or benefit. LO 6-2
42. Cass Corporation reported pretax book income of $10,000,000. During the current year, the reserve for bad debts increased by $100,000. In addition, tax depreciation exceeded book depreciation by $200,000. Cass Corporation sold a fixed asset and reported book gain of $50,000 and tax gain of $75,000. Finally, the company received $250,000 of tax-exempt life insurance proceeds from the death of one of its officers. Compute the company's current income tax expense or benefit. LO 6-2

LO 6-2 43. Grand Corporation reported pretax book income of $600,000. Tax depreciation exceeded book depreciation by $400,000. In addition, the company received $300,000 of tax-exempt municipal bond interest. The company's prior-year tax return showed taxable income of $50,000. Compute the company's current income tax expense or benefit.

LO 6-2 44. Akoto Corporation reported pretax book income of $2,000,000. Tax depreciation exceeded book depreciation by $500,000. During the year, the company capitalized $250,000 into ending inventory under §263A. Capitalized inventory costs of $150,000 in beginning inventory were deducted as part of cost of goods sold on the tax return. Compute the company's taxes payable or refundable.

LO 6-2 45. Choi Company determined that the book basis of its office building exceeded the tax basis by $800,000. This basis difference is properly characterized as:

a) A permanent difference.
b) A taxable temporary difference.
c) A deductible temporary difference.
d) A favorable book–tax difference.
e) Both (b) and (d) above are correct.

LO 6-2 46. Abbot Company determined that the book basis of its allowance for bad debts is $100,000. There is no corresponding tax basis in this account. The basis difference is properly characterized as:

a) A permanent difference.
b) A taxable temporary difference.
c) A deductible temporary difference.
d) A favorable book–tax difference.
e) Both (b) and (d) above are correct.

LO 6-2 47. Which of the following items is *not* a temporary book–tax basis difference?

a) Warranty reserve accruals.
b) Accelerated depreciation.
c) Capitalized inventory costs under §263A.
d) Nondeductible stock option compensation from exercising an ISO.
e) All of the above are temporary differences.

LO 6-2 48. Which of the following book–tax differences does *not* create a favorable temporary book–tax basis difference?

a) Tax depreciation for the period exceeds book depreciation.
b) Bad debts charged off in the current period exceed the bad debts accrued in the current period.
c) Inventory costs capitalized under §263A deducted as part of current-year tax cost of goods sold are less than the inventory costs capitalized in ending inventory.
d) Vacation pay accrued for tax purposes in a prior period is deducted in the current period.
e) All of the above create a favorable temporary book–tax difference.

LO 6-2 49. Lodge Inc. reported pretax book income of $5,000,000. During the year, the company increased its reserve for warranties by $200,000. The company deducted $50,000 on its tax return related to warranty payments made during the year. What is the impact on taxable income compared to pretax book income of the book–tax difference that results from these two events?

a) Favorable (decreases taxable income).
b) Unfavorable (increases taxable income).
c) Neutral (no impact on taxable income).

50. Which of the following book–tax basis differences results in a deductible temporary difference? LO 6-2
   a) Book basis of a fixed asset exceeds its tax basis.
   b) Book basis of a pension-related liability exceeds its tax basis.
   c) Prepayment of income included on the tax return but not on the income statement (the transaction is recorded as a liability on the balance sheet).
   d) All of the above result in a deductible temporary difference.
   e) Both (b) and (c) result in a deductible temporary difference.
51. Kumara Corporation reported pretax book income of $1,000,000. Kumara also reports an increase in the taxable temporary differences of $200,000, an increase in the deductible temporary differences of $50,000, and favorable permanent differences of $100,000. Assuming a tax rate of 21 percent, compute the company's deferred income tax expense or benefit. LO 6-2
52. Song Inc. reported pretax book income of $10,000,000. During the current year, the reserve for bad debts increased by $100,000. In addition, tax depreciation exceeded book depreciation by $200,000. Song Inc. sold a fixed asset and reported book gain of $50,000 and tax gain of $75,000. Finally, the company received $250,000 of tax-exempt life insurance proceeds from the death of one of its officers. Assuming a tax rate of 21 percent, compute the company's deferred income tax expense or benefit. LO 6-2
53. Li Corporation reported pretax book income of $600,000. Tax depreciation exceeded book depreciation by $400,000. In addition, the company received $300,000 of tax-exempt municipal bond interest. The company's prior-year tax return showed taxable income of $50,000. Assuming a tax rate of 21 percent, compute the company's deferred income tax expense or benefit. LO 6-2
54. Identify the following items as creating a temporary book–tax difference, a permanent book–tax difference, or no book–tax difference. LO 6-2

Item	Temporary Difference	Permanent Difference	No Difference
Reserve for warranties			
Accrued pension liability			
Goodwill not amortized for tax purposes but subject to impairment under ASC Topic 350			
Nondeductible meal expenses			
Life insurance proceeds			
Net capital loss carryover			
Nondeductible fines and penalties			
Accrued vacation pay liability paid within the first two and one-half months of the next tax year			

55. Which of the following items is *not* a permanent book–tax difference? LO 6-2
   a) Tax-exempt interest income.
   b) Tax-exempt insurance proceeds.
   c) Windfall tax benefits from the exercise of a nonqualified stock option (NQO).
   d) Nondeductible meal expenses.
   e) First-year expensing under §179.
56. Rimas Corporation reported pretax book income of $1,000,000. Included in the computation were favorable temporary differences of $200,000, unfavorable temporary differences of $50,000, and favorable permanent differences of $100,000. Compute the company's book equivalent of taxable income. Use this number to compute the company's total income tax provision or benefit. LO 6-2

LO 6-2 57. Burcham Corporation reported pretax book income of $600,000. Tax depreciation exceeded book depreciation by $400,000. In addition, the company received $300,000 of tax-exempt municipal bond interest. The company's prior-year tax return showed taxable income of $50,000. Compute the company's book equivalent of taxable income. Use this number to compute the company's total income tax provision or benefit.

LO 6-3 58. Arain Corporation has total deferred tax assets of $3,000,000 at year-end. Management is assessing whether a valuation allowance must be recorded against some or all of the deferred tax assets. What level of assurance must management have, based on the weight of available evidence, that some or all of the deferred tax assets will not be realized before a valuation allowance is required?

a) Probable.

b) More likely than not.

c) Realistic possibility.

d) Reasonable.

e) More than remote.

LO 6-3 59. Which of the following would *not* be considered positive evidence in determining whether Arain Corporation needs to record a valuation allowance for some or all of its deferred tax assets?

a) The company forecasts future taxable income because of its backlog of orders.

b) The company has unfavorable temporary differences that will create future taxable income when they reverse.

c) The company has tax-planning strategies that it can implement to create future taxable income.

d) The company has cumulative net income over the current and prior two years.

e) The company had a net operating loss carryover expire in the current year.

LO 6-3 60. As of the beginning of the year, Gratiot Company recorded a valuation allowance of $200,000 against its deferred tax assets of $1,000,000. The valuation allowance relates to a net operating loss carryover from the prior year. During the year, management concludes that the valuation allowance is no longer necessary because it forecasts sufficient taxable income to absorb the NOL carryover. What is the impact of management's reversal of the valuation allowance on the company's effective tax rate?

a) Increases the effective tax rate.

b) Decreases the effective tax rate.

c) No impact on the effective tax rate.

LO 6-3 61. Which of the following would be considered negative evidence in determining whether Gratiot Corporation needs to record a valuation allowance for some or all of its deferred tax assets?

a) The company forecasts future taxable income because of its backlog of orders.

b) The company has a cumulative net loss over the current and prior two years.

c) The company has unfavorable temporary differences that will create future taxable income when they reverse.

d) The company had a net operating loss carryover expire in the current year.

e) Both (b) and (d) constitute negative evidence in assessing the need for a valuation allowance.

LO 6-3 62. Saginaw Inc. completed its first year of operations with a pretax loss of $500,000. The tax return showed a net operating loss of $600,000, which the company will carry forward. The $100,000 book–tax difference results from excess tax depreciation over book depreciation. Management has determined that it should record a valuation allowance equal to the net deferred tax asset. Assuming the current tax expense is zero, prepare the journal entries to record the deferred tax provision and the valuation allowance.

63. Access the 2017 Form 10-Ks for General Motors, Inc. and Berkshire Hathaway. What was the impact of the Tax Cuts and Jobs Act on their income tax provision for 2017? Why was the impact in opposite directions (i.e., in one case the provision increased and in the other it decreased)? LO 6-3 research

64. Montcalm Corporation has total deferred tax assets of $3,000,000 at year-end. Of that amount, $1,000,000 results from the current expensing of an expenditure that the IRS might assert must be capitalized on audit. Management is trying to determine if it should not recognize the deferred tax asset related to this item under ASC 740-10 (FIN 48). What confidence level must management have that the item will be sustained on audit before it can recognize any portion of the deferred tax asset under ASC 740-10 (FIN 48)? LO 6-4
   a) Probable.
   b) More likely than not.
   c) Realistic possibility.
   d) Reasonable.
   e) More than remote.

65. Which of the following statements about uncertain tax positions (UTP) is correct? LO 6-4
   a) UTP applies only to tax positions accounted for under ASC 740 taken on a filed tax return.
   b) UTP applies to all tax positions accounted for under ASC 740, regardless of whether the item is taken on a filed tax return.
   c) UTP deals with both the recognition and realization of deferred tax assets.
   d) If a tax position meets the more-likely-than-not standard, the entire amount of the deferred tax asset or current tax benefit related to the tax position can be recognized under ASC 740.
   e) Statements (b), (c), and (d) are correct.

66. Cadillac Square Corporation determined that $1,000,000 of its research and development tax credit on its current-year tax return was uncertain but that it was more likely than not to be sustained on audit. Management made the following assessment of the company's potential tax benefit from the deduction and its probability of occurring. LO 6-4

Potential Estimated Benefit (000s)	Individual Probability of Occurring (%)	Cumulative Probability of Occurring (%)
$1,000,000	40	40
750,000	25	65
500,000	20	85
0	15	100

What amount of the tax benefit related to the uncertain tax position from the research and development tax credit can Cadillac Square Corporation recognize in calculating its income tax provision in the current year?

67. How would your answer to the previous problem change if management determined that there was only a 50/50 chance any portion of the $1,000,000 research and development tax credit would be sustained on audit? LO 6-4

LO 6-4

68. As part of its UTP assessment, Penobscot Company records interest and penalties related to its unrecognized tax benefit of $500,000. Which of the following statements about recording this amount is most correct?
   a) Penobscot must include the amount in its income tax provision.
   b) Penobscot must record the amount separate from its income tax provision.
   c) Penobscot can elect to allocate a portion of the amount to both its income tax provision and its general and administrative expenses provided the company discloses which option it has chosen.
   d) Penobscot can elect to record the entire amount as part of its income tax provision or separate from its income tax provision, provided the company discloses which option it has chosen.
   e) Statements (c) and (d) are both correct.

LO 6-5
research

69. What was Facebook's accounting effective tax rate for 2020? What items caused the company's accounting effective tax rate to differ from the "hypothetical" tax rate of 21 percent? What was the company's cash effective tax rate for 2020? What factors cause a company's cash tax rate to differ from its accounting effective tax rate? You can access Facebook's Form 10-K for 2020 at the company's website or the SEC EDGAR website.

LO 6-5

70. Beacon Corporation recorded the following deferred tax assets and liabilities:

Current deferred tax assets	$ 650,000
Current deferred tax liabilities	(400,000)
Noncurrent deferred tax assets	1,000,000
Noncurrent deferred tax liabilities	(2,500,000)
Net deferred tax liabilities	$ 1,250,000)

All of the deferred tax accounts relate to temporary differences that arose as a result of the company's U.S. operations. Which of the following statements describes how Beacon should disclose these accounts on its balance sheet?
   a) Beacon reports a net deferred tax liability of $1,250,000 on its balance sheet as noncurrent.
   b) Beacon nets the deferred tax assets and the deferred tax liabilities and reports a net deferred tax asset of $1,650,000 and a net deferred tax liability of $2,900,000 on its balance sheet.
   c) Beacon can elect to net the current deferred tax accounts and the noncurrent tax accounts and report a net current deferred tax asset of $250,000 and a net deferred tax liability of $1,500,000 on its balance sheet.
   d) Beacon is required to net the current deferred tax accounts and the noncurrent deferred tax accounts and report a net current deferred tax asset of $250,000 and a net deferred tax liability of $1,500,000 on its balance sheet.

LO 6-5

71. ASC 740 requires a company to disclose those components of its deferred tax assets and liabilities that are considered
   a) Relevant.
   b) Significant.
   c) Important.
   d) Major.

LO 6-5

72. Which of the following temporary differences creates a deferred tax asset?
   a) Allowance for bad debts.
   b) Goodwill amortization for tax, but not book, purposes.
   c) Cumulative excess of tax over book depreciation.
   d) Inventory capitalization under §263A.
   e) Both (a) and (d) create a deferred tax asset.

73. Which formula represents the calculation of a company's effective tax rate? LO 6-5
   a) Income taxes paid/Taxable income.
   b) Income taxes paid/Pretax income from continuing operations.
   c) Income tax provision/Taxable income.
   d) Income tax provision/Pretax income from continuing operations.
74. Which of the following items is *not* a reconciling item in the effective tax rate reconciliation in the income tax footnote? LO 6-5
   a) State income taxes.
   b) Foreign income taxes.
   c) Accrued pension liabilities.
   d) Dividends-received deduction.
   e) Tax-exempt municipal bond interest.
75. Hafnaoui Company reported pretax net income from continuing operations of $800,000 and taxable income of $500,000. The book–tax difference of $300,000 was due to a $200,000 favorable temporary difference relating to depreciation, an unfavorable temporary difference of $80,000 due to an increase in the reserve for bad debts, and a $180,000 favorable permanent difference from the receipt of life insurance proceeds. LO 6-5
   a) Compute Hafnaoui Company's current income tax expense.
   b) Compute Hafnaoui Company's deferred income tax expense or benefit.
   c) Compute Hafnaoui Company's effective tax rate.
   d) Provide a reconciliation of Hafnaoui Company's effective tax rate with its hypothetical tax rate of 21 percent.
76. Which of the following pronouncements should a company consult in computing its quarterly income tax provision? LO 6-5
   a) ASC Topic 740.
   b) ASC Topic 230.
   c) ASC Topic 718.
   d) ASC Topic 810.
   e) SarbOX §404.

COMPREHENSIVE PROBLEMS

Select problems are available with Connect®. Mc Graw Hill connect

77. You have been assigned to compute the income tax provision for Motown Memories Inc. (MM) as of December 31, 2022. The company's income statement for 2022 is provided below:

Motown Memories Inc. Statement of Operations at December 31, 2022	
Net sales	$50,000,000
Cost of sales	28,000,000
Gross profit	$22,000,000
Compensation	$ 2,000,000
Selling expenses	1,500,000
Depreciation and amortization	4,000,000
Other expenses	500,000
Total operating expenses	$ 8,000,000
Income from operations	$14,000,000
Interest and other income	1,000,000
Income before income taxes	$15,000,000

You identified the following permanent differences:

Interest income from municipal bonds	$50,000
Nondeductible entertainment expenses	20,000
Nondeductible fines	5,000

MM prepared the following schedule of temporary differences from the beginning of the year to the end of the year:

Motown Memories Inc.
Temporary Differences Scheduling Template

Taxable Temporary Differences	BOY Deferred Taxes	Current-Year Change	EOY Cumulative T/D	EOY Deferred Taxes
Accumulated depreciation	$(1,680,000)	$(1,000,000)	$(9,000,000)	**$(1,890,000)**

Deductible Temporary Differences	BOY Deferred Taxes	Current-Year Change	EOY Cumulative T/D	EOY Deferred Taxes
Allowance for bad debts	$ 42,000	$ 50,000	$ 250,000	$ 52,500
Reserve for warranties	21,000	20,000	120,000	25,200
Inventory §263A adjustment	50,400	60,000	300,000	63,000
Deferred compensation	10,500	10,000	60,000	12,600
Accrued pension liabilities	630,000	250,000	3,250,000	682,500
Total	**$753,900**	**$390,000**	**$3,980,000**	**$835,800**

Required:

a) Compute MM's current income tax expense or benefit for 2022.
b) Compute MM's deferred income tax expense or benefit for 2022.
c) Prepare a reconciliation of MM's total income tax provision with its hypothetical income tax expense of 21 percent in both dollars and rates.

78. You have been assigned to compute the income tax provision for Tulip City Flowers Inc. (TCF) as of December 31, 2022. The company's income statement for 2022 is provided below:

Tulip City Flowers Inc.
Statement of Operations at December 31, 2022

Net sales	$20,000,000
Cost of sales	12,000,000
Gross profit	$ 8,000,000
Compensation	$ 500,000
Selling expenses	750,000
Depreciation and amortization	1,250,000
Other expenses	1,000,000
Total operating expenses	$ 3,500,000
Income from operations	$ 4,500,000
Interest and other income	25,000
Income before income taxes	$ 4,525,000

You identified the following permanent differences:

Interest income from municipal bonds	$10,000
Nondeductible stock compensation	5,000
Nondeductible fines	1,000

TCF prepared the following schedule of temporary differences from the beginning of the year to the end of the year:

Tulip City Flowers Inc.
Temporary Differences Scheduling Template

Taxable Temporary Differences	BOY Deferred Taxes	Current-Year Change	EOY Cumulative T/D	EOY Deferred Taxes
Accumulated depreciation	$(1,050,000)	$(500,000)	$(5,500,000)	$(1,155,000)

Deductible Temporary Differences	BOY Deferred Taxes	Current-Year Change	EOY Cumulative T/D	EOY Deferred Taxes
Allowance for bad debts	$ 21,000	$ 10,000	$ 110,000	$ 23,100
Prepaid income	0	20,000	20,000	4,200
Deferred compensation	10,500	10,000	60,000	12,600
Accrued pension liabilities	105,000	100,000	600,000	126,000
Total	**$136,500**	**$140,000**	**$790,000**	**$165,900**

Required:

a) Compute TCF's current income tax expense or benefit for 2022.
b) Compute TCF's deferred income tax expense or benefit for 2022.
c) Prepare a reconciliation of TCF's total income tax provision with its hypothetical income tax expense of 21 percent in both dollars and rates.

79. Access the 2020 Form 10-K for Facebook, Inc., and answer the following questions.

Required:

a) Using information from the company's Income Statement and Income Taxes footnote, what was the company's effective tax rate for 2020? Show how the rate is calculated.
b) Using information from the Statement of Cash Flows, calculate the company's cash tax rate.
c) What does the company's Income Taxes note tell you about where the company earns its international income? Why does earning income in these countries cause the effective tax rate to decrease?
d) What item creates the company's largest deferred tax asset? Explain why this item creates a deductible temporary difference.
e) What item creates the company's largest deferred tax liability? Explain why this item creates a taxable temporary difference.
f) How does the company classify its income taxes payable related to its unrecognized tax benefits on the balance sheet?
g) How does the company treat interest and penalties related to its unrecognized tax benefits?

80. Spartan Builders Corporation is a builder of high-end housing with locations in major metropolitan areas throughout the Midwest. At June 30, 2022, the company has deferred tax assets totaling $10 million and deferred tax liabilities of $5 million, all of which relate to U.S. temporary differences. Reversing taxable temporary differences and taxable income in the carryback period can be used to support approximately $2 million of the $10 million gross deferred tax asset. The remaining $8 million of gross deferred tax assets will have to come from future taxable income.

The company has historically been profitable. However, significant losses were incurred in fiscal years 2020 and 2021. These two years reflect a cumulative loss of $10 million ($7 million of which was due to a write-down of inventory), with losses of $3 million expected in 2022. Beginning in fiscal 2023, management decided to get out of the metropolitan Chicago market, which had become oversaturated with new houses.

Evaluate the company's need to record a valuation allowance for the $10 million of gross deferred tax assets. What positive and negative evidence would you weigh?

UWorld Roger CPA Review

Sample CPA Exam questions from Roger CPA Review are available in Connect as support for the topics in this text. These Multiple Choice Questions and Task-Based Simulations include expert-written explanations and solutions and provide a starting point for students to become familiar with the content and functionality of the actual CPA Exam.

chapter

7 Corporate Taxation: Nonliquidating Distributions

Learning Objectives

Upon completing this chapter, you should be able to:

- **LO 7-1** Recognize the tax framework applying to property distributions from a corporation to a shareholder.
- **LO 7-2** Compute a corporation's earnings and profits and a shareholder's dividend income.
- **LO 7-3** Explain the taxation of stock distributions.
- **LO 7-4** Discern the tax consequences of stock redemptions.
- **LO 7-5** Describe the tax consequences of a partial liquidation to the corporation and its shareholders.

Sam Edwards/OJO Images/age fotostock

Storyline Summary

Taxpayer:	Jim Wheels (he/him/his)
Location:	East Lansing, Michigan
Status:	Co-owner of Spartan Cycle and Repair (75 percent)
Taxpayer:	Ginny Gears (she/her/hers)
Location:	East Lansing, Michigan
Status:	Co-owner of Spartan Cycle and Repair (25 percent)

Jim Wheels and Ginny Gears are old friends who met years ago at the Mid-Michigan Cycling Club. Members of the club, including Ginny, often found it difficult to get parts and have their bicycles repaired locally. Because of his experience from working at a bicycle shop during his undergraduate days, Jim was the club's local bike repair expert. Ginny majored in marketing at Michigan State University (MSU) and was eager to put marketing and management to work in a real business. Consequently, Jim and Ginny often discussed the feasibility of operating a high-end bicycle shop in East Lansing, Michigan.

A few years ago, Jim and Ginny decided to start Spartan Cycle and Repair (SCR). Their business had humble beginnings, as most start-up companies do. By borrowing from Jim's father, Walt, they raised $50,000 of capital needed to purchase inventory and the necessary repair tools. They also leased a vacant building on Grand River Avenue. On the advice of their accountant, Jim and Ginny organized their company as a C corporation, with Jim owning 75 percent of the corporation's stock and Ginny owning the remaining 25 percent. Jim's responsibilities include repairing bikes and deciding which bicycle brands to carry, while Ginny is responsible for managing and marketing the business. Jim works approximately 10 hours per week at the store and receives a modest salary of $15,000 per year. Ginny works half time at the store and currently receives a salary of $25,000 per year.

Since the company's inception, Jim and Ginny have used most of the company's profits to pay back the loan to Jim's father and expand the store's inventory and marketing activities. By the end of this year, SCR had become very successful, as evidenced by the significant amount of cash ($300,000) in the company's bank accounts. Over a latte at the local gourmet coffee shop, Jim and Ginny decided it was time to think about distributing some of the company's profits to reward their hard work. Jim admitted he liked the look of a dark green BMW that retailed for approximately $48,000. Ginny was a bit more restrained and wanted to put a down payment on a condominium in the newly developed Evergreen Commons being constructed near their store. The down payment would require $16,000. The latest proposal is for SCR to distribute $64,000 at year-end ($48,000 to Jim and $16,000 to Ginny).

(to be continued . . .)

At some point during the life of a company, especially in the case of a closely held business, the shareholders will likely want to distribute some of the company's accumulated profits. If the business is operated as a C corporation, the company can distribute its *after-tax* profits to its shareholders in the form of a **dividend, stock redemption,** or, in rare cases, a **partial liquidation.** This chapter addresses the tax consequences to the corporation and its shareholders when a C corporation makes distributions to its shareholders.[1]

LO 7-1 TAXATION OF PROPERTY DISTRIBUTIONS

The characterization of a distribution from a C corporation to a shareholder has important tax consequences to both the shareholders and the corporation. If the tax law characterizes the distribution as a dividend rather than compensation, the corporation may not deduct the amount paid in computing its taxable income. In addition, the shareholder must include the dividend received in gross income. The nondeductibility of the distribution by the corporation, coupled with the taxation of the distribution to the shareholder, creates *double taxation* of the corporation's income, first at the corporate level and then at the shareholder level. The double taxation of distributed corporate income has been a fundamental principle of the U.S. income tax since 1913.

Historically, tax planning focused on eliminating or mitigating one level of taxation on C corporation earnings. For example, if the distribution can instead be characterized as salary, bonus, interest, or rent, the corporation can deduct the amount paid in computing its taxable income, thereby avoiding the corporate income tax on this incremental payment. It is also important to recall that the corporate tax rate (21 percent) is significantly lower than the maximum individual tax rate (37 percent). However, the individual marginal tax rate on dividends is generally below the top individual tax rate. Hence, it is conceivable that some taxpayers may save taxes by choosing to have a business entity taxed as a C corporation. In other words, depending on the timing and form of distributions of profits, subjecting a business to double taxation may be preferable to operating the business as a flow-through entity and subjecting the income to a single tax at a higher individual rate.

LO 7-2 DETERMINING THE DIVIDEND AMOUNT FROM EARNINGS AND PROFITS

Overview

When a corporation distributes property to shareholders in their capacity as shareholders, the distributions are characterized as dividend income, return of capital, and/or capital gain. The portion characterized as dividend income is included in gross income. In contrast, a return of capital is not considered income, but rather a reduction in the shareholder's tax basis in the stock. If the nondividend portion of the distribution exceeds the tax basis of the stock, then the excess distribution (above basis) is taxed as a capital gain from the sale of the shares.[2]

Corporate distributions of "property" usually take the form of cash, but distributions can also consist of other tangible or intangible property. Special rules apply when a corporation distributes its own stock to its shareholders.[3]

Dividends Defined

A dividend is any distribution of property made by a corporation to its shareholders from earnings and profits (E&P). Congress created E&P to be a measure of the corporation's

[1]Corporations subject to the corporate tax are referred to as *C corporations* because Subchapter C (§§301–385) governs the tax consequences of distributions between a corporation and its shareholders. If Jim and Ginny had elected to operate their business through an S corporation or partnership, the entity-level taxation of the company's earnings would be eliminated.

[2]§301(c).

[3]§305.

economic earnings available for distribution to its shareholders. Hence, earnings and profits is similar in concept to financial accounting retained earnings. Corporations keep two separate E&P accounts. One is called **current earnings and profits** that is comparable to the economic income earned in the current period. The other account represents the undistributed earnings and profits accumulated in all prior years and is called **accumulated earnings and profits.**

Each year corporations compute their *current* E&P by making specific adjustments to taxable income (discussed below). When both current and accumulated E&P are positive, distributions can be treated as dividends up to the available amount of E&P (current plus accumulated). Any E&P that is not distributed to shareholders becomes the amount of *accumulated* E&P at the beginning of the next taxable year. Distributions reduce E&P but cannot produce (or increase) a deficit (a negative balance) in E&P. In other words, a corporation cannot distribute E&P if there is a deficit in E&P, and only losses can create a deficit in E&P. A corporation that makes a distribution in excess of its available E&P (i.e., a return of capital and/or capital gain to shareholders) must report the distribution on Form 5452 and include a calculation of its E&P balance to support the tax treatment.

Example 7-1

Jim owns 75 percent of the Spartan Cycle and Repair (SCR) stock, while Ginny owns the remaining 25 percent. Jim has a tax basis in his SCR stock of $24,000. Ginny's tax basis in her SCR stock is $10,000.

What if: Assume SCR has current earnings and profits (E&P) of $30,000 and no accumulated earnings and profits. At year-end, SCR makes a $64,000 distribution—a $48,000 distribution to Jim and a $16,000 distribution to Ginny.

What is the tax treatment of the distribution to Jim and Ginny?

Answer: Only $30,000 of the $64,000 distribution is treated as a dividend. The distribution is first deemed to be paid from current E&P to each shareholder in proportion to their ownership interest on the date of the distribution: $22,500 to Jim ($30,000 × 75%) and $7,500 to Ginny ($30,000 × 25%). The $34,000 distribution in excess of current E&P ($64,000 – $30,000) is then deemed to be paid from accumulated E&P in proportion to ownership interests. However, because there is no accumulated E&P, the distribution in excess of E&P is first treated as a return of capital and then capital gain once basis is exhausted.

Jim treats the $48,000 distribution for tax purposes as follows:

- $22,500 is treated as a dividend.
- $24,000 is a nontaxable reduction in his stock tax basis (return of capital).
- $1,500 is treated as gain from the deemed sale of his stock (capital gain).

Note that a return of capital cannot reduce a shareholder's stock basis below zero. Amounts paid in excess of stock basis result in gain recognition.

Ginny treats the $16,000 distribution for tax purposes as follows:

- $7,500 is treated as a dividend.
- $8,500 from E&P is a nontaxable reduction in her stock tax basis (return of capital).
- Ginny has no capital gain because the distribution did not exceed the tax basis of her SCR stock.

What is Jim's tax basis in his SCR stock after the distribution? What is Ginny's tax basis in her SCR stock after the distribution?

Answer: Jim has a zero basis in the SCR stock, while Ginny has a remaining tax basis of $1,500 ($10,000 – $8,500) in the SCR stock.

TAXES IN THE REAL WORLD Keeping Track of Tax Basis Is Important

When a corporation makes a distribution that is treated as a return of capital (i.e., a distribution in excess of E&P), it is incumbent on each shareholder to establish their basis for the stock in determining the extent to which the distribution is a nontaxable return of capital or a capital gain. The burden of proving the basis of the stock is on the shareholder, as a taxpayer, Mr. Visconti, ultimately discovered.

(continued)

To avoid income taxes on a corporate distribution, a shareholder must establish that the distribution is in respect to the corporation's stock, there is an absence of earnings and profits, and the stock basis is in excess of the distribution. The government charged Mr. Visconti with tax evasion for failing to pay capital gains taxes on a corporate distribution in excess of earnings and profits. At trial, focus was on whether the taxpayer could prove that the distributions did not exceed the stock basis.

Visconti argued the stock had a basis of $13.13 million. Checks were presented showing that Visconti paid $4.9 million to purchase the stock. Visconti also argued that the value of property contributed to the corporation increased the tax basis to $8.25 million. However, Visconti provided no evidence of the property's value or basis aside from his own estimate. In contrast, the government's evidence consisted of testimony of a CPA who testified that the property Visconti transferred to the corporation was only valued at $6.25 million. The government also presented bank records and a statement that Visconti submitted in divorce proceedings. These documents showed that the corporation had previously distributed $12.25 million to Visconti. Hence, the government argued that Visconti had a zero basis in his stock.

At trial, the district court ruled that Visconti's statements were insufficient to support the $8.25 million valuation or rebut the government's evidence. Hence, the court precluded Visconti's return-of-capital defense. On appeal, the Ninth Circuit Court held that the trial court did not abuse its discretion in finding that Visconti failed to establish a factual basis for a return-of-capital defense.

When a shareholder is unable to establish his basis for the stock, the IRS will treat the shareholder as having a zero basis in the stock. Hence, it pays for shareholders to be prepared and keep records of corporate contributions and distributions.

Source: United States v. Visconti, 122 AFTR2d 2018-5976 (9th Cir. 2018).

THE KEY FACTS

Adjustments to Taxable Income (Loss) to Compute Current E&P

- A corporation makes the following adjustments to taxable income to compute current E&P:
  - Include certain income that is excluded from taxable income.
  - Disallow certain expenses that are deducted in computing taxable income.
  - Deduct certain expenses that are not deductible in computing taxable income.
  - Defer deductions or accelerate income due to separate accounting methods required for E&P purposes.

Computing Earnings and Profits

The concept of earnings and profits has been part of the tax laws since 1916. Although Congress has never provided a precise definition, E&P is supposed to represent the economic income eligible for distribution to shareholders. Consistent with this rationale, E&P includes both taxable and nontaxable income, indicating that Congress intended E&P to represent a corporation's economic income. As a result, shareholders may be taxed on distributions of income even if the income was not taxable to the corporation.

A corporation begins the computation of current E&P with taxable income or loss. It then makes adjustments required by the Internal Revenue Code or the accompanying regulations and IRS rulings. These adjustments fall into four broad categories:

1. Certain nontaxable income is included in E&P.
2. Certain deductions do not reduce E&P.
3. Certain nondeductible expenses reduce E&P.
4. The timing of certain items of income and deduction is modified for E&P calculations because separate accounting methods are required for E&P purposes.[4]

Nontaxable Income Included in Current E&P Tax-exempt income represents economic income that can be distributed to shareholders. Thus, tax-exempt income is included in current E&P. Common examples of tax-exempt income included in current E&P are tax-exempt municipal interest and tax-exempt life insurance proceeds.

Example 7-2

SCR reported $5,000 of tax-exempt interest from its investment in City of East Lansing municipal bonds. What effect does the tax-exempt interest income have on current earnings and profits, if any?

Answer: The tax-exempt interest income is included in current earnings and profits thereby increasing current E&P by $5,000 because it reflects economic income.

[4]§312.

Deductible Expenses That Do Not Reduce Current E&P Deductions that require no cash outlay by the corporation or are carryovers from another tax year do not represent current economic outflows and cannot be used to reduce current E&P. Examples include the dividends-received deduction, net capital loss carryovers from a different tax year, net operating loss carryovers from a different tax year, and charitable contribution carryovers from a prior tax year.[5]

Nondeductible Expenses That Reduce Current E&P A corporation reduces its current E&P for certain expenditures that are not deductible in computing its taxable income but require a cash outflow. Examples of such expenses include:

- Federal income taxes paid or accrued (depending on the corporation's method of accounting).
- Expenses incurred in earning tax-exempt income (such income is included in E&P).
- Current-year charitable contributions in excess of the taxable income percentage limitation (there is no percentage limitation for E&P purposes).
- Premiums on life insurance contracts in excess of the increase in the policy's cash surrender value.
- Current-year net capital loss (there is no limit on capital losses for E&P purposes).
- Nondeductible meal expenses.
- Nondeductible entertainment expenses.
- Nondeductible lobbying expenses and political contributions.
- Nondeductible penalties and fines.
- Disallowed business interest expense.

Items Requiring Separate Accounting Methods for E&P Purposes A corporation must generally use the same accounting methods for computing both E&P and taxable income. For example, a gain or loss deferred for income tax purposes under the like-kind exchange rules (§1031) or the involuntary conversion rules is also deferred for calculating E&P. A corporation using the accrual method for income tax purposes generally must use the accrual method for E&P purposes. However, there are important differences between the accounting methods used to compute taxable income and current E&P. Hence, the adjustments to taxable income reflect differences in both the recognition and the timing of certain items of income and expense. The list of adjustments in deriving current E&P from taxable income is somewhat lengthy; some adjustments are positive and others are negative.

Some types of income deferred from current-year taxable income must be included in the computation of current E&P in the year in which the transaction occurs. For example, a corporation that defers gains under the installment method for income tax purposes must still include the deferred gain in current E&P. This difference reverses in future years when the installment payments are received, thereby triggering recognition of the deferred gain. In these years, the gain increases taxable income but is not included in current E&P.

Certain expenses currently deducted in the computation of taxable income are deferred in computing E&P.[6] For example, organizational expenditures, which can be

[5]The deduction allowed for employee exercises of nonqualified stock options reduces current E&P because the bargain element of the option reflects an economic cost to the corporation (even though it does not require a cash outflow from the corporation).

[6]§312(n) was added in 1984 to "ensure that a corporation's earnings and profits more closely conform to its economic income."

deducted currently or amortized for income tax purposes, must be capitalized for E&P purposes. Depreciation must be computed using the prescribed E&P method. For property acquired after 1986, the alternative depreciation system (ADS) must be used. This system requires that assets be depreciated using the asset depreciation range.[7] Also, bonus depreciation is not allowed for E&P purposes. This generally results in more accelerated depreciation for taxable income purposes than for E&P purposes. Further, amounts expensed under §179 (first-year expensing) must be amortized over five years for E&P purposes.

For any given year, adjustments in this category may increase or decrease current E&P because these adjustments are timing differences that reverse over time.

Example 7-3

This year, SCR reported taxable income of $10,000 and paid federal income tax of $2,100. SCR reported the following items of income and expense:

- $50,000 of depreciation, including bonus depreciation.
- $700 dividends-received deduction.
- $3,000 net operating loss carryover.
- $5,000 of tax-exempt interest.
- $6,000 of entertainment expense.
- $4,000 net capital loss from the current year.

For E&P purposes, depreciation computed under the alternative depreciation system is $30,000.

What is SCR's current E&P?

Answer: $26,600, computed as follows:

Taxable income	$ 10,000
Add:	
Tax-exempt interest income	5,000
Dividends-received deduction	700
NOL carryover	3,000
Excess of income tax depreciation over E&P depreciation	20,000
Subtract:	
Federal income taxes	(2,100)
Entertainment expense	(6,000)
Net capital loss for the current year	(4,000)
Current E&P	**$26,600**

What if: Assume that for taxable income purposes, SCR also reported a tax-deferred gain of $100,000 as the result of a §1031 (like-kind) exchange and deferred $75,000 of gain from an installment sale during the year. What is SCR's current E&P under these circumstances?

Answer: Current E&P would equal $101,600 ($26,600 + $75,000). Deferred gains from §1031 exchanges are not included in the computation of current E&P, but realized gain from current-year installment sales is included in current E&P. In future years, SCR would compute current E&P by reducing taxable income by any gain included in taxable income from the prior-year installment sale.

What if: Assume the original facts except that SCR also reported a $50,000 net capital loss for the current year (rather than a $4,000 loss). What is SCR's current E&P under these circumstances?

Answer: Current E&P would be a negative $19,400 ($26,600 + $4,000 − $50,000). E&P can be negative, but E&P cannot be driven below zero by distributions.

[7]§168(g)(2).

Exhibit 7-1 provides a summary of common adjustments to taxable income to compute current E&P. The IRC does not impose a statute of limitations on the computation of E&P. Hence, many corporations (public and private) may mistakenly fail to compute E&P until after years of operations. This delay makes the computation difficult because the annual adjustments necessary to derive the current E&P from taxable income may not have been well documented and because it is necessary to derive the current E&P for each year to calculate accumulated E&P.

EXHIBIT 7-1 Template for Computing Current Earnings and Profits

Taxable Income (Net Operating Loss)	
Add:	**Exclusions from Taxable Income** • Tax-exempt bond interest income. • Life insurance proceeds. • Federal tax refunds (if a cash-method taxpayer). • Increase in cash surrender value of corporate-owned life insurance policy.
Add:	**Deductions Allowed for Tax Purposes but Not for E&P** • Dividends-received deduction. • NOL deduction. • Net capital loss carryforwards. • Contribution carryforwards. • Organizational expenditures.
Subtract:	**Deductions Allowed for E&P Purposes but Not for Tax Purposes** • Federal income taxes paid or accrued. • Expenses of earning tax-exempt income. • Current-year charitable contributions in excess of the taxable income limitation. • Nondeductible premiums on life insurance policies. • Current-year net capital loss. • Penalties and fines. • Nondeductible portion of meal expense. • Entertainment expenses. • Disallowed lobbying expenses, dues, and political contributions. • Decrease in cash surrender value of corporate-owned life insurance policy. • Disallowed business interest expense.
Add or Subtract:	**Timing Differences Due to Separate Accounting Methods for Taxable Income and E&P** • Installment method. Add deferred gain under installment method in year of sale and subtract recognized gain in subsequent years. • Depreciation. Compare taxable income depreciation to E&P depreciation (other than §179 expense) under regular tax rules to E&P depreciation (bonus depreciation is not allowed). Add back difference if taxable income depreciation exceeds E&P depreciation. Subtract difference if E&P depreciation exceeds taxable income depreciation for the year. • §179 expense. Immediately deductible for taxable income purposes. Deductible over five years for E&P purposes. Add back in year of §179 expense but subtract in subsequent years. • Inventory. If LIFO is used for tax purposes, FIFO must be used for E&P calculations. • Gain or loss on sale of depreciable assets. Subtract greater taxable gain (lesser taxable loss) due to lower asset basis for taxable income purposes than for E&P purposes. This is a reversal of the depreciation deduction adjustment. • Long-term contracts. Percentage completion method is required for E&P. Compare the income recognized under both methods. Add back if more income is recognized under the completed contract method; subtract if more income is recognized under the percentage completion method. • Depletion. Must use the cost depletion method for E&P purposes. If using percentage depletion for taxable income, add back the difference if percentage depletion exceeds cost depletion for the year. Otherwise, subtract the excess of cost depletion over percentage depletion for the year.
Equals:	**Current Earnings and Profits**

Ordering of E&P Distributions

Corporations must refer to both current and accumulated E&P accounts in determining the amount of distributions that are deemed to be dividends. Distributions are designated as dividends in the following order:

1. Distributions are dividends up to the balance of current E&P.
2. Distributions in excess of current E&P are dividends up to the balance in accumulated E&P.

Under these ordering rules, whether a distribution is characterized as a dividend depends on whether the balances in these two accounts are positive or negative. As a result, there are only four possible scenarios:

1. Positive current E&P, positive accumulated E&P.
2. Positive current E&P, negative accumulated E&P.
3. Negative current E&P, positive accumulated E&P.
4. Negative current E&P, negative accumulated E&P.

Positive Current E&P and Positive Accumulated E&P Corporate distributions are deemed to be paid out of current E&P first. If distributions exceed current E&P, the amount distributed from current E&P is allocated pro rata to all the distributions made during the year. The amount of distributions in excess of current E&P come from accumulated E&P and distributions are allocated to the accumulated E&P in the chronological order in which the distributions were made.[8] This ordering of distributions is particularly important when distributions exceed current E&P and either the identity of the shareholders receiving the distributions changes or a shareholder's percentage ownership changes during the year. Because current E&P is calculated at year-end, it can be difficult to determine the dividend status of a distribution at the time of the distribution.

Example 7-4

What if: Assume SCR reported current E&P of $40,000 and the balance in accumulated E&P was $16,000. On December 31, SCR distributed $48,000 to Jim and $16,000 to Ginny. What amount of dividend income do Jim and Ginny report, and what is accumulated E&P for SCR at the beginning of next year?

Answer: Jim and Ginny report $42,000 and $14,000 of dividend income, respectively. The distribution is first deemed to be paid from current E&P to each shareholder in proportion to their ownership interest on the date of the distribution: $30,000 to Jim ($40,000 × 75%) and $10,000 to Ginny ($40,000 × 25%). The $24,000 distribution in excess of current E&P ($64,000 − $40,000) is then deemed to be paid from accumulated E&P ($16,000) in proportion to ownership interests ($12,000 to Jim and $4,000 to Ginny). The remaining distribution of $8,000 ($64,000 total minus $40,000 current E&P and $16,000 accumulated E&P) is a return of capital. Hence, Jim will reduce his stock basis by $6,000 and Ginny will reduce her stock basis by $2,000.

SCR has a zero balance in accumulated E&P at the beginning of the next year because all current and accumulated E&P was distributed during the current year.

What if: Assume that SCR's current E&P is $40,000 and its accumulated E&P is $15,000. Also, assume that Jim is the sole shareholder of SCR and that he received a $45,000 distribution on June 1. Assume that after the June distribution Jim sold all his SCR shares to Ginny for $12,000. Ginny received a $15,000 distribution on December 31. What are the amount and the character of each distribution?

Answer: Jim has a $45,000 dividend, and Ginny has a $10,000 dividend with a $5,000 return of capital. The $40,000 of current E&P is allocated between the two distributions in proportion to total distributions. Hence, $30,000 ($40,000 × $45,000/$60,000) is allocated to the first distribution and $10,000 ($40,000 × $15,000/$60,000) is allocated to the second distribution. After current E&P is exhausted, accumulated E&P is then allocated in chronological order. Thus, because Jim's distribution took place before Ginny's distribution, Jim's distribution ($15,000) is allocated to accumulated E&P, leaving $0 in remaining accumulated E&P to be allocated to Ginny's distribution. Because Ginny is allocated only $10,000 of E&P, the excess distribution of $5,000 ($15,000 − $10,000) is treated as a nontaxable reduction of her basis in the SCR stock. Ginny's basis is reduced to $2,000 ($12,000 − $10,000). Refer to Exhibit 7-2 to see how this fact pattern would be presented on a Form 5452.

[8] Reg. §1.316-2(b); Rev. Rul. 74-164.

EXHIBIT 7-2 Corporate Report of Nondividend Distributions

Form **5452** (Rev. October 2018)
Department of the Treasury Internal Revenue Service

Corporate Report of Nondividend Distributions

▶ For calendar year ending December 31, ________
▶ Attach to the corporation's income tax return.
▶ Go to *www.irs.gov/Form5452* for instructions and the latest information.

OMB No. 1545-0123

Name: SCR CORPORATION
Employer identification number: 00-0000000

A Has the corporation filed a Form 5452 for a prior calendar year? . . . ▶ ☐ Yes ☑ No
If "Yes," enter the applicable year(s) ________

B Are any of the distributions part of a partial or complete liquidation? . . . ▶ ☐ Yes ☑ No
If "Yes," attach explanation.

C Are any of the distributions from an S corporation's accumulated adjustments account? . . . ▶ ☐ Yes ☑ No
If "Yes," enter the balance at the beginning of the tax year ________

D Earnings and Profits (See **Supporting Information** in instructions.)

- Accumulated earnings and profits (since February 28, 1913) at the beginning of the tax year . . . ▶ $ 15,000
- Actual earnings and profits for the current tax year . . . ▶ $ 40,000

E Shareholders at Date of Last Dividend Payment

- Number of individuals 1
- Number of partnerships . . . .
- Number of corporations and other shareholders 1

F Corporate Distributions (see instructions)

Date Paid	Total Amount Paid (Common (C), Preferred (P), Other (O))	Amount Per Share	Amount Paid During Calendar Year From Earnings & Profits Since February 28, 1913: From the Current Year	Accumulated	Total	Percentage Taxable	Amount Paid During Calendar Year From Other Than Earnings & Profits Since February 28, 1913	Percentage Nontaxable
JUNE 1	$ 45,000 (C)	$ 1	$ 30,000	$ 15,000	$ 45,000	100 %	$	%
DEC 31	15,000 (C)	1	10,000		10,000	67	5,000	33
Totals	$ 60,000 (C)		$ 40,000	$ 15,000	$ 55,000		$ 5,000	

For Paperwork Reduction Act Notice, see the instructions. Cat. No. 11881T Form **5452** (Rev. 10-2018)

Source: irs.gov.

Positive Current E&P and Negative Accumulated E&P In this scenario, distributions deemed paid out of current E&P are taxable as dividends. Because accumulated E&P has a negative balance, distributions in excess of current E&P will be treated as a return of capital. If the nondividend distribution exceeds the stock basis, the excess is then treated as a capital gain.

Example 7-5

What if: Assume SCR reported current E&P of $60,000, but the balance in accumulated E&P is negative $20,000. On December 31, SCR distributed $48,000 to Jim and $16,000 to Ginny. Jim has a tax basis in his SCR stock of $24,000. Ginny's tax basis in her SCR stock is $10,000. What amount of income will Jim and Ginny report?

Answer: Jim and Ginny will report $45,000 and $15,000 of dividend income, respectively. The distribution is first deemed to be paid from current E&P ($45,000 to Jim and $15,000 to Ginny). No additional amount is treated as a dividend because current E&P has been exhausted and SCR has negative accumulated E&P.

What tax basis will Jim and Ginny have in their SCR stock after the distribution?

Answer: The distribution in excess of current E&P ($3,000 to Jim, $1,000 to Ginny) would be treated as a return of capital. Neither will recognize any gain because they both have sufficient tax basis in their SCR stock. Jim's tax basis in his SCR stock after the distribution would be $21,000 ($24,000 – $3,000), and Ginny's tax basis in her SCR stock after the distribution would be $9,000 ($10,000 – $1,000).

What is SCR's balance in accumulated E&P at the end of the year/beginning of next year.?

Answer: SCR has a $20,000 deficit (negative) balance in accumulated E&P at the end of the current year/beginning of the next year.

Negative Current E&P and Positive Accumulated E&P When current E&P is negative, the tax status of a distribution is determined by the available accumulated E&P on the *date* of the distribution. The available accumulated E&P is computed by allocating the negative current E&P up to the distribution date (but not including the distribution date) and then subtracting the allocated amount from accumulated E&P. The deficit in current earnings and profits can be prorated throughout the year using months or days, or the allocation can be made by closing the books and specifically identifying when the current earnings and profits was incurred. Distributions in excess of available E&P in this scenario are treated as return of capital, and any nondividend distribution in excess of stock basis is treated as a capital gain.

Example 7-6

What if: Assume SCR reported current E&P deficit (negative) of $20,000. However, the balance in accumulated E&P at the beginning of the year was $60,000. On July 1, SCR distributed $48,000 to Jim and $16,000 to Ginny. Jim has a tax basis in his SCR stock of $24,000. Ginny's tax basis in her SCR stock is $10,000. What amount of dividend income do Jim and Ginny report?

Answer: Jim and Ginny report $37,500 and $12,500 of dividend income, respectively. Because current E&P is negative, SCR must determine its available E&P on the distribution date. SCR prorates the full-year negative current E&P to June 30 [6 months/12 months × ($20,000) = ($10,000)]. The negative current E&P of $10,000 is subtracted from the balance in accumulated E&P on the date prior to the distribution ($60,000) to compute the available accumulated E&P as of the end of the day June 30 ($50,000). Because their distributions were made at the same time, Jim is allocated 75 percent of the total E&P (75% × $50,000 = $37,500) and Ginny is allocated the remaining 25 percent (25% × $50,000 = $12,500).

What tax basis do Jim and Ginny have in their SCR stock after the distribution?

Answer: $13,500 for Jim and $6,500 for Ginny. The amount in excess of available E&P ($10,500 to Jim, $3,500 to Ginny) is treated as a return of capital. Jim reduces the basis in his SCR stock to $13,500 ($24,000 – $10,500). Ginny reduces the basis in her SCR stock to $6,500 ($10,000 – $3,500).

What is SCR's balance in accumulated E&P at the end of the year?

Answer: Negative $10,000. Note that the distribution in excess of available E&P does not reduce E&P because it would generate a deficit in E&P. Only a loss can produce a deficit in E&P, as follows:

Accumulated E&P beginning balance	$ 60,000
Prorated negative current E&P, 1/1–6/30	(10,000)
Dividend distribution (July 1)	(50,000)
Prorated negative current E&P, 7/1–12/31	(10,000)
Accumulated E&P ending balance (deficit)	**$(10,000)**

Negative Current E&P and Negative Accumulated E&P When current E&P and accumulated E&P are both negative, none of the distribution is treated as a dividend. Distributions will be return of capital to extent of stock basis. Any distribution in excess of stock basis is treated as a capital gain.

Example 7-7

What if: Assume SCR reported current E&P of negative $50,000. The balance in accumulated E&P at the beginning of the year was negative $60,000. Jim has a tax basis in his SCR stock of $24,000. Ginny's tax basis in her SCR stock is $10,000. On December 31 of this year, SCR distributed $48,000 to Jim and $16,000 to Ginny. What amount of dividend income do Jim and Ginny report this year?

Answer: Neither Jim nor Ginny recognizes any dividend income from this distribution. Because current E&P and accumulated E&P are negative, the entire distribution would be treated as a return of capital/capital gain.

Will Jim or Ginny recognize any capital gain as a result of the distribution, and what is the tax basis in the SCR stock for Jim and Ginny at year-end?

Answer: Jim has a capital gain of $24,000, the amount by which the distribution exceeds the tax basis in his SCR stock ($48,000 − $24,000). Ginny has a capital gain of $6,000, the amount by which the distribution exceeds the tax basis in her SCR stock ($16,000 − $10,000). Both Jim and Ginny have a zero basis in their SCR stock at year-end.

What is SCR's balance in accumulated E&P at the end of the year?

Answer: A deficit (negative) balance of $110,000, the sum of the accumulated E&P deficit of $60,000 plus the negative current E&P of $50,000.

Exhibit 7-3 summarizes the rules for determining whether a distribution represents dividend income. When both balances are positive, the distribution is treated as a dividend to the extent of current E&P at year-end and then to the extent of the balance of accumulated E&P. A distribution in excess of current and accumulated E&P is treated as a return of capital/capital gain. When current E&P is negative and accumulated E&P is positive, distributions are dividend income to the extent of accumulated E&P after netting against the deficit in current E&P (up to the date of the distribution). The distribution reduces accumulated E&P but not below zero. When accumulated E&P is negative and current E&P is positive, distributions are dividend income to the extent of current E&P. Finally, when both balances are negative, the distribution is treated as a return of capital/capital gain and the deficits in E&P are unaffected.

EXHIBIT 7-3 Summary of E&P Status and Taxability of Cash Distributions

	Balance in Accumulated E&P at the Time of the Distribution	
Balance in Current E&P at the Time of the Distribution	**Negative**	**Positive**
Negative	Distributions are a return of capital/capital gain.	Distributions are dividend income to the extent of current E&P and the balance of accumulated E&P.[9]
Positive	Distributions are dividend income to the extent of current E&P.	Distributions are dividend income to the extent of accumulated E&P after netting against deficit in current E&P incurred up to the date of the distribution.

[9]When there are multiple distributions, current E&P is allocated to each distribution based on relative FMVs and AE&P is allocated chronologically.

Distributions of Noncash Property to Shareholders

THE KEY FACTS

Dividend Distributions

The amount of a distribution equals:

- Cash distributed.
- Increased by fair market value of noncash property distributed.
- Reduced by any liabilities assumed by the shareholder on property received.
- The amount distributed is a dividend to the extent of available E&P (see Exhibit 7-3).

On occasion, a shareholder will receive a distribution of property other than cash. The dividend sourcing rules, described in Exhibit 7-3, apply to both cash and noncash distributions. However, noncash distributions can be more complex for two reasons. First, any liability attached to the property affects the amount distributed, and second, any difference between the value and the tax basis of the property affects the calculation of E&P. In addition, noncash distributions can have income tax consequences to the distributing corporation. To begin, when noncash property is received, the shareholder determines the amount distributed as follows:

	Money received
+	Fair market value of other property received
−	Liabilities assumed by the shareholder on property received
	Amount distributed[10]

Example 7-8

What if: Assume that rather than distributing $16,000 of cash to Ginny, SCR distributes $15,000 in cash and a Fuji custom touring bike that has a fair market value of $1,000. Suppose that SCR has current E&P of $100,000 (including the impact of the distribution on current E&P) and no accumulated E&P. What amount of dividend income will Ginny report this year?

Answer: $16,000. Ginny would include the $15,000 plus the $1,000 fair market value of the bicycle in her gross income as a dividend.

As a general rule, a shareholder's tax basis in noncash property received as a dividend equals the property's fair market value.[11] Although liabilities affect the amount of the distribution, liabilities do not affect the new basis of the distributed property. In other words, the basis of the property received consists of the taxable distribution plus the liabilities assumed by the shareholder. The fair market value is determined as of the date of the distribution.

Example 7-9

What is Ginny's tax basis in the bicycle she received as a dividend in the previous example?

Answer: $1,000. Ginny has a tax basis in the bicycle of $1,000, the bicycle's fair market value.

Example 7-10

What if: Assume that, instead of distributing $48,000 in cash to Jim, SCR distributes a parcel of land that SCR previously purchased for $60,000. The land has a fair market value of $60,000 and a mortgage of $12,000 attached to it. Jim assumes the mortgage on the land. Suppose that SCR has current E&P of $100,000 and no accumulated E&P. How much dividend income does Jim recognize on the distribution?

Answer: $48,000. Jim recognizes dividend income in an amount equal to the land's fair market value of $60,000, less the mortgage he assumes on the land in the amount of $12,000.

What is Jim's tax basis in the land he receives?

Answer: $60,000. Jim receives a tax basis equal to the land's fair market value. Jim has a $60,000 basis in the land because he recognized $48,000 of income and assumed $12,000 of debt.

[10]§301(b).

[11]§301(d).

Effect of Noncash Property Distributions on Taxable Income When a corporation distributes noncash property to shareholders, the corporation recognizes a taxable gain on the distribution to the extent that the fair market value of the property distributed exceeds the corporation's adjusted tax basis in the property.[12] In contrast, if the fair market value of the property distributed is less than the corporation's adjusted tax basis in the property, the corporation does not recognize a deductible loss for computing taxable income.

Example 7-11

What if: Assume SCR has an adjusted tax basis of $650 in the Fuji custom touring bike (for both income tax and E&P purposes) that it distributes to Ginny (see the facts in Example 7-8). How much taxable gain, if any, does SCR recognize when it distributes the bicycle to Ginny? Recall the FMV of the bicycle is $1,000.

Answer: $350. SCR recognizes a taxable gain of $350 on the distribution of the bicycle to Ginny ($1,000 – $650). Because the bike is considered inventory, SCR would characterize the gain as ordinary income.

What if: Assume SCR has an adjusted tax basis of $1,200 in the Fuji custom touring bike that it distributes to Ginny. The bicycle's fair market value has declined to $1,000 because it is an outdated model. How much loss, if any, does SCR recognize when it distributes the bicycle to Ginny?

Answer: $0. SCR is not permitted to recognize a loss on the distribution of the bicycle to Ginny.

What if: Suppose SCR *sells* the bicycle to Ginny for $1,000. How much loss, if any, can SCR recognize if it sells the bicycle to Ginny?

Answer: $200. SCR is permitted to recognize a loss on the sale of property to a shareholder provided it does not run afoul of the related-person loss rules found in §267. To be a related person, Ginny must own *more than* 50 percent of SCR, which she does not in this scenario.

Liabilities The amount of any liability assumed by the shareholder can also affect the recognized gain. When a liability assumed by the shareholder is greater than the distributed property's fair market value, the property's fair market value is deemed to be the amount of the liability assumed by the shareholder.[13] If the liability assumed is less than the property's fair market value, the gain recognized on the distribution is still the excess of the property's fair market value over its tax basis (i.e., the liability is ignored by the distributing corporation).

Example 7-12

What if: Assume SCR distributes a parcel of land to Jim that SCR had purchased previously purchased for possible expansion. The land has a fair market value of $60,000 and a remaining mortgage of $12,000 attached to it. SCR has a tax basis in the land of $20,000, and Jim assumes the mortgage on the land. How much gain, if any, does SCR recognize when it distributes the land to Jim?

Answer: $40,000 ($60,000 – $20,000). Because the mortgage assumed by Jim is less than the land's fair market value, SCR recognizes gain in an amount equal to the excess of the land's fair market value over its tax basis.

What if: Assume the mortgage assumed by Jim is $75,000 instead of $12,000. The land has a fair market value of $60,000, and SCR has a tax basis in the land of $20,000. Jim will assume the mortgage on the land. How much gain, if any, does SCR recognize when it distributes the land to Jim?

Answer: $55,000 ($75,000 – $20,000). Because the mortgage assumed by Jim exceeds the land's fair market value, SCR treats the land's fair market value as $75,000 and recognizes gain in an amount equal to the excess of the mortgage assumed over its tax basis. Because the mortgage exceeds the value of the property, Jim is treated as receiving a distribution of $0 and will take a basis in the land of $75,000.

[12]§311.

[13]§311(b)(2) refers to §336(b).

THE KEY FACTS

Effect of Distributions on E&P

E&P is reduced by distributions as follows:

- Cash distributed.
- E&P adjusted tax basis of noncash *depreciated* property (fair market value less than or equal to its E&P adjusted tax basis).
- Fair market value of noncash *appreciated* property.
- Noncash property distributions are reduced by any liabilities assumed by the shareholder on property received.
- E&P reductions for distributions cannot cause E&P to drop below zero.

Effect of Noncash Property Distributions on E&P As we discuss below, noncash property distributions to shareholders can affect a corporation's current E&P and accumulated E&P.

Current E&P. Noncash property distributions can affect current E&P in two ways. First, current E&P is reduced by the income taxes paid (or payable) on the taxable gain (fair market value of property distributed in excess of the property's adjusted tax basis). Second, current E&P is increased to the extent the fair market value of the property distributed exceeds the E&P basis of the property. For most types of property, the corporation's E&P basis is the same as the corporation's taxable income basis, so the taxable gain on the distribution is equal to the current E&P gain on the distribution. However for certain types of property (e.g., inventory and depreciable assets), a corporation's income tax basis for the property is different from the E&P basis of the property (e.g., inventory may have a LIFO basis for taxable income purposes but must have a FIFO basis for E&P purposes and the adjusted basis of certain depreciable assets may differ for taxable income and E&P purposes because the accumulated depreciation for income tax is different from accumulated depreciation for E&P purposes). In these situations, the taxable gain will be different from the current E&P gain. When a corporation distributes property with a fair market value that is lower than the E&P basis of the property, the corporation does not deduct the loss in determining current E&P.

Accumulated E&P. To reflect the fact that a distribution reduces a corporation's economic resources to pay dividends in future years, a corporation reduces its accumulated E&P at the end of the current year. The amount of the reduction depends on whether the distributed property was appreciated or depreciated for E&P purposes. When a corporation distributes *appreciated* property (fair market value in excess of E&P adjusted tax basis), the distribution reduces accumulated E&P at year-end by the fair market value of the property distributed. However, when a corporation distributes *depreciated* property (E&P adjusted tax basis in excess of fair market value of the property), the distribution reduces accumulated E&P at the end of the year by the E&P adjusted tax basis of the property. When the distributed property is subject to a liability, the amount of the liability assumed by the shareholder(s) increases accumulated E&P essentially netting the liability against the distribution of the property. Recall, however, distributions cannot cause accumulated E&P to drop below zero and cannot increase a negative balance in E&P.

Example 7-13

What if: Assume the same facts as in Example 7-12. SCR distributed land to Jim that has a fair market value of $60,000 and a remaining mortgage of $12,000 attached to it. SCR has an income tax and E&P adjusted tax basis in the land of $20,000. Jim has assumed the mortgage on the land. SCR has current E&P of $100,000, which includes the net gain of $31,600 from distribution of the land ($40,000 gain less a related tax liability of $8,400) and accumulated E&P at the beginning of the year of $500,000. What is SCR's balance in accumulated E&P at the end of this year (i.e., the beginning of next year) as a result of the distribution of the land to Jim?

Answer: $552,000, computed as follows:

Accumulated E&P, beginning of this year	$ 500,000
Current E&P	100,000
Fair market value of land distributed	(60,000)
Liability assumed by Jim	12,000
Balance of accumulated E&P, at year-end (beginning of next year)	**$552,000**

[14]§312(a), (b).

What if: Assume SCR has current E&P of $40,000, which includes the net gain of $31,600 from the land distribution ($40,000 gain less a related tax liability of $8,400) and accumulated E&P of $500,000. What is SCR's beginning balance in accumulated E&P at the end of this year (i.e., the beginning of next year) as a result of the distribution of the land to Jim?

Answer: $492,000, computed as follows:

Accumulated E&P, beginning of this year	$ 500,000
Current E&P	40,000
Fair market value of land distributed	(60,000)
Liability assumed by Jim	12,000
Beginning balance, accumulated E&P, next year	**$492,000**

What if: Assume the land distributed to Jim has a tax and E&P basis to SCR of $75,000 instead of $20,000. SCR has current E&P of $100,000 ($15,000 loss on the distribution is not allowed in computing current E&P). SCR has accumulated E&P at the beginning of the year of $500,000. What is SCR's beginning balance in accumulated E&P at the beginning of next year after taking the distribution of the land into account?

Answer: $537,000, computed as follows:

Accumulated E&P, beginning of this year	$ 500,000
Current E&P	100,000
E&P basis of land distributed	(75,000)
Liability assumed by Jim	12,000
Balance of accumulated E&P at year-end (beginning of next year)	**$537,000**

TAXES IN THE REAL WORLD Tax Planning for Distributions

Visteon Corporation is a global technology company that designs, engineers, and manufactures innovative cockpit electronics and connected car solutions for the world's major vehicle manufacturers. During 2008 and 2009, weakened economic conditions triggered a global economic recession that severely impacted the automotive sector. Visteon filed voluntary petitions for reorganization relief in 2009, but the company has been profitable since it emerged from bankruptcy in 2010.

Visteon had two technology-focused core businesses: vehicle cockpit electronics and thermal energy management. The company's vehicle cockpit electronics product line includes audio systems, infotainment systems, driver information systems, and electronic control modules. In order to focus its operations on automotive cockpit electronics, Visteon sold a subsidiary at a pretax gain of approximately $2.3 billion. The sale was completed on June 9, 2015, and Visteon's net cash proceeds from the sale were approximately $2.7 billion. Visteon then announced a plan to return $2.5 billion–$2.75 billion of cash to its shareholders through a series of actions including a special distribution. Ultimately, Visteon actually distributed approximately $1.75 billion on January 22, 2016.

Is there a tax reason why Visteon might have delayed the distribution from 2015 until 2016?

One possibility is that Visteon had a large deficit in its accumulated E&P at the beginning of 2015 from prior losses. However, the gain on the sale of the subsidiary created significant 2015 current E&P. Recall that distributions are dividends to the extent of current E&P even when there is a deficit in accumulated E&P. If true, then Visteon's special distribution in 2015 would have been characterized entirely as a dividend to its shareholders. However, by waiting until 2016 to make the distribution, it is possible that a significant portion of the distribution was treated as a nontaxable return of capital to shareholders instead of a taxable dividend. This is because Visteon's available E&P (beginning-of-year accumulated E&P plus current E&P) was significantly less than the distribution amount.

Sources: Visteon Corporation 2014 and 2015 Forms 10-K and annual reports.

LO 7-3

STOCK DISTRIBUTIONS

Rather than distribute cash to its shareholders, a corporation may instead distribute additional shares of its own stock (or rights to acquire additional shares) to shareholders. A publicly held corporation is likely to distribute additional shares of stock to promote shareholder goodwill (it allows the corporation to retain cash and still provide shareholders with tangible evidence of their interest in corporate earnings) or to reduce the market price of its outstanding shares (the stock distribution reduces the price of shares by increasing their number, making the stock more accessible to a wider range of shareholders). For example, a 5 percent stock distribution will increase the number of shares outstanding by 5 percent. Hence, a shareholder holding 100 shares will own 105 shares after a 5 percent stock distribution. Corporations may also declare a **stock split,** in which the number of shares outstanding is increased by the ratio of the split. For example, a 2-for-1 stock split would double the number of shares outstanding. Hence, a shareholder holding 100 shares will own 200 shares after a 2-for-1 stock split. Stock splits are sometimes used by public corporations to keep stock prices accessible to a diverse group of investors.

Tax Consequences to Shareholders Receiving a Stock Distribution

Nontaxable Stock Distributions In theory, stock splits and pro rata stock distributions do not provide shareholders with any increase in value. This is because these distributions do not change a shareholder's interest in the corporation except that the shareholder now owns more pieces of paper (shares of stock). As a result, these distributions are generally not included in the shareholders' gross income.[15]

In a nontaxable stock distribution, each shareholder allocates a portion of their tax basis from the stock on which the distribution was issued to the newly issued stock based on the relative fair market value (FMV) of the stock.[16] In the case of a simple distribution of common stock or a stock split where the stock distributed is identical to the stock from which the distribution is made (same class and same fair market value), the new per-share tax basis is the original tax basis divided by the total number of shares held (including the new shares).

For example, assume a shareholder owns 100 shares of Acme Corporation stock, for which they paid $3,000. Acme declares a 100 percent stock distribution and sends the shareholder an additional 100 shares of stock. The shareholder will now own 200 shares of stock with the same tax basis of $3,000. The basis of each share of stock decreases from its original $30 per share ($3,000/100) to $15 per share ($3,000/200). The holding period of the new stock includes the holding period for which the shareholder held the old stock.[17]

Example 7-14

Jim has a tax basis in his SCR stock of $24,000. Ginny's tax basis in her SCR stock is $10,000. Jim owns 75 of the 100 shares of outstanding SCR stock, while Ginny owns the remaining 25 shares.

What if: Assume that SCR declares a 100 percent stock distribution. As a result, Jim will own 150 shares of SCR stock and Ginny will own the remaining 50 shares.

Is the stock distribution taxable to Jim and Ginny?

Answer: No. The stock distribution to Jim and Ginny is nontaxable because it is made pro rata to the shareholders (that is, the distribution did not change their proportional ownership of SCR).

[15]§305(a). To be nontaxable, a stock distribution must meet two conditions: (1) It must be made with respect to the corporation's common stock and (2) it must be pro rata with respect to all shareholders (i.e., the shareholders' relative equity positions do not change as a result of the distribution).

[16]§307.

[17]§1223(4).

What is the tax basis of each share of SCR stock now held by Jim and Ginny?

Answer: Jim's original tax basis of $24,000 is divided among 150 shares. Hence, each one of Jim's shares has a basis of $160. Ginny's original tax basis of $10,000 is divided among 50 shares. Hence, each one of Ginny's shares has a basis of $200.

THE KEY FACTS

Tax Consequences of Stock Distributions

- Pro rata stock distributions generally are nontaxable.
- Shareholders allocate basis from the pre-distribution shares of stock to the recently acquired shares of stock based on relative fair market value.
- Non–pro rata (disproportionate) stock distributions are treated as a property distribution that is taxed as a dividend up to the corporation's E&P.

Taxable Stock Distributions Non–pro rata (i.e., disproportionate) stock distributions generally are treated as a property distribution and characterized as dividends to the extent of the distributing corporation's E&P.[18] This makes sense because the recipient has now received something of value: an increase in the shareholder's claim on the corporation's income and assets. For example, a corporation may give its shareholders the choice between a cash or a stock distribution. In this case, shareholders who elect to receive stock in lieu of money will be treated as having received a property distribution equal to the fair market value of the stock received, and the shareholder will have a tax basis in the new stock equal to its fair market value.

Example 7-15

What if: Assume that SCR declares a 10 percent stock distribution but offers Jim and Ginny the choice between more stock or $100 per share in cash. Is the distribution taxable to Jim if he elects to receive 15 shares of stock worth $1,600? If Jim has received a taxable distribution, what is the character of the income?

Answer: Yes, Jim is taxed on $1,600, the fair value of the stock, because the distribution has the potential to change the proportionate ownership interests in SCR. If Jim elected the cash, he would be taxed on the cash distribution of $1,500. If Jim elected the stock, the distribution would be a property distribution treated as a dividend to the extent of SCR's earnings and profits.

STOCK REDEMPTIONS

LO 7-4

(continued from page 7-1. . .)

In the original storyline, Jim and Ginny raised some of the initial capital they needed to start SCR by borrowing $50,000 from Jim's father, Walt. An alternate strategy would have been to issue 25 additional shares of SCR stock to Walt in return for $50,000. This change in facts would reduce Jim's ownership percentage in SCR to 60 percent (75 shares/125 shares). Ginny's ownership percentage would decrease to 20 percent (25 shares/125 shares). Walt would own the remaining 20 percent. We will assume this change in facts to continue the storyline.

Walt does not participate in the management of the company. In fact, he was hoping to cash out of SCR when it became profitable and use the money to put a down payment on a condominium in a retirement community near Orlando, Florida. With the SCR stock valued at $5,000 per share ($125,000 in total), Walt saw an opportunity to realize his retirement dream. Jim and Ginny saw it as a chance to own all SCR's stock, eliminating a potential source of discord should Jim's father disapprove of the way they are managing the company.

By the end of this year, SCR will have sufficient cash to buy back some or all of Walt's shares of SCR stock. Jim and Ginny were wondering about the potential tax consequences to SCR and Walt under various redemption plans. In particular, Jim and Ginny wanted to know whether there was a tax difference between (1) buying back 5 of Walt's shares this year and the remaining 20 shares equally over the next four years (at 5 shares per year) and (2) buying back all 25 shares this year using an installment note that would pay Walt 20 percent of the purchase price in each of the next five years plus interest. ■

[18]§305(b). A technical discussion of all the rules that apply to determining whether a stock distribution is taxable is beyond the scope of this text.

Publicly held corporations buy back (redeem) their stock from existing shareholders for many and varied reasons. For example, a corporation may have excess cash and limited investment opportunities, or management may feel the stock is undervalued. Management may see a large redemption as a way to get shareholders or stock analysts to reconsider their valuation of the company or as a way to selectively buy out dissenting shareholders who have become disruptive. Reducing the number of outstanding shares also increases earnings per share (by reducing the number of shares in the denominator of the calculation) and potentially increases the stock's market price.[19]

Privately held corporations often use stock redemptions for other reasons, such as to shift ownership control from older to younger family members who do not have the resources to purchase shares directly or to buy out dissatisfied, disinterested, or deceased shareholders. In addition, redemptions of an ex-spouse's stock can provide liquidity in a divorce agreement and eliminate the individual from management or ownership in the company. Finally, redemptions can provide cash to satisfy estate taxes imposed on the estate of a deceased shareholder of the company.

The Form of a Stock Redemption

A stock redemption is an acquisition by a corporation of its stock from a shareholder in exchange for property. It is irrelevant whether the stock acquired by the corporation is cancelled, retired, or held as treasury stock.[20] The term *property* in this context has the same meaning as it does for distributions (i.e., cash and noncash property).

Stock redemptions take the form of an exchange in which the shareholders give up stock in the corporation for property, usually cash. If the form of the transaction is respected, shareholders compute gain or loss (capital gain or loss if the stock is held as an investment) by comparing the amount realized (money and the fair market value of other property received) with their tax basis in the stock exchanged.

Without any tax law restrictions, a sole shareholder of a corporation could circumvent the dividend rules by structuring distributions to have the form of an exchange (i.e., a stock redemption). For example, rather than have the corporation make a $100,000 dividend distribution, the shareholder could have the corporation buy back $100,000 of stock from the shareholder. If the shareholder had a tax basis of $60,000 in the stock redeemed, the amount of income reported on the shareholder's tax return would decrease from $100,000 (dividend) to $40,000 (capital gain). At present, both amounts would be taxed at the same preferential tax rate (20 percent is the highest capital gains tax rate), assuming the shareholder held the stock for more than a year. In contrast to a dividend, a capital gain can be offset with capital losses. Similar to a dividend, however, the sole shareholder would continue to own 100 percent of the corporation before and after the stock redemption.

Form is not always respected in a redemption, however. The tax law may determine (or the IRS may argue) that the transaction is, in substance, a distribution of earnings, the tax consequences of which should be determined under the dividend rules we discussed above.

The IRC provides both objective/mechanical tests (so-called **bright-line tests**) and subjective/judgmental tests to distinguish when a redemption should be treated as an exchange or a potential dividend.[21] The result is an intricate set of rules that the corporation and its shareholders must navigate carefully to ensure that the shareholders receive the tax treatment they desire. This is especially true in closely held family corporations, where the majority of stock is held by people related to each other through birth or marriage.

[19]It is also important to note that corporations are not taxed on gains or losses resulting from transactions in their own stock. §1032.

[20]§317(b).

[21]§302. The IRC also defines when sale treatment is appropriate in some special circumstances. For example, §303 defines when sale treatment is allowed for redemptions of stock to pay death taxes.

While individual shareholders prefer sale treatment, corporate shareholders generally have more incentive for dividend treatment. Dividends from domestic corporations are eligible for the dividends-received deduction (DRD) (usually 50 or 65 percent), whereas a capital gain is not eligible for the DRD. A corporation might prefer exchange treatment if the redemption results in a loss, if the corporation has capital loss carryovers, or if its stock tax basis as a percentage of the redemption price exceeds the DRD ratio.

Redemptions That Reduce a Shareholder's Ownership Interest

The IRC allows a shareholder to treat a redemption as an exchange if the transaction meets one of three change-in-ownership tests: the substantially disproportionate test, the complete termination test, or the not essentially equivalent to a dividend test.[22] These ownership tests consider the effect of each redemption from the shareholder's perspective.

Redemptions That Are Substantially Disproportionate The IRC states in §302(b)(2) that a redemption will be treated as an exchange if the redemption is "substantially disproportionate with respect to the shareholder." A shareholder meets this requirement by satisfying the three objective ("bright-line") *stock ownership tests:*

1. Immediately after the exchange, the shareholder owns less than 50 percent of the total combined voting power of all classes of stock entitled to vote.
2. The shareholder's percentage ownership of voting stock after the redemption is less than 80 percent of their percentage ownership before the redemption.
3. The shareholder's percentage ownership of the aggregate fair market value of the corporation's common stock (voting and nonvoting) after the redemption is less than 80 percent of their percentage ownership before the redemption.[23]

For example, suppose a shareholder owns 60 percent of a corporation's stock prior to a redemption. To satisfy the 80 percent test, this shareholder must own less than 48 percent of the outstanding stock after a redemption (60% × 80% = 48%). Note that in this instance the redemption would also satisfy the 50 percent test (48 percent is less than 50 percent). Note also, that a redemption reduces that number of shares outstanding, and this must be taken into account in calculating the ownership tests. In contrast, suppose the same shareholder owns 70 percent before a redemption. In this case, a redemption that satisfies the 80 percent reduction test (70% × 80% = 56%) will not satisfy the 50 percent test.

The determination as to whether a shareholder meets both the 50 percent and 80 percent tests is made on a shareholder-by-shareholder basis. If multiple shareholders have shares redeemed, some shareholders can satisfy the test while others do not. If a shareholder owns multiple classes of common stock (voting and nonvoting), the less-than-80-percent of fair market value test is applied to the shareholder's aggregate ownership of the common stock rather than on a class-by-class basis.

Example 7-16

What if: Assume Walt is not related to either Jim or Ginny. This year, SCR redeemed five shares of Walt's stock in exchange for $25,000. Walt has a tax basis in the five shares of SCR stock of $10,000 ($2,000 per share). What is the tax treatment of the stock redemption to Walt under §302(b)(2)?

Answer: $25,000 dividend to the extent of SCR's E&P. Prior to the redemption, Walt owned 20 percent of SCR (25/125 shares). After the redemption, his ownership percentage in SCR dropped to 16.67 percent (20/120 shares). This redemption does not satisfy the substantially disproportionate

(continued on page 7-20)

[22]§302(b)(1), (2), (3), respectively.

[23]§302(b)(2).

test. After the redemption, Walt owns less than 50 percent of SCR stock, but his ownership percentage after the redemption (16.67 percent) does not fall below 80 percent of his ownership percentage prior to the redemption (80% × 20% = 16%). Walt will not be able to treat the redemption as an exchange under this change-in-ownership test. Unless he can satisfy one of the other change-in-ownership tests, Walt will have a $25,000 dividend, assuming SCR has sufficient E&P, rather than a $15,000 capital gain ($25,000 – $10,000).

How many shares of stock would SCR have to redeem from Walt to guarantee exchange treatment under the substantially disproportionate test?

Answer: For Walt to meet the 80 percent test, SCR must redeem six shares of stock. The computation is made as follows:

$$\frac{25 - x}{125 - x} < 16\%, \text{ where } x \text{ is the number of shares to be redeemed}$$

Using some algebra, we can compute x to be 5.95, rounded up to six shares.[24] If SCR redeems six shares from Walt, his ownership percentage after the redemption will be 15.97 percent (19/119 shares), which now meets the 80 percent test. The redemption of this one additional share transforms the transaction from a $30,000 dividend (6 shares × $5,000) to an $18,000 capital gain ($30,000 – $12,000).

In determining whether the 50 percent and 80 percent tests are met, an individual shareholder must take into account the **constructive ownership** or stock attribution rules found in §318. Under certain circumstances, the stock attribution rules require that stock owned by other persons (individuals and entities) that are related to the redeeming shareholder are considered to be constructively owned (we also refer to this as indirect ownership) by the redeeming shareholder for purposes of determining whether the shareholder has met the change-in-stock-ownership tests. The purpose of the attribution rules is to prevent shareholders from dispersing stock ownership to either family members who have similar economic interests or entities controlled by the shareholder to avoid having a stock redemption characterized as a dividend.

Family attribution. Individuals are treated as owning the shares of stock owned by their spouse, children, grandchildren, and parents. Stock owned constructively through the family attribution rule cannot be reattributed to another family member through the family attribution rule.

Example 7-17

Return to the amended storyline in which Walt is Jim's father and, in exchange for contributing $50,000, he received 25 shares of SCR stock and 20 percent ownership of the company. This year, SCR redeems 6 shares of stock from Walt in exchange for $30,000. Walt has a tax basis in the 6 shares of stock redeemed of $12,000 ($2,000 per share). What is the tax treatment of the stock redemption to Walt under §302(b)(2)?

Answer: $30,000 dividend to the extent of SCR's E&P.

Prior to the redemption, Walt owned 20 percent of SCR (25/125 shares) directly. Under the family attribution rules, Walt is treated as constructively owning the shares of SCR stock owned by Jim (75 shares). In applying the substantially disproportionate change-in-stock-ownership tests, Walt is treated as owning 100 shares of SCR stock (25 + 75), or 80 percent of the SCR stock (100/125 shares). After the redemption, Walt's ownership percentage in SCR drops to 79 percent (94/119 shares). This redemption does not satisfy the substantially disproportionate test because Walt is deemed to own more than 50 percent of the SCR stock after the redemption. As a result, Walt will have a $30,000 dividend, assuming SCR has sufficient E&P, rather than an $18,000 capital gain ($30,000 – $12,000).

[24]Multiplying both sides by $(125 - x)$, we get $25 - x = 20 - .16x$. Moving x to the right side of the equation and the integers to the left side of the equation, we get $5 = .84x$. Solving for x, we get $x = 5.95$.

An interesting question relates to what happens to the tax basis of stock redeemed that is not used in determining the shareholder's tax consequences. This occurs in a redemption treated as a dividend, where the tax basis of the stock redeemed is not subtracted from the amount received from the corporation. Under the current rules, the tax basis of the stock redeemed is added to the tax basis of any shares still held by the shareholder.

Example 7-18

In the preceding example, SCR redeemed six shares of stock from Walt for $30,000, and the transaction was treated as a dividend because of the application of the family attribution rules. Walt had a tax basis in the 6 shares of stock redeemed of $12,000 ($2,000 per share), but this tax basis was not used in determining their taxable income from the transaction.

What is Walt's tax basis in the remaining 19 shares of SCR stock?

Answer: $50,000. Walt adds the unused $12,000 tax basis in the 6 shares redeemed to the tax basis of the remaining 19 shares. The tax basis in these remaining shares increases to $50,000, the original tax basis of the 25 shares.

If the shareholder no longer holds any shares, the tax basis transfers to the stock held by those persons who caused the shareholder to have dividend treatment under the attribution rules.[25]

Attribution from entities to owners or beneficiaries. Owners or beneficiaries of entities can be deemed to own shares of stock owned by the entity itself. Under these rules, partners are deemed to own a pro rata share of their partnership's stock holdings (i.e., a partner who has a 10 percent interest in a partnership is deemed to own 10 percent of any stock owned by the partnership). Beneficiaries are deemed to own a pro rata share of the stock owned by the trust or estate of which they are a beneficiary. Shareholders are deemed to own a pro rata share of their corporation's stock holdings, but only if they own at least 50 percent of the value of the corporation's stock. Other attribution rules, such as family attribution, apply in determining if this 50 percent test is met.

Example 7-19

What if: Assume that Walt is not Jim's father, and besides the 25 shares of SCR that he owns directly, he is a 40 percent partner in a partnership that also owns 25 shares in SCR. The other 60 percent of the partnership is owned by his neighbors, Fred and Ethel, who are unrelated to Walt. How many shares of SCR is Walt treated as owning directly and indirectly through the partnership?

Answer: 35 shares. Walt owns 25 shares directly and another 10 shares indirectly. Walt is treated as indirectly owning a pro rata share of SCR stock owned by the partnership; in this example, 40 percent times 25 shares is 10 shares.

What if: Assume now that Walt is a 40 percent shareholder in Acme Corporation, which owns 25 shares in SCR. The other 60 percent of Acme shares is owned by his neighbors, Fred and Ethel, who are unrelated to Walt. How many shares of SCR is Walt treated as owning indirectly through Acme Corporation?

Answer: 0 shares. None of the shares owned by Acme Corporation are attributed to Walt under the constructive ownership rules because Walt does not own at least 50 percent of the stock of Acme Corporation. Stock owned by a corporation (Acme in this example) is attributed to a shareholder only if the shareholder owns at least 50 percent of the corporation's stock. In this case, Walt owns only 40 percent of Acme, and, therefore, SCR shares owned by Acme are not attributed to Walt.

What if: Assume now that Walt is a 60 percent shareholder in Acme Corporation, which owns 25 shares in SCR. The other 40 percent of Acme shares is owned by his neighbors, Fred and Ethel, who are unrelated to Walt. How many shares of SCR is Walt treated as owning indirectly through Acme Corporation?

Answer: 15 shares. Walt is treated as indirectly owning a pro rata share of SCR stock owned by Acme; in this example, 60 percent times 25 shares. A portion of Acme's stock in SCR is attributed to Walt because Walt owns at least 50 percent of the stock of Acme Corporation.

[25]Reg. §1.302-2.

Attribution from owners or beneficiaries to entities. Entities can be deemed to own other stock owned by their owners or beneficiaries. Under these rules, a partnership is deemed to own 100 percent of the shares owned by its partners. A trust or estate is deemed to own 100 percent of the shares owned by its beneficiaries. A corporation is deemed to own 100 percent of the shares owned by a shareholder who owns at least 50 percent of the value of the corporation's stock (direct plus indirect (constructive) ownership). Stock that is deemed owned by an entity cannot be reattributed to the other owners in the entity under the entity-to-owner rules previously discussed (this is known as *sideways attribution*).

Example 7-20

What if: Assume that Walt owns 25 shares of SCR and he is a 40 percent partner in a partnership. The other 60 percent of the partnership is owned by Walt's neighbors, Fred and Ethel, who are unrelated to Walt. How many shares of SCR is the partnership treated as owning indirectly through Walt?

Answer: 25 shares. Stock in a corporation (SCR) is attributed from an owner in an entity (Walt) to the entity (the partnership) in full. Under the owner-to-entity attribution rule, all of Walt's 25 shares would be attributed to the partnership as long as Walt had any ownership interest in the partnership.

What if: Assume the same facts as in the previous what-if example except that the partnership is now Acme Corporation. How many shares of SCR is Acme treated as owning indirectly through Walt?

Answer: 0 shares. Because the entity (Acme) is a corporation, the owner in the entity (Walt) must own at least 50 percent of the stock of the entity (Acme) in order for there to be any attribution from the owner (Walt) to the entity (Acme).

What if: Assume the same facts as in the previous what-if example except that Walt owns 60 percent of Acme Corporation. How many shares of SCR is Acme Corporation treated as owning indirectly through Walt?

Answer: 25 shares. Because the entity (Acme) is a corporation and the owner (Walt) owns at least 50 percent of the entity (Acme), all of Walt's 25 shares in SCR are attributed to Acme Corporation.

Option attribution. A person having an option to purchase stock is deemed to indirectly own the stock that the option entitles the person to purchase.

Complete Redemption of the Stock Owned by a Shareholder A redemption will be treated as an exchange if it is in "complete redemption of all of the stock of the corporation owned by the shareholder."[26] This test seems redundant with the substantially disproportionate test discussed above; after all, a complete redemption seemingly satisfies the 50 percent and 80 percent tests. The difference is in the application of the family attribution rules discussed above.

The stock attribution rules also apply to a complete redemption. This presents a potential problem in family-owned corporations in which the only (or majority) shareholders are parents, children, and grandchildren. Parents who have all their stock redeemed will be will not be able to qualify for sale or exchange treatment if their children or grandchildren continue to own the remaining stock in the corporation because of the operation of the family attribution rules. To provide family members with relief in these situations, shareholders can waive (ignore) the family attribution rules in a complete redemption of their stock.[27] As usual, there are some strings attached.

The first requirement is that the shareholder has no interest in the corporation immediately after the exchange as a "shareholder, employee, director, officer or consultant."[28] These relations to the corporation are referred to as prohibited interests. The second

[26]§302(b)(3).

[27]§302(c)(2).

[28]§302(c).

requirement is that the shareholder does not acquire a prohibited interest within 10 years after the redemption, unless by inheritance (this is known as the *10-year look-forward rule*). Finally, the shareholder must agree to notify the IRS district director within 30 days if a prohibited interest is acquired within 10 years after the redemption. The shareholder can still be a creditor of the corporation (e.g., the parents can receive a corporate note in return for their stock if the corporation does not have the cash on hand to finance the redemption).

Example 7-21

Return to the amended storyline in which Walt is Jim's father and he owns 25 shares of SCR stock. Assume SCR redeemed all 25 of his shares this year for $125,000, and for the year SCR has current E&P of $500,000. Walt's tax basis in the SCR shares is $50,000 (25 × $2,000). Under the family attribution rules, Walt would still be treated as indirectly owning 75 percent of the SCR stock (Jim would own 75 of the remaining 100 shares in SCR). The $125,000 payment would be treated as a taxable dividend to the extent of SCR's E&P.

What happens to the unused $50,000 tax basis in the SCR stock redeemed?

Answer: The tax basis transfers to Jim's stock, giving Jim a tax basis in his SCR stock of $74,000 ($24,000 + $50,000).

How can Walt change the tax treatment of the complete redemption?

Answer: Because Walt has redeemed all his shares, he can waive the family attribution rules, provided he files an agreement with the IRS and does not retain a prohibited interest in SCR (e.g., as an employee or consultant). By waiving the family attribution rules, Walt will be treated as not owning any SCR stock and, thus, will be able to treat the redemption as an exchange and report a capital gain of $75,000 ($125,000 − $50,000).

Redemptions That Are Not Essentially Equivalent to a Dividend A redemption will also be treated as an exchange if it is "not essentially equivalent to a dividend."[29] This is a subjective determination that turns on the facts and circumstances of each case. To satisfy this requirement, there must be a "meaningful" reduction in the shareholder's ownership interest in the corporation as a result of the redemption.[30] Neither the IRS nor the courts provide any mechanical tests to make this determination. The courts generally look at the substance of the transaction to determine if the redemption is a sale or a disguised dividend. As a result of the potential for litigation, shareholder reliance on this test is typically a last resort.

Although the courts have held that a shareholder's interest can include the right to vote and exercise control, participate in current and accumulated earnings, or share in net assets on liquidation, the IRS generally looks at the change in voting power as the key factor. The shareholder's voting power must decrease and be below 50 percent as a result of the exchange before this test can be considered.[31] As before, the stock attribution rules apply to these types of redemptions. Shareholders generally turn to this test to provide exchange treatment for redemptions when they cannot meet any of the other tests discussed previously.

[29]§302(b)(1).

[30]*United States v. Davis,* 397 U.S. 301, 313 (1970).

[31]In Rev. Rul. 76-385, the IRS held that in the case of a "small, minority shareholder, whose relative stock interest is minimal and who exercises no control over the affairs of the corporation," any reduction in proportionate interest is "meaningful." In this ruling, the shareholder's ownership percentage decreased from .0001118% to .0001081%, which would not be considered a "meaningful" reduction by most standards. Because the reduction in stock ownership did not meet the substantially disproportionate tests of §302(b)(2), the shareholder's only hope for exchange treatment was to qualify under §302(b)(1).

TAXES IN THE REAL WORLD Form Sometimes Prevails over Substance

Jon Dickinson was a shareholder and CFO for Geosyntec Consultants, Inc. (GCI), a privately held corporation. With authorization from the GCI board of directors, Dickinson donated appreciated long-term GCI shares to a qualified charity, Fidelity Investments Charitable Gift fund (Gift Fund). GCI immediately redeemed the donated shares for cash (i.e., the Gift Fund sold stock back to the corporation for cash). Because the Gift Fund is a tax-exempt charity, it recognized no gain on the redemption. Dickinson, in turn, claimed a charitable contribution deduction for the fair market value of the donated stock. The IRS argued that the transaction should be recast as though GCI redeemed Dickinson's stock for cash and then Dickinson donated the cash to the charity. In this scenario, Dickinson would be taxed on the appreciation in the donated stock.

At trial, Dickinson presented contemporaneous evidence that he relinquished all ownership rights in the shares at the time of the donation. GCI's letters to the Gift Fund confirmed the ownership transfer, and the Gift Fund's letters to Dickinson explained that the charity had "exclusive legal control" over the donated shares. The Tax Court held that where control is relinquished, the form of the transaction (donation then redemption) takes precedence over the substance of the transaction (redemption then donation). In this case, the tax consequences follow from the form of the transaction regardless of whether the donation was closely followed by a redemption or whether there was a preexisting "understanding" that the stock would be redeemed. Thus, Dickinson was able to claim a donation for the appreciated stock and was not taxed on the redemption.

Source: Jon Dickinson, et ux. v. Comm'r, TC Memo 2020-128.

Example 7-22

What if: Assume Walt is not related to Jim or Ginny. This year, SCR redeemed five shares of his stock in exchange for $25,000. Walt has a tax basis in the five shares of SCR stock of $10,000 ($2,000 per share). Assume that SCR has sufficient E&P to cover any distribution. What is the tax treatment of the stock redemption to Walt under the *not essentially equivalent to a dividend* test?

Answer: $15,000 capital gain.

Prior to the redemption, Walt owned 20 percent of SCR (25/125 shares). After the redemption, his ownership percentage in SCR drops to 16.67 percent (20/120 shares). This redemption does not satisfy the substantially disproportionate test, which would treat the redemption as an exchange. Walt can argue that the redemption should be treated as an exchange because it was *not essentially equivalent to a dividend.* Walt's ownership percentage decreased (20 percent to 16.67 percent) and is below 50 percent after the redemption. However, the result Walt seeks (exchange treatment) is not guaranteed. For peace of mind, he might prefer having SCR redeem one additional share and have the certainty that the redemption will be treated as an exchange under §302(b)(2).

Example 7-23

What if: Assume Walt is Jim's father, and SCR redeemed five shares of his stock in exchange for $25,000. Walt has a tax basis in the five shares of SCR stock of $10,000 ($2,000 per share), and SCR has sufficient E&P to cover any distribution. What is the tax treatment of the stock redemption to Walt under the *not essentially equivalent to a dividend* test?

Answer: $25,000 dividend to the extent of SCR's E&P.

Prior to the redemption, Walt is treated as owning 80 percent of SCR (25 shares directly and 75 shares through Jim). After the redemption, his ownership percentage in SCR drops to 79 percent (95/120 shares). This redemption does not satisfy the *not essentially equivalent to a dividend* test because Walt is treated as owning more than 50 percent of the SCR stock.

Tax Consequences to the Distributing Corporation

The corporation distributing property to shareholders in a redemption generally recognizes gain on the distribution of appreciated property but is not permitted to recognize loss on the distribution of property with a fair market value less than its tax basis.[32]

If the redemption is treated as a distribution, the corporation reduces its accumulated E&P at the end of the year by the cash distributed and the greater of the fair market value or the adjusted tax basis of other property distributed.[33] If the redemption is treated as an *exchange,* the corporation reduces E&P at the date of distribution by the percentage of stock redeemed (i.e., if 60 percent of the stock is redeemed, E&P available at the time of the distribution is reduced by 60 percent), not to exceed the fair market value of the property distributed.[34] When dividend distributions and redemption distributions are made in the same taxable year, the dividend distributions are allocated to E&P first and then the redemptions reduce the remaining E&P on a per share basis.[35]

The distributing corporation cannot deduct expenses incurred in a stock redemption.[36] The corporation can, however, deduct interest on debt incurred to finance a redemption.

THE KEY FACTS

Stock Redemptions Treated as Exchanges

- A stock redemption is treated as an exchange if it meets one of the following three tests:
  - Substantially disproportionate with respect to the shareholders.
  - In complete termination of the shareholder's interest.
  - Not essentially equivalent to a dividend.
- The following attribution rules are used to determine if one of the three tests is met:
  - Family attribution.
  - Entity-to-owner attribution (pro rata).
  - Owner-to-entity attribution (100 percent).
  - Options.
- A corporation reduces its E&P as a result of a stock redemption as follows:
  - If the distribution is treated as an exchange, E&P is reduced by the lesser of (1) the amount distributed or (2) the percentage of stock redeemed times accumulated E&P at the redemption date.
  - If the distribution is treated as a distribution, E&P is reduced using the dividend rules.

Example 7-24

What if: Assume SCR redeemed all of the 25 shares owned by Walt in exchange for $125,000. The stock redeemed represents 20 percent of the total stock outstanding. Walt has a tax basis in his SCR shares of $50,000. Further assume that Walt treated the redemption as an exchange because he waived the family attribution rules and filed an agreement with the IRS.[37] As a result, Walt recognized a capital gain of $75,000 ($125,000 – $50,000). The redemption took place on December 31, on which date SCR had accumulated E&P at the end of the year (including current E&P for year) of $500,000. SCR did not make any distributions during the year.

By what amount does SCR reduce its E&P as a result of this redemption?

Answer: $100,000. SCR reduces E&P by the lesser of (1) $100,000 (20% × $500,000) or (2) $125,000, the amount paid to Walt in the redemption.

What if: Assume E&P was $1,000,000 at the end of the year. By what amount does SCR reduce its available E&P as a result of this redemption?

Answer: $125,000. SCR reduces E&P by the lesser of (1) $200,000 (20% × $1,000,000) or (2) $125,000, the amount paid to Walt in the redemption.

PARTIAL LIQUIDATIONS

LO 7-5

Corporations sometimes contract their operations either by distributing the stock of a subsidiary to their shareholders or by selling the business. In the case of a sale, the corporation may distribute the proceeds from the sale to its shareholders in partial liquidation of the corporation. The distribution may require the shareholders to tender shares of stock back to the corporation or may be pro rata to all the shareholders without an actual exchange of stock.

The tax treatment of a distribution received in a partial liquidation depends on the type of entity receiving the distribution.[38] All *noncorporate* shareholders (partnerships,

[32]§311(a), (b).

[33]§312(a), (b).

[34]§312(n)(7).

[35]See Rev. Rul. 74-338 and Rev. Rul. 74-339 for discussion of how to determine E&P when a corporation redeems stock and makes a distribution to shareholders during the year.

[36]§162(k).

[37]The requirements for this agreement are found in Reg. §1.302-4T.

[38]§302(b)(4).

THE KEY FACTS

Tax Consequences to Shareholders in a Partial Liquidation of a Corporation

- Noncorporate shareholders receive exchange treatment.
- Corporate shareholders determine their tax consequences using the change-in-stock-ownership rules that apply to stock redemptions.

LLCs, individuals, etc.) receive exchange treatment. This entitles the individual to sale or exchange treatment with respect to the gain or loss recognized on the actual or deemed exchange. If the shareholder is not required to tender stock to the corporation in return for the property received, the shareholder computes gain or loss recognized on the exchange by calculating the tax basis of the shares that would have been transferred to the corporation had the transaction been a stock redemption.

All *corporate* shareholders are subject to the change-in-stock-ownership rules that apply to stock redemptions. This usually results in dividend treatment because partial liquidations almost always involve pro rata distributions. Corporate shareholders generally prefer dividend treatment because of the availability of the dividends-received deduction, although the benefit of the dividends-received deduction is mitigated because a partial liquidating distribution to a corporate shareholder is treated as an extraordinary dividend under §1059 which requires corporations to reduce their stock basis by the amount of the dividends received deduction.

For a distribution to be in partial liquidation of the corporation, it must be either "not essentially equivalent to a dividend" (as determined at the corporate level) or the result of the termination of a "qualified trade or business."[39] The technical requirements to meet these requirements are beyond the scope of this text.

TAXES IN THE REAL WORLD A Partial Liquidation in Dutch Auction Tender Offer

XBiotech is a Canadian biotech company that trades on NASDAQ (XBIT). In December 2019, the company sold a subsidiary, True Human antibody Bermekimab, to Janssen Biotech, Inc. (Janssen), a subsidiary of Johnson & Johnson. Upon closing, XBiotech received $750 million, with the possibility that the company could also receive up to $600 million subject to other conditions. The company announced plans to use the sale proceeds for a new research program and to return remaining funds to shareholders.

In January 2020, the company announced that it planned to use $420 million to repurchase shares in a Dutch auction tender offer. In a Dutch auction tender offer, the company sets a price range for the offering, in this case $30–$33. Shareholders interested in tendering their shares offer a price where they are willing to sell. At expiration, the company adds up the shares tendered, starting at the minimum price, until they reach the number of shares they are seeking, in this case 33%. The highest price of that group is the price the company will pay for all shares tendered at or below that price.

According to the company, Canadian shareholders will treat the offer as a taxable dividend. However, U.S. shareholders who participate in the tender will be entitled to treat the offer as a redemption under §302. Specifically, the company indicated in the tender offer that it intends for the sale to be treated as a partial liquidation under §302(e). As a partial liquidation, noncorporate shareholders would be entitled to treat the redemption as a sale regardless of whether it qualifies as substantially disproportionate. Of course, the company suggests that shareholders should consult with tax advisers because treatment as a partial liquidation depends on the facts and circumstances, and the IRS may disagree with this position.

Source: Schedule TO (pages 39–40), filed with the SEC by XBiotech Inc. on January 14, 2020.

CONCLUSION

This chapter explains that a corporation can distribute cash and other property to its shareholders in alternative ways. The most common forms are dividend distributions and stock buybacks (redemptions). The form chosen to make such a distribution affects the tax consequences to the recipients (shareholders) as well as the corporation itself. In some cases, the tax laws or the tax administrators can ignore the form of the transaction and assess tax based on the substance of the transaction. This is common in the case of stock redemptions that can be taxed as dividend payments. The tax rules that apply to distinguishing between substance and form often are complex, and taxpayers and their tax advisers must evaluate them carefully before making a decision.

[39]§302(e).

Summary

Recognize the tax framework applying to property distributions from a corporation to a shareholder. LO 7-1

- Subchapter C of the Internal Revenue Code (IRC) provides guidelines and rules for determining the tax status of distributions from a C corporation to its shareholders.
- When a corporation distributes property to persons in their capacity as shareholders, all or a portion of the distribution could be characterized as a dividend.
- If the distribution is of property other than cash, the distributing corporation recognizes gain but not loss on the distribution.

Compute a corporation's earnings and profits and a shareholder's dividend income. LO 7-2

- The IRC defines a dividend as any distribution of property made by a corporation to its shareholders out of its current or accumulated earnings and profits (E&P).
- Similar in concept to financial accounting retained earnings, E&P is meant to represent accumulated economic income.
- A corporation must keep two E&P accounts: current E&P and accumulated E&P. Current E&P is computed on the last day of each tax year.
- The IRC and the related regulations list four basic types of adjustments that a corporation must make to its taxable income to compute current E&P.
  - Inclusion of income that is excluded from taxable income.
  - Disallowance of certain expenses that are deducted in computing taxable income.
  - Deduction of certain expenses that are excluded from the computation of taxable income.
  - Separate accounting methods required for E&P purposes that result in both positive and negative adjustments to taxable income.
- The shareholder recognizes a corporate distribution as dividend income up to the amount of E&P. The distribution is the sum of cash received plus the fair market value of property received less any liabilities assumed.
- Distributions reduce accumulated E&P but cannot produce a deficit in E&P.
- The distributing corporation recognizes gain, but not loss, on the distribution of noncash property.
- A corporation reduces accumulated E&P by the amount of cash distributed, the E&P basis of depreciated (loss) property distributed, and the fair market value of appreciated property distributed, net of any liability assumed by the shareholders.

Explain the taxation of stock distributions. LO 7-3

- The general rule is that a stock distribution (stock dividend or split) is not taxable.
- The basis of the "new" stock received is computed by allocating basis from the existing stock based on relative fair market value.
- The holding period of the new stock includes the holding period of the existing stock on which the new stock was distributed.
- Non–pro rata stock distributions usually are treated as taxable dividends to the recipients.

Discern the tax consequences of stock redemptions. LO 7-4

- If a redemption is treated as an exchange, the shareholder computes gain or loss by comparing the amount realized (money and property received) with the adjusted tax basis of the stock surrendered.
  - The character of the gain or loss is capital.
  - The basis of noncash property received is its fair market value.
  - The holding period of the property received begins at the date of receipt.
- If the redemption is treated as a dividend, the shareholder will recognize dividend income (to the extent of corporate E&P) equal to the cash and fair market value of other property received.
  - The basis of the property received is its fair market value.
- Redemptions can be treated as exchanges in transactions in which the shareholder's ownership interest in the corporation has been "meaningfully" reduced relative to other shareholders as a result of the redemption.

- There are three change-in-stock-ownership tests that entitle the shareholder to exchange treatment in a redemption.
- A redemption will be treated as an exchange if the redemption is "not essentially equivalent to a dividend."
  - This is a facts and circumstances determination (subjective).
  - To satisfy this requirement, the courts or IRS must conclude that there has been a "meaningful" reduction in the shareholder's ownership interest in the corporation as a result of the redemption.
- A redemption will be treated as an exchange if the redemption is "substantially disproportionate with respect to the shareholder," defined as follows:
  - Immediately after the exchange, the shareholder owns less than 50 percent of the total combined voting power of all classes of stock entitled to vote.
  - The shareholder's percentage ownership of voting stock after the redemption is less than 80 percent of the percentage ownership before the redemption.
  - The shareholder's percentage ownership of the aggregate fair market value of the corporation's common stock (voting and nonvoting) after the redemption is less than 80 percent of the percentage ownership before the redemption.
- A redemption will be treated as an exchange if the redemption is in "complete redemption of all of the stock of the corporation owned by the shareholder."
- In determining whether the change-in-stock-ownership tests are met, each shareholder's percentage change in ownership in the corporation before and after a redemption must take into account constructive ownership (attribution) rules.
- The attribution rules cause stock owned by other persons to be treated as owned by (attributed to) the shareholder for purposes of determining whether the shareholder has met any of the change-in-stock-ownership tests to receive exchange treatment.
  - Family attribution. Individuals are treated as owning the shares of stock owned by their spouse, children, grandchildren, and parents.
  - Attribution from entities to owners or beneficiaries.
    - Partners are deemed to own a pro rata share of their partnership's stock holdings (i.e., a partner who has a 10 percent interest in a partnership is deemed to own 10 percent of any stock owned by the partnership).
    - Shareholders are deemed to own a pro rata share of their corporation's stock holdings, but only if they own at least 50 percent of the value of the corporation's stock.
  - Attribution from owners or beneficiaries to entities.
    - Partnerships are deemed to own 100 percent of the stock owned by partners (i.e., a partnership is deemed to own 100 percent of the stock owned by a 10 percent partner).
    - Attribution to a corporation only applies to shareholders owning 50 percent or more of the value of the corporation's stock.
  - Option attribution. A person having an option to purchase stock is deemed to own the stock that the option entitles the person to purchase.
- Shareholders can waive the family attribution rules in a complete redemption of their stock if certain conditions are met.
  - The shareholder has not retained a prohibited interest in the corporation immediately after the exchange (e.g., as a shareholder, employee, director, officer, or consultant).
  - The shareholder does not acquire a prohibited interest within 10 years after the redemption, unless by inheritance (the 10-year look-forward rule).
  - The shareholder agrees to notify the IRS district director within 30 days if a prohibited interest is acquired within 10 years (by filing an agreement with the IRS).
- If the redemption is treated as a dividend by the shareholder, the corporation generally reduces its E&P by the cash distributed and the fair market value of other property distributed.
- If the redemption is treated as an exchange by the shareholder, the corporation reduces E&P at the date of distribution by the percentage of stock redeemed (i.e., if 50 percent of the stock is redeemed, E&P is reduced by 50 percent), not to exceed the fair market value of the property distributed.

Describe the tax consequences of a partial liquidation to the corporation and its shareholders. LO 7-5

- For a distribution to be a partial liquidation, it must be "not essentially equivalent to a dividend" (as determined at the corporate level, not the shareholder level). The distribution automatically meets this test if the distribution is the result of the termination of a "qualified trade or business."
- The tax treatment of a distribution received in partial liquidation of a corporation depends on the identity of the shareholder receiving it.
  - All noncorporate shareholders get exchange treatment.
  - All corporate shareholders are subject to the stock redemption change-in-ownership rules, which usually result in dividend treatment because partial liquidations are almost always pro rata distributions.

KEY TERMS

accumulated earnings and profits (7-3)
bright-line tests (7-18)
constructive ownership (7-20)
current earnings and profits (7-3)
dividend (7-2)
partial liquidation (7-2)
stock redemption (7-2)
stock split (7-16)

DISCUSSION QUESTIONS

Discussion Questions are available in Connect®.

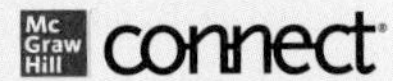

1. What is meant by the phrase "double taxation of corporate income"? LO 7-1
2. How does the double taxation of corporate distributions affect whether an individual chooses to operate a business as a C corporation or a flow-through entity? LO 7-1
3. Historically, taxpayers have implemented strategies to mitigate or eliminate the effects of double taxation. Why might taxpayers think twice before implementing such strategies today? Explain. LO 7-1
4. Why might a shareholder who is also an employee prefer receiving a dividend instead of compensation from a corporation? LO 7-1
5. What are the three potential tax treatments of a cash distribution to a shareholder? Are these potential tax treatments elective by the shareholder? LO 7-2
6. In general, what is the concept of earnings and profits (E&P) designed to represent? LO 7-2
7. How does the *current earnings and profits* account differ from the *accumulated earnings and profits* account? LO 7-2
8. Assume a calendar-year corporation has positive current E&P of $120 and a deficit in accumulated E&P of ($200). Under this circumstance, a cash distribution of $100 to the corporation's sole shareholder at year-end will not be treated as a dividend because total E&P is negative. True or false? Explain. LO 7-2
9. Assume a calendar-year corporation has a deficit in current E&P of ($120) and positive beginning accumulated E&P of $120. Under this circumstance, a cash distribution of $120 to the corporation's sole shareholder on June 30 will not be treated as a dividend because total E&P on December 31 is $0. True or false? Explain. LO 7-2
10. List the four general categories of adjustments that a corporation makes to taxable income or net loss to compute current E&P. What is the rationale for making these adjustments? LO 7-2
11. Assuming adequate amounts of corporate E&P, what is the formula for determining the amount of a noncash distribution a shareholder must include in gross income? LO 7-2
12. What income tax issues must a corporation consider before it makes a noncash distribution to a shareholder? LO 7-2
13. Assuming adequate E&P, will the shareholder's tax basis in noncash property received equal the amount included in gross income as a dividend (assuming adequate E&P)? Under what circumstances will the amounts be different, if any? LO 7-2

LO 7-2 14. A shareholder receives appreciated noncash property in a corporate distribution and assumes a liability attached to the property. How does the assumption of a liability affect the amount of dividend reported in gross income, assuming adequate E&P?

LO 7-2 15. A shareholder receives appreciated noncash property in a corporate distribution and assumes a liability attached to the property. How does this assumption affect the amount of gain the corporation recognizes? From the corporation's perspective, does it matter if the liability assumed by the shareholder exceeds the property's gross fair market value?

LO 7-2 16. When a shareholder receives a noncash distribution of property that is encumbered by a liability (the shareholder assumes the liability on the distribution), how does the shareholder determine the amount of the distribution?

LO 7-2 17. A corporation distributes *depreciated* noncash property to a shareholder. What impact does the distribution have on the corporation's earnings and profits

LO 7-2 18. A corporation distributes *appreciated* noncash property to a shareholder. What impact does the distribution have on the corporation's earnings and profits?

LO 7-3 19. Why might a corporation issue a stock distribution to its shareholders?

LO 7-3 20. What tax issue arises when a shareholder receives a nontaxable stock distribution?

LO 7-3 21. In general, what causes a stock distribution to be taxable to the recipient?

LO 7-4 22. What are the potential tax consequences to a shareholder who participates in a stock redemption?

LO 7-4 23. What stock ownership tests must be met before a shareholder receives exchange treatment under the substantially disproportionate change-in-stock-ownership test in a stock redemption? Why is a change-in-stock-ownership test used to determine the tax status of a stock redemption?

LO 7-4 24. What are the criteria necessary to meet the "not essentially equivalent to a dividend" change-in-stock-ownership test in a stock redemption?

LO 7-4 25. When might a shareholder have to rely on the "not essentially equivalent to a dividend" test in arguing that a stock redemption should be treated as an exchange for tax purposes?

LO 7-4 26. Explain why the tax law imposes constructive stock ownership rules on stock redemptions.

LO 7-4 27. Which members of a family are included in the family attribution rules? Is there any rationale for the family members included in the test?

LO 7-4 28. Ilya and Olga are brother and sister. Ilya owns 200 shares of stock in Parker Corporation. Is Olga deemed to own Ilya's 200 shares under the family attribution rules that apply to stock redemptions?

LO 7-4 29. Maria has all her stock in May Corporation redeemed. Under what conditions will Maria treat the redemption as an exchange and recognize capital gain or loss?

LO 7-4 30. What must a shareholder do to waive the family attribution rules in a complete redemption of stock?

LO 7-4 31. How does a corporation's adjustment to earnings and profits differ based on the tax treatment of a stock redemption to the shareholder (i.e., as either a dividend or exchange)?

LO 7-5 32. How does the tax treatment of a partial liquidation differ from a stock redemption?

LO 7-5 33. Reveille Corporation experienced a complete loss of its lumber mill as the result of a fire. The company received $2 million from the insurance company. Rather than rebuild, Reveille decided to distribute the $2 million to its two shareholders. No stock was exchanged in return. Under what conditions will the distribution meet the requirements necessary to be treated as a partial liquidation and not a dividend? Why does it matter to the shareholders?

PROBLEMS

Select problems are available in Connect®. connect

34. Gopher Corporation reported taxable income of $500,000 this year. Gopher paid a dividend of $100,000 to its sole shareholder, Sven Anderson. The dividend meets the requirements to be a qualified dividend, and Sven is subject to a tax rate of 15 percent on the dividend. What is the income tax imposed on the corporate income earned by Gopher and the income tax on the dividend distributed to Sven? LO 7-1

35. Bulldog Corporation reported taxable income of $500,000 this year, before any deduction for any payment to its sole shareholder and employee, Rojas. Bulldog chose to pay a bonus of $100,000 to Rojas at year-end. The bonus meets the requirements to be "reasonable" and is therefore deductible by Bulldog. Rojas is subject to a marginal tax rate of 35 percent on the bonus. What is the income tax imposed on the corporate income earned by Bulldog and the income tax on the bonus paid to Rojas? LO 7-1

36. Hawkeye Company reports current E&P of $300,000 this year and accumulated E&P at the beginning of the year of $200,000. Hawkeye distributed $400,000 to its sole shareholder, Ray, on December 31 of this year. Ray's tax basis in his Hawkeye stock before the distribution is $75,000. LO 7-2
    a) How much of the $400,000 distribution is treated as a dividend to Ray?
    b) What is Ray's tax basis in the Hawkeye stock after the distribution?
    c) What is Hawkeye's balance in accumulated E&P as of January 1 of next year?

37. Jayhawk Company reports current E&P of $300,000 and a deficit in accumulated E&P of ($200,000). Jayhawk distributed $400,000 to its sole shareholder, Rock, on the last day of the year. Rock's tax basis in the Jayhawk stock before the distribution is $75,000. LO 7-2
    a) How much of the $400,000 distribution is treated as a dividend to Rock?
    b) What is Rock's tax basis in the Jayhawk stock after the distribution?
    c) What is Jayhawk's balance in accumulated E&P on the first day of next year?

38. This year, Sooner Company reports a deficit in current E&P of ($300,000). Its accumulated E&P at the beginning of the year was $200,000. Sooner distributed $400,000 to its sole shareholder, Boomer, on June 30 of this year. Boomer's tax basis in the Sooner stock before the distribution is $75,000. LO 7-2
    a) How much of the $400,000 distribution is treated as a dividend to Boomer?
    b) What is Boomer's tax basis in the Sooner stock after the distribution?
    c) What is Sooner's balance in accumulated E&P on the first day of next year?

39. This year, Bobcat Company reports a deficit in current E&P of ($300,000) that accrued evenly throughout the year. At the beginning of the year, Bobcat's accumulated E&P was $200,000. Bobcat distributed $200,000 to its sole shareholder, Melanie, on June 30 of this year. Melanie's tax basis in the Bobcat stock before the distribution was $75,000. LO 7-2

    a) How much of the $200,000 distribution is treated as a dividend to Melanie?
    b) What is Melanie's tax basis in the Bobcat stock after the distribution?
    c) What is Bobcat's balance in accumulated E&P on the first day of next year?
    d) Prepare a draft of Bobcat's Form 5452 for this year. You may assume that the June 30 distribution was Bobcat's first and only distribution.

40. Lone Star Company is a calendar-year corporation, and this year Lone Star reported $100,000 in current E&P that accrued evenly throughout the year. At the beginning of the year, Lone Star's accumulated E&P was $12,000. At the beginning of the LO 7-2 tax forms

year, Lone Star's sole shareholder was Matt. Lone Star declared $30,000 in cash distributions on each of the following dates: March 31, June 30, September 30, and December 31.

a) How much of the $120,000 in total distributions will be treated as dividends?

b) Suppose that Matt sold half of the shares to Chris on June 1 for $40,000. How much dividend income will Matt recognize this year?

c) If Matt's basis in the Lone Star shares was $7,000 at the beginning of the year, how much capital gain will he recognize on the sale and distributions from Lone Star?

d) Prepare a draft of Lone Star's Form 5452 for this year.

LO 7-2 41. This year, Jolt Inc. reported $40,000 of taxable income before any charitable contribution deduction. Assume the 10% of taxable income limitation applies to the contribution because Jolt did not make the necessary election to use the 25% of taxable income limitation. Jolt contributed $10,000 this year to Goodwill Industries, a public charity. Compute the company's current E&P.

LO 7-2 42. Boilermaker Inc. reported taxable income of $500,000 this year and paid federal income taxes of $105,000. Not included in the company's computation of taxable income is tax-exempt income of $20,000, disallowed meals and entertainment expenses of $30,000, and disallowed expenses related to the tax-exempt income of $1,000. Boilermaker deducted depreciation of $100,000 on its tax return. Under the alternative (E&P) depreciation method, the deduction would have been $60,000. Compute the company's current E&P.

LO 7-2 43. Gator Inc. reported taxable income of $1,000,000 this year and paid federal income taxes of $210,000. Included in the company's computation of taxable income is gain from the sale of a depreciable asset of $50,000. The income tax basis of the asset was $100,000. The E&P basis of the asset using the alternative depreciation system was $175,000. Compute the company's current E&P.

LO 7-2 44. Paladin Inc. reported taxable income of $1,000,000 this year and paid federal income taxes of $210,000. The company reported a capital gain from sale of investments of $150,000, which was partially offset by a $100,000 net capital loss carryover from last year, resulting in a net capital gain of $50,000 included in taxable income. Compute the company's current E&P.

LO 7-2 45. Volunteer Corporation reported taxable income of $500,000 *from operations* this year. During the year, the company made a distribution of land to its sole shareholder, Rocky. The land's fair market value was $75,000 and its tax and E&P basis to Volunteer was $25,000. Rocky assumed a mortgage attached to the land of $15,000. The company had accumulated E&P of $750,000 at the beginning of the year.

a) Compute Volunteer's taxable income and federal income tax.

b) Compute Volunteer's current E&P.

c) Compute Volunteer's accumulated E&P at the beginning of next year.

d) What amount of dividend income does Rocky report because of the distribution?

e) What is Rocky's income tax basis in the land received from Volunteer?

LO 7-2 46. Tiger Corporation reported taxable income of $500,000 *from operations* this year. During the year, the company made a distribution of land to its sole shareholder, Mike. The land's fair market value was $75,000, and its tax and E&P basis to Tiger was $125,000. Mike assumed a mortgage attached to the land of $15,000. The company had accumulated E&P of $750,000 at the beginning of the year.

a) Compute Tiger's taxable income and federal income tax.

b) Compute Tiger's current E&P.

c) Compute Tiger's accumulated E&P at the beginning of next year.
d) What amount of dividend income does Mike report because of the distribution?
e) What is Mike's tax basis in the land he received from Tiger?

47. Illini Corporation reported taxable income of $500,000 *from operations* for this year. During the year, the company made a distribution of an automobile to its sole shareholder, Carly. The auto's fair market value was $30,000, and its adjusted tax basis to Illini was $0. The auto's E&P adjusted tax basis was $15,000. Illini had accumulated E&P of $1,500,000. LO 7-2
a) Compute Illini's taxable income and federal income tax.
b) Compute Illini's current E&P.
c) Compute Illini's accumulated E&P at the beginning of next year.
d) What amount of dividend income does Carly report because of the distribution?
e) What is Carly's tax basis in the auto received from Illini?

48. Beaver Corporation reported taxable income of $500,000 *from operations* this year. During the year, the company made a distribution of land to its sole shareholder, Eugenia. The land's fair market value was $20,000, and its income tax and E&P adjusted tax basis to Beaver was $50,000. Eugenia assumed a mortgage on the land of $25,000. Beaver Corporation had accumulated E&P of $1,500,000. LO 7-2
a) Compute Beaver's taxable income and federal income tax.
b) Compute Beaver's current E&P.
c) Compute Beaver's accumulated E&P at the beginning of next year.
d) What amount of dividend income does Eugenia report because of the distribution?

49. Tiny and Tim each owns half of the 100 outstanding shares of Flower Corporation. This year, Flower reported taxable income of $6,000. In addition, Flower received $20,000 of life insurance proceeds due to the death of an employee (Flower paid $500 in life insurance premiums this year). Flower had $5,000 of accumulated E&P at the beginning of the year. LO 7-2 tax forms research
a) What is Flower's current E&P?
b) Flower distributed $6,000 on February 15 and $30,000 on August 1. What total amount of dividends will Tiny and Tim report?
c) What amount of capital gain (if any) would Tiny and Tim report on the distributions in part (b) if their stock bases are $2,000 and $10,000, respectively?
d) What form would Flower use to report nondividend distributions?
e) On what form (line) would Tiny and Tim report nondividend distributions?

50. Hoosier Corporation declared a 2-for-1 stock split (shareholders received one share of stock for each share they already owned) to all shareholders of record on March 25 of this year. Hoosier reported current E&P of $600,000 and accumulated E&P of $3,000,000. The total fair market value of the stock distributed was $1,500,000. Barbara owned 1,000 shares of Hoosier stock with a tax basis of $100 per share. LO 7-3
a) What amount of taxable dividend income, if any, does Barbara recognize this year? Assume the fair market value of the stock was $150 per share on March 25 of this year.
b) What is the income tax basis in the new and existing stock Barbara owns in Hoosier Corporation, assuming the distribution is tax-free?
c) How does the stock distribution affect Hoosier's accumulated E&P at the beginning of next year?

LO 7-3 51. Badger Corporation declared a stock distribution to all shareholders of record on March 25 of this year. Shareholders will receive 1 share of Badger stock for each 10 shares of stock they already own. Madison owns 1,000 shares of Badger stock with a tax basis of $100 per share. The fair market value of the Badger stock was $110 per share on March 25 of this year.

a) What amount of taxable dividend income, if any, does Madison recognize this year?

b) What is the tax basis in Madison's new and existing stock in Badger Corporation, assuming the distribution is nontaxable?

c) How would you answer parts (a) and (b) if Badger offered shareholders a choice between receiving 1 additional share of Badger stock for each 10 Badger shares held or receiving $120 cash in lieu of an additional share of stock?

LO 7-4 52. Wildcat Company is owned equally by Evan and his sister Sara, each of whom holds 1,000 shares in the company. Sara wants to reduce her ownership in the company, and it was decided that the company will redeem 500 of her shares for $25,000 per share on December 31 of this year. Sara's tax basis in each share is $5,000. Wildcat has current E&P of $10,000,000 and at the beginning of the year accumulated E&P is $50,000,000.

a) What are the amount and character (capital gain or dividend) recognized by Sara because of the stock redemption?

b) What is the tax basis in the remaining 500 shares Sara owns in the company?

c) By what amount does Wildcat reduce its E&P because of the redemption?

LO 7-4 53. Flintstone Company is owned equally by Fred and his sister Wilma, each of whom holds 1,000 shares in the company. Wilma wants to reduce her ownership in the company, and it was decided that the company will redeem 250 of her shares for $25,000 per share on December 31 of this year. Wilma's tax basis in each share is $5,000. Flintstone has current E&P of $10,000,000 and accumulated E&P at the beginning of the year is $50,000,000.

a) What are the amount and character (capital gain or dividend) recognized by Wilma because of the stock redemption, assuming only the "substantially disproportionate with respect to the shareholder" test is applied?

b) Given your answer to part (a), what is the tax basis in the remaining 750 shares Wilma owns in the company?

c) By what amount does Flintstone reduce its E&P because of the redemption?

d) What other argument might Wilma make to treat the redemption as an exchange?

LO 7-4 54. Acme Corporation has 1,000 shares outstanding. Joan and Tin are married, and each of them owns 20 shares of Acme. Joan and Tin's daughter, Kara, also owns 20 shares of Acme. Joan is an equal partner with Jeri in the J&J partnership, and this partnership owns 60 shares of Acme. Jeri is not related to Joan or Tin. How many shares of Acme is Kara deemed to own under the stock attribution rules?

LO 7-4 55. Bedrock Inc. is owned equally by Barney and his wife Betty, each of whom holds 1,000 shares in the company. Betty wants to reduce her ownership in the company, and it was decided that the company will redeem 500 of her shares for $25,000 per share on December 31 of this year. Betty's tax basis in each share is $5,000. Bedrock has current E&P of $10,000,000 and accumulated E&P of $50,000,000.

a) What are the amount and character (capital gain or dividend) recognized by Betty because of the stock redemption, assuming only the "substantially disproportionate with respect to the shareholder" test is applied?

b) Given your answer to part (a), what is the tax basis in the remaining 500 shares Betty owns in the company?

c) By what amount does Bedrock reduce its E&P because of the redemption?

d) Can Betty argue that the redemption is "not essentially equivalent to a dividend" and should be treated as an exchange?

56. In the previous problem, assume that Betty and Barney are not getting along and have separated due to marital discord (although they are not legally separated). In fact, they cannot even stand to talk to each other anymore and communicate only through their accountant. Betty wants to argue that she should not be treated as owning any of Barney's stock in Bedrock because of their hostility toward each other. Can family hostility be used as an argument to void the family attribution rules? Consult Rev. Rul. 80-26; *Robin Haft Trust v. Comm'r,* 510 F.2d 43 (1st Cir. 1975); *Metzger Trust v. Comm'r,* 693 F.2d 459 (5th Cir. 1982); and *Cerone v. Comm'r,* 87 TC 1 (1986). LO 7-4 research

57. Boots Inc. is owned equally by Muhammad and his daughter Isabel, each of whom holds 1,000 shares in the company. Muhammad wants to retire from the company, and it was decided that the company will redeem all 1,000 of Muhammad's shares for $25,000 per share on December 31 of this year. Muhammad's tax basis in each share is $500. Boots Inc. has current E&P of $1,000,000 and at the beginning of the year accumulated E&P is $5,000,000. LO 7-4

a) What must Muhammad do to ensure that the redemption will be treated as an exchange?

b) If Muhammad remained as the chair of the board after the redemption, what are the amount and character of income (capital gain or dividend) that Muhammad will recognize this year?

c) If Muhammad treats the redemption as a dividend, what happens to the stock basis in the 1,000 shares redeemed?

58. In the previous problem, Isabel would like to have Muhammad stay on as a consultant after all his shares are redeemed. Boots would pay Muhammad a modest salary of $500 per month. Isabel wants to know if there is any *de minimis* rule such that Muhammad would not be treated as having retained a prohibited interest in the company because the salary is so small. Consult *Lynch v. Comm'r,* 801 F.2d 1176 (9th Cir. 1986), *reversing* 83 TC 597 (1984); *Seda v. Comm'r,* 82 TC 484 (1984); and *Cerone v. Comm'r,* 87 TC 1 (1986). LO 7-4 research

59. Limited Brands recently repurchased 68,965,000 of its shares, paying $29 per share. The total number of shares outstanding before the redemption was 473,223,066. The total number of shares outstanding after the redemption was 404,258,066. Assume your client owned 20,000 shares of stock in The Limited. What is the minimum number of shares she must tender to receive exchange treatment under the "substantially disproportionate with respect to the shareholder" change-in-ownership rules? LO 7-4 planning

60. Cougar Company is owned equally by Cat and a partnership that is owned equally by his father and two unrelated individuals. Cat and the partnership each owns 3,000 shares in the company. Cat wants to reduce his ownership in the company and decided that the company will redeem 1,500 of his shares for $25,000 per share. Cat's tax basis in each share is $5,000. What are the income tax consequences to Cat because of the stock redemption, assuming the company has earnings and profits of $10 million? LO 7-4

LO 7-4
planning

61. Oriole Corporation, a privately held company, has one class of voting common stock, of which 1,000 shares are issued and outstanding. The shares are owned as follows:

Larry	400
Ivan (Larry's son)	200
Gabi (Larry's daughter)	200
Cali (unrelated)	200
Total	1,000

Larry is considering retirement and would like to have the corporation redeem all his shares for $400,000.

a) What action is necessary if Larry wants to guarantee that the redemption will be treated as an exchange?

b) Could Larry act as a consultant to the company and still have the redemption treated as an exchange?

LO 7-4
research

62. Using the facts in the previous problem, Oriole Corporation proposes to pay Larry $100,000 and an installment note that pays $30,000 per year for the next 10 years plus a market rate of interest. Will this arrangement allow Larry to treat the redemption as an exchange? Consult §453(k)(2)(A).

LO 7-4

63. EG Corporation redeemed 200 shares of stock from one of its shareholders in exchange for $200,000. The redemption represented 20 percent of the corporation's outstanding stock. The redemption was treated as an exchange by the shareholder. By what amount does EG reduce its total E&P because of the redemption under the following E&P assumptions?

a) EG's total E&P at the time of the distribution was $2,000,000.

b) EG's total E&P at the time of the distribution was $500,000.

LO 7-4
research

64. Spartan Corporation redeemed 25 percent of its shares for $2,000 on July 1 of this year, in a transaction that qualified as an exchange under §302(a). Spartan's accumulated E&P at the beginning of the year was $2,000. Its current E&P is $12,000. Spartan made dividend distributions of $1,000 on June 1 and $4,000 on August 31. Determine the beginning balance in Spartan's accumulated E&P at the beginning of the next year. See Rev. Rul. 74-338 and Rev. Rul. 74-339 for help in making this calculation.

LO 7-4

65. Bonnie and Clyde are the only two shareholders in Getaway Corporation. Bonnie owns 60 shares with a basis of $3,000, and Clyde owns the remaining 40 shares with a basis of $12,000. At year-end, Getaway is considering different alternatives for redeeming some shares of stock. Evaluate whether each of the following stock redemption transactions will qualify for sale and exchange treatment.

a) Getaway redeems 10 of Bonnie's shares for $2,000. Getaway has $20,000 of E&P at year-end and Bonnie is unrelated to Clyde.

b) Getaway redeems 25 of Bonnie's shares for $4,000. Getaway has $20,000 of E&P at year-end and Bonnie is unrelated to Clyde.

c) Getaway redeems 10 of Clyde's shares for $2,500. Getaway has $20,000 of E&P at year-end and Clyde is unrelated to Bonnie.

LO 7-4
research

66. Brent, Matt, Chris, Brad, and Anwer are five unrelated shareholders who each owns 20 of the 100 outstanding shares of Aggie Corporation. On June 30 of this year, Aggie distributed $100,000 in cash to the shareholders. On September 30 of this

year, Aggie redeemed all Anwer's shares for $80,000. Aggie had $45,000 of accumulated E&P at the beginning of the year and reported $120,000 of current E&P at year-end. What is Aggie's accumulated E&P at the beginning of next year? Consult Rev. Rul. 74-338. (*Hint:* Determine the tax status of the redemption and then calculate the effect of the June distribution on current E&P.)

67. Nail Corporation made a distribution of $500,000 to Rusty in partial liquidation of the company on December 31 of this year. Rusty, an individual, owns 100 percent of Nail Corporation. The distribution was in exchange for 50 percent of Rusty's stock in the company. At the time of the distribution, the shares had a fair market value of $200 per share. Rusty's tax basis in the shares was $50 per share. Nail had total E&P of $8,000,000 at the time of the distribution. LO 7-5
    a) What are the amount and character (capital gain or dividend) of any income or gain recognized by Rusty because of the partial liquidation?
    b) Assuming Nail made no other distributions to Rusty during the year, by what amount does Nail reduce its total E&P because of the partial liquidation?

68. Wolverine Corporation made a distribution of $500,000 to Deer Inc. in partial liquidation of the company on December 31 of this year. Deer owns 100 percent of Wolverine Corporation. The distribution was in exchange for 50 percent of Deer's stock in the company. At the time of the distribution, the shares had a fair market value of $200 per share. Deer's tax basis in the shares was $50 per share. Wolverine had total E&P of $8,000,000 at the time of the distribution. LO 7-5
    a) What are the amount and character (capital gain or dividend) of any income or gain recognized by Deer because of the partial liquidation?
    b) Assuming Wolverine made no other distributions to Deer during the year, by what amount does Wolverine reduce its total E&P because of the partial liquidation?

COMPREHENSIVE PROBLEMS

Select problems are available in Connect®.

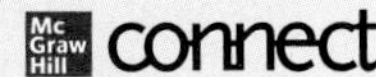

69. Lanco Corporation, an accrual-method corporation, reported taxable income of $1,460,000 this year. Included in the computation of taxable income were the following items:

    - MACRS depreciation of $200,000. Depreciation for earnings and profits purposes is $120,000.
    - A net capital loss carryover of $10,000 from last year.
    - A net operating loss carryover of $25,000 from last year.
    - $65,000 capital gain from the distribution of land to the company's sole shareholder (see below).

    Not included in the computation of taxable income were the following items:

    - Tax-exempt income of $5,000.
    - Life insurance proceeds of $250,000.
    - Excess current-year charitable contribution of $2,500 (to be carried over to next year).
    - Tax-deferred gain of $20,000 on a like-kind exchange.
    - Nondeductible life insurance premium of $3,500.
    - Nondeductible interest expense of $1,000 on a loan used to buy tax-exempt bonds.

Lanco's accumulated E&P at the beginning of the year was $2,400,000. During the year, Lanco made the following distributions to its sole shareholder, Luigi:

- June 30: $50,000.
- September 30: Parcel of land with a fair market value of $75,000. Lanco's adjusted tax basis in the land was $10,000. Luigi assumed an existing mortgage on the property of $15,000.

Required:

a) Compute Lanco's current E&P.

b) Compute the amount of dividend income reported by Luigi this year because of the distributions.

c) Compute Lanco's accumulated E&P at the beginning of next year.

70. Petoskey Stone Quarry Inc. (PSQ), a calendar-year, accrual-method C corporation, provides landscaping supplies to local builders in northern Michigan. PSQ has always been a family-owned business and has a single class of voting common stock outstanding. The 500 outstanding shares are owned as follows:

Nick	150
Abigail (Nick's daughter)	50
Charlie (Nick's son)	50
Sandler (Nick's father)	100
Amy (Sandler's sister)	150
Total shares	500

Nick serves as president of PSQ, and his father, Sandler, serves as chair of the board. Amy is the company's CFO, and Abigail and Charlie work as employees of the company. Sandler would like to retire and sell his shares back to the company. The fair market value of the shares is $500,000. Sandler's tax basis is $10,000. The redemption is tentatively scheduled to take place on December 31 of this year. At the beginning of the year, PSQ had accumulated earnings and profits of $2,500,000. The company projects current E&P of $200,000. The company intends to pay pro rata cash dividends of $300 per share to its shareholders on December 1 of this year.

Required:

a) Assume the redemption takes place as planned on December 31 and no elections are made by the shareholders.

1) What amount of dividend or capital gain will Sandler recognize because of the stock redemption?

2) How will the tax basis of Sandler's stock be allocated to the remaining shareholders?

b) What must Sandler and the other shareholders do to change the tax results you calculated in part (a)?

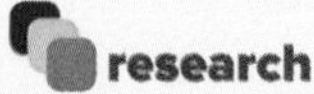

71. Thriller Corporation has one class of voting common stock, of which 1,000 shares are issued and outstanding. The shares are owned as follows:

Joe	400
Miguel (Joe's son)	200
Lili (Joe's daughter)	200
Vinnie (unrelated)	200
Total shares	1,000

Thriller Corporation has current E&P of $400,000 for this year and accumulated E&P on January 1 of this year of $60,000. During this year, the corporation made the following distributions to its shareholders:

03/31: Distributed $100 per share to each shareholder ($100,000 in total).

06/30: Distributed $100 per share to each shareholder ($100,000 in total).

09/30: Distributed $100 per share to each shareholder ($100,000 in total).

12/31: Redeemed all of Vinnie's shares for $250,000 in cash.

Required:

a) Determine the tax status of each distribution made this year.

b) Compute the corporation's accumulated E&P on January 1 of next year.

c) Joe is considering retirement and would like to have the corporation redeem all his shares for $100,000 plus a 10-year note with a fair market value of $300,000. What action must Joe consider to ensure that the redemption will be treated as an exchange? Could Joe still act as a consultant to the company?

d) Thriller Corporation must pay attorney fees of $5,000 to facilitate the stock redemptions. Is this fee deductible?

UWorld Roger CPA Review

Sample CPA Exam questions from Roger CPA Review are available in Connect as support for the topics in this text. These Multiple Choice Questions and Task-Based Simulations include expert-written explanations and solutions and provide a starting point for students to become familiar with the content and functionality of the actual CPA Exam.

chapter 8

Corporate Formation, Reorganization, and Liquidation

Learning Objectives

Upon completing this chapter, you should be able to:

LO 8-1 Review the taxation of property dispositions.

LO 8-2 Recognize the tax consequences to the parties to a tax-deferred corporate formation.

LO 8-3 Identify the different forms of taxable and tax-deferred acquisitions.

LO 8-4 Determine the tax consequences to the parties to a corporate acquisition.

LO 8-5 Calculate the tax consequences that apply to the parties to a complete liquidation of a corporation.

Sergey Ryzhov/123RF

Storyline Summary

Spartan Cycle and Repair

Privately held company located in East Lansing, Michigan, that sells and repairs high-end bicycles

Jim Wheels (he/him/his)

Co-owner of Spartan Cycle and Repair (75 percent)

Ginny Gears (she/her/hers)

Co-owner of Spartan Cycle and Repair (25 percent)

360 Air

Privately held company in East Lansing, Michigan, that sells snowboarding equipment

Al Pine (he/him/his)

Owner of 360 Air

Wolverine Cycles and Repair

Privately held company in Ann Arbor, Michigan
Sells and repairs high-end bicycles

Pam Peloton (she/her/hers)

Owner of Wolverine Cycles and Repair

Jim Wheels and Ginny Gears are excited about the growth of their business, Spartan Cycle and Repair (SCR). The business has a solid base of loyal customers and is showing a healthy profit, and now Jim and Ginny are ready for some new challenges. They have considered both expanding the bicycle business to a new geographic region and branching out into a new line of business. Given the seasonal nature of the demand for bicycle products and repair in Michigan, Jim and Ginny favor a complementary line of business that would provide them with a source of income during the winter months. Ginny is impressed with the growing popularity of snowboarding. Factors that have contributed to this growth include low equipment costs, easily attained skills, a "coolness" attractive to young people, and the sport's inclusion in the Olympic Games.

Jim and Ginny are aware of a small snowboarding store in East Lansing called 360 Air, which is also the name of a daring snowboarding maneuver. The business is owned and operated as a sole proprietorship by Al Pine, a rather free-spirited individual whose enthusiasm for the sport is not matched by business acumen.

Jim and Ginny feel that with some additional capital investment and marketing effort, they could turn Al's snowboarding business into a profitable operation. They set up a meeting with Al to discuss how they could become partners in his business enterprise.

After some negotiation, Jim, Ginny, and Al agree to jointly operate the snowboarding business as a corporation taxed as a C corporation. As part of incorporating the business, each individual will make a contribution of property or services to the corporation in return for stock. Al will contribute existing snowboard inventory, a building (with associated land), and a separate parcel of land in return for 50 percent of the stock in 360 Air. The corporation will assume the existing mortgage on the property. Jim will contribute cash in exchange for 40 percent of the stock, and Ginny will contribute marketing services in return for 10 percent of the stock.

Each of the parties wants to know the income tax implications of incorporating Al's ongoing business. In addition, Jim is wondering whether the manner in which they are intending to create the corporation is tax efficient and whether there are other issues they should consider that would lessen the current and future tax burdens of both the corporation and its new shareholders.

(to be continued . . .)

When creating a business, the owners must choose an organizational form for operations. The choice of tax entity affects whether and how the income or loss generated by the business is taxed at the entity level and the owner level. At some point during the life of a business, the owners may decide to change its tax status. In the case of an ongoing business, such as 360 Air, changing from proprietorship to corporate status will require the transfer of assets and liabilities by the owners in return for stock in the corporation. These property transfers have important tax implications. A transfer of assets or liabilities to a corporation in exchange for stock triggers realization of gains and losses and may cause shareholders to recognize gains in the year of the transfer. In addition, shareholders will need to calculate the tax basis of their stock, and the corporation will need to calculate the basis of the assets and liabilities received in the transfer.

LO 8-1

REVIEW OF THE TAXATION OF PROPERTY DISPOSITIONS

This section provides a brief review of tax rules that apply to transfers of property to a corporation in exchange for stock and other property. Before gain or loss is recognized (included in taxable income), it must first be realized. **Realization** generally occurs when a transaction takes place (that is, when there is an exchange of property rights between two persons).

Exhibit 8-1 provides a template for computing gain or loss realized by a party to a property transaction.

EXHIBIT 8-1 Computing Gain or Loss Realized in a Property Transaction

	Amount realized (received)
−	Adjusted tax basis of the property transferred
	Gain (+) or loss (−) realized

Source: §1001(a).

The **amount realized** is computed using the template in Exhibit 8-2.

THE KEY FACTS

Overview of the Taxation of Property Transactions

- Gain or loss is realized when a person engages in a transaction (an exchange of property rights with another person).
- Gain or loss realized is computed by subtracting the transferor's adjusted tax basis in the property exchanged from the amount realized in the exchange.
- Gain or loss realized is recognized (included in the computation of taxable income) unless exempted or deferred by a provision of the tax laws.

EXHIBIT 8-2 Computing the Amount Realized in a Property Transaction

	Cash received
+	Fair market value of other property received
+	Liabilities assumed by the transferee on the transferred property
–	Selling expenses incurred in the transaction
–	Liabilities assumed by the transferor on any property received in the exchange
	Amount realized

Source: §1001(b).

A property's **adjusted tax basis** is calculated using the template in Exhibit 8-3.

EXHIBIT 8-3 Computing a Property's Adjusted Tax Basis in a Property Transaction

	Acquisition basis
+	Capital improvements
–	Accumulated depreciation/Cost recovery
	Adjusted tax basis

Source: §1011.

The entire amount of gain or deductible loss realized is recognized unless otherwise excluded or deferred by other provisions of the law.[1] Gain or loss that is excluded from gross income will never be recognized. Gain or deductible loss that is deferred is merely postponed to a future period.

TAX-DEFERRED TRANSFERS OF PROPERTY TO A CORPORATION

LO 8-2

A realization event occurs when shareholders transfer cash and noncash property to a corporation in return for stock in the corporation. Transfers of assets to corporations occurs in the formation of a corporation, but it can also happen in subsequent transactions with an existing corporation. Unless the transfer meets certain requirements, the transaction is treated as a taxable sale or exchange of the shareholder's property to the corporation. That is, the taxpayer is treated as selling the property to the corporation for the corporation's stock (and any other property transferred from the corporation to the shareholder). The stock can be common or preferred, voting, or nonvoting.[2] We discussed the tax consequences of a sale or exchange of property in depth in the Property Dispositions chapter. To summarize, shareholders would recognize gain or loss by the difference between the value of the corporate stock and other assets received in the exchange and the adjusted tax basis of the assets contributed to the corporation.

[1]§1001(c). Realized losses must first be deductible to be recognized. Nondeductible losses are never recognized.

[2]A category of stock with different rights (e.g., voting rights, dividend rights, liquidation rights) is referred to as a class of stock.

In §351, Congress provides for the deferral of gain or loss on qualifying transfers of property to a corporation in exchange for stock in order to remove tax consequences as an impediment to conducting business in the corporate form. Congress justifies tax deferral because shareholders maintain an interest in the property transferred through a different form of ownership (i.e., from direct ownership to indirect ownership through stock). In other words, the shareholders making the transfer have not substantively disposed of their ownership of the property.

Gain or loss deferred in the transfer of property to a corporation in return for stock is reflected in the shareholder's adjusted tax basis in the stock received in exchange for the transferred property.[3] Consequently, when the shareholder defers a gain on the transfer, the stock basis will be lower than the fair market value of the stock by the amount of the gain. When the shareholder defers a loss on the transfer, the stock basis will be higher than the fair market value of the stock by the amount of the loss.

Transactions Subject to Tax Deferral

For shareholders to receive tax deferral in a transfer of property to a corporation, the transferors must meet all three requirements in §351 as follows:

1. One or more shareholders must transfer *property* to a corporation.
2. Shareholders who transfer property to the corporation (i.e., the transferors) must receive *stock* of the transferee corporation in exchange for the property they transfer.
3. Immediately after the transfer, the transferors, together, must *control* the corporation to which they transferred the property.

Each of these requirements is discussed below. When the requirements are met, deferral of gain or loss in a §351 transaction is mandatory. Section 351 applies to transfers of property to both C corporations and S corporations.

Section 351 applies only to those **persons** who transfer property to the corporation in exchange for stock (i.e., shareholders). A *person* is defined for tax purposes to include individuals, corporations, partnerships, and fiduciaries (estates and trusts).[4] Thus, §351 allows individuals like Al to form a corporation and also allows existing corporations, such as General Electric, to employ §351 when creating a subsidiary. Also, the corporation receiving the property in exchange for its own stock does not recognize gain or loss on the transaction.[5]

Meeting the Section 351 Tax Deferral Requirements

The shareholders transferring property (the *transferors*) to a corporation (the *transferee*) must meet several requirements for the transfer to be tax-deferred. Some of these requirements are not precisely defined in either the IRC or the regulations. As a result, much of what we understand about the parameters of §351 has developed over time as the IRS and the courts have interpreted the law. This incremental approach to understanding the meaning of the law is common throughout Subchapter C of the Internal Revenue Code.[6]

Section 351 Applies Only to the Transfer of Property to the Corporation

Property includes money, tangible assets, and intangible assets (e.g., company name, patents, customer lists, trademarks, and logos). Services are, however, excluded from the

[3]§358.

[4]§7701(a)(1).

[5]§1032. Note, however, that under GAAP a corporation will record contributed property at fair value for book purposes. Hence, a contribution of property under §351 will give rise to book–tax differences because different amounts of depreciation will be recorded for book and tax purposes.

[6]Subchapter C encompasses §§301–385 and provides the tax rules for the corporate transactions discussed in this chapter.

definition of property. Thus, a person who receives stock in return for services generally has compensation equal to the fair market value of the stock received.[7]

Example 8-1

As part of the formation of the corporation, Ginny received 10 percent of the stock in 360 Air, valued at $60,000, in exchange for services in setting up the corporation. Will Ginny recognize the $60,000 of value realized on the transaction?

Answer: Yes. Ginny must recognize compensation income of $60,000 as a result of this exchange because services are not considered property under §351.

What if: Suppose Ginny created a distinctive logo for the company and in exchange received 10 percent of the stock in 360 Air, valued at $60,000. Assume the adjusted tax basis of the slogan is zero because Ginny created it. Will Ginny recognize the $60,000 gain realized on the transfer of the slogan?

Answer: No. Ginny will not recognize the $60,000 gain realized because intangibles are considered property under §351.

The Property Transferred to the Corporation Must Be Exchanged for Stock of the Corporation When property is transferred to a corporation in exchange for stock and other property, only the portion of the property exchanged for stock will qualify for tax deferral. Property (other than stock in the transferee corporation) received by shareholders is referred to as **boot.** The receipt of boot will cause the shareholder (transferor) to recognize gain, but not loss, realized on the exchange. We will discuss the details of this computation later in the chapter.

The type of stock a shareholder can receive in a §351 exchange is quite flexible and includes voting or nonvoting and common or preferred stock. Stock for purposes of §351 does not include stock warrants, rights, or options.[8] Property transferred in exchange for debt of the corporation is not eligible for deferral under §351.

Example 8-2

What if: Suppose Ginny received a five-year note (debt) in 360 Air valued at $60,000 in exchange for contributing machinery. The original cost of the machinery was $70,000, and Ginny has depreciated it to a basis of zero. Will Ginny defer recognition of the $60,000 gain realized on the transfer of the machinery?

Answer: No. Section 351 provides for deferral only when the transferor of property receives stock in return. Ginny must recognize the entire $60,000 gain.

The Transferor(s) of Property to the Corporation Must Be in Control of the Corporation, in the Aggregate, Immediately after the Transfer Control for purposes of §351 is defined as the ownership of 80 percent or more of the total combined voting power of all voting stock that is issued and outstanding, and 80 percent or more of the total number of shares of each class of nonvoting stock.[9]

[7]An individual who receives stock subject to "restrictions" (e.g., they must remain with the company for a certain number of years) does not report compensation income until the restrictions attached to the stock are lifted (§83). Under §83(b), as an alternative the individual can elect to value the stock on the date received and report that amount as income.

[8]§351(g) identifies nonqualified preferred stock as boot but nonqualified preferred stock will count as equity for purposes of determining control of the corporation. Nonqualified preferred stock generally has characteristics that cause it to more resemble debt than equity.

[9]§368(c). Voting power is generally defined as the ability of the shareholders to elect members of the corporation's board of directors.

Whether the control test is met is based on the collective ownership of the shareholders transferring property to the corporation immediately after the transfer. Keep in mind that this group of shareholders (i.e., the transferors) is composed only of those who have transferred property, which does not include services, in exchange for stock. In addition, the aggregate ownership (not the change in ownership) of these shareholders immediately after the transfer must meet the 80 percent threshold.

ETHICS

Malik owns appreciated property and wants to use this property to start a business with Lance. Malik is considering making a contribution of the property to a newly organized corporation in exchange for 100 percent of the corporate stock. Malik then plans to give half of the stock to Lance in exchange for managing the business. Do you think this transaction will qualify for §351 treatment? Does it make any difference if Lance is Malik's son? Suppose Malik promises that the stock transfer won't occur for a month after making the contribution of property. Does this make any difference? Compare Rev. Rul. 54-96, with *Intermountain Lumber Co.,* 65 TC 1025 (1976).

Example 8-3

What if: Assume Ginny was hesitant to join with Jim and Al in the incorporation of 360 Air. Instead, after six months, Ginny changed her mind and received a 10 percent interest in 360 Air stock in exchange for intangibles that qualified as property under §351. The stock was valued at $60,000, and Ginny's adjusted tax basis in the intangibles was zero. Will Ginny defer recognition of the $60,000 gain realized on the exchange under §351?

Answer: No. Ginny is the only transferor and does not control (80 percent or more of) 360 Air immediately after the transfer. As a result, Ginny must recognize the $60,000 gain.

What if: Suppose Ginny joined with Jim and Al in forming 360 Air and received 25 percent of the corporation's stock in exchange for services. The stock was valued at $150,000. Al and Jim received the remaining 75 percent of the stock in the company in exchange for appreciated property. Will Al and Jim defer recognition of gain they realize on the exchange of the appreciated property under §351?

Answer: No. Taking into account only the stock received in exchange for property, Al and Jim do not collectively control 360 Air immediately after the transaction. Al and Jim own only 75 percent, not 80 percent. Consequently, the transaction is not eligible for deferral under §351, and all gain realized is recognized.

Generally, when a shareholder transfers both services and property to the corporation in exchange for stock, that shareholder is generally considered to be a transferor of property for purposes of the control test. However, if the primary purpose for the shareholder's transfer of property to the corporation is to qualify the exchange of another person under §351, that shareholder would be considered to be a transferor of property only if the value of the stock received for property is not of "relatively small value" compared to the value of the stock received for services.[10] The IRS has stated that, for ruling purposes, property will not be of "relatively small value" if it equals at least 10 percent of the value of the stock received for the services provided.[11]

Example 8-4

What if: Let's say Ginny joined with Jim and Al in the incorporation of 360 Air primarily to qualify Jim and Al for §351 treatment. Ginny received 25 percent of the corporation's stock in exchange for services and intangibles treated as property. The stock was valued at $150,000. The services were valued at $125,000 and the intangibles were valued at $25,000. Al and Jim received the remaining 75 percent of the stock in the company in exchange for appreciated property. Using the IRS standards

[10]Reg. §1.351-1(a)(1)(ii). Note that the determination of relative value is a factual issue.

[11]Rev. Proc. 77-37.

for rulings, will Al and Jim defer recognition of gain they realize on the exchange of the appreciated property under §351?

Answer: Yes. The stock Ginny received in exchange for the intangibles exceeds 10 percent of the value of the stock received for the services ($25,000/$125,000 = 20%). For purposes of determining control, Ginny will qualify as a transferor, and all of the stock received in 360 Air will qualify as having been received for property. Al, Jim, and Ginny will be treated as collectively receiving 100 percent of the 360 Air stock in exchange for property. Hence, Al and Jim will defer gain realized on their exchanges of property for stock. Ginny will recognize compensation of $125,000 on the exchange, but Ginny will defer recognizing any gain realized on the transfer of the intangibles.

What if: Assume Ginny's services were valued at $140,000 and the intangibles were valued at $10,000. Using the IRS standards for rulings, will Al and Jim defer recognition of gain they realize on the exchange of the appreciated property under §351?

Answer: No, because Ginny's primary purpose in transferring the intangible property was to qualify the transfer for deferral. The fair market value of the stock received for the intangibles is less than 10 percent of the stock received for services ($10,000/$140,000 = 7.14%). As a result, the IRS will not consider Ginny to be a transferor of property for ruling purposes, and none of Ginny's stock will count in the control test. Al, Jim, and Ginny are treated as having received collectively only 75 percent of 360 Air stock in exchange for property. Consequently, §351 does not apply to any of the transferors of the property to 360 Air.

This same rule applies to subsequent transfers of property by an existing shareholder to accommodate a new shareholder's transfer of property to an established corporation. The regulations state that stock received for property that is of "relatively small value" in comparison to the value of the stock already owned will not be considered issued in return for property (i.e., the shareholder making the contribution will not be included in the control test) if the "primary purpose" of the transfer is to qualify the exchange of another person under §351. The IRS has stated that, for ruling purposes, an existing shareholder must contribute property that has a fair market value of at least 10 percent of the value of the stock already owned to be included in the control test.[12]

Example 8-5

What if: Assume Jim and Ginny were 100 percent shareholders of SCR and wanted to bring Al on board as a 20 percent shareholder. Al will transfer appreciated property to SCR in return for stock in SCR valued at $100,000. Will Al defer recognizing any gain realized on the transfer under §351?

Answer: No. Al does not control SCR "immediately after" the exchange, taking into account only the stock Al owns in SCR.

What if: Suppose Jim agreed to make an additional property contribution to SCR at the same time as Al's transfer in order to help Al qualify his transfer under §351. Jim's 75 percent ownership interest in SCR was valued at $300,000 at the time of Al's transfer. Using the IRS standards for rulings, how much property (fair market value) must Jim contribute to SCR to have his ownership of stock in SCR counted in determining if Al qualifies for deferral under §351?

Answer: $30,000. For the "accommodation transfer" to be respected by the IRS, Jim must contribute property with a fair market value of 10 percent or more of the fair market value of his existing stock in SCR (10% × $300,000).

THE KEY FACTS

Requirements for Tax Deferral in a Corporate Formation

- Tax deferral applies to transfers of *property* to a corporation.
- The persons transferring property to a corporation must receive only stock in the corporation in return.
- The persons transferring property to a corporation must collectively control the corporation after the transaction.
- Control is defined as ownership of 80 percent or more of the corporation's voting stock and 80 percent or more of each class of nonvoting stock.

(continued)

Tax Consequences When a Shareholder Receives No Boot

As discussed above, when an exchange qualifies under §351, the shareholder's gain or loss realized on the exchange is deferred. This deferral is generally reflected in the shareholder's basis in stock received in the exchange (the deferred gain or loss is built into the stock's tax basis). When no boot is involved, the adjusted tax basis of stock received in a tax-deferred §351 exchange equals the adjusted tax basis of the property transferred less any liabilities assumed by the corporation.[13] The stock is said to have a **substituted basis.** That is, the

[12] Rev. Proc. 77-37.

[13] §358(a).

- Generally, all stock received by the transferor counts for the control test, unless the stock is received solely in exchange for services.

adjusted tax basis of the property transferred is substituted for the adjusted tax basis of the property received.[14] Exhibit 8-4 provides a template for computing the adjusted tax basis of stock received in a tax-deferred §351 transaction.

EXHIBIT 8-4 Computing the Adjusted Tax Basis of Stock Received in a Tax-Deferred Section 351 Transaction with No Boot

	Cash contributed
+	Adjusted tax basis of other property contributed
−	Liabilities assumed by the corporation on property contributed
	Adjusted tax basis of stock received

Source: §358(a).

Example 8-6

As part of the formation of 360 Air, Al transferred inventory, a building, and land to the corporation in return for 50 percent of the corporation's stock (50 shares). The property transferred to the corporation had the following fair market values and adjusted tax bases:

	FMV	Adjusted Tax Basis
Inventory	$ 25,000	$ 15,000
Building	150,000	60,000
Land	200,000	100,000
Total	$375,000	$175,000

In addition, the corporation assumed a mortgage of $75,000 attached to the building and land. The fair market value of the 360 Air stock Al received in the exchange was $300,000. Al realizes a gain of $200,000 on the transfer, computed as follows:

	Fair market value of 360 Air stock received	$ 300,000
+	Mortgage assumed by 360 Air	75,000
	Amount realized	$ 375,000
−	Adjusted tax basis of the property transferred	175,000
	Gain realized	$ 200,000

Assuming Al meets the requirements under §351 to defer recognizing the $200,000 gain realized, what is his tax basis in the 50 shares of 360 Air stock he receives in the exchange?

Answer: $100,000. Al's tax basis in the stock must reflect the gain he defers in the exchange. Al computes tax basis in the 360 Air stock as follows:

	Adjusted tax basis of property contributed	$ 175,000
−	Mortgage assumed by 360 Air	75,000
	Tax basis of 360 Air stock received	**$100,000**

If Al subsequently were to sell his 360 Air stock for its fair market value of $300,000, he would recognize a capital gain of $200,000 ($300,000 − $100,000), an amount equal to the gain he deferred previously.

What if: Assume Al did not meet the requirements under §351 and was required to recognize the $200,000 gain realized. What is Al's tax basis in the 50 shares of 360 Air stock received in the exchange?

Answer: $300,000. Al's tax basis in his stock equals its fair market value. If Al subsequently sells his 360 Air stock for $300,000, he will not recognize any further gain.

[14]§7701(a)(44) uses the term *exchanged basis property* for this type of property.

Tax Consequences When a Shareholder Receives Boot

A shareholder who receives property other than stock (boot) recognizes gains (but not losses) in an amount not to exceed the lesser of (1) the gain realized or (2) the fair market value of the boot received. We calculate the amount of gain recognized when boot is received in a §351 transaction by allocating the boot received to each contributed property using the relative fair market values of the properties.[15] The amount of gain recognized with respect to each asset is the lesser of the gain realized or the boot allocated to such asset. The character of the recognized gain (i.e., capital gain, §1231 gain, ordinary income) is determined by the character of the asset.

Example 8-7

What if: Suppose Al received 40 shares of 360 Air stock with a fair market value of $315,000 plus $60,000 in return for inventory, a building, and land used in his business and transferred to the corporation. The property transferred to the corporation had the following fair market values and adjusted bases:

	FMV	Adjusted Tax Basis	Gain Realized
Inventory	$ 25,000	$ 15,000	$ 10,000
Building	150,000	60,000	90,000
Land	200,000	100,000	100,000
Total	$375,000	$175,000	$200,000

What amount of gain does Al recognize on receipt of the $60,000 boot, and what is its character (ordinary income or §1231 gain)?

Answer: The $60,000 constitutes boot received and causes Al to recognize some or all of the gain realized on each asset in the transfer. Al apportions the $60,000 of boot to each of the properties transferred to the corporation based on their relative fair market values. Al recognizes gain on each property transferred in an amount equal to the lesser of the gain realized or the fair market value of the boot apportioned to the property. The computation is made for each property separately, as follows:

Inventory	
Fair market value of 360 Air stock and cash received	$ 25,000
Less adjusted tax basis of the inventory transferred	−15,000
(1) Gain realized	$ 10,000
(2) Boot apportioned (25/375 × $60,000)	4,000
Gain recognized: lesser of (1) or (2)	**$ 4,000**
Character of gain recognized: ordinary income	

Building	
Fair market value of 360 Air stock and cash received	$ 150,000
Less adjusted tax basis of the building transferred	−60,000
(1) Gain realized	$ 90,000
(2) Boot apportioned (150/375 × $60,000)	24,000
Gain recognized: lesser of (1) or (2)	**$ 24,000**
Character of gain recognized: §1231[16]	

(continued on page 8-10)

[15]In Rev. Rul. 68-55 and Rev. Rul. 85-164, the IRS adopted the proportionate method of allocating gain. However, neither the Code nor the regulations proscribe an allocation mechanism.

[16]If Al owned more than 50 percent of 360 Air after the transfer, the gain would be treated as ordinary income under §1239(a). Section 1239 converts §1231 gain to ordinary income if the transferor of the property owns more than 50 percent of the corporation and the property is depreciable in the hands of the transferee. The gain also could be unrecaptured §1250 gain subject to a maximum tax rate of 25 percent.

	Land	
	Fair market value of 360 Air stock and cash received	$ 200,000
−	Less tax basis of the land transferred	−100,000
	(1) Gain realized	$ 100,000
	(2) Boot apportioned (200/375 × $60,000)	32,000
	Gain recognized: lesser of (1) or (2)	**$ 32,000**
	Character of gain recognized: §1231	

Al recognizes total gain of $60,000 on this transfer ($4,000 + $24,000 + $32,000) and defers recognition of $140,000 of the $200,000 gain realized ($200,000 − $60,000).

What if: Suppose the land has a tax basis of $250,000. What amount of gain or loss would Al recognize?

Answer: The $60,000 of boot must still be apportioned among the assets based on relative fair market values. However, Al cannot recognize any of the realized loss on the land because boot only causes gain realized to be recognized. The recomputation for the land is as follows:

	Land	
	Fair market value of 360 Air stock and cash received	$200,000
−	Less adjusted tax basis of the building transferred	−250,000
	(1) Loss realized	($ 50,000)
	(2) Boot apportioned (200/375 × $60,000)	32,000
	No loss is recognized	

Al recognizes total gain of $28,000 from receipt of the building and inventory ($24,000 + $4,000). Al defers recognition of $72,000 of gain realized ($6,000 + $66,000) from receipt of the building and inventory and all of the $50,000 loss realized from receipt of the land.

Boot received in a §351 transaction receives a tax basis equal to its fair market value.[17] Al must adjust the tax basis in his 360 Air stock to take into account the boot received and the gain recognized. Exhibit 8-5 provides a template for computing stock basis when boot is received in a §351 transaction.

EXHIBIT 8-5 Computing the Tax Basis of Stock in a Section 351 Transaction When Boot Is Received

	Cash contributed
+	Adjusted tax basis of other property contributed
+	Gain recognized on the transfer
−	Fair market value of boot received
−	Liabilities assumed by the corporation on property contributed
	Tax basis of stock received

Source: §358(a)(1).

Example 8-8

Return to the original facts in Example 8-7, in which Al received $60,000 and recognized $60,000 gain in the exchange. What is Al's tax basis in the 360 Air stock?

Answer: $175,000. Al computes the tax basis in the 360 Air stock as follows:

	Adjusted tax basis of property contributed	$ 175,000
+	Gain recognized on the exchange	60,000
−	Fair market value of boot (cash) received	60,000
	Tax basis of stock received	**$175,000**

[17] §358(a)(2).

If Al subsequently sells the 360 Air stock for its current fair market value of $315,000, he would recognize a gain of $140,000 ($315,000 − $175,000), an amount equal to the gain he deferred in the exchange.

Assumption of Shareholder Liabilities by the Corporation

When a business is formed as a corporation in a §351 exchange, the newly formed corporation frequently assumes the outstanding liabilities of the business, such as accounts payable or mortgages. An important tax issue is whether the assumption of liabilities by the new corporation constitutes boot received by the shareholder transferring the liabilities to the corporation. After all, the shareholder does receive something other than stock in the transaction—that is, relief from debt.

Under the general rule, the corporation's assumption of a shareholder's liability attached to property transferred (e.g., the mortgage attached to the building and land transferred by Al to 360 Air) is *not* treated as boot received by the shareholder.[18] However, an exception to this general rule is described below.

Tax-Avoidance Transactions If *any* of the liabilities assumed by the corporation are contributed with the purpose of avoiding the federal income tax or if there is no corporate business purpose for the assumption, *all* liabilities assumed are treated as boot to the shareholder.[19] The "avoidance" motive may be present where the corporation assumes debt created by the shareholders immediately prior to the contribution of the encumbered assets. Completing this transaction is essentially equivalent to having the corporation pay the shareholder cash in exchange for the property. The "no business purpose" motive can also be present when shareholders have the corporation assume their personal liabilities (i.e., a home mortgage or car payments).

Example 8-9

What if: Suppose that when incorporating 360 Air, Jim transferred a parcel of land in exchange for 40 percent of the corporation's stock (40 shares valued at $80,000). The land's fair market value was $100,000, and its tax basis to Jim was $35,000. The land was subject to a $20,000 mortgage that 360 Air assumed on the transfer. Jim borrowed the $20,000 from a bank (using the land as collateral) shortly before transferring the land to 360 Air. Jim used the mortgage proceeds to pay for a new car. Assuming the transfer qualifies under §351 and that the mortgage has a tax-avoidance purpose, what gain or loss does Jim recognize on the transfer?

Answer: $20,000 gain recognized. Jim realized a $65,000 gain on the land transfer ($100,000 fair market value minus $35,000 basis). Because the mortgage has a tax-avoidance purpose, the $20,000 relief of debt is treated as boot received by Jim on the exchange. Consequently, he must recognize gain in the amount of the lesser of (1) the $65,000 realized gain or (2) the $20,000 boot received.

What if: Supposing the liability did not have a tax-avoidance purpose, what gain would Jim recognize on the exchange?

Answer: $0. Because the liability is not considered to be boot, Jim is allowed to defer the entire gain realized on the exchange.

Liabilities in Excess of Basis Even when liabilities are not treated as boot, under §357(c) the taxpayer is required to recognize gain to the extent the liabilities assumed by the corporation exceed the aggregate adjusted tax basis of the properties transferred by the shareholder. The character of §357(c) gain recognized should be based on the character of the transferred assets, but this rule is inadequate if the transfer includes two or more

[18]§357(a).

[19]§357(b).

assets of differing character. The regulations indicate that the character of the gain in this situation should be determined by allocating the gain according to the relative fair market value of the transferred assets. Some tax commentators argue that allocating the gain to assets based on their relative built-in gains is a more appropriate alternative method of allocating gain across the transferred assets because it does not allocate gain to loss assets.

ETHICS

Lisa is the sole proprietor of a business that manufactures solar panels. This week Lisa was approached to exchange her business assets for shares in Burns Power. As part of the exchange, Lisa is requiring Burns Power to assume the home equity loan on her home. Do you think that Lisa should argue that there is no tax-avoidance motive in this arrangement? Suppose that Lisa established her business five years ago by investing funds from a home equity loan. Does this make any difference?

Example 8-10

What if: Assume Al transferred inventory, a building, and land to 360 Air in return for 50 percent of the corporation's stock (50 shares) with a fair market value of $175,000. The corporation will assume a mortgage of $200,000 attached to the land and building. The properties transferred have fair market values and tax bases as follows:

	FMV	Adjusted Tax Basis
Inventory	$ 25,000	$ 15,000
Building	150,000	60,000
Land	200,000	100,000
Total	$375,000	$175,000

Al realizes a gain of $200,000 on the transfer, computed as follows:

	Fair market value of 360 Air stock received	$ 175,000
+	Mortgage assumed by 360 Air	200,000
	Amount realized	$ 375,000
–	Adjusted tax basis of the property transferred	175,000
	Gain realized	**$200,000**

What amount of gain, if any, does Al recognize on the transfer, assuming all of the other requirements of §351 are met?

Answer: $25,000, the excess of the mortgage assumed by 360 Air ($200,000) over the aggregate adjusted tax basis of the property Al transferred to the corporation ($175,000). Al defers gain of $175,000. The character of the $25,000 gain is determined by allocating the gain to the contributed assets and treating the gain in accordance with the character of each asset. For example, in this case 6.67 percent of the $25,000 gain ($25/$375) would be allocated to the inventory and taxed as ordinary income.

What is Al's tax basis in the 360 Air stock?

Answer: $0, computed as follows:

	Adjusted tax basis of property contributed	$175,000
+	Gain recognized on the exchange	25,000
–	Mortgage assumed by 360 Air	200,000
	Tax basis of stock received	**$ 0**

If Al sold his 360 Air stock for $175,000 (its current fair market value), he would recognize a gain of $175,000 ($175,000 – $0), an amount equal to the gain he deferred in the exchange.

There is a special exception for the assumption of liabilities the payment of which would give rise to a deduction. The assumption of such liabilities is disregarded in determining whether the liabilities assumed exceed basis.[20] Examples are a corporation assuming the accounts payable of a cash-method sole proprietorship and a subsidiary assuming "payment liabilities" (e.g., accrued vacation pay) of an accrual-method corporation.

Example 8-11

What if: Suppose Al transferred inventory, a building, and land to 360 Air in return for 50 percent of the corporation's stock (50 shares) with a fair market value of $175,000. The corporation will assume cash-method accounts payable of $200,000. The properties transferred have fair market values and tax bases as follows:

	FMV	Adjusted Tax Basis
Inventory	$ 25,000	$ 15,000
Building	150,000	60,000
Land	200,000	100,000
Total	$375,000	$175,000

Al realizes a gain of $200,000 on the transfer, computed as follows:

	Fair market value of 360 Air stock received	$ 175,000
+	Payables assumed by 360 Air	200,000
	Amount realized	$ 375,000
−	Adjusted tax basis of the property transferred	175,000
	Gain realized	**$200,000**

What amount of gain, if any, does Al recognize in the transfer, assuming all of the other requirements of §351 are met?

Answer: $0. Al defers recognition of the entire gain of $200,000. The assumption of the cash-method payables is disregarded in computing whether the liabilities assumed exceed the aggregate tax basis of the property transferred. The reason for disregarding the payables is that Al has no basis in this asset (the payables are not recognized by a cash-basis taxpayer). The corporation will recognize a deduction or an asset once payment is made on the payables.

What is Al's tax basis in the 360 Air stock?

Answer: $175,000, computed as follows:

	Adjusted basis of property contributed	$ 175,000
+	Gain recognized on the exchange	0
−	Payables assumed by 360 Air	0
	Tax basis of stock received	**$175,000**

If Al subsequently sells his 360 Air stock for $175,000 (its current fair market value), he will recognize a gain of $0 ($175,000 − $175,000). This result seems odd at first glance because the gain deferred before was $200,000. However, by transferring the payables to 360 Air, Al is forgoing a $200,000 deduction that he would have received if he paid off the liabilities while operating as a sole proprietorship. This $200,000 "loss" exactly offsets the $200,000 gain he realized when 360 Air assumed the payables, resulting in a net gain of $0.

Tax Consequences to the Transferee Corporation

The corporation receiving property in exchange for its stock does not recognize gain or loss realized on the transfer.[21] In transactions that do not qualify for §351, the corporation will have a fair market value tax basis in the property. In a §351 transaction, the corporation will

[20]§357(c)(3). Note that this exception is not available when the liabilities are used to create basis in assets, such as payables related to the purchase of tools.

[21]§1032.

have an adjusted tax basis in the property that equals the property's adjusted tax basis in the transferor's hands.[22] The transferred property is said to have a **carryover basis** (i.e., the corporation "carries over" the shareholder's basis and holding period in the transferred property).[23] To the extent the shareholder's adjusted tax basis carries over to the corporation and the property is §1231 property or a capital asset, the shareholder's holding period also carries over (it *tacks* to the property).[24] This could be important in determining if subsequent gain or loss recognized on the disposition of the property qualifies as a §1231 gain or loss or a long-term capital gain or loss.

If the shareholder recognizes gain as a result of the property transfer, either because the shareholder received boot or the liabilities assumed by the corporation in the exchange exceeded the adjusted tax basis of the property contributed by the shareholder, the corporation increases its tax basis in each asset by the gain recognized on that asset. Exhibit 8-6 provides a template for computing the tax basis of each asset received by the corporation in a §351 transaction.

EXHIBIT 8-6 Computing the Tax Basis of Each Asset Received by the Corporation in a Section 351 Transaction

	Adjusted tax basis of the asset contributed by the shareholder
+	Gain recognized by the shareholder on the transfer of the asset to the corporation
	Adjusted tax basis of the asset received

Source: §362(a).

Example 8-12

Let's return to the facts in Example 8-7 in which Al received 40 shares of 360 Air stock with a fair market value of $315,000 and $60,000 in return for his transfer of inventory, a building, and land to the corporation. The $60,000 received by Al constituted boot received and caused him to recognize gain on the transfer. The $60,000 was allocated to each of the properties transferred to the corporation based on their relative fair market values. Al recognized gain on each property transferred in an amount equal to the lesser of the gain realized or the fair market value of the boot allocated to the property. Al's tax results from this transaction can be summarized as follows:

	Adjusted Tax Basis	Gain Recognized
Inventory	$ 15,000	$ 4,000
Building	60,000	24,000
Land	100,000	32,000
Total	$175,000	$60,000

What tax basis does 360 Air take in each of the properties it receives from Al in the exchange?

Answer: 360 Air will carry over Al's adjusted tax basis in the property transferred and will increase the adjusted tax basis by gain recognized by Al on the transfer. The corporation's adjusted tax basis in each of the three properties is as follows:

	Adjusted Tax Basis	Gain Recognized	360 Air Adjusted Tax Basis
Inventory	$ 15,000	$ 4,000	$ 19,000
Building	60,000	24,000	84,000
Land	100,000	32,000	132,000
Total	$175,000	$60,000	$235,000

360 Air also will carry over Al's holding period in the building and land transferred because they are §1231 assets.

[22]§362(a).
[23]See §1223(2) and note that §7701(a)(43) refers to this type of property as *transferred basis property*.
[24]§1223(1).

Tax law limits the ability of a shareholder to transfer a built-in loss to a corporation in a §351 transaction. Without this limitation, a shareholder could create a duplicate loss, one loss for the shareholder and a second loss for the corporation. In particular, if the aggregate adjusted tax basis of property transferred to a corporation by a shareholder in a §351 transfer exceeds the aggregate fair market value of the assets, the aggregate adjusted tax basis of the assets in the hands of the transferee corporation cannot exceed their aggregate fair market value.[25] When determining whether the aggregate adjusted basis of the property transferred to a corporation exceeds the aggregate fair market value of the assets in a §351 transfer, gains recognized by the shareholders are included in the aggregate adjusted tax basis of the assets. The aggregate reduction in tax basis is allocated among the assets transferred in proportion to their respective built-in losses immediately before the transfer. As an alternative, the transferor and transferee can elect to have the transferor reduce her stock basis to fair market value (the duplicate loss is eliminated at either the corporate or shareholder level).

Example 8-13

What if: Assume Al transferred a building and land to the corporation in return for 50 percent of the corporation's stock (50 shares). The property transferred to the corporation had the following fair market values and adjusted tax bases:

	FMV	Adjusted Tax Basis
Building	$ 75,000	$100,000
Land	200,000	100,000
Total	$275,000	$200,000

The fair market value of the 360 Air stock Al received in the exchange was $275,000.

Assuming the transfer meets the requirements under §351 to defer recognizing the $75,000 net gain realized, what is Al's tax basis in the 50 shares of 360 Air stock received in the exchange?

Answer: $200,000. In this case, the aggregate fair market value of the property transferred to the corporation exceeds the aggregate adjusted tax basis of the property. As a result, Al's tax basis in the stock equals the aggregate adjusted tax basis of the property transferred.

What are the adjusted tax bases of the building and land held by 360 Air?

Answer: The building has a carryover basis of $100,000, and the land has a carryover basis of $100,000. Because the aggregate fair market value of the assets transferred to the corporation exceeds the aggregate adjusted tax basis of the property, 360 Air applies the general basis carryover rules. The building retains its built-in loss of $25,000 at the corporate level.

What if: Suppose Al transferred a building and land to the corporation in return for 50 percent of the corporation's stock (50 shares). The property transferred to the corporation had the following fair market values and adjusted bases:

	FMV	Adjusted Tax Basis
Building	$ 75,000	$200,000
Land	200,000	100,000
Total	$275,000	$300,000

The fair market value of the 360 Air stock Al received in the exchange was $275,000.

Assuming the transfer meets the requirements under §351 to defer recognizing the $25,000 net loss realized, what is Al's tax basis in the 50 shares of 360 Air stock he receives in the exchange?

Answer: $300,000. In this case, the aggregate adjusted tax basis of the property transferred to the corporation exceeds the aggregate fair market value of the property. Assuming he doesn't elect to reduce his stock basis to fair market value, Al's tax basis in the stock received will equal the adjusted basis of the assets transferred.

(continued on page 8-16)

[25]§362(e)(2).

What is the adjusted tax basis of the building and land held by 360 Air?

Answer: An aggregate adjusted tax basis of $275,000. Because the aggregate fair market value of the property transferred to the corporation is less than the aggregate adjusted tax basis of the property, 360 Air must reduce the aggregate adjusted tax basis of the property to their aggregate fair market value. The allocation is made to those assets that have a built-in loss; in this example, this includes only the building. The adjusted tax basis of the building will be reduced to $175,000 ($200,000 – $25,000 net built-in loss). The adjusted tax basis of the land will retain its carryover basis of $100,000. This adjustment eliminates the net $25,000 built-in loss at the corporate level.

What alternative election can Al and 360 Air make with respect to these basis reduction rules?

Answer: Al and the corporation can jointly elect to have Al reduce his stock basis to its fair market value of $275,000. The corporation would take a carryover basis of $200,000 in the building and a carryover basis of $100,000 in the land.

What if: Suppose Al transferred a building and land to the corporation in return for 40 percent of the corporation's stock (40 shares). The property transferred to the corporation had the following fair market values and adjusted bases:

	FMV	Adjusted Tax Basis
Building	$ 75,000	$200,000
Land	200,000	100,000
Total	$275,000	$300,000

In the exchange, Al received 360 Air stock worth $220,000 plus $55,000 in cash. Assuming the transfer qualifies under §351, how much gain or loss, if any, will Al recognize on the exchange?

Answer: $40,000 gain recognized. The cash (i.e., boot) is allocated between the building and land in proportion to the relative values, and gain is recognized to the lesser of boot received or realized gain. In this case, $40,000 of boot allocated to the land triggers $40,000 of recognized gain, calculated as follows:

		Building	Land
	Fair market value of stock received	$ 60,000	$160,000
+	Cash received (allocated by relative FMV)	+15,000	+40,000
	Amount realized	$ 75,000	$200,000
–	Adjusted tax basis of assets transferred	−200,000	−100,000
	Gain or (loss) realized	$(125,000)	$100,000
	Gain or (loss) recognized	**$ 0***	**$ 40,000**

*Realized loss is not recognized in a §351 exchange, even when boot is received.

What is Al's tax basis in the 40 shares of 360 Air stock received in the exchange?

Answer: $285,000. Assuming he does not elect to reduce his stock basis to fair market value, Al's tax basis in the stock received will equal the $300,000 adjusted basis of the assets less the $55,000 in cash received plus the $40,000 recognized gain.

What is the adjusted tax basis of the building and land held by 360 Air?

Answer: The aggregate basis is $275,000. Specifically, the basis in the building is $135,000 and the basis in the Land is $140,000. The aggregate tax basis of the assets in the hands of the transferee corporation must first be adjusted upward for any gain recognized by the transferor. Hence, 360 Air must first increase the aggregate basis by the $40,000 recognized gain from $300,000 to $340,000. After increasing the basis of the land for the gain recognized, the aggregate built-in loss is measured as the difference between the $340,000 aggregate basis ($200,000 + $100,000 + $40,000) and the $275,000 aggregate FMV of the transfer ($60,000 + $160,000 + $55,000). The $65,000 reduction in basis ($340,000 – 275,000) is allocated to the loss assets, but in this case the building is the only asset with a built-in loss and receives the reduction in basis.

		Building	Land
	Carryover basis	$200,000	$100,000
+	Gain recognized by Al		+40,000
–	Aggregate built-in loss ($340,000 – $275,000)	−65,000	
	Air 360 adjusted tax basis	$135,000	$140,000

Other Issues Related to Incorporating an Ongoing Business

Depreciable Assets Transferred to a Corporation To the extent a property's adjusted tax basis carries over from the shareholder, the corporation in effect steps into the shoes of the shareholder and continues to depreciate the carryover basis portion of the property's adjusted tax basis using the shareholder's depreciation schedule.[26] Any additional tax basis (from recognition of gain due to boot received) is treated as a separate asset and is subject to a separate depreciation election (i.e., this one physical asset is treated as two separate tax assets for depreciation purposes).

Example 8-14

Let's return to the facts in Examples 8-7 and 8-12. Recall that Al received 40 shares of 360 Air stock with a fair market value of $315,000 and $60,000 in return for his transfer of inventory, a building, and land to the corporation. The cash received by Al constituted boot received and caused him to recognize $60,000 of gain on the transfer. 360 Air takes Al's tax basis in the property and increases it by the gain recognized by Al on the transfer. The corporation's adjusted tax basis in each of the three properties is as follows:

	Adjusted Tax Basis	Gain Recognized	360 Air Adjusted Tax Basis
Inventory	$ 15,000	$ 4,000	$ 19,000
Building	60,000	24,000	84,000
Land	100,000	32,000	132,000
Total	$175,000	$60,000	$235,000

360 Air also will carry over Al's holding period in the building and land transferred because they are §1231 assets. How will 360 Air compute the depreciation deduction on the building for the year of the transfer? For this problem, let's assume that the transfer occurs on January 1. Furthermore, let's assume that Al originally purchased the building for $67,400 in September five years ago and has claimed $7,400 of straight-line depreciation over a 39-year recovery period using a mid-month convention.

Answer: 360 Air carries over Al's depreciation schedule for the building with respect to the $60,000 original basis, but 360 Air depreciates the additional $24,000 as a new asset. With respect to the carryover basis portion of the building, 360 Air uses Al's original cost of $67,400 in the building to calculate the depreciation computation. Al is entitled to ½ month of depreciation on the building in the year of transfer ($67,400 × .02564 × .5/12 = $72), and the corporation is entitled to the remaining 11.5 months of depreciation of $1,656 ($67,400 × .02564 × 11.5/12 = $1,656). The corporation treats the additional $24,000 of basis as a new asset and applies the proper depreciation rate to calculate the additional depreciation. Because the transfer took place in January, 360 Air would be entitled to 11.5 months of depreciation (recall the mid-month convention). Hence, 360 Air would claim additional depreciation of $591 ($24,000 × .02461 = $591) for a total depreciation deduction of $2,247 (i.e., $1,656 + $591).

Practitioners often advise against transferring appreciated property (especially real estate) into a closely held corporation. By doing so the shareholder creates two assets with the same built-in gain as the original property (the stock received in the hands of the shareholder and the building owned by the corporation). The federal government can now collect taxes twice on the same gain, once when the corporation sells the property received and a second time when the shareholder sells the stock. You will notice that Congress is not concerned by a duplication of gain result, only a duplication of loss result. By retaining the property outside the corporation, the shareholder can lease the property to the corporation, thereby reducing the corporation's taxable income through

[26]§168(i)(7)(B)(ii).

rent deductions. Note, however, that there may be valid state tax reasons to own the property inside a corporation, such as lower property taxes.

Contributions to Capital

A **contribution to capital** is a transfer of property to a corporation by a shareholder or nonshareholder for which no stock or other property is received in return. The corporation receiving the property is not taxed on the receipt of the property if the property is contributed by a shareholder.[27] If the property is contributed by a shareholder, the corporation takes a carryover tax basis in the property.[28] If the property is contributed by a nonshareholder (e.g., a city contributes land to induce a corporation to locate its operations there), the corporation recognizes the value of the contributed property as income and takes a fair market value basis in the property.

A capital contribution generally is not a taxable event to the shareholder because the shareholder does not receive any additional consideration in return for the transfer. A shareholder making a capital contribution gets to increase the tax basis in her existing stock in an amount equal to the tax basis of the property contributed.

TAXES IN THE REAL WORLD A Meaningless Gesture?

When a shareholder contributes assets or cash to a solely owned corporation, it would seem that §351 couldn't apply unless the transfer is made "solely in exchange for stock." Unfortunately, there is no other authority that directly addresses the tax consequences should a shareholder make a contribution to capital where the shareholder receives nothing in exchange for the property. Recently, the IRS "has become aware of transactions that purport to result in holding periods for corporate stock that are longer than the period of economic investment." Apparently, some enterprising consultants have attempted to utilize this absence of authority to argue that the contribution would not affect the holding period of the stock. Here's a version of the deal that worries the IRS:

> Shareholder creates corporation with negligible contribution on January 1, Year 1. On March 1, Year 1, Shareholder invests a substantial amount of money in property that appreciates in value. On August 1, Year 1, Shareholder transfers the appreciated property to Corporation for no consideration. On February 1, Year 2, Shareholder sells all of the stock in Corporation for a price that reflects the unrealized appreciation in the property, so that gain is recognized to Shareholder. Shareholder claims that all the stock has a holding period exceeding one year (from January 1, Year 1).

In a memorandum, the Office of Chief Counsel argues that despite the absence of any consideration, §351 applies to this transaction and the shareholder takes a bifurcated (split) basis in his shares with a short-term holding period for the amount representing the August contribution of property. The Chief Counsel argues that issuing stock to the sole shareholder represents a "meaningless gesture" that should not be used to alter the economic substance of the transaction.

The memorandum also provides a second illustration where the sole shareholder contributes cash instead of property. After the contribution, the corporation invests the cash in property that then appreciates and the shareholder again sells his shares. The Chief Counsel rejects the shareholder's argument that the gain on the sale of the shares is entirely long term, again arguing that issuing stock in exchange for the cash would be a meaningless gesture.

Suppose that in this latter illustration, the shareholder didn't make any additional contribution but instead had let the corporation borrow the funds to invest in the property. Do you think the subsequent sale of the shares be treated as long term or short term?

Source: AM 2020-005, available at www.irs.gov/pub/lanoa/am-2020-005.pdf.

[27]§118.

[28]§362(a)(2).

Section 1244 Stock

Stock is generally a capital asset in the hands of the shareholders, and gains or losses from sale or exchange are capital in nature. For individuals, long-term capital gains are taxed at a maximum tax rate of 20 percent. Losses can only offset capital gains plus $3,000 of ordinary income per year. Section 1244 allows a shareholder to treat a loss on the sale or exchange of stock that qualifies as §1244 stock as an ordinary loss.

Section 1244 applies only to individual shareholders who are the original recipients of the stock. The maximum amount of loss that can be treated as an ordinary loss under §1244 is $50,000 per year ($100,000 in the case of married, filing jointly shareholders). For shareholders to qualify for this tax benefit, the corporation from which they received stock must have been a small business corporation when the stock was issued. The Code defines a small business corporation as one in which the aggregate amount of money and other property received in return for the stock or as a contribution to capital did not exceed $1 million. In our story line, 360 Air qualifies as a small business corporation.

There is an additional requirement that for the five taxable years preceding the year in which the stock is sold, the corporation must have derived more than 50 percent of its aggregate gross receipts from an *active* trade or business. 360 Air meets this test as well. Section 1244 provides a tax benefit to entrepreneurs who create a risky start-up company that ultimately fails.

Example 8-15

What if: Assume Al received 50 shares of 360 Air stock (50 percent of the outstanding stock) with a fair market value of $300,000 in return for transferring a building and land to the corporation in a transaction that qualified under §351. As a result of the transfer, Al received a tax basis in the 50 shares of $200,000 ($4,000 per share). Suppose that over time the snowboarding business declined due to a change in weather patterns in Michigan. As a result, Al's 50 shares were worth $50,000 ($1,000 per share). Needing some cash, Al sold all 50 shares to Jim for $50,000 and recognized a $150,000 loss [$50,000 – ($4,000 × 50 shares)]. 360 Air qualifies as a small business corporation under §1244. Al has no capital gains in the year of the sale. How much of the loss can Al deduct if he held his stock at least five years, assuming current tax rules, and he is married, filing a joint tax return and does not have other capital gains or losses? What is the character of the loss (capital or ordinary)?

Answer: $103,000, $100,000 of which is ordinary loss and $3,000 of which is capital loss that can reduce up to $3,000 of ordinary income. The remaining $47,000 loss is carried forward as a capital loss.

What tax planning advice would you give Al to maximize the tax treatment of the loss from sale of the stock?

Answer: Section 1244 imposes an annual limit on the amount of the loss that can be treated as ordinary. To maximize the tax value of his loss, Al should sell enough shares of 360 Air stock to generate a $100,000 loss this year and sell the remaining amount to generate a $50,000 loss next year. In that way, the entire $150,000 loss will be treated as ordinary loss. Of course, delaying the sale of shares is risky because the stock could continue to lose value. Al would need to weigh the tax benefits of the delay against the risk of additional loss.

TAXABLE AND TAX-DEFERRED CORPORATE ACQUISITIONS

LO 8-3

(continued from page 8-2 . . .)

Jim Wheels and Ginny Gears are excited about their new business venture with Al Pine. It seems to solve their need to find a source of revenues during the winter months, when the demand for bicycles declines significantly. With that challenge met, Jim and Ginny have turned their attention to expanding their bicycle business to a new geographic region. At the recent Tour de Gaslight race sponsored by the Michigan Bicycle Racing

Association, Jim struck up a conversation with Pam Peloton, owner of Wolverine Cycles and Repair (WCR) in Ann Arbor, Michigan. Pam mentioned she is planning to move to Colorado and is looking to sell her business. Jim can see lots of synergies in buying WCR. He and Ginny are familiar with the biking community in Ann Arbor, and they understand the economics of operating a business in a college town. Ginny is also excited about the possibility of expanding their company to Ann Arbor.

A meeting has been set up with Pam to explore the possible acquisition of her business. Pam operates Wolverine Cycles and Repair as a C corporation, which gives Jim and Ginny the opportunity to consider buying the assets of the business directly or buying Pam's stock in the corporation. If they take the stock acquisition route, Jim and Ginny need to consider whether they want to operate their new company as a subsidiary of Spartan Cycle and Repair or in a lateral ownership arrangement (in which their two companies would be "brother-sister" corporations). Operating WCR as a subsidiary of SCR would allow Jim and Ginny to file a consolidated tax return with SCR. Pam is concerned about the tax consequences of each of these options, as are Jim and Ginny.

(to be continued . . .)

At some point in the life of a successful business, its owners likely will consider expanding its scope or geographic location. Businesses can grow internally through expansion or externally by acquiring an existing business. Jim and Ginny prefer to buy Pam's existing business to expand to a new geographic location. Because Pam operates the business as a C corporation, Jim and Ginny have multiple options. Jim and Ginny first need to consider whether they will personally acquire the business or have SCR acquire the business. Second, they must determine whether they will purchase the assets or the stock of the corporation. Finally, they need to determine the type of consideration to use in the acquisition (SCR stock or cash). Each of these options can result in different tax consequences for the buyer and the seller. Thus, besides negotiating a purchase price, Jim and Ginny will also need to negotiate the form of the transaction with Pam.

This section of the chapter considers the basic ways in which a corporation or its shareholders can acquire the stock or assets of another corporation and the tax consequences that follow the form of the acquisition. This is an extremely complicated and technical area of the tax law. A thorough discussion of all the ways in which an acquisition can take place likely would take up most or all of a semester. As a result, our discussion is limited to the basic types of corporate acquisitions.

THE KEY FACTS

Tax Model for Corporate Acquisitions

- The acquiring corporation can acquire the target corporation through either a stock or asset acquisition.
- The acquisition can be structured as either taxable or tax-deferred.
- Taxable asset acquisitions allow the acquiring corporation to step up the tax basis of the assets acquired to fair value.
- In stock acquisitions and tax-deferred asset acquisitions, the adjusted tax basis of the target corporation's assets remains at the assets' carryover basis (generally, cost less accumulated depreciation).

The Acquisition Tax Model

When negotiating an acquisition, management of the acquiring corporation must decide whether to acquire the target corporation's assets or stock and what consideration to use (equity, debt, and/or cash). The form of the transaction and the consideration paid will jointly determine the tax status of the transaction.[29] Nontax considerations, such as the ease of transferring stock or the existence of contingent liabilities, often dictate the form of an acquisition by a publicly traded corporation. In contrast, privately held corporations are more likely to make tax considerations a priority.

The shareholders of the target corporation must decide what consideration to demand in return for their stock or assets in the corporation. Cash provides liquidity and does not decline in value after the acquisition is announced, but it also causes the transaction to be fully or partially taxable to the seller. Receiving equity in the acquiring corporation may

[29]The form of the transaction and the consideration paid to shareholders does not affect the financial accounting treatment of the acquisition. ASC 805-10-25-1 requires that all business combinations be accounted for using the purchase method.

allow shareholders to defer paying tax on gain realized on the exchange, but the sellers must accept the risk that the acquiring corporation's stock will decline in value after the deal is announced or consummated.

The technical tax (and accounting) rules that apply to corporate acquisitions are extremely complex. Because the statutory language governing reorganizations is sparse, the IRS and courts often must decide whether the form of a tax-deferred reorganization transaction meets both the literal language of the statute and the substance of the judicial doctrines that underlie the reorganization provisions. As a result, the reorganization area is heavily laden with administrative and judicial pronouncements. Our goal is to provide you with a basic overview of the most common types of corporate acquisitions that you will see discussed in the business press.

Exhibit 8-7 summarizes the four basic types of transactions that can effect an acquisition of another company. The buyer can purchase either stock or assets in a transaction that is either taxable or tax-deferred (in whole or in part) to the seller. The buyer and seller must jointly and simultaneously decide on the form and consideration of the transaction.

EXHIBIT 8-7 Types of Corporate Acquisitions

	Asset Purchase	Stock Purchase
Taxable	Cash or debt generally (Cell 1)	Cash or debt generally (Cell 2)
Tax-Deferred Reorganization	Type A or Type C reorganization using equity (Cell 3)	Type B reorganization using voting equity only (Cell 4)

Often, the buyer and seller have different tax incentives (they want to be in different cells), and this requires both sides to negotiate a compromise arrangement that satisfies both parties. For example, the buyer likely prefers to acquire the target corporation's assets in a taxable asset transaction (cell 1). By purchasing the target corporation's assets in a taxable asset acquisition, the acquiring corporation gets a stepped-up tax basis in the assets equal to fair market value. To the extent the acquiring corporation can allocate the purchase price to depreciable or amortizable assets, this increases future depreciation or amortization deductions on the acquiring corporation's tax return. It is not uncommon in an acquisition involving publicly traded corporations for goodwill to comprise over 70 percent of the purchase price. If the acquiring corporation can achieve a tax basis in the goodwill, the basis can be amortized over 15 years.[30] If the acquiring corporation makes the acquisition using a tax-deferred technique (cell 3 or cell 4) or purchases stock (cell 2), then the tax basis of the acquired assets will not generally be stepped up to fair value and goodwill will have a zero tax basis. Hence, the acquiring company will be ineligible for increased depreciation and amortization deductions.

In contrast to the buyer, the seller likely prefers a tax-deferred transaction (cell 3 or cell 4) because any tax on the appreciation will be postponed. If deferral of the gain isn't possible, then the seller would prefer to sell the stock in a taxable transaction (cell 2) because any gain on the stock will be taxed as capital gains. However, neither of these options provides the acquiring corporation with a stepped-up tax basis in the assets, greatly reducing the future value of the acquisition to the buyer. The seller would likely be reluctant to sell the assets of the corporation in a taxable asset transaction (cell 1) because the seller would be required to pay both the corporate tax on appreciation of the assets and the individual capital gains tax on the appreciation of the stock. Of course, the buyer might be able to overcome the seller's reluctance by offering a sufficiently high purchase price.

[30]§197.

LO 8-4

TAX CONSEQUENCES TO A CORPORATE ACQUISITION

(continued from page 8-20 . . .)

As part of the negotiations with Pam, Jim and Ginny have examined WCR's balance sheet that compares adjusted tax basis with a recent valuation of the assets' fair market values. Pam has held the WCR stock for 10 years, and her tax basis in the stock is $50,000. WCR is an accrual-method taxpayer, and as a result, the payables have a tax basis. That is, the corporation deducted the expenses related to the payables when the expenses were accrued. These facts are summarized as follows:

	FMV	Adjusted Tax Basis	Appreciation
Cash	$ 10,000	$ 10,000	
Receivables	5,000	5,000	
Inventory	20,000	10,000	$ 10,000
Building	80,000	50,000	30,000
Land	120,000	60,000	60,000
Total	$235,000	$135,000	$100,000
Payables	$ 4,000	$ 4,000	
Mortgage*	31,000	31,000	
Total	$ 35,000	$ 35,000	

*The mortgage was attached to the building and land.

Jim and Ginny agree to pay Pam $300,000 for the business, an amount that is $100,000 more than the net fair market value of the assets less the liabilities listed on the balance sheet ($235,000 – $35,000). The additional $100,000 reflects an amount to be paid for the company's customer list, valued at $25,000, with the remaining $75,000 allocated to goodwill.

With the price apparently settled, Jim, Ginny, and Pam now must agree on the form the transaction will take.

(to be continued . . .)

Taxable Acquisitions

A corporation can acquire an ongoing business through the purchase of its stock or assets in return for cash, debt, equity, or a combination thereof. Cash purchases of stock are the most common form of corporate acquisition. Using cash to acquire another company has several nontax advantages; most notably, the acquiring corporation does not "acquire" the target corporation's shareholders in the transaction. There are disadvantages to using cash, particularly if the acquiring corporation must incur additional expensive debt to fund the purchase.

If SCR purchases the assets directly from WCR in return for cash (cell 1 in Exhibit 8-7), WCR will recognize gain or loss on the sale of each individual asset, including goodwill. If the sale results in WCR recognizing gain on self-created goodwill or other intangibles such as customer lists, these are capital assets that result in capital gains. In contrast, SCR will treat amounts allocated to purchased goodwill and other intangibles as assets eligible for amortization. WCR may cease to exist as a separate corporation and could liquidate by transferring the net after-tax proceeds received from SCR to its shareholder. If WCR liquidates, Pam recognizes gain or loss on the exchange of her WCR stock for the cash received.

Example 8-16

What if: Assume SCR will purchase WCR's assets for $300,000 and assume the company's liabilities of $35,000. WCR will realize $335,000 ($300,000 + $35,000), which it will allocate to each of the assets sold, as follows:

	Allocation	Adjusted Tax Basis	Gain Realized
Cash	$ 10,000	$ 10,000	$ 0
Receivables	5,000	5,000	0
Inventory	20,000	10,000	10,000
Building	80,000	50,000	30,000
Land	120,000	60,000	60,000
Customer list	25,000	0	25,000
Goodwill	75,000	0	75,000
Total	$335,000	$135,000	$200,000

What amount of gain or loss does WCR recognize on the sale of its assets, and what is the character of the gain or loss (ordinary income, §1231, or capital)?

Answer: WCR recognizes total gain of $200,000, and WCR pays a corporate-level tax of $42,000 ($200,000 × 21 percent). The character of the gain will be as follows:

	Gain Recognized	Character
Inventory	$ 10,000	Ordinary income
Building	30,000	Ordinary (§291) and §1231
Land	60,000	§1231
Customer list	25,000	Capital gain
Goodwill	75,000	Capital gain
Total	**$200,000**	

What if: Suppose that WCR opts to go out of existence (liquidate) by exchanging the $258,000 net amount realized after taxes ($300,000 – $42,000) for Pam's WCR stock. What amount of gain or loss will Pam recognize on the exchange of her WCR stock for the after-tax proceeds from the sale ($258,000)?

Answer: Pam recognizes a long-term capital gain of $208,000 ($258,000 – $50,000 stock basis) and pays a shareholder-level tax of $31,200 ($208,000 × 15%, assuming it is not subject to the net investment income tax and that Pam's total taxable income is not above the breakpoint for the 15%/20% capital gains tax rate). The total tax paid using this form of acquisition is $73,200 ($42,000 + $31,200). Pam is left with $226,800 after taxes ($300,000 – $42,000 – $31,200).

Although unattractive to Pam, this deal provides SCR (Jim and Ginny) with the maximum tax benefits. The building will have an increased tax basis of $30,000. The customer list and goodwill will have a tax basis of $25,000 and $75,000, respectively, and SCR can amortize these assets over 15 years on a straight-line basis.[31]

If SCR acquires WCR by acquiring Pam's stock for cash (cell 2 in Exhibit 8-7), WCR retains its tax and legal identity. The adjusted tax basis of WCR's assets, which will remain unchanged, will not reflect SCR's tax basis (purchase price) in WCR's stock.

[31]§197. Note that goodwill is not currently amortized for financial accounting purposes, and the determination of goodwill for accounting purposes under ASC 805-30-30-1 differs from the determination of goodwill for tax purposes under §1060. Hence, even a taxable acquisition can give rise to a book–tax difference because different amounts of goodwill exist for tax and book purposes.

Example 8-17

What if: Suppose instead that SCR purchases the WCR stock from Pam for $300,000. What amount of gain or loss does WCR recognize in this transaction?

Answer: WCR will not recognize gain on this form of acquisition because it has not sold any assets directly to SCR.

What amount and character of gain or loss does Pam recognize in this transaction?

Answer: Pam recognizes long-term capital gain of $250,000 ($300,000 – $50,000 stock basis) and pays a shareholder-level tax of $37,500 ($250,000 × 15%). Pam will be left with $262,500 after taxes ($300,000 – $37,500), which is $35,700 more than a direct asset sale ($262,500 – $226,800).

Although attractive to Pam, this deal will not be as attractive (from a tax perspective) as a direct asset sale to SCR (Jim and Ginny). Rather than $80,000, the building will retain its adjusted tax basis of $50,000. In addition, the customer list and goodwill will have a zero tax basis to WCR because they are self-created assets. The adjusted tax basis of WCR's other assets will remain at $135,000. SCR has a tax basis in the WCR stock equal to the purchase price of $300,000.

A tax-efficient outcome would be achieved if the acquisition could be structured so that (1) Pam can treat the transaction as a stock sale and pay a single level of capital gains tax on the gain recognized from the sale and (2) SCR can treat the transaction as an asset purchase and receive a step-up in basis of the assets to fair market value. This alternative is sometimes available in transactions where a corporate taxpayer purchases 80 percent or more of another corporation's stock within a 12-month period. In such cases, SCR can make a **§338(g) election** to treat the stock purchase as a deemed asset purchase.

Like most things that appear too good to be true, this election does not come without some cost. The calculation of these tax costs is extremely technical and beyond the scope of this text. In big-picture terms, WCR is treated as if it is selling its assets prior to the transaction and then repurchasing them at fair market value. This deemed sale of assets causes WCR to recognize gain on assets that have appreciated in value. SCR, as the buyer, bears this tax cost because the fair market value of WCR will be reduced by the tax paid. In almost all cases, this tax cost negates the tax benefits of getting a step-up in basis in WCR's assets and is rarely elected. For example, it rarely makes economic sense to pay income taxes on a $100 gain just to increase the basis of an asset by $100. The additional tax on the $100 gain would very likely outweigh the present value of the savings from an additional $100 of current and future depreciation deductions. However, this election might be tax-efficient if WCR has net operating losses or net capital losses that can be used to offset gain from the deemed sale of its assets.

If the target corporation is a subsidiary of the seller, the acquiring corporation and seller can make a joint **§338(h)(10) election** and have the seller report the gain from the deemed sale of the target corporation's assets on its tax return in lieu of reporting the actual gain from the sale of the target corporation stock. The technical rules that apply to §338(h)(10) elections are also beyond the scope of this text, but these elections often make sense when the seller has loss carryovers to offset any recognized gains. These elections, which are more common than the regular §338(g) election, often achieve tax savings to both parties to the transaction. For example, Dow Chemical sold its AgroFresh subsidiary to a group of investors in 2015. The buyer and seller made a joint §338(h)(10) election, which allowed AgroFresh to record a stepped-up tax basis for its asset. In this instance, the §338(h)(10) election provided almost $400 million in cash tax benefits from amortizing or depreciating the step-up in basis.

Tax-Deferred Acquisitions

As previously discussed, the tax law allows taxpayers to organize a corporation in a tax-deferred manner under §351. The tax law also allows taxpayers to *reorganize* their corporate structure in a tax-deferred manner. For tax purposes, the term **reorganization** encompasses acquisitions and dispositions of corporate assets (including the stock of subsidiaries) and a corporation's restructuring of its capital structure, place of incorporation, or company name. The Code provides tax deferral to the corporation(s) involved in the reorganization (the parties to the reorganization) and the shareholders if the transaction meets one of seven statutory definitions[32] and satisfies the judicial doctrines that underlie the reorganization statutes. As before, tax deferral in corporate reorganizations is predicated on the seller's receiving a continuing ownership interest in the assets transferred, in the form of equity in the acquiring corporation.

The statutory language governing corporate reorganizations is rather sparse. It should not be surprising, then, that the IRS and the courts frequently must interpret how changes in the facts related to a transaction's form affect its tax status. Our goal is to acquaint you with the basic principles that underlie all corporate reorganizations and provide you with an understanding of the most common forms of corporate acquisitions that are tax-deferred.

Judicial Doctrines That Underlie All Tax-Deferred Reorganizations

Continuity of Interest Tax deferral in a reorganization is based on the presumption that the shareholders of the acquired (target) corporation retain a continuing ownership (equity) interest in the target corporation's assets or historic business through their ownership of stock in the acquiring corporation. There is no **bright-line test** to establish whether **continuity of interest (COI)** has been met, although the regulations provide an example that says COI has been satisfied when the shareholders of the target corporation, in the aggregate, receive equity equal to 40 percent or more of the total value of the consideration received.[33]

Continuity of Business Enterprise For a transaction to qualify as a tax-deferred reorganization, the acquiring corporation must continue the target corporation's historic business or continue to use a *significant* portion of the target corporation's historic business assets in a business. This principle is called **Continuity of business enterprise (COBE).** For example, the regulations suggest that in an acquisition of a corporation with three equal business lines, an acquirer will meet COBE if one line of business is continued without interruption. Whether the historic business assets retained are "significant" is a facts-and-circumstances test, which adds to the administrative and judicial rulings that are part and parcel of the reorganization landscape. COBE does not apply to the historic business or assets of the acquiring corporation; the acquiring corporation can sell off its assets after the reorganization without violating the COBE requirement.

Business Purpose Test As early as 1935, the Supreme Court stated that transactions with "no business or corporate purpose" should not receive tax deferral even if they comply with the statutory requirements.[34] To meet the business purpose test, the acquiring corporation must be able to show a significant business purpose for engaging in the transaction (other than tax avoidance).

[32]The types of corporate reorganizations are defined in §368(a)(1).

[33]Reg. §1.368-1T(e)(2)(v), Example 10.

[34]*Gregory v. Helvering,* 293 U.S. 465 (1935).

Type A Asset Acquisitions

Type A reorganizations (cell 3 in Exhibit 8-7) are statutory **mergers** or **consolidations.**[35] In a merger, either the acquired (target) corporation or the acquiring corporation will cease to exist. For example, SCR could acquire the assets and liabilities of WCR by transferring SCR shares to Pam in exchange for her WCR stock, and WCR would no longer exist. This type of merger is an *upstream* or *forward* acquisition because the target is merged into the acquiring corporation. Alternatively, the target corporation could be the surviving entity, and this type of acquisition is a *downstream* or *reverse* acquisition. In a consolidation, two corporations (e.g., SCR and WCR) transfer their assets and liabilities to a newly formed corporation in return for stock in the new corporation, after which the original corporations (SCR and WCR) both cease to exist.

In a Type A reorganization, the target corporation shareholders defer recognition of gain or loss realized on the receipt of stock of the acquiring corporation. Similar to a §351 transaction, if a target corporation shareholder receives money or other property (boot) from the acquiring corporation or its acquisition subsidiary, the shareholder recognizes *gain* to the extent of the money and fair market value of other property received (not to exceed the gain realized). The shareholder's tax basis in the stock received is a *substituted basis* of the stock transferred plus any gain recognized less any money and the fair market value of other property received. The target corporation's assets remain the same at their (historic) adjusted tax basis in a Type A merger.

Exhibit 8-8 provides an illustration of a Type A merger. The consideration that can be paid to Pam is relatively flexible in a Type A merger; the only limitation on the consideration is that the transaction must satisfy the COI requirement (at least 40 percent of the consideration must be SCR stock). The stock used to satisfy the COI test can be voting or nonvoting, common or preferred.

EXHIBIT 8-8 Form of a Type A Merger

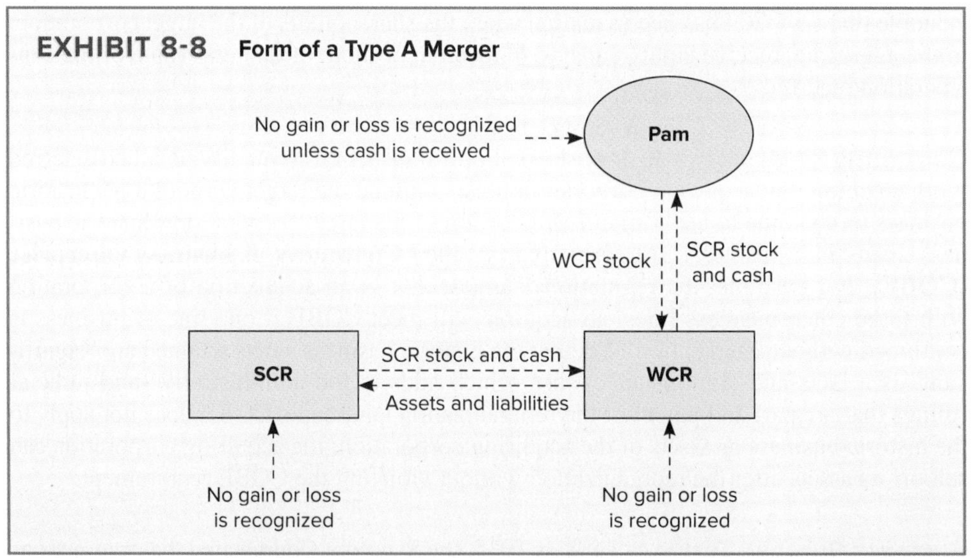

Example 8-18

What if: Assume WCR will merge into SCR in a Type A reorganization. Under the terms of the deal, SCR will pay Pam $300,000 in SCR stock, after which WCR will merge into SCR. Pam's tax basis in the WCR stock is $50,000. What amount of gain will Pam *realize* on the exchange of WCR stock for SCR stock?

Answer: $250,000 ($300,000 – $50,000)

[35]"Type A reorganizations" are so named because they are described in §368(a)(1)(A). Likewise, Type B and Type C reorganizations are described in subparagraphs (B) and (C) of §368, respectively.

What amount of gain will Pam *recognize* on the exchange of her WCR stock for SCR stock?

Answer: $0. Pam defers the entire $250,000 gain realized because only stock was transferred (no boot).

What is Pam's tax basis in the SCR stock?

Answer: $50,000. Because the entire gain is deferred, Pam's tax basis in the SCR stock is a substituted basis from the WCR stock. This preserves the gain deferred for future recognition if Pam should choose to sell the SCR stock in the future for $300,000.

What is the tax basis of each of the assets SCR receives from WCR in the merger?

Answer: SCR receives a carryover tax basis in each of the assets received (e.g., the tax basis of the goodwill and customer list will be zero).

What if: Suppose instead Pam wants some cash as well as SCR stock in the transaction. What is the maximum amount of cash Pam can receive from SCR and not violate the COI rule as illustrated in the regulations?

Answer: $180,000 ($300,000 × 60%). Pam can receive a maximum of 60 percent of the consideration in cash and not violate the COI rule under the regulations.

What if: Assume Pam receives $100,000 in cash plus $200,000 in SCR stock in exchange for all of her WCR stock in a Type A merger. What amount of gain will Pam *realize* on the exchange?

Answer: $250,000 ($300,000 – $50,000)

What amount of gain will Pam *recognize* on the exchange?

Answer: $100,000. Pam must recognize gain in an amount that is the lesser of the gain realized or the boot received. Pam defers the $150,000 gain.

What is Pam's tax basis in her SCR stock?

Answer: $50,000, computed as follows:

	Adjusted basis of WCR stock exchanged	$ 50,000
+	Gain recognized on the exchange	100,000
–	Fair market value of boot (cash) received	100,000
	Tax basis of stock received	**$ 50,000**

This calculation preserves the gain deferred for future recognition if Pam sells her SCR stock in the future for at least $200,000 ($200,000 – $50,000 = $150,000).

TAXES IN THE REAL WORLD What the Heck Is a SPAC?

When a private company wants its shares to be publicly traded, then historically it would hire an investment bank to provide advice, underwrite, and assist in issuing shares in the new public company. This process is called an initial public offering (IPO), and it involves regulatory review that can take months to finalize. Ultimately, there is no guarantee with an IPO that the company will ultimately go public if stock market conditions become unfavorable before the IPO is approved.

A reverse merger is a popular alternative to an IPO because the process is simpler, shorter, and less expensive. In a reverse merger, a private company becomes a public company by purchasing control of another public company. The shareholders of the private company receive sufficient stock in the public company to control its board of directors. Once the merger is complete, the firm has greater access to capital markets and can issue additional shares of stock to pursue corporate acquisitions, and investors gain the ability to liquidate their holdings.

The way a *special purpose acquisition company* (SPAC) works is that a *sponsor* creates a publicly listed *shell* corporation by selling shares to investors. This shell company does not operate a business, but instead only holds cash contributed by investors. The sponsor then looks for a private company to merge with the shell company in a reverse merger. When the sponsor identifies a target company and completes the merger, the target company gets the money in the shell company and the investors in the shell company get shares of the target company, which are publicly traded.

(continued on page 8-28)

Besides its speed and simplicity, a SPAC allows more speculative companies to get funding at an earlier stage than under an IPO. Rather than relying on reviews by the SEC and investment banks as in an IPO, investors in a SPAC rely on the sponsor who formed the SPAC to investigate the target company. This can allow the target company to become publicly traded using optimistic projections rather than the audited financial records that would be required to be reviewed in an IPO.

Reverse mergers are typically treated as Type A tax-deferred acquisitions. Hence, the target company retains all of its tax characteristics and tax attributes, as does the acquiring (SPAC) corporation. All that changes is the identity of the publicly traded corporation.

Sources: SEC Investor Alert, "What You Need to Know About SPACs—Updated Investor Bulletin," on the web at www.sec.gov/oiea/investor-alerts-and-bulletins/what-you-need-know-about-spacs-investor-bulletin.

There are several potential disadvantages to structuring the transaction as a statutory merger. Pam will become a shareholder of SCR, and the historic adjusted tax basis of WCR's assets and liabilities will carry over to SCR. Going back to the facts in Example 8-18, Pam will not owe any tax on the transaction, but she will not receive any cash. Finally, WCR will cease to exist as a separate corporation. Jim and Ginny expressed a desire to operate WCR as an independent corporation. To accomplish this, SCR will need to transfer the WCR assets and liabilities to a newly created subsidiary under §351. SCR will incur the additional cost to re-title the assets a second time and pay any state transfer tax on the transfer of the assets. Jim and Ginny can avoid this latter cost by employing a variation of a Type A reorganization called a *forward (upstream) triangular merger.*

Forward Triangular Merger In a forward triangular merger, the acquiring corporation creates a subsidiary corporation (called, perhaps, SCR Acquisition Subsidiary in our example) that holds stock of the acquiring corporation. The target corporation then merges into this subsidiary with its shareholders (Pam in this case) receiving stock of the acquiring corporation (SCR) in exchange for the stock of the target corporation (WCR). In our example, when the dust clears, WCR assets and liabilities are isolated in a wholly owned subsidiary of SCR. Exhibit 8-9 provides an illustration of a forward triangular merger for determining the tax consequences to the parties in our fictional transaction.

EXHIBIT 8-9 Form of a Forward Triangular Merger

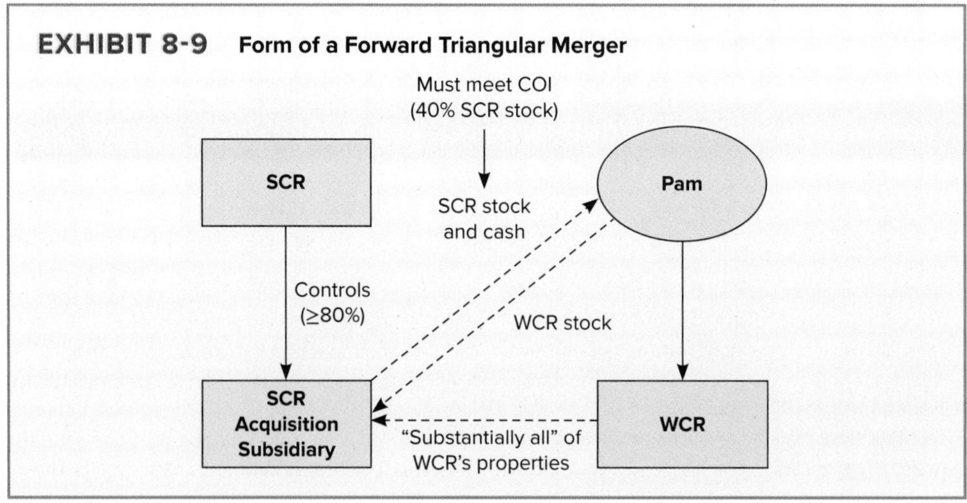

This type of merger is a common vehicle for effecting mergers when the parent corporation stock is publicly traded or the parent corporation is a holding company. For a forward triangular merger to be effective, the transaction must satisfy the requirements to be a straight Type A merger and one additional requirement: The acquisition subsidiary must acquire "substantially all" of the target corporation's properties in the exchange. In Rev. Proc. 77-37, the IRS announced in making rulings on triangular forward acquisitions, it would interpret "substantially all" to mean 90 percent of the fair market value of the target corporation's *net* properties and 70 percent of the fair market value of the target corporation's *gross* properties. For example, to qualify for an IRS ruling as a tax-deferred forward triangular merger, SCR would need to acquire 90 percent of WCR's net properties, or $270,000 (90% × $300,000). In addition, SCR would need to acquire 70 percent of WCR's gross value, or $234,500 ($335,000 × 70%).

Reverse Triangular Merger Another variation of a Type A reorganization is the *reverse (downstream) triangular merger*. Suppose that WCR holds valuable assets that cannot be easily transferred to another corporation (perhaps employment contracts or licenses). In this scenario, it would not be prudent to merge WCR into SCR or merge it into a subsidiary because these valuable assets would be lost when WCR ceased to exist. In a reverse triangular merger, the acquiring corporation still creates a subsidiary corporation that holds stock of the acquiring corporation. However, it is the acquisition subsidiary that merges into the target corporation. Again, the shareholders of the target corporation (Pam) receive stock of the acquiring corporation (SCR) in exchange for the stock of the target corporation (WCR). When the dust clears, however, the target corporation (WCR) is still intact, albeit as a wholly owned subsidiary of the acquiring corporation. Reverse triangular mergers are desirable because the transaction preserves the target corporation's existence. Exhibit 8-10 provides an illustration of a reverse triangular merger for determining the tax consequences to the parties in our fictional transaction.

EXHIBIT 8-10 Form of a Reverse Triangular Merger

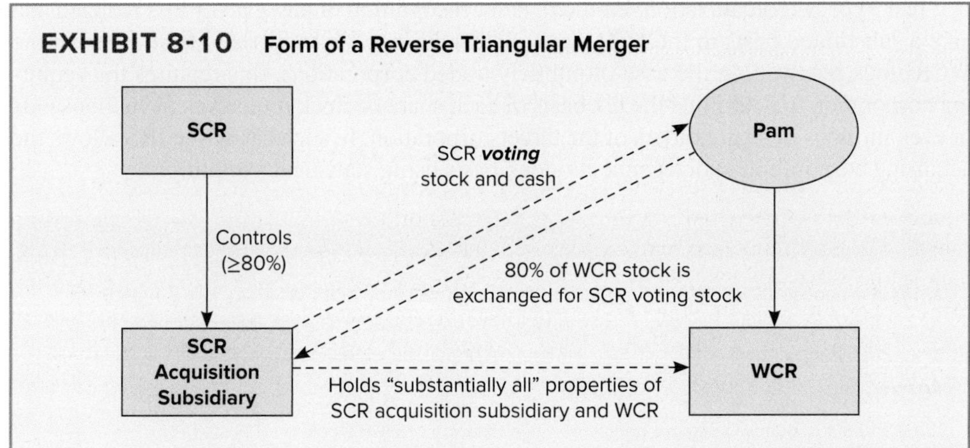

Three additional requirements must be met to satisfy the requirements for tax deferral in a reverse triangular merger. First, after the transaction the acquiring corporations must hold "substantially all" of the properties of both the target corporation and the acquisition subsidiary, excluding the property transferred to the shareholders. Second, in the exchange, the target corporation's shareholders must transfer an amount of stock in the target corporation that constitutes control of the target corporation (80 percent or more of the target stock). Finally, the target corporation's shareholders must receive *voting stock* of the acquiring corporation in return for target stock that constitutes control of the target corporation. For example, if the SCR Acquisition Subsidiary acquires 100 percent of WCR's stock in the exchange, at least 80 percent of the consideration the SCR Acquisition Subsidiary pays Pam must be in the form of SCR voting stock.

This last requirement often presents too high a hurdle in acquisitions in which the acquiring corporation wants to use a combination of cash and stock to acquire the target corporation. Publicly traded corporations are very sensitive to the amount of stock they use in an acquisition because of the negative effect it can have on the company's earnings per share (issuing additional stock increases the denominator in the earnings per share computation).

> **THE KEY FACTS**
>
> **Forms of a Tax-Deferred Asset Acquisition**
>
> - Statutory Type A merger
>   - Must meet state law requirements to be a merger or consolidation.
>   - Judicial requirements of COI, COBE, and business purpose must be met.
> - Forward triangular merger
>   - Must meet requirements to be a straight Type A merger.
>   - The target corporation merges into an acquisition subsidiary (80 percent or more shares owned by the acquiring corporation).
>   - The acquisition subsidiary must acquire "substantially all" of the target corporation's properties in the exchange.
> - Reverse triangular merger
>   - Must meet requirements to be a straight Type A merger.
>   - The acquisition subsidiary merges into the target corporation.
>   - The target corporation must hold "substantially all" of the acquisition subsidiary's properties and its own properties after the exchange.
>   - The acquisition subsidiary must receive in the exchange 80 percent or more of the target corporation's stock in exchange for voting stock of the acquiring corporation.

Type B Stock-for-Stock Reorganizations

Type B reorganizations (cell 4 in Exhibit 8-7) are often referred to as **stock-for-stock acquisitions.** The requirements for a tax-deferred Type B reorganization are very restrictive. In particular, the acquiring corporation (SCR) must acquire control (80 percent or more ownership) of the target corporation (WCR) using solely the voting stock of the acquiring corporation. Additional consideration of as little as $1 can taint the transaction and

THE KEY FACTS

Forms of a Tax-Deferred Stock Acquisition

- Stock-for-stock B reorganization
  - The acquiring corporation must exchange solely voting stock for stock of the target corporation.
  - The acquiring corporation must control (own 80 percent or more of) the target corporation after the transaction.
  - The target corporation shareholders take a substituted tax basis in the acquiring corporation stock received in the exchange.
  - The acquiring corporation takes a carryover tax basis in the target corporation stock received in the exchange.

EXHIBIT 8-11 Form of a Type B Reorganization

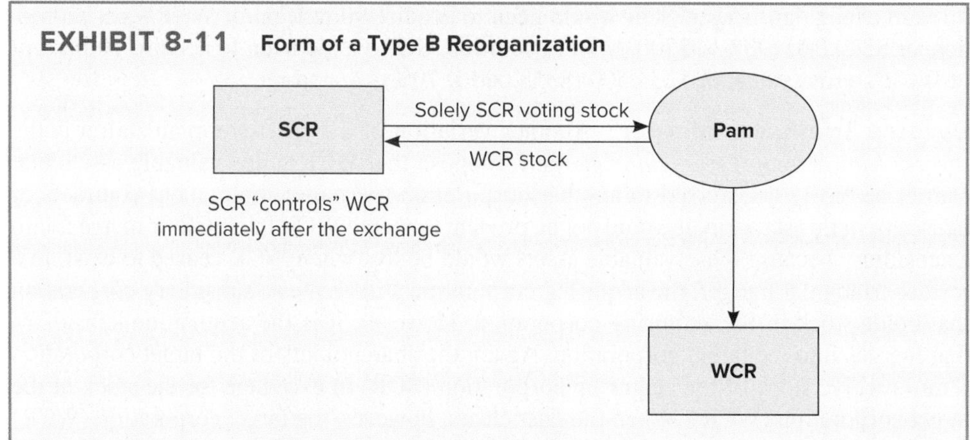

cause it to be fully taxable to the shareholders of the target corporation (Pam). Not surprisingly, Type B reorganizations are rare among publicly traded corporations. Exhibit 8-11 provides an illustration of the form of a Type B merger using our fictional example.

In a Type B reorganization, Pam will defer recognition of any gain or loss realized and take a substituted basis in the SCR stock. SCR takes a carryover basis (from Pam) in the WCR stock received. In the case of publicly traded corporations, this requires the acquiring corporation to determine the tax basis of each share of stock it receives from thousands or even millions of shareholders of the target corporation. In such cases, the IRS allows the acquiring corporation to determine its stock basis using statistical sampling.

Example 8-19

What if: Suppose SCR will exchange SCR voting stock for all of Pam's WCR stock in a Type B stock-for-stock reorganization. Pam's tax basis in WCR stock is $50,000. The fair market value of the SCR stock is $300,000. What amount of gain will Pam *realize* on the exchange of WCR stock for SCR stock?

Answer: $250,000 ($300,000 – $50,000)

What amount of gain will Pam *recognize* on the exchange of WCR stock for SCR stock?

Answer: $0. Pam defers the entire $250,000 gain realized because only SCR stock is received (no boot).

What is Pam's tax basis in the SCR stock?

Answer: $50,000. Because the entire gain is deferred, Pam's tax basis in the SCR stock is a substituted basis from the WCR stock. This preserves the gain deferred for future recognition if Pam should choose to sell the SCR stock in the future for its fair market value of $300,000.

What is SCR's tax basis in the WCR stock received in the exchange?

Answer: $50,000. SCR receives a substituted tax basis equal to Pam's basis in her WCR stock.

What is WCR's adjusted tax basis in the assets after the exchange?

Answer: The adjusted tax basis of WCR's assets remains the same (e.g., the tax basis of the goodwill and customer list will be zero).

What if: Suppose Pam received $10,000 plus $290,000 of SCR stock in the transaction. How does this change in facts affect Pam's tax consequences?

Answer: This transaction will not qualify as a Type B reorganization and the entire realized gain of $250,000 is recognized. For a Type B reorganization to be tax-deferred, Pam cannot receive any cash. Given her desire to move to Colorado, this limitation likely will be a deal breaker.

There are many variations of corporate acquisitions and reorganizations that we do not discuss in this chapter because of complexity. Suffice it to say that tax experts in mergers and acquisitions have a toolbox of ideas and alternatives that allow for countless ways to structure a transaction and achieve tax deferral for the parties to the reorganization. For the novice entering this field of taxation, such variety can be both exhilarating and exasperating. Our goal in this section is to provide you with a glimpse of this intricate area of taxation. A summary of the tax-deferred reorganizations discussed in this section, along with the other forms of tax-deferred reorganizations, is provided in Exhibit 8-12.

EXHIBIT 8-12 Summary of Tax-Deferred Corporate Reorganizations

Form of Reorganization	Description
Statutory Merger Type A	One corporation acquires the assets and liabilities of another corporation in return for stock or a combination of stock and cash. The acquisition is tax-deferred if the transaction satisfies the continuity of interest, continuity of business enterprise, and business purpose test requirements.
Forward Triangular	The acquiring corporation uses stock of its *parent* corporation to acquire the target corporation's stock, after which the target corporation merges into the acquiring corporation. To be tax-deferred, the transaction must meet the requirements to be a Type A merger. In addition, the acquiring corporation must use *solely* the stock of its parent corporation and acquire "substantially all" of the target corporation's property in the transaction.
Reverse Triangular	The acquiring corporation uses stock of its parent corporation to acquire the target corporation's stock, after which the acquiring corporation merges into the target corporation (which becomes a subsidiary of the parent corporation). To be tax-deferred, the transaction must satisfy three requirements: (1) the surviving corporation must hold "substantially all" of the properties of both the surviving and the merged corporations, (2) the target shareholders must transfer in the exchange an amount of stock in the target that constitutes control of the target (80 percent or more of the target's stock), and (3) the target shareholders must receive parent corporation voting stock in return.
Type B	The acquiring corporation uses its voting stock (or the voting stock of its parent corporation) to acquire control (80 percent voting power and 80 percent of nonvoting stock) of the target corporation. To be tax-deferred, the target shareholders must receive *solely* voting stock of the acquiring corporation.
Type C	The acquiring corporation uses its voting stock (or the voting stock of its parent corporation) to acquire "substantially all" of the target corporation's assets. The end result of a Type C reorganization resembles a Type A reorganization. The major difference between a Type C reorganization and a Type A reorganization is that state law governs the form of the Type A merger, while the Internal Revenue Code governs the form of the Type C reorganization.
Type D	Nondivisive Type D: A corporation transfers all or part of its assets to another corporation, and immediately after the transfer the shareholders of the transferor corporation own at least 50 percent of the voting power or value of the transferee corporation. Divisive Type D: A corporation transfers all or part of its assets to another corporation, and immediately after the transfer the shareholders of the transferor corporation own at least 80 percent of the transferee corporation.
Type E	Type E reorganizations are often referred to as recapitalizations. Stock in the corporation (e.g., common) is exchanged for a different class of stock (e.g., preferred) or securities (debt). Recapitalizations can range from an amendment in the corporate charter to a change in the redemption price or liquidating value of stock to an actual exchange of stock between the corporation and its shareholder(s).
Type F	Type F reorganizations are described as a "mere change in identity, form, or place of organization" of a single corporation. A corporation uses a Type F reorganization to change its corporate name or its state (country) of incorporation.
Type G	Type G reorganizations are often referred to as bankruptcy reorganizations. In a Type G reorganization, the corporation transfers all or a part of its assets to another corporation in a Title 11 case, and the stock of the corporation receiving the assets is distributed in a transaction that is tax-deferred.

Tax law also allows corporations to divide by transferring stock of a subsidiary to shareholders in a pro rata distribution (spin-off) or a non–pro rata distribution (split-off).[36] The technical details of these transactions are beyond the scope of this text.

[36]§355.

TAXES IN THE REAL WORLD Consolidations and Acquisitions in Oil

Innovations and unexpected events, such as recessions, can roil whole industries, resulting in waves of corporate acquisitions as firms try to retrench and reorganize. In 2017, the oil and gas industry was trying to recover from a recession and the fracking boom was about to upend the industry further.

One result was that Noble Energy (NYSE: NBL) agreed to exchange stock and cash to acquire Clayton Williams Energy Inc. (NYSE: CWEI). Under the agreement, CWEI shareholders would receive cash of $34.75 and approximately 3.722 NBL shares for each CWEI share. The ratio of cash and stock was to be adjusted so that the total value of the NBL stock issued would not be less than 75 percent of the total merger consideration. According to SEC filings, the qualification of the transaction as a "reorganization" within the meaning of §368(a) of the Internal Revenue Code of 1986 is a condition to the deal.

While fracking led to an earlier boom, the pandemic at the beginning of 2020 caused another severe recession for oil and gas. This time, however, Noble was the target and not the acquirer. On August 24, 2020, Noble Energy entered into a definitive agreement with Chevron (NYSE: CVX) under which Chevron would acquire all the outstanding shares of Noble in exchange for Chevron shares. Again, the deal depended on the transaction qualifying as a "reorganization" organized as a downstream triangular merger (Noble survives as a subsidiary of Chevron).

Sources: Clayton Williams Energy Inc. proxy dated March 23, 2017; and Nobel Energy proxy dated August 26, 2020.

LO 8-5

COMPLETE LIQUIDATION OF A CORPORATION

(continued from page 8-22 . . .)

After several years of trying to get 360 Air off the ground, Jim, Ginny, and even Al realize that there is not enough demand for snowboarding products in East Lansing to make their business venture profitable. Reluctantly, the three owners have decided to liquidate the corporation and have constructed the company's tax accounting balance sheet, which is reproduced below.

	FMV	Adjusted Tax Basis	Difference
Cash	$138,000	$138,000	
Receivables	2,000	2,000	
Inventory	10,000	12,000	$ (2,000)
Building	150,000	48,000	102,000
Land	200,000	100,000	100,000
Total	$500,000	$300,000	$200,000

The parties agree that 360 Air will sell off the inventory, building, and land and collect the remaining receivables. After the sale, 360 Air will pay taxes of $42,000 (21% × $200,000) on the gains and divide the remaining $458,000 in cash ($500,000 – $42,000) pro rata between the three shareholders (50 percent to Al, 40 percent to Jim, and 10 percent to Ginny). ■

The owners of a corporation may decide at some point to discontinue the corporation's business activities. They may make this decision because the corporation is not profitable, the officers and shareholders wish to change the organizational form of the business (e.g., to a flow-through entity), or the owners want to consolidate operations (e.g., a subsidiary is liquidated into the parent corporation).

A complete liquidation occurs when a corporation acquires all its stock from all its shareholders in exchange for all its net assets, after which the corporation ceases to do business. For tax purposes, a corporation files Form 966 ("Corporate Dissolution or Liquidation") to inform the IRS of its intention to liquidate its tax existence. The form should be filed within 30 days after the board of directors resolve to liquidate the corporation.

Tax Consequences to the Shareholders in a Complete Liquidation

The tax consequences to a shareholder in a complete liquidation depend on (1) whether the shareholder is incorporated and (2) what percentage of the corporation the shareholder owns. In general, all *noncorporate* shareholders receiving liquidating distributions have a fully taxable transaction.[37] The shareholders treat the property received as full payment in exchange for the stock transferred. They compute capital gain or loss by subtracting the stock's tax basis from the money and fair market value of property received in return. If a shareholder assumes the corporation's liabilities on property received as a liquidating distribution, this reduces the amount realized by the amount of the liabilities assumed when computing the realized gain or loss. The shareholder's tax basis in the property received equals the property's fair market value.

Example 8-20

As a result of the liquidation of 360 Air, Ginny received cash of $45,800 (representing her 10 percent ownership in the company's assets of $458,000 after all debts were paid). Ginny's tax basis in the 360 Air stock is $60,000.

What amount of gain or loss will Ginny *realize* and *recognize* on the exchange of 360 Air stock for 360 Air assets?

Answer: Ginny will realize a loss of $14,200, computed as the amount realized of $45,800 less the tax basis of $60,000. Ginny will recognize a $14,200 long-term capital loss. The entire amount could be deductible to the extent of Ginny's capital gains. Otherwise, Ginny can offset this loss against capital gains and deduct an additional $3,000 of net capital loss. Any unused capital loss would carry forward.

As a result of the complete liquidation of 360 Air, Jim received $183,200 cash (representing his 40 percent ownership in the company's assets of $458,000). Jim's tax basis in 360 Air is $240,000, an amount equal to the cash contributed when the corporation was formed.

What amount of gain or loss will Jim *realize* on the exchange of his 360 Air stock for 360 Air assets?

Answer: $56,800 loss, the amount realized ($183,200) less Jim's tax basis in the stock ($240,000).

What amount of loss will Jim *recognize* on the exchange, and what is the character of the loss?

Answer: $56,800 long-term capital loss. The entire amount could be deductible to the extent of Jim's capital gains. Otherwise, Jim can offset this loss against capital gains and deduct an additional $3,000 of net capital loss. Any unused capital loss would carry forward.

What if: Suppose that the land owned by 360 Air consists of two parcels, the building is located on parcel #1 which has a value of $50,000 and an adjusted basis of $40,000. Parcel #2 is an undeveloped tract of land with a value of $150,000 and an adjusted basis of $60,000. Suppose further that rather than sell parcel #2, 360 Air distributed parcel #2 and $79,000 cash to Al. This consideration represents Al's 50 percent interest in the net fair market value of the company (50% × $458,000). Al's tax basis in the 360 Air stock is $100,000. What amount of gain or loss will Al *realize* and *recognize* on the exchange of the 360 Air stock for 360 Air assets?

Answer: $129,000 realized and recognized gain. The gain is computed as the amount realized ($150,000 + $79,000 = $229,000) less Al's adjusted tax basis in the stock ($100,000). The gain is taxable as a long-term capital gain.

What is Al's tax basis in the land he receives in the liquidation?

Answer: $150,000. Al takes a tax basis in the land equal to its fair market value.

[37] §331.

Liquidating distributions to corporate shareholders are also taxable unless the corporation owns 80 percent or more of the stock (voting power and value). Corporate shareholders owning 80 percent or more of the stock of the liquidating corporation do not recognize gain or loss on the receipt of liquidating distributions.[38] This nonrecognition treatment is mandatory. The adjusted tax basis in the property transferred carries over to the corporate shareholder receiving the liquidating distribution.[39] This deferral provision allows a group of corporations under common control to reorganize their organizational structure without recognizing gain.

Example 8-21

What if: Suppose 360 Air was a 100-percent-owned subsidiary of SCR, and 360 Air is liquidated into SCR. SCR has a tax basis in its 360 Air stock of $300,000. What amount of gain or loss will SCR *realize* on the complete liquidation of 360 Air stock for 360 Air assets?

Answer: $200,000 ($500,000 – $300,000).

What amount of gain will SCR *recognize* on the exchange?

Answer: $0. The gain is not recognized because SCR owns 80 percent or more of 360 Air.

What is SCR's adjusted tax basis in the assets and liabilities it receives in the liquidation?

Answer: SCR will inherit a carryover tax basis in 360 Air's assets and liabilities.

Tax Consequences to the Liquidating Corporation in a Complete Liquidation

The tax consequences to the liquidating corporation depend on the tax treatment applied to the shareholder to whom the property was distributed.

Taxable Liquidating Distributions Typically, a liquidating corporation recognizes all gains and certain losses on taxable liquidating distributions of property to shareholders.[40] The liquidating corporation does not recognize loss if the loss property is distributed to a related person and either (1) the distribution is non pro rata (to the related person) or (2) the distributed asset is disqualified property.[41] A distribution of loss property is non pro rata unless the related person only receives in the distribution an interest in the loss property equal to the related party's ownership interest. A *related person* is defined as a shareholder who owns more than 50 percent of the value of the stock in the liquidating corporation.[42] *Disqualified property* is property acquired within five years of the date of distribution in a tax-deferred §351 transaction or as a nontaxable contribution to capital.

[38]§332(a). Corporate shareholders must meet the 80 percent ownership test from the time the plan is adopted until the plan is complete. Under §1504(a)(2), the corporation must own 80 percent or more of both voting power and value of the shares of the liquidating corporation. Besides corporate ownership, deferral also includes additional requirements for asset distributions.

[39]§334(b)(1).

[40]§336(a).

[41]§336(d)(1).

[42]§267(b) defines related persons and includes constructive ownership rules under §267(c).

Example 8-22

360 Air made taxable liquidating distributions to Jim, Ginny, and Al during the current year. Al owns 50 percent of the stock, Ginny owns 10 percent, and Jim owns 40 percent. Assume for purposes of this example that 360 Air made a pro rata distribution of each asset to its three shareholders. The company's tax accounting balance sheet at the time of the distribution is shown below:

	FMV	Adjusted Tax Basis	Difference
Cash	$138,000	$138,000	
Receivables	2,000	2,000	
Inventory	10,000	12,000	$ (2,000)
Building	150,000	48,000	102,000
Land	200,000	100,000	100,000
Total	$500,000	$300,000	$200,000

What amount of gain or loss does 360 Air recognize as a result of the distribution?

Answer: $200,000. 360 Air recognizes all gains and losses on the distribution of its assets in the following amounts and character:

	Gain (Loss) Recognized	Character
Inventory	$ (2,000)	Ordinary income
Building	102,000	Ordinary (§291) and §1231
Land	100,000	§1231
Net gain	**$200,000**	

Note that the gain or loss on the complete liquidation is identical to gains and losses that would result if 360 Air had sold all of its assets at fair market value.

What if: Assume Jim owned 60 percent of the stock and 360 Air proposed distributing the assets other than the land to Jim. The company's tax accounting balance sheet at the time of the distribution is shown below:

	FMV	Adjusted Tax Basis	Difference
Cash	$138,000	$138,000	
Receivables	2,000	2,000	
Inventory	10,000	12,000	$ (2,000)
Building	150,000	48,000	102,000
Land	200,000	100,000	100,000
Total	$500,000	$300,000	$200,000

What amount of gain or loss would 360 Air recognize as a result of the distribution?

Answer: $202,000 gain, as calculated below. 360 Air would recognize gains but could not recognize the $2,000 inventory loss because the distribution is non pro rata (Jim's interest in the inventory was only 60% but he received 100%) and the loss property is distributed to a related person (Jim owns more than 50 percent of the stock).

	Gain (Loss) Recognized	Character
Inventory	$ 0	
Building	102,000	Ordinary (§291) and §1231
Land	100,000	§1231
Net gain	**$202,000**	

(continued on page 8-36)

What if: Assume that Ginny owned 40 percent of the stock and that 360 Air proposed distributing the inventory, the building, and cash to Ginny. What amount of gain or loss would 360 Air recognize as a result of this distribution?

Answer: $200,000. 360 Air would now recognize the $2,000 loss on the distribution of the inventory because the inventory (loss property) was not distributed to a related person. To the extent loss property is distributed to an unrelated person, such as Ginny (she owns less than 50%), the loss is deductible even if the distribution of the loss property is non pro rata.

A second loss disallowance rule potentially applies to property acquired by the corporation in a §351 transaction or as a contribution to capital. The loss built in at the time of acquisition is not recognized if the property is distributed or sold after the corporation adopts a plan of liquidation and if a principal purpose of the §351 transaction or the contribution was to allow the liquidating corporation to recognize the loss.[43] This rule prevents a built-in loss (adjusted tax basis in excess of fair market value) from being recognized by treating the basis of the property distributed or sold as its fair market value at the time it was contributed to the corporation. This prohibited tax-avoidance purpose is presumed if the property is acquired within two years before the corporation adopts a plan of liquidation. The presumption can be overcome if the corporation can show that there was a corporate business purpose for contributing the property to the corporation.

Example 8-23

What if: Suppose Al transferred a building and land to 360 Air in return for 50 percent of the corporation's stock (50 shares) in a transaction that qualified under §351. The property transferred to the corporation had the following fair market values and adjusted tax bases:

	FMV	Adjusted Tax Basis
Building	$ 75,000	$100,000
Land	200,000	100,000
Total	$275,000	$200,000

In this case, the aggregate fair market value of the property transferred to the corporation exceeds the aggregate adjusted basis of the property. As a result, the building will retain its carryover basis of $100,000 and subsequent built-in loss of $25,000.

What if: If the building and land are either sold or distributed to Al in complete liquidation of his ownership of 360 Air stock within two years of the §351 transaction, will 360 Air be able to deduct the $25,000 loss on the distribution of the building?

Answer: It depends. Because the sale or liquidating distribution is made pursuant to a plan of complete liquidation adopted within two years of the §351 transaction, the presumption is that Al contributed the property to 360 Air for tax avoidance purposes (i.e., to allow the corporation to deduct the built-in loss). The corporation can rebut this presumption by demonstrating that the contribution of the property by Al had a corporate business purpose at the time of the §351 transaction. In addition, the corporation could argue that he did not have a tax avoidance motive because at the time of his original transfer, Al transferred assets with a net built-in gain.

[43]§336(d)(2).

Tax Deferred Liquidating Distributions The liquidating corporation does not recognize gain or loss on distributions of property to an 80 percent corporate shareholder.[44] If a shareholder receives tax deferral in the liquidation, the liquidating corporation cannot recognize any loss, even on distributions to shareholders who receive taxable distributions.[45]

Example 8-24

What if: Assume 360 Air was a 100-percent-owned subsidiary of SCR, and SCR liquidated 360 Air. SCR has a tax basis in its 360 Air stock of $300,000. The company's tax accounting balance sheet at the time of the distribution is shown below:

	FMV	Adjusted Tax Basis	Difference
Cash	$138,000	$138,000	
Receivables	2,000	2,000	
Inventory	10,000	12,000	$ (2,000)
Building	150,000	48,000	102,000
Land	200,000	100,000	100,000
Total	$500,000	$300,000	$200,000

What amount of gain or loss does 360 Air *recognize* as a result of the liquidation?

Answer: $0. 360 Air does not recognize any gain or loss on the liquidation.

What if: Suppose 360 Air was 80 percent owned by SCR and 20 percent owned by Jim. 360 Air distributed the inventory plus $90,000 to Jim in complete liquidation of his stock. Can 360 Air recognize the $2,000 inventory loss?

Answer: No. 360 Air cannot recognize the loss even though Jim is not a related person and has a taxable distribution. When one shareholder is not taxable on a liquidating distribution (SCR), the liquidating corporation cannot recognize any losses on the distribution of property to any shareholder.

THE KEY FACTS

Tax Consequences of a Complete Liquidation

- Shareholders other than corporations that own 80 percent or more of the liquidating corporation's stock recognize gain and usually loss in a complete liquidation of the corporation.
- Corporations that own 80 percent or more of the liquidating corporation's stock (vote and value) do not recognize gain or loss in a complete liquidation of the corporation.
- Shareholders recognizing gain or loss take a tax basis in property received in the complete liquidation equal to its fair market value.
- Corporate shareholders that defer recognizing gain or loss take an adjusted tax basis in property received in the complete liquidation equal to its carryover basis.

Liquidation-related expenses, including the cost of preparing and effectuating a plan of complete liquidation, are deductible by the liquidating corporation on its final Form 1120. Deferred or capitalized expenditures such as organizational expenditures also are deductible on the final tax return.

CONCLUSION

This chapter discussed some of the important tax rules that apply during the life cycle of a C corporation. As the storyline indicates, forming a corporation generally does not create any tax to any of the parties to the transaction. Gain or loss realized by the shareholders on the transfer of property to the corporation is deferred until a later date, when either the shareholder sells his ownership interest or the corporation liquidates. Subsequent acquisitions of new businesses or dispositions of existing businesses also can be achieved in a tax-deferred manner. However, failure to meet all the requirements can convert a tax-deferred transaction into a taxable transaction. A complete liquidation of a corporation generally is a fully taxable transaction to the shareholders and the liquidating corporation, except in the case where a subsidiary is liquidated into its parent corporation.

[44] §337(a).

[45] §336(d)(3).

Summary

LO 8-1 Review the taxation of property dispositions.

- A person realizes gain or loss as a result of engaging in a transaction, which is defined as an exchange of property rights with another person.
- Gain or loss realized is computed by subtracting the adjusted tax basis of property transferred in the exchange from the amount realized in the exchange.
- The amount realized is computed as cash received plus the fair market value of other property received plus any liabilities assumed by the transferee on the property transferred, reduced by selling expenses and any liabilities assumed by the transferor on property received in the exchange.
- The general tax rule is that gain or loss realized is recognized (included in the computation of taxable income) unless a specific tax rule exempts the gain or loss from being recognized (permanently) or defers such recognition until a future date.

LO 8-2 Recognize the tax consequences to the parties to a tax-deferred corporate formation.

- Section 351 applies to transactions in which one or more persons transfer property to a corporation in return for stock, and immediately after the transfer, these same persons control the corporation to which they transferred the property.
- If a transaction meets these requirements, the transferors of property (shareholders) do not recognize (defer) gain or loss realized on the transfer of the property to the corporation.
    - Shareholders contributing property to a corporation in a §351 transaction compute gain or loss realized by subtracting the adjusted tax basis of the contributed property from the fair market value of the consideration they receive in return (amount realized).
    - Gain, but not loss, is recognized when property other than the corporation's stock (boot) is received in the exchange.
    - Gain is recognized in an amount equal to the *lesser of* the gain realized or the fair market value of boot received.
    - The tax basis of stock received in the exchange equals the adjusted tax basis of the property transferred, less any liabilities assumed by the corporation on the property contributed (substituted basis).
    - The shareholder's stock basis is increased by any gain recognized and reduced by the fair market value of any boot received.
- The corporation receiving property for its stock in a §351 exchange does not recognize (excludes) gain or loss realized on the transfer.
    - The adjusted tax basis of the property received by the corporation equals the property's adjusted tax basis in the transferor's hands (carryover basis).
    - The asset's tax basis is increased by any gain recognized by the shareholder on the transfer of the property to the corporation.

LO 8-3 Identify the different forms of taxable and tax-deferred acquisitions.

- Corporations can be acquired in taxable asset or stock purchases.
- Corporations can be acquired in tax-deferred asset or stock purchases.
- To be tax-deferred, an acquisition must meet certain IRC and judicial doctrines to qualify as reorganization.
    - The judicial requirements, now summarized in the regulations, require continuity of interest, continuity of business enterprise, and business purpose.
- In a Type A tax-deferred acquisition, the target corporation's assets and liabilities are merged into the acquiring corporation (stock-for-assets exchange).
    - Type A acquisitions involving publicly traded corporations often use an acquisition subsidiary (triangular merger) to acquire the target corporation's assets and liabilities.
- In a Type B tax-deferred acquisition, the shareholders of the target corporation exchange their stock for stock of the acquiring corporation (stock-for-stock exchange).
    - Type B acquisitions prohibit the use of cash in the exchange.

Determine the tax consequences to the parties to a corporate acquisition. LO 8-4

- Shareholders participating in a taxable asset or stock transaction compute gain or loss realized by subtracting the adjusted basis of the stock they surrender to the acquiring corporation from the fair market value of the consideration they receive in the exchange.
- Shareholders participating in a tax-deferred reorganization defer gain and loss realized in the exchange unless cash (boot) is received.
  - Shareholders receiving boot recognize gain, but not loss, in an amount equal to the lesser of the gain realized or the fair market value of the boot received.
- The corporation does not recognize gain on the distribution of its own stock in exchange for property in a reorganization.
- The stock received in return for stock in a tax-deferred reorganization has a tax basis equal to the tax basis of the stock surrendered in the exchange (substituted basis).
- The shareholder's stock basis is increased by any gain recognized and reduced by cash or other boot received.
- The assets transferred to the corporation in a tax-deferred reorganization carry over the tax basis of the shareholders contributing the property (carryover basis).

Calculate the tax consequences that apply to the parties to a complete liquidation of a corporation. LO 8-5

- Noncorporate shareholders receiving a distribution in complete liquidation of their corporation recognize gain and (usually) loss in the exchange.
- Tax deferral is extended to corporate shareholders that own 80 percent or more of the liquidating corporation.
- The liquidating corporation recognizes gain and (usually) loss on the distribution of property to those shareholders who are taxable on the distribution.
- The liquidating corporation cannot deduct losses on property distributed to a related person if the distribution of loss property is non–pro rata or the loss property is disqualified property.
- A loss cannot be deducted on the distribution or sale of property after the corporation adopts the plan of liquidation, but only if the property was previously contributed to the corporation in a §351 transaction whose principal purpose was to avoid tax.
- The liquidating corporation cannot deduct losses on property distributed if one of the persons receiving the liquidation is not taxable on the distribution (a corporate shareholder owning 80 percent or more of the stock).
- The liquidating corporation does not recognize gain or loss on the distribution of property to a corporate shareholder owning 80 percent or more of the stock.
- The tax basis of each asset received by the shareholder in a taxable complete liquidation equals the asset's fair market value on the date of the distribution.
- The adjusted tax basis of each asset received by a corporate shareholder (owning 80 percent or more of the stock) in a tax-deferred complete liquidation carries over from the liquidating corporation.

KEY TERMS

§338(g) election (8-24)
§338(h)(10) election (8-24)
adjusted tax basis (8-3)
amount realized (8-3)
boot (8-5)
bright-line test (8-25)
carryover basis (8-14)
consolidations (8-26)
continuity of business enterprise (COBE) (8-25)
continuity of interest (COI) (8-25)
contribution to capital (8-18)
mergers (8-26)
persons (8-4)
realization (8-2)
reorganization (8-25)
stock-for-stock acquisitions (8-29)
substituted basis (8-7)

DISCUSSION QUESTIONS

Discussion Questions are available in Connect®. 

LO 8-1 1. Discuss the difference between realization and recognition in a property transaction.

LO 8-1 2. What information must a taxpayer gather to determine the *amount realized* in a property transaction?

LO 8-1 3. Distinguish between exclusion and deferral in a property transaction.

LO 8-1 4. Contrast how a taxpayer's tax basis in property received in a property transaction will be affected if the transaction results in gain exclusion versus gain deferral.

LO 8-1 5. What information must a taxpayer gather to determine the *adjusted tax basis* of property exchanged in a property transaction?

LO 8-2 6. Why does Congress provide tax deferral on the formation of a corporation?

LO 8-2 7. List the key statutory requirements that must be met before a corporate formation is tax deferred under §351.

LO 8-2 8. What is the definition of *control* for purposes of §351? Why does Congress require the shareholders to control a corporation to receive tax deferral?

LO 8-2 9. What is a *substituted basis* as it relates to stock received in exchange for property in a §351 transaction? What is the purpose of attaching a substituted basis to stock received in a §351 transaction?

LO 8-2 10. Explain whether the receipt of boot by a shareholder in a §351 transaction causes the transaction to be fully taxable.

LO 8-2 11. Explain whether a corporation's assumption of shareholder liabilities will always constitute boot in a §351 transaction.

LO 8-2 12. How does the tax treatment differ in cases where liabilities are assumed with a tax avoidance purpose versus where liabilities assumed exceed basis?

LO 8-2 13. What is a *carryover basis* as it relates to property received by a corporation in a §351 transaction? What is the purpose of attaching a carryover basis to property received in a §351 transaction?

LO 8-2 14. Under what circumstances does property received by a corporation in a §351 transaction not receive a carryover basis? What is the reason for this rule?

LO 8-2 15. How does a corporation depreciate an asset received in a §351 transaction in which no gain or loss is recognized by the transferor of the property?

LO 8-2 16. Are the tax consequences the same whether a shareholder contributes property to a corporation in a §351 transaction or as a capital contribution? Explain.

LO 8-2 17. Why might a corporation prefer to characterize an instrument as debt rather than equity for tax purposes? Are the holders of the instrument indifferent as to its characterization for tax purposes?

LO 8-2 18. Under what conditions is it advantageous for a shareholder to hold §1244 stock? Why did Congress bestow these tax benefits on holders of such stock?

LO 8-3 19. Explain when an acquiring corporation would prefer to buy the target corporation's assets directly in an acquisition.

LO 8-3 20. Do the shareholders of the target corporation usually prefer to sell the stock or the assets of the target corporation? Explain.

LO 8-3 21. What is the congressional purpose for allowing tax deferral on transactions that meet the definition of a corporate reorganization?

LO 8-3 22. Describe the advantages (if any) of using a reverse triangular form of reorganization in acquiring other corporations.

LO 8-3 23. What are the key differences in the tax law requirements that apply to forward versus reverse triangular mergers?

LO 8-3 24. What are the key differences in the tax law requirements that apply to a Type A stock-for-assets acquisition versus a Type B stock-for-stock acquisition?

25. How does the form of a regular §338(g) election compare and contrast to a §338(h)(10) election? LO 8-4
26. What tax benefits does the buyer hope to obtain by making a §338(g) or §338(h)(10) election? Describe how this election might affect the value offered for the target corporation. LO 8-4
27. In a stock acquisition, describe the difference (if any) between the *adjusted tax basis of assets* held by an acquired corporation and the *tax basis of the shares* held by a corporate acquirer. LO 8-4
28. What is the presumption behind the continuity of ownership interest (COI) requirement in a tax-deferred acquisition? How do the target shareholders determine if COI is met in a Type A reorganization? LO 8-4
29. W Corporation will acquire all of the assets and liabilities of Z Corporation in a Type A merger, after which W Corporation will sell off all of its assets and liabilities and focus solely on Z Corporation's business. Explain whether the transaction will be taxable because W Corporation fails the continuity of business enterprise (COBE) test. LO 8-4
30. Compare how a shareholder computes tax basis in stock received from the acquiring corporation in a forward triangular merger versus a Type B merger. LO 8-4
31. Do all shareholders receive the same tax treatment in a complete liquidation of a corporation? Explain. LO 8-5
32. Describe when a corporate shareholder must defer gains and losses on the receipt of distributions of property from the complete liquidation of a subsidiary corporation. LO 8-5
33. Is it true that a corporation recognizes all gains and losses on liquidating distributions of property to noncorporate shareholders? Explain. LO 8-5
34. Under what circumstances must a corporate shareholder recognize gains in a complete liquidation? LO 8-5
35. Under what circumstances will a liquidating corporation be allowed to recognize loss in a non–pro rata distribution? LO 8-5
36. Compare and contrast the built-in loss duplication rule as it relates to §351 with the built-in loss disallowance rule as it applies to a complete liquidation. LO 8-5

PROBLEMS

Select problems are available in Connect®.

37. Ramon incorporated his sole proprietorship by transferring inventory, a building, and land to the corporation in return for 100 percent of the corporation's stock. The property transferred to the corporation had the following fair market values and adjusted tax bases: LO 8-2

	FMV	Adjusted Tax Basis
Inventory	$ 10,000	$ 4,000
Building	50,000	30,000
Land	100,000	50,000
Total	$160,000	$84,000

The fair market value of the corporation's stock received in the exchange equaled the fair market value of the assets transferred to the corporation by Ramon.

a) What amount of gain or loss does Ramon *realize* on the transfer of the property to his corporation?
b) What amount of gain or loss does Ramon *recognize* on the transfer of the property to his corporation?
c) What is Ramon's basis in the stock received in the new corporation?

LO 8-2
planning

38. Carla incorporated her sole proprietorship by transferring inventory, a building, and land to the corporation in return for 100 percent of the corporation's stock. The property transferred to the corporation had the following fair market values and adjusted tax bases:

	FMV	Adjusted Tax Basis
Inventory	$ 20,000	$ 10,000
Building	150,000	100,000
Land	250,000	300,000
Total	$420,000	$410,000

The corporation also assumed a mortgage of $120,000 attached to the building and land. The fair market value of the corporation's stock received in the exchange was $300,000.

a) What amount of gain or loss does Carla *realize* on the transfer of the property to the corporation?
b) What amount of gain or loss does Carla *recognize* on the transfer of the property to her corporation?
c) What is Carla's basis in the stock received in the new corporation?
d) Would you advise Carla to transfer the building and land to the corporation? What tax benefits might be generated if Carla kept the building and land and leased it to the corporation?

LO 8-2

39. Ivan incorporated his sole proprietorship by transferring inventory, a building, and land to the corporation in return for 100 percent of the corporation's stock. The property transferred to the corporation had the following fair market values and adjusted tax bases:

	FMV	Adjusted Tax Basis
Inventory	$ 10,000	$15,000
Building	50,000	40,000
Land	60,000	30,000
Total	$120,000	$85,000

The fair market value of the corporation's stock received in the exchange equaled the fair market value of the assets transferred to the corporation by Ivan. The transaction met the requirements to be tax-deferred under §351.

a) What amount of gain or loss does Ivan *realize* on the transfer of the property to the corporation?
b) What amount of gain or loss does Ivan *recognize* on the transfer of the property to the corporation?
c) What is Ivan's basis in the stock received in the new corporation?
d) What is the corporation's adjusted tax basis in each of the assets received in the exchange?
e) Would the stock held by Ivan qualify as §1244 stock? Why is this determination important for Ivan?

LO 8-2

40. Zhang incorporated her sole proprietorship by transferring inventory, a building, and land to the corporation in return for 100 percent of the corporation's stock. The property transferred to the corporation had the following fair market values and adjusted tax bases:

	FMV	Adjusted Tax Basis
Inventory	$ 20,000	$ 10,000
Building	150,000	100,000
Land	230,000	300,000
Total	$400,000	$410,000

The corporation also assumed a mortgage of $100,000 attached to the building and land. The fair market value of the corporation's stock received in the exchange was $300,000. The transaction met the requirements to be tax-deferred under §351.

a) What amount of gain or loss does Zhang *realize* on the transfer of the property to the corporation?

b) What amount of gain or loss does Zhang *recognize* on the transfer of the property to the corporation?

c) What is Zhang's tax basis in the stock received in the exchange?

d) What is the corporation's adjusted tax basis in each of the assets received in the exchange?

Assume the corporation assumed a mortgage of $500,000 attached to the building and land. Assume the fair market value of the building is now $250,000 and the fair market value of the land is $530,000. The fair market value of the stock remains $300,000.

e) How much, if any, gain or loss does Zhang *recognize* on the exchange assuming the revised facts?

f) What is Zhang's tax basis in the stock received in the exchange?

g) What is the corporation's adjusted tax basis in each of the assets received in the exchange?

41. Sam and Devon agree to go into business together selling college-licensed clothing. According to the agreement, Sam will contribute inventory valued at $100,000 in return for 80 percent of the stock in the corporation. Sam's tax basis in the inventory is $60,000. Devon will receive 20 percent of the stock in return for providing accounting services to the corporation (these qualify as organizational expenditures). The accounting services are valued at $25,000. LO 8-2 planning

a) What amount of income gain or loss does Sam *realize* on the formation of the corporation? What amount, if any, does Sam *recognize*?

b) What is Sam's tax basis in the stock received in return for his contribution of property to the corporation?

c) What amount of income, gain, or loss does Devon *realize* on the formation of the corporation? What amount, if any, does Devon *recognize*?

d) What is Devon's tax basis in the stock received in return for the contribution of services to the corporation?

Assume Devon received 25 percent of the stock in the corporation in return for his services.

e) What amount of gain or loss does Sam *recognize* on the formation of the corporation?

f) What is Sam's tax basis in the stock received in return for the contribution of property to the corporation?

g) What amount of income, gain, or loss does Devon *recognize* on the formation of the corporation?

h) What is Devon's tax basis in the stock received in return for the contribution of services to the corporation?

i) What tax advice could you give Sam and Devon to change the tax consequences?

42. Jekyll and Hyde formed a corporation (Halloween Inc.) on October 31 to develop a drug to address split personalities. Jekyll will contribute a patented formula valued at $200,000 in return for 50 percent of the stock in the corporation. Hyde will contribute an experimental formula worth $120,000 and medical services in exchange for the remaining stock. Jekyll's tax basis in the patented formula is $125,000, whereas Hyde has a basis of $15,000 in his experimental formula. LO 8-2

a) Describe the tax consequences of the transaction.

b) Prepare the §351 statement that must be included with the return.

LO 8-2

43. Ramona and Hermione formed Wiley Corporation on January 2. Ramona contributed cash of $200,000 in return for 50 percent of the corporation's stock. Hermione contributed a building and land with the following fair market values and adjusted tax bases in return for 50 percent of the corporation's stock:

	FMV	Adjusted Tax Basis
Building	$ 75,000	$ 20,000
Land	175,000	80,000
Total	$250,000	$100,000

To equalize the exchange, Wiley Corporation paid Hermione $50,000 in addition to her stock.

a) What amount of gain or loss does Ramona *realize* on the formation of the corporation? What amount, if any, does Ramona *recognize*?
b) What is Ramona's tax basis in the stock received in return for the contribution of property to the corporation?
c) What amount of gain or loss does Hermione *realize* on the formation of the corporation? What amount, if any, does she *recognize*?
d) What is Hermione's tax basis in the stock received in return for the contribution of property to the corporation?
e) What adjusted tax basis does Wiley Corporation take in the land and building received from Hermione?

Assume Hermione's adjusted tax basis in the land was $200,000.

f) What amount of gain or loss does Hermione *realize* on the formation of the corporation? What amount, if any, does she *recognize*?
g) What adjusted tax basis does Wiley Corporation take in the land and building received from Hermione?

Assume Hermione's adjusted tax basis in the land was $250,000.

h) What amount of gain or loss does Hermione *realize* on the formation of the corporation? What amount, if any, does she *recognize*?
i) What adjusted tax basis does Wiley Corporation take in the land and building received from Hermione?
j) What election can Hermione and Wiley Corporation make to allow Wiley Corporation to take a carryover basis in the land?

LO 8-2
planning

44. This year, Jack O. Lantern incurred a $60,000 loss on the worthlessness of his stock in the Creepy Corporation (CC). The stock, which Jack purchased in 2005, met all of the §1244 stock requirements at the time of issue. In December of this year, Jack's wife, Jill, also incurred a $75,000 loss on the sale of Eerie Corporation (EC) stock that she purchased in July 2005 and that also satisfied all of the §1244 stock requirements at the time of issue. Both corporations are operating companies.

a) How much of the losses incurred on the two stock sales can Jack and Jill deduct this year, assuming they do not have capital gains in the current or prior years?
b) Assuming they did not engage in any other property transactions this year, how much of a net capital loss will carry over to next year for Jack and Jill?
c) What would be the tax treatment for the losses if Jack and Jill reported only $60,000 of taxable income this year, excluding the securities transactions?
d) What tax planning suggestions can you offer the Lanterns to increase the tax benefits of these losses?

LO 8-2

45. Breslin Inc. made a capital contribution of investment property to its 100-percent-owned subsidiary, Crisler Company. The investment property had a fair market value of $3,000,000 and a tax basis to Breslin of $2,225,000.

a) What are the tax consequences to Breslin Inc. on the contribution of the investment property to Crisler Company?

b) What is the tax basis of the investment property to Crisler Company after the contribution to capital?

46. Nareh joined Jim in forming DBJ Corp. Nareh contributed appreciated land for 90 percent of the stock in DBJ. Jim received 10 percent of the DBJ stock valued at $15,000. Determine Jim's tax consequences in each of the following alternative scenarios. LO 8-2
    a) Jim received the stock in exchange for providing computer-related services for the corporation. What amount of income or gain does Jim recognize on the exchange? What is Jim's basis in the stock received in the exchange?
    b) Jim contributed the rights to a patent he owned to DBJ in exchange for the DBJ stock. The patent was worth $15,000 and Jim's basis in the patent was $8,000. How much gain does Jim recognize on the exchange? What is Jim's basis in the DBJ stock?

47. Carole, Karmen, and Charles formed ABC Corporation. Carole received 60 percent of the stock in ABC Corporation in exchange for appreciated property, Karmen received 30 percent of the stock in ABC Corporation in exchange for legal services, and Charles received 10 percent of the stock in ABC Corporation in exchange for cash. LO 8-2
    a) Must Carole recognize the gain she realized on the transfer of the appreciated property?
    b) Suppose that, instead of receiving the entire 30 percent of the ABC Corporation stock in exchange for legal services, Karmen received 10 percent of the ABC Corporation stock in exchange for her legal services and she received 20 percent of the ABC Corporation stock in exchange for cash (i.e., she transferred both services and property to ABC Corporation). Must Carole recognize gain on the transfer of appreciated property?

48. Camila and Kelly invited Ben to join them in forming Aero, a plane-chartering company, as a corporation. Ben did not want to join at the time and declined their invitation. More than a year later, Ben changed his mind and transferred appreciated property to Aero in exchange for 45 percent of Aero stock. Is Ben required to recognize the realized gain on the transaction? LO 8-2

49. Kristine transferred investment property she has owned for six years to XYZ Corporation in exchange for 40 percent of the corporation's stock (40 shares valued at $160,000) at the time XYZ was incorporated. The property's adjusted tax basis was $90,000 and its fair market value was $160,000. Assume the transfer qualifies under §351. LO 8-2
    a) What gain or loss does Kristine recognize on the transfer?
    b) What is her basis in the stock received in the exchange?
    c) What is Kristine's holding period in the stock?

50. Jasmine transferred land she held as an investment (fair market value $140,000; basis $110,000) in exchange for 50 percent of Kandy Corporation stock (40 shares valued at $100,000) and $40,000 cash in a qualifying §351 exchange. What is the amount of gain Jasmine recognizes on the transfer and its character? LO 8-2

51. Jorge contributed land he held as an investment (fair market value $120,000; adjusted tax basis $55,000) and inventory (fair market value $80,000; adjusted tax basis $75,000) to ABC Corporation in exchange for 50 percent of the ABC stock (50 shares valued at $160,000) and $40,000 cash in a qualifying §351 exchange. LO 8-2
    a) What amount of gain does Jorge recognize on the exchange? What is the character of the gain? What would be Jorge's tax basis in his ABC stock after the exchange?
    b) Assume the same facts except that Jorge received $40,000 of business property from ABC instead of $40,000 cash. What is the amount of gain Jorge would recognize on the exchange and its character?
    c) Assume the original facts in this example except that the inventory had an adjusted tax basis of $90,000 so that Jorge realized a $10,000 loss on the inventory (he still realized a $65,000 gain on the land). How much gain or loss would Jorge recognize on the exchange?

LO 8-2

52. In forming Parts Inc. as a corporation, Candice transferred inventory to Parts Inc. in exchange for 30 percent of the corporation's stock (60 shares valued at $130,000). The inventory's fair market value was $147,000 and its adjusted tax basis to Candice was $75,000. The inventory was subject to a $17,000 liability that Parts Inc. assumed on the transfer. Candice borrowed the $17,000 from the bank (using the inventory as collateral) shortly before transferring the inventory to Parts Inc. and used the loan proceeds to pay for a family vacation to Europe.
    a) Assuming the transfer qualifies under §351 and that the liability has a tax-avoidance purpose, what gain or loss will Candice recognize on the transfer?
    b) Assuming the original facts, what is Candice's basis in the stock received in the exchange?
    c) Suppose the liability does not have a tax-avoidance purpose. What gain will Candice recognize on the transfer?
    d) Assuming the facts in part (c), what is Candice's basis in the stock received in the exchange?

LO 8-2

53. Johanne transferred investment property to S&J Corporation in exchange for 60 percent of the S&J Corporation stock (60 shares valued at $115,000). The property's fair market value was $190,000 and its adjusted tax basis to Johanne was $60,000. The investment property was subject to a $75,000 mortgage that S&J Corporation assumed on the transfer (not treated as boot).
    a) Assuming the transfer qualifies under §351, what is the amount of the gain Johanne must recognize on the exchange and its character?
    b) What is Johanne's tax basis in the S&J stock received in the exchange?
    c) Assume that in addition to the investment property, Johanne transferred inventory with a fair market value of $30,000 and an adjusted tax basis of $20,000 for additional S&J Corporation stock. What is the amount of gain Johanne must recognize on the exchange of the investment property and inventory for stock and its character?
    d) Assuming the facts in (c), what is Johanne's basis in the S&J stock received in the exchange?
    e) Assume the original facts except that the liability assumed by S&J Corporation would give rise to a deduction when paid. What is the amount of gain Johanne must recognize on the exchange and its character?
    f) Assuming the facts in (e), what is Johanne's basis in the S&J stock received in the exchange?

LO 8-2

54. When incorporating Spotfree, a cleaning company, Jayne transferred accounts receivable (fair market value $20,000 and $0 tax basis) and $12,000 of accounts payable from her cash-method sole proprietorship to Spotfree in exchange for Spotfree stock valued at $8,000. Assume the transfer qualifies under §351.
    a) What is the amount of the gain Jayne must recognize on the exchange and its character?
    b) What is Jayne's basis in the Spotfree stock received in the exchange?

LO 8-3
research

55. On January 21, 2020, FB Financial Corporation agreed to acquire Franklin Financial Network, Inc., a Tennessee bank corporation, in a tax-deferred acquisition. The Form 8-K for FB (NYSE ticker FBK, cik 00011649749) describes the transaction and was filed with the SEC on August 18, 2020. You can access the Form 8-K at the SEC's Investor website (www.sec.gov/ix?doc=/Archives/edgar/data/1649749/000119312520222966/d38613d8k.htm). Read "Item 2.01, Completion of Acquisition or Disposition of Assets" and determine which form of merger(s) was used to accomplish the acquisition.

56. On August 1, 2019, Salesforce completed its business combination with Tableau Software, Inc. The Form 8-K for Salesforce (NYSE ticker CRM) describes the transaction and was filed with the SEC on August 1, 2019. You can access the Form 8-K at the SEC's Investor website (www.sec.gov/Archives/edgar/data/1108524/000119312519169276/d764344d8k.htm). Read "Item 1.01, Entry into a Material Definitive Agreement" and determine which form of reorganization was used to complete the acquisition. LO 8-3

57. Amy and Brian were investigating the acquisition of a tax accounting business, Bottom Line Inc. (BLI). As part of their discussions with the sole shareholder of the corporation, Ernesto Young, they examined the company's tax accounting balance sheet. The relevant information is summarized as follows: LO 8-4

	FMV	Adjusted Tax Basis	Appreciation
Cash	$ 10,000	$ 10,000	
Receivables	15,000	15,000	
Building	100,000	50,000	$ 50,000
Land	225,000	75,000	150,000
Total	$350,000	$150,000	$200,000
Payables	$ 18,000	$ 18,000	
Mortgage*	112,000	112,000	
Total	$130,000	$130,000	

*The mortgage is attached to the building and land.

Ernesto was asking for $400,000 for the company. His tax basis in the BLI stock was $100,000. Included in the sales price was an unrecognized customer list valued at $100,000. The unallocated portion of the purchase price ($80,000) will be recorded as goodwill.

a) What amount of gain or loss does BLI recognize if the transaction is structured as a direct asset sale to Amy and Brian? What amount of corporate-level tax does BLI pay as a result of the transaction?

b) What amount of gain or loss does Ernesto recognize if the transaction is structured as a direct asset sale to Amy and Brian, and BLI distributes the after-tax proceeds [computed in question (a)] to Ernesto in liquidation of his stock?

c) What are the tax benefits, if any, to Amy and Brian as a result of structuring the acquisition as a direct asset purchase?

58. Using the same facts in problem 57, assume Ernesto agrees to sell his stock in BLI to Amy and Brian for $400,000. LO 8-4

a) What amount of gain or loss does BLI recognize if the transaction is structured as a stock sale to Amy and Brian? What amount of corporate-level tax does BLI pay as a result of the transaction?

b) What amount of gain or loss does Ernesto recognize if the transaction is structured as a stock sale to Amy and Brian?

c) What are the tax benefits, if any, to Amy and Brian as a result of structuring the acquisition as a stock sale?

59. Rather than purchase BLI directly (as in problems 57 and 58), Amy and Brian will have their corporation, Spartan Tax Services (STS), acquire the business from Ernesto in a tax-deferred Type A merger. Amy and Brian would like Ernesto to continue to run BLI, which he agreed to do if he could obtain an equity interest in STS. As part of the agreement, Amy and Brian propose to pay Ernesto $200,000 plus voting stock in STS worth $200,000. Ernesto will become a 10 percent shareholder in STS after the transaction. LO 8-4

a) Will the continuity of ownership interest (COI) requirements for a straight Type A merger be met? Explain.

b) What amount of gain or loss does BLI recognize if the transaction is structured as a Type A merger? What amount of corporate-level tax does BLI pay as a result of the transaction, assuming a tax rate of 21 percent?

c) What amount of gain or loss does Ernesto recognize if the transaction is structured as a Type A merger?

d) What is Ernesto's tax basis in the STS stock he receives in the exchange?

e) What is the adjusted tax basis of each of the BLI assets held by STS after the merger?

LO 8-4 60. Jakub and Sylvia propose to have their corporation, Wolverine Universal (WU), acquire another corporation, EMU Inc., in a tax-deferred triangular merger using an acquisition subsidiary of WU. The sole shareholder of EMU, Edie Eagle, will receive $250,000 plus $150,000 of WU voting stock in the transaction.

a) Can the transaction be structured as a forward triangular merger? Explain why or why not.

b) Can the transaction be structured as a reverse triangular merger? Explain why or why not.

LO 8-4 61. Jakub and Sylvia propose to have their corporation, Wolverine Universal (WU), acquire another corporation, EMU Inc., in a stock-for-stock Type B acquisition. The sole shareholder of EMU, Edie Eagle, will receive $400,000 of WU voting stock in the transaction. Edie's tax basis in the EMU stock is $100,000.

a) What amount of gain or loss does Edie recognize if the transaction is structured as a stock-for-stock Type B acquisition?

b) What is Edie's tax basis in the WU stock received in the exchange?

c) What is the tax basis of the EMU stock held by WU after the exchange?

LO 8-5 62. Shauna and Danielle decided to liquidate their jointly owned corporation, Woodward Fashions Inc. (WFI). After liquidating its remaining inventory and paying off its remaining liabilities, WFI had the following tax accounting balance sheet:

	FMV	Adjusted Tax Basis	Appreciation
Cash	$200,000	$200,000	
Building	50,000	10,000	$ 40,000
Land	150,000	90,000	60,000
Total	$400,000	$300,000	$100,000

Under the terms of the agreement, Shauna will receive the $200,000 cash in exchange for her 50 percent interest in WFI. Shauna's tax basis in her WFI stock is $50,000. Danielle will receive the building and land in exchange for her 50 percent interest in WFI. Danielle's tax basis in her WFI stock is $100,000. Assume for purposes of this problem that the cash available to distribute to the shareholders has been reduced by any tax paid by the corporation on gain recognized as a result of the liquidation.

a) What amount of gain or loss does WFI recognize in the complete liquidation?

b) What amount of gain or loss does Shauna recognize in the complete liquidation?

c) What amount of gain or loss does Danielle recognize in the complete liquidation?

d) What is Danielle's tax basis in the building and land after the complete liquidation?

LO 8-5 63. Tiffany and Carlos decided to liquidate their jointly owned corporation, Royal Oak Furniture (ROF). After liquidating its remaining inventory and paying off its remaining liabilities, ROF had the following tax accounting balance sheet:

	FMV	Adjusted Tax Basis	Appreciation (Depreciation)
Cash	$200,000	$200,000	
Building	50,000	10,000	$ 40,000
Land	150,000	200,000	(50,000)
Total	$400,000	$410,000	$(10,000)

Under the terms of the agreement, Tiffany will receive the $200,000 cash in exchange for her 50 percent interest in ROF. Tiffany's tax basis in her ROF stock is $50,000. Carlos will receive the building and land in exchange for his 50 percent interest in ROF. His tax basis in the ROF stock is $100,000. Assume for purposes of this problem that the cash available to distribute to the shareholders has been reduced by any tax paid by the corporation on gain recognized as a result of the liquidation.

a) What amount of gain or loss does ROF recognize in the complete liquidation?
b) What amount of gain or loss does Tiffany recognize in the complete liquidation?
c) What amount of gain or loss does Carlos recognize in the complete liquidation?
d) What is Carlos's adjusted tax basis in the building and land after the complete liquidation?

Assume Tiffany owns 40 percent of the ROF stock and Carlos owns 60 percent. Tiffany will receive $160,000 in the liquidation and Carlos will receive the land and building plus $40,000.

e) What amount of gain or loss does ROF recognize in the complete liquidation?
f) What amount of gain or loss does Tiffany recognize in the complete liquidation?
g) What amount of gain or loss does Carlos recognize in the complete liquidation?
h) What is Carlos's adjusted tax basis in the building and land after the complete liquidation?

64. Jefferson Millinery Inc. (JMI) decided to liquidate its wholly owned subsidiary, 8 Miles High Inc. (8MH). 8MH had the following tax accounting balance sheet: LO 8-5

	FMV	Adjusted Tax Basis	Appreciation
Cash	$200,000	$200,000	
Building	50,000	10,000	$ 40,000
Land	150,000	90,000	60,000
Total	$400,000	$300,000	$100,000

a) What amount of gain or loss does 8MH recognize in the complete liquidation?
b) What amount of gain or loss does JMI recognize in the complete liquidation?
c) What is JMI's adjusted tax basis in the building and land after the complete liquidation?

65. Jones Mills Inc. (JMI) decided to liquidate its wholly owned subsidiary, Most Help, Inc. (MH). MH had the following tax accounting balance sheet. LO 8-5

	FMV	Adjusted Tax Basis	Appreciation
Cash	$200,000	$200,000	
Building	50,000	10,000	$40,000
Land	150,000	200,000	(50,000)
Total	$400,000	$410,000	$(10,000)

a) What amount of gain or loss does MH recognize in the complete liquidation?
b) What amount of gain or loss does JMI recognize in the complete liquidation?
c) What is JMI's adjusted tax basis in the building and land after the complete liquidation?

COMPREHENSIVE PROBLEMS

Select problems are available in Connect®.

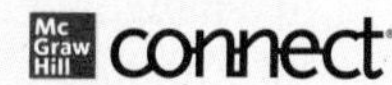

66. Several years ago, your client, Brooks Robertson, started an office cleaning service. His business was very successful, owing much to his legacy as the greatest defensive third baseman in major league history and his nickname, "The Human Vacuum Cleaner." Brooks operated his business as a sole proprietorship and used the cash method of accounting. Brooks was advised by his attorney that it is too risky to operate his business as a sole proprietorship and that he should incorporate to limit his liability. Brooks has come to you for advice on the tax implications of incorporation. His balance sheet is presented below. Under the terms of the incorporation, Brooks would transfer the assets to the corporation in return for 100 percent of the company's common stock. The corporation would also assume the company's liabilities (payables and mortgage).

Balance Sheet		
	Adjusted Tax Basis	**FMV**
Assets		
Accounts receivable	$ 0	$ 5,000
Cleaning equipment (net)	25,000	20,000
Building	50,000	75,000
Land	25,000	50,000
Total assets	$100,000	$150,000
Liabilities		
Accounts payable	$ 0	$ 10,000
Salaries payable	0	5,000
Mortgage on land and building	35,000	35,000
Total liabilities	$ 35,000	$ 50,000

Required:

Answer the following questions:

a) How much gain or loss (on a per-asset basis) does Brooks *realize* on the transfer of each asset to the corporation?

b) How much, if any, gain or loss (on a per-asset basis) does Brooks *recognize*?

c) How much gain or loss, if any, must the corporation recognize on the receipt of the assets of the sole proprietorship in exchange for the corporation's stock?

d) What tax basis does Brooks have in the corporation's stock?

e) What is the corporation's adjusted tax basis in each asset it receives from Brooks?

f) How would you answer the question in part (b) if Brooks had taken back a 10-year note worth $25,000 plus stock worth $75,000 plus the liability assumption?

g) Will Brooks be able to transfer the accounts receivable to the corporation and have the corporation recognize the income when the receivable is collected?

h) Brooks was depreciating the equipment (200 percent declining balance) and building (straight-line) using MACRS when it was held inside the proprietorship. How will the corporation depreciate the equipment and building? Assume Brooks owned the equipment for four years (seven-year property) and the building for six years.

i) Will the corporation be able to deduct the liabilities when paid? Will it matter which accounting method (cash or accrual) the corporation uses?

j) Would you advise Brooks to transfer the land and building to the corporation? What other tax strategy might you suggest to Brooks with respect to the realty?

67. Your client, Midwest Products Inc. (MPI), is a closely held, calendar-year, accrual-method corporation located in Fowlerville, Michigan. MPI has two operating divisions. One division manufactures lawn and garden furniture and decorative objects (furniture division), while the other division manufactures garden tools and hardware (tool division). MPI's single class of voting common stock is owned as follows:

	Shares	Adjusted Tax Basis	FMV
Iris Green	300	$2,000,000	$3,000,000
Rose Ruby	100	1,200,000	1,000,000
Lily White	100	800,000	1,000,000
Totals	500	$4,000,000	$5,000,000

The three shareholders are unrelated.

Outdoor Living Company (OLC), a publicly held, calendar-year corporation doing business in several midwestern states, has approached MPI about acquiring its furniture division. OLC has no interest in acquiring the tool division, however. OLC's management has several strong business reasons for the acquisition, the most important of which is to expand the company's market into Michigan. Iris, Rose, and Lily are amenable to the acquisition, provided it can be accomplished in a tax-deferred manner.

OLC has proposed the following transaction for acquiring MPI's furniture division. On April 30 of this year, OLC will create a whollly owned subsidiary, OLC Acquisition Inc. (OLC-A). OLC will transfer to the subsidiary 60,000 shares of OLC voting common stock and $2,000,000. The current fair market value of the OLC voting stock is $50 per share ($3,000,000 in total). Each of the three MPI shareholders will receive a pro rata amount of OLC stock and cash.

As part of the agreement, MPI will sell the tool division before the acquisition, after which MPI will merge into OLC-A under Michigan and Ohio state laws (a forward triangular merger). Pursuant to the merger agreement, OLC-A will acquire all of MPI's assets, including 100 percent of the cash received from the sale of the tool division ($2,000,000), and will assume all of MPI's liabilities. The cash from the sale of the tool division will be used to modernize and upgrade much of the furniture division's production facilities. OLC's management is convinced that the cash infusion, coupled with new management, will make MPI's furniture business profitable. OLC management has no plans to liquidate OLC-A into OLC at any time subsequent to the merger. After the merger, OLC-A will be renamed Michigan Garden Furniture Inc.

a) Determine whether the proposed transaction meets the requirements to qualify as a tax-deferred forward triangular merger. Consult Rev. Rul. 88-48 and Rev. Rul. 2001-25 in thinking about the premerger sale of the tool division assets.

b) Could the proposed transaction qualify as a reverse triangular merger if OLC-A merged into MPI? If not, how would the transaction have to be restructured to meet the requirements to be a reverse triangular merger?

68. Rex and Felix are the sole shareholders of Dogs and Cats Corporation (DCC). After several years of operation using the accrual method, they decided to liquidate the corporation and operate the business as a partnership. Rex and Felix hired a lawyer to draw up the legal papers to dissolve the corporation, but they need some tax advice from you, their trusted accountant. They are hoping you will find a way for them to liquidate the corporation while minimizing their total income tax liability.

Rex has a tax basis in his shares of $60,000 and Felix has a tax basis in his shares of $30,000. DCC's tax accounting balance sheet at the date of liquidation is as follows:

	Adjusted Tax Basis	FMV
Assets		
Cash	$ 30,000	$ 30,000
Accounts receivable	10,000	10,000
Inventory	10,000	20,000
Equipment	30,000	20,000
Building	15,000	30,000
Land	5,000	40,000
Total assets	$100,000	$ 150,000
Liabilities		
Accounts payable		$ 5,000
Mortgage payable—Building		10,000
Mortgage payable—Land		10,000
Total liabilities		$ 25,000
Shareholders' Equity		
Common stock—Rex (80%)		$ 100,000
Common stock—Felix (20%)		25,000
Total shareholders' equity		$ 125,000

a) Compute the gain or loss recognized by Rex, Felix, and DCC on a complete liquidation of the corporation assuming each shareholder receives a pro rata distribution of the corporation's assets and assumes a pro rata amount of the liabilities.

b) Compute the gain or loss recognized by Rex, Felix, and DCC on a complete liquidation of the corporation assuming that Felix received cash in lieu of his pro rata share of assets and liabilities.

Assume Felix received the accounts receivable and equipment and assumed the accounts payable for the following two questions.

c) Will Felix recognize any income when he collects the accounts receivable?

d) Will Felix be able to take a deduction when he pays the accounts payable?

Assume Rex is a corporate shareholder of DCC for the following two questions.

e) Compute the gain or loss recognized by Rex, Felix, and DCC on a complete liquidation of the corporation assuming each shareholder receives a pro rata distribution of the corporation's assets and assumes a pro rata amount of the liabilities.

f) Compute the gain or loss recognized by Rex, Felix, and DCC on a complete liquidation of the corporation assuming Felix receives $25,000 in cash and Rex receives the remainder of the assets and assumes all of the liabilities.

Assume the equipment was contributed by Rex to DCC in a §351 transaction two months prior to the liquidation. At the time of the contribution, the property's fair market value was $25,000.

g) Would the tax result change if the property was contributed one year ago? Two years ago? Three years ago?

69. Newman Corporation owns 90 shares of SP Corporation. The remaining 10 shares are owned by Kenny (an individual). After several years of operations, Newman decided to liquidate SP Corporation by distributing the assets to Newman and Kenny. The tax basis of Newman's shares is $10,000, and the tax basis of Kenny's shares is $7,000. SP reported the following balance sheet at the date of liquidation:

	Adjusted Tax Basis	FMV
Cash	$12,000	$ 12,000
Accounts receivable	8,000	8,000
Stock investment	2,000	10,000
Land	40,000	70,000
Total assets	$62,000	$100,000
Common stock—Newman (90%)		$ 90,000
Common stock—Kenny (10%)		10,000
Total shareholder equity		$100,000

a) Compute the gain or loss recognized by SP, Newman, and Kenny on a complete liquidation of the corporation, where SP distributes $10,000 of cash to Kenny and the remaining assets to Newman.
b) Compute the gain or loss recognized by SP, Newman, and Kenny on a complete liquidation of the corporation, where SP distributes the stock investment to Kenny and the remaining assets to Newman. Assume that SP's tax rate is zero.
c) What form needs to be filed with the liquidation of SP?

UWorld Roger CPA Review

Sample CPA Exam questions from Roger CPA Review are available in Connect as support for the topics in this text. These Multiple Choice Questions and Task-Based Simulations include expert-written explanations and solutions and provide a starting point for students to become familiar with the content and functionality of the actual CPA Exam.

chapter 9

Forming and Operating Partnerships

Learning Objectives

Upon completing this chapter, you should be able to:

LO 9-1 Describe tax flow-through entities and determine whether they are taxed as partnerships or S corporations.

LO 9-2 Resolve tax issues applicable to partnership formations and other acquisitions of partnership interests, including gain recognition to partners and tax basis for partners and partnerships.

LO 9-3 Determine the appropriate accounting periods and methods for partnerships.

LO 9-4 Calculate and characterize a partnership's ordinary business income or loss and its separately stated items, and demonstrate how to report these items to partners.

LO 9-5 Explain the importance of a partner's tax basis in her partnership interest and the adjustments that affect it.

LO 9-6 Apply the tax-basis, at-risk, passive activity loss, and excess business loss limits to losses from partnerships.

Gyorgy Barna/Shutterstock

Storyline Summary

Nicole Johnson (she/her/hers)

Location:	Salt Lake City, Utah
Status:	Managing member of Color Comfort Sheets LLC
Filing status:	Married to Tom Johnson
Marginal tax rate:	35 percent unless otherwise stated

Sarah Walker (she/her/hers)

Location:	Salt Lake City, Utah
Status:	Managing member of Color Comfort Sheets LLC
Filing status:	Married to Blaine Walker
Marginal tax rate:	24 percent unless otherwise stated

Chanzz Inc.

Location:	Salt Lake City, Utah
Business:	Managing sports franchises
Status:	Nonmanaging member of Color Comfort Sheets LLC
Filing status:	C corporation with a June 30 year-end
Marginal tax rate:	21 percent

In the Business Entities Overview chapter, we introduced you to Nicole Johnson, who decided to turn her sheet-making hobby into a full-time business called Color Comfort Sheets (CCS). In the Business Entities Overview chapter, she organized the business a a C corporation. However, for purposes of this chapter, we assume that in early 2021, Nicole decided to organize her new enterprise as a limited liability company. Once the business was organized, she turned her attention to raising capital for the business from other investors and a bank loan. Although her limited savings would clearly not be enough to get CCS started, she was willing to contribute a parcel of land in the industrial section of town that she had inherited five years ago from her grandfather. Her friend and mentor Sarah Walker offered to contribute time and money to help CCS get off the ground.

With Sarah on board, things seemed to be coming together nicely for Nicole. However, the amount her bank was willing to loan to CCS was not enough to fully capitalize it, and Nicole and Sarah were unable to invest any more cash into the business to make up the shortfall. Hoping to obtain the additional funding they needed, Nicole and Sarah visited Chance Armstrong, a successful local sports-team owner who had a reputation for being willing to take a chance on new ventures. After listening to Nicole and Sarah's proposal, Chance agreed to invest the additional cash needed to fully fund CCS. Rather than use his personal funds, however, Chance planned to have his closely held corporation, Chanzz Inc., invest in CCS. Unlike Nicole and Sarah, who would take an active role in managing CCS, Chanzz Inc., with everyone's agreement, would not play a part in running the company. By the end of March, CCS had cash, land on which to build its manufacturing facility and offices, and owners who were excited and willing to work hard to make it a successful company.

(to be continued . . .)

In this chapter, we review the options for operating a business with multiple owners as a **flow-through entity.** In addition, we explain the basic tax consequences of forming and operating business entities taxed as partnerships by examining the specific tax consequences of forming and operating Color Comfort Sheets as a limited liability company (LLC) taxed as a partnership.

LO 9-1 FLOW-THROUGH ENTITIES OVERVIEW

Income earned by flow-through entities is usually not taxed at the entity level. Instead, the *owners* of flow-through entities are taxed on the share of entity-level income allocated to them. Thus, unlike income earned by **C corporations,** income from flow-through entities is taxed only once—when it "flows through" to owners of these entities.[1]

Flow-through entities with multiple owners are governed by two somewhat different sets of rules in our tax system.[2] Unincorporated business entities such as **general partnerships, limited partnerships,** and **limited liability companies (LLCs)** are treated as partnerships under the rules provided in **Subchapter K** of the Internal Revenue Code unless they elect to be taxed as corporations.[3] In contrast, owners of entities that are taxed as corporations may elect to treat them as flow-through entities under the rules in **Subchapter S.** These corporations are called **S corporations.** See the Business Entities Overview chapter for further detail regarding the tax treatment of different entity types.

There are many similarities and a few important differences between the tax rules for partnerships and S corporations. Our focus in this chapter and the next is on the tax rules for partnerships. Then, in the S Corporations chapter, we turn our attention to the tax treatment of S corporations and their shareholders.

TAXES IN THE REAL WORLD Hedge Funds

We can scarcely read the financial press these days without encountering some reference to hedge funds. Hedge funds are private investment funds that have grown in popularity in recent years; they were estimated to have over $8.24 trillion in assets under management at the end of 2020.[4] According to a report by the Congressional Research Service, most hedge funds are organized as partnerships and their investors are taxed as limited partners.[5]

[1]The "check the box" rules determine how various legal entities should be classified for tax purposes. See the discussion in the Business Entities Overview chapter for a more detailed explanation of these rules.

[2]Unincorporated entities with one individual owner are taxed as *sole proprietorships*. The tax rules relevant to *sole proprietorships* are discussed in the Business Income, Deductions, and Accounting Methods chapter. In addition to sole proprietorships, other specialized forms of flow-through entities such as real estate investment trusts and regulated investment companies are authorized by the Internal Revenue Code. A discussion of these entities is beyond the scope of this chapter.

[3]Publicly traded partnerships may be taxed as corporations. The tax treatment of publicly traded partnerships is more fully developed in the Business Entities Overview chapter.

[4]"Private Fund Statistics, Fourth Calendar Quarter 2020," SEC Division of Investment Management (www.sec.gov), August 4, 2021.

[5]Congressional Research Service, "Taxation of Carried Interest," R46477, July 9, 2020.

Aggregate and Entity Concepts

When Congress adopted Subchapter K in 1954, it had to debate whether to follow an **entity approach** and treat tax partnerships as entities separate from their partners or to apply an **aggregate approach** and treat partnerships simply as an aggregation of the partners' separate interests in the assets and liabilities of the partnership. In the end, Congress decided to apply both concepts in formulating partnership tax law. For instance, one of the most basic tenets of partnership tax law—that partnerships don't pay taxes—reflects the aggregate approach. However, Congress also adopted other partnership tax rules that fall more squarely on the side of the entity approach. For example, the requirement that partnerships, rather than partners, make most tax elections represents the entity concept. Throughout this and the following chapter, we highlight examples where one or the other basic approach underlies a specific partnership tax rule.

PARTNERSHIP FORMATIONS AND ACQUISITIONS OF PARTNERSHIP INTERESTS

LO 9-2

Acquiring Partnership Interests When Partnerships Are Formed

When a partnership is formed, and afterwards, partners may transfer cash, other tangible or intangible property, and services to the partnership in exchange for an equity interest called a **partnership interest.** Partnership interests represent the bundle of economic rights granted to partners under the partnership agreement (or operating agreement for an LLC).[6] These rights include the right to receive a share of the partnership net assets if the partnership is liquidated, called a **capital interest,** and the right or obligation to receive a share of *future* profits or *future* losses, called a **profits interest.**[7] It is quite common for partners contributing property to receive both capital and profits interests in the exchange. Partners who contribute services instead of property frequently receive only profits interests. The distinction between capital and profits interests is important because the tax rules for partnerships are sometimes applied to them differently.

Contributions of Property Partnership formations are similar to other tax-deferred transactions, such as like-kind exchanges and corporate formations, because realized gains and losses from the exchange of contributed property for partnership interests are either fully or partially deferred for tax purposes, depending on the specifics of the transaction. The rationale for permitting taxpayers to defer realized gains or losses on property contributed to partnerships is identical to the rationale for permitting tax deferral when corporations are formed.[8] From a practical perspective, the tax rules in this area allow entrepreneurs to organize their businesses without having to pay taxes. In addition, these rules follow the aggregate theory of partnership taxation because they recognize that partners contributing property to a partnership still own the contributed property, albeit a smaller percentage, because other partners will also indirectly own the contributed property through their partnership interests.

> **THE KEY FACTS**
>
> **Property Contributions**
>
> - Partners don't generally recognize gain or loss when they contribute property to partnerships.
> - Initial tax basis for partners contributing property = Basis of contributed property − Liability securing contributed property + Partnership liabilities allocated to contributing partner + Gain recognized by the contributing partner.
> - Contributing partner's holding period in a partnership interest depends on the type of property contributed.

Gain and loss recognition. As a general rule, neither partnerships nor partners recognize gain or loss when they contribute property to partnerships.[9] This applies to property contributions when a partnership is initially formed and to subsequent property contributions. In this context, the term *property* is defined broadly to include a wide variety of both tangible and intangible assets but not services. The general rule facilitates contributions of property with **built-in gains,** meaning the fair market value is greater than the tax basis, but it

[6]The partnership books reflect partners' shares of the partnership's net assets in their individual capital accounts.

[7]An interest in the future profits or losses of a partnership is customarily referred to as a profits interest rather than a profits/loss interest.

[8]The Corporate Formation, Reorganization, and Liquidation chapter discusses the tax rules related to corporate formations.

[9]§721.

discourages contributions of property with **built-in losses,** meaning the fair market value is less than the tax basis. In fact, partners holding property with built-in losses are usually better off from a tax perspective selling the property, recognizing the associated tax loss, and contributing the cash from the sale to the partnership so it can acquire property elsewhere.

Example 9-1

What if: Assume Nicole contributes land to CCS with a fair market value of $120,000 and a basis of $20,000. What amount of gain or loss would she recognize on the contribution?

Answer: None. Under the general rule for contributions of appreciated property, Nicole will not recognize any of the $100,000 built-in gain from her land.

What if: Suppose Chanzz Inc. contributed equipment with a fair market value of $120,000 and a tax basis of $220,000 to CCS. What amount of the gain or loss would Chanzz Inc. recognize on the contribution?

Answer: None. Chanzz Inc. would not recognize any of the $100,000 built-in loss on the equipment. However, if Chanzz Inc. sold the property to an unrelated person and contributed $120,000 in cash instead of the equipment, it could recognize the $100,000 built-in tax loss. If, for some reason, the equipment Chanzz planned to contribute was uniquely suited to CCS's operations, Chanzz could obtain the same result by selling the equipment to Sarah and contributing the cash received from the sale to CCS. Sarah would then contribute the equipment to CCS.

Partner's initial tax basis in partnership interest. Among other things, partners need to determine the tax basis in their partnership interest to properly compute their taxable gains and losses when they sell their partnership interest. A partner's tax basis in a partnership interest is referred to as that partner's **outside basis.** In contrast, the partnership's basis in its assets is its **inside basis.** As we progress through this and the next chapter, you'll see other important reasons for calculating a partner's outside tax basis.

Calculating a partner's initial tax basis in a partnership interest acquired by contributing property and/or cash is relatively straightforward if the partnership doesn't have any liabilities. The partner will simply have a basis in the partnership interest equivalent to the tax basis of the property and cash contributed.[10] This rule ensures that realized gains and losses on contributed property are merely deferred until either the contributing partner sells the partnership interest or the partnership sells the contributed property.

Example 9-2

What if: Assume that Sarah contributed $120,000 in cash to CCS in exchange for her partnership interest and that CCS had no liabilities. What is Sarah's outside basis in her partnership interest after the contribution?

Answer: Sarah's basis is $120,000, the amount of cash she contributed to CCS.

What if: Assume Nicole contributed land with a fair market value of $120,000 and a basis of $20,000 and CCS had no liabilities. What is Nicole's outside tax basis in CCS?

Answer: Nicole's outside basis in CCS is $20,000, the basis of the property she contributed to CCS. If Nicole immediately sold her interest in CCS for $120,000 (the value of the land she contributed), she would recognize a gain of $100,000—exactly the amount she would have recognized if she had sold the land instead of contributing it to CCS.

When partnerships have liabilities, a few additional steps are required to determine each partners' tax basis in their respective partnership interests. First, all partners must include their shares of the partnership's liabilities in calculating their own outside bases because partnership tax law treats them as each borrowing their own proportionate shares of the partnership's liabilities and then contributing the borrowed cash to acquire their respective partnership interests.[11] You can understand the necessity for this basis increase by recalling that the basis of any purchased asset increases by the amount of any borrowed funds used to purchase it.

Partnerships may have either **recourse liabilities** or **nonrecourse liabilities** or both, and the specific approach to allocating partnership liabilities to individual partners differs

[10] §722.

[11] §752(a).

for each. These two types of liabilities are also frequently referred to in practice as recourse and nonrecourse debt. The fundamental difference between the two types of liabilities lies in the legal responsibility partners assume for ultimately paying the liability. Recourse liabilities are those for which at least one partner has economic risk of loss—that is, they may have to legally satisfy the liability with their own funds. For example, the unsecured liabilities of general partnerships, such as payables, are recourse liabilities because general partners are legally responsible for the liabilities of the partnership. Recourse liabilities are usually allocated to the partners who will ultimately be responsible for paying them.[12] The partners must consider their partner guarantees, other agreements, and state partnership or LLC statutes in making this determination.

Nonrecourse liabilities, in contrast, don't provide creditors the same level of legal recourse against partners. Nonrecourse liabilities such as mortgages are typically secured by real property and only give lenders the right to obtain the secured property in the event the partnership defaults on the liability. Because partners are responsible for paying nonrecourse liabilities only to the extent the partnership generates sufficient profits, such liabilities are generally allocated according to partners' profit-sharing ratios. We discuss an exception to this general rule later in the chapter.[13] The basic rules for allocating recourse and nonrecourse liabilities are summarized in Exhibit 9-1.

EXHIBIT 9-1 Basic Rules for Allocating Partnership Liabilities to Partners

Type of liability	Allocation Method
Recourse	Allocated to partners with ultimate responsibility for paying liability
Nonrecourse	Allocated according to partners' profit-sharing ratios

The legal structure of entities taxed as partnerships also influences the way partners characterize and allocate partnership liabilities. Recourse liabilities in limited partnerships are typically allocated only to general partners because, as we discuss in the Business Entities Overview chapter, limited partners are legally protected from a limited partnership's recourse creditors.[14] Limited partners, however, may be allocated recourse liabilities if they forgo their legal protection by guaranteeing some or all of the recourse liabilities. Similarly, LLC members generally treat LLC liabilities as nonrecourse liabilities because they, like corporate shareholders, are shielded from the LLC's creditors. However, like limited partners, LLC members may treat liabilities as recourse liabilities to the extent they contractually assume risk of loss by agreeing to be legally responsible for paying the liabilities.[15]

Example 9-3

Sarah and Chanzz Inc. initially each contributed $120,000, and CCS borrowed $60,000 from a bank when CCS was formed. The bank required Nicole, Sarah, and Chanzz Inc. to personally guarantee the bank loan. The terms were structured so each of the members would (1) be responsible for a portion of the liability equal to the percentage of CCS losses allocated to each member (one-third each) and (2) have no right of reimbursement from either CCS or the other members of CCS. How much of the $60,000 bank liability was allocated to each member?

(continued on page 9-6)

[12]Reg. §1.752-2. Under the regulations, partners' obligations for paying recourse liabilities are determined by assuming a hypothetical, worst-case scenario where partnership assets (including cash) become worthless, and the resulting losses are then allocated to partners. The partners who legally would be responsible for partnership recourse liabilities under this scenario must be allocated the recourse liabilities. A detailed description of this approach for allocating recourse liabilities is beyond the scope of this book.

[13]Reg. §1.752-3 provides the rules for allocating nonrecourse liabilities, some of which are beyond the scope of this text.

[14]Recall from the Business Entities Overview chapter that, in limited partnerships, general partners' liability is unlimited, whereas limited partners' liability is usually limited to the amount they have invested.

[15]It's actually quite common for banks and other lenders to require LLC members to personally guarantee loans made to LLCs.

Answer: Each member is allocated $20,000. The liability is treated as recourse liability because the members are personally guaranteeing it. Because each guarantees one-third of the liability, the $60,000 liability is allocated equally among them.

What if: Assuming the $60,000 bank loan is CCS's only liability, what is Sarah's outside basis in her CCS interest after taking her share of CCS's bank liability into account?

Answer: Sarah's basis is $140,000 ($120,000 + $20,000) and consists of her cash contribution plus her share of CCS's $60,000 bank loan.

Another step is needed to determine a partner's outside basis when the partnership assumes the *liability of the partner* secured by property the partner contributes to the partnership. Essentially, contributing partners must treat their own liability relief as deemed cash distributions from the partnership that reduce their individual outside bases.[16] If the liability securing the contributed property is a *nonrecourse liability,* the amount of the liability in excess of the basis of the contributed property is allocated solely to the contributing partner, and the remaining liability is allocated to all partners according to their profit-sharing ratios.[17]

Example 9-4

What if: Nicole contributed $10,000 of cash and land with a fair market value of $150,000 and basis of $20,000 to CCS when it was formed. The land was encumbered by a $40,000 nonrecourse mortgage executed three years before. Recalling that CCS already had a $60,000 bank loan before Nicole's contribution, what outside tax bases do Nicole, Sarah, and Chanzz Inc. have in their CCS interests?

Answer: Their outside bases are $36,666, $146,666, and $146,666, respectively. Nicole, Sarah, and Chanzz Inc. would determine their initial tax bases as illustrated in the table below:

Description	Nicole	Sarah	Chanzz Inc.	Explanation
(1) Basis in contributed land	$ 20,000			
(2) Cash contributed	10,000	$ 120,000	$ 120,000	Example 9-3
(3) Members' share of $60,000 recourse bank loan	20,000	20,000	20,000	Example 9-3
(4) Nonrecourse mortgage in excess of basis in contributed land	20,000			Nonrecourse liability > basis is allocated only to Nicole
(5) Remaining nonrecourse mortgage	6,666	6,666	6,666	33.33% × [$40,000 – (4)]
(6) Relief from mortgage liability	(40,000)			
Members' initial outside basis in CCS	**$36,666**	**$146,666**	**$146,666**	Sum of (1) through (6)

Although in many instances partners don't recognize gains on property contributions, there is an important exception to the general rule that may apply when property secured by a liability is contributed to a partnership. In these situations, the contributing partner recognizes gain *only if* the cash deemed to have been received from a partnership

[16]§752(b).

[17]Reg. §1.752-3(a)(2).

distribution exceeds the contributing partner's tax basis in the partnership interest prior to the deemed distribution.[18] Any gain recognized is generally treated as capital gain.[19]

Example 9-5

What if: Assume Sarah and Chanzz Inc., but *not* Nicole, personally guarantee all $100,000 of CCS's liabilities ($60,000 bank loan + $40,000 mortgage on land). How much gain, if any, would Nicole recognize on her contribution to CCS, and what would be the outside basis in her CCS interest?

Answer: Nicole would recognize $10,000 gain and have a $0 outside basis, computed as follows:

Description	Amount	Explanation
(1) Basis in contributed land	$ 20,000	Example 9-4
(2) Cash contributed	10,000	Example 9-4
(3) Nicole's share of liabilities	0	Sarah and Chanzz guaranteed all of CCS's liabilities, including the mortgage on land, thereby turning them into recourse liabilities that should be allocated only to Sarah and Chanzz.
(4) Liability relief	(40,000)	Nicole was relieved of mortgage on land.
(5) Liability relief in excess of basis in contributed land and cash	$(10,000)	Sum of (1) through (4)
(6) Capital gain recognized	10,000	(5) with opposite sign
Nicole's outside tax basis in CCS	**$ 0**	(5) + (6)

Partner's holding period in partnership interest. Because a partnership interest is a capital asset, the partner's holding period in the interest determines whether gains or losses from the disposition of the partnership interest are short-term or long-term capital gains or losses. The length of a partner's holding period for a partnership interest acquired by contributing property depends on the nature of the assets the partner contributed. When partners contribute capital assets or §1231 assets (§1231 assets are assets used in a trade or business and held for more than one year), the holding period of the contributed property "tacks on" to the holding period of the partnership interest.[20] Otherwise, it begins on the day the partnership interest is acquired.

Example 9-6

What if: Assume Nicole contributed only land held for investment that she had held for five years in exchange for her partnership interest. One month after contributing the property, she sold her partnership interest and recognized a capital gain. Is the gain long-term or short-term?

Answer: The gain is long-term because the five-year holding period of the land is tacked on to Nicole's holding period for her partnership interest. She is treated as though she held the partnership interest for five years and one month at the time she sells it.

Partnership's tax basis and holding period in contributed property. Just as partners must determine their outside basis in their partnership interests after contributing property, partnerships must establish their inside basis in the contributed property. Measuring both

[18]§731(a). However, §707(a)(2)(B) provides that deemed cash received from the relief of liability should be considered as sale proceeds rather than a distribution when circumstances indicate the relief of liability constitutes a disguised sale. Further discussion of disguised sale transactions is beyond the scope of this book.

[19]§731(a). This is equivalent to increasing what would have been a negative basis by the recognized gain to arrive at a zero basis. This mechanism ensures that partners will be left with an initial tax basis of zero any time they recognize gain from a property contribution.

[20]Reg. §1.1223-1(a).

the partner's outside basis and the partnership's inside basis is consistent with the entity theory of partnership taxation. To ensure built-in gains and losses on contributed property are ultimately recognized if partnerships sell contributed property, partnerships generally take a tax basis in the property equal to the contributing partner's tax basis in the property at the time of the contribution.[21] Like the tax basis of contributed property, a partnership retains the holding period of contributed assets.[22] In fact, the only tax attribute of contributed property that *doesn't* carry over to the partnership is the character of contributed property. Whether gains or losses on dispositions of contributed property are capital or ordinary usually depends on the manner in which the partnership uses contributed property.[23]

Example 9-7

What if: Assume CCS used the land Nicole contributed in its business for one month and then sold it for its fair market value of $150,000. What are the amount and character of the gain CCS would recognize on the sale? (See Example 9-4.)

Answer: CCS recognizes $130,000 of §1231 gain. Nicole held the land as a capital asset, and her basis in the land prior to the formation of CCS was $20,000. Because CCS receives a carryover basis in the land of $20,000, it recognizes $130,000 of gain when it sells the land for $150,000 ($110,000 in cash and $40,000 of liability relief minus $20,000 basis in land). Also, because CCS used the land in its business and because Nicole's five-year holding period carries over to CCS, the land qualifies as a §1231 asset to CCS, and CCS recognizes §1231 gain when the land is sold. Note that $130,000 of gain is recognized regardless of whether (1) Nicole sells the land, recognizes the gain, and contributes cash to CCS or (2) CCS sells the land shortly after it is contributed and recognizes the gain.

Unlike entities taxed as corporations, entities taxed as partnerships track the equity of their owners using a **capital account** for each owner. The methodology for maintaining owners' capital accounts depends on the approach these entities use to prepare their financial statements. For example, an entity preparing GAAP financial statements would track each owner's share of the equity using **GAAP capital accounts** maintained using generally accepted accounting principles.

In addition to tracking the inside basis of its assets for tax purposes, partnerships not required to produce GAAP financial statements may decide to use tax basis, as well as tax income and expense recognition rules, to maintain their books. Under this approach, a new partnership would prepare its initial balance sheet using the tax basis for its assets. In addition, it would create a **tax capital account** for each new partner, reflecting the tax basis of any property the partner contributed (net of any liability securing the property) and the partner's cash contributions. Because each new partner's tax capital account measures that partner's equity in the partnership using tax accounting rules, it will later be adjusted to include the partner's share of earnings and losses, contributions, and distributions.

Besides satisfying bookkeeping requirements, a partnership's tax basis balance sheet can provide useful tax-related information. For example, we can calculate each partner's share of the inside basis of partnership assets by adding each one's share of liabilities to their respective tax capital accounts. Interestingly, partners who acquire their interests by contributing property (without having to recognize any gain) will have an *outside basis* equal to their share of the partnership's total inside basis. However, as we discuss more fully in the Dispositions of Partnership Interests and Partnership Distributions chapter, partners' inside and outside bases will likely be different when they purchase existing partnership interests.

As another alternative to maintaining GAAP capital accounts, partnerships may also maintain their partners' capital accounts using accounting rules prescribed in the §704(b) tax regulations.[24] In fact, many partnership agreements require the partnership to

[21]§723.

[22]§1223(2).

[23]§702(b). However, §724 provides some important exceptions to this general rule for contributions of certain receivables, inventory, and capital loss property.

[24]Reg. §1.704-1(b)(2)(iv).

maintain **§704(b) capital accounts** for the partners in addition to tax basis capital accounts. Partnerships set up §704(b) capital accounts in much the same way as tax capital accounts, except that §704(b) capital accounts reflect the fair market value rather than the tax basis of contributed assets. Once a partnership begins operations, it can adjust §704(b) capital accounts so they continue to reflect the fair market value of partners' capital interests as accurately as possible. Partnerships may prefer this approach over simply maintaining tax capital accounts because §704(b) capital accounts may be a better measure of the true value of partners' capital interests.

(continued from page 9-2 . . .)

Before forming CCS, its members agreed to keep its books using the tax basis of contributed assets and tax income and expense recognition rules. After receiving the cash and property contributions from its members and borrowing $60,000 from Nicole's bank, CCS prepared the tax basis balance sheet in Exhibit 9-2.

Once CCS was organized in March 2021, it built a small production facility on the commercial land Nicole had contributed, purchased and installed the equipment needed to produce sheets, and hired and trained workers—all before the actual production and marketing of the sheets. After production began on July 1, 2021, CCS started selling its sheets to local specialty bedding stores, but this local market was limited. To create additional demand for their product, the members of CCS decided to draw on Sarah's marketing expertise to develop an advertising campaign targeted at home and garden magazines. All members of CCS agreed Sarah would receive, on December 31, 2021, an additional *capital interest* in CCS with a liquidation value of $20,000 *and* an increase in her profit-and-loss-sharing ratio from 1/3 to 40 percent (leaving the other members each with a 30 percent share of profits and losses), to compensate her for the time she would spend on this additional project. At this point, CCS's liability remained at $100,000.

(to be continued . . .)

EXHIBIT 9-2 **Color Comfort Sheets LLC**

Balance Sheet March 31, 2021		
	Tax Basis	**§704(b)/FMV***
Assets:		
Cash	$310,000	$310,000
Land	20,000	150,000
Totals	$330,000	$460,000
Liabilities and Capital:		
Long-term liabilities	$100,000	$100,000
Capital—Nicole	(10,000)	120,000
Capital—Sarah	120,000	120,000
Capital—Chanzz Inc.	120,000	120,000
Totals	$330,000	$460,000

*The §704(b)/FMV balance sheet is also provided to illustrate the difference in the two approaches to maintaining partners' capital accounts.

Contribution of Services So far we've assumed partners receive their partnership interests in exchange for contributed property. They may also receive partnership interests in exchange for services they provide to the partnership. For example, an attorney or other service provider might accept a partnership interest in lieu of cash payment for services provided as part of a partnership formation. Similarly, ongoing partnerships may compensate their employees with partnership interests to reduce compensation-related cash payments and motivate employees to behave more like owners. Unlike property contributions, services contributed in exchange for partnership interests may create immediate tax consequences to both the contributing partner *and* the partnership, depending on the nature of the partnership interest received.[25]

Capital interests. Partners who receive unrestricted capital interests in exchange for services have the right to receive a share of the partnership's capital if it liquidates.[26] Because capital interests represent a current economic entitlement amenable to measurement, partners receiving capital interests for services must treat the amount they would receive if the partnership were to liquidate, or the **liquidation value**[27] of the capital interest, as ordinary income at the time they receive their interest.[28] In addition, the tax basis in the capital interest received by the **service partner** will equal the amount of ordinary income recognized, and the holding period will begin on the date the service partner receives the capital interest. The partnership either deducts or capitalizes the value of the capital interest, depending on the nature of the services the partner provides. For example, a real estate partnership would capitalize the value of a capital interest compensating a partner for architectural drawings used for a real estate development project.[29] Conversely, the same partnership would deduct the value of a capital interest compensating a partner for providing property management services. When the partnership deducts the value of capital interests used to compensate partners for services provided, it allocates the deduction only to the partners *not* providing services, or **nonservice partners,** because they are the partners transferring capital to the new service partner.[30]

Example 9-8

What if: What are the income and deductions allocated to Sarah and CCS if Sarah receives a capital interest with a $20,000 liquidation value for her marketing services?

Answer: As summarized below, Sarah has $20,000 of ordinary income, and CCS receives a $20,000 ordinary deduction. However, this deduction must be split equally between Nicole and Chanzz Inc. because, in effect, they transferred a portion of their capital to Sarah.

Description	Sarah	Nicole	Chanzz Inc.	Explanation
(1) Ordinary income	$20,000			Liquidation value of capital interest
Ordinary deduction		$(10,000)	$(10,000)	Capital shift from nonservice partners (1) × .5

[25]Rev. Procs. 93-27 and 2001-43. In 2005, the Treasury issued Prop. Reg. §1.704-1, which will change certain elements of current tax law when it is adopted as a final regulation. The concepts and examples discussed here are consistent with both current law and the proposed regulation.

[26]Certain restrictions, such as vesting requirements, may be placed on partnership interests received for services. We limit our discussion here to unrestricted partnership interests.

[27]Proposed regulations in this area also allow the parties in this transaction to use the fair market value of partnership interests as a measure of value rather than liquidation value.

[28]The ordinary income recognized by the service partner is treated as a "guaranteed payment" by the service partner. Guaranteed payments are discussed more fully later in this chapter.

[29]§263(a).

[30]The preamble to Prop. Reg. §1.721-1(b) also applies the varying interest rule of §706(d)(1) to the admission of a service partner.

Profits interests. It's fairly common for partnerships to compensate service partners with profits rather than capital interests. Profits interests are fundamentally different from capital interests because the only economic benefit they provide is the right to share in the future profits of the partnership. Unlike capital interests, profits interests have no liquidation value at the time they are received. Nonservice partners generally prefer to compensate service partners with profits interests because they don't have to forgo their current share of capital in the partnership and may not ever have to give up anything if the partnership is ultimately unprofitable. Thus, a profits interest is more risky than a capital interest from the perspective of the service partner.

The tax rules applicable to profits interests differ from those pertaining to capital interests due to the fundamental economic differences between them. Because there is no immediate liquidation value associated with a profits interest, the service partner typically will not recognize income and the nonservice partners will not be allocated deductions.[31] However, future profits and losses attributable to the profits interest are allocated to the service partner (and away from the nonservice partners) as they are generated. At this point, the service partner will have a capital interest equal to the share of the undistributed profits of the partnership possessed by that service partner. In addition, the partnership must adjust liability allocations based on profit-and-loss-sharing ratios to reflect the service partner's new or increased share of profits and losses.

Example 9-9

What if: Assuming Sarah received only a profits interest for her marketing services instead of the capital interest she received in Example 9-8, what are the tax consequences to Sarah, Nicole, Chanzz Inc., and CCS?[32]

Answer: Sarah would not be required to recognize any income, and CCS would not deduct or capitalize any costs. As CCS generates future profits, Sarah will receive a greater share of the profits than she would have otherwise received, and the other two members will receive a correspondingly smaller share. In addition, Sarah will have a capital interest equal to her share of any undistributed future profits. Finally, with the increase in Sarah's profit-and-loss-sharing ratio from 1/3 to 40 percent, liability allocations among the partners will change to reflect Sarah's additional entitlement. Note that the liability allocations affect each partner's outside basis. The change in liability allocations is reflected in the table below:

Description	Sarah	Nicole	Chanzz Inc.	Explanation
(1) Increase in liability allocation	$5,334			Loss-sharing ratio increases from 1/3 to 40 percent, or 6.67 percent ($60,000 recourse bank loan × 6.67% increase in loss-sharing ratio) + ($20,000 nonrecourse mortgage not allocated solely to Nicole × 6.67% increase in profit-sharing ratio).
Decrease in liability allocation		$(2,667)	$(2,667)	(1) × .5

[31]Rev. Proc. 93-27 indicates that income is recognized by the service partner "if the profits interest relates to a substantially certain and predictable stream of income," if the partner disposes of the profits interest within two years, or "if the profits interest is a limited partnership interest in a 'publicly traded partnership'."

[32]It is common for partnerships to grant a profits interest without an accompanying capital interest.

Example 9-10

When compared with Example 9-9, what are the tax consequences to Sarah, Nicole, and Chanzz Inc. associated with the capital interest (liquidation value of $20,000) and profits interest Sarah receives for her marketing services?

Answer: The tax consequences associated with giving Sarah *both* a capital interest and a profits interest are summarized in the table below:

Description	Sarah	Nicole	Chanzz Inc.	Explanation
(1) Ordinary income	$20,000			Liquidation value of capital interest
Ordinary deduction		$(10,000)	$(10,000)	Capital shift from nonservice partners, (1) × .5
(2) Increase in liability allocation	5,334			Loss-sharing ratio increases from 1/3 to 40 percent, or 6.67 percent [($60,000 recourse bank loan × 6.67% increase in loss-sharing ratio) + ($20,000 nonrecourse mortgage not allocated solely to Nicole × 6.67% increase in profit-sharing ratio)].
Decrease in liability allocation		$(2,667)	$(2,667)	(2) × .5

TAXES IN THE REAL WORLD Carried Interests

In debates over tax policy, politicians in the news have frequently discussed *carried interests* as if everyone within earshot understands the term. However, judging from the public's confusion over the issue, not everyone does.

Carried interests are nothing more than profits interests granted to managing partners and key employees of private equity and other similar investment partnerships. Industry norms suggest that typical carried interests provide managing partners with a 20 percent (and sometimes greater) share of profits when partnership investments are eventually sold. When these investments have been held for the long term, gains from their sale allocated to carried interest holders are often taxed at favorable, long-term capital gains rates. However, under current law portfolio assets in investment funds must be held for more than three years before gains allocated to carried interest holders are eligible for long-term capital gains treatment.[33]

The benefits of these types of carried-interest arrangements are twofold: Any income managing partners receive is deferred until partnership investments are sold, and when the income is finally recognized, it is frequently taxed at favorable, long-term capital gains rates. To some politicians and their supporters, this result seems unfair given that carried interests are economically equivalent to deferred salary and thus should be taxed at higher ordinary rates.

Source: For a more detailed description of carried interests, see "Business Taxation: What Is Carried Interest and How Should It Be Taxed?" in *The Tax Policy Briefing Book* at www.taxpolicycenter.org.

Organizational Expenditures, Start-Up Costs, and Syndication Costs When partnerships are formed, they typically incur some costs that must be capitalized rather than expensed for tax purposes because they will benefit the partnership over its entire lifespan. This category of expenses includes **organizational expenditures** associated with legally forming a partnership (such as attorney and accountant fees), **syndication costs** to promote and sell partnership interests, and **start-up costs** that would normally be deducted as business expenses except that they are incurred before the start of active trade or business. However, with the exception of syndication costs,[34] which are not deductible, the partnership may elect to amortize these costs. The Property Acquisition and Cost

[33]§1061(a).

[34]Syndication costs are typically incurred by partnerships whose interests are marketed to the public. Thus, syndication expenses are unusual in closely held partnerships.

Recovery chapter provides additional detail about immediately expensing or amortizing business organizational expenditures and start-up costs.

Acquisitions of Partnership Interests after Formation

After a partnership has been formed and begins operating, new or existing partners can acquire partnership interests in exchange for contributing property and/or services, in which case the tax rules discussed above in the context of forming a partnership still apply. Or new partners may purchase partnership interests from existing partners. Partners who purchase their partnership interests don't have to be concerned with recognizing taxable income when they receive their interests. However, in each of these scenarios, they must still determine the initial tax basis and holding period in their partnership interests. Exhibit 9-3 summarizes the rules for determining the outside basis of partnership interests when they are received in exchange for contributed property or services or when they are purchased.

THE KEY FACTS

Acquisitions of Partnership Interests

- Contributing partner's tax basis and holding period in contributed property carry over to the partnership.
- If service partners report ordinary income, the partnership either expenses or capitalizes the amount depending on the nature of the services provided.
- The tax basis of a purchased partnership interest = Purchase price + Partnership liability allocated to partner, and the holding period begins on the purchase date.

EXHIBIT 9-3 Summary of Partner's Outside Basis and Holding Period by Acquisition Method

Acquisition Method	Outside Basis	Holding Period
Contribute Property	= Basis of contributed property − Liability relief + Liability allocation + Gain recognized.	If property contributed is a capital or §1231 asset, holding period includes holding period of contributed property; otherwise begins on date interest received.
Contribute Services	= Liquidation value of capital interest + Liability allocation. Equals liability allocation if only profits interest received.	Begins on date interest received.
Purchase	= Cost basis[35] + Liability allocation.	Begins on date interest purchased.

Example 9-11

CCS had overall operating losses from July 1, 2021 (when it began operating), through June 30, 2022. Because of the losses, Chanzz Inc. decided to sell its 30 percent interest in CCS (Chanzz Inc.'s original 1/3 interest in CCS was reduced to 30 percent at the end of 2021 when Sarah's interest was increased to compensate her for services provided) on June 30, 2022, to Greg Randall. Like Chanzz Inc., Greg will be a nonmanaging member and will guarantee a portion of CCS liabilities. Greg paid Chanzz Inc. $100,000 for his interest in CCS and was allocated a 30 percent share of CCS liabilities (CCS's liabilities remained at $100,000 on June 30, 2022). What are Greg's outside basis and holding period in CCS?

Answer: Greg's outside basis of $124,000 in CCS includes the $100,000 amount he paid to purchase the interest plus his $24,000 share of CCS's total $80,000 liabilities available to be allocated to all members ($60,000 recourse bank loan and $20,000 of nonrecourse mortgage remaining after allocating the first $20,000 to Nicole). Greg's holding period in his CCS interest begins on June 30, 2022.

PARTNERSHIP ACCOUNTING: TAX ELECTIONS, ACCOUNTING PERIODS, AND ACCOUNTING METHODS

LO 9-3

A newly formed partnership must adopt its required tax year-end and decide whether it intends to use either the cash or accrual method as its overall method of accounting. As discussed in the Business Income, Deductions, and Accounting Methods chapter, an entity's tax year-end determines the cutoff date for including income and deductions in a particular tax return, and its overall accounting method determines when income and

[35]§742.

deductions are recognized for tax purposes. Partnerships must frequently make other tax-related elections as well.

Tax Elections

New partnerships determine their accounting periods and make tax elections, including the election of overall accounting method, the election to expense a portion of organizational expenditures and start-up costs, and the election to expense tangible personal property. Who formally makes all these elections? In theory, either the partnership or the partners themselves could do so. However, with just a few exceptions, the partnership tax rules rely on the entity theory of partnership taxation and make the partnership responsible for tax elections.[36] In many instances, the partnership makes elections in conjunction with filing its annual tax return. For example, it selects an accounting method and determines whether to elect to amortize organizational expenditures or start-up costs by simply applying its elections in calculating ordinary business income on its first return. The partnership makes other tax elections by filing a separate document with the IRS, such as Form 3115, when it elects to change an accounting method.

Example 9-12

How will CCS elect its overall accounting method after it begins operations?

Answer: Nicole, Sarah, and Chanzz Inc. may jointly decide on an overall accounting method or, in their LLC operating agreement, they may appoint one of the members to be responsible for making this and other tax elections. Once they have made this decision, CCS makes the election by simply using the chosen accounting method when preparing its first return.

THE KEY FACTS

Partnership Accounting: Tax Elections, Accounting Periods, and Methods

- Partnerships are responsible for making most tax elections.
- A partnership's taxable year is the majority interest taxable year, the common taxable year of the principal partners, or the taxable year providing the least aggregate deferral to the partners.
- Partnerships are generally eligible to use the cash method for 2022 unless they have corporate partners and average gross receipts over the three prior years of greater than $27 million (this number is indexed for inflation).

Accounting Periods

Required Year-Ends Because partners include their share of partnership income or loss in their taxable year ending with the partnership taxable year, or within which the partnership taxable year falls, any partnership tax year other than that of the partners will result in some degree of tax deferral for some or all of the partners.[37] Exhibit 9-4 reflects the tax deferral a partner with a calendar year-end would receive if the corresponding partnership had a January 31 year-end.

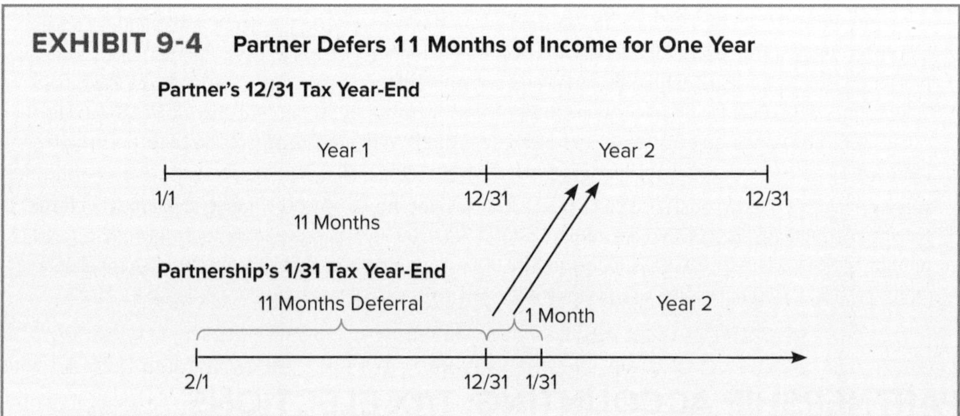

The partner reports the partnership's year 1 income earned from February 1 until January 31 in the partner's second calendar year (i.e., the year within which the partnership's January 31 year-end falls). As a result, the partner defers reporting for one year the

[36]§703(b). Certain elections are made at the partner level.

[37]§706(a).

11 months of income allocated from February 1 through December 31 of that partner's first calendar year.

The government's desire to reduce the aggregate tax deferral of partners (i.e., the sum of the deferrals for each individual partner) provides the underlying rationale behind the rules requiring certain partnership taxable year-ends. Partnerships are generally required to use one of three possible tax year-ends and, under certain circumstances, are allowed other alternative year-ends.[38] As illustrated in Exhibit 9-5, they must follow a series of steps to determine the appropriate year-end.

EXHIBIT 9-5 **Steps to Determine a Partnership's Year-End**

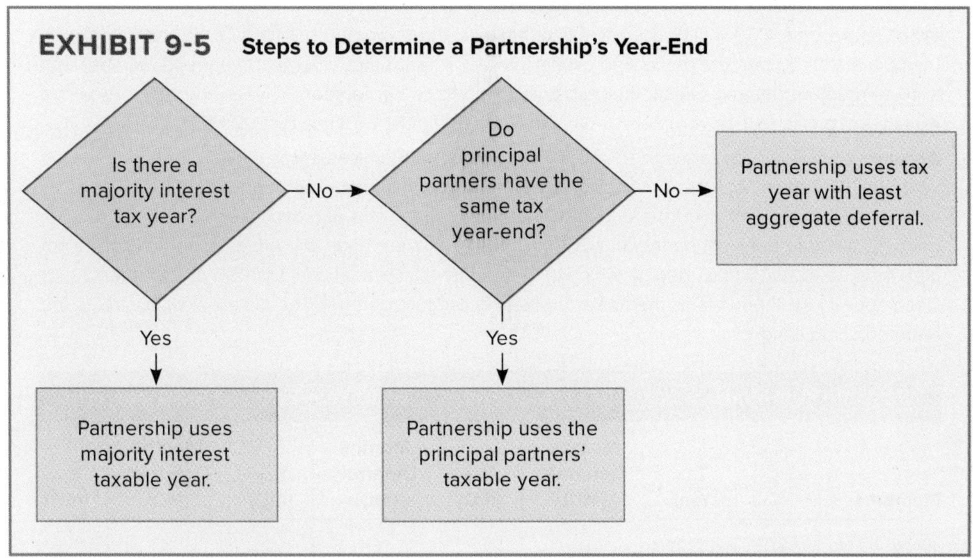

The first potential required tax year is the **majority interest taxable year,** the taxable year of one or more partners who together own more than 50 percent of the capital and profits interests in the partnership.[39] However, there may not be a majority interest taxable year when several partners have different year-ends. For example, if a partnership has two partners with 50 percent capital and profits interests and each has a different tax year, there will be no majority interest taxable year. In that case, the partnership next applies the principal partners test to determine its year-end.

Under the **principal partners** test, the required tax year is the taxable year the principal partners *all* have in common. For this purpose, principal partners are those who have a 5 percent or more interest in the partnership profits and capital.[40] Consider a partnership with two calendar-year partners, each with a 20 percent capital and profits interest, and 30 additional fiscal year-end partners, each with less than a 5 percent capital and profits interest. In this scenario, the required taxable year of the partnership is a calendar year, corresponding with the taxable year of the partnership's only two principal partners. If, as in the earlier example, the partnership had two 50 percent capital and profits partners with different tax years, it would then use the tax year providing the "least aggregate deferral" to the partners, unless it is eligible to elect an alternative year-end.[41]

The tax year with the **least aggregate deferral** is the one among the tax years of the partners that provides the partner group as a whole with the smallest amount of aggregate tax deferral. Under this approach, the total tax deferral is measured under each potential tax year mathematically by weighting each partner's months of deferral under the potential tax year by each partner's *profits* percentage and then summing the weighted months of deferral for all the partners.

[38]See Rev. Proc. 2002-38 and §444 for additional information concerning these options.

[39]§706(b)(1)(B)(i).

[40]§706(b)(3).

[41]Reg. §1.706-1(b)(3).

Example 9-13

When CCS began operating in 2021, it had two calendar-year-end members, Nicole and Sarah, and one member with a June 30 year-end, Chanzz Inc. What tax year-end must CCS use for 2021?

Answer: CCS must use the calendar year as its taxable year unless it was eligible for an alternative year-end. Although Chanzz Inc. had a June 30 taxable year, Nicole and Sarah both had calendar year-ends. Because Nicole and Sarah each initially owns 1/3 of the capital and profits of CCS, and together they own greater than 50 percent of the profits and capital of CCS, the calendar year is the required taxable year for CCS because it is the majority interest taxable year.

What if: Assume CCS initially began operating with three members: Nicole, a calendar-year-end member with a 20 percent profits and capital interest; Chanzz Inc., a June 30 year-end member with a 40 percent profits and capital interest; and Telle Inc., a September 30 year-end member with a 40 percent profits and capital interest. What tax year-end must CCS use for 2021?

Answer: CCS would be required to use a June 30 year-end unless it was eligible for an alternative year-end. CCS does not have a majority interest taxable year because no partner or group of partners with the same year-end owns more than 50 percent of the profits and capital interests in CCS. Also, because all three principal partners in CCS have different year-ends, the principal partner test is not met. As a result, CCS must decide which of three potential year-ends—June 30, September 30, or December 31—will provide its members the least aggregate deferral. The table below illustrates the required computations:

Possible Year-Ends			12/31 Year-End		6/30 Year-End		9/30 Year-End	
Members	**%**	**Tax Year**	**Months Deferral* (MD)**	**% × (MD)**	**Months Deferral* (MD)**	**% × (MD)**	**Months Deferral* (MD)**	**% × (MD)**
Nicole	20	12/31	0	0	6	1.2	3	.6
Chanzz Inc.	40	6/30	6	2.4	0	0	9	3.6
Telle Inc.	40	9/30	9	3.6	3	1.2	0	0
Total aggregate deferral				6		**2.4**		4.2

*Months deferral equals number of months between the proposed year-end and partner's year-end.

June 30 is the required taxable year-end because it provides members with the least aggregate tax deferral (2.4 is less than 6 and 4.2).

Accounting Methods

Although partnerships may use the accrual method freely, they may not use the cash method under certain conditions because it facilitates the deferral of income and acceleration of deductions. For example, partnerships with C corporation partners are generally not eligible to use the cash method[42] for 2022 unless their average annual gross receipts for the three prior taxable years do not exceed $27 million (this number is indexed for inflation) and they otherwise qualify.[43] Entities generally eligible to use the overall cash method of accounting must nevertheless use the accrual method to account for the purchase and sale of inventory in 2022 unless they have average annual gross receipts over the prior three years of $27 million (this number is indexed for inflation) or less.

[42]§448(a)(2). In addition, §448(a)(3) prohibits partnerships classified as "tax shelters" from electing the cash method.

[43]§448(b)(3). If a partnership has not been in existence for at least three years, this test is applied based on the number of years it has been in existence. See the Business Income, Deductions, and Accounting Methods chapter for more details on the gross receipts test.

Example 9-14

When CCS began operations, its members decided it should elect the cash method of accounting if eligible to do so. Would having a corporate member—Chanzz Inc.—prevent it from electing the cash method?

Answer: Not necessarily. Although Chanzz Inc. was a founding member of CCS, its ownership share would not affect the partnership's eligibility to use the cash method unless CCS's average annual gross receipts were to exceed the threshold that would require it to use the accrual method.

REPORTING THE RESULTS OF PARTNERSHIP OPERATIONS

LO 9-4

The first section in the Internal Revenue Code dealing with partnerships states emphatically that partnerships are flow-through entities: "A partnership as such shall not be subject to the income tax imposed by this chapter. Persons carrying on business as partners shall be liable for income tax only in their separate or individual capacities."[44] This feature of partnership taxation explains why entities taxed as partnerships are sometimes favored over entities taxed as corporations, whose shareholders are subject to a double tax—once when the income is earned and again when it is distributed to shareholders as a dividend or when the shares are sold.

TAXES IN THE REAL WORLD Publicly Traded Partnerships

Would it surprise you to know that many private equity firms are organized as partnerships for tax purposes? Even more surprising may be the fact that some well-known private equity funds—including Oaktree Capital Group and Oz Management—are publicly traded. Publicly traded firms are typically taxed as corporations even if they are legally structured as partnerships or, in the case of these private equity firms, as limited partnerships. However, relying on a provision in the tax code, these private equity funds are able to maintain their tax status as partnerships after their public offerings.[45] Thus, investors purchasing shares in these funds are buying investments that are subject to only one level of taxation but, like shares in a corporation, can be readily traded in a public securities market.

Ordinary Business Income (Loss) and Separately Stated Items

Although partnerships are not taxpaying entities, they are required to file information returns annually. They also distribute information to each partner detailing the amount *and* character of items of income and loss flowing through the partnership.[46] Partners must report these income and loss items on their tax returns even if they don't receive cash distributions from the partnership during the year.

When gathering this information for their partners, partnerships must determine each partner's share of **ordinary business income (loss)** and **separately stated items.** Partnership ordinary business income (loss) is all partnership income (loss) exclusive of any separately stated items of income (loss). Separately stated items share one common characteristic—they are treated differently from a partner's share of ordinary business income (loss) for tax purposes. To better understand why certain items must be separately disclosed to partners, consider how two particular separately stated items, dividend income and net capital losses, might affect an individual partner's tax liability. Qualified dividend income allocated to individual partners is taxed at either a 0 percent, 15 percent,

THE KEY FACTS

Reporting the Results of Partnership Operations

- Partnerships file annual information returns reporting their ordinary business income (loss) and separately stated items.
- Ordinary business income (loss) = Partnership overall income or loss exclusive of separately stated items.
- Separately stated items change partners' tax liabilities according to each partner's unique situation (e.g., tax bracket, capital gains/losses, etc.).

[44]§701.

[45]§7704.

[46]Other items, such as tax credits, may also flow through the partnership to partners.

or 20 percent rate, depending on individual partners' level of taxable income.[47] In a similar vein, individual partners without capital gains during the year may deduct up to $3,000 in net capital loss (i.e., capital losses in excess of capital gains) against their ordinary income, while other individual partners with capital gains may deduct more.[48] If a partnership's dividends and capital losses were simply buried in the computation of its overall income or loss for the year, the partner would be unable to apply these specific tax rules to their unique situation and determine their correct tax liability.

The tax code specifically enumerates several common separately stated items, including short-term capital gains and losses, long-term capital gains and losses, §1231 gains and losses, charitable contributions, and dividends.[49] Many more items are considered under regulations issued by the Treasury Department.[50] Exhibit 9-6 lists several other common separately stated items.

EXHIBIT 9-6 Common Separately Stated Items

- Interest income
- Guaranteed payments
- Net earnings (loss) from self-employment
- Tax-exempt income
- Net rental real estate income
- Investment interest expense
- Royalties
- §179 deduction

Example 9-15

After constructing a building and purchasing equipment in its first year of operations ending on December 31, 2021, CCS invested $15,000 of its remaining idle cash in stocks and bonds. CCS's books reflected an overall loss (computed on a tax basis) for the year of $80,000. Included in the $80,000 loss were $2,100 of dividend income, $1,200 of short-term capital gains, and a $20,000 deduction for the capital interest transferred to Sarah at the end of 2021 (see Example 9-10). How much ordinary business loss and what separately stated items are allocated to the CCS members for the taxable year ended December 31, 2021?

Answer: As reflected in the table below, CCS has $63,300 of ordinary business loss. In addition, it has $2,100 of dividend income, $1,200 in short-term capital gains, and $20,000 of ordinary deduction (related to the capital interest Sarah received) that are separately stated items. To Nicole, Sarah, and Chanzz Inc., CCS would report $21,100 of ordinary business loss, $700 of dividend income, and $400 of short-term capital gain. In addition, CCS would report $20,000 of ordinary income to Sarah for the capital interest she received, and a $10,000 deduction to Nicole and Chanzz Inc. reflecting the amount of partnership capital they relinquished.

Description	CCS	Nicole $\left(\frac{1}{3}\right)$	Sarah $\left(\frac{1}{3}\right)$	Chanzz Inc. $\left(\frac{1}{3}\right)$
2021 overall net tax loss	$(80,000)			
Less:				
Dividends	2,100			
Short-term capital gains	1,200			
Ordinary deduction for Sarah's capital interest	(20,000)			
Ordinary business loss	$(63,300)	$(21,100)	$(21,100)	$(21,100)
Separately stated Items:				
Dividends	2,100	700	700	700
Short-term capital gains	1,200	400	400	400
Ordinary income for capital interest to Sarah	20,000		20,000	
Ordinary deduction for capital interest to Sarah	(20,000)	(10,000)		(10,000)

[47]§1(h).

[48]§1211.

[49]§702.

[50]Reg. §1.702-1(a).

Nicole and Sarah will treat their shares of CCS's ordinary business loss as an *ordinary* loss and include it along with their shares of dividend income and short-term capital gain in their individual tax returns for the year.[51] Chanzz Inc. will also include its share of these items in its annual tax return. But because Chanzz is a C corporation, different tax rules apply to its share of dividend income and short-term capital gains. For example, Chanzz will be entitled to the 50 percent dividends-received deduction, while Nicole and Sarah will pay tax on their share of dividend income at individual capital gains rates.

Notice that the character of separately stated items is determined at the partnership level rather than at the partner level.[52] This treatment reflects the entity theory.

Example 9-16

What if: Assume Chanzz Inc. is an investments dealer rather than a sports franchise operator. How would Chanzz Inc. classify its share of the $1,200 gain from the securities sold by CCS during 2021?

Answer: Chanzz Inc. would classify its share of the $1,200 as short-term capital gains. Because the securities CCS sold were capital assets to CCS, the gain on the sale is a capital gain even though the securities would be inventory (an ordinary asset) if sold by Chanzz Inc. That is, we determine the character of the income at the partnership level, not the partner level.

Guaranteed Payments In addition to dividends, capital gains and losses, and other routine separately stated items, **guaranteed payments** are also a very common separately stated item for partners who receive them. As their name suggests, guaranteed payments are fixed amounts paid to partners regardless of whether the partnership shows a profit or loss for the year.[53] We can think of them—and some partnerships treat them—as economically equivalent to cash salary payments made to partners for services provided.[54] Specifically, they are typically deducted in computing a partnership's ordinary income or loss for the year. Though included in a partnership's ordinary business income (loss) computation, guaranteed payments must, nevertheless, be separately stated to the partners who receive them. This separate reporting serves the same purpose as providing W-2 forms to employees. Because guaranteed payments are similar to salary payments, partners treat them as ordinary income.

(continued from page 9-9. . .)

Because Sarah received an additional capital interest for marketing services she provided at the end of 2021, she held a 40 percent capital and profits interest, and Nicole and Chanzz Inc. each held a 30 percent capital and profits interest at the beginning of 2022. After Sarah's initial work in formulating a marketing strategy in 2021, Nicole suggested they hire a permanent employee to oversee product marketing. However, because they were unable to find a suitable candidate, Sarah continued to shoulder the product marketing responsibilities in addition to her normal role as a managing member of CCS. To compensate Sarah for her additional workload, all members of CCS agreed that CCS would provide Sarah a $10,000 guaranteed payment for her marketing efforts in 2022. Exhibit 9-7 provides CCS's income statement for 2022. ■

[51]Nicole and Sarah would report their share of ordinary business loss on Schedule E, their share of dividend income on Schedule B, and their share of short-term capital gain on Schedule D of Form 1040.

[52]§702(b).

[53]§707(c).

[54]Fringe benefits that partners receive for services provided such as medical insurance and group-term life insurance are also treated as guaranteed payments. In addition to compensating partners for services provided, guaranteed payments are also made to partners for the use of capital.

EXHIBIT 9-7 Color Comfort Sheets LLC

Income Statement December 31, 2022	
Sales revenue	$ 40,000
Cost of goods sold	(20,000)
Employee wages	(50,000)
Depreciation expense	(18,000)
Guaranteed payments	(10,000)
Miscellaneous expenses	(2,800)
Dividend income	500
Long-term capital gains	300
Overall net loss	$(60,000)

Example 9-17

Given CCS's operating results for 2022 presented in Exhibit 9-7, how much ordinary business loss and what separately stated items will it report on its return for the year? How will it allocate these amounts to its members?

Answer: The table below displays CCS's ordinary business loss and separately stated items and the allocation of these amounts to CCS's members:

Description	CCS	Nicole 30%	Sarah 40%	Chanzz Inc. 30% × 6/12*	Greg 30% × 6/12*
Sales revenue	$ 40,000				
Cost of goods sold	(20,000)				
Employee wages	(50,000)				
Depreciation expense	(18,000)				
Guaranteed payment to Sarah	(10,000)				
Miscellaneous expenses	(2,800)				
Ordinary business loss	$(60,800)	$(18,240)	$(24,320)	$(9,120)	$(9,120)
Separately stated to partners					
Dividends	500	150	200	75	75
Long-term capital gains	300	90	120	45	45
Guaranteed payment			10,000		

*As we noted in Example 9-11, Chanzz Inc. sold its 30 percent interest in CCS to Greg Randall on June 30, 2021. Therefore, the items related to Chanzz Inc.'s original 30 percent interest must be allocated between Chanzz Inc. and Greg Randall.[55]

THE KEY FACTS

Guaranteed Payments and Self-Employment Income

- Guaranteed payments are separately stated items, are treated as ordinary income by partners receiving them, and are either capitalized or expensed by partnerships.
- Guaranteed payments for services are always treated as self-employment income.
- Shares of ordinary business income (loss) are always treated as self-employment income (loss) by general partners and never treated as self-employment income (loss) by limited partners.
- Shares of ordinary business income (loss) may or may not be treated by LLC members as self-employment income (loss), depending on the extent of their involvement with the LLC.

Self-Employment Tax Individual partners, like sole proprietors, may be responsible for paying **self-employment taxes** in addition to income taxes on their share of business income from partnerships.[56] The degree to which partners are responsible for self-employment taxes depends on their legal status as general partners, limited partners, or LLC members and their business activities. General partners report guaranteed payments for services they provide and their share of ordinary business income (loss) as self-employment income (loss) because they are actively involved in managing the partnership. Limited partners, on the other hand, are generally not allowed under state law to participate in the management of limited partnerships. Therefore, their share of ordinary business income (loss) is conceptually more like investment income than trade or business income. As a result, ordinary business income (loss) allocated to limited partners is not subject to

[55]We assume here that the items are allocated based on the number of months the interest was held. See the Dispositions of Partnership Interests and Partnership Distributions chapter for additional detail regarding methods to account for partners' varying interests in a partnership when a partnership interest is sold.

[56]The Business Entities Overview chapter more fully discusses earned income and related self-employment taxes.

self-employment tax. However, if limited partners receive guaranteed payments for services provided to the partnership, they treat those payments as self-employment income.

Because LLC members may be either managing or nonmanaging members, the approach to taxing their share of ordinary business income (loss) for self-employment tax purposes does depend to some degree on their level of involvement in the LLC.[57] Tax rules in this area were developed before LLCs became popular, however, so the IRS has not issued any authoritative guidance to help LLCs decide whether to characterize their members' shares of ordinary business income (loss) as self-employment income (loss). However, a proposed regulation issued by the Treasury and later withdrawn can assist partnerships in drawing the line between aggressive and conservative positions in this area.[58] The proposed regulation provides that LLC members who have personal liability for the liabilities of the LLC by reason of being an LLC member, who have authority to contract on behalf of the LLC, *or* who participate more than 500 hours in the LLC's trade or business during the taxable year should be classified as general partners when applying the self-employment tax rules.

Historically, the lack of authoritative guidance in this area has resulted in a predictable diversity of practice. Indeed, some aggressive taxpayers and their advisers have ignored the proposed regulation entirely and claimed that managing members of LLCs or members providing significant services to their LLCs are similar to limited partners and shouldn't have to pay self-employment taxes at all. This approach has been invalidated by a string of court decisions.[59] These decisions follow the spirit of the proposed regulation in that they provide that LLC members either with management control or that actively participate in the trade or business of an LLC should be treated as general partners for self-employment tax purposes and be subject to self-employment tax on their share of ordinary business income.[60] The same criteria are used to determine if a loss is a self employment loss. If it is, it offsets other sources of self employment income in determining self employment tax.

Example 9-18

For *2022*, should CCS classify Sarah's $10,000 guaranteed payment as self-employment income?

Answer: Yes. The law is clear with respect to guaranteed payments to LLC members—they are always treated as self-employment income.

Using the proposed regulation, will CCS classify Sarah's $24,320 (see Example 9-17) share of ordinary business loss for *2022* as a self-employment loss?

Answer: Yes. Under the proposed regulations, an LLC member who has personal liability for LLC liabilities or the ability to contract on behalf of the LLC, or who spends more than 500 hours participating in the business of the LLC, is classified as a general partner when applying the self-employment tax rules. Given Sarah's status as a managing member of CCS, at least one but probably all three criteria for classifying her share of CCS's ordinary business loss as self-employment loss will apply. Although these rules have not been finalized and are therefore not authoritative, the IRS would likely follow them because they represent its current thinking on the matter. Applying the law this way, CCS will report a $14,320 self-employment loss ($24,320 share of ordinary business loss + $10,000 guaranteed payment) as a separately stated item to Sarah so she can properly compute her self-employment tax liability on her individual return. If Sarah has no other sources of self-employment income, Sarah would not be liable for self-employment tax. Otherwise, she would be able to use her self-employment loss from CCS to reduce or eliminate her self-employment income from other sources.

Example 9-19

Using the proposed regulation, will CCS classify Nicole's $18,240 (see Example 9-17) share of ordinary business loss for *2022* as a self employment loss?

Answer: Yes. Because Nicole, like Sarah, is involved in the day-to-day management of CCS, it will classify her entire share of ordinary business loss as a self employment loss, consistent with its

(continued on page 9-22)

[57]Guaranteed payments to LLC members are clearly subject to self-employment tax because they are similar to salary payments.

[58]Prop. Reg. §1.1402(a)-2.

[59]See *Renkemeyer, Campbell & Weaver, LLP v. Comm'r,* 136 TC 137 (2011); *Riether v. United States,* 919 F. Supp. 2d 1140 (D.N.M. 2012); *Castigliola,* TC Memo 2017-62.

[60]Of course, these cases also suggest that the opposite should also be true: LLC members without management control or that don't provide significant services should be treated as limited partners for self-employment tax purposes.

classification of Sarah's share of ordinary business loss, and report the amount as a separately stated item to Nicole.

Under the proposed regulation, will CCS treat Greg's $9,120 share of ordinary business loss for *2022* as a self employment loss?

Answer: Yes. CCS will treat Greg's share of ordinary business loss as a self employment loss because he has guaranteed a portion of CCS's liabilities. CCS's total self-employment loss is $41,680, consisting of Sarah's $14,320 self-employment loss (an amount that includes Sarah's share of ordinary business loss offset by her guaranteed payment), Nicole's $18,240 self-employment loss, and Greg's $9,120 self-employment loss.

Limitation on Business Interest Expense As explained in the Business Income, Deductions, and Accounting Methods chapter, the deduction for business interest expense is limited to the sum of (1) business interest income and (2) 30 percent of the adjusted taxable income of the taxpayer for the taxable year.[61] For entities taxed as partnerships, this limitation is applied at the partnership level first. Under this approach, any business interest expense of a partnership that is not disallowed due to the limitation is taken into account in determining the partnership's ordinary business income or loss for the year.

In contrast, disallowed business interest expense is allocated and separately stated to partners, reducing the basis in their partnership interests.[62] Subsequently, the disallowed business interest expense is carried forward indefinitely at the partner level until the partnership has excess business interest expense limitation to allocate to the partners. This will occur whenever the partnership's business interest expense limitation exceeds the partnership's business interest expense in a given year. Generally, partners may deduct their carried-forward disallowed interest expense from a given partnership in any future year to the extent they have excess business interest expense limitation (the adjusted taxable income equivalent is separately stated to partners[63]) from the same partnership.

The limitation on business interest expense does not apply to partnerships in 2022 with average annual gross receipts for the prior three years that do not exceed $27 million (indexed for inflation). As a result, the limitation on business interest expense will apply to only a relatively small number of large partnerships.

Deduction for Qualified Business Income As we more fully discuss in the Business Entities Overview chapter, noncorporate owners of flow-through entities, including partnerships, may deduct 20 percent of the qualified business income allocated to them from the entity subject to certain limitations. Qualified business income is the net business income from a qualified trade or business conducted in the United States. In a partnership setting, qualified business income would typically not include a partnership's ordinary business income from most service-related businesses and would also not include a partnership's investment income such as capital gains, dividends, and investment interest income.[64] Further, guaranteed payments received by partners for services provided to the partnership are, by definition, not considered to be qualified business income.

[61]§163(j).

[62]§163(j)(4).

[63]Under §163(j)(4)(A)(ii), a partner's share of adjusted taxable income is increased by the partner's distributive share of the partnership's "excess taxable income." Per §163(j)(4)(C), excess taxable income is mathematically equivalent to the amount of a partnership's excess business interest expense limitation divided by 30 percent.

[64]Section 199A(d)(2) excludes income from certain specified service trades or businesses from the definition of qualified business income. A specified service trade or business is defined as any trade or business involving the performance of services in the fields of health, law, accounting, actuarial science, performing arts, consulting, athletics, financial services, brokerage services, or any trade or business where the principal asset of such trade or business is the reputation or skill of one or more of its employees or which involves the performance of services that consist of investing and investment management trading, or dealing in securities, partnership interests, or commodities. The definition specifically excludes architecture and engineering from the definition. Reg. §1.199A-5 provides additional details regarding the definition of specified service trades or businesses. The specified service trade or business requirement does not apply to taxpayers with taxable income (before the deduction) below a certain threshold and the requirement phases in over a range of taxable income above the threshold [see §199A(d)(3)].

To facilitate a partner's calculation of the 20 percent deduction, partnerships must disclose certain items to the partners. First, the partnership must disclose each partner's share of qualified business income for the separate qualified trade or businesses within the partnership. Further, the partnership must also disclose for each qualified trade or business within the partnership any additional information required for the partners to calculate the limitations on the deduction applied at the partner level.[65]

Net Investment Income Tax

An individual partner's share of gross income from interest, dividends, annuities, royalties, or rents is included in the partner's net investment income when calculating the net investment income tax.[66] In addition, the partner's share of income from a trade or business that is a passive activity, income from a trade or business of trading financial instruments or commodities, and any net gain from disposing of property (other than property used in a trade or business that is not a passive activity) is also included in the partner's net investment income.[67]

Allocating Partners' Shares of Income and Loss

Partnership tax rules provide partners with tremendous flexibility in allocating overall profit and loss as well as specific items of profit and loss to partners, as long as partners agree to the allocations and they have "substantial economic effect." Partnership allocations designed to accomplish business objectives other than reducing taxes will generally have substantial economic effect.[68] If they are not defined in the partnership agreement or do not have substantial economic effect, allocations to partners must be made in accordance with the "partners' interests in the partnership."[69] According to tax regulations, the partners' interests in the partnership are a measure of the partners' economic arrangement and should be determined by considering factors such as their capital contributions, distribution rights, and interests in economic profits and losses (if different from their interests in taxable income and loss). Partnership allocations inconsistent with partners' capital interests or overall profit-and-loss-sharing ratios are called **special allocations.**

Although special allocations are made largely at the discretion of the partnership, certain special allocations of gains and losses from the sale of partnership property are mandatory. Specifically, when property contributed to a partnership with built-in gains (fair market value greater than tax basis) or built-in losses (tax basis greater than fair market value) is subsequently sold, the partnership must allocate, to the extent possible, the built-in gain or built-in loss (at the time of the contribution) solely to the contributing partner and then allocate any remaining gain or loss to all the partners in accordance with their profit-and-loss-sharing ratios.[70] This rule prevents contributing partners from shifting their built-in gains and built-in losses to other partners.

[65]Under §199A(b)(2)(B), the deduction cannot exceed the greater of 50 percent of the wages paid with respect to the qualified trade or business or the sum of 25 percent of the wages with respect to the qualified trade or business plus 2.5 percent of the unadjusted basis, immediately after acquisition, of all qualified property in the qualified trade or business. Partners are allocated their share of qualified wages and the unadjusted basis of qualified property so that they may properly calculate the limitations at their level. These limitations do not apply to taxpayers with taxable income (before the deduction) below a certain threshold, and the limitations phase in over a range of taxable income above the threshold [see §199A(b)(3)].

[66]§1411. The tax imposed is 3.8 percent of the lesser of (a) net investment income or (b) the excess of modified adjusted gross income over $250,000 for married-joint filers and surviving spouses, $125,000 for married-separate filers, and $200,000 for other taxpayers. Modified adjusted gross income equals adjusted gross income increased by income excluded under the foreign-earned income exclusion less any disallowed deductions associated with the foreign-earned income exclusion.

[67]§1411(c)(2)(A). For purposes of computing the net investment income tax, a partner's status as either active or passive with respect to an activity is determined according to the §469 passive activity loss rules explained later in this chapter.

[68]Reg. §1.704-1 defines the requirements allocations must satisfy to have substantial economic effect.

[69]§704(b).

[70]§704(c). In addition to requiring built-in gains and losses to be specially allocated to contributing partners, §704(c) also requires depreciation to be specially allocated to noncontributing partners. Tax regulations permit partners to choose among several methods for making these required special allocations. Further discussion of these methods is beyond the scope of this book.

Example 9-20

What if: Assume that at the beginning of 2022, Nicole and Sarah decide to organize CCS's marketing efforts by region. Nicole will take responsibility for marketing in the western United States, and Sarah will take responsibility for marketing in the eastern United States. All members agree that CCS's provision for allocating profits and losses in the operating agreement should be amended to provide Nicole and Sarah with better incentives. Specifically, CCS would like to allocate the first 20 percent of profits or losses from each region to Nicole and Sarah. Then, it will allocate any remaining profits or losses from each region among the members in proportion to their profits interests at the end of 2022—40 percent to Sarah and 30 percent each to Nicole and Greg. Will CCS's proposed special allocation of profits and losses be accepted by the IRS?

Answer: Yes. Because CCS is a partnership for federal income tax purposes, it can make special allocations to members, and because the allocations are designed to accomplish a business objective other than tax reduction, the IRS will accept them.[71]

What if: Assume that the land Nicole contributed to CCS had a fair market value of $150,000 and a tax basis of $20,000 (see original facts in Example 9-1) and was sold by CCS for $150,000 of consideration almost immediately after it was contributed. How would the resulting $130,000 gain be allocated among the members of CCS?

Answer: Nicole's built-in gain of $130,000 at the time of contribution must be allocated exclusively to her to prevent it from being shifted to other CCS members. Shifting the gain to other members could lower the overall tax liability of the CCS members if Sarah's and Greg's marginal tax rates are lower than Nicole's marginal tax rate, or it could increase it if their marginal rates are higher.

What if: Suppose CCS held the land Nicole contributed for one year and then sold it on March 31, 2022, for $180,000 instead of $150,000. How should the resulting $160,000 gain be allocated to Nicole, Sarah, and Chanzz Inc.?

Answer: The allocations are $139,000 to Nicole, $12,000 to Sarah, and $9,000 to Chanzz Inc., as reflected in the table below:

Description	CCS	Nicole 30%	Sarah 40%	Chanzz Inc. 30%
Total gain from sale of land	$160,000			
Less:				
Special allocation to Nicole of built-in gain	(130,000)	$ 130,000		
Post-contribution appreciation in land	30,000	9,000	$ 12,000	$ 9,000
Total gain allocations		**$139,000**	**$12,000**	**$9,000**

Partnership Compliance Issues

Although partnerships don't pay taxes, they are required to file **Form 1065,** U.S. Return of Partnership Income (shown in Exhibit 9-8), with the IRS by the 15th day of the third month after their year-end (March 15th for a calendar-year-end partnership). Partnerships may receive an automatic six-month extension to file by filing **Form 7004** with the IRS before the original due date of the return.[72] Page 1 of Form 1065 details the calculation of the partnership's ordinary business income (loss) for the year, and page 4, **Schedule K,** lists the partnership's ordinary business income (loss) and separately stated items. In addition to preparing Form 1065, the partnership is also responsible for preparing a Schedule K-1 for each partner detailing the partner's individual share of the partnership's ordinary business income (loss) and separately stated items for the year. Once prepared, Schedule K-1s are included with Form 1065 when it is filed, and they are also separately

[71]Reg. §1.704-1(b)(5), Example 10, suggests that this type of special allocation would not violate the substantial economic effect rules.

[72]Under §6698, late filing penalties apply if the partnership fails to file by the normal or extended due date for the return. For 2022 returns, the penalty is $220 ($210 for 2021 returns) times the number of partners in the partnership times the number of months (or fraction thereof) the return is late, up to a maximum of 12 months.

EXHIBIT 9-8 (PART I) Page 1 Form 1065 CCS's 2022 Ordinary Business Loss (on 2021 forms)

Form **1065** — Department of the Treasury, Internal Revenue Service

U.S. Return of Partnership Income

For calendar year 2021, or tax year beginning ________, 2021, ending ________, 20___.

▶ Go to *www.irs.gov/Form1065* for instructions and the latest information.

OMB No. 1545-0123 — **2021**

A Principal business activity: **Manufacturing**
B Principal product or service: **Textile Products**
C Business code number: **31400**

Type or Print:
Name of partnership: **Color Comfort Sheets**
Number, street, and room or suite no. If a P.O. box, see instructions.: **375 East 450 South**
City or town, state or province, country, and ZIP or foreign postal code: **Salt Lake City, UT 84608**

D Employer identification number: **000072359**
E Date business started: **April 1, 2021**
F Total assets (see instructions): $ **370,000**

G Check applicable boxes: (1) ☐ Initial return (2) ☐ Final return (3) ☐ Name change (4) ☐ Address change (5) ☐ Amended return
H Check accounting method: (1) ☑ Cash (2) ☐ Accrual (3) ☐ Other (specify) ▶
I Number of Schedules K-1. Attach one for each person who was a partner at any time during the tax year ▶ **3**
J Check if Schedules C and M-3 are attached ▶ ☐
K Check if partnership: (1) ☐ Aggregated activities for section 465 at-risk purposes (2) ☐ Grouped activities for section 469 passive activity purposes

Caution: Include **only** trade or business income and expenses on lines 1a through 22 below. See instructions for more information.

Income	1a	Gross receipts or sales	1a	40,000		
	b	Returns and allowances	1b			
	c	Balance. Subtract line 1b from line 1a			1c	40,000
	2	Cost of goods sold (attach Form 1125-A)			2	20,000
	3	Gross profit. Subtract line 2 from line 1c			3	20,000
	4	Ordinary income (loss) from other partnerships, estates, and trusts (attach statement)			4	
	5	Net farm profit (loss) (attach Schedule F (Form 1040))			5	
	6	Net gain (loss) from Form 4797, Part II, line 17 (attach Form 4797)			6	
	7	Other income (loss) (attach statement)			7	
	8	**Total income (loss).** Combine lines 3 through 7			8	20,000
Deductions (see instructions for limitations)	9	Salaries and wages (other than to partners) (less employment credits)			9	50,000
	10	Guaranteed payments to partners			10	10,000
	11	Repairs and maintenance			11	
	12	Bad debts			12	
	13	Rent			13	
	14	Taxes and licenses			14	
	15	Interest (see instructions)			15	
	16a	Depreciation (if required, attach Form 4562)	16a	18,000		
	b	Less depreciation reported on Form 1125-A and elsewhere on return	16b		16c	18,000
	17	Depletion **(Do not deduct oil and gas depletion.)**			17	
	18	Retirement plans, etc.			18	
	19	Employee benefit programs			19	
	20	Other deductions (attach statement)			20	2,800
	21	**Total deductions.** Add the amounts shown in the far right column for lines 9 through 20			21	80,800
	22	**Ordinary business income (loss).** Subtract line 21 from line 8			22	60,800
Tax and Payment	23	Interest due under the look-back method—completed long-term contracts (attach Form 8697)			23	
	24	Interest due under the look-back method—income forecast method (attach Form 8866)			24	
	25	BBA AAR imputed underpayment (see instructions)			25	
	26	Other taxes (see instructions)			26	
	27	**Total balance due.** Add lines 23 through 26			27	
	28	Payment (see instructions)			28	
	29	**Amount owed.** If line 28 is smaller than line 27, enter amount owed			29	
	30	**Overpayment.** If line 28 is larger than line 27, enter overpayment			30	

Sign Here

Under penalties of perjury, I declare that I have examined this return, including accompanying schedules and statements, and to the best of my knowledge and belief, it is true, correct, and complete. Declaration of preparer (other than partner or limited liability company member) is based on all information of which preparer has any knowledge.

▶ Signature of partner or limited liability company member ▶ Date

May the IRS discuss this return with the preparer shown below? See instructions. ☐ Yes ☐ No

Paid Preparer Use Only

Print/Type preparer's name	Preparer's signature	Date	Check ☐ if self-employed	PTIN
Firm's name ▶			Firm's EIN ▶	
Firm's address ▶			Phone no.	

For Paperwork Reduction Act Notice, see separate instructions. Cat. No. 11390Z Form **1065** (2021)

Source: irs.gov.

EXHIBIT 9-8 (PART II) Page 4 Form 1065 CCS's 2022 Schedule K (on 2021 forms)

Form 1065 (2021) Page 4

Section	Line	Schedule K Partners' Distributive Share Items		Line	Total amount
Income (Loss)	1	Ordinary business income (loss) (page 1, line 22)		1	(60,800)
	2	Net rental real estate income (loss) (attach Form 8825)		2	
	3a	Other gross rental income (loss)	3a		
	b	Expenses from other rental activities (attach statement)	3b		
	c	Other net rental income (loss). Subtract line 3b from line 3a		3c	
	4	Guaranteed payments: a Services 4a 10,000 b Capital 4b			
		c Total. Add lines 4a and 4b		4c	10,000
	5	Interest income		5	0
	6	Dividends and dividend equivalents: a Ordinary dividends		6a	500
		b Qualified dividends 6b 500 c Dividend equivalents 6c			
	7	Royalties		7	
	8	Net short-term capital gain (loss) (attach Schedule D (Form 1065))		8	
	9a	Net long-term capital gain (loss) (attach Schedule D (Form 1065))		9a	300
	b	Collectibles (28%) gain (loss)	9b		
	c	Unrecaptured section 1250 gain (attach statement)	9c		
	10	Net section 1231 gain (loss) (attach Form 4797)		10	
	11	Other income (loss) (see instructions) Type ▶		11	
Deductions	12	Section 179 deduction (attach Form 4562)		12	
	13a	Contributions		13a	
	b	Investment interest expense		13b	
	c	Section 59(e)(2) expenditures: (1) Type ▶ (2) Amount ▶		13c(2)	
	d	Other deductions (see instructions) Type ▶		13d	
Self-Employment	14a	Net earnings (loss) from self-employment		14a	(41,680)
	b	Gross farming or fishing income		14b	
	c	Gross nonfarm income		14c	20,000
Credits	15a	Low-income housing credit (section 42(j)(5))		15a	
	b	Low-income housing credit (other)		15b	
	c	Qualified rehabilitation expenditures (rental real estate) (attach Form 3468, if applicable)		15c	
	d	Other rental real estate credits (see instructions) Type ▶		15d	
	e	Other rental credits (see instructions) Type ▶		15e	
	f	Other credits (see instructions) Type ▶		15f	
International Transactions	16	Attach Schedule K-2 (Form 1065), Partners' Distributive Share Items-International, and check this box to indicate that you are reporting items of international tax relevance ☐			
Alternative Minimum Tax (AMT) Items	17a	Post-1986 depreciation adjustment		17a	
	b	Adjusted gain or loss		17b	
	c	Depletion (other than oil and gas)		17c	
	d	Oil, gas, and geothermal properties—gross income		17d	
	e	Oil, gas, and geothermal properties—deductions		17e	
	f	Other AMT items (attach statement)		17f	
Other Information	18a	Tax-exempt interest income		18a	
	b	Other tax-exempt income		18b	
	c	Nondeductible expenses		18c	
	19a	Distributions of cash and marketable securities		19a	
	b	Distributions of other property		19b	
	20a	Investment income		20a	500
	b	Investment expenses		20b	
	c	Other items and amounts (attach statement)			
	21	Total foreign taxes paid or accrued		21	

Form **1065** (2021)

Source: irs.gov.

EXHIBIT 9-8 (PART III) **2022 Schedule K-1 for Sarah Walker (on 2021 forms); CCS Operates as an LLC**

651121

☐ Final K-1 ☐ Amended K-1 OMB No. 1545-0123

Schedule K-1 (Form 1065) **2021**

Department of the Treasury
Internal Revenue Service

For calendar year 2021, or tax year

beginning / / 2021 ending / /

Partner's Share of Income, Deductions, Credits, etc. ▶ See back of form and separate instructions.

Part I Information About the Partnership

A Partnership's employer identification number
00072359

B Partnership's name, address, city, state, and ZIP code

Color Comfort Sheets

C IRS center where partnership filed return ▶ Ogden, UT

D ☐ Check if this is a publicly traded partnership (PTP)

Part II Information About the Partner

E Partner's SSN or TIN (Do not use TIN of a disregarded entity. See instructions.)
498-88-3426

F Name, address, city, state, and ZIP code for partner entered in E. See instructions.

Sarah Walker
540 Laurel Lane
Holladay, UT 84609

G ☒ General partner or LLC member-manager ☐ Limited partner or other LLC member

H1 ☒ Domestic partner ☐ Foreign partner

H2 ☐ If the partner is a disregarded entity (DE), enter the partner's:
TIN ______ Name ______

I1 What type of entity is this partner? Individual

I2 If this partner is a retirement plan (IRA/SEP/Keogh/etc.), check here ▶ ☐

J Partner's share of profit, loss, and capital (see instructions):

	Beginning	Ending
Profit	40 %	40 %
Loss	40 %	40 %
Capital	40 %	40 %

Check if decrease is due to sale or exchange of partnership interest . ▶ ☐

K Partner's share of liabilities:

	Beginning	Ending
Nonrecourse . .	$	$ 12,000
Qualified nonrecourse financing . .	$ 8,000	$ 8,000
Recourse . . .	$ 24,000	$ 24,000

Check this box if Item K includes liability amounts from lower tier partnerships ▶ ☐

L **Partner's Capital Account Analysis**

Beginning capital account . . .	$ 100,000
Capital contributed during the year . .	$ 20,000
Current year net income (loss) . . .	$ (24,000)
Other increase (decrease) (attach explanation)	$
Withdrawals and distributions . . .	$ ( )
Ending capital account	$ 96,000

M Did the partner contribute property with a built-in gain (loss)?
☐ **Yes** ☒ **No** If "Yes," attach statement. See instructions.

N **Partner's Share of Net Unrecognized Section 704(c) Gain or (Loss)**
Beginning . . . . $
Ending . . . . $

Part III Partner's Share of Current Year Income, Deductions, Credits, and Other Items

1	Ordinary business income (loss) (24,320)	14	Self-employment earnings (loss)	A (14,320)
2	Net rental real estate income (loss)			C 8,000
3	Other net rental income (loss)	15	Credits	
4a	Guaranteed payments for services 10,000			
4b	Guaranteed payments for capital	16	Schedule K-3 is attached if checked . . . . ▶ ☐	
4c	Total guaranteed payments 10,000	17	Alternative minimum tax (AMT) items	
5	Interest income			
6a	Ordinary dividends 200			
6b	Qualified dividends 200	18	Tax-exempt income and nondeductible expenses	
6c	Dividend equivalents			
7	Royalties			
8	Net short-term capital gain (loss)	19	Distributions	
9a	Net long-term capital gain (loss) 120			
9b	Collectibles (28%) gain (loss)	20	Other information	
9c	Unrecaptured section 1250 gain			A 200
10	Net section 1231 gain (loss)			Z See attached schedule
11	Other income (loss)			
12	Section 179 deduction	21	Foreign taxes paid or accrued	
13	Other deductions			

22 ☐ More than one activity for at-risk purposes*
23 ☐ More than one activity for passive activity purposes*
*See attached statement for additional information.

For IRS Use Only

For Paperwork Reduction Act Notice, see the Instructions for Form 1065. www.irs.gov/Form1065 Cat. No. 11394R Schedule K-1 (Form 1065) 2021

Source: irs.gov.

provided to all partners (each partner receives a Schedule K-1 with that partner's income and loss allocations). Beginning with returns filed for 2021, partnerships with income earned outside the United States will also be required to include Schedules K-2 and K-3 with their returns. These new schedules will provide partners with the uniform and detailed information they need to calculate their U.S. income tax liability stemming from the partnership's international operations and investments. Exhibit 9-8, parts I through III, displays CCS's return, showing the operating results we summarized in Example 9-17, and Sarah's actual Schedule K-1, reflecting the facts and conclusions in Examples 9-17 and 9-18.[73]

LO 9-5

ADJUSTING A PARTNER'S TAX BASIS IN PARTNERSHIP INTEREST

Earlier in this chapter, we discussed how partners measure their outside tax basis in their partnership interests when they contribute property or services to partnerships in exchange for their partnership interests, or when they purchase partnership interests from an existing partner. Unlike the basis in a stock or other similar investment, which is usually stable, the basis in a partnership interest is dynamic and must be *adjusted* as the partnership generates income and losses, changes its liability levels, and makes distributions to partners. These annual adjustments to a partner's tax basis are required to ensure partners don't double-count taxable income/gains and deductible expenses/losses, either when they sell their partnership interests or when they receive partnership distributions. They also ensure tax-exempt income and nondeductible expenses are not ultimately taxed or deducted.

Partners make the following adjustments to the basis in their partnership interests annually:

- Increase for actual and deemed cash contributions to the partnership during the year.[74]
- Increase for partner's share of ordinary business income and separately stated income/gain items.
- Increase for partner's share of tax-exempt income.
- Decrease for actual and deemed cash distributions during the year.[75,76]
- Decrease for partner's share of nondeductible expenses (fines, penalties, etc.).
- Decrease for partner's share of ordinary business loss and separately stated expense/loss items.[77]
- Decrease for partner's share of disallowed business interest expense.[78]

Partners first adjust their outside bases for items that increase basis, then for distributions, then by nondeductible expenses, and then by deductible expenses and losses to the extent any basis remains after prior adjustments.[79] Basis adjustments that decrease basis may never reduce a partner's tax basis below zero.[80]

Example 9-21

Given the events that affected CCS and its members during *2021*, what tax basis did Nicole, Sarah, and Chanzz Inc. have in their ownership interests at the end of 2021?

[73]We use 2021 forms because 2022 forms were unavailable at press time.

[74]Recall that partners are deemed to have made a cash contribution to the partnership when they are allocated an additional share of partnership liabilities.

[75]Recall that partners are deemed to have received a cash distribution from the partnership when they are relieved of partnership liabilities.

[76]Property distributions to partners are also treated as basis reductions. We discuss property distributions at length in the Dispositions of Partnership Interests and Partnership Distributions chapter.

[77]Per §704(d)(3)(B), a partner does not reduce the basis in her interest by her share of any appreciation in property contributed by the partnership to a charitable organization.

[78]§163(j)(4)(B)(iii).

[79]Reg. §1.704-1(d)(2).

[80]§705(a)(2).

Answer: Their tax bases in their CCS interests were $4,000, $152,000, and $114,000, respectively. Their individual tax basis calculations at the end of 2021 are illustrated in the table below:

Description	Nicole	Sarah	Chanzz Inc.	Explanation
(1) Initial tax basis (including liability)	$36,666	$ 146,666	$ 146,666	Example 9-4
(2) Dividends	700	700	700	Example 9-15
(3) Short-term capital gains	400	400	400	Example 9-15
(4) Liability reallocation (deemed cash contribution/distribution)	(2,667)	5,334	(2,667)	Example 9-10
(5) Sarah's capital interest	(10,000)	20,000	(10,000)	Examples 9-10, 9-15
(6) CCS's ordinary business loss	(21,100)	(21,100)	(21,100)	Example 9-15
Tax basis on 12/31/21	**$ 4,000**	**$152,000**	**$114,000**	Sum of (1) through (6)

What if: Suppose Sarah sold her LLC interest but forgot to include her share of short-term capital gains when computing her basis to determine her gain on the sale. What are the tax implications of Sarah's mistake?

Answer: Sarah would be double-taxed on the amount of the short-term capital gain. She was initially taxed on her share of the short-term capital gain allocation, and she will be taxed a second time when she recognizes $400 more long-term capital gain on the sale than she would have had she included her share of the gain in her basis.

What if: Assume Sarah was allocated $700 of tax-exempt municipal bond income instead of dividend income. What will happen if she neglects to increase her basis in CCS by the $700 tax-exempt income?

Answer: If Sarah were to sell her interest in CCS for a price reflecting the tax-exempt income received, she would, in effect, be converting tax-exempt income into taxable capital gain.

Example 9-22

In addition to the other events of *2022*, CCS increased its liabilities from $100,000 to $130,000 in the second half of the year. The $30,000 increase was attributable to accounts payable owed to suppliers. Unlike the case of the $60,000 bank loan, the members did not guarantee any of the accounts payable. Therefore, the accounts payable are considered a nonrecourse liability because CCS is an LLC. Given this information, what are Nicole's, Sarah's, and Greg's tax bases in their CCS interests at the end of *2022*?

Answer: The bases in their CCS interests are $0, $140,000, and $124,000, respectively. Nicole, Sarah, and Greg would determine their tax basis in CCS at the end of *2022* as illustrated in the table below:

Description	Nicole 30%	Sarah[81] 40%	Greg 30%	Explanation
(1) Tax basis on 1/1/22	$ 4,000	$ 152,000		Example 9-21
(2) Greg's purchase of Chanzz Inc.'s interest			$ 124,000	Example 9-11
(3) Dividends	150	200	75	Example 9-17
(4) Long-term capital gains	90	120	45	Example 9-17
(5) Increase in nonrecourse liability from accounts payable (deemed cash contribution)	9,000	12,000	9,000	$30,000 × member's profit-sharing ratio
(6) CCS's ordinary business loss	(18,240)	(24,320)	(9,120)	Example 9-17
Preliminary tax basis	(5,000)	140,000	124,000	Sum of (1) through (6)
Tax basis on 12/31/22	**$ 0***	**$140,000**	**$124,000**	*Nicole's basis can't go below zero.

[81]Recall that Sarah received a $10,000 cash guaranteed payment for services she performed in 2022. Cash guaranteed payments generally don't have a direct impact on the recipient partner's tax basis because they are similar to salary payments.

THE KEY FACTS

Partner's Basis Adjustments

- A partner will increase the tax basis in her partnership interest for:
  - Contributions.
  - Share of ordinary business income.
  - Separately stated income/gain items.
  - Tax-exempt income.
- A partner will decrease the tax basis in her partnership interest for:
  - Cash distributions.
  - Share of nondeductible expenses.
  - Share of ordinary business loss.
  - Separately stated expense/loss items.
  - Share of disallowed business interest expense
- A partner's tax basis may not be negative.

Cash Distributions in Operating Partnerships

Even after a partnership has been formed, partners are likely to continue to receive actual and deemed cash distributions. For example, excess cash may be distributed to partners to provide them with cash flow to pay their taxes or simply for consumption, and deemed cash distributions occur as partnerships pay down their liabilities. The principles underlying the calculation of a partner's tax basis highlight the fact that partners are taxed on income as the partnership earns it instead of when it distributes it. If cash is distributed when partners have a positive tax basis in their partnership interests, the distribution effectively represents a distribution of profits that have been previously taxed, a return of capital previously contributed by the partner to the partnership, a distribution of cash the partnership has borrowed, or some combination of the three. Thus, as long as a cash distribution does not exceed a partner's outside basis before the distribution, it reduces the partner's tax basis but is not taxable. However, as we highlighted in our discussion of property contributions earlier in this chapter, cash distributions (deemed or actual) in excess of a partner's basis are taxable gains and are generally treated as capital gains.[82]

Example 9-23

What if: In Example 9-22, we determined that Sarah's basis in her partnership interest was $140,000. Assume that in addition to the facts provided in that example, Sarah received a $10,000 distribution in *2022*. What will her basis in CCS (i.e., her outside basis) be at the end of the year?

Answer: Sarah's outside basis will be $130,000. After making only her positive adjustments for the year (positive adjustments come before negative adjustments such as distributions), she has an outside basis of $164,320, which is greater than the $10,000 distribution. Thus, the distribution is not taxable because it does not exceed her outside basis before adjusting for the distribution. Sarah will also reduce her outside basis by the $10,000 distribution in addition to the $24,320 reduction for her share of the ordinary business loss, leaving her with an ending outside basis of $130,000 ($164,320 – $10,000 – $24,320).

What problem will be created if Sarah does not reduce her basis by the $10,000 distribution?

Answer: After she receives the $10,000 distribution, the value of Sarah's interest will decrease by $10,000. If she doesn't reduce her tax basis by the distribution, selling her interest will produce a $10,000 artificial tax loss.

LO 9-6

LOSS LIMITATIONS

While partners generally prefer not to invest in partnerships with operating losses, these losses generate current tax benefits when partners can deduct them against other sources of taxable income. Unlike capital losses, which are of limited usefulness if taxpayers don't also have capital gains, ordinary losses from partnerships are deductible against any type of taxable income. However, they are deductible on the partner's tax return only when they clear four separate hurdles: (1) tax-basis, (2) at-risk amount, and (3) passive activity. In addition, for losses that clear each of the three hurdles, (4) partners are not allowed to deduct excess business losses, as described below.

Tax-Basis Limitation

A partner's outside or tax basis in the partnership interest limits the amount of partnership losses the partner can use to offset other sources of income. In theory, a partner's outside basis represents the amount a partner has invested in a partnership (or may have to invest to satisfy the partner's liability obligations). As a result, partners may not utilize partnership losses in excess of their investment or outside basis in their partnership interests. Any losses allocated in excess of their basis must be suspended and carried forward indefinitely until they have sufficient basis to utilize the losses.[83] Any suspended losses

[82]§731.

[83]§704(d).

remaining when partners sell or otherwise dispose of their interests are lost forever. Among other things, partners may create additional tax basis by making capital contributions, by guaranteeing more partnership liability, and by helping their partnership to become profitable.

Example 9-24

In Example 9-22 we discovered Nicole was allocated $5,000 of ordinary loss in excess of her tax basis for 2022, leaving her with a tax basis of $0 at the end of 2022. What does Nicole do with this loss?

Answer: Nicole will carry forward all $5,000 of ordinary loss in excess of her tax basis indefinitely until her tax basis in her CCS interest becomes positive. To the extent her tax basis increases in the future, the tax-basis limitation will no longer apply to her ordinary loss. Even then, however, the at-risk, passive activity loss, and/or excess business loss limitations may ultimately apply to constrain her ability to deduct the loss on her future tax returns.

What if: Assuming Nicole is allocated $4,000 of income from CCS in *2023*, how much of her $5,000 suspended loss will clear the tax basis hurdle in *2023*?

Answer: Nicole's basis will initially increase by $4,000. Then she can apply $4,000 of her suspended loss against this basis increase, leaving her tax basis at $0 and holding a remaining suspended loss of $1,000. The $4,000 loss clearing the tax-basis hurdle must still clear the at-risk, passive activity loss, and excess business loss hurdles before Nicole can deduct it on her return.

At-Risk Amount Limitation

The at-risk amount hurdle or limitation is more restrictive than the tax-basis limitation because it excludes a type of liability normally included in a partner's tax basis. We have already highlighted the distinction between recourse and nonrecourse liabilities and noted that partners allocated recourse liabilities have economic risk of loss, while partners allocated nonrecourse liabilities have no risk of loss. Instead, the risk of loss on nonrecourse liabilities is borne by lenders. The **at-risk rules** in §465 were adopted to limit the ability of partners to use nonrecourse liabilities as a means of creating tax basis to use losses from tax shelter partnerships expressly designed to generate losses for the partners. The at-risk rules limit partners' losses to their amount "at risk" in the partnership—their **at-risk amount.** Generally, a partner's at-risk amount is the same as the partner's tax basis except that, with one exception, the partner's share of certain nonrecourse liabilities is not included in the at-risk amount. Specifically, the only nonrecourse liabilities considered to be at risk are nonrecourse real estate mortgages from commercial lenders that are unrelated to borrowers. This type of liability is called **qualified nonrecourse financing.**[84] In addition to qualified nonrecourse financing, partners are considered to be at risk to the extent of cash and the tax basis of property contributed to the partnership. Further, partners are at risk for any partnership recourse liabilities allocated to them.

Partners apply the at-risk limitation after the tax-basis limitation. Any partnership losses that would otherwise have been allowed under the tax-basis limitation are further limited to the extent they exceed a partner's at-risk amount. Losses limited under the at-risk rules are carried forward indefinitely until the partner generates additional at-risk amounts to utilize the losses, or until they are applied to reduce any gain from selling the partnership interest.

THE KEY FACTS

Loss Limitations

- Partnership losses in excess of a partner's tax basis are suspended and carried forward until additional basis is created.
- Remaining partnership losses are further suspended by the at-risk rules to the extent a partner is allocated nonrecourse liabilities not secured by real property.
- If a partner is not a material participant or the partnership is involved in rental activities, losses remaining after application of the tax-basis and at-risk limitations may be used only against other passive income or when the partnership interest is sold.
- Losses remaining after applying the tax basis, at-risk, and passive activity loss limitations are only deductible to the extent they do not add to or create an excess business loss at the partner level.

Example 9-25

In Example 9-22, we discovered Nicole was allocated an ordinary business loss of $18,240. There we also learned that of this loss, $13,240 cleared the tax-basis hurdle and $5,000 did not. How much of the $13,240 ordinary business loss that clears the tax-basis hurdle will clear the at-risk amount hurdle?

(continued on page 9-32)

[84]§465(b)(6).

Answer: $4,240. The table below summarizes and compares Nicole's calculations to determine her tax-basis and at-risk limitations for 2021:

Example	Description	Tax Basis	At-Risk Amount	Explanation
9-22	(1) Nicole's tax basis on 1/1/22	$ 4,000	$ 4,000	Nicole's tax basis and at-risk amount are the same because she was allocated only recourse liability and qualified nonrecourse financing.
9-22	(2) Dividends	150	150	
9-22	(3) Long-term capital gains	90	90	
9-22	(4) Nonrecourse accounts payable	9,000	0	
	(5) Tax basis and at-risk amount before ordinary business loss	13,240	4,240	Sum of (1) through (4)
9-22	(6) Ordinary business loss	(18,240)		
	(7) Loss clearing the tax-basis hurdle	(13,240)		Loss limited to (5)
	Loss suspended by tax-basis hurdle	$ (5,000)		(6) – (7)
	(8) Loss clearing tax-basis hurdle		(13,240)	(7)
	(9) Loss clearing at-risk hurdle		**(4,240)**	Loss limited to (5)
	Loss suspended by at-risk hurdle		$ (9,000)	(8) – (9)

Although Nicole's $9,000 share of the nonrecourse accounts payable added in 2022 and her investment income of $240 allow her to create enough tax basis in her interest in 2022 to get $13,240 of her $18,240 ordinary business loss past the tax-basis limitation, she is not at risk with respect to her $9,000 share of accounts payable because an LLC's accounts payable are general nonrecourse liability. Therefore, $9,000 of the $13,240 ordinary business loss clearing the tax-basis hurdle is suspended under the at-risk limitation. As a result, Nicole has two separate losses to carry forward: a $5,000 ordinary loss limited by her tax basis in her CCS interest and a $9,000 ordinary loss limited by the at-risk rules, leaving $4,240 of ordinary loss that she may deduct on her 2022 return.

Passive Activity Loss Limitation

Prior to 1986, partners with sufficient tax basis and at-risk amounts were able to utilize ordinary losses from their partnerships to offset portfolio income (i.e., interest, dividends, and capital gains), salary income, and self-employment income from partnerships and other trades or businesses. During this time, a partnership tax shelter industry thrived by marketing to wealthy investors partnership interests designed primarily to generate ordinary losses they could use to shield other income from tax. To combat this practice, Congress introduced the **passive activity loss (PAL) rules.**[85] These rules were enacted as a backstop to the at-risk rules and are applied after the tax-basis and at-risk limitations. Thus, depending on their situation, partners may have to overcome *three separate hurdles* before finally reporting partnership ordinary losses on their returns. In a nutshell, the PAL rules limit the ability of partners in rental real estate partnerships and other partnerships they don't actively manage (passive activities) from using their ordinary losses from these activities (remaining after the application of the tax-basis and at-risk limitations) to reduce other sources of taxable income.

Passive Activity Defined The passive activity rules define a passive activity as "any activity which involves the conduct of a trade or business,[86] and in which the taxpayer does not materially participate."[87] According to the IRC and Treasury regulations, participants in

[85]§469. The passive activity loss rules apply primarily to individuals but also to estates, trusts, closely held C corporations, and personal service corporations.

[86]The term *trade or business* is also deemed to include property held for the production of income, such as rental property.

[87]irs.gov.

rental activities, including rental real estate,[88] and limited partners without management rights are automatically deemed to be passive participants. In addition, participants in all other activities are passive unless their involvement in an activity is "regular, continuous, and substantial." Clearly, these terms are quite subjective and difficult to apply. Fortunately, regulations provide more certainty in this area by enumerating seven separate tests for material participation.[89] An individual, other than a limited partner, can be classified as a material participant in activities, other than rental activities, by meeting any *one* of the seven tests in Exhibit 9-9.

EXHIBIT 9-9 Tests for Material Participation

1. The individual participates in the activity more than 500 hours during the year.
2. The individual's activity constitutes substantially all the participation in such activity by individuals.
3. The individual participates more than 100 hours during the year and the individual's participation is not less than any other individual's participation in the activity.
4. The activity qualifies as a "significant participation activity" (individual participates for more than 100 hours during the year) and the aggregate of all other "significant participation activities" is greater than 500 hours for the year.
5. The individual materially participated in the activity for any 5 of the preceding 10 taxable years.
6. The activity involves personal services in health, law, accounting, architecture, and so on, and the individual materially participated for any three preceding years.
7. Taking into account all the facts and circumstances, the individual participates on a regular, continuous, and substantial basis during the year.

TAXES IN THE REAL WORLD Donald Trump's Tax Losses

During his run for the presidency in the fall of 2016, the first page of Donald Trump's New York State resident tax return for 1995 was mailed anonymously to the *New York Times*. When the *Times* subsequently published the first page of President Trump's New York State return, it showed that he reported a loss for the year of nearly $16 million from "rental real estate, royalties, partnerships, S corporations, trusts, etc." Given President Trump's status as a real estate developer and owner, it is likely that a significant portion of this loss originated from rental real estate activities held in partnership form. These partnerships frequently generate losses because they are able to deduct depreciation, interest, and other operating costs in determining their taxable income.

President Trump's return also showed that he used the $16 million loss to offset business income of $3.4 million, $6,000 in wages, and $7.4 million in interest he reported earning the same year. For many taxpayers, losses from rental real estate are presumed to be passive losses and therefore may not be used to offset active and portfolio income. So, how was Donald Trump able to use the portion of his $16 million loss attributable to rental real estate to legally shelter his other sources of income? President Trump was likely able to take advantage of the "real estate professional" exception found in §469(c)(6) of the Code. This exception permits individuals that are heavily involved in real property trades or businesses to overcome the presumption that their losses from rental real estate are passive and then go on to establish that their losses are active under one of the material participation tests found in the tax regulations.

Income and Loss Baskets Under the passive activity loss rules, each item of a partner's income or loss from all sources for the year is placed in one of three categories, or "baskets." Losses from the *passive basket* are not allowed to offset income from other baskets. The three baskets are (see Exhibit 9-10):

1. *Passive activity income or loss*—income or loss from an activity, including partnerships, in which the taxpayer is not a material participant.

[88]Section 469(b)(7) provides an important exception to the general rule that all real estate activities are passive. To overcome this presumption, taxpayers must spend more than half their time working in trades or businesses materially participating in real estate activities and more than 750 hours materially participating in real estate activities during the year. This exception benefits partners that spend a substantial amount of time in partnership activities like real estate development and construction. Moreover, §469(i) permits individual taxpayers to treat up to $25,000 of losses from rental real estate as active losses each year.

[89]Reg. §1.469-5T.

2. *Portfolio income*—income from investments, including capital gains and losses, dividends, interest, annuities, and royalties.
3. *Active business income*—income from sources, including partnerships, in which the taxpayer is a material participant. For individuals, this includes salary and self-employment income.

EXHIBIT 9-10 Income and Loss Baskets

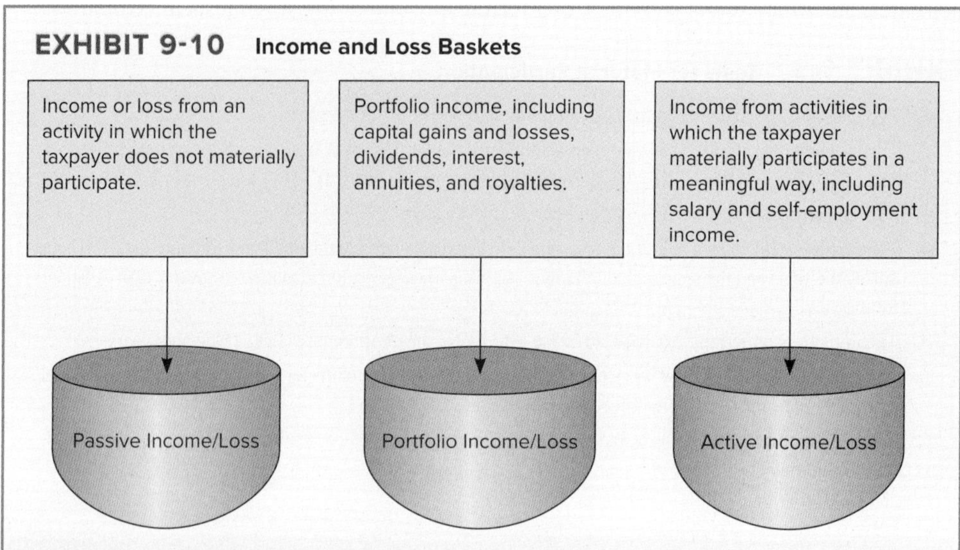

The impact of segregating a partner's income in these baskets is to limit their ability to apply passive activity losses against income in the other two baskets. In effect, passive activity losses are suspended and remain in the passive income or loss basket until the taxpayer generates current-year passive income, either from the passive activity producing the loss or from some other passive activity, or until the taxpayer sells the activity that generated the passive loss.[90] On the sale of the activity, the taxpayer would classify gain or loss from the sale as current-year passive income or loss, and they would treat a net passive loss from the activity (i.e., suspended prior-year passive losses, plus current-year passive losses, plus or minus any passive loss or income from the sale) as passive to the extent the taxpayer has passive income in the year from other activities. Finally, the taxpayer would treat any remaining net losses from the activity that had been sold as nonpassive losses.[91]

ETHICS

Several years ago, Lou, together with his friend Carlo, opened an Italian restaurant in their neighborhood. The venture was formed as an LLC, with Lou receiving a 75 percent ownership interest and Carlo receiving the remaining 25 percent ownership interest. While Lou was primarily responsible for operating the restaurant, Carlo came in only on weekends because he held a full-time job elsewhere. To document the time he spent in the restaurant, Carlo recorded the number of hours he had worked in a logbook at the end of every shift. This year, because of a downturn in the local economy, the restaurant showed a loss for the first time. To be able to deduct his share of this loss when he files his tax return, Carlo would like to establish that he worked more than 500 hours during the year and is therefore a material participant in the restaurant. His logbook shows that he worked for 502 hours during the year; however, he rounded up to the nearest hour at the end of every shift to simplify his record keeping. For example, if he worked 4 hours and 25 minutes during a shift, he wrote 5 hours in the logbook. Should Carlo claim that he is a material participant on the basis of the hours recorded in his logbook and deduct his share of the loss? What would you do?

[90]Under §469(k), this rule is even more restrictive for publicly traded partnerships. Passive activity losses from these partnerships may only be utilized to offset future passive income from the same partnership generating the passive activity loss.

[91]§469(g)(1)(A).

Example 9-26

As indicated in Example 9-22, Greg was allocated a $9,120 ordinary loss for 2022 and had a $124,000 tax basis at year-end *after* adjusting his tax basis in his CCS interest for the loss. Given that Greg was allocated $9,000 of nonrecourse liability from accounts payable during 2022, what is Greg's at-risk amount at the end of the year?

Answer: $115,000. Greg's at-risk amount is calculated by subtracting his $9,000 share of nonrecourse liability from his $124,000 tax basis.

Given Greg's status as a silent or nonmanaging member of CCS, how much of his $9,120 ordinary loss can he deduct in 2022 if he has no other sources of passive income?

Answer: None. Because Greg's tax basis and at-risk amount are large relative to his $9,120 ordinary loss, the tax-basis and at-risk hurdles don't limit his loss. However, Greg's $9,120 loss would be classified as a passive loss and suspended until Greg receives passive income from another source—hopefully CCS—or until he disposes of his interest in CCS.

What could Greg do to deduct any losses from CCS in the future?

Answer: He could satisfy one of the seven tests in Exhibit 9-9 to be classified as a material participant in CCS, thereby converting his future CCS losses from passive to active losses. Or he could become a passive participant in some other activity, producing trade or business income that could be offset by any future passive losses from CCS. Or he could sell his interest in CCS.

Excess Business Loss Limitation

Noncorporate taxpayers are not allowed to deduct an **excess business loss** for the year, including business losses from entities taxed as partnerships.[92] Rather, excess business losses are carried forward and used in subsequent years. The excess business loss limitation applies to losses that are otherwise deductible under the tax-basis, at-risk, and passive loss rules. An excess business loss for the year is the excess of the sum of business deductions for the year over the sum of aggregate business gross income or gain of the taxpayer plus a threshold amount. The threshold amount for losses reported in 2022 is $540,000 for married taxpayers filing jointly and $270,000 for other taxpayers. The amounts are indexed for inflation. In the case of partnership business losses, the provision applies at the partner level.

Example 9-27

From Example 9-25 we learned that Nicole would report $150 of dividend income and $90 of long-term capital gains from CCS on her 2022 tax return. Further, we learned that $4,240 of her $18,240 ordinary loss allocation from CCS for 2022 cleared both the tax-basis and at-risk hurdles, leaving a total of $14,000 ($9,000 + $5,000) ordinary loss suspended and carried forward. How much of the $4,240 of ordinary loss can Nicole actually deduct on her tax return, given her status as a managing member of CCS?

Answer: Because Nicole is a managing member of CCS, it is likely she will satisfy at least one of the seven tests for material participation in Exhibit 9-9. As a result, she will treat the $4,240 ordinary loss clearing the tax-basis and at-risk hurdles as an active loss. Because Nicole's $4,240 active business loss is less than the $540,000 threshold amount for married taxpayers filing jointly, she does not have an excess business loss and may fully deduct this loss on her tax return.

What if: Suppose that Nicole's share of the 2022 ordinary loss from CCS remaining after applying the tax basis and at-risk limitation was $544,000 rather than $4,240. How much of the loss would be deductible on her return?

Answer: $540,000. Deductible net business losses are limited to $540,000 for taxpayers married filing jointly. The $4,000 excess business loss would be carried forward and used in subsequent years.

What if: Assume Nicole was not a managing member of CCS during 2022 and could not satisfy one of the seven material participation tests in Exhibit 9-9. How much of the $4,240 ordinary loss could she deduct on her tax return, assuming she has no other sources of passive income?

Answer: None. Under this assumption, the $4,240 is a passive activity loss and suspended until Nicole either receives some passive income from CCS (or from some other source) or sells her interest in CCS. In the end, her entire $18,240 loss from 2022 would be suspended: $5,000 due to the tax-basis limitation, $9,000 due to the at-risk limitation, and $4,240 due to the passive activity loss limitation.

[92] §461(l).

CONCLUSION

This chapter explained the relevant tax rules pertaining to forming and operating partnerships. Specifically, we introduced important tax issues arising from partnership formations, including partner gain or loss recognition and the calculation of inside and outside basis. In addition, we explained accounting periods and methods, allocations of partners' ordinary income (loss) and separately stated items, basis adjustments, and loss limitation rules in the context of an operating partnership. Although it would seem that partnership tax law should be relatively straightforward given that partnerships don't pay taxes, by now you may have come to realize quite the opposite is true. The Dispositions of Partnership Interests and Partnership Distributions chapter continues our discussion of partnership tax law with a focus on dispositions of partnership interests and partnership distributions.

Summary

LO 9-1 Describe tax flow-through entities and determine whether they are taxed as partnerships or S corporations.

- Unincorporated business entities with more than one owner are taxed as partnerships unless they elect to be taxed as corporations.
- Owners of entities taxed as corporations may elect to have them treated as flow-through entities by filing an S election with the IRS.
- Though partnerships and S corporations are both flow-through entities, the tax rules that apply to them differ.
- Partnership tax rules reflect both the aggregate and entity concepts.

LO 9-2 Resolve tax issues applicable to partnership formations and other acquisitions of partnership interests, including gain recognition to partners and tax basis for partners and partnerships.

- As a general rule, partners don't recognize gain or loss when they contribute property to partnerships in exchange for a partnership interest.
- Partnership recourse liabilities are allocated to partners with ultimate responsibility for paying the liabilities, and nonrecourse liabilities are allocated to partners using profit-sharing ratios.
- Partners contributing property encumbered by a liability may have to recognize gain, depending on the basis of the property and the amount of the liability.
- Partners contributing property to a partnership will have an initial tax basis in their partnership interest equal to the basis of contributed property less any liability relief plus their share of any partnership liabilities and any gain they recognize.
- Partners receiving partnership interests by contributing capital assets or §1231 assets have a holding period in their partnership interest that includes the holding period of the contributed property. If they contribute any other type of property instead, their holding period begins on the date the partnership interest is received.
- Partnerships with contributed property have a tax basis and holding period in the property equal to the contributing partner's tax basis and holding period.
- Partners who receive capital interests in exchange for services must report the liquidation value of the capital interest as ordinary income, and the partnership either deducts or capitalizes an equivalent amount depending on the nature of the services provided.
- Partners who receive profits interest in exchange for services don't report any income. However, they share in any subsequent partnership profits and losses.
- Partners who purchase partnership interests have a tax basis in their interests equal to the purchase price plus their shares of partnership liabilities, and their holding periods begin on the date of purchase.

LO 9-3 Determine the appropriate accounting periods and methods for partnerships.

- Partnerships, rather than individual partners, are responsible for making most tax elections.
- The Code mandates that partners include their share of income (loss) or other partnership items for "any taxable year of the partnership ending within or with the taxable year of the partner."

- Partnerships must use a tax year-end consistent with the majority interest taxable year, the taxable year of the principal partners, or the year-end providing the least aggregate deferral for the partners.
- For 2022, partnerships with C corporation partners and average annual gross receipts over $27 million (indexed for inflation) may not use the cash method of accounting. Partnerships eligible to use the overall cash method of accounting must still use the accrual method to account for the purchase and sale of inventory in 2022 unless they have average annual gross receipts over the prior three years of $27 million (indexed for inflation) or less. Otherwise, partnerships may use either the cash or accrual method of accounting.

Calculate and characterize a partnership's ordinary business income or loss and its separately stated items, and demonstrate how to report these items to partners. **LO 9-4**

- Partnerships must file Form 1065, U.S. Return of Partnership Income, with the IRS annually and must provide each partner with a Schedule K-1 detailing the partner's share of ordinary business income (loss) and separately stated items.
- Separately stated items include short-term and long-term capital gains and losses, dividends, §1231 gains and losses, and other partnership items that may be treated differently at the partner level.
- The character of separately stated items is determined at the partnership rather than at the partner level.
- Guaranteed payments are typically fixed payments made to partners for services provided to the partnership. They are treated as ordinary income by partners who receive them and are either deducted or capitalized by the partnership depending on the nature of services provided.
- Guaranteed payments to any type of partner (or LLC member) and general partners' shares of ordinary business income (loss) are treated as self-employment income (loss).
- Limited partners' shares of ordinary business income (loss) are not treated as self-employment income (loss).
- Though the tax law is uncertain in this area, all or a portion of LLC members' shares of ordinary business income (loss) should be classified as self-employment income (loss) if members are significantly involved in managing the LLC.
- Partnerships provide a great deal of flexibility because they may specially allocate their income, gains, expenses, losses, and other partnership items, as long as the allocations have "substantial economic effect" or are consistent with partners' interests in the partnership. Special allocations of built-in gain or loss on contributed property to contributing partners are mandatory.

Explain the importance of a partner's tax basis in her partnership interest and the adjustments that affect it. **LO 9-5**

- Partners must make specified annual adjustments to the tax basis in their partnership interests to ensure that partnership taxable income/gain or deductible expense/loss items are not double-taxed or deducted twice and to ensure that partnership tax-exempt income or nondeductible expense is not taxed or deducted.
- Partners increase the tax basis in their interests by their actual or deemed cash contributions, shares of ordinary business income, separately stated income/gain items, and shares of tax-exempt income.
- Partners decrease the tax basis in their interests by their actual or deemed cash distributions, shares of ordinary business loss, separately stated expense/loss items, and shares of nondeductible expenses.
- A partner's tax basis in the partnership interest may never be reduced below zero.
- Cash distributions that are less than a partner's tax basis in her partnership interest immediately before the distribution are not taxable. However, cash distributions in excess of a partner's tax basis in her partnership interest immediately before the distribution are generally taxable as capital gain.

Apply the tax-basis, at-risk amount, passive activity loss, and excess business loss limits to losses from partnerships. **LO 9-6**

- In order for losses to provide tax benefits to partners, partnership losses must clear the tax-basis, at-risk, and passive activity loss hurdles (in that order).
- Partnership losses in excess of a partner's tax basis are suspended and may be utilized only when additional tax basis is created.

- Losses clearing the tax-basis hurdle may be utilized only to the extent of the partner's at-risk amount. A partner's at-risk amount generally equals that partner's tax basis (before any reduction for current-year losses) less the share of nonrecourse liability that is not secured by real estate.
- If a partner is not a material participant in the partnership or if the partnership is involved in rental activities, losses clearing the tax-basis and at-risk hurdles may be reported on the partner's tax return only when that partnership or other sources generate passive income or when the partnership interest is sold.
- If an individual partner is a material participant in the partnership, losses clearing the tax-basis and at-risk hurdles may only be reported on the partner's tax return for 2022 to the extent that the partner has business income from other sources plus a threshold amount of $540,000 for married taxpayers filing jointly and $270,000 for other taxpayers.

KEY TERMS

§704(b) capital accounts (9-9)
aggregate approach (9-3)
at-risk amount (9-31)
at-risk rules (9-31)
built-in gain (9-3)
built-in losses (9-4)
C corporations (9-2)
capital account (9-8)
capital interest (9-3)
entity approach (9-3)
excess business loss (9-35)
flow-through entity (9-2)
Form 1065 (9-24)
Form 7004 (9-24)
GAAP capital accounts (9-8)
general partnerships (9-2)
guaranteed payments (9-19)
inside basis (9-4)
least aggregate deferral (9-15)
limited liability companies (LLC) (9-2)
limited partnerships (9-2)
liquidation value (9-10)
majority interest taxable year (9-15)
nonrecourse liabilities (9-4)
nonservice partners (9-10)
ordinary business income (loss) (9-17)
organizational expenditures (9-12)
outside basis (9-4)
partnership interest (9-3)
passive activity loss (PAL) rules (9-32)
principal partners (9-15)
profits interest (9-3)
qualified nonrecourse financing (9-31)
recourse liabilities (9-4)
S corporation (9-2)
Schedule K (9-24)
self-employment taxes (9-20)
separately stated items (9-17)
service partner (9-10)
special allocations (9-23)
start-up costs (9-12)
Subchapter K (9-2)
Subchapter S (9-2)
syndication costs (9-12)
tax capital account (9-8)

DISCUSSION QUESTIONS

Discussion Questions are available in Connect®.

Mc Graw Hill connect

LO 9-1 1. What is a *flow-through entity,* and what effect does this designation have on how business entities and their owners are taxed?

LO 9-1 2. What types of business entities are taxed as flow-through entities?

LO 9-1 3. Compare and contrast the aggregate and entity concepts for taxing partnerships and their partners.

LO 9-2 4. What is a partnership interest, and what specific economic rights or entitlements are included with it?

LO 9-2 5. What is the rationale for requiring partners to defer most gains and all losses when they contribute property to a partnership?

LO 9-2 6. Under what circumstances is it possible for partners to recognize gain when contributing property to partnerships?

LO 9-2 7. What are *inside basis* and *outside basis,* and why are they relevant for taxing partnerships and partners?

LO 9-2 8. What are *recourse* and *nonrecourse liability,* and how is each generally allocated to partners?

9. How does the amount of liability allocated to a partner affect the amount of gain a partner recognizes when contributing property secured by a liability? LO 9-2
10. What is a tax-basis capital account, and what type of tax-related information does it provide? LO 9-2
11. Distinguish between a capital interest and a profits interest, and explain how partners and partnerships treat each when exchanging them for services provided. LO 9-2
12. How do partners who purchase a partnership interest determine the tax basis and holding period of their partnership interests? LO 9-2
13. Why do you think partnerships, rather than the individual partners, are responsible for making most of the tax elections related to the operation of the partnership? LO 9-3
14. If a partner with a taxable year-end of December 31 is in a partnership with a March 31 taxable year-end, how many months of deferral will the partner receive? Why? LO 9-3
15. In what situation will there be a common year-end for the principal partners when there is no majority interest taxable year? LO 9-3
16. Explain the least aggregate deferral test for determining a partnership's year-end and discuss when it applies. LO 9-3
17. When are partnerships eligible to use the cash method of accounting? LO 9-3
18. What is a partnership's ordinary business income (loss), and how is it calculated? LO 9-4
19. What are some common separately stated items, and why must they be separately stated to the partners? LO 9-4
20. Is the character of partnership income/gains and expenses/losses determined at the partnership or partner level? Why? LO 9-4
21. What are guaranteed payments, and how do partnerships and partners treat them for income and self-employment tax purposes? LO 9-4
22. How do general and limited partners treat their share of ordinary business income for self-employment tax purposes? LO 9-4
23. What challenges do LLCs face when deciding whether to treat their members' shares of ordinary business income as self-employment income? LO 9-4
24. How much flexibility do partnerships have in allocating partnership items to partners? LO 9-4
25. What are the basic tax-filing requirements imposed on partnerships? LO 9-4
26. In what situations do partners need to know the tax basis in their partnership interests? LO 9-5
27. Why does a partner's tax basis in a partnership interest need to be adjusted annually? LO 9-5
28. What items will increase a partner's basis in the partnership interest? LO 9-5
29. What items will decrease a partner's basis in the partnership interest? LO 9-5
30. What hurdles (or limitations) must partners overcome before they can ultimately deduct partnership losses on their tax returns? LO 9-6
31. What happens to partnership losses allocated to partners in excess of the tax basis in their partnership interests? LO 9-6
32. In what sense is the at-risk loss limitation rule more restrictive than the tax-basis loss limitation rule? LO 9-6
33. How do partners measure the amount they have at risk in the partnership? LO 9-6
34. In what order are the loss limitation rules applied to limit partners' losses from partnerships? LO 9-6
35. How do partners determine whether they are passive participants in partnerships when applying the passive activity loss limitation rules? LO 9-6
36. Under what circumstances can partners with passive losses from partnerships deduct their passive losses? LO 9-6

PROBLEMS

Select problems are available in Connect®.

LO 9-2

37. Joseph contributed $22,000 in cash and equipment with a tax basis of $5,000 and a fair market value of $11,000 to Berry Hill Partnership in exchange for a partnership interest.
    a) What is Joseph's tax basis in his partnership interest?
    b) What is Berry Hill's basis in the equipment?

LO 9-2

38. Lance contributed investment property worth $500,000, purchased three years ago for $200,000 cash, to Cloud Peak LLC in exchange for an 85 percent profits and capital interest in the LLC. Cloud Peak owes $300,000 to its suppliers but has no other liabilities.
    a) What is Lance's tax basis in his LLC interest?
    b) What is Lance's holding period in his interest?
    c) What is Cloud Peak's basis in the contributed property?
    d) What is Cloud Peak's holding period in the contributed property?

LO 9-2

39. Rania contributed equipment worth $200,000, purchased 10 months ago for $250,000 cash and used in her sole proprietorship, to Sand Creek LLC in exchange for a 15 percent profits and capital interest in the LLC. Rania agreed to guarantee all $15,000 of Sand Creek's accounts payable, but she did not guarantee any portion of the $100,000 nonrecourse mortgage securing Sand Creek's office building. Other than the accounts payable and mortgage, Sand Creek does not have any liabilities to other creditors.
    a) What is Rania's initial tax basis in her LLC interest?
    b) What is Rania's holding period in her interest?
    c) What is Sand Creek's initial basis in the contributed property?
    d) What is Sand Creek's holding period in the contributed property?

LO 9-2
planning

40. Harry and Sally formed the Evergreen Partnership by contributing the following assets in exchange for a 50 percent capital and profits interest in the partnership:

	Basis	Fair Market Value
Harry:		
Cash	$ 30,000	$ 30,000
Land	100,000	120,000
Totals	$130,000	$150,000
Sally:		
Equipment used in a business	200,000	150,000
Totals	$200,000	$150,000

    a) How much gain or loss will Harry recognize on the contribution?
    b) How much gain or loss will Sally recognize on the contribution?
    c) How could the transaction be structured in a different way to get a better result for Sally?
    d) What is Harry's tax basis in his partnership interest?
    e) What is Sally's tax basis in her partnership interest?
    f) What is Evergreen's tax basis in its assets?
    g) Following the format in Exhibit 9-2, prepare a tax basis balance sheet for the Evergreen partnership showing the tax capital accounts for the partners.

LO 9-2

41. Cosmo contributed land with a fair market value of $400,000 and a tax basis of $90,000 to the Y Mountain Partnership in exchange for a 25 percent profits and capital interest in the partnership. The land is secured by a $120,000 nonrecourse liability. Other than this nonrecourse liability, Y Mountain Partnership does not have any liability.
    a) How much gain will Cosmo recognize from the contribution?
    b) What is Cosmo's tax basis in his partnership interest?

42. When High Horizon LLC was formed, Maude contributed the following assets in exchange for a 25 percent capital and profits interest in the LLC: LO 9-2

	Basis	Fair Market Value
Maude:		
Cash	$ 20,000	$ 20,000
Land*	100,000	360,000
Totals	$120,000	$380,000

*Nonrecourse liability secured by the land equals $160,000.

Hiro, Harold, and Sofiya each contributed $220,000 in cash for a 25 percent profits and capital interest. LO 9-2

a) How much gain or loss will Maude and the other members recognize?
b) What is Maude's tax basis in her LLC interest?
c) What tax basis do Hiro, Harold, and Sofiya have in their LLC interests?
d) What is High Horizon's tax basis in its assets?
e) Following the format in Exhibit 9-2, prepare a tax basis balance sheet for High Horizon LLC showing the tax capital accounts for the members.

43. Kevan, Jerry, and Dave formed Albee LLC. Jerry and Dave each contributed $245,000 in cash. Kevan contributed the following assets: LO 9-2

	Basis	Fair Market Value
Kevan:		
Cash	$ 15,000	$ 15,000
Land*	120,000	440,000
Totals	$135,000	$455,000

*Nonrecourse liability secured by the land equals $210,000.

Each member received a one-third capital and profits interest in the LLC.

a) How much gain or loss will Jerry, Dave, and Kevan recognize on the contributions?
b) What is Kevan's tax basis in his LLC interest?
c) What tax basis do Jerry and Dave have in their LLC interests?
d) What is Albee LLC's tax basis in its assets?
e) Following the format in Exhibit 9-2, prepare a tax basis balance sheet for Albee LLC showing the tax capital accounts for the members. What is Kevan's share of the LLC's inside basis?
f) If the lender holding the nonrecourse liability secured by Kevan's land required Kevan to guarantee 1/3 of the liability and Jerry to guarantee the remaining 2/3 of the liability when Albee LLC was formed, how much gain or loss will Kevan recognize?
g) If the lender holding the nonrecourse liability secured by Kevan's land required Kevan to guarantee 1/3 of the liability and Jerry to guarantee the remaining 2/3 of the liability when Albee LLC was formed, what are the members' tax bases in their LLC interests?

44. Malak has decided to contribute some equipment she previously used in her sole proprietorship in exchange for a 10 percent profits and capital interest in Fast Choppers LLC. Malak originally paid $200,000 cash for the equipment. Since then, the tax basis in the equipment has been reduced to $100,000 because of tax depreciation, and the fair market value of the equipment is now $150,000. LO 9-2 research

a) Must Malak recognize any of the potential §1245 recapture when she contributes the machinery to Fast Choppers? [*Hint:* See §1245(b)(3).]

b) What cost recovery method will Fast Choppers use to depreciate the machinery? [*Hint:* See §168(i)(7).]

c) If Fast Choppers were to immediately sell the equipment Malak contributed for $150,000, how much gain would Malak recognize, and what is its character? [*Hint:* See §§1245 and 704(c).]

LO 9-2 research

45. Ansel purchased raw land three years ago for $200,000 to hold as an investment. After watching the value of the land drop to $150,000, he decided to contribute it to Mountainside Developers LLC in exchange for a 5 percent capital and profits interest. Mountainside plans to develop the property and will treat it as inventory, like all the other real estate it holds.

a) If Mountainside sells the property for $150,000 after holding it for one year, how much gain or loss does it recognize, and what is the character of the gain or loss? [*Hint:* See §724.]

b) If Mountainside sells the property for $125,000 after holding it for two years, how much gain or loss does it recognize, and what is the character of the gain or loss?

c) If Mountainside sells the property for $150,000 after holding it for six years, how much gain or loss does it recognize, and what is the character of the gain or loss?

LO 9-2 research

46. Claude purchased raw land three years ago for $1,500,000 to develop into lots and sell to individuals planning to build their dream homes. Claude intended to treat this property as inventory, like his other development properties. Before completing the development of the property, however, he decided to contribute it to South Peak Investors LLC when it was worth $2,500,000, in exchange for a 10 percent capital and profits interest. South Peak's strategy is to hold land for investment purposes only and then sell it later at a gain.

a) If South Peak sells the property for $3,000,000 four years after Claude's contribution, how much gain or loss is recognized, and what is its character? [*Hint:* See §724.]

b) If South Peak sells the property for $3,000,000 five and one-half years after Claude's contribution, how much gain or loss is recognized, and what is its character?

LO 9-2 research

47. Kamal contributed $10,000 in cash and a capital asset he had held for three years with a fair market value of $20,000 and tax basis of $10,000 for a 5 percent capital and profits interest in Green Valley LLC.

a) If Kamal sells his LLC interest 13 months later for $30,000 when the tax basis in his partnership interest is still $20,000, how much gain does he report, and what is its character?

b) If Kamal sells his LLC interest two months later for $30,000 when the tax basis in his partnership interest is still $20,000, how much gain does he report, and what is its character? [*Hint*: See Reg. §1.1223-3.]

LO 9-2

48. Connie recently provided legal services to the Winterhaven LLC and received a 5 percent interest in the LLC as compensation. Winterhaven currently has $50,000 of accounts payable and no other liabilities. The current fair market value of Winterhaven's capital is $200,000.

a) If Connie receives a 5 percent capital interest only, how much income must she report, and what is her tax basis in the LLC interest?

b) If Connie receives a 5 percent profits interest only, how much income must she report, and what is her tax basis in the LLC interest?

c) If Connie receives a 5 percent capital and profits interest, how much income must she report, and what is her tax basis in the LLC interest?

49. Mary and Scott formed a partnership that maintains its records on a calendar-year basis. The balance sheet of the MS Partnership at year-end is as follows: LO 9-2

	Basis	Fair Market Value
Cash	$ 60	$ 60
Land	60	180
Inventory	72	60
	$192	$300
Mary	$ 96	$150
Scott	96	150
	$192	$300

At the end of the current year, Kari will receive a one-third capital interest only in exchange for services rendered. Kari's interest will not be subject to a substantial risk of forfeiture, and the costs for the type of services she provided are typically not capitalized by the partnership. For the current year, the income and expenses from operations are equal. Consequently, the only tax consequences for the year are those relating to the admission of Kari to the partnership.

a) Compute and characterize any gain or loss Kari may have to recognize as a result of her admission to the partnership.
b) Compute Kari's basis in her partnership interest.
c) Prepare a balance sheet of the partnership immediately after Kari's admission showing the partners' tax capital accounts and capital accounts stated at fair market value.
d) Calculate how much gain or loss Kari would have to recognize if, instead of a capital interest, she received a profits interest.

50. Dave LaCroix recently received a 10 percent capital and profits interest in Cirque Capital LLC in exchange for consulting services he provided. If Cirque Capital had paid an outsider to provide the advice, it would have deducted the payment as compensation expense. Cirque Capital's balance sheet on the day Dave received his capital interest appears below: LO 9-2

	Basis	Fair Market Value
Assets:		
Cash	$150,000	$ 150,000
Investments	200,000	700,000
Land	150,000	250,000
Totals	$500,000	$1,100,000
Liabilities and capital:		
Nonrecourse liabilities	$100,000	$ 100,000
Tatsuki*	200,000	500,000
Robert*	200,000	500,000
Totals	$500,000	$1,100,000

*Assume that Tatsuki's basis and Robert's basis in their LLC interests equal their tax basis capital accounts plus their respective shares of nonrecourse liabilities.

a) Compute and characterize any gain or loss Dave may have to recognize as a result of his admission to Cirque Capital.
b) Compute each member's tax basis in his LLC interest immediately after Dave's receipt of his interest.
c) Prepare a balance sheet for Cirque Capital immediately after Dave's admission showing the members' tax capital accounts and their capital accounts stated at fair market value.

d) Compute and characterize any gain or loss Dave may have to recognize as a result of his admission to Cirque Capital if he receives only a profits interest.

e) Compute each member's tax basis in his LLC interest immediately after Dave's receipt of his interest if Dave receives only a profits interest.

LO 9-2

51. Last December 31, Ramon sold the 10 percent interest in the Del Sol Partnership that he had held for two years to Garrett for $400,000. Prior to selling his interest, Ramon's basis in Del Sol was $200,000, which included a $100,000 share of nonrecourse liabilities allocated to him.

a) What is Garrett's tax basis in his partnership interest?

b) If Garrett sells his partnership interest three months after receiving it and recognizes a gain, what is the character of his gain?

LO 9-3

52. Broken Rock LLC was recently formed with the following members:

Name	Tax Year-End	Capital/Profits %
George Allen	December 31	33.33%
Elanax Corp.	June 30	33.33
Elizabeth Cheam	December 31	33.34

What is the required taxable year-end for Broken Rock LLC?

LO 9-3

53. Granite Slab LLC was recently formed with the following members:

Name	Tax Year-End	Capital/Profits %
Nelson Black	December 31	22.0%
Brittany Jones	December 31	24.0
Lone Pine LLC	June 30	4.5
Red Spot Inc.	October 31	4.5
Pale Rock Inc.	September 30	4.5
Thunder Ridge LLC	July 31	4.5
Alpensee LLC	March 31	4.5
Lakewood Inc.	June 30	4.5
Streamside LLC	October 31	4.5
Burnt Fork Inc.	October 31	4.5
Snowy Ridge LP	June 30	4.5
Whitewater LP	October 31	4.5
Straw Hat LLC	January 31	4.5
Wildfire Inc.	September 30	4.5

What is the required taxable year-end for Granite Slab LLC?

LO 9-3

54. Tall Tree LLC was recently formed with the following members:

Name	Tax Year-End	Capital/Profits %
Eddie Robinson	December 31	40%
Pitcher Lenders LLC	June 30	25
Perry Homes Inc.	October 31	35

What is the required taxable year-end for Tall Tree LLC?

LO 9-3

55. Rock Creek LLC was recently formed with the following members:

Name	Tax Year-End	Capital/Profits %
Mark Banks	December 31	35%
Highball Properties LLC	March 31	25
Chavez Builders Inc.	November 30	40

What is the required taxable year-end for Rock Creek LLC?

56. Ryan, Dahir, and Bill have operated Broken Feather LLC for the last four years using a calendar year-end. Each has a one-third interest. Since they began operating, their busy season has run from June through August, with 35 percent of their gross receipts coming in July and August. The members would like to change their tax year-end and have asked you to address the following questions: LO 9-3 research
    a) Can they change to an August 31 year-end and, if so, how do they make the change? [*Hint:* See Rev. Proc. 2002-38.]
    b) Can they change to a September 30 year-end, and, if so, how do they make the change? [*Hint:* See §444.]

57. Ashlee, Hiroki, Kate, and Albee LLC each owns a 25 percent interest in Tally Industries LLC, which generates annual gross receipts of over $10 million. Ashlee, Hiroki, and Kate manage the business, but Albee LLC is a nonmanaging member. Although Tally Industries has historically been profitable, for the last three years losses have been allocated to the members. Given these facts, the members want to know whether Tally Industries can use the cash method of accounting. Why or why not? [*Hint:* See §448(b)(3).] LO 9-3 research

58. Turtle Creek Partnership had the following revenues, expenses, gains, losses, and distributions: LO 9-4

Sales revenue	$ 40,000
Long-term capital gains	2,000
Cost of goods sold	(13,000)
Depreciation—MACRS	(3,000)
Amortization of organization costs	(1,000)
Guaranteed payments to partners for general management	(10,000)
Cash distributions to partners	(2,000)

   a) Given these items, what is Turtle Creek's ordinary business income (loss) for the year?
   b) What are Turtle Creek's separately stated items for the year?

59. Georgio owns a 20 percent profits and capital interest in Rain Tree LLC. For the current year, Rain Tree had the following revenues, expenses, gains, and losses: LO 9-4

Sales revenue	$ 70,000
Gain on sale of land (§1231)	11,000
Cost of goods sold	(26,000)
Depreciation—MACRS	(3,000)
§179 deduction*	(10,000)
Employee wages	(11,000)
Nondeductible fines and penalties	(3,000)
Municipal bond interest	6,000
Short-term capital gains	4,000
Guaranteed payment to Sandra	(3,000)

*Assume the §179 property placed in service limitation does not apply.

   a) How much ordinary business income (loss) is allocated to Georgio for the year?
   b) What are Georgio's separately stated items for the year?

60. Richard Mendez and two friends from law school recently formed Mendez and Associates as a limited liability partnership (LLP). Income from the partnership will be split equally among the partners. The partnership will generate fee income primarily from representing clients in bankruptcy and foreclosure matters. While some attorney friends have suggested that partners' earnings will be self-employment income, other attorneys they know from their local bar association meetings claim just the opposite. After examining relevant authority, explain how you would advise Mendez and Associates on this matter. [*Hint:* See §1402(a)(13) and *Renkemeyer, Campbell & Weaver LLP v. Comm'r,* 136 TC 137 (2011).] LO 9-4

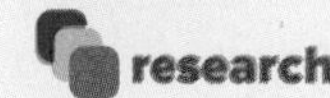

LO 9-4

61. The partnership agreement of the G&P general partnership states that Gary will receive a guaranteed payment of $13,000, and that Gary and Prudence will share the remaining profits or losses in a 45/55 ratio. For year 1, the G&P partnership reports the following results:

Sales revenue	$70,000
Gain on sale of land (§1231)	8,000
Cost of goods sold	(38,000)
Depreciation—MACRS	(9,000)
Employee wages	(14,000)
Cash charitable contributions	(3,000)
Municipal bond interest	2,000
Other expenses	(2,000)

a) Compute Gary's share of ordinary income (loss) and separately stated items to be reported on his year 1 Schedule K-1, including his self-employment income (loss).
b) Compute Gary's share of self-employment income (loss) to be reported on his year 1 Schedule K-1, assuming G&P is a limited partnership and Gary is a limited partner.
c) What do you believe Gary's share of self-employment income (loss) to be reported on his year 1 Schedule K-1 should be, assuming G&P is an LLC and Gary spends 2,000 hours per year working there full time?

LO 9-4
research

62. Hoki Poki, a cash-method general partnership, recorded the following items for its current tax year:

Rental real estate income	$ 2,000
Sales revenue	70,000
§1245 recapture income	8,000
Interest income	2,000
Cost of goods sold	(38,000)
Depreciation—MACRS	(9,000)
Supplies expense	(1,000)
Employee wages	(14,000)
Investment interest expense	(1,000)
Partner's medical insurance premiums paid by Hoki Poki	(3,000)

As part of preparing Hoki Poki's current-year return, identify the items that should be included in computing its ordinary business income (loss) and those that should be separately stated. [*Hint:* See Schedule K-1 and related preparer's instructions at www.irs.gov.]

LO 9-4
research

63. On the last day of its current tax year, Buy Rite LLC received $300,000 when it sold a machine it had purchased for $200,000 three years ago to use in its business. At the time of the sale, the basis in the equipment had been reduced to $100,000 due to tax depreciation taken. How much did the members' self-employment earnings from Buy Rite increase when the equipment was sold? [*Hint:* See §1402(a)(3).]

LO 9-4

64. Jhumpa, Stewart, and Kelly are all one-third partners in the capital and profits of Firewalker General Partnership. In addition to their normal share of the partnership's annual income, Jhumpa and Stewart receive an annual guaranteed payment of $10,000 each to compensate them for additional services they provide. Firewalker's income statement for the current year reflects the following revenues and expenses:

Sales revenue	$340,000
Interest income	3,300
Long-term capital gains	1,200
Cost of goods sold	(120,000)
Employee wages	(75,000)
Depreciation expense	(28,000)
Guaranteed payments	(20,000)
Miscellaneous expenses	(4,500)
Overall net income	$ 97,000

a) Given Firewalker's operating results, how much ordinary business income (loss) and what separately stated items [including the partners' self-employment earnings (loss)] will it report on its return for the year?
b) How will it allocate these amounts to its partners?
c) How much self-employment tax will each partner pay assuming none has any other source of income or loss?

65. This year, Darrel's distributive share from Alcove Partnership includes $6,000 of interest income, $3,000 of dividend income, and $70,000 ordinary business income. LO 9-4
a) Assume that Darrel materially participates in the partnership. How much of his distributive share from Alcove Partnership is potentially subject to the net investment income tax?
b) Assume that Darrel does not materially participate in the partnership. How much of his distributive share from Alcove Partnership is potentially subject to the net investment income tax?

66. This year, Agustin's distributive share from Eden Lakes Partnership includes $8,000 of interest income, $4,000 of net long-term capital gains, $2,000 net §1231 gain from the sale of property used in the partnership's trade or business, and $83,000 of ordinary business income. LO 9-4
a) Assume that Agustin materially participates in the partnership. How much of his distributive share from Eden Lakes Partnership is potentially subject to the net investment income tax?
b) Assume that Agustin does not materially participate in the partnership. How much of his distributive share from Eden Lakes Partnership is potentially subject to the net investment income tax?

67. Lane and Cal each owns 50 percent of the profits and capital of HighYield LLC. HighYield owns a portfolio of taxable bonds and municipal bonds, and each year the portfolio generates approximately $10,000 of taxable interest and $10,000 of tax-exempt interest. Lane's marginal tax rate is 35 percent, while Cal's marginal tax rate is 12 percent. To take advantage of the difference in their marginal tax rates, Lane and Cal want to modify their operating agreement to specially allocate all of the taxable interest to Cal and all of the tax-exempt interest to Lane. Until now, Lane and Cal had been allocated 50 percent of each type of interest income. LO 9-4 research
a) Is HighYield's proposed special allocation acceptable under current tax rules? Why or why not? [*Hint:* See Reg. §1.704-1(b)(2)(iii)(b) and (5) Example (5).]
b) If the IRS ultimately disagrees with HighYield's special allocation, how will it likely reallocate the taxable and tax-exempt interest among the members? [*Hint:* See Reg. §1.704-1(b)(5) Example (5)(ii).]

68. Mustafa's tax basis in his partnership interest at the beginning of the year was $10,000. If his share of the partnership liabilities increased by $10,000 during the year and his share of partnership income for the year is $3,000, what is his tax basis in his partnership interest at the end of the year? LO 9-5

69. Carmine was allocated the following items from Piccolo LLC for last year: LO 9-5

Ordinary business loss
Nondeductible penalties
Tax-exempt interest income
Short-term capital gain
Cash distributions

Rank these items in terms of the order in which they should be applied to adjust Carmine's tax basis in Piccolo for the year (some items may be of equal rank).

LO 9-5

70. Oscar, Felix, and Marv are all one-third partners in the capital and profits of Eastside General Partnership. In addition to their normal share of the partnership's annual income, Oscar and Felix receive annual guaranteed payments of $7,000 to compensate them for additional services they provide. Eastside's income statement for the current year reflects the following revenues and expenses:

Sales revenue	$420,000
Dividend income	5,700
Short-term capital gains	2,800
Cost of goods sold	(210,000)
Employee wages	(115,000)
Depreciation expense	(28,000)
Guaranteed payments	(14,000)
Miscellaneous expenses	(9,500)
Overall net income	$ 52,000

In addition, Eastside owed creditors $120,000 at the beginning of the year but managed to pay down its liabilities to $90,000 by the end of the year. All partnership liabilities are allocated equally among the partners. Finally, Oscar, Felix, and Marv had a tax basis of $80,000 in their interests at the beginning of the year.

a) What tax basis do the partners have in their partnership interests at the end of the year?

b) Assume the partners began the year with a tax basis of $10,000 and all the liabilities were paid off on the last day of the year. How much gain will the partners recognize when the liabilities are paid off? What tax basis do the partners have in their partnership interests at the end of the year?

LO 9-5

71. Pam, Sergei, and Mercedes are all one-third partners in the capital and profits of Oak Grove General Partnership. Partnership liabilities are allocated among the partners in accordance with their capital and profits interests. In addition to their normal share of the partnership's annual income, Pam and Sergei receive annual guaranteed payments of $20,000 each to compensate them for additional services they provide. Oak Grove's income statement for the current year reflects the following revenues and expenses:

Sales revenue	$476,700
Dividend income	6,600
§1231 losses	(3,800)
Cost of goods sold	(245,000)
Employee wages	(92,000)
Depreciation expense	(31,000)
Guaranteed payments	(40,000)
Miscellaneous expenses	(11,500)
Overall net income	$ 60,000

In addition, Oak Grove owed creditors $90,000 at the beginning of the year and $150,000 at the end, and Pam, Sergei, and Mercedes had a tax basis of $50,000 in their interests at the beginning of the year. Also, on December 31 of the current year, Sergei and Mercedes agreed to increase Pam's capital and profits interests from 1/3 to 40 percent in exchange for additional services she provided to the partnership. The current liquidation value of the additional capital interest Pam received is $40,000.

a) What tax basis do the partners have in their partnership interests at the end of the year?

b) If, in addition to the expenses listed above, the partnership donated $12,000 to a political campaign, what tax basis do the partners have in their partnership interests at the end of the year assuming the liquidation value of the additional capital interest Pam received at the end of the year remains at $40,000?

72. Laura Davis is a member in a limited liability company that has historically been profitable but is expecting to generate losses in the near future because of a weak local economy. In addition to the hours she works as an employee of a local business, she currently spends approximately 150 hours per year helping to manage the LLC. Other LLC members work approximately 175 hours per year each in the LLC, and the time Laura and other members spend managing the LLC has remained constant since she joined the company three years ago. Laura's tax basis and amount at risk are large compared to her share of projected losses; however, she is concerned that her ability to deduct her share of the projected losses will be limited by the passive activity loss rules. LO 9-6 research
   a) As an LLC member, will Laura's share of losses be presumed to be passive as they are for limited partners? Why or why not? [*Hint:* See §469(h)(2); *Garnett v. Comm'r,* 132 TC 368 (2009); and Prop. Reg. §1.469-5(e)(3)(i).]
   b) Assuming Laura's losses are not presumed to be passive, is she devoting sufficient time to the LLC to be considered a material participant? Why or why not?
   c) What would you recommend to Laura to help her achieve a more favorable tax outcome?

73. Alfonso began the year with a tax basis in his partnership interest of $30,000. His share of partnership liabilities at the beginning and end of the year consists of $4,000 of recourse liabilities and $6,000 of nonrecourse liabilities. During the year, he was allocated $40,000 of partnership ordinary business loss. Alfonso does not materially participate in this partnership, and he has $1,000 of passive income from other sources. LO 9-6
   a) How much of Alfonso's loss is limited by his tax basis?
   b) How much of Alfonso's loss is limited by his at-risk amount?
   c) How much of Alfonso's loss is limited by the passive activity loss rules?

74. Nareh began the year with a tax basis of $45,000 in her partnership interest. Her share of partnership liabilities consists of $6,000 of recourse liabilities and $10,000 of nonrecourse liabilities at the beginning of the year and $6,000 of recourse liabilities and $13,000 of nonrecourse liabilities at the end of the year. During the year, she was allocated $65,000 of partnership ordinary business loss. Nareh does not materially participate in this partnership, and she has $4,000 of passive income from other sources. LO 9-6
   a) How much of Nareh's loss is limited by her tax basis?
   b) How much of Nareh's loss is limited by her at-risk amount?
   c) How much of Nareh's loss is limited by the passive activity loss rules?

75. Juan Diego began the year with a tax basis in his partnership interest of $50,000. During the year, he was allocated $20,000 of partnership ordinary business income, $70,000 of §1231 losses, and $30,000 of short-term capital losses and received a cash distribution of $50,000. LO 9-5 LO 9-6 research
   a) What items related to these allocations does Juan Diego actually report on his tax return for the year? [*Hint:* See Reg. §1.704-1(d)(2) and Rev. Rul. 66-94.]
   b) If any deductions or losses are limited, what are the carryover amounts, and what is their character? [*Hint:* See Reg. §1.704-1(d).]

76. Farell is a member of Sierra Vista LLC. Although Sierra Vista is involved in a number of different business ventures, it is not currently involved in real estate either as an investor or as a developer. On January 1, year 1, Farell has a $100,000 tax basis in his LLC interest that includes his $90,000 share of Sierra Vista's general liabilities. By the end of the year, Farell's share of Sierra Vista's general liabilities have increased to $100,000. Because of the time he spends in other endeavors, Farell does not materially participate in Sierra Vista. His share of the Sierra Vista losses for year 1 LO 9-6

is $120,000. As a partner in the Riverwoods Partnership, he also has year 1, Schedule K-1 passive income of $5,000. Farell is single and has no other sources of business income or loss.

a) Determine how much of the Sierra Vista loss Farell will currently be able to deduct on his tax return for year 1, and list the losses suspended due to tax-basis, at-risk, and passive activity loss limitations.

b) Assuming Farell's Riverwoods K-1 indicates passive income of $30,000, determine how much of the Sierra Vista loss he will ultimately be able to deduct on his tax return for year 1, and list the losses suspended due to tax-basis, at-risk, and passive activity loss limitations.

c) Assuming Farell is deemed to be an active participant in Sierra Vista, determine how much of the Sierra Vista loss he will ultimately be able to deduct on his tax return for year 1, and list the losses suspended due to tax-basis, at-risk, and passive activity loss limitations.

d) Assuming Farell is deemed to be an active participant in Sierra Vista, and he also has a $280,000 loss from a sole proprietorship, determine how much total trade or business loss Farell will deduct on his return in year 1.

LO 9-6

77. Jenkins has a one-third capital and profits interest in the Maverick General Partnership. On January 1, year 1, Maverick has $120,000 of general liabilities and Jenkins has a $50,000 tax basis (including his share of Maverick's liabilities) in his partnership interest. During the year, Maverick incurred a $30,000 nonrecourse liability that is not secured by real estate. Because Maverick is a rental real estate partnership, Jenkins is deemed to be a passive participant in Maverick. His share of the Maverick losses for year 1 is $75,000. Jenkins is not involved in any other passive activities, and this is the first year he has been allocated losses from Maverick.

a) Determine how much of the Maverick loss Jenkins will currently be able to deduct on his tax return for year 1, and list the losses suspended due to tax-basis, at-risk, and passive activity loss limitations.

b) If Jenkins sells his interest on January 1, year 2, what happens to his suspended losses from year 1? [*Hint:* See §706(c)(2)(A); Reg. §1.704-1(d)(1); Prop. Reg. §1.465-66(a); and *Sennett v. Comm'r,* 80 TC 825 (1983).]

LO 9-6

78. Suki and Steve own 50 percent capital and profits interests in Lorinda LLC. Lorinda operates the local minor league baseball team and owns the stadium where the team plays. Although the liability incurred to build the stadium was paid off several years ago, Lorinda owes its general creditors $300,000 (at the beginning of the year) that is not secured by firm property or guaranteed by any of the members. At the beginning of 2022, Suki and Steve had a tax basis of $170,000 in their LLC interests, including their share of liabilities owed to the general creditors. Shortly before the end of the year, they each received a $10,000 cash distribution, even though Lorinda's ordinary business loss for the year was $400,000. Because of the time commitment to operate a baseball team, both Suki and Steve spent more than 1,500 hours during the year operating Lorinda. Both Suki and Steve are single, and neither of them has any business income or losses from other sources.

a) Determine how much of the Lorinda loss Suki and Steve will each be able to deduct on their current tax returns, and list their losses suspended by the tax-basis, at-risk, and passive activity loss limitations.

b) Assume that some time before receiving the $10,000 cash distribution, Steve is advised by his tax adviser that his marginal tax rate will be abnormally high during the current year because of an unexpected windfall. To help Steve utilize more of the losses allocated from Lorinda in the current year, his adviser recommends refusing the cash distribution and personally guaranteeing $100,000 of Lorinda's liabilities, without the right to be reimbursed by Suki. If Steve follows his adviser's recommendations, how much additional Lorinda loss can he deduct on his current tax return? How does Steve's decision affect the amount of loss Suki can deduct on her current return and the amount and type of her suspended losses?

79. Ray and Matias own 50 percent capital and profits interests in Alpine Properties LLC. Alpine builds and manages rental real estate, and Ray and Matias each works full time (over 1,000 hours per year) managing Alpine. Alpine's liabilities (at both the beginning and end of the year) consist of $1,500,000 in nonrecourse mortgages obtained from an unrelated bank and secured by various rental properties. At the beginning of the current year, Ray and Matias each had a tax basis of $250,000 in his respective LLC interest, including his share of the nonrecourse mortgage liability. Alpine's ordinary business losses for the current year totaled $600,000, and neither member is involved in other activities that generate passive income.

LO 9-6

a) How much of each member's loss is suspended because of the tax-basis limitation?
b) How much of each member's loss is suspended because of the at-risk limitation?
c) How much of each member's loss is suspended because of the passive activity loss limitation? [*Hint:* See §469(c)(7).]
d) If both Ray and Matias are single and Ray has a current-year loss of $50,000 from a sole proprietorship, how much trade or business loss can each deduct on his tax return in the current year?

COMPREHENSIVE PROBLEMS

Select problems are available in Connect®.

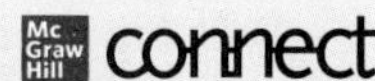

80. Aaron, Deanne, and Keon formed the Blue Bell General Partnership at the beginning of the current year. Aaron and Deanne each contributed $110,000, and Keon transferred an acre of undeveloped land to the partnership. The land had a tax basis of $70,000 and was appraised at $180,000. The land was also encumbered with a $70,000 nonrecourse mortgage for which no one was personally liable. All three partners agreed to split profits and losses equally. At the end of the first year, Blue Bell made a $7,000 principal payment on the mortgage. For the first year of operations, the partnership records disclosed the following information:

Sales revenue	$470,000
Cost of goods sold	410,000
Operating expenses	70,000
Long-term capital gains	2,400
§1231 gains	900
Charitable contributions	300
Municipal bond interest	300
Salary paid as a guaranteed payment to Deanne (not included in expenses)	3,000

a) Compute the adjusted basis of each partner's interest in the partnership immediately after the formation of the partnership.
b) List the separate items of partnership income, gains, losses, and deductions that the partners must show on their individual income tax returns that include the results of the partnership's first year of operations.

c) Using the information generated in answering parts (a) and (b), prepare Blue Bell's page 1 and Schedule K to be included with its Form 1065 for its first year of operations, along with Schedule K-1 for Deanne.

d) What are the partners' adjusted bases in their partnership interests at the end of the first year of operations?

81. The TimpRiders LP has operated a motorcycle dealership for a number of years. Amir is the limited partner, Francesca is the general partner, and they share capital and profits equally. Francesca works full time managing the partnership. Both the partnership and the partners report on a calendar-year basis. At the start of the current year, Amir and Francesca had bases of $10,000 and $3,000, respectively, and the partnership did not have any liabilities. During the current year, the partnership reported the following results from operations:

Net sales	$650,000
Cost of goods sold	500,000
Operating expenses	160,000
Short-term capital loss	2,000
Tax-exempt interest	2,000
§1231 gain	6,000

On the last day of the year, the partnership distributed $3,000 each to Amir and Francesca.

a) What outside basis do Amir and Francesca have in their partnership interests at the end of the year?

b) How much of their losses are currently not deductible by Amir and Francesca because of the tax-basis limitation?

c) To what extent does the passive activity loss limitation apply in restricting their deductible losses for the year?

d) Using the information provided, prepare TimpRiders's page 1 and Schedule K to be included with its Form 1065 for the current year. Also, prepare a Schedule K-1 for Amir and Francesca.

82. LeBron, Dennis, and Susan formed the Bar T LLC at the beginning of the current year. LeBron and Dennis each contributed $200,000 and Susan transferred several acres of agricultural land she had purchased two years earlier to the LLC. The land had a tax basis of $50,000 and was appraised at $300,000. The land was also encumbered with a $100,000 nonrecourse mortgage (i.e., qualified nonrecourse financing) for which no one was personally liable. The members plan to use the land and cash to begin a cattle-feeding operation. Susan will work full time operating the business, but LeBron and Dennis will devote less than two days per year to the operation.

All three members agree to split profits and losses equally. At the end of the first year, Bar T had accumulated $40,000 of accounts payable jointly guaranteed by LeBron and Dennis and had made a $9,000 principal payment on the mortgage. None of the members have passive income from other sources or business income from other sources. LeBron and Dennis are married, while Susan is single.

For the first year of operations, the partnership records disclosed the following information:

Sales revenue	$620,000
Cost of goods sold	380,000
Operating expenses	670,000
Dividends	1,200
Municipal bond interest	300
Salary paid as a guaranteed payment to Susan (not included in expenses)	10,000
Cash distributions split equally among the members at year-end	3,000

a) Compute the tax basis of each member's interest immediately after the formation of the LLC.
b) When does each member's holding period for his or her LLC interest begin?
c) What are Bar T's tax basis and holding period in its land?
d) What is Bar T's required tax year-end?
e) What overall methods of accounting were initially available to Bar T?
f) List the separate items of partnership income, gains, losses, deductions, and other items that will be included in each member's Schedule K-1 for the first year of operations. Use the proposed self-employment tax regulations to determine each member's self-employment income or loss.
g) What are the members' tax bases in their LLC interests at the end of the first year of operations?
h) What are the members' at-risk amounts in their LLC interests at the end of the first year of operations?
i) How much loss from Bar T, if any, will the members be able to deduct on their individual returns from the first year of operations?

UWorld Roger CPA Review

Sample CPA Exam questions from Roger CPA Review are available in Connect as support for the topics in this text. These Multiple Choice Questions and Task-Based Simulations include expert-written explanations and solutions and provide a starting point for students to become familiar with the content and functionality of the actual CPA Exam.

chapter

10 Dispositions of Partnership Interests and Partnership Distributions

Learning Objectives

Upon completing this chapter, you should be able to:

LO 10-1 Determine the tax consequences to the buyer and seller of the disposition of a partnership interest, including the amount and character of gain or loss recognized.

LO 10-2 List the reasons for distributions, and compare operating and liquidating distributions.

LO 10-3 Determine the tax consequences of proportionate operating distributions.

LO 10-4 Determine the tax consequences of proportionate liquidating distributions.

LO 10-5 Explain the significance of disproportionate distributions.

LO 10-6 Explain the rationale for special basis adjustments, determine when they are necessary, and calculate the special basis adjustment for dispositions and distributions.

Andresr/E+/Getty Images

Storyline Summary

Taxpayer:	Color Comfort Sheets LLC
Location:	Salt Lake City, Utah
Owners and interests:	Nicole Johnson (she/her/hers), managing member—30 percent interest
	Sarah Walker (she/her/hers), managing member—40 percent interest
	Greg Randall (he/him/his), nonmanaging member—30 percent interest

In January 2023,* Nicole and Sarah sit in the Color Comfort Sheets (CCS) LLC office discussing the current state of business affairs over a cup of coffee. They both agree they are not doing as well as they had hoped after two years of running the business. Their main topic of discussion this morning is how to turn the business around. Both women know the viability of the business is at stake if they can't figure out how to make it profitable . . . and soon.

As Nicole and Sarah brainstorm various ideas, Nicole's administrative assistant interrupts to announce a phone call from Olivia Winsted, the media mogul. Nicole takes the call. On her top-rated television talk show, Olivia occasionally promotes a product to her viewers based on her own successful experience using it. Apparently, one of Olivia's viewers sent her a set of Color Comfort sheets, and Olivia is so happy with the product that she wants to promote it on her show in about two weeks. Nicole and Sarah are, of course, thrilled with this news. Products Olivia has endorsed in the past have become wildly successful. The focus of Nicole and Sarah's meeting changes dramatically. Now they have to figure out how they can gear up for an immediate increase in production. Nicole and Sarah's analysis of the accounting records reveals that CCS is in a precarious cash position—the business is down to its last $10,000.

Nicole and Sarah immediately call Greg to fill him in on the news. Greg is as thrilled as they are to hear that Olivia will promote their sheets and agrees to kick in an additional $30,000. Nicole says she will contribute $30,000 and Sarah antes up another $40,000.

The following couple of weeks fly by in a whirlwind of work—phone calls, meetings with bankers, and production scheduling. Olivia's special guest for the show is the popular film star Tom Hughes, promoting his soon-to-be-released movie *Global Warfare*. Tom is good-natured and expresses interest in the sheets. During the show, he announces he will order a set as soon as the broadcast is over. Nicole and Sarah anticipate orders will roll in. Sure enough, before Olivia has even said goodbye to her studio audience, CCS's website traffic has picked up and the phone lines are hopping with new orders.

By the end of 2023, CCS's financial situation has completely turned around; business is booming, the accounting records show a healthy profit, and the members feel comfortable the trend will continue. Greg decides it is time to talk to Nicole and Sarah about cashing out his investment.

(to be continued. . .)

*To allow the storyline to continue from the previous chapter, this chapter begins in 2023 with CCS treated as a partnership for tax purposes. We assume the 2022 tax laws apply for 2023 and subsequent years.

This chapter explores the tax consequences associated with selling partnership interests and distributing partnership assets to partners. In the Business Entities Overview chapter, we learned that Color Comfort Sheets LLC actually elected to be taxed as a C corporation. In this chapter, we assume it did not make this election, leaving it to be taxed as a partnership.

LO 10-1

BASICS OF SALES OF PARTNERSHIP INTERESTS

As we've seen in preceding chapters, owners of various business entities receive returns on their investments, either when the business makes distributions or upon the sale of their business interest. Corporate shareholders may sell their stock to other investors or back to the corporation. Likewise, partners may dispose of their interest in several ways—by selling to a third party, selling to another partner, or transferring the interest back to the partnership. The payments in a disposition (sale) can come from either another owner of the partnership or a new partner; in either case, the sale proceeds come from outside the partnership.

Selling a **partnership interest** raises unique issues because of the flow-through nature of the entity. For example, is the interest a separate asset, or does the disposition represent the sale of the partner's share of each of the partnership's assets? To the extent the tax rules follow an entity approach, the interest is considered a separate asset and a sale of the partnership interest is very similar to the sale of corporate stock. That is, the partner simply recognizes capital gain or loss on the sale, based on the difference between the sales price and the partner's tax basis in the partnership interest. Alternately, to the extent the tax rules use the aggregate approach, the disposition represents a sale of the partner's share of each of the partnership's assets. This approach adds some complexity because of the differing character and holding periods of the partnership assets—ordinary, capital, and §1231. The selling partner also has the additional task of allocating the sales proceeds among the underlying assets in order to determine the gain or loss on each.

Rather than strictly following one approach, the tax rules end up being a mixture of the two approaches (see the Forming and Operating Partnerships chapter for a more detailed discussion of the entity and aggregate approaches). When feasible, the entity approach controls; however, if the result distorts the amount or character of income, then the aggregate approach dominates. We discuss the tax consequences of sales of partnership interests by first taking the perspective of the seller (partner), followed by a discussion from the perspective of the buyer (new investor).

Seller Issues

The seller's primary tax concern in a partnership interest sale is calculating the amount and character of gain or loss on the sale. The selling partner calculates the gain or loss as the difference between the amount realized and the **outside basis** in the partnership interest determined on the date of the sale.[1] Because selling partners are no longer responsible for their share of the partnership liabilities, any debt relief increases the amount that partners *realize* from the sale under general tax principles.

[1]Partners determine their outside basis as discussed in the Forming and Operating Partnerships chapter. Importantly, the outside basis includes the selling partner's share of distributive income for the year to the date of the sale.

Example 10-1

Last year, Chanzz Inc. sold its 30 percent interest in CCS on June 30 to Greg Randall, a wealthy local entrepreneur, to limit its exposure to any further losses. Greg anticipated that CCS would become profitable in the near future and paid Chanzz Inc. $100,000 for its interest in CCS. Chanzz's share of CCS liabilities as of June 30 was $24,000. Chanzz Inc.'s outside basis in its CCS interest at the sale date was $105,000 (including its share of CCS's liabilities). What amount of gain or loss did Chanzz recognize on the sale?

Answer: $19,000 gain, computed as follows:

Description	Amount	Explanation
(1) Cash and fair market value of property received	$100,000	
(2) Debt relief	24,000	
(3) Amount realized	$124,000	(1) + (2)
(4) Outside basis in CCS interest	105,000	
Recognized gain	**$ 19,000**	(3) − (4)

THE KEY FACTS

Sale of Partnership Interest

- Seller issues:
  - Gain or loss calculation.
    Amount realized:
    Cash and fair market value of property received
    Plus: Debt relief
    Less: Outside basis in partnership interest
    Equals: Realized gain or loss
  - Some of seller's gain or loss may be ordinary if hot assets are present inside the partnership.
  - Tax year closes with respect to selling partner when the entire interest is sold.
- Buyer issues:
  - Outside basis—cost of the partnership interest plus share of partnership's liabilities.
  - Inside basis—generally equals selling partner's inside basis at sale date.

The character of the gain or loss from a sale of a partnership interest is generally short-term or long-term capital gain or loss depending on the selling partner's holding period.[2] However, a portion of the gain or loss will be ordinary if a seller realizes any gain or loss attributable to **unrealized receivables** or **inventory items.**[3] Practitioners often refer to these assets that give rise to ordinary gains and losses as **hot assets.**[4] Let's discuss that term further because these assets are central to determining the tax treatment of many transactions in this chapter.

Hot Assets As you might expect, unrealized receivables include the right to receive payment for (1) "goods delivered, or to be delivered,"[5] or (2) "services rendered, or to be rendered."[6] For cash-method taxpayers, unrealized receivables include amounts earned but not yet received (accounts receivable). Accrual-method taxpayers, however, do not consider accounts receivable as unrealized receivables because they have already realized and recognized these items as ordinary income. Unrealized receivables also include items the partnership would treat as ordinary income if it sold the assets for its fair market value, such as depreciation recapture under §1245.[7]

[2]§§731, 741.

[3]§751(a). Partnerships are required to provide Form 8308, Report of a Sale or Exchange of Certain Partnership Interests, to all the parties to the sale as well as to the IRS. Selling partners include this form with their tax returns as well as a statement detailing the calculation of any ordinary gain from the sale of their interest. Practically speaking, these calculations are made with information provided by the partnership.

[4]There are actually two definitions of *inventory items* in §751. Section 751(a) *inventory items* are defined in §751(d) to include *all* inventory items. However, under §751(b), the definition includes only *substantially appreciated* inventory. For purposes of determining the character of gain or loss from the sale of partnership interests, the term *inventory items* includes all inventory as in §751(a). However, these two definitions have created some confusion when using the term *hot assets*. In this chapter, we use the term *hot assets* to refer to unrealized receivables and all inventory items as in §751(a). The definition under §751(b) becomes more relevant when determining the tax treatment in a disproportionate distribution (discussed only briefly later in the chapter).

[5]§751(c)(1).

[6]§751(c)(2).

[7]§751(c).

Inventory items include classic inventory, defined as property held for sale to customers in the ordinary course of business, but also, more broadly, any assets that are *not* capital assets or §1231 assets.[8] Under this definition, assets such as equipment or real estate used in the business but not held for more than a year and all accounts receivable are considered inventory. This broad definition means cash, capital assets, and §1231 assets are the only properties not considered inventory.[9]

Example 10-2

CCS's balance sheet last year as of the date of Chanzz's sale of its CCS interest to Greg follows:

Color Comfort Sheets LLC
June 30, 2022

	Tax Basis	FMV
Assets		
Cash	$ 27,000	$ 27,000
Accounts receivable	0	13,000
Investments	15,000	12,000
Inventory	1,000	1,000
Equipment (acc. depr. = $20,000)	80,000	86,000
Building	97,000	97,000
Land	20,000	150,000
Totals	$240,000	$386,000
Liabilities and capital		
Long-term debt	$100,000*	
Capital—Nicole	(49,000)	
—Sarah	108,000	
—Chanzz	81,000	
Totals	$240,000	

*Of the $100,000 of long-term debt, $20,000 is allocated solely to Nicole. The remaining $80,000 is allocated to all three owners according to their profit-sharing ratios (30 percent to Nicole, 40 percent to Sarah, and 30 percent to Greg).

Which of CCS's assets are considered hot assets under §751(a)?

Answer: The hot assets are accounts receivable of $13,000 and $6,000 depreciation recapture (§1245) potential ($86,000 – $80,000) in the equipment. The accounts receivable are unrealized receivables because CCS has not included them in income for tax purposes under CCS's cash accounting method. The depreciation recapture is also considered an unrealized receivable under §751(a). Inventory would be considered a hot asset; however, because the tax basis and fair market value are equal, it will not affect the character of any gain recognized on the sale.

[8]§751(d)(1).

[9]This broad definition of inventory includes all unrealized receivables except for recapture. Recapture items are excluded from the definition of inventory items simply because recapture is not technically an asset; rather, it is merely a portion of gain that results from the sale of property. Recapture is, however, considered an unrealized receivable (i.e., hot asset) under §751(a). This idea is important in determining whether inventory is substantially appreciated for purposes of determining the §751 assets for distributions, as we discuss later in the chapter.

Example 10-3

Review CCS's balance sheet as of the end of 2023.

Color Comfort Sheets LLC December 31, 2023	Tax Basis	FMV
Assets		
Cash	$390,000	$ 390,000
Accounts receivable	0	40,000
Inventory	90,000	200,000
Investments	60,000	105,000
Equipment (acc. depr. = $50,000)	150,000	200,000
Building (acc. depr. = $10,000)	90,000	100,000
Land—original	20,000	160,000
Land—investment	140,000	270,000
Totals	$940,000	$1,465,000
Liabilities and capital		
Accounts payable	$ 80,000	
Long-term debt	0	
Mortgage on original land	40,000	
Mortgage on investment land	120,000	
Capital—Nicole	119,000	
—Sarah	332,000	
—Greg	249,000	
Totals	$940,000	

What amount of CCS's assets are considered to be hot assets as of December 31, 2023?

Answer: The hot assets include inventory with a fair market value of $200,000 and unrealized receivables consisting of $50,000 of depreciation recapture potential on the equipment and $40,000 of accounts receivable.

When selling an interest in a partnership that holds hot assets, a partner modifies the calculation of the gain or loss to ensure the portion that relates to hot assets is properly characterized as ordinary income. The process for determining the gain or loss follows:

Step 1: Calculate the total gain or loss recognized by subtracting outside basis from the amount realized.

Step 2: Calculate the partner's share of gain or loss from hot assets as if the partnership sold these assets at their fair market value. This represents the ordinary portion of the gain or loss.

Step 3: Finally, subtract the ordinary portion of the gain or loss obtained in Step 2 from the total gain or loss from Step 1. This remaining amount is the capital gain or loss from the sale.[10,11]

[10]The partner must also determine if any portion of the capital gain or loss relates to collectibles (28 percent capital gain property) or to unrecaptured §1250 gains (25 percent capital gain property). This is typically referred to as the *look-through rule*.

[11]Any capital gain from the sale of a partnership interest is potentially subject to the 3.8 percent net investment income tax unless the gain is allocable to trade or business assets held by the partnership that generate trade or business income not subject to the tax. See Prop. Reg. §1.1411-7 for a detailed discussion of this concept.

Example 10-4

In Example 10-1, we are reminded that Chanzz Inc. sold its interest in CCS to Greg Randall for $100,000 cash on June 30, 2022. As a result, Chanzz recognized a gain of $19,000 on the sale. What was the character of Chanzz's gain?

Answer: $5,700 of ordinary income and $13,300 of capital gain, determined as follows:

Step 1: Determine the total gain or loss: $19,000 gain (from Example 10-1).

Step 2: Determine the ordinary gain or loss recognized from hot assets:

Asset	(1) Basis	(2) FMV	(3) Gain/Loss (2) – (1)	Chanzz's Share 30% × (3)
Accounts receivable	$ 0	$13,000	$13,000	$3,900
Equipment	80,000	86,000	6,000	1,800
Total ordinary income				**$5,700**

Step 3: Determine the capital gain or loss:

Description	Amount	Explanation
(1) Total gain	$ 19,000	From Step 1
(2) Ordinary income from §751(a)	5,700	From Step 2
Capital gain*	**$13,300**	(1) – (2)

*Because Chanzz sold its interest in CCS more than one year after it acquired its interest in CCS, this gain is long-term capital gain.

Example 10-5

What if: Assume the same facts as in Example 10-1, except Greg paid Chanzz only $82,800 cash for its interest in CCS. What would be the amount and character of Chanzz's gain or loss?

Answer: $5,700 of ordinary income and capital loss of $3,900, determined as follows:

Step 1: Determine the total gain or loss recognized:

Description	Amount	Explanation
(1) Cash and fair market value of property received	$ 82,800	
(2) Debt relief	24,000	Chanzz's share of CCS's allocable debt (30% × $80,000)
(3) Amount realized	$106,800	(1) + (2)
(4) Outside basis in CCS interest	105,000	
Gain recognized	$ 1,800	(3) – (4)

Step 2: Determine the ordinary gain or loss from hot assets:

Asset	(1) Basis	(2) FMV	(3) Gain/Loss (2) – (1)	Chanzz's Share 30% × (3)
Accounts receivable	$ 0	$13,000	$13,000	$ 3,900
Equipment	80,000	86,000	6,000	1,800
Total ordinary income				**$5,700**

Step 3: Determine the capital gain or loss:

Description	Amount	Explanation
(1) Total gain	$ 1,800	From Step 1
(2) Ordinary income from §751(a)	5,700	From Step 2
Capital loss*	**$(3,900)**	(1) – (2)

*Because Chanzz sold its interest in CCS more than one year after it acquired its interest in CCS, this loss is long-term capital loss.

ETHICS

Sarah recently sold her partnership interest for significantly more than her outside basis in the interest. Two separate appraisals were commissioned at the time of the sale to estimate the value of the partnership's hot assets and other assets. The first appraisal estimates the value of the hot assets at approximately $750,000, while the second appraisal estimates the value of these assets at approximately $500,000. Given that the partnership's inside basis for its hot assets is $455,000, Sarah intends to use the second appraisal to determine the character of the gain from the sale of her partnership interest. Is it appropriate for Sarah to ignore the first appraisal when determining her tax liability from the sale of her partnership interest?

Buyer and Partnership Issues

A new investor in a partnership is, of course, concerned with determining how much to pay for the partnership interest. However, a new partner's primary tax concerns are about the outside basis in the partnership interest and that partner's share of the inside basis of the partnership's assets. In general, for a sale transaction, the new investor's outside basis in this interest will be equal to the cost that investor paid for the partnership interest.[12] To the extent that the new investor shares in the partnership liabilities, his share of partnership liabilities increases his outside basis in his interest.

Example 10-6

When Greg Randall acquired Chanzz's 30 percent interest in CCS for $100,000 on June 30, 2022 (see Example 10-1), he guaranteed his share of CCS's liabilities just as Chanzz had done. As a result, Greg will be allocated his share of CCS's allocable liabilities in accordance with his 30 percent profit-sharing ratio. What is the outside basis of Greg's acquired interest?

Answer: $124,000, determined as follows:

Description	Amount	Explanation
(1) Initial tax basis in CSS	$100,000	Cash paid to Chanzz Inc.
(2) Share of CCS's liabilities	24,000	30% × CCS's allocable liabilities of $80,000
Outside basis in CSS	**$124,000**	(1) + (2)

The partnership experiences very few tax consequences when a partner sells their interest.[13] The sale does not generally affect a partnership's **inside basis** in its assets.[14]

[12]§1012. The outside basis in a partnership interest will depend, in part, on how the new investor obtains the interest. For example, a gift generally results in a carryover basis, whereas an inherited interest typically results in a basis equal to the fair market value as of the date of the decedent's death.

[13]Later in the chapter, we discuss situations in which the new investor's share of the partnership's asset bases is adjusted after a sale of a partnership interest under §754. Throughout this section, we assume that the partnership does not have a §754 election in effect.

[14]§743.

The new investor typically "steps into the shoes" of the selling partner to determine their share of the partnership's inside basis of the partnership assets. Consequently, the new investor's share of inside basis is equal to the selling partner's share of inside basis at the sale date. Recall from the preceding chapter that each partner has a tax capital account that reflects the tax basis of property and cash contributed by the partner, the partner's share of profits and losses, and distributions to the partner. In a sale of a partnership interest, the selling partner's tax capital account carries over to the new investor.[15]

Example 10-7

Refer to Example 10-2 for CCS's balance sheet as of June 30, 2022. What is Greg's share of CCS's inside basis in its assets immediately after purchasing Chanzz's 30 percent interest in CCS?

Answer: Greg's share is $105,000: the sum of Chanzz's tax capital account of $81,000 and its share of CCS's liabilities of $24,000. Greg simply steps into Chanzz's place after the acquisition. In Example 10-6, we determined Greg's outside basis in his interest to be $124,000. A sale of a partnership interest often results in a difference between the new investor's inside and outside bases because the outside basis in his interest is the price paid based on fair market value and the inside basis is generally the seller's share of tax basis in the partnership assets.

Varying Interest Rule If a partner's interest in a partnership increases or decreases during the partnership's tax year, the partnership income or loss allocated to the partner for the year must be adjusted to reflect their *varying interest* in the partnership.[16] Partners' interests increase when they contribute property or cash to a partnership[17] or purchase a partnership interest. Conversely, partners' interests decrease when they receive partnership distributions[18] or sell all or a portion of their partnership interests. Upon the sale of a partner's entire interest, the partnership tax year closes for the *selling* partner only. Regulations allow partners to choose between two possible methods for allocating income or loss to partners when their interests change during the year.[19] The first method allows the partnership to prorate income or loss to partners with varying interests, while the second method sanctions an interim closing of the partnership's books.

Example 10-8

CCS had a $60,000 overall business loss for the 2022 calendar year. The issue of how to allocate the 2022 loss between Chanzz Inc. and Greg was easily resolved because CCS's operating agreement specifies the proration method to allocate income or loss when members' interests in CCS change during the year. How much of CCS's 2022 loss will Chanzz be allocated under the proration method?

Answer: Chanzz is allocated a loss of $9,000, which includes its share of CCS's loss but for only one-half the year ($60,000 × 30% share × 6/12 months).[20] On the sale date, Chanzz decreases its outside basis in CCS by the $9,000 loss to determine its adjusted tax basis to use in calculating its gain or loss on the sale of its interest.

[15]An exception occurs when the selling partner contributes to the partnership property with a built-in loss. Only the contributing partner is entitled to that loss [see the Forming and Operating Partnerships chapter and §704(c)(1)(C)]. Therefore, when a new investor buys a partnership interest from a partner that contributed built-in loss property, the new investor reduces the inside basis and tax capital account by the amount of the built-in loss in the contributed property at the contribution date.

[16]§706(d)(1).

[17]If all partners simultaneously contribute property or cash with a value proportionate to their interests, their relative interests will not change.

[18]If all partners receive distributions with a value proportionate to their interests, their relative interests will not change.

[19]Reg. §1.706-1(c).

[20]Reg. §1.706-4(c)(3) requires the calendar-day convention when using the proration method. For the sake of mathematical simplicity, we use number of months here and elsewhere in the chapter when applying the proration method.

Example 10-9

What if: If CCS's overall loss through June 30 was $20,000, how much of the $60,000 overall loss for 2022 will Chanzz and Greg Randall be allocated under an interim closing of the books?

Answer: CCS will allocate $6,000 of loss (30% × $20,000) to Chanzz and $12,000 of loss (30% × $40,000) to Greg.

TAXES IN THE REAL WORLD Changing the Way Companies Dispose of a Business

Corporate takeovers seemed to be the transaction du jour during the 1990s, but many practitioners are predicting joint ventures will be the defining deal currently and in coming years. We regularly see articles in *The Wall Street Journal* describing how firms are starting up joint ventures or strategic alliances—or exiting them. For example, Volvo and Waymo announced in 2020 a $300 million joint venture to develop self-driving cars.

The increase in the number of joint ventures and their possible dissolution or disposition brings an increasing need to understand the partnership tax rules and regulations. More than ever before, corporate tax executives find they must advise senior management on the opportunities and pitfalls of structuring joint ventures and investments as partnerships or LLCs under Subchapter K of the Internal Revenue Code.

BASICS OF PARTNERSHIP DISTRIBUTIONS

LO 10-2

Like shareholders receiving corporate dividend distributions, partners often receive distributions of the partnership profits, known as **operating distributions.** Recall that owners of flow-through entities are taxed currently on their business income regardless of whether the business distributes it. As a result, partners may require cash distributions in order to make quarterly estimated tax payments on their shares of business income. Usually, the general partners (or managing members of LLCs) determine the amount and timing of distributions; however, the partnership (operating) agreement may stipulate some distributions.

Partners may also receive **liquidating distributions.** Because the market for partnership interests is much smaller than for publicly traded stock, partners may have a difficult time finding buyers for their interests. Partnership agreements also often limit purchasers of an interest to the current partner group, to avoid adding an unwanted partner. If the current partner group either cannot or does not want to purchase the interest, the partnership can instead distribute assets to terminate a partner's interest. These liquidating distributions are similar in form to corporate redemptions of a shareholder's stock. They can also terminate the partnership. We first explore the tax consequences of operating distributions and then examine the tax treatment for liquidating distributions.

LO 10-3

THE KEY FACTS

Operating Distributions

- **Gain or loss recognition:** Partners generally do not recognize gain or loss. One exception occurs when the partnership distributes money only and the amount is greater than the partner's outside basis in their interest.

(continued)

Operating Distributions

A distribution from a partnership is an operating distribution when the partners continue their interests afterwards. Operating distributions are usually made to distribute the business profits to the partners but can also reduce a partner's capital interest. The partnership may distribute cash or other assets. Let's look at the tax consequences of distributions of money, and then at the tax consequences of distributing property other than money.

Operating Distributions of Money Only The general rule for operating distributions states that a partnership does not recognize gain or loss on the distribution of property or money.[21,22] Nor do the general tax rules require a partner to recognize gain or loss when receiving distributed property or money.[23] The partner simply reduces the outside basis in the partnership interest by the amount of cash distributed and the inside basis of any property distributed. In general, the partnership's basis in its remaining assets remains unchanged.[24]

Example 10-10

- **Basis of distributed assets:** Partners generally take a carryover basis in distributed assets. If the partnership distribution includes property and the combined inside basis of the distributed property is greater than the partner's outside basis in their interest, the bases of the distributed property will be reduced.
- **Remaining outside basis:** In general, partners reduce outside basis by the amount of money distributed and the inside basis of distributed property.

What if: Suppose CCS makes its first distribution to the owners on December 31, 2023: $250,000 each to Nicole and Greg and $333,333 to Sarah. After taking into account their distributive shares of CCS's income for the year, the owners have the following predistribution bases in their CCS interests:

Owner	Outside Basis
Nicole	$205,000
Sarah	420,000
Greg	334,000

What are the tax consequences (gain or loss and basis in CCS interest) of the distribution to Sarah?

Answer: Sarah does not recognize any gain or loss on the distribution. She reduces her outside basis in her interest from $420,000 to $86,667 ($420,000 – $333,333) after the distribution.

The general rule of no gain is impractical when the partner receives a greater amount of money than their outside basis in their partnership interest. They cannot defer gain to the extent of the excess amount because the outside basis is insufficient for a full reduction. Therefore, the partner reduces their outside basis in their interest to zero[25] and recognizes gain (generally capital) to the extent the amount of money distributed is greater than their outside basis.[26] A partner *never* recognizes a loss from an *operating* distribution.

Example 10-11

What if: Suppose that in the December 31, 2023, distribution Nicole's distribution consists of $250,000 cash. Her outside basis in her CCS interest is $205,000 before the distribution. What are Nicole's gain or loss and basis in her CCS interest after the distribution?

Answer: Nicole has $45,000 capital gain and $0 basis in CCS. Because she receives only money in the distribution, she decreases her outside basis to $0 and must recognize a $45,000 capital gain ($250,000 distribution – $205,000 basis). She recognizes gain because she receives a cash distribution in excess of her outside basis in her CCS interest.

Operating Distributions That Include Property Other Than Money If a partnership makes a distribution that includes property *other than money,* the partners face the problem of determining how much outside basis in their interests to allocate to the

[21]For distribution purposes, money includes cash, deemed cash from reductions in a partner's share of liabilities, and the fair market value of certain marketable securities.

[22]§731(b).

[23]§731.

[24]However, if the partnership has a §754 election in effect or if there is a substantial basis reduction, the partnership basis of its remaining assets must be adjusted following a distribution according to §§734(b) and 755.

[25]§733.

[26]§731(a)(1).

distributed property.[27] Under the general rule, the partner takes a basis in the distributed property equal to the partnership's basis in the property. This is called a **carryover basis.**[28] The tax rules define the order in which to allocate outside basis in a partnership interest to the bases of distributed assets. First, the partner allocates the outside basis in their interest to any money received and then to other property as a carryover basis. The remainder is the partner's outside basis in the partnership interest after the distribution.

Example 10-12

What if: Suppose CCS's December 31, 2023 distribution to Sarah consists of $133,333 cash and investments (other than marketable securities) with a fair market value of $200,000 and an adjusted basis of $115,000. Sarah has a predistribution outside basis in her CCS interest of $420,000. What are the tax consequences (Sarah's gain or loss, basis of distributed assets, outside basis of CCS interest, and CCS's gain or loss) of the distribution?

Answer: Sarah recognizes no gain or loss on the distribution. To determine her bases in the distributed assets, she first allocates $133,333 to the cash and then takes a carryover basis in the investments so her basis in the investments is $115,000. Sarah reduces her outside basis in CCS by $248,333 ($133,333 cash + $115,000 basis of investments). Her outside basis in CCS after the distribution is $171,667 ($420,000 – $248,333). CCS does not recognize any gain or loss on the distribution.

When the partnership distributes property (other than money) with a basis that exceeds the remaining outside basis in the interest (after the allocation to any money also distributed), the partner assigns the remaining outside basis in the interest to the distributed assets,[29] and the partner's outside basis in the interest is reduced to zero.[30] The first allocation of outside basis in the interest goes to money, then to hot assets, and finally to other property.[31] In this case, the partner's basis in the property received in the distribution will be less than the property's basis in the hands of the partnership.

Example 10-13

What if: Suppose Nicole's December 31, 2023, distribution consists of $150,000 cash and investments (other than marketable securities) with a fair market value of $100,000 and an adjusted basis of $90,000 to CCS. Nicole's outside basis in her CCS interest is $205,000 before the distribution. What are Nicole's tax consequences (gain or loss, basis of distributed assets, and outside basis in CCS interest) of the distribution?

Answer: Nicole recognizes no gain or loss and takes a basis of $55,000 in the investments. Her outside basis in CCS is $0, computed as follows:

Description	Amount	Explanation
(1) Nicole's outside basis in CCS	$205,000	
(2) Cash distribution	150,000	
(3) Remaining basis	$ 55,000	(1) – (2); remaining outside basis to be allocated to the distributed investments
(4) Inside basis of investments	90,000	
(5) Basis in investments	55,000	Lesser of (3) or (4)
Nicole's outside basis in CCS	**$ 0**	(3) – (5)

[27]In this context, money includes certain marketable securities [§731(c)(1)(A)]. The special rules in §731(c) for the treatment of distributed marketable securities are beyond the scope of this book.

[28]§732(a).

[29]§732(a)(2).

[30]§733.

[31]If multiple assets are distributed, then the outside basis in a partnership interest will be allocated in accordance with §732(c). We discuss these rules later in conjunction with liquidating distributions.

Because a partner's outside basis in a partnership interest includes their share of the partnership liabilities, the outside basis in a partnership interest must reflect any changes in a partner's share of partnership liabilities resulting from a distribution. In essence, a partner treats a reduction of their share of liabilities as a distribution of cash.[32] If the partner increases their share of liabilities, the increase is treated as a cash contribution to the partnership.

Example 10-14

What if: Suppose Greg receives land held for investment with a fair market value of $250,000 (inside basis is $140,000) as his distribution from CCS on December 31, 2023. He agrees to assume the $120,000 mortgage on the land after the distribution. His outside basis in his CCS interest is $334,000 before considering the distribution. What are the tax consequences (gain or loss, basis of distributed assets, and outside basis in his CCS interest) of the distribution to Greg?

Answer: Greg does not recognize any gain or loss on the distribution. His basis in the land is $140,000 and his post-distribution outside basis in CCS is $278,000, determined as follows:

Description	Amount	Explanation
(1) Greg's predistribution outside basis	$ 334,000	
(2) Mortgage assumed by Greg	120,000	
(3) Greg's predistribution share of mortgage	36,000	(2) × 30% ownership
(4) Deemed cash contribution from debt assumption	$ 84,000	(2) − (3)
(5) Greg's outside basis in CCS after debt changes	418,000	(1) + (4)
(6) Greg's basis in distributed land	140,000	Carryover basis from CCS
Greg's post-distribution outside basis in CCS	**$278,000**	(5) − (6)

Greg must first consider the effects of changes in debt before determining the effects of the distribution. The tax rules treat him as making a net contribution of $84,000 cash to the partnership, the difference between the full mortgage he assumes and his predistribution share of the debt. Greg then allocates $140,000 of his outside basis in his CCS interest to the land and reduces his outside basis in CCS accordingly.

LO 10-4 Liquidating Distributions

In contrast to an operating distribution in which the partners retain a continuing interest in the partnership after the distribution, a liquidating distribution terminates a partner's interest in the partnership. Like operating distributions, a liquidating distribution can be made to just one partner or to multiple partners simultaneously. For example, if outside investors or current partners do not have sufficient cash or inclination to purchase a partner's interest, the partnership agreement often allows a partner wishing to cash out to receive a liquidating distribution from the partnership in lieu of selling the interest. On the other end of the spectrum, all the partners may agree at some point to end the partnership, because they have lost interest in continuing it or because it has not been profitable. In such cases, the partnership may distribute all its assets to the partners in a complete liquidation of the partnership. Once a partnership has been terminated in this manner, it must file a final return covering the period from the beginning of its tax year through the date of termination. Subsequently, it no longer has any tax filing obligations. A partnership termination is analogous to a complete corporate liquidation (discussed in the Corporate Formation, Reorganization, and Liquidation chapter).

The tax issues related to partnership liquidating distributions are basically twofold: (1) to determine whether the partner receiving the distribution recognizes gain or loss and (2) to allocate the partner's outside basis in their interest to the assets received in the liquidating distribution. The rationale behind the rules for liquidating distributions is simply to have the partner's outside basis in their interest carry over to the assets received by the partner. In some instances, the partner receiving the distribution will not recognize gain or loss on the distribution, and the tax basis in the distributed assets will be the same in

[32] §752(b).

the partner's hands as they were inside the partnership. Unfortunately, this simple outcome rarely occurs. Thus, the rules in this area stipulate when gain or loss must be recognized by partners receiving such distributions and describe how they must allocate their outside basis in their interests to the distributed assets received.

Gain or Loss Recognition in Liquidating Distributions In general, neither partnerships nor partners recognize gain or loss from liquidating distributions. However, there are exceptions. For example, when a terminated partner receives more money in the distribution than their outside basis in the interest, they will recognize gain.[33] See Example 10-11 for an illustration in the context of operating distributions.

In contrast to operating distributions, a partner may recognize a *loss* from a liquidating distribution, but only when two conditions are met: (1) The distribution includes only cash, unrealized receivables, and/or inventory *and* (2) the partner's outside basis in their partnership interest is greater than the sum of the *inside bases* of the distributed assets.[34] The loss on the distribution is a capital loss to the partner.

Commonly, the terminated partner's share of partnership debt decreases after a liquidating distribution. Any reduction in the partner's share of liabilities is considered a distribution of money to the partner and reduces the partner's outside basis in their interest available for allocation of basis to other assets, including inventory and unrealized receivables.

Example 10-15

What if: Suppose on December 31, 2023, CCS liquidates Greg's interest in the LLC by distributing to him cash of $206,000 and inventory with a fair market value of $103,000 (adjusted basis is $43,000). Greg's share of CCS's liabilities as of the liquidation is $66,000. On December 31, 2023, Greg's outside basis in CCS is $334,000, including his share of CCS's liabilities. What is Greg's gain or loss on the liquidation of his CCS interest?

Answer: Greg recognizes a capital loss of $19,000 from the liquidating distribution, computed as follows:

Description	Amount	Explanation
(1) Outside basis in CCS before distribution	$334,000	
(2) Debt relief	66,000	Deemed cash distribution
(3) Outside basis in CCS after considering debt relief	$268,000	(1) – (2)
(4) Basis of property distributed (cash + inventory)	249,000	($206,000 + $43,000)
Gain (loss) on distribution	**$(19,000)**	(4) – (3)

Greg recognizes a loss because he meets the two necessary conditions: (1) He receives only cash and inventory in the distribution *and* (2) the sum of the adjusted inside bases of the distributed assets is less than his outside basis in his CCS interest ($249,000 inside basis in assets versus $268,000 CCS outside basis after deemed cash distribution).

THE KEY FACTS

Gain or Loss Recognition in Liquidating Distributions

- **Generally:** Partners and partnerships do not recognize gain or loss.
- **Exceptions:**
  - **Gain:** Partner recognizes gain when partnership distributes money and the amount exceeds the partner's outside basis in the partnership interest.
  - **Loss:** Partner recognizes loss when two conditions are met: (1) Distribution consists of only cash and hot assets and (2) the partner's outside basis in the partnership interest exceeds the sum of the bases of the distributed assets.

Basis in Distributed Property A key theme of the partnership tax rules is the idea that the partnership acts merely as a conduit for the partners' business activities. Thus, the rules attempt to keep the basis of the assets the same regardless of whether the partner or the partnership has possession of them. Moving assets in and out of the partnership should therefore have few meaningful tax consequences. The primary objective of the basis rules in liquidating distributions is to allocate the partner's entire outside basis in the partnership interest to the assets the partner receives in the liquidating distribution. The allocation essentially depends on two things: (1) the partnership's bases in distributed assets relative to the partner's outside basis in the interest and (2) the type of property distributed—whether it is money, hot assets, or other property. For purposes of distributions, hot assets include unrealized receivables (including potential depreciation recapture) and inventory, as we've defined above. We discuss each of the possible scenarios in Exhibit 10-1 in turn.

[33]These rules are very similar to those for operating distributions. When a partner receives money only in complete termination of the partnership interest, any gain on distribution cannot be deferred through a basis adjustment. Therefore, the partner recognizes the gain.

[34]§731(a)(2).

EXHIBIT 10-1 Alternative Scenarios for Determining Basis in Distributed Property

Type of Property Distributed	Partner's Outside Basis Is *Greater* Than Inside Bases of Distributed Assets	Partner's Outside Basis Is *Less* Than Inside Bases of Distributed Assets
Money only	Scenario 1	Scenario 3
Money and hot assets	Scenario 1	Scenario 4
Other property included in distribution[35]	Scenario 2	Scenario 5

Partner's Outside Basis in an Interest Is Greater Than Inside Bases of Distributed Assets

Scenario 1: Distributions of money, inventory, and/or unrealized receivables. If the partnership distributes only money, inventory, and/or unrealized receivables (ordinary income property) and the partner's outside basis in the interest is greater than the sum of the inside bases of the distributed assets, the partner recognizes a capital loss.[36] The partner assigns a basis to the distributed assets equal to the partnership's inside basis in the assets, and the remaining outside basis in the interest is equal to the recognized loss.[37]

Example 10-16

What if: Suppose Greg has an outside basis in CCS of $334,000, including his share of liabilities of $66,000. In a liquidating distribution, he receives $159,000 cash and inventory with a fair market value and basis of $49,000. Will Greg recognize a gain or loss? Explain.

Answer: Greg will recognize a capital loss of $60,000 on the liquidation, computed as follows:

Description	Amount	Explanation
(1) Outside basis in CCS before distribution	$ 334,000	
(2) Debt relief	66,000	Deemed cash distribution
(3) Outside basis after considering debt relief	$ 268,000	(1) – (2)
(4) Basis of property distributed (cash + inventory)	208,000	($159,000 + $49,000)
Gain (loss) on distribution	**$ (60,000)**	(4) – (3)

In this case, Greg is unable to defer his loss without changing its character. Greg clearly cannot adjust the basis in the cash to defer the loss. *If* he were able to increase his basis in the distributed inventory, he could defer the loss. However, this would produce an ordinary loss of $60,000 when Greg sells the inventory.[38] Greg must recognize a $60,000 capital loss when he receives the liquidating distribution. This requirement ensures Greg does not convert a capital loss into an ordinary loss.

Scenario 2: Other property included in distributions. This scenario is similar to the first scenario except that property other than money, inventory, and unrealized receivables is also distributed. Recall that when other property is also distributed, the liquidating partner must allocate all the outside basis in that partner's interest to the distributed assets. We determined in Scenario 1 that when the partnership distributes only money and/or hot

[35]This category includes distributions that include other property in addition to or instead of either money or unrealized receivables or inventory. For example, the distributions in this category can include any combination of money, unrealized receivables, and inventory as long as other property is also distributed.

[36]§731(a)(2).

[37]§§732(c)(1), 731(a)(2). To prevent a partner from converting a capital loss from their investment into an ordinary loss, the tax law prohibits increasing their basis in unrealized receivables and inventory and requires the partner to recognize a capital loss.

[38]If the inventory distributed to Greg is also considered inventory in his hands, the eventual sale of the inventory will generate ordinary income. If the inventory is a capital asset to Greg, a sale of the asset within five years of the distribution will generate ordinary income. After five years, the gain or loss will be capital.

assets and the total inside basis of the distributed assets is less than the partner's outside basis in their interest, it is impossible to allocate the entire outside basis to the distributed assets without changing the character of a resulting loss. Thus, a partner never increases the bases of distributed hot assets. However, when the partnership distributes other property, in addition to money and/or hot assets, the partner can adjust the basis of the *other* property without converting ordinary gains to capital, and the liquidating partner will not currently recognize any gain or loss from the distribution.

Example 10-17

What if: Suppose CCS has no liabilities or hot assets and distributes $50,000 in cash and land with a fair market value of $160,000 and a basis of $20,000 to Greg in complete liquidation of his CCS interest. Greg has an outside basis in CCS of $268,000 prior to the distribution. What is Greg's recognized gain or loss on the distribution?

Answer: Greg does not recognize any gain or loss. He receives money and other property with a total basis of $70,000, which is less than his outside basis of $268,000. Greg first reduces his outside basis by the amount of money he receives, and he assigns his remaining outside basis to the land as follows:

Description	Amount	Explanation
(1) Outside basis in CCS before distribution	$268,000	
(2) Basis allocated to money distributed	50,000	
Remaining outside basis assigned to land	$218,000	(1) − (2)

Note that Greg increases the basis of the other property received in liquidation (land) from $20,000 to $218,000 in order to allocate his entire outside basis to the distributed assets. If Greg holds the distributed land as a personal use asset, he may never be able to receive a tax benefit for the basis increase.

Example 10-17 illustrates the required basis increase in a very simple situation. In reality, liquidating distributions may include several types of assets. In these situations, to allocate the outside basis in a partnership interest to the distributed assets, the partner implements the following, more detailed process:[39]

Step 1: The partner first determines their outside basis net of any debt relief, and then allocates that amount to any money, inventory, and unrealized receivables equal to the partnership's basis in these assets. The partner also assigns a basis to the other distributed property in an amount equal to the partnership's basis in those assets.

Step 2: The partner then allocates the remaining outside basis (full outside basis less the amounts assigned in Step 1) to the other distributed property that has unrealized appreciation to the extent of that appreciation. Thus, if an asset has an adjusted basis to the partnership of $500 and a fair market value of $700, the partner will allocate the first $200 of remaining basis to that asset.[40]

Step 3: The partner allocates any remaining basis to all other property in proportion to the relative *fair market values* of the other property.

$$\text{Basis allocation} = \text{Remaining basis} \times \frac{\text{FMV}_{\text{asset}}}{\text{Sum of FMV}_{\text{distributed other property}}}$$

[39] §732(c)(2).

[40] If the remaining outside basis in a partnership interest is insufficient to allocate the full amount of appreciation to the distributed assets in this step, then the partner will allocate the remaining basis in this step to the appreciated assets based on their relative appreciation.

Example 10-18

What if: Suppose CCS makes the following distribution to Greg in liquidation of his CCS interest:

Asset	CCS Tax Basis	Fair Market Value
Cash	$181,000	$181,000
Inventory	43,000	103,000
Investment A	5,000	12,000
Investment B	10,000	13,000

Greg's basis in his CCS interest as of the liquidation is $334,000, including his $66,000 share of CCS's liabilities. What is Greg's recognized gain or loss on the distribution? What are Greg's bases in the distributed assets following the liquidation?

Answer: Greg recognizes no gain or loss on the distribution. Greg's bases in the distributed assets are:

Cash	$181,000
Inventory	43,000
Investment A	21,120
Investment B	22,880
Total	$268,000

Because Greg receives other property in the distribution and the distributed asset bases are less than Greg's outside basis in CCS (Scenario 2), he will allocate his outside basis in CCS as follows:

First, Greg determines his allocable basis:

Description	Amount	Explanation
(1) Basis in CCS before distribution	$334,000	
(2) Debt relief	66,000	Greg's 30% share of CCS's liabilities
Allocable basis	$268,000	(1) – (2)

Next, Greg allocates his remaining outside basis in CCS of $268,000 to the distributed assets by following the allocation process.

Description	Amount	Explanation
Step 1:		
(1) Allocable basis	$268,000	See above
(2) Basis assigned to cash	181,000	
(3) Basis assigned to inventory	43,000	
(4) Initial basis assigned to Investment A	5,000	
(5) Initial basis assigned to Investment B	10,000	
(6) Required basis increase	$ 29,000	(1) – (2) – (3) – (4) – (5) Initial assignment of basis is less than Greg's allocable CCS basis
Step 2:		
(7) Additional basis assigned to Investment A	$ 7,000	Unrealized appreciation on Investment A (FMV of $12,000 less basis of $5,000)
(8) Additional basis assigned to Investment B	3,000	Unrealized appreciation on Investment B (FMV of $13,000 less basis of $10,000)
(9) Remaining required basis increase after Step 2	$ 19,000	(6) – (7) – (8)

Step 3:

In Step 3, Greg allocates the required remaining basis increase to the distributed investments based on their relative fair market values using:

$$\textbf{Basis allocation} = \textbf{Remaining basis} \times \frac{\textbf{FMV}_{\textbf{asset}}}{\textbf{Sum of FMV}_{\textbf{distributed other property}}}$$

(10) Additional basis allocated to other property: Investment A	$9,120	Basis allocation = $19,000 × ($12,000/$25,000) = $9,120
(11) Additional basis allocated to other property: Investment B	$9,880	Basis allocation = $19,000 × ($13,000/$25,000) = $9,880

Thus, Greg's bases in the investments are $21,120 (Investment A) and $22,880 (Investment B):

Description	Inv. A	Explanation	Inv. B	Explanation
(12) Initial basis assignment	$ 5,000	From (4) above	$ 10,000	From (5) above
(13) Basis assigned in Step 2	7,000	From (7) above	3,000	From (8) above
(14) Basis assigned in Step 3	9,120	From (10) above	9,880	From (11) above
Greg's bases in investments	**$21,120**	(12) + (13) + (14)	**$22,880**	(12) + (13) + (14)

Partner's Outside Basis in an Interest Is Less Than Inside Bases of Distributed Assets

Scenario 3: Distributions of money only. A partner recognizes a gain (generally capital) if the partnership distributes money (only) that exceeds the partner's outside basis in their interest. Example 10-11 illustrates the tax consequences for this scenario in the context of an operating distribution.

Scenario 4: Distributions of money, inventory, and/or unrealized receivables. In liquidating distributions when the partner's outside basis in their interest is less than the inside bases of the distributed assets and the partnership distributes money and property other than money, the partner reduces the basis in the noncash property distributed but does not recognize gain or loss. This basis reduction may apply to hot assets as well as other property because the tax law does not restrict *reducing* the basis of ordinary income assets. However, the tax law does prescribe a particular sequence for the required reductions.

If the partnership distributes only money, inventory, and unrealized receivables, the partner reduces the basis of the hot assets distributed, assuming money doesn't exceed basis. The required decrease in the basis of the distributed assets is equal to the difference between the partner's outside basis in their interest and the partnership's inside basis in the distributed assets. The partner first assigns basis to money and then to other assets received in an amount equal to the assets' inside bases. Then the partner allocates the required *decrease* to the assets with unrealized depreciation, to reduce or eliminate any existing losses built into the distributed assets.[41] Finally, the partner allocates any remaining required decrease to the distributed assets in proportion to their *adjusted bases* (AB), after considering the preceding steps and using the following equation:

$$\text{Basis allocation} = \text{Required decrease} \times \frac{\text{AB}_{\text{asset}}}{\text{Sum of AB}_{\text{distributed assets}}}$$

[41]If the required decrease is insufficient to allocate the full amount of depreciation to the distributed assets in this step, then the partner will allocate the remaining required decrease in this step to the depreciated assets based on their relative unrealized depreciation.

Example 10-19

What if: Suppose CCS makes the following distribution to Greg in liquidation of his CCS interest:

Asset	CCS Tax Basis	Fair Market Value
Cash	$256,000	$256,000
Inventory A	50,000	129,000
Inventory B	25,000	6,000
Total	$331,000	

Greg's basis in his CCS interest as of the liquidation is $334,000, including his $66,000 share of CCS's liabilities. What is Greg's recognized gain or loss on the distribution? What is Greg's basis in the distributed assets following the liquidation?

Answer: Greg does not recognize any gain or loss. His basis in the cash is $256,000; his basis in Inventory A is $10,714; and his basis in Inventory B is $1,286, computed as follows:

First, Greg reduces his outside basis in CCS by his $66,000 debt relief, such that his outside basis allocable to distributed assets is $268,000 ($334,000 – $66,000). He must allocate this remaining basis to the distributed assets using the following steps:

Description	Amount	Explanation
Step 1:		
(1) Allocable basis	$268,000	Basis in CCS of $334,000 – debt relief of $66,000
(2) Basis assigned to cash	256,000	
(3) Initial basis assigned to Inventory A	50,000	
(4) Initial basis assigned to Inventory B	25,000	
(5) Required basis decrease	$ (63,000)	(1) – (2) – (3) – (4): Initial assignment of basis exceeds Greg's allocable CCS basis
Step 2:		
(6) Required decrease to Inventory B	(19,000)	Unrealized depreciation on Inventory B (FMV of $6,000 less basis of $25,000)
(7) Remaining required basis decrease	$ (44,000)	(5) – (6)
(8) Interim adjusted basis of Inventory B	6,000	(4) + (6)

Step 3:

In Step 3, Greg decreases the basis of the inventory in proportion to their relative adjusted bases determined in Step 2 using the following allocation:

$$\textbf{Basis allocation} = \textbf{Required decrease} \times \frac{\textbf{AB}_{\textbf{asset}}}{\textbf{Sum of AB}_{\textbf{distributed assets}}}$$

(9) Required decrease to Inventory A	$(39,286)	Basis reduction = $(44,000) × ($50,000/$56,000)
(10) Required decrease to Inventory B	(4,714)	Basis reduction = $(44,000) × ($6,000/$56,000)
Final basis of Inventory A	**$10,714**	(3) + (9)
Final basis of Inventory B	**$ 1,286**	(8) + (10)

Example 10-20

What if: Suppose CCS makes the following distribution to Greg in liquidation of his CCS interest:

Asset	CCS Tax Basis	Fair Market Value
Cash	$242,000	$242,000
Accounts receivable	0	12,000
Inventory	72,000	120,000
Total	$314,000	

Greg's basis in his CCS interest as of the liquidation is $334,000, including his $66,000 share of CCS's liabilities. What is Greg's recognized gain or loss on the distribution? What is Greg's basis in the assets he receives in the liquidating distribution?

Answer: Greg does not recognize any gain or loss on the liquidation. His asset bases are:

Cash	$242,000
Accounts receivable	0
Inventory	26,000
Total	$268,000

Greg computes the basis as follows:

As a preliminary step to the allocation, he reduces his outside basis in CCS by his $66,000 debt relief, leaving an allocable outside basis of $268,000 ($334,000 – $66,000). He allocates this basis to the distributed assets using the following steps:

Description	Amount	Explanation
Step 1:		
(1) Allocable basis	$268,000	Basis in CCS of $334,000 – debt relief of $66,000
(2) Basis assigned to cash	242,000	
(3) Initial basis assigned to accounts receivable	0	
(4) Initial basis assigned to inventory	72,000	
(5) Required basis decrease	$ (46,000)	(1) – (2) – (3) – (4): Initial assignment of basis exceeds Greg's allocable CCS basis

Step 2: N/A because no assets have unrealized depreciation.

Step 3: In Step 3, Greg decreases the basis of the accounts receivable and inventory in proportion to their relative adjusted bases using the following reduction:

$$\textbf{Basis allocation} = \textbf{Required decrease} \times \frac{AB_{asset}}{\text{Sum of } AB_{distributed\ assets}}$$

(6) Required basis decrease to accounts receivable	$ 0	Basis reduction = $(46,000) × ($0/$72,000)
(7) Required basis decrease to inventory	(46,000)	Basis reduction = $(46,000) × ($72,000/$72,000)
Final basis of accounts receivable	0	(3) + (6)
Final basis of inventory	**$26,000**	(4) + (7)

Note that in this scenario, the tax rules recharacterize a portion ($46,000) of Greg's ultimate gain from capital gain to ordinary income. The sum of the bases of the distributed assets ($314,000) exceeds Greg's allocable outside basis in CCS ($268,000) by $46,000. Absent the allocation rules illustrated in Example 10-20, this would have been a capital gain to Greg. Instead, as we discuss below, the basis decrease to the hot assets will cause Greg to recognize any gain as ordinary upon sale of these assets.

Scenario 5: Other property included in distributions. Our final scenario is similar to Scenario 4 except the partnership distributes other property in addition to or instead of money and/or inventory and unrealized receivables. The terminating partner does not recognize gain or loss; rather, the partner first decreases the basis in the other property distributed before decreasing the basis in any distributed hot assets. The process for assigning basis to the distributed assets is similar to the method we described above, although the required basis decrease is applied first to other property before reducing the basis of any hot assets.[42] The procedure for determining the basis adjustment to other property is as follows:

Step 1: The partner first determines the outside basis in their interest net of any debt relief and then allocates that amount to any money, inventory, and unrealized receivables equal to the partnership's basis in these assets. The partner also assigns a basis to any other property equal to the partnership's basis in the other property distributed.

Step 2: The partner then allocates the required decrease (outside basis less partnership adjusted basis in distributed assets) to the other property that has unrealized depreciation to the extent of that depreciation to eliminate inherent losses. Thus, if an asset has an adjusted basis to the partnership of $700 and a fair market value of $600, the asset's basis is first reduced by $100 (unrealized depreciation).

Step 3: If any required decrease remains after accounting for the inherent losses in the distributed assets, the partner then allocates it to all other property in proportion to their *adjusted bases*. The adjusted bases used in this step are the bases from Step 2. We can determine the allocation as follows:

$$\text{Basis reduction} = \text{Required decrease} \times \frac{AB_{\text{asset}}}{\text{Sum of } AB_{\text{all distributed other property}}}$$

Example 10-21

What if: Suppose CCS makes the following distribution to Greg in liquidation of his CCS interest:

Asset	CCS Tax Basis	Fair Market Value
Cash	$187,000	$187,000
Inventory	70,000	162,000
Investment A	10,000	7,000
Investment B	10,000	18,000
Total	$277,000	

Greg's basis in his CCS interest as of the liquidation is $334,000, including his $66,000 share of CCS's liabilities. What is Greg's recognized gain or loss on the distribution? What is Greg's basis in the distributed assets following the liquidation?

[42] §732(c)(3).

Answer: Greg does not recognize any gain or loss. His asset bases are as follows:

Cash	$187,000
Inventory	70,000
Investment A	4,530
Investment B	6,470
Total	$268,000

Greg's basis in these assets is determined as follows:

Greg first determines his allocable basis of $268,000 by reducing his CCS basis ($334,000) for the deemed cash distribution relating to his $66,000 share of the reduction in CCS's debt.

Description	Amount	Explanation
Step 1:		
(1) Allocable basis	$268,000	Basis in CCS of $334,000 – debt relief of $66,000
(2) Basis assigned to cash	187,000	
(3) Initial basis assigned to Inventory	70,000	
(4) Initial basis assigned to Investment A	10,000	
(5) Initial basis assigned to Investment B	10,000	
(6) Required basis decrease	$ (9,000)	(1) – (2) – (3) – (4) – (5): Initial assignment of basis exceeds Greg's allocable CCS basis
Step 2:		
(7) Required basis decrease to Investment A	$ (3,000)	Unrealized depreciation on Investment A (FMV of $7,000 less basis of $10,000)
(8) Remaining required basis decrease	(6,000)	(6) – (7)
(9) Interim basis of Investment A	7,000	(4) + (7)

Step 3: In Step 3, Greg decreases the basis of the other property (Investments A and B) in proportion to their relative adjusted bases (after Step 2) using the following allocation:

$$\textbf{Basis reduction} = \textbf{Required decrease} \times \frac{\textbf{AB}_{\textbf{asset}}}{\textbf{Sum of AB}_{\textbf{all distributed other property}}}$$

(10) Required basis decrease to Investment A	$ (2,470)	Basis reduction = $(6,000) × ($7,000/$17,000)
(11) Required basis decrease to Investment B	(3,530)	Basis reduction = $(6,000) × ($10,000/$17,000)
Final basis of Investment A	**$ 4,530**	(9) + (10)
Final basis of Investment B	**$ 6,470**	(5) + (11)

Character and Holding Period of Distributed Assets For both operating and liquidating distributions, the character of distributed assets in the hands of the partner may stay the same as it was in the partnership in order to reduce the opportunity for converting ordinary income into capital gain with such distributions. Thus, if a partner sells certain assets with ordinary character after the distribution, the partner will recognize ordinary income from the sale.[43] These assets include §751(d) inventory and §751(c) unrealized receivables. For inventory items, the ordinary income "taint" will remain for five years after the distribution. For unrealized receivables, a subsequent sale at any time after the distribution will result in ordinary income. The reverse is not true, however. If a partnership distributes a capital asset that would be characterized as inventory in the hands of the terminating partner, the partner will have ordinary income from an eventual sale, not capital gain or loss. To ensure the character of any distributed long-term capital gain property retains its character to the partner, the partner's holding period generally includes the partnership's holding period.[44]

Example 10-22

Greg has decided to cash out his investment in CCS in order to invest in another project in which he can more actively participate. After speaking with Nicole and Sarah about different options, the three owners decide Greg can cash out using one of two options.

Option 1: CCS will liquidate Greg's interest by distributing cash of $242,000, accounts receivable worth $12,000 (adjusted basis is $0), and inventory worth $120,000 (adjusted basis is $72,000).

Option 2: Nicole and Sarah will purchase Greg's interest in CCS. Nicole agrees to purchase two-thirds of Greg's interest for $249,333 cash and Sarah agrees to purchase the remaining one-third for $124,667 cash.

Greg's basis in his 30 percent CCS interest is $334,000, including his share of CCS's liabilities of $66,000. Either event would occur on December 31, 2023, when CCS's balance sheet is as follows:

Color Comfort Sheets LLC
December 31, 2023

	Tax Basis	FMV
Assets		
Cash	$390,000	$ 390,000
Accounts receivable	0	40,000
Inventory	90,000	200,000
Investments	60,000	105,000
Equipment (cost = $200,000)	150,000	200,000
Building (cost = $100,000)	90,000	100,000
Land—original	20,000	160,000
Land—investment	140,000	270,000
Totals	$940,000	$1,465,000
Liabilities and capital		
Accounts payable	$ 80,000	
Long-term debt	0	
Mortgage on original land	40,000	
Mortgage on investment land	120,000	
Capital—Nicole	119,000	
—Sarah	332,000	
—Greg	249,000	
Totals	$940,000	

[43]§735(a).

[44]§735(b).

What are the tax consequences (amount and character of recognized gain or loss, basis in assets) for Greg under each option?

Answer: *Option 1:* Greg recognizes no gain or loss on the liquidating distribution. His bases in the distributed assets are:

Cash	$242,000
Accounts receivable	0
Inventory	26,000
Total	$268,000

Option 2: Greg recognizes ordinary income of $60,000 and a long-term capital gain of $46,000.

The tax consequences of both options are determined as follows:

Option 1: The distribution allows Greg to defer recognizing any gain or loss on the liquidation. Example 10-20 provides the details of the analysis. Greg has debt relief in an amount equal to his $66,000 share of CCS's liabilities. The debt relief is treated as a distribution of cash, so Greg reduces his outside basis in CCS by this amount from $334,000 to $268,000. The difference between the $314,000 sum of the inside bases of the distributed cash and inventory ($242,000 + $72,000) and his outside basis is $46,000 ($314,000 – $268,000) and represents a required *decrease* to the bases of assets distributed in liquidation. Greg follows the prescribed method illustrated in Example 10-20 to compute his asset bases (i.e., the accounts receivable will have a basis equal to zero and the inventory basis will be reduced by $46,000 from $72,000 to $26,000).

The basis reduction for these assets allows Greg to defer recognizing a $46,000 gain on the liquidation. The cost to accomplish the deferral is that if Greg sells the inventory and the accounts receivable immediately after the distribution, he will recognize ordinary income of $106,000, as follows:

Amount realized:		
Cash (equal to FMV of accounts receivable and inventory)	$ 12,000	
	120,000	$132,000
Less: Adjusted basis		
Accounts receivable	0	
Inventory	26,000	26,000
Ordinary income		$106,000

The $106,000 ordinary income is $46,000 greater than the inherent gain on these assets of $60,000 ($132,000 – $72,000) had the partnership sold the assets. If Greg selects Option 1, he will not recognize income on the liquidation until he sells the inventory and collects (or sells) the accounts receivable, thereby leaving himself flexibility on the timing of gain recognition.

Option 2: In this option, Greg sells his CCS interest to Nicole and Sarah and receives cash of $374,000 ($249,333 from Nicole and $124,667 from Sarah). Greg computes his total gain or loss as follows:

Amount realized:		
Cash	$374,000	
Debt relief	66,000	$440,000
Less: Basis in CCS interest		334,000
Realized and recognized gain		$106,000

Next, Greg determines the character of the gain from the sale by first identifying the gain related to hot assets.

Hot Asset—CCS	(1) Basis	(2) FMV	(3) Gain/Loss (2) – (1)	Greg's Share 30% × (3)
Accounts receivable	$ 0	$ 40,000	$ 40,000	$12,000
Inventory	90,000	200,000	110,000	33,000
Equipment	150,000	200,000	50,000	15,000
Total ordinary income				$60,000

(continued on page 10-24)

The final step for Greg is to determine the capital gain or loss by subtracting the ordinary portion from the total gain.

Total gain	$106,000
Less: ordinary income from §751(a)	(60,000)
Capital gain	$ 46,000

If he chooses Option 2, Greg will recognize $60,000 of ordinary income and $46,000 of capital gain in 2024.

Example 10-23

Given the tax consequences to Greg in the previous example, should he have CCS liquidate his interest (Option 1) or should he sell his interest (Option 2)?

Answer: Under Option 1 (the liquidation), Greg is able to defer all recognition of gain until he later sells the distributed assets. This provides him flexibility as to when he pays tax on the liquidating distribution. However, when he recognizes any income upon subsequent sales, the character of the income will be ordinary and taxed at ordinary rates. Under Option 2, Greg must recognize income immediately upon the sale: $60,000 of ordinary income and $46,000 of long-term capital gain. He has no future tax liability related to the liquidating distribution. The capital gain could be taxed at a rate as high as 23.8 percent (including the 3.8% net investment income tax). An additional consideration is that under Option 2 Greg receives cash, rather than a mix of cash and other assets. If he wants to immediately invest the proceeds in another venture, he may prefer a pure cash payment.

(continued from page 10-1 . . .)

Greg takes the liquidating distribution option (Option 1) offered by CCS to avoid recognizing a gain currently. Although this option doesn't give him as much cash as a sale would have, Greg figures it is enough for another investment and he can avoid paying tax on the distribution this year.

For the first time, CCS has only two owners—Nicole and Sarah. After liquidating Greg's interest, Nicole's interest has increased to 43 percent and Sarah's to 57 percent. Both women are happy with that outcome, although they are sorry to lose Greg's investment in the business. ■

LO 10-5 DISPROPORTIONATE DISTRIBUTIONS

Up to this point in the chapter, our distribution examples have either assumed or represented that each partner received a pro rata share of the partnership's unrealized appreciation in its ordinary assets, as specified in the partnership agreement based on the partner's capital interests. In practice, distributions may not always reflect each partner's proportionate share of the appreciation in hot assets.[45] Both operating and liquidating distributions can be **disproportionate distributions.** Without going into all the details of these complex rules, let's briefly discuss the implications of distributions in which partners receive either more or less than their share of the unrealized appreciation or losses in so-called hot assets [assets defined in §751(b) as **substantially appreciated inventory** and

[45]A thorough discussion of these issues is beyond the scope of this chapter. Therefore, we will abbreviate our discussion just to give a flavor for the issues and consequences of these disproportionate distributions.

unrealized receivables].[46] Note that the definition of hot assets for purposes of disproportionate distributions includes only *substantially appreciated* inventory, not *all* inventory [as is the case under §751(a), the definition we used to characterize the gain in dispositions of partnership interests]. Inventory is considered substantially appreciated if its fair market value is greater than 120 percent of its basis.

Suppose a partner receives less than their share of the appreciation in hot assets in a liquidating distribution. This may occur, for example, if a partner receives only cash in a liquidating distribution from a partnership with hot assets. Rather than only applying the rules we discussed above, the partner must treat part of the distribution as a sale or exchange.[47] Basically, the disproportionate distribution rules treat the partner as having sold their share of hot assets to the partnership in exchange for "cold" [non-§751(b)] assets. This deemed sale generates an ordinary gain or loss to the partner on the deemed sale, essentially equal to their share of the appreciation or depreciation in the portion of hot assets not distributed to them. From the partnership's perspective, the partnership is deemed to have purchased the hot assets from the partner in exchange for the distributed cold assets. Therefore, the *partnership* recognizes a capital or §1231 gain or loss equal to the remaining partners' inherent gain or loss in the distributed cold assets. The effects are reversed if a partner receives more than their share of the appreciation in a partnership's hot assets when the partner receives all or predominately hot assets in a distribution.[48] The rules are meant to ensure that partners cannot convert ordinary income into capital gain through distributions. Thus, they require that partners will ultimately recognize their share of the partnership ordinary income regardless of the form of their distributions.

THE KEY FACTS

Disproportionate Distributions

- **When?**
  When a distribution changes a partner's relative share of unrealized appreciation or losses in a partnership's hot assets.
- **Why?**
  To prevent partners from converting ordinary income into capital gains through distributions.
- **How?**
  Partner and partnership must treat part of the distribution as a sale or exchange, which may change the character and timing of income or losses that are recognized.

Example 10-24

What if: Suppose CCS distributes $328,000 in cash to Greg Randall on December 31, 2023, in complete liquidation of Greg's 30 percent interest in CCS. Greg's basis in his CCS interest before the distribution is $334,000. Assume CCS's balance sheet is as follows:

Color Comfort Sheets LLC
December 31, 2023

	Tax Basis	FMV
Assets		
Cash	$700,000	$ 700,000
Inventory	240,000	440,000
Totals	$940,000	$1,140,000
Liabilities and capital		
Liabilities	$240,000	
Capital—Nicole	119,000	
—Sarah	332,000	
—Greg	249,000	
Totals	$940,000	

(continued on page 10-26)

[46]Unrealized receivables include the accounts receivable of a cash-method taxpayer, the excess of the fair market value over basis of accounts receivable for accrual-method taxpayers, and depreciation recapture. The definition of substantially appreciated inventory is broader than simply goods primarily held for sale to customers. It also includes property that would not be classified as capital assets or §1231 assets if sold by the partnership. As a result, receivables are included as "inventory."

[47]§751(b).

[48]The partner would generally recognize capital gain on the deemed sale and the partnership would recognize ordinary income.

Is this distribution disproportionate? What are the implications of the distribution?

Answer: The CCS balance sheet as of December 31, 2023, indicates that CCS's inventory is a hot asset given that its fair market value is more than 120 percent of its basis ($440,000/$240,000 = 183.33%). Further, the CCS balance sheet indicates that the fair market value of Greg's share of the unrealized appreciation in CCS's hot assets for purposes of disproportionate distributions [§751(b)] is $60,000, or 30 percent of the $200,000 unrealized appreciation in inventory ($440,000 FMV – $240,000 adjusted basis). Because Greg receives only cash in the distribution, he has not received a proportionate share of the unrealized appreciation in CCS's hot assets. He could only have received a share of the appreciation in the hot assets if he had actually received hot assets in the distribution. Thus, the distribution will be disproportionate.

The tax law treats Greg as having sold his share of the hot assets for cold assets, and he will recognize ordinary income equal to his share of the appreciation on the hot assets not distributed, or $60,000. Absent this provision in the tax law, all of Greg's gains from the distribution would have been treated as capital gains. CCS does not recognize any gain or loss because it has no appreciation in the assets (cash) used to "purchase" the hot assets.

LO 10-6

SPECIAL BASIS ADJUSTMENTS

Recall that when an existing partner sells their partnership interest, the partnership's inside basis is generally unaffected by the sale. This creates a discrepancy between the new partner's outside basis in their interest (cost) and that partner's share of the partnership's inside basis, which artificially changes the potential income or loss at the partnership level. For example, earlier in the chapter we considered a scenario in which Greg Randall purchased Chanzz's 30 percent interest in CCS for $82,800 (see the *what-if* scenario in Example 10-5). Greg's outside basis in CCS after the acquisition is $106,800, reflecting the cash payment of $82,800 and his share of CCS's debt at the time of the acquisition, $24,000. However, Greg's share of CCS's inside basis in its assets is $105,000 (see Example 10-7). This is the outcome because the sale does not affect CCS's inside basis and Greg simply steps into Chanzz's shoes for determining his share of the inside basis. The discrepancy reflects Chanzz's unrecognized share in the net appreciation of CCS's assets (which Greg paid full value for) as of the sale date and causes Greg to be temporarily overtaxed when CCS sells these appreciated assets.

Example 10-25

What if: Assume that Greg acquires his 30 percent interest in CCS from Chanzz for $82,800 (see Example 10-5). Under this assumption, if CCS sells its accounts receivable for their fair market value of $13,000 (adjusted basis is $0) (see Example 10-2 for CCS's balance sheet as of June 30, 2022, the acquisition date), what are the amount and character of gain that Greg recognizes on the sale?

Answer: When CCS sells the accounts receivable, it recognizes $13,000 of ordinary income, of which $3,900 (30 percent) is allocated to Greg. However, when Chanzz sold its interest to Greg, Chanzz was already taxed on the $3,900 allocated portion of that ordinary income under §751(a), and Greg paid full value for his interest in the receivables when he acquired his 30 percent interest in CCS. This means Greg will be taxed on the $3,900 again in 2022, and his outside basis in CCS will increase by $3,900. Because Greg paid fair market value for his share of the receivables, he should not have any income when they are sold at fair market value. Eventually, when Greg disposes of his CCS interest, his ultimate gain (or loss) on the disposition will be $3,900 less because of the increase to his outside basis from this additional income; meanwhile, he is overtaxed on the receivables. Greg must report ordinary income today for an offsetting capital loss (or reduced capital gain) in the future when he disposes of his interest.

The tax rules allow the partnership to make an election for a **special basis adjustment** to eliminate discrepancies between partners' inside and outside bases and to correct the artificial income or loss at the partnership level.[49] For the most part, basis discrepancies arise in three situations: following *sales* of partnership interests, following *distributions* when a partner receives an asset that takes more or less basis outside the partnership than it had on the inside, and following *distributions* when a partner recognizes a gain or loss on the distribution. Once a partnership makes a §754 election, the partnership is required to

[49]§754. The election is made by including a written statement declaring that the partnership is making the §754 election with the partnership return when filed for the year the election is to take effect.

make special basis adjustments for all subsequent sales of partnership interests and partnership distributions. The election can be revoked only with permission from the IRS.

Even without a §754 election in effect, the partnership must adjust its bases if the partnership has a **substantial built-in loss** at the time a partner sells their partnership interest. A substantial built-in loss exists if the partnership's aggregate inside basis in its property exceeds the property's fair market value by more than $250,000 when a transfer of an interest occurs or when the purchasing partner would be allocated a loss of more than $250,000 if the partnership assets were sold for fair market value immediately after the sale.[50]

Similarly, a mandatory basis adjustment in partnership assets is required when a **substantial basis reduction** occurs in connection with a partnership distribution. A substantial basis reduction is triggered either when a partner recognizes a loss of more than $250,000 from a partnership distribution or when a partner takes a basis in distributed property exceeding the basis in that property prior to the distribution[51] by more than $250,000.

Although the election is made under §754, the actual authorization of the special basis adjustment is governed by two separate code sections, depending on which situation gives rise to the adjustment: (1) sale of partnership interest, §743(b), or (2) distributions, §734(b). These two sections determine the amount of the adjustment, and §755 then stipulates how the adjustment is allocated among partnership assets. The relationships among these code sections are depicted in Exhibit 10-2.

THE KEY FACTS

Special Basis Adjustments

- **How to elect?**
  Partnership makes a §754 election and then makes a special basis adjustment whenever (1) a new partner purchases a partnership interest or (2) a partner recognizes a gain or loss in a distribution or (3) a partner takes a basis in distributed property that differs from the partnership's basis in the property prior to the distribution.
- **When mandatory?**
  (1) When a partner sells a partnership interest and the partnership has a substantial built-in loss at the time of sale or (2) when a partnership has a substantial basis reduction from a distribution.
- **Why?**
  To prevent partners from being temporarily overtaxed or undertaxed after a partnership interest is transferred or after a distribution occurs.

EXHIBIT 10-2 Special Basis Adjustments

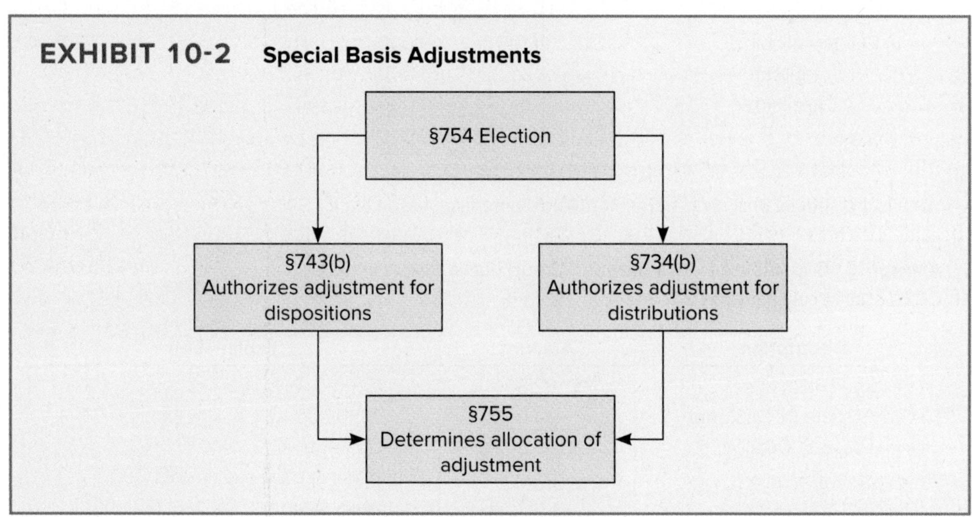

Special Basis Adjustments for Dispositions

The special basis adjustment the partnership makes when an existing partner sells their partnership interest is designed to give the new partner an inside basis in the partnership assets equal to their outside basis in the partnership interest. The basis adjustment in these cases applies *only* to the new partner. The inside bases of the continuing partners remain unchanged, so their income and losses will continue to be accurately allocated. The adjustment is equal to the difference between the new partner's outside basis in their interest and their share of the inside basis of the partnership's assets.[52] The new partner's outside basis is generally equal to the cost of their partnership interest plus their share of partnership liabilities.[53] The special basis adjustment must then be allocated to the assets under allocation rules in §755, which are beyond the scope of this text.

[50]§743(d). In this context, a transfer generally refers to sales, exchanges, or transfers at death, not gift transfers.

[51]§734(d).

[52]§743(b).

[53]A partner's share of inside basis is also labeled *previously taxed capital* [Reg. §1.743-1(d)]. The technical calculation is determined as follows (but generally equals the partner's tax capital account): (1) the amount of cash the partner would receive on liquidation after a hypothetical sale of all the partnership assets for their fair market value after the sale of the partnership interest, plus (2) the amount of taxable loss allocated to the partner from the hypothetical sale, less (3) the amount of taxable gain allocated to the partner from the hypothetical sale.

Example 10-26

What if: Suppose Greg acquired Chanzz's 30 percent interest in CCS on June 30, 2022, for $82,800. CCS's balance sheet as of the sale date is assumed to be as follows:

Color Comfort Sheets LLC
June 30, 2022

	Tax Basis	FMV
Assets		
Cash	$ 27,000	$ 27,000
Accounts receivable	0	13,000
Investments	15,000	12,000
Inventory	1,000	1,000
Equipment (cost = $100,000)	80,000	86,000
Building	97,000	97,000
Land	20,000	150,000
Totals	$240,000	$386,000
Liabilities and capital		
Long-term debt	$100,000	
Capital—Nicole	(49,000)	
—Sarah	108,000	
—Chanzz	81,000	
Totals	$240,000	

What is the special basis adjustment for Greg's purchase, assuming CCS has a §754 election in effect at the sale date?

Answer: $1,800, the difference between Greg's outside basis in his CCS interest and inside basis of CCS's assets, calculated as follows:

Description	Amount	Explanation
(1) Cash purchase price	$ 82,800	
(2) Greg's share of CCS debt	24,000	$80,000 × 30% (see Example 10-2)
(3) Initial basis in CCS	$106,800	(1) + (2)
(4) Greg's inside basis	105,000	Chanzz's tax capital ($81,000) plus share of CCS debt ($24,000) (see Example 10-7)
Special basis adjustment	**$ 1,800**	(3) − (4)

When a new partner's positive special basis adjustment is allocated to depreciable or amortizable assets, the new partner will benefit from additional depreciation or amortization. In some cases, the amounts can be quite substantial, and a new partner may be willing to pay more for a partnership interest with a §754 election in place than for a partnership interest without it.

TAXES IN THE REAL WORLD Sports Team Owners Garner Tax Deductions from Amortization

Professional sports team franchises are typically organized as partnerships for tax purposes. When a new owner purchases an interest in a professional sports team from an existing owner, the new owner is purchasing an interest in a business with assets that mainly consist of intangible assets such as goodwill, trademarks, licenses, broadcasting rights, and player contracts. As a result, the new owner usually receives a positive special basis adjustment that is allocated almost entirely to their share of these intangible assets. To be more specific, news sources report that 90 percent or more of the purchase price the new owner pays is typically allocated as a positive special basis adjustment to intangible assets. Because this special positive basis adjustment is amortizable over 15 years, the new owner will effectively be able to deduct nearly their entire investment in the team against their other sources of income over the remaining 15 years. Though this same tax advantage is available in other types of businesses taxed as partnerships, it has become somewhat controversial given the public visibility of professional sports teams and their owners.

Source: www.propublica.org/article/the-billionaire-playbook-how-sports-owners-use-their-teams-to-avoid-millions-in-taxes.

Special Basis Adjustments for Distributions

As with dispositions of partnership interests, partnership distributions may cause the partners' outside basis in their partnership interests to differ from their inside basis in partnership assets. This usually occurs when a partner recognizes a gain or loss on a distribution or when a partner's basis in the distributed property is different from the partnership's basis in the property prior to the distribution. In contrast to the special basis adjustment for sales of partnership interests, the special basis adjustment for distributions affects the common basis of *partnership* property and not merely one partner's basis adjustment.

The special basis adjustment can either increase or decrease the basis in the partnership assets. A **positive basis adjustment** will *increase* the basis in the partnership assets (1) when a partner receiving distributed property recognizes a gain on the distribution (for instance, in operating distributions where the partner receives money in excess of that partner's outside basis in their partnership interest) and (2) when a partner receiving distributed property takes a basis in the property less than the partnership's basis in the property. The positive adjustment will equal the sum of the gain recognized by the partners receiving a cash distribution in excess of their basis or the amount of the basis reduction in distributed property.

In Example 10-11, CCS distributed $250,000 cash to Nicole on December 31, 2023, as part of an operating distribution. Because Nicole's outside basis in her CCS interest before the distribution was $205,000 and she received only money in the distribution, Nicole was required to recognize a $45,000 gain on the distribution. If CCS had a §754 election in effect, it would have a positive special basis adjustment from the distribution of $45,000.

A **negative basis adjustment** will *decrease* the basis in partnership assets (1) when a partner receiving distributed property in a liquidating distribution recognizes a loss on the distribution and (2) when a partner receiving distributed property takes a basis in the property greater than the partnership's basis in the property.

The negative adjustment will equal the sum of the recognized loss or the amount of the basis increase in property distributed to partners. Recall from our previous discussion of distributions that negative adjustments can occur only in liquidating distributions. Only then does a partner recognize a loss or increase the distributed property's basis over its basis prior to the distribution.

In Example 10-15, CCS liquidated Greg's 30 percent interest by distributing cash of $206,000 and inventory with a fair market value of $103,000 (adjusted basis is $43,000). Because Greg's outside basis in his CCS interest after considering his debt relief ($268,000) was greater than the sum of the bases of the property distributed ($249,000), Greg recognized a loss of $19,000 on the liquidation. If CCS had a §754 election in effect at the time of this liquidation, CCS would have a negative basis adjustment of $19,000.

The allocation of the special basis adjustment among the partnership's remaining assets after a distribution is intended to offset any gain or loss any partners remaining in the partnership after the distribution would have recognized twice absent the adjustment. The process of allocating the adjustment for distributions is prescribed in §755, and these procedures are beyond the scope of this text.

CONCLUSION

The tax rules for partnership dispositions and distributions are among the most complex in the Internal Revenue Code. This chapter provided an overview of these rules and in some cases plunged into the complexity. We discussed the calculation of gains and losses from the sale of a partnership interest, as well as the basis implications of the purchase to a new investor. In doing so, we discussed how *hot assets* might affect the gain or loss. The chapter also explained the basic rules for determining the tax treatment of partnership distributions.

We illustrated how partnership elections might affect the partnership's basis in assets following partnership interest dispositions or distributions. In general, the tax rules are designed to avoid having business owners make decisions based on tax rules rather than on business principles; however, making this goal a reality provides for some challenging applications.

Summary

LO 10-1 Determine the tax consequences to the buyer and seller of the disposition of a partnership interest, including the amount and character of gain or loss recognized.

- Sellers are primarily concerned about their realized and recognized gain or loss on the sale of their partnership interest.
- Sellers' debt relief is included in the amount realized from the sale.
- Buyers' main tax concerns are determining their basis in the partnership interest they acquire and their inside bases of the partnership assets.
- The outside basis in a buyer's interest after an acquisition is generally equal to the cost that buyer paid plus the share of partnership liabilities allocated to that partner. A buyer's inside basis is generally the same as the seller's inside basis at the sale date.
- The sale of a partnership interest does not generally affect a partnership's inside basis in its assets.
- A partnership's tax year closes for the selling partner upon the sale of a partnership interest.
- Hot assets include unrealized receivables and inventory items.
- Unrealized receivables include the rights to receive payment for goods delivered or to be delivered, or services rendered or to be rendered, as well as items that would generate ordinary income if the partnership sold the asset for its fair market value, such as depreciation recapture.
- There are actually two definitions of inventory items. The first, under §751(a), applies to sales of partnership interests and includes all classic inventory items and assets that are *not* capital or §1231 assets. The second definition of inventory [§751(b)] applies primarily to distributions and includes only substantially appreciated inventory.
- Sellers classify gains and losses from the sale of partnership interests as ordinary to the extent the gain relates to hot assets.
- Hot assets are also important in determining whether a distribution is proportionate or disproportionate.

LO 10-2 List the reasons for distributions, and compare operating and liquidating distributions.

- Distributions from a flow-through entity are one mechanism to return business profits or capital to the owners of the entity.
- Distributions may also be used to liquidate an owner's interest in the business or to completely terminate the business.
- Operating distributions include distributions in which the owner retains an interest in the business.

LO 10-3 Determine the tax consequences of proportionate operating distributions.

- Partnerships do not generally recognize gain or loss on the distribution of property.
- Most operating distributions do not result in gain or loss to the partner receiving the distribution. Gains and losses are deferred through basis adjustments to the distributed assets and basis of the partnership interest.

- A partner recognizes a gain from an operating distribution if they receive a distribution of money that exceeds the basis in their partnership interest.
- Partners never recognize losses from operating distributions.

Determine the tax consequences of proportionate liquidating distributions. **LO 10-4**

- The tax issues in liquidating distributions are primarily twofold: (1) determining whether the liquidating partner recognizes a gain or loss and (2) allocating the liquidating partner's basis in the partnership interest to the distributed assets.
- A partner recognizes a gain only when receiving more money than that partner's basis in the partnership interest.
- A partner recognizes a loss only when the partnership distributes cash and hot assets and the partner's basis in the partnership interest is greater than the sum of the bases of the assets the partner receives in the distribution.
- In all other cases, a partner does not recognize gains or losses from a liquidating distribution; rather, the partner will simply allocate the basis in the partnership interest to the distributed assets.
- The key to the allocation process is to focus on two factors: (1) the type of property distributed and (2) whether the total basis in distributed assets is larger or smaller than the partner's basis in the partnership interest.
- The character of the distributed assets usually stays the same to the partner as in the partnership.

Explain the significance of disproportionate distributions. 

- Disproportionate distributions occur when the assets distributed in either operating or liquidating distributions do not represent the partner's proportionate share of the partnership's unrealized appreciation in its hot and cold assets.
- A disproportionate distribution causes a shift in the proportion of ordinary income and capital gain income from the partnership. Therefore, the rules require the partner to treat the disproportionate portion of a distribution as a sale or exchange.
- If a partner receives more cold assets than the proportionate share owned by that partner in a distribution, the partner will generally recognize ordinary income in an amount equal to that partner's share of the appreciation in the hot assets not distributed to the partner. If a partner receives more hot assets than the proportionate share owned, the partner will recognize capital gain equal to that partner's share of the appreciation in cold assets not distributed to the partner.
- The disproportionate distribution rules ensure that partners cannot convert ordinary income into capital gain through distributions.

Explain the rationale for special basis adjustments, determine when they are necessary, and calculate the special basis adjustment for dispositions and distributions. 

- Discrepancies between a partner's inside and outside bases may cause a partner to be overtaxed or undertaxed, at least temporarily. Special basis adjustment rules allow the partnership to eliminate discrepancies between inside and outside bases to correct any artificial income or loss at the partnership level.
- Basis discrepancies may occur following the acquisition of a partnership interest and following distributions where a partner receives more or less than their share of the inside basis in the partnership property.
- When purchasing a partnership interest, a new partner may receive a special basis adjustment equal to the difference between the new partner's outside basis in the partnership interest and their share of inside basis in the partnership's assets if the partnership has a §754 election in effect.
- A special basis adjustment is mandatory even without a §754 election in effect when a partnership has a substantial built-in loss at the time a partnership interest is transferred.
- When a partner recognizes a gain from a distribution or takes a basis in distributed property less than the partnership's basis in the property, the partnership will have a positive special basis adjustment to increase the basis in the partnership's assets.
- When a partner recognizes a loss from a liquidating distribution or takes a basis in distributed property greater than the partnership's basis in the property, the partnership will have a negative special basis adjustment to decrease the basis in partnership assets.

KEY TERMS

carryover basis (10-11)
disproportionate distributions (10-24)
hot assets (10-3)
inside basis (10-7)
inventory items (10-3)
liquidating distributions (10-9)
negative basis adjustment (10-29)
operating distributions (10-9)
outside basis (10-2)
partnership interest (10-2)
positive basis adjustment (10-29)
special basis adjustment (10-26)
substantial basis reduction (10-27)
substantial built-in loss (10-27)
substantially appreciated inventory (10-24)
unrealized receivables (10-3)

DISCUSSION QUESTIONS

Discussion Questions are available in Connect®.

LO 10-1 1. Joey is a 25 percent owner of Loopy LLC. He no longer wants to be involved in the business. What options does Joey have to exit the business?

LO 10-1 2. Compare and contrast the aggregate and entity approaches for a sale of a partnership interest.

LO 10-1 3. What restrictions might prevent a partner from selling their partnership interest to a third party?

LO 10-1 4. Explain how a partner's debt relief affects their amount realized in a sale of a partnership interest.

LO 10-1 5. Under what circumstances will the gain or loss on the sale of a partnership interest be characterized as ordinary rather than capital?

LO 10-1 6. What are *hot assets,* and why are they important in the sale of a partnership interest?

LO 10-1 7. For an accrual-method partnership, are accounts receivable considered unrealized receivables? Explain.

LO 10-1 8. Can a partnership have unrealized receivables if it has no accounts receivable?

LO 10-1 9. How do hot assets affect the character of gain or loss on the sale of a partnership interest?

LO 10-1 10. Under what circumstances can a partner recognize both gain and loss on the sale of a partnership interest?

LO 10-1 11. Absent any special elections, what effect does a sale of a partnership interest have on the partnership?

research LO 10-1 12. Generally, a selling partner's capital account carries over to the purchaser of the partnership interest. Under what circumstances will this not be the case?

LO 10-2 13. What distinguishes operating from liquidating distributions?

LO 10-3 14. Under what circumstances will a partner recognize a gain from an operating distribution?

LO 10-3 15. Under what circumstances will a partner recognize a loss from an operating distribution?

LO 10-3 16. In general, what effect does an operating distribution have on the partnership?

LO 10-3 17. If a partner's outside basis is less than the partnership's inside basis in distributed assets, how does the partner determine their basis of the distributed assets in an operating distribution?

LO 10-4 18. Under what conditions will a partner recognize gain in a liquidating distribution?

LO 10-4 19. Under what conditions will a partner recognize loss in a liquidating distribution?

LO 10-4 20. Describe how to determine the basis a partner has in distributed assets in cases in which a partnership distributes only money, inventory, and/or unrealized receivables in a liquidating distribution.

LO 10-4 21. How does a partner determine their basis in distributed assets when the partnership distributes other property in addition to money and hot assets?

22. SBT partnership distributes $5,000 cash and a parcel of land with a fair market value of $40,000 and a $25,000 basis to the partnership to Sam (30 percent partner). What factors must Sam and SBT consider in determining the tax treatment of this distribution? LO 10-5 planning

23. Discuss the underlying concern to tax policy makers in distributions in which a partner receives more or less than his share of the partnership's hot assets. LO 10-5

24. In general, how do the disproportionate distribution rules ensure that partners recognize their share of partnership ordinary income? LO 10-5

25. Why would a new partner who pays more for a partnership interest than the selling partner's outside basis want the partnership to elect a special basis adjustment? LO 10-6 planning

26. List two common situations that will cause a partner's inside and outside bases to differ. LO 10-6

27. Explain why a partnership might not want to make a §754 election to allow special basis adjustments. LO 10-6

28. When might a new partner have an upward basis adjustment following the acquisition of a partnership interest? LO 10-6

29. When are partnerships mandated to adjust the basis of their assets (inside basis) when a partner sells a partnership interest or receives a partnership distribution? LO 10-6

PROBLEMS

Select problems are available in Connect®.

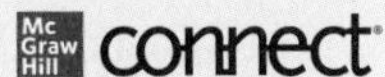

30. Jerry is a 30 percent partner in the JJM Partnership when he sells his entire interest to Lucia for $56,000 cash. At the time of the sale, Jerry's basis in JJM is $32,000. JJM does not have any debt or hot assets. What is Jerry's gain or loss on the sale of his interest? LO 10-1

31. Amina is a 30 percent partner in the AOM Partnership when she sells her entire interest to Hope for $72,000 cash. At the time of the sale, Amina's basis in AOM is $44,000 (which includes her $6,000 share of AOM liabilities). AOM does not have any hot assets. What is Amina's gain or loss on the sale of her interest? LO 10-1

32. Allison, Keesha, and Steven each owns an equal interest in KAS Partnership, a calendar-year-end, cash-method entity. On January 1 of the current year, Steven's basis in his partnership interest is $27,000. During January and February, the partnership generates $30,000 of ordinary income and $4,500 of tax-exempt income. On March 1, Steven sells his partnership interest to Juan for a cash payment of $45,000. The partnership has the following assets and no liabilities at the sale date: LO 10-1

	Tax Basis	FMV
Cash	$30,000	$30,000
Land held for investment	30,000	60,000
Totals	$60,000	$90,000

a) Assuming KAS's operating agreement provides for an interim closing of the books when partners' interests change during the year, what is Steven's basis in his partnership interest on March 1 just prior to the sale?

b) What are the amount and character of Steven's recognized gain or loss on the sale?

c) What is Juan's initial basis in the partnership interest?

d) What is the partnership's basis in the assets following the sale?

33. Gamila, James, Helen, and Carlos each owns an equal interest in GJHC Partnership, a calendar-year-end, cash-method entity. On January 1 of the current year, James's basis in his partnership interest is $62,000. For the taxable year, the partnership LO 10-1

generates $80,000 of ordinary income and $30,000 of dividend income. For the first five months of the year, GJHC generates $25,000 of ordinary income and no dividend income. On June 1, James sells his partnership interest to Robert for a cash payment of $70,000. The partnership has the following assets and no liabilities at the sale date:

	Tax Basis	FMV
Cash	$ 27,000	$ 27,000
Land held for investment	80,000	100,000
Totals	$107,000	$127,000

a) Assuming GJHC's operating agreement provides that the proration method will be used to allocate income or loss when partners' interests change during the year, what is James's basis in his partnership interest on June 1 just prior to the sale?

b) What are the amount and character of James's recognized gain or loss on the sale?

c) If GJHC uses an interim closing of the books, what are the amount and character of James's recognized gain or loss on the sale?

LO 10-1 34. At the end of last year, Milena, a 35 percent partner in the five-person LAMEC Partnership, has an outside basis of $60,000, including her $30,000 share of LAMEC debt. On January 1 of the current year, Milena sells her partnership interest to MaryLynn for a cash payment of $45,000 and the assumption of her share of LAMEC's debt.

a) What are the amount and character of Milena's recognized gain or loss on the sale?

b) If LAMEC has $100,000 of unrealized receivables as of the sale date, what are the amount and character of Milena's recognized gain or loss?

c) What is MaryLynn's initial basis in the partnership interest?

LO 10-1 35. Marco, Jaclyn, and Carrie formed Daxing Partnership (a calendar-year-end entity) by contributing cash 10 years ago. Each partner owns an equal interest in the partnership and has an outside basis in their partnership interest of $104,000. On January 1 of the current year, Marco sells his partnership interest to Ryan for a cash payment of $137,000. The partnership has the following assets and no liabilities as of the sale date:

	Tax Basis	FMV
Cash	$ 18,000	$ 18,000
Accounts receivable	0	12,000
Inventory	69,000	81,000
Equipment	180,000	225,000
Stock investment	45,000	75,000
Totals	$312,000	$411,000

The equipment was purchased for $240,000, and the partnership has taken $60,000 of depreciation. The stock was purchased seven years ago.

a) What are the *hot assets* [§751(a)] for this sale?

b) What is Marco's gain or loss on the sale of his partnership interest?

c) What is the character of Marco's gain or loss?

d) What are Ryan's inside and outside bases in the partnership on the date of the sale?

LO 10-1 36. Franklin, Jefferson, and Washington formed the Independence Partnership (a calendar-year-end entity) by contributing cash 10 years ago. Each partner owns an equal interest in the partnership and has an outside basis in his partnership interest of $104,000. On January 1 of the current year, Franklin sells his partnership interest to

Adams for a cash payment of $122,000. The partnership has the following assets and no liabilities as of the sale date:

	Tax Basis	FMV
Cash	$ 18,000	$ 18,000
Accounts receivable	0	12,000
Inventory	69,000	81,000
Equipment	180,000	225,000
Stock investment	45,000	30,000
Totals	$312,000	$366,000

The equipment was purchased for $240,000, and the partnership has taken $60,000 of depreciation. The stock was purchased seven years ago.

a) What is Franklin's overall gain or loss on the sale of his partnership interest?

b) What is the character of Franklin's gain or loss?

37. Travis and Alix Weber are equal partners in the Tralix Partnership, which does not have a §754 election in place. Alix sells one-half of her interest (25 percent) to Michael Tomei for $30,000 cash. Just before the sale, Alix's basis in her entire partnership interest is $75,000, including her $30,000 share of the partnership liabilities. Tralix's assets on the sale date are as follows: LO 10-1

	Tax Basis	FMV
Cash	$ 40,000	$ 40,000
Inventory	30,000	90,000
Land held for investment	80,000	50,000
Totals	$150,000	$180,000

a) What are the amount and character of Alix's recognized gain or loss on the sale?

b) What is Alix's basis in her remaining partnership interest?

c) What is Michael's basis in his partnership interest?

d) What is the effect of the sale on the partnership's basis in the assets?

38. Newton is a one-third owner of ProRite Partnership. Newton has decided to sell his interest in the business to Dunja for $50,000 cash plus the assumption of his share of ProRite's liabilities. Assume Newton's inside and outside bases in ProRite are equal. ProRite shows the following balance sheet as of the sale date: LO 10-1

	Tax Basis	FMV
Assets		
Cash	$ 80,000	$ 80,000
Receivables	25,000	25,000
Inventory	40,000	85,000
Land	30,000	20,000
Totals	$175,000	$210,000
Liabilities and capital		
Liabilities	$ 60,000	
Capital—Newton	38,333	
—Barbara	38,334	
—Liz	38,333	
Totals	$175,000	

What are the amount and character of Newton's recognized gain or loss?

LO 10-3 39. Coy and Matt are equal partners in the Matcoy Partnership. Each partner has a basis in his partnership interest of $28,000 at the end of the current year, prior to any distribution. On December 31, each receives an operating distribution. Coy receives $10,000 cash. Matt receives $3,000 cash and a parcel of land with a $7,000 fair market value and a $4,000 basis to the partnership. Matcoy has no debt or hot assets.

a) What is Coy's recognized gain or loss? What is the character of any gain or loss?
b) What is Coy's ending basis in his partnership interest?
c) What is Matt's recognized gain or loss? What is the character of any gain or loss?
d) What is Matt's basis in the distributed property?
e) What is Matt's ending basis in his partnership interest?

LO 10-3 40. Santiago and Lauren are equal partners in the PJenn Partnership. The partners formed the partnership seven years ago by contributing cash. Prior to any distributions, the partners have the following bases in their partnership interests:

Partner	Outside Basis
Santiago	$22,000
Lauren	22,000

On December 31 of the current year, the partnership makes a pro rata operating distribution of:

Partner	Distribution
Santiago	Cash $25,000
Lauren	Cash $18,000
	Property $7,000 (FMV)
	($2,000 basis to partnership)

a) What are the amount and character of Santiago's recognized gain or loss?
b) What is Santiago's remaining basis in his partnership interest?
c) What are the amount and character of Lauren's recognized gain or loss?
d) What is Lauren's basis in the distributed assets?
e) What is Lauren's remaining basis in her partnership interest?

LO 10-3 41. Adam and Alyssa are equal partners in the PartiPilo Partnership. The partners formed the partnership three years ago by contributing cash. Prior to any distributions, the partners have the following bases in their partnership interests:

Partner	Outside Basis
Adam	$12,000
Alyssa	12,000

On December 31 of the current year, the partnership makes a pro rata operating distribution of:

Partner	Distribution
Adam	Cash $16,000
Alyssa	Cash $8,000
	Property $8,000 (FMV)
	($6,000 basis to partnership)

a) What are the amount and character of Adam's recognized gain or loss?
b) What is Adam's remaining basis in his partnership interest?
c) What are the amount and character of Alyssa's recognized gain or loss?
d) What is Alyssa's basis in the distributed assets?
e) What is Alyssa's remaining basis in her partnership interest?

42. Rania has a $68,000 basis in her 50 percent partnership interest in the KD Partnership before receiving a current distribution of $6,000 cash and land with a fair market value of $35,000 and a basis to the partnership of $18,000. LO 10-3
    a) What are the amount and character of Rania's recognized gain or loss?
    b) What is Rania's basis in the land?
    c) What is Rania's remaining basis in her partnership interest?

43. Pam has a $27,000 basis (including her share of debt) in her 50 percent partnership interest in the Meddoc Partnership before receiving any distributions. This year Meddoc makes a current distribution to Pam of a parcel of land with a $40,000 fair market value and a $32,000 basis to the partnership. The land is encumbered with a $15,000 mortgage (the partnership's only liability). LO 10-3
    a) What are the amount and character of Pam's recognized gain or loss?
    b) What is Pam's basis in the land?
    c) What is Pam's remaining basis in her partnership interest?

44. Two years ago, Kimberly became a 30 percent partner in the KST Partnership with a contribution of investment land with a $10,000 basis and a $16,000 fair market value. On January 2 of this year, Kimberly has a $15,000 basis in her partnership interest, and none of her pre-contribution gain has been recognized. On January 2 Kimberly receives an operating distribution of a tract of land (not the contributed land) with a $12,000 basis and an $18,000 fair market value. LO 10-3

research
    a) What are the amount and character of Kimberly's recognized gain or loss on the distribution?
    b) What is Kimberly's remaining basis in KST after the distribution?
    c) What is KST's basis in the land Kimberly contributed after Kimberly receives this distribution?

45. Rufus is a one-quarter partner in the Adventure Partnership. On January 1 of the current year, Adventure distributes $13,000 cash to Rufus in complete liquidation of his interest. Adventure has only capital assets and no liabilities at the date of the distribution. Rufus's basis in his partnership interest is $18,500. LO 10-4
    a) What are the amount and character of Rufus's recognized gain or loss?
    b) What are the amount and character of Adventure's recognized gain or loss?
    c) If Rufus's basis is $10,000 at the distribution date rather than $18,500, what are the amount and character of Rufus's recognized gain or loss?

46. The Taurin Partnership (a calendar-year-end entity) has the following assets as of December 31 of the current year: LO 10-4

	Tax Basis	FMV
Cash	$ 45,000	$ 45,000
Accounts receivable	15,000	30,000
Inventory	81,000	120,000
Totals	$141,000	$195,000

On December 31, Taurin distributes $15,000 of cash, $10,000 (FMV) of accounts receivable, and $40,000 (FMV) of inventory to Emma (a one-third partner) in termination of her partnership interest. Emma's basis in her partnership interest immediately prior to the distribution is $40,000.
    a) What are the amount and character of Emma's recognized gain or loss on the distribution?
    b) What is Emma's basis in the distributed assets?
    c) If Emma's basis before the distribution was $55,000 rather than $40,000, what is Emma's recognized gain or loss and what is her basis in the distributed assets?

LO 10-4

47. Melissa, Nicole, and Miguel are equal partners in the Opto Partnership (a calendar-year-end entity). Melissa decides she wants to exit the partnership and receives a proportionate distribution to liquidate her partnership interest on January 1. The partnership has no liabilities and holds the following assets as of January 1:

	Tax Basis	FMV
Cash	$18,000	$18,000
Accounts receivable	0	24,000
Stock investment	7,500	12,000
Land	30,000	36,000
Totals	$55,500	$90,000

Melissa receives one-third of each of the partnership assets. She has a basis in her partnership interest of $25,000.

a) What are the amount and character of any recognized gain or loss to Melissa?
b) What is Melissa's basis in the distributed assets?
c) What are the tax implications (amount and character of gain or loss and basis of assets) to Melissa if her outside basis is $11,000 rather than $25,000?
d) What are the amount and character of any recognized gain or loss from the distribution to Opto?

LO 10-4
planning

48. Lonnie Davis has been a general partner in the Highland Partnership for many years and is also a sole proprietor in a separate business. To spend more time focusing on his sole proprietorship, he plans to leave Highland and will receive a liquidating distribution of $50,000 in cash and land with a fair market value of $100,000 (tax basis of $120,000). Immediately before the distribution, Lonnie's basis in his partnership interest is $350,000, which includes his $50,000 share of partnership debt. Highland Partnership does not hold any hot assets.

a) What are the amount and character of any gain or loss to Lonnie?
b) What is Lonnie's basis in the land?
c) What are the amount and character of Lonnie's gain or loss if he holds the land for 13 months as investment property and then sells it for $100,000?
d) What are the amount and character of Lonnie's gain or loss if he places the land into service in his sole proprietorship and then sells it 13 months later for $100,000?
e) Do your answers to parts (c) and (d) suggest a course of action that would help Lonnie to achieve a more favorable tax outcome?

LO 10-4

49. AJ is a 30 percent partner in the Trane Partnership, a calendar-year-end entity. On January 1, AJ has an outside basis in his interest in Trane of $73,000, which includes his share of the $50,000 of partnership liabilities. Trane generates $42,000 of income during the year and does not make any changes to its liabilities. On December 31, Trane makes a proportionate distribution of the following assets to AJ to terminate his partnership interest:

	Tax Basis	FMV
Inventory	$55,000	$65,000
Land	30,000	25,000
Totals	$85,000	$90,000

a) What are the tax consequences (gain or loss, basis adjustments) of the distribution to Trane?
b) What are the amount and character of any recognized gain or loss to AJ?
c) What is AJ's basis in the distributed assets?
d) If AJ sells the inventory four years after the distribution for $70,000, what are the amount and character of his recognized gain or loss?

50. Mikaere's basis in the Jimsoo Partnership is $53,000. In a proportionate liquidating distribution, Mikaere receives cash of $7,000 and two capital assets: (1) Land A with a fair market value of $20,000 and a basis to Jimsoo of $16,000 and (2) Land B with a fair market value of $10,000 and a basis to Jimsoo of $16,000. Jimsoo has no liabilities.  LO 10-4

   a) How much gain or loss will Mikaere recognize on the distribution? What is the character of any recognized gain or loss?
   b) What is Mikaere's basis in the distributed assets?
   c) If the two parcels of land had been inventory to Jimsoo, what are the tax consequences to Mikaere (amount and character of gain or loss and basis in distributed assets)?

51. Megan and Matthew are equal partners in the J & J Partnership (a calendar-year-end entity). On January 1 of the current year, they decide to liquidate the partnership. Megan's basis in her partnership interest is $100,000, and Matthew's is $35,000. The two partners receive identical distributions, with each receiving the following assets: LO 10-4

	Tax Basis	FMV
Cash	$30,000	$30,000
Inventory	5,000	6,000
Land	500	1,000
Totals	$35,500	$37,000

   a) What are the amount and character of Megan's recognized gain or loss?
   b) What is Megan's basis in the distributed assets?
   c) What are the amount and character of Matthew's recognized gain or loss?
   d) What is Matthew's basis in the distributed assets?

52. Markell's basis in the Markit Partnership is $58,000. In a proportionate liquidating distribution, Markell receives the following assets: LO 10-4

	Tax Basis	FMV
Cash	$ 8,000	$ 8,000
Land A	20,000	45,000
Land B	20,000	25,000

   a) How much gain or loss will Markell recognize on the distribution? What is the character of any recognized gain or loss?
   b) What is Markell's basis in the distributed assets?

53. Danner Inc. has a $395,000 capital loss carryover that will expire at the end of the current tax year if it is not used. Also, Danner Inc. has been a general partner in the Talisman Partnership for three years and plans to end its involvement with the partnership by receiving a liquidating distribution. Initially, all parties agreed that Danner Inc.'s liquidating distribution would include $50,000 in cash and land with a fair market value of $400,000 (tax basis of $120,000). Immediately before the distribution, Danner's basis in its partnership interest is $150,000, which includes its $100,000 share of partnership debt. Talisman Partnership does not hold any hot assets. LO 10-4  planning

   a) What are the amount and character of any gain or loss to Danner Inc.?
   b) What is Danner Inc.'s basis in the land?
   c) Can you suggest a course of action that would help Danner Inc. avoid the expiration of its capital loss carryover?

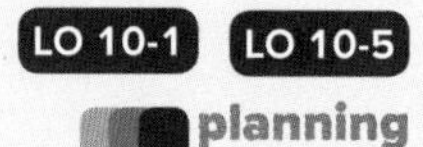

54. Bella Partnership is an equal partnership in which each of the partners has a basis in their partnership interest of $10,000. Bella reports the following balance sheet:

	Tax Basis	FMV
Assets		
Inventory	$20,000	$30,000
Land	10,000	15,000
Totals	$30,000	$45,000
Liabilities and capital		
Capital—Toby	$10,000	
—Kaelin	10,000	
—Andrew	10,000	
Totals	$30,000	

a) Identify the *hot assets* if Toby decides to sell his partnership interest. Are these assets "hot" for purposes of distributions?

b) If Bella distributes the land to Toby in complete liquidation of his partnership interest, what tax issues should be considered?

55. Fatima pays $120,000 cash for Brittany's one-third interest in the Westlake Partnership. Just prior to the sale, Brittany's basis in Westlake is $96,000. Westlake reports the following balance sheet:

	Tax Basis	FMV
Assets		
Cash	$ 96,000	$ 96,000
Land	192,000	264,000
Totals	$288,000	$360,000
Liabilities and capital		
Capital—Amy	$ 96,000	
—Brittany	96,000	
—Ben	96,000	
Totals	$288,000	

a) What are the amount and character of Brittany's recognized gain or loss on the sale?

b) What is Fatima's basis in her partnership interest? What is Fatima's inside basis?

c) If Westlake were to sell the land for $264,000 shortly after the sale of Brittany's partnership interest, how much gain or loss would the partnership recognize?

d) How much gain or loss would Fatima recognize if the land were sold for $264,000?

e) Suppose Westlake has a §754 election in place. What is Fatima's special basis adjustment? How much gain or loss would Fatima recognize on a subsequent sale of the land in this situation?

LO 10-1 LO 10-6

56. Elaine pays $40,000 cash for Martha's one-third interest in Lakewood Partnership. Just prior to the sale, Martha's basis in Lakewood is $140,000. Lakewood reports the following balance sheet:

	Tax Basis	FMV
Assets		
Cash	$ 50,000	$ 50,000
Land	370,000	70,000
Totals	$420,000	$120,000
Liabilities and capital		
Capital—Mary	140,000	
—Martha	140,000	
—Margaret	140,000	
Totals	$420,000	

Assume the land had been purchased several years ago and the partnership does not have a §754 election in place.

a) What are the amount and character of Martha's recognized gain or loss on the sale?
b) What is Elaine's basis in her partnership interest?
c) If Lakewood were to sell the land for $70,000 shortly after the sale of Martha's partnership interest, how much gain or loss would Elaine recognize?

57. Cliff's basis in his Aero Partnership interest is $11,000. Cliff receives a distribution of $22,000 cash from Aero in complete liquidation of his interest. Aero is an equal partnership with the following balance sheet: LO 10-4 LO 10-6

	Tax Basis	FMV
Assets		
Cash	$22,000	$22,000
Investment	8,800	8,800
Land	2,200	35,200
Totals	$33,000	$66,000
Liabilities and capital		
Capital—Chris	$11,000	
—Cliff	11,000	
—Cooper	11,000	
Totals	$33,000	

a) What are the amount and character of Cliff's recognized gain or loss? What is the effect on the partnership assets?
b) If Aero has a §754 election in place, what is the amount of the special basis adjustment?

58. Erin's basis in her Kiybron Partnership interest is $3,300. Erin receives a distribution of $2,200 cash from Kiybron in complete liquidation of her interest. Kiybron is an equal partnership with the following balance sheet: LO 10-4 LO 10-6

	Tax Basis	FMV
Assets		
Cash	$2,200	$2,200
Stock (investment)	1,100	2,200
Land	6,600	2,200
Totals	$9,900	$6,600
Liabilities and capital		
Capital—Erin	$3,300	
—Carl	3,300	
—Grace	3,300	
Totals	$9,900	

a) What are the amount and character of Erin's recognized gain or loss? What is the effect on the partnership assets?
b) If Kiybron has a §754 election in place, what is the amount of the special basis adjustment?

59. Helen's basis in Haywood Partnership is $270,000. Haywood distributes all the land to Helen in complete liquidation of her partnership interest. The partnership reports the following balance sheet just before the distribution: LO 10-4 LO 10-6

	Tax Basis	FMV
Assets		
Cash	$220,000	$220,000
Stock (investment)	480,000	220,000
Land	110,000	220,000
Totals	$810,000	$660,000
Liabilities and capital		
Capital—Charles	$270,000	
—Esther	270,000	
—Helen	270,000	
Totals	$810,000	

a) What are the amount and character of Helen's recognized gain or loss? What is the effect on the partnership assets?

b) If Haywood has a §754 election in place, what is the amount of the special basis adjustment?

LO 10-4 LO 10-6 60. Lauren's basis in Driftwood Partnership is $510,000. Driftwood distributes all the land to Lauren in complete liquidation of her partnership interest. The partnership reports the following balance sheet just before the distribution:

	Tax Basis	FMV
Assets		
Cash	$ 370,000	$ 370,000
Stock (investment)	910,000	370,000
Land	250,000	370,000
Totals	$1,530,000	$1,110,000
Liabilities and capital		
Capital—Esteban	$ 510,000	
—Kylie	510,000	
—Lauren	510,000	
Totals	$1,530,000	

a) What are the amount and character of Lauren's recognized gain or loss?

b) If Driftwood does not have a §754 election in place, what is the amount of the special basis adjustment, if any?

COMPREHENSIVE PROBLEMS

Select problems are available in Connect®.

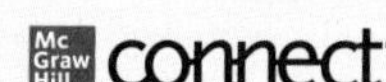

61. Joaquin is a 30 percent partner in the SBD Partnership, a calendar-year-end entity. As of the end of this year, Joaquin has an outside basis in his interest in SBD of $188,000, which includes his share of the $60,000 of partnership liabilities. On December 31, SBD makes a proportionate distribution of the following assets to Joaquin:

	Tax Basis	FMV
Cash	$ 40,000	$ 40,000
Inventory	55,000	65,000
Land	30,000	45,000
Totals	$125,000	$150,000

a) What are the tax consequences (amount and character of recognized gain or loss, basis in distributed assets) of the distribution to Joaquin if the distribution is an operating distribution?

b) What are the tax consequences (amount and character of recognized gain or loss, basis in distributed assets) of the distribution to Joaquin if the distribution is a liquidating distribution?

c) Compare and contrast the results from parts (a) and (b).

planning 62. Paolo is a 50 percent partner in the Capri Partnership and has decided to terminate his partnership interest. Paolo is considering two options as potential exit strategies. The first is to sell his partnership interest to the two remaining 25 percent partners, Giuseppe and Isabella, for $105,000 cash and the assumption of Paolo's share of Capri's liabilities. Under this option, Giuseppe and Isabella would each pay $52,500 for half of Paolo's interest. The second option is to have Capri liquidate Paolo's partnership interest with a proportionate distribution of the partnership assets. Paolo's basis in his partnership interest is $110,000, including Paolo's share of Capri's liabilities. Capri reports the following balance sheet as of the termination date:

	Tax Basis	FMV
Assets		
Cash	$ 80,000	$ 80,000
Receivables	40,000	40,000
Inventory	50,000	80,000
Land	50,000	60,000
Totals	$220,000	$260,000
Liabilities and capital		
Liabilities	$ 50,000	
Capital—Paolo	85,000	
—Giuseppe	42,500	
—Isabella	42,500	
Totals	$220,000	

a) If Paolo sells his partnership interest to Giuseppe and Isabella for $105,000, what are the amount and character of Paolo's recognized gain or loss?
b) Giuseppe and Isabella each has a basis in Capri of $55,000 before any purchase of Paolo's interest. What are Giuseppe's and Isabella's bases in their partnership interests following the purchase of Paolo's interest?
c) If Capri liquidates Paolo's partnership interest with a proportionate distribution of the partnership assets ($25,000 deemed cash from debt relief, $15,000 of actual cash, and half of the remaining assets), what are the amount and character of Paolo's recognized gain or loss?
d) If Capri liquidates Paolo's interest, what is Paolo's basis in the distributed assets?
e) Compare and contrast Paolo's options for terminating his partnership interest. Assume Paolo's marginal tax rate is 35 percent and his capital gains rate is 15 percent.

63. Carrie D'Lake, Reed A. Green, and Doug A. Divot share a passion for golf and decide to go into the golf club manufacturing business together. On January 2, 2022, D'Lake, Green, and Divot form the Slicenhook Partnership, a general partnership. Slicenhook's main product will be a perimeter-weighted titanium driver with a patented graphite shaft. All three partners plan to actively participate in the business. The partners contribute the following property to form Slicenhook:

tax forms

Partner	Contribution
Carrie D'Lake	Land, FMV $460,000 Basis $460,000, Mortgage $60,000
Reed A. Green	$400,000
Doug A. Divot	$400,000

Carrie had recently acquired the land with the idea that she would contribute it to the newly formed partnership. The partners agree to share in profits and losses equally. Slicenhook elects a calendar year-end and the accrual method of accounting.

In addition, Slicenhook received a $1,500,000 recourse loan from Big Bank at the time the contributions were made. Slicenhook uses the proceeds from the loan and the cash contributions to build a state-of-the-art manufacturing facility ($1,200,000), purchase equipment ($600,000), and produce inventory ($400,000). With the remaining cash, Slicenhook invests $45,000 in the stock of a privately owned graphite research company and retains $55,000 as working cash.

Slicenhook operates on a just-in-time inventory system so it sells all inventory and collects all sales immediately. That means that at the end of the year, Slicenhook does not carry any inventory or accounts receivable balances. During 2022, Slicenhook has the following operating results:

Sales		$1,126,000
Cost of goods sold		400,000
Interest income from tax-exempt bonds		900
Qualified dividend income from stock		1,500
Operating expenses		126,000
Depreciation (tax)		
§179 on equipment	$39,000	
Equipment	81,000	
Building	24,000	144,000
Interest expense on debt		120,000

The partnership is very successful in its first year. The success allows Slicenhook to use excess cash from operations to purchase $15,000 of tax-exempt bonds (you can see the interest income already reflected in the operating results). The partnership also makes a principal payment on its loan from Big Bank in the amount of $300,000 and a distribution of $100,000 to each of the partners on December 31, 2022.

The partnership continues its success in 2023 with the following operating results:

Sales		$1,200,000
Cost of goods sold		420,000
Interest income from tax-exempt bonds		900
Qualified dividend income from stock		1,500
Operating expenses		132,000
Depreciation (tax)		
Equipment	$147,000	
Building	30,000	177,000
Interest expense on debt		96,000

The operating expenses include a $1,800 trucking fine that one of its drivers incurred for reckless driving and speeding and meals expense of $6,000 (the meals were not provided by a restaurant).

By the end of 2023, Reed has had a falling out with Carrie and Doug and has decided to leave the partnership. He has located a potential buyer for his partnership interest, Indie Ruff. Indie has agreed to purchase Reed's interest in Slicenhook for $730,000 in cash and the assumption of Reed's share of Slicenhook's debt. Carrie and Doug, however, are not certain that admitting Indie to the partnership is such a good idea. They want to consider having Slicenhook liquidate Reed's interest on January 1, 2024. As of January 1, 2024, Slicenhook has the following assets:

	Tax Basis	FMV
Cash	$ 876,800	$ 876,800
Investment—tax exempts	15,000	18,000
Investment stock	45,000	45,000
Equipment—net of dep.	333,000	600,000
Building—net of dep.	1,146,000	1,440,000
Land	460,000	510,000
Total	$2,875,800	$3,489,800

Carrie and Doug propose that Slicenhook distribute the following to Reed in complete liquidation of his partnership interest:

	Tax Basis	FMV
Cash	$485,000	$485,000
Investment stock	45,000	45,000
Equipment—$200,000 cost, net of dep.	111,000	200,000
Total	$641,000	$730,000

Slicenhook has not purchased or sold any equipment since its original purchase just after formation.

a) Determine each partner's recognized gain or loss upon formation of Slicenhook.

b) What is each partner's initial tax basis in Slicenhook on January 2, 2022?

c) Prepare Slicenhook's opening tax basis balance sheet as of January 2, 2022.

d) Using the operating results, what are Slicenhook's ordinary income and separately stated items for 2022 and 2023? What amount of Slicenhook's income for each period would each of the partners receive?

e) Using the information provided, prepare Slicenhook's page 1 and Schedule K to be included with its Form 1065 for 2022. Also, prepare a Schedule K-1 for Carrie.

f) What are Carrie's, Reed's, and Doug's bases in their partnership interest at the end of 2022 and 2023?

g) If Reed sells his interest in Slicenhook to Indie Ruff, what are the amount and character of his recognized gain or loss? What is Indie's basis in the partnership interest?

h) What is Indie's inside basis in Slicenhook? What effect would a §754 election have on Indie's inside basis?

i) If Slicenhook distributes the assets proposed by Carrie and Doug in complete liquidation of Reed's partnership interest, what are the amount and character of Reed's recognized gain or loss? What is Reed's basis in the distributed assets?

j) Compare and contrast Reed's options for terminating his partnership interest. Assume Reed's marginal ordinary rate is 35 percent and his capital gains rate is 15 percent.

UWorld Roger CPA Review

Sample CPA Exam questions from Roger CPA Review are available in Connect as support for the topics in this text. These Multiple Choice Questions and Task-Based Simulations include expert-written explanations and solutions and provide a starting point for students to become familiar with the content and functionality of the actual CPA Exam.

chapter

11 S Corporations

Learning Objectives

Upon completing this chapter, you should be able to:

LO 11-1 Describe the requirements and process to elect S corporation status.

LO 11-2 Explain the events that terminate the S corporation election.

LO 11-3 Describe operating issues relating to S corporation accounting periods and methods, and explain income and loss allocations and separately stated items.

LO 11-4 Explain stock-basis calculations, loss limitations, determination of self-employment income, and fringe benefit rules that apply to S corporation shareholders.

LO 11-5 Apply the tax rules for S corporation operating distributions and liquidating distributions.

LO 11-6 Describe the taxes that apply to S corporations, estimated tax requirements, and tax return filing requirements.

Gyorgy Barna/Shutterstock

Storyline Summary

Taxpayers:	Nicole Johnson (she/her/hers), Sarah Walker (she/her/hers), and Chance Armstrong (he/him/his)
Location:	Salt Lake City, Utah
Status:	Shareholders of newly formed Color Comfort Sheets Inc. (CCS)
Situation:	Formed CCS as a corporation and have elected to have the entity taxed as an S corporation

In the Business Entities Overview chapter, we met Nicole Johnson, who turned her sheet-making hobby into a full-time business called Color Comfort Sheets (CCS). In this chapter, we assume Nicole formed CCS as a corporation, intending to elect S corporation tax status.

When starting the business, Nicole had cash to contribute to CCS but not enough to meet initial needs. She convinced her friend Sarah Walker to invest in CCS and fortunately, after listening to Nicole and Sarah's proposal, local sports team owner Chance Armstrong also agreed to invest. Nicole and Sarah would take an active role in managing CCS; Chance would not. Nicole contributed a parcel of land and cash in exchange for one-third of CCS's stock. Sarah and Chance each contributed cash for one-third of the stock. With funding in place, CCS began operating on January 1, 2021. However, with the excitement (and turmoil) of starting the new business, it took Nicole, Sarah, and Chance a while to talk with their accountant about electing S corporation status. After several discussions, they filed their S election on May 1, 2021. ■

In this chapter, we discuss the tax characteristics of an **S corporation,** a hybrid entity that shares some characteristics with C corporations and some with partnerships.[1] S corporations either are incorporated under state law, have the same legal protections as C corporations, and have elected S corporation status or, as we discuss in the Business Entities Overview chapter, they are noncorporate business entities (e.g., an LLC) that have elected to be treated as a corporation, and then elected S corporation status. S corporations are governed by the same corporate tax rules that apply in the organization, liquidation, and reorganization of C corporations. However, unlike a C corporation, an S corporation is a flow-through entity and shares many tax similarities with partnerships. For example, basis calculations for S corporation shareholders and partners are similar, the income or loss of an S corporation flows through to its owners, and distributions are generally not taxed to the extent of the owner's basis.

Throughout this chapter, we highlight the tax similarities between S corporations and C corporations and between S corporations and partnerships, while focusing on the unique rules that apply to S corporations. These rules are more complex for S corporations that were once C corporations with previously undistributed **earnings and profits (E&P).**

LO 11-1

S CORPORATION ELECTIONS

Formations

The same rules for forming and contributing property govern S and C corporations. As discussed earlier in the text, §351 and related provisions apply when one or more persons transfer property to a corporation (C or S) in return for stock, and immediately after the transfer, these persons control the corporation. These rules allow shareholders meeting the requirements to defer gains they realize when they transfer appreciated property to the corporation in exchange for stock. Note that similar rules apply to formations and property contributions to partnerships under §721. One important difference, however, is that partnership tax rules do not impose a control requirement to defer gains (see the Forming and Operating Partnerships chapter for partnership contributions).

THE KEY FACTS

S Corporation Qualification Requirements

- Only U.S. citizens or residents, estates, certain trusts, and certain tax-exempt organizations may be S corporation shareholders.
- S corporations may have no more than 100 shareholders.
- For purposes of the 100-shareholder limit, family members and their estates count as only one shareholder.

S Corporation Qualification Requirements

Unlike C corporations and partnerships, S corporations are limited as to type and number of owners (shareholders).[2] Only U.S. citizens or residents, estates, certain trusts, and certain tax-exempt organizations may be shareholders. No S or C corporations (legal corporations or treated as a corporation for tax purposes) or partnerships can be shareholders.[3] S corporations may have no more than 100 shareholders; family members and their estates count as one shareholder. Family members include a common ancestor (not more than six generations removed) and their lineal descendants and their lineal descendants' spouses (or former spouses).[4] Under this broad definition, great-grandparents, grandparents, parents, children, siblings, grandchildren, great-grandchildren, aunts, uncles, cousins, and the respective spouses are family members for this purpose. A practical implication of these limits is that large, publicly traded corporations cannot elect to be treated as S corporations.

[1]S corporations get their name from Subchapter S of the Internal Revenue Code, which includes code sections 1361–1379.

[2]§1361.

[3]Grantor trusts, qualified Subchapter S trusts, electing small business trusts, certain testamentary trusts, and voting trusts can own S corporation stock. A discussion of these trusts is beyond the scope of this chapter. Eligible tax-exempt shareholders include qualified retirement plan trusts or charitable, religious, educational, etc., organizations that are tax-exempt under §501. A single-owned LLC (not electing to be taxed as a corporation) owned by a permissible shareholder (e.g., an individual) may also be an S corporation shareholder. In this case, the LLC would be a disregarded entity and the LLC owner would be considered the shareholder.

[4]The common ancestor (living or not, owning shares or not) must not be more than six generations removed from the youngest generation of shareholder family members determined at the later of the S corporation election date or the date the first member of the respective family holds the S corporation's stock.

Example 11-1

What if: Suppose CCS was formed with Nicole Johnson, Sarah Walker, and Chanzz Inc., a legal corporation owned by Chance Armstrong, as shareholders. Would CCS be eligible to elect S corporation status?

Answer: No. Because one of its shareholders is a corporation (Chanzz Inc.), CCS would not be eligible to elect S corporation status.

What if: Suppose Nicole, Sarah, and Chance recruited 97 U.S. residents to become shareholders of CCS. Meanwhile, Nicole gave several of her CCS shares to her grandfather and his spouse as a wedding gift and to her first cousin as an MBA graduation gift. After the transfer, CCS had 103 shareholders. Can CCS elect S corporation status?

Answer: Yes. Nicole (descendant of common ancestor), her first cousin (descendant of common ancestor), her grandfather (common ancestor), and her grandfather's spouse (spouse of common ancestor) are treated as *one* shareholder for purposes of the 100-shareholder limit.

TAXES IN THE REAL WORLD Planning to Launch the Next Uber? May Want to Rethink That S Election

If you are planning to launch the next great start-up company with aspirations to create the next Uber, you may want to rethink an S corporation election. Many start-up companies with plans for uber growth (pun intended) seek outside investors through venture capital firms. Venture capital firms are generally organized as limited partnerships with an LLC or corporation serving as general partner. Either way, a limited partnership cannot be a shareholder in an S corporation. Thus, if you are planning to launch the next Uber, operating as an S corporation may not be a viable option. Note, however, an S corporation can receive funding from angel investors directly (high-net-worth individuals) and still maintain S corporation status as long as the 100-shareholder limit is not exceeded.

S Corporation Election

An eligible corporation must make an affirmative election to be treated as an S corporation.[5] In addition to meeting the shareholder requirements above, it must:

- Be a domestic corporation for tax purposes (created or organized in the United States or under U.S. law or the law of any state in the United States).
- Not be a specifically identified ineligible corporation.[6]
- Have only one class of stock.

A corporation is considered to have only one class of stock if all its outstanding shares provide identical distribution and liquidation rights. Differences in voting powers are permissible. In general, debt instruments do not violate the single-class-of-stock requirement unless they are treated as equity elsewhere under the tax law.[7] In addition, §1361 provides safe-harbor rules to ensure that debt obligations are not recharacterized as a second class of stock.[8]

THE KEY FACTS

S Corporation Election

- An eligible corporation must make an affirmative election to be treated as an S corporation.
- Eligible corporations meet the type and number of shareholder requirements, are domestic corporations for tax purposes, are not specifically identified as ineligible corporations, and have only one class of stock.
- To elect S corporation status, the corporation makes a formal election using Form 2553.

[5]§1362(a).

[6]Ineligible corporations include financial institutions using the reserve method of accounting under §585, insurance companies, corporations allowed a tax credit for income from Puerto Rico and from U.S. possessions under §936, corporations previously electing Domestic International Sales Corporation status, and corporations treated as a taxable mortgage pool.

[7]See §385 for factors considered in determining whether debt should be considered as equity for tax purposes.

[8]§1361(c)(5)(A) provides that straight debt issued during an S corporation year (i.e., not during a C corporation year) will not be treated as a second class of stock. Section 1361(c)(5)(A) defines straight debt as debt characterized by a written unconditional promise to pay on demand or on a specified date a certain sum in money if (1) the interest rate and interest payment dates are not contingent on profits, the borrower's discretion, or similar factors; (2) the debt is not convertible into stock; and (3) the creditor is an individual (other than a nonresident alien), an estate, a qualified trust, or a person who is actively and regularly engaged in the business of lending money.

Example 11-2

What if: Suppose Nicole were a resident of Toronto, Canada, and while she formed CCS in Canada under Canadian law, she still planned to do business in the United States. Is CCS eligible to elect S corporation status in the United States?

Answer: No. CCS would not be eligible for S corporation treatment because it was neither organized in the United States nor formed under U.S. laws.

What if: Suppose Nicole resided in Seattle and formed CCS under the state laws of Washington but planned to do a significant amount of business in Canada. Would CCS be eligible to elect S corporation status?

Answer: Yes, because CCS was formed under the laws of a U.S. state.

To formally elect S corporation status effective as of the beginning of the current tax year, the corporation uses **Form 2553,** Election by a Small Business Corporation, either in the prior tax year or on or before the 15th day of the third month of the current tax year.[9] Elections made after the 15th day of the third month of a year are effective at the beginning of the following year. All shareholders on the date of the election must consent to the election.

Example 11-3

What if: Suppose Nicole formed CCS as a C corporation in 2021 with a calendar tax year and finally got around to electing S corporation status on February 20, 2022. What is the earliest effective date of the S election?

Answer: January 1, 2022.

What if: Suppose Nicole formed CCS as a C corporation in 2021 with a calendar tax year and made the S election on March 20, 2022. When is the S election effective?

Answer: It is effective January 1, 2023, because Nicole made the election after March 15, 2022.

Even when the corporation makes the election on or before the 15th day of the third month of its tax year, the election will not be effective until the subsequent year if (1) the corporation did not meet the S corporation requirements for each day of the current tax year before it made the S election or (2) one or more shareholders who held the stock in the corporation during the current year and before the S corporation election was made did not consent to the election (e.g., a shareholder disposes of their stock in the corporation in the election year before the election is made and fails to consent to the S election).[10]

Example 11-4

What if: Suppose in 2021 Nicole formed CCS as a C corporation (calendar tax year) with Nicole, Sarah, and Chanzz Inc. (a C corporation) as shareholders. On January 2, 2022, Chanzz Inc. sold all its shares to Chance Armstrong. On January 31, 2022, CCS filed an S corporation election, with Nicole, Sarah, and Chance all consenting to the election. What is the earliest effective date of the S election?

[9]§1362(b). When the IRS determines that taxpayers have reasonable cause for making late elections, it has the authority to treat late elections as timely [§1362(b)(5)]. Rev. Proc. 2013-30 provides a simplified method to provide relief for late elections by submitting Form 2553 to the IRS with a statement that explains that (a) there was either reasonable cause for the late election or the late election was inadvertent and (b) the taxpayer acted diligently to correct the mistake upon discovery.

[10]§1362(b)(2). Requiring all shareholders who own stock in an S corporation during the year to consent to the election ensures that shareholders who dispose of their stock before the election do not suffer adverse tax consequences from an election to which they did not consent.

Answer: January 1, 2023. Because CCS had an ineligible shareholder (Chanzz Inc.) during 2022, the election is not effective until the beginning of 2023.

What if: Suppose in 2021 Nicole formed CCS as a C corporation (calendar tax year) with Nicole, Sarah, and Chance as shareholders. On January 30, 2022, Chance sold his shares to Nicole. On February 15, 2022, CCS filed an S election, with Nicole and Sarah consenting to the election. Chance, however, did not consent to the election. What is the earliest effective date of the S election?

Answer: January 1, 2023. Because Chance was a shareholder until January 30, 2022, and he did not consent to the S election in 2022, the S election is not effective until the beginning of 2023, the year after the election.

The timing of the election may be especially important for C corporations with net operating losses. The reason: Net operating losses attributable to C corporation years generally cannot be carried over to the S corporation. Thus, it may be beneficial to delay the S election until the corporation has utilized its net operating losses.[11]

S CORPORATION TERMINATIONS

LO 11-2

Once the S election becomes effective, the corporation remains an S corporation until the election is terminated. The termination may be voluntary or involuntary.

Voluntary Terminations

The corporation can make a *voluntary revocation* of the S election if shareholders holding more than 50 percent of the S corporation stock (including nonvoting shares) agree.[12] The corporation files a statement with the IRS revoking the election made under §1362(a) and stating the effective date of the revocation and the number of shares issued and outstanding. In general, voluntary revocations made on or before the 15th day of the third month of the year are effective as of the beginning of the year. A revocation after this period is effective the first day of the following tax year. Alternatively, an S corporation may specify the termination date as long as the date specified is on or after the date the revocation is made.[13]

Example 11-5

What if: Suppose CCS had been initially formed as an S corporation with a calendar year-end. After a couple of years, things were going so well that Nicole and Sarah (each one-third shareholders) wanted to terminate the S election and take CCS public. However, Chance (also a one-third shareholder) was opposed to the S election termination. Can Nicole and Sarah terminate the S election without Chance's consent?

Answer: Yes. To revoke the election, Nicole and Sarah need to own more than 50 percent of the shares, and together they own 66.7 percent.

What if: If Nicole and Sarah file the revocation on February 15, 2023, what is the effective date of the S corporation termination (assuming they do not specify one)?

Answer: January 1, 2023. If they file the S corporation revocation after March 15, 2023, it becomes effective January 1, 2024. Alternatively, CCS could have specified an effective date of the S corporation's termination (in 2023 or after) as long as it was on or after the date the revocation was made.

[11] Later in this chapter we discuss one exception to the rule that disallows net operating loss carryovers from C corporation to S corporation years. See the discussion of the S corporation built-in gains tax.

[12] §1362(d)(1)(B).

[13] §1362(d)(1)(D).

ETHICS

Suppose Chance Armstrong is a U.S. resident but a French citizen. His mother has recently been diagnosed with a terminal illness, and Chance has decided to move back to France to take care of his mother and her affairs. He anticipates that he will live in France for several years and that he will no longer be considered a U.S. resident. If you were Sarah or Nicole, how would you react to Chance's decision to move? Would you ignore the impact it may have on CCS's S corporation status? Would you pressure Chance to sell his CCS stock to you?

Involuntary Terminations

Involuntary terminations can result from failure to meet requirements (by far the most common reason) or from an excess of passive investment income.

Failure to Meet Requirements A corporation's S election is automatically terminated if the corporation fails to meet the requirements. The termination is effective on the date it fails the S corporation requirements. If the IRS deems the termination inadvertent, it may allow the corporation to continue to be treated as an S corporation if, within a reasonable period after the inadvertent termination, the corporation takes the necessary steps to meet the S corporation requirements.[14]

Example 11-6

What if: Suppose CCS was formed as a calendar-year S corporation with Nicole Johnson, Sarah Walker, and Chance Armstrong as equal shareholders. On June 15, 2022, Chance sold his CCS shares to his solely owned C corporation, Chanzz Inc. Is CCS's S election still in effect at the beginning of 2023? If not, when was it terminated?

Answer: No, the election was automatically terminated on June 15, 2022, when Chanzz Inc. became a shareholder because S corporations may not have corporate shareholders.

Excess of Passive Investment Income If an S corporation has *earnings and profits* from a previous C corporation year (or through a tax-deferred reorganization with a corporation that has earnings and profits), its election is terminated if the S corporation has passive investment income in excess of 25 percent of gross receipts for three consecutive years. If the S corporation has never operated as a C corporation or does not have C corporation earnings and profits (either by prior distribution of C corporation earnings and profits, or simply by not having earnings and profits at the effective date of the S election), this provision does not apply.

For purposes of the passive investment income test, **gross receipts** are the total amount of revenues received—including net capital gains from the sale of capital assets and gain (not offset by losses) from the sale of stock and securities—or accrued under the corporation's accounting method, *not* reduced by returns, allowances, cost of goods sold, or deductions. **Passive investment income (PII)** includes gross receipts from royalties, rents, dividends, interest (including tax-exempt interest), and annuities.[15] While net capital gain income is included in gross receipts, it is *not* considered passive investment income. S corporation election terminations due to excess passive investment income are effective on the first day of the year following the third consecutive tax year with excess passive investment income.

[14]§1362(f). Because the restrictions on S corporation ownership are so specific and exact, many S corporations require their shareholders, as a condition of stock ownership, to enter into a shareholder agreement. These agreements generally restrict the ability of shareholders to transfer their stock ownership to any disqualified shareholder.

[15]PII excludes certain rents (e.g., rents derived from the active trade or business of renting property, produced film rents, income from leasing self-produced tangible property, temporary parking fees, etc.).

Example 11-7

What if: Suppose CCS was initially formed as an S corporation with a calendar year-end. During its first three years, it reported passive investment income in excess of 25 percent of its gross receipts. Is CCS's S election terminated under the excess passive investment income test? If so, what is the effective date of the termination?

Answer: No, the excess passive investment income test does not apply to CCS in this situation because CCS has never operated as a C corporation; consequently, it does not have C corporation earnings and profits.

What if: Suppose CCS was initially formed as a C corporation with a calendar year-end. After a very profitable first year of operations, CCS elected S corporation status, effective January 1, 2022. During 2023, 2024, and 2025, it reported passive investment income in excess of 25 percent of its gross receipts and had undistributed earnings and profits from its C corporation year. Is CCS's S election terminated under the excess passive investment income test? If so, what is the effective date of the termination?

Answer: Yes, it is terminated. Because CCS has C corporation earnings and profits from 2021 and excess passive investment income for three consecutive years as an S corporation, its S election is terminated, effective January 1, 2026.

Short Tax Years

S corporation election terminations frequently create an S corporation *short tax year* (i.e., a reporting year less than 12 months) and a C corporation short tax year. The corporation must then allocate its income for the full year between the S and the C corporation years, using the number of days in each short year (the daily method). Or it may use the corporation's normal accounting rules to allocate income to the actual period in which it was earned (the specific identification method).[16] Both short tax year returns are due on the corporation's customary tax return due date (with normal extensions available).

Example 11-8

What if: Suppose CCS was formed as a calendar-year S corporation with Nicole Johnson, Sarah Walker, and Chance Armstrong as equal shareholders. On June 15, 2022, Chance sold his CCS shares (one-third of all shares) to his solely owned C corporation, Chanzz Inc., terminating CCS's S election on June 15, 2022. Assume CCS reported the following business income for 2022:

Period	Income
January 1 through June 14 (165 days)	$100,000
June 15 through December 31 (200 days)	265,000
January 1 through December 31, 2022 (365 days)	$365,000

If CCS uses the daily method of allocating income between the S corporation short tax year (January 1–June 14) and the C corporation short tax year (June 15–December 31), how much income will it report on its S corporation short tax year return and its C corporation short tax year return for 2022?

Answer: S corporation short tax year = $165,000 ($365,000/365 days × 165 days); C corporation short tax year = $200,000 ($365,000/365 days × 200 days).

(continued on page 11-8)

THE KEY FACTS

S Corporation Terminations and Reelections

- The S election may be revoked by shareholders holding more than 50 percent of the S corporation's stock (including nonvoting shares).

(continued)

[16]Use of the specific identification method requires that all shareholders at any time during the S corporation short year and the shareholders on the first day of the C corporation short year consent to the election using the specific identification method [§1362(e)(3)(A)]. However, an S corporation must use the specific identification method to allocate income between the short years (the per day allocation method is not allowed) if there is a sale or exchange of 50 percent or more of the corporation's stock during the year [§1362(e)(6)(D)].

- A corporation's S election is automatically terminated if (1) the S corporation fails to meet the S corporation requirements or (2) the S corporation has earnings and profits from a previous C corporation year and has passive investment income in excess of 25 percent of gross receipts for three consecutive years.
- A corporation losing its S corporation status must wait until the beginning of the fifth year after the election is terminated to elect S corporation status again.

What if: If CCS uses the specific identification method to allocate income, how much will it allocate to the S corporation short tax year and how much will it allocate to the C corporation short tax year?

Answer: S corporation short tax year, $100,000; C corporation short tax year, $265,000.

Note that if the entity wanted to minimize the income subject to taxation as a C corporation, it would use the daily method of allocating income.

S Corporation Reelections

After terminating or voluntarily revoking S corporation status, the corporation may elect it again, but it generally must wait until the beginning of the fifth tax year *after* the tax year in which it terminated the election.[17] Thus, if the election was terminated effective the first day of the tax year, the corporation must wait five full years to again become an S corporation.

Example 11-9

What if: Let's return to the facts of Example 11-8. CCS was formed as a calendar-year S corporation with Nicole Johnson, Sarah Walker, and Chance Armstrong as equal shareholders. On June 15, 2022, Chance sold his CCS shares (one-third of all shares) to his solely owned C corporation, Chanzz Inc., terminating CCS's S election on June 15, 2022. Absent permission from the IRS (see text below), what is the earliest date CCS may again elect to be taxed as an S corporation?

Answer: January 1, 2027. This is the fifth tax year after the year in which the termination became effective.

What if: Assume on February 1, 2022, CCS voluntarily elected to revoke its S corporation status effective January 1, 2023. Absent IRS permission, what is the earliest CCS may again elect to be taxed as an S corporation?

Answer: January 1, 2028. This is the fifth year after the year in which the termination became effective.

The IRS may consent to an earlier election under a couple of conditions: (1) if the corporation is now more than 50 percent owned by shareholders who were not owners at the time of termination or (2) if the termination was not reasonably within the control of the corporation or shareholders with a substantial interest in the corporation and was not part of a planned termination by the corporation or shareholders. Given the potential adverse consequences of an S election termination, the corporation should carefully monitor compliance with the S corporation requirements.

LO 11-3

OPERATING ISSUES

Accounting Methods and Periods

Like partnerships, S corporations determine their accounting periods and make accounting method elections at the entity level. An S corporation makes most of its elections (e.g., electing out of bonus depreciation) in conjunction with the filing of its annual tax return and some by filing a separate request with the IRS. (For example, an application to change accounting methods is filed on Form 3115, separate from the S corporation's tax return.) For an S corporation previously operating as a C corporation, all prior accounting methods carry over to the S corporation.

[17] §1362(g).

Recall that both C corporations and partnerships with C corporation partners face restrictions on using the cash method. S corporations do not. They may choose the cash, accrual, or a hybrid method unless selling inventory is a material income-producing factor for them. In that case, they generally must account for gross profit (sales minus cost of goods sold) using the accrual method, even if they are otherwise cash-method taxpayers.[18] Hence, they would use the hybrid method.

Tax laws also specify permissible tax years for S corporations, but they are a little less cumbersome than for partnerships. S corporations must use a calendar year-end unless they can establish a business purpose for an alternative year-end or a natural business year-end. For example, a business that receives 25 percent or more of gross receipts for the previous three years in the last two months of the year-end requested would qualify for a noncalendar year-end.[19]

THE KEY FACTS

Operating Issues

- S corporations are generally required to adopt a calendar tax year.
- S corporations allocate profits and losses to shareholders pro rata, based on the number of outstanding shares each shareholder owns on each day of the tax year.
- S corporations determine each shareholder's share of ordinary business income (loss) and separately stated items.
- Ordinary business income (loss) is all income (loss) exclusive of any separately stated items of income (loss). Separately stated items are tax items that are treated differently from a shareholder's share of ordinary business income (loss) for tax purposes.

Income and Loss Allocations

S corporations, like partnerships, are flow-through entities, and thus their profits and losses flow through to their shareholders annually for tax purposes. As we discussed in the Forming and Operating Partnerships chapter, partnerships have considerable flexibility in making special profit and loss allocations to their partners. In contrast, S corporations must allocate profits and losses pro rata, based on the number of outstanding shares each shareholder owns on each day of the tax year.[20]

An S corporation generally allocates income or loss items to shareholders on the last day of its tax year.[21] If a shareholder sells their shares during the year, they will report their share of S corporation income and loss allocated to the days they owned the stock (including the day of sale) using a pro rata allocation. If *all shareholders with changing ownership percentages* during the year agree, the S corporation can instead use its normal accounting rules to allocate income and loss (and other separately stated items, discussed below) to the specific periods in which it realized income and losses.

Example 11-10

What if: Assume CCS was formed as a calendar-year S corporation with Nicole Johnson, Sarah Walker, and Chance Armstrong as equal (one-third) shareholders. On June 14, 2022, Chance sold his CCS shares to Nicole. CCS reported the following business income for 2022:

Period	Income
January 1 through June 14 (165 days)	$100,000
June 15 through December 31 (200 days)	265,000
January 1 through December 31, 2022 (365 days)	$365,000

How much 2022 income is allocated to each shareholder if CCS uses the daily method of allocating income?

(continued on page 11-10)

[18]Section 471(c)(1) provides an exception to this general rule. Specifically, S corporations are not required to use the accrual method if (a) for 2022, they have average gross receipts of $27 million or less for the three prior tax years; (b) they choose not to keep an inventory; and (c) their method of accounting (i) treats inventory as nonincidental material or supplies deducted when first used or consumed or (ii) conforms to their financial accounting treatment for inventories. For these S corporations, the accrual method is not required for inventories.

[19]§1378(b). In addition, S corporations, like partnerships, have the option of electing an alternative taxable year under §444.

[20]§§1366(a), 1377(a).

[21]§1366(a).

Answer: Nicole's allocation is $188,333; Sarah's is $121,667; and Chance's is $55,000, calculated as follows.

Individual	(1) January 1–June 14	(2) June 15–December 31	(1) + (2) Total 2022 Allocation
Nicole	$55,000 ($365,000/365 × 165 × 1/3)	$133,333 ($365,000/365 × 200 × 2/3)	**$188,333**
Sarah	$55,000 ($365,000/365 × 165 × 1/3)	$66,667 ($365,000/365 × 200 × 1/3)	**121,667**
Chance	$55,000 ($365,000/365 × 165 × 1/3)	$0	**55,000**
Totals	$165,000	$200,000	$ 365,000

How much 2022 income is allocated to each shareholder if CCS uses its normal accounting rules to allocate income to the specific periods in which it was actually earned?

Answer: Nicole's allocation is $210,000 ($100,000 × 1/3 + $265,000 × 2/3); Sarah's is $121,667 ($365,000 × 1/3); and Chance's is $33,333 ($100,000 × 1/3).

Separately Stated Items

Like partnerships, S corporations are required to file tax returns (Form 1120-S, U.S. Income Tax Return for an S Corporation) annually. In addition, on Form 1120-S, Schedule K-1, they supply information to each shareholder detailing the amount *and* character of items of income and loss flowing through the S corporation.[22] Shareholders must report these income and loss items on their respective tax returns even if they do not receive cash distributions during the year.

S corporations determine each shareholder's share of ordinary business income (loss) and separately stated items. Like partnerships, **ordinary business income (loss)** (also referred to as *nonseparately stated income or loss*) is all income (loss) exclusive of any separately stated items of income (loss). **Separately stated items** are tax items that are treated differently from a shareholder's share of ordinary business income (loss) for tax purposes. The character of each separately stated item is determined at the S corporation level rather than at the shareholder level. The list of common separately stated items for S corporations is similar to that for partnerships, with a couple of exceptions. (For example, S corporations do not report self-employment income and do not have guaranteed payments.) Exhibit 11-1 lists several common separately stated items. See Form 1120-S,

EXHIBIT 11-1 Common Separately Stated Items

- Short-term capital gains and losses
- Long-term capital gains and losses
- §1231 gains and losses
- Dividends
- Interest income
- Charitable contributions
- Tax-exempt income
- Net rental real estate income
- Investment interest expense
- §179 deduction
- Foreign taxes
- §199A qualified business income, allocated wages, and unadjusted basis of qualified property (included in a statement attached to Schedule K-1)

[22]Other items, such as tax credits and informational items such as AMT adjustments, also flow through from the S corporation to its shareholders and are reported to shareholders on Form 1120-S, Schedule K-1.

Schedule K-1 (and related instructions) for a comprehensive list of separately stated items.[23] Similar to partners in a partnership, S corporation shareholders are allowed a 20 percent deduction for §199A qualified business income, calculated and subject to limitations at the shareholder level. See the Business Entities Overview chapter for a discussion of the deduction. Informational items related to the deduction calculation (e.g., §199A qualified business income; W-2 wages paid by the S corporation, including owner's compensation; and unadjusted basis of qualified property) are reported to shareholders in a statement included with Form 1120-S, Schedule K-1.

S corporations may hold stock in C corporations, and any dividends S corporations receive will flow through to their shareholders. However, S corporations are not entitled to claim the dividends-received deduction that is available to C corporations.

Assuming CCS operated as a C corporation in 2021 and an S corporation in 2022, Exhibit 11-2 presents the results of operations. CCS's S election was not effective until January 1, 2022, because the shareholders filed the S election after the required date for it to be effective in 2021.

EXHIBIT 11-2

Color Comfort Sheets
Income Statement
December 31, 2021 and 2022

	2021 C Corporation	2022 S Corporation
Sales revenue	$220,000	$ 520,000
Cost of goods sold	(50,000)	(115,000)
Salary to owners Nicole and Sarah	(70,000)	(90,000)
Employee wages	(45,000)	(50,000)
Depreciation expense	(15,000)	(20,000)
Miscellaneous expenses	(4,000)	(5,000)
Interest income (from investments)	3,000	6,000
Dividend income	1,000	3,000
Overall net income	$ 40,000	$ 249,000

Example 11-11

Given that CCS was a C corporation for tax purposes in 2021 and an S corporation in 2022, and its operating results in Exhibit 11-2, what amounts of ordinary business income and separately stated items are allocated to CCS's shareholders for 2021?

Answer: $0 ordinary business income and $0 separately stated items. Because CCS is a C corporation in 2021, its income does *not* flow through to its shareholders.

Based on the information in Exhibit 11-2, what amounts of ordinary business income and separately stated items are allocated to CCS's shareholders for 2022? Assume CCS has qualified property with an unadjusted basis of $300,000 for purposes of the deduction for qualified business income.

(continued on page 11-12)

[23]S corporations with average annual gross receipts for the prior three years that exceed $27 million in 2022 are subject to the 30 percent of taxable income limitation on the deduction for business interest expense. See the Business Income, Deductions, and Accounting Methods chapter. The limitation applies at the S corporation level, not at the shareholder level. In years where the adjusted taxable income limitation is binding, the disallowed business interest does not reduce S corporation income or reduce shareholder basis. Instead, the S corporation carries the disallowed business interest forward to the next year and applies the limitation calculation in that year. Any business interest deduction allowed reduces S corporation income (and shareholder basis). When the adjusted taxable income limitation applies but is not binding, the S corporation reports any excess taxable income to its shareholders as an information item so that shareholders can use the excess taxable income in calculating their deductible business interest expense from non–S corporation sources (e.g., from a sole proprietorship) if they are subject to the taxable income limitation.

Answer: See the following table for the allocations:

		Allocations		
Description	**CCS**	**Nicole 1/3**	**Sarah 1/3**	**Chance 1/3**
2022 overall net income less:	$249,000			
Dividends	3,000			
Interest income	6,000			
Ordinary Business Income	$240,000	**$80,000**	**$80,000**	**$80,000**
Separately Stated Items:				
Interest income	6,000	**2,000**	**2,000**	**2,000**
Dividends	3,000	**1,000**	**1,000**	**1,000**
Qualified Business Income				
Informational Items:				
§199A qualified business income	240,000	80,000	80,000	80,000
§199A allocated wages	140,000	46,667	46,667	46,666
§199A unadjusted basis of qualified property	300,000	100,000	100,000	100,000

Nicole, Sarah, and Chance will treat their shares of CCS's ordinary business income as *ordinary* income and include it, along with their shares of interest and dividend income, in their individual tax returns for the year.[24] Qualified business income does not include interest income because it was not allocable to the trade or business. Allocated wages include the $50,000 wages paid to employees and $90,000 wages paid to owners.

LO 11-4

SHAREHOLDER'S BASIS

Just as partners must determine their bases in their partnership interests, S corporation shareholders must determine their bases in S corporation stock to determine the gain or loss they recognize when they sell the stock, the taxability of distributions, and the deductibility of losses.

Initial Basis An S corporation shareholder calculates their *initial basis* upon formation of the corporation, like a C corporation shareholder. (See earlier discussion in text on corporate formation.) Specifically, the shareholder's basis in stock received in the exchange equals the tax basis of the property transferred, less any liabilities assumed by the corporation on the property contributed (*substituted basis*). The shareholder's stock basis is increased by any gain recognized; it is reduced by the fair market value of any property received other than stock.[25] If, on the other hand, the shareholder purchased the S corporation stock from another shareholder or the corporation, the new shareholder's basis is simply the purchase price of the stock.[26]

[24]Nicole, Sarah, and Chance would report their share of ordinary business income on Schedule E and their share of interest and dividend income on Schedule B of Form 1040.

[25]§358. This assumes the shareholder meets the §351 requirements. If the shareholder's exchange with the corporation does not meet these requirements, the shareholder's basis in the stock is its fair market value.

[26]If the shareholder acquires the stock by gift, their basis in the stock is the lesser of the donor's basis (increased for any gift taxes paid on the stock's appreciation) or the fair market value of the stock. In contrast, if the shareholder acquires the stock by bequest, their basis in the stock is the stock's fair market value on the date of the decedent's death adjusted to reflect any income in respect of the decedent.

Example 11-12

At the beginning of 2021, Nicole contributed $30,000 of cash and land with a fair market value of $130,000 and an adjusted basis of $125,000 to CCS. The land was encumbered by a $40,000 mortgage executed three years before. Sarah and Chance each contributed $120,000 of cash to CCS. What tax bases do Nicole, Sarah, and Chance have in their CCS stock at the beginning of 2021?

Answer: Nicole's basis is $115,000 ($30,000 cash + $125,000 adjusted basis of land – $40,000 mortgage assumed), Sarah's basis is $120,000, and Chance's basis is $120,000.

Annual Basis Adjustments While C corporation rules govern the initial stock basis of an S corporation shareholder, subsequent calculations more closely resemble the partnership rules. Specifically, an S corporation shareholder's stock basis is dynamic and must be *adjusted annually* to ensure that (1) taxable income/gains and deductible expenses/losses are *not* double-counted by shareholders either when they sell their shares or when they receive S corporation distributions (for example, because shareholders are taxed on the S corporation's income annually, they should not be taxed again when they receive distributions of the income) and (2) tax-exempt income and nondeductible expenses are not ultimately taxed or deducted.

S corporation shareholders make the following adjustments to their stock basis annually, in the order listed:

- Increase for any capital contributions to the S corporation during the year.
- Increase for shareholder's share of ordinary business income and separately stated income/gain items (including tax-exempt income).
- Decrease for distributions during the year.
- Decrease for shareholder's share of nondeductible expenses (e.g., fines and penalties).
- Decrease for shareholder's share of ordinary business loss and separately stated expense/loss items.[27]

As with a partnership, adjustments that decrease basis may never reduce an S corporation shareholder's tax basis below zero.[28]

S corporation shareholders are not allowed to include any S corporation debt in their stock basis. Recall that partners *are* allowed to include their share of partnership debt in the basis of their partnership interests. One implication of this difference is that, everything else equal, an S corporation shareholder's basis will be lower than a partner's basis, due to the exclusion of debt (however, see the discussion of *debt basis* for S corporation shareholders below).

THE KEY FACTS

S Corporation Shareholder's Basis Adjustments

- A shareholder will *increase* the tax basis in their stock for:
  - Capital contributions.
  - Share of ordinary business income.
  - Separately stated income/gain items.
  - Tax-exempt income.
- A shareholder will *decrease* the tax basis in their stock for:
  - Cash distributions.
  - Share of nondeductible expenses.
  - Share of ordinary business loss.
  - Separately stated expense/loss items.
- A shareholder's tax basis may not be negative.

Example 11-13

Given the shareholders' 2021 bases in their CCS stock in Example 11-12 (Nicole, $115,000; Sarah, $120,000; and Chance, $120,000), what basis does each have at the end of 2022, after taking into account the information in Exhibit 11-2 (but before taking into account any distributions, which are discussed below)?

(continued on page 11-14)

[27]Reg. §1.1367-1(g).

[28]§1367(a)(2).

Answer: Nicole, $198,000; Sarah, $203,000; and Chance, $203,000, computed as follows:

Description	Nicole	Sarah	Chance	Explanation
(1) Initial tax basis	$ 115,000	$ 120,000	$ 120,000	Example 11-12
(2) Ordinary business income	80,000	80,000	80,000	Example 11-11
(3) Interest income	2,000	2,000	2,000	Example 11-11
(4) Dividends	1,000	1,000	1,000	Example 11-11
Tax basis in stock at end of 2022	**$198,000**	**$203,000**	**$203,000**	(1) + (2) + (3) + (4)

Note that the shareholders do not include any portion of CCS's debt in their stock basis.

What if: Suppose that, in addition to the amounts in Exhibit 11-2, CCS also recognized $1,200 of tax-exempt interest income in 2022. Nicole's share of this separately stated item is $400. Taking this allocation into account, what is Nicole's stock basis at the end of 2022?

Answer: It is $198,400 ($198,000 + $400). The tax-exempt income allocated to Nicole as a separately stated item increases her tax basis to ensure that she is never taxed on her share of the tax-exempt income.

Loss Limitations

S corporations have loss-limitation rules similar to those for partnerships. For an S corporation shareholder to deduct a loss, the loss must clear three separate hurdles: (1) tax-basis, (2) at-risk amount, and (3) passive activity.[29] In addition, for losses that clear each of the three hurdles, S corporation shareholders are not allowed to deduct excess business losses as described below.

Tax-Basis Limitation S corporation shareholders may not deduct losses in excess of their stock basis. Recall they are not allowed to include debt in their basis; partners are. This restriction makes it more likely that the tax-basis limitation will apply to S corporation shareholders than to similarly situated partners. Losses not deductible due to the tax-basis limitation are not necessarily lost. Rather, they are suspended until the shareholder generates additional basis. The carryover period for the suspended loss is indefinite. However, if the shareholder sells the stock before creating additional basis, the suspended loss disappears unused.

Example 11-14

What if: Suppose at the beginning of 2023, Nicole's basis in her CCS stock was $14,000. During 2023, CCS reported a $60,000 ordinary business loss and no separately stated items. How much of the ordinary loss is allocated to Nicole?

Answer: The loss allocation is $20,000 ($60,000 × 1/3).

How much of the $20,000 loss clears the tax-basis hurdle for deductibility in 2023?

Answer: The amount of Nicole's basis in her CCS stock, or $14,000. The remaining $6,000 of loss does not clear the tax-basis hurdle; it is suspended until Nicole generates additional basis.

A shareholder can mitigate the disadvantage of not including S corporation debt in stock basis by loaning money directly to the S corporation. These loans create **debt basis,** separate from stock basis. Losses are limited first to the shareholder's tax basis in S corporation stock and *then* to the shareholder's basis in any direct loans made to the S corporation.[30]

[29] S corporations are also subject to the hobby loss rules in §183 that limit loss deductions for activities not engaged in for profit.

[30] §1366(d)(1)(B). These must be direct loans to the corporation. Thus, shareholders do not get debt basis when they guarantee a loan of the S corporation, although they would to the extent they had to "make good" on their guarantee obligation.

Specifically, if the total amount of items (besides distributions) that decrease the shareholder's basis for the year exceeds the shareholder's stock basis, the excess amount decreases the shareholder's debt basis. Like stock basis, debt basis cannot be decreased below zero. In subsequent years, any net increase in basis for the year restores first the shareholder's debt basis (up to the outstanding debt amount) and then the shareholder's stock basis. If the S corporation repays the debt owed to the shareholder before the shareholder's debt basis is restored, any loan repayment in excess of the shareholder's debt basis will trigger a taxable gain to the shareholder.

Example 11-15

What if: Suppose at the beginning of 2023, Nicole's basis in her CCS stock was $14,000. During 2023, Nicole loaned $8,000 to CCS, and CCS reported a $60,000 ordinary business loss and no separately stated items. How much of the $20,000 ordinary loss allocated to Nicole clears the tax-basis hurdle for deductibility in 2023?

Answer: All $20,000. The first $14,000 of the loss reduces her stock basis to $0, and the remaining $6,000 reduces her debt basis to $2,000 ($8,000 – $6,000).

What if: Suppose in 2024, CCS allocated $9,000 of ordinary business income to Nicole and no separately stated items. What are Nicole's CCS stock basis and debt basis at the end of 2024, assuming CCS did not pay back any debt?

Answer: Her stock basis is $3,000; her debt basis is $8,000. The income first restores debt basis to the outstanding debt amount and then increases her stock basis.

At-Risk Amount Limitation Like partners in partnerships, S corporation shareholders are subject to the *at-risk* rules. They may deduct S corporation losses only to the extent of their **at-risk amount** in the S corporation, as defined in §465. With one notable exception, an S corporation shareholder's at-risk amount is the sum of the shareholder's stock and debt bases. The primary exception relates to nonrecourse loans (i.e., loans that do not allow lenders to pursue anything other than the collateral securing the loans) and is designed to ensure that shareholders are deemed at risk only when they have an actual risk of loss. Specifically, an S corporation shareholder taking out a nonrecourse loan to make a capital contribution (either cash or other property) to the S corporation generally creates stock basis (equal to the basis of property contributed) in the S corporation but increases the amount at risk by only the net fair market value of the shareholder's property, if any, used as collateral to secure the nonrecourse loan.[31] The collateral's net fair market value is determined at the loan date.

Likewise, if the shareholder takes out a nonrecourse loan to make a direct loan to the S corporation, the loan creates debt basis but increases the amount at risk only by the net fair market value of the shareholder's property, if any, used as collateral to secure the nonrecourse loan. When the stock basis plus debt basis is different from the at-risk amount, S corporation shareholders apply the tax-basis loss limitation first, and then the at-risk limitation. Losses limited under the at-risk rules are carried forward indefinitely until the shareholder generates additional at-risk amounts to utilize them or sells the S corporation stock.

THE KEY FACTS

Loss Limitations

- S corporation losses in excess of a shareholder's tax basis and at-risk amount are suspended and carried forward until additional basis and amounts at risk are created.
- Upon S election termination, shareholders may create additional stock basis during the post-termination transition period to utilize losses limited by the basis or at-risk rules.
- The passive activity loss rules limit the ability of S corporation shareholders to deduct losses of the S corporation unless the shareholders are actively managing the business.

Post-Termination Transition Period Loss Limitation The voluntary or involuntary termination of a corporation's S election creates a problem for shareholders with suspended losses due to the basis and at-risk rules. The reason: These losses are generally not deductible after the S termination date. Shareholders can obtain some relief provided by §1366(d)(3), which allows them to treat any suspended losses existing at the S termination date as occurring on the last day of the **post-termination transition period (PTTP).** In general, the PTTP begins on the day after the last day of the corporation's last

[31]§465(b)(2)(B). In some circumstances (beyond the scope of this text), shareholders do not create stock basis (or debt basis) for capital contributions (or shareholder loans to the S corporation) that are funded by nonrecourse loans.

taxable year as an S corporation and ends on the later of (a) one year after the last S corporation day or (b) the due date for filing the return for the last year as an S corporation (including extensions).[32]

This rule allows the shareholder to create additional stock basis by making additional capital contributions during the PTTP and to utilize suspended losses based on their *stock* basis (but not debt basis) at the end of the period. Any suspended losses utilized at the end of the PTTP reduce the shareholder's basis in the stock. Any losses not utilized at the end of the period are lost forever.

Example 11-16

What if: Suppose CCS terminated its S election on July 17, 2023. At the end of the S corporation's short tax year ending on July 17, Nicole's stock basis and at-risk amounts were both zero (she has never had debt basis), and she had a suspended loss of $15,000. Nicole made additional capital contributions of $10,000 on February 20, 2024, and $7,000 on September 6, 2024. When does the PTTP end for CCS? How much loss may Nicole deduct, and what is her basis in the CCS stock at the end of the PTTP?

Answer: For loss deduction purposes, CCS's PTTP ends on September 15, 2024. That date represents (b) in the "later of (a) or (b)" alternative—(a) one year after the last S corporation day, which would be July 17, 2024, or (b) the due date for filing the return for the last year as an S corporation, including extensions, which would be September 15, 2024, assuming CCS extends its tax return. (Note that the short tax year S corporation return is due the same time as the short tax year C corporation return.) Nicole may deduct the entire $15,000 suspended loss because her basis at the end of the PTTP and before the loss deduction is $17,000. (That amount is calculated as a carryover basis of $0 on the last S corporation day plus $17,000 capital contributions during the PTTP.) Nicole's basis in CCS stock after the loss deduction is $2,000 ($17,000 basis at the end of the PTTP less the $15,000 loss deduction).

What if: Suppose Nicole made her second capital contribution on October 22, 2024, instead of September 6, 2024. How much loss can Nicole deduct, and what is her basis in CCS stock at the end of the PTTP?

Answer: The loss deduction is $10,000: Nicole's stock basis at the end of the PTTP and before her loss deduction is only $10,000 because the $7,000 capital contribution occurred after the end of the PTTP. Nicole's basis in the CCS stock at the end of the PTTP and after the loss deduction is zero ($10,000 basis less $10,000 loss deduction). Her basis then increases to $7,000 on October 22, 2024, but the $5,000 suspended loss is lost forever.

Passive Activity Loss Limitation S corporation shareholders, just like partners, are subject to the **passive activity loss (PAL) rules.** There are no differences in the application of these rules for S corporations; the definition of a passive activity, the tests for material participation, the income and loss baskets, and the passive activity loss carryover rules described in the Forming and Operating Partnerships chapter are exactly the same. Thus, as in partnerships, the passive activity loss rules limit the ability of S corporation shareholders to deduct losses unless they are involved in actively managing the business.[33]

Example 11-17

What if: Suppose in 2024, CCS incurred an ordinary business loss and allocated the loss equally to its shareholders. Assuming Nicole, Sarah, and Chance all had adequate stock basis and at-risk amounts to absorb the losses, which of the three shareholders would be least likely to deduct the loss due to the passive activity limitation rules?

Answer: Chance. Because he is not actively involved in managing CCS's business activities, any loss allocated to him is a passive activity loss.

[32]§1377(b)(1)(A). Section 1377(b) indicates that the PTTP also includes the 120-day period beginning on the date of a determination (not the date of the actual termination) that the corporation's S election had terminated for a previous taxable year.

[33]§469.

Excess Business Loss Limitation Taxpayers are not allowed to deduct an **excess business loss** for the year. Rather, an excess business loss is carried forward to subsequent years. The excess business loss limitation applies to losses that are otherwise deductible under the tax-basis, at-risk, and passive loss rules. An excess business loss for the year is the excess of aggregate business deductions for the year over the sum of aggregate business gross income or gain of the taxpayer plus a threshold amount indexed for inflation. The threshold amount for 2022 is $540,000 for married taxpayers filing jointly and $270,000 for other taxpayers.[34] In the case of partnership or S corporation business losses, the provision applies at the partner/shareholder level.

Self-Employment Income

You might wonder whether an S corporation shareholder's allocable share of ordinary business income (loss) is classified as self-employment income for tax purposes. The answer is no, even when the shareholder actively works for the S corporation.[35]

When a shareholder does work as an employee of and receives a salary from an S corporation, the S corporation treats this salary payment like that made to any other employee: For Social Security taxes, it withholds 6.2 percent of the shareholder's salary or wages subject to the wage limitation ($147,000 in 2022); for Medicare taxes, it withholds 1.45 percent of the shareholder's salary or wages (no limit); and for the additional Medicare tax, it withholds .9 percent of the shareholder's salary or wages above $200,000 (no limit).[36] In addition, the S corporation must pay its portion of the Social Security tax (6.2 percent of the shareholder's salary or wages subject to the $147,000 wage limitation in 2022) and Medicare tax (1.45 percent of the shareholder's salary or wages, regardless of the amount of salary or wages). In contrast to shareholder-employees, S corporations are not subject to the additional Medicare tax on employee salary or wages.

Because of this stark contrast between the treatment of ordinary business income and that of shareholder salaries, S corporation shareholders may desire to avoid payroll taxes by limiting or even eliminating their salary payments. However, if they work as employees, they are required to pay themselves a reasonable salary for the services they perform. If they pay themselves an unreasonably low salary, the IRS may attempt to reclassify some or all of the S corporation's ordinary business income as shareholder salary!

TAXES IN THE REAL WORLD The Benefits of an S Corporation

U.S. President Joe Biden appears to be a fan of S corporations. His 2017 and 2018 tax returns reveal that a large portion of his income came from an S corporation, CelticCapri Corp., that was established for his speaking and writing engagements after his book release of *Promise Me, Dad*. President Biden earned almost $3 million from CelticCapri but only reported $300,000 of compensation as CelticCapri's employee. By doing so, Biden avoided employment or self-employment taxes on the bulk of CelticCapri's earnings.

Source: Eric Yauch, "Biden Took 'Astounding' Tax Positions in Business Planning," *Taxnotes.com*, July 11, 2019.

[34]In 2020, the CARES Act suspended the excess business loss limitation for 2018, 2019, and 2020. Thus, taxpayers were able to deduct excess business losses arising from these years.

[35]Rev. Rul. 59-221.

[36]Although employee liability for the additional Medicare tax varies based on filing status ($250,000 combined salary or wages for married filing jointly; $125,000 salary or wages for married filing separate; $200,000 salary or wages for all other taxpayers), employers are required to withhold the additional Medicare tax on salary or wages above $200,000 irrespective of the taxpayer's filing status.

Net Investment Income Tax

Just like partners in a partnership, S corporation shareholders are subject to a 3.8 percent net investment income tax on their share of an S corporation's gross income from interest, dividends, annuities, royalties, rents, a trade or business that is a passive activity or a trade or business of trading financial instruments or commodities, and any net gain from disposing of property (other than property held in a trade or business in which the net investment income tax does not apply), less any allowable deductions from these items.[37,38] Likewise, any gain from the sale of S corporation stock (or distribution in excess of basis) is subject to the net investment income tax to the extent it is allocable to assets held by the S corporation that would have generated a net gain subject to the net investment income tax if all S corporation assets were sold at fair market value.[39]

Fringe Benefits

True to their hybrid status, S corporations are treated in part like C corporations and in part like partnerships with respect to tax deductions for qualifying employee fringe benefits.[40] For shareholder-employees who own 2 percent or less of the entity, the S corporation receives C corporation tax treatment. That is, it gets a tax deduction for qualifying fringe benefits, and the benefits are nontaxable to *all* employees. For shareholder-employees who own more than 2 percent of the S corporation, it receives partnership treatment.[41] That is, it gets a tax deduction, but the otherwise-qualifying fringe benefits are taxable to the shareholder-employees who own more than 2 percent.[42]

Fringe benefits taxable to this group include employer-provided health insurance[43] (§106), group-term life insurance (§79), meals and lodging provided for the convenience of the employer (§119), and benefits provided under a cafeteria plan (§125). Examples of benefits that are nontaxable to more-than-2-percent shareholder-employees (and partners in a partnership) include employee achievement awards (§74), qualified group legal services plans (§120), educational assistance programs (§127), dependent care assistance programs (§129), no-additional-cost services (§132), qualified employee discounts (§132), working-condition fringe benefits (§132), *de minimis* fringe benefits (§132), on-premises athletic facilities (§132), and medical savings accounts (§220).

[37]Interest, dividend, annuity, royalty, and rent income derived in the *ordinary* course of a trade or business that is not passive and does not involve financial instrument or commodity trading is exempt from the net investment income tax.

[38]The tax imposed is 3.8 percent of the lesser of (a) net investment income or (b) the excess of modified adjusted gross income over $250,000 for married-joint filers and surviving spouses, $125,000 for married-separate filers, and $200,000 for other taxpayers. Modified adjusted gross income equals adjusted gross income increased by income excluded under the foreign earned income exclusion less any disallowed deductions associated with the foreign earned income exclusion.

[39]See Prop. Reg. §1.1411-7.

[40]Qualifying fringe benefits are nontaxable to the employee. Other fringe benefits (nonqualifying) are taxed as compensation to employees.

[41]§1372(a).

[42]The §318 indirect stock ownership rules apply for purposes of determining which shareholders own more than 2 percent.

[43]Note, however, that shareholders who own more than 2 percent are allowed to deduct their insurance costs as for AGI deductions [§162(l)].

DISTRIBUTIONS

LO 11-5

S corporations face special rules when accounting for operating distributions of cash or other property and liquidating distributions.[44]

Operating Distributions

The rules for determining the shareholder-level tax consequences of operating distributions depend on the S corporation's history; specifically whether, at the time of the distribution, it has accumulated *earnings and profits* from a previous year as a C corporation. (See the discussion earlier in text of C corporation earnings and profits.) We consider both situations—with and without accumulated earnings and profits.

S Corporation with No C Corporation Accumulated Earnings and Profits

Two sets of historical circumstances could apply here: (1) An entity may have been an S corporation since inception or (2) it may have been converted from a C corporation but not have C corporation accumulated earnings and profits at the time of the distribution. In both cases, as long as there are no C corporation accumulated earnings and profits, the rules for accounting for the distribution are very similar to those applicable to distributions to partners. That is, shareholder distributions are nontaxable to the extent of the shareholder's stock basis determined after increasing the stock basis for income allocations for the year.[45] If a distribution exceeds the shareholder's stock basis, the shareholder has a capital gain equal to the excess distribution amount.

Example 11-18

What if: Suppose CCS has been an S corporation since its inception. On June 1, 2024, CCS distributed $30,000 to Nicole. Her basis in her CCS stock on January 1, 2024, was $20,000. For 2024, Nicole was allocated $15,000 of ordinary income from CCS and no separately stated items. What are the amount and character of income Nicole recognizes on the distribution, and what is her basis in her CCS stock after the distribution?

Answer: Nicole has $0 income from the distribution and $5,000 basis in stock after the distribution ($35,000 – $30,000). Her stock basis for determining the taxability of the distribution is $35,000, or her beginning basis of $20,000 plus the $15,000 income allocation for the year (which is taxable to Nicole).

What if: Assume the same facts except that CCS distributed $40,000 to Nicole rather than $30,000. What are the amount and character of income Nicole recognizes on the distribution, and what is her basis in her CCS stock after the distribution?

Answer: Nicole has a $5,000 long-term capital gain (she has held her CCS stock more than one year) and $0 basis in her stock (the distribution reduced her stock basis to $0).

What if: Suppose CCS began in 2021 as a C corporation and elected to be taxed as an S corporation in its second year of operations. In 2021, it distributed all its earnings and profits as a dividend, so it did not have any earnings and profits at the end of 2021. In 2022, it distributed $30,000 to Nicole when her basis in her stock was $35,000. What are the amount and character of income she recognizes on the distribution, and what is her basis in her CCS stock after the distribution?

Answer: Nicole has $0 income on the distribution and $5,000 basis in stock after the distribution ($35,000 – $30,000). Because CCS did not have C corporation earnings and profits at the time of the distribution, her outcome is the same as if CCS had been taxed as an S corporation since inception.

[44] The §302 stock redemption rules that determine whether a distribution in redemption of a shareholder's stock should be treated as a distribution or a sale or exchange apply to both C corporations and S corporations.

[45] §1368(d).

THE KEY FACTS

Cash Operating Distributions for S Corporations

- For S corporations without E&P: Distributions are nontaxable to the extent of the shareholder's stock basis. If a distribution exceeds the shareholder's stock basis, the shareholder has a capital gain equal to the excess distribution amount.
- For S corporations with E&P: Distributions are deemed to be paid from (1) the AAA (nontaxable to the extent of basis and taxed as capital gain thereafter), (2) existing accumulated E&P (taxable as dividends), and (3) the shareholder's remaining basis in the S corporation stock, if any (nontaxable to the extent of basis and taxed as capital gain thereafter).

S Corporation with C Corporation Accumulated Earnings and Profits When an S corporation has accumulated earnings and profits (E&P) from prior C corporation years, the distribution rules are a bit more complex. These rules are designed to ensure that shareholders cannot avoid tax on dividend distributions out of C corporation accumulated E&P by simply electing S corporation status and then distributing the accumulated E&P. For S corporations in this situation, the tax laws require the corporation to maintain an **accumulated adjustments account (AAA)** to determine the taxability of S corporate distributions. The AAA represents the cumulative income or losses for the period the corporation has been an S corporation. It is calculated as:

The beginning-of-year AAA balance
+ Separately stated income/gain items (excluding tax-exempt income)
+ Ordinary income
– Separately stated losses and deductions
– Ordinary losses
– Nondeductible expenses that are not capital expenditures (except deductions related to generating tax-exempt income)
– Distributions out of AAA[46]
= End-of-year AAA balance

Unlike a shareholder's stock basis, the AAA may have a negative balance. However, the reduction for distributions may not cause the AAA to go negative or to become more negative. Also, unlike stock basis, the AAA is a corporate-level account rather than a shareholder-specific account.

Example 11-19

CCS was originally formed as a C corporation and reported 2021 taxable income (and earnings and profits) of $40,000 (see Exhibit 11-2). Effective the beginning of 2022, it elected to be taxed as an S corporation. In 2022, CCS reported $249,000 of overall income (including separately stated items—see Exhibit 11-2). What is the amount of CCS's AAA for 2022 before considering the effects of distributions?

Answer: $249,000, computed as follows:

Description	Amount	Explanation
(1) Separately stated income	$ 9,000	$6,000 interest income + $3,000 dividend income (see Exhibit 11-2)
(2) Ordinary business income	240,000	Example 11-11
AAA before distributions	**$249,000**	(1) + (2)

What if: Assume that during 2022, CCS distributed $300,000 to its shareholders. What is CCS's AAA at the end of 2022?

Answer: AAA is $0 because the distribution cannot cause AAA to be negative.

What if: Instead of reporting $249,000 of income during 2022, assume that during 2022 CCS reported an ordinary business loss of $45,000, a separately stated charitable contribution of $5,000, and a $6,000 distribution to its shareholders. What is CCS's AAA at the end of 2022?

Answer: AAA is ($50,000). CCS decreases its AAA by the $45,000 business loss and the $5,000 charitable contribution. AAA before distributions is ($50,000). CCS does not decrease AAA by the $6,000 distribution to its shareholders because the distribution cannot cause AAA to be negative or make it more negative.

[46]§1368(e)(1)(C). If the current-year income and loss items net to make a negative adjustment to the AAA, the net negative adjustment from these items is made to the AAA *after* any AAA reductions for distributions (i.e., the reduction in AAA for distributions is made before the net negative adjustment for current-year income and loss items).

S corporation distributions are deemed to be paid from the following sources in the order listed:[47]

1. The AAA (to the extent it has a positive balance).[48]
2. Existing accumulated earnings and profits from years when the corporation operated as a C corporation.
3. The shareholder's stock basis.[49]

S corporation distributions from the AAA (the most common distributions) are treated the same as distributions when the S corporation does not have E&P. They are nontaxable to the extent of the shareholder's basis, and they create capital gains if they exceed the shareholder's stock basis. If an S corporation makes a distribution from accumulated E&P, the distribution is taxable to shareholders as a dividend. (See the discussion earlier in the text for the calculation of corporate E&P.) Once an S corporation's accumulated E&P is fully distributed, the remaining distributions reduce the shareholder's remaining basis in the S corporation stock (if any) and are nontaxable. Any excess distributions are treated as capital gain.

Example 11-20

What if: Assume at the end of 2022, before considering distributions, CCS's AAA was $24,000 and its accumulated E&P from 2021 was $40,000. Also assume Nicole's basis in her CCS stock is $80,000. If CCS distributes $60,000 on July 1 ($20,000 to each shareholder), what are the amount and character of income Nicole must recognize on her $20,000 distribution, and what is her stock basis in CCS after the distribution?

Answer: $12,000 dividend income and $72,000 stock basis after the distribution, computed as follows:

Description	Amount	Explanation
(1) Total distribution	$ 60,000	
(2) CCS's AAA beginning balance	24,000	
(3) Distribution from AAA	24,000	Lesser of (1) or (2)
(4) Distribution in excess of AAA	36,000	(1) – (3)
(5) Nicole's share of AAA distribution	8,000	(3) × 1/3 (nontaxable reduction of stock basis)
(6) Nicole's beginning stock basis	80,000	
(7) Nicole's ending stock basis	**72,000**	(6) – (5)
(8) CCS's E&P balance	40,000	
(9) Dividend distribution (from E&P)	36,000	Lesser of (4) or (8)
Nicole's share of dividend	**$12,000**	(9) × 1/3

[47]S corporations may elect to have distributions treated as being first paid out of existing accumulated earnings and profits from C corporation years to avoid the excess net passive income tax. We discuss the excess net passive income tax later in the chapter.

[48]Prior to 1983, S corporations' shareholders were taxed on undistributed taxable income as a deemed distribution. This undistributed income is referred to as *previously taxable income (PTI)*. For S corporations with PTI, distributions are considered to be paid out of PTI (if there is any remaining that has not been distributed) after any distributions out of their AAA. These distributions are also nontaxable to the extent of basis and reduce both the shareholder's basis and PTI.

[49]Technically, the distributions come from the Other Adjustments Account (OAA) and then any remaining shareholder equity accounts (e.g., common stock, paid-in capital). The OAA starts at zero at the S corporation's inception; is increased for tax-exempt income; and is decreased by expenses related to tax-exempt income, any federal taxes paid that are attributable to a C corporation tax year, and any S corporation distributions after the AAA and accumulated E&P have been reduced to zero. As with the AAA, the reduction for distributions may not cause the OAA to go negative or to increase a negative balance. Because from the shareholder's perspective distributions out of the OAA and equity accounts both reduce the shareholder's stock basis, we do not discuss the OAA or other equity accounts in detail.

Property Distributions At times, S corporations distribute appreciated property to their shareholders. When they do so, S corporations recognize gain as though they had sold the appreciated property for its fair market value just prior to the distribution.[50] (This rule contrasts with the partnership provisions for property distributions but is consistent with the C corporation rules.) Shareholders who receive the distributed property recognize their distributive share of the deemed gain and increase their stock basis accordingly. On the other hand, S corporations do not recognize losses on distributions of property whose value has declined.

For the shareholder, the amount of a property distribution is the fair market value of the property received (minus any liabilities the shareholder assumes on the distribution). The rules we described above apply in determining the extent to which the amount of the distribution is a nontaxable reduction of basis, a capital gain for a distribution in excess of basis, or a taxable dividend to the shareholder.[51] (See the rules for the taxability of distributions for S corporations with and without C corporation accumulated earnings and profits.) Shareholders take a fair market value basis in the property received in the distribution.

Example 11-21

What if: Assume that at the end of 2023, CCS distributes long-term capital gain property (fair market value of $24,000, basis of $15,000) to each shareholder (aggregate property distribution of $72,000 with an aggregate basis of $45,000). At the time of the distribution, CCS has no corporate E&P and Nicole has a basis of $10,000 in her CCS stock. How much gain, if any, does CCS recognize on the distribution? How much income does Nicole recognize as a result of the distribution?

Answer: CCS recognizes $27,000 of long-term capital gain, and Nicole recognizes $14,000 of long-term capital gain, computed as follows:

Description	Amount	Explanation
(1) FMV of distributed property	$ 72,000	
(2) CCS's basis in distributed property	45,000	
(3) CCS's LTCG on distribution	**$27,000**	(1) – (2)
(4) Nicole's share of LTCG from CCS	9,000	(3) × 1/3
(5) Nicole's stock basis after gain allocation	19,000	$10,000 beginning basis + (4)
(6) Distribution to Nicole	24,000	(1) × 1/3
(7) Nicole's stock basis after distribution	$ 0	(5) – (6), limited to $0
(8) LTCG to Nicole on distribution in excess of stock basis	5,000	(6) in excess of (5)
Nicole's total LTCG on distribution	**$14,000**	(4) + (8)

THE KEY FACTS
Property Distributions

- S corporations recognize gains but not losses when they distribute property to their shareholders.
- For shareholders, the amount of the distribution is the fair market value of the property received (minus any liabilities the shareholder assumes on the distribution).
- The rules for determining the taxability of property distributions at the shareholder level are the same as those for cash distributions.
- Shareholders take a fair market value basis in the property received in the distribution.

Post-Termination Transition Period Distributions Recall the special tax rules relating to suspended losses at the S corporation termination date. Similarly, §1371(e) provides for special treatment of any S corporation distribution *in cash* after an S election termination and during the post-termination transition period (PTTP). Such cash distributions are nontaxable to the extent they do not exceed the corporation's AAA balance and the individual shareholder's basis in the stock.

[50]§311(b). In addition, the S corporation may incur entity-level tax if the distributed property had built-in gains related to when the corporation converted to an S corporation. We discuss the built-in gains tax later in the chapter.

[51]Note that while S corporation shareholders reduce their stock basis by the fair market value of the property received, partners receiving property distributions from partnerships generally reduce the basis in their partnership interests by the adjusted basis of the distributed property.

The PTTP for post-termination distributions is generally the same as the PTTP for deducting suspended losses, discussed above. For determining the taxability of distributions, the PTTP generally begins on the day after the last day of the corporation's last taxable year as an S corporation; it ends on the later of (a) one year after the last S corporation day or (b) the due date for filing the return for the last year as an S corporation (including extensions).[52,53]

Liquidating Distributions

Liquidating distributions of a shareholder interest in an S corporation follow corporate tax rules rather than partnership rules. For a complete liquidation of the S corporation, the rules under §§331 and 336 (see discussion of C corporation liquidating distributions earlier in the text) govern the tax consequences. S corporations generally recognize gain *or* loss on each asset they distribute in liquidation (recall that S corporations recognize gain but not loss on operating distributions of noncash property). These gains and losses are allocated to the S corporation shareholders, increasing or decreasing their stock basis. In general, shareholders recognize gain on the distribution if the value of the property exceeds their stock basis; they recognize loss if their stock basis exceeds the value of the property.

Example 11-22

What if: Assume that at the end of 2024, CCS liquidates by distributing long-term capital gain property (fair market value of $20,000, basis of $12,000) to each shareholder (aggregate property distribution of $60,000 with an aggregate basis of $36,000). At the time of the distribution, CCS has no corporate E&P and Nicole has a basis of $25,000 in her CCS stock. How much gain or loss, if any, does CCS recognize on the distribution? How much gain or loss does Nicole recognize as a result of the distribution?

Answer: CCS recognizes $24,000 of long-term capital gain and Nicole recognizes $5,000 of net long-term capital loss, computed as follows:

Description	Amount	Explanation
(1) FMV of distributed property	$ 60,000	
(2) CCS's basis in distributed property	36,000	
(3) **CCS's LTCG on distribution**	**$24,000**	(1) – (2)
(4) Nicole's share of LTCG from CCS	8,000	(3) × 1/3
(5) Nicole's stock basis after gain allocation	33,000	$25,000 beginning basis + (4)
(6) Distribution to Nicole	20,000	(1) × 1/3
(7) Nicole's LTCL on liquidating distribution	(13,000)	(6) – (5)
Nicole's net LTCL on distribution	**(5,000)**	(4) + (7)

[52]§1377(b)(1)(A). For purposes of the taxability of distributions, the PTTP also includes (1) the 120-day period that begins on the date of any determination (court decision, closing agreement, and so on) from an IRS audit that occurs after the S election has been terminated and adjusts the corporation's income, loss, or deduction during the S period and (2) the 120-day period beginning on the date of a determination (not the date of the actual termination) that the corporation's S election had terminated for a previous taxable year [§1377(b)(1)(B), (C)].

[53]In addition to the general rules that apply to PTTP distributions, there is a special rule that applies to distributions from an "eligible terminated S corporation" that occur *after* the PTTP. Specifically, distributions from an eligible terminated S corporation that occur after the PTTP are treated as paid *pro rata* from its accumulated adjustments account and from its earnings and profits. An eligible terminated S corporation is any C corporation that (i) was an S corporation on December 21, 2017; (ii) revoked its S corporation election during the two-year period beginning on December 22, 2017; and (iii) had the same owners on December 22, 2017, and on the revocation date (in identical proportions).

LO 11-6

S CORPORATION TAXES AND FILING REQUIREMENTS

Although S corporations are flow-through entities generally not subject to tax, three potential taxes apply to S corporations that previously operated as C corporations: the built-in gains tax, excess net passive income tax, and LIFO recapture tax. The built-in gains tax is the most common of the three and will be our starting point.

THE KEY FACTS

Built-in Gains Tax

- The built-in gains tax applies only to S corporations that have a net unrealized built-in gain at the time they convert from C corporations and that recognize net built-in gains during the built-in gains tax recognition period.
- The net unrealized built-in gain represents the net gain (if any) that the corporation would recognize if it sold each asset at its fair market value.
- Recognized built-in gains (losses) include the gain (loss) for any asset sold during the year [limited to the unrealized gain (loss) for the specific asset at the S conversion date].
- The net recognized built-in gain is limited to the lowest of (a) the net recognized built-in gain less any net operating loss (NOL) and net capital loss carryovers, (b) the net unrealized built-in gain not yet recognized, and (c) the corporation's taxable income for the year using the C corporation tax rules.

Built-in Gains Tax

Congress enacted the built-in gains tax to prevent C corporations from avoiding corporate taxes on sales of appreciated property by electing S corporation status. The **built-in gains tax** applies only to an S corporation that has a *net unrealized built-in gain* at the time it converts from a C corporation. Further, for the built-in gains tax to apply, the S corporation must subsequently recognize net built-in gains during the **built-in gains tax recognition period.**[54] The built-in gains tax recognition period is the five-year period beginning with the first day of the first taxable year the corporation operates as an S corporation.

What exactly is a **net unrealized built-in gain?** Measured on the first day of the corporation's first year as an S corporation, it represents the net gain (if any) the corporation would recognize if it sold each asset at its fair market value. For this purpose, we net gains and losses to determine whether indeed there is a net unrealized gain at the conversion date. The corporation's accounts receivable and accounts payable are also part of the computation: Under the cash method, accounts receivable are gain items and accounts payable are loss items. If the S corporation has a net unrealized gain at conversion, it must compute its net recognized built-in gains for each tax year during the applicable built-in gain recognition period to determine whether it is liable for the built-in gains tax.

Example 11-23

CCS uses the accrual method of accounting. At the beginning of 2022, it owned the following assets (but leased its manufacturing facility and its equipment):

Asset	Fair Market Value (FMV)	Adjusted Basis (AB)	Built-in Gain (Loss)
Cash	$ 80,000	$ 80,000	$ 0
Accounts receivable	20,000	20,000	0
Inventory (FIFO)	130,000	110,000	20,000
Land	100,000	125,000	(25,000)
Totals	$330,000	$335,000	$ (5,000)

What is CCS's net unrealized built-in gain when it converts to an S corporation on January 1, 2022?

Answer: CCS has $0 net unrealized built-in gain. It has a net unrealized built-in loss, so it is not subject to the built-in gains tax.

What if: Suppose CCS's inventory is valued at $155,000 instead of $130,000. What is its net unrealized built-in gain?

Answer: $20,000. The $45,000 built-in gain on the inventory is netted against the $25,000 built-in loss on the land.

Recognized built-in gains for an S corporation year include (1) the gain for any asset sold during the year (limited to the unrealized gain for the specific asset at the S conversion date) and (2) any income received during the current year attributable to pre–S corporation years (such as collection on accounts receivable for cash-method S corporations). Likewise, recognized built-in losses for a year include (1) the loss for any asset sold during the year (limited to the unrealized loss for the specific asset at the S conversion date) and (2) any deduction during the current year attributable to pre–S corporation years (such as

[54]§1374.

deductions for accounts payable for cash-method S corporations). The net recognized built-in gain for any year is limited to *the least of:*

1. The net of the recognized built-in gains and losses for the year.
2. The net unrealized built-in gains as of the S election date less the net recognized built-in gains in previous years. (This restriction ensures the net recognized built-in gains during the recognition period do not exceed the net unrealized gain at the S conversion date.)
3. The corporation's taxable income for the year, using the C corporation tax rules exclusive of the dividends-received deduction and net operating loss deduction.

If taxable income limits the net recognized built-in gain for any year [item (3) above], the excess gain is treated as a recognized built-in gain in the next tax year, *but only if* the next tax year is in the built-in gains tax recognition period. After the net recognized built-in gain to be taxed has been determined using the limitations above, it should be reduced by any net operating loss (NOL) or net capital loss carryovers from prior C corporation years.[55] This base is then multiplied by the corporate tax rate (21 percent) to determine the built-in gains tax. The built-in gains tax paid by the S corporation is allocated to the shareholders as a loss. The character of the allocated loss (ordinary, capital, §1231) depends on the nature of assets that give rise to the built-in gains tax. Specifically, the loss is allocated proportionately among the character of the recognized built-in gains resulting in the tax.[56] For planning purposes, the S corporation should consider when to recognize built-in losses to reduce its exposure to the built-in gains tax. That is, the company could seek to recognize built-in losses in years with recognized built-in gains in order to avoid the built-in gains tax.

Example 11-24

What if: Suppose CCS had a net unrealized built-in gain of $20,000. In addition to other transactions in 2022, CCS sold inventory it owned at the beginning of the year; that inventory had built-in gain at the beginning of the year of $40,000 (FMV $150,000; cost basis $110,000). If CCS had been a C corporation in 2022, its taxable income would have been $200,000. How much built-in gains tax must CCS pay in 2022?

Answer: It must pay $4,200 ($20,000 × 21%) in built-in gains tax. CCS must pay a 21 percent tax on the least of (a) $40,000 (recognized built-in gain on inventory), (b) $20,000 (initial net unrealized gain), and (c) $200,000 (taxable income computed as if CCS were a C corporation for 2022). It will reduce the amount of ordinary business income it would otherwise allocate to its shareholders by $4,200—the amount of the built-in gains tax—because the entire amount of the tax is due to inventory sales.

What if: Assume the same facts as above (an initial net unrealized gain of $20,000) except CCS sold two assets that had built-in gains at the time CCS became an S corporation. CCS sold a capital asset with a built-in gain of $10,000 and inventory with a built-in gain of $40,000. CCS will still pay a $4,200 built-in gains tax. This tax will be allocated as a loss to its shareholders. What is the character of the $4,200 loss?

Answer: It is an $840 capital loss [$4,200 × ($10,000 capital gain/$50,000 total recognized built-in gain)] and a $3,360 ordinary loss [$4,200 × ($40,000 ordinary income from inventory sale/$50,000 total recognized built-in gain)].

What if: Assume that in addition to the initial facts in the example, CCS also had a net operating loss from 2021 (the year it operated as a C corporation) of $15,000. CCS has no NOLs from tax years beginning before 2018. How much built-in gains tax will CCS have to pay in 2022?

Answer: It will pay $1,050 ($5,000 × 21%). CCS is allowed to offset $15,000 of the $20,000 recognized portion of the initial net unrealized gain by its $15,000 net operating loss carryover from 2021. Note that because CCS's net operating loss originated after 2017, the net operating loss deduction could not exceed 80 percent of CCS's taxable income, determined before the post-2017 net operating loss deduction ($20,000 × 80% = $16,000). Thus, the full $15,000 net operating loss can be used to offset the $20,000 built-in gain.

(continued on page 11-26)

[55]Net capital loss carryovers only reduce built-in gains that are capital gains. For net operating losses originating in tax years beginning after 2017, the net operating loss deduction is limited to 80 percent of taxable income, determined after deducting pre-2018 NOLs but before deducting the post-2017 NOLs. The 80 percent of taxable income limitation only applies for tax years beginning after 2020.

[56]§1366(f)(2).

What if: Suppose CCS had a net unrealized built-in gain of $20,000. In addition to other transactions in 2022, CCS sold inventory it owned at the beginning of the year; that inventory had built-in gain at the beginning of the year of $40,000 (FMV $150,000; AB $110,000). If CCS had been a C corporation in 2022, its taxable income would have been $4,000. How much built-in gains tax would CCS have to pay in 2022?

Answer: $840 ($4,000 × 21%). CCS must pay a 21 percent tax on the least of (a) $40,000 (recognized built-in gain on inventory), (b) $20,000 (initial net unrealized gain), and (c) $4,000 (taxable income computed as if CCS were a C corporation for 2022). Because the tax was limited due to the taxable income limitation, the excess gain of $16,000 ($20,000 recognized built-in gain minus $4,000 gain on which CCS paid tax) is treated as a recognized built-in gain in 2023.

Excess Net Passive Income Tax

THE KEY FACTS

Excess Net Passive Income Tax

- The excess net passive income tax applies only to S corporations that previously operated as C corporations *and* at the end of the year have accumulated earnings and profits from a prior C corporation year.
- This tax applies when passive investment income exceeds 25 percent of gross receipts.
- Passive investment income includes gross receipts from royalties, rents, dividends, interest (including tax-exempt interest), and annuities.

If an S corporation previously operated as a C corporation *and* has accumulated earnings and profits at the end of the year from a prior C corporation year, it may be subject to the **excess net passive income tax.**[57] Congress created this tax to encourage S corporations to distribute their accumulated earnings and profits from prior C corporation years. It does not apply to S corporations that never operated as a C corporation, or to S corporations without earnings and profits from prior C corporation years.

The tax is levied on the S corporation's **excess net passive income,** computed as follows:

$$\text{Excess net passive income} = \text{Net passive investment income} \times \frac{\text{Passive investment income} - (25\% \times \text{Gross receipts})}{\text{Passive investment income}}$$

Note that an S corporation has excess net passive income only when (1) it has net passive investment income and (2) its passive investment income exceeds 25 percent of its gross receipts. For purposes of determining excess net passive income, *gross receipts* is the total amount of revenues (including passive investment income) received or accrued under the corporation's accounting method, and not reduced by returns, allowances, cost of goods sold, or deductions. Gross receipts include net capital gains from the sales or exchanges of capital assets and gains from the sales or exchanges of stock or securities (losses do not offset gains). As defined previously in the chapter, passive investment income includes gross receipts from royalties, rents, dividends, interest (including tax-exempt interest), and annuities. **Net passive investment income** is passive investment income decreased by any expenses connected with producing that income.

The excess net passive income tax is imposed on excess net passive income at the corporate tax rate (21 percent). For purposes of computing the tax, excess net passive income is limited to taxable income computed as if the corporation were a C corporation (excluding net operating losses). The formula for determining the tax is:

$$\text{Excess net passive income tax} = 21\% \times \text{Excess net passive income}$$

Each item of passive investment income that flows through to shareholders is reduced by an allocable share of the excess net passive income tax. The portion of the tax allocated to each item of passive investment income is the amount of the item divided by the total amount of passive investment income.

The IRS may waive the excess net passive income tax in some circumstances—for example, if the S corporation determined in good faith it did not have accumulated earnings and profits at the end of the tax year and within a reasonable period distributed earnings and profits it identified later.[58]

[57] §1375.

[58] §1375(d).

Example 11-25

During 2022, CCS reported the following income (see Exhibit 11-2):

Description	2022 (S Corporation)
Sales revenue	$ 520,000
Cost of goods sold	(115,000)
Salary to owners Nicole and Sarah	(90,000)
Employee wages	(50,000)
Depreciation expense	(20,000)
Miscellaneous expenses	(5,000)
Interest income	6,000
Dividend income	3,000
Overall net income	$ 249,000

What are CCS's passive investment income, net passive investment income, and gross receipts for 2022?

Answer: The amounts are $9,000 passive income ($6,000 interest income + $3,000 dividends); $9,000 net passive investment income (because CCS has $0 expenses in producing passive investment income); and $529,000 gross receipts ($520,000 sales revenue + $3,000 dividends + $6,000 interest income).

What is CCS's excess net passive income tax in 2022, if any?

Answer: Zero. CCS has accumulated earnings and profits from 2021 (see Exhibit 11-2), but it owes zero excess net passive income tax because its passive investment income is less than 25 percent of its gross receipts [$9,000 < $132,250 ($529,000 × 25%)].

What if: Suppose CCS has passive investment income of $180,000 ($120,000 interest + $60,000 dividends), expenses associated with the passive investment income of $20,000, and gross receipts of $700,000 ($520,000 + $180,000). Also, if CCS were a C corporation, its taxable income would have been $249,000; assume it had accumulated earnings and profits of $40,000. What is CCS's excess net passive income tax, if any? What effect, if any, would the excess net passive income tax have on interest and dividends allocated to the shareholders?

Answer: The base for the tax is limited to the lesser of (a) excess net passive income of $4,444 [($180,000 passive investment income − $20,000 expenses associated with passive investment income) × ($180,000 − 25% × $700,000)/$180,000] or (b) $249,000 (CCS's taxable income if it had been a C corporation). Thus, the base for the tax is limited to $4,444, and the tax is $933 (21% × $4,444).

Interest and dividends allocated to the shareholders will be reduced by the excess net passive income tax. The interest income allocated to shareholders will be reduced by $622 [$933 tax × ($120,000 interest/$180,000 total passive investment income)], and dividend income will be reduced by $311 [$933 × ($60,000 dividend/$180,000)].

What if: Suppose CCS has passive investment income of $180,000, expenses associated with the passive investment income of $20,000, and gross receipts of $700,000 ($520,000 + $180,000). Also, if CCS were a C corporation, its taxable income would have been $2,000; assume it had accumulated earnings and profits of $40,000. What is CCS's excess net passive income tax, if any?

Answer: The base for the tax is limited to the lesser of (a) excess net passive investment income of $4,444 [$160,000 × ($180,000 − 25% × $700,000)/$180,000] or (b) $2,000 (taxable income if CCS had been a C corporation). So the tax is $420 (21% × $2,000).

Remember, if an S corporation pays the net excess passive income tax for three years in a row, its S election will be terminated by the excess passive income test.

LIFO Recapture Tax

C corporations that elect S corporation status and use the LIFO inventory method are subject to the **LIFO recapture tax.** The purpose of this tax is to prevent former C corporations from avoiding built-in gains tax by using the LIFO method of accounting for their inventories.

Specifically, a LIFO method S corporation would not recognize built-in gains unless the corporation invaded its LIFO layers during the built-in gains tax recognition period.

The LIFO recapture tax requires the C corporation to include the **LIFO recapture amount** in its gross income in the last year it operates as a C corporation.[59] That amount equals the excess of the inventory basis computed using the FIFO method over the inventory basis computed using the LIFO method at the end of the corporation's last tax year as a C corporation. In addition to being included in gross income (and taxed at the C corporation's tax rate), the LIFO recapture amount also increases the corporation's adjusted basis in its inventory at the time it converts to an S corporation. The basis increase reduces the amount of net unrealized gain subject to the built-in gains tax.

The corporation pays the LIFO recapture tax (technically a C corporation tax) in four annual installments. The first installment is due on or before the due date (not including extensions) of the corporation's last *C corporation* tax return. The final three annual installments are due each year on or before the due date (not including extensions) of the *S corporation*'s tax return.

The LIFO recapture tax does not preclude the S corporation from using the LIFO method, but it obviously does accelerate the gain attributable to differences between LIFO and FIFO for inventory existing at the time of the S corporation election.

Example 11-26

What if: Suppose CCS uses the LIFO method of accounting for its inventory and elected S corporation status effective January 1, 2023. Assume that at the end of 2022, the basis of the inventory under the LIFO method was $90,000. Under the FIFO method, the basis of the inventory would have been $100,000. Finally, CCS's taxable income in 2022 was $40,000. What amount of LIFO recapture tax must CCS pay?

Answer: CCS must pay $2,100 [($100,000 FIFO inventory basis – $90,000 LIFO inventory basis) × 21%, the corporate tax rate]. CCS would increase its basis in its inventory by $10,000, to $100,000, as of the end of 2022, its last year as a C corporation. This would reduce the unrealized net built-in gain on the inventory.

When is CCS required to pay the tax?

Answer: CCS must pay $525 by April 15, 2023 (the unextended due date of the C corporation tax return); March 15, 2024; March 15, 2025; and March 15, 2026. March 15 is the annual tax return due date for calendar-year-end S corporation returns without extensions (see discussion below).

Estimated Taxes

The estimated tax rules for S corporations generally follow the rules for C corporations: S corporations with a federal income tax liability of $500 or more due to the built-in gains tax or excess net passive income tax must estimate their tax liability for the year and pay it in four quarterly estimated installments. However, an S corporation is not required to make estimated tax payments for the LIFO recapture tax.[60]

THE KEY FACTS

S Corporation Estimated Tax and Filing Requirements

- S corporations owing the built-in gains tax or excess net passive investment income tax (but not the LIFO recapture tax) must pay the tax based on estimated tax rules similar to C corporations.
- S corporations file Form 1120-S to report the results of their operations for the year. They request a filing extension on Form 7004.

Filing Requirements

S corporations are required to file **Form 1120-S** with the IRS by the 15th day of the third month after the S corporation's year-end (e.g., March 15 for a calendar-year-end S corporation). S corporations may receive an automatic six-month extension by filing **Form 7004** with the IRS prior to the original due date of the return.[61] Thus, the extended due date of an S corporation tax return is generally September 15.

Exhibit 11-3 presents page 1 of CCS's Form 1120-S (for its 2022 activities), CCS's partial Schedule K, and Nicole's Schedule K-1 (we use 2021 forms because 2022 forms were unavailable at the time this book went to press). Note the K-1 of the 1120-S is

[59]§1363(d).

[60]Rev. Proc. 94-61.

[61]Under §6698, late-filing penalties apply if the S corporation fails to file by the normal or extended due date for the return.

EXHIBIT 11-3, PART I CCS's 2022 Form 1120-S (on 2021 form)

Form **1120-S** — Department of the Treasury, Internal Revenue Service

U.S. Income Tax Return for an S Corporation

▶ Do not file this form unless the corporation has filed or is attaching Form 2553 to elect to be an S corporation.
▶ Go to *www.irs.gov/Form1120S* for instructions and the latest information.

OMB No. 1545-0123 — 2021

For calendar year 2021 or tax year beginning , 2021, ending , 20

A S election effective date: January 1, 2022	Name: Color Comfort Sheets	D Employer identification number: 24-4681012
B Business activity code number (see instructions): 314000	TYPE OR PRINT — Number, street, and room or suite no. If a P.O. box, see instructions: 375 East 450 South	E Date incorporated: January 1, 2021
C Check if Sch. M-3 attached ☐	City or town, state or province, country, and ZIP or foreign postal code: Salt Lake City, UT 84103	F Total assets (see instructions): $ 370,000

G Is the corporation electing to be an S corporation beginning with this tax year? See instructions. ☑ Yes ☐ No

H Check if: (1) ☐ Final return (2) ☐ Name change (3) ☐ Address change (4) ☐ Amended return (5) ☐ S election termination

I Enter the number of shareholders who were shareholders during any part of the tax year ▶ 3

J Check if corporation: (1) ☐ Aggregated activities for section 465 at-risk purposes (2) ☐ Grouped activities for section 469 passive activity purposes

Caution: Include **only** trade or business income and expenses on lines 1a through 21. See the instructions for more information.

Income	1a	Gross receipts or sales	1a	520,000		
	b	Returns and allowances	1b			
	c	Balance. Subtract line 1b from line 1a			1c	520,000
	2	Cost of goods sold (attach Form 1125-A)			2	115,000
	3	Gross profit. Subtract line 2 from line 1c			3	405,000
	4	Net gain (loss) from Form 4797, line 17 (attach Form 4797)			4	
	5	Other income (loss) (see instructions—attach statement)			5	
	6	**Total income (loss).** Add lines 3 through 5 ▶			6	405,000
Deductions (see instructions for limitations)	7	Compensation of officers (see instructions—attach Form 1125-E)			7	90,000
	8	Salaries and wages (less employment credits)			8	50,000
	9	Repairs and maintenance			9	
	10	Bad debts			10	
	11	Rents			11	
	12	Taxes and licenses			12	
	13	Interest (see instructions)			13	
	14	Depreciation not claimed on Form 1125-A or elsewhere on return (attach Form 4562)			14	20,000
	15	Depletion **(Do not deduct oil and gas depletion.)**			15	
	16	Advertising			16	
	17	Pension, profit-sharing, etc., plans			17	
	18	Employee benefit programs			18	
	19	Other deductions (attach statement)			19	5,000
	20	**Total deductions.** Add lines 7 through 19 ▶			20	165,000
	21	**Ordinary business income (loss).** Subtract line 20 from line 6			21	240,000
Tax and Payments	22a	Excess net passive income or LIFO recapture tax (see instructions)	22a			
	b	Tax from Schedule D (Form 1120-S)	22b			
	c	Add lines 22a and 22b (see instructions for additional taxes)			22c	
	23a	2021 estimated tax payments and 2020 overpayment credited to 2021	23a			
	b	Tax deposited with Form 7004	23b			
	c	Credit for federal tax paid on fuels (attach Form 4136)	23c			
	d	Add lines 23a through 23c			23d	
	24	Estimated tax penalty (see instructions). Check if Form 2220 is attached ▶ ☐			24	
	25	**Amount owed.** If line 23d is smaller than the total of lines 22c and 24, enter amount owed			25	
	26	**Overpayment.** If line 23d is larger than the total of lines 22c and 24, enter amount overpaid			26	
	27	Enter amount from line 26: **Credited to 2022 estimated tax ▶** **Refunded ▶**			27	

Sign Here — Under penalties of perjury, I declare that I have examined this return, including accompanying schedules and statements, and to the best of my knowledge and belief, it is true, correct, and complete. Declaration of preparer (other than taxpayer) is based on all information of which preparer has any knowledge.

Signature of officer | Date | Title | May the IRS discuss this return with the preparer shown below? See instructions. ☐ Yes ☐ No

Paid Preparer Use Only

Print/Type preparer's name	Preparer's signature	Date	Check ☐ if self-employed	PTIN
Firm's name ▶			Firm's EIN ▶	
Firm's address ▶			Phone no.	

For Paperwork Reduction Act Notice, see separate instructions. Cat. No. 11510H Form **1120-S** (2021)

Source: irs.gov.

EXHIBIT 11-3, PART II CCS's 2022 Partial Schedule K (on 2021 form)

Schedule K — Shareholders' Pro Rata Share Items

Section	Line	Description			Line	Total amount
Income (Loss)	1	Ordinary business income (loss) (page 1, line 21)			1	240,000
	2	Net rental real estate income (loss) (attach Form 8825)			2	
	3a	Other gross rental income (loss)	3a			
	b	Expenses from other rental activities (attach statement)	3b			
	c	Other net rental income (loss). Subtract line 3b from line 3a			3c	
	4	Interest income			4	6,000
	5	Dividends: **a** Ordinary dividends			5a	3,000
		b Qualified dividends	5b	3,000		
	6	Royalties			6	
	7	Net short-term capital gain (loss) (attach Schedule D (Form 1120-S))			7	
	8a	Net long-term capital gain (loss) (attach Schedule D (Form 1120-S))			8a	
	b	Collectibles (28%) gain (loss)	8b			
	c	Unrecaptured section 1250 gain (attach statement)	8c			
	9	Net section 1231 gain (loss) (attach Form 4797)			9	
	10	Other income (loss) (see instructions) Type ▶			10	

Source: irs.gov.

EXHIBIT 11-3, PART III Nicole's 2022 Schedule K-1 (on 2021 form)

671121

Schedule K-1 (Form 1120-S) 2021
Department of the Treasury
Internal Revenue Service
For calendar year 2021, or tax year beginning / / 2021 ending / /

Shareholder's Share of Income, Deductions, Credits, etc. ▶ See separate instructions.

☐ Final K-1 ☐ Amended K-1 OMB No. 1545-0123

Part I Information About the Corporation

A Corporation's employer identification number: 24-4681012

B Corporation's name, address, city, state, and ZIP code:
Color Comfort Sheets
375 East 450 South
Salt Lake City, UT 84103

C IRS Center where corporation filed return: Ogden, UT

D Corporation's total number of shares
Beginning of tax year: 3,000
End of tax year: 3,000

Part II Information About the Shareholder

E Shareholder's identifying number: 123-45-6789

F Shareholder's name, address, city, state, and ZIP code:
Nicole Johnson
811 East 8320 South
Sandy, UT 84094

G Current year allocation percentage: 33.333333 %

H Shareholder's number of shares
Beginning of tax year: 1000
End of tax year: 1000

I Loans from shareholder
Beginning of tax year: $
End of tax year: $

For IRS Use Only

Statement on Qualified Business Income Items:

Line 17, Code V:
QBI income: $80,000
QBI wages: $46,667
QBI unadjusted basis: $100,000

* Not a specified service trade or business

Part III Shareholder's Share of Current Year Income, Deductions, Credits, and Other Items

Line	Item	Amount
1	Ordinary business income (loss)	80,000
2	Net rental real estate income (loss)	
3	Other net rental income (loss)	
4	Interest income	2,000
5a	Ordinary dividends	1,000
5b	Qualified dividends	1,000
6	Royalties	
7	Net short-term capital gain (loss)	
8a	Net long-term capital gain (loss)	
8b	Collectibles (28%) gain (loss)	
8c	Unrecaptured section 1250 gain	
9	Net section 1231 gain (loss)	
10	Other income (loss)	
11	Section 179 deduction	
12	Other deductions	
13	Credits	
14	Schedule K-3 is attached if checked . . . . ▶ ☐	
15	Alternative minimum tax (AMT) items	
16	Items affecting shareholder basis	
17	Other information	A 3,000; V STMT
18	☐ More than one activity for at-risk purposes*	
19	☐ More than one activity for passive activity purposes*	

* See attached statement for additional information.

For Paperwork Reduction Act Notice, see the Instructions for Form 1120-S. www.irs.gov/Form1120S Cat. No. 11520D Schedule K-1 (Form 1120-S) 2021

Source: irs.gov.

different from the K-1 of the partnership Form 1065. In contrast to the 1065 Schedule K-1, the 1120-S Schedule K-1 does not report self-employment income, does not allocate entity-level debt to shareholders, and does not allow for shareholders to have profit-and-loss-sharing ratios that are different from shareholders' percentage of stock ownership.

COMPARING C AND S CORPORATIONS AND PARTNERSHIPS

Exhibit 11-4 compares tax consequences for C corporations, S corporations, and partnerships discussed in this chapter.

EXHIBIT 11-4 Comparison of Tax Consequences for C and S Corporations and Partnerships

Tax Characteristic	C Corporation	S Corporation	Partnership/LLC
Forming or contributing property to an entity	No gain or loss on contribution of appreciated or depreciated property if transferors of property have control (as defined in §351) after transfer.	Same as C corporation.	Same as C and S corporations except no control requirement (§721 applies to partnerships).
Type of owner restrictions	No restrictions.	Only individuals who are U.S. citizens or residents, certain trusts, and tax-exempt organizations.	No restrictions.
Number of owner restrictions	No restrictions.	Limited to 100 shareholders. (Family members and their estates count as one shareholder.)	Must have more than one owner.
Election	Default status if corporation under state law.	Must formally elect to have corporation taxed as S corporation.	Default status if unincorporated; must have more than one owner.
Income and loss allocations	Not allocated to shareholders.	Income and loss flow through to owners based on ownership percentages.	Income and loss flow through to owners but may be allocated based on something other than ownership percentages (special allocations).
Entity debt included in stock (or partnership interest) basis	No	Generally no. However, loans made from shareholder to corporation create debt basis. Losses may be deducted to extent of stock basis and then debt basis.	Yes. All entity liabilities are allocated to basis of partners.
Loss limitations	Losses remain at corporate level.	Losses flow through but subject to tax-basis limitation, at-risk limitation, passive activity limitations, and excess business loss limitation.	Same as S corporations.
Self-employment income status of ordinary income allocations	Not applicable.	Not self-employment income.	May be self-employment income depending on partner's status.
Salary to owners permitted	Yes	Yes	Generally no. Salary-type payments are guaranteed payments subject to self-employment tax.
Fringe benefits	Can pay nontaxable fringe benefits to owners.	Can pay nontaxable fringe benefits to owners who own 2 percent or less of stock.	May not pay nontaxable fringe benefits to owners.
Operating distributions: Owner tax consequences	Taxable as dividends to extent of earnings and profits.	Generally not taxable to extent of owner's basis.	Same as S corporations.
Operating distributions: Entity tax consequences	Gain on distribution of appreciated property; no loss on distribution of depreciated property.	Same as C corporations.	Generally no gain or loss on distribution of property.
Liquidating distributions	Corporation and shareholders generally recognize gain or loss on distributions.	Same as C corporations.	Partnership and partners generally do not recognize gain or loss on liquidating distributions.

(*continued*)

EXHIBIT 11-4 *(concluded)*

Tax Characteristic	C Corporation	S Corporation	Partnership/LLC
Entity-level taxes	Yes, based on corporate tax rate schedule.	Generally no, but may be required to pay built-in gains tax, excess passive investment income tax, or LIFO recapture tax if converting from C to S corporation.	No
Tax year	Last day of any month or 52/53-week year.	Generally calendar year.	Based on tax year of owners.

CONCLUSION

This chapter highlights the rules specific to S corporations and compared S corporations to C corporations and partnerships. S corporations are true hybrid entities: They share characteristics with C corporations (the tax rules that apply in organizing and liquidating a corporation). They also share characteristics with partnerships (the flow-through of the entity's income and loss to its owners, ability to make nontaxable distributions to the extent of the owner's basis, and basis calculations for owners).

Although many S corporation attributes follow from the C corporation or partnership rules, several specific attributes unique to S corporations may be particularly important in choosing an entity form or operating an S corporation in a tax-efficient manner. These attributes include unique S corporation taxes, the rules for how debt enters into the basis calculations and loss limitation rules for S corporations, and the rules for how distributions are taxed for S corporations previously operating as C corporations.

Summary

LO 11-1 Describe the requirements and process to elect S corporation status.

- Shareholders of S corporations are able to defer realized gains when they contribute property to the corporation if they have control of the corporation after the contribution.
- S corporations are limited in the type of owners they may have. Only individuals who are U.S. citizens or residents, certain trusts, and certain tax-exempt organizations may be shareholders of S corporations.
- S corporations may have no more than 100 shareholders. For this purpose, family members and their estates count as one shareholder. Family members include a common ancestor and their lineal descendants and their lineal descendants' spouses (or former spouses).
- S corporations may have only one class of stock. The stock may have differences in voting rights between shares, but all stock must have identical rights with respect to corporate distribution and liquidation proceeds.
- The S corporation election is made on Form 2553. All shareholders on the date of the election must consent to the election.
- To be effective for the current year, the election must be filed in the prior tax year or on or before the 15th day of the third month of the year. Even then, the election may not be effective in certain circumstances.

LO 11-2 Explain the events that terminate the S corporation election.

- The S corporation election may be voluntarily revoked by shareholders owning more than 50 percent of the S corporation stock. In general, revocations made on or before the 15th day of the third month of the year are effective as of the beginning of the year, and revocations after that date are effective on the first day of the next year. Alternatively, the shareholders may choose an alternate date that is not before the revocation election is filed.

- An S corporation's election is automatically terminated on the date it fails to meet the S corporation requirements.
- If an S corporation has earnings and profits from a previous C corporation year, its S election is terminated if it has passive investment income in excess of 25 percent of gross receipts for three consecutive years.
- When an S corporation election is terminated midyear, the corporation files a short tax year return for the period it was an S corporation and a short tax year return for the portion of the year it was a C corporation. It can allocate the income on a per-day basis, or it may specifically identify the income to each period.
- When an S corporation's S election is terminated, it may not reelect S status until the beginning of the fifth tax year after the tax year in which the election was terminated.

Describe operating issues relating to S corporation accounting periods and methods, and explain income and loss allocations and separately stated items. LO 11-3

- When C corporations elect to become S corporations, all prior accounting methods carry over to the S corporation.
- S corporations are generally required to use a calendar tax year.
- Income and losses are allocated to S corporation shareholders pro rata based on the number of outstanding shares each shareholder owns on each day of the tax year, or, with shareholder consent, it may use its normal accounting rules to allocate income and loss to the shareholders.
- S corporations determine their ordinary business income and separately stated items for the year and allocate these to the shareholders during the year.
- Separately stated items are tax items treated differently at the shareholder level than a shareholder's share of ordinary business income.

Explain stock-basis calculations, loss limitations, determination of self-employment income, and fringe benefit rules that apply to S corporation shareholders. LO 11-4

- An S corporation shareholder's initial basis in their stock is generally the basis of the property contributed to the corporation minus liabilities assumed by the corporation on the contribution.
- S corporation shareholders adjust their stock basis annually. They increase it for (in this order) capital contributions to the S corporation during the year, the shareholder's share of ordinary business income, and separately stated income/gain items. They decrease it for distributions during the year, the shareholder's share of nondeductible expenses, and the shareholder's share of ordinary business loss and separately stated expense/loss items. The basis may not be reduced below zero.
- S corporation shareholders are not allowed to include the S corporation's debt in their stock basis. However, they are allowed to create *debt basis* for the amount of loans they make directly to the S corporation. Debt basis can absorb S corporation losses (see below).
- For an S corporation shareholder to deduct them, S corporation losses must clear three separate hurdles: (1) tax-basis limitation in stock (and debt), (2) at-risk amount limitation, and (3) passive activity loss limitation. In addition, for losses that clear each of the three separate hurdles, S corporation shareholders are not allowed to deduct excess business losses.
- Losses suspended at a particular level remain suspended until the shareholder creates additional tax-basis or at-risk amounts, clears the passive loss hurdle, or sells their stock in the S corporation.
- If a shareholder's stock and debt bases are reduced by loss allocations and then increased by subsequent income allocations, the income allocation first increases the debt basis to the debt's outstanding amount before increasing the stock basis.
- When an S corporation's S election is terminated, S corporation shareholders can deduct their share of S corporation losses on the last day of the post-termination transition period as long as the losses are able to clear the three loss limitation hurdles.
- Allocation of ordinary business income is not self-employment income to S corporation shareholders.
- If S corporation shareholders are employees of the corporation, their wages are subject to employment taxes.

- S corporation shareholders are subject to the net investment income tax on their share of an S corporation's gross income from interest, dividends, annuities, royalties, rents, a trade or business that is a passive activity or a trade or business of trading financial instruments or commodities, and generally any net gain from disposing of property, less any allowable deductions from these items.
- Many fringe benefits that are nontaxable to other S corporation employees are taxable to employees who own more than 2 percent of the S corporation.

LO 11-5 Apply the tax rules for S corporation operating distributions and liquidating distributions.

- Operating distributions from S corporations without accumulated earnings and profits from C corporation years are nontaxable to the extent of the shareholder's basis and then taxable as capital gain to the extent they exceed the shareholder's stock basis.
- Operating distributions from S corporations with accumulated earnings and profits from C corporation years are a nontaxable reduction in stock basis to the extent of the S corporation's accumulated adjustments account, a dividend to the extent of the corporation's earnings and profits, and then a nontaxable return of capital to the extent of the stock basis. Amounts in excess of the stock basis are capital gain.
- The accumulated adjustments account represents the cumulative income or losses for the period the corporation has been an S corporation.
- When S corporations distribute appreciated property to shareholders, they must recognize gain on the distribution (the gain is allocated to the shareholders). When they distribute loss property, they are not allowed to deduct the losses. In either case, the fair market value of the property (reduced by liabilities) is the amount of the distribution to the shareholders.
- When an S election is terminated, cash distributions during the post-termination transition period are nontaxable to the shareholder to the extent of the S corporation's accumulated adjustments account and the shareholder's stock basis.
- S corporations making liquidating distributions recognize gain or loss on the distributions. The gains or losses are allocated to the shareholders. The shareholders compare the amount received in the liquidating distribution to their stock basis to determine if they recognize gain or loss on the distributions.

LO 11-6 Describe the taxes that apply to S corporations, estimated tax requirements, and tax return filing requirements.

- S corporations that were formerly C corporations may be required to pay the built-in gains tax. The tax applies if the S corporation had a net unrealized built-in gain at the time it converted to an S corporation. It must pay the tax when it recognizes these net built-in gains during its first five years operating as an S corporation.
- The base for the tax is limited to the least of (1) the net of the recognized built-in gains and losses for the year, (2) the net unrealized built-in gains as of the date of the S election date less the net recognized built-in gains in previous years, and (3) the corporation's taxable income for the year using the C corporation tax rules [excluding the dividends-received deduction and net operating loss (NOL) deduction]. The base is then reduced by any NOL or net capital loss carryovers from prior C corporation years.
- S corporations that were formerly C corporations and have C corporation earnings and profits must pay the excess net passive income tax when their passive investment income exceeds 25 percent of their gross receipts.
- The formula for the excess net passive income tax is 21 percent (the corporate tax rate) × {Net passive investment income × [Passive investment income − (25% × Gross receipts)]/Passive investment income}.
- C corporations that elect to be taxed as S corporations and that use the LIFO method of accounting for inventories must pay the LIFO recapture tax. The tax is the C corporation's tax rate times the excess of the inventory valued under the LIFO method over the inventory valued under the FIFO method at the time the S election became effective. The corporation pays one-quarter of the tax on its final C corporation tax return and the final three installments on its S corporation tax return for the first three years it is an S corporation.
- S corporations that must pay the built-in gains tax or the excess passive income tax generally must pay estimated taxes in four quarterly installments. They are not required to make estimated tax payments for the LIFO recapture tax.

- S corporations file Form 1120-S by the 15th day of the third month after the tax year-end (generally March 15).
- S corporations may receive a six-month extension by filing Form 7004.
- On Form 1120-S, S corporations report ordinary business income and separately stated items on Schedule K. Each shareholder's portion of items on Schedule K is reported to the shareholder on their Schedule K-1.

KEY TERMS

accumulated adjustments account (AAA) (11-20)
at-risk amount (11-15)
built-in gains tax (11-24)
built-in gains tax recognition period (11-24)
debt basis (11-14)
earnings and profits (E&P) (11-2)
excess business loss (11-17)
excess net passive income (11-26)
excess net passive income tax (11-26)
Form 1120-S (11-28)
Form 2553 (11-4)
Form 7004 (11-28)
gross receipts (11-6)
LIFO recapture amount (11-28)
LIFO recapture tax (11-27)
net passive investment income (11-26)
net unrealized built-in gain (11-24)
ordinary business income (loss) (11-10)
passive activity loss (PAL) rules (11-16)
passive investment income (PII) (11-6)
post-termination transition period (PTTP) (11-15)
S corporation (11-2)
separately stated items (11-10)

DISCUSSION QUESTIONS

Discussion Questions are available in Connect®.

1. In general terms, how are C corporations different from and similar to S corporations? LO 11-1
2. What are the limitations on the number and type of shareholders an S corporation may have? How are these limitations different from restrictions on the number and type of shareholders C corporations or partnerships may have? LO 11-1
3. Why can't large, publicly traded corporations be treated as S corporations? LO 11-1
4. How do the tax laws treat family members for purposes of limiting the number of owners an S corporation may have? LO 11-1
5. Super Corp. was organized under the laws of the state of Montana. It issued common voting stock and common nonvoting stock to its two shareholders. Is Super Corp. eligible to elect S corporation status? Why or why not? LO 11-1
6. Karen is the sole shareholder of a calendar-year-end C corporation she formed last year. If she elects S corporation status this year on February 20, when will the election become effective and why? What if she had made the election on March 20? LO 11-1
7. JB Corporation is a C corporation owned 80 percent by Jacob and 20 percent by Bauer. Jacob would like JB to make an S election, but Bauer is opposed to the idea. Can JB elect to be taxed as an S corporation without Bauer's consent? Explain. LO 11-1
8. In what circumstances could a calendar-year C corporation make an election on February 1, year 1, to be taxed as an S corporation in year 1 but not have the election effective until year 2? LO 11-1
9. Theodore, Alvin, and Simon are equal shareholders of Timeless Corp. (an S corporation). Simon wants to terminate the S election, but Theodore and Alvin disagree. Can Simon unilaterally elect to have the S election terminated? If not, what would Simon need to do to have the S election terminated? LO 11-2
10. Juanita is the sole shareholder of Belize Corporation (a calendar-year S corporation). She is considering revoking the S election. It is February 1, year 1. What options does Juanita have for timing the effective date of the S election revocation? LO 11-2
11. Describe the circumstances in which an S election may be involuntarily terminated. LO 11-2

LO 11-2 12. Describe a situation in which a former C corporation that elected to be taxed as an S corporation may have its S election automatically terminated, but a similarly situated corporation that has always been taxed as an S corporation would not.

LO 11-2 13. When a corporation's S election is terminated midyear, what options does the corporation have for allocating the annual income between the S corporation short year and the C corporation short year?

LO 11-2 14. On June 1, year 1, Jasper Corporation's S election was involuntarily terminated. What is the earliest Jasper may be taxed as an S corporation again? Are there any exceptions to the general rule? Explain.

LO 11-3 15. Apple Union (AU), a C corporation with a March 31 year-end, uses the accrual method of accounting. If AU elects to be taxed as an S corporation, what will its year-end and method of accounting be (assuming no special elections)?

LO 11-3 16. Compare and contrast the method of allocating income or loss to owners for partnerships and for S corporations.

LO 11-3 17. Why must an S corporation report separately stated items to its shareholders? How is the character of a separately stated item determined? How does the S corporation report this information to each shareholder?

LO 11-3 18. How do S corporations report dividends they receive? Are they entitled to a dividends-received deduction? Why or why not?

LO 11-4 19. Shawn receives stock in an S corporation when it is formed in a tax-deferred transaction by contributing land with a tax basis of $50,000 and encumbered by a $20,000 mortgage. What is Shawn's initial basis in his S corporation stock?

LO 11-4 20. Why is a shareholder's basis in an S corporation stock adjusted annually?

LO 11-4 21. What adjustments are made annually to a shareholder's basis in S corporation stock, and in what order? What impact do these adjustments have on a subsequent sale of stock?

LO 11-4 22. Can a shareholder's basis in S corporation stock ever be adjusted to a negative number? Why or why not?

LO 11-4 23. Describe the three hurdles a taxpayer must pass if they want to deduct a loss from their share in an S corporation. What other loss limitation rule may impact the deductibility of losses from an S corporation?

LO 11-4 24. Is a shareholder allowed to increase their basis in S corporation stock by their share of the corporation's liabilities, as partners are able to increase the basis of their ownership interest by their share of partnership liabilities? Explain.

LO 11-4 25. How does a shareholder create *debt basis* in an S corporation? How is debt basis similar and dissimilar to stock basis?

LO 11-4 26. When an S corporation shareholder has suspended losses due to the tax-basis or at-risk amount limitation, are they allowed to deduct the losses if the S corporation status is terminated? Why or why not?

LO 11-4 27. When considering C corporations, the IRS checks to see whether salaries paid are too large. In S corporations, however, it usually must verify that salaries are large enough. Account for this difference.

LO 11-4 28. How does the tax treatment of employee fringe benefits reflect the hybrid nature of the S corporation?

LO 11-4 29. If a corporation has been an S corporation since inception, describe how its operating distributions to its shareholders are taxed to the shareholders.

LO 11-4 30. How are the tax consequences of a cash distribution different from those of a noncash property distribution to both the S corporation and the shareholders?

LO 11-5 31. What role does debt basis play in determining the taxability of operating distributions to S corporation shareholders?

LO 11-5 32. What does the accumulated adjustments account represent? How is it adjusted year by year? Can it have a negative balance?

33. If an S corporation with accumulated E&P makes a distribution, from what accounts (and in what order) is the distribution deemed to be paid? LO 11-5
34. Under what circumstances could a corporation with earnings and profits make a nontaxable distribution to its shareholders after the S election termination? LO 11-5
35. How do the tax consequences of S corporation liquidating distributions differ from the tax consequences of S corporation operating distributions at both the corporate and shareholder levels? LO 11-5
36. When is an S corporation required to pay a built-in gains tax? LO 11-6
37. When is an S corporation required to pay the excess net passive income tax? LO 11-6
38. Is the LIFO recapture tax a C corporation tax or an S corporation tax? Explain. LO 11-6
39. When must an S corporation make estimated tax payments? LO 11-6
40. On what form does an S corporation report its income to the IRS? When is the tax return due? What information does the S corporation provide to shareholders to allow them to complete their tax returns? LO 11-6
41. Compare and contrast S corporations, C corporations, and partnerships in terms of tax consequences at formation, shareholder restrictions, income allocation, basis calculations, compensation to owners, taxation of distributions, and accounting periods. LO 11-6

PROBLEMS

Select problems are available in Connect®.

42. Janelle wants to create an S corporation called J's Dance Shoes (JDS). Describe how the items below affect her eligibility for an S election. LO 11-1
    a) Because Janelle wants all her shareholders to have an equal say in the future of JDS, she gives them equal voting rights and decides shareholders who take a more active role in the firm will have priority in terms of distribution and liquidation rights.
    b) Janelle decides to incorporate under the state laws of Utah because that is where she lives. Once she gets her business up and running, however, she plans on doing extensive business in Mexico.
43. Lucy and Ricky Ricardo live in Los Angeles, California. After they were married, they started a business named ILL Corporation (a C corporation). For state law purposes, the shares of stock in ILL Corp. are listed under Ricky's name only. Ricky signed Form 2553 electing to have ILL taxed as an S corporation for federal income tax purposes, but Lucy did not sign. Given that California is a community property state, is the S election for ILL Corp. valid? LO 11-1

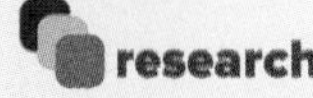

44. Maria has been operating Mansfield Park as a C corporation and decides she would like to make an S election. What is the earliest the election will become effective under each of these alternative scenarios? LO 11-1
    a) Maria is on top of things and makes the election on January 1, 2022.
    b) Maria is mostly on top of things and makes the election on January 15, 2022.
    c) Maria makes the election on February 10, 2022. She needed a little time to convince a C corporation shareholder to sell its stock to a qualifying shareholder. That process took all of January, and she was glad to have it over with.
    d) Maria makes the election on March 14, 2022.
    e) Maria makes the election on February 5, 2022. One of the shareholders refused to consent to the S election. They sold their shares (on January 15, 2022) to another shareholder who consented to the election.
45. Missy is 1 of 100 unrelated shareholders of Dalmatian, an S corporation. She is considering selling her shares. Under the following alternative scenarios, would the S election be terminated? Why or why not? LO 11-2

a) Missy wants to sell half her shares to a friend, a U.S. citizen, so they can rename their corporation 101 Dalmatians.
b) Missy's mother's family wants to be involved with the corporation. Missy splits half her shares evenly among her aunt, uncle, grandfather, and two cousins.
c) Missy sells half her Dalmatian stock to her husband's corporation.

LO 11-2

46. Cathy, Heathcliff, and Isabelle are equal shareholders in Wuthering Heights (WH), an S corporation. Heathcliff has decided he would like to terminate the S election. In the following alternative scenarios, indicate whether the termination will occur, and indicate the date if applicable (assume no alternative termination dates are selected).
   a) Cathy and Isabelle both decline to agree to the termination. Heathcliff files the termination election anyway on March 14, 2022.
   b) Isabelle agrees with the termination, but Cathy strongly disagrees. The termination is filed on February 16, 2022.
   c) The termination seems to be the first thing all three could agree on. They file the election to terminate on March 28, 2022.
   d) The termination seems to be the first thing all three could agree on. They file the election to terminate on February 28, 2022.
   e) Knowing the other two disagree with the termination, on March 16, 2022, Heathcliff sells 1 of his 50 shares to his maid, who recently moved back to Bulgaria, her home country.

LO 11-2

47. Assume the following S corporations, gross receipts, passive investment income, and corporate E&P. Will any of these corporations have its S election terminated due to excessive passive income? If so, in what year? All became S corporations at the beginning of year 1.
   a) Clarion Corp.

Year	Gross Receipts	Passive Investment Income	Corporate Earnings and Profits
1	$1,353,458	$250,000	$321,300
2	1,230,389	100,000	321,300
3	1,139,394	300,000	230,000
4	1,347,039	350,000	100,000
5	1,500,340	400,000	0

   b) Hanson Corp.

Year	Gross Receipts	Passive Investment Income	Corporate Earnings and Profits
1	$1,430,000	$247,000	$138,039
2	700,380	200,000	100,000
3	849,000	190,000	100,000
4	830,000	210,000	80,000
5	1,000,385	257,390	80,000

   c) Jelena Corp.

Year	Gross Receipts	Passive Investment Income	Corporate Earnings and Profits
1	$1,000,458	$250,000	$0
2	703,000	300,480	0
3	800,375	400,370	0
4	900,370	350,470	0
5	670,000	290,377	0

d) Nazmul Corp.

Year	Gross Receipts	Passive Investment Income	Corporate Earnings and Profits
1	$1,100,370	$250,000	$500
2	998,000	240,000	400
3	800,350	230,000	300
4	803,000	214,570	200
5	750,000	200,000	100

48. Hughie, Dewey, and Louie are equal shareholders in HDL, an S corporation. HDL's S election terminates under each of the following alternative scenarios. When is the earliest it can again operate as an S corporation? LO 11-2
   a) The S election terminates on August 1, year 2, because Louie sells half his shares to his uncle Walt, a citizen and resident of Scotland.
   b) The S election terminates effective January 1, year 3, because on August 1, year 2, Hughie and Dewey vote (2 to 1) to terminate the election.

49. Winkin, Blinkin, and Nod are equal shareholders in SleepEZ, an S corporation. In the conditions listed below, how much income should each report from SleepEZ for 2022 under both the daily allocation and the specific identification allocation methods? Refer to the following table for the timing of SleepEZ's income. LO 11-3

Period	Income
January 1 through March 15 (74 days)	$125,000
March 16 through December 31 (291 days)	345,500
January 1 through December 31, 2022 (365 days)	$470,500

   a) There are no sales of SleepEZ stock during the year.
   b) On March 15, 2022, Blinkin sells his shares to Nod.
   c) On March 15, 2022, Winkin and Nod each sells his shares to Blinkin.

Use the following information to complete problems 50 and 51:

UpAHill Corporation (an S Corporation)
Income Statement
December 31, Year 1 and Year 2

	Year 1	Year 2
Sales revenue	$175,000	$310,000
Cost of goods sold	(60,000)	(85,000)
Salary to owners Jack and Jill	(40,000)	(50,000)
Employee wages	(15,000)	(20,000)
Depreciation expense	(10,000)	(15,000)
Miscellaneous expenses	(7,500)	(9,000)
Interest income (unrelated to business)	2,000	2,500
Qualified dividend income	500	1,000
Overall net income	$ 45,000	$134,500

50. Jack and Jill are owners of UpAHill, an S corporation. They own 25 and 75 percent, respectively. LO 11-3

   a) What amount of ordinary income and separately stated items are allocated to them for years 1 and 2 based on the information above? Assume that UpAHill Corporation has $100,000 of qualified property (unadjusted basis) in both years.
   b) Complete UpAHill's Form 1120-S, Schedule K, for year 1.
   c) Complete Jill's Form 1120-S, Schedule K-1, for year 1.

LO 11-3 LO 11-4

51. Assume Jack and Jill, 25 and 75 percent shareholders, respectively, in UpAHill Corporation, have tax bases in their shares at the beginning of year 1 of $24,000 and $56,000, respectively. Also assume no distributions were made. Given the income statement above, what are their tax bases in their shares at the end of year 1?

Use the following information to complete problems 52 and 53:

Falcons Corporation (an S Corporation)
Income Statement
December 31, Year 1 and Year 2

	Year 1	Year 2
Sales revenue	$300,000	$430,000
Cost of goods sold	(40,000)	(60,000)
Salary to owners Julio and Milania	(40,000)	(80,000)
Employee wages	(25,000)	(50,000)
Depreciation expense	(20,000)	(40,000)
Section 179 expense	(30,000)	(50,000)
Interest income (related to business)	12,000	22,500
Municipal bond income	1,500	4,000
Government fines	0	(2,000)
Overall net income	$158,500	$174,500
Distributions	$ 30,000	$ 50,000

LO 11-3

52. Julio and Milania are owners of Falcons Corporation, an S corporation. Each owns 50 percent of Falcons Corporation. In year 1, Julio and Milania each received distributions of $15,000 from Falcons Corporation.
   a) What amount of ordinary income and separately stated items are allocated to them for year 1 based on the information above? Assume that Falcons Corporation has $200,000 of qualified property (unadjusted basis).
   b) Complete Falcons's Form 1120-S, Schedule K, for year 1.
   c) Complete Julio's Form 1120-S, Schedule K-1, for year 1.

LO 11-3

53. In year 2, Julio and Milania each received distributions of $25,000 from Falcons Corporation.
   a) What amount of ordinary income and separately stated items are allocated to them for year 2 based on the information above? Assume that Falcons Corporation has $200,000 of qualified property (unadjusted basis).
   b) Complete Falcons's Form 1120-S, Schedule K, for year 2.
   c) Complete Milania's Form 1120-S, Schedule K-1, for year 2.

LO 11-4

54. Harriet, Herm, and Ronde formed an S corporation called Innovet. Harriet and Herm both contributed cash of $25,000 to get things started. Ronde was a bit short on cash but had a parcel of land valued at $60,000 (basis of $50,000) that he decided to contribute. The land was encumbered by a $35,000 mortgage. What tax bases will each of the three have in their stock of Innovet?

LO 11-4

55. Sunita is a one-third owner in Bikes-R-Us, an S corporation that experienced a $45,000 loss this year (year 1). If her stock basis is $10,000 at the beginning of the year, how much of this loss clears the hurdle for deductibility (assume the at-risk limitation equals the tax-basis limitation)? If she cannot deduct the whole loss, what happens to the remainder? Is she able to deduct her entire loss if she sells her stock at year-end?

LO 11-4

56. Assume the same facts as in the previous problem, except that at the beginning of year 1 Sunita loaned Bikes-R-Us $3,000. In year 2, Bikes-R-Us reported ordinary income of $12,000. What amount is Sunita allowed to deduct in year 1? What are her stock and debt bases in the corporation at the end of year 1? What are her stock and debt bases in the corporation at the end of year 2?

57. Birch Corp., a calendar-year corporation, was formed three years ago by its sole shareholder, James, who has operated it as an S corporation since its inception. Last year, James made a direct loan to Birch Corp. in the amount of $5,000. Birch Corp. has paid the interest on the loan but has not yet paid any principal. (Assume the loan qualifies as debt for tax purposes.) For the year, Birch experienced a $25,000 business loss. What amount of the loss clears the tax-basis limitation, and what is James's basis in his Birch Corp. stock and Birch Corp. debt in each of the following alternative scenarios? LO 11-4
   a) At the beginning of the year, James's basis in his Birch Corp. stock was $45,000 and his basis in his Birch Corp. debt was $5,000.
   b) At the beginning of the year, James's basis in his Birch Corp. stock was $8,000 and his basis in his Birch Corp. debt was $5,000.
   c) At the beginning of the year, James's basis in his Birch Corp. stock was $0 and his basis in his Birch Corp. debt was $5,000.

58. Timo is the sole owner of Jazz Inc., an S corporation. On October 31, 2022, Timo executed an unsecured demand promissory note of $15,000 and transferred the note to Jazz (Jazz could require Timo to pay it $15,000 on demand). When Timo transferred the note to Jazz, his tax basis in his Jazz stock was $0. On January 31, 2023, Timo paid the $15,000 to Jazz as required by the promissory note. For the taxable year ending December 31, 2022, Jazz incurred a business loss of $12,000. How much of the loss clears the stock and debt basis hurdles for deductibility? LO 11-4 research

59. Chandra was the sole shareholder of Pet Emporium, which was originally formed as an S corporation. When Pet Emporium terminated its S election on August 31, 2021, Chandra had a stock basis and an at-risk amount of $0. Chandra also had a suspended loss from Pet Emporium of $9,000. What amount of the suspended loss is Chandra allowed to deduct, and what is her basis in her Pet Emporium stock, at the end of the post-termination transition period under the following alternative scenarios (assume Pet Emporium files for an extension to file its tax returns)? LO 11-4
   a) Chandra makes capital contributions of $7,000 on August 30, 2022, and $4,000 on September 14, 2022.
   b) Chandra makes capital contributions of $5,000 on September 1, 2022, and $5,000 on September 30, 2022.
   c) Chandra makes a capital contribution of $10,000 on August 31, 2022.
   d) Chandra makes a capital contribution of $10,000 on October 1, 2022.

60. Dejan owns stock in two S corporations, Blue and Green. He actively participates in the management of Blue but maintains ownership in Green only as a passive investor. Dejan has no other business investments. Both Blue and Green anticipate a loss this year, and Dejan's basis in his stock of both corporations is $0. All else equal, if Dejan plans on making a capital contribution to at least one of the corporations this year, to which firm should he contribute in order to increase his chances of deducting the loss allocated to him from the entity? Why? LO 11-4 planning

61. In the past several years, Shakira had loaned money to Shakira Inc. (an S corporation) to help the corporation keep afloat in a downturn. Her stock basis in the S corporation is now $0, and she has deducted $40,000 in losses, reducing her debt basis from $100,000 to $60,000. Things appear to be turning around this year, and Shakira Inc. repaid Shakira $20,000 of the $100,000 outstanding loan. What is Shakira's income, if any, on the partial loan repayment? LO 11-4 planning

62. Adam Fleeman, a skilled carpenter, started a home improvement business with Tom Collins, a master plumber. Adam and Tom are concerned about the payroll taxes they will have to pay. Assume they form an S corporation and each earns a salary of $80,000 from the corporation; in addition, they expect their share of business profits to be $60,000 each. How much Social Security tax and Medicare tax (or self-employment tax) will Adam, Tom, and their corporation have to pay on their salary and profits? LO 11-4

LO 11-4 

63. Using the facts in problem 62, could Adam and Tom lower their payroll tax exposure if they operated their business as a partnership? Why or why not?

LO 11-4

64. This year, Justin B.'s share of S corporation income includes $4,000 of interest income, $5,000 of dividend income, and $40,000 of net income from the corporation's professional service business activity.
    a) Assume that Justin B. materially participates in the S corporation. How much of his S corporation income is potentially subject to the net investment income tax?
    b) Assume that Justin B. does not materially participate in the S corporation. How much of his S corporation income is potentially subject to the net investment income tax?

LO 11-4

65. Friends Jackie (0.5 percent owner), Jermaine (1 percent owner), Marlon (2 percent owner), Janet (86 percent owner), and Tito (10.5 percent owner) are shareholders in Jackson 5 Inc. (an S corporation). As employees of the company, each receives health insurance ($10,000 per year benefit), dental insurance ($2,000 per year benefit), and free access to a workout facility located at company headquarters ($500 per year benefit). What are the tax consequences of these benefits for each shareholder and for Jackson 5 Inc.?

LO 11-5

66. Maple Corp., a calendar-year corporation, was formed three years ago by its sole shareholder, Jian, who immediately elected S corporation status. On December 31 of the current year, Maple distributed $30,000 cash to Jian. What are the amount and character of gain Jian must recognize on the distribution in each of the following alternative scenarios?
    a) At the time of the distribution, Jian's basis in his Maple Corp. stock was $35,000.
    b) At the time of the distribution, Jian's basis in his Maple Corp. stock was $8,000.
    c) At the time of the distribution, Jian's basis in his Maple Corp. stock was $0.

LO 11-5

67. Oak Corp., a calendar-year corporation, was formed three years ago by its sole shareholder, Glover, and has always operated as a C corporation. However, at the beginning of this year, Glover made a qualifying S election for Oak Corp., effective January 1. Oak Corp. did not have any C corporation earnings and profits on that date. On June 1, Oak Corp. distributed $15,000 to Glover. What are the amount and character of gain Glover must recognize on the distribution, and what is his basis in his Oak Corp. stock in each of the following alternative scenarios?
    a) At the time of the distribution, Glover's basis in his Oak Corp. stock was $35,000.
    b) At the time of the distribution, Glover's basis in his Oak Corp. stock was $8,000.
    c) At the time of the distribution, Glover's basis in his Oak Corp. stock was $0.

LO 11-5

68. On January 1, 2022, Janna has a tax basis of $15,000 in her Mimikaki stock (Mimikaki has been an S corporation since inception). In 2022, Janna was allocated $20,000 of ordinary income from Mimikaki. What are the amount and character of gain she recognizes from end-of-the-year distributions in each of the following alternative scenarios, and what is her stock basis following each distribution?
    a) Mimikaki distributes $10,000 to Janna.
    b) Mimikaki distributes $20,000 to Janna.
    c) Mimikaki distributes $30,000 to Janna.
    d) Mimikaki distributes $40,000 to Janna.

LO 11-5

69. Assume the following year 2 income statement for Johnstone Corporation, which was a C corporation in year 1 and elected to be taxed as an S corporation beginning in year 2. Johnstone's earnings and profits at the end of year 1 were $10,000. Marcus is Johnstone's sole shareholder, and he has a stock basis of $40,000 at the end of year 1. What is Johnstone's accumulated adjustments account at the end of

year 2, and what amount of dividend income does Marcus recognize on the year 2 distribution in each of the following alternative scenarios?

Johnstone Corporation
Income Statement
December 31, Year 2

	Year 2 (S Corporation)
Sales revenue	$150,000
Cost of goods sold	(35,000)
Salary to owners	(60,000)
Employee wages	(50,000)
Depreciation expense	(4,000)
Miscellaneous expenses	(4,000)
Interest income	10,000
Overall net income	$ 7,000

a) Johnstone distributed $6,000 to Marcus in year 2.
b) Johnstone distributed $10,000 to Marcus in year 2.
c) Johnstone distributed $16,000 to Marcus in year 2.
d) Johnstone distributed $26,000 to Marcus in year 2.

70. At the end of the year, before distributions, Bombay (an S corporation) has an accumulated adjustments account balance of $15,000 and accumulated E&P of $20,000 from a previous year as a C corporation. During the year, Nicolette (a 40 percent shareholder) received a $20,000 distribution (the remaining shareholders received $30,000 in distributions). What are the amount and character of gain Nicolette must recognize from the distribution? What is her basis in her Bombay stock at the end of the year? (Assume her stock basis is $40,000 after considering her share of Bombay's income for the year but before considering the effects of the distribution.) LO 11-5

71. Pine Corp., a calendar-year corporation, was formed three years ago by its sole shareholder, Alejandro, who has always operated it as a C corporation. However, at the beginning of this year, Alejandro made a qualifying S election for Pine Corp., effective January 1. Pine Corp. reported $70,000 of C corporation earnings and profits on the effective date of the S election. This year (its first S corporation year), Pine Corp. reported business income of $50,000. Alejandro's basis in his Pine Corp. stock at the beginning of the year was $15,000. What are the amount and character of income or gain Alejandro must recognize on the following alternative distributions, and what is his basis in his Pine Corp. stock at the end of the year? LO 11-5

a) Alejandro received a $40,000 distribution from Pine Corp. at the end of the year.
b) Alejandro received a $60,000 distribution from Pine Corp. at the end of the year.
c) Alejandro received a $130,000 distribution from Pine Corp. at the end of the year.
d) Alejandro received a $150,000 distribution from Pine Corp. at the end of the year.

72. Carolina Corporation, an S corporation, has no corporate E&P from its years as a C corporation. At the end of the year, it distributes a small parcel of land to its sole shareholder, Shadiya. The fair market value of the parcel is $70,000, and its tax basis is $40,000. Shadiya's basis in her stock is $14,000. Assume Carolina Corporation reported $0 taxable income before considering the tax consequences of the distribution. LO 11-5

a) What amount of gain or loss, if any, does Carolina Corporation recognize on the distribution?
b) How much gain must Shadiya recognize (if any) as a result of the distribution, what is her basis in her Carolina Corporation stock after the distribution, and what is her basis in the land?

c) What is your answer to part (a) if the fair market value of the land is $25,000 rather than $70,000?

d) What is your answer to part (b) if the fair market value of the land is $25,000 rather than $70,000?

LO 11-5

73. Miley decided to terminate the S corporation election of her solely owned corporation on October 17, 2021 (effective immediately), in preparation for taking it public. Miley had previously elected S corporation status on January 1, 2020. At the time of the election, the corporation had an accumulated adjustments account balance of $150,000 and $450,000 of accumulated E&P from prior C corporation years, and Miley had a basis in her S corporation stock of $135,000. During 2022, Miley's corporation reported $0 taxable income or loss. Also, during 2022 the corporation made distributions to Miley of $80,000 and $60,000. How are these distributions taxed to Miley assuming the following?

a) Both distributions are in cash. The first was paid on June 15, 2022, and the second was paid on November 15, 2022.

b) Both distributions are in cash. The first was paid on June 15, 2022, and the second was paid on September 30, 2022.

c) Assume the same facts as in part (b), except the June 15 distribution was a property (noncash) distribution (fair market value of distributed property equal to basis).

LO 11-6

74. Alabama Corporation, an S corporation, liquidates this year by distributing a parcel of land to its sole shareholder, Mark Ingram. The fair market value of the parcel is $50,000, and its tax basis is $30,000. Mark's basis in his stock is $25,000.

a) What amount of gain or loss, if any, does Alabama Corporation recognize on the distribution?

b) How much gain must Mark recognize (if any) as a result of the distribution, and what is his basis in the land?

c) What is your answer to part (a) if the fair market value of the land is $20,000 rather than $50,000?

d) What is your answer to part (b) if the fair market value of the land is $20,000 rather than $50,000?

LO 11-6

75. Rivendell Corporation uses the accrual method of accounting and has the following assets as of the end of 2021. Rivendell converted to an S corporation on January 1, 2022.

Asset	Adjusted Basis	FMV
Cash	$ 40,000	$ 40,000
Accounts receivable	30,000	30,000
Inventory	130,000	60,000
Land	100,000	125,000
Totals	$300,000	$255,000

a) What is Rivendell's net unrealized built-in gain at the time it converted to an S corporation?

b) Assuming the land was valued at $200,000, what would be Rivendell's net unrealized gain at the time it converted to an S corporation?

c) Assuming the land was valued at $125,000 but that the inventory was valued at $85,000, what would be Rivendell's net unrealized gain at the time it converted to an S corporation?

LO 11-6

76. Virginia Corporation is a calendar-year corporation. At the beginning of 2022, its election to be taxed as an S corporation became effective. Virginia Corp.'s balance sheet at the end of 2021 reflected the following assets (it did not have any earnings and profits from its prior years as a C corporation).

Asset	Adjusted Basis	FMV
Cash	$ 20,000	$ 20,000
Accounts receivable	40,000	40,000
Inventory	90,000	200,000
Land	150,000	175,000
Totals	$300,000	$435,000

In 2022, Virginia Corp. reported business income of $50,000 (this would have been its taxable income if it were still a C corporation). What is Virginia's built-in gains tax in each of the following alternative scenarios?

a) During 2022, Virginia Corp. sold inventory it owned at the beginning of the year for $100,000. The basis of the inventory sold was $55,000.

b) Assume the same facts as in part (a), except Virginia Corp. had a net operating loss carryover of $24,000 from its time as a C corporation.

c) Assume the same facts as in part (a), except that if Virginia Corp. were a C corporation, its taxable income would have been $1,500.

77. Tempe Corporation is a calendar-year corporation. At the beginning of 2022, its election to be taxed as an S corporation became effective. Tempe Corp.'s balance sheet at the end of 2021 reflected the following assets (it did not have any earnings and profits from its prior years as a C corporation): LO 11-6

Asset	Adjusted Basis	FMV
Cash	$ 20,000	$ 20,000
Accounts receivable	40,000	40,000
Inventory	160,000	200,000
Land	150,000	120,000
Totals	$370,000	$380,000

Tempe Corp.'s business income for the year was $40,000 (this would have been its taxable income if it were a C corporation). During 2022, Tempe Corp. sold all of the inventory it owned at the beginning of the year for $210,000.

a) What is its built-in gains tax in 2022?

b) Assume the original facts, except that if Tempe Corp. were a C corporation, its taxable income would have been $7,000. What is its built-in gains tax in 2022?

c) Assume the original facts, except the land was valued at $140,000 instead of $120,000. What is Tempe Corp.'s built-in gains tax in 2022?

78. Wood Corporation was a C corporation in 2021 but elected to be taxed as an S corporation in 2022. At the end of 2021, its earnings and profits were $15,500. The following table reports Wood Corp.'s (taxable) income for 2022 (its first year as an S corporation). LO 11-6

Wood Corporation Income Statement December 31, 2022	
Sales revenue	$150,000
Cost of goods sold	(35,000)
Salary to owners	(60,000)
Employee wages	(50,000)
Depreciation expense	(4,000)
Miscellaneous expenses	(4,000)
Interest income	8,000
Qualified dividend income	2,000
Overall net income	$ 7,000

What is Wood Corporation's excess net passive income tax for 2022?

LO 11-6

79. Calculate Anaheim Corporation's excess net passive income tax in each of the following alternative scenarios:

   a) Passive investment income, $100,000; expenses associated with passive investment income, $40,000; gross receipts, $120,000; taxable income if a C corporation, $40,000; corporate E&P, $30,000.

   b) Passive investment income, $100,000; expenses associated with passive investment income, $70,000; gross receipts, $120,000; taxable income if a C corporation, $1,200; corporate E&P, $30,000.

   c) Passive investment income, $100,000; expenses associated with passive investment income, $40,000; gross receipts, $120,000; taxable income if a C corporation, $40,000; corporate E&P, $0.

LO 11-5 LO 11-6 planning

80. Inuk is the sole shareholder of Tex Corporation. Inuk first formed Tex as a C corporation. However, in an attempt to avoid having Tex's income double-taxed, Inuk elected S corporation status for Tex several years ago. On December 31, 2022, Tex reports $5,000 of earnings and profits from its years as a C corporation and $50,000 in its accumulated adjustments account from its activities as an S corporation (including its 2022 activities). Inuk discovered that for the first time Tex was going to have to pay the excess net passive income tax. Inuk wanted to avoid having to pay the tax, but he determined the only way to avoid the tax was to eliminate Tex's E&P by the end of 2022. He determined that, because of the distribution ordering rules (AAA first), he would need to have Tex immediately (in 2022) distribute $55,000 to him. This would clear out Tex's accumulated adjustments account first and then eliminate Tex's C corporation earnings and profits in time to avoid the excess net passive income tax. Inuk was not sure Tex could come up with $55,000 of cash or property in time to accomplish his objective. Does Inuk have any other options to eliminate Tex's earnings and profits without first distributing the balance in Tex's accumulated adjustments account?

LO 11-6 planning

81. Farve Inc. recently elected S corporation status. At the time of the election, the company had $10,000 of accumulated earnings and profits and a net unrealized gain of $1,000,000 associated with land it had invested in (although some parcels had an unrealized loss). In the next couple of years, most of the income the company expects to generate will be in the form of interest and dividends (approximately $200,000 per year). However, in the future, the company will want to liquidate some of its current holdings in land and possibly reinvest in other parcels. What strategies can you recommend for Farve Inc. to help reduce its potential tax liability as an S corporation?

LO 11-6

82. Until the end of year 0, Magic Carpets (MC) was a C corporation with a calendar year-end. At the beginning of year 1, it elected to be taxed as an S corporation. MC uses the LIFO method to value its inventory. At the end of year 0, under the LIFO method, its inventory of rugs was valued at $150,000. Under the FIFO method, the rugs would have been valued at $170,000. How much LIFO recapture tax must MC pay, and what is the due date of the first payment under the following alternative scenarios?

   a) MC's regular taxable income in year 0 was $65,000.

   b) MC's regular taxable income in year 0 was $200,000.

COMPREHENSIVE PROBLEMS

Select problems are available in Connect®.

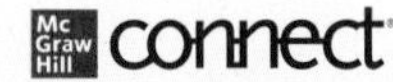

planning

83. Knowshon, sole owner of Moreno Inc., is contemplating electing S status for the corporation (Moreno Inc. is currently taxed as a C corporation). Provide recommendations related to Knowshon's election under the following alternative scenarios:

   a) At the end of the current year, Moreno Inc. has a net operating loss of $800,000 carryover from 2021. Beginning next year, the company expects to return to profitability. Knowshon projects that Moreno will report profits of $400,000, $500,000, and $600,000 over the next three years. What suggestions do you have regarding the timing of the S election? Explain.

b) How would you answer part (a) if Moreno Inc. had been operating profitably for several years and thus had no net operating loss?

c) While several of Moreno Inc.'s assets have appreciated in value (to the tune of $2,000,000), the corporation has one property—some land in a newly identified flood zone—that has declined in value by $1,500,000. Knowshon plans on selling the loss property in the next year or two. Assume that Moreno does not have a net operating loss. What suggestions do you have for timing the sale of the flood zone property, and why?

84. Barry Porter and Winnie Weeks are considering making an S election on March 1, 2023, for their C corporation, Omniocular. However, first they want to consider the implications of the following information: **planning**

- Winnie is a U.S. citizen and resident.
- Barry is a citizen of the United Kingdom but a resident of the United States.
- Barry and Winnie each owns 50 percent of the voting power in Omniocular. However, Barry's stock provides him with a claim on 60 percent of the Omniocular assets in liquidation.
- Omniocular was formed under Arizona state law, but it plans on eventually conducting some business in Mexico.

a) Is Omniocular eligible to elect S corporation status? If so, when is the election effective?

For the remainder of the problem, assume Omniocular made a valid S election effective January 1, 2023. Barry and Winnie each owns 50 percent of the voting power and has an equal claim on Omniocular's assets in liquidation. In addition, consider the following information:

- Omniocular reports on a calendar tax year.
- Omniocular's earnings and profits as of December 31, 2022, were $55,000.
- Omniocular's 2022 taxable income was $15,000.
- Omniocular's assets at the end of 2022 are as follows:

Omniocular Assets
December 31, 2022

Asset	Adjusted Basis	FMV
Cash	$ 50,000	$ 50,000
Accounts receivable	20,000	20,000
Investments in stocks and bonds	700,000	700,000
Investment in land	90,000	100,000
Inventory (LIFO)	80,000*	125,000
Equipment	40,000	35,000
Totals	$980,000	$1,030,000

*$110,000 under FIFO accounting.

- On March 31, 2023, Omniocular sold the land for $42,000.
- In 2023, Omniocular sold all the inventory it had on hand at the beginning of the year. This was the only inventory it sold during the year.

Other Income/Expense Items for 2023	
Sales revenue	$155,000
Salary to owners	(50,000)
Employee wages	(10,000)
Depreciation expense	(5,000)
Miscellaneous expenses	(1,000)
Interest income	40,000
Qualified dividend income	65,000

- Assume that if Omniocular were a C corporation for 2023, its taxable income would have been $88,500.

b) How much LIFO recapture tax is Omniocular required to pay, and when is it due?
c) How much built-in gains tax, if any, is Omniocular required to pay?
d) How much excess net passive income tax, if any, is Omniocular required to pay?
e) Assume Barry's basis in his Omniocular stock was $40,000 on January 1, 2023. What is his stock basis on December 31, 2023?

For the following questions, assume that after electing S corporation status, Barry and Winnie had a change of heart and filed an election to terminate Omniocular's S election, effective August 1, 2024.

- In 2024, Omniocular reported the following income/expense items:

Description	January 1—July 31, 2024 (213 days)	August 1—December 31, 2024 (153 days)	January 1—December 31, 2024
Sales revenue	$ 80,000	$185,000	$265,000
Cost of goods sold	(40,000)	(20,000)	(60,000)
Salaries to Barry and Winnie	(60,000)	(40,000)	(100,000)
Depreciation expense	(7,000)	(2,000)	(9,000)
Miscellaneous expenses	(4,000)	(3,000)	(7,000)
Interest income	6,000	5,250	11,250
Overall net income (loss)	$(25,000)	$125,250	$100,250

f) For tax purposes, how would you recommend Barry and Winnie allocate income between the short S corporation year and the short C corporation year if they would like to minimize double taxation of Omniocular's income?
g) Assume in part (f) that Omniocular allocates income between the short S and C corporation years in a way that minimizes the double taxation of its income. If Barry's stock basis in his Omniocular stock on January 1, 2024, is $50,000, what is his stock basis on December 31, 2024?
h) When is the earliest tax year in which Omniocular can be taxed as an S corporation again?

85. Agustina, Bobby, and Claudia are equal owners in Lafter, an S corporation that was a C corporation several years ago. While Agustina and Bobby actively participate in running the company, Claudia has a separate day job and is a passive owner. Consider the following information for 2022:

- As of January 1, 2022, Agustina, Bobby, and Claudia each has a basis in Lafter stock of $15,000 and a debt basis of $0. On January 1, the stock basis is also the at-risk amount for each shareholder.
- Bobby and Claudia also are passive owners in Aggressive LLC, which allocated business income of $14,000 to each of them in 2022. Neither has any other source of passive income (besides Lafter, for Claudia).

- On March 31, 2022, Agustina lends $5,000 of her own money to Lafter.
- Anticipating the need for basis to deduct a loss, on April 4, 2022, Bobby takes out a $10,000 loan to make a $10,000 capital contribution to Lafter. Bobby uses his automobile ($12,000 fair market value) as the sole collateral for his loan (nonrecourse).
- Lafter has an accumulated adjustments account balance of $45,000 as of January 1, 2022.
- Lafter has C corporation earnings and profits of $15,000 as of January 1, 2022.
- During 2022, Lafter reports a business loss of $75,000, computed as follows:

Sales revenue	$ 90,000
Cost of goods sold	(85,000)
Salary to Agustina	(40,000)
Salary to Bobby	(40,000)
Business (loss)	$(75,000)

- Lafter also reported $12,000 of tax-exempt interest income.

a) What amount of Lafter's 2022 business loss of $75,000 are Agustina, Bobby, and Claudia allowed to deduct on their individual tax returns? What are each owner's stock basis and debt basis (if applicable) and each owner's at-risk amount with respect to the investment in Lafter at the end of 2022?

- During 2023, Lafter made several changes to its business approach and reported $18,000 of business income, computed as follows:

Sales revenue	$208,000
Cost of goods sold	(90,000)
Salary to Agustina	(45,000)
Salary to Bobby	(45,000)
Marketing expense	(10,000)
Business income	$ 18,000

- Lafter also reported a long-term capital gain of $24,000 in 2023.
- Lafter made a cash distribution on July 1, 2023, of $20,000 to each shareholder.

b) What amount of gain/income does each shareholder recognize from the cash distribution on July 1, 2023?

86. While James Craig and his former classmate Paul Dolittle both studied accounting at school, they ended up pursuing careers in professional cake decorating. Their company, Good to Eat (GTE), specializes in custom-sculpted cakes for weddings, birthdays, and other celebrations. James and Paul formed the business at the beginning of 2022, and each contributed $50,000 in exchange for a 50 percent ownership interest. GTE also borrowed $200,000 from a local bank. Both James and Paul had to personally guarantee the loan. Both owners provide significant services for the business. The following information pertains to GTE's 2022 activities:

- GTE uses the cash method of accounting (for both book and tax purposes) and reports income on a calendar-year basis.
- GTE received $450,000 of sales revenue and reported $210,000 of cost of goods sold (it did not have any ending inventory).
- GTE paid $30,000 compensation to James, $30,000 compensation to Paul, and $40,000 of compensation to other employees (assume these amounts include applicable payroll taxes, if any).
- GTE paid $15,000 of rent for a building and equipment, $20,000 for advertising, $14,000 in interest expense, $4,000 for utilities, and $2,000 for supplies.

- GTE contributed $5,000 to charity.
- GTE received a $1,000 qualified dividend from a great stock investment (it owned 2 percent of the corporation distributing the dividend), and it recognized $1,500 in short-term capital gain when it sold some of the stock.
- On December 1, 2022, GTE distributed $20,000 to James and $20,000 to Paul.
- GTE has qualified property of $300,000 (unadjusted basis).

Required:

a) Assume James and Paul formed GTE as an S corporation.

- Complete GTE's Form 1120-S, page 1; Form 1120-S, Schedule K; and Paul's Form 1120-S, Schedule K-1 (note that you should use 2021 tax forms).
- Compute the tax basis of Paul's stock in GTE at the end of 2022.
- What amount of Paul's income from GTE is subject to FICA or self-employment taxes?
- What amount of income, including its character, will Paul recognize on the $20,000 distribution he receives on December 1?
- What amount of tax does GTE pay on the $1,000 qualified dividend it received?

b) Assume James and Paul formed GTE as an LLC.

- Complete GTE's Form 1065, page 1; Form 1065, Schedule K; and Paul's Form 1065, Schedule K-1 (note that you should use 2021 tax forms).
- Compute the tax basis of Paul's ownership interest in GTE at the end of 2022.
- What amount of Paul's income from GTE is subject to FICA or self-employment taxes?
- What amount of income, including its character, will Paul recognize on the $20,000 distribution he receives on December 1?
- What amount of tax does GTE pay on the $1,000 qualified dividend it received?

c) Assume James and Paul formed GTE as a C corporation.

- Complete GTE's Form 1120, page 1 (note that you should use the 2021 tax form).
- Compute the tax basis of Paul's stock in GTE at the end of 2022.
- What amount of Paul's income from GTE is subject to FICA or self-employment taxes?
- What amount of income, including its character, will Paul recognize on the $20,000 distribution he receives on December 1?
- What amount of tax does GTE pay on the $1,000 qualified dividend it received?

UWorld Roger CPA Review

Sample CPA Exam questions from Roger CPA Review are available in Connect as support for the topics in this text. These Multiple Choice Questions and Task-Based Simulations include expert-written explanations and solutions and provide a starting point for students to become familiar with the content and functionality of the actual CPA Exam.

chapter

12 State and Local Taxes

Learning Objectives

Upon completing this chapter, you should be able to:

LO 12-1 Describe the primary types of state and local taxes.

LO 12-2 Determine whether a business has sales tax nexus and calculate its sales tax withholding responsibilities.

LO 12-3 Identify whether a business has income tax nexus and determine its state income tax liabilities.

Robert Dziewulski/dziewul/123RF

Storyline Summary

Taxpayer:	Ken Brody (he/him/his)
Location:	Idaho
Status:	Sole owner of Wild West River Runners Inc., a C corporation
Situation:	Ken owns retail stores in Idaho and Wyoming that sell merchandise locally; operates a Wyoming-based Internet store; and provides services in Idaho, Tennessee, Washington, and Wyoming. He must determine the company's state and local tax liabilities.

Ken Brody owns Wild West River Runners Incorporated (Wild West), an Idaho C corporation. Wild West offers guided white-water rafting adventures in Idaho, Tennessee, Washington, and Wyoming. It also operates retail stores in Idaho and Wyoming and an Internet-based retail store based in Wyoming. Wild West's retail stores sell only locally (they never ship merchandise), but the salesclerks often refer customers to the Internet store (www.wildwestriverrunners.com). Most employees are seasonal (teachers or college students). During the off-season, a few guides make sales visits with Ken and operate the retail stores. Also during the off-season, Ken attends the annual 10-day Raft and River Show in Phoenix, Arizona, and travels the country promoting Wild West's guided river adventures.

Wild West's Form 1120, U.S. Corporation Income Tax Return, shows federal taxable income for the current year of $53,289, and it must calculate its state and local tax liabilities. Because Wild West operates a multistate business, it must identify the states in which it must collect sales tax, collect the sales tax and remit it to the respective states, determine the states in which it must file income tax returns, and file income tax returns reflecting its taxable income for each state in which it must file. ■

Like a lot of other businesses, Wild West is a multistate operation. From a business perspective, multistate businesses generally have access to a larger economic base than those operating in a single state. However, with this economic opportunity come complexity and additional tax burdens.

LO 12-1

STATE AND LOCAL TAXES

The primary purpose of state and local taxes is to raise revenue to finance state and local governments. All 50 states and the District of Columbia have some combination of three primary revenue sources: sales and use tax, income or franchise tax, and property tax.[1] This chapter focuses on sales and use taxes (i.e., excise taxes levied on the sale or use of tangible personal property within a state) and taxes based on *net* income (i.e., income taxes).[2]

Like federal tax law, state tax law includes the following:

- Legislative law (state constitution and tax code).
- Administrative law (regulations and rulings).
- Judicial law (tax court cases).

While businesses deal with a single federal tax code, there are different tax codes or laws for each state. This makes state tax research particularly challenging. State tax agencies, such as the California Franchise Tax Board and the New York Department of Finance and Taxation, administer the law and promulgate regulations for their particular states.[3] Federal and state courts interpret the law when a state's tax authority and businesses cannot agree on its interpretation or constitutionality. Because of constitutionality questions, judicial law plays a significantly more important role in state tax law than in federal tax law. It is impractical, if not impossible, to study each individual state statute in one text. Instead, this chapter addresses the most important state and local tax principles at a conceptual level.

The most important question Wild West, or any other business, must answer is whether it is subject to a state's taxing regime. The answer depends on the business's state of **commercial domicile** and whether the business has **nexus** (either sales tax nexus or income tax nexus) in that state. We will discuss both sales tax nexus and income tax nexus in this chapter. Commercial domicile is the state where a business is headquartered and directs its operations; this location may be different from the place of incorporation.[4] A business must always collect and remit sales tax from its customers and pay income tax in the state where it is domiciled. **Nondomiciliary businesses**—businesses not domiciled or headquartered in a state—are subject to taxing authorities only where they have nexus. Nexus is the sufficient (or minimum) connection between a business and a state that subjects the business to the state's tax system.

Wild West's commercial domicile is Idaho because it is headquartered there. Consequently, it must collect and remit Idaho sales tax and pay Idaho income tax. Yet, as detailed in Exhibit 12-1, it has activities and sales in other states, and therefore it must collect sales tax and pay income tax in the states in which it has nexus.

[1]State and local jurisdictions may also tax or levy the following: personal property, capital stock, business licensing, transfer, incorporation, excise, severance, payroll, disability, unemployment, fuel, and telecommunication.

[2]This chapter discusses corporate income and franchise taxes interchangeably. Franchise taxes are imposed for the right to conduct business within a state. Most franchise taxes (such as the California Franchise Tax) are calculated based on net income.

[3]A great resource for guidance and forms from specific states can be found on the Federation of Tax Administrators website, www.taxadmin.org/state-tax-forms.

[4]Some companies (e.g., Adobe Inc.) are incorporated in one state (e.g., Delaware) but domiciled or headquartered in another (e.g., California). These companies pay taxes in both states (although sometimes just a capital stock tax applies in the state of incorporation if there are no activities other than incorporation within a state).

EXHIBIT 12-1 **Wild West's Activities and Sales by State**

Wild West In-State Activities					
State	**Sale of Goods**	**Sale of Services**	**Employees**	**Property**	**Commercial Domicile**
Arizona	✓				
California	✓				
Colorado	✓				
Idaho	✓	✓	✓	✓	✓
Tennessee	✓	✓	✓	✓	
Washington	✓	✓	✓	✓	
Wyoming	✓	✓	✓	✓	

Wild West Sales				
State	**Goods**	**Services**	**Total**	**Transactions**
Arizona	$ 89,242	$ 0	$ 89,242	215
California	132,045	0	132,045	489
Colorado	75,002	0	75,002	163
Idaho	167,921	625,003	792,924	1,043
Tennessee	45,331	357,061	402,392	753
Washington	41,982	377,441	419,423	812
Wyoming	185,249	437,755	623,004	941
Totals	$736,772	$1,797,260	$2,534,032	4,416

When a business sells tangible personal property that is included in a state's sales tax base, it must collect and remit the **sales tax** on a periodic basis if it has sales tax nexus in that state.[5] Exhibit 12-2 provides an overview of who bears the burden of sales taxes (i.e., who must pay and who must collect and remit sales tax to the state). Sales tax liability accrues on certain sales of tangible personal property within the state. For example, Wild West's Idaho retail store collects sales tax on goods sold in Idaho stores and remits the tax

EXHIBIT 12-2 **State Sales and Use Tax Process**

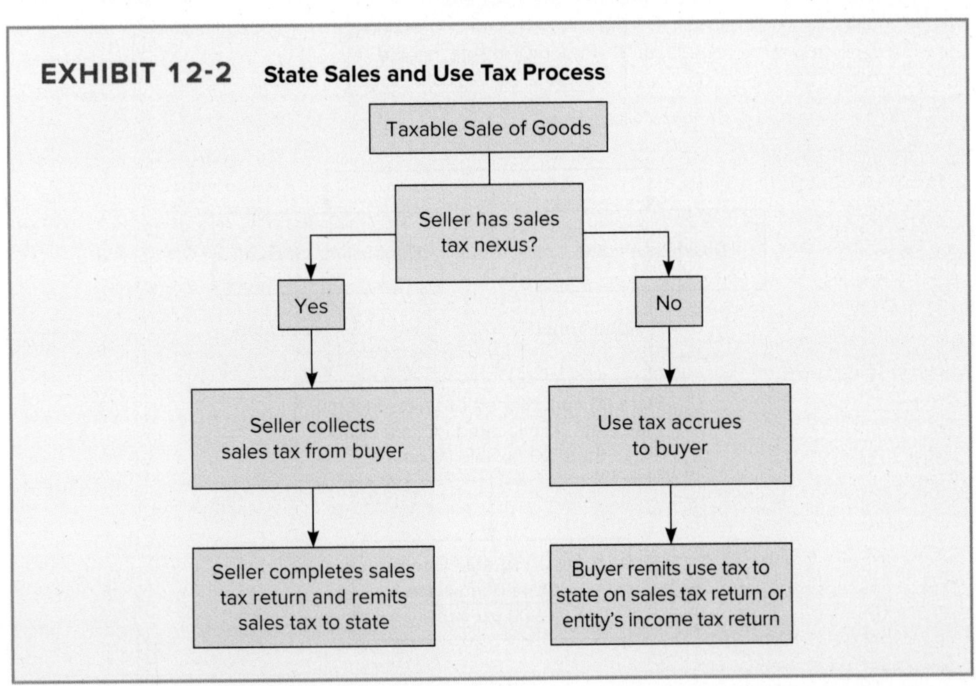

[5]Businesses remit the sales taxes collected from customers to the state on a sales tax return, which is filed on a monthly, quarterly, or annual basis depending on the size of the liability and the state law thresholds.

to the Idaho Department of Revenue. **Use tax** liability accrues in the state where purchased property will be used when no sales tax was paid at the time of purchase. The use tax applies only when a seller in one state ships goods to a customer in a different state and the seller is not required to collect the sales tax (i.e., the seller does not have sales tax nexus in the state to which the goods are shipped). For example, Colorado customers ordering through Wild West's Wyoming-based Internet store (which has no Colorado sales tax nexus) are required to accrue and remit the Colorado use tax (i.e., usually through their personal income tax returns).[6] Businesses with sales tax nexus in a state are legally responsible for remitting the sales tax even when they fail to collect it, and they generally record the sales tax liability on their financial statements.

Businesses engaged in **interstate commerce** must also deal with income tax–related issues. If a business meets certain requirements creating income tax nexus, it may be required to remit income tax to that state. The general process of determining a business's state income tax liability is highlighted in Exhibit 12-3. The **state tax base** is computed by making adjustments to federal taxable income. The adjustments are necessary to account for differences between federal income tax laws and state income tax laws. Then we divide the state tax base into **business income** and **nonbusiness income.** Business income (i.e., income from business activities) is subject to **apportionment** among states where income tax nexus and a filing requirement exist, based on the extent of the business's activities and property in various states. Nonbusiness income (i.e., all income except business income—generally investment income) is subject to **allocation,** or assignment directly to the business's state of commercial domicile. For states in which the business has income tax nexus and a filing requirement, state taxable income is the sum of the business income apportioned to that state plus the nonbusiness income allocated to that state. The business computes its state tax liability for that particular state by multiplying state taxable income by the state's tax rate.

Let's now look in more depth at sales tax and net income–based taxes, the nexus requirements, and the calculation of each tax.

EXHIBIT 12-3 **State Income Tax Process**

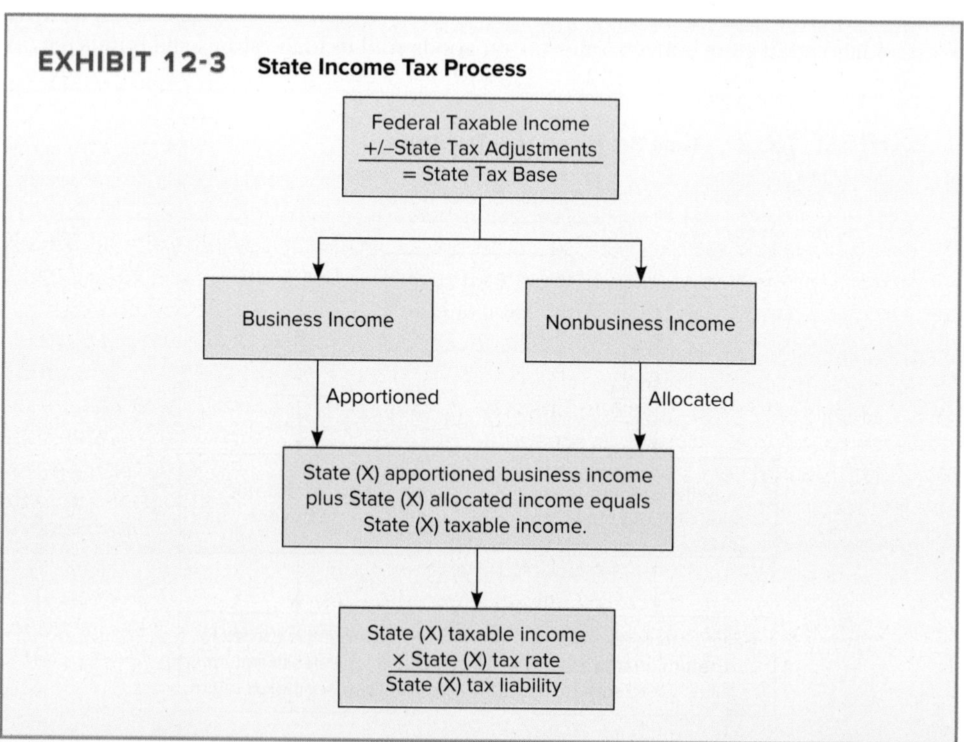

[6]Individuals remit their use tax by adding their use tax liability to a line on their individual income tax return. Businesses remit their use tax by adding it to any sales tax collected from customers on their sales and use tax return.

SALES AND USE TAXES

LO 12-2

Forty-five states and the District of Columbia impose sales taxes; Alaska, Delaware, Montana, New Hampshire, and Oregon do not. Sales tax must be collected on the state's sales tax base. Generally, sales of tangible personal property are subject to the tax. Most states also tax restaurant meals, rental car usage, hotel room rentals (often at higher tax rates than general sales), and some services (which vary widely by state). Purchases of inventory for resale are generally exempt from the sales tax.[7] For example, Wild West's rafting equipment purchases for resale are exempt from sales tax because inventory is taxed when sold, but the office furniture purchased for use in the business is taxable because it represents a final sale. Items that are included in the sales tax base vary from state to state. Many states exempt food (except prepared restaurant food) because taxing food is considered to be regressive; that is, it imposes a proportionally higher tax burden on lower-income taxpayers, who spend a greater proportion of their income on food and other necessities. Most states also exempt sales of real property, intangible property, and services. However, many states are expanding the types of services subject to sales tax in order to increase their sales tax revenue.[8]

TAXES IN THE REAL WORLD Is It Candy or Is It Food?

Items subject to the sales tax vary from state to state. Historically, New York taxed the sale of large marshmallows but exempted the sale of small marshmallows. Large and small marshmallows were treated differently because large marshmallows were considered to be candy, which was included in the sales tax base, while small marshmallows were considered to be a food ingredient and therefore excluded from the sales tax base. Currently, all marshmallows are taxed as a food ingredient.

The Washington state legislature passed a law subjecting candy to sales tax a few years ago. Any item containing flour was considered a food item, not candy. As a result, Twix bars were exempt because the cookie has flour as an ingredient, while Starburst candy was subject to sales tax. Within a year, Washington voters repealed the tax on candy through a ballot initiative.

Sales Tax Nexus

Have you ever wondered why sometimes you pay sales tax on goods purchased over the Internet and sometimes you don't? The answer is it depends on whether the seller has **sales tax nexus** in the state where the goods are being shipped to. A business is required to collect sales tax from customers in a state only if it has sales tax nexus in the destination state. For example, if you purchase a book from a local bookstore, you will pay sales tax, but if you purchase the book from some online sellers, you won't pay sales tax unless the book is being shipped to a state where the seller has sales tax nexus. As a result, understanding when a business has sales tax nexus can be extremely important for profitability, business modeling, and compliance. Exhibit 12-4 provides an excerpt from the 2020 annual report for Wayfair, a prominent online seller, in which it describes how the Court's Wayfair decision is not expected to have a significant impact on its business.

The Commerce Clause of the U.S. Constitution gives Congress the authority "[t]o regulate Commerce with foreign Nations, and among the several States, and with the Indian Tribes." The purpose of the Commerce Clause is to place limits on taxation to enhance or increase interstate commerce. Because Congress has never exercised its Commerce Clause right with respect to sales tax, the courts have historically determined sales tax nexus thresholds. Businesses that establish sales tax nexus with a state but fail to properly collect sales tax and remit it to the state can create significant liabilities that may need to be disclosed for financial reporting purposes.[9]

THE KEY FACTS

Sales Tax Nexus

- Nexus is the sufficient connection between a business and a state that allows a state to levy a tax on the business.
- Historically, sales tax nexus was established through the physical presence of salespeople or property within a state.
- On June 21, 2018, the Supreme Court ruled that economic nexus is also established for an online seller when either $100,000 of sales or 200 sales transactions are made to customers within a state during a year.

[7]Most states grant a reseller's certificate, which exempts purchases of inventory for resale from sales tax.

[8]For example, Connecticut taxes services such as tax preparation.

[9]Sales tax liabilities are ASC Topic 450 contingencies.

EXHIBIT 12-4 Excerpt from Wayfair's 2020 Annual Report

From the Form 10-K

Collection of Sales or Other Similar Taxes

Wayfair has historically collected and remitted sales tax based on the locations of its physical operations. On June 21, 2018, the U.S. Supreme Court rendered a 5-4 majority decision in South Dakota v. Wayfair Inc., 17-494. Among other things, the Court held that a state may require an out-of-state seller with no physical presence in the state to collect and remit sales taxes on goods the seller ships to consumers in the state, overturning existing court precedent. Several states and other taxing jurisdictions have presented, or indicated that they may present, Wayfair with sales tax assessments. The aggregate assessments received as of December 31, 2020 are not material to Wayfair's business and Wayfair does not expect the Court's decision to have a significant impact on its business.

Source: Wayfair 2020 Annual Report.

Prior to June 21, 2018, sales tax nexus was established through a business having *physical presence* within a state. Physical presence was established through either (1) salespeople (or independent contractors representing a business) entering a state to obtain sales or (2) tangible property (such as a company-owned truck that made deliveries) being located within a state.[10] In *National Bellas Hess* (1967), the U.S. Supreme Court held that an out-of-state mail-order company (nondomiciliary) did not have a sales tax collection responsibility because it lacked physical presence (even though it mailed catalogs and advertised in the state).[11] Subsequently, in *Quill Corp.* (1992), the U.S. Supreme Court reaffirmed that out-of-state (nondomiciliary) businesses must have a physical presence in the state before the state may require a business to collect sales tax from in-state customers.[12]

On June 21, 2018, the U.S. Supreme Court reversed its physical presence standard for online sellers in favor of an economic nexus standard in its *Wayfair* decision.[13] The new economic nexus standard allows a state to impose a sales tax collection responsibility on businesses (including non-U.S. businesses) when the following six criteria are met: (1) businesses selling less than $100,000 in sales or having less than 200 sales transactions are excluded; (2) no retroactive tax is collected; (3) there is a single, state-level administration of sales taxes; (4) there is a simplified tax rate structure; (5) there are uniform definitions and other rules; and (6) the state provides software for sales tax collection and provides immunity to businesses that rely on the software. Currently, all states imposing a sales tax have now adopted the new economic nexus standard for sales tax. Missouri's law will not be effective until January 1, 2023.

Even after the *Wayfair* decision, it remains unclear whether the physical presence and economic sales tax nexus standards now apply simultaneously or whether the economic nexus standard has completely replaced the physical presence standard for all businesses. For example, does a business that has a physical presence in a state but has less than $100,000 in sales or 200 sales transactions have sales tax nexus in that state? A strict reading of most of these newly implemented economic nexus laws indicates that online sellers meeting the economic standard are treated as if they have a physical presence within the state. For this reason, many professionals believe that the nexus standards apply simultaneously—but only time will help businesses resolve this question.

[10]*Scripto, Inc. v. Carson,* 362 U.S. 207 (1960). Scripto hired independent salespeople to represent the company in Florida. The Supreme Court held that these salespeople were agents of Scripto, who established the physical presence necessary to create sales tax nexus.

[11]*Nat'l Bellas Hess, Inc. v. Dep't of Rev. of the State of Ill.,* 386 U.S. 753 (1967).

[12]*Quill Corp. v. North Dakota,* 504 U.S. 298 (1992).

[13]*South Dakota v. Wayfair, Inc.,* 138 S. Ct. 2080 (2018).

Example 12-1

Wild West sends promotional brochures from Idaho to its Arizona and Colorado clients. Wild West generated current-year sales of $89,242 on 215 sales transactions and $75,002 on 163 sales transactions within Arizona and Colorado, respectively. Prior to the *Wayfair* decision, Wild West didn't collect Arizona or Colorado sales tax or file sales tax returns. Wild West has neither employees nor property in Arizona or Colorado. Assume that Arizona and Colorado both adopted the new economic nexus standard under *Wayfair*. Does Wild West have sales tax nexus in Arizona and/or Colorado?

Answer: Yes in Arizona and no in Colorado. Wild West has met the new economic nexus standard of $100,000 in sales or 200 sales transactions within Arizona because of its 215 sales transactions, but not in Colorado, where it had only 163 sales transactions and its sales revenue from those transactions was less than $100,000. Wild West has economic sales tax nexus in Arizona, but not in Colorado, Therefore, Wild West has an Arizona sales tax collection responsibility.

What if: Assume that in addition to mailing promotional brochures, Ken visits Colorado on promotional trips. Does Wild West have sales tax nexus in Colorado under these circumstances?

Answer: Probably yes. Prior to Colorado adopting the new economic nexus standard, the presence of Wild West's representatives would have created physical presence nexus. Colorado law now treats online sellers that meet the economic nexus standard as if they had physical presence in that state. So Wild West should probably assume that the physical presence of the promotional trips creates sales tax nexus in Colorado.

What if: Assume the original facts except that Wild West had $110,000 in sales and 250 sales transactions with Colorado customers during the year. Does Wild West have sales tax nexus in Colorado under these circumstances?

Answer: Yes. The new economic nexus standard has been met because Wild West exceeds both $100,000 in sales and 200 sales transactions in Colorado during the year.

Sales Tax Liability

Typically, sellers with sales tax nexus collect sales tax from their customers at the time of sale. For example, Wild West collects sales tax on river rafting equipment it sells from its retail store but not on river guiding *services* it provides. If the seller doesn't have sales tax nexus and chooses not to collect the sales tax, then the customer is responsible for remitting a use tax (at the same tax rate as sales tax) to the state in which the property is located and used. If the buyer is charged a sales tax in another state, the buyer will have a use tax liability for the incremental amount if the state where the property is located and used has a higher sales tax rate than the state where the item was purchased.

Example 12-2

Wild West generated current-year sales of $75,002 within Colorado on its 163 sales transactions to Colorado customers. Wild West received $3,500 from a customer named Casey Jarvie residing in Boulder, Colorado. Of this amount, $500 was for personal rafting equipment shipped to Boulder, where the sales tax rate is 8.845 percent. The remaining $3,000 was payment for a four-day river raft adventure on the Salmon River in Idaho. Colorado adopted the new economic nexus standard. Does Wild West have a responsibility to collect sales tax from Casey?

Answer: No. Wild West is below the economic nexus standard, has no physical presence, and does not have sales tax nexus in Colorado; therefore, it has no Colorado sales tax collection requirement.

Because Wild West has no sales tax collection responsibility, does Casey have a use tax liability to the state of Colorado? If so, in what amount?

(continued on page 12-8)

Answer: Yes. Casey is responsible for remitting $44.23 of use tax ($500 × 8.845%) on his personal Colorado state income tax return for the purchase of the personal rafting equipment in Colorado. He is not required to pay Colorado use tax on the river raft adventure purchase because Wild West provided an out-of-state service (no sales tax is due on the services in Idaho either).

What if: If Casey had Wild West hold the goods until he arrived in Burley, Idaho, to pick them up at the time of the trip (assume the sales tax rate in Burley, Idaho, is 6 percent), would Wild West have sales tax collection responsibility? If so, what is the sales tax amount? Would Casey have a Colorado use tax liability?

Answer: Yes. Because Wild West has physical presence in Idaho, it is required to collect $30 ($500 × 6%) of sales tax and remit it to Idaho. Casey would also have a $14.23 Colorado use tax liability ($44.23 reduced by the $30 remitted to Idaho) in this scenario.

ETHICS

Jill is a Virginia resident who purchased $1,500 of personal use items from various small Internet retailers during the year. None of these retailers meets the new economic nexus standard and they do not collect sales taxes from Jill. While completing her personal tax return using a popular software package, Jill was asked to report her online purchases. After entering these purchases, she noticed that $75 of "use tax" was added to her state tax liability. Jill has never paid this tax in the past. She decided to delete the online purchase information she had previously entered. What do you think of Jill's failure to report her Virginia use tax?

Many states have now implemented marketplace seller rules for companies like Amazon, eBay, and Etsy. Rather than applying the economic nexus standard to the small reseller, these states apply the economic nexus standard at the marketplace level. This forces the marketplace to collect and remit sales tax.

Large companies often must file sales tax returns in all 45 states, and the District of Columbia, that have sales taxes.[14] This administrative burden is further increased by the fact that more than 7,500 tax jurisdictions (including counties, cities, school districts, and other divisions) impose sales taxes, and several hundred jurisdictions have rates change annually at various times throughout the year.[15] The sales tax administrative burden can also be large for small businesses. For example, a local pizzeria that delivers can sometimes be subject to a half-dozen sales tax rates if its delivery services cross city, county, or even school district boundaries.

ETHICS

Oklahoma has notice and reporting requirements that require nondomiciliary businesses without sales tax nexus to report all the necessary information to help the Department of Revenue collect its use tax from resident individuals and domiciliary businesses. Assume you are responsible for resolving sales tax issues for an online retailer from another state. You believe that Oklahoma's notice and reporting requirements are unconstitutional based on a seminar you attended and the advice of your accounting firm. Would you recommend that your company comply with these notice and reporting laws? Would your opinion change if the court issued an injunction prohibiting the state from enforcing the new law?

[14]Some counties or political subdivisions of states without state sales taxes (such as Kenai Peninsula Borough in Alaska) impose a county or local sales tax.

[15]Software companies provide sales tax solutions that help companies with the administrative burden. However, they generally fail to indemnify or compensate businesses against errors in their software that result in uncollected sales taxes, which creates a liability for the business.

Example 12-3

Recall from Exhibit 12-1 that Wild West has sales in Arizona, California, Colorado, Idaho, Tennessee, Washington, and Wyoming. Also recall that it has property and employees in Idaho, Tennessee, Washington, and Wyoming. In which states does Wild West have sales tax nexus and, therefore, sales tax collection responsibility?

Answer: Wild West's physical presence of employees and real and personal property create sales tax nexus in Idaho, Tennessee, Washington, and Wyoming. Additionally, under the new economic nexus standard for sales taxes, Wild West will have sales tax nexus in Arizona and California. Wild West will have under $100,000 in sales and less than 200 sales transactions with Colorado customers and will not have sales tax nexus in Colorado.

Using the sales data provided in Exhibit 12-1, how much sales tax must Wild West remit? Assume the following (hypothetical) sales tax rates: Arizona, 8.6 percent; California, 9.5 percent; Idaho, 6 percent; Tennessee, 9.25 percent; Washington, 7.7 percent; and Wyoming, 6 percent.

Answer: It must remit $48,835, computed as follows:

State	(1) Taxable Sales	(2) Rate	(1) × (2) Sales Tax Due
Arizona	$ 89,242	8.60%	$ 7,675
California	132,045	9.50%	12,544
Idaho	167,921	6.00%	10,075
Tennessee	45,331	9.25%	4,193
Washington	41,982	7.70%	3,233
Wyoming	185,249	6.00%	11,115
Totals	**$661,770**		**$48,835**

Remember, services are not generally subject to sales tax.

TAXES IN THE REAL WORLD Groupon

Have you ever bought a restaurant meal from Groupon? Did you know there is a tax issue complicating these types of purchases? Suppose you pay $25 for a $50 voucher good at your favorite restaurant. You just scored a great deal. Groupon collects the $25 and pays the restaurant $12.50. You show up and order $50 worth of food, and the server brings you the bill. How much sales tax should the restaurant collect from you on the prepared food (which is a taxable item)? You received $50 worth of prepared food (one possible tax base), but you paid only $25 (another possible tax base), and the restaurant received only $12.50 (a third possible tax base). What is the nature of the $12.50 retained by Groupon? Did it provide a good (taxable) or a service (not taxable)? Most restaurants currently collect tax on the entire $50 benefit you received. However, some states have started providing guidance.

INCOME TAXES

LO 12-3

Forty-four states impose an income tax on corporations; South Dakota and Wyoming impose no corporate income tax and Nevada, Ohio, Texas, and Washington impose a gross-receipts tax.[16] Forty-three states tax individuals on income earned through partnerships and S corporations.[17] This chapter focuses on C corporations, but the same

[16]Several states (such as California and New York) impose a franchise tax rather than an income tax. Because franchise taxes are generally based upon net income, they are essentially the same as income taxes.

[17]These states tax individuals, including the income that flows through from partnerships and S corporations (although New Hampshire and Tennessee tax only dividends and interest). The following states do not tax individuals: Alaska, Florida, Nevada, South Dakota, Texas, Washington, and Wyoming.

principles generally apply to flow-through entities. Most states imposing income-based taxes conform to an entity's federal tax status. For example, most states treat an S corporation as a flow-through entity and tax only the owner of the entity. However, a few states impose minimum taxes on flow-through entities. For example, California imposes a minimum tax of $800 or a 1.5 percent tax on the income of all flow-through entities, including partnerships (and LLCs taxed as partnerships) and S corporations.

Businesses must pay income tax in their state of commercial domicile (i.e., where they are headquartered). For example, Wild West is both incorporated and domiciled in Idaho and is therefore subject to Idaho's income tax regime. Until a few decades ago, many businesses believed they were virtually exempt from state income taxes in states other than their state of commercial domicile. However, in *Complete Auto Transit,* the U.S. Supreme Court spelled out four criteria for determining whether states can tax nondomiciliary businesses and whether the tax imposed is discriminatory against nondomiciliary businesses (i.e., businesses domiciled in another state).[18] First, a sufficient connection, or **income tax nexus,** must exist between the state and the business. Second, a state may tax only a fair portion of a business's income. Businesses must be able to divide or apportion income among the states where an income tax filing requirement exists. Third, the tax cannot be constructed to discriminate against nonresident businesses. For example, states cannot impose a higher tax rate on nondomiciliary businesses than domiciliary businesses. Fourth, the taxes paid must be fairly related to the services the state provides the business. For example, states provide businesses access to their courts, economic base, infrastructure, and so forth.

Businesses must answer the following questions to determine their state income tax liabilities:

- In which state(s) does it have income tax nexus?
- If income tax nexus exists, is the company protected from paying income taxes by Public Law 86-272?
- If the business is related to other entities, should it file separate state income tax returns, or should it include the activities of the related entities on a single state income tax return?
- What adjustments to federal taxable income must the business make to calculate state taxable income for each state in which it is required to file?
- If it has income tax nexus in more than one state, how is income divided among the various states in which the business is required to file tax returns?

THE KEY FACTS

Income Tax Nexus

- Income tax nexus is created through physical presence of salespeople or property.
- Sellers of tangible personal property, even when income tax nexus exists, can be protected from an income tax liability under Public Law 86-272.
  - As long as in-state activities are limited to solicitation.
- Several states are now asserting economic income tax nexus.

Income Tax Nexus

Income tax nexus can be created through either physical presence or economic factors.[19] Historically, income tax nexus has been created through the physical presence of salespeople or property in that state. Physical presence in a state always creates income tax nexus in that state. More recently, states are pursuing nexus through economic presence to capture additional tax revenue. However, even when physical presence or economic presence creates income tax nexus for sellers of tangible personal property, these sellers may be protected from paying income taxes if their activities within a state are limited to certain "protected" activities as described by **Public Law 86-272.**

[18]*Complete Auto Transit, Inc. v. Brady,* 430 U.S. 274 (1977).

[19]Until 1959, there was a common and persistent belief among businesses that state tax accrued only in the business's state of commercial domicile. In 1959, the U.S. Supreme Court allowed Minnesota to tax an Iowa-based business [*Nw. States Portland Cement Co. v. Minnesota,* 358 U.S. 450 (1959)]. As discussed in the next section, Congress passed Public Law 86-272 seven months later.

Economic Presence Many states assert that because they provide the infrastructure for nonresident companies to do business in the state (e.g., Internet, phone connections, and roads), nonresident companies doing business in the state have an economic presence in the state and thus have **economic income tax nexus** in the state, even when they don't have a physical presence in the state.[20] For example, West Virginia asserted income tax nexus and an income tax liability on a business (MBNA Bank) that merely solicited credit card customers through advertising and phone calls without having physical presence (employees or property) in the state. The West Virginia Supreme Court upheld the assertion, and the U.S. Supreme Court denied MBNA's *writ of certiorari*. However, some experts believe West Virginia's law to be unconstitutional and that the U.S. Supreme Court's refusal to hear the case was designed to urge Congress to resolve the uncertainty surrounding income tax nexus issues. Economic presence is most often measured through the factor presence test (see the Taxes in the Real World box Factor Presence Nexus).

TAXES IN THE REAL WORLD Economic Income Tax Nexus

While several states have asserted economic income tax nexus through state courts, the Multistate Tax Commission (MTC) adopted the Factor Presence Nexus Standard in 2002 (MTC Policy Statement 02-02). The MTC is an intergovernmental state tax agency created by the Multistate Tax Compact. Factor Presence asserts that if any business exceeds any of the following criteria for a given state, it is deemed to have economic income tax nexus:

- $50,000 of property,
- $50,000 of payroll,
- $500,000 of sales, or
- 25 percent of total property, payroll, or sales.

In 2021, the MTC updated its Statement on P.L. 86-272 for the first time in 20 years. The MTC now claims that many Internet-based transactions are unprotected activities creating income tax nexus. These standards are attempts change the game by making Public Law 86-272 irrelevant, and it should make all companies not filing income tax returns in a state concerned because of potential income tax liabilities.

Example 12-4

What if: Assume Wild West's Internet store receives and fills an order from a West Virginia customer. Wild West has no physical presence in West Virginia. Does Wild West have economic income tax nexus in West Virginia?

Answer: Unlikely, but perhaps. West Virginia's assertion that economic presence creates income tax nexus could happen. If a court were to uphold the MTC's Statement on P.L. 86-272 or the West Virginia sales exceed $500,000 or 25 percent of sales from all sources, it could create economic nexus.

Protection under Public Law 86-272 Public Law 86-272 protects or places limits on states' power to impose income taxes on certain nondomiciliary businesses. Businesses that sell only tangible personal property within a state are protected from paying income taxes, even in a state where income tax nexus exists, if they meet all of the criteria

[20]The Supreme Court's *Quill* decision, which has now been vacated, gave credibility to the concept of economic presence creating income tax nexus. In *Quill*, the court said that while physical presence was required for sales tax nexus, "nexus for other taxes may be different." States have interpreted that nexus for other taxes, including an income tax, could be created through economic presence. Several more recent cases have given de facto income tax nexus to businesses without the requisite physical presence [*Geoffrey, Inc. v. S.C. Tax Comm'n*, 313 S.C. 15 (1993); *Lanco, Inc. v. Dir., Div. of Taxation*, 188 N.J. 380, 908 A.2d 176 (2006); *Tax Comm'r of W. Va. v. MBNA Am. Bank, N.A.*, 640 S.E.2d 226 (W. Va. 2006)].

listed below. One common strategy businesses protected by Public Law 86-272 use is to file a "zero" income tax return in the protected state to start the statute of limitations running—businesses list their name and address and write "protected by Public Law 86-272" on the top of page 1 of the income tax return. Businesses that provide services along with selling tangible personal property, or that sell real property or intangibles, are not protected by Public Law 86-272 and therefore are subject to a state's income tax. Businesses are protected from paying income taxes, even when income tax nexus exists, if (and only if) *all* the following apply:

- The tax is based on net income.[21]
- The taxpayer sells only tangible personal property in that state.
- The taxpayer's in-state activities are limited to solicitation of sales (see the discussion below for the definition of *solicitation*).
- The taxpayer participates in interstate commerce.
- The taxpayer is nondomiciliary.
- The taxpayer approves orders outside the state.
- The taxpayer delivers goods from outside the state through a common carrier.[22]

Example 12-5

What if: Assume that Wild West sends employees into Oregon to visit retail stores and solicit orders of rafting equipment only. Does the presence of Wild West's employees in Oregon create income tax nexus in Oregon? If income tax nexus exists, would Wild West have an income tax filing requirement in Oregon?

Answer: Yes. The physical presence of representatives creates income tax nexus. However, because Wild West is a seller of tangible personal property in Oregon, its Oregon activities are protected under Public Law 86-272. Thus, while income tax nexus is created for Wild West in Oregon, Wild West has no obligation to file an Oregon income tax return.

What if: Assume that Ken or other Wild West sales representatives enter Oregon to solicit customers for both rafting equipment and white-water adventures. Does the presence of Wild West's employees create income tax nexus in Oregon? If income tax nexus exists, would Wild West have an income tax filing requirement in Oregon?

Answer: Yes. The physical presence of representatives creates income tax nexus. Additionally, because solicitation of services is not a protected activity under Public Law 86-272, Wild West will have to file an income tax return in Oregon.

Solicitation. Public Law 86-272 protects **solicitation** of tangible personal property but doesn't clearly define the term *solicitation*. In *Wisconsin v. Wrigley,* however, the U.S. Supreme Court addressed the definition.[23] Wrigley, a chewing gum manufacturer, based in Chicago, Illinois, had sales representatives and a regional manager in Wisconsin. Sales meetings in Wisconsin were held both in the manager's basement and in a rented hotel space. The sales representatives had company cars, a stock of gum, display racks, and promotional literature. The sales activities included handing out promotional materials, free samples, and free display racks; replacing stale gum; handling billing disputes; and occasionally filling orders from their stock of gum and issuing an agency stock check (a bill) to customers. All other orders were sent to Illinois for acceptance and were filled by a common carrier from outside of Wisconsin. In *Wrigley,* the U.S.

[21]Taxes calculated based on gross receipts or other bases are not protected by Public Law 86-272.

[22]"Common carrier" is a general term referring to delivery businesses (such as FedEx, UPS, DHL, or USPS).

[23]*Wis. Dep't of Rev. v. William Wrigley, Jr. Co.,* 505 U.S. 214 (1992).

Supreme Court determined the following activities performed within Wisconsin met the definition of solicitation:

- Soliciting by any form of advertising.
- Carrying samples and promotional materials for display or distribution without charge.
- Passing inquiries or complaints to the home office.
- Checking a customer's inventory for reorder.
- Maintaining a sample room for two weeks or less; this is known as the **trade show rule.**
- Recruiting, training, and evaluating sales reps using homes or hotels.
- Owning or furnishing personal property and autos used in sales activities.

The U.S. Supreme Court held the following activities do *not* meet the definition of solicitation and, therefore, create an income tax filing requirement with the state in which they take place:

- Making repairs.
- Collecting delinquent accounts.
- Investigating creditworthiness.
- Installing or supervising the installation of property.
- Providing training for employees other than sales representatives.
- Approving or accepting orders.
- Repossessing property.
- Securing deposits.
- Maintaining an office (other than an in-home office).

If sales representatives know and understand these solicitation rules, they can help businesses avoid income tax liability in states where a business wants to avoid paying income taxes.

TAXES IN THE REAL WORLD Independent Contractors Create Nexus

One of the biggest current issues for out-of-state retailers is the manner in which warranty work is performed. For example, assume you buy a new laptop for school from an online retailer because the price is unbeatable. Two months later you are told by customer support that the hard drive needs to be replaced and you need to ship the computer from Lawrence, Kansas, to Austin, Texas, for repair. You respond that you cannot go a week without your computer, so the retailer agrees to have a local repair shop in Kansas do the repair for you. Many companies wrongly assume that hiring an independent representative to do in-state warranty work does not create income tax nexus. The hiring of the independent contractor is an agency relationship that creates income tax nexus for the out-of-state Texas retailer in Kansas. The MTC issued guidance (MTC Nexus Bulletin 95-1) on this issue more than two decades ago—and taxpayers challenging the ruling have lost time and time again. Retailers with these issues quickly find themselves liable for both current and past income taxes as well as for sales taxes.

Example 12-6

Assume Wild West's Oregon sales representatives give store employees free white-water gloves and pass on customer complaints to the home office. Do these activities create an income tax filing requirement for Wild West in Oregon?

(continued on page 12-14)

Answer: No. Even though the presence of sales representatives creates income tax nexus, giving samples (without charge) and passing on customer complaints, suggestions, and customer inquiries are protected sales activities under Public Law 86-272. Therefore, Wild West is protected from an Oregon income tax filing requirement.

What if: While in Oregon, several sales representatives accept checks for down payments on merchandise, repair faulty merchandise, and perform credit checks. Do these activities create an income tax filing requirement for Wild West in Oregon?

Answer: Yes. Each of these activities is an unprotected sales activity, and any or all of these activities will create an Oregon income tax filing requirement for Wild West.

Example 12-7

What if: Assume that Ken and other Wild West employees visit Colorado retail stores and hold slideshows about summer rafting trips. After the slideshows, Ken and the other guides interact with and gather information from potential white-water rafting customers. Do these solicitation activities create an income tax filing requirement?

Answer: Yes. The presence of sales representatives creates income tax nexus. Additionally, because Wild West is soliciting for services, rather than tangible personal property, Public Law 86-272 does not protect them from Colorado's income tax.

Does a one-time sales activity violation create a potential income tax filing requirement? Technically, yes. However, the *Wrigley* decision indicates that *de minimis* (i.e., immaterial) activities may be excluded. The decision whether an activity is *de minimis* is a subjective one, however, based on relevant facts and circumstances.

Example 12-8

Assume that Wild West's sales representatives occasionally investigate creditworthiness and occasionally repossess property in Oregon. Can Wild West avoid income tax liability?

Answer: Possibly. Even though the physical presence of sales representatives in Oregon creates income tax nexus and the sales representatives performed unprotected activities, Wild West could argue that these unprotected activities are *de minimis* because they are not material to its overall operations within Oregon. However, these activities put Wild West at risk and could lead to an income tax liability.

Now that we've explored income tax nexus, let's determine Wild West's income tax nexus and filing requirements.

Example 12-9

Wild West is domiciled in Idaho and has physical presence through property and employees whose activities exceed protected solicitation in Idaho, Tennessee, Washington, and Wyoming. Recall from Exhibit 12-1 that Wild West has sales in the following states: Arizona, California, Colorado, Idaho, Tennessee, Washington, and Wyoming. Where does Wild West have income tax nexus?

Answer: Wild West has income tax nexus in Idaho, Tennessee, Washington, and Wyoming. It has income tax nexus in Idaho because of commercial domicile, physical presence of retail stores (where orders are accepted), and the provision of services. Wild West has income tax nexus in Tennessee and Washington because of the provision of services. Wild West has income tax nexus in Wyoming because of the physical presence of retail stores, Internet-based store, and the provision of services.

Where does Wild West have an income tax filing requirement?

Answer: Wild West has an income tax filing requirement in Idaho, Tennessee, Washington, and Wyoming. Wild West will file income tax returns in Idaho and Tennessee. Wild West will not file in Wyoming because Wyoming does not impose a corporate income tax. Washington imposes a gross receipts tax (business and occupation tax) rather than an income tax. Wild West will file a Washington gross receipts tax return, as we discuss in Example 12-21.

Entities Included on Income Tax Return

When a business operates as more than one legal entity, the way it files its tax return(s) becomes an issue. Some states require a **separate tax return** for each entity with an income tax filing requirement in the state, and others require a **unitary tax return** (i.e., one tax return) for a group of related entities.[24]

Separate Tax Returns A separate-return state requires only those businesses with an income tax filing requirement in the state to file an income tax return. This is generally true even when a group of companies file together on a federal consolidated tax return.[25] Historically, many states east of the Mississippi River (except Illinois) were separate-return states; however, many states have begun shifting away from separate-return requirements over the last decade. Today, 28 states impose taxes on unitary groups.

Example 12-10

Wild West has income tax nexus in Tennessee because its employees provide services within the state and it owns property there. Must Wild West file a Tennessee income tax return?

Answer: Yes. Wild West must file a Tennessee income tax return because it has income tax nexus in Tennessee and it exceeds the protections offered by Public Law 86-272.

What if: Assume that Tennessee is a separate return state and Wild West splits into two separate corporations: one that runs retail stores (Wild West Retail) and one that provides the guided rafting services (Wild West Services). How would the split affect Wild West's Tennessee income tax filing requirements (even though Tennessee recently became a unitary state, answer the question as though Tennessee is still a separate-return state)?

Answer: Wild West would file two separate income tax returns: one for Wild West Retail and one for Wild West Services. Both companies would have income tax nexus in Tennessee because Wild West Retail's stores do more than solicit sales of tangible personal property and Wild West Service's activities are not protected activities under Public Law 86-272.

THE KEY FACTS

Entities Included on a Tax Return

- Separate-return states require a separate return for each entity that has an income tax filing requirement in the state.
- Unitary states require members of a unitary group to file a single tax return reflecting the combined income of the unitary group if any member of the unitary group has an income tax filing requirement.
  - Any of three factors characterizes a unitary group: functional integration, centralization of management, and economies of scale.

While separate tax returns are simple, the income reported on separate tax returns can easily be manipulated through related-entity transactions (i.e., through transfer pricing, for example). A historical tax planning technique was to use passive investment companies (PICs), in which a company simply created a subsidiary and transferred ownership of its trademarks and patents to an entity within a state that did not tax royalties, interest, and other similar types of intangible income (e.g., within a state such as Delaware or Nevada that does not tax these items). The PIC then charged a royalty for use of the intangible, which generated a deductible business expense in the state used and created income in a little- or no-tax state. States have implemented laws to fight this type of planning, and many other states have responded by adopting unitary filing requirements. Such "tax planning" opportunities are not available if the related entities are required to file a unitary tax return.

Unitary Tax Returns Historically, only states west of the Mississippi River, and Illinois, were unitary-return states. However, since 2004, the following states have adopted unitary return filing requirements: Colorado, Connecticut, Georgia, Kentucky, Maine, Massachusetts, Michigan, Minnesota, New Hampshire, New Jersey, New Mexico, New York, Ohio, Rhode Island, Tennessee, Vermont, and Wisconsin. Whether a business must file one tax return with other businesses or entities depends on whether these businesses are considered to be a "unitary" group of entities.

[24]The separate versus unitary discussion is a complex and complicated discussion even at the graduate tax level. However, a basic understanding of the terminology and concepts can be useful for all accounting professionals.

[25]Some states also allow combined reporting, a setting where more than one corporation file together on the same income tax return. However, the tax is calculated as if each corporation filed a separate return and was taxed separately.

In *Mobil,* the U.S. Supreme Court identified the following three factors that can be used to establish whether a group of businesses is unitary:

- Functional integration (vertical or horizontal integration or knowledge transfer).
- Centralization of management (interlocking directors, common officers, or rotation of management between companies).
- Economies of scale (group discounts or other efficiencies due to size).[26]

The unitary concept considers the integration and flow of value, rather than the business's legal form and ownership structure, in establishing which companies file a tax return together. Taxpayers must consider each of the three factors to determine whether multiple businesses will be treated as one for state tax purposes.

The important concept here is that companies filing a federal consolidated tax return may have to file separately for state purposes, and companies not filing a federal consolidated tax return may be required to file as a unitary group in some states.[27] A unitary tax return group includes all members meeting the unitary criteria—whether they have an income tax filing requirement in that state or not.[28] Unitary businesses usually have a flow of value between the various businesses. For example, raw materials or components can flow between businesses or one entity may borrow funds from another. The unitary concept pervades activities in the entire state income tax computation, including computing taxable income, computing apportionment percentages (discussed later in the chapter), and identifying income tax return filing requirements. The primary difference between separate and unitary states is that separate-return states tax the entire apportioned income of each separate business by requiring each business entity to file a separate tax return while unitary-return states tax the entire unitary group using a smaller apportioned percentage.

Example 12-11

What if: As in the previous example, assume Wild West is divided into two separate corporations: Wild West Retail (WWR) and Wild West Services (WWS). Ken owns and manages both companies. The rafting services company purchases all its rafting equipment from the retail stores company. Guides for the rafting company stop at the retail store before trips so customers can purchase any necessary gear, and the store refers customers looking for guided rafting to the rafting services company. Assume the two companies use the same marketing and accounting firms and receive discounts for having multiple bank accounts and insurance policies. Using the *Mobil* factors (i.e., functional integration, centralization of management, and economies of scale), are WWR and WWS part of a unitary group in a unitary state like Idaho?

Answer: Yes. WWR and WWS would likely be considered a unitary group and thus would combine income and file a single unitary tax return in each unitary state. The two companies likely share some integration in that their customer bases have significant overlap, and WWS purchases its equipment from WWR. They share centralization of management in that both are owned and operated by the same individual (Ken). The two companies have some economies of scale because they receive discounts for using the same accounting, banking, insurance, and marketing vendors. Businesses do not have to meet all three factors to be considered a unitary group, but WWR and WWS probably do. As a result, WWR and WWS would likely file a unitary (single) Idaho income tax return.

State Taxable Income

Companies doing business in multiple states must identify the tax return due dates, procedures for filing tax return extensions, and other administrative requirements specific to each state. Businesses must also calculate state taxable income for each state in which

[26]*Mobil Oil Corp. v. Comm'r of Taxes,* 445 U.S. 425 (1980).

[27]In some cases, different divisions of a single corporation can be separated, and in others a partnership and corporation can be joined.

[28]Entities without an income tax filing requirement will usually have apportionment factors that are zero. While their incomes increase the unitary group's income, their zero apportionment factors decrease the apportionment factors to the state. Therefore, the inclusion of entities without an income tax filing requirement is usually considered to be nondiscriminatory.

they must file tax returns. Federal taxable income before special deductions (Form 1120, Page 1, Line 28) is generally the starting point for computing state taxable income. Just as corporations reconcile from book income to taxable income to compute federal income tax (see the Corporate Operations chapter), businesses must reconcile from federal taxable income to state taxable income to compute state taxable income. This requires them to identify **federal/state adjustments** or differences for *each specific state* before apportioning the income to a particular state in which they have an income tax filing requirement.

Rather than starting from scratch, most states conform to the federal tax law in some way. Most "piggyback" their state tax laws on the federal tax laws (state tax codes generally follow the Internal Revenue Code).[29] Idaho generally conforms to the current Code. Consequently, Wild West will not report many federal/state adjustments. Other states adopt a specific version of the Code (i.e., the Code as of a specific date). For example, California adopts the Code as of January 1, 2015. This method requires more federal/state adjustments because every subsequent change to the Internal Revenue Code results in less conformity between the state law and the federal tax law. Corporations should carefully examine federal/state adjustments because states may not fully conform with recent federal tax law changes including bonus depreciation, deemed repatriation, interest deductions, and international provisions, including the participation exemption, global intangible low-taxed income (GILTI), and foreign-derived intangible income (FDII). Income tax software helps practitioners correctly calculate the federal/state adjustments necessary to compute state taxable income.

Because states cannot tax federal interest income (interest from Treasury notes, for example), all states require a negative adjustment (reduction in federal taxable income in adjusting to state taxable income) for federal interest income. Most states require a positive adjustment for state income tax deductions because they *do not* allow businesses to deduct state income taxes, and they require a positive adjustment for state and local bond interest income if the bond is from another state (i.e., they tax out-of-state bond interest income).[30]

States' tax instruction booklets generally describe common federal/state tax adjustments applicable for that state, but these descriptions are often incomplete and particularly problematic for states with low federal tax conformity. While it is impractical to identify all potential federal/state adjustments, Exhibit 12-5 provides a list of common federal/state adjustments and identifies each as a positive adjustment (state income increasing) or a negative adjustment (state income decreasing).

EXHIBIT 12-5 Common Federal/State Adjustments

Positive Adjustments (Increasing Taxable Income)

State and local income taxes
State and local bond interest income from bonds in other states
Federal dividends-received deduction
Federal income tax refunds (only in states where federal tax is allowed as a deduction)
Intercompany expenses associated with related persons (for separate-return states)*
MACRS depreciation over state depreciation
Federal bonus depreciation

Negative Adjustments (Decreasing Taxable Income)

U.S. obligation interest income (T-bills, notes, and bonds)
State dividends-received deduction
Foreign dividend gross-up
State income tax refunds included on federal return
State depreciation over federal depreciation

*Approximately 20 separate-return states require a positive adjustment of intercompany royalties, interest, and other expenses between related persons. The disallowance prevents companies from extracting profits from high-tax states and placing them in low- or no-tax states.

[29]Also, states may conform or not conform to administrative authority such as Treasury Regulations, Revenue Procedures, and Revenue Rulings.

[30]Thirty-three of the 46 states with an income tax require a positive adjustment for state and local income tax expenses deducted on the federal return.

Example 12-12

Wild West properly included, deducted, or excluded the following items on its federal tax return in the current year:

Item	Amount	Federal Treatment
Idaho income tax	$27,744	Deducted on federal return
Tennessee income tax	18,152	Deducted on federal return
Washington gross receipts tax	6,201	Deducted on federal return
Idaho bond interest income	5,000	Excluded from federal return
Federal T-note interest income	1,500	Included on federal return

Given federal taxable income of $53,289, what is Wild West's state tax base for Idaho and for Tennessee?

Answer: The Idaho state tax base is $97,685; for Tennessee it is $102,685. Bases are calculated as follows:

Federal Taxable Income	Idaho	Tennessee	Source
Wild West	$ 53,289	$ 53,289	Storyline
Positive Adjustments			
Idaho income tax	$ 27,744	$ 27,744	Idaho tax is not deducted.
Tennessee income tax	18,152	18,152	Tennessee tax is not deducted.
Washington gross receipts tax	0	0	Washington tax is not a positive adjustment because it is not an income-based tax.
State bond interest	0	5,000	States exempt their own interest only.
Total positive adjustments	$ 45,896	$ 50,896	
Negative Adjustments			
Federal interest	($ 1,500)	($ 1,500)	Federal interest is not taxable for state purposes.
Total negative adjustments	($ 1,500)	($ 1,500)	
State tax base	**$97,685**	**$102,685**	Federal + Positive − Negative

THE KEY FACTS

Dividing Income among States with Income Tax Nexus

- Business income is apportioned based on some combination of the following factors:
  - Sales
  - Payroll
  - Property
- Nonbusiness income is allocated.
- Investment income is allocated to the state of commercial domicile.
- Rents and royalties are generally allocated to the state where the property is used.

Dividing State Tax Base among States

All state taxable income is taxed in the state of commercial domicile unless the business is taxable in more than one state. An interstate business must separate its business income (earned from business operations) from nonbusiness income (primarily from investments, including rents and royalties). The business must fairly *apportion* its business income among the states in which it conducts business in a manner that creates income tax filing requirements, whereas it *allocates* or assigns nonbusiness income to a specific state (usually the state of commercial domicile).[31]

Business Income Business income includes all revenues earned in the ordinary course of business—sales less cost of goods sold and other expenses. Business income is fairly apportioned or divided across the states with an income tax filing requirement.[32] If

[31]The Multistate Tax Commission (MTC) has provided guidance on the division of income between states in Article IV of its Compact. The Compact can be found at www.mtc.gov. Also, see the Uniform Division of Income Tax Purposes Act that many states have adopted. Some states are treating all income as business income, and therefore have no separation of business and nonbusiness income.

[32]*Complete Auto Transit, Inc. v. Brady,* 430 U.S. 274 (1977).

a business has income tax nexus or a filing requirement with more than one state, it has the right to apportion income to that state—even if the state does not actually impose a tax (e.g., Wyoming).[33]

Example 12-13

Recall from Example 12-12 that Wild West's Idaho and Tennessee state tax bases were $97,685 and $102,685, respectively. Wild West's federal tax return shows the following items of investment income: dividends of $6,000, interest income of $16,005 (which includes $14,505 of bank interest and $1,500 of federal government interest but excludes $5,000 from Idaho bond interest), and rental income of $18,000. What is Wild West's business income for Idaho and Tennessee?

Answer: Idaho and Tennessee business income amounts are $59,180 and $59,180, respectively, calculated as follows:

Description	Idaho	Tennessee	Explanation
(1) State tax base	$ 97,685	$102,685	Example 12-12
(2) Dividends	6,000	6,000	Federal tax return
(3) Interest income	14,505	19,505	$14,505 (bank interest) + $5,000 of Idaho bond interest (for Tennessee only)
(4) Rental income	18,000	18,000	Federal tax return
(5) Nonbusiness income	$ 38,505	$ 43,505	(2) + (3) + (4)
Business income	**$59,180**	**$ 59,180**	(1) − (5)

Apportionment formula. States set the apportionment formula for income based on some combination of the following factors: sales, payroll, and property. For each state in which it establishes income tax nexus, the business calculates the factors as the ratio of (1) total sales, payroll, or property in a specific state to (2) total sales, payroll, or property everywhere. The sales factor is calculated as follows:

$$\text{Sales factor in state } X = \frac{\text{Total sales in state } X}{\text{Total sales in all states}}$$

The sales factor includes all gross business receipts net of returns, allowances, and discounts.[34] The general rules for determining the amount of sales to include in the sales factor calculation are:

- Sales of tangible personal property are sourced to the destination state (i.e., the state where the personal property is delivered and used).
- If the business does not have income tax nexus in the destination state, sales are generally "thrown back" to the state from which the property is shipped; this is called the **throwback rule.**[35] For example, if Wild West ships goods from Idaho to Montana, where it does not have income tax nexus, the sales are treated as if they are Idaho sales.

[33]Creating income tax nexus in states without an income tax creates "nowhere income"—income that is not taxed anywhere.

[34]There is substantial variation in the apportionment factor across states.

[35]Some states don't have a throwback rule and some states such as California have a double-throwback rule. This rule applies to drop shipments from a state without income tax nexus. For example, if a California company ships goods from Arizona into Colorado and the company has income tax nexus in neither Arizona nor Colorado, the sales are thrown back from Colorado into Arizona and then thrown back again from Arizona to California.

- Dock sales should be sourced to the good's ultimate destination (e.g., sales picked up by an out-of-state buyer at the seller's in-state dock rather than being shipped to the buyer's out-of-state location).
- Sales of services are generally apportioned to the state in which the services are performed (California and Illinois are exceptions to this general rule, but the list of states that apportion services to the state in which the services are consumed is growing).
- Government sales are sourced in the state from which they were shipped.

TAXES IN THE REAL WORLD Sourcing Receipts from Sales of Services and Intangible Property

The last 20 years have seen a shift from the use of the equally weighted three-factor formula to the adoption of a single sales-factor formula for apportionment purposes. This shift has made the method of calculating the sales factor more important for both taxpayers and tax administrators. Additionally, over the same period, there has been a significant shift from a goods-based economy to an intangibles- and service-based economy. Consequently, many states have changed their apportionment method for services. While sales of services were traditionally sourced to the state from which the services were provided, many states have now shifted the sourcing to the market (state) where the services are consumed—a destination approach. This means that, in many cases, two states are trying to tax the same services. For example, if an Idaho-based marketing firm creates a campaign for a California-based retailer, both states may assert the right to tax the transaction. Idaho will source the sale to the state in which the marketing campaign was created (Idaho) and California will source the sale to the state where the services will be used (California). Alternatively, if the facts were reversed, neither state would assert the right to tax the sale.

Example 12-14

Recall from Exhibit 12-1 that Wild West reported sales of $2,534,032. The sales are split between goods and services and sourced by state as follows:

Wild West Sales

State	Goods	Services	Total
AZ	$ 89,242	$ 0	$ 89,242
CA	132,045	0	132,045
CO	75,002	0	75,002
ID	**167,921**	**625,003**	**792,924**
TN	**45,331**	**357,061**	**402,392**
WA	41,982	377,441	419,423
WY	185,249	437,755	623,004
Totals	**$736,772**	**$1,797,260**	**$2,534,032**

Recall from Example 12-9 that Wild West has income tax nexus in Idaho, Tennessee, Washington, and Wyoming. Washington has a gross receipts tax and Wyoming does not tax corporations. What are the sales apportionment factors for Idaho and Tennessee?

Answer: The apportionment factors for Idaho and Tennessee are 31.29 percent and 15.88 percent, respectively, calculated from figures in the Total column in the sales table above:

Idaho $\frac{\$792,924}{\$2,534,032} = 31.29\%$

Tennessee $\frac{\$402,392}{\$2,534,032} = 15.88\%$

Note the Arizona, California, and Colorado sales are thrown back to Wyoming because the sales were made through the Internet store based in Wyoming and Wild West does not have an income tax filing requirement in Arizona, California, or Colorado.

Payroll is generally defined as total compensation paid to employees.[36] The payroll factor is calculated as follows:

- Payroll includes salaries, commissions, bonuses, and other forms of compensation.
- Payroll does not include amounts paid to independent contractors.
- Payroll for each employee is apportioned to a single state (payroll for employees who work in more than one state is sourced to the state where they perform the majority of services).

Example 12-15

Wild West's payments for wages are $737,021, sourced to the states as follows:

Payroll State	Wild West Wages
Idaho	**$201,032**
Tennessee	**148,202**
Washington	115,021
Wyoming	272,766
Total	**$737,021**

What are the payroll apportionment factors for Idaho and Tennessee?

Answer: The payroll apportionment factors for Idaho and Tennessee are 27.28 percent and 20.11 percent, respectively, calculated from the payroll table above:

Idaho $\frac{\$201,032}{\$737,021} = 27.28\%$

Tennessee $\frac{\$148,202}{\$737,021} = 20.11\%$

Property generally includes both real and tangible personal property, but not intangible property.[37] The general rules for determining the property factors are:

- Use the average property values for the year [(beginning + ending)/2].
- Value property at historical cost rather than adjusted basis (do not subtract accumulated depreciation in determining value).
- Include property in transit (such as inventory) in the destination state.

[36]The payroll definition varies by state.

[37]Property definitions may vary slightly by state.

- Include only business property (values of rented investment properties are excluded).
- Include rented or leased business property by multiplying the annual rent by 8 and adding this value to the average owned-property factor.[38]

Example 12-16

The historical cost of Wild West's property (before subtracting accumulated depreciation) owned at the beginning and end of the year and rented during the year, by state, is as follows:

Property			
State	**Beginning**	**Ending**	**Rented**
Idaho	$1,042,023	$1,203,814	$36,000
Tennessee	502,424	531,984	0
Washington	52,327	65,829	60,000
Wyoming	1,420,387	1,692,373	0
Total	$3,017,161	$3,494,000	$96,000

What are the property apportionment factors for Idaho and Tennessee?

Answer: The property apportionment factors for Idaho and Tennessee are 35.07 percent and 12.85 percent, respectively, computed as follows:

Property and Rents Total					
	Owned Property			**Rented Property**	
State	**Beginning**	**Ending**	**Average**	**Rents × 8**	**Total**
Idaho	**$1,042,023**	**$1,203,814**	**$1,122,919**	**$288,000**	**$1,410,919**
Tennessee	**502,424**	**531,984**	**517,204**		**517,204**
Washington	52,327	65,829	59,078	$480,000	539,078
Wyoming	1,420,387	1,692,373	1,556,380		1,556,380
Total	**$3,017,161**	**$3,494,000**	**$3,255,581**		**$4,023,581**

Idaho $\frac{\$1,410,919}{\$4,023,581} = 35.07\%$

Tennessee $\frac{\$517,204}{\$4,023,581} = 12.85\%$

The average amount for each state from the subtotal property table is added to the inclusion amount from the subtotal rent table to reach the total property numerator for each state.

Historically, most states used an equally weighted three-factor apportionment formula, which was required by the Model Tax Compact (MTC). This method adds together the sales, payroll, and property factors and divides the total by 3 to arrive at the apportionment factor (percentages) for each state. Over time most states shifted to a double-weighted sales factor (doubling the sales factor and then adding the payroll and property factors, and dividing the total by 4). Currently, 28 states have moved to a single-weighted sales factor formula that eliminates the payroll and property factors altogether. California is an example of a state that requires corporations to use a single-weighted sales factor. All else equal, increasing the weight of the sales factor in the apportionment formula tends to decrease the tax liabilities of in-state businesses and increases the tax liabilities of out-of-state businesses. This result occurs because in-state businesses tend to

[38]The annual rent is multiplied by 8 to approximate the value of the rental property.

have higher payroll and property factors relative to their sales factors where headquartered, and out-of-state businesses tend to have higher sales factors than payroll and property factors in nondomiciliary states.

TAXES IN THE REAL WORLD Apportionment: The *Gillette* Decision

On December 31, 2015, the California Supreme Court reversed the California Court of Appeals decision in *Gillette Co. v. Franchise Tax Board* [196 Cal. Rptr. 3d 486, 363 P.3d 94 (2015)]. The California Court of Appeals had held that a taxpayer could apportion its income to California using the Model Tax Compact's evenly weighted three-factor formula, despite statutory language mandating the use of a three-factor, double-weighted sales formula for most corporations for the years at issue.

The California Supreme Court reversed this decision and concluded that the California Legislature may properly preclude a taxpayer from relying on the Model Tax Compact's election provision. On October 12, 2016, the U.S. Supreme Court denied the *Gillette* appeal. The Minnesota, Oregon, and Texas Supreme Courts recently reached the same decision as California. Similarly, the Michigan Appellate Court reversed a 2015 decision favoring IBM, and the Michigan Supreme Court denied the consolidated appeal of IBM and 50 other companies.[39]

The U.S. Supreme Court has denied *writ of certiorari* in these cases, and it is unclear whether taxpayers can ultimately win this argument. As a result, the single-weighted sales factor formula or methodology appears to be constitutional and will likely see continued growth and adoption by the remaining states.

Example 12-17

Wild West must apportion its business income to Idaho and Tennessee. Its Idaho sales, payroll, and property factors are 31.29 percent, 27.28 percent, and 35.07 percent, respectively. Its Tennessee sales, payroll, and property factors are 15.88 percent, 20.11 percent, and 12.85 percent, respectively. These factors are aggregated from Examples 12-14, 12-15, and 12-16. What are Wild West's apportionment factors in both states if they use a double-weighted sales factor?

Answer: The apportionment factors for Idaho and Tennessee are 31.23 percent and 16.18 percent, respectively.

Factor	Idaho	Tennessee	Explanation
(1) Sales	31.29%	15.88%	Example 12-14
(2) Sales	31.29	15.88	Example 12-14
(3) Payroll	27.28	20.11	Example 12-15
(4) Property	35.07	12.85	Example 12-16
Apportionment factor	**31.23%**	**16.18%**	[(1) + (2) + (3) + (4)]/4

What if: Assume Tennessee uses an equally weighted three-factor apportionment formula. What is Wild West's Tennessee apportionment factors?

Answer: The apportionment factor for Tennessee is 16.28 percent. Tennessee's apportionment factor would now be calculated as follows:

Factor	Tennessee	Explanation
(1) Sales	15.88%	
(2) Payroll	20.11	
(3) Property	12.85	
Apportionment factor	**16.28%**	[(1) + (2) + (3)]/3

What if: Assume Idaho uses a single-weighted sales factor apportionment formula. What would Wild West's apportionment factor be?

Answer: The apportionment factor for Idaho would be 31.29 percent. Idaho's apportionment factor would now simply be Wild West's Idaho sales factor. No payroll or property factor would be needed for Idaho.

[39]*Int'l Bus. Machines Corp. v. Dep't of Treasury,* Docket No. 327359, 316 Mich. App. 346 (July 21, 2016).

Nonbusiness Income We've said nonbusiness income includes all income except business income. Common types of nonbusiness income and the rules for allocating each type to specific states include:[40]

- Allocate interest and dividends to the state of commercial domicile (except interest on working capital, which is business income).
- Allocate rental income to the state where the property generating the rental income is located.
- Allocate royalties to the state where the property is used (if the business has income tax nexus in that state; if not, allocate royalties to the state of commercial domicile).
- Allocate capital gains from investment property to the state of commercial domicile.
- Allocate capital gains from selling rental property to the state where the rental property is located.

Example 12-18

Wild West reports nonbusiness income as follows:

Wild West			
Description	**Idaho**	**Tennessee**	**Explanation**
Dividends	$ 6,000	$ 6,000	From Example 12-13
Interest	14,505	19,505	From Example 12-13
Rental income	18,000	18,000	From Example 12-13
Allocable total	$38,505	$43,505	

Wild West's commercial domicile is in Idaho. Its rental income is for real property located in Wyoming. To which state(s) should the firm allocate its nonbusiness income?

Answer: $20,505 to Idaho and $18,000 to Wyoming, calculated as follows:

Wild West		
State	**Amount**	**Explanation**
Idaho	**$20,505**	$6,000 dividends + $14,505 interest income
Tennessee	0	
Washington	0	
Wyoming	**18,000**	Rental income
Total	$ 38,505	

State Income Tax Liability

It is relatively easy to calculate a business's state taxable income and state tax after separating business and nonbusiness income, apportioning business income, and allocating nonbusiness income. Specifically, state taxable income is calculated by multiplying business income by the apportionment factor and then adding any nonbusiness income allocated to the state.

[40]Multistate Tax Compact, Article IV, Division of Income, para. 4. Note that a few states treat all income as business income.

Example 12-19

What if: Assume Idaho and Tennessee have a flat income tax rate of 7.6 percent and 6.5 percent, respectively. What is Wild West's income tax liability for Idaho and Tennessee?

Answer: Its income tax liabilities in Idaho and Tennessee are $2,963 and $622, respectively, computed as follows:

Description	Idaho	Tennessee	Explanation
(1) State tax base	$97,685	$102,685	Example 12-12
(2) Allocable income	(38,505)	(43,505)	Example 12-18
(3) Business income	$59,180	$ 59,180	(1) – (2)
(4) Apportionment factor	31.23%	16.18%	Example 12-17
(5) Apportioned income	$18,482	$ 9,575	(3) × (4)
(6) Allocable income	20,505	0	Example 12-18
(7) State taxable income	$38,987	$ 9,575	(5) + (6)
(8) Tax rate	7.6%	6.5%	
Tax liability	**$ 2,963**	**$ 622**	(7) × (8)

Nonincome-Based Taxes

Several states have nonincome-based taxes (other than sales tax). Washington has the business and occupation (B&O) tax, which is a gross receipts tax. Texas has the margin tax, the lesser of a gross margin tax or gross receipts tax (e.g., many states are treating the Texas margin tax as a tax based on net income). Many states are imposing nonincome-based taxes to increase revenues from nondomiciliary businesses because the nexus for nonincome-based taxes is different.

Remember that Public Law 86-272 only protects businesses from the imposition of income-based taxes. Therefore, physical or economic presence is all that is necessary for the imposition of a nonincome-based tax. While nonincome-based taxes are largely beyond the scope of this text, recognizing that a different nexus standard exists for nonincome-based taxes is vitally important.

Example 12-20

What if: The Texas margin tax is calculated on the least of (1) revenue less cost of goods sold, (2) 70 percent of sales revenue, (3) revenue minus compensation, or (4) revenue minus $1 million. Assume that Wild West sends employees into Texas to visit retail stores and solicit orders of rafting equipment. Would the presence of Wild West employees create nonincome-based tax nexus for the Texas margin tax?

Answer: Yes. Because the tax is nonincome-based (it is not based on *net* income), Wild West is not protected by Public Law 86-272. Therefore, the physical presence of salespeople soliciting sales of tangible personal property creates a nonincome-based tax nexus (but it would *not* have created an income tax filing requirement if the tax were based on net income).

Some states impose nonincome-based taxes on all businesses, not just the businesses taxable at the federal level. For example, Texas imposes the margin tax on C corporations, S corporations, partnerships, and sole proprietorships that have limited liability. The calculation of a nonincome-based tax is detailed in Example 12-21.

Example 12-21

Wild West has nexus in Washington and is subject to that state's business and occupation (B&O) tax. The tax is .471 percent of gross receipts for retailers and 1.5 percent of gross receipts on services. Wild West's gross receipts from retail sales and services in Washington are $41,982 and $377,441, respectively (from Exhibit 12-1). Calculate Wild West's B&O tax.

(continued on page 12-26)

Answer: Wild West's B&O tax is $5,860, calculated as follows:

Activity	(1) Receipts	(2) Rate	(1) × (2) Tax
Retailing	$ 41,982	0.471%	$ 198
Services	377,441	1.500%	5,662
B&O tax			**$5,860**

CONCLUSION

In this chapter, we discussed the fundamentals of state and local taxation with an emphasis on sales tax nexus, income tax nexus, sales tax, and net income-based corporate taxes. State and local taxes currently make up a significant portion of many businesses' total tax burden and also consume a significant portion of the tax department's time.

Sales tax nexus was traditionally established through physical presence but has shifted to economic sales tax nexus under the *Wayfair* decision. Companies selling tangible personal property must collect sales tax from their customers (where sales tax nexus exists) and remit it to the various states. Income tax nexus can be created through either physical or economic presence. However, even when income tax nexus exists, sellers of tangible personal property are protected from income tax filing requirements by Public Law 86-272 if certain criteria are met.

Businesses subject to multijurisdictional taxation—taxation by more than one government—have many issues in common. A business located in San Diego, California, but also doing business in Tucson, Arizona, will be subject to California and Arizona tax. If it also does business in Rosarito, Mexico, it will be subject to both U.S. and Mexico federal taxes. State and local taxation and international taxation bring up many of the same issues. For both, businesses must determine which jurisdiction has the right to tax a transaction (nexus) and how to divide income among different jurisdictions. The next chapter examines the taxation of multinational transactions.

Summary

LO 12-1 Describe the primary types of state and local taxes.

- The primary purpose of state and local taxes is to raise revenue.
- Like federal tax law, state tax law is composed of legislative, administrative, and judicial law.
- Judicial law plays a more important role in state tax law than federal tax law because constitutionality is a primary concern for state tax laws.
- The most important question any taxpayer must answer is whether it is subject to a state's taxing regime.
- Nexus is the connection between a business and a state sufficient to subject the business to the state's tax system. We cover two types of nexus: sales tax nexus and income tax nexus.
- When a business sells tangible personal property, sales and/or use tax is due. If the seller has sales tax nexus, the seller must collect and remit the tax to the state. Otherwise, the buyer is responsible for paying the use tax.
- Businesses engaged in interstate commerce that have income tax nexus and an income tax filing requirement must pay income tax.

LO 12-2 Determine whether a business has sales tax nexus and calculate its sales tax withholding responsibilities.

- Forty-five states and the District of Columbia impose sales taxes. The items subject to sales tax vary from state to state.

- Businesses are required to collect sales tax on sales only if they have sales tax nexus in that state.
- For nondomiciliary businesses, sales tax nexus may be created through either economic activity or physical presence.

Identify whether a business has income tax nexus and determine its state income tax liabilities. LO 12-3

- Forty-four states impose an income tax on corporations, and 43 states impose an income tax on income from partnerships and S corporations.
- Businesses must pay income tax in their state of commercial domicile, and nondomiciliary firms may be subject to tax if they have income tax nexus in the state.
- Income tax nexus can be created through either physical or economic presence. Income tax nexus creates an income tax filing requirement unless a business is protected by Public Law 86-272. Public Law 86-272 protects sellers of tangible personal property from the income tax filing requirement—even when income tax nexus exists—if the business activities within the state are limited to solicitation. However, recent changes to the MTC's Statement on P.L. 86-272 suggest indicate that a push towards economic nexus may have arrived.
- Businesses divide or apportion their income among the states where they have established income tax nexus.
- Some states require a separate income tax return for each entity with income tax nexus, and others require a unitary (single) tax return for a group of related entities as long as one of the entities has established income tax nexus in the state.
- Businesses must calculate state taxable income for each state in which they must file a tax return—this requires businesses to identify federal/state adjustments.
- Firms adjust federal taxable income to arrive at their state taxable base.
- The state taxable base of an interstate business is generally separated into business and nonbusiness income: Business income is apportioned across states using a general formula, and nonbusiness income is allocated to specific states using specific rules.
- Business income is apportioned using some combination of sales, payroll, and property factors.

KEY TERMS

allocation (12-4)
apportionment (12-4)
business income (12-4)
commercial domicile (12-2)
economic income tax nexus (12-11)
federal/state adjustments (12-17)
income tax nexus (12-10)
interstate commerce (12-4)
nexus (12-2)
nonbusiness income (12-4)
nondomiciliary businesses (12-2)
Public Law 86-272 (12-10)
sales tax (12-3)
sales tax nexus (12-5)
separate tax return (12-15)
solicitation (12-12)
state tax base (12-4)
throwback rule (12-19)
trade show rule (12-13)
unitary tax return (12-15)
use tax (12-4)

DISCUSSION QUESTIONS

Discussion Questions are available in Connect®.

1. Why do states and local jurisdictions assess taxes? LO 12-1
2. Compare and contrast the relative importance of judicial law to state and local and federal tax law. LO 12-1
3. Describe briefly the nexus concept and explain its importance to state and local taxation. LO 12-1
4. What is the difference, if any, between the state of a business's commercial domicile and its state of incorporation? LO 12-1
5. What types of property sales are subject to sales tax, and why might a state choose to exclude the sales of certain types of property from the sales tax base? LO 12-1
6. In what circumstances would a business be subject to income taxes in more than one state? LO 12-1

LO 12-1 7. Describe how the failure to collect sales tax can result in a larger tax liability for a business than failing to pay income taxes.

LO 12-2 8. Discuss why restaurant meals, rental cars, and hotel receipts are often taxed at a higher-than-average sales tax rate.

LO 12-2 9. Compare and contrast general sales tax nexus rules under the *Quill* and *Wayfair* decisions.

LO 12-2 10. What is the difference between a sales tax and a use tax?

LO 12-2 11. Renée operates Scandinavian Imports, a furniture shop in Olney, Maryland, that ships goods to customers in all 50 states. Scandinavian Imports also appraises antique furniture and has recently conducted in-home appraisals in the District of Columbia, Maryland, Pennsylvania, and Virginia. Online appraisals have been done for customers in California, Minnesota, New Mexico, and Texas. Determine where Scandinavian Imports has sales tax nexus.

LO 12-2 12. Web Music, located in Gardnerville, Nevada, is a new online music service that allows inexpensive legal music downloads. Web Music prides itself on having the fastest download times in the industry. It achieved this speed by leasing server space from 10 regional servers dispersed across the country. Discuss where Web Music has sales tax nexus.

LO 12-2 13. Discuss possible reasons why the Commerce Clause was included in the U.S. Constitution.

LO 12-2 14. Describe the administrative burden businesses face in collecting sales taxes.

LO 12-3 15. Compare and contrast the rules determining where domiciliary and nondomiciliary businesses must file state income tax returns.

LO 12-3 16. Lars operates Keep Flying Incorporated, a used airplane parts business, in Laramie, Wyoming. Lars employs sales agents who visit mechanics in all 50 states to solicit orders. All orders are sent to Wyoming for approval, and all parts are shipped via common carrier. The sales agents are always on the lookout for wrecked, abandoned, or salvaged aircraft with rare parts because they receive substantial bonuses for purchasing and salvaging these parts and shipping them to Wyoming. Discuss the states where Keep Flying has income tax nexus.

LO 12-3 17. Explain changes in the U.S. economy that have made Public Law 86-272 partially obsolete. Provide an example of a company for which Public Law 86-272 works well and one for which it does not.

LO 12-3 18. Climb Higher is a distributor of high-end climbing gear located in Paradise, Washington. Its sales personnel regularly perform the following activities in an effort to maximize sales:

- Carry swag (free samples) for distribution to climbing shop employees.
- Perform credit checks of new customers to reduce delivery time of the first order of merchandise.
- Check customer inventory for proper display and proper quantities.
- Accept returns of defective goods.

Identify which of Climb Higher's sales activities are protected and unprotected activities under the *Wrigley* Supreme Court decision.

LO 12-3 19. Describe a situation in which it would be advantageous for a business to establish income tax nexus in a state.

LO 12-3 20. States are arguing for economic income tax nexus; provide at least one reason for and one reason against the validity of economic income tax nexus.

LO 12-3 21. Explain the difference between separate-return states and unitary-return states.

LO 12-3 22. Explain the rationale for the factors (functional integration, centralization of management, and economies of scale) that determine whether two or more businesses form a unitary group under the *Mobil* decision.

LO 12-3 23. Compare and contrast the reasons why book/tax and federal/state adjustments are necessary for interest income.

24. Compare and contrast the ways a multistate business divides business and nonbusiness income among states. LO 12-3
25. Contrast the treatment of government sales and dock sales for the sales apportionment factor. LO 12-3
26. Most states have increased the weight of the sales factor for the apportionment of business income. What are some of the possible reasons for this change? LO 12-3
27. Compare and contrast federal/state tax differences and book/federal tax differences. LO 12-3

PROBLEMS

Select problems are available in Connect®.

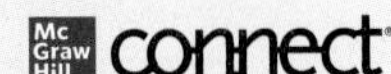

28. Crazy Eddie Incorporated manufactures baseball caps and distributes them across the northeastern United States. The firm is incorporated and headquartered in New York and sells to customers in Connecticut, Delaware, Massachusetts, New Jersey, New York, Ohio, and Pennsylvania. It has sales reps only where discussed in the scenarios below. Determine whether Crazy Eddie has sales tax nexus in each of the following states, assuming these states have adopted *Wayfair:* LO 12-2
    a) Crazy Eddie is incorporated and headquartered in New York. It also has property, employees, salespeople, and intangibles in New York.
    b) Crazy Eddie has a warehouse, personal property, and employees in Connecticut.
    c) Crazy Eddie has two customers in Delaware. Crazy Eddie receives orders over the phone and ships goods to its Delaware customers using FedEx.
    d) Crazy Eddie has independent sales representatives in Massachusetts who distribute baseball-related items for over a dozen companies.
    e) Crazy Eddie has salespeople who visit New Jersey. They follow procedures that comply with Public Law 86-272 by sending orders to New York for acceptance. The goods are shipped to New Jersey by FedEx.
    f) Crazy Eddie provides graphic design services to another manufacturer located in Ohio. While the services are performed in New York, Crazy Eddie's designers visit Ohio at least quarterly to deliver the new designs and receive feedback.
    g) Crazy Eddie receives online orders from its Pennsylvania clients. Because the orders are so large, the goods are delivered weekly on Crazy Eddie's trucks.
29. Brad Carlton operates Carlton Collectibles, a rare-coin shop in Washington, D.C., that ships coins to collectors in all 50 states. Carlton also provides appraisal services upon request. During the last several years, the appraisal work has been done either in the D.C. shop or at the homes of private collectors in Maryland and Virginia. Determine the jurisdictions in which Carlton Collectibles has sales tax nexus, assuming these states have enacted *Wayfair* legislation. LO 12-2
30. Melanie operates Mel's Bakery in Foxboro, Massachusetts, and has retail stores in Connecticut, Maine, Massachusetts, New Hampshire, and Rhode Island. Mel's Bakery also ships specialty breads nationwide upon request. Determine Mel's Bakery's sales tax collection responsibility and calculate the sales tax liability for Massachusetts, Connecticut, Maine, New Hampshire, Rhode Island, and Texas, based on the following information: LO 12-2
    a) The Massachusetts stores have $500,000 in sales. Massachusetts's sales tax rate is 5 percent; assume it exempts food items.
    b) The Connecticut retail stores have $400,000 in sales ($300,000 from in-store sales and $100,000 from catering) and $10,000 in delivery charges for catering activities. Connecticut sales tax is 6 percent and excludes food products but taxes prepared meals (catering). Connecticut also imposes sales tax on delivery charges on taxable sales.

c) Mel's Bakery's Maine retail store has $250,000 of sales ($200,000 for take-out and $50,000 of in-store sales). Maine has a 5 percent sales tax rate and a 7 percent sales tax rate on prepared food; it exempts other food purchases.

d) The New Hampshire retail stores have $250,000 of dine-in sales. New Hampshire is one of five states with no sales tax. However, it has a room and meals tax rate of 8 percent. New Hampshire considers any food or beverage served by a restaurant for consumption on or off the premises to be a meal.

e) Mel's Bakery's Rhode Island stores earn $300,000 in sales. The Rhode Island sales tax rate is 7 percent and its restaurant surtax is 1 percent. Rhode Island considers Mel's Bakery to be a restaurant because its retail store has seating.

f) One of Mel's Bakery's best customers relocated to Texas, which imposes an 8.25 percent state and local sales tax rate but exempts bakery products. This customer entertains guests regularly and made 10 orders totaling $15,000 of food items this year. Assume Texas only has a sales threshold of $500,000 to establish an economic nexus.

LO 12-2

31. Cuyahoga County, Ohio, has a sales tax rate of 8 percent. Determine the state, local, and transit (a local transportation district) portions of the rate. You can find resources on the State of Ohio website, including the following link: www.tax.ohio.gov/Portals/0/tax_analysis/tax_data_series/sales_and_use/salestaxmap.pdf.

LO 12-2

32. Kai operates the Surf Shop in Laie, Hawaii, which designs, manufactures, and customizes surfboards. Hawaii has a hypothetical 4 percent excise tax rate, technically paid by the seller. However, the state also allows "tax on tax" to be charged, which effectively means a customer is billed 4.166 percent of the sales price. Determine the sales tax the Surf Shop must collect and remit—or the use tax liability the customer must pay—for each of the following orders:

a) Kalani, a Utah customer, places an Internet order for a $1,000 board that will be shipped to Provo, Utah, where the local sales tax rate is 6.85 percent.

b) Nick, an Alabama resident, comes to the retail shop on vacation and has a $2,000 custom board made. Nick uses the board on vacation and then has the Surf Shop ship it to Tuscaloosa, Alabama, where the sales tax rate is 9 percent.

c) Jim, a Michigan resident, places an order for a $2,000 custom board at the end of his vacation. Upon completion, the board will be shipped to Ann Arbor, Michigan, where the sales tax rate is 6 percent.

d) Scott, a Nebraska resident, sends his current surfboard to the Surf Shop for a custom paint job. The customization services come to $800. The board is shipped to Lincoln, Nebraska, where the sales tax rate is 7.25 percent.

LO 12-2
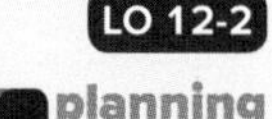

33. Last year, Reggie, a Los Angeles, California, resident, began selling autographed footballs through Trojan Victory (TV) Incorporated, a California corporation. TV has never collected sales tax. Last year it had sales as follows: California ($100,000), Arizona ($10,000), Oregon ($15,000), New York ($50,000), and Wyoming ($1,000). Most sales are made over the Internet and shipped by common carrier. Determine how much sales tax TV should have collected in each of the following situations:

a) California treats the autographed footballs as tangible personal property subject to an 8.25 percent sales tax rate. Answer for California.

b) California treats the autographed footballs as part tangible personal property ($50,000) and part services ($50,000), and tangible personal property is subject to an 8.25 percent sales tax rate. Answer for California.

c) TV has no property or other physical presence in New York (10.25 percent) or Wyoming (5 percent). Answer for New York and Wyoming.

d) TV has Reggie deliver a few footballs to fans in Arizona (5.6 percent sales tax rate) and Oregon (no sales tax) while attending football games there. Answer for Arizona and Oregon.

e) Related to part (d), can you make any suggestions that would decrease TV's Arizona sales tax liability?

34. LeMond Incorporated, a Wisconsin corporation, runs bicycle tours in several states. LeMond also has a Wisconsin retail store and an Internet store that ships to out-of-state customers. The bicycle tours operate in Colorado, North Carolina, and Wisconsin, where LeMond has employees and owns and uses tangible personal property. LeMond has real property only in Wisconsin and logs the following sales: LO 12-2

LeMond Sales

State	Goods	Services	Total
Arizona	$ 34,194	$ 0	$ 34,194
California	110,612	0	110,612
Colorado	25,913	356,084	381,997
North Carolina	16,721	225,327	242,048
Oregon	15,431	0	15,431
Wisconsin	241,982	877,441	1,119,423
Totals	$444,853	$1,458,852	$1,903,705

Assume the following hypothetical tax rates: Arizona (5.6 percent), California (7.75 percent), Colorado (8 percent), North Carolina (6.75 percent), Oregon (no sales tax), and Wisconsin (5 percent). How much sales tax must LeMond collect and remit, assuming these states, except California, have adopted *Wayfair* legislation?

35. Kashi Corporation is the U.S. distributor of fencing (sword fighting) equipment imported from Europe. It is incorporated in Virginia and headquartered in Arlington, Virginia; it ships goods to all 50 states. Kashi's employees attend regional and national fencing competitions, where they maintain temporary booths to market their goods. Determine whether Kashi has income tax nexus and a filing requirement in the following situations: LO 12-3 planning

a) Kashi is incorporated and headquartered in Virginia. It also has property, employees, salespeople, and intangibles in Virginia. Determine whether Kashi has income tax nexus in Virginia.

b) Kashi has employees who live in Washington, D.C., and Maryland, but they perform all their employment-related activities in Virginia. Does Kashi have income tax nexus in Washington, D.C., and Maryland?

c) Kashi has two customers in North Dakota. It receives their orders over the phone and ships goods to them using FedEx. Determine whether Kashi has income tax nexus in North Dakota.

d) Kashi has independent sales representatives in Illinois who distribute fencing and other sports-related items for many companies. Does Kashi have income tax nexus in Illinois?

e) Kashi has salespeople who visit South Carolina for a regional fencing competition for a total of three days during the year. They send all orders to Virginia for credit approval and acceptance, and Kashi ships the goods into South Carolina by FedEx. Determine whether Kashi has income tax nexus in South Carolina.

f) Kashi has sales reps who visit California for a national fencing competition and several regional competitions for a total of 17 days during the year. They send all orders to Virginia for credit approval and acceptance. The goods are shipped by FedEx into California. Does Kashi have income tax nexus in California?

g) Kashi receives online orders from its Pennsylvania client. Because the orders are so large, the goods are delivered weekly on Kashi's trucks. Does Kashi have income tax nexus in Pennsylvania?

h) In addition to shipping goods, Kashi provides fencing lessons in Virginia and Maryland locations. Determine whether Kashi has income tax nexus in Virginia and Maryland.

i) Given that Kashi ships to all 50 states, are there locations that would decrease Kashi's overall state income tax burden if income tax nexus were created there?

LO 12-3 36. Gary Holt LLP provides tax and legal services regarding the tax-exempt bond issues of state and local jurisdictions. Gary typically provides the services from his New York offices. However, for large issuances he and his staff occasionally travel to another state to complete the work. Determine whether the firm has income tax nexus in the following situations:

a) Gary Holt LLP is a New York partnership and headquartered in New York. It also has property and employees in New York. Does it have income tax nexus in New York?

b) Gary Holt LLP has employees who live in New Jersey and Connecticut and perform all their employment-related activities in New York. Does it have income tax nexus in New Jersey and/or Connecticut?

c) Gary Holt LLP has two customers in California. Gary personally travels there to finalize the Alameda County bond issuance. Does it have income tax nexus in California?

LO 12-3 37. Root Beer Inc. (RBI) is incorporated and headquartered in Seattle, Washington. RBI runs an Internet business, www.makerootbeer.com, and sells bottling equipment and other supplies for making homemade root beer. It also has an Oregon warehouse from which it ships goods. Determine whether RBI has income tax nexus in the following situations:

a) RBI is incorporated and headquartered in Washington and has property and employees in Oregon and Washington. Determine whether RBI has income tax nexus in Oregon and Washington.

b) RBI has hundreds of customers in California but no physical presence (no employees or property). Does it have income tax nexus in California?

c) RBI has 500 New York customers but no physical presence (no employees or property). Determine whether RBI has income tax nexus in New York.

LO 12-3 38. Rockville Enterprises manufactures woodworking equipment and is incorporated and based in Evansville, Indiana. All of its real property is in Indiana. Rockville Enterprises employs a large sales force that travels throughout the United States. Determine whether each of the following is a protected activity in nondomiciliary states under Public Law 86-272:

a) Rockville Enterprises advertises in Wisconsin using television, radio, and newspapers.

b) Rockville Enterprises's employees in Illinois check the credit of potential customers.

c) Rockville Enterprises maintains a booth at an industry trade show in Arizona for 10 days.

d) Sales representatives check the inventory of a Tennessee customer to make sure it has enough stock and that the stock is properly displayed.

e) Rockville Enterprises holds a management seminar executive retreat for corporate executives over four days in Florida.

f) Sales representatives supervise the repossession of inventory from a customer in Maine that is not making payments on time.

g) Rockville Enterprises provides automobiles to Idaho and Montana sales representatives.

h) An Alabama sales representative accepts a customer deposit on a large order.

i) Colorado sales reps carry display racks and promotional materials that they place in customers' retail stores without charge.

LO 12-3 research 39. Software Incorporated is a sales and use tax software vendor that provides customers with a license to download and use its software on their machines. Software retains ownership of the software. It has customers in New Jersey and West Virginia. Determine whether Software has economic income tax nexus in these states based on the following decisions: *Lanco, Inc. v. Director, Division of Taxation,* 188 N.J. 380, 908 A.2d 176 (2006), and *Tax Commissioner of West Virginia v. MBNA America Bank, N.A.,* 640 S.E.2d 226 (W. Va. 2006).

LO 12-3 research 40. Peter Inc., a Kentucky corporation, owns 100 percent of Suvi Inc., a Mississippi corporation. Peter and Suvi file a consolidated federal tax return. Peter has income tax nexus in Kentucky and South Carolina; Suvi has income tax nexus in Mississippi and South Carolina. Kentucky, Mississippi, and South Carolina are separate-return states. In which states must Peter and Suvi file tax returns? Can they file a consolidated return in any states? Explain. (*Hint:* Use South Carolina Form SC 1120 and the related instructions.)

41. Use California Publication 1061 (2020) to identify the various tests California uses to determine whether two or more entities are part of a unitary group. The publication can be found here: www.ftb.ca.gov/forms/2020/2020-1061-publication.pdf. LO 12-3 research

42. Bulldog Incorporated is a Georgia corporation. It properly included, deducted, or excluded the following items on its federal tax return in the current year: LO 12-3

Item	Amount	Federal Treatment
Georgia income taxes	$25,496	Deducted on federal return
Tennessee income taxes	13,653	Deducted on federal return
Washington gross receipts tax	3,105	Deducted on federal return
Georgia bond interest income	10,000	Excluded from federal return
Federal T-note interest income	4,500	Included on federal return
Bonus depreciation	15,096	Deducted on federal return

Use Georgia's Corporate Income Tax Form 600 and Instructions to determine what federal/state adjustments Bulldog needs to make for Georgia. Bulldog's federal taxable income was $194,302. Calculate its Georgia state tax base and complete Schedule 1, page 1, of Form 600 for Bulldog.

43. Herger Corporation does business in California, Nevada, and Oregon and has income tax nexus in these states as well. Herger's California state tax base was $921,023 after making the required federal/state adjustments. Herger's federal tax return contains the following items: LO 12-3

Item	Amount
Federal T-note interest income	$ 5,000
Nevada municipal bond interest income	3,400
California municipal bond interest income	6,000
Interest expense related to T-note interest income	1,400
Royalty income	100,000
Travel expenses	9,025

Determine Herger's business income.

44. Bad Brad sells used semitrucks and tractor trailers in the Texas panhandle. Bad Brad has sales as follows: LO 12-3

Bad Brad	
State	**Sales**
Colorado	$ 234,992
New Mexico	675,204
Oklahoma	402,450
Texas	1,085,249
Total	$2,397,895

Bad Brad is a Texas corporation. Answer the questions in each of the following alternative scenarios.

a) Bad Brad has income tax nexus in Colorado, New Mexico, Oklahoma, and Texas. What are the Colorado, New Mexico, Oklahoma, and Texas sales apportionment factors?

b) Bad Brad has income tax nexus in Colorado and Texas. Oklahoma and New Mexico sales are shipped from Texas (a throwback state). What are the Colorado and Texas sales apportionment factors?

c) Bad Brad has income tax nexus in Colorado and Texas. Oklahoma and New Mexico sales are shipped from Texas (a throwback state); $200,000 of Oklahoma sales were to the federal government. What are the Colorado and Texas sales apportionment factors?

d) Bad Brad has income tax nexus in Colorado and Texas. Oklahoma and New Mexico sales are shipped from Texas (assume Texas is a nonthrowback state). What are the Colorado and Texas sales apportionment factors?

LO 12-3 45. Nicole's Salon, a Louisiana corporation, operates beauty salons in Arkansas, Louisiana, and Tennessee. The salons' payrolls by state are as follows:

Nicole's Salon	
State	**Payroll**
Arkansas	$ 130,239
Louisiana	309,192
Tennessee	723,010
Total	$1,162,441

What are the payroll apportionment factors for Arkansas, Louisiana, and Tennessee in each of the following alternative scenarios?

a) Nicole's Salon has income tax nexus in Arkansas, Louisiana, and Tennessee.

b) Nicole's Salon has income tax nexus in Arkansas, Louisiana, and Tennessee, but $50,000 of the Arkansas amount is paid to independent contractors.

LO 12-3 46. Delicious Dave's Maple Syrup, a Vermont corporation, has property in the following states:

	Property	
State	**Beginning**	**Ending**
Maine	$ 923,032	$ 994,221
Massachusetts	103,311	203,109
New Hampshire	381,983	283,021
Vermont	873,132	891,976
Total	$2,281,458	$2,372,327

What are the property apportionment factors for Maine, Massachusetts, New Hampshire, and Vermont in each of the following alternative scenarios?

a) Delicious Dave's has income tax nexus in each of the states.

b) Delicious Dave's has income tax nexus in each of the states, but the Maine total includes $400,000 of investment property that Delicious rents out (unrelated to its business).

c) Delicious Dave's has income tax nexus in each of the states, but it also pays $50,000 to rent property in Massachusetts.

LO 12-3 47. Susie's Sweet Shop has the following sales, payroll, and property factors:

Item	Iowa	Missouri
Sales	69.20%	32.01%
Payroll	88.00%	3.50%
Property	72.42%	24.04%

What are Susie's Sweet Shop's Iowa and Missouri apportionment factors under each of the following alternative scenarios?

a) Iowa and Missouri both use a three-factor apportionment formula.

b) Iowa and Missouri both use a four-factor apportionment formula that double-weights sales.

c) Iowa uses a three-factor formula and Missouri uses a single-factor apportionment formula (based solely on sales).

48. Brady Corporation is a Nebraska corporation, but it owns business and investment property in surrounding states as well. Determine the state where each item of income is allocated. LO 12-3
    a) $15,000 of dividend income.
    b) $10,000 of interest income.
    c) $15,000 of rental income for South Dakota property.
    d) $20,000 of royalty income for intangibles used in South Dakota (where income tax nexus exists).
    e) $24,000 of royalty income from Kansas (where income tax nexus does not exist).
    f) $15,000 of capital gain from securities held for investment.
    g) $30,000 of capital gain on real property located in South Dakota.
49. Ashton Corporation is headquartered in Pennsylvania and has a state income tax base there of $500,000. Of this amount, $50,000 was nonbusiness income. Ashton's Pennsylvania apportionment factor is 42.35 percent. The nonbusiness income allocated to Pennsylvania was $32,000. Assuming a Pennsylvania corporate tax rate of 8.25 percent, what is Ashton's Pennsylvania state tax liability? 

COMPREHENSIVE PROBLEMS

Select problems are available in Connect®. 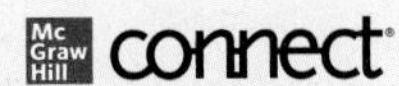

50. Cloud computing is the use of hosted computer facilities through the Internet. Gmail, RIA Checkpoint, and even your iPhone are some applications of cloud computing. Please research the following questions. 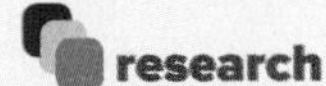
    a) If HP provides a customized bundle of servers, storage, network and security software, and business application software to a customer in Washington State, how is it taxed?
    b) Is HP leasing tangible personal property, which is taxable, or providing a nontaxable service?
    c) Is the buyer of HP's product subject to Washington sales tax?
    d) Is HP subject to Washington's B&O tax?
51. Sharon Inc. is headquartered in State X and owns 100 percent of Carol Corp., Josey Corp., and Janice Corp., which form a single unitary group. Assume sales operations are within the solicitation bounds of Public Law 86-272. Each of the corporations has operations in the following states:

Domicile State	Sharon Inc. State X (throwback)	Carol Corp. State Y (throwback)	Josey Corp. State Z (nonthrowback)	Janice Corp. State Z (nonthrowback)
Dividend income	$ 1,000	$ 200	$ 300	$ 500
Business income	50,000	30,000	10,000	10,000
Sales: State X	70,000	10,000	10,000	10,000
State Y		40,000	5,000	
State Z		20,000	20,000	10,000
State A	20,000			
State B	10,000			10,000
Property: State X	50,000	20,000		10,000
State Y		80,000		
State Z			25,000	20,000
State A	50,000			
Payroll: State X	10,000	10,000		
State Y		40,000		
State Z			3,000	10,000
State A				10,000

Compute the following for State X assuming a tax rate of 15 percent.

a) Calculate the State X apportionment factor for Sharon Inc., Carol Corp., Josey Corp., and Janice Corp.

b) Calculate the business income apportioned to State X.

c) Calculate the taxable income for State X for each company.

d) Determine the tax liability for State X for the entire group.

52. Happy Hippos (HH) is a manufacturer and retailer of New England crafts headquartered in Camden, Maine. HH provides services and has sales, employees, property, and commercial domicile as follows:

Happy Hippos In-State Activities

State	Sales	Employees	Property	Services	Commercial Domicile
Connecticut	✓	✓		✓	
Maine	✓	✓	✓	✓	✓
Massachusetts	✓	✓			
New York	✓				
Rhode Island	✓	✓			
Vermont	✓	✓	✓	✓	

HH's sales of goods and services by state are as follows:

Happy Hippos Sales

State	Goods	Services	Total
Connecticut	$ 78,231	$ 52,321	$130,552
Maine	292,813	81,313	374,126
Massachusetts	90,238		90,238
New York	129,322		129,322
Rhode Island	98,313		98,313
Vermont	123,914	23,942	147,856
Totals	$812,831	$157,576	$970,407

HH has federal taxable income of $282,487 for the current year. Included in federal taxable income are the following income and deductions:

- $12,000 of Vermont rental income.
- City of Orono, Maine, bond interest of $10,000.
- $10,000 of dividends.
- $2,498 of state tax refund included in income.
- $32,084 of state net income tax expense.
- $59,234 of federal depreciation.

Other relevant facts include:

- Assume that the New York sales are to a single customer who is a retailer and can provide a valid New York reseller's certificate.
- Maine state depreciation for the year was $47,923, and Maine doesn't allow deductions for state income taxes.
- The employees present in Connecticut, Massachusetts, and Rhode Island are salespeople who perform only activities protected by Public Law 86-272.
- Assume that each of the states is a separate-return state.

HH's payroll is as follows:

Payroll	
State	**Wages**
Connecticut	$ 94,231
Maine	392,195
Massachusetts	167,265
Rhode Island	92,391
Vermont	193,923
Total	$940,005

HH's property is as follows:

Property			
State	**Beginning**	**Ending**	**Rented**
Maine	$ 938,234	$ 937,652	
Vermont	329,134	428,142	$12,000
Total	$1,267,368	$1,365,794	$12,000

Required:

a) Determine the states in which HH has sales tax nexus, assuming these states have passed *Wayfair* legislation.

b) Calculate the sales tax HH must remit assuming the following (hypothetical) sales tax rates:

- Connecticut (6 percent)
- Maine (8 percent)
- Massachusetts (7 percent)
- New York (8.875 percent)
- Rhode Island (5 percent)
- Vermont (9 percent)

c) Determine the states in which HH has income tax nexus and an income tax filing requirement.

d) Determine HH's state tax base for Maine, assuming federal taxable income of $282,487.

e) Calculate business and nonbusiness income.

f) Determine HH's Maine apportionment factors using the three-factor method (assume that Maine is a throwback state).

g) Calculate HH's business income apportioned to Maine.

h) Determine HH's allocation of nonbusiness income to Maine.

i) Determine HH's Maine taxable income.

j) Calculate HH's Maine income tax liability, assuming a Maine income tax rate of 5 percent.

UWorld Roger CPA Review

Sample CPA Exam questions from Roger CPA Review are available in Connect as support for the topics in this text. These Multiple Choice Questions and Task-Based Simulations include expert-written explanations and solutions and provide a starting point for students to become familiar with the content and functionality of the actual CPA Exam.

chapter

13 The U.S. Taxation of Multinational Transactions

Learning Objectives

Upon completing this chapter, you should be able to:

- **LO 13-1** Describe the basic U.S. framework for taxing multinational transactions and the role of the foreign tax credit limitation.
- **LO 13-2** Apply the U.S. source rules for common items of gross income and deductions.
- **LO 13-3** Explain the role of income tax treaties in international tax planning.
- **LO 13-4** Identify creditable foreign taxes and compute the foreign tax credit limitation.
- **LO 13-5** Compare the advantages and disadvantages of the different forms of doing business outside the United States.
- **LO 13-6** Explain the basic U.S. anti-deferral tax regime and identify common sources of subpart F income.

Karin Dreyer/Tetra images/Getty Images

Storyline Summary

Detroit Doughnut Depot (3D)

Privately held company located in Detroit, Michigan. Operated as a C corporation for U.S. tax purposes. Makes and sells fresh baked goods, homemade sandwiches, and premium coffee and tea drinks.

Owner:	Lily Green (she/her/hers)
Filing status:	Married filing jointly
Marginal tax rate:	24 percent

Lily Green was excited about the growth of her coffee and baked goods business since she opened her store in downtown Detroit in 2015. From its humble beginnings, the Detroit Doughnut Depot (3D) had attracted a solid base of loyal customers who appreciated the freshness and organic ingredients that set the company's products apart from its competitors. Many of Lily's customers were commuters from nearby Windsor, Canada. They often asked Lily whether she ever considered opening a store in Windsor, where they thought she would find a receptive customer base. Lily was intrigued by the idea of "going global" with her business, but she knew she needed to find someone to help her understand the U.S. and Canadian income tax implications of expanding her business to Windsor. Her first questions dealt with how and when she would be subject to Canadian tax and whether her Canadian activities also would be subject to U.S. tax. ■

Lily Green is about to take part in a growing trend of expansion by U.S. businesses into international markets. In 1983, gross receipts of non-U.S. subsidiaries of U.S. multinational corporations totaled approximately $720 billion; by 2019, that number exceeded $7.7 trillion, over a tenfold increase.[1] Net income increased from $57 billion in 1983 to $1.5 trillion in 2019. Companies such as Google Inc. and Apple Inc. report a significant amount of revenue from international operations. For example, Alphabet Inc. (Google) reported revenue from its international operations of $97 billion in the calendar year ended 2020, approximately 53 percent of its total revenue.[2] Apple Inc. reported net sales of $365.8 billion in fiscal 2021, approximately 63 percent of which came from outside the United States.

As dramatic as the outflow of investment from the United States has been, the inflow of investment by non-U.S. businesses and individuals into the United States has been just as impressive. According to the U.S. Bureau of Economic Analysis, the total amount of foreign-owned assets in the United States increased by more than 1,000 percent between 1989 and 2020, to $32.3 trillion.[3] U.S. subsidiaries of non-U.S. companies currently employ 7.9 million Americans.[4] Familiar non–U.S. headquartered companies with large U.S. operations include BP Global (United Kingdom), Toyota Motor Corporation (Japan), Honda Motor Corporation (Japan), Nissan Group (Japan), Nestlé S.A. (Switzerland), Sony Corporation (Japan), GlaxoSmithKline PLC (United Kingdom), Volkswagen AG (Germany), Samsung Group (South Korea), BMW AG (Germany), Bridgestone Corporation (Japan), Bayer AG (Germany), and Philips Electronics N.V. (Netherlands).

This chapter provides a basic overview of the income tax consequences related to transactions that span more than one national tax jurisdiction (in our storyline, the United States and Canada). We focus primarily on the U.S. tax rules that apply to **outbound transactions,** involving the establishment of a **foreign branch** or formation of a foreign corporation, where a U.S. person engages in a transaction that occurs outside the United States or involves a non-U.S. person.[5] We also discuss briefly the U.S. tax rules that apply to **inbound transactions,** where a non-U.S. person engages in a transaction that occurs within the United States or involves a U.S. person. Most of the U.S. income tax rules that apply to multinational transactions are found in subchapter N of the Internal Revenue Code (IRC) (§§861–999).

LO 13-1

THE U.S. FRAMEWORK FOR TAXING MULTINATIONAL TRANSACTIONS

When a U.S. person engages in a transaction that involves a country outside the United States, there arises the issue as to which tax authority or authorities have jurisdiction (i.e., the legal right) to tax that transaction. All governments (national, state, and local) must adopt a basis on which to claim the right to tax income. The criteria they choose to assert their right to tax a person or transaction is called **nexus.** At the national level, governments most often determine nexus by either the taxpayer's citizenship or residence, called **residence-based jurisdiction,** or the geographic source of income, called **source-based jurisdiction.**

THE KEY FACTS

Basic Framework for U.S. Taxation of Multinational Transactions

- The United States taxes citizens and residents on their worldwide income and nonresidents on their U.S. source income.
- U.S. corporations owning 10 percent or more of a foreign corporation receive a 100 percent dividends-received deduction for dividends received from these corporations.

(continued)

[1]Bureau of Economic Analysis, *U.S. Direct Investment Abroad: Financial and Operating Data for U.S. Multinational Companies,* available at www.bea.gov.

[2]As a reference point, Google Inc. reported a *loss* of $42.3 million in 2005 from international operations.

[3]Bureau of Economic Analysis, *U.S. Net International Investment Position Year 2020* (updated September 30, 2021), available at www.bea.gov.

[4]Global Business Alliance, data available at www.globalbusiness.org.

[5]As used in this chapter, a "person" includes an individual, corporation, partnership, trust, estate, or association. §7701(a)(1). The "United States," as used in this context, includes only the 50 states and the District of Columbia. §7701(a)(9).

Once nexus has been established, a government must decide how to allocate and apportion a person's income and expenses to its tax jurisdiction. Under a residence-based approach, a country taxes the worldwide income of the person earning the income. Under a source-based approach, a country taxes only the income earned within its boundaries. When applying a source-based approach, a government must develop source rules to allocate and apportion income and expenses to its jurisdiction. Within the United States, states use apportionment formulas that take into account sales, property, and payroll, or some combination of these factors, to apportion income and expenses to their tax jurisdiction.[6]

Income earned by a citizen or resident of one country that has its source in another country can be taxed by both countries. The country where the taxpayer resides can assert residence-based jurisdiction, whereas the country where the income is earned can apply geographic source–based jurisdiction. To mitigate such double taxation and to promote international commerce, governments often allow their residents a tax credit for foreign income taxes paid on *foreign source* income. National governments also enter into income tax treaties with other national governments to mitigate the double taxation of income earned by residents of one country in the other country. Under a treaty, both countries may agree not to tax income earned within their boundaries by a resident of the other country.

The United States applies both residence-based jurisdiction and source-based jurisdiction in asserting its right to tax income. The U.S. government taxes *citizens* and *residents* on their worldwide income, regardless of source (i.e., residence-based jurisdiction).[7] In the Tax Cuts and Jobs Act (TCJA), enacted on December 22, 2017, Congress replaced the worldwide approach with a more territorial approach for U.S. corporations owning 10 percent or more of a foreign corporation. The TCJA allows these 10 percent U.S. corporate shareholders a 100 percent dividends-received deduction to the extent the earnings distributed do not exceed a "normal rate of return" (defined as 10 percent) on the foreign corporation's tangible assets. In contrast, the U.S. government only taxes *nonresidents* on income that is "U.S. source" or is connected with the operation of a U.S. trade or business (i.e., source-based jurisdiction).

- A noncitizen is treated as a U.S. resident for income tax purposes if the individual is a permanent resident (has a green card) or meets a substantial presence test.
- Nonresident income is characterized as either ECI or FDAP income.
  - ECI income is taxed on a net basis using the U.S. graduated tax rates.
  - FDAP income is taxed on a gross basis through a flat withholding tax.
- The U.S. allows citizens and residents a tax credit for foreign income taxes paid on foreign source income.
- U.S. corporations do not receive a foreign tax credit on dividend income from foreign corporations eligible for the 100 percent dividends-received deduction.
- The foreign tax credit is limited to the percentage of foreign source taxable income to total taxable income times the pre-credit income tax on total taxable income.

U.S. Taxation of a Nonresident

U.S. source income earned by a nonresident is classified into two categories for U.S. tax purposes: (1) **effectively connected income (ECI)** and (2) **fixed and determinable, annual or periodic (FDAP) income.** Income that is effectively connected with a U.S. trade or business is subject to *net taxation* (i.e., gross income minus deductions) at the U.S. tax rate. A nonresident reports such income and related deductions on a U.S. tax return, either a Form 1120F for a nonresident corporation or a Form 1040NR for a nonresident individual. FDAP income, which generally is passive income such as dividends, interest, rents, or royalties, is subject to a *withholding tax* regime applied to gross income. The payor of the FDAP income withholds the tax at the statutory rate (30 percent under U.S. tax law), unless reduced under a treaty arrangement, and remits it to the government. The recipient of the FDAP income usually does not have to file a tax return and does not reduce the FDAP income by any deductions. Most countries, including Canada, apply a similar tax regime to U.S. persons earning income within their jurisdiction.[8]

[6]See the State and Local Taxes chapter for a more thorough discussion of how states apportion income.

[7]The United States is one of two countries, the other being Eritrea, that applies full worldwide taxation based on citizenship as well as residency.

[8]Canada applies a 25 percent withholding tax rate on dividends, rents, and royalties unless reduced under a treaty. Under the U.S.–Canada income tax treaty, the withholding tax on shareholders owning less than 10 percent of a corporation's stock is 15 percent, and 5 percent otherwise.

Example 13-1

Lily decided to open a store in Windsor, Canada, from which she will sell baked goods and sandwiches prepared in her U.S. store and transported daily across the border. She elected to operate the store as an unincorporated division, or branch, of Detroit Doughnut Depot (3D) for Canadian tax purposes. Will 3D be subject to tax in Canada on any taxable income it earns through its Windsor store?

Answer: Yes. 3D will have nexus in Canada because it operates a business there (residence-based jurisdiction). As a result, Canada and the province of Ontario will tax the branch's Canadian-source taxable income.

How will Canada tax 3D's Canadian-source taxable income?

Answer: Canada will apply the appropriate corporate tax rate(s) to the branch's taxable income (gross income less deductions). For 2022, the general Canadian corporate net tax rate is a flat 15 percent after abatements. The province of Ontario also will impose an income tax between 3.2 and 11.5 percent on the branch's taxable income.

What if: Assume 3D does not operate a business in Canada but owns 5 percent of the stock in a Canadian corporation that pays 3D a C$100 dividend each year.[9] How will Canada tax 3D on the dividend income it receives from its investment in the stock of the Canadian company?

Answer: Canada will apply a flat withholding tax of 15 percent on the gross amount of the dividend. This is the rate imposed under the U.S.–Canada income tax treaty.[10]

Definition of a Resident for U.S. Tax Purposes

An individual who is not a U.S. citizen is characterized for U.S. tax purposes as either a **resident alien** or a **nonresident alien.** An individual becomes a U.S. resident by satisfying one of two tests found in the Code.[11] Under the first test, sometimes referred to as the *green card test,* if an individual possesses a permanent resident visa ("green card") at any time during the calendar year, that individual is treated as a resident. Under the second test, sometimes referred to as the *substantial presence test,* an individual who is *physically present* in the United States for 31 days or more during the current calendar year *and* the number of days of physical presence during the current calendar year, plus one-third times the number of days of physical presence during the first preceding year, plus one-sixth times the number of days of physical presence during the second preceding year, equals or exceeds 183 days, becomes a U.S. resident.[12] As we will discuss later in the chapter, these rules often are modified by treaties between the United States and other countries to limit instances in which an individual might be taxed as a resident by more than one country.

As always, there are a number of exceptions. For example, international students and teachers generally are exempt from the physical presence test for five and two years, respectively. Individuals who are present in the United States during the current year for less than 183 days and who establish that they have a "closer connection" to another country can elect to be exempt from the physical presence test.[13] Other exemptions apply to individuals who experience unexpected medical conditions while in the United States and to commuters from Canada and Mexico who have a U.S. employer.

The residence of a corporation for U.S. tax purposes generally is determined by the entity's country of incorporation. Other countries may determine the residency of

[9]The national currency of Canada is the Canadian dollar, abbreviated C$.

[10]Article X of the U.S.–Canada income tax treaty.

[11]§7701(b).

[12]For purposes of this test, a full day is considered any part of a day.

[13]An individual usually satisfies the closer connection test by demonstrating that they have a "tax home" in another country. A tax home is defined as the taxpayer's regular place of business or *regular place of abode.*

corporations for tax purposes using different standards. For example, the United Kingdom (UK) also typically treats businesses incorporated in the UK as residents for UK tax purposes. However, the UK also considers companies incorporated outside of the UK to be UK tax residents if their central management and control are located in the UK.

Example 13-2

What if: Assume that for quality-control purposes, Lily has decided to do all the baking for her Windsor store in Detroit. Every morning a Windsor employee drives a van to Detroit and picks up the baked goods for sale in Windsor. One of her Windsor employees, Stan Lee Cupp, made the two-hour trip on 132 different days during 2022. He was not physically present in the United States prior to 2022. Will Stan be considered a U.S. resident in 2022 applying only the substantial presence test? Stan is a Canadian citizen and resident.

Answer: No. Although he is physically present in the United States for more than 30 days in 2022, Stan does not satisfy the 183-day test when applying the formula [132 + (1/3 × 0) + (1/6 × 0) = 132].

What if: Assume Stan continues to be physically present in the United States for 132 days in 2023 and again in 2024. Will Stan be considered a U.S. resident in 2023 or 2024 applying only the substantial presence test?

Answer: 2023: No. He does not satisfy the 183-day test when applying the formula [132 + (1/3 × 132) + (1/6 × 0) = 176].

2024: Yes. He now satisfies the 183-day test when applying the formula [132 + (1/3 × 132) + (1/6 × 132) = 198].

Does Stan qualify for any exceptions that allow him to avoid being treated as a U.S. resident in 2024?

Answer: Yes. Stan can avoid being treated as a U.S. resident under the closer connection test because he was physically present in the United States for less than 183 days in 2024 and his tax home is in Canada. If Stan is in the United States for 183 days or more, he will have to rely on the U.S.–Canada income tax treaty to avoid being considered a U.S. resident for income tax purposes (to be discussed in more detail later in the chapter).

Overview of the U.S. Foreign Tax Credit System

For U.S. taxpayers subject to worldwide taxation of their income, the United States mitigates the double taxation of foreign source income by allowing U.S. taxpayers to claim a **foreign tax credit (FTC)** for foreign income taxes paid on *foreign source* income not eligible for exemption from U.S. tax. Generally, the United States taxes foreign source income to the extent the foreign taxing jurisdiction did not tax the income at a rate equal to or greater than the U.S. tax rate of 21 percent. The United States does not allow a current-year credit for taxes paid in excess of the U.S. tax rate, however. The United States attempts to achieve this residual tax approach through the **foreign tax credit limitation,** which is computed as follows:

$$\frac{\text{Foreign source taxable income}}{\text{Total taxable income}} \times \text{Precredit U.S. tax on total taxable income}$$

For tax years beginning after December 31, 2017, the foreign tax credit limitation is computed separately for foreign branch income along with three additional categories of foreign source income. We first address the foreign branch income category because it is the most straightforward. We discuss the other categories of foreign source income later in this chapter. Generally, taxpayers can carry any unused (excess) FTC for the current year back to the previous tax year and then forward to the next 10 tax years.

Example 13-3

Lily's store in Windsor is an immediate success and reports taxable income on its Canadian operations of C$50,000 for 2022. 3D paid a combined national and provincial income tax of C$9,100 on its taxable income. Because 3D operates the Windsor store as a branch, it also must report the income on its U.S. corporate income tax return along with taxable income from its Detroit operations.[14]

Assuming a translation rate of C$1:US$0.80, 3D reports the Canadian taxable income on its U.S. tax return as $40,000 and reports the Canadian income taxes as $7,280. 3D also reports taxable income from its U.S. operations of $160,000. The company's U.S. income tax on $200,000 of taxable income from all sources is $42,000 before any credit for the income taxes paid to Canada. 3D's income from its Windsor operations is classified as "foreign branch income" for foreign tax credit purposes (we discuss the significance of foreign branch income later in the chapter).

Using the above facts, what is the foreign tax credit limitation that applies to 3D's Canadian income taxes for 2022?

Answer: $8,400, computed as $40,000/$200,000 × $42,000,

where:

$40,000 = Foreign source taxable income
$200,000 = Taxable income from all sources
$42,000 = Pre-credit U.S. tax on total taxable income

What is 3D's net U.S. tax after subtracting the available foreign tax credit?

Answer: $34,720, computed as $42,000 – $7,280. 3D has an "excess foreign tax credit limitation" of $1,120 (i.e., $8,400 FTC limitation – $7,280 Canadian income taxes). That is, 3D could have incurred an additional $1,120 of foreign taxes and received a foreign tax credit for them as well.

What is 3D's average tax rate on its taxable income from all sources for 2022?

Answer: 21 percent, computed as ($7,280 + $34,720)/$200,000.

What if: Assume 3D pays Canadian income taxes of C$12,800 ($10,240) for 2022 (a Canadian tax rate of 26.5 percent). What is its net U.S. tax after subtracting the available foreign tax credit?

Answer: $33,600, computed as $42,000 – $8,400.

The foreign tax credit limitation limits the foreign tax credit to $8,400. 3D now has an "excess foreign tax credit" of $1,840 ($10,240 – $8,400), which 3D can carry forward 10 years.

Given the above scenario, what is 3D's average tax rate on its taxable income from all sources for 2022?

Answer: 21.92 percent, computed as ($10,240 + $33,600)/$200,000. The FTC limitation prevents 3D from getting a current-year tax credit on income taxes paid in excess of the U.S. rate of 21 percent.

LO 13-2

U.S. SOURCE RULES FOR GROSS INCOME AND DEDUCTIONS

Many of the U.S. tax rules that apply to multinational transactions require taxpayers to determine the jurisdictional (i.e., geographic) source (U.S. or foreign) of their gross income.[15] The source rules determine whether income and related deductions are from sources within or without the United States. All developed countries have source-of-income rules, although most practitioners consider the U.S. rules to be the most complex in the world.

[14]Because 3D is a "small corporation," the Ontario tax rate is 3.2 percent, which, added to the federal tax rate of 15 percent, creates a combined tax rate of 18.2 percent. Large corporations are subject to a combined tax rate of 26.5 percent if operating in Ontario.

[15]The U.S. federal income tax source rules are found in §§861–865 and the accompanying regulations.

The U.S. source-of-income rules are important to *non-U.S. persons* because they limit the scope of U.S. taxation to only their U.S. source income. For *U.S. persons,* the primary purpose of the U.S. source-of-income rules is to calculate *foreign source taxable income* in the numerator of the foreign tax credit limitation. Except in the case of dividends from foreign corporations eligible for the 100 percent dividends-received deduction, the United States imposes a tax on the worldwide income of U.S. persons, regardless of its source or the U.S. person's residence. The United States cedes *primary jurisdiction* to foreign governments to tax U.S. persons on income earned outside the United States while retaining the *residual* right to tax foreign source income to the extent it has not been "fully taxed" by the foreign government. The net result is that the United States taxes foreign source income earned by U.S. persons at a rate that theoretically reflects the difference between the U.S. tax rate and the foreign tax rate imposed on the income.

THE KEY FACTS

Source Rules

- The source rules determine whether income and deductions are treated as U.S. source or foreign source.
- For a U.S. taxpayer, the source rules primarily determine foreign taxable income in the calculation of the foreign tax credit limitation.
- For a non-U.S. taxpayer, the source rules determine what income is subject to U.S. taxation.

U.S. persons must understand the source-of-income rules in other situations. For example, U.S. citizens and residents employed outside the United States may be eligible to exclude a portion of their *foreign source earned income* from U.S. taxation under §911.[16] In addition, U.S. persons who pay U.S. source FDAP income to foreign payees (e.g., interest or dividends) usually are required to withhold U.S. taxes on such payments.[17] U.S. corporations receive a 100 percent dividends-received deduction (DRD) on the "foreign-source portion" of dividends received from 10 percent-or-more-owned foreign corporations.

The source-of-income rules are definitional in nature; they do not impose a tax liability, create income, or allow a deduction. Although the primary focus of the source rules is on where the economic activity that generates income takes place, the U.S. government also uses the source rules to advance a variety of international tax policy objectives.

Source-of-Income Rules

The Internal Revenue Code defines nine classes of gross income from sources within the United States[18] and nine classes of gross income from sources outside the United States.[19] A summary of the general rules that apply to common sources of income follows. A detailed discussion of all the exceptions to these rules is beyond the scope of this text.

Interest As a general rule, the taxpayer looks to the residence of the party *paying* the interest (i.e., the borrower) to determine the geographic source of interest received. A borrower's residence is established at the time the interest is paid. Factors that determine an individual's residence include the location of the individual's family; whether the person buys a home, pays foreign taxes, and engages in social and community affairs; and the length of time spent in a country. Under these general rules, interest income is U.S. source income if it is paid by the United States or the District of Columbia, a noncorporate U.S. resident, or a U.S. corporation. Although interest income paid by a U.S. bank to a nonresident (e.g., an international student attending a U.S. university) is U.S. source income, such interest is exempt from U.S. withholding or other income taxation.[20] This exception is designed to attract foreign capital to U.S. banks.

[16]If certain conditions are met, a U.S. individual can exclude up to $112,000 of foreign earned income from U.S. taxation in 2022 plus additional earnings equal to excess "foreign housing expenses" under §911.

[17]§1441.

[18]§861(a).

[19]§862(a).

[20]§§871(i)(2)(A), 881(d).

Example 13-4

3D was dissatisfied with the 1 percent interest rate it received on its checking account at Bank of America in Detroit. Lily's investment adviser suggested the company invest $50,000 in five-year bonds issued by the Canadian government with an annual interest rate of 3 percent. During 2022, 3D received C$1,500 in interest from the bonds. Per the U.S.–Canada treaty, the Canadian government did not withhold taxes on the payment.

What is the source, U.S. or foreign, of the interest Lily receives on the bonds?

Answer: Foreign source. The source of interest income depends on the residence of the borrower at the time the interest is paid. The Canadian government is considered a resident of Canada for U.S. source rule purposes.

Dividends In general, the source of dividend income is determined by the residence of the corporation paying the dividend. Residence usually is determined by the corporation's country of incorporation or organization (in some countries, such as the United Kingdom, a corporation's residence may also be determined by where its central management is located).

Example 13-5

As part of diversifying its investment portfolio, 3D purchased 200 shares of Scotiabank (Bank of Nova Scotia, Canada). In 2022, Scotiabank paid 3D dividends of C$400. Scotiabank withheld C$60 in taxes (15 percent) on the payment.

What is the source, U.S. or foreign, of the dividend 3D receives on the stock?

Answer: Foreign source. The source of dividend income depends on the residence of the payor of the dividend. Scotiabank is headquartered in Toronto, Canada, and is a resident of Canada for U.S. source rule purposes.

Compensation for Services The source of compensation received for "labor or personal services" is determined by the location where the service is performed. The IRS and the courts have held that the term includes activities of employees, independent contractors, artists, entertainers, athletes, and even corporations offering "personal services" (e.g., accounting). The IRC provides a limited **commercial traveler exception,** in which personal service compensation earned by nonresidents within the United States is *not* treated as U.S. source if the individual meets the following criteria:

- The individual was present in the United States for not more than 90 days during the current taxable year;[21]
- Compensation for the services does not exceed $3,000; and
- The services are performed for a nonresident alien, foreign corporation, or foreign partnership or for the foreign office of a domestic corporation.[22]

The United States frequently modifies the limitations on length of stay and compensation through treaty agreements. In most cases, the 90-day limit is extended to 183 days, and no dollar limit is put on the amount of compensation received.

Compensation for services performed within and outside of the United States must be allocated between U.S. and foreign sources. An individual who receives compensation,

[21]For purposes of this test, a full day is considered to be any part of a day.

[22]§861(a)(3)(A)–(C).

other than compensation in the form of fringe benefits, as an employee for labor or personal services performed partly within and partly outside the United States is required to source such compensation on a *time basis.* An individual who receives compensation as an employee for labor or personal services performed partly within and partly outside the United States in the form of fringe benefits (e.g., additional amounts paid for housing or education) is required to source such compensation on a *geographic basis;* that is, determined by the employee's principal place of work.

Example 13-6

What if: Assume that for quality-control purposes Lily decided to do all the baking for her Windsor store in Detroit. Every morning a Windsor employee drives a truck to Detroit and picks up the baked goods for sale in Windsor. One of her Windsor employees, Stan Lee Cupp, made the 2-hour trip on 120 different days during 2022 (240 hours spent in the United States). 3D paid Stan a salary of C$50,000 during 2022. He worked a total of 1,920 hours during 2022. Assume the translation rate is C$1:US$0.80. How much U.S. source compensation does Stan have in 2022? Base your computation on hours worked.

Answer: $5,000 (C$50,000 × 240/1,920 × $0.80). Stan sources his salary for U.S. tax purposes based on where he performed the services. Using hours worked, Stan spent 12.5 percent of his time performing services in the United States (240/1,920).

Using only the exception found in the IRC, will Stan be subject to U.S. tax on his U.S. source wages in 2022?

Answer: Yes. Stan fails the commercial traveler exception. He is in the United States for more than 90 days during 2022.

What if: Assume Stan limits his trips to 90 days during 2022 (180 hours spent in the United States). Using only the IRC exception, will Stan be subject to U.S. tax on his U.S. source salary in 2022?

Answer: Yes. Stan still fails the commercial traveler exception. Although he is in the United States for not more than 90 days, his U.S. source salary is $3,750 (C$50,000 × 180/1,920 × $0.80), which exceeds $3,000.

As we discuss later in the chapter, the U.S.–Canada income tax treaty significantly liberalizes the commercial traveler exception, thus allowing Stan to spend more time in the United States without being taxed by the U.S. government on his U.S. source wages.

Rents and Royalties Rent has its source where the property generating the rent is located. Royalty income has its source where the intangible property or rights generating the royalty are used. Royalties include payments related to intangibles such as patents, copyrights, secret processes and formulas, goodwill, trademarks, trade brands, and franchises. An intangible is "used" in the country that protects the owner against its unauthorized use.

Example 13-7

In 2022, 3D rented its Windsor store from a Canadian owner for C$2,500 per month, for a total of C$30,000. Under the U.S.–Canada income tax treaty, 3D must withhold U.S. taxes at a 30 percent rate on rent payments that flow from the United States to Canada if the rent is U.S. source income. Will 3D have to withhold taxes on the rent payments it makes in 2022?

Answer: No. The rent is considered foreign source income because the store that is rented is located in Canada.

TAXES IN THE REAL WORLD Taxing Professional Golfers

One of the issues that the IRS has struggled with is whether to characterize fees paid to foreign professional golf and tennis players pursuant to on-course/on-court endorsement contracts (e.g., contracts that require wearing a company's logo or using its equipment) as income from royalties or income from personal services, or both. A Tax Court case dealing with a well-known professional golfer illustrates the complexities of this issue.

The first case involved Retief Goosen, a PGA tour member and winner of the 2001 U.S. Open Championship.* Mr. Goosen was a citizen of South Africa and a resident of the United Kingdom, but he spent most of his time competing in the United States and Europe.

Mr. Goosen entered into several endorsement and appearance agreements with sponsors that allowed the sponsor to use his name and likeness to advertise and promote the sponsor's products or in connection with advertising and promoting a specific tournament or event. The "on-course" endorsement agreements required him to wear or use the sponsor's products during golf tournaments, whereas the "off-course" endorsement agreements did not have this requirement.

Mr. Goosen reported all his prize money from golf tournaments and appearance fees in the United States as "effectively connected" income taxable in the United States. He characterized his endorsement fees from on-course endorsements as 50 percent royalty income and 50 percent personal services income. He sourced the personal services income from the on-course endorsement fees to the United States based on the number of days he played within the United States over the total number of days he played golf for the year. Mr. Goosen characterized his endorsement fees from the off-course endorsement agreements as 100 percent royalty income. The IRS argued that the sponsors primarily paid Mr. Goosen to perform personal services, which included playing golf and carrying or wearing the sponsors' products.

The Tax Court awarded a partial victory to both parties. The court found that Mr. Goosen's name had a value beyond his golf skills and abilities for which his sponsors paid a substantial amount of money for the right to use his name and likeness. The sponsors also valued Mr. Goosen's play at tournaments, as evidenced by the fact that the sponsors conditioned the full endorsement fee on his playing in 36 tournaments a year. The court thus held that his performance of services and the use of his name and likeness were equally important and characterized 50 percent of the endorsement fees from the on-course endorsement agreements as royalty income and 50 percent of the fees as personal services income.

The court held that Mr. Goosen's earnings from playing golf in the United States were effectively connected U.S. source income. The on-course endorsement and appearance fees and his on-course royalty income also were held to be U.S. source effectively connected income because payment depended on whether he played a specified number of tournaments. Both categories of income were taxed at U.S. tax rates.

The court held that income Mr. Goosen received from off-course endorsement agreements did not depend on whether he played in golf tournaments. Thus, the income was not effectively connected with a U.S. trade or business and was thus subject to a 30 percent withholding tax to the extent it was treated as U.S. source income.

**Retief Goosen v. Comm'r,* 136 TC No. 27 (June 9, 2011).

Gain or Loss from Sale of Real Property In general, gain or loss from the sale of real property (i.e., realty) has its source where the property is located.

Gain or Loss from Sale of Purchased Personal Property Under the general rule, gain or loss from the sale of purchased personal (nonrealty) property, including intangible assets and stock, has its source based on the seller's residence. There are many exceptions to this general rule. In particular, gross income (i.e., sales minus cost of goods sold) from the sale of purchased inventory is sourced where title passes. Title is deemed to pass at the time when, and the place where, the seller's rights, title, and interest in the property are transferred to the buyer.

Gain or Loss from Sale of Manufactured Inventory Gain or loss from the sale of manufactured inventory has its source based on the physical location of the assets used to produce the inventory.

Source-of-Deduction Rules

After determining the source of gross income as being from U.S. or foreign sources, a taxpayer may be required to **allocate** and **apportion** allowable deductions to gross income from each geographical source to compute taxable income from U.S. and foreign sources. For a U.S. taxpayer, this allocation and apportionment process identifies the foreign source deductions that are subtracted from foreign source gross income in computing foreign source taxable income in the numerator of the foreign tax credit (FTC) limitation computation. A non-U.S. taxpayer with gross income that is effectively connected with a U.S. trade or business must identify the U.S. source deductions that are subtracted from U.S. gross income to compute U.S. taxable income.

U.S. and non-U.S. taxpayers can have different motivations in seeking to deduct (or not deduct) expenses from either foreign source or U.S. source gross income. A U.S. taxpayer seeking to maximize the foreign tax credit limitation will want to allocate as few deductions to foreign source gross income as possible, the goal being to make the ratio of foreign source taxable income to taxable income from all sources as close to 100 percent as possible (or whatever ratio is needed to absorb any excess credits). Non-U.S. taxpayers operating in a low-tax-rate country (i.e., a tax rate less than the U.S. rate) have a tax incentive to allocate as many deductions to U.S. source income as possible to minimize their U.S. tax liability. Non-U.S. taxpayers operating in a high-tax-rate country (i.e., a tax rate greater than the U.S. rate) have a worldwide tax incentive to allocate as many deductions to foreign source income as possible to minimize their worldwide tax liability.

ETHICS

International Contractors, Inc., has been hired by the U.S. government to build roads and bridges in Spartania, a country with which the United States recently signed a treaty. To facilitate the issuance of visas and licenses to begin construction, an official from the Spartanian government asked for 100 "facilitating payments" (also known as "grease payments") of $5,000 each from the company. These payments were customary in Spartania and did not violate Spartanian law. The company intended to expense the $500,000 payment in its financial statements. It was not clear if these payments violated the Foreign Corrupt Practices Act. To avoid IRS and possible Department of Justice scrutiny, the company's tax director suggested that the payment be described as "taxes and licenses" on the tax return (line 17 of Form 1120) without further details. What do you think of the tax director's advice? What tax and other consequences might result from taking this advice?

General Principles of Allocation and Apportionment The IRC provides very broad language in describing how to allocate deductions to U.S. and foreign source gross income. The regulations attempt to match deductions with the gross income such deductions were incurred to produce.[23] Matching usually is done based on the "factual relationship" of the deduction to gross income. Deductions that can be directly associated with a particular item of income (e.g., machine depreciation with manufacturing gross profit) are referred to as **definitely related deductions.** Deductions not directly associated with a particular item of gross income (e.g., medical expenses, property taxes, standard deduction) are referred to as **not definitely related deductions** and are allocated to all gross income.

[23]Reg. §1.861-8 provides the general rules for allocating and apportioning deductions to U.S. and foreign source gross income.

The regulations require the taxpayer to first allocate (i.e., associate) deductions to the class or classes of gross income such deductions were incurred to produce. The taxpayer then apportions the deductions between, in most cases, foreign source and U.S. source gross income. The regulations allow the taxpayer to apportion deductions using a method that reflects the factual relationship between the deduction and the grouping of gross income. Examples include units sold, gross sales or receipts, and gross income.

Example 13-8

Return to the facts in Example 13-3. Lily's store in Windsor reported taxable income on its Canadian operations of C$50,000 for 2022. For U.S. tax purposes, foreign source taxable income was $40,000 (C$50,000 × 0.80). 3D paid a combined national and provincial income tax of C$9,100 ($7,280) on its taxable income (at a tax rate of 18.2 percent). The company reported the $40,000 taxable income on its U.S. corporate income tax return along with $160,000 of taxable income from its Detroit operations. 3D's U.S. income tax on $200,000 of taxable income is $42,000 before any credit for the income taxes paid to Canada.

Included in the computation of taxable income was a deduction of $50,000 for advertising that 3D incurred to promote its stores in Detroit and Windsor. 3D elected to apportion the advertising deduction based on sales. For 2022, Detroit sales were $400,000 and Windsor sales were C$125,000 ($100,000). How much of the $50,000 advertising deduction does 3D apportion to its foreign source taxable income for FTC purposes?

Answer: $10,000, computed as $100,000/$500,000 × $50,000,

where:

$100,000 = Canadian sales
$500,000 = Total sales
$50,000 = Advertising deduction

Using the above facts, what is the foreign tax credit limitation that applies to 3D's Canadian income taxes for 2022?

Answer: $6,300, computed as ($40,000 − $10,000)/$200,000 × $42,000,

where:

$40,000 = Foreign source taxable income *before* apportionment of any advertising deduction
$10,000 = Apportioned advertising deduction
$200,000 = Taxable income from all sources
$42,000 = Pre-credit U.S. tax on taxable income from all sources

Apportioning some of the advertising deduction to the numerator of 3D's FTC limitation ratio reduces the amount of foreign income taxes that are creditable in 2022. 3D gets a foreign tax credit of $6,300 because the FTC limitation is less than the foreign taxes paid. 3D now has a foreign tax credit carryforward of $980 ($7,280 − $6,300).

Special Apportionment Rules Special apportionment rules apply to nine categories of deductions, most notably interest expense, research and experimentation, state and local income taxes, losses on property disposition, and charitable contributions.[24] These special apportionment rules are very complicated, and the details are beyond the scope of this text. However, the basic rules for apportioning interest expense and research and experimentation costs are discussed below.

[24]The other deductions are stewardship expenses attributable to dividends received, supportive expenses, net operating losses, and legal and accounting fees.

Interest expense is allocated to all gross income based on the assets that generated such income. Interest expense is apportioned based on average tax book value for the year. Assets are attributed to income based on the source and type of income they generate, have generated, or may reasonably be expected to generate. A taxpayer using the tax book value method can elect to use the alternative depreciation system (ADS)[25] on U.S. assets solely for purposes of apportioning interest expense.

Example 13-9

Expanding on the facts in Example 13-8, 3D borrowed $100,000 from Bank of America in Detroit and paid interest expense of $6,000 in 2022. 3D apportions this interest expense between U.S. and foreign source income using average tax book value. 3D's U.S. assets had an average tax book value of $250,000, and its foreign assets had an average tax book value of $50,000 in 2022. How much of the $6,000 interest deduction does 3D apportion to its foreign source taxable income for FTC purposes? Assume the limitation on business interest does not apply.

Answer: $1,000, computed as $50,000/$300,000 × $6,000,

where:

$50,000 = Average tax book value of Canadian assets

$300,000 = Total average tax book value of all of 3D's assets

$6,000 = Interest expense

Taking into account the apportioned advertising deduction and interest deduction determined in the previous example, what is the foreign tax credit limitation that applies to 3D's Canadian income taxes for 2022?

Answer: $6,090, computed as ($40,000 – $10,000 – $1,000)/$200,000 × $42,000,

where:

$40,000 = Foreign source taxable income before apportioned advertising and interest expense

$10,000 = Apportioned advertising expense

$1,000 = Apportioned interest expense

$200,000 = Taxable income from all sources

$42,000 = Pre-credit U.S. tax on taxable income from all sources

Allocation of a portion of the interest expense to the numerator of 3D's FTC limitation ratio further reduces the amount of foreign taxes that are creditable in 2022. 3D now has an excess foreign tax credit of $1,190 ($7,280 – $6,090).

Research and experimentation (R&E) expenditures must be apportioned between U.S. and foreign source income using the sales method. Under this method, taxpayers apportion 50 percent of R&E expenditures based on where the research is conducted, and they apportion the remaining 50 percent based on the proportion of U.S. and foreign sales to worldwide sales. State and local income taxes are allocated to the gross income with respect to which such state income taxes are imposed. Charitable contributions and the dividends-received deductions generally are allocated to U.S. source income. The allocation and apportionment rules of these deductions are complex and beyond the scope of this text.

The foreign tax credit limitation is computed on Form 1118 (corporations) or Form 1116 (individuals). Exhibit 13-1 presents a completed Form 1118 for the cumulative facts in Examples 13-3, 13-8, and 13-9. This is a 2021 form because the 2022 form was not available when we went to press.

[25]This alternative approach to calculating tax depreciation is more fully described in the Property Acquisition and Cost Recovery chapter.

EXHIBIT 13-1 Form 1118: Foreign Tax Credit—Corporations, Schedules A, B, and H for 3D Corporation (cumulative facts from Examples 13-3, 13-8, and 13-9)

Form **1118** (Rev. December 2021) Department of the Treasury Internal Revenue Service

Foreign Tax Credit—Corporations

▶ Attach to the corporation's tax return.

▶ Go to *www.irs.gov/Form1118* for instructions and the latest information.

OMB No. 1545-0123

Attachment Sequence No. 118

For calendar year 20 , or other tax year beginning , 20 , and ending , 20

Name of corporation: **3D Corporation**

Employer identification number

Use a separate Form 1118 for each applicable category of income (see instructions).

a Separate Category (Enter code—see instructions.) ▶ **FB**

b If code 901j is entered on line a, enter the country code for the sanctioned country (see instructions) ▶

c If one of the RBT codes is entered on line a, enter the country code for the treaty country (see instructions) ▶

Schedule A **Income or (Loss) Before Adjustments** *(Report all amounts in U.S. dollars. See* **Specific Instructions.***)*

	1. EIN or Reference ID Number (see instructions)*	2. Foreign Country or U.S. Possession (enter two-letter code—use a separate line for each) (see instructions)	Gross Income or (Loss) From Sources Outside the United States: 3. Inclusions Under Sections 951(a)(1) and 951A (see instructions) (a) Exclude Gross-Up	3. (b) Gross-Up (section 78)	4. Dividends (see instructions)	5. Interest
A		CN				
B						
C						
Totals (add lines A through C) ▶						

	6. Gross Rents, Royalties, and License Fees	7. Sales	8. Gross Income From Performance of Services	9. Currency Gain	10. Currency Gain Code (see instructions)	11. Other (attach schedule)	12. Total (add columns 3(a) through 9 and 11)
A		40,000					40,000
B							
C							
Totals		40,000					40,000

13. Allocable Deductions

	(a) Dividends Received Deduction (see instructions)	(b) Deduction Allowed Under Section 250(a)(1)(A)—Foreign Derived Intangible Income	(c) Deduction Allowed Under Section 250(a)(1)(B)—Global Intangible Low-Taxed Income	Rental, Royalty, and Licensing Expenses: (d) Depreciation, Depletion, and Amortization	(e) Other Allocable Expenses	(f) Expenses Allocable to Sales Income	(g) Expenses Allocable to Gross Income From Performance of Services
A						10,000	
B							
C							
Totals						10,000	

	13. Allocable Deductions (continued): (h) Currency Loss	(i) Currency Loss Code (see instructions)	(j) Other Allocable Deductions (attach schedule) (see instructions)	(k) Total Allocable Deductions (add columns 13(a) through 13(h) and 13(j))	14. Apportioned Share of Deductions (enter amount from applicable line of Schedule H, Part I, column (b), and Schedule H, Part II, column (d))	15. Net Operating Loss Deduction	16. Total Deductions (add columns 13(k) through 15)	17. Total Income or (Loss) Before Adjustments (subtract column 16 from column 12)
A				10,000	1,000		11,000	29,000
B								
C								
Totals				10,000	1,000		11,000	29,000

*For section 863(b) income, NOLs, income from RICs, high-taxed income, section 951A, and reattribution of income by reason of disregarded payments, use a single line (see instructions). Also, for reporting branches that are QBUs, use a separate line for each such branch.

For Paperwork Reduction Act Notice, see separate instructions. Cat. No. 10900F Form **1118** (Rev. 12-2021)

Source: irs.gov.

EXHIBIT 13-1 Form 1118: Foreign Tax Credit—Corporations, Schedules A, B, and H for 3D Corporation (cumulative facts from Examples 13-3, 13-8, and 13-9) *(continued)*

Form 1118 (Rev. 12-2021) Page 2

Schedule B Foreign Tax Credit *(Report all foreign tax amounts in U.S. dollars.)*

Part I—Foreign Taxes Paid, Accrued, and Deemed Paid *(see instructions)*

	1. Credit Is Claimed for Taxes (check one): ☑ Paid ☐ Accrued		2. Foreign Taxes Paid or Accrued (attach schedule showing amounts in foreign currency and conversion rate(s) used) — Tax Withheld at Source on:					
	Date Paid	Date Accrued	(a) Dividends	(b) Distributions of Previously Taxed Earnings and Profits	(c) Branch Remittances	(d) Interest	(e) Rents, Royalties, and License Fees	(f) Other
A	various							
B								
C								
Totals (add lines A through C) ▶								

	2. Foreign Taxes Paid or Accrued (continued) — Other Foreign Taxes Paid or Accrued on:				
	(g) Sales	(h) Services Income	(i) Other	(j) Total Foreign Taxes Paid or Accrued (add columns 2(a) through 2(i))	3. Tax Deemed Paid (see instructions)
A	7,280			7,280	
B					
C					
Totals	7,280			7,280	

Part II—Separate Foreign Tax Credit *(Complete a **separate** Part II for **each** applicable category of income.)*

1a	Total foreign taxes paid or accrued (total from Part I, column 2(j))	1a	7,280		
b	Foreign taxes paid or accrued by the corporation during prior tax years that were suspended due to the rules of section 909 and for which the related income is taken into account by the corporation during the current tax year (see instructions)	1b			
2	Total taxes deemed paid (total from Part I, column 3)	2			
3	Reductions of taxes paid, accrued, or deemed paid (enter total from Schedule G, Part I)	3	( )		
4	Taxes reclassified under high-tax kickout	4			
5	Enter the sum of any carryover of foreign taxes (from Schedule K, line 3, column (xiv), and from Schedule I, Part III, line 3) plus any carrybacks to the current tax year	5			
6	Total foreign taxes (combine lines 1a through 5)			6	7,280
7	Enter the amount from the applicable column of Schedule J, Part I, line 11 (see instructions). If Schedule J is **not** required to be completed, enter the result from the "Totals" line of column 17 of the applicable Schedule A			7	29,000
8a	Total taxable income from all sources (enter taxable income from the corporation's tax return)	8a	200,000		
b	Adjustments to line 8a (see instructions)	8b			
c	Subtract line 8b from line 8a			8c	200,000
9	Divide line 7 by line 8c. Enter the resulting fraction as a decimal (see instructions). If line 7 is greater than line 8c, enter 1			9	.145
10	Total U.S. income tax against which credit is allowed (regular tax liability (see section 26(b)) minus any American Samoa economic development credit)			10	42,000
11	Multiply line 9 by line 10			11	6,090
12	Increase in limitation (section 960(c))			12	
13	Credit limitation (add lines 11 and 12) (see instructions)			13	6,090
14	**Separate foreign tax credit** (enter the smaller of line 6 or line 13). Enter here and on the appropriate line of Part III ▶			14	6,090

Form **1118** (Rev. 12-2021)

Form 1118 (Rev. 12-2021) Page 3

Schedule B Foreign Tax Credit *(Report all foreign tax amounts in U.S. dollars.) (continued)*

Part III—Summary of Separate Credits *(Enter amounts from Part II, line 14, for **each** applicable category of income. **Do not** include taxes paid to sanctioned countries.)*

1	Credit for taxes on section 951A category income	1			
2	Credit for taxes on foreign branch category income	2	6,090		
3	Credit for taxes on passive category income	3			
4	Credit for taxes on general category income	4			
5	Credit for taxes on section 901(j) category income (combine all such credits on this line)	5			
6	Credit for taxes on income re-sourced by treaty (combine all such credits on this line)	6			
7	Total (add lines 1 through 6)			7	
8	Reduction in credit for international boycott operations (see instructions)			8	
9	**Total foreign tax credit** (subtract line 8 from line 7). Enter here and on the appropriate line of the corporation's tax return ▶			9	6,090

Source: irs.gov.

EXHIBIT 13-1 Form 1118: Foreign Tax Credit—Corporations, Schedules A, B, and H for 3D Corporation (cumulative facts from Examples 13-3, 13-8, and 13-9) *(continued)*

Form 1118 (Rev. 12-2021) Page **11**

Schedule H **Apportionment of Certain Deductions** *(Complete only once for all categories of income.) (continued)*

Part II—Interest Deductions, All Other Deductions, and Total Deductions

	(a) Average Value of Assets—Check Method Used: ☑ Tax book value ☐ Alternative tax book value		**(b)** Interest Deductions		**(c)** All Other Deductions (attach schedule) (see instructions)	**(d)** Totals (add the amounts from columns (b)(iii), (b)(iv), and (c))
	(i) Nonfinancial Corporations	**(ii)** Financial Corporations	**(iii)** Nonfinancial Corporations	**(iv)** Financial Corporations		**Additional note:** With respect to each applicable statutory grouping, enter the amount in column (d) of line 3a(2), 3b(2), 3c(2), 3d(2), 3e(2), or 3f(2) below in column 14 of the corresponding Schedule A.
1a Totals (see instructions)	300,000		6,000			
b Amounts specifically allocable under Temporary Regulations section 1.861-10T(e)						
c Other specific allocations under Temporary Regulations section 1.861-10T						
d Assets excluded from apportionment formula						
2 Total to be apportioned (subtract the sum of lines 1b, 1c, and 1d from line 1a)	300,000		6,000			
3 Apportionment among statutory groupings (see instructions):						
a Enter code FB						
(1) Section 245A dividend	0		0			
(2) Other	50,000		1,000			
(3) Total line a	50,000		1,000			
b Enter code						
(1) Section 245A dividend						
(2) Other						
(3) Total line b						
c Enter code						
(1) Section 245A dividend						
(2) Other						
(3) Total line c						
d Enter code						
(1) Section 245A dividend						
(2) Other						
(3) Total line d						
e Enter code						
(1) Section 245A dividend						
(2) Other						
(3) Total line e						
f Enter code						
(1) Section 245A dividend						
(2) Other						
(3) Total line f						
4 **Total foreign** (add lines 3a(3), 3b(3), 3c(3), 3d(3), 3e(3), and 3f(3)) ▶	50,000		1,000			

Section 904(b)(4) Adjustments

5 Expenses Allocated and Apportioned to Foreign Source Section 245A Dividend. Enter the sum of amounts in column (d) of lines 3a(1), 3b(1), 3c(1), 3d(1), 3e(1), and 3f(1). Include this line 5 result as a negative amount on Schedule B, Part II, line 8b	**5**	
6 Enter expenses allocated and apportioned to U.S. source section 245A dividend. Include this line 6 amount as a negative amount on Schedule B, Part II, line 8b	**6**	

Form **1118** (Rev. 12-2021)

Source: irs.gov.

OPERATING ABROAD THROUGH A FOREIGN CORPORATION

The Tax Cuts and Jobs Act (TCJA of 2017) made significant changes to the taxation of foreign source income earned through a foreign corporation owned by *domestic corporations* that meet certain ownership requirements. In particular, U.S. corporations that meet the definition of a *U.S. shareholder* of such foreign corporation (i.e., owns 10 percent or more of the voting power or value of the foreign corporation) are eligible for a 100 percent dividends-received deduction (also known as a *participation exemption*) on earnings remitted by the foreign corporation that have not previously been subject to the deemed dividend rules of subpart F or GILTI (to be discussed later in the chapter).[26] Any foreign income taxes paid on income eligible for the exemption are not creditable or deductible on the U.S. shareholder's U.S. tax return.

The enactment of this deduction moves the United States toward a territorial tax system for corporations and puts the United States in line with most other countries in the taxation of foreign source active trade or business income.

[26]§§245A, 951(a), 951A(a).

Example 13-10

Assume the same facts as Example 13-3 except that Detroit Donut Depot (3D) decides to operate its Windsor operations through a wholly owned Canadian corporation rather than as a foreign branch. In 2022, the Canadian corporation reported taxable income of C$50,000 and paid a combined national and provincial income tax of C$9,100 on its taxable income. The C$50,000 is not subject to U.S. taxation because it is active trade or business income earned through a foreign corporation. In 2023, the Canadian subsidiary pays a dividend of C$10,000 to the U.S. corporation. The dividend is subject to a 5 percent withholding tax (C$500) under the U.S.–Canada treaty. How much of the dividend is subject to U.S. taxation, and are any of the foreign taxes imposed on the income distributed creditable?

Answer: $0 income is subject to U.S. taxation and $0 foreign taxes are creditable. The dividend is eligible for a 100 percent dividends-received deduction, and any Canadian taxes paid on such income are not creditable or deductible on 3D's U.S. tax return.

Foreign-Derived Intangible Income Current tax rules give U.S. C corporations that sell goods and services an incentive to export such products and services from the United States, and to hold intellectual property in the United States. For tax years beginning after December 31, 2017, gross profit derived from certain export sales or services provided to persons outside the United States, referred to as **foreign-derived intangible income (FDII),** is eligible for a tax deduction equal to 37.5 percent of FDII, which reduces the effective tax rate imposed on such income to 13.125 percent (21 percent × 62.5 percent).[27] The FDII deduction is computed on Form 8993, Section 250 Deduction for Foreign-Derived Intangible Income and Global Intangible Low-Taxed Income.

The computation of FDII is extremely complex, as are many of the international tax provisions. In general terms, the deduction applies to income from sales of property intended for foreign use or services provided to any person not located in the United States in excess of a "normal return" on U.S. assets used in the production of the product or services. A normal return is defined as 10 percent of **qualified business asset investment (QBAI).** QBAI is defined as the tax basis of depreciable property used in the production of the products sold (to both U.S. and foreign customers), assuming straight-line depreciation.

Example 13-11

Assume 3D, a Detroit-based C corporation, had $175,000 of net income (gross income less allocated deductions) from sales of baked goods to U.S. customers and $25,000 of net income from sales of baked goods to the Canadian store for sale to Canadian customers in 2022. Also assume 3D had QBAI of $300,000. What is 3D's deduction for FDII in 2022?

Answer: $7,969. 3D has net income of $170,000 in excess of 10 percent of QBAI [$200,000 − (.10 × $300,000)]. Of that amount, $21,250 ($25,000/$200,000 × $170,000) is considered FDII and eligible for the 37.5 percent deduction. The FDII deduction allowed in computing 3D's taxable income is $7,969 ($21,250 × 37.5 percent). The actual calculation is much more complex than this and is beyond the scope of this text.

TREATIES

LO 13-3

A tax treaty is a bilateral agreement between two contracting countries in which each agrees to modify its own tax laws to achieve reciprocal benefits. The general purpose of an income tax treaty is to eliminate or reduce the impact of double taxation so that residents paying taxes to one country will not have the full burden of taxes in the other country. The United States signed its first income tax treaty with France in 1939. The United States now has income tax treaties with 67 countries as of the date we went to press. Exhibit 13-2 provides a list of the countries with which the United States has

[27] §250.

EXHIBIT 13-2 Countries with Which the United States Has Income Tax Treaties

Australia	India	Philippines
Austria	Indonesia	Poland
Bangladesh	Ireland	Portugal
Barbados	Israel	Romania
Belgium	Italy	Russian Federation
Bulgaria	Jamaica	Slovak Republic
Canada	Japan	Slovenia
China, People's Republic of	Kazakhstan	South Africa
Commonwealth of Independent States[a]	Korea, Republic of	Spain
Cyprus	Latvia	Sri Lanka
Czech Republic	Lithuania	Sweden
Denmark	Luxembourg	Switzerland
Egypt	Malta	Thailand
Estonia	Mexico	Trinidad and Tobago
Finland	Morocco	Tunisia
France	Netherlands	Turkey
Germany	New Zealand	Ukraine
Greece	Norway	United Kingdom
Hungary	Pakistan	Venezuela
Iceland		

[a]Armenia, Azerbaijan, Belarus, Georgia, Kyrgyzstan, Moldova, Tajikistan, Turkmenistan, and Uzbekistan.
Source: Internal Revenue Service, "Publication 901: U.S. Tax Treaties," www.irs.gov/pub/irs-pdf/p901.pdf.

THE KEY FACTS

Treaties

- Treaties are designed to encourage cross-border trade by reducing or eliminating the double taxation of such income by the countries that are party to the treaty.
- Treaties define whether and when a resident of one country has nexus in the other country.
- Treaties reduce or eliminate the withholding tax imposed on cross-border payments such as interest, dividends, and royalties.

income tax treaties. U.S. treaties generally do not affect the U.S. taxation of U.S. citizens, residents, and domestic corporations because such taxpayers are taxed on a worldwide basis.

Treaties reduce or eliminate the tax on income earned in one contracting country by a resident of the other contracting country. For example, most U.S. treaties provide a low withholding tax rate or an exemption from tax on various types of investment income (i.e., interest, dividends, gains from sale of stock, and royalties) that otherwise would be subject to a high withholding tax.[28] For individuals, U.S. treaties often provide exemption from taxation by the host country on wages or self-employment income earned in the treaty country, provided the individual does not spend more than 183 days in that other country. U.S. businesses generally are not taxed on business profits earned in the host treaty country unless they conduct that business through a **permanent establishment.** A permanent establishment generally is a fixed place of business such as an office or factory, although employees acting as agents can create a permanent establishment. Treaties also provide "tiebreaker" rules for determining the country in which an individual will be considered a resident for treaty purposes.

Example 13-12

What if: Lily is trying to determine whether 3D would be subject to Canadian taxation under two different scenarios: (1) she opens a store in Windsor and operates it as a branch of 3D or (2) she prepares the baked goods in Detroit and ships them to Windsor-area grocery stores using the company's van. Article VII of the U.S.–Canada income tax treaty states that the business profits of a U.S. resident are taxed in Canada only if the business operates in Canada through a permanent establishment.

[28]Absent a treaty, the United States imposes a withholding tax rate of 30 percent on payments of FDAP income to nonresidents.

Article V defines a permanent establishment as including a place of management, a branch, an office, a factory, and a workshop. Under the U.S.–Canada treaty, will 3D be subject to Canadian tax on taxable income earned through its Windsor store?

Answer: Yes. A branch is defined as a permanent establishment. Canada can tax 3D's Canadian source taxable income under Article VII of the U.S.–Canada treaty.

Under the U.S.–Canada treaty, will 3D be subject to Canadian tax on taxable income earned by selling goods to grocery stores in Windsor directly?

Answer: No. 3D does not have a permanent establishment in Canada on these sales. Canada will not tax income from these sales under Article VII of the U.S.–Canada treaty.

Example 13-13

What if: Assume that for quality-control purposes Lily decided to do all the baking for her Windsor store in Detroit. Every morning a Windsor employee drives a van to Detroit and picks up the baked goods for sale in Windsor. One of her Windsor employees, Stan Lee Cupp, made the two-hour trip on 200 different days during 2022. Article IV of the U.S.–Canada income tax treaty states that, in cases where an individual is considered a resident of both countries under their respective tax laws, the individual will be considered a resident of the country in which they have a permanent home. Stan has a home only in Canada, and Canada still considers him to be a Canadian resident. Will Stan be considered a U.S. resident in 2022 applying only the substantial presence test?

Answer: Yes. Stan is physically present in the United States for more than 30 days in 2022 and satisfies the 183-day test when applying the formula [200 + (1/3 × 0) + (1/6 × 0) = 200].

Will Stan be considered a U.S. resident in 2022 under the U.S.–Canada treaty?

Answer: No. Under the tiebreaker rules in the U.S.–Canada treaty, Stan is considered to be a resident only of Canada for income tax purposes because that is where he has his permanent home. The United States can tax Stan only on income that is considered to be from U.S. sources.

Example 13-14

What if: Return to the facts in Example 13-6. Stan made the 2-hour trip from Windsor to Detroit and back on 120 different days during 2022 (240 hours). 3D paid Stan a salary of C$50,000 ($40,000) during 2022. He worked a total of 240 days (1,920 hours) during 2022. Article XV of the U.S.–Canada income tax treaty states that a Canadian resident individual earning wages in the United States will be exempt from U.S. tax on his or her U.S. source wages if the wages do not exceed $10,000 or the individual is present in the United States for no more than 183 days. Under the U.S.–Canada treaty, will Stan be subject to U.S. tax on his U.S. source compensation in 2022?

Answer: No. Stan is exempt from U.S. tax on his wages because under the apportionment rules for compensation (discussed in Example 13-6), he has only $5,000 of U.S. source compensation, computed as (240/1,920) × $40,000,

where:

240 = Number of hours worked in the United States

1,920 = Total number of hours worked

$40,000 = Total compensation in U.S. dollars

What if: Assume Stan received wages from 3D of $100,000 in 2022. Under the U.S.–Canada treaty, will Stan be subject to U.S. tax on his U.S. source compensation in 2022?

Answer: No. Even though Stan has U.S. source wages of $12,500 (240/1,920 × $100,000), Stan was in the United States for less than 184 days, and therefore he is exempt from U.S. tax on his U.S. source compensation.

LO 13-4

FOREIGN TAX CREDITS

THE KEY FACTS

Foreign Tax Credits

- Only income taxes can be claimed as a credit on a U.S. tax return.
- The current-year foreign tax credit cannot exceed the FTC limitation.
- The FTC limitation is applied to four separate categories (baskets) of foreign source income: passive, general, foreign branch, and GILTI.

The United States taxes the worldwide income of U.S. partnerships, trusts and estates, U.S. citizens, and resident aliens. U.S. corporations continue to be taxed on all income other than dividends received from foreign corporations eligible for the 100 percent dividends-received deduction (DRD). As we have discussed, U.S. persons earning foreign source income may be subject to multiple taxation on such income by the United States and the country in which the individual resides or where the income is earned. For example, a U.S. citizen who earns income in France may be subject to taxation by both governments. Without any relief from such multiple taxation, U.S. taxpayers would have little incentive to do business outside the United States.

FTC Limitation Categories of Taxable Income

Earlier in the chapter, when we discussed the foreign tax credit, we assumed that all foreign source income was from one category (foreign branch income). However, as a policy matter, the U.S. government must decide whether, and to what extent, U.S. taxpayers should segregate foreign source income subject to different tax rates and compute a separate FTC limitation for different categories of foreign source income. Since 1976, the United States has required persons claiming the foreign tax credit to segregate foreign source income by category of income. Practitioners often refer to each income category as an **FTC basket.** Historically, there were two primary categories of FTC income: **passive category income** and **general category income.**[29] Beginning in 2018, two more categories of FTC income were added: foreign branch income and **global intangible low-taxed income (GILTI).** The "basket" approach is intended to limit blending opportunities (i.e., high-tax foreign source income and low-tax foreign source income) to income that is in the same category.

Passive Category Income Passive category income generally is investment-type income that traditionally is subject to low foreign taxes, usually in the form of withholding taxes. Passive category income includes interest, dividends not eligible for the 100 percent DRD, rents, royalties, and annuities.

General Category Income Income not treated as passive category income, foreign branch income, or GILTI is defined as general category income.

Foreign Branch Income Foreign branch income generally is defined to be business profits earned through one or more unincorporated qualified business units (branches). Earlier in the chapter, we discussed and illustrated how the foreign tax credit limitation applies to foreign branch income.

GILTI Income A new category of foreign source income to be discussed later in this chapter.

Example 13-15

What if: Suppose 3D's branch operations in Windsor generated C$50,000 ($40,000) of taxable income and paid Canadian tax of C$9,250 ($7,400). The branch income meets the definition of qualified branch income for FTC purposes. In addition, 3D received a dividend of C$1,000 ($800) from its stock investment in Scotiabank. Under the U.S.–Canada treaty, Scotiabank withheld C$150 ($120) in taxes (15 percent) on the payment. The withholding tax is eligible for the foreign tax credit, and the dividend meets the definition of passive category income for FTC purposes. 3D has taxable income from all

[29]§904(d).

sources of $200,000 (including the dividend) in 2022 and a pre-credit U.S. income tax of $42,000. In computing its FTC for 2022, can 3D combine the branch income with the dividend in calculating its FTC limitation? Assume the exchange rate is C$1:$0.80.

Answer: No. The branch income and the dividend cannot be blended because they are in different income categories for FTC limitation purposes.

How much of the $7,520 ($7,400 + $120) in Canadian taxes can 3D claim as an FTC in 2022?

Answer: $7,520.

3D must compute separate FTC limitations for the branch income and the dividend, as follows:

Branch income: $40,000/$200,000 × $42,000 = $8,400

Dividend income: $800/$200,000 × $42,000 = $168

3D can take a credit for the full amount of the withholding tax on the dividend and a full credit for taxes paid on the branch income because the foreign taxes associated with each FTC basket are less than the FTC limitation for each basket.

What if: Assume the branch income is subject to Canadian income tax of C$13,240 ($10,600). How much of the $10,720 in Canadian taxes can 3D take as a credit in 2022?

Answer: $8,520, computed as $8,400 + $120.

The FTC for the branch income is now limited to $8,400, as computed previously. 3D can carry forward the excess FTC of $2,200 ($10,600 − $8,400) for 10 years.

Creditable Foreign Taxes

The foreign tax credit is available only for foreign taxes the United States considers to be *income* taxes in the U.S. sense. In general, a tax resembles the U.S. concept of an income tax when it is applied to net income.[30] Taxes that do not qualify as income taxes include property taxes, customs taxes, sales taxes, and value-added taxes. U.S. taxpayers can deduct noncreditable foreign taxes. On an annual basis, U.S. taxpayers also can elect to deduct foreign income taxes in lieu of claiming the credit. This election might make sense if the taxpayer does not expect to be able to use the credit during the 10-year carryforward period. Foreign taxes generally are translated into U.S. dollars using the average exchange rate for the year, regardless of when the tax is actually paid.[31] U.S. taxpayers can elect to translate withholding taxes using the exchange rate on the day the tax is withheld. This election makes translation of the withholding tax consistent with the translation of the payment (e.g., dividend, interest, royalty) into U.S. dollars, which is done using the exchange rate on the date of payment, which is referred to as the **spot rate.**

Direct Taxes Direct foreign income taxes are income taxes paid directly by the U.S. taxpayer.[32] For example, the income taxes 3D pays to the Canadian government on its branch operations in Windsor are direct foreign income taxes and are eligible for a credit on the company's U.S. tax return.

In Lieu of Taxes Taxes that do not qualify as income taxes can still be creditable if they are imposed in lieu of an income tax.[33] The most common example is a withholding tax imposed on gross income such as dividends, interest, and royalties. These taxes technically do not meet the definition of an income tax because they are imposed on gross, rather than net, income. Governments impose these taxes for administrative purposes in lieu of requiring the recipient of the income to file an income tax return.

[30]There has been much litigation and many IRS rulings over whether a tax paid to another country qualifies as an income tax in the U.S. sense. See Reg. §1.901-2(a)(1) for the definition of a tax "in the U.S. sense."

[31]§986(a)(1)(A).

[32]Direct foreign income taxes are creditable under §901.

[33]In lieu of income taxes are creditable under §903.

LO 13-5

PLANNING FOR INTERNATIONAL OPERATIONS

The organizational form through which a U.S. person does business or invests outside the United States affects the timing and scope of U.S. taxation of foreign source income or loss reported by the business or investment. U.S. corporations conducting international operations directly (e.g., through a branch) or through a flow-through entity (such as a partnership) are subject to U.S. tax or receive a U.S. tax benefit currently on income or loss from those operations. Foreign source income earned by a foreign corporation owned by U.S. persons (e.g., a Canadian subsidiary of a U.S. corporation) generally is not subject to U.S. taxation until such income is repatriated to the U.S. shareholder as interest, rent, royalty, or a management fee (i.e., U.S. taxation of such income is deferred to a future period). Dividends paid to domestic corporations from 10-percent-or-more-owned foreign corporations are exempt from U.S. taxation because they are eligible for a 100 percent DRD.

The organizational form chosen can help a U.S. person reduce worldwide taxation by:

- Exempting from U.S. taxation income not subject to the subpart F or GILTI deemed dividend rules.
- Reducing foreign taxes in high-tax jurisdictions through tax-deductible payments (e.g., rent, interest, royalties, and management fees) to lower-tax jurisdictions.
- Taking advantage of tax incentives provided by host jurisdictions (e.g., a tax holiday on profits for a specified time period).
- Using transfer pricing to shift profits from a high-tax jurisdiction to a low-tax jurisdiction.
- Taking advantage of tax treaties to reduce withholding taxes on cross-border payments.

Hybrid entities such as limited liability companies can provide the U.S. investor with the legal advantages of the corporate form (i.e., limited liability, continuity of life, transferability of interests) and the tax advantages of the partnership or branch form (e.g., flow-through of losses and flow-through of foreign taxes to individual investors).

Each organizational form offers a U.S. person investing abroad with advantages and disadvantages. Most U.S. businesses operate abroad through either a subsidiary or hybrid entity. Corporation status provides the U.S. investor with protection against liabilities of the subsidiary, entitles the subsidiary to treaty benefits in its dealings outside the country of incorporation, and generally insulates the subsidiary's business income from U.S. taxation until such income is repatriated back to the United States. Conversely, losses incurred in the subsidiary are not currently deductible on the investor's U.S. tax return.

THE KEY FACTS

Organizational Forms for Conducting International Operations

- A U.S. taxpayer doing business outside the United States can choose between a branch, partnership, corporation, or hybrid entity.
- A hybrid entity is an entity that is treated as a flow-through entity for U.S. tax purposes and a corporation for foreign tax purposes (or vice versa).
- A U.S. taxpayer elects the U.S. tax status of a hybrid entity by checking the box on Form 8832.
- "Per se" entities are not eligible for the check-the-box election.

Check-the-Box Hybrid Entities

Through regulations, the U.S. Treasury allows U.S. taxpayers to elect the *U.S. tax status* of eligible entities by checking the box on Form 8832, Entity Classification Election. Where the U.S. person owns 100 percent of the entity, that person can choose corporation status or branch status; the latter often is referred to as a **disregarded entity** because it is disregarded for U.S. tax purposes. Where more than one U.S. person owns the entity, the taxpayers can choose corporation status or partnership status. Such an entity is referred to as a hybrid entity. A multiple-person-owned hybrid entity for which corporation status is elected is referred to as a **reverse hybrid entity.** Certain designated "per se" foreign entities are not eligible for this elective treatment. These ineligible entities tend to be entities that can be publicly traded in their host countries (e.g., a German A.G., Dutch N.V., U.K. PLC, Spanish S.A., or Canadian corporation). The entire list is printed in the Instructions to Form 8832. In Canada, a

U.S. corporation or individual must operate through an unlimited liability company (ULC) organized under the laws of Nova Scotia, Alberta, or British Columbia to achieve the benefits of operating through a hybrid entity.

Hybrid entities offer U.S. investors much flexibility in avoiding the U.S. anti-deferral rules found in subpart F, which we discuss in the next section. However, there are drawbacks to operating through a hybrid entity. In particular, a hybrid entity organized outside the United States may not be eligible for treaty benefits because it is not recognized as a resident of the United States by the host country. For example, the U.S.–Canada treaty does not extend treaty benefits to distributions from a ULC to its U.S. investors. Distributions from a Nova Scotia ULC to its U.S. parent company in the form of dividends or royalties will be subject to a 25 percent withholding tax instead of a 5 percent or 10 percent withholding tax, respectively, under the U.S.–Canada treaty. Exhibit 13-3 lists the advantages and disadvantages of operating outside the United States through different organizational forms.

EXHIBIT 13-3 Advantages and Disadvantages of Operating Outside the United States in Different Organizational Forms

Branch

Advantages

- Foreign losses are currently deductible on the U.S. tax return.
- Foreign taxes imposed on income earned through the branch are eligible for the direct foreign tax credit.
- A branch qualifies as a permanent establishment and is eligible for treaty benefits.

Disadvantages

- Profits are subject to immediate U.S. taxation.
- The U.S. corporation must have 100 percent control over its international operations (joint ventures are not available).

Subsidiary

Advantages

- Separate entity status insulates the U.S. parent corporation against certain types of liabilities.
- Distributions from 10-percent-or-more owned foreign corporations are eligible for a 100 percent DRD when distributed as a dividend.
- Certain payments (e.g., management fees, royalties) made to the U.S. parent corporation may be deductible in the host country only if the payor is a corporation.

Disadvantages

- Losses are not deductible on the U.S. tax return for tax purposes.
- Certain foreign source income may be subject to the subpart F and GILTI rules, which increase the administrative costs of operating as a subsidiary.

Hybrid Entity Treated as a Flow-Through Entity

Advantages

- Foreign losses are currently deductible on the U.S. tax return.
- Foreign taxes imposed on income earned through the hybrid entity are eligible for the direct foreign tax credit.
- The U.S. corporation can operate as a joint venture.
- Certain payments (e.g., management fees, royalties, interest) made to the U.S. parent corporation are deductible in the foreign jurisdiction.

Disadvantages

- Profits are subject to immediate U.S. taxation.
- Dividend, interest, and royalty payments to the United States are not eligible for reduced treaty withholding taxes.

Example 13-16

Lily expects her Canadian operations to be profitable for the foreseeable future. She has plans to expand her operations throughout the province of Ontario and hopefully throughout all of Canada. Lily is trying to decide whether she should change the organizational form of her Canadian operations from a branch to a corporation or perhaps a hybrid entity. Can Lily organize her Canadian operations as a hybrid entity in Ontario for U.S. tax purposes?

Answer: No. Hybrid entities (unlimited liability companies) in Canada can be organized only in the provinces of Nova Scotia, Alberta, and British Columbia.

What are the primary income tax reasons for organizing the Canadian operations as a corporation for U.S. tax purposes?

Answer: There are several. Operating as a corporation allows for exemption from U.S. taxation on income earned by the Canadian operations when it is distributed to 3D as a dividend. In addition, 3D can loan money or lease its trademarks to the Canadian corporation and transfer income from Canada to the United States in the form of tax-deductible interest expense or royalty payments.

Are there any compelling nontax reasons for organizing the Canadian operations as a corporation for U.S. tax purposes?

Answer: Yes. Corporate form limits 3D's liability in Canada to its Canadian assets. In addition, operating as a corporation allows the company to hold itself out as a Canadian business to its customers and borrow money directly from Canadian banks.

When drawing an organizational chart of a multinational company, we often designate the different organizational forms with symbols. Exhibit 13-4 shows the symbols for each of the common organizational forms U.S. taxpayers use to do business outside the United States and their tax status for U.S. tax purposes (we will refer back to this exhibit in Exhibit 13-5).

EXHIBIT 13-4 Symbols for Different Organizational Forms and Their U.S. Tax Status

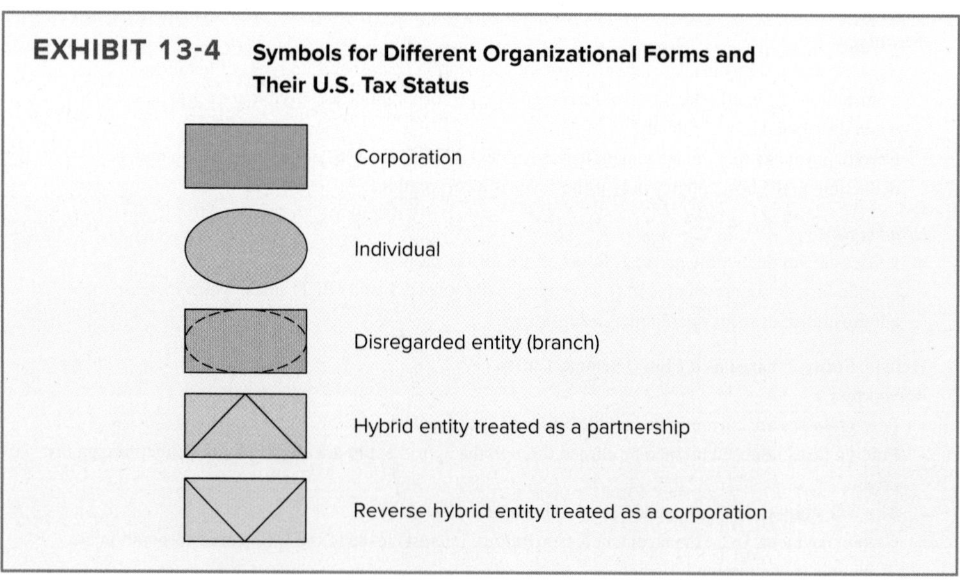

LO 13-6

U.S. ANTI-DEFERRAL RULES

Deferral of U.S. taxation on all foreign source income earned through a foreign subsidiary would invite tax planning strategies that shift income to low-tax countries to minimize worldwide taxation. U.S. individuals and corporations could transfer investment assets to subsidiaries located in low- or no-tax countries, called **tax havens,** and earn low-tax or tax-exempt income until such time as the money was repatriated to the United States.

The United States has debated whether to allow full deferral on all foreign earnings since 1937, when the U.S. government enacted its first "anti-deferral" rules applying to foreign personal holding companies. Congress, with urging from President Kennedy, enacted more expansive anti-deferral rules in subpart F of subchapter N of the IRC in 1962.[34]

In a nutshell, subpart F requires certain *U.S. shareholders* in a **controlled foreign corporation (CFC)** to include in their gross income their pro rata share of specified categories of "tainted" income earned by the CFC during the current year—**subpart F income** and global intangible low-taxed income (GILTI)—regardless of whether such income is repatriated as a dividend (i.e., the income is treated as if it were paid out to the shareholders as a deemed dividend at the end of the CFC's taxable year). The deemed dividend is translated into U.S. dollars using the average exchange rate for the year. The technical rules that determine the amount of the deemed dividend to be included in income are among the most complex provisions in the IRC.

THE KEY FACTS

U.S. Anti-Deferral Rules

- Income described in subpart F of subchapter N of the IRC defines income that is not eligible for deferral from U.S. taxation when earned by a foreign corporation.
- Subpart F income generally includes foreign personal holding company income and foreign base company sales income.
- Subpart F applies only to U.S. shareholders of a CFC.
- *De minimis* and full inclusion rules apply to exclude or increase the amount of a CFC's income subject to the deemed dividend regime of subpart F.
- In addition to subpart F income, U.S. shareholders of a CFC must also include their share of GILTI in their gross income.

Definition of a Controlled Foreign Corporation

A controlled foreign corporation (CFC) is defined as any foreign corporation in which U.S. shareholders collectively own more than 50 percent of the total combined voting power of all classes of stock entitled to vote or the total value of the corporation's stock on any day during the CFC's tax year.[35] For purposes of subpart F, a U.S. shareholder is any U.S. person who owns or is deemed to own 10 percent or more of the voting power or value of the corporation's stock.[36] The term **United States person** means a citizen or resident of the United States, a domestic partnership, a domestic corporation, or any U.S. estate or trust, but it excludes certain residents of U.S. possessions.

Indirect (constructive) ownership rules are used in the calculation of both the 50 percent test for determining CFC status and the 10 percent test for determining who is a U.S. shareholder.[37] These rules are similar to the indirect ownership rules found in §318 (see the Corporate Taxation: Nonliquidating Distributions chapter) and include family attribution (spouse, children, grandchildren, and parents), entity-to-owner attribution, and owner-to-entity attribution. A detailed discussion of the other attribution rules is beyond the scope of this chapter.

Example 13-17

What if: Assume Lily decided to partner with a Canadian investor, Maurice Richard, to expand her operations into Quebec through a Canadian corporation to be called Quebec Doughnut Depot (QDD). As part of the creation of QDD, Maurice contributed enough cash to the corporation to become a 50 percent shareholder in the corporation, with Lily owning the remaining 50 percent. Will QDD be a controlled foreign corporation (CFC) for U.S. tax purposes?

Answer: No. Lily is the only U.S. person who qualifies as a U.S. shareholder for purposes of determining whether QDD is a CFC for U.S. tax purposes. Because Lily owns only 50 percent of QDD (not *more than* 50 percent), the corporation is not considered a CFC.

What if: Suppose Lily organized QDD with her spouse, Red, and Maurice, with each owning one-third of the company's stock. Will QDD be a CFC for U.S. tax purposes?

(*continued on page 13-26*)

[34]§§951–965.

[35]§957(a).

[36]§951(b).

[37]§958(b).

Answer: Yes. Lily and Red are both U.S. persons who qualify as U.S. shareholders for purposes of determining whether QDD is a CFC for U.S. tax purposes (each owns at least 10 percent of the QDD stock). Because they collectively own more than 50 percent of QDD, the corporation is a CFC.

What if: Suppose Lily organized QDD with her spouse, Red, and Maurice, with Lily owning 49 percent, Red owning 2 percent, and Maurice owning 49 percent of the company's stock. Will QDD be a CFC for U.S. tax purposes?

Answer: Yes. Lily is deemed to own Red's 2 percent stock interest in QDD under the family attribution rules, making her a U.S. shareholder owning 51 percent of QDD's stock.

Definition of Subpart F Income

Subpart F income generally can be characterized as low-taxed passive income or as portable income earned by a CFC. Passive income, otherwise referred to as **foreign personal holding company income,** includes interest, dividends, rents, royalties, annuities, gains from the sale of certain foreign property, foreign currency exchange rate gains, net income from certain commodities transactions, and income equivalent to interest. There are complex exceptions involving payments between CFCs in the same country, export financing interest, and rents and royalties derived in the active conduct of a trade or business. Subpart F income does not include dividends, interest, rents, and royalties received by one CFC from a related CFC to the extent the payment is attributable to non–subpart F income of the payor. That is, the taxpayer "looks through" the payment to the income from which it was paid.

Example 13-18

What if: Assume that 3D organized its Windsor operations as a wholly owned Canadian subsidiary, Canadian Doughnut Depot Company (CDD). Now suppose CDD reported taxable income from its bakery operations of C$75,000 in 2022. CDD also purchased 1,000 shares of stock (less than 1 percent) in Thorntons PLC, a United Kingdom corporation that makes fine chocolate. During 2022, CDD received dividends of £1,000, which translated into C$1,500.[38] Thorntons withheld £100 (C$150) of U.K. taxes on the payment (a 10 percent withholding tax under the U.K.–Canada treaty). Does the dividend from Thorntons to CDD constitute subpart F income to 3D in 2022?

Answer: Yes. Dividends from investments by a CFC in a non-CFC are considered foreign personal holding company income under subpart F.

Also included in subpart F income is **foreign base company sales income,** which is defined as income derived by a CFC from the sale or purchase of personal property (e.g., inventory) to or from a related person (a U.S. shareholder owning more than 50 percent of the CFC or a corporation that is 50-percent-or-more owned by the CFC) when the property is manufactured and sold outside the CFC's country of incorporation.[39] Similar rules apply to foreign base company services income.

Together, a CFC's foreign personal holding company income, foreign base company sales income, and foreign base company services income are defined as a CFC's **foreign base company income.** For most CFCs, foreign base company income represents the largest single category of subpart F income.

This category of subpart F income was included because many countries offer incentives to multinational corporations to locate holding companies or sales companies within their borders by imposing no or a low tax on investment income or export sales. These companies are referred to as base companies because they operate primarily as profit centers and are located in a different country than where the economic activity (i.e., manufacture, sales, or service) takes place.

[38]The currency of the United Kingdom is the pound sterling, abbreviated £.

[39]§954(d).

Without any anti-deferral rules, a U.S. multinational corporation could shift profits to a foreign base company by selling goods to the base company at an artificially low transfer price. The base company could then resell the goods at a higher price to the ultimate customer in a different country. The profit earned by the base company would be subject to the lower (or no) tax imposed by the tax haven country. The base company thus would become a depository for the multinational company's excess funds, which could be invested in an active business or in passive investment assets outside the United States.

Example 13-19

What if: Assume in 2022 that 3D set up a corporation in the Cayman Islands through which it intended to transfer its products from the United States to its operations in Canada. Under this plan, 3D would "sell" its products, made in the United States, to the subsidiary in the Cayman Islands at a low transfer price, after which the Cayman Islands subsidiary would resell the products to CDD at a high transfer price. The goal would be to locate as much profit as possible in a low-tax country (the Cayman Islands has no corporate income tax). Will profit from the sale of goods from the Cayman Islands subsidiary to CDD constitute subpart F income to 3D in 2022?

Answer: Yes. The Cayman Islands profit is considered foreign base company sales income under subpart F because the goods are manufactured outside the Cayman Islands by a related person (3D) and sold outside the Cayman Islands. 3D will be treated as having received a deemed dividend equal to the profit from the Cayman Islands subsidiary.

Several exceptions serve to exclude all or a portion of a CFC's subpart F income from current taxation to the U.S. shareholders. A *de minimis rule* excludes all gross income from being treated as foreign base company income if the sum of the CFC's gross foreign base company income is less than the lesser of 5 percent of gross income or $1 million. A *full inclusion rule* treats all the CFC's gross profit as foreign base company income if more than 70 percent of the CFC's gross income is foreign base company income. In addition, a taxpayer can *elect* to exclude "high-tax" subpart F income from the deemed dividend rules. High-tax subpart F income is taxed at an effective tax rate that is 90 percent or more of the highest U.S. statutory rate. For a U.S. corporation, the current rate is 18.9 percent (90% × 21%). The calculation of the effective tax rate is complex and beyond the scope of this text.

Example 13-20

Return to the facts in Example 13-18, in which CDD reported taxable income from its bakery operations of C$75,000 in 2022 and received dividends of £1,000 from Thorntons PLC, which translated into C$1,500. Assume CDD has gross income of C$125,000 in 2022. In Example 13-18, we determined that the dividend constitutes subpart F income for U.S. tax purposes. Will 3D have a deemed dividend of this subpart F income in 2022?

Answer: No. The dividend is less than the lesser of 5 percent of CDD's gross income ($6,250) or $1 million and is not subject to the deemed dividend rules under the *de minimis rule*.

Only those U.S. shareholders who own stock in the CFC on the last day in the CFC's taxable year are treated as having received their pro rata share of any subpart F deemed dividend.

The computation of the deemed dividend related to subpart F income is exceptionally complicated and requires the CFC to allocate both deductions and taxes paid to subpart F gross income. The formula for this computation can be found in worksheets in the instructions to Form 5471, Information Return of U.S. Persons with Respect to Certain Foreign Corporations. In addition, the U.S. shareholder receives a foreign tax credit for income taxes paid on the subpart F income.[40]

[40]§960.

Subpart F income of the CFC treated as a deemed dividend under subpart F becomes *previously taxed earnings and profits* and subsequently can be distributed to the shareholders without being included in the shareholder's income a second time. A foreign currency gain or loss on repatriation of such income is included in (deducted from) the shareholders' income.

Planning to Avoid Subpart F Income

U.S. multinational corporations expanding outside the United States often use hybrid entities as a tax-efficient means to avoid the subpart F rules. Tax aligning a U.S. corporation's international supply chain has become a frequent objective in international tax planning. Accomplishing this goal requires the formation of a foreign holding company (Foreign HoldCo) treated as a corporation for U.S. tax purposes (and thus eligible for deferral from U.S. taxation). The holding company owns the stock of hybrid entities set up to conduct each of the components of the company's foreign operations: financing (FinanceCo), manufacturing (OpCo), distribution (DistribCo), and intellectual property (IPCo). The holding company is strategically located in a country that lightly taxes dividend income paid by the hybrid entities. The hybrid entities also are strategically located in countries that tax the income from such operations (e.g., interest or royalties paid by the operating company to the finance company or intellectual property company) at a low tax rate.

For instance, Ireland taxes manufacturing and intellectual property income at 12.5 percent. Because these operations are conducted through hybrid entities, transactions between the entities (e.g., payments of interest, rents, or royalties from one entity to another), which otherwise would create subpart F income, are ignored for U.S. tax purposes but respected for foreign tax purposes because the hybrid entity is treated as a corporation in the country in which it is organized. This allows for the free flow of cash between foreign operations without the intrusion of the U.S. tax laws and the reduction of taxes in high-tax countries through cross-border payments that are deductible in the country in which the hybrid entity is located. Exhibit 13-5 illustrates a template for such an international operation.[41]

EXHIBIT 13-5 A Tax-Aligned International Organizational Chart (see Exhibit 13-4 for explanation of symbols)

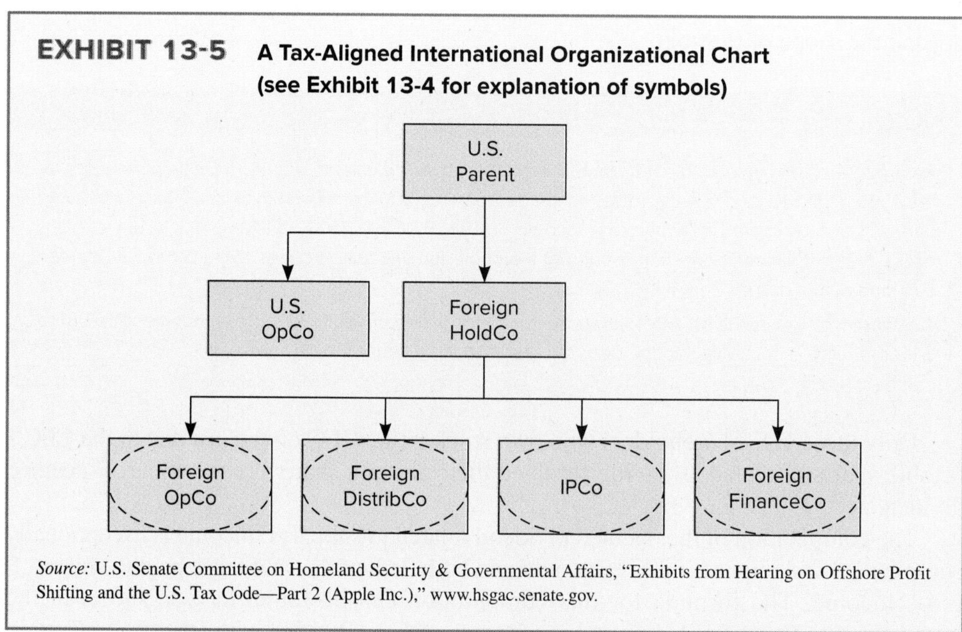

Source: U.S. Senate Committee on Homeland Security & Governmental Affairs, "Exhibits from Hearing on Offshore Profit Shifting and the U.S. Tax Code—Part 2 (Apple Inc.)," www.hsgac.senate.gov.

[41]In hearings held on May 21, 2013, Senator Carl Levin accused Apple Inc. of avoiding billions of U.S. taxes by structuring its overseas operations to route royalty income to low-tax jurisdictions. See www.hsgac.senate.gov/subcommittees/investigations/hearings/offshore-profit-shifting-and-the-us-tax-code_-part-2 for more details.

TAXES IN THE REAL WORLD Apple Inc.'s $37 Billion Repatriation Tax

As part of the transition toward a territorial tax system in the Tax Cuts and Jobs Act of 2017, Congress enacted a one-time deemed repatriation tax on unrepatriated earnings and profits of U.S. multinational companies that were previously deferred from U.S. taxation. Congress enacted this deemed repatriation tax to prevent earnings that had been deferred from U.S. taxation under the previous tax rules to avoid permanent exemption from U.S. taxation under the new 100 percent DRD rules. The repatriation tax is calculated as 15.5 percent times the component of earnings that is considered cash and cash equivalents and 8 percent times the component of earnings that is considered "illiquid" (for example, a building). The U.S. corporation determines its earnings as the greater of the earnings on November 2, 2017, or year-end (December 31, 2017, for a calendar-year corporation).

Apple Inc. had, by most estimates, unrepatriated earnings subject to the repatriation tax of more than $250 billion, almost all of which was in cash. The company announced in its Form 10-K for September 28, 2018, that its repatriation tax was $37.3 billion! The good news for Apple Inc. is that the tax law gives companies subject to the repatriation tax eight years in which to pay the tax, interest-free! Had Apple Inc. distributed its foreign earnings under the pre-TCJA rules, it would have incurred a U.S. tax of more than $75 billion, so the deemed repatriation tax saved the company a significant amount of potential future taxes—which, of course, would only have been paid if Apple Inc. actually repatriated the earnings.

Global Intangible Low-Taxed Income

The tax rules that apply to a category of foreign earnings known as Global Intangible Low-Taxed Income (GILTI) add an additonal anti-deferral regime on top of the existing subpart F income regime for U.S. shareholders in CFCs. These rules apply to a CFC's "nonroutine" GILTI. Most of the details of this tax are beyond the scope of this text. You should understand, however, that the goal of the GILTI tax is to subject CFC income (other than subpart F income) that exceeds a "normal rate of return" (10 percent of its invested foreign assets or QBAI) to treatment similar to subpart F income (deemed dividend).

All U.S. shareholders include their share of pretax GILTI in their gross income. U.S. *corporate* shareholders are then allowed a deduction equal to 50 percent of GILTI

TAXES IN THE REAL WORLD Corporate Inversions

In the years leading up to the passage of the Tax Cuts and Jobs Act in 2017, a number of large corporations headquartered in the United States such as Allergan, Mylan, and Johnson Controls changed their tax residence from the United States to tax haven countries like Ireland and the Netherlands through cross-border mergers with foreign corporations. These transactions were commonly referred to as "corporate inversions." To a great extent, the international provisions adopted as part of the TCJA were designed to deter new inversions and incentivize inverted companies to return to the United States. These international rule changes included a reduction in U.S. corporate tax rates from 35 percent to 21 percent, the creation of a new 37.5 percent deduction for foreign-derived intangible income reported in the United States, and the introduction of a new tax levied on the U.S. shareholders of controlled foreign corporations with GILTI (foreign earnings of controlled foreign corporations that exceed a 10 percent return on certain foreign assets).

Though it will take some time before the full impact of the TCJA is fully understood, it appears that it may indeed be having the intended impact on corporate location decisions. For example, Mylan and Allergan PLC, both inverted pharmaceutical companies, returned to the United States in 2020. Mylan returned by way of a merger with a subsidiary of Pfizer, Inc., and Allergan PLC through a sale to AbbVie Inc.

for 2018 through 2025, which decreases to 37.5 percent beginning in 2026. As a result, the effective tax rate on GILTI when U.S. *corporate* shareholders are allowed the 50 percent deduction is 10.5 percent for tax years prior to 2026. U.S. *corporate* shareholders are also eligible for an FTC of up to 80 percent of foreign taxes paid on their share of GILTI; however, as noted earlier in the chapter, the foreign tax credit limitation is applied separately to income in the GILTI basket and any excess foreign tax credits are not eligible to be carried back or forward. For U.S. corporate shareholders, the U.S. tax on GILTI generally will be zero if the foreign tax rate paid on the GILTI is at least 13.125 percent. In contrast, U.S. *individual* shareholders will typically be taxed on GILTI at rates as high as 40.8 percent (the 37 percent rate on ordinary income plus the 3.8 percent rate on net investment income) because they are not eligible for any deduction or FTC on their share of GILTI.[42] Many U.S. multinational companies with significant offshore intangibles (e.g., Apple, Microsoft, Alphabet, and Coca-Cola) will be subject to the new tax. Taxpayers compute their GILTI on Form 8992, U.S. Calculation of Global Intangible Low-Taxed Income, and the related deduction is computed on Form 8993, Section 250 Deduction for Foreign-Derived Intangible Income and Global Intangible Low-Taxed Income.

BASE EROSION AND PROFIT-SHIFTING INITIATIVES AROUND THE WORLD

The Organization for Economic Cooperation and Development (OECD) has embarked on a "base erosion and profit shifting" (BEPS) initiative. Its goal is to provide "governments with solutions for closing the gaps in existing international rules that allow corporate profits to 'disappear' or be artificially shifted to low/no tax environments, where little or no economic activity takes place."[43] The BEPS initiative, which began in 2013, was prompted by estimates that governments around the world were losing between $100 and $240 billion per year in tax revenues due to aggressive tax planning by multinational corporations. The OECD issued 15 "actions" in October 2015 that focused on transfer pricing, harmful tax practices, and treaty shopping and urged more transparent reporting ("country-by-country reporting" of income and taxes paid). Adoption of these actions by governments around the world will dramatically change the way multinational corporations plan their international operations and develop their information systems, as well as the way taxing agencies audit the tax returns filed by these corporations.

More recently, the OECD, issued its "Statement on a Two Pillar Solution to the Address the Tax Challenges Arising from the Digitalization of the Economy" in October 2021.[44] This action is a continuation of the BEPS initiative it had begun earlier and focuses on two specific areas that it refers to as "pillars". The first, "Pillar One" would shift tax revenues to the countries where companies sell to customers as opposed to where the companies are located, and the second, "Pillar Two", establishes a global 15 percent

[42]U.S. individual shareholders may elect under §962 to have their GILTI inclusions taxed as if they had been received by domestic corporations. This election, however, also requires that a portion of subsequent distributions of GILTI to an electing shareholder be taxed as dividend income.

[43]Organization for Economic Cooperation and Development (OECD), "Reforms to the International Tax System for Curbing Avoidance by Multinational Enterprises," May 10, 2015, www.oecd.org/ctp/oecd-presents-outputs-of-oecd-g20-beps-project-for-discussion-at-g20-finance-ministers-meeting.htm.

[44]Organization for Economic Cooperation and Development (OECD), "Statement on a Two-Pillar Solution to Address the Tax Challenges Arising from the Digitalisation of the Economy," October 8, 2021, www.oecd.org/tax/beps/statement-on-a-two-pillar-solution-to-address-the-tax-challenges-arising-from-the-digitalisation-of-the-economy-october-2021.pdf.

minimum tax rate on large corporations with profits reported in OECD countries that agree to participate.

As of the date we go to press, 137 OECD countries have signed on to this new approach to international taxation. The impact of this transformational agreement will not be immediate, however. To conform, each of these countries will be required to enact substantial changes to their current tax laws.

Consistent with the BEPS objectives, the IRC includes a **base erosion and anti-abuse tax (BEAT)** minimum tax. Under this provision, U.S. corporations with annual average gross receipts of at least $500 million for the three tax-year periods ending with the preceding tax year are required to pay a minimum tax amount of 10 percent (12.5 percent for tax years beginning after December 31, 2025) of a corporation's modified taxable income determined by adding back to regular taxable income cross-border outbound payments such as interest, royalties, and rents.[45] Because it is a minimum tax, the BEAT will only apply when the minimum tax amount exceeds a corporation's regular income tax liability. In effect, the BEAT serves as a minimum tax on outbound payments made by U.S. corporations to related foreign persons that reduce the U.S. tax base. The BEAT only applies when the "base erosion" deductions exceed 3 percent of total deductions. The details of this tax are beyond the scope of this text.

In addition, the European Union (EU) has aggressively gone after U.S. multinational companies for special arrangements with low-tax countries such as Ireland and Luxembourg that lowered the tax paid in these countries through transfer pricing. The European Commission ruled in September 2016 that Apple Inc. had received more than $14.5 billion of "illegal" tax benefits from Ireland and demanded that the Irish government recoup these lost taxes. However, the European Union's General Court announced in July 2020 that it was overturning this decision because there was not sufficient evidence to show that Apple had broken EU rules. This did not end the battle, however, because the European Commission subsequently announced it would appeal the decision to a higher court. At the date of publication, the issue remains unresolved.

CONCLUSION

In this chapter we discussed some of the important U.S. tax rules that apply to U.S. persons who expand their business operations outside the United States. As the storyline indicates, a U.S. business that wants to expand its markets outside the United States must decide on an organizational form through which to conduct its business. Establishing a physical presence in another country generally subjects the profits of the business to taxation in the host country and potentially in the United States as well.

Treaties between the United States and other countries can provide beneficial tax treatment to a U.S. company's operations, employees, and cross-border payments. Where a cross-border transaction is subject to both foreign and U.S. taxation, the United States provides relief in the form of a foreign tax credit for foreign income taxes paid on foreign income that is reported on a U.S. tax return. These credits can be reduced by the foreign tax credit limitation. By operating through a foreign corporation, a U.S. corporation can repatriate foreign source income to the United States as a dividend and avoid residual U.S. taxation by receiving a 100 percent dividends-received deduction. Certain types of income are not subject to exemption if earned through a controlled foreign corporation (CFC). The use of hybrid entities outside the United States provides U.S. companies with the ability to shift income and move cash across jurisdictions without being subject to deemed dividends under subpart F.

[45]§59A.

Summary

LO 13-1 Describe the basic U.S. framework for taxing multinational transactions and the role of the foreign tax credit limitation.

- Countries most often determine nexus by either the geographic source of the income (source-based jurisdiction) or the taxpayer's citizenship or residence (residence-based jurisdiction).
  - Under a residence-based approach, a country taxes the worldwide income of the person earning the income.
  - Under a source-based approach, a country taxes only the income earned within its boundaries.
- The U.S. government taxes citizens and residents on their worldwide income, regardless of source (residence-based jurisdiction).
  - An individual who is not a citizen will be treated as a U.S. resident for income tax purposes if they are considered a permanent resident (have a green card) or satisfy a substantial presence test.
- The U.S. government only taxes nonresidents on income that is "U.S. source" or is connected with the operation of a U.S. trade or business (source-based jurisdiction).
- To alleviate (mitigate) potential double taxation and to promote international commerce, governments often allow their residents a tax credit for foreign income taxes paid on foreign source income or exempt dividends from foreign corporations from U.S. taxation.
- Dividends remitted to U.S. corporate shareholders from 10-percent-or-more-owned foreign corporations qualify for a 100 percent dividends-received deduction and are exempt from residual U.S. taxation.

LO 13-2 Apply the U.S. source rules for common items of gross income and deductions.

- The U.S. source rules determine whether income and related deductions are from sources within or outside of the United States.
  - The U.S. source-of-income rules are important to non-U.S. persons because they limit the scope of U.S. taxation of their worldwide income.
  - For U.S. persons, the primary purpose of the U.S. source-of-income rules is to calculate foreign source taxable income in the numerator of the foreign tax credit limitation.
- The Internal Revenue Code defines eight classes of gross income from sources within the United States and eight classes of gross income from sources outside of the United States.
  - As a general rule, the taxpayer looks to the borrower's residence to determine the geographic source of interest received.
  - In general, the source of dividend income is determined by the residence of the corporation paying the dividend.
  - The source of compensation received for labor or personal services is determined by the location where the service is performed.
  - Rent has its source where the property generating the rent is located.
  - Royalty income has its source where the intangible property or the rights generating the royalty are used.
- After determining the source of gross income as being from U.S. or foreign sources, a taxpayer may be required to allocate and apportion allowable deductions to gross income from each geographical source to compute taxable income from U.S. and foreign sources.
  - The IRC provides very broad language in describing how to allocate deductions to U.S. and foreign source gross income.
  - The regulations attempt to match deductions with the gross income such deductions were incurred to produce, usually based on the "factual relationship" of the deduction to gross income.
  - Special apportionment rules apply to nine categories of deductions, most notably interest, research and experimentation, state and local income taxes, losses on property disposition, and charitable contributions.

Explain the role of income tax treaties in international tax planning. LO 13-3

- A tax treaty is a bilateral agreement between two contracting countries in which each agrees to modify its own tax laws to achieve reciprocal benefits.
- The general purpose of an income tax treaty is to eliminate or reduce (mitigate) the impact of double taxation so that residents paying taxes to one country will not have the full burden of taxes in the other country.
- The United States currently has income tax treaties with over sixty countries.
- Most U.S. treaties provide a low withholding tax rate or an exemption from tax on various types of investment income (interest, dividends, gains from the sale of stock, and royalties) that would otherwise be subject to a high withholding tax.

Identify creditable foreign taxes and compute the foreign tax credit limitation. LO 13-4

- The foreign tax credit is available only for foreign taxes the United States considers to be income taxes.
- Creditable foreign income taxes can be direct or "in lieu of" income taxes.
- Taxpayers must compute a separate FTC limitation for each category ("basket") of foreign source taxable income.
    - Passive category income generally is investment-type income that traditionally is subject to low foreign taxes (usually in the form of withholding taxes).
    - Foreign branch income is business profit earned through unincorporated operations located outside the United States.
    - GILTI is a new category of income based on returns in excess of a fixed rate of return on certain assets held by foreign corporations.
    - Income not treated as passive category income, foreign branch income, or GILTI is defined as general category income. General category income includes gross income from an active trade or business, financial services income, and shipping income.
    - A taxpayer computes the FTC limitation by multiplying the ratio of foreign source taxable income to taxable income from all sources by its pre-credit U.S. tax, as follows:

$$\frac{\text{Foreign source taxable income}}{\text{Taxable income from all sources}} \times \text{Pre-credit U.S. tax}$$

Compare the advantages and disadvantages of the different forms of doing business outside the United States. LO 13-5

- A U.S. person can do business outside the United States through a branch, partnership, corporation, or hybrid entity.
- A hybrid entity is an entity that is treated as a flow-through entity for U.S. tax purposes and a corporation for foreign tax purposes (or vice versa).
- A U.S. taxpayer elects the U.S. tax status of a hybrid entity by "checking the box" on Form 8832.
    - Certain designated per se foreign entities are not eligible for this elective treatment.

Explain the basic U.S. anti-deferral tax regime and identify common sources of subpart F income. LO 13-6

- Subpart F requires certain U.S. shareholders in a controlled foreign corporation (CFC) to include in their current gross income their pro rata share of specified categories of "tainted" income earned by the CFC during the current year (*subpart F income*).
- A controlled foreign corporation is defined as any foreign corporation in which U.S. shareholders collectively own more than 50 percent of the total combined voting power of all classes of stock entitled to vote or the total value of the corporation's stock on any day during the CFC's tax year.
    - Constructive ownership rules are used in the calculation of both the 50 percent test for determining CFC status and the 10 percent test for determining who is a U.S. shareholder.
- Subpart F income generally can be characterized as low-taxed passive income or "portable" income earned by a CFC.
    - Foreign personal holding company income includes interest, dividends, rents, royalties, and gains from the sale of certain foreign property.

  - Foreign base company sales income is income derived by a CFC from the sale or purchase of personal property to (or from) a related person when the property is manufactured and sold outside the CFC's country of incorporation.
- There are several exceptions that serve to exclude all or a portion of a CFC's subpart F income from current taxation to the U.S. shareholders.
  - A *de minimis rule* excludes all gross income from being treated as foreign base company income if the sum of the CFC's gross foreign base company income is less than the lesser of 5 percent of gross income or $1 million.
  - A *full inclusion rule* treats all of the CFC's gross income as foreign base company income if more than 70 percent of the CFC's gross income is foreign base company income.
  - GILTI is high-return income earned through a foreign corporation.

KEY TERMS

allocate (13-11)
apportion (13-11)
base erosion and anti-abuse tax (BEAT) (13-31)
commercial traveler exception (13-8)
controlled foreign corporation (CFC) (13-25)
definitely related deductions (13-11)
disregarded entity (13-22)
effectively connected income (ECI) (13-3)
fixed and determinable, annual or periodic (FDAP) income (13-3)
foreign base company income (13-26)
foreign base company sales income (13-26)
foreign branch (13-2)
foreign personal holding company income (13-26)
foreign tax credit (FTC) (13-5)
foreign tax credit limitation (13-5)
foreign-derived intangible income (FDII) (13-17)
FTC basket (13-20)
general category income (13-20)
global intangible low-taxed income (GILTI) (13-20)
hybrid entity (13-22)
inbound transaction (13-2)
nexus (13-2)
nonresident alien (13-4)
not definitely related deductions (13-11)
outbound transaction (13-2)
passive category income (13-20)
permanent establishment (13-18)
qualified business asset investment (QBAI) (13-17)
residence-based jurisdiction (13-2)
resident alien (13-4)
reverse hybrid entity (13-22)
source-based jurisdiction (13-2)
spot rate (13-21)
subpart F income (13-25)
tax haven (13-25)
United States person (13-25)

DISCUSSION QUESTIONS

Discussion Questions are available in Connect®.

McGraw Hill connect

LO 13-1 1. Distinguish between an outbound transaction and an inbound transaction from a U.S. tax perspective.

LO 13-1 2. What are the major U.S. tax issues that apply to an inbound transaction?

LO 13-1 3. What are the major U.S. tax issues that apply to an outbound transaction?

LO 13-1 4. How does a residence-based approach to taxing worldwide income differ from a source-based approach to taxing the same income?

LO 13-1 5. Henri is a resident of the United States for U.S. tax purposes and earns $10,000 from an investment in a French company. Will Henri be subject to U.S. tax under a residence-based approach to taxation? A source-based approach?

LO 13-1 6. What are the two categories of income that can be taxed by the United States when earned by a nonresident? How does the United States tax each category of income?

LO 13-1 7. Maria is not a citizen of the United States, but she spends 180 days per year in the United States on business-related activities. Under what conditions will Maria be considered a resident of the United States for U.S. tax purposes?

8. Natasha is not a citizen of the United States, but she spends 200 days per year in the United States on business. She does not have a green card. True or False: Natasha will always be considered a resident of the United States for U.S. tax purposes because of her physical presence in the United States. Explain. LO 13-1
9. Why does the United States allow U.S. taxpayers to claim a credit against their pre-credit U.S. tax for foreign income taxes paid? LO 13-1
10. What role does the foreign tax credit limitation play in U.S. tax policy? LO 13-1
11. Why are the income source rules important to a U.S. citizen or resident? LO 13-2
12. Why are the income source rules important to a U.S. nonresident? LO 13-2
13. Carol receives $500 of dividend income from Microsoft Inc., a U.S. company. True or False: Absent any treaty provisions, Carol will be subject to U.S. tax on the dividend regardless of whether she is a resident or nonresident. Explain. LO 13-2
14. Pavel, a citizen and resident of Russia, spent 100 days in the United States working for his employer, Yukos Oil, a Russian corporation. Under what conditions will Pavel be subject to U.S. tax on the portion of his compensation earned while working in the United States? LO 13-2
15. What are the potential U.S. tax benefits from engaging in an export sale? LO 13-2
16. True or False: A taxpayer will always prefer deducting an expense against U.S. source income and not foreign source income when filing a tax return in the United States. Explain. LO 13-2
17. Distinguish between *allocation* and *apportionment* in sourcing deductions in computing the foreign tax credit limitation. LO 13-2
18. Distinguish between a *definitely related deduction* and a *not definitely related deduction* in the allocation and apportionment of deductions to foreign source taxable income. LO 13-2
19. Briefly describe the method for apportioning interest expense to foreign source taxable income in the computation of the foreign tax credit limitation. LO 13-2
20. What is the primary goal of the United States in negotiating income tax treaties with other countries? LO 13-3
21. What is a *permanent establishment,* and why is it an important part of most income tax treaties? LO 13-3
22. Why is a treaty important to a nonresident investor in U.S. stocks and bonds? LO 13-3
23. Why is a treaty important to a nonresident worker in the United States? LO 13-3
24. Why does the United States use a "basket" approach in the foreign tax credit limitation computation? LO 13-4
25. True or False: All dividend income received by a U.S. taxpayer is classified as passive category income for foreign tax credit limitation purposes. Explain. LO 13-4
26. True or False: All foreign taxes are creditable for U.S. tax purposes. Explain. LO 13-4
27. What is a hybrid entity for U.S. tax purposes? Why is a hybrid entity a popular organizational form for a U.S. company expanding its international operations? What are the potential drawbacks to using a hybrid entity? LO 13-5
28. What is a "per se" entity under the check-the-box rules? LO 13-5
29. What are the requirements for a foreign corporation to be a *controlled foreign corporation* for U.S. tax purposes? LO 13-6
30. Why does the United States not allow exclusion of all foreign source income earned by a controlled foreign corporation? LO 13-6
31. True or False: A foreign corporation owned equally by 11 U.S. individuals can never be a controlled foreign corporation. Explain. LO 13-6
32. What is foreign base company sales income? Why does the United States include this income in its definition of subpart F income? LO 13-6

LO 13-6 33. True or False: Subpart F income is always treated as a deemed dividend to the U.S. shareholders of a controlled foreign corporation. Explain.

LO 13-6 34. What is global intangible low-tax income (GILTI)? How and when is the GILTI of controlled foreign corporations taxed?

LO 13-6 35. True or False: All outbound payments from a U.S. corporation to a related foreign subsidiary are subject to the BEAT minimum tax. Explain.

PROBLEMS

Select problems are available in Connect®.

LO 13-1 36. Diya, a citizen and resident of Country A, received a $1,000 dividend from a corporation organized in Country B. Which statement best describes the taxation of this income under the two different approaches to taxing foreign income?

a) Country B will not tax this income under a residence-based jurisdiction approach but will tax this income under a source-based jurisdiction approach.

b) Country B will tax this income under a residence-based jurisdiction approach but will not tax this income under a source-based jurisdiction approach.

c) Country B will tax this income under both a residence-based jurisdiction approach and a source-based jurisdiction approach.

d) Country B will not tax this income under either a residence-based jurisdiction approach or a source-based jurisdiction approach.

LO 13-1 37. Spartan Corporation, a U.S. corporation, reported $2 million of pretax income from its business operations in Spartania, which were conducted through a foreign branch. Spartania taxes branch income at 15 percent, and the United States taxes corporate income at 21 percent.

a) If the United States provided no mechanism for mitigating double taxation, what would be the total tax (U.S. and foreign) on the $2 million of branch profits?

b) Assume the United States allows U.S. corporations to exclude foreign source income from U.S. taxation. What would be the total tax on the $2 million of branch profits?

c) Assume the United States allows U.S. corporations to claim a deduction for foreign income taxes. What would be the total tax on the $2 million of branch profits?

d) Assume the United States allows U.S. corporations to claim a credit for foreign income taxes paid on foreign source income. What would be the total tax on the $2 million of branch profits? What would be your answer if Spartania taxed branch profits at 30 percent?

LO 13-1 38. Lars is a citizen and resident of Belgium. He has a full-time job in Belgium and has lived there with his family for the past 10 years. In 2020, Lars came to the United States for the first time. The sole purpose of his trip was business. He intended to stay in the United States for only 180 days, but he ended up staying for 210 days because of unforeseen problems with his business. Lars came to the United States again on business in 2021 and stayed for 180 days. In 2022 he came back to the United States on business and stayed for 70 days. Determine if Lars meets the U.S. statutory definition of a resident alien in 2020, 2021, and 2022 under the substantial presence test.

LO 13-1 research 39. Use the facts in problem 38. If Lars meets the statutory requirements to be considered a resident of both the United States and Belgium, what criteria does the U.S.–Belgium treaty use to "break the tie" and determine Lars's country of residence? Look at Article 4 of the 2007 U.S.–Belgium income tax treaty, which you can find on the IRS website, www.irs.gov.

40. How does the U.S.–Belgium treaty define a *permanent establishment* for determining nexus? Look at Article 5 of the 2007 U.S.–Belgium income tax treaty, which you can find on the IRS website, www.irs.gov. LO 13-1 research

41. Mackinac Corporation, a U.S. corporation, reported total taxable income of $5 million. Taxable income included $1.5 million of foreign source taxable income from the company's branch operations in Canada. All of the branch income is foreign branch income. Mackinac paid Canadian income taxes of $375,000 (as translated) on its branch income. Compute Mackinac's allowable foreign tax credit. LO 13-1

42. Waco Leather Inc., a U.S. corporation, reported total taxable income of $5 million. Taxable income included $1.5 million of foreign source taxable income from the company's branch operations in Mexico. All of the branch income is foreign branch income. Waco paid Mexican income taxes of $300,000 on its branch income. Compute Waco's allowable foreign tax credit. LO 13-1

43. Valley View Inc., a U.S. corporation, formed a wholly owned Mexican corporation to conduct manufacturing and selling operations in Mexico. In its first year of operations, the Mexican corporation reported taxable income of Mex$5,000,000 and paid Mexican income tax of Mex$1,500,000 on its taxable income. In the second year of its operations, the Mexican subsidiary pays a dividend of Mex$2,000,000 to Valley View Inc. The dividend is subject to a 10 percent withholding tax (Mex$200,000) under the U.S.–Mexico treaty. Assume the currency translation rate for both years is Mex$1:US$.05. LO 13-2
    a) Assuming that Valley View Inc.'s Mexican subsidiary does not have any subpart F income or global intangible low-tax income (GILTI), how much taxable income would Valley View Inc. report in U.S. dollars from its Mexican subsidiary's first year of operations?
    b) How much of the dividend from the Mexican subsidiary is subject to U.S. taxation, and are any of the Mexican taxes imposed on the income distributed creditable in the U.S.?
    c) If Valley View Inc. only held 5 percent of the Mexican corporation stock, how much of the dividend from the Mexican corporation would be subject to U.S. taxation, and would any of the Mexican taxes imposed on the income distributed be creditable in the U.S.?

44. Petoskey Stone Inc., a U.S. corporation, received the following sources of income during the current year. Identify the source of each item as either U.S. or foreign. LO 13-2
    a) Interest income from a loan to its German subsidiary.
    b) Dividend income from Granite Corporation, a U.S. corporation.
    c) Royalty income from its Irish subsidiary for use of a trademark.
    d) Rent income from its Canadian subsidiary for its use of a warehouse located in Wisconsin.

45. Carmen SanDiego, a U.S. citizen, is employed by General Motors Corporation, a U.S. corporation. On April 1, 2022, GM relocated Carmen to its Brazilian operations for the remainder of 2022. Carmen was paid a salary of $120,000 and was employed on a 5-day-week basis. As part of her compensation package for moving to Brazil, Carmen also received a housing allowance of $25,000. Carmen's salary was earned ratably over the 12-month period. During 2022 Carmen worked 260 days, 195 of which were in Brazil and 65 of which were in Michigan. How much of Carmen's total compensation is treated as foreign source income for 2022? Why might Carmen want to maximize her foreign source income in 2022? LO 13-2

46. Sam Smith is a citizen and bona fide resident of Great Britain (United Kingdom). During the current year, Sam received the following income: LO 13-2
    - Compensation of $30 million from performing concerts in the United States.
    - Cash dividends of $10,000 from a French corporation's stock.

- Interest of $6,000 on a U.S. corporation bond.
- Interest of $2,000 on a loan made to a U.S. citizen residing in Australia.
- Gain of $80,000 on the sale of stock in a U.S. corporation.

Determine the source (U.S. or foreign) of each item of income Sam received.

Income	Source
Income from concerts	
Dividend from French corporation	
Interest on a U.S. corporation bond	
Interest of $2,000 on a loan made to a U.S. citizen residing in Australia	
Gain of $80,000 on the sale of stock in a U.S. corporation	

LO 13-2

47. Spartan Corporation, a U.S. company, manufactures green eyeshades for sale in the United States and Europe. All manufacturing activities take place in Michigan. During the current year, Spartan sold 10,000 green eyeshades to European customers at a price of $10 each. Each eyeshade costs $4 to produce. For each independent scenario, determine the source of the gross income from sale of the green eyeshades.
    a) All of Spartan's production assets are located in the United States.
    b) Half of Spartan's production assets are located outside the United States.

LO 13-2 planning

48. Falmouth Kettle Company, a U.S. corporation, sells its products in the United States and Europe. During the current year, selling, general, and administrative (SG&A) expenses included:

Personnel department	$ 500
Training department	350
President's salary	400
Sales manager's salary	200
Other general and administrative	550
Total SG&A expenses	$2,000

Falmouth had $12,000 of gross sales to U.S. customers and $3,000 of gross sales to European customers. Gross income (sales minus cost of goods sold) from domestic sales was $3,000, and gross profit from foreign sales was $1,000. Apportion Falmouth's SG&A expenses to foreign source income using the following methods:
    a) Gross sales.
    b) Gross income.
    c) If Falmouth wants to maximize its foreign tax credit limitation, which method produces the better outcome? Assume the FDII deduction does not apply.

LO 13-2 planning

49. Owl Vision Corporation (OVC) is a North Carolina corporation engaged in the manufacture and sale of contact lenses and other optical equipment. The company handles its export sales through sales branches in Belgium and Singapore. The average tax book value of OVC's assets for the year was $200 million, of which $160 million generated U.S. source income and $40 million generated foreign source income. OVC's total interest expense was $20 million. What amount of the interest expense will be apportioned to foreign source income under the tax book value method?

LO 13-2 planning

50. Riverbend Semiconductor Corporation (RSC) is an Arizona corporation engaged in the manufacture and sale of semiconductors and other computer equipment. RSC spent $3 million on research and experimentation costs, and all its research and experimentation activity was conducted in the United States. The company handles its export sales through sales branches in Ireland and Taiwan. Total foreign sales from the foreign branches were $8 million and worldwide sales were $20 million.

What amount of the total research and experimentation expense will be apportioned to foreign source income?

51. Coleen is a citizen and bona fide resident of Ireland. During the current year, she received the following income: LO 13-3 research
    - Cash dividends of $2,000 from a U.S. corporation's stock.
    - Interest of $1,000 on a U.S. corporation bond.
    - Royalty of $100,000 from a U.S. corporation for use of a patent she developed.
    - Rent of $3,000 from U.S. individuals renting her cottage in Maine.

    Identify the U.S. withholding tax rate on the payment of each item of income under the U.S.–Ireland income tax treaty and cite the appropriate treaty article. You can access the 1997 U.S.–Ireland income tax treaty on the IRS website, www.irs.gov.

Income	Withholding Tax Rate	Treaty Article
Cash dividends of $2,000		
Interest of $1,000		
Royalty of $100,000		
Rent of $3,000		

52. Gameco, a U.S. corporation, operates gambling machines in the United States and abroad. Gameco conducts its operations in Europe through a Dutch B.V., which is treated as a branch for U.S. tax purposes. Gameco also licenses game machines to an unrelated company in Japan. During the current year, Gameco paid the following foreign taxes, translated into U.S. dollars at the appropriate exchange rate: LO 13-4

Foreign Taxes	Amount (in $)
National income taxes	1,000,000
City (Amsterdam) income taxes	100,000
Value-added tax	150,000
Payroll tax (employer's share of social insurance contributions)	400,000
Withholding tax on royalties received from Japan	50,000

Identify Gameco's creditable foreign taxes.

53. Sombrero Corporation, a U.S. corporation, operates through a branch in Espania. Management projects that the company's pretax income in the next taxable year will be $100,000: $80,000 from U.S. operations and $20,000 from the Espania branch. Espania taxes corporate income at a rate of 30 percent. LO 13-4 planning
    a) If management's projections are accurate, what will be Sombrero's excess foreign tax credit in the next taxable year? Assume all of the income is foreign branch income.
    b) Management plans to establish a second branch in Italia. Italia taxes corporate income at a rate of 10 percent. What amount of income will the branch in Italia have to generate to eliminate the excess credit generated by the branch in Espania?

54. Chapeau Company, a U.S. corporation, operates through a branch in Champagnia. The source rules used by Champagnia are identical to those used by the United States. For 2022, Chapeau has $2,000 of gross income: $1,200 from U.S. sources and $800 from sources within Champagnia. The $1,200 of U.S. source income and $700 of the foreign source income are attributable to manufacturing activities in Champagnia (foreign branch income). The remaining $100 of foreign source income is passive category interest income. Chapeau had $500 of expenses other than taxes, all of which are allocated directly to manufacturing income ($200 of which is apportioned to foreign sources). Chapeau paid $150 of income taxes to Champagnia on its manufacturing income. The interest income was subject to a 10 percent withholding tax of $10. Compute Chapeau's allowable foreign tax credit in 2022. LO 13-4

LO 13-5 research

55. Identify the "per se" companies for which a check-the-box election cannot be made for U.S. tax purposes in the countries listed below. Consult the Instructions to Form 8832, which can be found on the "Forms & Instructions" site on the IRS website, www.irs.gov.
    a) Japan
    b) Germany
    c) Netherlands
    d) United Kingdom
    e) People's Republic of China

LO 13-5 research

56. Eagle Inc., a U.S. corporation, intends to create a *Limitada* (limited liability company) in Brazil in 2022 to manufacture pitching machines. The company expects the operation to generate losses of US$2,500,000 during its first three years of operations. Eagle would like the losses to flow through to its U.S. tax return and offset its U.S. profits.
    a) Can Eagle "check the box" and treat the *Limitada* as a disregarded entity (branch) for U.S. tax purposes? Consult the Instructions to Form 8832, which can be found on the "Forms & Instructions" site on the IRS website, www.irs.gov.
    b) Assume management's projections were accurate and Eagle deducted $75,000 of branch losses on its U.S. tax return from 2022–2024. On January 1, 2025, the fair market value of the *Limitada*'s net assets exceeded Eagle's tax basis in the assets by US$5 million. What are the U.S. tax consequences of checking the box on Form 8832 and converting the *Limitada* to a corporation for U.S. tax purposes?

LO 13-6

57. Identify whether the corporations described below are controlled foreign corporations.
    a) Shetland PLC, a U.K. corporation, has two classes of stock outstanding, 75 shares of class AA stock and 25 shares of class A stock. Each class of stock has equal voting power and value. Angus owns 35 shares of class AA stock and 20 shares of class A stock. Angus is a U.S. citizen who resides in England.
    b) Mihai and Gina, both U.S. citizens, own 5 percent and 10 percent, respectively, of the voting stock and value of DaVinci S.A., an Italian corporation. Mihai and Gina are also equal partners in Roma Corporation, an Italian corporation that owns 50 percent of the DaVinci stock.
    c) Pierre, a U.S. citizen, owns 45 of the 100 shares outstanding in Vino S.A., a French corporation. Pierre's father, Pepe, owns 8 shares in Vino. Pepe also is a U.S. citizen. The remaining 47 shares are owned by non-U.S. individuals.

LO 13-6

58. USCo owns 100 percent of the following corporations: Dutch N.V., Germany A.G., Australia PLC, Japan Corporation, and Brazil S.A. During the year, the following transactions took place. Determine whether these transactions result in Subpart F income.
    a) Germany A.G. owns an office building that it leases to unrelated persons. Germany A.G. engaged an independent managing agent to manage and maintain the office building and performs no activities with respect to the property.
    b) Dutch N.V. leased office machines to unrelated persons. Dutch N.V. performed only incidental activities and incurred nominal expenses in leasing and servicing the machines. Dutch N.V. is not engaged in the manufacture or production of the machines and does not add substantial value to the machines.
    c) Dutch N.V. purchased goods manufactured in France from an unrelated contract manufacturer and sold them to Germany A.G. for consumption in Germany.
    d) Australia PLC purchased goods manufactured in Australia from an unrelated person and sold them to Japan Corporation for use in Japan.

59. USCo manufactures and markets electrical components. USCo operates outside the United States through a number of CFCs, each of which is organized in a different country. These CFCs derived the following income for the current year. Determine the amount of income that USCo must report as a deemed dividend under Subpart F in each scenario. LO 13-6

a) F1 has gross income of $5 million, including $200,000 of foreign personal holding company interest and $4.8 million of gross income from the sale of inventory that F1 manufactured at a factory located within its home country.

b) F2 has gross income of $5 million, including $4 million of foreign personal holding company interest and $1 million of gross income from the sale of inventory that F2 manufactured at a factory located within its home country.

COMPREHENSIVE PROBLEMS

Select problems are available in Connect®.

60. Spartan Corporation manufactures quidgets at its plant in Sparta, Michigan. Spartan sells its quidgets to customers in the United States, Canada, England, and Australia.

Spartan markets its products in Canada and England through branches in Toronto and London, respectively. Spartan reported total gross income on U.S. sales of $15,000,000 and total gross income on Canadian and U.K. sales of $5,000,000, split equally between the two countries. Spartan paid Canadian income taxes of $600,000 on its branch profits in Canada and U.K. income taxes of $700,000 on its branch profits in the United Kingdom. Spartan financed its Canadian operations through a $10 million capital contribution, which Spartan financed through a loan from Bank of America. During the current year, Spartan paid $600,000 in interest on the loan.

Spartan sells its quidgets to Australian customers through its wholly owned Australian subsidiary. Spartan reported gross income of $3,000,000 on sales to its subsidiary during the year. The subsidiary paid Spartan a dividend of $670,000 on December 31 (the withholding tax is 0 percent under the U.S.–Australia treaty). Spartan paid Australian income taxes of $330,000 on the income repatriated as a dividend.

a) Compute Spartan's foreign source gross income and foreign tax (direct and withholding) for the current year.

b) Assume 20 percent of the interest paid to Bank of America is allocated to the numerator of Spartan's FTC limitation calculation. Compute Spartan Corporation's FTC limitation using your calculation from part (a) and any excess FTC or excess FTC limitation (all of the foreign source income is put in the foreign branch FTC basket).

61. Windmill Corporation manufactures products in its plants in Iowa, Canada, Ireland, and Australia. Windmill conducts its operations in Canada through a 50-percent-owned joint venture, CanCo. CanCo is treated as a corporation for U.S. and Canadian tax purposes. An unrelated Canadian investor owns the remaining 50 percent. Windmill conducts its operations in Ireland through a wholly owned subsidiary, IrishCo. IrishCo is a controlled foreign corporation for U.S. tax purposes. Windmill conducts its operations in Australia through a wholly owned hybrid entity, KiwiCo. KiwiCo is treated as a branch for U.S. tax purposes and a corporation for Australian tax purposes. Windmill also owns a 5 percent interest in a Dutch corporation, TulipCo.

During 2022, Windmill reported the following foreign source income from its international operations and investments.

	CanCo	IrishCo	KiwiCo	TulipCo
Dividend income				
Amount	$45,000	$28,000		$20,000
Withholding tax	2,250	1,400		3,000
Interest income				
Amount	30,000			
Withholding tax	0	0		
Branch income				
Taxable income			$93,000	
AUS income taxes			31,000	

Note: CanCo and KiwiCo derive all of their earnings from active business operations.

a) Classify the income received by Windmill into the appropriate FTC baskets.

b) Windmill has $1,250,000 of U.S. source gross income. Windmill also incurred SG&A of $300,000 that is apportioned between U.S. and foreign source income based on the gross income in each basket. Assume KiwiCo's gross income is $200,000. Compute the FTC limitation for each basket of foreign source income.

62. Euro Corporation, a U.S. corporation, operates through a branch in Germany. During 2022, the branch reported taxable income of $1,000,000 and paid German income taxes of $300,000. In addition, Euro received $50,000 of dividends from its 5 percent investment in the stock of Maple Leaf Company, a Canadian corporation. The dividend was subject to a withholding tax of $5,000. Euro reported U.S. taxable income from its manufacturing operations of $950,000. Total taxable income was $2,000,000. Pre-credit U.S. taxes on the taxable income were $420,000. Included in the computation of Euro's taxable income were "definitely allocable" expenses of $500,000, 50 percent of which were related to the German branch taxable income.

Complete pages 1 and 2 of Form 1118 for just the foreign branch income reported by Euro. You can use the fill-in form available on the IRS website, www.irs.gov.

research

63. USCo, a U.S. corporation, has decided to set up a headquarters subsidiary in Europe. Management has narrowed its location choice to either Spain, Ireland, or Switzerland. The company has asked you to research some of the income tax implications of setting up a corporation in these three countries. In particular, management wants to know what tax rate will be imposed on corporate income earned in the country and the withholding rates applied to interest, dividends, and royalty payments from the subsidiary to USCo.

To answer the tax rate question, consult KPMG's *Corporate Tax Rates Table 2011–2021,* which you can access at https://home.kpmg.com/xx/en/home/services/tax/tax-tools-and-resources/tax-rates-online/corporate-tax-rates-table.html. To answer the withholding tax questions, consult the treaties between the United States and Spain, Ireland, and Switzerland, which you can access at www.irs.gov (type in "treaties" as your search word).

UWorld Roger CPA Review

Sample CPA Exam questions from Roger CPA Review are available in Connect as support for the topics in this text. These Multiple Choice Questions and Task-Based Simulations include expert-written explanations and solutions and provide a starting point for students to become familiar with the content and functionality of the actual CPA Exam.

chapter 14

Transfer Taxes and Wealth Planning

Learning Objectives

Upon completing this chapter, you should be able to:

LO 14-1 Describe federal transfer taxes.

LO 14-2 Calculate the federal gift tax.

LO 14-3 Compute the federal estate tax.

LO 14-4 Understand how income and transfer taxation interact to affect wealth planning.

Ekaterina Kholyavskaya/THIETVU/mangostar/123RF

Storyline Summary

Taxpayers:	Harry (he/him/his) and Bob (he/him/his) Smith, brothers, ages 63 and 69, respectively. Frank's Frozen Pizzas Inc. (FFP) is a family business organized as a C corporation.
Description:	Harry is married to his second spouse, Wilma (she/her/hers), age 38, and has a daughter, Dina (age 35, she/her/hers); a son-in-law, Steve (he/him/his); and a grandson, George (age 6, he/him/his). Bob, a widower, is recently deceased and has a son, Nate (age 28, he/him/his).
Location:	Ann Arbor, Michigan
Status:	Harry and Bob were both previously employed by FFP and they inherited the FFP shares from their father in 1990. Bob retired from FFP and subsequently died this year.
Current situation:	Harry is planning to retire as CEO of FFP. Nate is Bob's executor.

Harry and Bob Smith were brothers and owners of a small privately held corporation, Frank's Frozen Pizzas Inc. (FFP). Their father, Frank, established the business 40 years ago, and Harry and Bob each inherited half of FFP's outstanding shares upon Frank's death. At the time of Frank's death in 1990, FFP was worth about \$1 million, but the business is now debt-free and has a value of \$9 million. FFP's success didn't come easily. Over the years, Harry and Bob were employed as executive officers and worked long, hard hours. After the death of his spouse in 2005, Bob retired on his FFP pension. Since that time, Harry has served as CEO of FFP. Both Harry and Bob have transferred some of their FFP shares to other family members. Bob has given 20 percent of the shares in FFP to his son, Nate, and Harry has transferred a like amount to a trust established for Dina (his daughter) and George (his grandson).

Harry recently decided that he wants to retire from FFP and spend more time traveling and enjoying his family. Harry believes that Nate would like to assume responsibilities as CEO, and Dina has agreed to support Nate's decisions. Harry plans to begin an orderly transfer of his FFP stock to Dina to provide a future source of support for her and George. Besides his FFP stock, Harry has accumulated considerable personal assets to help maintain his lifestyle during retirement. Although Wilma, Harry's spouse, owns significant assets, Harry also wants to provide for Wilma's eventual support. Finally, while Harry believes taxes and lawyers are necessary evils, he wants to avoid any unnecessary fees or taxes associated with the transfer of his assets. Hence, Harry would like advice on how to make his gifts in the most tax-efficient manner possible.

(to be continued . . .)

LO 14-1

INTRODUCTION TO FEDERAL TRANSFER TAXES

In this chapter, we explain the structure of the federal transfer taxes and begins with background on transfer taxes. We then describe details of the federal gift and estate taxes and conclude with a description of wealth planning.

Beginnings

In 1916 Congress imposed an estate tax on transfers of property at death. Transfers at death are dictated by the **last will and testament** of the deceased, and such transfers are called **testamentary transfers.** The transfer tax system was expanded in 1924 to include a gift tax on lifetime transfers called **inter vivos transfers** (*inter vivos* is from the Latin meaning "during the life of"). Eventually, a generation-skipping tax was also added to prevent people from avoiding taxes by transferring assets to younger generations (making transfers to grandchildren rather than to children). Together, this trio of taxes represents one way of reducing the potential wealth society's richest families might accumulate over several generations. (Recall that neither gifts nor inheritances are included in recipients' gross income.)

Common Features of Integrated Transfer Taxes

The two primary federal transfer taxes, the gift tax and the estate tax, were originally enacted separately and operated independently. In 1976 they were combined into a *unified* transfer tax scheme that applies a progressive tax rate schedule to cumulative transfers. In other words, the gift and estate taxes now are integrated to operate in unison.

This integrated formula takes into account the cumulative effect of transfers in previous periods when calculating the tax on a transfer in a current period. Likewise, it takes lifetime transfers into account to compute the tax on assets transferred at death. As you'll see in the tax formulas, taxable transfers in prior years are added to the current-year transfers, and the tax is computed on total (cumulative) transfers. The tax on the prior-year transfers is subtracted from the total tax to avoid taxing prior-year transfers twice. This calculation ensures that the current transfers will be taxed at a marginal tax rate as high as or higher than the rate applicable to the prior-year transfers. Exhibit 14-1 presents the unified transfer tax rate schedule for estate and gift taxes that has been in effect since 2013. As presented in Exhibit 14-1, the transfer tax rate is progressive on taxable transfers up to $1 million at which point the tentative tax is $345,800. Over $1 million, the rate is a flat 40 percent.

EXHIBIT 14-1 Unified Transfer Tax Rates*

Tax Base Equal to or Over	Not Over	Tentative Tax	Plus	of Amount Over
$ 0	$ 10,000	$ 0	18%	$ 0
10,000	20,000	1,800	20	10,000
20,000	40,000	3,800	22	20,000
40,000	60,000	8,200	24	40,000
60,000	80,000	13,000	26	60,000
80,000	100,000	18,200	28	80,000
100,000	150,000	23,800	30	100,000
150,000	250,000	38,800	32	150,000
250,000	500,000	70,800	34	250,000
500,000	750,000	155,800	37	500,000
750,000	1,000,000	248,300	39	750,000
1,000,000		345,800	40	1,000,000

THE KEY FACTS

Common Features of the Unified Transfer Taxes

- Property transfers, whether made by gift or at death, are subject to transfer tax using a progressive tax rate schedule.
- The applicable credit exempts cumulative transfers of up to $12.06 million.
- Each transfer tax allows a deduction for transfers to charities and surviving spouses (the charitable and marital deductions, respectively).

Another common feature of the integrated transfer taxes is the **applicable credit.** This credit, previously known as the *unified credit,* was enacted in 1977, and it applies to both the gift tax and the estate tax. The credit is designed to prevent the application of transfer tax to taxpayers who either would not accumulate a relatively large amount of property transfers during their lifetime and/or would not have a relatively large transfer passing to heirs upon their death. The value of cumulative taxable transfers a person can make without exceeding the applicable credit is called the **exemption equivalent** or, alternately, the *applicable exclusion amount.*

Exhibit 14-2 presents the applicable exclusion amounts for both the estate and gift taxes since 1986. Except for the period between 2004 and 2010 (inclusive), the base exclusion amount has been the same for both the estate and gift taxes. Beginning in 2011, the base amount was set at $5 million and is indexed for inflation. In 2018, Congress increased the base exclusion amount from $5 million to $10 million for the years 2018 through 2025. The base exclusion amount is scheduled to revert to $5 million in 2026.[1]

EXHIBIT 14-2 The Exemption Equivalent/Applicable Exclusion Amount

Year of Transfer	Gift Tax	Estate Tax
1986	$ 500,000	$ 500,000
1987–1997	600,000	600,000
1998	625,000	625,000
1999	650,000	650,000
2000–2001	675,000	675,000
2002–2003	1,000,000	1,000,000
2004–2005	1,000,000	1,500,000
2006–2008	1,000,000	2,000,000
2009–2010*	1,000,000	3,500,000
2011	5,000,000	5,000,000
2012	5,120,000	5,120,000
2013	5,250,000	5,250,000
2014	5,340,000	5,340,000
2015	5,430,000	5,430,000
2016	5,450,000	5,450,000
2017	5,490,000	5,490,000
2018	11,180,000	11,180,000
2019	11,400,000	11,400,000
2020	11,580,000	11,580,000
2021	11,700,000	11,700,000
2022	12,060,000	12,060,000

*The estate tax was optional for decedents dying in 2010. In lieu of the estate tax, executors could opt to have the adjusted tax basis of the assets in the gross estate carry over to the heirs of the decedent. The applicable credit and exemption are zero for taxpayers who opt out of the estate tax in 2010.

The value of the applicable credit depends on both the transfer tax rates and the exemption equivalent that apply in the year of the transfer. Because the tax rates can change over time and because the exemption equivalent changes with inflation adjustments, we can best calculate the applicable credit by tracking the exemption equivalent and converting it into the applicable credit using the *current* tax rate schedule. Consequently, in 2022, the amount of the applicable credit for a transfer made in 2011 will be $1,945,800 ($345,800 on the first million and 40 percent on the remaining four million) regardless of the amount of the actual applicable credit in 2011. In other words, the applicable credit for the current year is always calculated using the tax rate schedule for the current year.

The exemption equivalent is $12.06 million for transfers made in 2022. Under the tax rate schedule for 2022, the applicable credit would be $4,769,800. The amount is calculated

[1]If the exclusion amount at the time of a taxpayer's death is less than the cumulative exclusion amount used to reduce gift taxes in earlier periods, Reg. §20.2010-2(c) provides that the exclusion amount at the time of death governs for purposes of computing the estate tax. For example, suppose a taxpayer made taxable gifts of $9 million that were fully sheltered from gift tax by an exclusion, but the basic exclusion amount on the taxpayer's death was only $6.8 million. In this case, the taxpayer's estate tax would be computed using the $9 million exclusion amount allowed in computing the gift tax payable on the prior gift.

in three steps, as follows: (1) the tax on the first million is $345,800; (2) the tax on the next $11.06 million is calculated at 40 percent or $4.424 million; (3) the total tax is the sum of the two parts $4,424,000 + $345,800 = $4,769,800.

A third common feature of the unified tax system is the application of two deductions. Each transfer tax provides an unlimited deduction for charitable contributions and a generous **marital deduction** for transfers to a spouse. The marital deduction allows almost unfettered transfers between spouses. In contrast to the income tax where a married couple can elect to file a single joint return, both individuals are required to file separate transfer tax returns.

A final important feature of the transfer taxes is the valuation of transferred property. Property transferred via gift or at death is valued at fair market value. While fair market value is simple in concept, it is very complicated to apply. For purposes of the transfer taxes, fair market value is defined by the *willing-buyer, willing-seller rule* as follows:

> The price at which such property would change hands between a willing buyer and a willing seller, neither being under any compulsion to buy or to sell, and both having reasonable knowledge of the relevant facts.[2]

Fair market value is determined based on the facts and circumstances for each individual property. Determining value is relatively simple for properties that have an active market. For example, stocks and bonds traded on exchanges or over the counter are valued at the mean of the highest and lowest selling prices. Unfortunately, the valuation of many other properties, especially realty, is very difficult. The large number of court cases resolving contentious values testifies to the difficulties in applying the willing-buyer, willing-seller rule.

LO 14-2

THE FEDERAL GIFT TAX

The gift tax is levied on individual taxpayers for all *taxable* gifts made during a calendar year. As noted above, each *individual* who makes a gift in excess of the annual exclusion amount must file a gift tax return (Form 709) by April 15 of the following year.[3] Exhibit 14-3 presents the complete formula for the federal gift tax in two parts. In the first part, taxable gifts are calculated for each donee, and in the second, the gift tax is calculated using aggregate taxable gifts to all donees. We begin the first part by identifying transfers that constitute gifts.

EXHIBIT 14-3 The Federal Gift Tax Formula

	***Part 1:* Calculate taxable gifts for each individual donee:**
	Total Current Gifts
Minus	½ of split gifts (other half included in spouse's current gifts)
Plus	½ of split gifts by spouse
Minus	Annual exclusion ($16,000 per donee)
Minus	Marital and charitable deductions
Equals	Current Taxable Gifts
	***Part 2:* Sum taxable gifts for all donees and calculate tax:**
	Total Current Taxable Gifts
Plus	Prior taxable gifts
Equals	Cumulative taxable gifts
Times	Current tax rates
Equals	Cumulative tax
Minus	Tax at current rates on prior taxable gifts
Minus	Unused applicable credit at current rates
Equals	Gift tax payable

[2]Reg. §25.2512-1.

[3]A gift tax return reporting taxable gifts must be filed by April 15 following year-end if a taxpayer has made *any* taxable gifts during the current calendar year *or wishes to elect* gift-splitting. When taxpayers request extensions for their individual income tax returns, they also receive a six-month extension for filing their gift tax returns.

Transfers Subject to Gift Tax

The gift tax is imposed on lifetime transfers of property for less than **adequate consideration.** Typically, a gift is made in a personal context such as between family members, but the satisfaction of an obligation to support is not considered a gift. For example, tuition payments for a dependent child's education satisfy a support obligation. On the other hand, transfers motivated by affection or other personal motives, including transfers associated with marriage, are gratuitous and potentially subject to the tax. The gift tax is imposed once a gift has been completed, and this occurs when the **donor** relinquishes control of the property and the **donee** accepts the gift.[4] For example, deposits made to a joint bank account are not complete gifts because the donor (depositor) can withdraw the deposit at any time. The gift will be complete at the time the donee withdraws cash from the account.

THE KEY FACTS

Gifts Excluded from the Gift Tax

- Incomplete and revocable gifts.
- Payments for support obligations or debts.
- Contributions to political parties or candidates.
- Medical and educational expenses paid on behalf of an unrelated individual.

TAXES IN THE REAL WORLD Gifts or Compensation?

In the 1990s, Burt Kroner was in the business of credit counseling. During this period, Kroner was introduced to Haring, a "high-net-worth British citizen with residences and business interests in various non-U.S. jurisdictions." Haring invested in Kroner's credit counseling business and hired him to assist with investing in discounted privately held mortgages. Unfortunately, Kroner was prohibited from participating in these investments due to a noncompete agreement.

In 2005, Mr. Haring experienced a "liquidity event" with respect to these mortgage investments, and Kroner received a two-to-three-minute phone call from Haring to inform him of a "surprise" bank transfer. Haring's tax attorneys drafted a note stating that the transfers were gifts. The note was signed by Haring and dated January 18, 2005.

Despite not having personal contact with Haring since 2002, over the period 2005–2007 Kroner received $24.875 million in wire transfers from Haring that were coordinated by Haring's attorney. Based on the note and a call with Haring, Kroner's tax attorney advised him that the transfers were excludable from income as gifts. The IRS audited Kroner's returns and disagreed with his characterization. The dispute landed in the Tax Court.

The court stated that to qualify as a gift requires "detached and disinterested" generosity. When a donee has rendered services to a donor, a payment for the services is not a gift even if the transferor had no legal compulsion to pay the remuneration. Despite warning Kroner that Haring's intention in making the transfers was critical evidence, Haring refused to testify. Instead, Kroner relied on his testimony and Haring's note to establish the intent of the transfers.

After observing the candor, sincerity, and demeanor of the witnesses, the court found Kroner's story unconvincing. The court described the testimony as self-serving and evasive. The court noted that Haring did not draft the note and that there was no credible evidence to suggest that it came from detached and disinterested generosity.

Source: Burt Kroner v. Comm'r, TC Memo 2020-73.

In some instances, a donor may relinquish some control over transferred property but retain other powers that can influence the enjoyment or disposition of the property. If the retained powers are important, the transfer will not be a complete gift.[5] For example, a transfer of property to a trust will not be a complete gift if the grantor retains the ability to revoke the transfer. If the grantor releases the powers, then the gift will generally be complete at that time because the property is no longer subject to the donor's control. For example, a distribution of property from a revocable trust is a complete gift because the grantor no longer has the ability to revoke the distribution.

[4]Under Reg. §25.2511-2, a gift is complete only when the donor has departed with control of property so that he has no power to change the disposition of the property. If property is subject to a reserved power, the gift may be wholly or partially incomplete depending on the scope of the power. Also, if a donee refuses or disclaims a gift under §2518, the gift is incomplete.

[5]Section 2514 addresses the treatment of general powers of appointment.

Example 14-1

On July 12 of this year, Harry transferred $250,000 of FFP stock to a new trust. He gave the trustee directions to pay income to Dina for the next 20 years and then remit the remainder to Dina's son George. Harry named a bank as trustee but retained the power to revoke the trust in case he should need additional assets after retirement. Is the transfer of the stock a complete gift?

Answer: No. Harry retains sufficient control that the transfer of the stock to the trust is an incomplete gift.

What if: Suppose $11,000 of trust income was distributed to Dina at year-end. Is the transfer of the cash to Dina a complete gift?

Answer: Yes. With the payment, Harry has relinquished control over the $11,000, and, thus, it is a complete gift.

What if: Suppose Harry releases his power to revoke the trust at a time when the shares of FFP in the trust are valued at $225,000. Would this release cause the transfer of the stock to be a complete gift, and, if so, what is the amount of the gift?

Answer: Yes. By releasing his powers, Harry has relinquished control over the entire trust, and the value of the trust at that time, $225,000, would be a complete gift.

There are several important exceptions to the taxation of gifts. For example, political contributions are not gifts. Also, the payment of medical or educational expenses on behalf of another individual is not considered a gift if the payments are made directly to the health care provider or to the educational institution. To avoid confusing a division of property with a gift, a transfer of property in conjunction with a divorce is not considered to be a gift if the property is transferred within three years of the divorce under a written property settlement. Also, special rules apply to transfers of certain types of property, such as life insurance and jointly held property. To make a complete gift of a life insurance policy, the donor must give the donee all the incidents of ownership, including the power to designate beneficiaries.

Special rules apply to the purchase or transfer of property with joint (i.e., multiple) owners. The two most common forms of joint ownership are **joint tenancy** (also called **joint tenancy with right of survivorship**) and **tenancy in common.** In joint tenancy, each owner owns an equal share of the property, whereas ownership proportions can vary for property held as tenants-in-common. When property is purchased or ownership is transferred, each of the joint owners is responsible for providing or receiving their proportionate share of funds. When one of the joint owners provides a disproportionate share of funds, that owner is treated as having made a gift to the other owners. The gift is the amount necessary to pay for the other party's interest in the property. For example, suppose the donor pays $80,000 toward the purchase of $100,000 in realty held in equal proportions with the donee (i.e., the donee provides only $20,000 of the purchase price). The donor is deemed to make a gift of $30,000 to the donee, the difference between the value of the joint interest ($100,000 ÷ 2 = $50,000) and the consideration provided by the donee ($20,000).

ETHICS

Carol is a retired engineer who has three adult children and several grandchildren. This year Rudy, Carol's youngest son, approached Carol for a $40,000 business loan. Although Rudy had no collateral for the loan and did not sign any written promise to repay the money, Carol still transferred the funds to Rudy's account. Do you think Carol should file a gift tax return for the transfer? Suppose Carol has no intention of demanding repayment but has not told anyone so. Does this make any difference?

Example 14-2

This year Harry helped purchase a residence for use by Dina and her spouse Steve. The price of the residence was $250,000, and the title named Harry and Steve joint tenants with the right of survivorship. Harry provided $210,000 of the purchase price and Steve the remaining $40,000. Has Harry made a complete gift, and if so, in what amount?

Answer: Yes, Harry made a complete gift to Steve of $85,000, calculated by subtracting the amount paid by Steve from the price of his ownership interest ($125,000 – $40,000).

What if: Suppose Steve didn't provide any part of the purchase price for his half interest in the property. What is the amount of the gift?

Answer: In this case, Harry made a complete gift to Steve of half the purchase price, $125,000.

Valuation Gifts are taxed at the fair market value of the donated property on the date the gift becomes complete. Remember that despite the valuation of a gift at fair market value, the donee generally takes a carryover basis for income tax purposes.[6]

Valuation of remainders and other temporal interests. Assigning value to unique property is difficult enough, but sometimes we must also assign a value to a stream of payments over time or a payment to be made in the future. The right to currently enjoy property or receive income payments from property is called a **present interest.** In contrast, the right to receive income or property in the future is called a **future interest.** A present right to possess and/or collect income from property may not be permanent; if the right is granted for a specific period of time or until the occurrence of a specific event, it is a **terminable interest.** For example, the right to receive income payments from property for 10 years is a terminable interest. Another terminable interest is the right to possess property and/or receive income for the duration of someone's life, and this right is called a **life estate.** The person whose life determines the duration of the life estate is called the *life tenant.*

At the end of a terminable interest, the property will pass to another owner, the person holding the future interest. In a **reversion,** it returns to the original owner. If it goes to a new owner, the right to the property is called a **remainder** and the owner is called a **remainderman.** For example, the right to own property after a 10-year income interest has ended is a future interest held by the remainderman. The right to property after the termination of a life estate is also called a remainder.

Future interests are common when property is placed in a trust. **Trusts** are legal entities established by a person called the **grantor.** Trusts are administered by a **trustee** and generally contain property called the **corpus** (principal) of the trust. The trustee has a **fiduciary duty** to manage the property in the trust for the benefit of a **beneficiary** or beneficiaries. This duty requires the trustee to administer the trust in an objective and impartial manner and not favor one beneficiary over another.

Because a future interest is essentially a promise of a future payment, we estimate the value of the remainder by discounting the future payment to a present value using a market rate of interest. For example, suppose property worth $100 is placed in a trust with the income to be paid to an income beneficiary each year for 10 years, after which time the property accumulated in the trust will be distributed. The remainder is a future interest with a value we estimate by calculating the present value of a payment of $100 in 10 years as follows:

$$\text{Value of remainder} = \frac{\text{Future payment}}{(1 + r)^n}$$

where r is the market rate of interest and n is the number of years. The interest rate used for this calculation is published monthly by the Treasury as the §7520 rate.[7] If the §7520 rate is 6 percent, we calculate the value of a remainder of $100 placed in trust for 10 years as follows:

$$\text{Value of remainder} = \frac{\$100}{(1 + .06)^{10}} = \frac{\$100}{1.791} = \$55.83$$

THE KEY FACTS

Valuation of Remainders and Income Interests

- Future interests are valued at present value, calculated by estimating the time until the present interest expires.
- The present value calculation uses the §7520 interest rate published by the Treasury.
- If the present interest is measured by a person's life (a life estate), then we estimate the delay by reference to the person's life expectancy as published in IRS tables.
- The value of a present interest, such as an income interest or life estate, is determined by subtracting the value of the remainder interest from the total value of the property.

[6]The carryover basis may be increased for any gift tax paid (after 1976) on the appreciation of the property.

[7]The §7520 rate is 120 percent of the applicable federal mid-term rate in effect during the month of the transaction. The IRS publishes this rate each month in a Revenue Ruling. For example, in Revenue Ruling 2022-1, the IRS announced that this rate was 0.53% for January, 2022.

The value of property consists of the present interest (the right to income) and the future interest (the remainder). Hence, once we have estimated the value of the remainder, we compute the value of the income interest as the difference between the value of the remainder and the total value of the property.

Value of income interest = Total value − Value of remainder
= $100 − $55.83
= $44.17

If the terminable interest is a life estate, the valuation of the remainder is a bit more complicated because payment of the remainder is delayed by the duration of the life estate. To estimate this delay, the calculation is based on the number of years the life tenant is expected to live. To facilitate the calculation, the regulations provide a table (Table S) that calculates the discount factor by including the life tenant's age at the time of transfer. Exhibit 14-4 includes a portion of Table S from the regulation with interest rates by column and the age of the life tenant by row.

EXHIBIT 14-4 Discount Factors for Estimating the Value of Remainders

Regulation §20.2031-7(d)(7)
Table S.—Based on Life Table 2000CM Single Life Remainder Factors
Applicable on or after May 1, 2009

	Interest rate									
Age	4.2%	4.4%	4.6%	4.8%	5.0%	5.2%	5.4%	5.6%	5.8%	6.0%
0	.06083	.05483	.04959	.04501	.04101	.03749	.03441	.03170	.02931	.02721
1	.05668	.05049	.04507	.04034	.03618	.03254	.02934	.02652	.02403	.02183
2	.05858	.05222	.04665	.04178	.03750	.03373	.03042	.02750	.02492	.02264
3	.06072	.05420	.04848	.04346	.03904	.03516	.03173	.02871	.02603	.02366
4	.06303	.05634	.05046	.04530	.04075	.03674	.03319	.03006	.02729	.02483
5	.06547	.05861	.05258	.04726	.04258	.03844	.03478	.03153	.02866	.02610
6	.06805	.06102	.05482	.04935	.04453	.04026	.03647	.03312	.03014	.02749
⋮										
35	.19692	.18423	.17253	.16174	.15178	.14258	.13408	.12621	.11892	.11217
36	.20407	.19119	.17931	.16833	.15818	.14879	.14009	.13204	.12457	.11764
37	.21144	.19838	.18631	.17515	.16481	.15523	.14635	.13811	.13046	.12335
38	.21904	.20582	.19357	.18222	.17170	.16193	.15287	.14444	.13661	.12932
⋮										
86	.79825	.79044	.78278	.77524	.76783	.76055	.75340	.74636	.73944	.73264
87	.80921	.80176	.79443	.78722	.78014	.77316	.76630	.75956	.75292	.74638
88	.81978	.81268	.80569	.79880	.79203	.78536	.77880	.77234	.76598	.75971
89	.82994	.82317	.81651	.80995	.80349	.79712	.79085	.78467	.77859	.77259

Source: Reg. §20.2031-7(d)(7) Table S.

Example 14-3

Harry transferred $500,000 of FFP stock to the DG Trust, whose trustee is directed to pay income to Dina for her life and, upon Dina's death, pay the remainder to George (or his estate). At the time of the gift, Dina was 35 years old and the §7520 interest rate was 5.8 percent. What are the values of the gift of the life estate and of the remainder interest?

Answer: Harry made a $59,460 gift of the remainder to George and a $440,540 gift of the life estate to Dina. Under Table S (see Exhibit 14-4), the percentage of the property that represents the value of George's remainder is .11892. Thus, George's remainder is valued at $59,460 ($500,000 × .11892). Dina's life estate (the income interest) is the remaining value of $440,540 ($500,000 − $59,460).

The Annual Exclusion One of the most important aspects of the gift tax is the **annual exclusion,** which operates to eliminate "small" gifts from the gift tax base. The amount of the exclusion has been revised upward periodically over the years and is now indexed for inflation.[8] In 2022, the annual exclusion amount is $16,000.

The annual exclusion is available to offset gifts made to *each* donee regardless of the number of donees in any particular year. For example, in 2022 a donor could give $16,000 in cash to each of 10 donees without exceeding the annual exclusion. One important limitation to the annual exclusion is that it applies only to gifts of *present* interests; that is, with limited exceptions, a gift of a future interest is not eligible for an annual exclusion.

Example 14-4

When Harry transferred $500,000 of FFP stock to the DG Trust (Example 14-3), he simultaneously made two taxable gifts: a life estate to Dina and a remainder to George. What is the amount of the taxable gift of the life estate to Dina and the remainder interest to George, after taking the annual exclusion into account?

Answer: Dina's life estate is a present interest and would qualify for the annual exclusion. However, George's remainder is a future interest and will not qualify for the annual exclusion. Harry would file a Form 709 to report total taxable gifts of $484,000, consisting of a $424,540 taxable gift to Dina ($440,540 less the annual exclusion of $16,000) and a taxable gift of $59,460 to George (no annual exclusion is available for a future interest).

Description	Dina	George	Harry's Gift Tax Return
Current gifts	$440,540	$59,460	$500,000
Annual exclusion	−16,000	−0	−16,000
Taxable gifts	$424,540	$59,460	$484,000

THE KEY FACTS

Annual Exclusion

- In 2022, gifts of present interests qualify for an annual exclusion of $16,000 per donee.
- A present interest is the ability to use property or receive income presently.
- Gifts of future interests placed in trust for a minor can also qualify for the exclusion.

The prohibition on annual exclusions for gifts of future interests means that most gifts will qualify for an annual exclusion only if the donee has a present interest (the ability to immediately use the property or the income from it). However, a special exception applies to future interests given to "minors" (defined as individuals under the age of 21). Gifts in trust for a minor are future interests if the minor does not have the ability to access the income or property until reaching the age of majority. These gifts will still qualify for the annual exclusion as long as the property can be used to support the minor and any remaining property is distributed to the child once they reach age 21.[9]

Example 14-5

Harry transferred $48,500 of cash to the George Trust. The trustee of the George Trust has the discretion to distribute income or corpus (principal) for George's benefit and is required to distribute all assets to George (or his estate) not later than George's 21st birthday. Is this gift eligible for the annual exclusion? If so, what is the amount of the taxable gift?

Answer: Yes, Harry will be entitled to an annual exclusion for the transfer despite the fact that George's interest is a future one because the gift is in trust for the support of a minor and the property must distribute the assets to George once he reaches age 21. The amount of the gift is $48,500, reduced to a taxable gift of $32,500 after applying the $16,000 annual exclusion.

[8] The exclusion is indexed for inflation in such a way that the amount of the exclusion only increases in increments of $1,000. The annual exclusion was $10,000 from 1981 through 2001, but was $11,000 for 2002 through 2005, $12,000 for 2006 through 2008, $13,000 for 2009 through 2012, $14,000 from 2012 through 2017, $15,000 from 2018 through 2021, and $16,000 in 2022.

[9] §2503(c). The courts have created another exception to the present interest rule called *Crummey power.* [See *Clifford Crummey v. Comm'r,* 397 F.2d 82 (9th Cir. 1968).] A discussion of this exception is beyond the scope of this text.

Taxable Gifts

In Part 1 of the formula in Exhibit 14-3, **current gifts** are accumulated for each donee, and this amount includes all gifts completed during the calendar year for each individual. Current gifts do not include transfers exempted from the tax, such as political contributions. Several adjustments are made to calculate current **taxable gifts** for each donee. As we've seen, each taxpayer is allowed an annual exclusion applied to the cumulative gifts of present interests made during the year to *each* donee. Next, if a married couple elects to split gifts (discussed below), half of each gift is included in the current gifts of each spouse. The marital deduction for gifts to spouses and the charitable deduction for gifts to charity are the last adjustments to calculate taxable gifts for each donee. We discuss each in turn.

Gift-Splitting Election Married couples have the option to *split gifts,* allowing them to treat *all* gifts made in a year as if each spouse had made one-half of each gift. In a **community-property state,** both spouses automatically own equal shares in most property acquired during the marriage.[10] Hence, a gift of community property is divided between the spouses equally. In **common-law states,** one spouse can own a disproportionate amount of property because the spouse earns most of the income. The gift-splitting election provides a mechanism for married couples in common-law states to achieve the same result as couples receive automatically in community-property states.[11]

Example 14-6

Wilma and Harry live in Michigan, a common-law state. For the holidays, Wilma gave cash gifts of $35,000 to Steve and $41,000 to Dina. Wilma and Harry did not elect to split gifts. What is the amount of Wilma's taxable gifts?

Answer: $44,000. After using her annual exclusion (both gifts are present interests), Wilma has made taxable gifts of $19,000 to Steve ($35,000 – $16,000) and $25,000 to Dina ($41,000 – $16,000).

What if: Suppose Wilma and Harry elect gift-splitting this year. How would your answer change?

Answer: Wilma and Harry each made taxable gifts of $6,000. Under gift-splitting, Wilma and Harry are each treated as making a current gift of $17,500 to Steve and $20,500 to Dina. After the annual exclusion, both Wilma and Harry made a $1,500 taxable gift to Steve [($35,000 ÷ 2) – $16,000 = $1,500]. In addition, both Wilma and Harry made a $4,500 taxable gift to Dina [($41,000 ÷ 2) – $16,000 = $4,500].

What if: Suppose Wilma and Harry lived in Texas (a community-property state), and Wilma made the same gifts from community property.

Answer: Even without electing gift-splitting, Wilma and Harry will each be treated as making a taxable gift of $6,000. Under state law, each spouse is automatically treated as gifting half the value of any gifts made from community property. After the annual exclusion, both Wilma and Harry made a $1,500 taxable gift to Steve [($35,000 ÷ 2) – $16,000], and each made a $4,500 taxable gift to Dina [($41,000 ÷ 2) – $16,000].

THE KEY FACTS

Marital Deduction

- Gifts of property to a spouse may be deducted in computing taxable gifts.
- Transfers of terminable interests in property, such as a life estate, will not generally qualify for the deduction.
- The deduction is limited to the value of property included in taxable gifts.

Besides increasing the application of the annual exclusion, a gift-splitting election also increases the likelihood that taxable gifts will be taxed at lower tax rates or any gift tax will be offset by applicable credits. To utilize gift-splitting, each spouse must be a citizen or resident of the United States, be married at the time of the gift, and not remarry during the remainder of the calendar year. The election is made by both spouses by consenting on each other's gift tax return. Split gifts are computed separately in each return, and the tax is calculated for each spouse separately on their respective returns. Taxpayers make this election annually, and it applies to all gifts completed by either spouse during the calendar year. As a result of the election, both spouses share joint and several liability for any gift tax due.

Marital Deduction The marital deduction was originally enacted to equalize the treatment of spouses residing in common-law states with those residing in community-property

[10]Depending upon state law, the ownership of property acquired by either spouse prior to a marriage is not automatically divided equally between the spouses. In other words, property owned prior to the marriage is not necessarily community property and continues to belong to the original owner.

[11]There are nine community-property states: Arizona, California, Idaho, Louisiana, Nevada, New Mexico, Texas, Washington, and Wisconsin.

states. In community-property states, the ownership of most property *acquired* during a marriage is automatically divided between the spouses. In common-law states, one spouse can own a disproportionate amount of property if that spouse earns most of the income. Absent the marital deduction, in a common-law state, a transfer between spouses to equalize the ownership of property would be treated as a taxable gift. However, because transfers to spouses are eligible for a marital deduction, no taxable gift results from such a transfer.

The marital deduction is subject to two limits. First, the amount is limited to the value of the gift after the annual exclusion. Second, transfers of **nondeductible terminable interests** do not qualify for a marital deduction. A nondeductible terminable interest is a property interest transferred to the spouse that terminates when some event occurs or after a specified amount of time, when the property is transferred to another.

Example 14-7

After his decision to retire, Harry gave Wilma a piece of jewelry that is a family heirloom valued at $50,000. What is the amount of the taxable gift from this transfer?

Answer: Zero. This gift will qualify for an annual exclusion, and the amount remaining after subtracting the annual exclusion qualifies for the marital deduction. The taxable gift is calculated below:

Description	Amount
Current gift	$ 50,000
Less: Annual exclusion	−16,000
Less: Marital deduction	−34,000
Taxable gift	$ 0

What if: Suppose Harry transferred $200,000 to a trust with directions to pay income to Wilma for her life (a life estate). After Wilma's death, the corpus of the trust would then pass to Dina (the remainder). What is the amount of this taxable gift if Wilma is age 38 at the time and the §7520 interest rate is 5 percent?

Answer: The total taxable gift is $184,000. This transfer is actually two gifts, a gift of a present interest to Wilma (a life estate) and a future interest to Dina (the remainder). The gift of the remainder is valued at $34,340 using Wilma's age and the §7520 interest rate from Table S in Exhibit 14-4 ($200,000 × .17170). The remainder does not qualify for an annual exclusion because it is a future interest. The gift of the life estate is a present interest valued at $165,660 ($200,000 − $34,340), and it qualifies for the annual exclusion. The taxable gifts are calculated below:

Description	Dina (remainder)	Wilma (life estate)
Current gifts	$34,340	$165,660
Less: Annual exclusion (life estate)	−0	−16,000
Less: Marital deduction	−0	−0
Taxable gift	$34,340	$149,660

When the life estate is given to a spouse, it does not qualify for the marital deduction because it will terminate upon a future event (Wilma's death) and then pass to another person (Dina).

The limitation on the deductible terminable interests ensures that property owned by a married couple is subject to a transfer tax when the property is eventually transferred from the couple (as opposed to between the spouses).[12] If a life estate were eligible for a marital deduction, it would not be taxed at the time of the gift, nor would any value be taxed upon the spouse's death (the life estate disappears with his or her death). Hence, a marital deduction is available only for spousal transfers that will eventually be included in the recipient spouse's estate.[13]

[12]Qualified terminable interest properties (QTIPs for short) are an exception to the nondeductibility of terminable interest property. To qualify, the taxpayer must agree to have qualifying terminable interests included in the estate of the spouse. A detailed discussion of this election is beyond the scope of this text.

[13]To be eligible for the marital deduction, the spouse must be entitled to all of the income from the property payable at least annually, and no person has the power to appoint any part of the property to anyone other than the spouse until the death of the spouse.

Charitable Deduction The amount of the charitable deduction is also limited to the value of the gift after subtracting the annual exclusion. Requirements for an organization to qualify as a charity for purposes of the gift tax charitable deduction are quite similar to those for the income tax deduction (i.e., the entity must be organized for religious, charitable, scientific, educational, or other public purposes, including governmental entities). Unlike the income tax deduction, however, the charitable deduction has no income tax percentage limitation. In addition, as long as the qualifying charity receives the donor's entire interest in the property, no gift tax return need be filed (assuming the donor has no other taxable gifts). Finally, a transfer to a charity also qualifies for an income tax deduction (subject to the AGI percentage limits on the income tax charitable deduction).

Example 14-8

Harry donated $155,000 in cash to State University. What is the amount of the taxable gift?

Answer: Zero. The gift qualifies for the charitable gift tax deduction, as calculated below.

Description	Amount
Current gift	$ 155,000
Less: Annual exclusion	−16,000
Less: Charitable deduction	−139,000
Taxable gift	$ 0

Note that Harry can also claim an income tax deduction for the transfer.

Computation of the Gift Tax

Part 2 of the formula in Exhibit 14-3 provides the method for calculating the gift tax. It begins by summing the taxable gifts made for all donees during a calendar year.

Example 14-9

Harry and Wilma did not make any gifts from community property and did not elect to gift-split this year (see Example 14-6). What is the value of Harry's current taxable gifts this year?

Answer: Harry made $585,500 of taxable gifts, calculated using Part 1 of the formula in Exhibit 14-3 as follows:

Gifted Property	Donee	Value	Explanation
1. Residence	Steve	$ 85,000	Example 14-2
Less: Annual exclusion		−16,000	
2. DG Trust—life estate	Dina	440,540	Example 14-3
Less: Annual exclusion		−16,000	
3. DG Trust—remainder	Dina	59,460	Example 14-3
4. George Trust	George	48,500	Example 14-5
Less: Annual exclusion		−16,000	
5. Jewelry	Wilma	50,000	Example 14-7
Less: Annual exclusion		−16,000	
Less: Marital deduction	Wilma	−34,000	
6. Donation	State University	155,000	Example 14-8
Less: Annual exclusion		−16,000	
Less: Charitable deduction	State University	−139,000	
Harry's current taxable gifts		**$ 585,500**	

The amounts of the marital and charitable deductions are limited to the value of the property included in taxable gifts.

Will Wilma be required to file a gift tax return this year? If so, what is the amount of her taxable gifts?

Answer: Wilma must also file a gift tax return this year because her current gifts exceed the available annual exclusion amounts. Wilma's taxable gifts sum to $44,000, calculated as follows:

Gifted Property	Donee	Value	Explanation
1. Cash gift	Steve	$ 35,000	Example 14-6
Less: Annual exclusion		−16,000	
2. Cash gift	Dina	41,000	Example 14-6
Less: Annual exclusion		−16,000	
Wilma's current taxable gifts		**$ 44,000**	

What if: What is the amount of Harry and Wilma's taxable gifts if they elect to gift-split?

Answer: Harry and Wilma each made $306,750 of taxable gifts, calculated as follows:

				Gift-Splitting	
Gifted Property	**Harry**	**Wilma**	**Donee**	**Harry**	**Wilma**
1. Gift of a residence	$ 85,000		Steve	$ 42,500	$ 42,500
Less: Annual exclusion	−16,000			−16,000	
2. Cash gift		$ 35,000	Steve	17,500	17,500
Less: Annual exclusion		−16,000			−16,000
3. Transfer to DG trust	440,540		Dina	220,270	220,270
Less: Annual exclusion	−16,000			−16,000	
4. Cash gift		41,000	Dina	20,500	20,500
Less: Annual exclusion		−16,000			−16,000
5. DG Trust—remainder	59,460		George	29,730	29,730
6. George Trust	48,500		George	24,250	24,250
Less: Annual exclusion	−16,000			−16,000	−16,000
7. Gift of jewelry	50,000		Wilma	50,000	
Less: Annual exclusion	−16,000			−16,000	
Less: Marital deduction	−34,000			−34,000	
8. Donation to State U	155,000		State U	77,500	77,500
Less: Annual exclusion	−16,000			−16,000	−16,000
Less: Charitable deduction	−139,000			−61,500	−61,500
Total	**$ 585,500**	**$ 44,000**		**$306,750**	**$306,750**

Note that absent gift-splitting, Harry and Wilma made taxable gifts totaling $629,500 ($585,500 + $44,000), but under gift-splitting that reduced to $613,500 ($306,750 + $306,750) because Wilma was able to use an additional $16,000 annual exclusion for her portion of the gift to the George Trust. Neither Harry nor Wilma was able to use any additional annual exclusions for the gifts to Steve and Dina because they had already used annual exclusions to these two donees. If they were to elect to gift-split, Harry and Wilma would be jointly and severally liable for the gift taxes.

Tax on Current Taxable Gifts The first step to computing the gift tax on current taxable gifts is to add prior taxable gifts to current taxable gifts. The purpose of adding gifts from previous periods is to increase the tax base and thereby increase the marginal tax rate applied to current gifts. To prevent double taxation of prior taxable gifts, the gift tax on prior taxable gifts is subtracted from the tax on total transfers. Two elements of the tax on prior taxable gifts are important to understand. First, the tax is calculated on prior taxable gifts ignoring whether any applicable credit was claimed on the gifts in the prior year. Second, the tax on prior taxable gifts is computed using the *current* tax rate schedule (the tax rates for the year of the prior transfer are not relevant). The difference between the tax on cumulative taxable gifts and prior taxable gifts is the tax on the current taxable gifts.

Applicable Credit The last adjustment in the formula is for the *unused* portion of the applicable credit. Recall that the applicable credit is calculated using the current tax rate schedule applied to the exemption equivalent ($12.06 million for 2022). The exemption equivalent can change over time because it is indexed for inflation. Thus, as the exemption equivalent changes, the applicable credit on the exemption equivalent also changes.

Example 14-10

Assume that Harry made a taxable gift of $1,500,000 in 2007. At that time, the exemption equivalent for the gift tax was $1 million, so Harry paid gift taxes on $500,000. Harry has not made any taxable gifts since 2007. This year, however, Harry made taxable gifts of $585,500. What is Harry's gift tax on the transfer?

Answer: Harry will report cumulative taxable gifts of $2,085,500, but he will not owe any gift tax this year. The calculation is as follows:

Current taxable gifts	$ 585,500	
Prior taxable gifts	1,500,000	
Cumulative taxable gifts	$2,085,500	
Tax on cumulative taxable gifts (at current rates)		$ 780,000
Less: Current tax on prior taxable gifts ($1.5 million)		−545,800
Tax on current taxable gifts		$ 234,200
Applicable credit on current taxable gifts		−234,200
Gift tax due		$ 0

What is Harry's unused exemption equivalent?

At the end of 2022, Harry has $10,474,500 of unused exemption equivalent remaining ($12,060,000 − $1,000,000 − $585,500). Harry used $1 million of his exemption equivalent in 2007, and this year he used another $585,500 (the amount of exemption equivalent necessary to offset the current taxable gift).

What if: Suppose Harry made a taxable gift of $3,500,000 in 2007, and at that time, the exemption equivalent was $1 million. What should Harry report this year as his cumulative taxable gifts, gift tax on cumulative taxable gifts, gift tax on current taxable gifts, applicable credit for current tax on prior taxable gifts, and gift tax due? What is Harry's unused exemption equivalent?

Answer: Harry should report cumulative taxable gifts of $4,085,500 and gift tax on cumulative gifts of $1,580,000. Harry, however, owes no gift tax because of the applicable credit. The calculation is as follows:

Current taxable gifts	$ 585,500	
Prior taxable gifts	3,500,000	
Cumulative taxable gifts	$4,085,500	
Tax on cumulative taxable gifts (at current rates)		$ 1,580,000
Less: Current tax on prior taxable gifts ($3.5 million)		−1,345,800
Tax on current taxable gifts		234,200
Applicable credit on current taxable gifts		−234,200
Gift tax due		$ 0

At the end of 2022, Harry would have $10,474,500 of exemption equivalent remaining ($12,060,000 − $1,000,000 − $585,500). Note that Harry paid gift tax in 2007 because his taxable gifts far exceeded the exemption equivalent of $1 million in 2007. However, the amount of gift tax that was paid in 2007 is not relevant for calculating Harry's current tax. All calculations in the current year are made using the current tax rate schedule (not the one that applied in prior years).

What are Wilma's gift tax due and unused exemption equivalent?

Answer: Zero gift tax due. Wilma has used $44,000 of her exemption equivalent. Hence, at the end of 2022, Wilma has $12,016,000 ($12,060,000 – $44,000) of exemption equivalent remaining.

Wilma's current taxable gifts	$44,000	
Prior taxable gifts	+0	
Cumulative taxable gifts	$44,000	
Tax on cumulative taxable gifts (at current rates)		$ 9,160
Less: Current tax on prior taxable gifts		–0
Tax on current taxable gifts		$ 9,160
Applicable credit on current taxable gifts		–9,160
Gift tax due		$ 0

Example 14-11

What if: Suppose that Harry made a taxable gift of $8 million in 2011 (when the exemption equivalent was $5 million) and made current taxable gifts of $20 million. In this example, Harry has cumulative transfers of $28 million, and because he used $5 million of exemption equivalent in 2011, he has an unused exemption equivalent of $7.06 million ($12.06 million minus $5 million). The unused applicable credit is $2.824 million, calculated by subtracting the tax on the $5 million previously used exemption ($1,945,800) from the tax on the $12.06 million current exemption ($4,769,800). The gift tax due is calculated below using the tax formula in Exhibit 14-3:

Gift Tax Calculation Tracking the Applicable Credit on the Unused Exemption Equivalent

Description	Tax Amounts
Gift tax on cumulative transfers of $28 million	$11,145,800
Less gift tax on $8 million of prior taxable gifts	–3,145,800
Less gift tax on unused exemption equivalent of $7.06 million	–2,824,000
Gift tax due	$ 5,176,000

The gift tax formula requires donors to keep track of the unused applicable credit to calculate the tax due. Fortunately, there is a shortcut method for calculating the gift tax when cumulative taxable transfers exceed $1 million. Rather than track the tax on the exemption equivalent, instead subtract gifts from prior periods and the unused exemption equivalent from the cumulative taxable transfers to calculate the taxable transfers in the current period. If the cumulative transfers exceed $1 million, the tax is computed using a flat 40% tax rate. Here's how the shortcut works in this example:

Gift Tax Calculation Using the Shortcut

Description	Exemption Equivalent
Cumulative taxable transfers ($8 million plus $20 million)	$28,000,000
Less total taxable gifts in prior periods	–8,000,000
Less ***unused*** exemption equivalent ($12.06 – $5 million)	–7,060,000
Taxable transfers in this period	$12,940,000
Times marginal tax rate (40%)	× 40%
Gift tax on current gifts at the current tax rate	$ 5,176,000

To recap, rather than track the tax on the exemption equivalent, subtract taxable gifts from prior periods and the unused exemption equivalent from total taxable transfers. As long as taxable transfers exceed $1 million, the tax is calculated by multiplying the difference by the marginal tax rate, 40 percent.

Exhibit 14-5 presents the first page of the 2021 gift tax return Form 709 (using the 2022 exemption equivalent) for Harry Smith (Form 709 for 2022 was not available as of press date).

EXHIBIT 14-5 Page 1 of Form 709 Gift Tax Return for Harry Smith

Form **709**

Department of the Treasury
Internal Revenue Service

United States Gift (and Generation-Skipping Transfer) Tax Return

▶ Go to *www.irs.gov/Form709* for instructions and the latest information.
(For gifts made during calendar year 2021)
▶ See instructions.

OMB No. 1545-0020

2021

Part 1—General Information

1 Donor's first name and middle initial	2 Donor's last name	3 Donor's social security number
HARRY	SMITH	000-00-0000
4 Address (number, street, and apartment number)		5 Legal residence (domicile)
2813 ELMWOOD		WASHTENAW, MICHIGAN
6 City or town, state or province, country, and ZIP or foreign postal code		7 Citizenship (see instructions)
ANN ARBOR, MI 48109		USA

Line	Item	Yes	No
8	If the donor died during the year, check here ▶ ☐ and enter date of death ______, ______.		
9	If you extended the time to file this Form 709, check here ▶ ☐		
10	Enter the total number of donees listed on Schedule A. Count each person only once ▶		
11a	Have you (the donor) previously filed a Form 709 (or 709-A) for any other year? If "No," skip line 11b	✓	
b	Has your address changed since you last filed Form 709 (or 709-A)?		✓
12	**Gifts by husband or wife to third parties.** Do you consent to have the gifts (including generation-skipping transfers) made by you and by your spouse to third parties during the calendar year considered as made one-half by each of you? (See instructions.) (If the answer is "Yes," the following information must be furnished and your spouse must sign the consent shown below. **If the answer is "No," skip lines 13–18.**)		✓
13	Name of consenting spouse — 14 SSN		
15	Were you married to one another during the entire calendar year? See instructions		
16	If line 15 is "No," check whether ☐ married ☐ divorced or ☐ widowed/deceased, and give date. See instructions ▶		
17	Will a gift tax return for this year be filed by your spouse? If "Yes," mail both returns in the same envelope		
18	**Consent of Spouse.** I consent to have the gifts (and generation-skipping transfers) made by me and by my spouse to third parties during the calendar year considered as made one-half by each of us. We are both aware of the joint and several liability for tax created by the execution of this consent. **Consenting spouse's signature ▶** **Date ▶**		
19	Have you applied a DSUE amount received from a predeceased spouse to a gift or gifts reported on this or a previous Form 709? If "Yes," complete Schedule C		✓

Part 2—Tax Computation

Line	Item	Line	Amount
1	Enter the amount from Schedule A, Part 4, line 11	1	585,500
2	Enter the amount from Schedule B, line 3	2	1,500,000
3	Total taxable gifts. Add lines 1 and 2	3	2,085,500
4	Tax computed on amount on line 3 (see *Table for Computing Gift Tax* in instructions)	4	780,000
5	Tax computed on amount on line 2 (see *Table for Computing Gift Tax* in instructions)	5	545,800
6	Balance. Subtract line 5 from line 4	6	234,200
7	Applicable credit amount. If donor has DSUE amount from predeceased spouse(s) or Restored Exclusion Amount, enter amount from Schedule C, line 5; otherwise, see instructions	7	4,769,800
8	Enter the applicable credit against tax allowable for all prior periods (from Sch. B, line 1, col. C)	8	345,800
9	Balance. Subtract line 8 from line 7. Do not enter less than zero	9	4,424,000
10	Enter 20% (0.20) of the amount allowed as a specific exemption for gifts made after September 8, 1976, and before January 1, 1977. See instructions	10	0
11	Balance. Subtract line 10 from line 9. Do not enter less than zero	11	4,424,000
12	Applicable credit. Enter the smaller of line 6 or line 11	12	234,200
13	Credit for foreign gift taxes (see instructions)	13	
14	Total credits. Add lines 12 and 13	14	234,200
15	Balance. Subtract line 14 from line 6. Do not enter less than zero	15	0
16	Generation-skipping transfer taxes (from Schedule D, Part 3, col. G, total)	16	
17	Total tax. Add lines 15 and 16	17	0
18	Gift and generation-skipping transfer taxes prepaid with extension of time to file	18	
19	If line 18 is less than line 17, enter **balance due.** See instructions	19	
20	If line 18 is greater than line 17, enter **amount to be refunded**	20	

Attach check or money order here.

Sign Here

Under penalties of perjury, I declare that I have examined this return, including any accompanying schedules and statements, and to the best of my knowledge and belief, it is true, correct, and complete. Declaration of preparer (other than donor) is based on all information of which preparer has any knowledge.

May the IRS discuss this return with the preparer shown below? See instructions. ☐ Yes ☐ No

Signature of donor | Date

Paid Preparer Use Only

Print/Type preparer's name	Preparer's signature	Date	Check ☐ if self-employed	PTIN
Firm's name ▶			Firm's EIN ▶	
Firm's address ▶			Phone no.	

For Disclosure, Privacy Act, and Paperwork Reduction Act Notice, see the instructions for this form. Cat. No. 16783M Form **709** (2021)

Source: irs.gov.

(continued from page 14-1. . .)
Early this year Bob was injured in an auto accident. Unable to recover from his injuries, he died after two days in the hospital. Bob is survived by his son Nate, who is also the executor of Bob's estate. Nate is now collecting his father's assets, and he would like help in preparing Bob's federal estate tax return. ■

THE FEDERAL ESTATE TAX

LO 14-3

The estate tax is designed to tax the value of property owned or controlled by an individual at death, the decedent. Because federal gift and estate taxes are integrated, taxable gifts affect the tax base for the estate tax. Exhibit 14-6 presents the estate tax formula.

EXHIBIT 14-6 The Federal Estate Tax Formula

	Gross estate
Minus	Expenses, debts, and losses
Equals	Adjusted gross estate
Minus	Marital and charitable deductions
Equals	Taxable estate
Plus	Adjusted taxable gifts
Equals	Cumulative taxable transfers (the tax base)
Times	Current tax rates
Equals	Tax on cumulative transfers
Minus	Gift taxes payable on adjusted taxable gifts at current rates
Equals	Tentative tax
Minus	Full applicable credit calculated using current tax rates
Equals	Gross estate tax

The Gross Estate

Property possessed by or owned (titled) by a decedent at the time of death is generally referred to as the **probate estate** because the transfer of this property is carried out by a probate court. **Probate** is the process of gathering property possessed by or titled in the name of a decedent at the time of death, paying the debts of the decedent, and transferring the ownership of any remaining property to the decedent's **heirs.** Property in the probate estate can include cash, stocks, jewelry, clothing, and realty owned by or titled in the name of the deceased at the time of death. The person appointed by the court to carry out the will is called the **executor.** If the decedent does not have a valid will at the time of death, the person is said to die *intestate*.

The **gross estate** is broader than the probate estate. The gross estate consists of (1) the fair market value of property possessed or owned by a decedent at death *plus* (2) the value of certain automatic property transfers that take effect at death.[14] Property transfers that take effect only at death are not in the probate estate because the transfer takes place just as death occurs. Hence, the probate court does not need to effect a transfer. Establishing a trust to hold the title to property is another method of avoiding probate. The ownership of property transferred to these living trusts automatically vests in a designated beneficiary upon the occurrence of an event, such as death of the donor.

[14]§2033. The principle of increasing the gross estate for transfers taking effect at death began with gifts in contemplation of death. So-called deathbed gifts were a device used to avoid the estate tax in the years before enactment of the gift tax.

Example 14-12

What if: Nate took an inventory of his father's property in preparation for distributing assets according to Bob's will. Nate must report this preliminary inventory of personal and investment property to the probate court. Bob's property includes the following:

Property	Fair Market Value
Auto	$ 33,000
Clothes, furniture, and personal effects	48,000
Smith painting (original cost/initial estimated value)	25,000
Checking and savings accounts	75,250
FFP stock	19,500,000
Residence	400,000
Other investments	8,200
Total	$20,089,450

What amount of this property is included in Bob's gross estate?

Answer: Bob's gross estate includes the value of *all* the above property, or $20,089,450, because he owned these assets at his death (i.e., these assets are included in Bob's probate estate). In this example, Bob's gross estate and his probate estate are identical, but this would not be the case if Bob owned property that transferred automatically on his death.

What if: Suppose Bob was also entitled to a pension distribution of $15,000 but had not yet received the check at the time of his death. Would this value also be included in Bob's probate estate and therefore gross estate?

Answer: Yes. Although Bob had not received the check, he was legally entitled to the property at the time of his death, and therefore it will be included in both his probate estate and his gross estate.

TAXES IN THE REAL WORLD Income in Respect of a Decedent

Individual retirement accounts are one of the most common properties inherited from a decedent, and retirement accounts owned by the decedent are included in the gross estate. When the retirement account consists of income accrued by the decedent but untaxed at the time of death, the untaxed income is called income in respect of a decedent (IRD). Because this income was never included in the decedent's gross income (i.e., not subject to income tax during the decedent's life), distributions from the inherited retirement account are included in the gross income of the beneficiary who inherits the account.

For example, suppose that at Bob's death he owned a traditional IRA (all pretax) worth $1 million, and Nate was the beneficiary of Bob's IRA. The $1 million would be included in Bob's gross estate, and when Nate takes a distribution from the IRA, the distribution would be included in Nate's gross income. However, when Nate takes a distribution from the IRA, he would be eligible to claim a deduction for the estate tax imposed on the IRA. The deduction is allowed as an itemized deduction under §691(c) but is not subject to the 2 percent of AGI limitation under §67 and was *not* one of the itemized deductions temporarily eliminated by TCJA in 2017.

The purpose of the IRD deduction is to prevent the double taxation of inherited property representing income that was accrued but untaxed at the time of the decedent's death. Examples of IRD include retirement plan assets, IRAs, unpaid interest and dividends, and accrued but unpaid salary. Most items of IRD are eventually distributed to beneficiaries, and the beneficiaries then include the IRD in their gross income. In the case of a traditional IRA or retirement plan where the assets have not yet been included in gross income, distributions are taxed to the beneficiary when the property is distributed from the IRA or retirement plan.

To understand the operation of an IRD deduction, suppose that Bob died with no lifetime gifts and an estate worth $20 million that includes an IRA worth $1 million. In 2022, the estate tax on this estate would total $3,176,000, and $400,000 of this tax would be attributable to the IRA. If the $1 million were immediately distributed to Nate, he would include $1 million in gross income and claim a $400,000 IRD as a miscellaneous itemized deduction. If Nate only received a distribution of $10,000 from the IRA, he would only include $10,000 in gross income and claim a deduction for $4,000 [(10,000/1,000,000) × $400,000].

Specific Inclusions Besides property in the probate estate, the gross estate also includes property transferred automatically at the decedent's death. These automatic transfers can occur without the help of a probate court because the ownership transfers by law at the time of death. For example, property can be transferred automatically through a living trust.

Certain automatic property transfers are specifically included in the gross estate because, while the decedent didn't own the property at death, they controlled the ultimate disposition of the property. That is, the decedent effectively determined who would receive the property at the time of death. Joint ownership of property is the most common form of automatic transfer, but the amounts included in the gross estate vary with the form of joint ownership. Property held in joint tenancy with right of survivorship legally transfers to the surviving tenant upon the joint tenant's death. For example, joint bank accounts are commonly owned in joint ownership with right of survivorship. In contrast, tenants in common hold divided rights to property and have the ability to transfer these rights during their life or upon death. Property held by tenants in common, such as real estate, does not automatically transfer at death and thus must be transferred via probate. Although the decedent's interest in jointly owned property (with the right of survivorship) ceases at death, the value of the interest the decedent held in this property is still included in the gross estate.[15]

Example 14-13

Nate and his father jointly own two parcels of real estate not included in the inventory above. One parcel is a vacation home in Colorado. Nate owns this property jointly with Bob and the title is held in joint ownership with the right of survivorship. Will this property be included in Bob's probate estate and/or gross estate?

Answer: The property will *not* be included in Bob's *probate* estate, but it will be included in Bob's *gross* estate. When Bob died, Nate automatically became the sole owner of the property without going through probate. However, the property will be included in Bob's gross estate because it is an automatic transfer that is specifically included in the gross estate by law.

The second parcel of land is real estate in west Texas that Nate and Bob hold as equal tenants in common. Will it be necessary to use probate to transfer ownership of Bob's share to the beneficiary named in Bob's will?

Answer: Yes, ownership must be transferred through probate. The value of Bob's one-half interest in the west Texas real estate is also included in his gross estate.

Another example of an automatic transfer is insurance on the life of the decedent. Proceeds of life insurance paid due to the death of the decedent are specifically included in the gross estate if either of two conditions is met. The proceeds are included in the gross estate if (1) the decedent owned the policy or had "incidents of ownership" such as the right to designate the beneficiary or (2) the decedent's estate or executor is the beneficiary of the insurance policy (that is, the executor must use the insurance proceeds to discharge the obligations of the estate).

Example 14-14

Bob owned and paid annual premiums on an insurance policy that, on his death, was to pay the beneficiary of his choice $500,000. Bob named Nate as the beneficiary, and the insurance company paid Nate $500,000 after receiving notification of Bob's death. Will Bob's gross estate include the value of the insurance proceeds paid to Nate?

(continued on page 14-20)

[15]§2040. There are a number of other transfers that are specifically included in the gross estate. For example, §§2036–2039 and §2041 address transfers with retained life estates, transfers taking place at death, revocable transfers, annuities, and powers of appointment. A discussion of these provisions is beyond the scope of this text.

Answer: Yes. The $500,000 of insurance proceeds is specifically included in Bob's estate despite the fact that it was paid directly to Nate and did not go through probate.

What if: Suppose Bob transferred ownership of the policy to Nate four years prior to his death. Nate had the power to designate the beneficiary of the policy, and he also paid the annual premiums. Will Bob's gross estate include the value of the insurance proceeds paid to Nate?

Answer: No. Bob had no incidents of ownership at his death (Nate controlled who would be paid the proceeds upon Bob's death), and the proceeds were not paid to his estate.

Value of jointly owned property included in the gross estate. The proportion of the value of jointly owned property included in the gross estate depends upon the type of ownership. When a decedent's interest is a tenancy in common (there is no right of survivorship), a proportion of the value of the property is included in the gross estate that matches the decedent's ownership interest. For example, consider a decedent who owned a one-third interest in property as a tenant in common. If the entire property is worth $120,000 at the decedent's death, then $40,000 is included in the gross estate.

The amount includable for property held as joint tenancy with the right of survivorship depends upon the marital status of the owners. When property is jointly owned by a married couple with the right of survivorship, *half the value* of the property is automatically included in the estate of the first spouse to die.[16] For *unmarried* co-owners, the value included in the decedent's gross estate is determined by the decedent's contribution to the total cost of the property. For example, consider a decedent who provided two-thirds of the total cost of property held as joint tenants with the right of survivorship. If the entire property is worth $240,000 at the decedent's death, then two-thirds ($160,000) is included in the gross estate.

Example 14-15

Bob and Nate originally purchased the Colorado vacation home seven years ago for $200,000 and held it as joint tenants with the right of survivorship. This property is not included in the list of property in Bob's probate estate because the title passes automatically to Nate upon Bob's death. Bob provided $150,000 of the purchase price, and Nate provided the remaining $50,000. The property was worth $400,000 at Bob's death. How much is included in his gross estate?

Answer: Bob's gross estate includes $300,000. For property held in joint tenancy with the right of survivorship, the amount included in the gross estate is equal to the proportion of the purchase price provided by the decedent. Bob provided 75 percent ($150,000 ÷ $200,000 = 75%). Hence, his gross estate will include $300,000 (75% × $400,000) of the value of the vacation home.

What if: Suppose Bob was married and owned the home with a spouse as joint tenants with the right of survivorship. What amount would be included in Bob's gross estate?

Answer: Bob's gross estate includes $200,000. For property held with a spouse in joint tenancy with the right of survivorship, the amount included in the gross estate is half the value of the property at death.

What if: The west Texas land Bob and Nate owned is valued at $500,200. They owned it as tenants in common, with Bob holding a one-quarter interest and Nate holding the rest. What amount is included in Bob's gross estate?

Answer: The amount included in the estate is $125,050 ($500,200 × 25%) because Bob owned a one-quarter interest in the property.

Exhibit 14-7 summarizes the rules for determining the value of jointly owned property included in a decedent's gross estate.

[16]In some states, joint tenancy with a right of survivorship between spouses is referred to as a *tenancy by the entirety*.

EXHIBIT 14-7 **Amount of Jointly Owned Property Included in Gross Estate**

Ownership Form	Marital Status of Co-owners	Amount in Gross Estate
Community property (discussed above)	Married	Half the fair market value
Joint tenancy with right of survivorship	Married	Half the fair market value
Joint tenancy with right of survivorship	Unmarried	Percentage of fair market value determined by decedent's contribution to total cost of the property
Tenancy in common	Married or unmarried	Percentage of fair market value determined by decedent's interest in the property

Transfers within three years of death. Certain transfers, such as transfers of life insurance policies, made within three years of the decedent's death are also included in the decedent's gross estate, valued as of the time of death. Without this provision, a simple but effective estate tax planning technique would be to transfer ownership in a life insurance policy just prior to the decedent's death. This strategy, called a *deathbed gift,* would reduce the decedent's transfer taxes on the life insurance by the difference between its proceeds from the policy (the value at death) and its value on the date transferred. Only certain transfers are specifically included under this provision, and they are often difficult to identify.

Gift taxes paid on transfers within three years of death. Gift taxes paid on any taxable gifts during the three-year period preceding the donor's death are also included in the decedent's gross estate. This inclusion provision prevents donors from escaping estate tax on the value of gift taxes paid within three years of death. In other words, the amount of gift taxes paid is included in the estate because it would have been included in the estate had the decedent kept the property until death.

Example 14-16

What if: Suppose Bob owned a life insurance policy and transferred all incidents of ownership in the policy to his son one year before dying from a fatal disease. Also suppose that Bob paid $40,000 of gift taxes on the transfer and the policy paid his son $3 million on Bob's death. What amount would be included in Bob's gross estate?

Answer: $3,040,000. Bob's estate would include proceeds of the policy ($3 million) because Bob transferred the incidents of ownership within three years of his death. The value of the transfer would also include the gift taxes paid ($40,000) when Bob transferred the policy.

Valuation Property is included in the gross estate at the *fair market value* on the date of the decedent's death. Virtually all the factors (and controversies) regarding valuation that we've already discussed for the gift tax also apply to the valuation of property for estate tax purposes. There are special use valuations that can apply to certain farming property and close businesses if this property constitutes a substantial portion of the gross estate, but a discussion of these rules is detailed beyond the scope of this text.

Example 14-17

At his death, Bob owned an original landscape painting made in the late 1800s by one of his ancestors, Tully Smith. Bob purchased the Smith painting for $25,000 in 1980, and last year an expert estimated it was worth $210,000. Nate has now had the painting appraised by another expert, who estimates its value at $250,000 based upon a painting by the same artist that sold at auction last month. What value should be placed on the painting for inclusion in the gross estate?

Answer: Nate should value the painting at $250,000, according to its specific characteristics and attributes (such as age, condition, history, authenticity, and so forth). Of course, the IRS might disagree with this value and seek to value the painting at a higher amount.

Future interests owned by the decedent at death, such as reversions and remainders, are also included in the gross estate. These interests are valued using the same techniques used to value future interests for gift tax purposes (explained previously).

Example 14-18

THE KEY FACTS

Valuation of Assets

- Property is included in the estate at its fair market value at the date of the decedent's death.
- The executor can elect to value the estate on an alternate valuation date, six months after death, if it reduces the gross estate and estate tax.

At the time of his death, Bob owned a reversion in a trust (a future interest in the property) he established for his favorite cousin, Becky. Under the terms of the trust, Becky is entitled to income for her life (a life estate), and Bob (or his heir) is entitled to the reversion. At the time of Bob's death, the trust assets were valued at $100,000, Becky was 35, and the §7520 interest rate was 6 percent. Should this reversion be included in Bob's gross estate, and, if so, what value is placed on the future interest?

Answer: Bob's reversion interest is included in his estate because this is a property right he owned at his death. Under Table S in the regulations (Exhibit 14-4), based upon Becky's age and the current interest rate at the time of Bob's death, the percentage of the property that represents the value of Bob's reversion is 11.217 percent. Thus, his reversion is valued at $11,217 ($100,000 × .11217).

What if: Suppose the trust was established for George, age 6. Would this influence the value of Bob's reversion interest?

Answer: Yes. Under Table S in the regulations and based upon George's age and the current interest rate, the portion of the property that represents the value of Bob's reversion is 2.749 percent. Thus, Bob's reversion is valued at $2,749 ($100,000 × .02749).

The executor of an estate, however, can elect—irrevocably—to have all the property in the gross estate valued on an **alternative valuation date.** The alternate date for valuing the estate is six months after the date of death or on the date of sale or distribution of the property (if this occurs before the end of the six-month period). This election is available only if it reduces the value of the gross estate and the combined estate and generation-skipping taxes.[17]

Example 14-19

What if: Bob's shares of FFP are included in his estate at a value of $19.5 million. Suppose the value of the shares plummet to $5 million several months after Bob's death. Further suppose that the drop in value causes the value of Bob's estate to drop from $28 million to $13.5 million and consequently reduces the tax on Bob's estate. Could Nate, as executor of Bob's estate, opt to value these shares at the lower value for estate tax purposes?

Answer: Yes. Nate could elect to value the shares on the alternative valuation date, six months after Bob's death. Bob's estate qualifies for this election because it reduces the value of the entire gross estate and the estate tax. Besides reducing the estate tax, the election would also reduce the tax basis of the property for beneficiaries.

Gross Estate Summary So far we've seen that the decedent's gross estate consists of the assets subject to probate as well as certain assets transferred outside probate. These latter assets include property owned by the decedent in joint tenancy with the right of survivorship as well as life insurance. The gross estate also includes certain property transferred by the decedent within three years of death and certain future interests owned by the decedent.

[17]Under §2032, the alternative valuation election is made on the estate tax return and is irrevocable on the due date. The election applies to all the property in the gross estate. The executor can also make a protective election to use the alternate valuation date in case it is later determined that the estate and estate tax would decrease under the election.

Example 14-20

Given previous examples, what is the value of Bob's gross estate?

Answer: The value of Bob's gross estate is $21,250,717, calculated as follows:

Property	Value	Explanation
Auto	$ 33,000	Example 14-12
Personal effects	48,000	Example 14-12
Smith painting	250,000	Example 14-17
Checking and savings accounts	75,250	Example 14-12
FFP shares	19,500,000	Example 14-12
Residence	400,000	Example 14-12
Other investments	8,200	Example 14-12
Life insurance proceeds	500,000	Example 14-14
Colorado vacation home	300,000	Examples 14-13 and 14-15
West Texas land	125,050	Examples 14-13 and 14-15
Reversion interest in Becky Trust	11,217	Example 14-18
Gross estate	**$21,250,717**	

The Taxable Estate

Referring to the federal estate tax formula in Exhibit 14-6, we calculate the **taxable estate** in two steps. The first step consists of subtracting from the gross estate the deductions allowed for administrative expenses, debts of the decedent, and losses incurred during the administration of the estate. These deductions are allowed because Congress intends to tax the amount transferred to beneficiaries. This step results in the **adjusted gross estate.** In the second step, the adjusted gross estate is reduced for transfers to a decedent's spouse (i.e., the marital deduction) and to charities (i.e., the charitable deduction). These deductions result in the taxable estate. We discuss each type of deduction next.

Administrative Expenses, Debts, Losses, and State Death Taxes Debts included in or incurred by the estate, such as mortgages and accrued taxes, are deductible. Expenses incurred in administering the estate, such as executor fees, attorney fees, and the like, are also deductible. Funeral expenses are deductible if reasonable in amount. Likewise, casualty and theft losses are deductible. These losses must be incurred during the administration of the estate; otherwise, any deductions belong to the new owner of the property. Finally, death taxes imposed by the state are also deductible.[18]

Example 14-21

Nate paid $6,685 in funeral expenses for his father's services, and during the administration of his father's estate, he paid executor fees of $4,032 and attorney fees of $9,500. In addition, Nate discovered Bob owed debts totaling $100,500. Because Michigan has no state death or inheritance taxes, no amounts were owed to the state. What is Bob's adjusted gross estate (gross estate minus expenses and debts)?

(continued on page 14-24)

[18]Sections 2053, 2054, and 2058 address expenses, losses, and state death taxes, respectively.

Answer: Bob's adjusted gross estate is $21,130,000, calculated as follows:

Gross estate (from Example 14-20)		$ 21,250,717
Funeral expenses	$ 6,685	
Executor fees and expenses	4,032	
Attorney fees	9,500	
Debts of the decedent	100,500	
Total expenses and debts		−120,717
Adjusted gross estate		**$21,130,000**

What if: Suppose that during the administration of Bob's estate a storm damaged the Colorado vacation home. Bob's share of the casualty loss to the home was $25,000. Would this be deductible in calculating Bob's taxable estate?

Answer: Yes, the executor can deduct this loss on the estate tax return. Note that personal (nonbusiness) casualty and theft losses are not deductible on income tax returns.

The estate may collect income earned during its administration and, therefore, the estate will need to file an estate *income* tax return. The executor has the option of deducting administration expenses (but not funeral expenses) on either the estate tax return or the estate's *income* tax return. While no double deduction is available, the choice is relatively simple. If the estate owes no estate taxes, then the executor should claim the deduction on the estate income tax return. If the estate owes estate taxes, the marginal estate tax rate is likely to be higher than the marginal income tax rate. Hence, it should probably claim the deduction on the estate tax return.

THE KEY FACTS

Estate Tax Deductions

- Estate tax deductions include the debts of the decedent, funeral expenses, and the costs of administering the estate, including casualty losses.
- The value of property interests bequeathed to a surviving spouse is deductible if the interest is not terminable.
- The value of property bequeathed to a qualified charity is deductible.

Marital and Charitable Deductions To avoid taxing a married couple's estate twice, Congress provides a deduction for bequests to a surviving spouse. To qualify for the marital deduction, the transferred property must be included in the estate of the deceased spouse. That is, the surviving spouse must receive the property from the decedent and control its ultimate disposition. For example, property that passes to the surviving spouse as a result of joint tenancy with the right of survivorship qualifies for the marital deduction, as would a direct bequest from the decedent. In contrast, transfers of property rights that are terminable do not generally qualify for the estate marital deduction (as discussed earlier, terminable interests are treated similarly for gift tax purposes). For example, suppose the decedent bequeaths the surviving spouse the right to occupy the decedent's residence until such time as the spouse remarries. The value of the right to possess the residence is a terminable interest and is not eligible for the marital deduction.[19] In general, the estate tax marital deduction is unlimited in amount. Hence, no tax would be imposed on a decedent who leaves their entire estate to a spouse.[20]

Charitable contributions of property are also deductible without any limitation. Charities are defined to include the usual public organizations (i.e., corporations organized exclusively for religious, charitable, scientific, literary, or educational purposes) but exclude certain nonprofit cemetery organizations. Interestingly, foreign charities qualify for the charitable deduction under the estate and gift tax but not under the income tax. No deduction is allowed unless the charitable bequest is specified under the last will and testament or

[19]The restriction on the estate tax deduction for terminable interests is drafted consistent with the gift tax deduction. As noted previously, *qualified terminable interest properties* (QTIPs for short) are an exception to the nondeductibility of terminable interest property. To qualify, the executor must agree to have qualifying terminable interests included in the estate of the surviving spouse. A detailed discussion of this exception is beyond the scope of this text.

[20]There are other credits that could also apply, but these are beyond the scope of this text. The credit for taxes on prior transfer is designed to adjust the tax for property that was subjected to estate tax within the last 10 years. There is also a credit for pre-1977 gift taxes paid on certain pre-1977 gifts that must be included in the gross estate. Both of these credits are equitable adjustments for potential multiple transfer taxes associated with sequential deaths and multiple inclusions, respectively. Prior to 2005, there was a credit for state death taxes.

is a transfer of property by the decedent before their death that is subsequently included in the decedent's estate. The amount of any bequest must be mandatory, although another person such as the executor can be given discretion to identify the charitable organization.

Example 14-22

Not long after Bob's death, Nate gathered the Smith family for a reading of Bob's will. The will was relatively simple because Bob was unmarried at the time of his death. Bob had an adjusted gross estate of $21,130,000 and left all of his property to Nate, with two exceptions. Bob bequeathed his reversion (future) interest in the trust (value of $11,217) to Becky, and he bequeathed the Smith painting (value of $250,000) to the Midwest Museum in Ann Arbor (a qualified charity). Are either of these bequests deductible in calculating Bob's taxable estate? What is Bob's taxable estate?

Answer: Bequests are not deductible unless made to spouses or charitable organizations. The bequest to the museum qualifies for the charitable deduction because the museum is a qualified charity. Because Bob was unmarried at his death, the other bequests do not qualify for the marital deduction. Bob's taxable estate is $20,880,000, calculated as follows:

Description	Amount
Adjusted gross estate	$ 21,130,000
Charitable deduction	−250,000
Taxable estate	**$20,880,000**

What if: Suppose Bob was married at the time of his death and left a portion of his FFP stock, valued at $4.5 million, to the surviving spouse. What amount of this transfer, if any, would qualify for the marital deduction?

Answer: Bob's estate would be entitled to a marital deduction of $4.5 million, the value of the entire spousal bequest. In the extreme, if Bob had left *all his property* to his spouse, the taxable estate would be reduced to zero.

Computation of the Estate Tax

Three additional steps are necessary to calculate the estate tax liability from the taxable estate. First, the taxable estate is increased by **adjusted taxable gifts** (defined below) to compute cumulative lifetime transfers (i.e., the estate tax base). The objective of adding previously taxed transfers to the taxable estate is to allow the estate tax base to reflect all transfers, both during life and at death. Second, a tentative tax is computed on cumulative lifetime transfers and reduced by the tax payable on adjusted taxable gifts (computed using the current tax rates). Finally, this tentative tax is then reduced by the applicable credit.

In contrast to the gift tax formula, the estate tax formula allows a reduction only for taxes *payable* on adjusted taxable gifts. Recall that the gift tax formula reduces the tax on cumulative transfers by the gift taxes on all prior transfers rather than the gift taxes payable. Taxes payable on adjusted taxable gifts are a hypothetical amount computed using the past amount of applicable credit but the current tax rate schedule. Another difference between the gift tax formula and the estate tax formula is that the entire applicable credit (not just the unused portion) reduces the tentative tax (because all prior transfers are included in the tax base). These differences are illustrated below.

Adjusted Taxable Gifts Adjusted taxable gifts are prior taxable gifts reduced by prior gifts that are already included in the gross estate. For example, the value of life insurance transferred within three years of death would not be included in adjusted taxable gifts, but the value of the life insurance proceeds paid at death would be included in the estate. Despite increasing cumulative transfers, adjusted taxable gifts are not subject to double tax because the tentative tax on cumulative transfers is reduced by taxes payable on adjusted taxable gifts calculated under the current tax rate schedule. It is important to note that although adjusted taxable gifts were made in prior years, all tax calculations are made using the *current* rate schedule.

Example 14-23

After reviewing all Bob's records, Nate determined that Bob's only taxable gift was his gift of FFP stock in 2009. This transfer resulted in a taxable gift of $1 million, the tax on which was entirely offset by the applicable credit. What is the amount of cumulative transfers subject to estate tax, and what is Bob's tentative estate tax?

Answer: Bob's estate includes $21,880,000 of cumulative taxable transfers, and Bob's tentative estate tax is $8,697,800, calculated as follows:

Description	Amount	Explanation
Adjusted taxable gifts	$ 1,000,000	Prior gift
Taxable estate	20,880,000	Taxable transfers in estate
Cumulative taxable transfers	**$21,880,000**	Total taxable transfers
Tentative tax	**$ 8,697,800**	Tax from current tax rate schedule

What if: Suppose Bob had not made any taxable gifts prior to his death. Without the prior gifts, what would be Bob's tentative estate tax?

Answer: Without the gift of stock, Bob's tentative tax would be $8,297,800, calculated as follows:

Description	Amount
Adjusted taxable gifts	$ 0
Taxable estate	20,880,000
Cumulative taxable transfers	$20,880,000
Tentative tax	**$ 8,297,800**

Note that Bob's tentative tax has decreased by $400,000. This is the amount of tax on the $1 million 2009 gift at the top marginal rate (40 percent).

What if: Suppose that Bob's 2009 taxable gift was $4 million and the gift tax exemption equivalent in 2009 was $1 million. What is the amount of the reduction of taxes payable on adjusted taxable gifts?

Answer: $1.2 million. The adjusted taxable gift of $4 million would result in a tax of $1,545,800 under the current rate schedule. However, because the transfer was made in 2009, the tax would be reduced by $345,800. This is the amount of the applicable credit for an exemption equivalent of $1 million calculated using the current tax rate schedule. The calculation would be made as follows:

Description	Amount
Current tax on adjusted taxable gifts	$ 1,545,800
Applicable credit ($1 million at current tax rate)	−345,800
Current taxes payable on adjusted taxable gifts	**$1,200,000**

Note that the credit is 40 percent of the gift in excess of the exemption equivalent ($4,000,000 – $1,000,000 = $3,000,000). The $4 million prior taxable transfer is included in the calculation of Bob's cumulative taxable transfers and the tentative estate tax is calculated as before.

Description	Amount
Adjusted taxable gifts	$ 4,000,000
Taxable estate	20,880,000
Cumulative taxable transfers	$24,880,000

Description	Amount
Tax on cumulative transfers	$ 9,897,800
Taxes payable on adjusted taxable gifts	−1,200,000
Tentative estate tax	$ 8,697,800

Hence, the adjusted taxable gift increases the amount of Bob's estate subject to the top estate tax rate. Adjusted taxable gifts are not subject to an additional transfer tax at the time of Bob's death for two reasons. First, the tax payable on adjusted taxable gifts is deducted when computing the tentative tax. Second, the estate tax on the $1 million of adjusted taxable gifts that is not offset by the taxes payable will be offset by the applicable credit when computing the gross estate tax.

THE KEY FACTS

Adjusted Taxable Gifts and the Applicable Credit

- Adjusted taxable gifts are added to the taxable estate to determine cumulative taxable transfers, and the tax is computed on cumulative taxable transfers.
- Adjusted taxable gifts are not subject to double tax because the tax on cumulative transfers is reduced for taxes payable on adjusted taxable gifts.
- Taxes payable on adjusted taxable gifts are a hypothetical tax computed using the current rate schedule applied to gifts not included in the gross estate.
- The applicable credit eliminates transfer taxes on estates with relatively small cumulative lifetime and testamentary transfers (total transfers under the exemption equivalent).

Applicable Credit Besides subtracting the credit for tax on adjusted taxable gifts, we reduce the gross estate tax by several other credits.[21] The most important is the applicable credit because it eliminates the estate tax on cumulative transfers up to the exemption equivalent ($12.06 million in 2022). Hence, estate taxes are imposed only on relatively large estates. The objective of the applicable credit is to prevent the application of transfer tax to taxpayers who either would not accumulate a relatively large amount of property transfers during their lifetime and/or would not have a relatively large value of assets to pass to heirs upon their death.

The shortcut to calculating the gift tax can also be used to calculate the estate tax if total taxable transfers exceed $1 million. Rather than compute the tax on the adjusted taxable gifts and the resulting tentative tax, instead compute the tax using 40 percent times the cumulative taxable transfers after subtracting the unused exemption equivalent and adjusted taxable gifts. This shortcut works if the taxable transfers exceed $1 million because the tax can be calculated by multiplying the taxable amount by the marginal tax rate, 40 percent.

Example 14-24

Bob died on February 7 of 2022. What amount of estate tax must be paid on his estate, given his prior taxable gift of $1 million? What is the due date for Bob's estate tax return?

Answer: Estate tax of $3,928,000 is due after applying the applicable credit, computed as follows:

Description	Amount
Tentative tax (from Example 14-23)	$ 8,697,800
Less: Applicable credit	4,769,800
Estate tax due	**$3,928,000**

Bob's executor must file the estate tax return (Form 706 in Exhibit 14-8) or request an extension of time within nine months of Bob's death (by November 7 of 2022).

Using the shortcut method, the estate tax is calculated as follows:

Shortcut to Estate Tax Calculation

Description	Exemption Equivalent
Cumulative taxable transfers ($1 million plus $20.88 million)	$ 21,880,000
Less total taxable gifts in prior periods	−1,000,000
Less unused exemption equivalent	−11,060,000
Taxable transfers in this period	$ 9,820,000
Times marginal tax rate (40%)	×40%
Estate tax on estate at the current tax rate	$ 3,928,000

What if: Suppose Bob did not make any taxable gifts during his life. What amount of estate tax would be owed upon his death?

Answer: Bob's estate would owe $3,528,000, computed as follows:

Description	Amount
Tentative tax (from Example 14-23)	$ 8,297,800
Less: Applicable credit	4,769,800
Estate tax due	**$3,528,000**

In this case, the absence of gifts prior to Bob's death (no adjusted taxable gifts) would result in a $400,000 savings. The reason is that over his lifetime, Bob made fewer taxable transfers ($1 million in fact).

What if: Suppose Bob's 2009 taxable gift was $4 million (instead of $1 million) and the gift tax exemption equivalent in 2009 was $1 million. What amount of estate tax would be owed upon Bob's death?

Answer: Bob's estate would owe $3,928,000, computed as follows:

Description	Amount
Tentative tax (from Example 14-23)	$ 8,697,800
Less: Applicable credit	4,769,800
Estate tax due	**$3,928,000**

(continued on page 14-28)

[21]Other transfers that are required to be included in the gross estate are described in §2035(a). A discussion of these transfers is beyond the scope of this text.

Bob's estate tax is not increased by the amount of the adjusted taxable gifts in excess of $1 million because these gifts were taxed in 2009. The taxes payable on adjusted taxable gifts eliminate the potential for double taxation. The portion of the 2009 gift that was not taxed in 2009 (recall that $1 million was offset by the applicable credit) is now subject to tax, however.

Using the shortcut method, Bob's estate tax could be calculated as follows:

Shortcut to Estate Tax Calculation

Description	Exemption Equivalent
Cumulative taxable transfers ($4 million plus $20.88 million)	$ 24,880,000
Less total taxable gifts in prior periods	−4,000,000
Less unused exemption equivalent	−11,060,000
Taxable transfers in this period	$ 9,820,000
Times marginal tax rate (40%)	×40%
Estate tax on estate at the current tax rate	$ 3,928,000

The applicable credit for a surviving spouse is based on the current exemption equivalent increased by the amount of the **deceased spousal unused exclusion (DSUE).** Under §2010(c)(5) the DSUE is irrevocably elected by the decedent's executor on a timely filed Form 706, and it is reduced to the extent that the deceased spouse used any of the applicable credit. For example, suppose a deceased spouse died in 2013 without using any of the $5.25 million applicable credit available in that year. If a DSUE election was made by the deceased spouse's executor, the surviving spouse's estate would be entitled to an exemption equivalent in 2022 of $17.31 million ($12.06 million plus $5.25 million). If the deceased spouse had used $2 million of the 2013 exemption equivalent prior to their death, then the surviving spouse would only be entitled to an exemption equivalent of $15.31 million ($12.06 million plus $3.25 million).

Besides eliminating transfer taxes for relatively small cumulative transfers, the exemption equivalent also acts as the transfer requirement for filing an estate return. That is, an estate tax return (Form 706) must be filed if the gross estate plus adjusted taxable gifts equals or exceeds the exemption equivalent. Exhibit 14-8 presents the first page of Form 706 for Bob Smith. The deadline for the estate tax return is nine months after the decedent's death.[22]

Example 14-25

What if: Using the facts in Example 14-24, suppose Bob's spouse died in 2015, at which time they left a gross estate of $5 million to Bob. Bob's spouse had never made a taxable gift, and the executor of the spouse's estate claimed a marital deduction for the $5 million transfer and made a portability election for the unused spousal exclusion of $5.43 million. What amount of estate tax would be owed upon Bob's death?

Answer: $1.756 million. Bob's estate would be entitled to claim an applicable credit based on the combination of the current exemption equivalent and the deceased spouse's unused 2015 exemption, or $17.49 million ($5.43 million + $12.06 million). Bob's estate would be entitled to an applicable credit equal to the current tax on $17.49 million of $6,941,800. Bob's estate tax would be computed as follows:

Description	Amount
Tentative tax	$ 8,697,800
Less: Applicable credit	6,941,800
Estate tax due	**$1,756,000**

[22]A six-month extension to file the estate tax return is automatically granted by the IRS. However, an estimate of the tax due must be paid on the due date of the return. In addition, an election for DSUE (called a portability election) must be made on a timely filed estate tax return regardless of whether the estate is otherwise required to file an estate tax return. Reg. §20.2010-2(a)(1) indicates that the IRS will not grant an extension of time to file an estate tax return merely to make a portability election.

EXHIBIT 14-8 Page 1 of Form 706 Estate Tax Return for Bob Smith

Form **706** (Rev. August 2019) Department of the Treasury Internal Revenue Service

United States Estate (and Generation-Skipping Transfer) Tax Return

▶ Estate of a citizen or resident of the United States (see instructions). To be filed for decedents dying after December 31, 2018.

▶ Go to *www.irs.gov/Form706* for instructions and the latest information.

OMB No. 1545-0015

Part 1—Decedent and Executor

1a Decedent's first name and middle initial (and maiden name, if any) BOB	1b Decedent's last name SMITH			2 Decedent's social security no. 000 00 0000
3a City, town, or post office; county; state or province; country; and ZIP or foreign postal code ANN ARBOR WASHTENAW COUNTY MICHIGAN 48109	3b Year domicile established 1990	4 Date of birth 1940		5 Date of death 2022
6a Name of executor (see instructions) NATE SMITH	6b Executor's address (number and street including apartment or suite no.; city, town, or post office; state or province; country; and ZIP or foreign postal code) and phone no. 6500 TRAIL ROAD ANN ARBOR, MICHICAN 48109 Phone no. (000) 000-0000			
6c Executor's social security number (see instructions)				

6d If there are multiple executors, check here ☐ and attach a list showing the names, addresses, telephone numbers, and SSNs of the additional executors.

7a Name and location of court where will was probated or estate administered WASHTENAW COUNTY PROBATE COURT	7b Case number 00-12345

8 If decedent died testate, check here ▶ ☑ and attach a certified copy of the will. 9 If you extended the time to file this Form 706, check here ▶ ☐

10 If Schedule R-1 is attached, check here ▶ ☐ 11 If you are estimating the value of assets included in the gross estate on line 1 pursuant to the special rule of Reg. section 20.2010-2(a)(7)(ii), check here ▶ ☐

Part 2—Tax Computation

Line	Description			Line	Amount
1	Total gross estate less exclusion (from Part 5—Recapitulation, item 13)			1	21,250,717
2	Tentative total allowable deductions (from Part 5—Recapitulation, item 24)			2	370,717
3a	Tentative taxable estate (subtract line 2 from line 1)			3a	20,880,000
b	State death tax deduction			3b	0
c	Taxable estate (subtract line 3b from line 3a)			3c	20,880,000
4	Adjusted taxable gifts (see instructions)			4	1,000,000
5	Add lines 3c and 4			5	21,880,000
6	Tentative tax on the amount on line 5 from Table A in the instructions			6	8,697,800
7	Total gift tax paid or payable (see instructions)			7	0
8	Gross estate tax (subtract line 7 from line 6)			8	8,697,800
9a	Basic exclusion amount	9a	12,060,000		
b	Deceased spousal unused exclusion (DSUE) amount from predeceased spouse(s), if any (from Section D, Part 6—Portability of Deceased Spousal Unused Exclusion)	9b	0		
c	Restored exclusion amount (see instructions)	9c	0		
d	Applicable exclusion amount (add lines 9a, 9b, and 9c)	9d	12,060,000		
e	Applicable credit amount (tentative tax on the amount in line 9d from Table A in the instructions)	9e	4,769,800		
10	Adjustment to applicable credit amount (May not exceed $6,000. See instructions.)	10	0		
11	Allowable applicable credit amount (subtract line 10 from line 9e)			11	4,769,800
12	Subtract line 11 from line 8 (but do not enter less than zero)			12	3,928,000
13	Credit for foreign death taxes (from Schedule P). (Attach Form(s) 706-CE.)	13			
14	Credit for tax on prior transfers (from Schedule Q)	14			
15	Total credits (add lines 13 and 14)			15	0
16	Net estate tax (subtract line 15 from line 12)			16	3,928,000
17	Generation-skipping transfer (GST) taxes payable (from Schedule R, Part 2, line 10)			17	0
18	Total transfer taxes (add lines 16 and 17)			18	3,928,000
19	Prior payments (explain in an attached statement)			19	0
20	Balance due (or overpayment) (subtract line 19 from line 18)			20	3,928,000

Under penalties of perjury, I declare that I have examined this return, including accompanying schedules and statements, and to the best of my knowledge and belief, it is true, correct, and complete. Declaration of preparer (other than the executor) is based on all information of which preparer has any knowledge.

Sign Here

▶ Signature of executor ▶ Date

▶ Signature of executor ▶ Date

Paid Preparer Use Only

Print/Type preparer's name	Preparer's signature	Date	Check ☐ if self-employed	PTIN
Firm's name ▶			Firm's EIN ▶	
Firm's address ▶			Phone no.	

For Privacy Act and Paperwork Reduction Act Notice, see instructions. Cat. No. 20548R Form **706** (Rev. 8-2019)

Source: irs.gov.

LO 14-4

WEALTH PLANNING CONCEPTS

Wealth planning coordinates both income and transfer tax strategies with nontax objectives. Before we explore transfer tax strategies, we briefly review the generation-skipping tax and outline income taxation of fiduciary entities. While these topics are certainly important, we note them only in passing because their complexity is beyond the scope of this text.

The Generation-Skipping Tax

The **generation-skipping tax (GST)** is a supplemental tax designed to prevent the avoidance of transfer taxes (both estate and gift tax) through transfers that skip a generation of recipients. For example, a grandparent could give a life estate in property to a child, with the remainder to a grandchild. When the child dies and the grandchild inherits the property, no transfer tax is imposed because nothing remains in the child's estate (the life estate terminates at death). In this way, the grandparent pays one transfer tax (on the initial gift) to transfer the property down two generations.

The GST is triggered by the transfer of property to someone more than one generation younger than the donor or decedent—a grandchild rather than a child. A transfer to a grandchild is not subject to GST, however, if the grandchild's parents are dead. The GST is very complex and can be triggered directly by transfers or indirectly by a termination of an interest. Fortunately, the GST is not widely applicable because it does not generally apply to transfers that qualify for an annual gift tax exclusion, and each donor/decedent is entitled to a relatively generous aggregate exemption ($12.06 million in 2022).

Income Tax Considerations

A **fiduciary** entity is a legal entity that takes possession of property for the benefit of a person. An **estate** is a legal entity, such as an estate or trust, that comes into existence upon a person's death to transfer the decedent's real and personal property. Likewise, a **trust** is also a legal entity whose purpose is to hold and administer the corpus for other persons (*beneficiaries*). While an estate exists only until the assets of the decedent are distributed, a trust may have a prolonged or even indefinite existence. Because these entities can exist for many years, special rules govern the taxation of income realized on property they hold. These rules are complex and relate to how fiduciaries account for income under state law. A detailed discussion is beyond the scope of this text, but we provide an overview below.

The trust or testamentary instrument (or, in the absence of an instrument, state law) determines how income and expenses are allocated between beneficiaries—under fiduciary accounting rules, income belongs to income beneficiaries and corpus (principal) belongs to the remainderman. For example, an instrument may allocate gains on the sale of assets to corpus and rental receipts to trust accounting income. Likewise, depreciation expense may be allocated to accounting income, whereas repairs may be allocated to corpus. Accounting income is important because it determines how much income can be (or must be) distributed. Trusts and estates may have discretion whether to accumulate income within the entity (for future distribution) or make current distributions.[23] Income retained by the entity is taxed as income to the entity, and consequently, the trust or estate must file an income tax return. In contrast, income distributed currently by the entity is taxed as income to the beneficiary. To accomplish this flow-through of income, trusts and estates are granted an income tax deduction for current distributions of income, and this deduction depends, in part, on accounting income.

To better understand how taxable income is divided between a trust or estate and its beneficiaries, it is helpful to first summarize the formula for determining taxable income.[24]

[23]Regulations under §§651–652 make a distinction between simple trusts and complex trusts. **Simple trusts** must distribute all trust accounting income currently (and cannot make charitable contributions), whereas **complex trusts** are not required by the trust instrument to distribute income currently.

[24]Subchapter J (§§641–692) contains the provisions governing income taxation of trusts and estates.

With few exceptions, the formula for calculating taxable income for a trust or an estate is analogous to the individual income tax formula. Gross income for the entity is determined in the same manner as gross income for an individual. For example, trusts are generally taxed on realized income, but they can exclude certain items from gross income, such as municipal interest, and make elections to defer certain items, such as installment gains.

Trusts and estates can also deduct expenses similar to an individual. For example, they may deduct trade or business expenses, interest, taxes, and charitable contributions. Lastly, trusts and estates are allowed a deduction for distributions of income to beneficiaries. It is this **distribution deduction** that operates to eliminate the potential for double taxation of income.

The maximum amount of the distribution deduction is the lesser of the amount actually distributed or **distributable net income (DNI).** DNI is calculated by adjusting taxable income before the distribution deduction for certain items of income and deduction. The calculation of DNI, and consequently taxable income, can be complicated by items such as net operating losses, net capital losses, charitable contributions, multiple beneficiaries, and discretionary (versus mandatory) distributions. Suffice it to say that the calculation of income tax for a trust or estate can be a very complicated matter.

While granting a trust or estate discretion over distributions complicates the calculation of taxable income, it might appear that this discretion also provides an opportunity to split income (by creating yet another taxpayer). However, the income tax rates applying to trusts and estates, provided in Appendix C in this text, are generally as high as or higher than the tax rates for individual beneficiaries. Hence, the potential income tax benefits from splitting income between these entities and beneficiaries are typically negligible.

Transfer Tax Planning Techniques

Transfer tax planning strategies are the same as those employed for income tax planning: timing, shifting, and conversion. Like income tax planning, wealth planning is primarily concerned with accomplishing the client's goals in the most efficient and effective manner after considering *both* tax and nontax costs. For the most part, wealth planning is directed to maximizing after-tax wealth to be transferred from an older generation to a younger generation. A critical constraint in this process, however, is determining how tax strategies can achieve the client's ultimate (tax and nontax) goals. Before attempting to integrate tax and nontax considerations, let's survey a few basic techniques for transfer tax planning.

THE KEY FACTS

Basic Wealth Planning Techniques

- A serial gift strategy saves gift taxes by converting a potentially large taxable transfer into multiple smaller transfers that qualify for the annual exclusion.
- Testamentary transfers allow a step-up in tax basis to fair market value, thereby eliminating income tax on unrealized appreciation.
- Lifetime gifts eliminate transfer taxes on post-gift appreciation.

Serial Gifts A **serial gift** strategy converts a large taxable transfer into a tax-exempt transfer by dividing it into multiple lifetime gifts. As long as the gifts qualify as present interests and do not exceed the annual exclusion, the transfers are exempt from all transfer taxes. Although serial gifts are an easy and low-cost planning strategy, this technique is limited in scope because only $16,000 per donee ($32,000 for married donors electing gift-splitting) can be transferred in 2022 (the amount is indexed for inflation) without any transfer tax. Hence, serial gifts can move significant amounts of wealth only if employed by multiple donors over multiple years and multiple donees.

Example 14-26

Suppose Harry and Wilma decide to begin transferring wealth to Dina and George. To what extent can serial gifts accomplish this goal without triggering gift taxes?

Answer: Harry and Wilma could each make annual gifts of $16,000 to Dina and George. These gifts would remove $64,000 per year from the Smiths' estate without triggering any transfer taxes (gift tax or generation-skipping tax). They could include any type of property as long as Dina and George can presently enjoy the property or income generated by it.

Step-Up in Tax Basis Timing is an important component in tax planning. Generally, a good tax planning strategy delays payment of tax, thereby reducing the present value of the tax paid. While deferral is important, transfer tax planning must also consider the potential appreciation of assets transferred and the effect of the income tax that could apply if and when the appreciation is realized. Gifted property generally retains the donor's basis in the property, meaning the donee takes a **carryover basis,** whereas inherited property takes a tax basis of fair market value. The advantage of gifting property is that the donor eliminates the transfer tax on any additional future appreciation on the gifted property. The disadvantage is that the unrealized appreciation of the gifted property will eventually be taxed (although at the donee's income tax rate). Thus, gifting appreciating property reduces future transfer taxes but at the cost of additional future income taxes imposed on the donee. In contrast, for inherited property, past appreciation (up to the date of death) will never be subject to income tax but instead is subject to transfer tax at the time of the transfer.

Example 14-27

What if: Suppose Harry currently owns 30 percent of the outstanding shares of FFP. These shares have a basis of $300,000 but are worth in excess of $2.7 million. Suppose Harry intends to transfer his FFP shares to his daughter Dina, who, in turn, intends to sell them after Harry's death (in three years). It is important to consider the extent to which income tax considerations influence whether Harry gifts these shares or holds them until his death.

Assume the transfer (whether by gift or inheritance) will be taxed at the top transfer rate of 40 percent, while when Dina sells the shares in three years, the gain will be taxed at a capital gains tax rate of 20 percent (ignoring the net investment income tax). Also assume the FFP shares will not appreciate and the prevailing interest rate is 6 percent. What is the total tax savings if Harry delays the transfer of the shares until his death three years hence?

Answer: The total tax savings is $686,280 if Harry delays the transfer until his death rather than gifting the shares to Dina immediately. See the following discussion and computations:

Description	Gift	Inheritance	Explanation
Gift tax paid	$1,080,000		40% × $2.7 million
Time value of gift tax	× 1.191		$(1.06)^3$
Future value of gift tax	$1,286,280		Value of gift tax paid
Estate tax paid		$1,080,000	40% × $2.7 million
Dina's capital gain tax of 20%	480,000	0	Gain of $2.4 million on gift due to carryover basis
Total taxes paid	$1,766,280	$1,080,000	$686,280 of tax savings

If a sale is planned, then the step-up in tax basis becomes critical to avoid being taxed on the accumulated appreciation. In this scenario, a testamentary transfer provides a step-up in tax basis and delays payment of the transfer tax for three years.

What if: Suppose Dina has no interest in selling the family business and intends to eventually transfer the shares to George. Moreover, suppose Harry believes the FFP shares will appreciate to $3.5 million within three years. To what extent should income tax considerations influence whether Harry transfers these shares immediately via gift or in three years via testamentary transfer? Estimate the total tax savings if Harry transfers the shares immediately rather than delaying the transfer until his death.

Answer: The tax savings is $113,720 if Harry transfers property immediately rather than delaying the transfer until his death. See the following discussion and computations:

Description	Gift	Inheritance	Explanation
Gift tax paid	$1,080,000		40% × $2.7 million
Time value of gift tax	× 1.191		$(1.06)^3$
Future value of gift tax	$1,286,280		Value of gift tax paid
Estate tax paid		$1,400,000	40% × $3.5 million
Total taxes paid	$1,286,280	$1,400,000	$113,720 of tax savings

If Dina plans to hold the shares indefinitely and the property is rapidly appreciating, then an inter vivos gift avoids having future appreciation taxed in Harry's estate. Although a gift of the shares would accelerate the imposition of transfer taxes, any unused applicable credit could minimize the amount of taxes due on the transfer. In this scenario, transfer via gift reduces total transfer taxes even though the gift tax is paid three years before an estate tax would be due.

Timing becomes critical in determining how to trade off income tax savings (step-up in tax basis) against transfer tax costs (paying gift tax now or paying estate taxes on additional appreciation later). Most tax advisers will suggest that elderly clients sell business assets or investments with unrealized losses because upon death the basis of these assets will be adjusted downward to fair market value. In other words, the adjustment to basis can be a step-down as well as a step-up, and a sale allows the loss to be deducted.

Integrated Wealth Plans

A client can have many nontax goals associated with the ultimate disposition of wealth, and some are very personal. It is often difficult to ascertain and prioritize them for planning purposes. However, an effective wealth plan must identify and integrate these personal objectives with tax costs. Often, the primary nontax objective of wealth planning is to preserve value during the transfer of control (management) of business assets. Thus, an essential nontax element of any effective wealth plan is to identify a safe mechanism to support the older generation in a specific lifestyle while transferring control to the younger generation.

Trusts are common vehicles for tax planning, in large part because these entities can be structured to achieve a great variety of tax and nontax objectives, including the support of specific beneficiaries.[25] The trustee is responsible for managing property in the trust, but the grantor can also give the trustee discretionary powers to provide flexibility. These powers can include the discretion to distribute income or corpus among beneficiaries. In addition, grantors can retain powers, including the ability to revoke the trust, select the trustee (original or successor), terminate beneficial interests, and add to the corpus. The most important aspect of an irrevocable trust is that the provisions (including powers and guidelines for the exercise of discretionary powers) cannot be changed once the trust instrument has been executed.

Specific types of trusts are common to many wealth transfer plans. For example, a **life insurance trust** is funded with an irrevocable transfer of a life insurance policy, and the trustee is given the power to name beneficiaries and redesignate them in case of divorce or death. Upon the death of the grantor, the amount of the policy is paid into the trust but not included in the grantor's estate. Moreover, an immediate cash distribution from the trust is not taxable income to the beneficiaries.

Example 14-28

Harry is planning to purchase a $2 million life insurance policy. He wants to use the proceeds to support Wilma after his death and have any remaining funds paid to his surviving children. How might Harry structure a trust to accomplish these goals?

Answer: Harry could transfer the policy to an irrevocable trust that directs the trustee to hold the policy and pay the premiums until Harry's death. At that time, the trustee could be directed to invest the $2 million proceeds and pay income to Wilma for the remainder of her life or until she remarries. At Wilma's death or remarriage, the trust terminates and pays the remaining funds to Harry's surviving children or their estates.

What if: Suppose Harry transfers the policy to an irrevocable trust and dies four years later. Will the use of this trust trigger any estate taxes at that time?

Answer: Harry's transfer of the policy to the trust will be a taxable gift at the time of the transfer to the extent of the value of the transfer. However, the $2 million proceeds from the policy will not be included in Harry's estate upon his death because the gift was not made within three years of Harry's death.

[25]Trusts are also popular because the trust property transfers outside probate, thereby avoiding both the costs and the publicity associated with probate.

Donors often use partnerships to transfer assets and for the control of a business in a systematic manner that also provides them with income and security. One specific form of partnership, the **family limited partnership,** divides a family business into various ownership interests, representing control of operations and future income and appreciation of the assets. Prior to restrictions enacted by Congress, these limited partnerships were sometimes used to transfer appreciation to members of a younger generation while allowing the older generation to effectively retain control of the business. Obviously, the intent of estate and gift taxes is to recognize transfers of assets that also represent control of the assets. Hence, it is not surprising that Congress revised the law to restrict the ability of family limited partnerships to effectively transfer appreciation in business assets and operations to younger generations without also transferring control.

CONCLUSION

In this chapter we learned to identify taxable transfers whether made during life (inter vivos transfers) or at death (testamentary transfers). We also learned how to calculate gift and estate taxes and described some fundamental transfer tax planning techniques. The simplest and most effective wealth planning technique is serial gifting. As long as the gifts are restricted to present interests under the annual exclusion, serial gifting avoids all transfer taxes. Other methods, such as family limited partnerships, can also be effective under the proper circumstances. In all cases, however, wealth planning should be carefully coordinated with other needs and objectives.

Summary

LO 14-1 Describe federal transfer taxes.

- Congress imposes a tax on transfers of property whether the transfer is a gift or occurs at death.
- The unified transfer tax scheme provides for a progressive tax rate schedule that applies to cumulative transfers. That is, transfers in all prior periods are taken into account when calculating the tax for a transfer in a current period.
- The applicable (unified) credit offsets transfer tax on cumulative lifetime transfers (the exemption equivalent) of $12.06 million for gifts and transfers at death made during 2022.
- Each transfer tax shares two common deductions: an unlimited deduction for charitable contributions and a marital deduction that allows almost unfettered transfers between spouses.
- Property transfers are valued at fair market value, defined as the value paid by a willing buyer to a willing seller. The determination of fair market value often depends upon the facts and circumstances surrounding the property.

LO 14-2 Calculate the federal gift tax.

- Lifetime transfers of property for no (or inadequate) consideration are taxed as gifts if the transfer is complete and irrevocable.
- Contributions to political parties or candidates, and medical and educational expenses paid on behalf of an unrelated individual, are excluded from gift taxation.
- Gifts are taxed at the fair market value of the donated property on the date the gift becomes complete, and small gifts are reduced by the annual exclusion ($16,000 in 2022) if they are present interests.

- With gift-splitting, married couples can elect to treat all gifts made in a year as if each spouse made one-half of each gift.
- Taxable gifts are calculated by adjusting current gifts for exclusions and gift-splitting, and then deducting the marital deduction (for qualifying gifts to a spouse) and the charitable deduction.
- Transfers of terminable interests in property, such as a life estate, will not generally qualify for the marital deduction.
- The gift tax on cumulative taxable gifts is computed by adding prior taxable gifts to current taxable gifts.
- The gift tax on cumulative gifts is reduced by the gift tax on prior taxable gifts and is calculated using the current rate schedule and ignoring any exemption equivalent used in prior years. The gift tax is then reduced by the *unused* portion of the exemption equivalent as converted into the applicable credit using the current tax rate schedule.

Compute the federal estate tax. **LO 14-3**

- The gross estate includes property owned by the decedent at death (the probate estate) and certain property transfers taking effect at death.
- Property the decedent owned jointly is included in the gross estate. The value of the decedent's interest is included when property is held in joint tenancy, whereas half the value of the property is included when held with a spouse in joint tenancy with the right of survivorship.
- Temporal interests begin or end with the passage of time. The value of a future interest, such as a remainder, can be determined from IRS tables, and the value of a present interest, such as a life estate, is calculated as the difference between the value of the future interest and the current value of the property.
- The gross estate is reduced by administrative expenses, debts of the decedent, and losses incurred during the administration of the estate, resulting in the adjusted gross estate.
- The adjusted gross estate is reduced for certain transfers to a surviving spouse (the marital deduction) and for transfers to charities (the charitable deduction), resulting in the taxable estate.
- The taxable estate is increased by adjusted taxable gifts to determine cumulative transfers.
- The tentative estate tax is calculated on cumulative transfers as reduced by the tax payable on adjusted taxable gifts calculated using the current rate schedule.
- The estate tax due is the tentative tax reduced by the full applicable credit.
- An estate is allowed to increase the exemption equivalent by the amount of a deceased spousal unused exclusion (DSUE) if an irrevocable election is made on the deceased spouse's timely filed estate tax return.

Understand how income and transfer taxation interact to affect wealth planning. **LO 14-4**

- The generation-skipping tax is a supplemental tax designed to prevent the avoidance of transfer taxes (both estate and gift taxes) through transfers that skip a generation of recipients.
- Trusts and estates are taxpayers taxed on accumulated (undistributed) income via a fiduciary income tax return.
- Because trust and estate income tax rates are generally as high as or higher than the tax rates for individual beneficiaries, the income tax benefits from splitting income between these entities and beneficiaries are typically negligible.
- A serial gift strategy saves gift taxes by converting a potentially large taxable transfer into a tax-exempt transfer of multiple smaller gifts that qualify for the annual exclusion of the donor.
- Testamentary transfers allow a step-up in tax basis to fair market value, thereby eliminating the income tax on unrealized appreciation. In contrast, appreciation of property transferred via inter vivos transfers may be eventually realized and taxed as income. However, a gift eliminates transfer taxes on expected future appreciation.

KEY TERMS

adequate consideration (14-5)
adjusted gross estate (14-23)
adjusted taxable gifts (14-25)
alternative valuation date (14-22)
annual exclusion (14-9)
applicable credit (14-2)
beneficiary (14-7)
carryover basis (14-32)
common-law states (14-10)
community-property states (14-10)
complex trust (14-30)
corpus (14-7)
current gifts (14-10)
deceased spousal unused exclusion (DSUE) (14-28)
distributable net income (DNI) (14-31)
distribution deduction (14-31)
donee (14-5)
donor (14-5)
estate (14-30)
executor (14-17)
exemption equivalent (14-3)
family limited partnership (14-34)
fiduciary (14-30)
fiduciary duty (14-7)
future interest (14-7)
generation-skipping tax (GST) (14-30)
grantor (14-7)
gross estate (14-17)
heirs (14-17)
inter vivos transfers (14-2)
joint tenancy (14-6)
joint tenancy with right of survivorship (14-6)
last will and testament (14-2)
life estate (14-7)
life insurance trust (14-33)
marital deduction (14-4)
nondeductible terminable interests (14-11)
present interest (14-7)
probate (14-17)
probate estate (14-17)
remainder (14-7)
remainderman (14-7)
reversion (14-7)
serial gift (14-31)
simple trust (14-30)
taxable estate (14-23)
taxable gifts (14-10)
tenancy in common (14-6)
terminable interest (14-7)
testamentary transfers (14-2)
trust (14-7, 14-30)
trustee (14-7)

DISCUSSION QUESTIONS

Discussion Questions are available in Connect®.

LO 14-1 1. Identify the features common to the gift tax formula and the estate tax formula.

LO 14-1 2. Explain why Congress felt it necessary to enact a gift tax to complement the estate tax.

LO 14-1 3. Describe the applicable credit and the purpose it serves in the gift and estate tax.

LO 14-1 4. Fredi is retired and living on a pension and has accumulated almost $1 million of property. Fredi would like to leave this property to her children. However, Fredi is afraid that the federal estate tax will appropriate much of her wealth. Explain whether this fear is well-founded.

LO 14-1 5. Define fair market value for transfer tax purposes.

LO 14-2 6. Describe the requirements for a complete gift, and contrast a gift of a present interest with a gift of a future interest.

LO 14-2 7. Describe the property transfers that qualify as gifts and define transfers that are not gifts for transfer tax purposes.

LO 14-2 8. Describe a situation in which a transfer of cash to a trust might be considered an incomplete gift.

LO 14-2 9. Identify two types of transfers for inadequate consideration that are specifically excluded from imposition of the gift tax.

LO 14-2 10. Under what circumstances will a deposit of cash to a bank account held in joint tenancy be considered a complete gift?

LO 14-2 11. Explain how a purchase of realty could result in a taxable gift.

LO 14-2 12. Describe the conditions for using the annual exclusion to offset an otherwise taxable transfer.

LO 14-2 13. List the conditions for making an election to split gifts.

LO 14-2 14. Describe the limitations on the deduction of transfers to charity.

15. Explain the purpose of adding prior taxable gifts to current taxable gifts and show whether these prior gifts could be taxed multiple times over the years. LO 14-2
16. Explain why the gross estate includes the value of certain property transferred by the decedent at death, such as property held in joint tenancy with the right of survivorship, even though this property is not subject to probate. LO 14-3
17. Identify the factors that determine the proportion of the value of property held in joint tenancy with the right of survivorship that will be included in a decedent's gross estate. LO 14-3
18. Ahmad owns a condo in Hawaii that he plans on using for the rest of his life. However, to ensure his sister Jana will own the property after his death, Ahmad deeded the remainder of the property to her. He signed the deed transferring the remainder in July 2009 when the condo was worth $250,000 and his life estate was worth $75,000. Ahmad died in January of this year, at which time the condo was worth $300,000. What amount, if any, is included in Ahmad's gross estate? Explain. LO 14-3 research
19. Paul is a widower with several grown children. He is considering transferring his residence into a trust for his children and retaining a life estate in it. Comment on whether this plan will prevent the value of the home from being included in Paul's gross estate when he dies. LO 14-3
20. Explain how a remainder and an income interest are valued for transfer tax purposes. LO 14-3
21. Explain why the fair market value of a life estate is more difficult to estimate than an income interest. LO 14-3
22. Describe a reason why transfers of terminable interests should not qualify for the marital deduction. LO 14-3
23. Adjusted taxable gifts are included in cumulative taxable transfers for calculating the estate tax. Explain whether including these gifts in the estate tax base will subject the gifts to double taxation. LO 14-3
24. People sometimes confuse the applicable credit with the exemption equivalent. Describe how these terms differ and how they are related. LO 14-3
25. Describe a reason why a generation-skipping tax was necessary to augment the estate and gift taxes. LO 14-4
26. Explain why an effective wealth transfer plan likely necessitates cooperation between lawyers, accountants, and investment advisers. LO 14-4
27. Describe how to initiate the construction of a comprehensive and effective wealth plan. LO 14-4
28. List two questions you might pose to a client to find out whether a program of serial gifts would be an advantageous wealth transfer plan. LO 14-4
29. A client in good health wants to support the college education of her teenage grandchild. The client holds various properties but proposes to make a gift of cash in the amount of the annual exclusion. Explain to the client why a direct gift of cash may not be advisable and what property might serve as a reasonable substitute. LO 14-4
30. An elderly client has a life insurance policy worth $40,000 that upon death pays $250,000 to a sole grandchild (or their estate). The client retains ownership of the policy. Outline the costs and benefits of transferring ownership of the policy to a life insurance trust. LO 14-4
31. Identify the sections in the Internal Revenue Code that authorize the use of qualified terminable interest property (QTIPs) for gift and estate tax purposes, respectively. LO 14-4 research
32. Under what conditions can an executor or trustee elect to claim a marital deduction for a transfer of a terminable interest to a spouse? LO 14-4 research
33. Explain how a transfer of property as a gift may have income tax implications to the donee. LO 14-4

PROBLEMS

Select problems are available in Connect®. 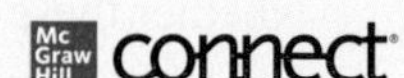

LO 14-2 34. Raquel transferred $100,000 of stock to a trust, with income to be paid to her nephew for 18 years and the remainder to her nephew's children (or their estates). Raquel named a bank as independent trustee but retained the power to determine how much income, if any, will be paid in any particular year. Is this transfer a complete gift? Explain.

LO 14-2 35. This year Gerry's friend, Dewey, was disabled. Gerry paid $15,000 to Dewey's doctor for medical expenses and paid $12,500 to State University for college tuition for Dewey's son. Has Gerry made taxable gifts and, if so, in what amounts?

LO 14-2 36. This year Omar and Mike purchased realty for $180,000 and took title as equal tenants in common. However, Mike was able to provide only $40,000 of the purchase price, and Omar provided the remaining $140,000. Has Omar made a complete gift to Mike and, if so, in what amount?

LO 14-2 37. Last year Nate opened a savings account with a deposit of $15,000. The account was in the name of Nate and Derrick, joint tenancy with the right of survivorship. Derrick did not contribute to the account, but this year he withdrew $5,000. Has Nate made a complete gift and, if so, what is the amount of the taxable gift and when was the gift made?

LO 14-2 38. Barry transfers $1,000,000 to an irrevocable trust with income to Robin for her life and the remainder to Maurice (or his estate). Calculate the value of the life estate and the remainder if Robin's age and the prevailing interest rate result in a Table S discount factor of .27 for the remainder.

LO 14-2 39. This year Jim created an irrevocable trust to provide for Ted, his 32-year-old nephew, and Ted's family. Jim transferred $70,000 to the trust and named a bank as the trustee. The trust was directed to pay income to Ted until he reaches age 35, and at that time the trust is to be terminated and the corpus is to be distributed to Ted's two children (or their estates). Determine the amount, if any, of the current gift and the taxable gift. If necessary, you may assume the relevant interest rate is 6 percent and Jim is unmarried.

LO 14-2 40. This year Colleen transferred $100,000 to an irrevocable trust that pays equal shares of income annually to three cousins (or their estates) for the next eight years. At that time, the trust is to be terminated and the corpus of the trust will revert to Colleen. Determine the amount, if any, of the current gifts and the taxable gifts. If necessary, you may assume the relevant interest rate is 6 percent and Colleen is unmarried. What is your answer if Colleen is married and elects to gift-split with the spouse?

LO 14-2 41. Sly is a widower and wants to make annual gifts of cash to each of his four children and six grandchildren. How much can Sly transfer to his children this year if he makes the maximum gifts eligible for the annual exclusion? What is the amount of the total transfer if Sly is married and elects gift-splitting, assuming his spouse makes no other gifts?

LO 14-2 42. Jack and Liz live in a community-property state and their vacation home is community property. This year they transferred the vacation home to an irrevocable trust that provides their son, Tom, a life estate in the home and the remainder to their daughter, Laura. Under the terms of the trust, Tom has the right to use the vacation home for the duration of his life, and Laura will automatically own the property after Tom's death. At the time of the gift, the home was valued at $500,000, Tom was 35 years old, and the §7520 rate was 5.4 percent. What is the amount, if any, of the taxable gifts? Would your answer be different if the home was not community property and Jack and Liz elected to gift-split?

43. David placed $80,000 in trust with income to Steve for his life and the remainder to Lil (or her estate). At the time of the gift, given the prevailing interest rate, Steve's life estate was valued at $65,000 and the remainder at $15,000. What is the amount, if any, of David's taxable gifts? LO 14-2

44. Stephen transferred $17,500 to an irrevocable trust for Graham. The trustee has the discretion to distribute income or corpus for Graham's benefit but is required to distribute all assets to Graham (or his estate) not later than Graham's 21st birthday. What is the amount, if any, of the taxable gift? LO 14-2

45. For the holidays, Marty gave a watch worth $25,000 to Sobia and jewelry worth $40,000 to Natalie. Has Marty made any taxable gifts this year and, if so, in what amounts? Does it matter if Marty is married and lives in a community-property state? LO 14-2

46. This year Jeff earned $850,000 and used it to purchase land in joint tenancy with a right of survivorship with Mary. Has Jeff made a taxable gift to Mary and, if so, in what amount? What is your answer if Jeff and Mary are married? LO 14-2

47. Laura is married to Willy. This year Laura transfers $500,000 into an irrevocable trust with the income to be paid annually to Willy for life (a life estate) and the remainder to Jenny. Calculate the amount of the taxable gifts from the transfers. LO 14-2

48. Red transferred $5,000,000 of cash to State University for a new sports complex. Calculate the amount of the taxable gift. LO 14-2

49. In 2010 Casey made a taxable gift of $5 million to both Stephanie and Linda (a total of $10 million in taxable gifts). Calculate the amount of gift tax due this year and Casey's unused exemption equivalent under the following alternatives. LO 14-2

    a) This year Casey made a *taxable gift* of $1 million to Stephanie. Casey is not married, and the 2010 gift was the only other taxable gift he has ever made.
    b) This year Casey made a *taxable gift* of $15 million to Stephanie. Casey is not married, and the 2010 gift was the only other taxable gift he has ever made.
    c) This year Casey made a *gift* worth $15 million to Stephanie. Casey married Helen last year, and they live in a common-law state. The 2010 gift was the only other taxable gift Casey or Helen has ever made. Casey and Helen elect to gift-split this year.

50. Tom Hruise was an entertainment executive who had a fatal accident on a film set. Tom's will directed his executor to distribute his cash and stock to his spouse, Kaffie, and the real estate to a church, The First Church of Methodology. The remainder of Tom's assets were to be placed in trust for three children. Tom's estate consisted of the following: LO 14-3

Assets	
Personal assets	$ 800,000
Cash and stock	24,000,000
Intangible assets (film rights)	71,500,000
Real estate	15,000,000
	$111,300,000
Liabilities	
Mortgage	$ 3,200,000
Other liabilities	4,100,000
	$ 7,300,000

    a) Tom made a taxable gift of $8 million in 2011. Compute the estate tax for Tom's estate.
    b) Fill out lines 1 through 12 in part 2 of Form 706 for Tom's estate.

LO 14-3 51. Hal and Wendy are married, and they own a parcel of realty, Blackacre, as joint tenants with the right of survivorship. Hal owns an additional parcel of realty, Redacre, in his name alone. Suppose Hal should die when Blackacre is worth $800,000 and Redacre is worth $750,000. What value of realty would be included in Hal's probate estate, and what value would be included in Hal's gross estate?

LO 14-3 52. Walter owns a whole-life insurance policy worth $52,000 that directs the insurance company to pay the beneficiary $250,000 on Walter's death. Walter pays the annual premiums and has the power to designate the beneficiary of the policy (it is currently his son, James). What value of the policy, if any, will be included in Walter's estate upon his death?

LO 14-3 53. Many years ago James and Sergio purchased property for $450,000. Although they are listed as equal co-owners, Sergio was able to provide only $200,000 of the purchase price. James treated the additional $25,000 of his contribution to the purchase price as a gift to Sergio. If the property is worth $900,000 at Sergio's death, what amount would be included in Sergio's estate if the title to the property was tenants in common? What if the title was joint tenancy with right of survivorship?

LO 14-3 54. Terry transferred $500,000 of real estate into an irrevocable trust for her son, Lee. The trustee was directed to retain income until Lee's 21st birthday and then pay him the corpus of the trust. Terry retained the power to require the trustee to pay income to Lee at any time and the right to the assets if Lee predeceased her. What amount of the trust, if any, will be included in Terry's estate?

LO 14-3 55. Last year Robert transferred a life insurance policy worth $450,000 to an irrevocable trust with directions to distribute the corpus of the trust to a grandson, Danny, upon graduation from college, or to Danny's estate upon death. Robert paid $40,000 of gift tax on the transfer of the policy. Early this year, Robert died, and the insurance company paid $4 million to the trust. What amount, if any, is included in Robert's gross estate?

LO 14-3 research 56. Willie purchased a whole-life insurance policy on his brother, Benny. Under the policy, the insurance company will pay the named beneficiary $1 million upon the death of the insured, Benny. Willie names Tess the beneficiary, and upon Benny's death, Tess receives the proceeds of the policy, $1 million. Identify and discuss the transfer tax implications of this arrangement.

LO 14-3 57. Jimmy owns two parcels of real estate, Tara and Sundance. Tara is worth $240,000 and Sundance is worth $360,000. Jimmy plans to bequeath Tara directly to his spouse Lois and leave her a life estate in Sundance. What amount of value will be included in Jimmy's gross estate and taxable estate should he die now?

LO 14-3 58. Banele had a taxable estate of $15.5 million when they died this year. Calculate the amount of estate tax due (if any) under the following alternatives.

a) Banele's prior taxable gifts consist of a taxable gift of $1 million in 2005.

b) Banele's prior taxable gifts consist of a taxable gift of $1.5 million in 2005.

c) Explain how the tax calculation would change if Banele made a $1 million taxable gift in the year prior to their death.

LO 14-2 tax forms 59. Brad and Angelina are a married couple who have three children, Fred, Bridget, and Lisa. Two of the three children, Fred and Bridget, are from Brad's previous marriages. On Christmas this year, Brad gave each of the three children a cash gift of $10,000, and Angelina gave Lisa an additional cash gift of $40,000. Brad also gave stock worth $60,000 (adjusted basis of $10,000) to the Actors Guild (an "A" charity).

a) Brad and Angelina have chosen to split gifts. Calculate Brad's gift tax. Assume that Angelina has no previous taxable gifts, but Brad reported previous taxable gifts of $2 million in 2009 when he used $345,800 of applicable credit and paid $435,000 of gift taxes.

b) Fill out parts 1 and 4 of Form 709 for Brad.

60. Jones is seriously ill and has $6 million of property that he wants to leave to his four children. Jones is considering making a current gift of the property (rather than leaving the property to pass through a will). Assuming any taxable transfer will be subject to the highest transfer tax rate, determine how much gift tax Jones will owe if the transfers are made now. How much estate tax will be saved if Jones dies after three years, during which time the property appreciates to $6.8 million? Besides transfer taxes, what other tax and financial factors should Jones consider in making this choice? LO 14-4 planning

61. Oisha gave a parcel of realty to Julie valued at $210,000 (Oisha purchased the property five years ago for $88,000). Compute the amount of the taxable gift on the transfer, if any. Suppose several years later Julie sold the property for $216,000. What is the amount of her gain or loss, if any, on the sale? LO 14-4

62. Several years ago Doug invested $21,000 in stock. This year he gave his daughter Tina the stock on a day it was valued at $20,000. She promptly sold it for $19,500. Determine the amount of the taxable gift, if any, and calculate the amount of taxable income or gain, if any, for Tina. Assume Doug is not married and does not support Tina, who is 28. LO 14-4 research

63. Roberta is considering making annual gifts of $16,000 of stock to each of four children. Roberta expects to live another five years and to leave a taxable estate worth approximately $18 million. Roberta requests that you justify the gifts by estimating the estate tax savings from making the gifts. LO 14-4

64. Harold and Maude were married and lived in a common-law state. Maude died in 2018 with a taxable estate of $25 million and left it all to Harold. Maude's executor filed a timely estate tax return claiming the marital deduction for the property left to Harold including a valid portability election. Harold died this year, leaving the entire $25 million to their three children. Calculate how much estate tax is due from Harold's estate under the following two alternatives. LO 14-4
    a) Assume that neither Harold nor Maude had made any taxable gifts prior to this year.
    b) Assume that Harold and Maude each made a $1 million taxable gift in 2011 and offset the gift tax at that time with the applicable credit.

COMPREHENSIVE PROBLEMS

Select problems are available in Connect®.

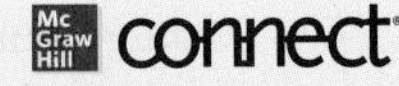

65. Vince and Millie are married. Vince dies this year with a gross estate of $25 million and no adjusted prior gifts. Calculate the amount of estate tax due (if any) under the following *alternative* conditions: planning
    a) Vince leaves his entire estate to Millie.
    b) Vince leaves $10 million to Millie and the remainder to charity.
    c) Vince leaves $10 million to Millie and the remainder to his son, Paul.
    d) Vince leaves $10 million to Millie and the remainder to a trust whose trustee is required to pay income to Millie for her life and the remainder to Paul.

66. Diego is a single individual who owns a life insurance policy worth $1.5 million that will be worth $8 million upon his death. This year Diego transferred the policy and all incidents of ownership to an irrevocable trust that pays income annually to Diego's two children for 15 years and then distributes the corpus to the children in equal shares.
    a) Calculate the amount of gift tax due (if any) on the transfer of the insurance policy. Assume that Diego has made only one prior taxable gift of $12 million in January of 2018.

b) Diego died unexpectedly this year after transferring the policy. At the time of death, Diego's probate estate was $25 million, to be divided in equal shares between Diego's two children. Calculate the amount of cumulative taxable transfers for estate tax purposes.

67. Jack is single and made his first taxable gift of $1,000,000 in 2008. Jack made additional gifts in 2009, at which time he gave $1,750,000 to each of his three children and an additional $1,000,000 to State University (a charity). The annual exclusion in 2009 was $13,000. Recently Jack has been in poor health and would like you to estimate his estate tax should he die this year. Jack estimates his taxable estate (after deductions) will be worth $20.4 million at his death.

68. Montgomery has decided to engage in wealth planning and has listed the value of his assets below. The life insurance has a cash surrender value of $120,000, and the proceeds are payable to Montgomery's estate. The Walen Trust is an irrevocable trust created by Montgomery's brother 10 years ago and contains assets currently valued at $800,000. The income from the trust is payable to Montgomery's faithful butler, Walen, for his life, and the remainder is payable to Montgomery or his estate. Walen is currently 37 years old, and the §7520 interest rate is currently 5.4 percent. Montgomery is unmarried and plans to leave all his assets to his surviving relatives.

Property	Value	Adjusted Basis
Auto	$ 20,000	$ 55,000
Personal effects	75,000	110,000
Checking and savings accounts	250,000	250,000
Investments	2,500,000	770,000
Residence	1,400,000	980,000
Life insurance proceeds	1,000,000	50,000
Real estate investments	10,125,000	2,800,000
Walen Trust	800,000	80,000

a) Calculate the amount of the estate tax due (if any), assuming Montgomery dies this year and has never made any taxable gifts.

b) Calculate the amount of the estate tax due (if any), assuming Montgomery dies this year and made one taxable gift in 2006. The taxable gift was $1 million, and Montgomery used his 2006 applicable credit to avoid paying any gift tax.

c) Calculate the amount of the estate tax due (if any), assuming Montgomery dies this year and made one taxable gift in 2006. The taxable gift was $5 million, and Montgomery used his $1 million 2006 applicable credit to reduce the gift tax in 2006. Montgomery plans to bequeath his investments to charity and leave his remaining assets to his surviving relatives.

UWorld Roger CPA Review

Sample CPA Exam questions from Roger CPA Review are available in Connect as support for the topics in this text. These Multiple Choice Questions and Task-Based Simulations include expert-written explanations and solutions and provide a starting point for students to become familiar with the content and functionality of the actual CPA Exam.

Appendix A

Tax Forms

The tax forms can be found in the Instructor Resources and Additional Student Resources, as well as additional forms at www.irs.gov/forms-instructions. The Additional Student Resources can be accessed directly by students in the eBook Table of Contents. They can also be assigned by instructors within Connect.

Appendix B

Tax Terms Glossary

83(b) election a special tax election that employees who receive restricted stock or other property with ownership restrictions can make to accelerate income recognition from the normal date when restrictions lapse to the date when the restricted stock or other property is granted. The election also accelerates the employer's compensation deduction related to the restricted stock or other property.

§179 expense an incentive for small businesses that allows them to immediately expense a certain amount of tangible personal property placed in service during the year.

§197 intangibles intangible assets that are purchased that must be amortized over 180 months regardless of their actual useful lives.

§291 depreciation recapture the portion of a corporate taxpayer's gain on real property that is converted from §1231 gain to ordinary income.

§338(g) election an election by a corporate buyer of 80 percent or more of a corporation's stock to treat the acquisition as an asset acquisition and not a stock acquisition.

§338(h)(10) election a joint election by the corporate buyer and corporate seller of the stock of a subsidiary of the seller to treat the acquisition as a sale of the subsidiary's assets by the seller to the buyer.

§481 adjustment a change to taxable income associated with a change in accounting methods.

§704(b) capital accounts partners' capital accounts maintained using the accounting rules prescribed in the Section 704(b) regulations. Under these rules, capital accounts reflect the fair market value of property contributed to and distributed property from partnerships.

§1231 assets depreciable or real property used in a taxpayer's trade or business owned for more than one year.

§1231 look-back rule a tax rule requiring taxpayers to treat current year net §1231 gains as ordinary income when the taxpayer has deducted a §1231 loss as an ordinary loss in the five years preceding the current tax year.

§1245 property tangible personal property and intangible property subject to cost recovery deductions.

§1250 property real property subject to cost recovery deductions.

12-month rule regulation that allows prepaid business expenses to be currently deducted when the contract does not extend beyond 12 months and the contract period does not extend beyond the end of the tax year following the year of the payment.

30-day letter the IRS letter received after an audit that instructs the taxpayer that they have 30 days to either (1) request a conference with an appeals officer or (2) agree to the proposed adjustment.

90-day letter the IRS letter received after an audit and receipt of the 30-day letter that explains that the taxpayer has 90 days to either (1) pay the proposed deficiency or (2) file a petition in the U.S. Tax Court to hear the case. The 90-day letter is also known as the *statutory notice of deficiency.*

Abandoned spouse a married taxpayer who lives apart from their spouse for the last six months of the year (excluding temporary absences), who files a tax return separate from their spouse, and who maintains a household for a qualifying child.

Accelerated death benefits early receipt of life insurance proceeds that are not taxable under certain circumstances, such as the taxpayer is medically certified with an illness that is expected to cause death within 24 months.

Accountable plan an employer's reimbursement plan under which employees must submit documentation supporting expenses to receive reimbursement and reimbursements are limited to legitimate business expenses.

Accounting method the procedure for determining the taxable year in which a business recognizes a particular item of income or deduction, thereby dictating the timing of when a taxpayer reports income and deductions.

Accounting period a fixed period in which a business reports income and deductions.

Accrual method a method of accounting that generally recognizes income in the period earned and recognizes deductions in the period that liabilities are incurred.

Accrued market discount a ratable amount of the market discount at the time of purchase (based on the number of days the bond is held over the number of days until maturity when the bond is purchased) that is treated as interest income when a bond with market discount is sold before it matures.

Accumulated adjustments account (AAA) an account that reflects the cumulative income or loss for the time the corporation has been an S corporation.

Accumulated earnings and profits undistributed earnings and profits from years prior to the current year.

Accumulated earnings tax a tax assessed on C corporations that retain earnings without a business reason to do so.

Acquiescence issued after the IRS loses a trial-level or circuit court case when the IRS has decided to follow the court's adverse ruling in the future. It does not mean that the IRS agrees with the court's ruling. Instead, it simply means that the IRS will no longer litigate this issue.

Acquisition indebtedness debt secured by a qualified residence that is incurred in acquiring, constructing, or substantially improving the residence but only to the extent that the amount borrowed does not exceed certain borrowing limitations.

Action on decisions IRS pronouncement that explains the background reasoning behind an IRS acquiescence or nonacquiescence.

Active participant in a rental activity an individual who owns at least 10 percent of a rental property and participates in the process of making management decisions, such as approving new tenants, deciding on rental terms, and approving repairs and capital expenditures.

Ad valorem taxes taxes based on the value of property.

Additional Medicare tax a tax imposed at a rate of .9 percent for salary or wages or net self-employment earnings in excess of $200,000 ($125,000 for married filing separate; $250,000 of combined salary or wages or net self-employment earnings for married filing joint).

Adequate consideration a price paid that is equal in value to the service or property received.

Adjusted basis an asset's carrying value for tax purposes at a given point in time, measured as the initial basis (for example, cost) plus capital improvements less depreciation or amortization. Also called *adjusted tax basis*.

Adjusted gross estate gross estate reduced by administrative expenses, debts of the decedent, losses incurred during the administration of the estate, and state death taxes.

Adjusted gross income (AGI) gross income less deductions for AGI. AGI is an important reference point that is often used in other tax calculations.

Adjusted tax basis an asset's carrying value for tax purposes at a given point in time, measured as the initial basis (for example, cost) plus capital improvements less depreciation or amortization.

Adjusted taxable gifts cumulative taxable gifts from previous years other than gifts already included in the gross estate valued at date of gift values.

Affiliated group two or more "includible" corporations that are related through common stock ownership and eligible to file a U.S. consolidated tax return. An affiliated group consists of a parent corporation that owns directly 80 percent or more of the voting stock and value of another corporation and one or more subsidiary corporations that meet the 80 percent ownership requirement collectively. Includible corporations are taxable U.S. C corporations, excluding real estate investment trusts; regulated investment companies; and life insurance companies.

After-tax rate of return a taxpayer's before-tax rate of return on an investment minus the taxes paid on the income from the investment. The formula for an after-tax rate of return that is taxed annually is the before-tax rate of return × (1 − marginal tax rate) [i.e., $r = R \times (1 - t)$]. A taxpayer's after-tax rate of return on an investment held for more than one tax period is $r = (FV/I)^{1/n} - 1$, where r is the after-tax rate of return, FV is the after-tax future value of the investment, I is the original investment amount, and n is the number of periods the investment is held.

Aggregate approach a theory of taxing partnerships that ignores partnerships as entities and taxes partners as if they directly owned partnership net assets.

Alimony a support payment of cash made to a former spouse. The payment must be made under a written separation agreement or divorce decree that does not designate the payment as something other than alimony, the payment must be made when the spouses do not live together, and the payments must cease no later than when the recipient dies.

All-events test requires that income or expenses are recognized when (1) all events have occurred that determine or fix the right to receive the income or liability to make the payments and (2) the amount of the income or expense can be determined with reasonable accuracy.

All-inclusive income concept a definition of income that says that gross income means all income from whatever source derived.

Allocate as used in the sourcing rules, the process of associating a deduction with a specific item or items of gross income for purposes of computing foreign source taxable income.

Allocation the method of dividing or sourcing nonbusiness income to specific states.

Allowance method method used for financial reporting purposes; under this method, bad debt expense is based on an estimate of the amount of the bad debts in accounts receivable at year-end.

Alternative minimum tax (AMT) a tax on a broader tax base than the base for the "regular" tax; the additional tax paid when the tentative minimum tax (based on the alternative minimum tax base) exceeds the regular tax (based on the regular tax base). The alternative minimum tax is designed to require taxpayers to pay some minimum level of tax even when they have low or no regular taxable income as a result of certain tax breaks in the tax code.

Alternative minimum tax (AMT) base alternative minimum taxable income minus the alternative minimum tax exemption.

Alternative minimum tax (AMT) exemption a deduction to determine the alternative minimum tax base that is phased out based on alternative minimum taxable income.

Alternative minimum tax adjustments adjustments (positive or negative) to regular taxable income to arrive at the alternative minimum tax base.

Alternative minimum tax system a secondary or parallel tax system calculated on an *alternative* tax base that more closely reflects economic income than the regular income tax base. The system was designed to ensure that taxpayers generating economic income pay some *minimum* amount of income tax each year.

Alternative valuation date the date six months after the decedent's date of death.

Amortization the method of recovering the cost of intangible assets over a specific time period.

Amount realized the value of everything received by the seller in a transaction (cash, FMV of other property, and relief of liabilities) less selling costs.

Annotated tax services a tax service arranged by code section. For each code section, an annotated service includes the code section; a listing of the code section history; copies of congressional committee reports that explain changes to the code section; a copy of all the regulations issued for the specific code section; the service's unofficial explanation of the code section; and brief summaries (called annotations) of relevant court cases, revenue rulings, revenue procedures, and letter rulings that address issues specific to the code section.

Annual exclusion amount of gifts allowed to be made each year per donee (regardless of the number of donees) to prevent the taxation of relatively small gifts ($16,000 per donee per year currently).

Annualized income method a method for determining a corporation's required estimated tax payments when the taxpayer earns more income later in the year than earlier in the year. Requires corporations to base their first and second required estimated tax installments on their income from the first three months of the year, their third installment based on their taxable income from the first six months of the year, and the final installment based on their taxable income from the first nine months of the year.

Annuity a stream of equal payments over time.

Applicable credit also known as the *unified credit,* the amount of current tax on the exemption equivalent; designed to prevent transfer taxation of smaller cumulative transfers.

Apportion as used in the sourcing rules, the process of calculating the amount of a deduction that is associated with a specific item or items of gross income for purposes of computing foreign source taxable income.

Apportionment the method of dividing business income of an interstate business among the states where nexus exists.

Arm's-length amount price in transactions among unrelated taxpayers, where each transacting party negotiates for their own benefit.

Arm's-length transactions transactions among unrelated taxpayers, where each transacting party negotiates for their own benefit.

Articles of incorporation a document, filed by a corporation's founders with the state, describing the purpose, place of business, and other details of the corporation.

Articles of organization a document, filed by a limited liability company's founders with certain states, describing the purpose, place of business, and other details of the company.

Assignment of income doctrine the judicial doctrine holding that earned income is taxed to the taxpayer providing the service, and that income from property is taxed to the individual who owns the property when the income accrues.

At-risk amount an investor's risk of loss in a worst-case scenario. In a partnership, an amount generally equal to a partner's tax basis exclusive of the partner's share of nonrecourse debt.

At-risk rules tax rules limiting the losses flowing through to partners or S corporation shareholders to their amount "at risk" in the partnership.

Average tax rate a taxpayer's average level of taxation on each dollar of taxable income. Specifically,

$$\text{Average tax rate} = \frac{\text{Total tax}}{\text{Taxable income}}$$

B

Bargain element (of stock options) the difference between the fair market value of the employer's stock and the amount employees pay to acquire the employer's stock.

Barter clubs organizations that facilitate the exchange of rights to goods and services between members.

Base erosion and anti-abuse tax (BEAT) a 10 percent minimum tax imposed on a U.S. corporation's payments of interest and royalties to a related foreign party.

Basis a taxpayer's unrecovered investment in an asset that provides a reference point for measuring gain or loss when an asset is sold.

Before-tax rate of return a taxpayer's rate of return on an investment before paying taxes on the income from the investment.

Beneficiary person for whom trust property is held and administered.

Bonds debt instruments issued for a period of more than one year with the purpose of raising capital by borrowing.

Bond discount the result of issuing bonds for less than their maturity value.

Bond premium the result of issuing bonds for more than their maturity value.

Bonus depreciation additional depreciation allowed in the acquisition year for tangible personal property with a recovery period of 20 years or less.

Book (financial reporting) income the income or loss corporations report on their financial statements using applicable financial accounting standards.

Book equivalent of taxable income a company's pretax income from continuing operations adjusted for permanent differences.

Book–tax difference a difference in the amount of an income item or deduction item taken into account for book purposes compared to the amount taken into account for the same item for tax purposes.

Boot property given or received in an otherwise nontaxable transaction such as a like-kind exchange that may trigger gain to a party to the transaction. The term *boot* derives from a trading expression describing additional property a party to an exchange might throw in "to boot" to equalize the exchange.

Brackets a subset (or portion) of the tax base subject to a specific tax rate. Brackets are common to graduated taxes.

Bright-line test technical rules found in the tax law that provide the taxpayer with objective tests to determine the tax consequences of a transaction.

Built-in gain the difference between the fair market value and tax basis of property owned by an entity when the fair market value exceeds the tax basis.

Built-in gains tax a tax levied on S corporations that were formerly C corporations. The tax applies to net unrealized built-in gains at the time the corporation converted from a C corporation to the extent the gains are recognized during the built-in gains tax recognition period. The applicable tax rate is 21 percent.

Built-in gains tax recognition period the first five years a corporation operates as an S corporation after converting from a C corporation.

Built-in losses the difference between the fair market value and tax basis of property owned by an entity when the tax basis exceeds the fair market value.

Bunching itemized deductions a common planning strategy in which a taxpayer pays two years' worth of itemized expenses in one year to exceed the standard deduction in that year.

Business activity a profit-motivated activity that requires a relatively high level of involvement or effort from the taxpayer to generate income.

Business income income derived from business activities.

Business purpose doctrine the judicial doctrine that allows the IRS to challenge and disallow business expenses for transactions with no underlying business motivation.

Business tax credits nonrefundable credits designed to provide incentives for taxpayers to hire certain types of individuals or to participate in certain business activities.

C

C corporations a corporate taxpaying entity with income subject to taxation. Such a corporation is termed a "C" corporation because the corporation and its shareholders are subject to the provisions of Subchapter C of the Internal Revenue Code.

Cafeteria plan an employer plan that allows employees to choose benefits from a menu of nontaxable fringe benefits or receive cash compensation in lieu of the benefits.

Capital account an account reflecting a partner's share of the equity in a partnership. Capital accounts are maintained using tax accounting methods or other methods of accounting, including GAAP, at the discretion of the partnership.

Capital asset in general, an asset other than an asset used in a trade or business or an asset such as an account or note receivable acquired in a business from the sale of services or property.

Capital gain property any asset that would have generated a long-term capital gain if the taxpayer had sold the property for its fair market value.

Capital interest an economic right attached to a partnership interest giving a partner the right to receive cash or property in the event the partnership liquidates. A capital interest is synonymous with the liquidation value of a partnership interest.

Carryover basis the basis of an asset the transferee takes in property received in a nontaxable exchange. The basis of the asset carries over from the transferor to the transferee.

Cash method the method of accounting that recognizes income in the period in which cash, property, or services are received and recognizes deductions in the period paid.

Cash tax rate the tax rate computed by dividing a company's taxes paid during the year by its pretax income from continuing operations.

Cashless exercise a technique where options are exercised and at least a portion of the shares are sold in order to facilitate the purchase.

Ceiling limitation that is the maximum amount for adjustments to taxable income (or credits). The amounts in excess of the ceiling are either lost or carried to another tax year.

Certainty one of the criteria used to evaluate tax systems. Certainty means taxpayers should be able to determine when, where, and how much tax to pay.

Certificate of deposit (CD) an interest-bearing debt instrument offered by banks and savings and loans. Money removed from the CD before maturity is subject to a penalty.

Certificate of limited partnership a document limited partnerships must file with the state to be formally recognized by the state. The document is similar to articles of incorporation or articles or organization.

Certificate of organization a document, filed by a limited liability company's founders with certain states, describing the purpose, place of business, and other details of the company.

Character of income a type of income that is treated differently for tax purposes from other types of income. Common income characters (or types of income) include ordinary, capital, and qualified dividend.

Charitable contribution limit modified taxable income taxable income for purposes of determining the 10 percent of taxable income deduction limitation for corporate charitable contributions. Computed as taxable income before deducting (1) any charitable contributions, (2) the dividends-received deduction, and (3) capital loss carrybacks.

Child tax credit a $2,000 tax credit, subject to an AGI phase-out, for each qualifying child who is under age 17 at the end of the year and claimed as a dependent of the taxpayer, and a $500 credit, also subject to the AGI phase-out, for other qualified dependents claimed as dependents of the taxpayer.

Circular 230 regulations issued by the IRS that govern tax practice and apply to all persons practicing before the IRS. There are five parts of Circular 230: Subpart A describes who may practice before the IRS (e.g., CPAs, attorneys, enrolled agents) and what practicing before the IRS means (tax return preparation, representing clients before the IRS, etc.). Subpart B describes the duties and restrictions that apply to individuals governed by Circular 230. Subparts C and D explain sanctions and disciplinary proceedings for practitioners violating the Circular 230 provisions. Subpart E concludes with a few miscellaneous provisions (such as the Circular 230 effective date).

Citator a research tool that allows one to check the status of several types of tax authorities. A citator can be used to review the history of the case to find out, for example, whether it was subsequently appealed and overturned, and to identify subsequent cases that cite the case. Citators can also be used to check the status of revenue rulings, revenue procedures, and other IRS pronouncements.

Civil penalties monetary penalties imposed when tax practitioners or taxpayers violate tax statutes without reasonable cause—for example, as the result of negligence, intentional disregard of pertinent rules, willful disobedience, or outright fraud.

Claim of right doctrine judicial doctrine that states that income has been realized if a taxpayer receives income and there are no restrictions on the taxpayer's use of the income (for example, the taxpayer does not have an obligation to repay the amount).

Cliff vesting a qualified plan provision allowing for benefits to vest all at once after a specified period of time has passed.

Collectibles a type of capital asset that includes a work of art, a rug or antique, a metal or gem, a stamp or coin, an alcoholic beverage, or other similar items held for investment for more than one year.

Commercial domicile the state where a business is headquartered and directs operations; this location may be different from the place of incorporation.

Commercial traveler exception a statutory exception that exempts nonresidents from U.S. taxation of compensation from services if the individual is in the United States 90 days or less and earns compensation of $3,000 or less.

Common-law states the 41 states that have not adopted community property laws.

Community property states nine states (Arizona, California, Idaho, Louisiana, Nevada, New Mexico, Texas, Washington, and Wisconsin) that automatically equally divide the ownership of property acquired by either spouse during a marriage.

Community property systems systems in which state laws dictate how the income and property are legally shared between a husband and a wife.

Complex trust a trust that is not required by the trust instrument to distribute income currently.

Consolidated tax return a combined U.S. income tax return filed by an affiliated group of corporations.

Consolidations the combining of the assets and liabilities of two or more corporations into a new entity.

Constructive ownership rules that cause stock not owned by a taxpayer to be treated as beneficially owned by the taxpayer for purposes of meeting certain stock ownership tests.

Constructive receipt doctrine the judicial doctrine that provides that a taxpayer must recognize income when it is actually or constructively received. Constructive receipt is deemed to have occurred if the income has been credited to the taxpayer's account or if the income is unconditionally available to the taxpayer, the taxpayer is aware of the income's availability, and there are no restrictions on the taxpayer's control over the income.

Continuity of business enterprise (COBE) a judicial (now regulatory) requirement that the acquiring corporation continue the target corporation's historic business or continue to use a "significant" portion of the target corporation's historic business assets to be tax-deferred.

Continuity of interest (COI) a judicial (now regulatory) requirement that the transferors of stock in a reorganization collectively retain a continuing ownership (equity) interest in the target corporation's assets or historic business to be tax-deferred.

Contribution to capital a shareholder's or other person's contribution of cash or other property to a corporation without receipt of an additional equity interest in the corporation.

Controlled foreign corporation (CFC) a foreign corporation that is more than 50 percent owned by U.S. shareholders.

Convenience one of the criteria used to evaluate tax systems. Convenience means a tax system should be designed to facilitate the collection of tax revenues without undue hardship on the taxpayer or the government.

Corporation business entity recognized as a separate entity from its owners under state law.

Corpus the principal or property transferred to fund a trust or accumulated in the trust.

Correspondence examination an IRS audit conducted by mail and generally limited to one or two items on the taxpayer's return. Among the three types of audits, correspondence audits are generally the most common, the most narrow in scope, and the least complex. The IRS typically requests supporting documentation for one or more items on the taxpayer's return (e.g., documentation of charitable contributions deducted).

Cost depletion the method of recovering the cost of a natural resource that allows a taxpayer to estimate or determine the number of units that remain in the resource at the beginning of the year and allocate a pro rata share of the remaining basis to each unit of the resource that is extracted or sold during the year.

Cost recovery the method by which a company expenses the cost of acquiring capital assets. Cost recovery can take the form of depreciation, amortization, or depletion.

Covenants not to compete a contractual promise to refrain from conducting business or professional activities similar to those of another party.

Criminal penalties penalties commonly charged in tax evasion cases (i.e., willful intent to defraud the government). They are imposed only after normal due process, including a trial. Compared to civil cases, the standard of conviction is higher in a criminal trial (beyond a reasonable doubt). However, the penalties are also much higher, such as fines up to $100,000 for individuals plus a prison sentence.

Current earnings and profits a year-to-year calculation maintained by a corporation to determine if a distribution is a dividend. Earnings and profits are computed for the current year by adjusting taxable income to make it more closely resemble economic income.

Current gifts gifts completed during the calendar year that are not already exempted from the gift tax.

Current income tax expense (benefit) the amount of taxes paid or payable (refundable) in the current year.

Current tax liability (asset) the amount of taxes payable (refundable) in the current year.

D

***De minimis* fringe benefits** a nontaxable fringe benefit that allows employees to receive occasional or incidental benefits tax-free.

Debt basis the outstanding principal of direct loans from an S corporation shareholder to the S corporation. Once taxpayers deduct losses to the extent of their stock basis, they may deduct losses to the extent of their debt basis. When the debt basis has been reduced by losses, it is restored by income/gain allocations.

Deceased spousal unused exclusion (DSUE) amount of unused applicable credit from predeceased spouse.

Deductible temporary differences book–tax differences that will result in tax deductible amounts in future years when the related deferred tax asset is recovered.

Deduction for qualified business income subject to limitations, equal to 20 percent of the taxpayer's qualified business income.

Deductions amounts that are subtracted from gross income in calculating taxable income.

Deductions above the line for AGI deductions or deductions subtracted from gross income to determine AGI.

Deductions below the line from AGI deductions or deductions subtracted from AGI to calculate taxable income.

Deferral items, deferred income, or deferrals realized income that will be taxed as income in a subsequent year.

Deferred like-kind exchange a like-kind exchange where the taxpayer transfers like-kind property before receiving the like-kind property in exchange. The property to be received must be identified within 45 days and received within 180 days of the transfer of the property given up.

Deferred tax asset the expected future tax benefit attributable to deductible temporary differences and carryforwards.

Deferred tax liability the expected future tax cost attributable to taxable temporary differences.

Defined benefit plans employer-provided qualified plans that spell out the specific benefit employees will receive on retirement.

Defined contribution plans employer-provided qualified plans that specify the maximum annual contributions employers and/or employees may contribute to the plan.

Definitely related deductions deductions that are associated with the creation of a specific item or items of gross income.

Depletion the cost recovery method to allocate the cost of natural resources as they are removed.

Depreciation the cost recovery method to allocate the cost of tangible personal and real property over a specific time period.

Depreciation recapture the conversion of §1231 gain into ordinary income on a sale (or exchange) based on the amount of accumulated depreciation on the property at the time of sale or exchange.

Determination letters rulings requested by the taxpayer, issued by local IRS directors, and generally not controversial. An example of a determination letter is the request by an employer for the IRS to rule that the taxpayer's retirement plan is a "qualified plan."

DIF (Discriminant Function) system the DIF system assigns a score to each tax return that represents the probability that the tax liability on the return has been underreported (a higher score = a higher likelihood of underreporting). The IRS derives the weights assigned to specific tax return attributes from historical IRS audit adjustment data from the National Research Program. The DIF system then uses these (undisclosed) weights to score each tax return based on the tax return's characteristics. Returns with higher DIF scores are then reviewed to determine if an audit is the best course of action.

Direct conversions when a taxpayer receives noncash property rather than a cash payment as a replacement for property damaged or destroyed in an involuntary conversion.

Direct write-off method required method for deducting bad debts for tax purposes. Under this method, businesses deduct bad debt only when the debt becomes wholly or partially worthless.

Disability insurance sometimes called sick pay or wage replacement insurance. It pays the insured for wages lost due to injury or disability.

Discharge of indebtedness debt forgiveness.

Discount factor the factor based on the taxpayer's rate of return that is used to determine the present value of future cash inflows (e.g., tax savings) and outflows (taxes paid).

Disproportionate distributions partnership distributions that change the partners' relative ownership of hot assets.

Disqualifying disposition the sale of stock acquired using incentive stock options prior to satisfying certain holding period requirements. Failing to satisfy the holding period requirements converts the options into nonqualified stock options.

Disregarded entities unincorporated entity with one owner that is considered to be the same entity as the owner.

Disregarded entities (international tax) entities with one owner that are treated as flow-through entities for U.S. income tax purposes.

Distributable net income (DNI) the maximum amount of the distribution deduction by fiduciaries and the maximum aggregate amount of gross income reportable by beneficiaries.

Distribution deduction deduction by fiduciaries for distributions of income to beneficiaries that operates to eliminate the potential for double taxation of fiduciary income.

Dividend a distribution to shareholders of money or property from the corporation's earnings and profits.

Dividends-received deduction (DRD) a corporate deduction for part or all of a dividend received from another corporation.

Document perfection program a program under which all tax returns are checked for mathematical and tax calculation errors.

Donee person receiving a gift.

Donor person making a gift.

Double taxation the tax burden when an entity's income is subject to two levels of tax. Income of C corporations is subject to double taxation. The first level of tax is at the corporate level, and the second level of tax on corporate income occurs at the shareholder level.

DRD modified taxable income taxable income for purposes of applying the taxable income limitation for the dividends-received deduction. Computed as the dividend-receiving corporation's taxable income before deducting the dividends-received deduction, the net operating loss deduction, and capital loss carrybacks.

Dwelling unit property that provides a place suitable for people to occupy (live and sleep).

Dynamic forecasting the process of forecasting tax revenues that incorporates into the forecast how taxpayers may alter their activities in response to a tax law change.

E

Earmarked tax a tax assessed for a specific purpose (e.g., for education).

Earned income compensation and other forms of income received for providing goods or services in the ordinary course of business.

Earned income credit a refundable credit designed to help offset the effect of employment taxes on compensation paid to low-income taxpayers and to encourage lower-income taxpayers to seek employment.

Earnings and profits (E&P) a measure of a corporation's earnings that is similar to its economic earnings. Corporate dividends are taxable to shareholders to the extent they come from earnings and profits.

Economic income tax nexus the concept that businesses without a physical presence in the state may establish income tax nexus in the state through an economic presence there.

Economic performance test the requirement that must be met for an accrual method taxpayer to deduct an expense currently. The specific event that satisfies the economic performance test varies based on the type of expense.

Economic substance doctrine judicially based doctrine that requires transactions to meaningfully change a taxpayer's economic position *and* have a substantial purpose (apart from a federal income tax purpose) in order for a taxpayer to obtain tax benefits.

Economy one of the criteria used to evaluate tax systems. Economy means a tax system should minimize its compliance and administration costs.

Educational assistance benefits a nontaxable fringe benefit that allows an employer to provide a certain amount of education benefits on an annual basis.

Effective tax rate the taxpayer's average rate of taxation on each dollar of total income (taxable and nontaxable income). Specifically,

$$\text{Effective tax rate} = \frac{\text{Total tax}}{\text{Total income}}$$

Also (for income tax footnote purposes), the tax rate computed by dividing a company's income tax provision (expense or benefit) for the year by its pretax income from continuing operations.

Effectively connected income (ECI) net income that results from the conduct of a U.S. trade or business by a nonresident.

Employee a person who is hired to provide services to a company on a regular basis in exchange for compensation and who does not provide these services as part of an independent business.

Employment taxes taxes consisting of the Old Age, Survivors, and Disability Insurance (OASDI) tax, commonly called the Social Security tax, and the Medical Health Insurance (MHI) tax, known as the Medicare tax.

Enacted tax rate the statutory tax rate that will apply in the current or a future period.

Entity approach a theory of taxing partnerships that treats partnerships as entities separate from partners.

Equity one of the criteria used to evaluate a tax system. A tax system is considered fair or equitable if the tax is based on the taxpayer's ability to pay; taxpayers with a greater ability to pay tax pay more tax.

Escrow account (mortgage-related) a holding account with a taxpayer's mortgage lender. The taxpayer makes mortgage payments to the lender that include payment for the interest and principal and payments for property taxes. The lender maintains the payments for property taxes in the escrow account and uses the funds in the account to pay the property taxes when the taxes are due.

Estate fiduciary legal entity that comes into existence upon a person's death and is empowered by the probate court to gather and transfer the decedent's real and personal property.

Estimated tax payments quarterly tax payments that a taxpayer makes to the government if the tax withholding is insufficient to meet the taxpayer's tax liability.

Ex-dividend date the relevant date for determining who receives a dividend from a stock. Anyone purchasing stock before this date will receive current dividends. Otherwise, the purchaser must wait until subsequent dividends are declared before receiving them.

Excess business loss excess of aggregate business deductions for the year over aggregate business gross income or gain of an individual taxpayer plus a threshold amount depending on filing status.

Excess net passive income net passive investment income × passive investment income in excess of 25 percent of the S corporation's gross receipts divided by its passive investment income.

Excess net passive income tax a tax levied on an S corporation that has accumulated earnings and profits from years in which it operated as a C corporation if the corporation reports excess net passive income.

Exchange traded funds (ETF) diversified portfolios of securities owned and managed by a regulated investment company similar to mutual funds except they are traded on exchanges and the shares trade throughout the day like ordinary stock listings.

Excise taxes taxes levied on the retail sale of particular products. They differ from other taxes in that the tax base for an excise tax typically depends on the *quantity* purchased rather than a monetary amount.

Exclusions or excluded income realized income that is exempted from income taxation.

Executor the person who takes responsibility for collecting the assets of the decedent, paying the decedent's debts, and distributing the remaining assets to the rightful heirs.

Exemption equivalent the amount of cumulative taxable transfers a taxpayer can make without exceeding the applicable credit.

Exercise date the date employees use their stock options to acquire employer stock at a discounted price.

Exercise price the price at which holders of stock options may purchase stock in the corporation issuing the option.

Explicit taxes taxes directly imposed by a government.

F

Face value a specified final amount paid to the owner of a coupon bond on the date of maturity. The face value is also known as the *maturity value*.

Facts and circumstances test a test used to make a subjective determination such as whether the amount of salary paid to an employee is reasonable. The test requires the taxpayer and the IRS to consider all the relevant facts and circumstances surrounding the situation in order to make a decision. The relevant facts and circumstances are situation-specific.

Family limited partnership a partnership designed to save estate taxes by dividing a family business into various ownership interests representing control of operations and future income and appreciation of the assets.

Favorable book–tax difference a book–tax difference that requires a subtraction from book income in determining taxable income.

Federal short-term interest rate the quarterly interest rate used to determine the interest charged for tax underpayments (federal short-term rate plus 3 percent).

Federal/state adjustments amounts added to or subtracted from federal taxable income when firms compute taxable income for a particular state.

FICA taxes FICA (Federal Insurance Contributions Act) taxes is a term used to denote both the Social Security and Medicare taxes upon earned income. For self-employed taxpayers, the terms "FICA tax" and "self-employment tax" are synonymous.

Fiduciary a person or legal entity that takes possession of property for the benefit of beneficiaries.

Fiduciary duty a requirement that a fiduciary act in an objective and impartial manner and not favor one beneficiary over another.

Field examinations the least common audit. The IRS conducts these audits at the taxpayer's place of business or the location where the taxpayer's books, records, and source documents are maintained. Field examinations are generally the broadest in scope and most complex of the three audit types. They can last many months to multiple years and generally are limited to business returns and the most complex individual returns.

Filing status filing status places taxpayers into one of five categories (married filing jointly, married filing separately, qualifying widow or widower, head of household, and single) by marital status and family situation as of the end of the year. Filing status determines whether a taxpayer must file a tax return, appropriate tax rate schedules, standard deduction amounts, and certain deduction and credit limitation thresholds.

Final regulations regulations that have been issued in final form, and, thus, until revoked, they represent the Treasury's interpretation of the Code.

First-in, first-out (FIFO) method an accounting method that values the cost of assets sold under the assumption that the assets are sold in the same order in which they are purchased (i.e., first purchased, first sold).

Fiscal year a year that ends on the last day of a month other than December.

Fixed and determinable, annual or periodic (FDAP) income U.S. source passive income earned by a nonresident.

Flat tax a tax in which a single tax rate is applied throughout the tax base.

Flexible spending accounts (FSA) a plan that allows employees to contribute before-tax dollars that may be used for unreimbursed medical expenses or dependent care.

Flipping a term used to describe the real estate investment practice of acquiring a home, repairing or remodeling the home, and then immediately, or soon thereafter, selling it (presumably at a profit).

Floor limitation a minimum amount that an expenditure (or credit or other adjustment to taxable income) must meet before any amount is allowed.

Flow-through entities legal entities, like partnerships, limited liability companies, and S corporations, that do not pay income tax. Income and losses from flow-through entities are allocated to their owners.

For AGI deductions deductions that are subtracted from gross income to determine AGI.

For the convenience of the employer benefits nontaxable benefits employers provide to employees and employee spouses or dependents in the form of meals or lodging if provided on the employer's premises and provided for a purpose that is helpful or convenient for the employer.

Foreign base company income the sum of CFC's foreign personal holding company income, foreign base company sales income, and foreign base company services income.

Foreign base company sales income gross profit from the sale of personal property by (to) a U.S. corporation to (from) a CFC, where the product was manufactured outside the country of incorporation of the CFC and resold outside the country of incorporation of the CFC.

foreign branch an unincorporated division of a U.S. corporation located outside the United States.

Foreign personal holding company income a category of foreign source passive income that includes interest, dividends, rents, royalties, and gains from the sale of certain foreign property.

Foreign tax credit (FTC) a credit for income taxes paid to a foreign jurisdiction.

Foreign tax credit limitation the limit put on the use of creditable foreign taxes for the current year.

Foreign-derived intangible income (FDII) net income from certain export sales, services, and licensing of intangibles that is eligible for a 37.5 percent deduction by U.S. corporations.

Form 1065 the form partnerships file annually with the IRS to report partnership ordinary income (loss) and separately stated items for the year.

Form 1098 the form used by taxpayers to report the annual amount of interest and related expenses paid on a mortgage when the amount paid totals $600 or more.

Form 1120-S the form S corporations file annually with the IRS to report S corporation ordinary income (loss) and separately stated items for the year.

Form 2553 the form filed to elect S corporation status.

Form 7004 the form C corporations, partnerships, and S corporations file to receive an automatic extension to file their annual tax return.

Form W-2 a form filed by the employer for each employee detailing the income, Social Security, and Medicare wages and taxes withheld. Additionally, state income, state taxes withheld, dependent care benefits, and many other tax-related items are reported.

Form W-4 a form used by a taxpayer to supply their employer with the information necessary to determine the amount of tax to withhold from each paycheck.

Fringe benefits noncash benefits provided to an employee as a form of compensation. As a general rule, fringe benefits are taxable. However, certain fringe benefits are excluded from gross income.

From AGI deductions deductions subtracted from AGI to calculate taxable income.

FTC basket a category of income that requires a separate FTC limitation computation.

Full-month convention a convention that allows owners of intangibles to deduct an entire month's amortization in the month of purchase and month of disposition.

Future interest the right to receive property in the future.

GAAP capital accounts partners' capital accounts maintained using generally accepted accounting principles (GAAP).

General category income foreign source income that is not considered passive category income for foreign tax credit purposes (generally income from an active trade or business).

General partnership (GP) a partnership with partners who all have unlimited liability with respect to the liabilities of the entity.

Generation-skipping tax (GST) supplemental transfer tax designed to prevent the avoidance of estate and gift taxes through transfers that skip a generation of recipients.

Gift a transfer of property where no, or inadequate, consideration is paid for the property.

Gift tax the tax paid on a gift.

Global intangible low-taxed income (GILTI) a new category of income added by the Tax Cuts and Jobs Act that relates to "high return" income earned by a U.S. corporation's CFC and subject to a low foreign tax rate.

***Golsen* rule** the rule that states that the U.S. Tax Court will abide by the rulings of the circuit court that has appellate jurisdiction for a case.

Graded vesting a qualified plan rule that requires an increasing percentage of plan benefits to vest with each additional year of employment.

Graduated taxes taxes in which the tax base is divided into a series of monetary amounts, or brackets, where each successive bracket is taxed at a different (gradually higher or gradually lower) percentage rate.

Grant date the date on which employees receive stock options to acquire employer stock at a specified price.

Grantor person creating a trust.

Gross estate property owned by the decedent at death and certain property transfers taking effect at death.

Gross income realized income minus excluded and deferred income.

Gross receipts (for S corporations) the total amount of revenues (including passive investment income) received or accrued under the corporation's accounting method, not reduced by returns, allowances, cost of goods sold, or deductions. Gross receipts include net capital gains from the sales or exchanges of capital assets and gains from the sale or exchange of stock or securities (losses do not offset gains).

Gross receipts test determines if a business qualifies as a "small" business under an annual gross receipts test if its average annual gross receipts for the three prior taxable years does not exceed an indexed threshold set at $27 million for 2022. For purposes of the test, includes total sales (net of returns and allowances but not cost of goods sold), amounts received for services, and income from investments (including tax-exempt interest).

Group-term life insurance term life insurance provided by an employer to a group of employees.

Guaranteed payments payments made to partners or LLC members that are guaranteed because they are not contingent on partnership profits or losses. They are economically similar to shareholder salary payments.

H

Half-year convention a depreciation convention that allows owners of tangible personal property to take one-half of a year's worth of depreciation in the year of purchase and in the year of disposition regardless of when the asset was actually placed in service or sold.

Head of household one of five primary filing statuses. A taxpayer may file as head of household if they are unmarried as of the end of the year *and* pays more than half of the cost to maintain a household for a qualifying person who lives with the taxpayer for more than half of the year; or they pay more than half the costs to maintain a household for a parent who qualifies as the taxpayer's dependent.

Health and accident insurance fringe benefits often offered through employers, including health insurance, group-term life insurance, and accidental death and dismemberment policies.

Health savings accounts accounts that allow individuals covered by a high-deductible plan to set aside amounts to pay for qualified medical and dental expenses for the taxpayer, spouse, and dependents.

Heirs persons who inherit property from the deceased.

Home office deductions deductions relating to the use of an office in the home. A taxpayer must meet strict requirements to qualify for the deduction.

Horizontal equity one of the dimensions of equity. Horizontal equity is achieved if taxpayers in similar situations pay the same tax.

Hot assets unrealized receivables or inventory items defined in §751(a) that give rise to ordinary gains and losses. The exact definition of hot assets depends on whether it is in reference to dispositions of a partnership interest or distributions.

Hybrid entity an entity for which an election is available to choose the entity's tax status for U.S. tax purposes.

I

Impermissible accounting method an accounting method prohibited by tax laws.

Implicit taxes indirect taxes that result from a tax advantage the government grants to certain transactions to satisfy social, economic, or other objectives. They are defined as the reduced before-tax return that a tax-favored asset produces because of its tax-advantaged status.

Imputed income income from an economic benefit the taxpayer receives indirectly rather than directly. The amount of the income is based on comparable alternatives.

Inbound transaction a transaction conducted by a foreign person that is subject to U.S. taxation.

Incentive stock options (ISO) a type of stock option that allows employees to defer the bargain element for regular tax purposes until the stock acquired from option exercises is sold. The bargain element is taxed at capital gains rates provided the stock is retained long enough to satisfy certain holding period requirements. Employers cannot deduct the bargain element as compensation expense.

Income effect one of the two basic responses that a taxpayer may have when taxes increase. The income effect predicts that when taxpayers are taxed more (e.g., tax rate increases from 25 to 28 percent), they will work harder to generate the same after-tax dollars.

Income tax a tax in which the tax base is income. Income taxes are imposed by the federal government and by most states.

Income tax nexus the connection between a business and a tax jurisdiction sufficient to subject the business to the tax jurisdiction's income tax.

Income tax provision refers to the income tax expense or (benefit) reported on a company's financial statement and is composed of the current income tax expense or (benefit) and the deferred income tax expense or (benefit). These components may also be referred to as the current income tax provision and the deferred tax provision, respectively.

Independent contractor a person who provides services to another entity, usually under terms specified in a contract. The independent contractor has more control over how and when to do the work than does an employee.

Indirect conversions receipt of money or other property as a replacement for property that was destroyed or damaged in an involuntary conversion.

Individual retirement account (IRA) a tax-advantaged account in which individuals who have earned income can save for retirement.

Information matching program a program that compares the taxpayer's tax return to information submitted to the IRS from other taxpayers (e.g., banks, employers, mutual funds, brokerage companies, mortgage companies). Information matched includes items such as wages (e.g., Form W-2 submitted by employers), interest income (e.g., Form 1099-INT submitted by banks), dividend income (e.g., Form 1099-DIV submitted by brokerage companies), and so forth.

Inheritance a transfer of property when the owner is deceased (the transfer is made by the decedent's estate).

Initial public offering (IPO) the first sale of stock by a company to the public.

Inside basis the tax basis of an entity's assets and liabilities.

Installment sales sales for which taxpayers receive payment in more than one period.

Institutional shareholder an entity such as an investment company, mutual fund, brokerage, insurance company, pension fund, investment bank, and endowment fund, with large amounts to invest in corporate stock.

Intangible assets assets that do not have physical characteristics. Examples include goodwill, covenants not to compete, organizational expenditures, and research and experimentation expenses.

Inter vivos transfers gifts made by a donor during their lifetime.

Internal Revenue Code of 1986 the codified tax laws of the United States. Although the Code is frequently revised, there have been only three different codes since the Code was created in 1939 (i.e., the IRC of 1939, IRC of 1954, and IRC of 1986).

Interpretative regulations the most common regulations; they represent the Treasury's interpretation of the Code and are issued under the Treasury's general authority to interpret the Code.

Interstate commerce business conducted between parties in two or more states.

Inventory items (for sale of partnership interest purposes) classic inventory defined as property held for sale to customers in the ordinary course of business, but also assets that are not capital assets or §1231 assets, which would produce ordinary income if sold by the entity. There are actually two definitions of inventory items in §751. The §751(a) inventory items are defined in §751(d) to include all inventory items. The §751(b) definition includes only substantially appreciated inventory.

Investment activity a profit-seeking activity that is intermittent or occasional in frequency, including the production or collection of income or the management, conservation, or maintenance of property held for the production of income.

Investment income income received from portfolio-type investments. Portfolio income includes capital gains and losses, interest, dividend, annuity, and royalty income not derived in the ordinary course of a trade or business. When computing the deductibility of investment interest expense, however, capital gains and dividends subject to the preferential tax rate are not treated as investment income unless the taxpayer elects to have this income taxed at ordinary tax rates.

Investment interest expense interest paid on borrowings or loans that are used to fund portfolio investments. Individuals are allowed an itemized deduction for qualified investment interest paid during the year.

Involuntary conversions direct or indirect conversions of property through natural disaster, government condemnation, or accident that allows a taxpayer to defer realized gain if certain requirements are met.

IRS allocation method allocates expenses associated with rental use of the home between rental use and personal use. The percentage of total expenses allocated to rental use is the ratio of the number of rental use days for the property to the total days the property was used during the year.

Itemized deductions certain types of expenditures that Congress allows taxpayers to deduct as from AGI deductions.

J

Joint tenancy joint ownership of property by two or more people.

Joint tenancy with right of survivorship title to property that provides the co-owners with equal rights to it and that automatically transfers to the survivor(s) at the death of a co-owner.

K

Kiddie tax a tax imposed at parents' marginal tax rate on a child's unearned income.

L

Last will and testament the document that directs the transfer of ownership of the decedent's assets to the heirs.

Last-in, first-out (LIFO) method an accounting method that values the cost of assets sold under the assumption that assets are sold in the reverse order in which they are purchased (i.e., last purchased, first sold).

Late filing penalty a penalty assessed if a taxpayer does not file a tax return by the required date (the original due date plus extension).

Late payment penalty a tax penalty equal to .5 percent of the amount of tax owed for each month (or fraction thereof) that the tax is not paid.

Least aggregate deferral an approach to determine a partnership's required year-end if a majority of the partners don't have the same year-end and if the principal partners don't have the same year-end. As the name implies, this approach minimizes the combined tax deferral of the partners.

Legislative grace the concept that taxpayers receive certain tax benefits only because Congress writes laws that allow taxpayers to receive the tax benefits.

Legislative regulations the rarest type of regulation, issued when Congress specifically directs the Treasury Department to create regulations to address an issue in an area of law. In these instances, the Treasury is actually writing the law instead of interpreting the Code. Because legislative regulations actually represent tax law instead of an interpretation of tax law, legislative regulations have more authoritative weight than interpretative and procedural regulations.

Life estate the right to possess property and/or collect income from property for the duration of someone's life.

Life insurance trust a trust that is funded with an irrevocable transfer of a life insurance policy and that gives the trustee the power to redesignate beneficiaries.

LIFO recapture amount the excess of a C corporation's inventory basis under the FIFO method in excess of the inventory basis under the LIFO method in its final tax year as a C corporation before it becomes an S corporation.

LIFO recapture tax a tax levied on a C corporation that elects to be taxed as an S corporation when it is using the LIFO method for accounting for inventories.

Like-kind exchange a nontaxable (or partially taxable) trade or exchange of assets that are similar or related in use.

Limited liability company (LLC) a type of flow-through entity for federal income tax purposes. By state law, the owners of the LLC have limited liability with respect to the entity's debts or liabilities. Limited liability companies are generally taxed as partnerships for federal income tax purposes.

Limited partnership (LP) a partnership with at least one general partner with unlimited liability for the entity's debts and at least one limited partner with liability limited to the limited partner's investment in the partnership.

Liquidating distribution a distribution that terminates an owner's interest in the entity.

Liquidation value the amount a partner would receive if the partnership were to sell all its assets, pay its debts, and distribute its remaining assets to the partners in exchange for their partnership interests.

Listed property business assets that are often used for personal purposes. Depreciation on listed property is limited to the business-use portion of the asset.

Local taxes taxes imposed by local governments (cities, counties, school districts, etc.).

Long-term capital gains or losses gains or losses from the sale of capital assets held for more than 12 months.

Luxury automobiles automobiles on which the amount of annual depreciation expense is limited because the cost of the automobile exceeds a certain threshold. The definition excludes vehicles with gross vehicle weight exceeding 6,000 pounds.

M

M adjustments book–tax differences that corporations report on the Schedule M-1 or M-3 of Form 1120 as adjustments to book income to reconcile to taxable income.

Majority interest taxable year the common tax year of a group of partners who jointly hold greater than 50 percent of the profits and capital interests in the partnership.

Marginal tax rate the tax rate that applies to the *next additional increment* of a taxpayer's taxable income (or to deductions). Specifically,

$$\text{Marginal tax rate} = \frac{\Delta \text{ Tax}}{\Delta \text{ Taxable income}}$$

$$= \frac{(\text{New total tax} - \text{Old total tax})}{(\text{New taxable income} - \text{Old taxable income})}$$

where "old" refers to the current tax and "new" refers to the revised tax after incorporating the additional income (or deductions) in question.

Marital deduction the deduction for transfers of qualified property to a spouse.

Market discount the difference between the amount paid for a bond in a market purchase rather than at original issuance when the amount paid is less than the maturity value of the bond.

Market premium the difference between the amount paid for a bond in a market purchase rather than at original issuance when the amount paid is greater than the maturity value of the bond.

Marriage benefit the tax savings married couples receive by filing a joint return relative to the tax they would have paid had they each filed as single taxpayers. This typically occurs when one spouse is either not working or earns significantly less than the other spouse.

Marriage penalty the extra tax cost a married couple pays by filing a joint return relative to what they would have paid had they each filed as single taxpayers. This typically occurs when both spouses earn approximately the same amount of income.

Married filing jointly one of five primary filing statuses. A taxpayer may file jointly if they are legally married as of the end of the year (or one spouse died during the year and the surviving spouse did not remarry) and both spouses agree to jointly file. Married couples filing joint returns combine their income and deductions and share joint and several liability for the resulting tax.

Married filing separately one of five primary filing statuses. When married couples file separately, each spouse reports the income they received during the year and the deductions they paid on a tax return separate from the other spouse.

Maturity the amount of time to the expiration date, or maturity date, of a debt instrument. The maturity of a debt instrument is generally the life of the instrument, at which point a payment of the face value is due or the instrument terminates.

Maturity value the amount paid to a bondholder when the bond matures and the bondholder redeems the bond for cash.

Maximum 15 percent rate amount threshold for the 15 percent rate to apply to long-term capital gains. Any 0/15/20 percent capital gains included that result in taxable income above the maximum zero rate amount and up to the maximum 15 percent rate amount are taxed at 15 percent. The threshold is based on a taxpayer's filing status and income.

Maximum zero percent rate amount threshold for the zero percent rate to apply to long-term capital gains. Any 0/15/20 percent capital gains included in taxable income up to the maximum zero percent amount are taxed at 0 percent. It is based on a taxpayer's filing status and income level.

Medicare tax the Medical Health Insurance (MHI) tax. This tax helps pay medical costs for qualifying individuals. The Medicare tax rate for employees and employers is 1.45 percent on salary or wages. An additional Medicare tax of .9 percent is assessed on employees (not employers) on salary or wages in excess of $200,000 ($125,000 for married filing separate; $250,000 of combined salary or wages for married filing joint). Self-employed taxpayers pay both the employee and employer Medicare tax and additional Medicare tax.

Mergers the acquisition by one (acquiring) corporation of the assets and liabilities of another (target) corporation. No new entity is created in the transaction.

Mid-month convention a convention that allows owners of real property to take one-half of a month's depreciation during the month when the property was placed in service and in the month it was disposed of.

Mid-quarter convention a depreciation convention for tangible personal property that allows for one-half of a quarter's worth of depreciation in the quarter of purchase and in the quarter of disposition. This convention must be used when more than 40 percent of tangible personal property is placed into service in the fourth quarter of the tax year.

Minimum tax credit credit available in certain situations for the alternative minimum tax paid. The credit can be used only when the regular tax exceeds the tentative minimum tax.

Mixed-motive expenditures activities that involve a mixture of business and personal objectives.

Modified Accelerated Cost Recovery System (MACRS) the current tax depreciation system for tangible personal and real property. Depreciation under MACRS is calculated by finding the depreciation method, the recovery period, and the applicable convention.

Municipal bonds the common name for state and local government debt.

Mutual fund a diversified portfolio of securities owned and managed by a regulated investment company.

N

Negative basis adjustment (for special basis adjustment purposes) the sum of the recognized loss and the amount of the basis increase made by an owner receiving the distribution.

Net capital gain the excess of net long-term capital gain for the taxable year over net short-term capital loss for such year.

Net capital loss carryback the amount of a corporation's net capital loss from one year that it uses to offset net capital gains in any of the three preceding tax years.

Net capital loss carryover the amount of a corporation's or an individual's net capital loss from one year that it may use to offset net capital gains in future years.

Net earnings from self-employment the amount of earnings subject to self-employment income taxes. The amount is 92.35 percent of a taxpayer's self-employment income.

Net investment income (for determining deductibility of investment interest expense) gross investment income reduced by deductible investment expenses.

Net investment income tax a 3.8 percent tax on the lesser of (a) net investment income or (b) the excess of modified adjusted gross income over $250,000 for married-joint filers and surviving spouses, $125,000 for married-separate filers, and $200,000 for other taxpayers.

Net long-term capital gain the excess of long-term capital gains for the taxable year over the long-term capital losses for such year.

Net long-term capital loss the excess of long-term capital losses for the taxable year over the long-term capital gains for such year.

Net operating loss (NOL) the excess of allowable deductions over gross income.

Net operating loss carryback the amount of a pre-2018 net operating loss that a corporation elects to carry back to the two previous years to offset taxable income in those years.

Net operating loss carryover the amount of a current-year net operating loss that is carried forward for up to 20 years to offset taxable income in those years (20 years for pre-2018 losses; unlimited for post-2017 losses).

Net passive investment income passive investment income less any expenses connected with producing it.

Net short-term capital gain the excess of short-term capital gains for the taxable year over the short-term capital losses for such year.

Net short-term capital loss the excess of short-term capital losses for the taxable year over the short-term capital gains for such year.

Net unearned income unearned income in excess of a specified threshold amount of a child under the age of 19 or under the age of 24 if a full-time student.

Net unrealized built-in gain the net gain (if any) an S corporation that was formerly a C corporation would recognize if it sold each asset at its fair market value. It is measured on the first day of the corporation's first year as an S corporation.

Nexus the connection between a business and a tax jurisdiction sufficient to subject the business to the tax jurisdiction's tax system. Also, the connection that is required to exist between a jurisdiction and a potential taxpayer such that the jurisdiction asserts the right to impose a tax.

No-additional-cost services a nontaxable fringe benefit that provides employer services to employees with little cost to the employer (e.g., airline tickets or phone service).

Nonacquiescence issued after the IRS loses a trial-level or circuit court case when the IRS has decided to continue to litigate this issue.

Nonbusiness income all income except for business income—generally, investment income and rental income.

Nondeductible terminable interests transfers of property interests to a spouse that do not qualify for a marital deduction because the interest of the spouse terminates when some event occurs or after a specified amount of time and the property is then transferred to another person.

Nondomiciliary business a business operating in a state other than its commercial domicile.

Nonqualified deferred compensation compensation provided for under a nonqualified plan allowing employees to defer compensation to a future period.

Nonqualified stock options (NQO) a type of stock option requiring employees to treat the bargain element from options exercised as ordinary income in the tax year options are exercised. Correspondingly, employers may deduct the bargain element as compensation expense in the tax year options are exercised.

Nonrecaptured net §1231 loss a net §1231 loss that is deducted as an ordinary loss in one year and has not caused subsequent §1231 gain to be taxed as ordinary income.

Nonrecognition provisions tax laws that allow taxpayers to permanently exclude income from taxation or to defer recognizing realized income until a subsequent period.

Nonrecourse debt debt for which no partner bears any economic risk of loss. Mortgages on real property are a common form of nonrecourse debt.

Nonrefundable credits tax credits that reduce a taxpayer's gross tax liability but are limited to the amount of gross tax liability. Any credit not used in the current year is lost.

Nonresident alien a non-U.S. citizen who does not meet the criteria to be treated as a resident for U.S. tax purposes.

Nonservice partner a partner who receives a partnership interest in exchange for property rather than services.

Nontaxable fringe benefits an employer-provided benefit that may be excluded from an employee's income.

Not definitely related deductions deductions that are not associated with a specific item or items of gross income in computing the foreign tax credit limitation.

O

Office examinations the second most common audit. As the name suggests, the IRS conducts these audits at the local IRS office. These audits are typically broader in scope and more complex than correspondence examinations. Small businesses, taxpayers operating sole proprietorships, and middle- to high-income individual taxpayers are more likely, if audited, to have office examinations.

Operating distributions payments from an entity to its owners that represent a distribution of entity profits. Distributions generally fall into the category of operating distributions when the owners continue their interests in the entity after the distribution.

Operating income the annual income from a trade or business or rental activity.

Operating loss the annual loss from a trade or business or rental activity.

Option exercise the use of a stock option to acquire employer stock at a specified price.

Ordinary and necessary an expense that is normal or appropriate and that is helpful or conducive to the business activity.

Ordinary asset an asset created or used in a taxpayer's trade or business (e.g., accounts receivable or inventory) that generates ordinary income (or loss) on disposition.

Ordinary business income (loss) a partnership's or S corporation's remaining income or loss after separately stated items are removed. It is also referred to as nonseparately stated income (loss).

Ordinary income property property that if sold would generate income taxed at ordinary rates.

Organizational expenditures expenses that are (1) connected directly to the creation of a corporation or partnership, (2) chargeable to a capital account, and (3) generally amortized over 180 months (limited immediate expensing may be available).

Original issue discount (OID) a type of bond issued for less than the maturity or face value of the bond.

Outbound transaction a transaction conducted outside the United States by a U.S. person that is subject to U.S. taxation.

Outside basis an investor's tax basis in the stock of a corporation or the interest in a partnership or LLC.

P

Partial liquidation a distribution made by a corporation to shareholders that results from a contraction of the corporation's activities.

Partnership agreement an agreement among the partners in a partnership stipulating the partners' rights and responsibilities in the partnership.

Partnership interest an intangible asset reflecting the economic rights a partner has with respect to a partnership, including the right to receive assets in liquidation of the partnership (called a *capital interest*) and the right to be allocated profits and losses (called a *profits interest*).

Passive activity loss (PAL) rules tax rules designed to limit taxpayers' ability to deduct losses from activities in which they don't materially participate against income from other sources.

Passive category income foreign source personal holding company income, such as interest, dividends, rents, royalties, annuities, and gains from sale of certain assets, that is combined in computing the FTC limitation.

Passive investment income (PII) royalties, rents, dividends, interest (including tax-exempt interest), annuities, and gains from the sale or exchange of stock or securities.

Passive investments direct or indirect investments (other than through a C corporation) in a trade or business or rental activity in which the taxpayer does not materially participate.

Payment liabilities liabilities of accrual method businesses for which economic performance occurs when the business actually *pays* the liability for, among others, workers' compensation; tort; breach of contract or violation of law; rebates and refunds; awards, prizes, and jackpots; insurance, warranties, and service contracts provided *to* the business; and taxes.

Percentage depletion a method of recovering the cost of a natural resource that allows a taxpayer to recover or expense an amount based on a statutorily determined percentage.

Permanent book–tax differences items of income or deductions for either book purposes or tax purposes during the year but not both. Permanent differences do not reverse over time, so over the long run, the total amount of income or deduction for the item is different for book and tax purposes.

Permanent establishment generally, a fixed place of business through which an enterprise carries out its business. Examples include a place of management, a branch, an office, and a factory.

Permissible accounting method accounting method allowed under the tax law. Permissible accounting methods are adopted the first time a taxpayer uses the method on a tax return.

Person an individual, trust, estate, partnership, association, company, or corporation.

Personal expenses expenses incurred for personal motives. Personal expenses are not deductible for tax purposes.

Personal holding companies closely held corporations generating primarily investment income.

Personal holding company tax penalty tax on the undistributed income of a personal holding company.

Personal property all tangible property other than real property.

Personal property taxes a tax on the fair market value of all types of tangible and intangible property, except real property.

Point one percent of the principal amount of a loan. A home buyer might pay points to compensate the lender for services or for a lower interest rate.

Portfolio investments investments producing dividends, interest, royalties, annuities, or capital gains.

Positive basis adjustment (for special basis adjustment purposes) the sum of the gain recognized by the owners receiving distributed property and the amount of any required basis reduction.

Post-termination transition period (PTTP) the period that begins on the day after the last day of a corporation's last taxable year as an S corporation and generally ends on the later of (a) one year after the last S corporation day or (b) the due date for filing the return for the last year as an S corporation (including extensions).

Preferential tax rate a tax rate that is lower than the tax rate applied to ordinary income.

Present interest right to presently enjoy property or receive income from the property.

Present value the concept that $1 today is worth more than $1 in the future. For example, assuming an investor can earn a 5 percent after-tax return, $1 invested today should be worth $1.05 in one year. Hence, $1 today is equivalent to $1.05 in one year.

Primary authorities official sources of the tax law generated by the legislative branch (i.e., statutory authority issued by Congress), judicial branch (i.e., rulings by the U.S. district courts, U.S. Tax Court, U.S. Court of Federal Claims, U.S. circuit courts of appeals, or U.S. Supreme Court), or executive/administrative branch (i.e., Treasury or IRS pronouncements).

Principal partner a partner having a 5 percent or more interest in partnership capital or profits.

Principal residence the main place of residence for a taxpayer during the taxable year.

Private letter rulings IRS pronouncements issued in response to a taxpayer request for a ruling on specific issues for the taxpayer. They are common for proposed transactions with potentially large tax implications. For the requesting taxpayer, a private letter ruling has very high authority. For all other taxpayers, private letter rulings have little authoritative weight.

Private nonoperating foundations privately sponsored foundations that disburse funds to other charities.

Private operating foundations privately sponsored foundations that actually fund and conduct charitable activities.

Probate the process in the probate court of gathering property possessed by or titled in the name of a decedent at the time of death, paying the debts of the decedent, and transferring the ownership of any remaining property to the decedent's heirs.

Probate estate property possessed by or titled in the name of a decedent at the time of death.

Procedural regulations regulations that explain Treasury Department procedures as they relate to administering the Code.

Production of income a for-profit activity that doesn't rise to the level of a trade or business.

Profits interest an interest in a partnership giving a partner the right to share in future profits but not the right to share in the current value of a partnership's assets. Profits interests are generally not taxable in the year they are received.

Progressive tax rate structure a tax rate structure that imposes an increasing marginal tax rate as the tax base increases. As the tax base increases, both the marginal tax rate and the taxes paid increase.

Proportional tax rate structure also known as a *flat tax,* this tax rate structure imposes a constant tax rate throughout the tax base. As the tax base increases, the taxes paid increase proportionally.

Proposed regulations regulations issued in proposed form; they do not carry the same authoritative weight as temporary or final regulations. All regulations are issued in proposed form first to allow public comment on them.

Public Law 86-272 federal law passed by Congress that provides additional protection for sellers of tangible personal property against income tax nexus.

Q

Qualified business asset investment (QBAI) the tax basis of tangible personal property used in a trade or business that forms the basis for determining the deductions allowed for foreign-derived intangible income and global low-taxed intangible income.

Qualified business income (QBI) net business income from a qualified trade or business conducted in the United States. This is the tax base for the deduction for qualified business income.

Qualified dividends paid by domestic or certain qualified foreign corporations that are eligible for lower capital gains rates.

Qualified education expenses consist of tuition and related costs for enrolling the taxpayer, spouse, or a dependent at a postsecondary institution of higher education.

Qualified education loans loans whose proceeds are used to pay qualified education expenses.

Qualified employee discounts a nontaxable fringe benefit that provides a discount on employer goods (not to be discounted below the employer's cost) and services (up to a 20 percent discount) to employees.

Qualified equity grant a broad-based equity grant of either stock options or restricted stock units by a private corporation. Eligible employees may make an inclusion deferral election that may defer the income attributable to the qualified equity for up to five years.

Qualified nonrecourse financing nonrecourse debt secured by real property from a commercial lender unrelated to the borrower.

Qualified replacement property property acquired to replace property damaged or destroyed in an involuntary conversion. It must be of a similar or related use to the original property even if the replacement property is real property (e.g., rental real estate for rental real estate).

Qualified residence the taxpayer's principal residence and one other residence.

Qualified retirement accounts plans meeting certain requirements that allow compensation placed in the account to be tax-deferred until the taxpayer withdraws money from the account.

Qualified retirement plans employer-sponsored retirement plans that meet government-imposed funding and antidiscrimination requirements.

Qualified small business stock stock received at original issue from a corporation with a gross tax basis in its assets both before and after the issuance of no more than $50,000,000 and with 80 percent of the value of its assets used in the active conduct of certain qualified trades or businesses.

Qualified trade or business for purposes of the deduction for qualified business income, any trade or business other than a specified trade or business.

Qualified transportation fringe benefits a nontaxable fringe benefit provided by employers in the form of mass transit passes, parking, or company-owned carpool benefits.

Qualifying child an individual who qualifies as a dependent of a taxpayer by meeting a relationship, age, residence, and support test with respect to the taxpayer.

Qualifying relative an individual who is not a qualifying child of another taxpayer and who meets a relationship, support, and gross income test and thus qualifies to be a dependent of another taxpayer.

Qualifying widow or widower one of five primary filing statuses. Applies for up to two years after the year in which the taxpayer's spouse dies (the taxpayer files married filing jointly in the year of the spouse's death) as long as the taxpayer remains unmarried and maintains a household for a dependent child.

Question of fact a research question that hinges upon the facts and circumstances of the taxpayer's transaction.

Question of law a research question that hinges upon the interpretation of the law, such as interpreting a particular phrase in a code section.

R

Real property land and structures permanently attached to land.

Real property taxes a tax on the fair market value of land and structures permanently attached to land.

Realization gain or loss that results from an exchange of property rights in a transaction.

Realization principle the proposition that income only exists when there is a transaction with another party resulting in a measurable change in property rights.

Realized gain or loss the difference between the amount realized and the adjusted basis of an asset sold or otherwise disposed of.

Realized income income generated in a transaction with a second party in which there is a measurable change in property rights between parties.

Reasonable in amount an expenditure is reasonable when the amount paid is neither extravagant nor exorbitant.

Recognized gains or losses gains or losses included in gross income on a taxpayer's tax return. This is usually the realized gain or loss unless a nonrecognition provision applies.

Recourse debt liability held by a partnership for which at least one partner has economic risk of loss.

Recovery period a length of time prescribed by statute in which business property is depreciated or amortized.

Recurring item an election under economic performance to currently deduct an accrued liability if the liability is expected to persist in the future and either it is not material or a current deduction better matches revenue.

Refinance when a taxpayer pays off a current loan with the proceeds of a second loan.

Regressive tax rate structure a tax rate structure that imposes a decreasing marginal tax rate as the tax base increases. As the tax base increases, the taxes paid increase, but the marginal tax rate decreases.

Regulations the Treasury Department's official interpretation of the Internal Revenue Code. Regulations are the highest authority issued by the IRS.

Related-person transaction financial activities among family members, among owners and their businesses, or among businesses owned by the same owners.

Remainder the right to ownership of a property that transfers to a new owner, the remainderman, following a temporary interest.

Remainderman the person entitled to a remainder interest.

Reorganization a tax-deferred transaction (acquisition, disposition, recapitalization, or change of name or place of incorporation) that meets one of the seven statutory definitions found in §368(a)(1).

Requisite service period the period or periods during which an employee is required to provide service in exchange for an award under a share-based payment arrangement (ASC Topic 718, Glossary).

Research and experimentation (R&E) costs expenses for research including costs of research laboratories (salaries, materials, and other related expenses). Taxpayers amortize research and development costs over not less than 60 months from the time benefits are first derived from the research.

Residence-based jurisdiction taxation of income based on the taxpayer's residence.

Resident alien an individual who is not a U.S. citizen but is treated as a resident for U.S. tax purposes.

Restricted stock stock employees receive as compensation that may be sold only after the passage of time or after certain performance targets are achieved. Because employees are not entitled to immediately sell the restricted stock they receive, the value of the stock is generally not taxable to employees or deductible by employers until the selling restrictions lapse.

Return of capital the portion of proceeds from a sale (or distribution) representing a return of the original cost of the underlying property.

Revenue procedures second in administrative authoritative weight after regulations. Revenue procedures are much more detailed than regulations and explain in greater detail IRS practice and procedures in administering the tax law. Revenue procedures have the same authoritative weight as revenue rulings.

Revenue rulings second in administrative authoritative weight after regulations. Revenue rulings address the specific application of the Code and regulations to a specific factual situation. Revenue rulings have the same authoritative weight as revenue procedures.

Reverse hybrid entity a "check-the-box" entity owned by multiple persons for which corporation status is elected.

Reversion terms by which ownership of property returns to the original owner following a temporary interest.

Rollover a transfer of funds from a qualified retirement plan to another qualified retirement plan, from a qualified retirement plan to a Roth or traditional IRA, or from a traditional IRA to a Roth IRA.

Roth 401(k) a type of defined contribution plan that allows employees to contribute on an after-tax basis and receive distributions tax-free.

Roth IRA an individually managed retirement plan permitting individuals to contribute on an after-tax basis and receive distributions tax-free.

S corporation a corporation under state law that has elected to be taxed under the rules provided in Subchapter S of the Internal Revenue Code. Under Subchapter S, an S corporation is taxed as a flow-through entity.

Safe-harbor provision provision of the tax law that reduces or eliminates a taxpayer's liability under the law if the taxpayer meets certain requirements.

Salary a fixed regular payment by an employer to an employee in exchange for the employee's services; usually paid on a monthly basis, but typically expressed as an annual amount.

Sales tax a tax imposed on the retail price of goods (plus certain services). Retailers are responsible for collecting and remitting the tax; typically, sales tax is collected at the point of sale.

Sales tax nexus the connection between a business and a tax jurisdiction sufficient to subject the business to the tax jurisdiction's sales tax.

Same-day sale a phrase used to describe a situation where a taxpayer exercises stock options and then immediately sells the stock received through the option exercise.

Schedule C a schedule on which a taxpayer reports the income and deductions for a sole proprietorship.

Schedule K a schedule filed with a partnership's annual tax return listing its ordinary income (loss) and its separately stated items.

Schedule M adjustments book–tax differences that corporations report on the Schedule M-1 or M-3 of Form 1120 as adjustments to book income to reconcile to taxable income.

Secondary authorities unofficial tax authorities that interpret and explain the primary authorities, such as tax research services, tax articles, newsletters, and textbooks. Secondary authorities may be very helpful in understanding a tax issue, but they hold little weight in a tax dispute (hence, the term *unofficial* tax authorities).

Self-employment taxes Social Security and Medicare taxes paid by the self-employed on a taxpayer's net earnings from self-employment. For self-employed taxpayers, the terms "self-employment tax" and "FICA tax" are synonymous.

SEP IRA a simplified employee pension (SEP) that is administered through an individual retirement account (IRA). Available to self-employed taxpayers.

Separate tax return a state tax return methodology requiring that each related entity with nexus must file a separate tax return.

Separately stated items income, expenses, gains, losses, credits, and other items that are excluded from a partnership's or S corporation's operating income (loss) and disclosed to partners in a partnership or shareholders of an S corporation separately because their tax effects may be different for each partner or shareholder.

Serial gift transfer tax strategy that uses the annual exclusion to convert a potentially large taxable transfer into a tax-exempt transfer by dividing it into multiple inter vivos gifts spread over several periods or donees.

Service partner a partner who receives a partnership interest by contributing services rather than cash or property.

Settlement statement a statement that details the monies paid out and received by the buyer and seller in a real estate transaction.

Short-term capital gains or losses gains or losses from the sale of capital assets held for one year or less.

Simple trust a trust that must distribute all accounting income currently and cannot make charitable contributions.

Sin taxes taxes imposed on the purchase of goods (e.g., alcohol, tobacco products, etc.) that are considered socially less desirable.

Single one of five primary filing statuses. A taxpayer files as single if they are unmarried as of the end of the year and does not qualify for any of the other filing statuses. A taxpayer is considered single if they are unmarried or legally separated from their spouse under a divorce or separate maintenance decree.

Single-member LLC a limited liability company with only one member. Single-member LLCs with individual owners are taxed as sole proprietorships and as disregarded entities otherwise.

Social Security tax the Old Age, Survivors, and Disability Insurance (OASDI) tax. The tax is intended to provide basic pension coverage for the retired and disabled. Employees pay Social Security tax at a rate of 6.2 percent on the wage base (employers also pay 6.2 percent). Self-employed taxpayers are subject to a Social Security tax at a rate of 12.4 percent on their net earnings from self-employment. The base on which Social Security taxes are paid is limited to an annually determined amount of wages and/or net earnings from self-employment.

Social security wage base limitation limit on the amount of employee compensation and/or net earnings from self-employment subject to the social security tax. The amount is provided annually and is indexed for inflation.

Sole proprietorship a business entity that is not legally separate from the individual owner of the business. The income of a sole proprietorship is taxed and paid directly by the owner.

Solicitation selling activities or activities ancillary to selling that are protected under Public Law 86-272.

Source-based jurisdiction taxation of income based on where the income is earned.

Special allocations allocations of income, gain, expense, loss, etc., that are allocated to the owners of an entity in a manner out of proportion with the owners' interests in the entity. Special allocations can be made by entities treated as partnerships for federal income tax purposes.

Special basis adjustment an optional (sometimes mandatory) election to adjust the entity asset bases as a result of an owner's disposition of an interest in the entity or distributions from the entity to its owners.

Specific identification method an elective method for determining the cost of an asset sold. Under this method, the taxpayer specifically chooses the assets that are to be sold.

Specified service trade or business any trade or business involving the performance of services in the fields of health, law, consulting, athletics, financial services, brokerage services, or any trade or business where the principal asset of such trade or business is the reputation or skill of one or more of its employees or owners, or which involves the performance of services that consist of investing and investment management trading, or dealing in securities, partnership interests, or commodities. Architecture and engineering services (their services build things) are specifically excluded from the definition of specified service trade or business.

Spot rate the foreign currency exchange rate on a specific day.

Spousal IRA an IRA account for the spouse with the lesser amount of earned income. Contributions in this account belong to this spouse no matter where the funds for the contribution came from.

Standard deduction a fixed deduction offered in lieu of itemized deductions. The amount of the standard deduction depends on the taxpayer's filing status.

Stare decisis a doctrine meaning that a court will rule consistently with (a) its previous rulings (i.e., unless, due to evolving interpretations of the tax law over time, it decides to overturn an earlier decision) and (b) the rulings of higher courts with appellate jurisdiction (i.e., the courts to which its cases are appealed).

Start-up costs expenses that would be classified as business expenses except that the expenses are incurred before the business begins. These costs are generally capitalized and amortized over 180 months, but limited immediate expensing may be available.

State tax a tax imposed by one of the 50 U.S. states.

State tax base the federal taxable income plus or minus required state adjustments.

Statements on Standards for Tax Services (SSTS) standards of practice for tax professionals issued by the AICPA. Currently, there are seven SSTS that describe the tax professional standards when recommending a tax return position, answering questions on a tax return, preparing a tax return using data supplied by a client, using estimates on a tax return, taking a tax return position inconsistent with a previous year's tax return, discovering a tax return error, and giving tax advice to taxpayers.

Static forecasting the process of forecasting tax revenues based on the existing state of transactions while ignoring how taxpayers may alter their activities in response to a tax law change.

Statute of limitations defines the period in which the taxpayer can file an amended tax return or the IRS can assess a tax deficiency for a specific tax year. For both amended tax returns filed by a taxpayer and proposed tax assessments by the IRS, the statute of limitations generally ends three years from the *later* of (1) the date the tax return was actually filed or (2) the tax return's original due date.

Step-transaction doctrine judicial doctrine that allows the IRS to collapse a series of related transactions into one transaction to determine the tax consequences of the transaction.

Stock redemption a property distribution made to shareholders in return for some or all of their stock in the distributing corporation that is not in partial or complete liquidation of the corporation.

Stock split a stock redemption in which a corporation exchanges a ratio of shares of stock (e.g., 2 for 1) for each share held by the shareholder.

Stock-for-stock acquisitions an exchange of solely voting stock by the acquiring corporation in exchange for stock of the target corporation, after which the acquiring corporation controls (owns 80 percent or more of) the target corporation. Often referred to as a "Type B reorganization."

Strike price the price at which holders of stock options may purchase stock in the corporation issuing the option.

Structural tax rate the tax rate computed by dividing a company's income tax provision adjusted for nonrecurring permanent differences by its pretax income from continuing operations.

Subchapter K the portion of the Internal Revenue Code dealing with partnerships tax law.

Subchapter S the portion of the Internal Revenue Code containing tax rules for S corporations and their shareholders.

Subpart F income income earned by a controlled foreign corporation that is not eligible for deferral from U.S. taxation.

Substance-over-form doctrine judicial doctrine that allows the IRS to consider the transaction's substance regardless of its form and, where appropriate, reclassify the transaction according to its substance.

Substantial authority the standard used to determine whether a tax practitioner may recommend and a taxpayer may take a tax return position without being subject to IRS penalty under IRC §6694 and IRC §6662, respectively. A good CPA evaluates whether supporting authority is substantial or not based upon the supporting and opposing authorities' weight and relevance. Substantial authority suggests that the probability that the taxpayer's position will be sustained upon audit or litigation is in the 35 to 40 percent range or above.

Substantial basis reduction negative basis adjustment of more than $250,000 resulting from a distribution from an entity taxed as a partnership to its owners.

Substantial built-in loss exists when a partnership's adjusted basis in its property exceeds the property's fair market value by more than $250,000 when a transfer of an interest occurs or if the purchasing partner would be allocated a loss of more than $250,000 if the partnership assets were sold for fair market value immediately after the transfer.

Substantially appreciated inventory (for partnership disproportionate distributions purposes) inventory with a fair market value that exceeds its basis by more than 120 percent.

Substituted basis the transfer of the tax basis of stock or other property given up in an exchange to stock or other property received in return.

Substitution effect one of the two basic responses that a taxpayer may have when taxes increase. The substitution effect predicts that, when taxpayers are taxed more, rather than work more, they will substitute nontaxable activities (e.g., leisure pursuits) for taxable ones because the marginal value of taxable activities has decreased.

Sufficiency a standard for evaluating a good tax system. Sufficiency is defined as assessing the aggregate size of the tax revenues that must be generated and ensuring that the tax system provides these revenues.

Syndication costs costs partnerships incur to promote the sale of partnership interests to the public. Syndication expenses must be capitalized and are not amortizable.

T

Tax a payment required by a government that is unrelated to any specific benefit or service received from the government.

Tax accounting balance sheet a balance sheet that records a company's assets and liabilities at their tax bases instead of their financial accounting bases.

Tax avoidance the legal act of arranging one's transactions or affairs to reduce taxes paid.

Tax base the item that is being taxed (e.g., purchase price of a good, taxable income, etc.).

Tax basis the amount of a taxpayer's unrecovered cost of or investment in an asset; *see also* adjusted tax basis.

Tax benefit rule holds that a refund of an amount deducted in a previous period is only included in income to the extent that the deduction reduced taxable income.

Tax bracket a range of taxable income taxed at a specified rate.

Tax capital accounts partners' capital accounts initially determined using the tax basis of contributed property and maintained using tax accounting income and expense recognition principles.

Tax carryovers tax deductions or credits that cannot be used on the current-year tax return and that can be carried forward to reduce taxable income or taxes payable in a future year.

Tax Court allocation method allocates expenses associated with rental use of the home between rental use and personal use. Property taxes and mortgage interest are allocated to rental use of the home based on the ratio of the number of rental use days to the total days in the year. All other expenses are allocated to rental use based on the ratio of the number of rental use days to total days the property was used during the year.

Tax credits items that directly reduce a taxpayer's tax liability.

Tax evasion the willful attempt to defraud the government (i.e., by not paying taxes legally owed). Tax evasion falls outside the confines of legal tax avoidance.

Tax haven generally, a country offering very favorable tax laws for foreign businesses and individuals.

Tax rate the level of taxes imposed on the tax base, usually expressed as a percentage.

Tax rate schedule a schedule of progressive tax rates and the income ranges to which the rates apply that taxpayers may use to compute their gross tax liability.

Tax return preparers any person or entity who prepares for compensation, or who employs one or more persons to prepare for compensation, all or a substantial portion of any tax return or claim for refund.

Tax shelter an investment or other arrangement designed to produce tax benefits without any expectation of economic profits.

Tax tables IRS-provided tables that specify the federal income tax liability for individuals with taxable income within a specific range. The tables differ by filing status and reflect tax rates that increase with taxable income.

Tax treaties agreements negotiated between countries that describe the tax treatment of entities subject to tax in both countries (e.g., U.S. citizens earning investment income in Spain). The U.S. president has the authority to enter into a tax treaty with another country after receiving the Senate's advice.

Tax year a fixed period in which a business reports income and deductions, generally 12 months.

Tax-deferred transactions transactions where at least a portion of the realized gain or loss is not currently recognized.

Taxable estate adjusted gross estate reduced by the marital deduction and the charitable deduction.

Taxable fringe benefits a noncash fringe benefit provided by employers to an employee that is included in taxable income (e.g., auto allowance or group-term life over $50,000).

Taxable gifts the amount left after adjusting current gifts for gift splitting, annual exclusions, the marital deduction, and the charitable deduction.

Taxable income the tax base for the income tax.

Taxable temporary differences book–tax differences that will result in taxable amounts in future years when the related deferred tax liability is settled.

Technical advice memorandums rulings issued by the IRS national office, requested by an IRS agent, and generated for completed transactions.

Temporary book–tax differences book–tax differences that reverse over time such that, over the long term, corporations recognize the same amount of income or deductions for the items on their financial statements as they recognize on their tax returns.

Temporary regulations regulations issued with a limited life (three years for regulations issued after November 20, 1988). During their life, temporary regulations carry the same authoritative weight as final regulations.

Tenancy in common ownership in which owners hold divided rights to property and have the ability to transfer these rights during their life or upon their death.

Tentative minimum tax (TMT) the tax on the AMT tax base under the alternative minimum tax system.

Terminable interest a right to property that terminates at a specified time or upon the occurrence of a specified event, such as a life estate.

Testamentary transfers transfers that take place upon the death of the donor.

Third-party intermediaries people or organizations that facilitate the transfer of property between taxpayers in a like-kind exchange. Typically, the intermediary receives the cash from selling the property received from the taxpayer and uses it to acquire like-kind property identified by the taxpayer.

Throwback rule the rule that sales into a state without nexus are included with sales from the state the property was shipped from.

Topical tax services a tax service arranged by subject (i.e., topic). Topical services identify tax issues that relate to each topic and then explain and cite authorities relevant to the issue (code sections, regulations, court cases, revenue rulings, etc.).

Trade or business a profit-motivated activity characterized by a sustained, continuous, high level of individual involvement or effort.

Trade show rule a rule that permits businesses to have physical presence at conventions and trade shows, generally up to two weeks a year, without creating income tax nexus.

Traditional 401(k) a popular type of defined contribution plan with before-tax employee and employer contributions and taxable distributions.

Traditional IRA an individually managed retirement account with deductible contributions and taxable distributions.

Transfer taxes taxes on the transfer of wealth from one taxpayer to another. The estate and gift taxes are two examples of transfer taxes.

Travel expenses expenditures incurred while "away from home overnight," including the cost of transportation, meals, lodging, and incidental expenses.

Treasury bond a debt instrument issued by the U.S. Treasury at face value, at a discount, or at a premium, with a set interest rate and maturity date that pays interest semiannually. Treasury bonds have terms of 30 years.

Treasury note a debt instrument issued by the U.S. Treasury at face value, at a discount, or at a premium, with a set interest rate and maturity date that pays interest semiannually. Treasury notes have terms of 2, 5, or 10 years.

Trust fiduciary entity created to hold and administer the property for other persons according to the terms of a trust instrument.

Trustee the person responsible for administering a trust.

U

U.S. circuit courts of appeals the first level of appeals courts after the trial-level courts. There are 13 U.S. circuit courts of appeal: 1 for the Federal Circuit and 12 assigned to hear cases that originate from a specific circuit (e.g., the 11th Circuit Court of Appeals only hears cases originating within the 11th Circuit).

U.S. Constitution the founding law of the United States, ratified in 1789.

U.S. Court of Federal Claims one of the three trial-level courts. It is a national court that only hears monetary claims against the federal government.

U.S. district court one of three trial-level courts. It is the only court that allows a jury trial. There is at least one district court in each state.

U.S. savings bonds debt instruments issued by the U.S. Treasury at face value or at a discount, with a set maturity date. Interest earned from U.S. bonds is paid either at maturity or when the bonds are converted to cash before maturity.

U.S. Supreme Court the highest court in the United States. The Supreme Court hears only a few tax cases a year with great significance to a broad cross-section of taxpayers or cases litigating issues in which there has been disagreement among the circuit courts. For most tax cases, the Supreme Court refuses to hear the case (i.e., the *writ of certiorari* is denied) and, thus, litigation ends with the circuit court decision.

U.S. Tax Court a national court that only hears tax cases and where the judges are tax experts. The U.S. Tax Court is the only court that allows tax cases to be heard *before* the taxpayer pays the disputed liability and the only court with a small claims division (hearing claims involving disputed liabilities of $50,000 or less).

Uncertain tax position a tax return position for which a corporation does not have a high degree of certainty as to its tax consequences.

Underpayment penalty the penalty that applies when taxpayers fail to adequately prepay their tax liability. The underpayment penalty is determined by multiplying the federal short-term interest rate plus 3 percentage points by the amount of tax underpayment per quarter.

Unearned income income from property that accrues as time passes without effort on the part of the owner of the property.

Unemployment tax the tax that pays for temporary unemployment benefits for individuals terminated from their jobs without cause.

Unfavorable book–tax difference any book–tax difference that requires an add-back to book income in computing taxable income. This type of adjustment is unfavorable because it increases taxable income relative to book income.

Uniform cost capitalization (UNICAP) rules specify that inventories must be accounted for using full absorption rules to allocate the indirect costs of productive activities to inventory.

Unitary tax return a state tax return methodology requiring the activities of a group of related entities to be reported on a single tax return. The criteria for determining whether a group of entities must file a unitary tax return are functional integration, centralization of management, and economies of scale.

United States person a citizen or resident of the United States, a domestic corporation, a domestic partnership, or any U.S. estate or trust.

Unrealized receivables any rights to receive payment for (1) goods delivered, or to be delivered, or (2) services rendered, or to be rendered. Unrealized receivables also include other assets to the extent that they would produce ordinary income if sold for their fair market value.

Unrecaptured §1250 gain a type of §1231 gain derived from the sale of real estate held by a noncorporate taxpayer for more than one year in a trade or business or as rental property attributable to tax depreciation deducted at ordinary tax rates. This gain is taxable at a maximum 25 percent capital gains rate.

Unrelated business income income from a trade or business, regularly carried on, that is not substantially related to the charitable, educational, or other purpose that is the basis of the organization's exemption.

Use tax a tax imposed on the retail price of goods owned, possessed, or consumed within a state that were *not* purchased within the state.

V

Valuation allowance the portion of a deferred tax asset for which management determines it is more likely than not that a tax benefit will not be realized on a future tax return.

Value-added tax a tax imposed on the producer of goods (and services) based on the value added to the goods (services) at each stage of production. Value-added taxes are common in Europe.

Vertical equity one of the dimensions of equity. Vertical equity is achieved when taxpayers with greater ability to pay tax pay more tax relative to taxpayers with a lesser ability to pay tax.

Vesting the process of becoming legally entitled to receive a particular benefit without risk of forfeiture; gaining ownership.

Vesting date the date on which the taxpayer becomes legally entitled to receive a particular benefit without risk of forfeiture.

Vesting period period of employment over which employees earn the right to own and exercise stock options.

W

Wages a payment by an employer to an employee in exchange for the employee's services; typically expressed in an hourly, daily, or piecework rate.

Wash sale the sale of an investment if that same investment (or substantially identical investment) is purchased within 30 days before or after the sale date. Losses on wash sales are deferred.

Wherewithal to pay the ability or resources to pay taxes due from a particular transaction.

Withholdings taxes collected and remitted to the government by an employer from an employee's wages.

Working condition fringe benefits a nontaxable fringe benefit provided by employers that would be deductible as an ordinary and necessary business expense if paid by an employee (e.g., reimbursement for professional dues).

Writ of certiorari a document filed to request the U.S. Supreme Court to hear a case.

Z

Zero-coupon bond a type of bond issued at a discount that pays interest only at maturity.

Appendix C

Tax Rates

2022 Tax Rate Schedules

Individuals

Schedule X—Single

If taxable income is over:	But not over:	The tax is:
$ 0	$ 10,275	10% of taxable income
$ 10,275	$ 41,775	$1,027.5 plus 12% of the excess over $10,275
$ 41,775	$ 89,075	$4,807.5 plus 22% of the excess over $41,775
$ 89,075	$170,050	$15,213.5 plus 24% of the excess over $89,075
$175,050	$215,950	$34,647.5 plus 32% of the excess over $170,050
$215,950	$539,900	$49,335.50 plus 35% of the excess over $215,950
$539,900	—	$162,718 plus 37% of the excess over $539,900

Schedule Z—Head of Household

If taxable income is over:	But not over:	The tax is:
$ 0	$ 14,650	10% of taxable income
$ 14,650	$ 55,900	$1,465 plus 12% of the excess over $14,650
$ 55,900	$ 89,050	$6,415 plus 22% of the excess over $55,900
$ 89,050	$170,050	$13,708 plus 24% of the excess over $89,050
$170,050	$215,950	$33,148 plus 32% of the excess over $170,050
$215,950	$539,900	$47,836 plus 35% of the excess over $215,950
$539,900	—	$161,218.5 plus 37% of the excess over $539,900

Schedule Y-1—Married Filing Jointly or Qualifying Widow(er)

If taxable income is over:	But not over:	The tax is:
$ 0	$ 20,550	10% of taxable income
$ 20,550	$ 83,550	$2,055 plus 12% of the excess over $20,550
$ 83,550	$178,150	$9,615 plus 22% of the excess over $83,550
$178,150	$340,100	$30,427 plus 24% of the excess over $178,150
$340,100	$431,900	$69,295 plus 32% of the excess over $340,100
$431,900	$647,850	$98,671 plus 35% of the excess over $431,900
$647,850	—	$174,253.5 plus 37% of the excess over $647,850

Schedule Y-2—Married Filing Separately

If taxable income is over:	But not over:	The tax is:
$ 0	$ 10,275	10% of taxable income
$ 10,275	$ 41,775	$1,027.5 plus 12% of the excess over $10,275
$ 41,775	$ 89,075	$4,807.5 plus 22% of the excess over $41,775
$ 89,075	$170,050	$15,213.5 plus 24% of the excess over $89,075
$170,050	$215,950	$34,647.5 plus 32% of the excess over $170,050
$215,950	$323,925	$49,335.5 plus 35% of the excess over $215,950
$323,925	—	$87,126.75 plus 37% of the excess over $323,925

Estates and Trusts

If taxable income is over:	But not over:	The tax is:
$ 0	$ 2,750	10% of taxable income
$ 2,750	$ 9,850	$275 plus 24% of the excess over $2,750
$ 9,850	$13,450	$1,979 plus 35% of the excess over $9,850
$13,450		$3,239 plus 37% of the excess over $13,450

Tax Rates for Net Capital Gains and Qualified Dividends

	Taxable Income				
Rate*	Married Filing Jointly	Married Filing Separately	Single	Head of Household	Trusts and Estates
0%	$0–$83,350	$0–$41,675	$0–$41,675	$0–$55,800	$0–$2,800
15%	$83,351–$517,200	$41,676–$258,600	$41,676–$459,750	$55,801–$488,500	$2,801–$13,700
20%	$517,201+	$258,601+	$459,751+	$488,501+	$13,701+

*This rate applies to the net capital gains and qualified dividends that fall within the range of taxable income specified in the table (net capital gains and qualified dividends are included in taxable income last for this purpose).

Basic Standard Deduction Amounts*

Filing Status	2021 Amount	2022 Amount
Married Filing Jointly	$25,100	$25,900
Qualifying Widow or Widower	$25,100	$25,900
Married Filing Separately	$12,550	$12,950
Head of Household	$18,800	$19,400
Single	$12,550	$12,950

*For individuals claimed as a dependent on another return, the 2022 standard deduction is the greater of (1) $1,150 or (2) $400 plus earned income not to exceed the standard deduction amount of those who are not dependents.

Amount of Each Additional Standard Deduction for Taxpayers Who Are Age 65 or Blind

	2021 Amount	2022 Amount
Married taxpayers	$1,350	$1,400
Single taxpayer or head of household	$1,700	$1,750

Exemption Amount*

2021	2022
$4,300	$4,400

*Used for qualifying relative gross income test.

Corporations

Rate	Taxable Income
21%	All

Code Index

Page numbers followed by n refer to footnotes.

Subject Index

Page numbers followed by n refer to footnotes.

A

B

C

D

E

G

J

M

N

O

P

T

U